Butterworths
BUSINESS AND LAW DICTIONARY

Butterworths Reference Works

Australian Current Law
Australian Legal Words and Phrases
Butterworths Encyclopaedic Australian Legal Dictionary (Online and CD-ROM)
Butterworths Australian Legal Dictionary (Hardcover and CD-ROM)
Butterworths Concise Australian Legal Dictionary
Butterworths Environmental Management and Law Dictionary
Halsbury's Laws of Australia
Federal Statutes Annotations
New South Wales Statutes Annotations
Queensland Legislation Case Annotations
Victorian Statutes Annotations

If you have any queries and suggestions regarding Butterworths Business and Law Dictionary, please call and let us know, or drop us a line via e-mail.

We welcome your comments and hope to enhance and improve this publication to assist you in your legal studies.

Butterworths Australia
Ph: (02) 9422 2222
E-mail address: dictionary@butterworths.com.au

Butterworths
BUSINESS AND LAW DICTIONARY

Editors

The Honourable Justice Ipp
of the Supreme Court of Western Australia

W S Weerasooria LLB(Hons) PhD(Lond)
Associate Professor of Banking Law Monash University
Barrister and Solicitor, Victoria
Consultant Minter Ellison, Melbourne

General Editors

The Honourable Dr Peter E Nygh LLD(Syd) SJD(Mich)
Visiting Professor of Law University of New South Wales

Peter Butt BA LLM(Hons)(Syd)
Associate Professor Faculty of Law University of Sydney
Solicitor, New South Wales, High Court of Australia
Consultant Mallesons Stephen Jaques
Foundation Director Centre for Plain Legal Language

Butterworths

Sydney — Adelaide — Brisbane — Canberra — Hobart — Melbourne — Perth
1997

AUSTRALIA	BUTTERWORTHS Tower 2, 475–495 Victoria Avenue, Chatswood NSW 2067	
	111 Gawler Place, Adelaide, SA 5000	
	Oxley House, 25 Donkin Street, West End, Qld 4101	
	53–55 Northbourne Avenue, Canberra ACT 2601	
	461 Bourke Street, Melbourne, Vic 3000	
	Suite 32, Hyatt Centre, 23 Plain Street, East Perth, WA 6004	
	On the Internet at: www.butterworths.com.au	
ARGENTINA	ABELEDO-PERROT SA Buenos Aires	
AUSTRIA	REED ELSEVIER LEGAL DIVISION Vienna	
	VERLAG ORAC Vienna	
CANADA	BUTTERWORTHS CANADA LTD Toronto	
CZECH REPUBLIC	NAKLADATELSTVI ORAC, SPOL S R O Prague	
FRANCE	EDITIONS DU JURIS-CLASSEUR Paris	
HONG KONG	BUTTERWORTHS ASIA Hong Kong	
INDIA	BUTTERWORTHS INDIA LTD New Delhi	
IRELAND	BUTTERWORTH (IRELAND) LTD Dublin	
ITALY	GIUFFRÈ EDITORE SPA Milan	
MALAYSIA	MALAYAN LAW JOURNAL SDN BHD Kuala Lumpur	
NEW ZEALAND	BUTTERWORTHS OF NEW ZEALAND LTD Wellington	
POLAND	WYDAWNICTWA PRAWNICZE PWN Warsaw	
	WYDAWNICTWO PRAWNICZE Warsaw	
SINGAPORE	BUTTERWORTHS ASIA & MALAYAN LAW JOURNAL Singapore	
SOUTH AFRICA	BUTTERWORTH PUBLISHERS (PTY) LTD Durban	
SWITZERLAND	STAEMPFLI VERLAG AG Berne	
UNITED KINGDOM	BUTTERWORTH & CO (PUBLISHERS) LTD London and Edinburgh	
USA	LEXIS-NEXIS Miamisburg, Ohio	
	LEXIS LAW PUBLISHING Charlottesville, Virginia	

National Library of Australia Cataloguing-in-Publication entry

---

Butterworths Business and Law Dictionary

ISBN 0409 314005

©1997 Reed International Books Australia Pty Limited trading as Butterworths
Reprinted 1999.

The book is copyright. Except as permitted under the Copyright Act 1968 (Cth), no part of this publication may be reproduced by any process, electronic or otherwise, without the specific written permission of the copyright owner. Neither may information be stored electronically in any form whatsoever without such permission.

Inquiries should be addressed to the publishers.
Printed in Australia by Star Printery Pty Ltd.

Contributors

A-Khavari, Afshin BSc LLB(UNSW) Associate Lecturer in Law University of Sydney *Foreign Relations, Insurance, Maritime Law*

Adams, Richard H T BE(Civil)(Syd) LLB(QUT) CPEng MIE Aust RPEQ MAIBS Nationally Accredited Building Surveyor, Barrister of the Supreme Court of Queensland, Partner Codesafe, Principal Universal Texts *Building and Construction*

Atwood, John LLB(Hons)(QUT) Deputy Director of Research Administrative Review Council *Aboriginals and Torres Strait Islanders, Constitutional Law*

Babb, Lloyd A BA LLB LLM Barrister of the Supreme Court of New South Wales *Courts and Judicial System*

Barkehall-Thomas, Susan J BA LLB(Hons) Barrister and Solicitor of the Supreme Court of Victoria, of the Federal Court, and of the High Court, Assistant Lecturer in Law Monash University *Real Property*

Bates, Dr Gerry LLB(Hons) PhD(Birm) Environmental Law Consultant Senior Lecturer in Law University of Sydney *Environmental Law*

Beckmann, Matthew T OFM BA LLB Solicitor of the Supreme Court of Queensland, Registered Migration Agent, Victorian Immigration Advice and Rights Centre Inc *Citizenship and Migration*

Beerworth, Dr Ellen BA(R-MWC) MA(UVa) LLB(ANU) PhD(Macq) Solicitor of the Supreme Court of New South Wales, Freehill Hollingdale & Page *Product Liability*

Bennett, Judith BA(Hons) LLB(Syd) Solicitor of the Supreme Courts of New South Wales and Victoria, Consultant, Plain Law Documents, Precedents Manager Middletons Moore & Bevins *Legal Terminology*

Berecry, Grahame J Dip Law (SAB) Registrar, Equity Division, Supreme Court of New South Wales *Courts and Judicial System*

Best, Roderick BA LLM Solicitor of the Supreme Court of New South Wales, Manager, Legal Services New South Wales TAFE Commission *Real Property*

Bicego, Carl BEc LLB(Hons)(Macq) LLM(Dalhousie) *Environmental Law, Conflict of Laws*

Blay, Professor Sam LLB(Ghana) LLM(ANU) PhD(Tas) former Dean of Law University of Tasmania, Professor of Law University of Technology Sydney *Damages, Negligence, Tort*

Bourke, Geoffrey John LLB(Syd) Solicitor of the Supreme Court of New South Wales, Senior Lecturer College of Law, Principal Bourke & Bourke Solicitors *Legal Practitioners*

Brazil, Raymond MA(Syd) LLB(Hons)(UTS) Solicitor of the Supreme Court of New South Wales *Public Health*

Burton, Gregory BCL(Oxon) BA(Hons) LLB(Hons)(Syd) Barrister of the Supreme Courts of New South Wales and Queensland, of the High Court of Australia, of the Federal Court, and of Ireland, Barrister and Solicitor of the Supreme Courts of Victoria, the Australian Capital Territory, and Western Australia, Arbitrator, Mediator *Bailment, Personal Property*

Carlton, Suzanne E JD(Seattle U) BA(UCLA) Solicitor and Barrister of the Supreme Court of South Australia, Judge's Associate District Court of South Australia *Courts and Judicial System*

Chambers, Dr Robert BEd LLB(Alberta) DPhil(Oxon) Barrister and Solicitor of the Province of Alberta, Lecturer, Law School, University of Melbourne *Restitution, Trusts*

Chidiac, Emil DipCom DipTrans(Lond) DipCoDir(UNE) MA(Hons)(UWS) ACIS AFAIM AICM AMIQ CMAHRI FAICD FSSE FTMA MIIA(AUST) MIL(Lond) JP, Accountant, Accredited Internal Auditor, Chartered Secretary, Incorporated Linguist, Accredited Interpreter and Translator *Economics, Taxation and Revenue*

Clyde, Ian J BA LLB Solicitor of the Supreme Court of New South Wales, Human Rights and Equal Opportunity Commission *Civil and Political Rights*

Cremean, Dr Damien J LLB(Hons)(Melb) PhD(Mon) Barrister of the Supreme Courts of Victoria and New South Wales, Senior Lecturer in Law Deakin University, Deputy Chairperson Domestic Building Tribunal Victoria *Building and Construction*

Cuffe, Natalie A LLB(Hons)(QUT) Associate Lecturer, Law Reference Librarian, Griffith University *Real Property*

Devereux, Dr John A BA LLB(Hons)(Qld) DPhil(Oxon) Barrister of the Supreme Court of Queensland, Senior Lecturer in Law Griffith University *Real Property*

Earl, Lisa BComm LLB(Hons) Solicitor of the Supreme Court of New South Wales *Criminal Law*

Edgeworth, Brendan J LLB MA(Sheff) Senior Lecturer, Faculty of Law, University of New South Wales *Defamation*

© Butterworths

Edwards, Jane LLB M ED(Admin) Barrister and Solicitor of the Supreme Court of Victoria, Senior Lecturer in Law University of Melbourne, Senior Member Veterans' Review Board *Contract*

Ehrlich, David P BComm LLB(NSW) LLM(Syd) Solicitor of the Supreme Court of New South Wales *Conflict of Laws, Succession*

Emmett, Arthur R QC BA LLM One of Her Majesty's Counsel, Challis Lecturer in Roman Law University of Sydney *Latin Words and Phrases, Roman Law*

Enright, Ian BA(Hons) LLB(Syd) LLM(Lond) Solicitor of the Supreme Court of New South Wales and of England, Partner Ebsworth & Ebsworth *Insurance*

Eyland, David W BA(Hons)(UNSW) Captain Royal Australian Artillery *Weapons and Dangerous Goods*

Favretto, John D Dip Law (SAB) Solicitor of the Supreme Court of New South Wales and of the High Court of Australia, Accredited Specialist Criminal Law, Senior Principal Lawyer Office of the Director of Public Prosecutions NSW *Criminal Law*

Finch, Andrew J BComm LLB Solicitor of the Supreme Court of New South Wales, Allen Allen & Hemsley *Corporations*

Finlay-Jones, Jenny BA LLM(Syd) Solicitor of the Supreme Court of New South Wales and the High Court of Australia, Lecturer in Law University of Newcastle *Courts and Judicial System*

Fitzgerald, Brian BA(GU) LLB(Hons)(QUT) BCL(Oxon) Barrister of the Supreme Court of Queensland and of the High Court of Australia, Barrister and Solicitor of the Supreme Court of the Australian Capital Territory, Lecturer in Law Griffith University *Constitutional Law*

Ford, H A J SJD(Harv) LLD Hon(Melb) LLM(Melb) Professor Emeritus of Commercial Law University of Melbourne Barrister and Solicitor of the Supreme Court of Victoria *Corporations*

Gayford, Matthew BA Lieutenant Royal Australian Artillery *Defence*

Gilpin, Dr Alan BSc(Econ) PhD CEng FIEAust FInstE Consultant and the Adviser, Environmental Planning *Economics, Environment*

Glasson, Robert Dudley BA LLB(Hons)(Syd) Solicitor of the Supreme Court of New South Wales, Research Assistant, Common Law Division, Supreme Court of New South Wales, Associate Lecturer in Law University of Sydney *Constitutional Law*

Gormly, Julian F BA(Hons)(NSW) LLB(Syd) Barrister of the Supreme Court of New South Wales *Courts and Judicial System*

Guthleben, Catherine LLB(Hons) LLM(Adel) Barrister and Solicitor of the Supreme Courts of South Australia and New South Wales *Real Property*

Halabi, Abdel K BBus Grad Dip Ed Grad Dip Bus MBus(Mon) ACA Lecturer in Accounting Faculty of Business and Economics Monash University *Accounting*

Hanson, Cameron BJuris(UNSW) *Contract, Criminal Law*

Harb, James LLB(Hons)(UTS) Solicitor of the Supreme Court of New South Wales, Ebsworth & Ebsworth, *Carriers, Conflict of Law, Insurance*

Harrison, Joanne BLegS Grad Dip Law (Court Policy and Admin) Solicitor of the Supreme Court of New South Wales, Registrar Supreme Court of New South Wales *Courts and Judicial System*

Healey, Deborah J LLM(Hons)(Syd) Solicitor of the Supreme Court of New South Wales, Senior Associate Allen Allen & Hemsley, *Sale of Goods, Trade and Commerce*

Hill, Peter A BA(Hons) LLB(Syd) Legal Practitioner of the Supreme Court of New South Wales *Conflict of Laws*

Hinde, G W LLM(NZ) LLD(Auckland) Emeritus Professor of Law, University of Auckland *Corporations*

Hinde, M S BCom LLB(Auckland) Barrister and Solicitor of the High Court of New Zealand *Corporations*

Ho, Leanne BA LLB(Syd) A Mus A

Hockley, John James BSc(Hons) Dip Ed PhD(UNE) LLB(UNSW) LLM(Melb) Dip Int Tax(Harv) Barrister of the Supreme Courts of New South Wales, Victoria, Queensland, South Australia, Western Australia, Tasmania, and the Northern Territory *Real Property*

Horton, Jonathan BA(ANU) *Primary Industry*

Howie, Judge R N QC Judge of the District Court of New South Wales *Criminal Law*

Hyam, Alan A LFAIVLE Barrister of the Supreme Court of New South Wales, of the Northern Territory, and of the High Court of Australia *Agency, Auction, Real Property*

Ingleby, Dr Richard S MA(Oxon) LLM(Cantab) DPhil(Oxon) Barrister of the Supreme Court of Victoria, Professorial Associate Faculty of Law University of Melbourne *Courts and Judicial System*

Islam, Dr M Rafiqul BA(Hons) MA LLB(Raj B'Desh) LLM(Mon) PhD(Mon) Senior Lecturer School of Law Macquarie University *Conflict of Laws, Foreign Relations*

Contributors

Johnstone, Ian M BA(UNE) LLB(Syd) Solicitor of the Supreme Court of New South Wales, Partner A W Simpson & Co Armidale *Latin Words and Phrases*

Jonson, Paul T BA(Hons) LLB(Syd) Grad Dip Leis St(KCAE) Solicitor of the Supreme Court of New South Wales and of the High Court of Australia, Senior Lecturer School of Leisure and Tourism Studies, University of Technology Sydney *Entertainment, Sport and Tourism*

Kercher, Bruce BA LLB(Syd) LLM(NSW) PhD(Macq) Associate Professor School of Law Macquarie University *Australian Legal History*

Khoury, Daniel BJuris LLM(Mon) Dip Ed(Tertiary)(Mon) Grad Dip Tax Law(RMIHE) Barrister of the Supreme Court of Victoria, Senior Lecturer in Law Victoria University of Technology *Contract*

Khoury, Fadi BEc LLB(Syd) Legal Practitioner of the Supreme Court of New South Wales, Tax Consultant Arthur Andersen *Banking and Finance, Corporations*

Lamb, Anthony J BA LLB(UNSW) Solicitor of the Supreme Court of New South Wales, Senior Legal Officer NSW Land Titles Office *Real Property*

Law, James D BEc LLB(Macq) Solicitor of the Supreme Court of New South Wales, Chartered Accountant, Tax Consultant KPMG *Superannuation, Taxation and Revenue*

Lee, Edmund BSc(Hons) M Env Law(Syd) Research Associate Australian Centre for Environmental Law *Environmental Law*

Leeming, Mark J BA(Hons) LLB(Hons)(Syd) Barrister of the Supreme Court of New South Wales *Constitutional Law*

Lees, Merryl A BA(Mon) LLB(Syd) Solicitor of the Supreme Court of New South Wales, Human Rights and Equal Opportunity Commission *Civil and Political Rights*

Leis, Susan BA(N'castle) Grad Dip Ed(NewCAE) BLegS(Macq) Solicitor of the Supreme Court of New South Wales, Solicitor and Barrister of the Supreme Court of the Australian Capital Territory, Accredited Specialist Criminal Law, Associate Lecturer in Law University of Newcastle, Solicitor Newcastle Legal Centre *Criminal Law*

Levingston, John BA LLB(ANU) Solicitor of the Supreme Courts of New South Wales, Victoria, and the Australian Capital Territory, and of the High Court and Federal Court of Australia, Principal Levingstons *Insurance*

Lipton, Jacqueline D BA(Melb) BA(Hons)(La Trobe) LLB(Hons)(Melb) LLM(Mon) Barrister and Solicitor of the Supreme Court of Victoria and of the High Court of Australia, Lecturer Faculty of Law Monash University *Guarantees and Indemnities*

Lloyd, Bruce L BEc LLB(Hons)(ANU) Solicitor of the Supreme Court of New South Wales, Senior Associate Clayton Utz *Intellectual Property*

Lloyd, Dianne RN RPN BA LLB(UTS) Publishing Editor, Halsbury's Laws of Australia *Mental Health*

Lo, Stefan BA LLB(Syd)

Lusk, Michael A BSc LLB(Hons)(Macq) *Constitutional Law, Intellectual Property*

Lyster, Rosemary BA LLB LLM(Natal) Lecturer School of Law University of Sydney *Environmental Law*

McDonald, Ian J BA(Hons) MA Dip Ed LLB(Syd) Solicitor of the Supreme Court of New South Wales, Legal Officer Australian Copyright Council *Intellectual Property*

McKay, Dr Jennifer M BA(Hons) LLB PhD GCLP Solicitor of the Supreme Court of South Australia, Senior Lecturer University of South Australia *Police and Emergency Services, Water*

McLachlan, Ian BSc LLB(Hons)(Macq) *Courts and Judicial System*

McNicol, Andrew D BComm LLB(Melb) LLM(Mon) ACA Barrister and Solicitor of the Supreme Court of Victoria and the High Court of Australia, Chartered Accountant, Lecturer in Taxation Law Faculty of Business and Economics Monash Univeristy *Taxation and Revenue*

McNicol, Suzanne B LLB(Hons) BA(Melb) BCL(Oxon) Barrister and Solicitor of the Supreme Court of Victoria, Associate Professor in Law Monash University *Evidence*

Moore, Dr Marilyn A MB BS(Tas) FRANZCP Consultant Psychiatrist *Medicine*

Nader, Jonar C President of the Australian Information Technology Society, Lecturer, Journalist, Broadcaster, Author, Consumer Manager Asia Pacific South IBM Corp *Technology*

Naghdy, Hajir BMaths Student-at-Law *Constitutional Law*

Neate, Graeme BA LLB(Hons)(ANU) Barrister and Solicitor of the Supreme Court of the Australian Capital Territory and the Northern Territory, Solicitor of the Supreme Court of New South Wales and of Queensland, Chairperson of the Aboriginal and Torres Strait Islander Land Tribunals, Member of the Land Court of Queensland, Member of the National Native Title Tribunal *Aboriginal and Torres Strait Islanders*

Nickel, Bruce W BA LLB(Qld) Barrister of the Supreme Court of Queensland and of the High Court of Australia *Succession*

North, Jon BA LLM Solicitor of the Supreme Court of New South Wales and the High Court of Australia, Partner Allen Allen & Hemsley *Corporations*

Oakman, Mark LLB(UTS) Solicitor of the Supreme Court of the Australian Capital Territory, Barrister of the Supreme Court of New South Wales, NSW Department of Industrial Relations *Employment Law*

Ozen, Ertunc BA LLB(Macq) Solicitor of the Supreme Court of New South Wales, Western Aboriginal Legal Service *Criminal Law*

Pakula, Jennifer BA LLB Solicitor of the Supreme Court of New South Wales *Leases and Tenancies, Perpetuities, Real Property*

Payne, Michelle BJuris LLB(UWA) Barrister and Solicitor of the Supreme Court of Western Australia, McLeod & Co Barristers and Solicitors *Environmental Law*

Peters, Associate Professor Pam H BA(Hons)(Melb) MA(Hons)(Syd) School of English, Linguistics and Media Macquarie University *Phonetic Pronunciations*

Pinto, Dale A M BBus(Dist)(Curtin) P GradDipBus (Dist)(Curtin) MTax(Hons)(Syd) CPA FTIA FTMA AIMM AAANZ Senior Lecturer School of Business Law Curtin University of Technology *Superannuation, Taxation and Revenue*

Piotrowicz, Dr Ryszard LLB(Hons)(Dund) Dip Int Law-(Thess) PhD(Glasg) Dean and Senior Lecturer Faculty of Law University of Tasmania *Damages, Negligence, Tort*

Price, David C Dip Law BEc LLB(Hons) Solicitor of the Supreme Court of New South Wales, Mallesons Stephen Jaques *Criminal Law*

Poke, Ashley R BComm LLB Barrister and Solicitor of the Supreme Court of Victoria, Attorney and Counsellor-at-Law of the Supreme Court of the State of New York, Solicitor of the Supreme Court of England and Wales, Senior Associate Mallesons Stephen Jaques *Corporations*

Powers, Lindsay M BA LLM(Syd) Solicitor of the Supreme Court of New South Wales, Victoria, Queensland, Australian Capital Territory, and of the Federal and High Courts of Australia, Partner Minter Ellison *Bankruptcy*

Raff, Murray J BJuris LLB(Hons)(Mon) Barrister and Solicitor of the Supreme Court of Victoria, Lecturer in Property Law, and Environment and Planning Law, Faculty of Law University of Melbourne *Real Property*

Rahman, Wahida BComm LLB MComm(Rajshahi) LLM(Syd) Barrister of the Supreme Court of Bangladesh *Conflict of Laws, Succession*

Roberts, Susan Mary BA LLB(Hons)(ANU) Solicitor of the Supreme Court of New South Wales, Human Rights and Equal Opportunity Commission *Civil and Political Rights*

Robertson, Donald B BEc(Hons) LLB(Hons) LLM(Columbia U) Barrister and Solicitor of the Supreme Court of Victoria, Solicitor of the Supreme Court of New South Wales and Queensland, of the Federal and High Court of Australia, Partner Freehill Hollingdale & Page *Equity, Estoppel, Trade and Commerce, Trusts*

Rollinson, Michael LLB(Syd) Barrister of the Supreme Court of New South Wales *Contracts*

Rowland, Stuart BTh(SCD) BLitt(Melb) Barrister of the Supreme Courts of Victoria and Queensland *Religion*

Rowland, Tracey A BA(Hons) LLB(QLD) BLitt MA Dip Mod Lang(Melb) Commonwealth Scholar Gonville & Caius College Cambridge University *Administrative Law, Jurisprudence*

Rutgers, Danielle J BEc LLB(Macq) Officer Australian Competition and Consumer Commission *Sale of Goods, Trade and Commerce*

Sangha, Bibi BA(Law) LLM(Lon) Barrister of Lincoln's Inn and of the Australian Capital Territory, Advocate and Solicitor Malaysia, Lecturer in Law Flinders University *Contract, Partnerships and joint ventures, Voluntary Associations*

Shaflender, Leonid BBus LLB(UTS) *Entertainment, Sport and Tourism*

Shorten, Dr Ann R BA MEd(Melb) LLB(Hons) PhD-(Mon) Barrister and Solicitor of the Supreme Court of Victoria, Senior Lecturer in Education, Monash University *Education and Research*

Smith, Derek BA LLB(Syd) Solicitor of the Supreme Court of New South Wales, NSW Department of Community Services *Social Welfare*

Sourdin, Dr Tania M BA LLB(UNSW) LLM(UTS) PhD(UTS) Solicitor of the Supreme Court of New South Wales, Deputy Registrar Supreme Court of New South Wales *Courts and Judicial System*

Tehan, Maureen F BA LLM(Melb) LLB(Hons)(Mon) Barrister and Solicitor of the Supreme Courts of Victoria, South Australia, Western Australia, and the High Court of Australia, Legal Practitioner of the Supreme Court of the Northern Territory of Australia, Lecturer Faculty of Law University of Melbourne *Real Property*

Walker, Fiona C BA LLB(Syd) Enforcement Division Australian Competition and Consumer Commission *Sale of Goods, Trade and Commerce*

Waller, Kevin AM Barrister, Former State Coroner and Magistrate *Coroners*

Waye, Vicky LLM(Adel) Grad Dip Leg Prac Barrister and Solicitor of the Supreme Court of South Australia, and of the High Court of Australia, Senior Lecturer Faculty of Law University of Adelaide *Courts and Judicial System*

Webb, Rose BEc LLB(Hons)(ANU) LLM(Syd) Solicitor of the Supreme Court of New South Wales *Corporations*

Weerasooria, W S LLB(Hons) PhD(Lond) Associate Professor of Banking Law Monash University, Barrister and Solicitor of the Supreme Court of Victoria, Consultant Minter Ellison Melbourne *Banking and Finance*

West, Andrew BCom LLM(Qld) Barrister of the Supreme Court of Queensland and of the High Court of Australia *Aviation, Carriers, Highways, Roads and Bridges, Maritime Law, Transport*

Whelan, Mark A BA LLB Solicitor of the Supreme Court of New South Wales, Accredited Specialist Family Law and Personal Injury, Lecturer in Law University of Newcastle *Family Law*

Whelan, Jennifer L BA LLB(Syd) Solicitor of the Supreme Court of New South Wales, Human Rights and Equal Opportunity Commission *Civil and Political Rights*

Wright, David BComm LLB Enforcement Division, Australian Competition and Consumer Commission *Sale of Goods, Trade and Commerce*

Wyburn, Mary BA(NSW) LLB(Hons)(Syd) LLM(Lond) Solicitor of the Supreme Court of New South Wales and of the High Court of Australia, Lecturer Faculty of Economics University of Sydney *Intellectual Property*

Yallop, Associate Professor Colin L MA(Camb) PhD(Macq) School of English, Linguistics and Media Macquarie University *Phonetic Pronunciations*

Yen, Stephen BEc LLB(Syd) Barrister and Solicitor of the Supreme Court of the Australian Capital Territory *Family Law*

Yeng, Boh L BA LLB(UNSW) Solicitor of the Supreme Court of New South Wales *Betting, Gaming and Lotteries*

Butterworths Editorial

Managing Editor
Michael Horton BA LLB(UNSW)
Solicitor of the Supreme Court of New South Wales

Legal Editors

Linda Barach BA LLB(Macq)
Priscilla Brown LLB(Hons)(UTS)
Leanne Ho BA A Mus A LLB(Syd)
Susan Mary Hunt BA(UQ) LLB(ANU)
Solicitor of the Supreme Court of New South Wales

Wolfgang Laggner BA MTax(Melb)
Hajir Naghdy BSc
Matthew K P Olliffe BA LLB(UNSW)
Legal Practitioner of the Supreme Court of New South Wales

Editorial Research

Lara A Andreasen BA(Macq)
Brian Boys BA LLB(Macq)
Andrew M Brown
Connie Chen BCom LLB(Syd)
Judith Edwards BA(Qld) LLB(UNSW)
Enis Easaw-Mamutil BA LLB(Leicester)
Peter Galland BA LLB
Matthew Gayford BA(UNSW)
Sundip P Ghedia BA LLB(Macq)
Deepinderpal Kaur Grewal BComm(UNSW)

Juliette S Hromas BA LLB(Hons)
Solicitor of the Supreme Court of New South Wales
Simon Ioannou BEc(Hons)(Mon) DipComm(LIFS)
Stefan Lo BA LLB(Syd)
Sapna Malhotra
Damien MacRae BEc(UNSW)
Craig Pacey
Ros Parsons BA LLB(Macq)
Harjeet Rana
Daniel Sinclair
Boh Yeng BA LLB(UNSW)

Foreword

The rapid pace of change is possibly the greatest constant for the business community of the late 1990s. With change comes a rapid expansion in the words and phrases that are used to describe new concepts and refine existing ones. These terms need to be precisely understood by all to ensure that a common language is being used.

The *Butterworths Business and Law Dictionary* will be the the first port of call for anyone in business, commercial or corporate life wanting to understand the complex and diverse terminology used in business and the law. It will also be an invaluable shelf reference for company secretaries and others involved in corporate administration who are faced with meeting the rigorous demands of corporate compliance.

The main features of the Dictionary are its comprehensiveness, the clarity with which the terms are defined and its practical focus. Abundant case and statute references will also assist the reader who needs to have more than a quick answer.

The Dictionary covers company and commercial law, as well as banking and finance terms. Its scope is as wide as the practice of modern business and includes words and phrases in such diverse areas as accounting, economics, taxation, negotiable instruments, sale of goods and trade practices.

The editors and the many contributors are to be congratulated on the quality of this new Dictionary for which there is an acute need. Our Institute is proud to be associated with its publication.

Don Munro FCIS
President
Chartered Institute of Company Secretaries
   in Australia Ltd

Chartered Secretaries

Contents

Page

Contributors	v
Butterworths Editorial	xi
Foreword	xiii
Contents	xv
Series Preface	xvi
Preface	xvii
International Phonetic Alphabet Symbols for Australian English	xix
How to Use	xx
Table of Abbreviations	xxv
Definitions	1
Appendixes	475
A — International Currency Units	475
B — Currencies traded by Australian banks	481
C — World Central Banks	482
D — World Stock Exchanges	487
E — Australian Stock Exchange Addresses	490
F — Recognised Futures Exchanges	491
G — Australian Prime Ministers	492
H — Australian Federal Treasurers	493
I — Reserve Bank Governors	494

Series Preface

Butterworths Specialist Dictionaries are a series of dictionaries designed to provide professionals, legal practitioners, students, and other interested readers, with easy-to-use reference works for words and phrases in their specific fields.

Each Specialist Dictionary is drawn from a central database of legal and professional terms. The database has been compiled from contributions by more than 120 experts from diverse backgrounds. It has been supervised by ourselves as General Editors and our 11 specialist Consultant Editors. Currently the database contains approximately 22 megabytes of information. It is available as a continually growing subscription service called *Butterworths Encyclopaedic Australian Legal Dictionary*, updated monthly on Butterworths Online. It is also available on the *Australian Legal Research Library CD-Rom*.

Law is often complex and its terminology confusing. A knowledge of legal words and phrases is essential to an understanding of how law affects life. Butterworths Specialist Dictionaries are designed to illuminate those words and phrases in each main area of contemporary law.

Peter Nygh   **Peter Butt**

May 1997

Preface

Butterworths Business and Law Dictionary gives definitions of words and phrases used in the Australian business and commercial context. It is one of a series of Specialist Dictionaries, designed to serve both the non-legally trained professional who needs to know something of the law in his or her field, and the legal practitioner who needs to know something of the unique language used in that field.

Major changes have occurred in the last 20 years in the business and commercial environment, and the dictionary takes into account words that have arisen as a result of financial and business deregulation. Important reports such as the Hilmer Report into national competition policy and the Wallis Inquiry into the banking and finance industry, the recommendations of which were handed down in April this year, will continue to reshape our commercial world.

Technological developments have led to the globalisation of commerce. Computer technology destroys geographical boundaries, and any work wanting to deal seriously with modern business must have an eye to the global environment.

While the drafting and compilation of the terms was a cooperative effort from all our contributors, the Honourable Mr Justice Ipp supervised the company law terms, and Associate Professor Weerasooria supervised the banking and financial terms.

The entries have been selected and structured to reflect the various strategies and policies that businesses pursue to achieve their objectives. It contains the nuts and bolts of business practice, the concepts, techniques, and methods used in business, marketing, finance, production, and personnel, and the industrial, economic, and banking environment of business. Extensive cross referencing and abbreviations of terms adds to its value as a reference guide.

The Honourable Mr Justice Ipp   **Associate Professor W S Weerasooria**

May 1997

International Phonetic Alphabet Symbols for Australian English

(a) Vowels

i as in 'peat'	/pit/	ɔ as in 'port'	/pɔt/
ɪ as in 'pit'	/pɪt/	ʊ as in 'put'	/pʊt/
ɛ as in 'pet'	/pɛt/	u as in 'pool'	/pul/
æ as in 'pat'	/pæt/	ɜ as in 'pert'	/pɜt/
a as in 'part'	/pat/	ə as in 'apart'	/ə'pat/
ɒ as in 'pot'	/pɒt/	y as in French 'rue'	/ry/
ʌ as in 'but'	/bʌt/		

(b) Diphthongs

aɪ as in 'buy'	/baɪ/	oʊ as in 'hoe'	/hoʊ/
eɪ as in 'bay'	/beɪ/	ɪə as in 'here'	/hɪə/
ɔɪ as in 'boy'	/bɔɪ/	ɛə as in 'hair'	/hɛə/
aʊ as in 'how'	/haʊ/	ʊə as in 'tour'	/tʊə/

(c) Consonants

(i) Plosives

		(iii) Affricatives	
p as in 'pet'	/pɛt/	tʃ as in 'choke'	/tʃoʊk/
b as in 'bet'	/bɛt/	dʒ as in 'joke'	/dʒoʊk/
t as in 'tale'	/teɪl/	*(iv) Nasals*	
d as in 'dale'	/deɪl/	m as in 'mile'	/maɪl/
k as in 'came'	/keɪm/	n as in 'neat'	/nit/
g as in 'game'	/geɪm/	ŋ as in 'sing'	/sɪŋ/

(ii) Fricatives

		(v) Semi-vowels	
f as in 'fine'	/faɪn/	j as in 'you'	/ju/
v as in 'vine'	/vaɪn/	w as in 'woo'	/wu/
θ as in 'thin'	/θɪn/	*(vi) Laterals*	
ð as in 'then'	/ðɛn/	l as in 'last'	/last/
s as in 'seal'	/sil/		
z as in 'zeal'	/zil/		
ʃ as in 'show'	/ʃoʊ/		
ʒ as in 'measure'	/mɛʒə/		
h as in 'heat'	/hit/		
r as in 'rain'	/reɪn/		

(d) Stress

' as in 'clatter'	/'klætə/
ˌ as in 'multimillionaire'	/ˌmʌltimɪljə'nɛə/

Reproduced with kind permission from the Macquarie Dictionary

© Butterworths

How to Use

This key relates to the sample Dictionary entries on the following page.

1. **Also known as** — provides synonymous terms. In this example the term '**Holder of a bill**' is indicated as being synonymous with '**bearer of a bill**'.
2. **See also reference** — refers to another term that provides further information in relation to the term.
3. **Lat** — denotes that the term is Latin or of Latin derivation. The following abbreviations indicate derivation of a term from other languages:

Aborig	Aboriginal	LF	Law French
AF	Anglo-French	OE	Old English
Ar	Arabic	OF	Old French
Fr	French	ON	Old Norse
German	German	Scand	Scandinavian
Gk	Greek	Sp	Spanish
Heb	Hebrew	Welsh	Welsh
It	Italian		

4. **Numbered definitions** — where there are a number of general definitions of a term, these are numbered. In this example, there are three general definitions.
5. **Legislative authority** — where appropriate, terms are supported by authority and, where it exists, the authority is Australian. In this example, the (CTH) Bills of Exchange Act 1909 s 48(1) is authority for the definition.
6. **Context statement** — where a definition relates to a particular area of the law its context is indicated by an italicised statement (in this example the context is '*Courts and judicial system*'). The Butterworths subject classification (which appears in *Halsbury's Laws of Australia* and *Australian Current Law*) is used for the Dictionary. The Butterworths subject classification is reproduced on page xxii.
7. **See reference** — where the full definition of a term is found under another term a see reference is provided, cross referencing to that term. In this example the definition is found under '**Tacking**'.
8. **Bullet point** — a cross reference to Butterworths *Australian Legal Words and Phrases* is indicated by a bullet point ('•'). *Australian Legal Words and Phrases* provides an index to over 100,000 words and phrases from case law and legislation. In many instances, it is impossible to provide within the Dictionary the full set of statutory references for a term across the jurisdictions. This link to *Australian Legal Words and Phrases* allows users to find legislative and judicial definitions across all jurisdictions where they exist. In this example the bullet point indicates that the word '**Horticulture**' is found in *Australian Legal Words and Phrases*. This phrase is located on pages 156-7 of *Australian Legal Words and Phrases*. Page 157 is reproduced on page xxiii.
9. **Judicial authority** — where appropriate, terms are supported by authority and, where it exists, the authority is Australian. In this example, the case *Griffiths v Kerkemeyer* (1977) CLR 161; 15 ALR 387 is authority for the definition.
10. **Definitional sentence** — the first sentence of each term is the definitional sentence. This sentence captures the general meaning of the term.
11. **Phonetic fonts** — phonetic characters are provided that indicate the pronunciations of Latin terms. For an explanation of how these phonetic pronunciations operate see the 'International Phonetic Alphabet Symbols for Australian English' on page xix.

© Butterworths

How to Use

The following extract is illustrative only, designed to give samples of the type of information and what it denotes.

Butterworths Business and Law Dictionary   Hos

Holder of a bill The payee or indorsee of a bill who is in possession of it or, in the case of a bill which is payable to bearer, the bearer of it: (CTH) Bills of Exchange Act 1909 s 4. A bearer is a person in possession of a bill which is payable to bearer: s 4. The holder of a bill, who has a right to sue, may sue in that person's own name: s 43(1)(a); *Stock Motor Ploughs Ltd v Forsyth* (1932) 32 SR (NSW) 259 at 262; 49 WN(NSW) 61. Also known as 'bearer of a bill'. See also **Holder; Holder for value; Holder in due course.**

Honorary consul A resident citizen of a host state who administers the daily functions of a consulate together with his or her own private business. Except in relation to arrest and detention, an honorary consul enjoys the same freedom of communication and movement, and the same degree of judicial immunity as a career consul. See also **Consul; Consular immunity.**

Honorary degree A degree granted by a university in the exercise of its powers to admit persons to degrees without examination: for example (VIC) Monash University Act 1958 s 23(2)(b). See also **Honoris causa.**

Honoris causa /ɒnɔrɪs kaʊsa/ *Lat* – in order to show esteem and respect. The granting of an honorary degree by a university to a distinguished scholar or public figure. See also **Honorary degree.**

Honour 1. An historical term synonymous with **feodum.** 2. A courtesy title given to judges, legislators and ministers 3. Acceptance of a bill of exchange for payment.

Bills of exchange and other negotiable instruments The act of the drawee accepting a bill which has been presented to him or her for acceptance or the act of the drawee or the acceptor paying the amount due on a bill which has been presented by the holder of it for payment. Non-acceptance of a bill presented for acceptance is known as 'dishonour by non-acceptance': (CTH) Bills of Exchange Act 1909 s 48(1). See also **Dishonour by non-acceptance; Presentation for acceptance; Presentation for payment.**

Courts and judicial system A title of courtesy given to judges, legislators and ministers as in 'His or Her Honour', 'Your Honour' or 'The Honourable Justice'. In court the judge should always be addressed as 'Your Honour'. Out of court the judge may be addressed as 'Judge' or in the case of the Chief Justice, 'Chief'. See also **Worship.**

Legal history A group of holdings in medieval times, forming a large estate under one lord who held directly from the king. The term is used in the Domesday book, often interchangeably with feodum. See also **Feodum.**

Honour clause A clause that declares that an agreement is not to be legally binding, with the result that the agreement is binding in honour only: for example *Rose and Frank Co v J R Crompton & Bros Ltd* [1923] 2 KB 261. An honour clause indicates that the mutual intention of the parties was not to enter contractual relations. See also **Contract; Expressed intention; Intention; Term.**

Hopkinson v Rolt, rule in See Tacking.

Horizontal arrangement In competition law, an arrangement entered into by corporations on the same functional level in a distribution chain. It is contrasted with a vertical arrangement. See also **Arrangement; Competition; Vertical arrangement.**

Horticulture See Agriculture

Hospital expenses Reasonable costs incurred as a consequence of spending time in hospital. In negligence law, a plaintiff who has suffered personal injuries requiring care in hospital has a right to recover damages for reasonable expenses thus incurred, including medical, hospital and nursing care. The amount recoverable may depend on whether the plaintiff's expenses are to some extent defrayed by care in an institution requiring less or no outlay from the plaintiff: *Griffiths v Kerkemeyer* (1977) 139 CLR 161; 15 ALR 387. The expenses recoverable may affect entitlement to Commonwealth benefits: for example (CTH) Health Insurance Act 1973 s 18. See also **Damages recoverable.**

Hospital order An order requiring a person suffering from a mental illness, psychopathic disorder, subnormality, or severe subnormality, and who has been convicted of an offence, to be detained in a hospital for medical treatment. Examples are orders made under (CTH) Crimes Act 1914 s 20BS and (TAS) Mental Health Act 1963 s 48(1) authorising the detention of a person in an institution. See also **Detention; Orders for detention.**

Hospitium /hɒspɪʃɪʊm/ *Lat* – hospitality; the relationship between a host and his or her guest. An inn or guest-house. An innkeeper is strictly liable for damage caused to the goods of a traveller in the hospitium of the inn: *Williams v Linnit*; *Irving v Heferen* [1995] 1 Qd R 255. See also **Guest; Inn; Innkeeper; Innkeeper's liability.**

Hostage taking Seizing or threatening a person in order to put pressure on a third person to act in a particular manner: International Convention Against the Taking of Hostages 1979 art 1.

Conflict of laws Any state may detain and prosecute an alleged offender on its territory, regardless of the locality of the hostage taking, on the basis that it is a *delicta jurius gentium* (a crime against all humanity) and thus a crime of universal jurisdiction: *United States v Yunis* 681 F Supp 896 (1988). See also **Hijacking; Terrorism; Universal jurisdiction.**

Hostes humani generis /hɒsteɪz hʊmani dʒɛnərɪs/ *Lat* – enemies of the human race. See also **Pirate; Jurisdiction.**

Hostile intent The mental element which may render an otherwise innocent act criminal or tortious. In

Butterworths Subject Classification

Aboriginals and Torres Strait Islanders
Administrative law
Agency
Animals
Arbitration
Auction
Aviation
Bailment
Banking and finance
Bankruptcy
Betting, gaming and lotteries
Bills of exchange and other negotiable instruments
Building and construction
Carriers
Charities
Citizenship and migration
Civil and political rights
Conflict of laws
Constitutional law
Consumer credit
Consumer protection
Contempt
Contract
Coroners
Corporations
Courts and judicial system
Criminal law
Damages
Deeds and other instruments
Defamation
Defence
Dependencies
Education and research
Employment
Energy and resources
Entertainment, sport and tourism
Environment
Equity
Estoppel
Evidence
Family law
Foreign relations
Guarantees and indemnities
Highways, roads and bridges

Industrial law
Insurance
Intellectual property
Leases and tenancies
Legal practitioners
Limitation of actions
Liquor
Local government
Maritime law
Media and communications
Medicine
Mental health
Mortgages and securities
Negligence
Partnerships and joint ventures
Perpetuities and accumulations
Personal property
Police and emergency services
Practice and procedure
Primary industry
Prisons
Product liability
Professions and trades
Public administration
Public health
Real property
Receivers
Religion
Restitution
Sale of goods
Social welfare and services
Statutes
Succession
Superannuation
Taxation and revenue
Time
Tort
Trade and commerce
Transport
Trusts
Voluntary associations
Water
Weapons and dangerous goods
Weights and measures
Workers' compensation

Horticulture — (NSW) Local Government Act 1919 s 118 — *Blacktown City Council v Grah* (1990) 69 LGRA 303
Horticulture — (NSW) Local Government Act 1919 s 514A — *Wym Pty Ltd v Sutherland Shire Council* (1990) 69 LGRA 322
Horticulture — (SA) Development Control Regulations 1982 reg 4
Hortizontal single spindle disc grinder — (TAS) Industrial Safety, Health, and Welfare (Administrative and General) Regulations 1979 reg 15
Hose dispensing unit — (NSW) Consumer Protection (Safer Goods) Regulation 1976 cl 66
Hospital — (ACT) Drugs of Dependence Act 1989 s 3
Hospital — (ACT) Inebriates Act 1900 (NSW) s 2A
Hospital — (ACT) Medical Services (Fees) Act 1984 s 2
Hospital — (ACT) Stamp Duties and Taxes Act 1987 s 4
Hospital — (ACT) Workmen's Compensation Ordinance 1951 s 6(1) — *Tanner v Marquis Jackson* (1974) 3 ACTR 32
Hospital — (CTH) Health Insurance Act 1973 s 3
Hospital — (CTH) National Health Act 1953 ss 67, 84
Hospital — (CTH) Racial Discrimination Act 1975 s 3
Hospital — (CTH) Superannuation (Salary) Regulations
Hospital (planning scheme) — *Dilettoso v Watson* (1984) 54 LGRA 31
Hospital (will) — *Executor Trustee and Agency Co (SA) Ltd v Warbey* [1971] SASR 255
Hospital (drug rehabilitation centre under planning scheme) — *Franceschini v Melbourne & Metropolitan Board of Works* (1980) 57 LGRA 284
Hospital (retirement village) — *Ku-ring-gai Municipal Council v Geoffrey Twibill & Associates* (1979) 39 LGRA 154
Hospital (planning scheme) — *Ku-ring-gai Old People's Welfare Co Ltd v Ku-ring-gai Municipal Council* [1976] 2 NSWLR 232
Hospital (home for aged persons) — *Ku-ring-gai Old People's Welfare Co Ltd v Ku-ring-gai Municipal Council* (1976) 34 LGRA 363
Hospital — (NSW) Adoption Information Act 1990 s 4
Hospital — (NSW) Anatomy Act 1977 s 4(1)
Hospital — (NSW) Human Tissue Act 1983 s 4
Hospital — (NSW) Inebriates Act 1912 s 9(3)
Hospital — (NSW) Marine (Boating Safety — Alcohol and Drugs) Act 1991 s 3(1)
Hospital — (NSW) Mental Health Act 1990 s 3
Hospital — (NSW) Motor Vehicles (Third Party Insurance) Act 1942 s 24(1)
Hospital — (NSW) Public Hospitals Act 1929 s 3
Hospital — (NSW) Summary Offences Act 1988 s 3(1)
Hospital — (NSW) Traffic Act 1909 s 2
Hospital — (NT) Community Welfare Act 1983 s 4
Hospital — (NT) Hospital Management Boards Act 1980 s 4
Hospital — (NT) Medical Services Act 1982 s 5
Hospital — (NT) Mental Health Act 1980 s 4
Hospital — (NT) Poisons and Dangerous Drugs Act 1983 s 6
Hospital — (QLD) Health Act 1937 s 5
Hospital — (QLD) Hospitals Foundation Act 1982 s 4
Hospital — (QLD) Mental Health Services Act 1974 s 5(1)
Hospital — (QLD) Transplantation and Anatomy Act 1979 s 4(1)
Hospital — (SA) Development Control Regulations 1982 reg 4
Hospital — (SA) Hospitals Act 1934 s 49
Hospital (rateable property) — (SA) Local Government Act 1934 s 5 — *Helping Hand Centre Inc v City of Adelaide* (1971) 1 SASR 470
Hospital (planning scheme) — (SA) Planning Act 1982 s 47(5) — *Dilettoso v Watson* (1984) 36 SASR 272
Hospital — (SA) Sexual Reassignment Act 1988 s 3
Hospital — (SA) South Australian Health Commission Act 1976 ss 6, 44

Table of Abbreviations

A'asia	Australasia
AAT	Administrative Appeals Tribunal
ABC	Australian Broadcasting Corporation
ABT	Australian Broadcasting Tribunal
ACT	Australian Capital Territory
Adv Op	Advisory Opinion
AF	Anglo-French
AG	Aktiengesellschaft
A-G(Cth)	Attorney-General (Commonwealth)
A-G(Qld)	Attorney-General (State)
AIRC	Australian Industrial Relations Commission
ALRC	Australian Law Reform Commission Discussion Papers
am	amended
am	ante meridiem
AMAA	Australian Media Accreditation Authority
Antn	Annotation
ANZ Banking Group Ltd	Australia and New Zealand Banking Group Limited
AO	Adults only
App	Appendix
apptd	appointed
Ar	Arabic
art	Article
ASC	Australian Securities Commission
Assn	Association
Assoc	Associate
Aust	Australia
Aust TS	Australian Treaty Series
AUSTEL	Australian Telecommunications Authority
BC	Borough Council
BFSP	British Foreign State Papers
BHP Co Ltd	Broken Hill Proprietary Company Limited
BR	Business Rule
Bros	Brothers
C	United Kingdom Command Papers to 1900
CA	Court of Appeal (UK)
CA(Vic)	Court of Appeal (jurisdiction follows)
CC	County Council
CC	County Court
CC(Vic)	County Court of Victoria
CCA(NSW)	Court of Criminal Appeal (jurisdiction follows)
CCR	Court for the consideration of Crown Cases Reserved
Cd	United Kingdom Command Papers 1900-1918

© Butterworths

Ch	Chancery Court or Division
ch	chapter
CIM(NSW)	Chief Industrial Magistrate's Court of New South Wales
cl	clause
Cmd	United Kingdom Command Papers 1919-1956
Cmnd	United Kingdom Command Papers 1957-current
Cmr	Commissioner
Co	Company
controller apptd	Controller appointed
Co-op	Co-operative
C of Petty Sessions	Court of Petty Sessions
Corp	Corporation
Ct of Sess	Court of Sessions
Cth	Commonwealth
CTS	Children's Television Standards
CTV	Cable Television
DC	District Court (jurisdiction follows)
DC(US)	United States District Court
DCT	Deputy Commissioner of Taxation
dec'd	deceased
def	definition
Dept	Department
DFDAT	Defence Force Discipline Appeal Tribunal
D-G	Director-General
Div	Division
Div Ct	Divisional Court
DPP(NSW)	Director of Public Prosecutions (jurisdiction follows)
ECOSOC Res	ECOSOC Resolution
ed	edition
EOC	Equal Opportunity Commission
Eq	Equity Court or Division
ERC(Vic)	Employee Relations Commission of Victoria
ERDC(SA)	Environment Resources and Development Court of South Australia
ex	Example
Ex	Exemption
Ex	Exhibit
Exch	Exchequer Court or Division
Ex rel	ex relatione
f	folio
FACTS	Federation of Australian Commercial Television Stations
Fam C of A	Family Court of Australia
Fam C of WA	Family Court of Western Australia
FARB	Federation of Australian Radio Broadcasters
FCT	Federal Commissioner of Taxation
Fed	Federation
Fed C of A	Federal Court

Table of Abbreviations

Fed C of Bkty	Federal Court of Bankruptcy
Fed C of Canada	Federal Court of Canada
fig	figure
FR	Federal Court Rule
Fr	French
G	German
GA Res	Resolution of United Nations General Assembly
Gaz	Gazette
GIO(NSW)	Government Insurance Office (jurisdiction follows)
Govt	Government
Gk	Greek
HC of A	High Court of Australia
HC(UK)	High Court of the United Kingdom
Heb	Hebrew
HL	House of Lords
HREOC	Human Rights and Equal Opportunity Commission
IAC of WA	Industrial Appeal Court of Western Australia
IC of NSW	Industrial Court of New South Wales
IC of Qld	Industrial Court of Queensland
IC of SA	Industrial Court of South Australia
IC(SA)	Industrial Commission of South Australia
IC(Tas)	Industrial Commission of Tasmania
id	the same
ILO	International Labour Organisation
IMP	Imperial
(in liq)	in liquidation
Inc	Incorporated
(in prov liq)	in provisional liquidation
Insp	Inspector
insrt	inserted
Int	International
(in vol liq)	in voluntary liquidation
IRC	Commissioner of Inland Revenue (UK)
IRC(NSW)	Industrial Relations Commission of New South Wales
IRC of A	Industrial Relations Court of Australia
IRC of SA	Industrial Relations Court of South Australia
IRC(Qld)	Industrial Relations Commission of Queensland
IRC(SA)	Industrial Relations Commission of South Australia
IRC(Vic)	Industrial Relations Commission of Victoria
IRT	Immigration Review Tribunal
It	Italian
KB	King's Bench Court or Division
Lat	Latin
LEC(NSW)	Land and Environment Court of New South Wales
LF	Law French
LNTS	League of Nations Treaty Series
Loc Ct	Local Court

© Butterworths

Loc Govt Ct	Local Government Court
LR	Listing Rule(s)
Ltd	Limited
LVC(NSW)	Land and Valuation Court of New South Wales
Mag Ct	Magistrate's Court
MC	Municipal Council
MCA	Media Council of Australia
Mfg	Manufacturing
Minister for	Minister of State for...
ms	manuscript(s)
MV	Motor Vessel
NB	take careful note
NCSC	National Companies & Securities Commission
NL	no liability
No	number
NSW	New South Wales
NT	Northern Territory
NZ	New Zealand
O	Order
OE	Old English
OF	Old French
OL	Outline
ON	Old Norse
op cit	in the work cited
Ord	Ordinance(s)
OTC	Overseas Telecommunications Commission
p	page
para	paragraph
PC	Judicial Committee of the Privy Council
PEC(Qld)	Planning and Environment Court of Queensland
PGR	Parental guidance recommended
Plc	Public Limited Company
pm	post meridiem
Pr	Precedent
Pt	Part
Pte	Private
Pty	Proprietary
Pty Ltd	Proprietary Limited
QB	Queen's Bench Court or Division
QGIG	Queensland Government Industrial Gazette
Qld	Queensland
R	Rex, Regina, The King, The Queen
r	rule
receiver and manager apptd	receiver and manager appointed
reg'd	registered
reg(s)	regulation(s)
Repat	Repatriation

xxviii

Table of Abbreviations

Rly	Railway
RMPAT(Tas)	Resource Management and Planning Appeal Tribunal of Tasmania
s	section
SA	South Australia
SBS	Special Broadcasting Service
Scand	Scandinavian
Sch	Schedule
SCR	Supreme Court Rule
SC Res	Resolution of United Nations Security Council
SC(Tas)	Supreme Court (jurisdiction follows)
SC(US)	United States Supreme Court
Sp	Spanish
SPS	Satellite Program Services
SR	Statutory Rule(s)
SS	Steamship
SSAT	Social Security Appeals Tribunal
Stat	United States Statutes at Large
subcl	subclause(s)
Subdiv	Subdivision(s)
subpara	subparagraph(s)
subs	subsection(s)
subs	substituted
TAC	Television Advertising Conditions
t/as	trading as
Tas	Tasmania
TPAT(WA)	Town Planning Appeals Tribunal of Western Australia
TPC	Trade Practices Commission
TPS	Television Program Standards
TPT	Trade Practices Tribunal
UDC	Urban District Council
UK	United Kingdom
UKTS	United Kingdom Treaty Series
Uni	University
unrptd	unreported
UNTS	United Nations Treaty Series
US	United States
USA	United States of America
VAES	Video and Audia Entertainment Information Services
VAS	Value Added Services
Vic	Victoria
vol	volume(s)
vol admin apptd	voluntary administrator appointed
WA	Western Australia

A

A1 An expression used in a general sense meaning excellent or physically fit. It is derived from Lloyd's Register of British and Foreign Shipping which awarded varying classification marks to vessels listed in the register.

AAA 1. Affirmative Action Agency. 2. A triple-A credit-rating in respect of the creditworthiness and reliability of a corporation, financial institution, government or country. It is the top rating given by all major rating agencies. See also **Affirmative action program**; **Bond rating agencies**.

AARF See **Australian Accounting Research Foundation**.

AAS See **Accounting Standards**.

AASB See **Australian Accounting Standards Board**.

•**AAT** See **Administrative Appeals Tribunal**.

AB See **Aktiebolag**.

Ab initio /æb ɪnɪʃioʊ/ *Lat* – from the beginning. For example, the term is used to describe contracts which are null and void from the beginning, as distinct from those which are voidable. See also **Null and void**; **Void**; **Void ab initio**.

•**Abandonment** The action or process of surrendering, forsaking, giving up completely or finally, or leaving something or someone unprotected.

Contract The relinquishment or discharge of a contract by giving up one's rights in it: *DTR Nominees Pty Ltd v Mona Homes Pty Ltd* (1978) 138 CLR 423; 19 ALR 223. See also **Delay**; **Discharge**; **Estoppel**.

Courts The relinquishment of an interest or claim. Abandonment of action occurs when proceedings are ceased or when an appeal is withdrawn: (NSW) Supreme Court Rules Pt 51 r 5(5).

Maritime law The complete relinquishment of an interest, claim, or thing. 1. In marine insurance, the right of an assured to completely relinquish his or her right to the insured object and treat the loss as if it were an actual total loss: (CTH) Marine Insurance Act 1909 s 69. 2. In maritime law, the breaking of a voyage in order to carry out repairs. See also **Assured**.

Abatement A reduction; diminution; decrease.

Equity A reduction; a diminution. For example, if the fund out of which a general legacy is payable is insufficient, the legacy will reduce ('abate') rateably, in accordance with the equitable maxim 'equality is equity': *Re Farmer* [1939] Ch 573. See also **Equitable compensation**; **Specific performance**.

Real property 1. Reduction *pro rata* of a charge or rent in response to altered or diminished use and enjoyment of a right or premises. 2. The exercise of a self-help remedy when hindered in the use or exercise of a *profit*

à prendre or easement. See also **Easement**.

Tort Prevention, reduction, elimination, or control. For example, control by a method designed to minimise the effects of noise: (QLD) Noise Abatement Act 1978 s 6(1).

Abatement of purchase money A deduction made from an amount due under a contract of sale, whether by way of a discount for prompt payment of the purchase price or as compensation where the goods supplied are not of the warranted quality or description: for example *Mondel v Steel* (1841) 8 M & W 858; 151 ER 1288. Once a party has obtained an abatement of purchase-money for breach of contract, he or she is precluded from bringing an action to recover damages in respect of that breach: *Mondel v Steel*. See also **Abatement**; **Discount**.

•**Ability** Skills, aptitude, qualifications, or experience, or any combination of these: (CTH) Public Service Act 1922 s 82(1). See also **Merit**.

Abnormal hazard In an insurance contract for a flying club, an expression comprising two words in common use in the English language that is to be given its ordinary meaning and not read down by attempting to form a class with the list of words preceding it. Flying at a low altitude in contravention of the (CTH) Air Navigation Regulations and level with cliff tops involves abnormal hazards: *McLean v McLean*; *Australian Aviation Underwriting Pool* (1977) 15 SASR 306.

Abnormal income amount The amount of assessable income of certain taxpayers, such as authors, inventors, and entertainers, which is subject to concessional taxation by way of averaging under (CTH) Income Tax Assessment Act 1936 Div 16A. See also **Assessable income**; **Average income**.

Abnormal item In the formulation of profit and loss accounts for a particular period, an item which is included in operating profit or loss, but which is considered abnormal by reason of its size and effect on results: Applicable Accounting Standard AASB 1018. Abnormal items are incurred outside normal operations and are not of a recurring nature. For example, the sale or abandonment of a key business or the condemnation, expropriation or destruction of company property may give rise to an abnormal item on the profit-loss account.

Abnormal loss Waste, spoilage, or shrinkage beyond the normal rate for the company, capable of being reduced or eliminated by improving the efficiency of the company's operations. See also **Abnormal item**; **Abnormal profit**.

Abnormal profit Profits arising from items which, by reason of their size or effect on the item, are abnormal. The profit and loss statement of a company may show 'operating profit and loss before abnormal items' and then subtract 'abnormal items' as a separate line. This is

© Butterworths

required by Applicable Accounting Standard AASB 1018, but not by Corporations Regulations Sch 5 cl 6(1). See also **Abnormal item**.

Abnormal return Income from an investment which is larger than would otherwise be expected in that industry.

Aboriginal and Torres Strait Islander Commercial Development Corporation A statutory body corporate established to assist and enhance Aboriginal and Torres Strait Islander self-management and economic self-sufficiency, and to advance the commercial and economic interests of Aboriginal people and Torres Strait Islanders: (CTH) Aboriginal and Torres Strait Islander Commission Act 1989 s 145. See also **Aboriginal person**; **Aboriginal and Torres Strait Islander Commission**.

Aboriginal and Torres Strait Islander Commission *Abbr* – ATSIC A Commonwealth statutory corporation that functions to formulate, implement, and monitor the effectiveness of government programs for Aboriginal people and Torres Strait Islanders. See also **Aboriginal person**.

•**Aboriginal land 1.** Land held by an Aboriginal land trust for an estate in fee simple, or land the subject of a deed of grant in trust held in escrow by an Aboriginal land council: (CTH) Aboriginal Land Rights (Northern Territory) Act 1976 s 3. **2.** Land transferred under the (QLD) Aboriginal Land Act 1991 for the benefit of Aboriginal people without a land claim being made under the Act, or land claimed and granted under the Act to a group of Aboriginal people. See also **Aboriginal lease**.

Aboriginal land rights Statutory title to land granted to Aboriginal groups by legislation. Aboriginal people are entitled to land rights when they have common spiritual affiliations to a site on the land, being affiliations that place the group under a primary spiritual responsibility for that site and the land, and are entitled by Aboriginal tradition to forage as of right over the land (for example (CTH) Aboriginal Land Rights (Northern Territory) Act 1976 s 3(1); *Northern Land Council v Commonwealth* (1986) 161 CLR 1; 64 ALR 493) or when land is claimable crown land (for example (NSW) Aboriginal Land Rights Act 1983 s 36(1); *Darkingung Local Aboriginal Land Council v Minister for Natural Resources* [1985] 1 NSWLR 104; (1985) 58 LGRA 298). See also **Native title**.

•**Aboriginal lease** A lease in perpetuity, or for a specified term of years, granted to a group of Aboriginal people under (QLD) Aboriginal Land Act 1991 ss 60, 64. See also **Aboriginal person**.

•**Aboriginal person** In legislation, a member of the Aboriginal race of Australia (for example (CTH) Aboriginal and Torres Strait Islander Heritage Protection Act 1984 s 3); or a descendant of an indigenous inhabitant of Australia; or a person who identifies as an Aboriginal person and is accepted by the Aboriginal community as an Aboriginal person.

Aboriginal title See **Native title**.

•**Aborigine** See **Aboriginal person**.

Abortive company An attempt to float a company by offering its shares to the public which fails because the minimum number of shares are not subscribed for. See also **Minimum subscription**.

Above and below the line A phrase descriptive of financial transactions in the annual Budget Statement given by the Australian Federal Treasurer. Above the line transactions comprise outlays and revenues, the difference between which is the budget balance, by way of surplus or deficit. Below the line transactions are those undertaken to utilise a surplus or finance a deficit. See also **Budget**.

Above par A market price that is higher than its face value, especially in relation to shares, debentures, and other company securities. See also **Share price index**.

•**Abridged financial information** Information derived from the accounts of a multi-member superannuation fund, and in a form prescribed under (CTH) Occupational Superannuation Standards Regulations reg 18H. Abridged financial information may need to be included in the information that a superannuation fund may need to provide to its members under Pt II Div 2. See also **Superannuation fund**.

•**Abrogate** To annul, cancel, or repeal. For example, rights, duties, and obligations may be abrogated by legislation.

Absence of intention to benefit In restitution, the state of mind of a person who provides an enrichment to another but has no intention to benefit the recipient, such as where the provider is unaware of the transfer, is aware but powerless to prevent the transfer, is incapable of forming the intention to transfer, or has positively decided that the recipient should not enjoy the benefit of the property transferred. It may provide a justification for restitution of the enrichment: for example *Australia and New Zealand Banking Group Ltd v Westpac Banking Corp* (1988) 164 CLR 662; 78 ALR 157. See also **Restitution**.

•**Absent from duty** The state of being away from or not attending a duty, or of refusing to perform or complete a duty.

Employment The status of an employee who physically attends work but refuses to perform all or a significant part of his or her duties. See also **Award**; **Part performance**.

•**Absolute** Complete; unconditional. See also **Absolute assignment**.

Absolute acceptance In contract law, unequivocal acceptance of all the terms of an offer. Absolute acceptance is required before a binding contract can be formed: *Appleby v Johnson* (1874) LR 9 CP 158. See also **Acceptance**; **Contract**; **Conditional acceptance**; **Offer**; **Terms and conditions**.

Absolute assignment An assignment of the whole of a debt or other legal chose in action to an assignee. An absolute assignment by writing of any debt or chose in action (of which express notice has been given to the debtor) transfers to the assignee all legal rights and remedies in relation to the chose in action assigned:

(NSW) Conveyancing Act 1919 s 12; (VIC) Property Law Act 1958 s 134. See also **Assignment**; **Chose in action**.

Absolute bill of sale A common law conveyance of a chattel given otherwise than as security for the payment of money. Ownership does not revert to the grantor: *Swift v Pannell* (1883) 24 Ch D 210; *Malick v Lloyd (Official Assignee)* (1913) 16 CLR 483; 30 WN (NSW) 104. See also **Bill of sale**.

Absolute gift A complete and unconditional gift good against the whole world.

Absolute liability Legal responsibility for a breach of law, not dependent on any particular state of mind, and for which no defence is available except act of God. By comparison strict liability allows the defence of honest and reasonable mistake. *Goodes v General Motors Holdens' Pty Ltd* [1972] VR 386; (1970) 27 LGRA 287. See also **Strict liability**.

Absolute obligation A promise that the promisor must perform notwithstanding some frustrating event. If performance of that obligation is impossible, the promisor must pay damages for breach of contract: *Taylor v Caldwell* (1863) 3 B & S 826; 122 ER 309. See also **Dependent obligation**; **Frustrating event**; **Frustration**.

•**Absolutely free** In the context of the constitutional requirement that interstate trade and commerce shall be absolutely free, trade and commerce that is free from interstate discriminatory burdens of a protectionist kind: Commonwealth Constitution s 92; *Cole v Whitfield* (1988) 165 CLR 360; 78 ALR 42. See also **Freedom of interstate trade, commerce and intercourse**; **Interstate trade and commerce**; **Trade**; **Trade and commerce**.

Absorption costing A method of valuing manufactured trading stock under (CTH) Income Tax Assessment Act 1936 s 31(1) that includes (absorbs) into the cost of stock material and direct labour costs, fixed and variable production overheads, and ancillary costs such as advertising, sales, and general administrative costs. See also **Common cost**; **Trading stock**.

Abuse of power Generally, the misuse or improper exercise of a power.

Administrative law The exercise by an administrator of a discretionary power conferred by statute so as to exceed the scope of the power conferred. The types of abuse of power include: taking an irrelevant consideration into account; failing to take a relevant consideration into account; exercising a power in bad faith or for an improper purpose; making a decision so unreasonable that no reasonable person could have reached it; acting under dictation; or applying policy inflexibly. These types of abuse of power, described as 'improper exercise of power' are codified in (CTH) Administrative Decisions (Judicial Review) Act 1977 ss 5(1)(e), (2), 6(1)(e), (2). See also **Bad faith**; **Ultra vires**.

Corporations The exercise by a person of a power conferred on him or her for a purpose outside the purposes for which the power was granted. Such exercise is invalid. Generally, an exercise of power which is an abuse of power is voidable, while an exercise in excess of power is void: *ANZ Executors Trustee Co Ltd v Qintex Australia Ltd* [1991] 2 Qd R 360; (1990) 2 ACSR 676; Corporations Law s 161(3).

Abuse of process The misuse or unjust or unfair use of court process and procedure.

Practice and procedure Abuse of process includes instituting or maintaining proceedings that will clearly fail, proceedings unjustifiably oppressive or vexatious in relation to the defendant, and generally any process that gives rise to unfairness: *Walton v Gardiner* (1993) 177 CLR 378; 112 ALR 289. Where an abuse of process occurs, the court is required to stay the proceedings to avoid a miscarriage of justice.

Tort An action on the case arising when a person uses the process of the court predominantly for an ulterior and improper purpose, causing damage to the plaintiff as a result: *Varawa v Howard Smith Co Ltd* (1911) 13 CLR 35.

Abuttal 1. Adjoining or adjacent. 2. The sides of land that adjoin or abut onto the neighbouring land. 3. That part of the land in physical contact with adjoining land.

•**Academic period** For fringe benefits tax purposes, a period in relation to an educational institution, consisting of a term or semester of the academic year, or an academic year of the institution where the academic year is not divided into semesters: (CTH) Fringe Benefits Tax Assessment Act 1986 s 136(1). An academic period relates to the taxation of benefits provided by an employer or an associate of the employer for the education of children of overseas employees: s 65A. See also **Fringe benefit**; **Fringe benefits tax**.

ACCC See **Australian Competition and Consumer Commission**.

ACCC representative action An application by the Australian Competition and Consumer Commission (ACCC) on behalf of persons affected by conduct in breach of (CTH) Trade Practices Act 1974 Pts IVA, V. The ACCC may make an application with the consent of persons suffering or likely to have suffered loss or damage: (CTH) Trade Practices Act 1974 s 87(1B); *Trade Practices Commission v Frendship Aloe Vera Pty Ltd* (1988) 82 ALR 557; *Trade Practices Commission v J & R Enterprises Pty Ltd* (1991) 99 ALR 325; ATPR ¶46-069. See also **Australian Competition and Consumer Commission**.

Accede 1. To consent to something. 2. To enter a treaty or accord. 3. To come into office. See also **Accession**.

Accelerated depreciation A concessional taxation treatment for the depreciation of assets, by which the cost of depreciable property may be claimed over a shorter period of time than would otherwise be the case, by allowing a higher depreciation rate than normal. See also **Depreciable property**; **Depreciated value**; **Depreciation**; **Plant**.

Accelerated expenditure The practice of bringing forward the planned expenditure of a taxpayer to an earlier year of income to increase the allowable deductions which can be claimed in that earlier year of income. See also **Allowable deduction**.

•**Acceleration** The situation where, by reason of default or other cause defined in the relevant contract, the whole (or a greater than normal part) of an advance or other payment becomes immediately due and payable. See also **Acceleration clause; Mortgage; Personal property; Securities.**

•**Acceleration clause** A term found in contracts for the lease, hire, or hire-purchase of goods, which accelerates the payment of rent by the lessee, hirer, or hire-purchaser on the occurrence of specified events: for example *O'Dea v Allstates Leasing System (WA) Pty Ltd* (1983) 152 CLR 359; 45 ALR 632. The distinction between liquidated damages and penalties applies to acceleration clauses. There is no penalty where the acceleration clause does not impose an additional or different liability on breach; nor where the clause is in an instalment contract where the whole sum is to be payable immediately on the lessee's failure to make punctual payment; nor where a sum is payable on a certain event which does not involve a breach of contract: *O'Dea v Allstates Leasing System (WA) Pty Ltd.* See also **Agreed damages clause; Instalment contract; Liquidated damages; Penalty; Relief against forfeiture.**

Accelerator A process by which changes in the demand for consumer goods may bring about even larger variations in the demand for the capital equipment used to make them. For example, the effect of a 10 per cent increase in consumer demand may lead to a 100 per cent increase in demand for the relevant capital equipment when a normal 10 per cent per annum replacement program is augmented by a 10 per cent increase in capacity, thus doubling the orders for equipment. See also **Multiplier.**

•**Acceptable rate of interest** In consumer credit law, an annual percentage rate that the credit provider agrees to accept so long as the debtor performs all contractual obligations: for example (VIC) Credit Act 1987 (repealed) s 5(1); (QLD) Credit Act 1987 (repealed) s 7(1) (replaced by Uniform Consumer Credit Code). In a loan contract or continuing credit contract where there is an acceptable rate of interest, the contract must state that rate of interest: for example (NSW) Credit Act 1984 (repealed) ss 5(1), 39(2) (replaced by Uniform Consumer Credit Code). See also **Annual percentage rate; Continuing credit contract; Credit provider.**

•**Acceptance** The act of assenting to, agreeing; receiving or taking something offered.

Bills of exchange and other negotiable instruments The signification by a drawee of assent to the order of a drawer, requiring the drawee to sign the bill and an expression that the drawee's promise will be performed only by money payment: (CTH) Bills of Exchange Act 1909 s 22(1), (2). A drawee is not liable until acceptance. See also **Assent by the drawee; Bill of exchange; Conditional acceptance; General acceptance; Local acceptance; Partial acceptance; Qualified acceptance; Signification.**

Contract **1.** The act of agreeing or assenting. Acceptance is one of the three elements which form a contract (the others being offer and consideration). A binding contract results when an offer is accepted. The offeree must have knowledge of the offer and an intention to accept: *Carter v Hyde* (1923) 33 CLR 115; *R v Clarke* (1927) 40 CLR 227. Acceptance may be express or implied from conduct, but must correspond with the offer, be unequivocal and, as a general rule, be communicated to the offeror: *Ballas v Theophilos (No 2)* (1957) 98 CLR 193; *Farmers' Mercantile Union & Chaff Mills Ltd v Coade* (1921) 30 CLR 113. **2.** An election by the promisee to terminate further performance of the contract: for example *Bowes v Chaleyer* (1923) 32 CLR 159. Acceptance of repudiation must be communicated to the promisor, but the promisee need not otherwise act on the repudiation. See also **Agreement; Contract; Discharge; Election; Offer; Postal acceptance rule; Repudiation; Termination.**

Acceptance credit An arrangement in which a bank lends its credit by accepting bills drawn on it by a customer who then discounts the bill with a market dealer or with another bank. An alternative arrangement having the same function occurs where the bank draws a bill payable to the customer. Both types of bill are referred to commercially as 'accommodation bills'. See also **Accommodation bill; Bill line facility.**

Acceptance fee A commission or fee charged by a bank or merchant bank for drawing bills of exchange under a line of credit. This is an extra expense for the borrower. See also **Bill of exchange.**

Acceptance in blank See **Indorsement in blank**.

Acceptance of service Where a solicitor or agent empowered to accept service, agrees to receive service of a process on behalf of a party. It is assumed that the served documents will be brought to the notice of the party: *Ditfort v Temby* (1990) 97 ALR 409 at 415-7.

Acceptance or payment for honour supra protest The intervention and undertaking by a person (not already liable on a bill of exchange) to accept or pay the bill protested for dishonour after the protest (*supra protest*); the intervention being for the honour of a party liable on the bill, or the person for whose account the bill is drawn: (CTH) Bills of Exchange Act 1909 ss 70(1), 73(1). See also **Acceptance; Bill of exchange; Dishonour; Notarial act of honour; Referee in case of need.**

Accepting house A firm, usually a well-known merchant bank, that accepts bills of exchange and facilitates money lending as a result; a select group of UK merchant banks such as Hambros, Hill Samuel, Rothschild, Morgan Grenfell, which organise the lending of money with the Bank of England. They receive slightly better discount rates from the bank. See also **Acceptance; Acceptance credit; Bill line facility.**

Acceptor The drawee of a bill of exchange who signs the bill presented by the holder, intending to become bound to the personal primary liability on the bill: (CTH) Bills of Exchange Act 1909 s 28(1). See also **Acceptance; Assent by the drawee; Bill of exchange; Drawer.**

•**Access** *Lat – accessus –* a coming to; an approach to. **1.** The privilege or power of approach, admission, or entrance. **2.** The act of coming into contact with. **3.** The means of approach or admittance.

Employment Any reasonable means of approaching

work: *Australian Paper Manufacturers Ltd v Conyers* [1962] SR (NSW) 682 at 684; *Andriolo v G & G Constructions Pty Ltd* (1989) Aust Torts Reports ¶68,478. Access may not include approaches while engaged in work: *Trimp v SA Butler Pty Ltd* (1964) 81 WN (Pt 1) (NSW) 511; [1964-5] NSWR 1031; *Australian Iron & Steel Pty Ltd v Luna* (1969) 123 CLR 365; [1970] ALR 257; 44 ALJR 52. However, it may: *Bertram v Armstrong & De Mamiel Constructions Pty Ltd* (1978) 23 ACTR 15. Approaching work in this context also entails egress: *Bertram v Armstrong & De Mamiel Constructions Pty Ltd*.

Real property Freedom over land or property: *Scott v Pape* (1886) 31 Ch D 554; *Colls v Home and Colonial Stores Ltd* [1904] AC 179 at 205. Access is usually a freedom to approach one parcel of land by crossing another parcel: for example *Draper v South Australian Railways Cmr* [1903] SALR 150; *Thomas v Bergin* [1986] 2 Qd R 478. The freedom can be characterised as either a licence (*Davis v Northern Territory Housing Commission* (1984) 71 FLR 85), or as an easement (*Liverpool City Council v Irwin* [1977] AC 239). See also **Easement**; **Licence**.

Access regime The regime established by (CTH) Trade Practices Act 1974 Pt IIIA, intended to ensure access to essential services such as transport and communications services: ss 44 B, 44H(4). The Minister may declare certain services (s 4HH) and if a party cannot make satisfactory arrangements with the provider of a declared service, the dispute may be arbitrated by the Australian Competition and Consumer Commission (ACCC) (s 44S). The ACCC may make a binding determination, which may include requiring the provider to provide access to the service: s 44 V(2). See also **Australian Competition and Consumer Commission**.

Access to information In taxation law, the right of the Commissioner of Taxation and any authorised taxation officer to have full and free access to all buildings, places, books, documents, and other papers for the purpose of the administration of taxation laws ((CTH) Income Tax Assessment Act 1936 s 263), and to require provision of information, production of books or documents, or attendance to give evidence (s 264). This power must be exercised for the purposes of the (CTH) Income Tax Assessment Act 1936: *Industrial Equity Ltd v DCT (NSW)* (1990) 170 CLR 649; 96 ALR 337. See **Freedom of information**.

Accession *Lat – accessio –* increase. Generally, addition or increase.

Bailment A doctrine derived from Roman law entitling an owner of a chattel to any improvement of the chattel which cannot be physically detached without destruction or serious injury to the whole so formed: *McKeown v Cavalier Yachts Pty Ltd* (1988) 13 NSWLR 303 at 311; *Rendell v Associated Finance Ltd* [1957] VR 604. See also **Appropriation**; **Confusion**.

ACCI See **Australian Chamber of Commerce and Industry**.

•**Accident** Generally, something that happens without intention or design: *Australian Casualty Co Ltd v Federico* (1986) 160 CLR 513; 66 ALR 99.

Carriers An unintended and unexpected occurrence that produces loss or damage. In a bill of lading, accident is often recognised as an exception releasing the carrier of the goods from liability for damage caused by the accident. See also **Bill of lading**; **Cargo**; **Charterparty**; **Goods**; **Master**; **Negligence**.

Insurance In an insurance policy, a mishap or untoward event that is not expected or designed: *Australian Casualty Co Ltd v Federico* (1986) 160 CLR 513; 66 ALR 99. See also **Accident insurance**.

Accident benefit A payment under an insurance policy for loss, detriment, injury, or specified consequences derived from an accident. See also **Accident**.

Accident compensation An amount paid in either a lump sum or by progressive payments to compensate a person for a loss or reduction of earning capacity and associated expenses as a result of an accident. See also **Accident**; **Workers' compensation**.

Accident Compensation Tribunal A tribunal established under (VIC) Accident Compensation Act 1985 s 39 (repealed) with exclusive jurisdiction to inquire into, hear and determine any question or matter in relation to (VIC) Workers Compensation Act 1958: s 40. The tribunal was disbanded under (VIC) Accident Compensation (WorkCover) Act 1992 s 64.

•**Accident insurance** A form of insurance in which an insured, to recover, must prove that the injury or loss was caused by an accident. Policies providing coverage against accidents include workers' compensation, public liability, and sickness and accident insurance policies. See also **Accident**; **Insurance**; **Insurance contract**; **Life insurance**; **Public liability**; **Workers' compensation**.

•**Accident pay** An amount paid under an award to ensure that a worker receives full pay for any period during which the worker is on workers' compensation: *Re Dispute-Building Trades re Accident Pay* [1971] AR (NSW) 241. See also **Accident**; **Workers' compensation**.

•**Accommodation bill** 1. A bill of exchange, the purpose of which is to provide financial support or credit (accommodation) to a person. 2. For the purposes of (CTH) Bills of Exchange Act 1909 s 64(3), a bill of exchange in which the party providing the accommodation is the acceptor. 3. A bill of exchange signed by an accommodation party: *Coles Myer Finance Ltd v FCT* (1991) 28 FCR 7; 98 ALR 411. See also **Acceptor**; **Accommodation party**; **Bill of exchange**.

Accommodation land Land acquired for the purpose of improving adjoining or adjacent land. Accommodation land may be acquired for the erection of buildings for sale or letting. See also **Holding**.

Accommodation line An insurance contract which insurance brokers or agents would not typically underwrite but which is undertaken for the purposes of engendering goodwill, or as a means of subsequently securing better contracts. See also **Goodwill**.

•**Accommodation party** A party to a bill of exchange who signed the bill as drawer, acceptor, or indorser without receiving value, for the purpose of lending its name to another: (CTH) Bills of Exchange Act 1909 s 33(1). See also **Acceptor; Accommodation bill; Drawer; Holder; Indorser.**

• **Accord** An agreement made in 1983 between the Australian Labor Party and the Australian Council of Trade Unions on policies to manage prices and incomes. The aim of the accord was to reduce inflation and maintain economic growth, employment, and living standards. Under the accord, unions limited wage claims in return for government support for wage-fixing principles, price controls, and beneficial industrial legislation. The accord was re-negotiated many times to implement policy changes, such as enterprise bargaining, and to adjust to changing economic circumstances. See also **Australian Council of Trade Unions; Enterprise bargaining; Wage fixation; Wage indexation.**

Accord and satisfaction A contract of compromise where the bargained-for consideration is an actual release of a cause of action: *Butler v Fairclough* (1917) 23 CLR 78. See also **Accord executory; Consideration; Contract of compromise.**

Accord executory A contract of compromise where the bargained-for consideration is a promise of release of a cause of action: *Butler v Fairclough* (1917) 23 CLR 78. See also **Accord and satisfaction; Consideration; Contract of compromise.**

• **Account** In banking and finance, a facility or arrangement by which a cash dealer accepts deposits or allows withdrawals of currency, pays cheques or payment orders drawn on the cash dealer by another person, or collects cheques or payment orders on behalf of another person: (CTH) Financial Transaction Reports Act 1988 s 3(1). See also **Account of profits; Account stated; Blocked account; Cash dealer; Clayton's case, rule in; Right of combination; Current account; Debt; Joint account; Non-callable deposit account; Overdraft account; Partnership account; Savings account; Trust account; Unclaimed moneys.**

• **Account charge** In consumer credit legislation, and in relation to a continuing credit contract, a term with two meanings. **1.** In relation to the period of 12 months after the contract is made, the total sum payable by the debtor to the credit provider as the fixed fee for entering the contract, and any amount payable as the fixed annual fee for that period: (NSW) Credit Act 1984 (repealed) s 5(1) (now replaced by Uniform Consumer Credit Code). **2.** In relation to any other period of 12 months, any amount that, under the contract, is payable by the debtor as the fixed annual fee for that period: s 5(1). See also **Continuing credit contract.**

Account executive A full-time employee of a stock exchange member organisation who meets the requirements of the exchange with respect to background and knowledge of the securities business. Also known as 'registered representative trader' or 'customers broker'. See also **Securities; Stock exchange.**

Account keeping fee A periodic fee, usually levied monthly by financial institutions like banks, on transaction accounts maintained by customers. The fee is a fixed amount and not dependent on the number of transactions which pass through the account. See also **Acceptance fee.**

Account of profits An action in equity for the computation and payment to an applicant of profits made from a wrong done to the applicant. See also **Account; Account stated; Unjust enrichment.**

Account party A person who requests a bank to perform the service undertaken in a letter of credit. Also known as 'applicant'. See also **Letter of credit.**

Account payable The amounts payable as the result of purchases. The term normally refers to the purchase on credit of goods or services.

Account payee Words written on a cheque putting a bank on inquiry if the cheque is not paid into the payee's account, even if the cheque appears to be regularly indorsed. Also known as 'account payee only'. See also **Cheque; Crossing; Not negotiable.**

Account sales A statement provided to a consignor of goods by the consignee detailing particulars such as the amount of sales of the consigned goods, the amount of unsold merchandise, consignee expenses incurred, the consignee's commission, and the net amount due to the consignor. See also **Consignee; Consignor.**

Account stated 1. An account containing several items of claim on both sides set against one another so that a balance can be calculated and paid. **2.** An account between two parties containing entries on both sides where a set-off has been effected and the balance agreed to be the only amount payable. The consideration for the promise to pay the balance is the discharge of the items on each side: *Siqueira v Noronha* [1934] AC 332. At common law it is called *insimul computassent* (they accounted together), being the 'real account stated': *Re Laycock v Pickles* (1863) 4 B & S 497; 122 ER 546. **2.** A mere acknowledgment of a debt, where there in fact may be no debt, consideration, or binding promise: *Siqueira v Noronha* [1934] AC 332. A promise to pay may be inferred by law from an account statement. Such an admission is of evidential value only and the existence and validity of the debt itself may be examined despite the admission: *Perry v Attwood* (1856) LJQB 408. **3.** An account consisting of a claim by one party which the other party has for valuable consideration agreed to accept: *Irving v Veitch* (1837) 3 M 7 W 90; 150 ER 1069. See also **Account; Debt.**

• **Accountable** Responsible; liable. For example, a person who enters into a contract becomes legally accountable to the other party for the performance of the obligations undertaken. Failure to render performance makes the party in breach liable in law to compensate the other party: *Hungerfords v Walker* (1989) 171 CLR 125; 84 ALR 119.

Accountancy The organised classification, recording, and analysis, in financial terms, of all transactions and events affecting an organisation or individual; the study of the discipline of accounting. See also **Accounting; Transaction.**

• **Accountant** A person who practises and is skilled in the profession of accountancy. See also **Accountancy.**

Accountant's lien The right of an accountant to retain, as a lien, books, and documents of a client that he or she has worked on until payment for the work done is received: *Re Gleebs Pty Ltd (in liq)* [1933] VLR 293. See also **Lien**.

Accounting The process of identifying, measuring, recording and communicating economic information to permit informed judgments and decisions by the users of the information. Identifying involves observing economic events and determining which events are relevant to a particular business. Accounting transactions are measured in dollar values to allow the comparison of the value of diverse objects. Recording is the process of systematically maintaining a record of all transactions which have affected business operations. It involves classification and summarisation of information. Communication is the process of preparing and distributing accounting reports to potential users of accounting information. See also **Absorption costing; Accounting period; Accounting record; Balance sheet; Consolidated profit and loss account; Matching principle; Profit and loss statement**.

Accounting beta A device to measure the risk of a security within a portfolio. Beta measures the extent to which the returns on a security vary with movements in the whole market. As market movements cannot be avoided by diversification into more assets, the beta is an index of the non-diversifiable risk. The beta coefficient for the market as a whole is one. Securities with a beta less than one are said to be less risky than the market, and conversely a beta greater than one means the security is more risky than the market risk. Beta can be measured from accounting data (accounting beta) as well as from market data (market beta). See also **Beta factor**.

Accounting costs Costs considered as recorded costs only. As with a financial analysis, the recording of accounting costs is vital to an enterprise for the purpose of management, balance sheets, reporting, taxation and continuous assessment of viability and profit. It is, however, a narrow exercise within the context of economic assessment, and social and environmental analysis. Accounting costs may be contrasted with economic costs which take external effects and opportunity cost into account. See also **Financial analysis; Opportunity cost**.

Accounting earnings The total returns, revenues, or receipts derived from all sources of investment of time, effort, and capital from one's business. Accounting earnings are reported as revenue in a profit and loss account. Net earnings refers to earnings in excess of any expenditures incurred in producing those earnings. Accounting earnings can also be expressed before or after any applicable income tax.

Accounting method The means of recording and explaining transactions and events engaged in by a person carrying on a business. The method of accounting used in calculating a taxpayer's taxable income should correctly reflect the amount of assessable income derived and allowable deductions incurred for each year: *Henderson v FCT* (1970) 119 CLR 612; 1 ATR 596. The two recognised methods for calculating a person's taxable income are the cash (or receipts) basis and the accruals (or earnings) basis. See also **Accruals accounting; Assessable income; Allowable deduction; Cash basis of accounting; Taxable income**.

Accounting party The party in court that claims an account or makes a claim which involves taking an account.

•**Accounting period** A period of time selected by a business for the purpose of comparing its business performance over time: *Henderson & Sons v FCT* (1924) 34 CLR 294. See also **Accounting; Accounting record; Accounting standards; Balance sheet; Consolidated profit and loss account; Controlled foreign company; Financial year; Matching principle; Profit and loss statement**.

Accounting postulate An underlying assumption derived from observing the economic and social climate and which encompasses the purpose of measuring and recording economic data which is served by accounting information. Accounting postulates are crucial to the development of accounting principles. See also **Accounting; Accounting principle; Accounting record; Balance sheet; Consolidated profit and loss account; Matching principle; Profit and loss statement**.

Accounting principle A professionally enforced rule used to provide guidance in relation to the measurement, classification, or interpretation of economic information and the communication of the results through the use of financial statements. An accounting principle is characterised as a principle because no alternative rule is generally recognised or accepted as authoritative in the situation governed by the principle. See also **Accounting; Accounting postulate; Accounting record; Balance sheet; Consolidated profit and loss account; Matching principle; Profit and loss statement**.

•**Accounting record** Generally, records of a person carrying on a business, which record and explain, for reporting or managerial purposes, relevant transactions engaged in by the person in carrying on that business. It includes invoices, receipts, orders for the payment of money, bills of exchange, cheques, promissory notes, vouchers and other documents of prime entry, and such working papers and other documents as are necessary to explain the methods and calculations by which accounts are made up: Corporations Law s 9. See also **Accounting standards; Accounts**.

Accounting standards A body of rules regulating the format and content of financial statements. Australian accounting standards emanate from the Australian Accounting Standards Board (AASB) and are of two kinds: AASB standards (which apply, principally, to companies, certain non-companies and disclosing entities which are trusts) and AAS standards (which apply to public sector and most non-corporate private sector reporting entities). Standards are developed by the Australian Accounting Research Foundation. Company directors must ensure that the company's financial statements are made out in accordance with applicable accounting standards: Corporations Law s 298. If the financial statements would not otherwise give a true and fair view of the company's activities, the directors must add such information and explanation as will give a true and fair view of the relevant matters: s 299. See also **Accounting period; General purpose financial report**.

Accounting Standards Review Board See **Australian Accounting Standards Board**.

•**Accounts** **1.** Ledgers, journals, profit and loss accounts and balance sheets, and statements attached to these: (CTH) Insurance Act 1973 s 3. **2.** In bankruptcy, records of the administration of a debtor's affairs and property. Trustees in bankruptcy and controlling trustees must keep proper accounts: (CTH) Bankruptcy Act 1966 ss 173, 210(2). **3.** Investigations into a transaction or matter relevant to proceedings before the court. The court has general power to direct that accounts be taken: (CTH) Bankruptcy Act 1966 s 30(2). **4.** In company law, the profit and loss account and balance sheet for an entity together with statements, reports (other than a directors' or auditors' report), and notes intended to be read with the profit and loss account or balance sheet: Corporations Law s 9. **5.** For taxation purposes, ledgers, journals, profit and loss accounts, and balance-sheets, statements, reports, and notes attached to or intended to be read with any of these: (CTH) Taxation Administration Act 1953 s 8J. See also **Accounting; Accounting period; Accounting record; Accounting standards; Balance sheet; Consolidated profit and loss account; Controlling trustee; Debtor; Financial statement; Profit and loss statement; Trustee in bankruptcy.**

Accounts, falsification of See **Falsification of accounts.**

Accounts, partner's duty to render See **Partner's duty to render accounts.**

Accounts payable Debts owed by an entity for the purchase of goods or services rendered. Accounts payable are expenses incurred but not paid and are recorded as a current liability on the balance sheet at the end of a particular accounting period. See also **Accounting period; Accounts receivable; Balance sheet; Creditor.**

Accounts receivable Debts owed to an entity for the sale of goods or services. Accounts receivable are income items not yet received and are recorded as a current asset on the balance sheet at the end of a particular accounting period. See also **Accounting period; Accounts payable; Balance sheet; Creditor.**

Accredited mediator A neutral third party appointed by agreement or court order to facilitate settlement-oriented negotiations between the parties to a dispute. Court rules may allow a court to refer proceedings or part of proceedings to a mediator. See also **Alternative Dispute Resolution; Mediation; Mediator.**

Accrual An item of income or an expense, for which it can reasonably be considered that a right exists to the income, or an obligation has arisen to make payment in respect of an expense, although the income has not been received or the expense actually paid: *Australia and New Zealand Banking Group Ltd v FCT* (1994) 48 FCR 268; 119 ALR 727. See also **Accruals accounting; Income; Losses and outgoings.**

•**Accrual of cause of action** For the purpose of determining whether an action falls within a limitation period, the occurrence of a wrong to a party which gives rise to a cause of action to the party. In contract, the cause of action accrues on breach of contract: *Howell v Young* (1826) 5 B & C 259; 108 ER 97. In tort, the cause of action accrues when the tortious act is committed. See also **Limitation period; Limitation of actions.**

Accrual period The period, generally six months, over which income from a qualifying security, such as a zero-coupon bond or annuity, will be attributed to the issuer or acquirer of the security under (CTH) Income Tax Assessment Act 1936 Div 16A s 159GQA. See also **Zero-coupon bond**.

Accruals accounting A form of accounting introduced in 1983 by the Commonwealth government for statutory authorities, which is widely used in the private sector. It is a method of accounting for assessable income, under which trading, some professional, and certain other income is included in taxable income when the income is earned (that is, usually on completion of the obligation giving rise to the income) even if there has been no actual or constructive receipt: *Henderson v FCT* (1970) 119 CLR 612; 1 ATR 596. It is not the actual receipt, but the right to receive income which governs derivation of income under this method. Accruals accounting considers the overall asset and liability position during an accounting period, recording commitments that will require cash in the future, expenses incurred but not yet paid and income earned but not yet received. Also known as 'accruals basis of accounting'. See also **Accounting method; Assessable income; Cash basis of accounting; Constructive receipt; Derived; Personal service.**

Accruals tax A tax introduced by the Commonwealth Government in 1990 to ensure that income earned by Australian companies in tax havens such as the Cook Islands is taxed by the Australian Taxation Office at the Australian rate of tax, even though the funds might never be returned to Australia. Accruals taxes for similar purposes have been introduced by the United States, Japan, Britain, Germany, France, Canada, and New Zealand. See also **Company rate of tax**.

•**Accrued credit charge** In consumer credit legislation, and in relation to a credit sale contract or a loan contract at a particular time, the greater of the minimum credit charge and the amount of any credit charge which has accrued at that time, calculated according to a prescribed method: (NSW) Credit Act 1984 (repealed) s 5(1) (replaced by Uniform Consumer Credit Code). See also **Credit charge; Credit sale contract; Minimum credit charge.**

Accrued expense An expense which has been incurred in an accounting period but is either not yet paid or has not yet been billed. An accrued expense is included as a liability in the financial statements at the end of a particular accounting period or at the end of the financial year. See also **Accounts; Accounting period; Balance sheet; Financial statement; Financial year.**

Accrued interest 1. Interest accounted or debited but not yet due for payment. **2.** Accumulating interest that has not been paid to the person who owns the principal amount. In a liquidation, any accrued interest on the capital is repayable to relevant shareholders after payment of creditors, but in advance of the repayment of capital generally: *Re Life Funds of Australia Ltd* (1977) 2 ACLR 444. See also **Interest**.

Accrued liability A liability enforceable on either a short-term or long-term basis depending upon the nature of the liability and the terms of the agreement. The liability is accrued and included in the financial statements for the end of a particular accounting period or the end of the financial year. See also **Accounting period**; **Financial statement**; **Financial year**.

Accrued revenue See **Accrual**.

•**Accrued right** In contract law, a right that survives termination of the contract, being unconditionally acquired. Rights that arise from the partial execution of the contract and causes of action that have accrued from its breach continue unaffected following termination. Two types of rights survive termination: the right to damages and the right to receive performance of accrued contractual obligations: *McDonald v Dennys Lascelles Ltd* (1933) 48 CLR 457. See also **Damages**; **Performance**; **Termination**.

Accruing debt A debt not yet actually payable, but that is represented by an existing obligation: *Webb v Stenton* (1883) 11 QBD 518 at 527. See also **Debt**.

Accumulated losses Losses carried forward by a company from past financial periods to the present one (that is, the accumulation of losses recorded by an entity over a number of accounting periods); the opposite of retained profits. The level of accumulated losses (or retained profits) at the beginning of the financial year must be included in the profit and loss statement: Corporations Regulations Sch 5 cl 6. See also **Retained profit**.

•**Accumulated profits** An amount showing in a company's profit account carried forward from one year's accounts to the next. Accumulated profits are profits left after paying dividends, taxes, and putting some funds to the company's reserves. Accumulated profits are simply profits that are amassed or collected and not distributed, including amounts standing to the credit of the profit and loss account of a company: *Federal Cmr of Taxation v Miller Anderson Ltd* (1946) 73 CLR 341. See also **Accumulated losses**.

Accumulation In relation to income, the process of heaping up, or laying by, income, irrespective of whether it is reinvested as capital or not. Accumulation does not apply to unapplied income heaped up or laid aside, irrespective of whether or not it is actually reinvested at that time. See also **Accumulated profits**.

•**Accumulation fund** See **Defined contribution scheme**.

Accumulation index A stock market index which reveals the total return on the equities in terms of dividends and capital gain over a period of time, showing the investor which sections of the market are giving the best returns. See also **Australian Accumulation Index**.

Accumulation plan See **Defined contribution scheme**.

ACDC See **Australian Commercial Disputes Centre**.

ACICA See **Australian Centre for International Commercial Arbitration**.

Acid test ratio A ratio of liquid assets to current liabilities which gives an indication of a company's solvency. See also **Asset**; **Contingent asset**.

ACIP See **Advisory Council on Industrial Property**.

Acknowledgment of debt A written, signed admission that a debt is due: *Bucknell v Commercial Banking Co of Sydney Ltd* (1937) 58 CLR 155. Acknowledgment or part-payment of a debt may extend the limitation period for claims in respect of the debt: for example (NSW) Limitation Act 1969 s 54; (VIC) Limitation of Actions Act 1958 s 24; (QLD) Limitation of Actions Act 1974 s 35. See also **Debt**; **Limitation of actions**; **Part-payment of debt**.

ACN See **Australian Company Number**.

•**Acquiescence** 1. Abstaining from interference while one's rights are being violated: *Ramsden v Dyson* (1866) LR 1 HL 129. 2. Refraining from seeking relief, once it is known that rights exist, for such a period that abandonment or release of the rights has occurred: *Mehmet v Benson* (1965) 113 CLR 295; [1965] ALR 903. 3. Delay by a plaintiff where to give relief would involve prejudice to the defendant or a third party: *Mehmet v Benson* (1965) 113 CLR 295; [1965] ALR 903. 4. Sometimes, mere delay: *Boyns v Lackey* (1958) 58 SR (NSW) 395; 75 WN (NSW) 451. See also **Consent**; **Laches**; **Waiver**.

Contract 1. Abstaining from interference or objection while one's rights are being violated: *Duke of Leeds v Earl of Amherst* (1846) 2 Ph 117 at 124; 41 ER 886. A person who acquiesces in a violation of his or her rights is prevented from later complaining of the violation: *Ramsden v Dyson* (1866) LR 1 HL 129; *Glasson v Fuller* [1922] SASR 148. A person may be so prevented on the grounds of election, estoppel, or waiver: *Commonwealth v Verwayen* (1990) 170 CLR 394; 95 ALR 321. 2. Delay or laches amounting to affirmation of or assent to a violation of an equitable right. See also **Election**; **Estoppel**; **Laches**; **Waiver**.

Tort Tacitly, agreeing to allow a person to perform an otherwise tortious act upon the one acquiescing. Acquiescence normally operates as a complete defence to an action in tort, depriving the victim of the right of action on the ground that he or she has acquiesced in the activity: for example *Balmain New Ferry Co Ltd v Robertson* (1906) 4 CLR 379. See also **Consent**.

•**Acquire** 1. Generally, to acquire ownership of, an interest in, or the benefit of, goods or services. 2. To obtain, directly or indirectly, ownership of any legal or equitable interest in shares or assets: Corporations Law s 51. 3. To receive the supply of services including accepting those services: (CTH) Trade Practices Act 1974 s 4(1); *Castlemaine Tooheys Ltd v Williams & Hodgson Transport Pty Ltd* (1986) 162 CLR 395; 68 ALR 376. See also **Acquisition**; **Entitlement to shares**; **Services**; **Takeover**.

•**Acquisition** 1. Obtaining ownership or possession of a thing. 2. The thing acquired.

Taxation and revenue For capital gains tax purposes, a change of the beneficial ownership of an asset: (CTH) Income Tax Assessment Act 1936 ss 160M(1)-(1A). Such a change of ownership gives rise to an acquisition by the person who beneficially owns the asset immediately after the change. For an acquisition of an asset to occur there must generally be a disposal of the asset to another person. The term 'disposal' is extensively dealt with in (CTH) Income Tax Assessment Act 1936 ss 160M(1)-(13), 160MA. However, (CTH) Income Tax Assessment Act 1936 s 160M(5) provides that certain events can give rise to an acquisition without a disposal; for example, an issue or allotment of shares is an acquisition by the person to whom the shares are issued but is not a disposal by the company issuing the shares: (CTH) Income Tax Assessment Act 1936 s 160 M(5)(a). See also **Asset**; **Capital gain**; **Capital gains tax**; **Capital loss**.

Trade and commerce In relation to a merger, obtaining ownership of any legal or equitable interest in a corporation or other assets: (CTH) Trade Practices Act 1974 ss 4(4), 50. See also **Competition law**; **Indirect acquisition**; **Merger**; **Restrictive trade practices**; **Share**.

Acquisition of company shares, financial assistance See **Financial assistance for acquisition of a company's shares**.

Acquittance An acknowledgment of the payment of a sum of money or a debt due in writing.

Acre A measure of area of land equivalent to approximately 4050 square metres (43,560 square feet). An acre is divided into four roods or 160 perches. The term is still in common use, although it has been replaced by the metric measurement of the hectare since 1973.

•**Act** See **Legislation**.

ACT See **Australian Capital Territory**.

Act in law An act done by law or by the force of law, whether it is willing or not. Any act which a person is compelled to do, or does under statutory compulsion is an act in law: *Piggot v Middlesex County Council* [1909] 1 Ch 134 at 142.

Act in pais /ækt ɪn peɪ/ *LF* – act in the country. An act in pais includes an ordinary conveyance, as distinguished from an act done in court, which is a matter of record.

Act of bankruptcy An act of the kind listed in (CTH) Bankruptcy Act 1966 s 40(1) that a creditor must prove to the court to make someone bankrupt. See also **Bankruptcy**; **Bankruptcy notice**; **Creditor's petition**; **Relation-back doctrine**.

•**Act of God** An event or occurrence due to natural causes which occurs independently of human intervention and either could not be foreseen, or if foreseen, could not be reasonably guarded against: *Commissioner of Railways (WA) v Stewart* (1936) 56 CLR 520. Examples include a storm or earthquake. See also **Force majeure clause**; **Frustration**; **Strict liability**.

•**Act of Parliament** A body of law passed by the legislature, and given royal assent by the Crown. The passing of an Act of Parliament by a State Parliament requires the agreement to a proposed law on the part of each of the elements of that Parliament. Also known as 'Act', 'primary legislation', or 'statute'. See also **House of Representatives**; **Legislation**; **Parliament**.

Act of third party An act by a person who is not a party to an action or transaction. An act of a third party may operate as a defence, or entitle a defendant to contribution or indemnity against the third party. In negligence, if the act of a third party amounts to a *novus actus interveniens* (intervening cause), breaking the chain of causation, the defendant is not liable for the consequences of that act: *Mahony v J Kruschich (Demolitions) Pty Ltd* (1985) 156 CLR 522; 59 ALR 722. See also **Contribution**; **Indemnity**; **Novus actus interveniens**.

ACTA See **Australian Credit Transfer Agency Pty Ltd**.

•**Acting in concert** In trade practices law, conduct undertaken by two or more persons knowingly: (CTH) Trade Practices Act 1974 s 45D. Acting in concert does not involve conduct that merely occurs simultaneously for whatever reason; rather, conduct that is the result of communication, which is contemporaneous, and has community of purpose: *J-Corp Pty Ltd v Australian Builders Labourers Federated Union of Workers (WA Branch)* (1992) 111 ALR 502; 46 IR 263. See also **Cartel**; **Collusion**; **Competition law**; **Contract, arrangement or understanding**; **Exclusionary provision**; **Secondary boycott**.

Acting in good faith Acting honestly without fraud, collusion, or participation in wrongdoing. Generally, acting in good faith is no defence to a tort, such as defamation: *Baltinos v Foreign Language Publications Pty Ltd* (1986) 6 NSWLR 85. Also known as 'acting bona fide'. See also **Bona fide**; **Interference with contractual relations**.

Actio in personam /æktioʊ ɪn pɜːsoʊnæm/ *Lat*. In Roman law, an action based on a contractual or delictual obligation. See also **In personam**.

Actio in rem /æktioʊ ɪn rɛm/ *Lat*. In Roman law, an action in which a right is asserted to a certain thing possessed by the defendant.

•**Actio personalis moritur cum persona** /æktioʊ pɜːsoʊnalɪs mɒrɪtʊə kʊm pɜːsoʊnə/ *Lat* – a personal right of action dies with the person.

•**Action** Any proceeding in a court: (NSW) Limitation Act 1969 s 11. 'Action' is a generic term and in its proper legal sense includes suits by the Crown: *Bradlaugh v Clarke* (1883) 8 App Cas 354 at 361-2. See also **Proceeding**.

Action, abandonment of See **Abandonment**.

Action for loss of services An action at common law *per quod servitium amisit* (by reason of which his or her services were lost) for damages by a person entitled to services from the injured person, against the third party who has deprived him or her of those services through some wrongful act. The plaintiff must have had a legal right or interest in the services of the injured party. See also **Master**; **Servant**.

Action for price A civil proceeding maintained by a seller against a buyer for the price of goods sold. A seller may maintain an action for price against the buyer only where the property has passed or where, under the contract of sale, the price is payable 'on a day certain' irrespective of delivery: (NSW) Sale of Goods Act 1923 s 51. See also **Action**; **Action of debt**.

Action goods Goods whose supply and defect is alleged in a strict product liability claim under (CTH) Trade Practices Act 1974 Pt VA: (CTH) Trade Practices Act 1974 s 75AA. Ships, aircraft or other vehicles, animals and fish, minerals, trees and crops, and gas and electricity are all examples of possible action goods: (CTH) Trade Practices Act 1974 s 4(1). See also **Goods**.

Action of covenant An action seeking specific performance or damages for breach of an agreement under seal. See also **Assumpsit; Contract; Covenant; Parol contract**.

Action of debt An action to recover a sum certain for an executed consideration. The common law conceived an action to recover a debt due not merely as one for damages for breach of contract, but for the detention of a sum of money: *Young v Queensland Trustees Ltd* (1956) 99 CLR 560. The plaintiff in an action to recover debt is not required to show that any loss or damage was caused by the breach, and the defendant bears the onus of establishing payment by way of discharge as a defence to the action. Historically the action was an alternative to *assumpsit*: *Pavey & Matthews Pty Ltd v Paul* (1987) 162 CLR 221; 69 ALR 577. Also known as an 'action for indebtedness' or ' action for debt due', See also **Assumpsit; Breach of contract; Damages; Discharge; Executed consideration; Liquidated damages**.

Action on the award An action brought in a court by a party to an arbitration award to enforce it by means of a court order, where another party has refused to perform the award. See also **Alternative dispute resolution; Award; Commercial arbitration legislation; Convention on the Recognition and Enforcement of Foreign Arbitral Awards 1958**.

Active management Participation by directors in the day to day operations of a company. Generally directors, whether executive or non-executive, have a duty to take an active part in the management of a company: *Daniels (formerly practising as Deloitte, Haskin & Sells) v Anderson* (1995) 16 ACSR 607; 10 ACLC 933; *Dorchester Finance Co Ltd v Stebbing* [1989] BCLC 498. See also **Director; Passive management**.

Active trustee A trustee with positive trust duties to perform in addition to the duties of preserving the trust assets and conveying them as instructed: *Herdegen v FCT* (1988) 84 ALR 271; 20 ATR 24. See also **Trustee**.

Activity costing Activity-based accounting, being the collation of financial and operational information about significant activities in a business. The aims are to avoid quite arbitrary allocations of overhead costs, to separate operations, and to achieve a more accurate statement of the actual costs, both gross and marginal, incurred in different lines of production.

•**Activity in the nature of a business** Conduct having the character or essence of a trading or commercial enterprise, often involving competition, trade, or dealings with other persons, capital, plant, and employees: *State Authorities Superannuation Board v FCT* (1988) 21 FCR 535; 85 ALR 125. See also **Competition**.

Acts Interpretation Act 1901 A statute providing rules for the interpretation of all Commonwealth Acts: (CTH) Acts Interpretation Act 1901 s 2(1). The rules address matters such as the commencement of Acts, the interpretation of words in Acts, the repeal and expiration of Acts, the calculation of distance and time, and the citation of Acts. See also **Act of parliament**.

ACTU See **Australian Council of Trade Unions**.

Actual authority Generally a grant of authority to act within the confines of the grant.

Agency In agency law, authority granted to an agent by a principal under a consensual agreement or contract to which they alone are parties: *Freeman & Lockyer v Buckhurst Park Properties (Mangal) Ltd* [1964] 2 QB 480. The scope of actual authority is ascertained by applying ordinary principles of construction of contracts, including any proper implications from the express words used, the usages of the trade, and the course of business between the parties. Actual authority may be divided into express and implied authority, and is to be contrasted with apparent or ostensible authority. See also **Agency; Agent; Apparent authority; Construction; Express authority; Implied authority; Principal; Warranty of authority**.

Corporations The express or implied authority given to a person (usually a company officer) by a company, to engage in particular conduct on behalf of the company. Actual authority to act for a company is governed by Corporations Law s 164, the company's constitution (for example Corporations Law Table A reg 66) and the board of directors. See also **Apparent authority; Implied authority**.

Actual fraud At common law, deceit with an intention to deceive or reckless indifference as to the truth or falsity of a representation: *Derry v Peek* (1889) 14 App Cas 337. Actual fraud is distinguished from equitable fraud, which focuses on the conscience and motives of the party. See also **Fraud**.

Actual income threshold amount The amount of income earned by a bankrupt after bankruptcy, which is excluded from assessment when a trustee assesses the bankrupt's liability to make contributions to the bankrupt's estate: (CTH) Bankruptcy Act 1966 ss 139K, 139S. The amount is calculated by reference to a base income threshold amount set out in the (CTH) Social Security Act 1991, with additional allowances for dependants. See also **Bankrupt; Base income threshold amount; Income of bankrupt**.

Actual insolvency Where the liabilities of an individual or business exceed their assets. See also **Insolvency**.

Actual intention In contract law, the intention subjectively held by the parties to a contract. When the court determines what the parties intended by a contract, their actual intention is not generally considered relevant: *Codelfa Construction Pty Ltd v State Rail Authority of NSW* (1982) 149 CLR 337; 41 ALR 367. This rule protects the integrity of the bargain and controls evidence in the court, avoiding time wasted in hearing what the parties thought their contract meant. See also **Construction; Implied intention; Intention**.

•**Actual knowledge** The knowledge that a person as a matter of fact had or has with regard to a course of events or a particular situation. The test of actual knowledge is

•Actual market exchange rate The on-demand airmail buying rate for a foreign currency available at the Commonwealth Bank of Australia: (CTH) Veterans' Entitlements Act 1986 s 5Q(1).

•Actual money price In the context of customs duty, monetary consideration required to be paid to a seller that is determined according to facts rather than hypothetically: *Carmody v Sarah Coventry Pty Ltd* (1974) 3 ALR 374; (CTH) Customs Act 1901 s 154. See also **Customs duty**.

Actual net benefit In relation to an eligible termination payment, the amount of the eligible termination payment reduced by the tax payable by the taxpayer in relation to that termination payment: (CTH) Income Tax Assessment Act 1936 s 27A(1). See also **Eligible Termination Payment**.

Actual notice 1. Actual knowledge; notice that is shown to have been received by a person directly and personally. 2. In contract law, notice that brings home to the mind of a reasonably intelligent and careful reader such knowledge as fairly, and in a business sense, amounts to notice of a contract: *Greenwood v Leather Shod Wheel Co* [1900] 1 Ch 421. See also **Constructive notice**; **Notice**.

•**Actuary** A person who computes insurance risks and premiums and solves other problems in the areas of superannuation and investment. In Australia, an actuary qualifies as a fellow or accredited member of the Institute of Actuaries of Australia: for example (CTH) Superannuation Guarantee (Administration) Act 1992 s 6(1). See also **Insurance**.

Actus reus /æktʊs rɪʊs/ *Lat* – a guilty act. Voluntary actions or omissions constituting a crime; the physical element of an offence: *Ryan v R* (1967) 121 CLR 205; [1967] ALR 577. The actus reus may be a positive act or a failure to act. See also **Absolute liability**; **Strict liability**.

Ad hoc /æd hɒk/ *Lat* – for a special purpose or occasion. Used to describe a body, committee or argument, often with the disparaging implication of hasty improvisation.

Ad idem /æd ɪdɛm/ *Lat* – tallying in the essential point. There must be *consensus ad idem* in a valid contract. See also **Consensus ad idem**.

Ad infinitum /æd ɪnfənaɪtəm/ *Lat* – to infinity; forever.

Ad interim /æd ɪntərɪm/ *Lat* – in the meantime.

Ad libitum /æd lɪbɪtʊm/ *Lat* – extemporaneously; freely; ad lib.

AD policy An accident policy or a disability policy taken out with a life assurance company: (CTH) Income Tax Assessment Act 1936 s 110(1). See also **AD premium**.

AD premium A premium received by a life assurance company in respect of an accident policy or disability policy: (CTH) Income Tax Assessment Act 1936 s 110(1). See also **AD policy**.

Ad valorem /æd vælɔrəm/ *Lat* – according to the value. An *ad valorem* rate is a rate of tax that is not fixed but for which the rate of tax payable will vary depending on the value of the dutiable transaction or item. See also **Land tax**; **Stamp duty**; **Tax**.

Ad valorem freight Freight rates calculated in proportion to the value of the goods shipped and generally based on the cost of those goods. The calculation of freight charges in this way has the advantage of adjusting the burden of the charges according to the value of the goods carried. See also **Ad valorem**; **Freight**.

Ad valorem tax See **Ad valorem**.

Adaptation right In copyright law, the copyright owner's exclusive right to make an adaptation of a work: (CTH) Copyright Act 1968 s 31(1)(a)(vi). See also **Copyright**; **Work**.

ADB See **Asian Development Bank**.

Additional dispute resolution See **Alternative dispute resolution**.

Add-on In industrial law, an enterprise agreement that is additional to an existing industrial award. That is, it extends or modifies the award, rather than replacing it with a comprehensive 'stand-alone' agreement regulating the collective employer-employee relationship. See also **Enterprise agreement**; **Enterprise bargaining**; **Industrial award**.

Add-on contract A credit sale contract which provides for the consolidation of the amount payable under the contract with amounts owed to the credit provider under previous credit sale contracts. The previous contracts are discharged upon the debtor entering into the new credit sale contract: for example (NSW) Credit Act 1984 (repealed) s 37 (replaced by Uniform Consumer Credit Code). See also **Credit provider**; **Credit sale contract**.

•**Address** A private residence, place of business, or official address: (NSW) Justices Act 1902 s 48BA(7). In relation to a natural person, it includes the address of the person's sole or principal place of business, and in relation to a registered business, the address of the place where the business is. In the case of a corporation, it means the address of the corporation's registered office: for example (SA) Packages Act 1967 (repealed) s 4(1). See also **Corporation**.

•**Address for service** The place where a document can be served. In court proceedings, the plaintiff and defendant in their initial documents nominate the place where they will receive documents such as pleadings, or notices for discovery and interrogatories: (NSW) Supreme Court Rules Pt 9. See also **Indorsement**; **Originating process**.

Adduce To tender; to bring forward; to seek to have admitted as evidence anything that a party seeks to rely on to prove or disprove an element of the case.

Ademption Lat – *ademptio* – a taking away; revocation.

Insurance A common law principle in marine insurance law arising in relation to abandonment by which, if a change in circumstances reduces a total loss to a partial loss before an action is commenced, a marine assured can only recover for the partial loss: *Patterson v Ritchie* (1815) 4 M & S 393; 105 ER 879. See also **Marine insurance**.

Adequacy of consideration In contract law, adequacy in the value of consideration by comparison with the value of the promise which it is said to support. For consideration to be good or valuable, it must be sufficient, but need not be adequate. A purely nominal consideration will suffice to make a contract binding: *Cavallari v Premier Refrigeration Co Pty Ltd* (1952) 85 CLR 20. Adequacy may be relevant to issues of economic duress, undue influence, unconscionability, enforceability of a promise in restraint of trade, and the availability of specific performance. See also **Consideration; Contract; Nominal consideration; Sufficiency of consideration**.

ADF See **Approved deposit fund**.

Adhesion See **Standard form contract**.

•**Adjournment** A court order by which proceedings are postponed, interrupted, or continued at a different time or place before the same court.

ADJR Act See **Administrative Decisions (Judicial Review) legislation**.

•**Adjudication** The determination of the rights and liabilities in dispute between two or more parties by the final imposition of a decision or judgment of a court of law, tribunal, or as a result of a decision of a person otherwise sitting in judgment: *Commissioner of Police v Brady* [1954] SASR 314 at 316-18. See also **Judgment**.

Adjustable events Events occurring after the balance date of a set of financial statements and requiring adjustments to those financial statements. There are three types of adjustable events: events that contribute to determining an amount attributable to financial statement items where the amount was uncertain at the period end; events that produce a contrasting assessment of the amount allocated to a financial statement item, if known at that date; and statutory requirements imposing a particular adjustment. See also **Non-adjustable events**.

Adjustable term debenture A debenture issued on terms that the principal is repayable at the end of a specified term, or on notice given by the lender after a defined part of that term has expired. For example, a debenture for two years repayable on 30 days notice given after 12 months. See also **Debenture**.

•**Adjustment** The process of determining the amount due to an assured who has suffered loss covered by a policy of insurance and the proportion of the loss to be borne by each underwriter. In marine insurance law, unless otherwise agreed, an adjustment is governed by the law of the place of the ship's destination or delivery of cargo: *Simonds v White* (1824) 2 B & C 805; 107 ER 582. See also **Average; Underwriter**.

•**Adjustment agreement** See **Cash settled futures contract**.

Administered pricing Pricing by a seller of a good or service which is kept constant for a period of time and over a long series of transactions. Administered pricing has emerged as the most common form of pricing, replacing day-to-day haggling and bargaining. It applies to wages and salaries as much as to goods and services. The inflexibility of prices means that it is production and stock which are adjusted to meet changes in demand. For the consumer, it means that prices remain steady. Even in fruit and vegetable markets, vulnerable to seasonal factors, there is a day-to-day stability in prices.

•**Administration** 1. In succession, the management of a deceased estate by a person duly authorised to act as executor or administrator depending on whether the appointment was made by will or by the court. 2. An order bringing the general administration of a deceased estate or trust under the court's control, where there is a question between the trustees and beneficiaries. 3. The performance of the executive function of government, as compared with the judicial and legislative functions of government: *Glenister v Dillon* [1976] VR 550. 4. The management of a business or other organisation. See also **Administration bond; Administrator; Executive; Trust**.

Administration bond A guarantee made by a third party, often an insurance company, to make good any loss in the event of the administrator appointed under the grant of administration failing to properly administer the deceased estate. Such a bond is required by the court before issuing the grant of administration when it considers the beneficiaries need special protection (for example, where the administrator lives abroad or the appointment is disputed). The amount of the bond is usually equal to the value of the estate being administered but may be fixed on an individual basis in some jurisdictions: for example (NSW) Wills, Probate and Administration Act 1898 s 65. Bonds are not required in Queensland, Victoria, or Western Australia: (VIC) Administration and Probate (Amendment) Act 1977 s 41; (QLD) Succession Act 1981 s 51; (WA) Administration Act 1903 ss 26, 143. See also **Administrator**.

•**Administration component** An additional amount required to be paid by an employer who has failed to provide sufficient levels of superannuation support to an employee: (CTH) Superannuation Guarantee (Administration) Act 1992 ss 17, 32. See also **Superannuation guarantee charge**.

•**Administration order** An order directing that, during the period for which it is in force, the affairs, business and property of a person are to be managed by an appointed administrator. For example, in Victoria, the Board may make an administration order appointing a person as an administrator of an estate under specific circumstances: (VIC) Guardianship and Administration Board Act 1986 ss 3, 46, 60. In the law of bankruptcy, the court may order the appointment of an administrator of the estate of a deceased debtor: (CTH) Bankruptcy Act 1966 Pt XI. See also **Administrator**.

•**Administrative action** In administrative law, any action taken in relation to administration by a government body, authority, or organ. An action may include a decision or act, the refusal or failure to make a decision or to perform an act, the formulation of a proposal or intention, or the making of a recommendation: (VIC) Ombudsman Act 1973 s 2. See also **Administration; Decision.**

Administrative appeal An appeal from a decision of a statutory authority in which the appellant seeks a review of the merits of the decision or questions its legality. An appeal may be based on statutory entitlements or may seek common law remedies.

• **Administrative Appeals Tribunal** Abbr – AAT A statutory tribunal that conducts external merits review of the administrative decisions of government departments and authorities. Such a tribunal exists at the Commonwealth level and in Victoria and the Australian Capital Territory: (CTH) Administrative Appeals Tribunal Act 1975; (VIC) Administrative Appeals Tribunal Act 1984; (ACT) Administrative Appeals Tribunal Act 1989. See also **Administrative law; Tribunal.**

Administrative decisions (judicial review) legislation Abbr – AD(JR) Act Legislation designed to codify the common law grounds for judicial review of the actions of administrators, and to simplify the procedure for gaining review at the federal level: (CTH) Administrative Decisions (Judicial Review) Act 1977. The Act applies to decisions of an administrative character made under an enactment. An aggrieved person may apply for judicial review of the decision on several grounds, including that the decision breached the rules of natural justice; the procedures required to be observed in making the decision were not observed; the decision-maker did not have jurisdiction or the decision was not authorised; the decision involved an error of law whether or not the error appears on the face of the record; the decision was affected by fraud; there was no evidence or other material to justify the decision; there was an improper exercise of power; or the decision was otherwise contrary to law: ss 5(1), 6(1). See also **Abuse of power; Fraud; Grounds for review; Natural justice.**

• **Administrative fund** The fund established by a body corporate for the purposes of financing the control, management, and administration of the common property for the benefit of the proprietors in a strata title scheme: for example (QLD) Building Units and Group Titles Act 1980 s 7(1). See also **Body corporate.**

Administrative law The legal principles governing the relationship between the government and the governed. The exercise of power by administrators, including the state (the Crown), ministers, departmental officers, tribunals, boards, and commissions must be based on legal authority.

• **Administrator** Generally, a person who directs or manages the affairs of another.

Corporations A person appointed in a voluntary administration under Corporations Law Pt 5.3A to determine whether a company should come under administration according to an approved deed of company arrangement, be wound up, or revert to normal operation. See also **Committee of creditors.**

Admiralty court A court established in England in about 1360 that exercised jurisdiction in admiralty actions, including bottomry and *respondentia*, flotsam, jetsam, lagan, prize, towage, salvage, and maritime collisions. See also **Admiralty jurisdiction; Admiralty law; Court of Admiralty; Towage.**

Admiralty jurisdiction Jurisdiction over admiralty matters. A distinguishing feature of the admiralty jurisdiction is that it allows an aggrieved person to proceed by way of an action in rem, an action directed against the property in question (which is usually a ship). It is in contrast to an action in personam, which lies against a particular person. The (CTH) Admiralty Act 1988 conferred admiralty jurisdiction on the Federal Court of Australia and the various courts of the Territories and States. See also **Admiralty court; Admiralty law.**

Admiralty law The body of legal rules that govern ships and shipping. Its rules cover maritime liens, limitation of liability of ship owners, issues of fault, and compensation in relation to collisions, salvage, and insurance. See also **Admiralty court; Admiralty jurisdiction; International Maritime Organisation; Maritime lien.**

Admissible evidence Evidence received, or capable of being received by a court or tribunal of fact for the purpose of proving a fact in issue, because it is relevant to the proceedings in which it is tendered or adduced. The rules governing admissibility of evidence are found in statute (for example (CTH) Evidence Act 1995), the common law, and the rules of court (for example (CTH) High Court Rules O 37). The most common form of admissible evidence is oral testimony of an eye-witness who is available for cross-examination: *Myers v DPP* [1965] AC 1001. Evidence will only be admissible when it is relevant to a fact in issue: (CTH) Evidence Act 1995 s 56; *R v Stephenson* [1976] VR 376. See also **Evidence.**

Admission of facts A voluntary acknowledgment made as to the existence of the truth of certain facts which are inconsistent with a party's claims in an action; a statement, oral or written, which suggests an unfavourable inference to the party making the statement. If a party admits a fact in a pleading, the fact is taken as established for the purposes of the proceeding: *British Thomson-Houston Co Ltd v British Insulated & Helsby Cables Ltd* [1924] 1 Ch 203 at 210.

• **Adoption 1.** An action signifying acceptance or approval **2.** Incorporation.

Contract Acceptance of a contractual obligation by which the adopter would not otherwise be legally bound. For example, a person may adopt a contract on which his or her signature has been forged, or which was entered into on his or her behalf by an agent acting in excess of authority: *Coastal Estates Pty Ltd v Melevende* [1965] VR 433. See also **Affirmation; Mistake; Misrepresentation; Fraud.**

ADR See **Alternative dispute resolution.**

ADRs See **Australian Design Rules.**

ADS See **Australian Stock Exchange Ltd.**

Adv Frt See **Advance freight.**

Advance Bank Australia Established in 1985, a bank originating in the New South Wales Permanent Building Society which in turn had its origins in the New South Wales Group of Cooperative Societies founded in 1937. The Advance Bank is the fourth largest listed bank in Australia. It engages in retail banking, corporate banking, funds management, insurance and financial services. It has more than 200 branches throughout Australia. In 1990, the bank's subsidiary in the Australian Capital Territory, Civic Advance Bank, merged with the former Canberra Building Society to form Canberra Advance Bank.

Advance freight *Abbr* – Adv Frt, AF Freight paid by a consignor in exchange for handing over to the consignor the original bill of lading, or on presentation of the shipping order signed by the master of the vessel acknowledging receipt of the goods onto the ship. Advance freight must be specifically provided for in the contract of carriage since, as a general rule, freight is not payable until it is earned, that is until the vessel has arrived at its port of destination and the goods consigned have been delivered. The advantage to the carrier of advance freight is that the carrier may retain it, even if the cargo is lost, unless the loss is the carrier's fault: for example *A Coker & Co Ltd v Limerick Steamship Co Ltd* [1918-19] All ER 1099. A shipper of goods under a bill of lading, who is required to pay advance freight, has an insurable interest in so far as the freight is not repayable in case of loss: (CTH) Marine Insurance Act 1909 s 18. See also **Bill of lading; Carrier; Consignment; Contract of carriage; Freight; Insurable interest; Shipping note.**

Advance note A draft for wages given to a seaman by the owner of the ship upon the signing of articles of agreement. It is redeemable against the shipowner after the ship has sailed with the seaman on board. The note is negotiable and enables the seaman to purchase a kit while giving the shipowner a measure of security that the seaman will in fact join the ship.

Advance on freight An advance of money by a consignor to the master of a ship for the purpose of paying disbursements while the ship is in port. Often, it is later deducted from the total freight due under the charterparty or bill of lading. See also **Bill of lading; Charterparty; Freight.**

Advancement clause A clause inserted in a trust instrument or testamentary instrument which authorises the trustee or executor to make an advance out of a capital fund in which a named beneficiary or minor has a vested, presumptive, or contingent interest for the purpose of advancing or establishing that person in life: *Re Gosset's Settlement* (1854) 19 Beav 529; 52 ER 456.

Adventure A form of speculation in which goods are sent abroad by the owner at the owner's risk, in the charge of a person authorised to act as agent of the owner in disposing of the goods on the best possible terms. Adventures are rarely entered into today. See also **Agent.**

Adversarial system A mode of dispute resolution in which the competing claims of the parties are presented, usually by legal representatives who have no interest in the outcome of the dispute, to an impartial and disinterested third party with the power to impose an authoritative determination. Some tribunals are required to place as little emphasis on the adversarial approach as possible: for example (NSW) Independent Commission Against Corruption Act 1988 s 17. See also **Court.**

Adverse opinion report An opinion expressed by an auditor in the form of a written report. An auditor gives an adverse opinion report whenever there is a significant departure from accepted accounting principles or when the financial statements fail to provide a fair and true presentation of the business operations: AUP3. See also **Qualified audit report; Qualified opinion.**

•**Advertisement** *Lat – adverto –* to turn to. A means by which attention is directed to a particular good or service, or through which notice, advice, or information about the good or service is conveyed. An advertisement may constitute the making of a statement or a representation: *Guthrie v Universal Telecasters (Qld)* (1977) 16 ALR 247; *Hartnell v Sharp Corp* (1975) 5 ALR 493; ATPR ¶40-003. See also **Advertisement offer; Advertising.**

Advertisement offer A holding out or representation made to a person, in an advertisement, for their acceptance or refusal. See also **Advertisement; Invitation to treat.**

•**Advertising** The trade or profession of creating advertisements. See also **Advertisement; Advertisement offer.**

Advertising, comparative See **Comparative advertising.**

Advertising substantiation The proof of the truth of an advertisement. If an advertiser is able to prove that claims made about a product or service are true, the advertisement is capable of substantiation. See also **Advertising; Advertisement.**

•**Advice note 1.** A notice given by a consignor to a consignee with respect to goods to be consigned showing details such as the quantity to be consigned. **2.** A notice sent by a carrier to a consignee intimating that the goods will be arriving soon (or have arrived) and advising the consignee to prepare for the receipt of the goods without undue delay from the warehouse, customs buildings, or other point of delivery. The note indicates that unless the goods are collected within the specified time, the carrier will no longer hold the goods as carrier and will only be liable for loss caused by negligence. See also **Carrier; Consignee; Consignment; Negligence.**

Advising bank A bank through which the issuing bank in a documentary credit transaction advises the beneficiary of the establishment of the credit.

•**Advisory Committee** See **Companies and Securities Advisory Committee.**

Advisory Council on Industrial Property *Abbr* – ACIP A non-statutory body established in July 1994 to advise the relevant Minister and the Australian Industrial Property Organisation (AIPO) on industrial property policy and the AIPO's administration. The Minister appointed 10 members to the Council on 18 July 1994 for a maximum of three years. The council comprises executives and a corporate solicitor of Australian technology companies, a solicitor, a patent attorney, and, as ex-officio members, the Deputy Secretary and Chief Science Adviser of the relevant department, and the Director General of the AIPO. See also **Australian Industrial Property Organisation**.

Advocacy The art of conducting or presenting proceedings before a court. An advocate's work comprises argument or making speeches (called 'addressing'), questioning witnesses, and preparation and planning for these tasks.

Advocate A legal practitioner or person who presents or defends a case on behalf of a client before a court or tribunal. Both barristers and solicitors may act as advocates: for example (NSW) Legal Profession Act 1987 s 38L(1). See also **Advocacy**; **Barrister**; **Legal professional privilege**; **Solicitor**.

AF See **Advance freight**.

AFCUL See **Australian Federation of Credit Unions**.

• **Affairs** In corporations law, the activities, business, or concerns of a corporation: *Johns v Connor* (1992) 35 FCR 1; 107 ALR 465. The 'affairs of a body corporate' are defined in Corporations Law s 53 for the purposes of certain provisions of the Corporations Law to include matters such as the promotion, formation, membership, control, business, trading transactions, dealings, properties, liabilities, profits, receipts, losses, outgoings, and expenses of a company. It also encompasses the internal management of the company. Generally the expression has been given a wide interpretation: *Bond Corp Holdings Ltd v Sulan* (1990) 3 WAR 49; 2 ACSR 435; *Australian Securities Commission v Lucas* (1992) 27 ALD 67; 36 FCR 165; 7 ACSR 676. The 'business affairs of a body corporate' include any of the body's affairs and matters concerned with ascertaining the corporations with which the body is or has been connected: Corporations Law s 53AA. 'Examinable affairs' of a corporation are defined in Corporations Law s 9 for the purposes of an examination before the court under Corporations Law ss 596A -597B. See also **Corporation**.

Affected In relation to (CTH) Income Tax Assessment Act 1936 s 80B(5), a description of rights carried by shares which are affected by arrangement. It includes an arrangement which affects the rights of a person to sell or otherwise dispose of the beneficial interest held in shares: *K Porter & Co Pty Ltd v FCT* (1977) 19 ALR 510. See also **Shareholder**.

• **Affidavit** /æfədeɪvət/ *Lat* – he or she has sworn; he or she has made an oath. A written statement, made by a person who has sworn or affirmed before a person authorised to administer the oath that the contents of the statement are true, which may be used to support certain legal applications or as a substitute for oral testimony in court proceedings: for example (CTH) Acts Interpretation Act 1901 s 27; (CTH) High Court Rules O 39 r 9(3); (VIC) Rules of the Supreme Court O 43 r 1; (TAS) Evidence Act 1910 s 145. Under legislation, an affidavit includes a statutory declaration ((CTH) Bankruptcy Act 1966 s 5), a transparency or certified copy of an affidavit ((QLD) Evidence Act 1977 s 115), and an affirmation, declaration or promise ((CTH) Acts Interpretation Act 1901 s 27; (NSW) Interpretation Act 1987 s 21). See also **Affidavit evidence**; **Affidavit or statement of financial circumstances**; **Affirmation**.

Affidavit evidence Evidence put before a court by the successful tendering of an affidavit, as opposed to oral evidence. The deponent may be cross-examined as to the content of the evidence that he or she swore or affirmed by affidavit: for example (CTH) Judiciary Act 1903 s 77 H; (VIC) Rules of the Supreme Court O 40 r 2. See also **Affidavit**.

Affidavit or statement of financial circumstances An affidavit or statement required to be filed by parties to family law proceedings, dealing with property and spousal maintenance and setting out comprehensive particulars in relation to the parties' financial affairs including their ownership of property, superannuation rights, interests in trusts and deceased estates, and liabilities: (CTH) Family Law Rules O 17. If a party does not adequately comply with the statutory requirements for the affidavit, a court may refuse to proceed with a hearing and may give directions for the further conduct of the proceedings: *In the Marriage of Morgan* (1982) FLC ¶91-225. See also **Affidavit**; **Maintenance**.

• **Affiliation** In trade and commerce, 'sponsorship' or 'approval', requiring a positive link between a supplier and another person or body: *McDonald's System of Australia Pty Ltd v McWilliams Wines Pty Ltd* (1979) 28 ALR 236; 41 FLR 436. It is not a representation of affiliation merely to use an expression or name that is associated with another business or product, although such conduct may be misleading or deceptive: *McDonald's System of Australia Pty Ltd v McWilliam's Wines Pty Ltd*. It is an offence for a supplier to represent that the supplier has an affiliation that it does not have: (CTH) Trade Practices Act 1974 s 53(d); (NSW) Fair Trading Act 1987 s 44(g). See also **Approval**; **False representation**; **Misleading or deceptive conduct**; **Sponsorship**.

Affirmation 1. Confirmation; ratification. 2. A solemn declaration that is asserted to be true.

Contract An election to continue performance of contractual obligations: for example *Tropical Traders Ltd v Goonan* (1964) 111 CLR 41. An affirmation must be unambiguous, and will not be found unless unequivocal words or conduct are present: *Hawker Pacific Pty Ltd v Helicopter Charter Pty Ltd* (1991) 22 NSWLR 298. See also **Election**; **Rescission**; **Waiver**.

Evidence A solemn declaration by a witness or interpreter that the evidence or interpretation he or she gives will be truthful: (CTH) Evidence Act 1995 Sch. A witness must usually take an oath or make an affirmation before giving evidence: for example *Wendo v R* (1963) 109 CLR 559; (1964) ALR 292; (CTH) Evidence Act 1995 s 21(1). A person who is to be a witness may make an affirmation instead of taking an oath where the person has no religious belief or where it is not reasonably practicable to administer an appropriate oath as required by the person's particular faith: for example (CTH) Evidence Act 1995 s 23; (NSW) Evidence Act 1995 s 23; (VIC) Evidence Act 1958 s 102; (QLD) Oaths Act 1867 s 5A; *R v Kemble* [1990] 3 All ER 116. See also **Jurat**.

• **Affirmative action program** A program to be implemented by an employer, designed to ensure that appropriate action is taken to eliminate discrimination by the employer against women in relation to workplace matters, and to promote equal opportunity for women in employment: (CTH) Affirmative Action (Equal Employment Opportunity for Women) Act 1986 s 3.

Affirmative disclosure The confirmation of the true situation. In the context of consumer protection legislation, the Minister or the Australian Competition and Consumer Commission (ACCC) may seek orders following breach of the (CTH) Trade Practices Act 1974 Pt V requiring disclosure of correct information or advertisements in accordance with set terms: (CTH) Trade Practices Act 1974 s 80A: *Annand & Thompson Pty Ltd v Trade Practices Commission* (1979) 25 ALR 227; 40 FLR 165. An order seeking corrective advertising may also be pursued, in appropriate cases, under the general power to grant mandatory injunctions: (CTH) Trade Practices Act 1974 s 80; *Janssen Pharmaceutical Pty Ltd v Pfizer Pty Ltd* (1985) 6 IPR 227; *Makita (Aust) Pty Ltd v Black & Decker (A'asia) Pty Ltd* (1990) ATPR ¶41-030. See also **Corrective advertising**.

Affirmative dispute resolution See **Alternative dispute resolution**.

Affreightment A contract entered into between a consignor and a carrier under which the latter undertakes to carry goods to a specific destination for the consignor who is to pay the freight as a reward. In the case of a carrier by sea, the contract will be by way of charterparty or bill of lading. See also **Bill of lading**; **Carrier**; **Charterparty**; **Consignor**; **Freight**.

•**AFIC** See **Australian Financial Institutions Commission**.

Aforementioned Mentioned before or earlier, previously mentioned. See also **Aforesaid**.

Aforesaid Said before, previously stated. See also **Aforementioned**.

After acquired property Property acquired by a bankrupt on or after the date of bankruptcy and before discharge, which is otherwise divisible among the bankrupt's creditors: (CTH) Bankruptcy Act 1966 s 116. See also **After acquired property**; **Bankrupt**; **Deed of arrangement**; **Deed of assignment**; **Divisible property**; **Income of bankrupt**.

After tax profit The aggregate of the operating profit and extraordinary items of an entity for a given accounting period after deducting the income tax expense. See also **Extraordinary items**; **Operating revenue**.

After the commencement of this section A phrase inserted in an amended statutory provision so that the amended provision only operates from the date when the original section in the statute was enacted: *Byrne v Gray* [1956] VLR 520 at 523.

•**Age of majority** The age at which a person obtains adult status as a fully responsible citizen with full legal capacity. The age of majority at common law was 21 years, but has been lowered to 18 years by legislation: for example (NSW) Minors (Property and Contracts) Act 1970 s 9. Also known as 'full age', 'adult', 'full capacity', '*sui juris*', and 'coming of age': (QLD) Age of Majority Act 1974 (repealed) s 5(2). See also **Necessaries**.

•**Age pension** A pension paid by the Commonwealth Government to a person who has reached the pension age and has been an Australian resident for 10 years or has a qualifying residence exemption. A man, and a woman born on or after 1 January 1949, reaches pension age when he or she turns 65: (CTH) Social Security Act 1991 ss 23(5A), 23(5D). The pension age for women born before 1 July 1935 is 60 (s 23(5B)) and the age for women born between 1 July 1935 and 1 January 1949 increases gradually from 60 to 65 (s 23(5C)). The rate of pension payable varies according to such factors as whether the person is living with another as a spouse on a genuine domestic basis, and the person's income and assets: (CTH) Social Security Act 1991 ss 43, 1064. See also **Benefit**.

Ageing accounts receivable A method of analysing the outstanding amount of accounts receivable according to the length of time they have been overdue. The time is measured either from the date of invoice or 30 days from the date of statement. The method provides a means of monitoring, among other things, old accounts to determine whether a debt has become uncollectable, and thus a doubtful or bad debt. See also **Allowance for bad debts**; **Accounts receivable**; **Doubtful debts**.

•**Agency** A relationship involving authority or capacity in one person (the agent) to create or affect legal relations between another person (the principal) and third parties: *International Harvester Co of Australia Pty Ltd v Carrigan's Hazeldene Pastoral Co* (1958) 100 CLR 644; 32 ALJ 160. A relationship of agency is created either by the express or implied agreement of principal and agent, by the subsequent ratification by the principal of the agent's acts done on behalf of the principal, by operation of law, pursuant to statute, or by estoppel under the doctrine of apparent (or ostensible) authority. See also **Agent**; **Agency by estoppel**; **Agency of necessity**; **Apparent authority**; **Capacity**; **Express agency**; **Implied agency**; **Implied authority**; **Power of attorney**; **Principal**; **Ratification**; **Third party**.

Agency by estoppel An estoppel that arises where one person (the principal) by words or conduct holds out to another (the third party) that a particular person has been authorised as agent, and in reliance on that representation, the third party enters into transactions with the agent within the scope of the agent's apparent (or ostensible) authority: *Lysaght Bros & Co Ltd v Falk* (1905) 2 CLR 421. The person so holding out is estopped from denying the fact of agency. See also **Actual authority**; **Agency**; **Agent**; **Apparent authority**; **Estoppel**; **Principal**; **Third party**.

Agency cheque A third party payment service offered to the customers of a non-bank financial institution (NBFI). The NBFI may establish an account with its bank. Cheques drawn on that account by the NBFI will be authorised to be completed by the NBFI's customers to whom cheque books for that account are issued by the NBFI. The facility gives indirect access to the clearing system to the NBFI's customers. (CTH) Cheques and Payment Orders Act 1986 s 100 gives legal force to this commercial reality by giving special status to those agency cheques that are 'signed by the customer'. See also **Cheque**; **Clearance of cheque**; **Customer of a bank**; **Non-bank financial institution**; **Payment order**.

Agency clause 1. A clause in an agreement with a licensed agent for the performance of services for a commission, fee, gain, or reward. **2.** A clause that specifies the extent of the authority of an agent to act on behalf of the principal. **3.** A clause in a document, not in itself an agency agreement, which provides for, or makes reference to, the creation of a relationship of agent and principal. See also **Agency; Express agency; Express authority; Scope of authority.**

Agency cost The cost of resolving conflicts of interest amongst stockholders, bondholders, and managers. An example of an agency cost is the cost of providing managers with an incentive to increase shareholder wealth and control their performance. Agency costs are borne by stockholders.

Agency of necessity A relationship of principal and agent by which the authority to act on behalf of another is deemed or implied by reason of emergency: *Bank of New South Wales v Owston* (1878) 4 App Cas 270: *China-Pacific SA v Food Corp of India* [1982] AC 939. The agent must have acted reasonably, in good faith and without the opportunity to obtain the consent of the principal: *China-Pacific SA v Food Corp of India*; *Baker v Burns Philp and Co Ltd* (1944) 45 SR (NSW) 1. See also **Agency; Agent.**

Agency, termination of See **Termination of agency.**

Agenda /ədʒɛndə/ *Lat* – things which need to be done; items of business to be transacted at a meeting.

Agent In its strict legal sense, a person with an authority or capacity to create or affect legal relations between a principal and third parties: *International Harvester Co of Australia Pty Ltd v Carrigan's Hazeldene Pastoral Co* (1958) 100 CLR 644; 32 ALJ 160; *Petersen v Moloney* (1951) 84 CLR 91. Generally speaking, what a person may do himself or herself, the person may do by an agent: *Christie v Permewan Wright & Co Ltd* (1904) 1 CLR 693. A principal may be vicariously liable for the agent's tortious conduct, such as negligence: *Kooragang Investments Pty Ltd v Richardson & Wrench Ltd* [1982] AC 462; (1981) 36 ALR 142; *Beach Petroleum NL v Johnson* (1993) 43 FCR 1; 115 ALR 411. See also **Agency; Auctioneer; Broker; Capacity; Del credere agent; Factor; Fiduciary; Forwarding agent; General agent; Insurance agent; Mercantile agent; Principal; Special agent; Third party.**

Agent, air cargo See **Air cargo agent.**

Agent of necessity See **Agency of necessity.**

Agent's lien A lien held by an agent on the goods and chattels of the agent's principal in the agent's possession in respect of all claims against the principal arising out of the agent's employment, whether for remuneration earned, or for expenses or liabilities incurred. See also **Agency; Agent; General lien; Lien; Particular lien; Principal; Remuneration.**

Agent's signature The signature of an agent; when taken with the words of a contract or words added to the signature, it can have a variety of effects. If the signature is representative of the person signing in the capacity of agent, no personal liability accrues. Examples of such accompanying phrases are 'as agents', 'on behalf of', 'for' and 'on account of': for example *J S Robertson (Aust) Pty Ltd v Martin* (1956) 94 CLR 30; 30 ALJ 114. However, where the accompanying phrase is descriptive solely, for example 'as purchaser', personal liability may arise: *Public Trustee v Taylor* [1978] VR 289; (1977) 43 LGRA 108. See also **Agency; Agent; Signature.**

•**Aggravation** An increase in the gravity, severity, or seriousness of something.

Tort An increase in the gravity of an injury suffered by a person as the result of mental distress brought about by the insulting and humiliating manner in which another has committed a tort. The court acknowledges aggravation in an award of increased general compensatory damages: *Henry v Thompson* [1989] 2 Qd R 412; (1989) Aust Tort Reports ¶80-265. See also **Exemplary damages.**

•**Aggregate lot entitlement** The sum of the lot entitlements on a building units plan: (QLD) Building Units and Group Titles Act 1980 s 7(1).

Aggregate unit entitlement See **Aggregate lot entitlement.**

•**Aggrieved** In administrative law, a person having a genuine legal grievance arising from a decision or determination which adversely affects their interests: (CTH) Administrative Decisions (Judicial Review) Act 1977 s 3(4). In an application for the review of an administrative decision, standing depends on the applicant establishing that he or she is a 'person aggrieved': ss 5-7. The interests affected may be business interests: *Ralkan Agricultural Co Pty Ltd v Aboriginal Development Commission* (1982) 43 ALR 535. Individuals may be aggrieved if their rights against third parties are affected by the decision or determination: *Tooheys Ltd v Minister for Business and Consumer Affairs* (1981) 36 ALR 64. A person may be aggrieved where their employment, or posting as an employee, is affected: *Stammers v Broadbridge* (1987) 73 ALR 523.

•**Aggrieved person** A person whose interests are adversely affected by a decision or determination to which the (CTH) Administrative Decisions (Judicial Review) Act 1977 applies: (CTH) Administrative Decisions (Judicial Review) Act 1977 s 3(4). The grievance may be in relation to a decision which directly or indirectly affects an existing or future legal right: *Tooheys Ltd v Minister for Business and Consumer Affairs* (1981) 4 ALD 277 at 290; 36 ALR 64 at 79. Where the interest affected does not amount to a legal right, a person who suffers a grievance beyond the suffering experienced by an ordinary member of the public may be a person aggrieved: *Tooheys Ltd v Minister for Business and Consumer Affairs*. See also **Locus standi.**

Civil and political rights In the context of anti-discrimination legislation, a person who is the victim or subject of discriminatory conduct and is able to initiate a complaint under anti-discrimination legislation. See also **Discrimination.**

Agio A fee charged for changing money of one currency to another or for changing gold or silver or negotiable instruments (for example, cheques) into cash; the difference between the two values such as between the interest charged by banks on loans and the interest paid by banks on deposits. See also **Cheque**; **Currency**; **Money**.

Agreed damages clause A term quantifying the damages payable in the event of breach. The function of an agreed damages clause is to overcome the requirement of proof of loss in a claim for damages; the clause fixes the amount recoverable by the plaintiff, without the need for litigation. See also **Liquidated damages**; **Penalty**; **Primary obligation**; **Secondary obligation**; **Term**.

Agreed fact A fact that the parties to a proceeding have agreed is not, for the purposes of the proceeding, to be disputed: (CTH) Evidence Act 1995 s 191(1).

• **Agreed return** In relation to the performance of a contract by a party, the performance by another party, contemplated by the contract as consideration for the first mentioned performance: (NSW) Frustrated Contracts Act 1978 s 5(3). An amount equal to the value of the agreed return is required to be paid to the performing party where full performance is received by the other party prior to frustration (except where performance involved the payment of money): (NSW) Frustrated Contracts Act 1974 s 10. See also **Consideration**; **Frustration**; **Performance**.

Agreed value clause A clause contained in a bill of lading that limits the liability of the carrier for loss of or damage to the goods carried. The limitation is usually a sum agreed upon between the parties and set either as a lump sum in money, or by use of a formula allowing an agreed amount per unit of the goods shipped. See also **Agreed damages clause**; **Bill of lading**.

Agreed value policy An insurance policy which provides for the payment of a fixed sum in the event of loss irrespective of whether there has been any fluctuations in value during the currency of the policy. The mere fact that the insured declares the value of the property in a proposal or in the policy does not make it an agreed value policy; the purpose of the insured doing so is simply to give the insurer information about the risk being covered: *Carreras Ltd v Cunard Steamship Co Ltd* [1918] 1 KB 118. An agreed value policy is still an indemnity policy: *British Traders' Insurance Co Ltd v Monson* (1964) 111 CLR 86; [1964] ALR 845. See also **Agreed value clause**.

• **Agreement** In contract law, the stage at which the negotiations between the parties are complete. The traditional approach to establish agreement between the parties requires offer and acceptance, which is a clear indication by one party (the offeror) of a willingness to be bound on certain terms accompanied by a communication by the other party (the offeree) to the offeror of an unqualified assent to that offer: *MacRobertson Miller Airline Services v Cmr of State Taxation (WA)* (1975) 133 CLR 125; 8 ALR 131. See also **Acceptance**; **Contract**; **Offer**; **Term**.

Agreement between the Commonwealth of Australia and the States and Territories of Australia in relation to the adoption of Uniform Trade Measurement Legislation 1990 See **Trade Measurement Agreement 1990**.

Agreement by speciality See **Specialty**.

Agreement Concerning the International Classification of Goods and Services for the Purposes of the Registration of Marks 1957 An international agreement to adopt, for the purposes of the registration of marks, a single classification of goods and services: Agreement Concerning the International Classification of Goods and Services for the Purposes of the Registration of Marks 1957 art 2. The agreement consists of a list of classes, and an alphabetical list of goods and services with an indication of the classes into which they fall: art 1. Australia has adopted the agreement and its revisions but is yet to implement the classification scheme in Australia. See also **Goods and services**; **Trade mark**.

Agreement Concerning the International Deposit of Industrial Designs and Revisions 1925 An agreement providing for an international deposit of designs: Agreement Concerning the International Deposit of Industrial Designs and Revisions 1925 art 4(1). A design registered and deposited at the international bureau has the same effect in each designated state as if all the formalities for that state had been complied with: art 7. Australia is not a member of the Agreement but recognises Convention applications on the basis of an application made under that agreement: (CTH) Designs Act 1906 s 48(3). See also **International Convention for the Protection of Industrial Property 1883**.

Agreement establishing the European Bank for Reconstruction and Development 1991 An agreement signed in 1990 in Paris for the establishment of the European Bank for Reconstruction and Development. The main purpose of the bank is to foster the transition of Central and Eastern European countries towards open market-oriented economies and the promotion of private and entrepreneurial initiative by assisting structural and sectoral economic reforms: Agreement establishing the European Bank for Reconstruction and Development 1991 art 2.

Agreement for lease An agreement enforceable in equity, but not in law, as an obligation to grant a lease: *Walsh v Lonsdale* (1881) 21 Ch D 9. See also **Lease**.

Agreement to sell Lat – *aggregatio mentium*. The consent or concurrence of the minds of two or more parties in respect of the sale of a subject matter. An agreement as to price during negotiations does not amount to agreement to sell in the sense that a binding contract has been formed: *Clifton v Palumbo* [1944] 2 All ER 497 at 499. See also **Consensus ad idem**; **Contract**.

• **Agriculture** The use or cultivation of land for any purpose of husbandry or horticulture, including the raising of livestock and the growing of crops. Growing plants in pots rather than in the ground may still be properly described as agriculture: *Wym Pty Ltd v Sutherland Shire Council* (1990) 69 LGRA 322.

AGS See **Australian Government Solicitor**.

AIBF See **Australian Institute of Banking and Finance**.

Aid and abet To assist and to encourage.

Criminal law To assist in the commission of a crime

without actually participating in the offence itself. An accused who aids and abets must be shown to have been in some way linked in purpose with the person actually committing the principal offence, and the accused's words or conduct must encourage or render more likely the commission of the crime by the principal: *R v Russell* [1933] VLR 59.

Trade and commerce To encourage another to commit a contravention, resulting in ancillary liability for a contravention of legislation: (CTH) Trade Practices Act 1974 ss 75B(1)(a), 80. See also **Ancillary liability**.

Aid to production or export of goods A grant of money to assist or reward production or export of goods: Commonwealth Constitution s 91. The aid is pecuniary and does not include the provision of other non-pecuniary benefits or advantages to assist or reward the production of goods: *Seamen's Union of Australia v Utah Development Co* (1978) 144 CLR 120; 22 ALR 291. It can occur either before or after the production or export of goods has taken place. The Australian States are allowed to provide this aid with the permission of both Houses of the Commonwealth Parliament: Commonwealth Constitution s 91. However, such permission is not required where the assistance or reward is non-pecuniary: *Seamen's Union of Australia v Utah Development Co.* See also **Export; Parliament; Pecuniary; Production**.

AIDS litigation Product liability litigation commenced in Australia and elsewhere against blood suppliers and hospitals, brought by persons seeking damages for personal injury caused by contracting the disease Acquired Immune Deficiency Syndrome (AIDS) from transfused blood contaminated with the human immunodeficiency virus (HIV): for example *Dwan v Farquhar* [1988] 1 Qd R 234; (1987) Aust Tort Reports ¶80-096; *E v Australian Red Cross Society* (1991) 31 FCR 299; 105 ALR 53.

•**Aids to manufacture** Goods for use by a manufacturer in the course of carrying on a business: *Genex Corp Pty Ltd v Commonwealth* (1991) 30 FCR 193; 101 ALR 161. The goods must be used mainly for the purpose of that business: (CTH) Sales Tax (Exemptions and Classifications) Act 1935 Sch 1 cl 1. Aids to manufacture include the machinery, implements, and apparatus used while processing or treating manufactured goods. They must be used in, wrought into, or attached to the manufactured goods. See also **Aid to production or export of goods; Manufacture**.

AIPO See **Australian Industrial Property Organisation**.

Air cargo agent A person who creates relations between two other people, one of whom is in control of cargo that is to be transported by air to a destination, and the other of whom is an aircraft operator who is willing to transport that cargo. Air cargo agency (and air passenger agency) is regulated by the International Air Transport Association. There are also regional associations. There is a program for the accreditation of agents in Australia. Activities under the program including licensing agents, regulating professional conduct, reputation and competence, and setting standards for financial requirements and documentation. Air cargo agents must use the standard form cargo agency agreement and air consignment and air waybill conditions of contract. See also **Agent; Air waybill; Sea cargo agent**.

Air carrier A body or person who carries persons, baggage, or cargo by air. An air carrier's liability is governed by international conventions such as the Convention for the Unification of Certain Rules relating to International Carriage by Air 1929. See also **Carrier**.

Air consignment note See **Air waybill**.

Air law The part of international law governing civil aviation and institutions involved in the operation and use of aircraft (excluding hovercraft and military aviation). Air law includes rules of customary and general international law, mainly emanating from bilateral and multilateral treaties on civil aviation. See also **Convention on International Civil Aviation 1944; International Civil Aviation Organisation**.

•**Air pollution 1.** The artificial introduction of substances or energy into the air resulting in deleterious effects on humans, living resources, ecosystems, or material property, and interfering with amenities and other legitimate uses of the environment: Convention on Long-Range Transboundary Air Pollution 1979 art 1(a). **2.** In air pollution control legislation, a contamination of the atmosphere by the discharge or emission of particulates or gases; the emission into air of any air impurity: (NSW) Clean Air Act 1961 s 5(1). See also **Pollution**.

Air transport undertaking A business undertaking to carry passengers and goods by air in exchange respectively for fares and freight. The person or corporation carrying on such a business may be a common carrier, but will more usually be a private carrier. See also **Common carrier; Fare; Freight; Goods**.

Air waybill *Abbr* – AWB A document made as evidence of the contract of carriage entered into between the consignor of goods to be carried by air and the carrier. An air waybill shows details of the goods being carried, and the ownership of those goods. Also known as 'air consignment note'. See also **Consignor; Contract of carriage; Goods**.

AIRC See **Australian Industrial Relations Commission**.

Airline over-booking The practice of airline operators by which more passengers are allowed to be booked onto an aircraft than there are seats available, in anticipation that not all persons who have booked a seat will actually seek to board the aircraft. This practice may constitute misleading and deceptive conduct by airlines where the traveller is reasonably led to believe a booking is confirmed: (CTH) Trade Practices Act 1974 s 52; *Re Sullivan* (unrptd, FC, Pincus J, G78/85, 1 Sep 1986); *British Airways Board v Taylor* [1976] 1 All ER 65. See also **Misleading or deceptive conduct**.

Airline ticket A document prepared by or on behalf of a carrier by air and tendered to the intending passenger in return for the fare. It is later presented by the passenger to the carrier in order to obtain carriage by air between the point of embarkation and the point of disembarkation nominated in the ticket. Such a ticket is not an agreement or any memorandum of agreement for the purposes of stamp duty legislation, but is merely an offer by the carrier to carry a passenger which offer is subsequently accepted by the passenger's conduct: *MacRobertson Miller Airline Services v Cmr of State Taxation (WA)* (1975) 133 CLR 125; 8 ALR 131. See also **Carrier; Offer.**

• **Airline transport fringe benefit** A taxable fringe benefit arising where free or discounted travel in passenger aircraft on a standby basis is provided to employees of either airlines or travel agents by an employer in those industries: (CTH) Fringe Benefits Tax Assessment Act 1986 s 32. See also **Fringe benefit; Fringe benefits tax.**

• **Airport** An aerodrome; an area of land used for the landing, take off, storage, servicing and maintenance of aircraft, and for receiving passengers and goods for carriage by air: (CTH) Airports (Surface Traffic) Act 1960 (repealed) s 31; (CTH) Airports (Business Concessions) Act 1959 (repealed) s 3; (CTH) Customs Act 1901 s 4. See also **Convention on International Civil Aviation 1944.**

Aktiebolag *Abbr* – AB *Scand.* The Swedish equivalent of a company limited by shares. There are no private limited liability companies in Sweden. See also **Company limited by shares.**

Aktiengesellschaft *Abbr* – AG *German.* The Austrian, German, and Swiss equivalent of a public company limited by shares. See also **Company limited by shares; Public company.**

Aktieselskab *Abbr* – A/s The Danish equivalent of a public limited liability company. See also **Limited company.**

• **Alcoholic liquor** A beverage which contains more than 1.15 per cent ethanol by volume at 20 degrees celsius or a beverage, for the purposes of sale, held out to be beer, wine, or spirits: (NSW) Liquor Act 1982 s 4(1). Ale, beer, brandy, cider, perry, mead, porter, stout, rum, whisky, and wine are commonly included under the term.

Aleatory contract A contract in which the promisor's obligation to perform becomes enforceable on the occurrence of a fortuitous event which neither party desires to occur and in respect of which there is no promise of occurrence: for example *United Dominions Trust (Commercial) Ltd v Eagle Aircraft Services Ltd* [1968] 1 All ER 104; *Aldwell v Bundey* (1876) 10 SALR 118. The main example is an insurance contract. See also **Contract; Insurance contract.**

Alias /ˈeɪliəs/ *Lat* – otherwise; at another time or at other times. An assumed name. Often used with the implication that the assumption of an alternative name is for criminal purposes. Pl – *Aliases.*

Alibi /ˈæləbaɪ/ *Lat* – elsewhere. A claim by a person charged with an offence to the effect that the person was somewhere other than the place where the crime was committed at the time of the commission of the offence and, therefore, could not be guilty of the offence. An accused person has the evidentiary onus in respect of an alibi: *R v Johnson* [1961] 1 WLR 1478.

• **Alien 1.** A person who was born outside of Australia, whose parents were not Australian, and who has not been naturalised as an Australian: *Pochi v Macphee* (1982) 151 CLR 101; 43 ALR 261. **2.** A person with no relationship with the state, or a citizen or subject of a foreign state: *Nolan v Minister for Immigration and Ethnic Affairs* (1988) 165 CLR 178; 80 ALR 561.

• **Alienation** The transfer of value from one person to another: *Ord Forrest Pty Ltd v FCT* (1974) 130 CLR 124; 2 ALR 403 at 407. Although 'alienation' is wide enough to cover all transfers of property, it is usually understood to apply only to transfers of property effected by action of the transferor, and not those occurring automatically due to the operation of law: *Australian Trade Commission v Film Funding & Management Pty Ltd* (1989) 14 IPR 461; 24 FCR 595; 87 ALR 49. See also **Assignment; Nemo dat quod non habet; Property; Sale.**

Alienation of income The transfer by one person to another, of the right to receive income so that the income is derived for taxation purposes by that other person. To be an effective alienation for taxation purposes, the right transferred must be a presently existing right to income, not a mere expectancy: *Norman v FCT* (1963) 109 CLR 9; [1964] ALR 131. See also **Assignment.**

Aliquot /ˈælɪkwɒt/ *Lat* – several; so many. In the phrase 'aliquot part', aliquot means contained in a greater quantity an integral number of times.

Aliquot share Strictly denotes an equal share, but in law is used to describe any definite share or interest in property. The interest of a tenant in common is often described as an aliquot share even where the shares in the tenancy in common are unequal. See also **Aliquot; Tenancy in common; Undivided share.**

All financial resources concept The notion that a statement of changes in financial position is more informative and useful when it reports on all additions of financial resources to business operations and all distribution of resources as well as the changing composition of resources.

All Ordinaries Index A weighted share price index summarising the price movements on the Australian stock market. It is calculated using the market prices of the shares of over 300 Australian companies listed on the Sydney and Melbourne stock exchanges. The combined market value of these companies accounts for nearly 90 per cent of the value of all shares listed on those exchanges. Each stock is weighted by multiplying the number of shares in each company by the current price per share to give a total market value or market capitalisation. The index was first established in January 1980 and is calculated continuously each day by the Australian Stock Exchange. The Fifty Leaders sub-index is composed of the top fifty stocks by capitalisation and is reviewed annually. The Twenty Leaders sub-index contains 20 of Australia's largest companies. See also **Australian Stock Exchange Ltd; Share price index.**

All Ordinaries Index option Introduced by the Australian Stock Exchange in 1985, a means by which an investor may invest in the whole stock market making it possible to hedge against the risk of market-wide movements. It was designed to assist all those holding shares whether as portfolio managers, underwriter, or individual shareholders. See also **Option.**

•**All reasonable precautions** A common phrase in a liability insurance policy requiring the insured to be concerned to protect the insured property from loss or damage and to take such steps to protect the property as he or she thinks reasonable, having regard to dangers which he or she recognises: *Legal and General Insurance Australia Ltd v Eather* (1986) 6 NSWLR 390. The condition will be breached where the insured deliberately courted a danger which he or she recognised, by refraining from taking any measures at all, or by only taking measures that the insured knew would be inadequate: *Albion Insurance Co Ltd v Body Corporate Strata Plan No 4303* [1983] 2 VR 339. See also **Assured**; **Accident insurance**; **Condition**; **Indemnity**; **Liability insurance**.

All Resources Index A share price index which measures the performance of companies in the resources area of the Australian economy. It embraces over 90 per cent of Australia's largest companies involved in the mining and exploration of natural resources.

All risks insurance Insurance, effected mainly in relation to particular items of property, providing cover in respect of any losses of an accidental or fortuitous character and not merely risks of a specified class: *London & Provincial Leather Processes Ltd v Hudson* [1939] 2 KB 724. The meaning of the phrase is a matter of construction: *Queensland Government Railways v Manufacturers' Mutual Insurance* [1969] 1 Lloyd's Rep 214. All risks insurance does not cover losses caused by inherent vice, wear and tear, or events that were inevitable: *British & Foreign Marine Insurance Co Ltd v Gaunt* [1921] 2 AC 41. The onus of proof rests upon the plaintiff to prove that the loss was caused by some event covered by the general expression: *British & Foreign Marine Insurance Co Ltd v Gaunt*. Because of the wide ambit of cover, insurers may try to restrict their liability through exclusion clauses. See also **All risks policy**; **Construction**; **Exclusion clause**; **Inherent vice**; **Insurance**.

All risks policy An insurance policy covering accidental loss, damage, or destruction resulting from a wide range of causes other than those specifically excluded in the policy. The policy does not cover damage which is a result of ordinary wear and tear or depreciation: *British & Foreign Marine Insurance Co Ltd v Gaunt* [1921] 2 AC 41. See also **All risks insurance**.

Alligator spread A commodity traders' expression for a commission that is so large that it 'eats the clients' or 'chews up the client's cash'.

•**Allocate 1.** To set apart, designate, or assign a number of the available shares in a company to particular persons: *TC Newman (Qld) Pty Ltd v DHA Rural (Qld) Pty Ltd* [1988] 1 Qd R 308; 12 ACLR 257. **2.** To apportion or assign an expense or income to various accounts, departments, or periods depending upon the nature of each account and the policy adopted in determining the allocation. See also **Share**.

•**Allocated annuity** An annuity under which an annuitant has an account on which he or she may regularly draw within certain statutory limits: (CTH) Occupational Superannuation Standards Regulations 1987 regs 3E-3F. Allocated annuities also offer access to the capital sum invested and may run out during the purchaser's lifetime. See also **Allocated pension**; **Annuity**; **Life insurance**; **Pension**.

Allocated fund A type of superannuation fund where both the employer and employee contributions are allocated for payment at set rates. The accumulated interest and contributions then form benefits payable to members.

•**Allocated pension** A payment made from a superannuation fund from contributions or eligible termination payments which have been rolled over from another fund. The allocated pension is payable until death or until the funds run out. Beneficiaries can decide whether to draw only the income generated from the balance in the fund, or to use capital as well. Also known as 'cash-back' or 'rollover pension '. See also **Allocated annuity**.

Allocation system A system of assigning the risk and cost of loss to particular persons, employed by courts and legislatures in decisions concerning the sources of compensation to a plaintiff. Rather than merely shifting the loss from the victim to the tortfeasor, such a scheme recognises that many wrongdoers do not have the financial resources to recompense their victims, and that some activities, although dangerous, are beneficial to a larger section of the public. It may place the burden of loss on insurers, or attach liability to those who can most easily absorb the cost of loss. Also known as 'loss spreading' or 'loss distribution'. See also **Compensation**.

Allocative efficiency The flow of goods and services which is likely to maximise the consumption benefits for society over time. Allocative inefficiencies may occur as a result of monopoly, price controls, and other regulations, or simply the maldistribution of income in which there is a divergence between effective demand and basic human needs. See also **Optimisation**.

Allonge A piece of paper pasted on the side of a negotiable instrument, when there is no room for indorsement on the instrument itself. See also **Indorsement**; **Negotiable instrument**.

All-or-none *Abbr* – AON A qualification by an intending purchaser of shares to a stockbroker that the whole order must be executed at the same time. In the absence of sufficient quantity of the stock at the proper price the purchase cannot be made. An AON order may take all day to execute, or it may never happen at all. See also **Sharebroker**.

•**Allotment 1.** A distribution or apportionment. **2.** A separate parcel of land.

Allotment letter The letter by which a company accepts an application for securities. The letter states how many shares have been allotted and is evidence of the allotment of those shares. See also **Allotment**.

Allotment of shares See **Allotment**.

Allottee In corporations law, the person to whom shares have been allotted. An allottee of shares only becomes a member of the issuing company when the person's name is entered on the company register: *Federal Cmr of Taxation v St Helens Farm ACT Ltd* (1981) 146 CLR 336; 34 ALR 23. See also **Allotment**; **Share**.

•**Allowable capital expenditure** Expenditure of a capital nature incurred by a taxpayer allowable as a deduction to mining operators or primary producers under specific provisions of the (CTH) Income Tax Assessment Act 1936. Capital expenditure is not an allowable deduction for income tax purposes under the general deduction provisions: (CTH) Income Tax Assessment Act 1936 s 51. Allowable capital expenditure includes expenditure in carrying on mining operations; expenditure on plant for use primarily in the treatment of minerals; on buildings or plant for the maintenance or storage of plant; on acquiring mining or prospecting rights, or information in certain circumstances; and on certain start-up costs of a mining company: s 122A. Exchange losses on borrowed money spent on prescribed mining operations are not allowable capital expenditure: *Robe River Mining Co Pty Ltd v FCT* (1989) 21 FCR 1; 88 ALR 50. Similarly, some capital expenditure is allowable to primary producers in relation, for example, to extension of telephone lines, grape vines, and soil and water conservation: (CTH) Income Tax Assessment Act 1936 ss 70, 75 AA, 75A, 75B, 75D. See also **Allowable deduction**; **Capital**.

•**Allowable deduction** A deduction allowable under (CTH) Income Tax Assessment Act 1936: s 6(1). Taxable income is arrived at by subtracting allowable deductions from assessable income: s 48. See also **Apportionment**; **Assessable income**; **Business**; **Capital**; **Depreciation**; **Exempt income**; **Incurred**; **Taxable income**.

•**Allowance** 1. In relation to employment, payments made to an employee to compensate the employee for any disabilities, additional skills, or other aspects of the work. 2. A grant of something additional to ordinary wages for the purpose of meeting particular requirements connected with the service rendered by the employee as compensation for unusual conditions of that service: *Mutual Acceptance Co Ltd v FCT* (1944) 69 CLR 389. Examples are isolation allowances and dirt allowances (for unusually dirty or offensive work). See also **Remuneration**; **Wage**.

Allowance for bad debts An estimate of bad debts expected to eventuate in an accounting period. The allowance is recorded as an expense in the profit and loss account by debiting bad debts and crediting allowance for bad debts. The credit appears on the balance sheet as a liability against accounts receivable. Also known as 'provision for bad debts'. See also **Bad debt**.

Alongside A maritime term used in contracts of affreightment. Cargo is not brought alongside the ship in which it is to be carried until it is lying within reach of the ship's tackle. Prior to being brought alongside, the cargo remains at the risk and expense of the consignor or charterer. In relation to the position of a vessel, a charterparty may contain a clause providing for the cargo to be brought alongside another vessel, in which case the term implies having the two vessels in such proximity that the cargo can be offered over the ship's rail: *Brenda Steamship Co v Green* (1900) 69 LJQB 445. The term does not necessarily require actual contact between the two vessels, but it does suggest close contiguity: *Palgrave Brown & Son Ltd v Owners of SS Turid* [1922] 1 AC 397; 22 All ER 622. See also **Affreightment**; **Alongside date**; **Cargo**; **Charterer**; **Charterparty**; **Consignor**.

Alongside date In maritime law, a date stipulated in the bill of lading or charterparty by which cargo must be brought alongside a ship for loading. See also **Alongside**; **Bill of lading**; **Cargo**; **Charterparty**.

ALRC See **Australian Law Reform Commission**.

Alter ego /ɔltə igoʊ/ *Lat* – one's other self; a very close friend.

•**Alteration** Generally, a change, modification, or amendment.

Deeds and other instruments In relation to a deed or bond, a modification to the writing in an instrument, whether by interlineation, addition, erasure, or by drawing a pen through a line. A writing may be altered in any way before it is signed without affecting the validity of the instrument. See also **Bond**; **Cancellation**; **Deed**; **Obligee**; **Void**.

•**Alternate director** A person appointed by a director to act for or on behalf of that director when that director is absent or unable to act at any time: Corporations Law s 238. See also **Director**; **Directors' duties**; **Table A articles**.

Alternative dispute resolution *Abbr* – ADR
The decision making process by which matters are resolved outside the usual court-based litigation model. The aim of ADR is to encourage parties in conflict to arrive at compromise solutions with the assistance of a neutral person. ADR includes processes such as assisted negotiation, expert appraisal, mediation, conciliation, evaluation, and arbitration: for example (QLD) Supreme Court of Queensland Act 1991 ss 100A, 100B. See also **Arbitration**; **Counselling**; **Court-appointed expert**; **Mediation**; **Negotiation**.

Alternative projects In environmental impact assessment, an examination of alternative locations, methods, and techniques for a particular project, including the alternative of not proceeding. It may be demonstrated that a project is not actually needed if demand-management approaches (for example, curbing the demand for water or electricity) are adopted or strengthened.

Alternative remedies Remedies that can be obtained by means other than litigation. An example of an alternative remedy is alternative dispute resolution which may involve mediation or arbitration and bypasses the court system. See also **Arbitration**; **Out of court settlement**; **Mediation**.

Always afloat *Abbr* – aa In maritime law, a clause generally included in a charterparty providing that the ship chartered must berth for loading and discharging cargo without touching the sea bed or river bed. Sometimes the clause will allow for an exception where the ship touches harmless ground during low tide. A clause in the form 'load in the customary manner, always afloat' gives the charterer the right to refuse to load the vessel except when it is afloat: *Carlton SS Co Ltd v Castle Mail Packet Co Ltd* [1898] AC 486. A clause providing for loading and discharge 'in any dock or at any wharf or place the charterer may direct where she can always safely lie afloat' allows the master to refuse to take the ship into any place where in the master's reasonable judgment the ship could not always safely lie afloat: *Steam Ship Boveric Co Ltd v Howard Smith & Sons Pty Ltd* (1901) 27 VLR 347. See also **Charterparty**.

- **Amalgamated organisation** In relation to amalgamation of employer or employee organisations, the organisation of which members of the deregistered organisation have become members: (CTH) Industrial Relations Act 1988 ss 234, 253Q. See also **Amalgamation**; **Employee organisation**; **Employer organisation**.

- **Amalgamation** Generally, a joining, merging, or union of two separate things to create a new thing.

  Corporations A process where one company takes over or merges with another company, or a number of companies unite with one or more other companies by merging or taking control. See also **Control**; **Merger**.

  Industrial law The joining of two or more existing industrial organisations to form a new organisation, or the absorption of one or more organisations by another organisation: for example (CTH) Industrial Relations Act 1988 ss 233-253ZG; (NSW) Industrial Relations Act 1996 s 283(3). See also **Amalgamated organisation**; **Industrial organisation**.

- **Amalgamation day** The day fixed by the Australian Industrial Relations Commission as the day on which an amalgamation of employer or employee organisations is to take effect. On that day, the amalgamated organisation must be registered; the deregistering organisations must be deregistered; and the members of the deregistering organisations become members of the amalgamated organisation: (CTH) Industrial Relations Act 1988 ss 234, 253Q. See also **Amalgamated organisation**; **Amalgamation**; **Australian Industrial Relations Commission**; **Employee organisation**; **Employer organisation**.

- **Ambiguity** Generally, in the context of language, uncertainty or doubt.

  Contract In the construction of contracts, uncertainty or doubt as to the meaning of the parties' language. Ambiguity may be patent, being on the face of the document, or latent, in which case a word or description, superficially referring to one person or thing, is found to be equally applicable to more than one person or thing. Extrinsic evidence may be used to resolve both a patent ambiguity and a latent ambiguity: *Matthews v Smallwood* [1910] 1 Ch 777; *Codelfa Construction Pty Ltd v State Rail Authority of NSW* (1982) 149 CLR 337; 41 ALR 367. See also **Construction**; **Extrinsic evidence**.

  Trade and commerce Language that is doubtful, uncertain, or capable of double meaning. Language is ambiguous when it is reasonably capable of being understood in more than one sense: *City of Sioux Falls v Henry Carlson Co Inc* 258 NW 2d 676 (SD 1977) at 679. Ambiguity of language is to be distinguished from unintelligibility and inaccuracy. Ambiguous statements will be misleading or deceptive and will contravene (CTH) Trade Practices Act s 52 if any one or more of the reasonably possible meanings are misleading or deceptive or likely to mislead or deceive. If a word or term is ambiguous and one meaning is false, then the word or term is deceptive: *Rhodes Pharmacal Co Inc v FTC* 1952-1953 Trade Cases. A statement that a product stops perspiration, when in fact perspiration stopped only temporarily is ambiguous: *Carter Products Inc v FTC* 186 F 2d 821 (1951). See also **Misleading or deceptive conduct**.

Ambit The area of dispute or disagreement between the parties to an industrial dispute that may be found from the claims and counter claims of the parties and taken in the general context of those claims. The ambit of a dispute generally restricts the jurisdiction of the Australian Industrial Relations Commission to make or vary an award: for example *R v Commonwealth Conciliation and Arbitration Commission; Ex parte Australian Boot Trades Employees' Federation* (1966) 114 CLR 548. See also **Log of claims**; **Paper dispute**.

Ambush marketing A marketing activity conducted by a business in which it links, without proper authorisation, its name, goods, or services with a particular sporting event. This may be misleading and deceptive conduct, infringement of copyright, or passing off. See also **Copyright**; **Misleading or deceptive conduct**; **Passing off**.

Amended Hague Rules 1979 The rules relating to contracts of carriage of goods by sea and establishing an international liability regime, defining the rights and liabilities of the owner of such goods, the consignee, and the charterparties or carrier of those goods. The Amended Hague Rules 1979 apply to interstate and international transactions. Also known as 'Hague-Visby Rules'. See also **Bill of Lading**; **Consignee**; **Carriage by sea**; **Carrier**; **Charterparty**; **Cost insurance freight contract**; **Free on board**; **International Convention for the Unification of Certain Rules of Law relating to Bills of Lading 1924**.

Amended statement of claim A statement of claim which has been amended since the commencement of proceedings. An amendment to the statement of claim to plead a cause of action accruing since the commencement of the proceeding cannot be made unless the other party consents or under the rules of court there is authority to allow the amendment. See also **Statement of claim**.

- **Amending Act** An Act of Parliament that amends an earlier Act. An amending Act may operate by substituting, inserting, omitting, or repealing words or provisions in the original Act. See also **Act of Parliament**; **Amendment**.

- **Amendment** 1. A change or alteration to a document; for example, amending a statement of claim. 2. A change to an existing statute made by an amending Act. If the court is satisfied that the later Act is to bring about an alteration in the operation of an earlier Act, the later Act will be treated as an amending Act: for example *R v Wheeldon* (1978) 18 ALR 619 at 622-3. See also **Act of Parliament**; **Amended statement of claim**; **Amending Act**.

Amends, offer of See **Offer of amends**.

American Depository Receipt *Abbr* – ADR A certificate issued in the United States by a trustee bank or similar organisation confirming that it holds non-securities. Most Australian ADRs represent several shares each. They are used to facilitate the trading of foreign shares in United States markets. During recent years, dozens of non-companies have set up listed ADR programs. A number of Australian companies have ADRs listed on the New York and American stock exchanges and with the National Association of Securities Dealers and Quotations. See also **American Stock Exchange Market Value Index**.

American option An option that can be exercised at or before its maturity date.

American Standard Code for Information Interchange *Abbr* – ASCII An internationally-agreed seven-bit coding system that changes standard letters of the alphabet (A to Z and a to z), decimal numbers (0 to 9), and symbols (such as the question mark) into binary form that a computer can transmit to ensure hardware and software compatibility through standardisation. ASCII that uses seven bits also engages an eighth bit as the check digit for error detection. The lowest character is NUL (0000 0000), and the highest is the DEL (0111 1111).

American Stock Exchange *Abbr* – AMEX Located in New York, the second largest stock exchange in the United States, preceded by the New York Stock Exchange. Until 1953, it was known as 'the kerb Exchange'.

American Stock Exchange Market Value Index An index that measures the aggregate market value changes in all common shares, American Depository Receipts, and warrants listed on the American Stock Exchange. The index is calculated at intervals throughout the day and at the close of business. A percentage change in the index is equal to the percentage change in the market value since the last close. See also **American Depository Receipt**.

Amiable compositeur *Fr* – friendly arbiter or compositor. A person appointed as an arbitrator who may, by agreement of the parties, settle the dispute *ex aequo et bono* (on the basis of what is fair and right) subject to the rules of procedural fairness and the provisions of the arbitration agreement, rather than by applying the settled laws of a fixed legal system. See also **Alternative dispute resolution; Commercial arbitration legislation; Ex aequo et bono**.

AMIEU Australian Meat Industry Employees' Union.

Amortisation The process of allocating the cost or value of intangible assets that have no physical qualities (such as patents, copyright, and goodwill) over an appropriate period as an expense or as product cost. See also **Depreciation**.

Amortising swap An interest rate swap in which interest obligations are calculated on a declining nominal principal amount.

•**Amount due** An amount that is owing but not necessarily yet payable: *Clyne v DCT* (1981) 150 CLR 1; 35 ALR 567; 81 ATC 4429; (CTH) Income Tax Assessment Act 1936 s 218. Income tax assessed becomes an amount due when a notice of assessment has been delivered to the taxpayer. See also **Assessment**.

•**Amount financed** Generally in consumer credit law, the principal advanced by a credit provider, plus interest, insurance charges, and stamp duty: (NSW) Credit Act 1984 (repealed) s 5(1), Sch 2 cl 1, Sch 4 cl 1 (replaced by Uniform Consumer Credit Code). See also **Credit provider**.

•**Amusement parlour** A building used for recreation or amusement purposes, usually containing a number of amusement devices. The installation of two coin-operated amusement machines in a fish and chip shop does not convert that place into an amusement parlour: *Blount v Gianevsky* [1980] VR 156; 42 LGRA 294. Similarly, marking bingo cards in a building does not make the building an amusement parlour: *TJ Torode Holdings Pty Ltd v Shire of Morwell* (1985) 14 APA 347.

Ancillary liability In consumer protection legislation, conduct which does not itself contravene the legislation, but which constitutes attempting, assisting, conspiring at, or being in any way knowingly concerned in, or a party to, a contravention. See also **Aid and abet; Corrective advertising; Counsel; Inducement; Information disclosure; Trade practices legislation**.

Ancillary privilege The privilege afforded to incidental communications between the defendant and employees involved in the mechanical production of the published matter, such as secretaries and telephonists, if it is reasonable and in the usual course of business. Ancillary privilege only arises in cases where the communication to persons toward whom it is ultimately directed is itself privileged in defamation law: *Bryanston Finance Ltd v de Vries* [1975] QB 703; *Holding v Jennings* [1979] VR 289.

Annexure stamp An official mark on the principal document to indicate that there are additional documents attached or appended. An example is a schedule annexed to a will: *Watson v Arundel* Ir Rep 10 Eq 299.

Annual company return See **Annual return**.

•**Annual general meeting** *Abbr* – AGM A meeting of all shareholders which a company (except a proprietary company) is required to hold at least once every calendar year: Corporations Law s 245(1). See also **General Meeting**.

Annual holiday loading An amount payable to an employee who takes annual holiday leave, payable at 17.5 per cent of the weekly wages. No loading is payable if the employee takes an annual holiday in advance, but the 17.5 per cent entitlement becomes payable on the date the holiday leave accrues. See also **Annual leave**.

•**Annual leave** A paid leave of absence from work for the purpose of granting a worker an annual holiday: for example (NSW) Annual Holidays Act 1944 s 3. See also **Annual holiday loading**.

•**Annual national payroll** The total amount of salaries and wages paid by an organisation during the year for work performed by its employees in Australia. For superannuation purposes, the annual national payroll determines the contributions payable by employers based on a percentage of the payroll in accordance with the superannuation levy. For taxation purposes, the amount helps determine the payroll tax due, which is based on the total annual payroll above a stipulated threshold. For training levy purposes, it determines the amount that must be spent on staff training by employers to qualify as meeting eligible staff training requirements. See also **Salary; Taxation; Wage**.

- **Annual percentage rate** In consumer protection law, an interest rate which applies to credit sale contracts and loan contracts, and which must be stated in those contracts. It is calculated in accordance with a prescribed formula provided in the uniform credit legislation. Apart from loan contracts secured by a mortgage over land, a credit sale contract or loan contract must not refer to more than one annual percentage rate or a right to increase that rate, or state that a different rate is to be used: (NSW) Credit Act 1984 (repealed) ss 10, 35, 36, 40, Sch 6 (replaced by Uniform Credit Code). See also **Credit sale contract; Uniform credit legislation**.

- **Annual report** A report in which information is provided annually, containing the financial statements, auditor's report, directors' report, and other relevant and necessary information given by the management of a company, regarding its business operations. See also **Auditor's report; Director's report**.

- **Annual return** A document that every Australian company is required to lodge annually with the Australian Securities Commission. The return must be in a prescribed form, reporting on the company's annual general meeting, indicating its registered office, reporting on its accounts, and giving particulars of its secured indebtedness share capital, its members (subject to exceptions) and directors, and certain certificates: (CTH) Corporations Regulations regs 3.8.01-3.8.03, Form 316. See also **Accounting standards; Annual general meeting**.

- **Annual value 1.** For water rating purposes, the net value of premises to the owner after all proper deductions have been made: *West Middlesex Waterworks v Coleman* (1885) 14 QBD 529. **2.** The gross annual rental, or a specified proportion of that rental, that land might reasonably be expected to realise if leased on the condition that the landlord is liable for the payment all rates, taxes, and other outgoings: (SA) Valuation of Land Act 1971 s 5(1). See also **Full annual value; Rent; Yearly value**.

Annualise To present a change in an economic or financial variable over a short period as a rate of change over a year. For example, the rate of unemployment or inflation over a period of three months may be presented as an equivalent rate per annum.

- **Annuitant 1.** The holder of a policy of insurance for the payment of an annuity on a human life: *Re Profits and Income Insurance Co Ltd* [1929] 1 Ch 262. **2.** A person who receives an annuity: (WA) Transfer of Land Act 1893 s 4(1). See also **Annuity; Deferred annuity; Income**.

- **Annuity** Generally, an annual payment that is made to a person for life or for a fixed number of years. The term has various legal uses:

Bankruptcy An amount calculated by reference to yearly or other regular periods, paid as an investment return or under some other arrangement. See also **Bankruptcy; Divisible property**.

Taxation and revenue An investment, generally by way of a single outlay of money or other property which returns a fixed annual sum over a fixed number of years: (CTH) Income Tax Assessment Act 1936 s 26(c); *Atkinson v FCT* (1951) 84 CLR 298. See also **Allocated annuity; Deferred annuity; Fixed term annuity; Immediate annuity; Indexed annuity; Joint annuity; Life insurance; Pension; With-profits annuity**.

Annulment The act of rendering something void, often from the beginning.

Bankruptcy The process of ending a bankruptcy by which the bankruptcy order is set aside: (CTH) Bankruptcy Act 1966 ss 74, 154. See also **Automatic discharge; Bankruptcy; Composition; Debtor's petition; Sequestration order**.

Answers to interrogatories A response to another party's notice to answer interrogatories: for example by affidavit ((CTH) High Court Rules O 32 r 6(1)). The answers must relate to matters in issue in the proceedings. Answers must be in writing and verified.

- **ANTA** See **Australian National Training Authority**.

Antarctic Treaty 1959 An international multilateral agreement allowing freedom of scientific research and movement on and around the Antarctic continent, signed in Washington on 1 December 1959. Under the treaty, the Antarctic is declared nuclear free (Antarctic Treaty 1959 art 5), is demilitarised (art 1), and is given over to research (art 2). The treaty is implemented in Australia by the (CTH) Antarctic Treaty Act 1960.

Antecedent negotiations Negotiations or arrangements conducted or made with a consumer by a person in the course of a business by which the consumer was induced to acquire the goods or that otherwise promoted the acquisition of the goods by the consumer: (CTH) Trade Practices Act 1974 ss 74A(2)(c), (d).

Ante-date An ante-dated negotiable instrument is not invalid for that reason only: (CTH) Bills of Exchange Act 1909 s 18(2); (CTH) Cheques and Payment Orders Act 1986 s 16(2). See also **Negotiable instrument; Post-date**.

Anticipation Assigning, charging, or otherwise dealing with income before it is earned or becomes due.

Anticipatory breach A breach of contract of a kind entitling the promisee to terminate the contract before the time appointed for the promisor's performance. The promisee's termination is justified if the words or conduct of the promisor, or the promisor's actual position, give rise to a repudiation of obligation or indicate that the promisor was wholly and finally disabled from performing the contract: *Progressive Mailing House Pty Ltd v Tabali Pty Ltd* (1985) 157 CLR 17; 57 ALR 609. Also known as 'prospective breach'. See also **Breach of contract; Failure of performance; Repudiation; Termination**.

Anti-discrimination legislation A generic term given to legislation making discrimination in various areas of public life unlawful. The most common prohibited grounds of discrimination are: sex, marital status, pregnancy, family responsibilities, race, colour, ethnic origin, disability, age, sexual preference, political opinion, and religion: for example (CTH) Racial Discrimination Act 1975; (CTH) Sex Discrimination Act 1984; (CTH) Human Rights and Equal Opportunity Commission Act 1986; (CTH) Disability Discrimination Act 1992. See also **Anti-discrimination tribunal; Discrimination.**

• **Anti-discrimination tribunal** A tribunal formed under State law, usually principally to hear and determine allegations that anti-discrimination legislation has been contravened: (NSW) Anti-Discrimination Act 1977 Pt 7A; (VIC) Equal Opportunity Act 1995 Div 3 Pt 9; (QLD) Anti-Discrimination Act 1991 Ch 9 Pt 2; (SA) Equal Opportunity Act 1984 Div II Pt II; (WA) Equal Opportunity Act 1984 Pt VIII. The Australian Capital Territory and the Northern Territory have a Discrimination Commissioner and an Anti-Discrimination Commissioner respectively. See also **Anti-discrimination legislation; Anti-discrimination tribunal; Discrimination.**

Anti-Dumping Authority A federal authority established by (CTH) Anti-Dumping Authority Act 1988 s 4. The authority has broad powers to do all things necessary or convenient in connection with the performance of its functions in relation to dumping: (CTH) Anti-Dumping Authority Act 1988 s 6. See also **Anti-dumping duty.**

Anti-dumping duty A duty imposed on the produce or manufactured goods of another country, other than New Zealand, with the objective of discouraging the dumping of those goods on the Australian market: (CTH) Customs Tariff (Anti-Dumping) Act 1975. See also **Anti-dumping Authority.**

Antitrust The United States generic term for the area of competition law, derived from the structures adopted by American business in the 19th century to overcome instability in cartels (pooling arrangements) caused by cheating on the cartels. In Australia, the area is usually referred to as 'restrictive trade practices' ((CTH) Trade Practices Act 1974 Pt IV), and in Europe, as ' competition law'. See also **Cartel; Competition law; Restrictive trade practices; Trade practices legislation.**

Anton Piller injunction See **Anton Piller order.**

• **Anton Piller order** An ex parte interlocutory mandatory injunction, first used in cases involving bootleg copies of musical records and tapes. It compels a defendant to permit the plaintiff to inspect the defendant's premises for the purpose of discovering and removing any material relevant to the plaintiff's case. It is named after the decision in *Anton Piller KG v Manufacturing Processes Ltd* [1976] 1 Ch 55. Also known as 'Anton Piller injunction'. See also **Ex parte injunction; Interlocutory injunction.**

• **Any other person** In relation to who may apply for an injunction to restrain a breach of consumer protection legislation, these words have been interpreted literally: *Phelps v Western Mining Corp Ltd* (1987) 20 ALR 183; 33 FLR 327. The effect is that there is no standing requirement under the legislation; it is not necessary for an applicant to show that a proprietary interest has been affected or to establish special damage: *World Series Cricket v Parish* (1977) 161 ALR 181; ATPR ¶ 40-040. Not only a consumer but a trader may apply to restrain a competitor engaging in conduct which contravenes the legislation: *Hornsby Building Information Centre Pty Ltd v Sydney Building Information Centre Ltd* (1978) 140 CLR 216; 18 ALR 639; (CTH) Trade Practices Act 1974 s 80(1); (NSW) Fair Trading Act 1987 s 65. See also **Injunction.**

ANZCERTA See **Australia-New Zealand Closer Economic Relations Trade Agreement.**

ANZUS A cooperative tripartite security agreement between Australia, New Zealand, and the United States which came into force under the Security Treaty (ANZUS Treaty) 1951 on 29 April 1952. By agreement, the Treaty arrangement that created ANZUS ceased to exist on 30 June 1977.

AOM See **Australian Options Market.**

APCA See **Australian Payments Clearing Association Ltd.**

Apparent alteration A change to the text of a negotiable instrument, which is apparent upon inspection: *Automobile Finance Co of Australia Ltd v Law* (1933) 49 CLR 1; [1934] VLR 17. See also **Holder in due course; Material alteration; Negotiable instrument.**

Apparent authority The authority of an agent as it appears to others, regardless of any limit to the agent's authority agreed between principal and agent; to be distinguished from actual authority: *Metal Manufacturers Ltd v Lewis* (1988) 13 ACLR 357. Apparent authority operates by way of estoppel; any person giving the impression that an agent has authority is estopped from denying that the agent had authority: *Roma Corp Ltd v Proved Tin and General Investments Ltd* [1952] 2 QB 147. Also known as 'ostensible authority'. See also **Actual authority; Agency; Agency by estoppel; Apparent partner; Express authority; Implied authority; Principal.**

Partnerships and joint ventures In the context of partnerships, a partner acting within the scope of apparent authority acts on behalf of the firm and binds the other partners: *Polkinghorne v Holland* (1934) 51 CLR 143; [1934] SASR 475. Where a person acts with apparent authority the firm is bound provided that: the transaction is within the scope of the kind of business carried on by the partnership (*Polkinghorne v Holland* (1934) 51 CLR 143; [1934] SASR 475); the transaction is effected in the usual way (*Goldberg v Jenkins* (1889) 15 VLR 36); and the other party to the transaction either knows or believes that the person acting is a partner and believes that the person is acting with authority (*Construction Engineering (Aust) Pty Ltd v Hexyl Pty Ltd* (1985) 155 CLR 541; 58 ALR 411). See also **Apparent partner; Holding out.**

Apparent partner A person who represents him or herself as a partner in a partnership, or who knowingly allows others to so represent him or her: *Tower Cabinet Co v Ingram* [1949] 2 KB 397. Where the constitution of a firm changes, a person continuing to deal with the firm is entitled to treat all apparent members of the old firm as still being members until he or she receives notice of the change: (NSW) Partnership Act 1892 s 36. See also **Firm; Holding out; Partner; Partnership**.

•**Appeal** **1.** In the narrow sense an application to a higher court to reconsider or rehear the decision of a lower court, on the ground that there has been an error in the decision of the lower court, available on a question of law only or for mistakes of fact or law. An appeal may be as of right, or may depend on the higher court consenting to the appeal. The higher court may dismiss the appeal by affirming the decision of the lower court, or uphold the appeal and reverse or modify the decision of the lower court, or remit the matter to the lower court for reconsideration in the light of principles set out by the higher court. A right of appeal may be created, limited, or abolished by statute. **2.** More broadly, includes an appeal by way of re-hearing. An appeal includes an application in relation to a case in which a decision has been made to a court higher in the judicial hierarchy for a new trial: (CTH) Judiciary Act 1903 s 2. **3.** An appeal from an executive authority to another executive authority or to a court: *Re Dash; Ex parte Australian Sporting Club Ltd* (1947) 47 SR (NSW) 283. See also **Appeal as of right; Appeal by leave; Appeal de novo; Australia Acts; High Court of Australia; Privy Council**.

Appeal as of right An appeal which an appellant may pursue without the need to obtain the leave of the court determining the appeal. See also **Appeal; Appeal by leave**.

Appeal by leave An appeal which can only be pursued once leave has been granted by the court with jurisdiction to determine the appeal. Whether or not a court grants leave will often depend upon the merits of the matter, and the issue as to leave and the determination of the appeal is dealt with at one and the same time: *Bailey v DPP(NSW)* (1988) 78 ALR 116. See also **Appeal; Appeal as of right**.

Appeal de novo An appeal conducted by way of a complete rehearing of the information or complaint so that the prosecution commences again by leading evidence to prove the charge: *Sweeney v Fitzhardinge* (1906) 4 CLR 716; *R v Longshaw* (1990) 20 NSWLR 554. The court must rehear the whole matter and not simply review the decision of the original court: *Hodder* (1986) 33 A Crim R 295; *Budget Nursery Pty Ltd v Cmr of Taxation* (1989) 42 A Crim R 81. See also **Appeal; Rehearing**.

Appeal time For income tax purposes, the period allowed to a taxpayer to lodge an application for review or appeal with the Administrative Appeals Tribunal or Federal Court against an assessment or an objection decision made by the Commissioner of Taxation: (CTH) Taxation Administration Act 1953 ss 14zzc, 14zzn. See also **Administrative Appeals Tribunal; Appeal; Assessment; Federal Court; Objection; Decision**.

Appearance The formal submission by a party to the court's jurisdiction as evidenced by a memorandum or notice of appearance. See also **Ex parte; Entering an appearance**.

•**Appellant** A party who appeals against a judicial decision which is not in that party's favour. See also **Appeal**.

Appellate jurisdiction The jurisdiction of a court to hear and determine an appeal from a decision of a court or other decision maker lower in the judicial hierarchy: for example Commonwealth Constitution s 73. The exercise of appellate jurisdiction may be regulated by statute (for example (CTH) Family Law Act 1975 s 94) or by rules of court. See also **Appeal**.

Appertaining Belonging: *McDonald v Deputy Federal Cmr of Land Tax for NSW* (1915) 20 CLR 231 at 234-5.

•**Applicant** The person or persons making an application. See also **Account party**.

Intellectual property In the context of plant breeder's rights, the person shown as the applicant on the application form for plant breeder's rights: (CTH) Plant Breeder's Rights Act 1994 s 3(1).

•**Application** The act of making a request.

Application for appointment of a provisional liquidator An application made by a company, the Australian Securities Commission, or a contributory or creditor for the appointment of a provisional liquidator after the filing of a winding up application: (CTH) Corporations Law s 472(2); (CTH) Federal Court Rules O 71 r 48. The application may be made on an ex parte basis or in the presence of the company: *Riviana (Aust) Pty Ltd v Laospac Trading Pty Ltd* (1986) 10 ACLR 865 at 866. Mere insolvency is not sufficient to justify the appointment: *Re McLennan Holdings Pty Ltd* (1983) 7 ACLR 732. There must be a demonstrated useful purpose, urgency, a great jeopardy to the assets of the company, or irresponsible behaviour by the directors. The provisional liquidator exercises such powers as are conferred on him by the (CTH) Corporations Law s 472(4), or as specified by the court. See also **Application; Provisional liquidator**.

Application for expedition Application by notice of motion supported by affidavit seeking to have a matter heard earlier than would normally be the case thus giving it priority over matters commenced prior to or entered into a hearing list before the matter the subject of the application. Evidence is required to show that the circumstances are such that this matter should displace matters in priority to it: *Braham v Braham* (unrptd, SC(NSW), McLelland J, No 1449 of 1987, 27 April 1987). See also **Application**.

Application for shares An acceptance of an offer made by a company to subscribe to a primary issue of shares. Unless the offer is an excluded offer (Corporations Law s 66(3)) a prospectus must accompany an application form to subscribe for shares: Corporations Law s 1018(1). See also **Application; Prospectus; Subscription**.

Application money Where an enterprise invites applications for securities, the amount per share, debenture or other security offered which the enterprise specifies as the amount to accompany an application. Any application must be held by the corporation in trust for the applicant in a bank account established solely for the purpose of depositing application money: Corporations Law s 1043. See also **Application**; **Prospectus**; **Subscription moneys**.

Application of partnership property The use of assets belonging to a partnership. The application must be exclusively for the purposes of the partnership in accordance with the partnership agreement: for example (NSW) Partnership Act 1892 s 20(1). See also **Application**; **Partnership property**.

• **Applied industrially** In the context of designs, generally a design that is applied to more than 50 articles, either by a process, or in the course of production, or if it is applied to one or more articles (other than handmade articles) manufactured in lengths or pieces: (CTH) Copyright Regulations 1969 reg 17. The (CTH) Copyright Act 1968 s 77 contains certain defences to infringement of copyright where a design has been applied industrially. The circumstances in which a design is taken to be applied industrially in the regulation are not exhaustive, and the application of a design to fewer than 50 items may still constitute an application which is 'industrial' for the purposes of (CTH) Copyright Act 1968 s 77: for example *Press-Form Pty Ltd v Henderson's Ltd* (1993) 40 FCR 274; 112 ALR 671; 26 IPR 113. A design may be applied industrially even though the relevant articles are hand-made, provided that there is an 'element of system' in their manufacture: *Kevlacat Pty Ltd v Trailcraft Marine Pty Ltd* (1987) 79 ALR 534; 11 IPR 77. See also **Copyright**; **Work**.

Applied to an article A design must be 'applied to an article' ((CTH) Designs Act 1906 s 4(1); *Design No 29076, Class 14, Registered by Wolanski, Re* (1953) 88 CLR 278; 27 ALJ 588), capable of distinguishing the article with the design from the fundamental form of the article: for example *Re Application by Comshare Inc* (1991) 23 IPR 145. An article must have some function or utility other than merely carrying the design: *Re Application by TDK Electronics Co Ltd* (1983) 1 IPR 529. See also **Applied industrially**.

• **Appoint** To authorise a person to fulfil a particular role or perform a particular task: *Gollin & Co Ltd v Karenlee Nominees Pty Ltd* (1983) 153 CLR 455; 49 ALR 135. Appointment usually requires nothing more than communication between appointor and prospective appointee: *Gollin & Co Ltd v Karenlee Nominees Pty Ltd*. However, where one party is entitled under a contract to appoint a third person who will have authority to do something that will be contractually binding on the other parties to the contract, the appointment will only be valid where it has been communicated to those other parties: *Gollin & Co Ltd v Karenlee Nominees Pty Ltd*. See also **Appointment**.

• **Appointment** The nomination, selection, or assignment of a person to perform a function or enjoy a right.

Employment Nomination or assignment of a person to an office, post, or function. It includes re-appointment: (CTH) Acts Interpretation Act 1901 s 33(4A). See also **Appoint**.

• **Apportion** To divide into a specific fraction or share. In real property law, apportion is used in reference to dividing up land after a settlement has been reached. In contract law, it is used in reference to dividing up a contract into several distinct parts or sections. See also **Apportionment**.

Apportionable deduction A deduction allowed or allowable for: money paid before 1 July 1991 on shares in management and investment companies; gifts to specified institutions or funds, such as charities; and rates or land tax incurred in gaining or producing assessable income or carrying on a business for that purpose: (CTH) Income Tax Assessment Act 1936 ss 6(1), 77F, 78(4), (5), 72. Apportionable deductions are concessional deductions because they are not necessarily directly related to income-producing activities. See also **Assessable income**; **Eligible taxable income**.

• **Apportionment** The division of rights or the allocation of responsibilities.

Taxation and revenue For income tax purposes, the dissection or allocation of losses and outgoings to ascertain whether the expenditure is an allowable deduction to the extent to which it is incurred in the course of gaining or producing assessable income; or not allowable to the extent that it is of a capital, private or domestic nature, or was incurred in the gaining of exempt income: (CTH) Income Tax Assessment Act 1936 s 51(1); *Ronpibon Tin NL v FCT* (1949) 78 CLR 47; 4 AITR 236. See also **Allowable deduction**; **Assessable income**; **Capital**; **Exempt income**; **Incurred**; **Loss**; **Outgoings**.

Tort In relation to blame for the commission of a tort, the due sharing of responsibility between two or more parties for the same damage. The law assesses the contribution of each individual at fault for the commission of a tort, and apportions liability accordingly. The apportionment of blame determines the apportionment of damages or the amount of contribution: *Pennington v Norris* (1956) 96 CLR 10. See also **Contribution**; **Contributory negligence**; **Fault**.

Apportionment legislation The provisions in force in all Australian States and Territories which allow a plaintiff to recover damages despite having suffered damage partly as a result of his or her own fault. Before the legislation, the defence of contributory negligence would have barred such a plaintiff from recovering: for example *Cayzer, Irvine & Co v Carron Co* (1884) 9 App Cas 873. Under the legislation, a plaintiff can now recover damages, reduced to the extent that the court considers 'just and equitable': for example (VIC) Wrongs Act 1958 s 26(1). The court thus apportions the responsibility of the parties to the action. See also **Contributory negligence**; **Fault**; **Just and equitable**; **Negligence**.

Appraisement An estimation of the worth or value of an object or property, or of the chances of success in litigation. An appraisement considers not only the price, as a valuation does, but also the quality or excellence of the thing appraised: *Pappa v Rose* (1872) 7 CP 525.

Appreciation An increase in the real value of an asset.

• **Apprentice** A person undertaking vocational training as a probationary apprentice, an indentured apprentice, or a trainee apprentice in any trade or calling which falls within legislation governing vocational education and training: (NSW) Industrial and Commercial Training Act 1989 s 4(1). See also **Apprenticeship**; **Indenture**; **Trainee**.

•**Apprenticeship** A statutory arrangement for the provision of vocational education and training: for example (NSW) Industrial and Commercial Training Act 1989 Pt 3 Div 2. See also **Apprentice**; **Trainee**.

Apprenticeship contract See **Apprenticeship**.

Approbate and reprobate To approve, then subsequently reject a course of action. A person may not approbate and reprobate, meaning that, having a choice between two inconsistent courses of action and having chosen one, he or she is treated as having made an election from which he or she cannot resile: *Randwick Municipal Council v Broten* [1964-65] NSWR 1445; 10 LGRA 309. For example, when a party to a contract has a right to terminate for breach, he or she must elect to either terminate or continue performance and seek damages: *United Australia Ltd v Barclays Bank Ltd* [1941] AC 1. See also **Election**; **Waiver**.

Approbation See **Approbate and reprobate**; **Election**.

•**Appropriation 1.** The act of taking to oneself the property of another, either lawfully or unlawfully. **2.** The power to transfer property. The term has various legal uses:

Contract An act which indicates an intention to confer ownership of particular property on a person, sometimes out of a larger amount: *Akron Tyre Co Pty Ltd v Kittson* (1951) 82 CLR 477 at 484; [1951] ALR 277. See also **Accession**; **Confusion**.

Real property The compulsory acquisition of Crown land by a statutory acquiring authority. See also **Acquisition**.

Trusts An administrative power which permits the transferral or appropriation of specific assets to a beneficiary in satisfaction of his or her share in a trust estate: *Long v Comptroller of Stamps* [1964] VR 796 at 800.

Appropriation of payments The allocation of a payment to satisfy a specific part of a debt. A debtor and creditor may contract to appropriate payments in a specified way, thus it is common to agree that interest owed be repaid before the principal. In the absence of a prior agreement, the debtor may expressly or impliedly appropriate any payment at the time of payment, but failing any such appropriation the creditor may apply the payment as he or she chooses: *Deeley v Lloyds Bank Ltd* [1912] AC 756 at 783. In the case of current accounts the rule in *Clayton's case* requires payments to be appropriated to the oldest part of a debt: *Devaynes v Noble (Clayton's case)* (1816) 1 Mer 572; 35 ER 781 at 7931. See also **Clayton's case, rule in**; **Current account**.

•**Approval** The action of approving or sanctioning, or giving approbation: *McDonald's System of Australia Pty Ltd v McWilliams Wines Pty Ltd (No 2)* (1979) 28 ALR 236; 41 FLR 455. See also **Affiliation**; **Misleading or deceptive conduct**; **False representation**; **Sponsorship**.

Approval, on See **On approval**.

Approved accounting standard *Abbr* – AAS An accounting standard that has been approved by the Australian Accounting Standards Board (AASB) and gazetted. The AASB has the power to make and approve standards: Corporations Law s 32. See also **Australian Accounting Standards**; **Accounts**.

•**Approved auditor** A person entitled to audit superannuation funds, approved deposit funds, or pooled superannuation trusts: (CTH) Superannuation Industry (Supervision) Act 1993 s 10. See also **Approved deposit fund**; **Auditor**; **Complying superannuation fund**; **Non complying superannuation fund**; **Superannuation fund**.

•**Approved cash carrier** A cash dealer declared by the Australian Transaction Reports and Analysis Centre to be an approved cash carrier, where it is satisfied that the dealer maintains records containing reportable details of significant transactions: (CTH) Financial Transaction Reports Act 1988 s 8A. An approved cash carrier is relieved of the requirement of reporting significant cash transactions under this Act. See also **Cash dealer**.

•**Approved deposit fund** *Abbr* – ADF A fund used to invest and provide retirement benefits to individual taxpayers which is subject to a concessional tax regime. An approved deposit fund is an indefinitely continuing fund. It is maintained by a trustee approved by the Insurance and Superannuation Commissioner for the purpose of receiving eligible termination payments, benefits rolled over from other funds, and superannuation guarantee payments: (CTH) Superannuation Industry (Supervision) Act 1993 s 10. See also **Approved deposit fund tax**; **Eligible Termination Payment**; **Insurance and Superannuation Commissioner**; **Rollover**; **Superannuation fund**; **Superannuation guarantee charge**.

Approved deposit fund tax The income tax payable on the income of or the contribution to an approved deposit fund: (CTH) Income Tax Assessment Act 1936 ss 289, 290. A concessional rate of tax applies if the fund complies with (CTH) Superannuation Industry (Supervision) Act 1993; the top marginal tax rate applies to individuals for the year if it is a non-complying fund: (CTH) Income Tax (Rates) Act 1986 s 27. When contributions and accumulated earnings are withdrawn from an approved deposit fund by a depositor, the amount withdrawn is an eligible termination payment and is subject to tax at that point. See also **Approved deposit fund**; **Eligible Termination Payment**; **Marginal tax rate**.

•**Approved securities organisation** A body corporate which operates a stock exchange and which has been approved by the Minister under an application under Corporations Law s 770. The Minister must be satisfied that the body has included certain matters in its business rules and listing rules and that appropriate fidelity arrangements have been made. A stock market is unauthorised unless it is operated by a 'securities exchange' (subject to some specific exemptions): Corporations Law s 767, 770. A 'securities exchange' is defined as an 'approved securities organisation' and a 'local stock market': Corporations Law s 9. Also known as 'securities exchange'. See also **Local stock exchange**; **Securities exchange**; **Stock exchange**; **Stock market**.

Approving holding company A listed company of which a body corporate is a subsidiary. Alternatively it is the ultimate holding company of a body corporate, where a body corporate is not a subsidiary of a listed corporation but where its ultimate holding company is incorporated in Australia or in an external Territory: Corporations Law s 9. The term 'approving holding company' is used in Corporations Law s 205(9)(b), which authorises the giving of financial assistance by a company for the purposes of or in connection with the acquisition of fully-paid shares in the company or its holding company, provided the shares are to be held for the benefit of participating employees and the financial assistance is given in accordance with a scheme approved by the company and any approving holding company in general meeting. See also **Employee share scheme**; **Holding company**.

Appurtenant *OF* – holding through. A term used to describe a subsidiary right that becomes attached to an estate in land by express or implied grant or by prescription, such as a profit or an easement. See also **Easement**; **Prescription**.

APRA See **Australasian Performing Right Association**.

APS Australian Public Service. See also **Public service**.

Arbitrable dispute A dispute which may be resolved by arbitration. It must be a justiciable issue, triable civilly. Generally, if the dispute can be compromised lawfully by way of accord and satisfaction, it is arbitrable. See also **Accord and satisfaction**; **Alternative dispute resolution**; **Arbitration**.

Arbitrage Trading in currencies, commodities or securities between two or more markets to take profitable advantage of any differences in the prices quoted. Also known as 'arbitraging'. See also **Arbitrage transaction**.

•**Arbitrage transaction** A dealing with the purpose of profiting from exchange or interest rate differentials. Arbitrage transactions are outside the prohibition on short-selling: Corporations Law s 846(3)(b). See also **Arbitrage**; **Securities**.

Arbitraging See **Arbitrage**.

•**Arbitral award** A term with the same meaning as 'award', used in the Convention on the Recognition and Enforcement of Foreign Arbitral Awards (New York Convention) 1958 art 1(2). See also **Alternative dispute resolution**; **Award**; **Convention on the Recognition and Enforcement of Foreign Arbitral Awards 1958**.

Arbitral power An administrative or quasi-judicial power to make awards. The power is not judicial: *Waterside Workers' Federation of Australia v JW Alexander Pty Ltd* (1918) 25 CLR 434; *R v Kirby; Ex parte Boilermakers' Society of Australia* (1956) 94 CLR 254.

Arbitral tribunal See **Arbitration tribunal**.

Arbitrary taxation Liability for taxation imposed without reference to ascertainable criteria of sufficiently general application which indicate the objects and subject matter of the tax (*MacCormick v FCT* (1984) 158 CLR 622 at 639; 52 ALR 53) or as a result of some administrative decision based upon individual preference unrelated to any test laid down by legislation (*Deputy Cmr of Taxation v Truhold Benefit Pty Ltd* (1985) 158 CLR 678 at 684; 59 ALR 431). While taxation imposed arbitrarily in this sense will not be valid (*MacCormick v FCT* at (CLR) 639, 640), taxation imposed arbitrarily in the sense of a harsh or unreasonable incidence unrelated to the quantity or value of its subject matter or objects will be valid (*Deputy Federal Cmr of Taxation v Truhold* at 684). See also **Incontestable taxation**.

•**Arbitration 1.** The system of determining disputes by a private tribunal constituted for that purpose by the agreement of the disputants (common law or ordinary arbitration). **2.** A method of deciding issues by arbitral tribunals otherwise than by agreement between the parties, resort to which may be optional or compulsory, and in the constitution of which the disputants have no choice (statutory arbitration). **3.** The system of permanent public arbitral tribunals for settling industrial disputes, constituted not by the choice of the parties but by public authority (for example, industrial arbitration).

Industrial law A system of compulsory conciliation and arbitration used by the States and the Commonwealth to regulate industrial relations within their respective jurisdictions. An arbitrator is empowered to make a binding decision, but is not bound to administer the rules of evidence strictly: *Australian Boot Trade Employees Federation v Harbor & Co* (1910) 10 CLR 266. However, the right to be heard is an essential feature distinguishing arbitration: *Hammond v Wolt* [1975] VR 108 at 112. Mediation or any other process where the purpose is to bring the parties to an agreement, rather than to establish the rights of the parties, is not arbitration: *Waterside Workers' Federation of Australia v J W Alexander Ltd* (1918) 25 CLR 434 at 463; *Norths Ltd v McCaughan Dyson Capel Cure Ltd* (1988) 12 ACLR 739 at 747-8. See also **Compulsory arbitration**.

Trade and commerce The reference, usually by agreement, to a person (the arbitrator) or to persons other than a court of competent jurisdiction, of a dispute or difference between at least two parties, for determination after hearing both sides in a judicial manner. Commercial arbitration is governed by substantially uniform legislation in every Australian jurisdiction (for example (NSW) Commercial Arbitration Act 1984; (VIC) Commercial Arbitration Act 1984; (QLD) Commercial Arbitration Act 1990) and the common law. See also **Alternative Dispute Resolution**; **Arbitrator**; **Commercial dispute resolution**; **Mediation**; **Statutory arbitration**.

Arbitration bond Mutual bonds executed by persons, the bonds containing a condition to abide by an award. See also **Arbitration**; **Award**; **Bond**.

Arbitration clause A clause in a contract by which the parties agree to refer future disputes to arbitration, whether or not the arbitrator is named. It is to be contrasted with an arbitration submission.

Conflict of laws A clause included in a written international agreement between two parties which provides that disputes that arise between the parties are to be resolved by arbitration. The clause often sets out the manner of appointment of the arbitrator and of proceedings. Often the clause provides that if arbitration is not acceded to, any claims will be treated as waived and absolutely barred: *Atlantic Shipping & Trading Co Ltd v Louis Dreyfus & Co* [1922] 2 AC 250. In some agreements, the arbitration clause is merely collateral to the main clauses of the agreement: *Skips A/S Nordheim v Syrian Petroleum Co Ltd 'The Varenna'* [1983] 3 All ER 645. An arbitral decision is final and binding on the parties. The legal regime of arbitration clauses in Australia is governed by the (CTH) International Arbitration Act 1974. Arbitration clauses are frequently found in bilateral air service agreements, charterparties, contracts for the sale of ships, and other similar agreements. See also **Alternative dispute resolution**; **Arbitration**; **Arbitration submission**; **Arbitration tribunal**; **Arbitrator**; **Charterparty**.

Insurance A clause in a contract of insurance requiring disputes in relation to the contract to be submitted to arbitration. A compulsory arbitration clause is now rendered void in relation to contracts subject to the (CTH) Insurance Contracts Act 1984 s 43; (CTH) Carriage of Goods by Sea Act 1991 s 11. However, once a dispute has arisen, the parties may agree to submit it to arbitration: (CTH) Insurance Contracts Act 1984 s 43(2). A compulsory arbitration clause is also rendered void in relation to insurance contracts caught by various State legislation. See also **Arbitration**; **Insurance contract**.

Arbitration submission The reference of an actual present dispute to a particular arbitrator for settlement. It is to be contrasted with an arbitration clause. See also **Alternative dispute resolution**; **Arbitration clause**; **Arbitration tribunal**; **Arbitrator**.

Arbitration tribunal A tribunal with the function of arbitrating disputes referred to it, either voluntarily or by compulsion, as a result of a statute or court order requiring or authorising arbitration. In international law, a sole arbitrator or a panel of arbitrators: UNCITRAL Model Law on International Commercial Arbitration 1985 art 2. See also **Alternative dispute resolution**; **Arbitration**; **Arbitrator**; **UNCITRAL Model Law on International Commercial Arbitration 1985**.

•**Arbitrator** A person to whom a dispute or difference is referred to be resolved by arbitration. The arbitrator's decision is termed an 'award'. Also known as 'referee' or 'umpire'. See also **Alternative dispute resolution**; **Arbitration**; **Arbitration clause**; **Award**; **Evidence**.

Arbitrator advocate An arbitrator who, having discharged the duties of an arbitrator, appears at the hearing of the dispute before an umpire as an advocate for the party who appointed him or her as arbitrator. See also **Alternative dispute resolution**; **Arbitration**; **Arbitration tribunal**; **Arbitrator**.

Arbitrator's lien The right of an arbitrator or umpire to retain possession of the arbitration agreement and the award until the amount of his or her charges for the arbitration are paid: *R v South Devon Railway Co* (1850) 15 QB 1043; 117 ER 754. The lien does not extend to documents handed to the arbitrator in the course of the reference of the dispute: *Ponsford v Swaine* (1861) 1 John & H 433; 70 ER 816. See also **Alternative dispute resolution**; **Arbitration**; **Arbitrator**; **Award**.

ARBN See **Australian Registered Body Number**.

Architect's negligence Breach of the duty of care owed by an architect. An architect is liable to anyone whom it could reasonably have been expected might be physically injured as a result of his or her negligence. The duty is owed independently of the contract of employment, and extends to those who actually use the building after its construction: *Voli v Inglewood Shire Council* (1963) 110 CLR 74; [1963] ALR 657. See also **Duty of care**.

Archive A collection of documents or other material of historical significance or public interest in the custody of a body (either incorporated or unincorporated), for the purpose of conservation and preservation, provided that the body does not maintain and operate the collection for profit: (CTH) Copyright Act 1968 s 10(1), (4). In copyright law, an archive includes archival material in the custody of the Australian Archives, the Archives Office of New South Wales, the Public Record Office in Victoria, or the Archives Office in Tasmania: s 10. In copyright law, a person who for the time being has the immediate care and control of a non-profit archive, and persons authorised by him or her, may make certain copies of copyright materials without obtaining permission from the copyright owner: for example ss 48A–53, 110 A110B. See also **Copyright**.

Areeda and Turner test A test, named after two eminent United States competition law analysts, which tests the pricing policy of firms for the presence of predation. As a general rule, monopolistic pricing below short run marginal cost constitutes predatory or exclusionary practice. This form of pricing is neither allocatively efficient nor consistent with competition on its merits, since the monopolist incurs losses by selling the good or service. It is predatory to the extent that there is a strong likelihood that the conduct is being engaged in with the purpose of driving out rivals or preventing entry, with the expectation of recouping losses in the absence of those rivals. Areeda and Turner allow an exception to their rule when the below marginal cost price equals or exceeds average cost. Because of the difficulty of measuring marginal costs, they allow average costs to be used as a surrogate benchmark. See also **Antitrust**; **Competition law**; **Marginal cost**; **Predatory conduct**; **Predatory pricing**.

•**Arising out of or in the course of employment** A phrase often used in workers' compensation legislation to determine entitlement to compensation; generally, an injury that arises out of or in the course of employment is compensable. The words 'out of' point to the origin or cause of the injury, and imports some kind of causal relationship with employment, but do not necessitate direct or physical causation. See also **Course of employment**; **Workers' compensation**.

•**Arm's length transaction** A transaction in which the parties act severally and independently in forming the bargain and in which neither of the parties has the ability to exert personal influence or control over the other: *Granby Pty Ltd v FCT* (1995) 129 ALR 503; *Australian Trade Commission v WA Meat Exports Pty Ltd* (1987) 11 ALD 52; 75 ALR 287.

Equity A commercial relationship between the persons, where neither is under a legal duty to act for the benefit of the other: *Commercial Bank of Australia Ltd v Amadio* (1983) 51 CLR 447; 46 ALR 402. See also **Equity**.

Taxation and revenue For income tax purposes, where parties are not dealing with each other at arm's length in transactions in relation to an international agreement, the Commissioner of Taxation may adjust the incidence of tax applicable to such dealings: (CTH) Income Tax Assessment Act 1936 s 136AD. Whether parties have dealt at arm's length depends not only on the relationship between the parties but also on the nature of the dealing: *Hains (dec'd), Re; Barnsdall v FCT* (1988) 81 ALR 173; 19 ATR 1352. See also **Fair dealing**; **International agreement**.

•**Arrangement** Generally, an agreement, plan, or compact, the legal effect of which depends on the context in which it is used:

Corporations An agreement modifying rights between persons regardless of whether they are in dispute about their rights. Under Corporations Law Pt 5.1, an arrangement includes a reorganisation of share capital of a company by the consolidation of shares of different classes or by the division of shares into shares of different classes: s 9. See also **Compromise**.

Trade and commerce In competition law, something less than a binding agreement; a plan arranged between two or more parties which may not be enforceable at law: *Top Performance Motors Pty Ltd v Ira Berk (Qld) Pty Ltd* (1975) 5 ALR 465. See also **Contract, arrangement or understanding**; **Substantially lessening competition**.

Arrangement for bonus issue A consensual agreement or understanding under which bonus shares are issued in order to provide money or other property to any person: *Federal Cmr of Taxation v Lutovi Investments Pty Ltd* (1978) 140 CLR 434; 22 ALR 519. Such an arrangement may be informal and the parties may be free to withdraw from it or act inconsistently with it, notwithstanding their adoption of it: *Federal Cmr of Taxation v Lutovi Investments Pty Ltd*. However, a number of piecemeal steps that are not part of a conscious plan cannot amount to an arrangement: *Trustee of Estate of Grant (dec'd) and Williamson v FCT* (1981) 39 ALR 594. See also **Arrangement**; **Bonus share issue**.

Arrangement, scheme of See **Scheme of arrangement**.

•**Arrears** A term commonly used to describe sums overdue and payable in respect of periods of time, for example unpaid rent, unpaid interest, and unpaid maintenance: *Queen Anne's Bounty v Tithe Redemption Commission* [1938] Ch 229. See also **Maintenance**; **Mortgagee's power of sale**; **Relief against forfeiture**; **Voting share**.

•**Arrest** The seizure or touching of a person's body with a view to his or her restraint: for example *Lewis v Norman* [1982] 2 NSWLR 649 at 655. An arrest occurs where a person is in the company of an investigating official for the purpose of being questioned and the official believes that there is sufficient evidence to establish that the person has committed an offence that is to be the subject of the questioning, or whenever it is plain by what is said and done by the police officer that the suspect is no longer a free person: for example (CTH) Crimes Act 1914 s 23b(2); (VIC) Crimes Act 1958 s 464(1); *R v O'Donoghue* (1988) 34 A Crim R 397. See also **Arrest warrant**.

•**Arrest warrant** A document issued by an official, usually a judge or a magistrate, authorising that a person be arrested and brought before a court: (NSW) Justices Act 1902 s 23; (VIC) Magistrates' Court Act 1989 s 28 See also **Arrest**.

Arson Generally, a colloquial expression referring to the unlawful setting fire to property.

Insurance In marine insurance law, to avoid liability for loss due to arson, a defendant insurer must prove on the balance of probabilities that the ship or cargo was destroyed by the plaintiff, or that the plaintiff connived at its destruction: *Slattery v Mance* [1962] 1 QB 676. See also **Balance of probabilities**.

•**Articled clerk** A law clerk employed under written articles of agreement by which the clerk agrees to serve a master solicitor, in consideration of the master solicitor providing practical training sufficient to entitle the clerk to qualify for admission to the legal profession.

•**Articles** See **Articled clerk**; **Articles of association**.

Articles of Agreement of the International Monetary Fund 1945 Terms and conditions drawn up at the United Nations Monetary and Financial Conference, Bretton Woods (New Hampshire), 1-22 July 1944 for creation of the International Monetary Fund. The Articles of Agreement of the International Monetary Fund 1945 came into force generally on 27 December 1945 and for Australia on 5 August 1947. The Agreement was first amended at Rio de Janeiro in 1968 and entered into force 28 July 1969. In 1976 further amendments were made to the Agreement which came into force on 1 April 1978. The Agreement is implemented in Australia by the (CTH) International Monetary Agreements Act 1947. Also known as 'International Monetary Agreement'. See also **International Monetary Fund**.

•**Articles of association** The rules adopted by a company on incorporation that govern the internal affairs of a company: *Re Amtrao Pty Ltd* (1994) 13 ACSR 654; 12 ACLC 486. The articles of association set out items such as: the relationship between the shareholders and the directors; method of appointment of directors; procedures for allotment and transfer of shares; declaration of dividends; and the rights and obligations of company members. Along with the memorandum of association, the articles of association comprise the company constitution. See also **Australian Securities Commission**; **Company constitution**; **Memorandum of association**; **Table A articles**; **Table B articles**.

Articles of partnership See **Partnership agreement**.

Artificial person An entity recognised by law but which is not a real person, for example, a company. See also **Company**.

•**AS** The Greek equivalent of a joint stock company. See also **Joint Stock Company**.

AS 2124-1992 The current edition of the General Conditions of Contract prepared by the Standards Association of Australia ('Standards Australia'). Earlier editions were AS 2124-1981 and AS 2124-1986. This contract is accompanied by AS 2125-1992 (general conditions of tendering and form of tender). These standard forms are frequently amended by the parties or qualified by other provisions in the contract documents: *Mitsui Construction Co Ltd v A-G(Hong Kong)* (1986) 33 BLR 1 at 18. There are standard form subcontracts which are used in conjunction with the standard form contracts: for example SCNPWC 3, SCJCC A-1994 and AS 2545-1993. See also **AS 2545-1993**; **Building Contract**; **Incorporation**; **Standard form contract**.

AS 2545-1993 A standard form contract commonly used in the Australian construction industry, published by the Standards Association of Australia in 1993. See also **AS 2124-1992**; **Building Contract**; **Construction**; **Standard form contract**; **Subcontract**.

As soon as reasonably possible As quickly as the task at hand is capable of being done in the circumstances: *Lindner v Wright* (1976) 14 ALR 105.

•**Asbestos** A group of fibrous minerals, actinolite, amosite, chrysolite, crocidolite, fibrous anthophyllite, tremolite, or any material containing those minerals: (ACT) Building Act 1972 s 5(1). Prolonged inhalation of asbestos fibres may give rise to a form of pneumoconiosis known as asbestosis. A proportion of those exposed may acquire a rare but fatal form of cancer, mesothelioma. Regulations in Australia and overseas specify the number of fibres per unit volume of air. Removal of asbestos from buildings is mandatory but when removed the activity is regulated for health reasons: for example (CTH) National Occupational Health and Safety Commission Act 1985; (CTH) Asbestos: Code of Practice 1988; (NSW) Occupational Health and Safety Act 1983; (NSW) Factories, Shops and Industries Act 1962. See also **Air pollution**.

ASC See **Australian Securities Commission**.

ASC certificate See **Certificate of incorporation**.

ASC instrument See **Australian Securities Commission Instrument**.

•**ASC law** See **Australian Securities Commission law**.

ASCII See **American Standard Code for Information Interchange**.

ASCPA See **Australian Society of Certified Practising Accountants**.

ASEAN See **Association of South East Asian Nations**.

Asian Development Bank *Abbr* – ADB A multilateral development finance institution with membership from Asian and developed countries that aims to foster economic growth and cooperation in the Asia and Pacific region, and to contribute to accelerating the process of economic development of the developing member countries in the region: (CTH) Asian Development Bank Act 1966 Sch 1 art 1; Agreement Establishing the Asian Development Bank 1965 art 1.

Asia-Pacific Development Centre A regional autonomous institution established in 1980. Its main objectives are to assist the member states in overcoming their development problems through independent study and analysis of development alternatives; and formulating proper development strategies, policies, and programs of action. The centre encourages the member states to think regionally and act nationally in seeking solutions to their development problems. Its headquarters are in Kuala Lumpur.

Asia-Pacific Economic Cooperation *Abbr* – APEC A forum for economic cooperation in the greater Asia-Pacific region, intended to achieve regional and national economic progress.

ASIO See **Australian Security Intelligence Organisation**.

Ask price The price at which the vendor of shares is prepared to sell his or her shares in the share market. See also **Bid-ask spread**.

Assent by the drawee A phrase expressing a drawee's intention to sign a bill of exchange as acceptor which results in proper signature of the bill. See also **Acceptance**; **Acceptor**; **Bill of exchange**; **Drawee**; **Sign**; **Signification**.

•**Assessable income** All the amounts included in assessable income under the provisions of the (CTH) Income Tax Assessment Act 1936 s 6(1). Allowable deductions are subtracted from a taxpayer's assessable income to determine that taxpayer's taxable income: ss 6(1), 17. See also **Allowable deduction**; **Exempt income**; **Income**; **Net capital gain**; **Statutory income**; **Taxable income**.

•**Assessed annual value** Land value assessed on an annual basis in the manner prescribed by law: for example (NSW) Valuation of Land Act 1916 s 7; (TAS) Land Valuation Act 1971 s 3. Used for rating and valuation purposes. See also **Valuation**.

•**Assessment** The ascertainment of a taxpayer's taxable income, the amount of tax payable on that income, and the completion of the process by which the liability to tax is specified by service of a notice of assessment: (CTH) Income Tax Assessment Act 1936 s 6(1); *Batagol v FCT* (1963) 109 CLR 243. See also **Self assessment**; **Gross tax payable**; **Net tax payable**; **Tax return**; **Taxable income**.

•**Assessment of costs** The system by which the amount of legal costs payable as between barrister and client, solicitor and client, or between the parties to legal proceedings is assessed, where an order for the payment of costs has been made by a court of tribunal in those proceedings, rather than taxed by an officer of the court: for example (NSW) Legal Profession Act 1987 Pt 11 Div 6. Where a costs agreement exists between a barrister or solicitor and the client, the client's entitlement to have legal costs assessed may be restricted: (NSW) Legal Profession Act 1987 s 208C. See also **Costs agreement**.

Assessment of damages The process of estimating and quantifying the reasonable monetary value of a plaintiff's loss. In tort law, the aim in assessing damages is to put the plaintiff in the position he or she would have been in had the tort not been committed: *Todorovic v Waller* (1981) 150 CLR 402; 37 ALR 481. In contract law, damages will be assessed on the basis of both loss of bargain (expectation loss) and damage suffered, including expenditure incurred, in reliance on the contract (reliance loss): *Gates v City Mutual Life Assurance Society Ltd* (1986) 160 CLR 1; 63 ALR 600. Also known as 'measure of damages' or 'quantum of damages'. See also **Damages; Expectation interest; Heads of damage**.

• **Assessor 1.** A person appointed as a judicial officer to advise a court or tribunal on questions of technical or scientific knowledge, for example in relation to planning and environmental appeals: (NSW) Land and Environment Court Act 1979 s 12. See also **Member**.

• **Asset** An item, whether tangible or intangible, having economic value to its owner which, if not already in the form of money, can be converted into money to the owner's benefit. Assets are service potential or future economic benefits controlled by an entity as a result of past transactions or other past events: Statement of Accounting Concepts SAC 4. See also **Balance sheet; Contingent asset; Property**.

Accounting Service potential or future economic benefits controlled by an entity as a result of past transactions or other past events: Statement of Accounting Concepts SAC 4. See also **Balance sheet; Contingent asset; Property**.

Taxation and revenue For capital gains tax purposes, any form of property, including: an option, debt, a chose in action, any other right whether legal or equitable and whether or not a form of property; goodwill or any other form of incorporeal property; currency of a foreign country; a taxpayer's interest in a partnership asset of a partnership in which the taxpayer is a partner; and so much of a taxpayer's interest in a partnership as is not an interest in a partnership asset: (CTH) Income Tax Assessment Act 1936 s 160A. See also **Capital gains tax; Chose in action; Corporeal property; Partnership**.

Asset allocation The process of dividing investments between the various asset classes as part of an investment strategy. The decision as to how an investment should be allocated is based on the relative risk and return of each of the asset classes, the tax implications of the investment on both return and the investors personal tax situation, and the investment strategy of the investor or manager: (CTH) Superannuation Industry (Supervision) Regulations 1994 reg 2.61. See also **Asset class**.

Asset backed security A financial instrument which is secured by other assets such as a mortgage of land or chattels. See also **Asset; Security; Securitisation arrangement**.

Asset backing The net assets of a company divided by the number of issued shares. For example, if the ABC company has $100 million net assets and 100,000 shares issued, the asset backing is $1000 per share. See also **Asset; Share**.

Asset class For investment purposes, the category of an asset according to differences in its investment characteristics. The major asset classes are cash, fixed-interest securities, property, and equities, although these classes can be further broken down to reflect different characteristics within the classes. The asset classes differ in terms of risk, return, liquidity, and tax effect. See also **Asset; Asset allocation**.

Asset disposal Disposal of an asset by way of sale, loss or destruction. An actual or deemed change in the legal and beneficial ownership of an asset is deemed to effect a disposal of the asset by the person who owned it immediately before the change and an acquisition by the person who owned it immediately after the change: (CTH) Income Tax Assessment Act 1936 ss 160L, 160M. When an asset is disposed of during the financial year the amount received for such a disposal is consideration received on disposal of assets. This consideration is offset against the closing written down value of the asset as at the date of disposal. If the amount received is less than the original purchase price, a capital loss is incurred which can be used to reduce capital gains. The calculation is shown on the depreciation schedule in which the asset was originally recorded. See also **Asset**.

Asset information Certain information which the directors of a company are required to include in the company's financial statements with respect to the value of the assets of the company. Corporations Law s 294(4) requires the directors to take reasonable steps to find out if the value of any non-current asset exceeds the amount that would have been reasonable for the company to spend to acquire the asset at the end of the financial year. Unless adequate provision for writing down the value of that asset is made, the directors must include such information and explanation in the company's financial statements as will prevent those statements from being misleading because of an overstatement of the value of the assets. See also **Asset**.

Asset revaluation reserves A capital account created when assets are revalued beyond their carrying amount. The reserves are credited with the accumulated increments to value. If the value decreases, the decrement is debited to the previous increment. If the decrement is bigger than the previous increments, the difference is charged as an expense to the profit and loss account: Applicable Accounting Standard AASB 1010. 'Accounting for the revaluation of non-current assets' refers to the transfers of amounts to and from the asset revaluation reserve account.

Asset stripping Purchasing a company that is undervalued and selling off some or all of its assets. See also **Corporate crime**.

• **Assignment** A transfer of rights or liabilities such as those that arise under an instrument, chose in action, or debt.

Contract **1.** An arrangement in which one of the original parties to a contract transfers his or her benefits and obligations under the contract to a third party. Assignments of a contract may be effected: by contract of novation, where the debtor, creditor, and assignee each agree that in future the debtor is to regard the assignee as the creditor (for example *Robinson v Po-*

dosky [1905] St R Qd 118 at 122; *Olsson v Dyson* (1969) 120 CLR 365 at 388); by equitable assignment, by which the creditor assigns the benefit of a contractual right owed by the debtor to an assignee by demonstrating an intention to assign (for example *Comptroller of Stamps (Vic) v Howard-Smith* (1936) 54 CLR 614); or by statutory assignment, in which the creditor assigns a right to a debtor by complying with the statutory requirements (for example (NSW) Conveyancing Act 1919 s 12; (VIC) Property Law Act 1958 s 134). **2.** An assignment of debt is the transfer by a debtor to a third party of any obligations under a debt owed to another person. See also **Absolute assignment; Debt; Equitable assignment; Novation.**

Deeds and other instruments The transfer of a legal interest or property. At law, assignment of a legal chose in action requires: an absolute transfer, in writing and signed by the assignor, with express notice given to the person from whom the assignor is entitled to receive the debt: for example (NSW) Conveyancing Act 1919 s 12. Equity will consider a voluntary assignment valid ('complete') where the intending donor has done what is sufficient to enable an effectual legal transfer without further action on his or her part: *Milroy v Lord* (1862) 4 De GF & J 264; [1861-73] All ER Rep 783; *Corin v Patton* (1990) 169 CLR 540; 92 ALR 1. A purported assignment for value that fails at law will take effect as an immediate equitable assignment, on the basis that equity regards as done that which ought to be done: *Federal Cmr of Taxation v Betro Harrison Constructions Pty Ltd* (1978) 20 ALR 647. See also **Assignment; Chose in action; Debt.**

Tort The transferral of a right to sue or of the damages to be recovered. A right of action in tort is not generally assignable, in order to prevent maintenance and champerty. See also **Maintenance.**

Assignment inter vivos A transfer of property or some interest or right in the property from the transferor to the transferee during the life of the transferor, usually involving the whole interest in a chattel, estate, or other asset (such as a negotiable instrument) unless specifically qualified in some way. See also **Inter vivos.**

• **Associate** *Lat* – associates; joined to. A person or entity related to or connected with another. A person or entity may be an associate to another in various legal contexts:

Consumer protection A person holding money or property on behalf of another or a wholly owned subsidiary of a body corporate: for example (VIC) Fair Trading Act 1985 s 35A; (QLD) Fair Trading Act 1989 s 102.

Corporations The relationship existing between an entity or person and another, arising either automatically due to the relationship of the one to the other, or on the facts based on a relevant agreement or concerted activity. See also **Associated company; Associated entity; Entitlement to shares; Takeover.**

Taxation and revenue **1.** For a natural person: a relative; a partner; a trustee of a trust estate under which the person or an associate benefits or is capable of benefiting; and a company under the control of the person or associate: (CTH) Income Tax Assessment Act 1936 s 26AAB(14)(a). **2.** For a company: a partner or an associate of a partner; a trustee of a trust estate under which the company or associate of the company benefits or is capable of benefiting; another person or associate of the other person who controls the company; and another company which is under the control of the company or that company's associate: (CTH) Income Tax Assessment Act 1936 s 26AAB(14)(b). Also known as 'associated person', 'associated company'. See also **Associated company; Associated entity; Company; Partner; Partnership; Attributable Taxpayer; Trust; Trustee.**

• **Associate director** In company law, a person appointed as a director, usually with more limited powers and duties than other directors. See also **Director; Directors' duties.**

• **Associate member** In futures trading, a form of membership of the Sydney Futures Exchange (SFE), comprising three types of membership; full associate member, introducing broker associate member (normally referred to as an 'introducing broker') and market associate member. The rights and obligations attaching to each type of associate membership differ. See also **Full associate member; Introducing broker; Market associate member; Sydney Futures Exchange.**

• **Associated company** A body corporate linked with another body corporate in terms of control of operations: Corporations Law s 3. Whether an associate or company is an associate of another is relevant in determining entitlements to shares for the purposes of Corporations Law Ch 6, so that the aggregate entitlements of associates must comply with, for example, the notice provisions in Ch 6. Wide definitions of 'associates' are provided in Corporations Law ss 11-17. For example, one company may be associated with another if certain types of agreements exist between the two bodies or if the companies are acting in concert. More generally companies may be considered to be associated when one company has an interest in another: for example (CTH) Re Export Market Development Grants Act 1974 s 3; *Bassarab Holdings Pty Ltd v Australian Trade Commission* (1991) 24 ALD 793; (QLD) Stamp Act 1894 s 49C(2); *KLDE Pty Ltd v Cmr of Stamp Duties (Qld)* (1984) 155 CLR 288; 56 ALR 337. See also **Associate.**

• **Associated entity** In bankruptcy, a natural person, partnership, trust, or private company associated with a bankrupt in the ways mentioned in (CTH) Bankruptcy Act 1966 ss 5B, 5C, 5D, 5E: (CTH) Bankruptcy Act 1966 s 5(1). A trustee in bankruptcy investigating the affairs of a bankrupt can have access to the records of an associated entity: s 77A. See also **Associate; Associated company; Bankrupt; Trustee in bankruptcy.**

• **Association** Any group of persons who have agreed to join together in pursuit of one or more common objects or purposes: *Smith v Anderson* (1880) 15 Ch D 247. Also known as 'society'. See also **Club; Company; Cooperative-company; Credit union; Domestic tribunal; Partnership; Voluntary non-profit association.**

Association, articles of See **Articles of association.**

Association, memorandum of See **Memorandum of association.**

Association of South East Asian Nations
Abbr – ASEAN An association of South East Asian nations which was formed in 1967 to promote regional cooperation. Based in Jakarta, ASEAN has as its goals the acceleration of economic growth, cultural development and social progress, the promotion of collaboration and mutual assistance in matters of common interest, and the continuing stability of the South East Asian region: ASEAN Declaration 1967 arts 1-7.

Associations incorporation laws Legislation in each jurisdiction which provides for the incorporation by registration of non-profit associations: for example (QLD) Associations Incorporation Act 1981. This gives an association separate legal status as a body corporate: for example (VIC) Associations Incorporation Act 1981 s 14. See also **Incorporation; Separate legal personality**.

Assumpsit /æsʌmpsɪt/ *Lat* – he or she promised or undertook. Assumpsit was a general contractual remedy arising from a promise where a person assumed and took on himself or herself to perform some act or pay something for another. It was subsequently abolished by the (UK) Judicature Act 1873. The term is now used mainly to refer to an action which lay where a party claimed damages for breach of simple contract. See also **Contract; Promise; Remedy; Simple contract**.

•**Assurance 1.** In relation to the sale of land, a conveyance or other instrument by which an estate in land is disposed of, otherwise than by will: (NSW) Conveyancing Act 1919 s 7. **2.** Another term for insurance, generally used in relation to contracts of life insurance. See also **Assured; Conveyance; Estate; Insurance; Life insurance**.

•**Assured** A person or body who agrees to pay money to an insurer to insure against loss; a person who makes a contract of insurance with an insurer: *Wadsley v City Mutual Life Assurance Society Ltd* [1971] VR 140. Also known as 'insured'. See also **Disclosure; Insurance contract; Insurer; Materiality; Uberrimae fidei**.

Assured payment system *Abbr* – APS An arrangement in an exchange-for-value system under which completion of timely settlement of a payment instruction is supported by an irrevocable and unconditional commitment from a third party typically being a bank, syndicate of banks, or clearing house. See also **Exchange- for-value settlement system**.

ASX See **Australian Stock Exchange Ltd**.

ASX Business Rules See **Australian Stock Exchange Business Rules**.

ASX Continuing Listing Rules See **Australian Stock Exchange Continuing Listing Rules**.

ASX listing See **Australian Stock Exchange listing**.

ASX Listing Rules See **Australian Stock Exchange Listing Rules**.

ASX Settlement and Transfer Corporation See **Securities clearing house**.

Asymmetric information A situation where there is a lack of balance or symmetry between the information available to consumers regarding a product or service and the information available to the producer or supplier. Producers and suppliers tend to have more information regarding their product than do consumers. See also **Consumer; Supplier**.

At a discount At a price lower than par value; lower than normal.

At a premium At a price higher than par value; higher than normal.

•**At arm's length** See **Arm's length transaction**.

At best In relation to instructions to a broker or financial institution, an abbreviation for 'at the lowest possible price' in respect of a buying order, and 'at the highest possible price' in respect of a selling order. See also **At discretion**.

At call Used with reference to invested funds which can be withdrawn on demand, without notice.

•**At discretion** In respect of an instruction to a broker to buy or sell shares. An instruction by a buyer or seller of securities quoted on a stock exchange giving the broker discretion as to the price at which to buy or sell. See also **At best; At limit; At market; At par**.

At large, damages See **Damages at large**.

At limit In respect of an instruction to a broker to buy or sell shares, a specified limit on either the highest price that may be paid, or the lowest price at which a sale may be made. See also **At best; At discretion; At market; At par**.

At market An indorsement on an instruction to a broker that an order to buy or sell is to be executed promptly on the trading floor at the best possible price. See also **At best; At discretion; At limit; At par**.

At par Stocks and shares, the market price of which is the same as the nominal or face value. See also **At best; At discretion; At limit; At market; Par value**.

At sight Payable on demand. A bill of exchange drawn at sight is payable on demand, without delay.

At the money option A put or call option where the current (or spot) price of the underlying asset is equivalent to the strike (or exercise) price of the option. See also **Option; Spot price; Strike price**.

At your risk An indorsement that the rates quoted are subject to change.

Atlantic Shipping clause In relation to an arbitration agreement, a provision in the agreement barring all claims unless a claim is put forward in writing and an arbitrator appointed within a limited period. It takes its name from *Atlantic Shipping & Trading Co Ltd v Louis Dreyfus & Co* [1922] 2 AC 250. Such a clause is an effective bar to a claim made after the stated period has expired: *Atlantic Shipping & Trading Co Ltd v Louis Dreyfus & Co*. The court may extend the time for doing any act or taking any proceeding in or in relation to an arbitration: (NSW) Commercial Arbitration Act 1984 s 48(1) ; (QLD) Commercial Arbitration Act 1990 s 48(1); (VIC) Commercial Arbitration Act 1984 s 48(1). An arbitrator who is given express power to extend time may exercise it in the appropriate case: *Timmerman's Graan-en Maalhandel en Maalderij BV v Sachs* [1980] 1 Lloyd's Rep 194. See also **Alternative dispute resolution; Arbitration; Arbitrator**.

•**ATM** See **Automatic teller machine**.

•**Attachment** The use of a court order by a creditor to intercept the payment of a debt owed to a debtor by a third party. See also **Bankruptcy Court; Creditor's petition; Debtor**.

Attachment of debts See **Garnishment**.

Attachment of earnings See **Garnishment**.

Attempting to pervert the course of justice The offence at common law and under statute of doing an act that has a tendency to, and is intended to, pervert the administration of public justice, whether or not proceedings have been commenced: *R v Rogerson; Nowytarger & Paltos* (1992) 174 CLR 268; 107 ALR 225. It includes fabricating evidence (*R v St Jean* (1903) 20 WN (NSW) 211), bribing police to hinder the prosecution (*R v Matthews & Ford* [1972] VR 3), and improperly securing a plea of guilty by another person (*Meissner v R* (1995) 130 ALR 547).

Attendant term The length of a lease determined by the leased property being held 'upon trust to attend an inheritance'. Such a lease term protects the beneficiary against unknown encumbrances created after the lease commences, but before the trust property vests in that beneficiary. See also **Lease; Leasehold; Term lease; Term of years**.

Attest Generally, to give evidence or witness. To witness by signature the execution of a deed or document: *Ellison v Vukicevic* (1986) 7 NSWLR 104; *Wickham v Marquis of Bath* (1865) LR 1 Eq 17 at 24. Documents that require attesting include deeds and wills.

Deeds and other instruments A deed is not properly attested unless the signature of each person who signs the deed is witnessed by at least one person not a party to the deed: (NSW) Conveyancing Act 1919 s 38; (QLD) Property Law Act 1974 s 45(2); *Mostyn v Mostyn* (1989) 16 NSWLR 635. See also **Deed; Delivery; Execution**.

Attested copy A copy of a document verified as correct.

•**Attorn** 1. A submission to another's authority: *Henry v Geoprosco International Ltd* [1975] 2 All ER 702; [1974] Lloyd's Rep 536 at 538. 2. An agreement not to contest another's authority: *Aldred v Australian Building Industries Pty Ltd* (1987) 48 NTR 59.

•**Attorney** A person appointed by another to represent or act in place of that person. See also **Advocate; Barrister; Solicitor**.

•**Attorney-General** *Abbr* – A-G The first law officer of the Crown, with the function of enforcing the law and advising and acting for the Crown in all matters to which the Crown is a party. The A-G exercises some of the prerogative powers of the Crown, such as the power to grant consent (fiat) to a relator action, to file an *ex officio* indictment and to file a *nolle prosequi* (no bill). The Commonwealth Government appoints an Attorney-General, as does each State Government. See also **Australian Government Solicitor; Crown; Fiat; Solicitor-General**.

•**Attributable cost** In relation to performance received under a frustrated contract: the reasonable cost of performance where there is no incidental gain to the performing party; or the reasonable cost of performance less the value of any incidental gain; or where the reasonable cost less incidental gain exceeds the proportionate allowance, the proportionate allowance: (NSW) Frustrated Contracts Act 1978 s 11(1). An amount calculated by reference to the attributable cost must be paid to the performing party if the contract is frustrated after the other party has received partial performance not involving the payment of money. See also **Frustration; Incidental gain; Part performance; Performance; Subtantial performance**.

Attributable income The quantum of taxable income derived by a controlled foreign corporation (CFC) during a period if certain statutory assumptions are made: (CTH) Income Tax Assessment Act 1936 ss 382, 383. Attributable income derived by the CFC for the purposes of (CTH) Income Tax Assessment Act 1936 Pt X Div 7 is included in the assessable income of an attributable taxpayer. See also **Assessable income; Attributable taxpayer; Controlled foreign company**.

Attributable taxpayer 1. In the context of a controlled foreign corporation, an Australian entity which with any associates satisfies either of the control tests in (CTH) Income Tax Assessment Act 1936 ss 349-355, 361(1)(a), (b): (CTH) Income Tax Assessment Act 1936 s 317. The s 361(1)(a) test uses a 10 per cent control interest requirement. **2.** In the context of a controlled foreign trust, an Australian entity which together with any associates holds at least a 10 per cent control interest in the foreign trust (s 361(2)). The tests for determining the level of Australian entity (and associated) control are contained in ss 349-355. An attributable taxpayer is taxed on an accrual basis in respect of the taxpayers' share of the income derived by a controlled foreign corporation or controlled foreign trust. See also **Accruals accounting; Controlled foreign company**.

•**Attributable value** In contract law, an amount equal to the value of the proportionate allowance for performance, reduced by the lost value of that performance. Lost value, in relation to performance received under a frustrated contract, refers to the amount (if any) by which the frustration reduced the value of that performance. That value is assessed as at the time immediately before the frustration of the contract and on the basis that the contract would not be frustrated: (NSW) Frustrated Contracts Act 1978 s 11(1). See also **Frustration; Performance**.

•**Auction** A public sale at which any type of real or personal property, including livestock, is sold, usually to the highest bidder. See also **Auctioneer; Auction advertisement; Bid; Bidder; Dutch auction; Reserve price**.

Auction advertisement A public notice or announcement appearing in a newspaper, catalogue, magazine, brochure, handbill, or other publication, in the electronic media, or on a sign or poster, notifying of an intention to sell certain property by auction on the day, and at the time and place specified. See also **Auction**.

Auction conditions The conditions, usually imposed by a seller, governing the conduct of an auction and the relationship between the auctioneer, seller, bidders, and particularly the highest bidder. The auction conditions may be exhibited or read out at the auction, or incorporated in the contract for sale. A seller may accept the standard auction conditions recommended and used by the auctioneer. See also **Auction**; **Auctioneer**; **Bid**; **Incorporation**.

•**Auction sale** See **Auction**.

•**Auctioneer** A person who conducts sales by auction: for example (NSW) Property, Stock and Business Agents Act 1941 s 3(1). See also **Agency**; **Agent**; **Auction**; **Auctioneers licence**; **Auctioneers lien**; **Authority**; **Bid**; **Provincial auctioneer**.

•**Auctioneer's licence** A licence required by statute enabling a person to legally carry on business as an auctioneer: for example (VIC) Auction Sales Act 1958 s 4. In all jurisdictions except New South Wales legislation specifies the type of licence required. Some licences entitle the licensee to act only as an employee or to undertake auctions of particular types of property. The qualifications required by an applicant in order to be eligible for a particular licence generally relate to minimum age, educational qualifications, and experience; in addition, the applicant must be a fit and proper person to hold such a licence: for example (QLD) Auctioneers and Agents Act 1971 s 39. See also **Auction**; **Auctioneer**; **Fit and proper person**.

Auctioneer's lien An auctioneer's entitlement to retain property, goods, and documents held on behalf of the seller, until payment of the auctioneer's remuneration and any expenses or liabilities properly incurred. See also **Auction**; **Auctioneer**; **Deposit**; **Lien**; **Remuneration**.

Auction-rated preference stock A type of floating rate preferred stock where the dividend is reset by auction every 49 days.

•**Audit** The official and systematic examination of the financial statements of an accounting entity with verification by reference to witnesses and vouchers: *Shire of Frankston and Hastings v Cohen* (1960) 102 CLR 607; ALR 249. See also **Accounting standards**; **Audit committee**; **Auditor**; **Auditor's report**; **Auditing standards**.

•**Audit committee** A committee of directors, usually non-executive directors, appointed in a large company to assist the board of directors in checking arrangements made by the company's full-time managers regarding the audit of the company's accounts and the reports to members. A listed company is required to state, in its annual report, whether or not it has an audit committee and if not, why not: Australian Stock Exchange Listing Rule 4.11.2. See also **Audit**; **Australian Stock Exchange Continuing Listing Rules**.

Audit Guide A professional statement issued by the Auditing Standards Board intended to provide detailed practical assistance in implementing Statements of Auditing Standards (AUSs) and Statements of Auditing Practice (AUPs), and to stimulate discussion on matters of auditing theory and practice, including industry-specific guidance to auditors. Guides do not extend or limit the application of AUSs or AUPs and should be read in conjunction with those statements. See also **Auditing standards**; **Statement of Auditing Standards**.

Audit risk The risk that an auditor may express an inappropriate opinion on financial information that is materially misstated: Statement of Auditing Practice (AUP) 12 para 7. See also **Auditing standards**; **Auditor's report**; **Control risk**; **Detection risk**; **Inherent risk**.

•**Auditing** See **Audit**.

Auditing Discussion Paper A professional statement issued by the Auditing Standards Board and intended to focus on basic auditing concepts and questions of policy. Papers do not extend or limit the application of Statements of Auditing Standards or Practice. See also **Statement of Auditing Standards**.

Auditing Guidance Release A professional statement issued by the Auditing Standards Board (ASB) providing guidance concerning the application of the Statement of Auditing Standards and Statements of Auditing Practice. A release does not establish new principles and does not amend existing statements. Issuance will normally be appropriate where a principle in an existing statement requires explanation. See also **Statement of Auditing Standards**.

Auditing standards Professional standards describing the basic principles which govern the auditor's professional responsibilities and which must be complied with whenever an audit is carried out. Auditing standards are set out in Statement of Auditing Standards AUS 1. See also **Audit**; **Audit Guide**; **Auditing Standards Board**; **Statement of Auditing Standards**.

Auditing Standards Board The board of the Australian Accounting Research Foundation with responsibility for the development and maintenance of Statements of Auditing Standards, Statements of Auditing Practice and other publications. The Board consists of members nominated by the accounting professional bodies and are supported by full-time technical staff of the Foundation. See also **Auditing standards**.

•**Auditor** A person who examines accounting records and systems to ascertain whether the records are accurate and whether accounting systems are operating efficiently. Every company, other than certain small proprietary companies (Corporations Law ss 325(1)), must appoint an external auditor to audit the company's financial affairs and to provide a report to the members and directors: s 331A(1), (3). See also **Audit**; **Auditing standards**.

Auditor's negligence Breach of the duty of care owed by an accountant appointed to ascertain the true financial position of a company by examining the company's books. See also **Auditor**; **Auditors report**; **Duty of care**; **Liability to third parties**; **Negligent misrepresentation**; **Pure economic loss**.

Auditor's report 1. A report made to members of a company by an external auditor on the company's financial statements, accounting records, and other relevant records: Corporations Law s 331A(1). **2.** A report by an auditor to a company's directors for lodgment with the Australian Securities Commission (ASC): s 331A(3). See also **Audit; Auditors report; Audit risk; Internal control structure; Qualified audit report.**

AUS See **Statement of Auditing Standards.**

•**AusAID** See **Australian Agency for International Development.**

•**AUSTEL** See **Australian Telecommunications Authority.**

•**AUSTRAC** See **Australian Transaction Reports and Analysis Centre.**

Austraclear An unlisted public company that acts as a central depository and clearing house for securities traded in the Australian money markets. It began operations in 1984. Initially, transactions processed through it were limited to bearer securities, such as bills of exchange and commercial paper. In 1989 its scope was extended to include registered securities issued by semi-government bodies, banks and corporations, and by 1993 its daily turnover of around A$25 billion represented 90 per cent of the national turnover of fixed-interest securities issued by these bodies. As the central depository and registry for semi-government and private sector paper, Austraclear facilitates trading in these securities by removing the need for a physical transfer of paper. Austraclear electronically records book-entry changes in ownership or entitlement as securities are traded or pledged as collateral. Austraclear is governed by its own regulations. Its members include all of the banks and authorised money market dealers as well as large government and semi-government bodies, insurance and superannuation companies, securities dealers, building societies, trustee companies, custodians, and large corporations. See also **Australian Financial Markets Association; Clearing house; Securities.**

•**Australasia** Australia, New Zealand, and the Fiji Islands: (CTH) Bills of Exchange Act 1909 s 4. See also **Australia; Inland bill; Inland note.**

Australasian Mechanical Copyright Owners Society *Abbr* – AMCOS A non-profit company, limited by guarantee, established in 1979 by the Australian Music Publishers Association Ltd (AMPAL) to administer various copyright rights on behalf of its music publisher members. AMCOS represents most music publishers in Australia and in New Zealand, and, by way of reciprocal agreements, most overseas music publishers. The licensing schemes offered by AMCOS include the licensing of cover versions of musical works (based on the scheme provided under (CTH) Copyright Act 1968 ss 54-64; agreements in respect of photocopying of copyright music and lyrics by schools; the licensing of rights in production music libraries produced by AMCOS member publishers; and, agreements with broadcasters which extend the ephemeral reproduction rights under (CTH) Copyright Act 1968 s 47. AMCOS also has a substantial database of owners of copyright in music which has been recorded, and offers a research service to advertising agencies, film production companies, and other users of copyright music. See also **Copyright.**

Australasian Performing Right Association *Abbr* – APRA A non-profit company, limited by guarantee, incorporated in 1926 to act as a collecting society on behalf of members in respect of the public performance of their copyright musical works and associated lyrics. APRA also administers the broadcast and cable diffusion rights in such works. Authors, composers, music publishers and other music copyright owners whose work is being broadcast or performed in public are entitled to become members. APRA's voluntary licence schemes are offered both on behalf of its members and on behalf of the members of affiliated overseas organisations. See also **Copyright.**

•**Australia** A constitutional monarchy with the Queen of Australia as the Head of State. Australia is a federation in which the governmental powers are divided between the Commonwealth or Federal Government and the six State governments (New South Wales, Victoria, Queensland, South Australia, Western Australia, Tasmania). There are two self governing mainland Territories (Australian Capital Territory, Northern Territory), and seven external territories. See also **Commonwealth of Australia; Federal system.**

Australia Acts Two constitutionally significant Acts passed in 1986 in substantially the same form, one by the Australian Commonwealth Parliament and the other by the United Kingdom Parliament: (IMP) Australia Act 1986; (CTH) Australia Act 1986. The Acts terminated the power of the United Kingdom Parliament to legislate for Australia, and restrictions on the legislative powers of the States arising from the doctrine of repugnancy: (CTH) Australia Act 1986 ss 1, 3. See also **Privy Council.**

Australia and New Zealand Banking Group *Abbr* – ANZ A banking group established in 1970 when the Australia and New Zealand Bank merged with the English, Scottish and Australian Bank. The history of these earlier banks goes back to 1834 and 1852 respectively. ANZ provides a range of financial services in its home market of Australia, New Zealand and the Pacific Islands. The group encompasses ANZ Grindlays Bank Plc and Esanda Finance Corporation. See also **Australian banking system.**

Australia card National identity card, to be carried by every citizen as part of a national identity scheme proposed by the Commonwealth Government in 1986. Production of the card would have been required for many activities such as opening a bank account or claiming social security benefits. The proposal was withdrawn after strong public opposition to mandatory identity cards. A system of tax file numbers was introduced instead in 1989: (CTH) Income Tax Assessment Act 1936 Pt 5A. See also **Tax file number.**

Australia Day 26 January. Australia Day is a public and bank holiday prescribed by statute: for example (NSW) Banks and Bank Holidays Act 1912 s 15, Sch 4; (VIC) Public Holidays Act 1993 s 6(b).

•**Australia Post** See **Australian Postal Corporation.**

Australian Accounting Research Foundation *Abbr* – AARF A body established in 1966 by the Institute of Chartered Accountants in Australia and the Australian Society of Accountants, with the principal objective of improving the quality of financial reporting and auditing in Australia. The foundation plays an important role in the development of accounting and auditing standards. See also **Accounting standards**.

• **Australian Accounting Standards** *Abbr* – AAS Rules which set out procedures to be followed in the preparation of financial statements. See also **Approved accounting standard; Australian Accounting Standards Board; Financial statement**.

Australian Accounting Standards Board *Abbr* – AASB A board established under (CTH) Australian Securities Commission Act 1989 Pt 12 with various functions including developing a conceptual framework for evaluating proposed accounting standards; reviewing, developing and amending proposed accounting standards; and consulting the public as to whether a proposed accounting standard should be adopted. The AASB succeeded the Accounting Standards Review Board (ASRB) in 1991. See also **Australian Securities Commission Law; Corporations Law**.

Australian Accumulation Index *Abbr* – AAI Published routinely in the *Australian Financial Review*, an index measuring what returns an investor might have received over a period of time. Constructed by the Australian Stock Exchange, the index includes the total return on stock income from dividends as well as capital gains or losses. It allows an investor to identify which sections of the market are giving the best returns. See also **Australian Stock Exchange Ltd**.

Australian Agency for International Development *Abbr* – AusAID An agency possessing management autonomy implementing government international aid in a coordinated and responsive fashion, AusAID administers the development cooperation program within the Department of Foreign Affairs and Trade, which includes the Australian Centre for International Agricultural Research. The government's aid policy attempts to meet the social justice objectives of equity, equality, access, and participation through meeting short-term needs and promoting long-term development of economic and human resources. See also **Australian Centre for International Agricultural Research; Commonwealth Scientific and Industrial Research Organisation; Department of Foreign Affairs and Trade**.

Australian and New Zealand Agricultural Council A Commonwealth-State ministerial council with New Zealand representatives established to examine and review agricultural problems and to promote cooperation in matters of common interest.

Australian Associated Stock Exchanges An organisation of Australian stock exchanges which was established in 1937 to consider matters of mutual interest and to promote uniform stock exchange regulations such as Listing Rules. The organisation was superseded in 1987 by the Australian Stock Exchange Ltd. See also **Australian Stock Exchange Ltd; Australian Stock Exchange listing rules**.

• **Australian Bank** A specialist bank lending to companies and private individuals. It was a wholly-owned subsidiary of the State Bank of Victoria. Following the merger between the Commonwealth Banking Corp and the State Bank of Victoria in 1991, the Australian Bank became a wholly-owned subsidiary of the former. It was then intended to undertake an orderly winding down of the operations of the bank with the eventual relinquishment of its banking licence. The Australian Bank was established in 1981 as the first new trading bank licensed in Australia in 50 years. See also **Commonwealth Banking Corporation; State Bank of Victoria; Trading Bank**.

Australian Bankers Association *Abbr* – ABA A national association representing Australian banks. Its functions are to promote the interests of the banking industry, improve the efficiency of the banking system in the public interest, and undertake research on matters affecting the industry. Most banking groups operating in Australia are represented by the association. Over 20 task forces and working groups address a variety of banking matters. The ABA collaborates closely with the government and agencies such as the Australian Taxation Office and the Australian Payments Clearing Council. See also **Australian banking system; Australian Payments Clearing Association Ltd; Australian Taxation Office**.

Australian Banking Industry Ombudsman Scheme A voluntary scheme of the banking industry to facilitate the resolution of disputes between individual customers and their banks at no cost to the customer. The Ombudsman has the power to make recommendations and awards are binding on the banks but not on the complainant, who retains the right to take legal action if he or she does not accept the Ombudsman's ruling. See also **Banking service; Commercial judgment; Mediation**.

Australian banking system A banking system comprising a central bank, the Reserve Bank of Australia, the Commonwealth Banking Corporation, a number of cheque-issuing commercial banks and various other special, state-owned and foreign-owned banks. See also **Australia and New Zealand Banking Group; Australian Bankers Association; Commonwealth Banking Corporation; National Australia Bank; Westpac Banking Corporation**.

• **Australian Capital Territory** *Abbr* – ACT One of Australia's two internal Territories. It became a self governing Territory in 1988: (CTH) Australian Capital Territory (Self-Government) Act 1988.

Australian Centre for International Agricultural Research *Abbr* – ACIAR A body established in 1982 to formulate programs and policies for identifying and finding solutions to agricultural problems in developing countries as well as funding and conducting training schemes, development activities and agricultural research centres having regard to the need for developing countries and persons to share in the research: (CTH) Australian Centre for International Agricultural Research 1982 ss 4, 5. Through both bilateral Country Programmes and multilateral Global Programmes the ACIAR makes a special contribution of Australia's agricultural expertise. ACIAR is part of the Development Cooperation program within the Department of Foreign Affairs and Trade which is administered by the Australian Agency for International Development. See also **Australian Agency for International Development; Commonwealth Scientific and Industrial Research Organisation; Department of Foreign Affairs and Trade.**

Australian Centre for International Commercial Arbitration *Abbr* – ACICA A company established in 1985 in Melbourne to conduct and provide facilities for domestic and international commercial arbitrations. See also **Alternative dispute resolution; Arbitration; Institute of Arbitrators Australia.**

Australian Chamber of Commerce and Industry *Abbr* – ACCI A national association of employers and employer organisations, formed in 1992, that advises employers on industrial and employment matters and may represent employers or employer organisations before the Australian Industrial Relations Commission. It was formerly the 'Confederation of Australian Industry'. See also **Australian Industrial Relations Commission; Employer; Employer organisation.**

•**Australian Code for the Transport of Dangerous Goods by Road and Rail** A code establishing standards to be observed when transporting dangerous goods. The code covers the packaging, marking, bulk transport, and handling of dangerous goods containers. The code has been adopted in legislation dealing with dangerous goods in all jurisdictions: for example (NSW) Dangerous Goods Regulation 1978 cl 176. See also **Dangerous goods.**

Australian Commercial Disputes Centre *Abbr* – ACDC A non-profit company incorporated in Sydney in 1986 to promote methods of dispute resolution designed to meet the needs of the business community for cheaper, speedier resolutions than are provided by litigation and arbitration. See also **Alternative dispute resolution; Arbitration; Commercial.**

•**Australian Company Number** *Abbr* – ACN A unique number allocated to every company incorporated in Australia: Corporations Law s 120(1). The ACN, which a company must have, can also be the company name: s 372(1). See also **Australian Registered Body Number; Company seal.**

Australian Competition and Consumer Commission *Abbr* – ACCC Federal regulatory agency formed in late 1995 by the merger of the Trade Practices Commission and the Prices Surveillance Authority: (CTH) Trade Practices Act 1974 s 6A. The principle functions and responsibilities of the ACCC are enforcement, determination of authorisation and notification applications, dissemination of information, law reform and research, compliance with directions by the Minister, assessment of the effect on competition of the allocation of subscription television licences, and informal consultation: (CTH) Trade Practices Act 1974 ss 28, 29. The ACCC is also responsible for enforcing the Competition Code, for prices surveillance, inquiries, and monitoring under the (CTH) Prices Surveillance Act 1983 and (CTH) Competition Policy Reform Act 1995, and for assessment of the effect on competition of the allocation of subscription television licences, and informal consultation ((CTH) Trade Practices Act 1974 ss 28, 29). See also **ACCC representative action; Australian Competition Tribunal; Prices Surveillance Authority; Trade Practices Commission.**

Australian Competition Tribunal A Commonwealth tribunal which reviews determinations of the Australian Competition and Consumer Commission (formerly the Trade Practices Commission) on applications or revocations of authorisation or notification, and hears applications for a declaration in relation to the effect of certain acquisitions outside Australia: (CTH) Trade Practices Act 1974 ss 50A, 101, 101A. The Tribunal was established as the 'Trade Practices Tribunal' under the (CTH) Trade Practices Act 1974 and renamed in 1995. See also **Australian Competition and Consumer Commission; Authorisation; Notification; Restrictive trade practices; Trade practices legislation.**

Australian Conciliation and Arbitration Commission A former industrial tribunal constituted under the (CTH) Conciliation and Arbitration Act 1904 (repealed). It was replaced by the Australian Industrial Relations Commission. See also **Australian Industrial Relations Commission.**

Australian Council of Trade Unions *Abbr* – ACTU An organisation established in May 1927 to assist the interests of affiliated trade unions especially in relation to interstate disputes. See also **Trade Union.**

Australian Credit Transfer Agency Pty Ltd *Abbr* – ACTA A company that is a wholly owned subsidiary of the Australian Vice-Chancellors' Committee. The ACTA was established to assess applications for credit transfer and the recognition of prior learning. It is currently located in Adelaide. See also **Credit; Credit transfer.**

Australian Dairy Corporation A statutory body established by the (CTH) Dairy Produce Act 1986 to promote and enhance the profitable production and marketing of Australian dairy produce. The functions of the Corporation are to improve the marketability of dairy produce, to promote its consumption, to control its export, to deal in dairy produce, to assist manufacturers of dairy produce by way of loans, and to advise the Minister on matters relating to marketing dairy produce. See also **Dairy produce.**

Australian Design Rules *Abbr* – ADRs Rules issued by the Commonwealth Government and adopted by the Australian Transport Advisory Council, with which new vehicles sold in Australia must comply: (NT) Motor Vehicle Act 1949 s 5(1). The purposes of the rules are to provide detailed performance specifications for safety standards in vehicles, so as to reduce accidents and injury; to place the responsibility for the safety of new vehicles on manufacturers and importers rather than purchasers; to provide a check on the safety aspects of a vehicle type before a manufacturer begins volume production; and to reduce the impact of vehicle noise, smoke, and emissions on the community and the environment.

Australian Environment Standards Council A Commonwealth body set up in 1993 to establish national goals and standards and promote other environment protection measures for Australia, such as developing national standards for air and water. It was set up under the Intergovernmental Agreement on the Environment.

Australian Federation of Credit Unions *Abbr* – AFCUL A Sydney based trade association established in 1966 to represent the interests of the credit union industry. See also **Australian Financial Institutions Commission; Credit union**.

Australian Financial Futures Market *Abbr* – AFFM Part of the Australian Stock Exchange, a market launched in 1985 to provide investors with a range of futures contracts. The Australian Futures Contract (AFC) covers a number of listed Australian companies. AFCs are based on ordinary shares, all contracts being cash-settled. The Gold Index Contract was introduced in 1987, being the only futures contract based on Australian gold mining stocks. It is based on the shares of 28 leading gold mining companies which constitute the ASX Gold Index. In the same year, the Twenty Leaders Index Contract was launched, being based on the ASX Twenty Leaders Share Price Index comprised exclusively of blue-chip companies. See also **Sydney Futures Exchange**.

Australian Financial Institutions Commission *Abbr* – AFIC A state and territory body created in 1992, undertaking the prudential supervision of building societies, credit unions and other non-bank financial institutions. AFIC administers the financial institutions scheme: (QLD) Australian Financial Institutions Commission Act 1992 s 6(1). See also **Building society; Credit Union; Financial institutions scheme; Non-bank financial institution**.

Australian Financial Markets Association *Abbr* – AFMA An association established in the mid-1980s to formalise dealing procedures and to set dealing standards, market conventions and trading principles to serve as a guide to appropriate financial market conduct. AFMA liaises regularly with the Reserve Bank of Australia, the Sydney Futures Exchange and Austraclear about market matters. See also **Austraclear; Reserve Bank of Australia; Sydney Futures Exchange**.

•**Australian Government Solicitor** *Abbr* – AGS A body corporate performing solicitor functions on behalf of the Commonwealth, including acting for such person or body as the Attorney-General may request: (CTH) Judiciary Act 1903 ss 55E(1), (3). See also **Attorney-General; Solicitor-General**.

Australian Industrial Court *Abbr* – AIC A federal court that exercised the judicial power of the Commonwealth in relation to industrial awards under the (CTH) Conciliation and Arbitration Act 1904 (repealed). The AIC was abolished in 1977, and its jurisdiction and functions transferred to the Federal Court of Australia (Industrial Division). Now replaced by the Industrial Relations Court of Australia. See also **Federal Court of Australia (Industrial Division)**.

Australian Industrial Property Organisation *Abbr* – AIPO A non-statutory organisation uniting the statutorily distinct Patent Office, Trademarks Office, and Designs Office. See also **Designs Office; Patent Office; Trade mark**.

Australian Industrial Registry A federal registry established by the (CTH) Industrial Relations Act 1988 s 62. Its functions are to keep a register of industrial organisations, to act as the registry for the Australian Industrial Relations Commission, and to advise and assist organisations about their rights and obligations under the (CTH) Industrial Relations Act 1988. It is directed by the Industrial Registrar. See also **Australian Industrial Relations Commission; State industrial authority**.

•**Australian Industrial Relations Commission** *Abbr* – AIRC A federal tribunal established under (CTH) Industrial Relations Act 1988 s 8 to prevent and settle industrial disputes by conciliation and arbitration, and to exercise any other functions conferred on it by other legislation: (CTH) Industrial Relations Act 1988 s 89. It may only conciliate and arbitrate; it is not a general regulatory body. See also **Australian Conciliation and Arbitration Commission; Australian Industrial Court; Australian Industrial Relations Commissioner; Australian industrial system; Compulsory arbitration; Federal Court of Australia (Industrial Division); Industrial award; Industrial tribunal**.

Australian Industrial Relations Commissioner A commissioner appointed to the Australian Industrial Relations Commission: (CTH) Industrial Relations Act 1988 s 9. See also **Australian Industrial Relations Commission**.

Australian industrial system The systems of industrial tribunals established under the laws of the Commonwealth and of each of the six States, considered together or functioning in parallel. The industrial tribunals exercise the power to regulate terms and conditions of employment by arbitration. To promote comity and consistency, the Commonwealth and States have provided for the reference of disputes between the federal and State systems. Federal legislation and awards prevail over inconsistent State legislation and awards: Commonwealth Constitution s 109. See also **Federal industrial system; Industrial tribunal; State industrial system**.

•**Australian industry** The use of labour and capital to produce goods or services in Australia. The term refers to the sum total of that industry in Australia and not simply to a element of that industry in a particular part of the country: (CTH) Customs Tariff (Anti-Dumping) Act 1975 s 8; *Swan Portland Cement Ltd v Minister for Science, Customs and Small Business* (1989) 88 ALR 196.

Australian Institute of Bankers See **Australian Institute of Banking and Finance**.

Australian Institute of Banking and Finance *Abbr* – AIBF The banking and finance industry's principal professional association. It was established in 1886 to assist bankers' career prospects through formal education and professional development. It monitors banking and finance education at tertiary level to ensure that courses are relevant and of high standard and conducts regular professional development activities in all capital cities. Until 1995 it was known as the 'Australian Institute of Bankers'. See also **International Banks and Securities Association of Australia**.

Australian Law Reform Commission *Abbr* – ALRC A statutory body established by (CTH) Australian Law Reform Commission Act 1973 (repealed) s 5 and now existent under (CTH) Australian Law Reform Commission Act 1996. The ALRC has the following functions: to review laws with a view to the systematic development and reform of federal laws; to consider proposals for the making of federal laws; to consider proposals relating to the consolidation of federal laws or the repeal of federal laws which are obsolete or unnecessary; and to consider proposals for uniformity between laws of the Territories and the States: (CTH) Australian Law Reform Commission Act 1996 s 21. See also **Attorney-General; Consolidation**.

•**Australian Legal Aid Office** *Abbr* – ALAO Formerly, a Commonwealth body providing legal aid services in relation to Federal, State, and Territory law to persons the government considered it had a special responsibility to, such as pensioners, Aboriginal persons, ex-servicemen, and newcomers to Australia. See also **Legal aid**.

Australian Loan Council *Abbr* – ALC A council of Commonwealth, State, and Northern Territory ministers which determines the amount of public borrowing that may be undertaken during the current financial year, and the distribution of the amount raised between the governments concerned. See also **Public Sector Borrowing Requirement**.

•**Australian Meat and Livestock Corporation** A statutory body established by the (CTH) Australian Meat and Livestock Corporation Act 1977 (repealed) to promote and control the export of meat and livestock from Australia, and to further the interests of the industry. It also aims to promote and protect trade and commerce in meat and livestock among the States and Territories, to improve the production of meat and livestock, and to encourage the consumption of meat. The Corporation continues in existence under (CTH) Meat and Livestock Industry Act 1995 s 53.

Australian Merchant Bankers Association See **International Banks and Securities Association of Australia**.

Australian Minerals and Energy Council A Commonwealth-State ministerial council appointed to examine and review problems and policies relating to minerals and energy, and to promote cooperation in matters of common interest. The Council is supported by an advisory committee and a standing joint study group.

Australian National Training Authority *Abbr* – ANTA A body corporate established to assist the Ministerial Council set up under the Statement entitled 'A National Vocational Education and Training System' agreed on by the Commonwealth and the States on 21 July 1992 and to administer national programs in vocational education and training: (CTH) Australian National Training Authority Act 1992 ss 4(1), 5(1), 6(1), Sch. The ANTA prepares draft strategic national plans for the Ministerial Council and collaborates with state training agencies to enable the efficient and effective provision of vocational education and training: (CTH) Australian National Training Authority Act 1992 s 6(2), (3). It is also responsible for the allocation of funds made available by the Commonwealth to the States and Territories for vocational education and training: (CTH) Australian National Training Authority Act 1992 ss 11-16.

•**Australian Options Market** *Abbr* – AOM An organised market, opened in February 1976, for the trading of call and put options, and located on the trading floor of the Australian Stock Exchange. See also **Call option; Clearing house; Put option; Share index option**.

Australian Payments Clearing Association Ltd *Abbr* – APCA A limited liability company established in 1992 to oversee and manage the development and operation of the Australian payment clearance system. Shareholders are the Reserve Bank, banks and the industry bodies of building societies and credit unions. The costs of running APCA are met by members in shares broadly proportional to their relative importance in the payments system. Other interested groups or individuals may join as associate members. Its prime objectives are: to optimise the efficiency, reliability, and security of the Australian payment system; preserve the integrity of the payments system; minimise and control risks in the payments system; ensure principles of equity and competitive neutrality are applied in determining participation in the payments system; and provide timely and well-based information on developments in the payments system. See also **Australian Payments System Council**.

Australian Payments System Council A council established by the Commonwealth government in 1984 to oversee the evolution of Australia's payments systems, essentially to ensure fair competition in the provision of payments services. Specific tasks allocated to the council were to facilitate access by non-bank financial institutions to the cheque clearing system, monitor the development of domestic payments systems, promote the implementation of standards for electronic funds transfer systems and foster interconnections between the funds transfer system and the various participants. The council is chaired by an officer of the Reserve Bank of Australia. See also **Australian Payments Clearing Association Ltd; Clearing house; Clearing House Interbank Payments System; Non-bank financial institution; Reserve Bank of Australia**.

Australian Postal Corporation A statutory corporation established by the (CTH) Australian Postal Corporation Act 1989, supplying postal services within Australia and between Australia and places outside Australia, and carrying on activities relating to postal services outside Australia. Australia Post has a monopoly of most postal services: (CTH) Australian Postal Corporation Act 1989 ss 3, 12-18, 29. Also known as 'Australia Post'.

Australian Press Council An unincorporated association established in 1976 and funded by the newspaper industry. It administers a system of self-regulation of the conduct and activities of publishers. See also **Financial journalist**.

•**Australian primary standard of measurement** A standard of measurement maintained by the Commonwealth Scientific and Industrial Research Organisation. It allows measurements of physical quantities for which there are Australian legal units of measurement to be made in terms of those units: (CTH) National Measurement Act 1960 ss 3(1), 8(1).

Australian Public Service Management Advisory Board A body established under the (CTH) Public Service Act 1922 s 22 that advises the Commonwealth Government on significant issues relating to the management of the Australian Public Service. It is constituted by the Secretary to the Department, the Public Service Commissioner, the Secretary to the Department of Finance, and four other persons nominated by the Prime Minister. One member is to be appointed after consultation with the Australian Council of Trade Unions, and one is to have management expertise in the private sector. See also **Australian Council of Trade Unions; Company secretary; Public service.**

Australian Register of Company Charges The register kept by the Australian Securities Commission (ASC) of charges against the property of a company: Corporations Law s 263. The register is open for public inspection: s 271. A charge which is registered on the Australian Register of Company Charges is generally enforceable in priority to an unregistered, or later registered, charge: s 280. See also **Charge; Register of charges; Floating charge; Fixed charge.**

Australian Registered Body Number The number assigned to a body which is not incorporated as a company within Australia but which is registered under Corporations Law Pt 4.1. See also **Australian Company Number; Foreign Company; Registrable Australian body; Recognised company.**

Australian Resources Development Bank *Abbr* – ARDB A specialised bank enabling Australian enterprises to participate more fully in the development of Australia's natural resources. It provides finance for major development projects by providing direct loans, investing in equity capital, and refinancing loans made by trading banks. The bank obtains funds by accepting deposits and by borrowing on the Australian and overseas capital markets. It was established in 1967, equity capital being subscribed by the major trading banks, and given the status of a bank under the (CTH) Banking Act 1959. See also **Australian banking system.**

Australian savings bonds First issued by the Commonwealth government in 1976, 'Aussie bonds' offered a specified rate of interest and terms of up to eight years. They were introduced as a means of funding the Commonwealth government budget deficit and became the most popular form of saving by Australians. They can be redeemed at any time or sold in the secondary market before maturity. See also **Bond; Treasury bond.**

Australian Securities Commission *Abbr* – ASC The regulatory authority charged with the sole administration of corporations and securities regulation in Australia, established by (CTH) Australian Securities Commission Act 1989 s 7. See also **Administrative Appeals Tribunal; Australian Securities Commission Law; Corporations and Securities Panel; Corporations Law.**

Australian Securities Commission instrument An instrument made by the Australian Securities Commission (ASC) giving effect to the ASC's powers (for example, exempting or modifying the law with respect to particular corporations) that are gazetted in the ASC gazette. All instruments which have been or must be gazetted are published in ASC Digest Vol 3 No 3. See also **Australian Securities Commission.**

Australian Securities Commission Law *Abbr* – ASC Law The (CTH) Australian Securities Commission Act 1989 which established the Australian Securities Commission (ASC) and defined its powers and duties. Section 58 of the Corporations Act of each State and the Northern Territory applies certain provisions of the (CTH) Australian Securities Commission Act 1989 as a law of each jurisdiction, allowing it to be cited as the 'Australian Securities Commission Law' of the jurisdiction. The (CTH) Australian Securities Commission Act 1989 gives the ASC powers and duties in the Australian Capital Territory. The ASC Law established a Corporations and Securities Panel, a Companies and Securities Advisory Committee, a Companies Auditors and Liquidators Disciplinary Board, an Australian Accounting Standards Board and a Parliamentary Joint Committee on Corporations and Securities. See also **Australian Accounting Standards Board; Australian Securities Commission; Companies and Securities Advisory Committee; Companies Auditors and Liquidators Disciplinary Board; Corporations and Securities Panel.**

Australian Securities Commission On Time *Abbr* – ASCOT The comprehensive national corporate database of the Australian Securities Commission located at Morwell, Victoria. ASCOT holds all Australian company information on all Australian companies, foreign companies and other bodies registered in Australia. One-stop searching for information about these companies and bodies is possible from any Australian Securities Commission business centre in Australia. See also **Australian Securities Commission.**

Australian Security Intelligence Organisation *Abbr* – ASIO Australian intelligence agency responsible for obtaining, correlating, and evaluating intelligence relevant to national security: (CTH) Australian Security Intelligence Organisation Act 1979 s 17(1). ASIO may make security assessments on individuals and provide these to agencies of the government: s 37.

Australian Share Price Index See **Share Price Index.**

Australian Society of Certified Practising Accountants *Abbr* – ASCPA A professional body (previously the Australian Society of Accountants) having, among others, the object of supporting, protecting and advancing the character, status and interests of the accountancy profession generally and particularly of accountants being members of the Society. See also **Institute of Chartered Accountants in Australia.**

• **Australian Stock Exchange** See **Australian Stock Exchange Ltd.**

• **Australian Stock Exchange Business Rules** The constitution of, and rules made by, a body corporate that conducts a stock exchange, other than listing rules: Corporations Law s 761. Business Rules deal with various matters including the standards of training and experience and the required level of character and integrity for membership, the disciplining of members and the conditions governing dealings in securities by members. See also **Approved securities organisation; Australian stock exchange listing rules.**

Australian Stock Exchange Continuing Listing Rules Listing rules of the Australian Stock Exchange (ASX) requiring continuous disclosure of certain information of listed companies: ASX Listing Rules rule 3. An example is ASX Listing Rules rule 3.1, which provides that a listed company must immediately notify the ASX of any information concerning the company of which it is aware and which a reasonable person would expect to have a material effect on the price or value of the securities of the company. There are exceptions to this rule: ASX Listing Rules rule 3.1.1-3.1.3. See also **Australian stock exchange listing.**

Australian Stock Exchange listing The placement of an issuer of securities on the official list of the Australian Stock Exchange (ASX). This allows the company to trade its securities on the market at the ASX. To be listed the company must comply with the listing rules of the ASX. See also **Australian stock exchange listing rules.**

Australian Stock Exchange listing rules *Abbr* – ASX Listing Rules The regulations or by-laws governing the admission to or removal from the official list of the securities exchange, or stock exchange of bodies corporate, governments, unincorporated bodies or other persons, for the purpose of the quotation on the stock market of the securities exchange or stock exchange of securities, and the activities or conduct of those included in the list: Corporations Law s 603. See also **Australian Stock Exchange Ltd; Australian Stock Exchange listing.**

Australian Stock Exchange Ltd *Abbr* – ASX A company incorporated on 1 April 1987 as a company limited by guarantee in accordance with the (CTH) Australian Stock Exchange and National Guarantee Fund Act 1987. Each State capital city exchange is a subsidiary company of Australian Stock Exchange Ltd which replaced Australian Associated Stock Exchanges Ltd. The ASX sets uniform trading rules, listing requirements and ethical standards. The subsidiaries are still known by their original names, for example the Melbourne Stock Exchange. The Australian Options Market and the Australian Financial Futures Market are part of the ASX. See also **Stock exchange.**

Australian Stock Exchange quoted security A marketable security in a class of marketable securities listed for quotation on the Australian Stock Exchange (ASX), regulated by the ASX Listing Rules: Corporations Law ss 761, 1097 A(1). A temporary suspension of quotation of the security does not prevent it from being listed for quotation: Corporations Law s 1097A(3).

Australian Stock Exchange Share Price Indices See **Share Price Index.**

Australian Taxation Office *Abbr* – ATO The body headed by the Commissioner of Taxation with the responsibility for the administration of Commonwealth tax laws including income tax, sales tax, and fringe benefits tax: (CTH) Taxation Administration Act 1953 s 3A. See also **Fringe benefits tax; Income taxation; Sales tax.**

•**Australian Telecommunications Authority** *Abbr* – AUSTEL A regulatory authority established under the (CTH) Telecommunications Act 1991. It has overall responsibility in three areas: economic and technical regulation of the telecommunications industry, including the promotion of fair and efficient conduct in the industry and the implementation of government industry policies; advising and assisting the telecommunications industry; and reporting to and advising the Minister on the industry. AUSTEL may exercise its general powers is by giving directions to the carriers: ss 34 - 46.

Australian Trade Commission A commission established to encourage trade between Australia and other countries. The Australian Trade Commission represents Australian trading and commercial interests in foreign countries, assists Australian organisations in trade negotiations, promotes Australian export trade, makes available to Australian organisations information relating to current or future opportunities for Australian export trade, and supports and facilitates investment likely to enhance Australian export trade: (CTH) Australian Trade Commission Act 1985 s 8. The commission is a body corporate with a seal, and it may sue or be sued: (CTH) Australian Trade Commission Act 1985 s 7.

Australian Transaction Reports and Analysis Centre *Abbr* – AUSTRAC A body established under the (CTH) Financial Transaction Reports Act 1988 to receive and analyse information: (CTH) Financial Transaction Reports Act 1988 ss 35, 38(1). The principal object of this legislation is to facilitate the administration and enforcement of taxation laws: (CTH) Financial Transaction Reports Act 1988 s 4(1). The legislation provides for the reporting of certain financial transactions and transfers, and imposes certain obligations in relation to the opening of accounts with cash dealers. For example, where a cash dealer has reasonable grounds to suspect that information about a transaction may be relevant to an investigation of tax evasion, the dealer must report this information to the AUSTRAC: (CTH) Financial Transaction Reports Act 1988 s 16(1). See also **Account; Cash dealer; International funds transfer instruction; Significant cash transaction.**

Australia-New Zealand Closer Economic Relations Trade Agreement *Abbr* – ANZCERTA A trade agreement between Australia and New Zealand concluded and entered into force on 1 January 1983. It contains 26 articles covering a wide spectrum of technical trading details with six annexures dealing with various trading commodities of common interest. The closer economic ties are intended to improve the socio-economic well-being and living standard of their peoples through the expansion of trans-Tasman trade, investment, marketing, movement of people, tourism, transport, and the harmonisation of legal regimes governing these areas.

AUSTUDY 1. A federal government scheme to grant benefits in the form of financial assistance to Australian citizens or permanent residents enrolled as students in an educational institution undertaking a course of study which forms part of a secondary or tertiary course: (CTH) Student and Youth Assistance Act 1973 s 7.

Authenticated signature fiction A principle by which words on a document will be deemed to be a person's signature when that person expressly or impliedly acknowledges the writing as an authenticated expression of the contract. This principle has no application to a document which is not in some way or other recognisable as a note or memorandum of a concluded agreement: *Pirie v Saunders* (1961) 104 CLR 149.

• **Author 1.** The generic term for human creator of an original work; the person who originates or gives existence to something: *Sands & McDougall Pty Ltd v Robinson* (1917) 23 CLR 49. **2.** In relation to a photograph, generally the author is the person who took the photograph: (CTH) Copyright Act 1968 s 10(1). **3.** The person whose mind conceives the relevant shape, configuration, pattern or ornamentation applicable to the article in question and reduces it to visible form: *Chris Ford Enterprises Pty Ltd v B H & J R Badenhop Pty Ltd* (1985) 7 FCR 75; 4 IPR 485; 60 ALR 400. See also **Copyright; Design right; Maker; Material form; Original work.**

• **Authorisation** In trade practices law, the sanction given by the Australian Competition and Consumer Commission to engage in conduct otherwise prohibited under (CTH) Trade Practices Act 1974 Pt IV. See also **Australian Competition and Consumer Commission; Australian Competition Tribunal; Clearance; Notification; Pre-merger consultation; Pre-merger notification.**

Authorised act In tort, an act authorised by an employer or necessarily involved in performing work for an employer. See also **Strict liability; Vicarious liability.**

Authorised buy-back The acquisition by the company of shares in itself authorised by Corporations Law s 206 B: Corporations Law s 205(1A). Corporations Law Pt 2.4 Div 4B regulates five types of authorised buy-back: odd-lot buy-backs, employee share scheme buy-backs, on-market buy-backs, equal access buy-backs, and selective buy-backs. See also **Employee share scheme buy-back; Equal access buy-back scheme; Odd-lot buy- back; On-market buy-back; Selective buy-back; Share buy-back.**

Authorised capital The amount of share capital stated in the memorandum of association of a company, which is the maximum amount of capital that the company is authorised to raise by issuing its shares. The memorandum must state the manner in which the company's authorised capital is divided into shares of a 'nominal' or 'par' value. Also known as 'nominal capital' or 'nominal share capital'. See also **Capital; Share.**

• **Authorised dealer** A member of a group of specialist securities dealers operating in the official short-term money market, enjoying a special relationship with the Reserve Bank of Australia, including a lender-of-last resort or line of credit facility. The group was established in 1959, primarily to stimulate trading in securities and to provide an avenue through which monetary policy could be implemented. Interest rates are influenced by the authorised dealers. See also **Reserve Bank of Australia.**

• **Authorised insurer** An insurer authorised or registered under (CTH) Insurance Act 1973 Pt III or (CTH) Life Insurance Act 1995 Pt III to carry on insurance business or life insurance business in Australia. See also **Insurer; Life Insurance; Registered Insurer.**

Authorised investment In the context of Victorian legal practitioners legislation, a term deposit, debenture, or deposit stock of a bank; a document issued by a bank relating to money deposited with the bank that recognises that the bearer is entitled to payment of a sum from the bank; a loan to the Treasurer repayable on demand; a Commonwealth, State or public authority security guaranteed by the Commonwealth or a State; specified deposits with a body corporate; or specific bills of exchange and specified investments: (VIC) Legal Profession Practice (Guarantee Fund) Act 1993 s 4.

Authorised reduction of capital The return of capital that has been paid in, or reduction of liability to pay capital as allowed under Corporations Law s 195. See also **Capital; Maintenance of capital.**

Authorised share capital See **Authorised capital**.

• **Authority 1.** In agency law, the power, right, or permission that an agent has or appears to have to do acts or make contracts with third parties on the principal's behalf. The scope of authority determines which of the agent's acts bind the principal. In general, a principal is responsible for all acts of the agent within the agent's authority. **2.** A case, statute or other highly regarded legal text relied upon and cited as a foundation for legal principle or for an exposition of the law. See also **Actual authority; Agency; Agent; Apparent authority; Express authority; Implied authority; Irrevocable authority; Principal; Revocation of authority; Third party.**

Authority to act The express or implied power of a legal practitioner as agent of the client to bind the client in dealings with third parties. See also **Express authority; Implied authority; Retainer.**

Authority to call meeting A document in the form prescribed by the (CTH) Bankruptcy Act 1966 and signed by a debtor which authorises a registered trustee in bankruptcy or solicitor to call a meeting of creditors under the: s 188 (CTH) Bankruptcy Act 1966 s 188. This is the first step taken by a debtor seeking an arrangement with creditors to avoid being made bankrupt. If the authority is given to a registered trustee, control of the debtor's property and affairs temporarily passes to the trustee: s 189. See also **Bankrupt; Controlling trustee; Debtor; Trustee; Part X.**

• **Authority to complete** The authority given by a principal to an agent to complete a transaction on behalf of the principal. An agent authorised to sign documents necessary to complete an agreement is not authorised to sign a contract that varies substantially from the original agreement: *Marriott v General Electric Co Ltd* (1935) 53 CLR 409.

Automated bond system *Abbr* – ABS A computerised system that since 1976 has matched all orders of listed non-convertible bonds on the New York Stock Exchange. The system quotes prices and allows subscribing members to enter and execute orders through terminals in their offices. See also **Bond**.

Automated Land Titles System *Abbr* – ALTS
A computerised system of land registration introduced under the (NSW) Real Property (Computer Register) Amendment Act 1979 which commenced the conversion of manual folios to computer folios, with all new titles being issued in the form of computer folios. Under the system the primary record of registration is now maintained on computer files rather than in books. Title references have been changed to 'folio identifiers', and the certificate of title no longer includes a title diagram, referring instead to the relevant deposited plans. The system commenced operation in October 1983. Similar systems now operate in other States and Territories.

Automated teller machine See **Automatic teller machine**.

Automatic crystallisation The crystallisation of a floating charge on the occurrence of a particular event, usually specified in the document creating the charge, without the need for any action to be taken by the chargor or the chargee. See also **Automatic crystallisation clause; Floating charge**.

Automatic crystallisation clause A clause in a document creating a floating charge which provides for crystallisation of the charge on the occurrence of a specified event without the need for any further action on the part of the chargor or the chargee: for example *Deputy Federal Cmr of Taxation v Horsburgh* (1984) 54 ALR 397. Such clauses are recognised as valid in Australian contract law: *Fire Nymph Products v The Heating Centre Pty Ltd* (1992) 10 ACLC 629. See also **Automatic crystallisation; Floating charge**.

Automatic discharge **1.** Termination of a contract on the breach of a clause of the contract that purports to be self-executing: for example *Westralian Farmers Ltd v Commonwealth Agricultural Service Engineers Ltd* (1938) 54 CLR 361. **2.** The discharge of a person from bankruptcy by the operation of (CTH) Bankruptcy Act 1966 s 149. See also **Discharge; Discharge of bankruptcy; Termination**.

Automatic stabiliser An element of fiscal policy which tends to automatically adjust or modify the level of spending in an economy. In Australia, when money incomes rise, the progressive nature of the income tax system brings taxpayers into higher brackets, decreasing the level of spending and dampening inflation. In a recession, increased unemployment leads to a greater volume of social security payments, tending to sustain a certain level of spending and economic activity.

Automatic teller machine *Abbr* – ATM A computer used by banks and other financial institutions to provide banking services to customers during and outside business hours. See also **Cash dispenser**.

Autonomy The principle that a letter of credit is a separate transaction from the sale or other contract on which it may be based, and banks are in no way concerned with or bound by such contracts, even if the letter of credit contains a reference to such contracts. See also **Letter of credit**.

Available market The ability of a buyer or seller to buy or sell other goods of the same quality and description as is provided for by the contract: for example *Francis v Lyon* (1907) 4 CLR 1023. The concept of an available market is applicable to both non-acceptance and non-delivery in the context of contracts for the sale of goods. See also **Non-acceptance; Non-delivery; Sale of goods**.

•**Average** The apportionment of loss incurred in mercantile transactions, such as contracts of affreightment or insurance, between the persons suffering the loss and other persons concerned or interested; the contribution payable by such others to the person so suffering the loss. See also **Underinsurance**.

Average adjuster An expert in the practice of general average and marine insurance. The functions of an average adjuster include adjusting the general average contributions payable by shipowners and cargo owners, calculating or adjusting claims on policies of insurance, dividing recoveries from third parties and proceeds of sale, and arbitrating disputes.

Average clause A clause in an insurance contract providing that if at the time of the loss the value of the insured subject matter exceeds the amount of cover, the insurer is deemed to be his or her own insurer for the difference in the value, and thus must bear a proportion of the loss. Also known as 'co-insurance clause'. See also **Average**.

Average cost method A method of costing inventory where the sum of the beginning inventory at cost price, plus the cost of additional purchases of inventory, is divided by the total units available for sale during the period. This average is then multiplied by the number of units of inventory remaining at the end of the period to determine the cost of inventory and subsequently the cost of goods sold. See also **Common cost; Inventory; Marginal cost; Net acquisition cost; Opportunity cost**.

•**Average income** A concept applicable to certain categories of taxpayers who have fluctuating incomes, including primary producers, authors, inventors and sportspersons. In relation to primary producers, for the purpose of the average income rebate, the average income is the average of the income of the current year of income and up to four years of income before current year: (CTH) Income Tax Assessment Act 1936 s 149. For a year to be eligible as the first average year, the taxable income of the second average year must not be greater than the taxable income of the first average year. Under (CTH) Income Tax Assessment Act 1936 Div 16A 'average eligible taxable income' is used in calculating abnormal income and concessional tax liability: (CTH) Income Tax Assessment Act 1936 s 151. Tax loss years are not included in the average. See also **Average income rebate; Taxable income; Tax loss**.

Average income rebate A rebate available to primary producers where the rate of tax applicable to the current year of income is greater than the rate of tax applicable to the average income of the primary producer over the last five income years of that person: (CTH) Income Tax Assessment Act 1936 s 156. The rebate has the effect of applying the average rate of tax to the current year income. See also **Average income; Income; Primary producer; Rebate**.

Average return on investment The amount earned for a given period (expressed as operating profits after taxes), in direct proportion to the average capital (the sum at the beginning of the period and the end of the period divided by two) invested for the period. The amount calculated is expressed as a percentage. See also **Operating revenue**.

•**Average weekly earnings** *Abbr* – AWE An estimate of the average total weekly earnings for adults working full-time in Australia for the latest period for which such an estimate was published by the Australian Statistician: (CTH) Child Support (Assessment) Act 1989 s 5; (CTH) Social Security Act 1991 s 17(1). See also **Average weekly ordinary time earnings**.

•**Average weekly ordinary time earnings** *Abbr* – AWOTE The average weekly earnings of employed salary and wage earners (both full-time and part-time) as compiled by the Australian Bureau of Statistics. See also **Average weekly earnings; Bona fide redundancy payment; Rebate**.

•**Averaging 1.** The concept under income taxation legislation which reduces the tax impact of large fluctuations in income earned by a taxpayer in a particular year. See also **Abnormal income amount; Average income**.

Aviation insurance Insurance that covers risks associated with air travel. Contracts in respect of aircraft engaged in commercial operations are exempt from the legislative requirements: (CTH) Insurance Contracts Act 1984 s 9(3).

•**Avoid** To set aside, undo, or invalidate. For example, a provision in a contract giving a party an option to avoid the contract upon breach of the terms of the contract allows the party to set it aside and not be bound by the contract upon breach. See also **Void contract**.

Avoidance See **Tax avoidance**.

•**Award 1.** The determination and order of an arbitrator, resolving a dispute referred to arbitration. **2.** A document that affects legal rights, but which is not legislation or subordinate legislation: *R v Hamilton Knight; Ex parte Commonwealth Steamship Owners Assn* (1952) 86 CLR 283. See also **Alternative dispute resolution; Arbitration; Arbitrator; Award wage; Industrial award; Interim award; UNCITRAL Model Law on International Commercial Arbitration 1985**.

Award wage The rate of wages that an applicable industrial award states an employee is to receive. See also **Industrial award; Minimum wage; Wage**.

AWB See **Air waybill**.

AWE See **Average weekly earnings**.

•**AWOTE** See **Average Weekly Ordinary Time Earnings**.

B

Back In payment systems, to adopt liability, usually by signing on the back of a completed negotiable instrument: *Freedman & Co v Dan Che Lin* (1905) 7 WALR 179. See also **Backer; Holder; Indorsement; Negotiable instrument**.

Back freight An extra charge that a consignor of cargo must pay to the carrier to cover expenses arising from additional transport or storage of the goods if normal delivery at the intended port was prevented: *Gaudet v Brown (Cargo ex Argos)* (1873) LR 5 PC 134 at 165 See also **Agency of necessity; Consignor; Freight**.

Backdate To put an earlier date on; to apply retrospectively.

Insurance To make an insurance policy valid from the time that interim cover commenced. See also **Indemnity; Insurance; Interim cover**.

Backdoor listing Stock exchange listing achieved by purchasing the shell of an already listed company and injecting the business of an unlisted company into it. See also **Australian Stock Exchange Listing Rules; Listed body; Underwriting commission**.

•**Backer** The person who 'backs', or offers security for, a negotiable instrument. See also **Back; Indorser; Negotiable instrument**.

Back-to-back Matching or corresponding; mutually converse. **1.** A back-to-back credit arrangement is an arrangement for financing the purchase of goods that are first supplied to an intermediary, who then supplies them to the ultimate purchaser. The ultimate purchaser applies for a letter of credit to be issued in favour of the intermediary. **2.** Descriptive of loans where one loan, such as a parallel loan, made in one currency in one country, is offset against a loan in another currency in another country. See also **Credit; Futures contract; Letter of credit; Parallel loan**.

Backwardation A futures market situation in which prices are progressively lower in the future delivery months compared with the nearest delivery month. See also **Contango; Normal backwardation**.

•**Bad debt** A debt incurred by a person in the course of business, which cannot be collected, or is considered to be unable to be collected. To be a bad debt for income tax purposes, the debt must be legally or beneficially owned or owing to the person writing it off: *AGC (Advances) Ltd v FCT* (1975) 132 CLR 175; 5 ALR 208. See also **Assessable income; Business; Debt; Incurred; Write-off method**.

Bad debts recovered The collection of the whole or part of accounts receivable previously thought of as uncollectable and written-off as bad debts. The amount recovered if previously allowed as a deduction will be included as assessable income of a taxpayer: (CTH) Income Tax Assessment Act 1936 s 63(3). If a taxpayer has sold goods, sales tax paid can be credited to the taxpayer when uncollectable amounts have been written-off as bad debts. However, the taxpayer must pay sales tax on recovery of bad debts: (CTH) Sales Tax Assessment Act 1992 s 57. See also **Allowable deduction; Assessable income; Bad debt; Sales tax**.

Bad faith A description of conduct by a contracting party that is contrary to community expectations, in that it is outrageous given the relationship between the parties. A court may award damages in tort for loss or damage caused by an act done in bad faith: for example *Reynard Constructions (ME) Pty Ltd v Minister for Public Works* (1992) 26 NSWLR 234; 9 BCL 40; *Gibson v Parkes District Hospital* (1991) 26 NSWLR 9; Aust Torts Reports ¶81-140. See also **Abuse of power; Good faith**.

Contract Where a promisor is subject to an express or implied obligation of good faith, performance in bad faith constitutes a breach of contract: for example *Shepard v Felt and Textiles of Australia Ltd* (1931) 45 CLR 359. See also **Breach of contract; Fraud**.

•**Bail** The right to be released from custody granted to a person charged with an offence, on the condition that he or she undertakes to return to the court at some specified time, and any other conditions that the court may impose: for example (NSW) Bail Act 1978 s 7; (TAS) Bail Act 1994 s 8. Under the statutory schemes that now regulate bail applications in every jurisdiction, there may be a right to release on bail, a presumption in favour of bail, no presumption or a presumption against bail, depending on the offence: for example (NSW) Bail Act 1978 ss 8-9.

•**Bailee** A person in possession of goods belonging to another: (SA) Unclaimed Goods Act 1987 s 3(1). See also **Bailee's duties; Bailee estoppel; Bailee's lien; Bailee's remedies; Bailment**.

Bailee's duties The duties of a person in possession of the goods of another to: deliver the bailed chattels to the bailor on termination of the bailment or in accordance with the bailor's instructions (unless the bailee can demonstrate some lawful excuse for not doing so, such as inability to do so despite reasonable care); take reasonable care of the bailed chattels; and carry out whatever the purpose and terms of the bailment are: *Sydney City Council v West* (1965) 114 CLR 481 at 494-8; [1966] ALR 538; *Jackson v Cochrane* [1989] 2 Qd R 23; *Crouch v Jeeves (1938) Pty Ltd* (1946) 46 SR (NSW) 242. See also **Bailee's remedies; Bailment; Bailor; Carrier; Conversion**.

Bailee's estoppel Estoppel of a bailor's claim that the bailee breached his or her duty to the bailor that arises where the bailee can show that the bailed goods were delivered to the true owner: *Edwards v Amos* (1945) 62 WN (NSW) 204. See also **Bailee's duties; Bailee's remedies; Bailment; Bailor's remedies; Jus tertii**.

Bailee's lien Special property of a bailee in the bailed chattels for the amount agreed to be paid, or, failing agreement, a reasonable amount, in respect of work requested by the bailor to be done on the bailed chattels: *Standard Electronic Apparatus Laboratories Pty Ltd v Stenner* [1960] NSWR 447; 77 WN (NSW) 833. See also **Bailment; Lien**.

Bailee's remedies The remedies that flow from a bailee's right, based on the bailee's possession of the bailed chattel, to maintain an action in conversion, detinue, trespass, or replevin in respect of the bailed chattel for its full value. Any damages received above the bailee's interest in the bailed chattel will be held on trust for the bailor: *Goldsbrough Mort & Co Ltd v Maurice* (1937) 58 CLR 773; [1939] ALR 233 at 798-9; *Hepburn v A Tomlinson (Hauliers) Ltd* [1966] AC 451. A bailee may even maintain an action in conversion, detinue, or trespass against the bailor for wrongful premature termination of the bailment: *City Motors (1933) Pty Ltd v Southern Aerial Super Service Pty Ltd* (1961) 106 CLR 477; (1962) ALR 184; *Standard Electronic Apparatus Laboratories Pty Ltd v Stenner* [1960] NSWR 447; (1960) 77 WN (NSW) 833. A bailee also has the right to sue in negligence for damage to the goods (including temporary damage), but the damages will be limited to those which the bailee has suffered consistent with the bailee's limited interest in the bailed chattels: *McCauley v Karooz* (1944) 61 WN (NSW) 165; *Goldsbrough Mort & Co Ltd v Maurice*; *Hepburn v Tomlinson (Hauliers) Ltd*. See also **Bailee's lien; Bailment; Conversion; Detinue**.

Bailment OF – *bailler* – to deliver. The delivery of personal chattels by the owner of the chattels (the 'bailor') into the possession of another person (the 'bailee') upon an express or implied promise that they will be redelivered to the bailor, or dealt with in a stipulated way: *Hobbs v Petersham Transport Co Pty Ltd* (1971) 124 CLR 220; [1971] ALR 675 at 238. Bailment requires re-delivery of the bailed chattel at the end of the bailment in its original state unless altered with the consent of the bailor: *Chapman Bros v Verco Bros & Co Ltd* (1933) 49 CLR 306 at 314, 316, 317-8. See also **Bailee; Bailment at will; Bailment by concealment; Bailor; Constructive bailment; Contractual bailment**.

Bailment at will A bailment where the bailor may repossess the bailed goods at any time without the bailee's consent and so end the bailment: *Manders v Williams* (1849) 4 Ex 339; 154 ER 1242. Also known as 'revocable bailment'. See also **Bailment; Contractual bailment; Gratuitous bailment**.

Bailment by attornment The situation that arises when, without any change in custody or physical transfer of a chattel, a person such as a seller or a seller's agent acknowledges by attornment that he or she holds the chattel as bailee for another person such as a buyer: for example *Gamer's Motor Centre (Newcastle) Pty Ltd v Natwest Wholesale Australia Pty Ltd* (1987) 163 CLR 236; 72 ALR 321. See also **Bailment; Constructive possession; Custody; Sub-bailment**.

Bailment by concealment The situation in which a person unknowingly comes into possession of chattels, such as when goods are lost on an occupier's land: for example *Parker (1983) v British Airways Board* [1982] QB 1004. See also **Bailment; Possession**.

Bailment for reward See **Contractual bailment**.

•**Bailor** The person who delivers possession of chattels to another under a bailment: *Hobbs v Petersham Transport Co Pty Ltd* (1971) 124 CLR 220; [1971] ALR 675 at 238. See also **Bailment; Bailor's duties; Bailor's remedies**.

Bailor's duties Obligations imposed on a bailor by the terms of contract between bailor and bailee as to the bailment, including terms as to the fitness for purpose of items bailed under a bailment for reward for a specific purpose, and by the law of negligence: *Derbyshire Building Co Pty Ltd v Becker* (1962) 107 CLR 633; [1962] ALR 796; *Hoey v Hardie* (1912) 12 SR (NSW) 268. See also **Bailee; Bailee's remedies; Bailment; Bailor**.

Bailor's remedies The right of a bailor to damages for negligence on the part of the bailee where the bailed chattels are lost or damaged owing to absence of reasonable care on the part of the bailee, or for unauthorised use of the bailed chattels by the bailee: *McKenna & Armistead Pty Ltd v Excavations Pty Ltd* (1957) 57 SR (NSW) 515; *Penfolds Wines Pty Ltd v Elliott* (1946) 74 CLR 204; [1946] ALR 517 at 222-231; *Sydney City Council v West* (1965) 114 CLR 481 at 494-498; [1966] ALR 538. A bailor may also claim damages in an action in contract for loss or damage to chattels caused by a common carrier, who is strictly liable for such loss or damage: *Commissioner for Railways (NSW) v Quinn* (1946) 72 CLR 345; *Penfolds Wines Pty Ltd v Elliott*; *Sydney City Council v West*. Furthermore, a bailor has an action in trespass, conversion, detinue, or replevin against the bailee for non-delivery or knowing misdelivery of the bailed chattels at the end of the bailment and ancillary loss. In addition, the bailor has a co-extensive right to sue with the bailee in trespass, conversion, detinue, or replevin for a wrongful taking of the bailed chattels from the bailee's possession, because the wrongful taking is inconsistent with the continuance of the bailment: *Penfolds Wines Pty Ltd v Elliott*; *Sydney City Council v West*. Where the bailor has no immediate right to possession, the bailor's relief under the general law is by way of an 'action on the case' for special damage of a permanent, not temporary, kind to the chattel: *Gilchrist Watt & Sanderson Pty Ltd v York Products Pty Ltd* [1970] 2 NSWR 156; (1970) 44 ALJR 269; *Penfolds Wines Pty Ltd v Elliott*; *Sydney City Council v West*. See also **Bailment; Conversion; Detinue; Carrier**.

Bait advertising The advertising of a product or service at a lower than normal price, where the product is unavailable at that price, or available only in limited quantities. See also **Fair trading legislation; Trade practices legislation**.

Balance date The date at the end of the accounting period or financial year applicable to a particular set of financial statements (being the profit and loss account, the balance sheet and the cash flow statement): Applicable Accounting Standard ASRB 1002.10. In Australia, June 30 marks the end of the financial year. See also **Accounting period; Balance sheet; Cash flow statement; Financial statement; Profit and loss account**.

Bal   *Butterworths Business and Law Dictionary*

•**Balance of convenience** The weighing of the disadvantages of taking an action against the disadvantages of not taking that action.

Tort The principle that a plaintiff placed in an emergency situation by a defendant's negligence, who assumes a risk of injury to avoid an inconvenience, is not contributorily negligent if the conduct is reasonable in the circumstances. The test is whether on balance the risk of injury is less than the inconvenience: *Caterson v Cmr for Railways* (1973) 128 CLR 99; [1972-73] ALR 1393. See also **Contributory negligence**.

Balance of payments A record of the monetary transactions between Australia and the rest of the world, including payments for transactions and the movement of money into and out of the country.

•**Balance of probabilities** The weighing up or comparison of competing possibilities. A fact is proved to be true on the balance of probabilities if its existence is more probable than not, or if it is established by a preponderance of probability (*Rejfek v McElroy* (1965) 112 CLR 517; [1966] ALR 270; for example (CTH) Evidence Act 1995 s 140(1)), or to the reasonable satisfaction of the tribunal of fact (*Briginshaw v Briginshaw* (1938) 60 CLR 336). See also **Beyond reasonable doubt; Burden of proof; Civil law; Fact; Standard of proof**.

Balance order An order obtained by a liquidator calling on contributories in the course of the winding up of a company.

•**Balance sheet** A financial statement of a company that sets out the assets and liabilities of the enterprise and the shareholder equity in the enterprise at a given date. See also **Accounting period; Accounting standards; Asset; General purpose financial report; Liability; True and fair view**.

Balance sheet date The date at which a balance sheet is prepared. The balance sheet is prepared 'as at' a certain date, as opposed to the profit and loss statement which is prepared for a period of time ending on that date. See also **Balance date; Balance sheet; Balance sheet disclosure**.

Balance sheet disclosure An explanation or note attached to the balance sheet or embodied in the report, containing a fact, opinion, or detail required in interpretation of the firm's financial position as at a certain point in time. See also **Balance sheet; Financial position; Note**.

Balance sheet risk In banking, the potential risk to earnings and capital resulting from changes in interest rates, liquidity conditions, and the impact of exchange rate fluctuations on foreign currency capital provisions. See also **Interest rate; Operating risk; Trading risk**.

Balancing charge An amount included in assessable income where the consideration on disposal or loss of a unit of depreciated property exceeds the depreciated value of that property: (CTH) Income Tax Assessment Act 1936 s 59(2). A balancing charge may be deducted successively against the cost of replacement plant, other plant acquired during the year or the opening depreciated value of existing plant provided certain conditions are satisfied: (CTH) Income Tax Assessment Act 1936 s 59(2A)-(2E). The excess of consideration above the original cost of the property may be ordinary assessable income or a capital gain. See also **Assessable income; Balancing deduction; Capital gain; Depreciation**.

Balancing deduction An allowable deduction amounting to the excess of depreciated value of depreciable property over the consideration received on disposal or loss of that property: (CTH) Income Tax Assessment Act 1936 s 59(1). See also **Allowable deduction; Balancing charge; Depreciation**.

Balloon payment A large final repayment of monies due on a loan, much larger than the preceding payments, which discharges a debt that was owing. See also **Debt; Debt adjusting**.

Bancassurance The merger of banking and insurance services into one group.

•**Bank** A body corporate authorised to carry on banking business in Australia ((CTH) Banking Act 1959 s 5(1)), a person who carries on State banking within the meaning of Commonwealth Constitution s 51(xiii), the Reserve Bank of Australia or someone who carries on the business of banking outside Australia: for example: (CTH) Cheques and Payment Orders Act 1986 s 3(1). See also **Banker; Banking business; Building society; Corporation; Customer of a bank; Reserve Bank of Australia**.

•**Bank account** An account maintained by a bank for a customer recording the deposits and withdrawals of the customer to or from that account. There is a statutory obligation on banks to verify the identity of customers opening new accounts: (CTH) Financial Transaction Reports Act 1988 s 22. See also **Account; Australian Transaction Reports and Analysis Centre; Bank passbook**.

Bank account debits tax See **Debits tax**.

•**Bank bill** A discounted bank-accepted bill of exchange; a short-term borrowing facility guaranteed by a bank. A bank bill resembles a cheque drawn by a borrower who seeks funds from a bank. See also **Bank bill future; Bill of exchange; Discount**.

Bank bill future A futures contract representing an agreement to buy or sell bills with a given face value at a specified price on a given month in the future. See also **Bank bill; Futures contract; Futures exchange**.

Bank charge A monetary charge made by a bank for performing services for a customer. See also **Bank fees inquiry**.

Bank cheque See **Banker's draft**.

Bank confirmation A report supplied by a bank in answer to a request submitted by an auditor in respect of a client who is a customer of the bank. It confirms the client's account balance and other related information held by the bank. See also **Banker's opinion**.

Bank customer See **Customer of a bank**.

Bank fees inquiry An inquiry conducted by the Prices Surveillance Authority in 1995 into fees and charges imposed on retail accounts by banks and other financial institutions and by retailers on electronic funds transfer at point of sale (EFTPOS) transactions. See also **Banking service; Electronic funds transfer at point of sale; Prices Surveillance Authority.**

Bank for International Settlements *Abbr* – BIS Established at Basle, Switzerland in 1930, the bank's original functions were to promote central bank cooperation, maintain the gold standard, and solve German reparation problems. See also **Capital adequacy guidelines.**

Bank guarantee See **Performance bond.**

Bank inquiry An inquiry conducted in 1990-91 by the House of Representatives Standing Committee on Finance and Public Administration, under the chairmanship of Mr Stephen Martin MHR, into the performance and behaviour of banks in Australia. See also **Australian banking system; Bank fees inquiry; Code of banking practice.**

Bank Interchange and Transfer System *Abbr* – BITS An automated electronic funds transfer system for effecting high value, same day funds transfers between financial institutions.

•**Bank manager** Ordinarily, the manager of a branch of a bank: *Union Bank of Australia Ltd v Whitelaw* [1906] VLR 711. See also **Branch manager; Clearance.**

Bank manuals Instruction manuals of individual banks prepared for the information, guidance, and direction of their staff in the conduct of the bank's business. Bank manuals are usually divided under sections, headings, and captions according to the diverse activities of the bank. Such manuals and instructions are 'no doubt counsels of perfection, but the fact that they are not always entirely complied with does not convict the bank of negligence, though no doubt, where the rules are not kept the matter needs attention': *Orbit Mining and Trading Co Ltd v Westminster Bank Ltd* [1963] 1 QB 794 at 826. A disregard of instructions or a total lack of instructions about a bank's business can be evidence of negligence: *Marfani & Co Ltd v Midland Bank Ltd* [1968] 2 All ER 573; *Selangor United Rubber Estates Ltd v Cradock (No 3)* [1968] 2 All ER 1073. Bank manuals are also relevant in considering whether any particular transaction comes within the business of that bank: *Woods v Martins Bank Ltd* [1959] 1 QB 55. Also known as 'Standing orders', 'Bank internal rules', or 'Regulations'.

Bank money The amount of credit a bank extends to a customer in excess of what is available to it in cash. Bank money is money and not fictitious book entries: *Warner v Elders Rural Finance Ltd* (1993) 113 ALR 517; 41 FCR 399; *Abram v Bank of New Zealand* (1993) ATPR ¶41-218. See also **Credit; Loan; Money.**

Bank nationalisation The unsuccessful attempt by the Labor government under Prime Minister J B Chifley in 1947 to pass legislation nationalising all private banks in Australia other than State-owned banks. The banking industry successfully challenged the validity of the legislation (the (CTH) Banking Act (repealed) 1947) before the High Court, which held that the legislation was beyond the constitutional powers of the Commonwealth with respect to banking, thereby invalidating the government's nationalisation scheme: *Bank of New South Wales v Commonwealth* (1948) 76 CLR 1. See also **Banking business; Privy Council; Ultra vires.**

•**Bank note** A promissory note for a specified amount, payable to the bearer on demand and intended to be used as equivalent to money. See also **Legal tender; Note.**

Bank of America Australia A subsidiary of the San Francisco based Bank of America. It engages in capital market activities and offers banking and custodian services to institutions.

Bank of China A foreign bank authorised to establish a branch bank in Australia in 1985 through the renewal of an old banking authority. The original authority was held by a Taiwan based bank and lapsed in 1972.

Bank of Credit and Commerce International *Abbr* – BCCI A major international bank which collapsed in 1991 with considerable losses. An investigation by Price Waterhouse revealed that the losses had been systematically concealed for many years by means of fictitious deposits and loans, unrecorded transactions and falsified records. BCCI links were worldwide.

Bank of England The central bank of the British banking system. It was established as a joint-stock company in 1694. The (UK) Bank Charter Act 1844 gave the bank a virtual monopoly of note issues. In 1946, the bank was nationalised, the capital being acquired by the British government whose monetary policy the bank carries out. With some qualifications, the Treasury is able to direct the bank. In turn, the bank is able to direct any or all of the commercial banks. It manages the national debt and floats new loans for the government. It is also the lender-of-last-resort for the money market and conducts open-market operations.

Bank of Melbourne A retail bank created in 1989 from the Victorian RESI-Statewide Building Society with listing on the Australian Stock Exchange. In addition to its retail banking operations, the bank operates as a mortgage lender in respect of residential and investment property. It does not operate in the larger corporate banking area.

Bank of New Zealand *Abbr* – BNZ A regional bank located in Australia and New Zealand, owned substantially by the New Zealand government. The BNZ undertakes retail, business, corporate and investment banking.

Bank of Queensland Originating in 1874 as The Brisbane Permanent Benefit Building and Investment Society, a bank which has evolved through a series of amalgamations becoming the Bank of Queensland Limited in 1970. The bank provides complete trading and savings bank facilities together with management services for the Security Permanent Building Society. Operations are conducted through branches and agencies located in Queensland. The bank also has a network of agent banks throughout Australia and overseas.

Bank of Singapore Australia A foreign bank which commenced operations in Australia in 1986. It is a wholly-owned subsidiary of the Oversea-Chinese Banking Corporation (OCBC), incorporated in the Republic of Singapore. The OCBC is one of the 'big four' local

Singapore banks, offering a full range of retail and commercial banking services.

Bank of Tokyo Australia A wholly-owned subsidiary of the Bank of Tokyo established in Australia in 1985. The bank provides services in the areas of foreign exchange, money markets and capital markets, international trade finance and corporate and retail banking.

Bank of Western Australia A bank established in its current form in 1990 as a public company limited by shares under the (WA) Bank of Western Australia Act 1990. It is an agency through which the State of Western Australia engages in State banking: s 22. Notwithstanding this, the bank lacks the status, immunities, and privileges of the Crown, and the State is not liable for the bank's acts, omissions, or obligations: s 23. The bank must ensure that its policy is directed to the greatest advantage of the State and that it promotes the balanced economy of the State. See also **Banking business**; **Crown immunity**; **Public company**; **Reserve Bank of Australia**.

Bank ombudsman See Australian Banking Industry Ombudsman Scheme.

Bank overdraft See Overdraft.

Bank passbook A small book given by a bank to its customer in which deposits and withdrawals are recorded. The book is normally retained by the customer. See also **Bank account**; **Bank statement**; **Deposit**.

Bank reconciliation A schedule reconciling the cash book balance of a business with the bank statement balance. The difference is made up of unpresented cheques, bank charges, outstanding deposits, interest paid, interest received, and other charges made directly to the bank account. See also **Bank statement**.

Bank securities Different types of securities made available by banks to customers in normal banking business, such as: interest bearing term deposits which are not transferable; negotiable certificates of deposit which are transferable; convertible certificates of deposit; and bank accepted bills. See also **Banker's acceptance**; **Term deposit**.

Bank statement A computer printout of a customer's bank account supplied to the customer at regular intervals and containing an opening and closing balance and the intervening debits and credits. A bank statement or passbook is prima facie evidence against both the bank and the customer of the account balance: *Akrokerri (Atlantic) Mines Ltd v Economic Bank* [1904] 2 KB 465; *MacDermott v Bank of Australasia* (1873) 4 AJR 37. A bank has a duty to maintain accurate accounts; if a customer is misled and alters his or her position in reliance on an inaccurate account the bank will be prevented from correcting the error when discovered: *Lloyd's Bank Ltd v Brooks* (1950) 6 LDB 161. See also **Account**; **Bank passbook**; **Credit**; **Debt**.

•**Banker** A person who carries on the business of banking, that is, accepting deposits from the public and lending to the public: *Commissioner of State Savings Bank of Victoria v Permewan, Wright & Co Ltd* (1914) 19 CLR 457; VLR 81 at 470-1. See also **Banker-customer relationship**; **Banking business**; **Credit**; **Debit**.

Banker-customer relationship The relationship, normally contractual, between a bank and its customer: *Aschkenasy v Midland Bank Ltd* (1934) 51 TLR 34; *Stewart v Bank of Australasia* (1883) 9 VLR(L) 240; *Tai Hing Cotton Mill Ltd v Lu Chong Hing Bank Ltd* [1986] AC 80. Apart from contract, the legal relationship of banker and customer is that of debtor and creditor (the banker being the debtor and the customer the creditor) with the added obligation on the banker to honour the customer's cheques when there is sufficient credit in his or her account at the bank: *Foley v Hill* [1848] 2 HL Cas 28; 9 ER 1002; *Joachimson v Swiss Bank Corp* [1921] 3 KB 110; *Bank of New South Wales v Laing* [1954] AC 135. The general relationship between the parties is not of a fiduciary nature: *National Westminster Bank Ltd Plc v Morgan* [1985] 1 AC 686. A bank is under no duty to repay the money of a customer unless the customer makes a demand at the branch of the bank where the account is kept: *Joachimson v Swiss Bank Corp*. A cheque drawn by the customer normally constitutes the demand: *London Joint Stock Bank Ltd v Macmillan and Arthur* [1918] AC 777 at 789. See also **Banker**; **Cheque**; **Customer of a bank**.

Banker's acceptance A United States equivalent of a bank-accepted bill of exchange. A banker's acceptance is a negotiable money market instrument. A fee is charged by the bank for providing the acceptance facility, while the bill itself is discounted at the prevailing market rate. See also **Acceptance**; **Bill of exchange**.

•**Bankers' books** Certain documentation kept by a bank, including ledgers, day books, cash books, and account books.

Banker's draft A written order for the payment of money on demand drawn by or on behalf of a bank upon itself and payable at any office of the bank. A banker's draft is treated as equivalent to cash because of the certainty of payment: for example *W J Alan and Co Ltd v El Nasr Export and Import Co* [1972] 2 QB 189 at 210. Also known as 'bank cheque'.

Banker's lien A bank's right to retain all negotiable instruments and securities deposited with it by its customer or by a third person on the customer's behalf until debts are discharged: *National Australia Bank Ltd v KDS Construction Services Pty Ltd (in liq)* (1987) 163 CLR 668; 76 ALR 27. It is binding on customers whether they know of it or not. See also **Banking business**; **Right of combination**; **Law merchant**; **Lien**; **Pledge**; **Set-off**.

Banker's opinion Information given in confidence by one bank to another as to the respectability and financial standing of a customer. In Australia, banker's opinions are justified by a combination of banking practice and customer's implied consent: *Commercial Banking Co of Sydney Ltd v RH Brown & Co* (1972) 126 CLR 337; 46 ALJR 297; ALR 393. Also known as 'status opinion' or 'credit reference' See also **Credit rating**; **Liability**.

Banker's standard of care The standard of care required of a reasonable person involved in the business of banking. Whether in any given case a bank has acted without negligence is necessarily a question of fact. It is impossible to lay down general rules or statements which will determine what is negligence and what is not. Each case must be decided on its own circumstances: *Commissioners of Taxation v English Scottish and Australian Bank* [1920] AC 683; *Commercial Bank of Australia Ltd v Flannagan* (1932) 47 CLR 461. It has been held that it is not our way of life either in trade or banking or in private relationships to be always on the alert against dishonesty: *Orbit Mining and Trading Co Ltd v Westminster Bank Ltd* [1963] 1 QB 794 at 815. To require a thorough inquiry into the history of each cheque would render banking business as ordinarily carried on impossible and customers would often be left for long periods without available money: *Commissioners of Taxation v English Scottish and Australian Bank* at 690; *Lloyds Bank Ltd v Chartered Bank of India Australia and China* [1929] 1 KB 40 at 59. Bank officials need not play the role of amateur detectives or subject an account to microscopic examination: *Lloyds Bank Ltd v Chartered Bank of India, Australia and China* at 73. The officials of a bank doing their duty need not be abnormally suspicious. Moneys must be paid out, among a multiplicity of other transactions, with reasonable dispatch: *Penmount Estates Ltd v National Provincial Bank Ltd* (1945) 173 LT 344 at 346. There is no duty on a bank to research the history of its customers with such intensity as to make it liable if it fails to discover that a particular professional qualification (of a customer) has ceased to exist: *Day v Bank of New South Wales* (1978) 18 SASR 163; 19 ALR 32 at 171. Advice that a bank cheque is 'as good as cash' will constitute a breach of a banker's duty of care if it is not qualified with a warning about forged, counterfeit, lost, or stolen cheques: *Lyritzis v Westpac Banking Corp* (1994) ATPR ¶41-360.

Bankers Trust Australia An investment bank and a subsidiary of Bankers Trust New York Corporation. It was among the first 16 foreign banks invited to take up banking authorities in 1985.

Banking authority A written instruction given by a customer to the bank regarding the operation of the bank account. Banks have standard printed authority forms ('mandate forms') for this purpose. The mandate form will normally mention the authority given to the authorised signatories, and the authority given to the bank as to how it should act. The specimen signature of the authorised signatories will also appear in the form. See also **Blacklight facility; Signature; Standing order**.

Banking business The accepting of deposits from and lending to the public: *Commissioner of State Savings Bank of Victoria v Permewan Wright & Co Ltd* (1914) 19 CLR 457; VLR 81. See also **Banker; Banking service; Reserve Bank of Australia**.

Banking Code See **Code of Banking Practice**.

Banking Commission See **Royal Commission into the Monetary and Banking System**.

Banking custom Usages and practices of banks that have been judicially recognised as customs enforceable at law. Illustrations of such customs are the banker's lien (*Brandao v Barnett* (1846) 12 Cl & Fin 787; 8 ER 1622), and banks' right to charge compound interest (*National Bank of Greece SA v Pinios Shipping Co No 1 (The Maira)* [1990] 1 AC 637). See also **Bank's right to compound interest; Banking practice; Bank manuals; Banker's lien**.

Banking industry ombudsman scheme See **Australian Banking Industry Ombudsman Scheme**.

Banking mandate See **Banking authority**.

Banking ombudsman See **Australian Banking Industry Ombudsman Scheme**.

Banking power The legislative power of the Commonwealth to make laws with respect to banking (other than State banking), State banking extending beyond the limits of the State concerned, the incorporation of banks, and the issue of paper money: Commonwealth Constitution s 51(xiii). See also **Banking business**.

Banking practice Practices in the banking industry, some of which have been recognised by the courts as constituting 'a custom or usage of bankers'. While banking customs are derived from the practice of bankers, not all matters of practice have been judicially recognised as banking usage or custom. The practice of bankers is relevant when considering the standard of care to be exercised by banks in the conduct of their business: *Bank of Baroda Ltd v Punjab National Bank Ltd* [1944] AC 176. What is relevant is not the practice of an individual bank but the practice of banks generally: *Rosenhain v Commonwealth Bank of Australia Ltd* (1922) 31 CLR 46; [1922] VLR 787. In deciding disputes, the Australian banking industry ombudsman will also consider not only banking law but good banking practice. See also **Australian Banking Industry Ombudsman Scheme; Bank manuals; Code of Banking Practice; Banking custom**.

Banking service 1. A deposit, loan, or other banking facility provided by a bank to a customer, but not including a service in relation to a bill of exchange, a variation of a term or condition of a facility, or a debt to a bank that arises as a result of a withdrawal of more than the amount by which an account is in credit without the approval of the bank: (CTH) Code of Banking Practice s 1.1. **2.** For the purposes of the Australian Banking Industry Ombudsman Scheme, a financial service provided by a bank in the ordinary course of its business to an individual. See also **Australian Banking Industry Ombudsman Scheme; Banking business; Code of Banking Practice**.

Banknote A document, either a promissory note or a bill of exchange, issued by a bank, payable to the bearer on demand and intended for circulation as money. No person or State may issue banknotes in Australia: (CTH) Reserve Bank Act 1959 s 44. The Reserve Bank through its Note Issue Department is the sole issuer of banknotes and these are called Australian notes and are legal tender throughout Australia: s 34. See also **Banker; Bill of exchange**.

•**Bankrupt** A person against whose estate a sequestration order has been made or who has become bankrupt by presenting a debtor's petition to the registrar in Bankruptcy: (CTH) Bankruptcy Act 1966 s 5(1). See also **Annulment; Bankruptcy; Deed of assignment; Discharge of bankruptcy; Registrar in Bankruptcy; Sequestration order**.

•**Bankruptcy** **1.** Jurisdiction or proceedings under or by virtue of (CTH) Bankruptcy Act 1966 ss 27, 5(1). **2.** The state of a person's affairs after becoming a bankrupt. **3.** The process by which the State takes possession of the property of a bankrupt through the Official Trustee in Bankruptcy or a registered trustee and such property is realised and subject to certain priorities, distributed rateably amongst the persons to whom the debtor owes money: (CTH) Bankruptcy Act 1966. See also **Act of bankruptcy; Bankrupt; Creditor; Discharge of bankruptcy; Income of bankrupt; Insolvency; Official trustee in bankruptcy.**

Bankruptcy, commencement of See **Commencement of bankruptcy.**

Bankruptcy court A court that has jurisdiction to make persons bankrupt and to deal with matters arising under the (CTH) Bankruptcy Act 1966. See also **Bankruptcy; Federal Court of Australia.**

Bankruptcy jurisdiction Jurisdiction to try offences under the (CTH) Bankruptcy Act 1966 on indictment or summarily: s 273(2); *Pearce v Cocchiaro* (1977) 14 ALR 440.

Bankruptcy notice A notice served on a debtor requiring the payment of a judgment debt. A debtor who fails to comply with a bankruptcy notice commits an act of bankruptcy and can then be made bankrupt: (CTH) Bankruptcy Act 1966 s 40(1)(g). See also **Act of bankruptcy; Bankrupt; Debtor; Judgment debt; Registrar in bankruptcy.**

Bankruptcy power The legislative power of the Commonwealth to make laws with respect to bankruptcy and insolvency: Commonwealth Constitution s 51(xvii). See also **Bankruptcy; Insolvency.**

Bank's customer See **Customer of a bank.**

Bank's internal rules See **Bank manuals.**

Bank's right to compound interest The legal right of banks to levy compound interest on their lending to customers. This right has been judicially recognised as a 'usage of bankers' and is implied in the banker-customer relationship. The customer's acquiescence or implied consent is not required for the bank to exercise this right. This right continues even after the bank's demand for payment, until the date of judgment: *National Bank of Greece SA v Pinios Shipping Co No 1 (The Maira)* [1990] AC 637; *Bank of New South Wales v Brown* (1983) 151 CLR 514; 45 ALR 225. See also **Interest.**

Bank's subsidiary A wholly owned subsidiary of a bank can be regarded as the bank's alter ego: *Amalgamated Investment and Property Co Ltd v Texas Commerce International Bank Ltd* [1982] 1 QB 84 at 122.

•**Banning order** An order excluding a person from the security industry (Corporations Law ss 835, 836) or the futures industry (ss 1199, 1199A). See also **Australian Securities Commission; Futures industry; Securities industry.**

Banque Nationale de Paris Abbr – BNP Established in 1881 for the purpose of financing the wool trade between Australia and France, a trading bank offering a complete range of banking services. It is one of the fifteen largest banks in the world and the largest of all European banks. Prior to 1984, BNP was the only major international bank in the world with an Australian trading bank licence.

•**Bans clause** A term of an award (except grievance procedures) that, to any extent, prohibits engaging in conduct that would hinder, prevent, or discourage the observance of an award, working in accordance with an award, or the acceptance of, or offering for, work in accordance with the award: (CTH) Industrial Relations Act 1988 s 4. See also **Award; Industrial relations.**

•**Bar association** An association of legal practitioners practising as barristers representative of the practising bar: *Wentworth v New South Wales Bar Assn* (1992) 176 CLR 239; 106 ALR 624. See also **Bar council; Barrister.**

•**Bar council** The governing body of a bar association. The rules or articles of a bar association usually provide for its business to be managed by elected members of the association.

Barclays Bank Australia Granted a full banking authority in 1985, Barclays Bank Australia offers a banking service to the corporate, commercial and high net worth individual markets. The Barclays Group is one of the world's oldest and largest banking organisations, tracing its origins back to London in 1736. Barclays has been present in Australia since 1972 when it established a merchant bank. The Barclays Australasia Consensus Earning Profile Report provides earnings forecasts on Australia's top 100 and New Zealand's top 25 companies for the next two years. The companies included in the report cover more than 85 per cent of the Australian and New Zealand share market capitalisation.

Bare negative pledge A negative pledge given to an unsecured lender. A bare negative pledge in isolation is not a security but a contractual promise: *Pullen v Abalcheck Pty Ltd* (1990) 3 ACSR 246; 8 ACLC 1087. See also **Charge; Negative pledge; Security.**

Bare power In relation to a discretionary trust, the fiduciary power of a trustee to appoint property with no obligation to exercise the power by distributing among the objects of the trust: *Brown (1988) v Higgs* (1803) 8 Ves Jun 561; 32 ER 473. Also known as 'revocable bailment'. See also **Discretionary trust; Fiduciary; Power of appointment; Trust power; Trustee.**

Bare trust 1. A trust where the trustee holds the property without any beneficial interest in the property and without any further duty to perform in relation to the trust, except to convey the trust property on demand to the beneficiaries of the trust, or to deal with the property as directed by the beneficiaries: *Herdegen v FCT* (1988) 84 ALR 271. **2.** A resulting trust flowing from the provision by a beneficiary of the purchase money for a property. See also **Beneficial interest; Beneficiary; Resulting trust; Trust.**

Bareboat charterparty A charterparty agreement where the shipowner agrees to pass to the charterer for a period of time, possession of the ship and control of the master of the ship, but there is no passing of control of a crew for the ship. Where control of the crew is also passed, it is called a demised charterparty instead. See also **Charterparty**.

Bargain 1. To negotiate over the terms of a purchase or contract in an effort to obtain more favourable terms. 2. A mutual undertaking, contract, or agreement. See also **Agreement; Bargaining power; Contract; Purchase**.

Bargain basement Money market transactions that take place above or below the generally available market level. They are attractive to the participant depending on whether the transaction is a borrowing or a lending.

Bargaining power The ability of a party to a transaction to achieve results desired by that party. Bargaining power is derived from the resources and advantages a party may have such as the existence of equally attractive alternatives to the transaction, financial resources, and negotiation skills.

Barrier to entry A market condition such that potential entrants to the market face costs greater than the market incumbents. See also **Contestable market; Competition; Market; Market power**.

•**Barrister** A class of legal practitioner who is by law or custom limited to advocacy and advisory work, in any field of the law. The bar is comprised of junior counsel or 'members of the outer bar' and senior or Queen's Counsel. Also known as 'counsel'. See also **Bar council; Queen's Counsel; Solicitor**.

•**Barter** Exchange of goods and commodities for other goods instead of money. Barter was a characteristic of primitive communities but is not unknown in modern times when trading with countries that are short of hard, convertible currencies. Sometimes, it is also known as 'compensation trading' or 'counter-purchase'. See also **Counter trade; Sell; Swap**.

Base income threshold amount An amount that fixes the level of a bankrupt's post-bankruptcy income that need not be taken into account when determining the level of contributions to be made to the bankrupt's estate. See also **Actual income threshold amount; Bankrupt; Contribution assessment period; Income of bankrupt**.

Basel Committee on Banking Supervision A committee of banking supervisory authorities established by the central bank Governors of the Group of Ten countries in 1975. It formulated an international agreement on minimum capital adequacy standards for banks that has been adopted by central banks in the majority of developed countries including Australia. It consists of senior representatives of bank supervisory authorities and central banks from Belgium, Canada, France, Germany, Italy, Japan, Luxembourg, Netherlands, Sweden, Switzerland, the United Kingdom, and the United States. It usually meets at the Bank for International Settlements in Basel, Switzerland. See also **Bank for International Settlements; Capital adequacy guidelines; Reserve Bank of Australia**.

Basel concordat An agreement, first formulated in 1975 and revised in 1983, by the Bank for International Settlements (BIS) that sets out the principles governing the supervision of banks' foreign branches and representation by the parent and host authorities. The concordat deals with the responsibilities of the central bank of the host country as the prudential supervisor of the foreign bank's branch or subsidiary. See also **Bank for International Settlements; Basel Committee on Banking Supervision; Prudential supervision; Reserve Bank of Australia**.

Basic banking product An account provided by a bank for customers which provides basic transaction services, without fees, or with a low level of fees. See also **Banking service**.

Basis In a futures market, the difference between the price of a cash instrument being hedged and the price of the futures contract (that is the difference between the futures price and the spot price). See also **Futures contract; Futures contract; Spot price**.

•**Basis clause** In insurance law, a clause by which the insured agrees to the truth or existence of specific matters forming the basis of the insured's insurance contract. Basis clauses are now deprived of effect for insurance contracts: (CTH) Insurance Contracts Act 1984: s 24. See also **Insurance contract; Warranty**.

Basis point One gradation on a scale representing 0.01 per cent; 100 basis points equals 1 per cent. The basis point scale is used in particular to express variations in the yield of bonds. Fixed income yields vary often and the basis point scale easily expresses these changes. For example, the difference between 12.83 and 12.88 is five basis points. See also **Bond**.

Basis risk The possibility that an imperfectly matched hedge could produce a loss by the deviation of the basis from its predicted value. See also **Basis; Bond**.

Basis swap A swap agreement in which the interest benchmarks are based on different instrument types. See also **Interest rate swap**.

Basket purchase The acquisition of a group of assets for a lump sum without classifying such assets into classes. However, the cost of assets is recorded in the assets register when the purchase is made. Also known as 'lock, stock and barrel purchase', ' walk in walk out purchase', and 'lump sum purchase'. See also **Asset; Consumer Price Index; Lump sum**.

Battery A trespass to the person consisting in an intentional act that directly causes a physical interference with the body of the plaintiff, without lawful justification or the plaintiff's consent. A battery is actionable 'per se' (without proof of damage): *Collins v Wilcock* [1984] 1 WLR 1172.

Battle of forms The process of exchanging documents of differing terms by parties in pre-contractual negotiations, the documents constituting offers and counter offers. See also **Acceptance; Contract; Counter offer; Offer; Pre-contractual statement**.

Baumol-Willig rule A proposed rule in trade practices law designed to assess the price at which supply should be given. According to the rule, the supplier should not be forced to receive less than the price that makes the supplier indifferent as to whether the other components of the final product are provided by itself or others. The supplier has the right to calculate its price as component price equals direct incremental cost of supplying the component plus contribution foregone by the supplier because of the competitor's use of the component: *Telecom Corp of New Zealand Ltd v Commerce Communications* [1992] 3 NZLR 429. See also **Essential facility doctrine; Marginal cost**.

BCA See **Building Code of Australia**.

Bear A dealer in shares who, believing prices are about to fall, sells shares in the hope of buying them back again at a lower price, thereby making a profit. See also **Bear market; Securities**.

Bear market A market in which prices are falling. See also **Bear; Bull market**.

Bear spread In futures markets, a market strategy involving buying a nearby contract and selling a deferred contract, to take advantage of a weakening market. In a declining market, the deferred month contract will usually fall in price faster than those expiring earlier. If an investor in gold anticipates that gold prices will decline but needs to reduce exposure should the market rally, the investor may, for example, buy a nearby June contract and simultaneously sell a more distant February contract. If in mid-May with prices edging downward the June-February spread changes and the carrying charge narrows, the investor liquidates the spread, earning a profit. See also **Butterfly spread; Option; Trading spread**.

Bear straddle In futures markets, selling nearby months while buying distant months. See also **Butterfly spread; Option; Straddle option; Trading spread**.

•**Bearer** The person in possession of a negotiable instrument that is payable to bearer: (CTH) Bills of Exchange Act 1909 s 4; (CTH) Cheques and Payment Orders Act 1986 s 3(1). A bill may be payable to the bearer in its origin or become so by an indorsement in blank: (CTH) Bills of Exchange Act 1909 ss 13(3), 37(f), 39(1). See also **Bearer bill; Bearer debenture; Cheque; Indorsement in blank; Negotiable instrument**.

Bearer bill A bill expressed to be made payable to bearer. A bill on which the only or last indorsement is an indorsement in blank is payable to the bearer: (CTH) Bills of Exchange Act 1909 s 13(3). See also **Bearer; Bill of exchange; Indorsement; Indorsement in blank; Order bill; Payee**.

Bearer bill of lading A bill of lading used where the goods are deliverable to the bearer of the bill. See also **Bill of lading; Order bill of lading**.

Bearer debenture A debenture expressed to be payable to its bearer. A bearer debenture may be transferred by delivery without advising the issuing company: *Edelstein v Schuler & Co* [1902] 2 KB 144. See also **Debenture; Negotiable instrument**.

•**Bearer security** A written instrument issued on the basis that the person entitled to the claim represented by the instrument will be the holder of the instrument. See also **Debenture; Securities; Share**.

Bed and breakfast deal A term used in London financial circles for an arrangement between two parties in which one party sells shares to the other on one day, and then buys them back the next day. The purpose is to establish a profit or loss so as to minimise tax.

Bench 1. The place in court where the judge or judges sit. When a judge is 'on the bench' the court is sitting and court etiquette applies. **2.** Judicial office. When a person is first appointed as a judge, he or she is said to have been 'elevated to the bench'. **3.** The court. That is, the presiding judge, or where more than one judge is sitting, one, some, or all of the presiding judges. A question 'from the bench' is a question from the judge or one of the judges. **4.** Issued by a judge. For example, a bench warrant. See also **Court; Full court; Judge**.

Benchmark rate A rate used by banks as a yardstick for measuring and setting other interest rates on which they accept deposits or lend money to customers. See also **Prime rate**.

•**Beneficial interest** An interest in property recognised by the courts of equity: *DKLR Holding Co (No 2) Pty Ltd v Cmr of Stamp Duties* [1980] 1 NSWLR 510 at 518-519. See also **Asset; Beneficiary; Derived; Equitable interest; Nominee shareholder; Trust**.

•**Beneficial owner** A person who holds or is entitled to a beneficial or equitable interest in property, such as a person for whose benefit a trust is created: for example *Custom Credit Corp Ltd v Ravi Nominees Pty Ltd* (1992) 8 WAR 42; Corporations Law s 1097.

Corporation The person recognised in equity as being the owner of shares, but who does not hold the legal title because the shares are registered in the name of another. See also **Beneficial ownership; Relevant interest; Share; Takeover**.

•**Beneficial ownership** Ownership conferring the use and benefit of property. The concept has two main uses in the (CTH) Income Tax Assessment Act 1936. See also **Acquisition; Asset; Beneficial interest; Beneficial owner; Tax loss**.

Beneficial property See **Beneficial interest**.

Beneficiary A person who, by being in a particular kind of legal (including equitable) relationship, receives or is to receive a benefit, profit, or advantage.

Finance The person in whose favour a letter of credit is addressed. See also **Letter of credit**.

Superannuation In relation to a superannuation fund, scheme, or trust, a person who has a beneficial interest in the fund, scheme or trust: (CTH) Superannuation Industry (Supervision) Act 1993 s 10. See also **Superannuation fund**.

Trusts A beneficial owner of property who does not hold the legal title, but for whose benefit the legal title is held by a trustee under a trust arrangement. Also known as *'cestui que trust'*. See also **Beneficial interest; Beneficial owner; Legal title; Trust; Trustee**.

•**Benefit** An advantage or profit; a gain.

Restitution Anything of economic value, including an asset, chose in action, money, property, service, and the discharge or decrease of a liability. See also **Enrichment; Free acceptance; Incontrovertible benefit; Restitution; Unjust enrichment**.

Taxation and revenue For the purposes of fringe benefits tax legislation; any right, privilege, service, or facility. See also **Annuity**; **Fringe benefit**; **Reasonable benefit limit**.

•**Berth** A wharf or quay where a vessel can load or discharge cargo: *Leonis Steamship Co v Rank* [1908] 1 KB 499.

Berth charter See **Dock charter**.

Berth charterparty See **Dock charter**.

Berth clause A clause contained in a charterparty, that stipulates that a ship is to await its turn to berth before lay days are to commence. See also **Charterparty**; **Lay day**.

Berth note A form of contract signed by the master of a vessel and endorsed by the owners, charterers, or agents. A berth note is used when individual port cargo is booked, and provides information such as the tonnage and nature of the cargo, the ports for loading and unloading, and the number of lay days to be allowed. See also **Agent**; **Cargo**; **Charterer**; **Lay day**; **Master**; **Owner**; **Tonnage**.

Besloten Vennootschap met beperkte aansprakelijkheid *Abbr* – BV Netherlands equivalent of a private limited liability company. See also **Company**; **Limited company**; **Private company**.

Best alternative to negotiated agreement *Abbr* – BATNA In the context of a negotiation or mediation, the most satisfactory outcome a party could hope to achieve in the event that the mediation does not result in settlement of the dispute. See also **Alternative dispute resolution**; **Bottom line**; **Mediation**.

Best endeavours clause A clause in a contract requiring a party to do what may reasonably be done in the circumstances, having regard to the nature, capacity, qualifications, and responsibilities of the party, to bring about a certain result: *Transfield Pty Ltd v Arlo International Ltd* (1980) 30 ALR 201; 144 CLR 83. See also **Contract**; **Implied term**; **Salvage agreement**.

Best interests of employer, duty to act in See **Duty to act in best interests of employer**.

Best rent The highest rent that can reasonably be obtained. See also **Current annual open market rental**; **Lease**; **Mortgagor**; **Mortgagee in possession**.

Best-efforts underwriting The underwriting of a public offer of new securities where the underwriting undertakes to use its best efforts to sell the securities by a given date. The underwriter, unlike the usual underwriting agreement, makes no guarantee it will sell or buy all of the securities in the offer, leaving the risk with the issuer. See also **Underwriter**.

Bestolen Venootschap met Beperkte Aansprakelijkheid *Abbr* – BVBA The Belgian equivalent of a limited liability company. See also **Limited company**; **Private company**.

Beta factor A measure of the volatility of a particular security or group of securities. The beta factor for the market as a whole is 1.0. A high beta factor (exceeding 1.0) indicates that in the past the relevant security has been, on average, more volatile than the market as a whole; while it has moved in the same direction as the market, it has moved further. Beta factors may be less than 1.0. By weighing the beta factors of securities in a portfolio, a beta factor for the whole portfolio may be calculated. The beta factor is a guide to probable future behaviour. See also **Accounting beta**; **Historical beta**.

Betterment Unearned or excess increase in value. The concept of betterment affects a variety of legal spheres.

Environment Increase in the value of land resulting from a change in zoning or town planning controls, or a scheme that has been carried out by a statutory authority.

•**Beyond reasonable doubt** A standard of proof. In criminal proceedings a court must not find the charge proved if it is not satisfied beyond reasonable doubt that the accused committed the offence charged: for example (CTH) Evidence Act 1995 s 141(1). See also **Balance of probabilities**; **Burden of Proof**; **Standard of proof**.

Bid In relation to an auction, an offer for property, the bidder being the offeror: *AGC (Advances) Ltd v McWhirter* (1977) 1 BPR 9454. See also **Acceptance**; **Auction**; **Auctioneer**; **Fictitious bid**; **Knock down**; **Offer**; **Contract**.

Bid-ask spread In relation to securities and futures markets, the difference between the bid price and the ask price. See also **Ask price**; **Bid**.

Bidder At an auction, a person who makes an offer to purchase the property auctioned at a certain price. There is no requirement at common law as to how a bid should be made, but the onus is on the bidder to ensure that an effective bid is made and that it is communicated to the auctioneer: *Richards v Phillips* [1969] 1 Ch 39 at 52. Any bid, being merely an offer, can be withdrawn before it has been accepted, usually before the fall of the hammer: *Payne v Cave* (1789) 3 Term Rep 148; 100 ER 502. This is expressly provided in legislation, with reference to the sale of goods by auction: for example (NSW) Sale of Goods Act 1923 s 60; (QLD) Sale of Goods Act 1896 s 59; (SA) Sale of Goods Act 1895 s 57. When a bid is accepted by an auctioneer, the offer is converted into an oral contract for sale, between the seller and the bidder: *Phillips v Butler* [1945] Ch 358; [1945] 2 All ER 258. See also **Auction**.

Bidding, competitive See **Competitive bidding**.

Big bang The changes that occurred in the trading practices on the London Stock Exchange which culminated in the introduction of electronic trading on 27 October 1986. These changes which deregulated the UK stockmarket included the abolition of stock jabbers and the removal of fixed commissions. Automated share trading was also introduced on that day. See also **Deregulation**.

Big Board A colloquial term for the New York Stock Exchange. See also **New York Stock Exchange**.

Big four 1. The four largest Australian commercial banks: National Australia Bank (NAB), Commonwealth Bank (Commonwealth), Westpac Banking Corp (Westpac), and Australia and New Zealand Banking Group (ANZ). 2. The four largest UK commercial banks:

Barclays, Lloyds, Midland, and National Westminster. **3.** The four largest Japanese securities firms: Daiwa, Nikko, Nomura, and Yamaichi.

Big Mac Index A price index created by the British financial journal *The Economist* as a guide to the validity of exchange rates. The McDonald Big Mac hamburger is produced to an identical formula in more than 50 countries and is subject to none of the distribution and transport costs that might distort its price. Thus a Big Mac should cost the same everywhere, if the exchange rates are reflecting the price differences between countries. An international comparison indicates which currencies may be under-valued or over-valued. See also **Currency; Exchange rate; Selling and distribution expense.**

Bilateral contract A contract formed by the exchange of mutual or reciprocal promises. The offer is made in the form of a promise to be accepted by a counter-promise. See also **Acceptance; Consideration; Contract; Executory contract; Offer; Unilateral contract.**

•**Bill** A legislative document in the form of a proposed Act of Parliament. Commonwealth bills require approval by the House of Representatives and the Senate and assent by the Governor-General ('royal assent'). State bills require approval by the relevant houses (or house in Queensland) and the assent of the State Governor. A bill tabled before parliament may be amended extensively before enactment. See also **Bill of exchange; Legislation; Parliament.**

Bill acceptance facility agreement An agreement between a drawer of a bill of exchange and a person or financial institution for the acceptance of bills of exchange upon presentment by the drawee to the person or financial institution.

Bill line facility A credit facility with a bank in which a contract with the bank calls for the issuing of new bills on the maturation of outstanding ones. See also **Acceptance credit.**

•**Bill of exchange** An unconditional order in writing addressed by one person (the 'drawer') to another (the 'drawee') signed by the drawer, requiring the drawee to pay on demand, or at a fixed future time, a sum of money to a specified person or to the bearer: (CTH) Bills of Exchange Act 1909 s 8; *Levine v Bank of Adelaide* (1875) 9 SALR 119. A bill of exchange is a negotiable instrument. See also **Acceptor; Accommodation bill; Bearer; Demand bill; Drawer; Negotiable instrument; Order bill.**

•**Bill of exchange drawn on a banker payable otherwise than on demand** A bill of exchange drawn on a banker, other than a cheque. Under the (CTH) Bills of Exchange Act 1909 a cheque is a bill of exchange drawn on a banker payable on demand: (CTH) Bills of Exchange Act 1909 s 78(1). A bill of exchange drawn on a bank payable otherwise than on demand is payable 'at a fixed or determinable future time': (CTH) Bills of Exchange Act 1909 s 8. See also **Bill of Exchange; Maturity date.**

•**Bill of lading** The written evidence of a contract for the carriage and delivery of goods sent by sea, between a carrier and a consignor of goods ('shipper'), for certain freight. Although the bill of lading does not constitute the contract between the carrier and the shipper of goods, it does represent evidence of its terms: *SS Ardennes (Cargo owners) v SS Ardennes (Owners)* [1951] 1 KB 55. See also **Affreightment; Bearer bill of lading; Carrier; Charterparty; Clean bill of lading; On board bill of lading.**

•**Bill of sale** A document intended to give effect to the transfer of title to an article to another person without transferring actual possession to that person. A bill of sale may be a transfer of an article absolutely by way of sale, gift, or settlement or it may be a transfer by way of security, to be redeemed on repayment of the money secured by it: *Malick v Lloyd (official assignee)* (1913) 16 CLR 483; 30 WN (NSW) 104. In consumer protection law, it is essentially the mortgage of an article. See also **Chattel security; Credit; Trader's bill of sale; Wool lien.**

Bill of special crossing A cheque that bears two parallel transverse lines across the front of the cheque (with or without the addition of the words 'not negotiable' between the lines), and with the name of a banker specified on the face of the cheque: (CTH) Bills of Exchange Act 1909 s 82. See also **Crossing.**

Bill payable at sight A bill of exchange where payment is due immediately upon presentation of the bill. See also **Payable on demand.**

Bill payable on demand See **Demand bill.**

Bill payable to bearer See **Bearer bill.**

Bill payable to order See **Order bill.**

Billable hours Those hours available to a legal practitioner to be occupied in the actual performance of work on behalf of a client. See also **Partner.**

•**Billing cycle** In consumer credit law and in relation to a continuing credit contract, the period applied in accordance with the contract as the billing cycle for that contract. See also **Chargeable amount; Continuing credit contract; Credit charge; Notice of terms.**

Bills of exchange legislation Legislation regulating bills of exchange. The (CTH) Bills of Exchange Act 1909 governed all bills of exchange, cheques, and promissory notes until 1 July 1987. Since then, it covers only bills of exchange and promissory notes: (CTH) Cheques and Payment Orders Act 1986. See also **Bill of exchange; Cheque; Law Merchant; Promissory note.**

Binder agreement 1. An authority given by an insurer to an insurance intermediary to enter into, as agent for the insurer, contracts of insurance on behalf of the insurer: (CTH) Insurance Contracts Act 1984 s 11(1). **2.** An authority given by an insurer to an insurance intermediary to deal with and settle, as agent for the insurer, claims against the insurer: (CTH) Insurance (Agents and Brokers) Act 1984 s 9. Also known as a 'Bordereaux agreement'. See also **Insurance agent; Insurance broker.**

Binding nature of contract At common law there are three essential elements of a binding contract: agreement (being determined by the rules on offer and acceptance), consideration (except where the contract is made by deed), and intention to create legal relations. Once a binding contract has been formed, all the parties are bound to fulfil their obligations under it. Failure to do so may give rise to an order for specific performance or may create an obligation to pay damages. See also **Acceptance**; **Agreement**; **Consideration**; **Contract**; **Damages**; **Offer**; **Specific performance**.

Biological process In patent law, a method or process for any medical or veterinary treatment, including a merely cosmetic medical treatment, or genetic modification, of humans, animals, or micro-organisms. Subject to the exclusion of processes for the biological generation of human beings, novel and inventive biological processes are prima facie patentable subject matter. It is generally sufficient to demonstrate that the product of the claimed process is an artificially created state of affairs of economic significance. Where the product is a new organism, no objection can be taken to a claim defining the alleged invention on the ground that it is directed to something living: (CTH) Patents Act 1990 s 18(2); *National Research Development Corp v Cmr of Patents* (1959) 102 CLR 252; (1961) 78 RPC 134; *Ranks Hovis McDougall Ltd's Application* [1976] AOJP 3915; *Joos v Cmr of Patents* (1972) 126 CLR 611; (1972-73) ALR 831; *Genentech Inc v Wellcome Foundation* [1989] RPC 147. See also **Patentability**.

Black economy That part of the economy that is not reflected in the national accounts because it involves cash payments or payments in kind for goods and services which are not declared by the receiver or the payer for income tax purposes. See also **Black market**.

Black Friday Any sudden collapse on the stock market. It takes its name from Friday 24 September 1869 when for the first time there was a major collapse on the US stock market. See also **Black Monday**.

Black list A list containing the names of persons, natural and corporate, who are proscribed for specific purposes. See also **Boycott**.

Black market The illegal trading in goods and provisions whose availability is restricted or controlled. This usually arises in a time of war as a response to rationing.

Black Monday A record collapse of share prices on the New York Stock Exchange on Monday 19 October 1987 which triggered falls in sharemarket prices throughout the world. The Dow-Jones Industrial Average fell by some 40 per cent. The following day, known as Black Tuesday, witnessed remarkable falls in share prices on the Australian sharemarket. The falls on both stock exchanges were more rapid than that occurring during the Great Depression of 1929. In the United States, the Brady Commission attempted to identify the several causes. See also **Portfolio insurance**.

Blacklight facility Method by which the bank verifies its customer's signature by placing an ultra violet ink signature on the customer's passbook. The ultra violet signature shows up when placed under black light. See also **Banking authority**; **Signature**.

•**Blackmail 1.** A general term covering a number of statutory offences involving obtaining money and other property by using threats of violence, threats to accuse of a crime, or other menacing conduct: for example (NSW) Crimes Act 1900 s 100; (SA) Criminal Law Consolidation Act 1935 s 160. **2.** An offence in the Australian Capital Territory, Victoria, and Tasmania of making an unwarranted demand with menaces with a view to gain or to cause a loss: for example (VIC) Crimes Act 1958 s 87(1); (ACT) Crimes Act 1900 s 112(1). See also **Corrupt conduct**.

Blank An omission of something fundamental in the structure of a bill of exchange: for example, the name of the payee on an order bill, the amount of the bill, or the date (when that is important to determine the bill's maturity). See also **Bill of exchange**; **Maturity date**; **Order bill**.

Blank, acceptance in See **Indorsement in blank**.

Blank cheque A cheque form issued by a bank which has been signed by the customer without filling in the name of the payee or the amount payable. See also **Cheque**; **Cheque book**.

Blank, endorsement in See **Indorsement in blank**.

Blank transfer A document executed by an owner of real property or shares evidencing an intention to convey the property to a transferee not named in the instrument. A blank transfer is often used as a form of security and held by the mortgagee. See also **Conveyance**; **Mortgage**.

Blind trust A trust in which the beneficiary is unable to inspect the trust instruments (including the trust accounts). The principle of a blind trust is contrary to the usual obligation to keep a beneficiary informed. See also **Trust**; **Trust account**.

Block discounting An early acceptance of settlement of a liability for a discount. This may occur where the seller of goods on hire purchase discounts the rights on the hire purchase agreement and accepts the present value of those rights from a finance company, with an adjustment discounting the value of those rights because of the collection risk, rather than waiting for the customer's payments by instalments as stipulated in the agreement. This system exchanges an early settlement in return for discounting of the liability. Also known as 'factoring'. See also **Discount**; **Factoring arrangement**; **Hire purchase**.

Block house A dealer's firm that acts primarily in block trades. See also **Block trade**.

Block trade The purchase and sale by brokers of 'blocks of shares', with a broker acting as the intermediary and negotiator between the buyers and the sellers. A block trade in the United States is a trade greater than 10,000 units. See also **Block house**; **Exchange distribution**; **Specialist block purchase**; **Specialist block sale**.

•**Blocked account** An account from which withdrawals may be made only for certain purposes or in defined conditions. See also **Account**.

Blue chip security A share in a large, soundly-based public company that is thought to be a safe investment. See also **Dow Jones averages**; **Securities**.

Blue collar worker A person employed to do unskilled manual labour, semi-skilled production operations, or as a craftsperson, typically remunerated on a weekly wage basis rather than an annual salary.

Blue sky law Investor protection laws in various states of the United States regulating the public offering of securities. See also **Prospectus**; **Securities and Exchange Commission**.

•**Board fringe benefit** A fringe benefit where an employee is entitled under an industrial award or an employment arrangement to accommodation and at least two meals a day: (CTH) Fringe Benefits Tax Assessment Act 1986 ss 35, 136(1). See also **Fringe Benefits Tax**.

•**Board of directors** Corporate organ comprising the directors elected by the shareholders of a company and having various functions including: appointing and rewarding the chief executive; setting goals, formulating strategy, and approving business plans; approving annual budgets and key management decisions; monitoring management performance and business results; setting and reviewing policies for shareholder communication and approving reports to shareholders; and setting and reviewing budgetary control and conformance strategies: for example Corporations Law Sch 1 Table A art 66. Also known as 'company board'. See also **Actual authority**; **Chairman of the board**; **Directing mind and will**; **Director**; **Seal**.

Board of directors meeting Subject to the company's constitution, the meeting in which the directors collectively exercise the powers or functions entrusted to them by the company's constitution: for example Corporations Law Sch 1 Table A reg 66; *Northside Developments Pty Ltd v Registrar-General* (1990) 170 CLR 146 at 205; 93 ALR 385 at 425. See also **Board of directors**; **Directors' resolution**; **Extraordinary general meeting**; **Table A articles**.

•**Board of Reference** A board appointed under (CTH) Industrial Relations Act 1988 s 131 by an award or order of the Australian Industrial Relations Commission to allow, approve, fix, determine, or deal with, in a specified manner, a matter or thing that may from time to time arise under the award. The High Court has upheld the validity of the boards: *R v Hegarty; Ex parte Corporation of City of Salisbury* (1981) 147 CLR 617; (1981) 36 ALR 275. See also **Australian Industrial Relations Commission**; **Award**.

Board of Review, Income Tax See **Income Tax Board of Review**.

•**Body** The physical structure of a person or animal; an entity; a group of people or things. Body has legal significance in both physical and non physical senses.

Voluntary associations For the purposes of the Corporations Law, an organisation that is a society or association: Corporations Law s 9. See also **Association**; **Body corporate**; **Collective body**; **Society**.

•**Body corporate** An artificial legal entity having separate legal personality. It includes bodies created by common law (such as a corporation sole and corporation aggregate), by statute (such as the Australian Securities Commission) and by registration pursuant to statute (such as a company, building society, credit union, trade union, and incorporated association).

Corporations A company or other body registrable under the Corporations Law: Corporations Law s 9. See also **Company**; **Corporation**; **Corporation aggregate**; **Corporation sole**; **Separate legal personality**.

Body of a deed The main and operative part of a deed, essential to its validity, as opposed to the recitals which outline the factual matrix surrounding the deed foundation and are not essential.

•**Bona fide** /bouna faɪdi/ *Lat* – in good faith; with sincerity. **1.** In law, to do something in good faith or with an honest intention. For example, 'the bona fide and proper exercise of the power': *Wayde v New South Wales Rugby League* (1994) 180 CLR 459; 61 ALR 225. **2.** In common usage, true, genuine, sincere, not a fake. However, this is not a correct legal usage. See also **Duty to disclose**; **Fiduciary duty**; **Good faith**; **Mala fide**; **Notice**; **Uberrimae fidei**.

Bona fide purchase A defence to an equitable proprietary claim or restitutionary personal claim which is available to a defendant who has acquired the legal title to the property in question from a third party for valuable consideration in good faith and without notice of the plaintiff's claim: *Lipkin Gorman v Karpnale Ltd* [1991] 2 AC 548. See also **Good faith exchange**; **Purchaser**.

•**Bona fide redundancy payment** A payment made to a taxpayer because of the dismissal of the taxpayer from employment due to bona fide redundancy: (CTH) Income Tax Assessment Act 1936 ss 27A(1), 27F. A bona fide redundancy payment made to a taxpayer on or after 1 July 1994 is exempt from tax providing it does not exceed a certain limit: s 27 CB. The limit is indexed annually to movements in average weekly ordinary time earnings: s 27A(20). See also **Average Weekly Ordinary Time Earnings**; **Eligible Termination Payment**.

Bona fides /bɒnə faɪdeɪz/ *Lat* – good faith; honest intention; absence of intent to defraud; absence of deliberate wrongdoing. See also **Bona fide**.

Bona vacantia /bɒnə vækæntiə/ *Lat* – unclaimed goods; property that has no owner: *Dyke v Walford* (1848) 5 Moo PCC 434; 13 ER 557. While goods with no owner generally belong to the first finder, *bona vacantia* belong to the Crown: for example *Dyke v Walford*; (NSW) Wills, Probate and Administration Act 1898 s 61B(7)-(8).

Corporations Property of a dissolved company which has not yet been claimed by creditors or contributories.

•**Bond** An instrument under seal, usually in the form of a deed poll, by which a person (the 'obligor') binds himself or herself to another (the 'obligee') to pay a specified sum of money at some fixed date. It is a form of specialty debt, being evidenced in writing in the form of a deed. Since execution of a deed imports consideration, consideration is not necessary for a valid bond: *Squire v Whitton* (1848) 1 HL Cas 333; 9 ER 785. See also **Arbitration bond**; **Collateral**; **Deed**; **Double bond**; **Obligee**.

Bond rating agencies Firms or institutions that provide informed and considered judgments on the quality of corporate, municipal, and other bonds for those interested in the merits of particular issues. Ratings are essentially a ranking of bond issues according to the probability of default. Agencies must not engage in the market or be connected with investors or issues. The first rating agency in the United States was that of John Moody, set up in 1909. Standard and Poor began rating corporate bonds in 1923 and municipal bonds in 1940. Ratings are primarily based on the reputation of the institution issuing the bond and are usually on the scale AAA (small risk) to D (already in default). Australian Ratings is a subsidiary of Standard and Poor and adopted an identical rating system in 1991. See also **AAA**; **Fallen angel**; **Investment grade bond**; **Junk bond**.

Bond store A storage space licensed to contain goods on which duty is yet to be paid.

Bond swap The simultaneous sale of one bond issue and the purchase of another. Swaps may occur for tax purposes, to decrease risks or to produce profits. See also **Bond**; **Callable swap**; **Debt-equity swap**; **Off market swap**.

Bond washing A transaction used by owners of securities seeking to avoid taxation under which the sale and repurchase of securities is arranged to take place before and after the payment of a dividend, with the result that a person, other than the owner of the securities, receives the dividend.

Bondsman A person bound by a bond, such as a guarantor or surety.

Bonus dividend An abnormal and unusual dividend declared out of profits. See also **Bonus share issue**; **Dividend**.

Bonus issue See **Bonus share issue**.

Bonus option An option to take up unissued shares given as a bonus. See also **Share**.

•**Bonus payment** A payment by way of division of the profits of an industry or business, that is additional to the payment of a just wage. See also **Allowance**; **Certified agreement**; **Enterprise flexibility agreement**; **Industrial agreement**; **Industrial award**; **Wage**.

Bonus share dividend A dividend paid to a shareholder where the entitlement to receive the dividend is satisfied in whole or in part by the issue of a share usually in the company paying the dividend.

Bonus share issue The distribution of undistributed profits of a company in the form of share capital: *BTR Nylex Ltd v Churchill International Inc* (1992) 9 ACSR 361. See also **Dividend**; **Share**.

Bonus shares See **Bonus share issue**.

•**Book** Generally, bound leaves of paper containing printed material; leaves fastened together as a volume but not in a way that the leaves may be taken out and substituted: for example, *Hearts of Oak Assurance Co v James Flower* [1936] 1 Ch 76; *Re Tomline's Will Trusts* (1931) 1 Ch 521.

Corporations Any register, documents, accounting record, or other record of information relating to an accounting entity: Corporations Law s 9. Accounting records would include invoices, receipts, orders, cheques, and other such documents necessary to explain the calculations by which accounts are made up: Corporations Law s 9. Both books of original entry (journals) and ledgers are included. In some contexts books may be constituted by paper documents, electronically, or on computer disk: for example (WA) Gaming Commission Act 1987 s 3(1). See also **Book debt**.

Intellectual property For the purposes of parallel importation, 'book' is defined to exclude items whose main content is music, computer software manuals, and periodical publications: (CTH) Copyright Act 1968 s 44A(9). See also **Author**; **Copyright**; **Literary work**.

•**Book debt** A debt becoming due to a business entrepreneur in the normal course of carrying on the business, as distinct from either a debt due on transactions unconnected with the business or a debt that is merely incidental to the conduct of the business: *Waters v Widdows* (1983) 54 ALR 691. See also **Assignment**; **Charge**.

•**Book of account** A record where the operations and transactions of a business are recorded in monetary terms, forming part of the accounting system. The books of account include books of original entry (journal) and ledgers.

Book value In accounting, the value of an asset as recorded in the books of an enterprise. See also **Book value per share**; **Capital loss**; **Depreciated value**; **Valuation**.

Book value per share The asset value of each of the company's securities. The number is the total assets with debts and liabilities deducted divided by the number of securities. See also **Book value**; **Capital loss**; **Depreciated value**; **Share**.

Books closing date The specified time and date set by a company for the lodgment of transfers for the purpose of determining the holders of the company's securities who are entitled to dividends, interest, new securities, and rights to priority of applications for issues of securities, or any other particular entitlements.

Boom market A market (for example, in securities) in which buying demand is greatly in excess of selling pressure thus causing prices to rise dramatically. Also known as 'bull market'. See also **Bear**.

•**Borrower** A person to whom money is lent. Borrowing necessarily implies repayment at some time and under some circumstances: *Re Southern Brazilian Rio Grande Do Sul Railway Co Ltd* [1905] 2 Ch 78 at 83. See also **Debtor**; **Money lender**.

•**Borrowing corporation** A body corporate that is or will be under a liability to repay any money received by it in response to an invitation or offer to subscribe for or buy debentures of the body corporate or an offer of debentures as consideration for acquisition under a takeover scheme, of the shares in a body corporate: Corporations Law s 9. See also **Debenture trust deed**; **Financial corporation**; **Money market corporation**.

Both to blame A principle established under the International Convention for the Unification of Certain Rules of Law Respecting: (1) Collisions Between Vessels; and (2) Assistance and Salvage at Sea 1910 that if two ships collide, both are to blame for damage to their respective cargoes to the extent that each is to blame for the accident: (CTH) Navigation Act 1912 s 259(1); *Union Steamship Co of New Zealand Ltd v The Ship 'Caradale'* (1937) 56 CLR 277; [1937] ALR 142. A ship that has not contributed by any fault to such loss or damage is not liable. See also **Apportionment; Both to blame clause; Cargo.**

Both to blame clause   *Abbr* – B B clause   A clause often inserted in a charterparty or bill of lading in order to ensure that the 'both to blame' concept applies to the contract. Also known as a 'both to blame collision clause'. See also **Bill of lading; Both to blame; Charterparty.**

Bottom line   In relation to a party to a negotiation, the least that the party would be prepared to accept in any negotiated settlement. See also **Alternative dispute resolution; Best alternative to negotiated agreement; Mediation.**

Bottom-up forecasting   The analysis of individual securities ratings and performances before assessing wider issues such as industry and economic trends. The assumption is that individual securities can do well even if the specific industry does not. See also **Economic impact study; Index of Leading Indicators.**

•**Bought position**   **1.** In relation to a commodity agreement or a futures contract that is a commodity agreement, the position of a person who has an obligation, whether or not enforceable, to accept delivery in accordance with the agreement: Corporations Law ss 9, 55. **2.** In relation to a futures contract that is an adjustment agreement, the position of a person who has an obligation to pay the difference if the value of the agreement at a particular future time is less than its value at an earlier time, and who has the right to receive the difference if the former value is greater than the latter: Corporations Law s 9. See also **Cash settled futures contract; Commodity agreement.**

Bounced cheque   A customer's cheque that is dishonoured by a bank for want of funds to meet it. See also **Dishonour.**

•**Bounty**   An inducement to achieve a particular trading target. The Commonwealth Parliament has power with respect to bounties on the production or export of goods, but the bounties must be uniform throughout the Commonwealth: Commonwealth Constitution s 51(iii). Also known as 'subsidy'. See also **Prize; Subsidy; Trade and commerce.**

Bovill's Act   The (UK) Law of Partnership (Amendment) Act 1865 (28 & 29 Vict c 86), repealed but substantially re-enacted by the (UK) Partnership Act 1890. The Act confirmed the common law principle that the fact that a person shares in the profits of a business does not of itself make the person a partner in the business. The principle is embodied in Australia in the partnership legislation (for example (NSW) Partnership Act 1892 s 2(3)) which provides that the receipt by a person of a share of profits of a business is prima facie evidence that the person is a partner in the business, but does not of itself make the person a partner in the business. See also **Partnership; Partnership Acts.**

•**Boycott**   To cease dealings with, in order to intimidate or coerce. Boycott has domestic and international implications.
Industrial law   To combine in refusing to have any dealings with a person, to punish or coerce the person into a particular course of conduct; in particular, to refuse any commercial dealings such as acquiring or supplying goods, services, or labour. See also **Boycotting agreement; Secondary boycott.**

Boycott contravention   A contravention of (CTH) Industrial Relations Act 1988 s 162. See also **Boycott; Secondary boycott.**

Boycotting agreement   An agreement between an employer and employees (or the employees' union) that the employer will refrain from trading with another person, where the agreement is entered into for the purpose of settling an industrial dispute between the employers and employees in connection with that trade. See also **Boycott; Collusion; Industrial dispute; Restraint of trade.**

Bracket creep   The situation where a taxpayer is pushed into a higher marginal rate of tax because of income increasing with inflation, but the tax rates remaining at the same nominal level. See also **Income taxation; Progressive tax.**

Brainstorming   Discussing an idea or problem, usually in small groups, where all participants volunteer their understanding of the problem, and suggest a diverse range of potential solutions with the aim of reaching a solution by consensus.

•**Branch**   In relation to an industrial organisation, any section, division, chapter, or other group within the industrial organisation that has an executive or governing body, or officers: for example (QLD) Industrial Relations Act 1990 s 5. See also **Industrial organisation; Trade union.**

•**Branch manager**   In banking, an officer of the bank empowered to enter into contracts and perform acts that are within the scope of the business of the bank. Naturally, his or her authority will be more restricted than that of other senior management because it extends only to dealings with the business of the branch. A branch manager is the bank itself when acting within the scope of his or her authority. His or her knowledge is the bank's knowledge: *McMahon v Brewer* (1897) 18 LR (NSW) Eq 88. See also **Bank manager.**

•**Branch register**   **1.** The register of an Australian company kept outside Australia which shows who the members of the company are: Corporations Law s 216K. **2.** In relation to registered foreign companies with a share capital, a register of members kept in Australia. Also known as 'Australian register'. See also **Principal Australian register.**

•**Breach**   **1.** Breaking through a boundary, as in breach of close. **2.** The invasion of a legal right, the infraction of a law or the violation of a legal obligation.

Breach date rule   The general rule in the assessment of damages for breach of contract that the date of assessment is the time of breach, on the basis of the loss or damage suffered at that time: *Wenham v Ella* (1972) 127 CLR 454. See also **Anticipatory breach**; **Damages**; **Inflation**.

•**Breach of confidence** In equity, the failure of a confidant to preserve the confidential character of information which has been communicated in circumstances giving rise to an obligation of confidence: *Coco v A N Clarke (Engineers) Ltd* [1969] RBC 41; *Moorgate Tobacco Co Ltd v Philip Morris Ltd (No 2)* (1984) 156 CLR 414; 56 ALR 193. Protection may also flow from the (CTH) Privacy Act 1988. See also **Confidential information**; **Confidential relationship**; **Duty of confidence**; **Fiduciary duty**; **Privacy**.

Breach of contract The failure of a party to a contract to perform a contractual obligation; or an anticipatory breach. The commission of a breach of contract by the promisor provides the promisee with a right to claim damages. See also **Anticipatory breach**; **Contract**; **Damages**; **Failure of performance**; **Performance**; **Time stipulation**.

Breach of covenant The contravention of a positive or negative covenant by the covenantor. Where there is a breach of a positive covenant, the covenantee can enforce the covenant in an action for specific performance: *Butler v Powis* (1845) 8 Jur 859. Where there is a breach of a negative covenant, the covenantee may enforce the covenant by injunction: *Cole v Sims* (1854) 5 De G M & G 1; 43 ER 768. See also **Covenant**; **Deed**.

Breach of duty of care Negligent or careless conduct, or failure to act, of a person who owes a duty of care to another and who fails to maintain the standard of care necessary to fulfil that duty. Breach of the duty of care alone is insufficient to ground an action for negligence. See also **Duty of care**; **Negligence**.

•**Breach of statutory duty** A cause of action against a person who breaches a duty imposed on that person by statute. A person who suffers loss as a result of the breach has a right to claim damages in compensation for the loss. Generally, a remedy for such breach is not available to an individual directly, because statutes themselves impose penalties. However, there are many exceptions, sometimes express but frequently implied, allowing individuals to sue for breach of a statutory duty. In order for the cause of action to arise, the statute must be for the benefit of a class of the public rather than the benefit of the public as a whole: *Groves v Wimborne (Lord)* [1898] 2 QB 402. An example is the duty to fence in dangerous machinery under (NSW) Factories, Shops and Industries Act 1962 s 27: *Sovar v Henry Lane Pty Ltd* (1967) 116 CLR 397; ALR 609. See also **Common law damages**; **Statutory duty**.

•**Breach of trust** The failure of a trustee to meet the obligations of a trustee. The trustee legislation in each State governs the right to bring an action for breach of trust, and includes provisions giving the court power to excuse a breach of trust where the trustee has acted honestly and reasonably and ought fairly to be excused for breaching the trust and omitting to obtain court direction in the matter: for example (NSW) Trustee Act 1925 s 85. See also **Beneficiary**; **Mingling of trust property**; **Restitution**; **Trust account**; **Wilful default**.

Breach of warranty The non-fulfilment of the type of contractual term known as a warranty. A breach of warranty usually allows the party not in default to sue for damages, but does not avoid or enable the avoidance of the contract. See also **Breach of contract**; **Warranty**; **Warranty of authority**.

•**Breakdown** In a machine insurance policy, the actual breaking of any part of a machine while it is in use, arising from mechanical or electrical defects in the machine causing sudden stoppage of the machine's functions, and necessitating its repair or replacement: *Sun Alliance & London Insurance Group v Northwest Iron Co Ltd* [1974] 2 NSWLR 625. Breakdown does not include a wasting away or wearing out of the relevant part of a machine caused by or naturally resulting from ordinary use: *Sun Alliance & London Insurance Group v North West Iron Co Ltd*. However, it includes the case where a defect is discovered in the course of ordinary maintenance and a competent person correctly perceives the problem and reasonably decides not to operate the machine further: *Sun Alliance & London Insurance Group v North West Iron Co Ltd*. See also **Force majeure**; **Insurance contract**; **Off-hire clause**.

Breakdown clause A clause contained in a charterparty whereby, if time is lost due to the vessel being inoperative, it automatically goes 'off hire' until it returns to seaworthiness. The clause may allow a certain time in respect of an agreed-upon breakdown, after which no charter fees are payable until the vessel is in commission again. See also **Charterparty**; **Off-hire clause**.

Break-even analysis A type of economic analysis with the object of establishing the point where total revenue equals total costs and profit equals zero.

Breakeven point The revenue level at which a business neither makes a profit nor incurs a loss. At the breakeven point, the business revenue derived equals the total of both fixed and variable expenses. See also **Profit**.

•**Breaking bulk** Unpacking something contained; misappropriating property.

Maritime law The opening of the cargo being carried by a ship so as to unload it: for example (TAS) Marine Act 1976 s 4(1). Bulk may be broken in order to sell the cargo or to take samples. A clause may be included in a charterparty or bill of lading requiring the freight to be paid before breaking bulk. See also **Bill of lading**; **Cargo**; **Charterparty**; **Freight**.

Bretton Woods Agreement An agreement on the aims of post-war monetary policy reached at an international monetary and financial conference held at Bretton Woods in New Hampshire, United States in 1944. See also **International Monetary Fund**; **Articles of Agreement of the International Bank for Reconstruction and Development 1945**.

Bretton Woods Conference See **United Nations Monetary and Financial Conference**.

•**Bribe** A gift to a person as an inducement to that person to breach a duty owed to a third party: *Attorney-General (Hong Kong) v Reid* [1994] 1 AC 324 at 330. When a bribe is offered and accepted in money or in kind, the money or property constituting the bribe belongs in law to the recipient: *Attorney-General for Hong Kong v Reid*. However, he or she must pay and account for the bribe to the person to whom the duty was owed: *Attorney-General for Hong Kong v Reid*. A bribe is a type of secret profit. See also **Secret profits**.

•**Bribery** The common law offence of giving or offering a bribe to a public officer to induce the officer to act otherwise than in accordance with his or her duty: *Day v Rugala* (1978) 20 ACTR 3; *Thiess v TCN Channel Nine Pty Ltd (No 5)* [1994] 1 Qd R 156 at 180. The offence is complete whether or not the offer is accepted: *Herscu v R* (1991) 173 CLR 276; 103 ALR 1; *R v Allen* (1992) 27 NSWLR 398; 62 A Crim R 251; *R v Glynn* (1994) 33 NSWLR 139; 71 A Crim R 537. See also **Bribe; Corruption; Secret Commission**.

Bridge finance 1. A temporary loan advanced by a bank or other lending body to tide a customer over a period of difficulty, for example while buying one property and selling another when there is a mismatch in timing. **2.** Large temporary loans made by investment banking firms to clients involved in corporate takeovers. See also **Junk bond; Loan**.

British banking Traditionally, three categories of banks operate in the United Kingdom. First, deposit banks or clearing banks with their network of branches, which includes the 'Big Four', Barclays, Lloyds, Midland, and National Westminster. Second, merchant or investment banks such as Hambros, Morgan Grenfell, and Kleinwort Benson. Third, United Kingdom offices of foreign banks, many of which concentrate on international banking. These include major American, Asian, and European banks operating through branches and representative offices. See also **Merchant Bank**.

British banking system A banking system comprising a central bank, the Bank of England established in 1964 which supervises the banking system and carries out the monetary policy of the British government, merchant banks, the National Savings Bank and the commercial banks, much of whose business is conducted by Barclays, Lloyds, Midland, National Westminster, and the Scottish banks. In Britain, there are about 300 recognised banks in all including foreign banks. There are over 14,000 bank branches throughout the nation. See also **Bank of England**.

Broadbanding In industrial relations, the practice of bringing together in a single classification or occupation a number of jobs that previously had separate individual classifications. It reduces the number of job classifications within an enterprise or award, creating a more streamlined employment structure. Broadbanding often involves establishing a small number of skill-based levels, to replace numerous job classifications based on the particular task done by the worker. See also **Industrial award**.

Brocage See **Brokerage**.

Brokage See **Brokerage**.

•**Broker** A mercantile agent employed to make contracts for the purchase or sale of property or goods, who usually contracts in the name of the principal and is not entrusted with possession of the goods or documents of title: *Milford v Hughes* (1846) 16 M&W 174; 153 ER 1148.

See also **Agency; Agent; Factor; Mercantile agent; Principal; Securities business**.

Brokerage The fee charged by a broker for the broker's services. Also known as 'brocage' or 'brokage'. See also **Agent; Broker; Commission; Good faith; Insurance broker**.

Brokerage clause A clause contained in a charter-party, setting out the rate of commission due to a broker for brokerage services at the conclusion of the charter-party. See also **Broker; Charterparty; Commission**.

Broker's slip In insurance law, a document prepared by an insurance broker containing details of the risk for which he or she will arrange or has arranged cover. Also known as 'broker's placing slip'. See also **Broker; Brokerage; Co-insurance; Insurance contract**.

Bubble Act The (UK) Bubble Act 1720 (6 Geo I c 18) under which the predecessors of the modern business corporation appeared. The term 'bubble company' developed at that time to describe the sudden appearance and the insubstantial nature of many of the new companies. The term 'South Sea Bubble' is generally used to refer to this boom at the beginning of the 18th century. The Act was passed in an effort to control the abuses occurring during the boom. It was England's first attempt at general company legislation. The Act was finally repealed in 1825. An important result of the Bubble Act was the development of the deed of settlement company. The deed of settlement company served as the model for the internal constitution of the registered company when it appeared in 1844. See also **Corporations law; Deed of settlement company**.

Bucket shop An unauthorised office for gambling in stocks or speculating on markets. Traditionally a bucket shop was a shop that sold goods outside the official system and was therefore able to undercut the market. A travel agency that sells cheap airline tickets, but provides no additional services, is known as a bucket shop. See also **Bucketing; Trade**.

Bucketing The failure of a broker to execute trades on a recognised futures exchange when instructed to do so by a client. Normally the broker or an associated company will take a principal position against the client. The orders are normally telexed offshore to create the illusion that they are being executed, when in fact they are not. Bucketing is prohibited by Corporations Law ss 1258, 1260. See also **Sydney Futures Exchange**.

•**Budget** An estimate of expected expenditure and income, for a specific period of time.

Corporations A financial and quantitative statement, prepared in advance, of the policy to be pursued by a company or other organisation during a defined period of time, to serve specified objectives.

•**Building** Generally, a substantial structure or edifice with a roof and walls. Its meaning is relevant in several legal contexts.

Building and construction **1.** For planning purposes, any building, part of a building, structure or part thereof, or fixture attached to land: (NSW) Local Government Act 1993 s 3, Dictionary; (NSW) Environmental Planning and Assessment Act 1979 s 4(1).

Generally it does not include a movable dwelling or structure unless it can be fixed on site: *Hay Shire Council v Crease* [1973] 1 NSWLR 545; *Aquatic Airways Pty Ltd v Warringah Shire Council* (1990) 71 LGRA 10. Erection and use of buildings is controlled by environmental planning legislation and other instruments as falling within the term 'development'. **2.** A structure or part of a structure: (NSW) Housing Act 1976 s 4.

Insurance A structure with a roof and a support for that roof: *Hilderbrandt v Stephen* [1964] NSWR 740. Whether a structure constitutes a building is a question of fact and degree: *Lavy v London County Council* [1895] QB 577. The term may also be used to include a fence, wall, provision for lighting, heating, refrigeration, water supply, drainage and sewerage, and any other appurtenance of a building: for example (NSW) Housing Act 1912 s 2(1).

•**Building Code of Australia** *Abbr* – BCA A uniform set of technical requirements for the design and construction of buildings and other structures throughout Australia. The objective of the BCA is to ensure that acceptable standards of structural sufficiency, fire safety, health, and amenity are maintained for the benefit of the community. See also **Building regulations**.

•**Building contract** A contract in which one person (the 'contractor') agrees to perform building or engineering works for another (the 'proprietor' or 'employer'). See also **Subcontract; Supplier**.

Building mortgage A mortgage given to secure sums advanced to finance the construction of a building on land the subject of the mortgage. Progressive sums are advanced as progress payments fall due under a building contract, with the extent of security over the land increasing as the value of the land and building increases. Where the final amount to be secured under such a mortgage is ascertainable, a building mortgage may be an exception to the rule that further advances may not be tacked to the original advances by a mortgagee who has notice of a subsequent intervening mortgage: *Matzner v Clyde Securities Ltd* [1975] 2 NSWLR 293. See also **Mortgage; Tacking**.

•**Building regulations** Technical requirements for the design and construction of buildings and other structures, and procedures for administration of these requirements by local government authorities, private building surveyors, or other authorised persons or bodies, prescribed by State and Territory legislation: for example (NSW) Local Government Act 1993; (VIC) Building Act 1993; (QLD) Building Act 1975. The technical provisions are largely governed by the Building Code of Australia, which forms part of State and Territory building legislation. Building regulations are generally administered by local government authorities: *Sutherland Shire Council v Heyman* (1985) 157 CLR 424; 60 ALR 1. See also **Building Code of Australia**.

•**Building society** A society registered or incorporated as a building society, cooperative housing society or similar society under a law relating to such societies that is in force in a State or Territory: (CTH) Privacy Act 1988 s 6(1). Building societies are non-profit, non-bank financial institutions that apply the funds generated by members' deposits and the money raised from issuing its shares to providing financial accommodation to its members for the purchase of residential buildings or for residential development. See also **Financial institutions scheme; Society**.

Building society account For the purposes of the (CTH) Social Security Act 1991, an account maintained by a person with an organisation registered as a permanent building society under a law of a State or Territory into which moneys received on deposit by the organisation from the person are paid: (CTH) Social Security Act 1991 s 23(1).

•**Bull** A dealer in shares who, believing prices are about to rise, buys shares in the hope of selling them back again at a higher price, thereby making a profit; the opposite of a bear. A bull aims to make a profit on the shares without ever paying for them. See also **Bear; Boom-market**.

Bull market A market in which prices are rising. See also **Bear market**.

Bullet loan A loan that requires a one-time payment of principal and interest at its termination. It is not expected to be repaid gradually (in instalments) but in a single lump sum at the end of its term. It is similar to a balloon maturity loan, the main difference being that unlike the latter, a bullet loan has no identified source of repayment. To pay off such a loan the borrower may have to refinance, liquidate assets, or sell collateral. The term originated in the United States. Also known as 'single payment loan'. See also **Loan**.

Bullion The bulk form of precious metals, such as gold or silver. See also **Cash dealer; Goods; London Gold Market**.

Bundling The provision by a bank of a number of products to customers as a composite product. See also **Banking business; Banking service**.

Bunker clause A clause contained in a charterparty, stipulating that the charterer of the vessel must pay for the fuel contained in the bunkers at the port of delivery of the vessel, and that the owner must pay for the remaining fuel at the time of redelivery. In this context, the fuel is referred to as the 'bunker'. See also **Charterer; Charterparty**.

Burden of a contract The liability to perform one's obligations created by a contract with another. The burden of a contract can only be assigned with the consent of both parties to the contract as well as the person to whom the burden is being assigned: *Tolhurst v Associated Portland Cement Manufacturers (1900) Ltd* [1902] 2 KB 660 at 668. See also **Assignment; Performance**.

•**Burden of proof** Under the common law accusatorial system, the duty of one party (usually the party bringing the proceedings against another) to make out the case against the other party and to prove to the court that the case has been established. The burden of proof has two components: the evidential burden and the legal burden: *Purkess v Crittenden* (1965) 114 CLR 164 at 167-8; [1966] ALR 98. The evidential burden denotes which party has the burden of establishing a prima facie case on an issue; the legal burden denotes which party will lose on an issue in cases of doubt. The legal burden lies on the party who alleges or asserts an issue: *Currie v Dempsey* (1967) 2 NSWR 532; 69 SR (NSW) 116 at 125. In criminal cases, the prosecution generally bears both the legal and the evidential burden in relation to all facts in issue which relate to the guilt of the accused: *Woolmington v DPP* [1935] AC 462 at 481; *R v Falconer* (1990) 171 CLR 30; 96 ALR 545. In civil cases the plaintiff generally bears both the legal and evidential burden in relation to all facts in issue which relate to establishing the cause of action: for example *Munce v Vinidex Tubemakers Pty Ltd* [1974] 2 NSWLR 235. Also known as 'onus of proof'. See also **Balance of probabilities; Beyond reasonable doubt; Evidential burden; Legal burden; Standard of proof**.

•**Business** An activity undertaken as a commercial enterprise on a going concern basis, or engaged in for the purpose of profit on a continuous and repetitive basis: *Hope v Bathurst City Council* (1980) 144 CLR 1; 29 ALR 577.

Industrial law A trade, manufacture, undertaking, or calling of employers: (CTH) Industrial Relations Act 1988 s 189(3).

Partnerships and joint ventures A trade, occupation, or profession: for example, (NSW) Partnership Act 1892 s 45. Work that is entirely exploratory or preparatory cannot be characterised as constituting or forming part of a business, nor can the participants be described at that stage as carrying on or conducting a business: *Pioneer Concrete Services Ltd v Galli* [1985] 1 VR 675; 4 IPR 227. See also **Carrying on business; Enterprise**.

Taxation and revenue Any profession, trade, employment, vocation, or calling, but not occupation as an employee: (CTH) Income Tax Assessment Act 1936 s 6(1). See also **Business day; Business income**.

Business affairs Matters which relate to the activities of a business undertaking which is carried on in an organised manner with the purpose of obtaining profits or gains (whether or not they are actually obtained). A one-off commercial transaction which is entered into by an individual in relation to his or her domestic situation is generally the personal affairs of that person rather than business affairs.

Business asset Property whether tangible or intangible used for the purpose of earning income, usually otherwise than as an employee, or otherwise producing a profit.

Corporations An asset that forms part of a business undertaking as opposed to an individual's personal estate. Business assets include goodwill, plant, fixtures, fittings, stock-in-trade and book debts: *Re Chetkovich* [1965] ALR 342.

Business combination Any business transaction where one company combines with or obtains control over another company, regardless of whether the control is formal legal control or not. A conglomerate business combination occurs when companies participating in different industries combine. A horizontal business combination occurs when companies combine that have similar products or are competing in the same market. A vertical business combination involves companies combining where the output from one can be substituted as the input for the other. See also **Amalgamation; Control**.

Business Council of Australia *Abbr* – BCA A national business research and liaison group formed in 1983 as a result of a merger of the Australian Industries Development Association and the Business Round Table.

Business cycle Trade cycle. Alternating periods of trade boom and slump, especially characteristic of 19th century business activity in Britain when cycles of this nature occurred at fairly regular intervals. The period 1792-1913 revealed an average of eight year intervals between one boom and the next. During boom periods, employment, wages, prices, profits and production all rose together, only to decline during the ensuing slump. During the 20th century, the characteristics changed. The whole of the period 1919-1939 was characterised by slump upon which was superimposed the Great Depression of 1929-1935. The effects were worldwide with some 25 million unemployed. For some 30 years following the 1939-45 war, the developed world experienced full employment; from about 1975, the situation deteriorated with rising unemployment.

•**Business day** A work day. Business day is defined frequently in statutes, with minor variations. **1.** Any day other than Christmas Day, Good Friday, a Sunday, or a bank holiday: (CTH) Bills of Exchange Act 1909 ss 98(3)-(5). Saturday is regarded as a bank holiday. **2.** A day that is not a Saturday, Sunday or a public or bank holiday: Corporations Law s 9. **3.** A day other than a public or bank holiday, weekend (including a long weekend), or court holiday: for example (CTH) Insurance Contracts Act 1984 s 11. **4.** A day other than a Saturday, Sunday, or public holiday in the place concerned: (CTH) Fringe Benefits Tax Assessment Act 1986 s 136; (CTH) Income Tax Assessment Act 1936 s 51AGB(1). See also **Business**.

Business efficacy Acheiving desired commercial results. A court will imply a term in a written contract where it is necessary to do so to give it business efficacy: for example *Butts v O'Dwyer* (1952) 87 CLR 267. See also **Commercial contract; Implied term**.

Business finance The provision of funds to assist a company or enterprise during an adverse period of mismatch between receipts and payments. The sources of short-term finance include trade and consumer credit, running down of internal financial assets, factoring of invoices, selective reduction of inventories, intercompany loans, overdrafts, term loans, commercial bills, or promissory notes. The sources of long-term finance include corporate debentures, bonds and mortgages, share issues and calls, leasing arrangements, tax exempt financing, and long-term borrowing from banks and institutions.

•**Business income** Income or profits derived from carrying on any profession, trade, employment, vocation, or calling, excluding income derived from occupation as an employee. See also **Business**.

Business judgment rule The rule that the business judgment of the directors of a company, as long as it is exercised in good faith and not for improper purposes, is not open to review by the courts: *Harlowe's Nominees Pty Ltd v Woodside (Lakes Entrance) Oil Co NL* (1968) 121 CLR 483. See also **Directors' duties**.

Business Migration Program *Abbr* – BMP A program of migration to encourage investors, executives, and entrepreneurs to migrate to Australia. Applicants must pass the business skills points test. See also **Business skills points test**.

• **Business name** The name, style, title, or designation under which a business is carried on: for example (NSW) Business Names Act 1962 s 4; (VIC) Business Names Act 1962 s 4; (QLD) Business Names Act 1962 s 3. See also **Company name**.

Business opportunity doctrine See **Corporate opportunity doctrine**.

• **Business premises** Premises at which a business is undertaken or carried on: (CTH) Fringe Benefits Tax Assessment Act 1986 s 136. The term is significant in the context of legislation regulating commercial tenancy agreements. See also **Business; Premises; Shop premises**.

• **Business records** Records documenting the operation of a business, particularly its financial transactions and status. See also **Accounting record**.

• **Business rules** See **Australian stock exchange business rules**.

• **Business skills points test** A points test used to determine eligibility to obtain a visa under the Business Migration Program. Applicants must obtain a requisite number of points as set out in (CTH) Migration Regulations 1994 Sch 7. Points are awarded for the size of the annual turnover, employee levels, labour costs, total business assets, applicant's age and language skills, government sponsorship, and net personal assets. See also **Business Migration Program**.

Business trust See **Trading trust**.

• **Business undertaking** A venture where a person, trust, joint venture, government agency, or other entity engages in economic activity: for example (QLD) Queensland Development Corporation Act 1994 s 3; Corporations Regulations Sch 5 cl 1(1). See also **Business**.

Butterfly deposit An arrangement that enables a depositor to be guaranteed a minimum interest rate, while having the opportunity to take advantage of fluctuations in foreign exchange markets.

Butterfly spread 1. In an options market, a situation in which an investor holds both a bullish and a bearish spread, with one of the options in each spread having the same strike price. The purpose is to manage risk. **2.** In a futures market, a straddle position in three delivery months in the pattern of one-two-one. An example is an agreement to sell one futures contract maturing in December, to buy two futures contracts maturing in March, and to sell one futures contract maturing in June. Again, the purpose is to manage risk.

Butterworths Australia One of Australia's largest legal reference information publishers. Founded in 1818 as a law bookselling and publishing business in London, Butterworths began distributing law publications in Australia from Sydney in 1910. Butterworths Australia currently publishes a wide range of legal books, journals, loose-leaf publications, newsletters, and encyclopedias in paper form. In the electronic sphere, Butterworths Australia has developed the largest database of legal information in the Southern Hemisphere, providing an expanding array of CD-Rom 'libraries' and on-line services. Butterworths Australia is part of the Butterworths group, which also has branches in New Zealand, Singapore, Malaysia, Hong Kong, Canada, South Africa, and the United Kingdom. See also **Law reports; On-line**.

Buy on opening An order placed with a broker to buy a futures or option contract at the market price on opening. See also **Futures contract; Option**.

• **Buy-back** The purchase by a company of shares in itself: Corporations Law s 9. Buy-backs are prohibited under the Corporations Law (s 205), although there are exceptions (s 206 B). See also **Buy-back arrangement; Buy-back authorisation; Buy-back covenant; Buy-back scheme; Maintenance of capital**.

Buy-back arrangement In relation to a deed regarding prescribed interests, an arrangement made to ensure that the management company can comply with a buy-back covenant contained in the deed: Corporations Law s 9. When offering prescribed interests, the deed under which they may be offered (s 1065) must have an adequate buy-back arrangement which is maintained at all times: s 1069(1)(d). See also **Buy-back; Buy-back authorisation; Buy-back covenant; Buy-back scheme**.

• **Buy-back authorisation** The required approval of the shareholders of a company for a company buy-back where the 10 per cent in 12 months limit is breached or there is a selective 10 per cent back: Corporations Law ss 206D(1), 206E(1). See also **Buy-back; Buy-back arrangement; Buy-back covenant; Buy-back scheme**.

• **Buy-back covenant** In relation to a deed regarding prescribed interests, a covenant binding the management company, if asked by the holder of the prescribed interest to which the deed relates, to buy the prescribed interest, or cause it to be bought at the price agreed to in the deed: Corporations Law s 9. See also **Buy-back; Buy-back arrangement; Buy-back authorisation; Buy-back scheme**.

Buy-back provision See **Buy-back**.

• **Buy-back scheme** Formerly, a type of permitted buy-back where the company makes uniform offers to each shareholder to buy back a uniform proportion of each shareholder's ordinary shares: Corporations Law s 206FB (repealed). Each shareholder has equal access to the offers. Now known as 'equal access buy-back scheme'. See also **Share buy-back; Equal access buy-back scheme; Authorised buy-back**.

• **Buyer** A person who buys or agrees to buy goods: for example (NSW) Sale of Goods Act 1923 s 5(1); (VIC) Goods Act 1958 s 3(1); (QLD) Sale of Goods Act 1896 s 3(1). See also **Goods; Purchaser; Seller**.

Buyer in possession after sale The situation where a person who has bought or agreed to buy goods is in possession of the goods or of the documents of title to the goods: (NSW) Sale of Goods Act 1923 s 28(1). See also **Buyer; Possession; Seller**.

Buyer level injury See **Price discrimination**.

Buyer's option The right to purchase something within a given period of time, under conditions agreed in advance of the actual sale.

Buyer's representative clause In maritime law, a clause contained in an agreement for the sale of a vessel by which the seller allows the buyer's representative to board the vessel before delivery in order to assess the vessel's manoeuvrability, capabilities, and general operation. The representative boards the vessel at the sole risk and expense of the buyer.

Buyer's right to examine goods The right of a purchaser not to accept goods unless and until he or she has had a reasonable opportunity of examining them for the purpose of ascertaining whether they are in conformity with the contract: for example (NSW) Sale of Goods Act 1923 s 37(1). See also **Buyer; Contract; Seller**.

Buying hedge A long hedge; a hedging transaction in which futures contracts are bought to provide protection against the possible increased cost of commodities.

Buying in In a share market, action taken by a stockbroker when a client fails to deliver certain shares by a certain date.

Buying straw hats in winter A strategy of buying that goes against the market trend.

C

Cabotage Trade or navigation in coastal waters.

Aviation The right of an aircraft of a state to remuneration for taking on and then dropping off passengers, mail and cargo in another state. A state has the right to refuse permission for cabotage: Convention on International Civil Aviation 1944 art 7, scheduled in (CTH) Air Navigation Act 1920 s 4, Sch 1. In Australia, permission to claim cabotage for unscheduled flights must be sought from the secretary to the Department of Transport and Communications: (CTH) Air Navigation Act 1920 s 14.

Maritime law The carriage of freight and passengers between any two ports in the same country. It does not matter that the ports are on different coasts, provided that the different coasts are all coasts of the same country.

Trade and commerce A statutory monopoly granted to shipping companies and trade unions, restricting Australian coastal shipping to Australian-flag vessels. In the late 1980s, this monopoly came under close scrutiny on the grounds that, as a matter of fairness, shipping should not remain shielded from international competition when manufacturing and export industries had been required to adjust to competitive international trading conditions.

Cairns Group of Fair Trading Nations A group of 14 nations established in 1986 to lobby for fair trade in agriculture, active within the General Agreement on Tariffs and Trade (GATT). Australia was instrumental in the formation of the Cairns Group, whose first meeting was held in Canberra. The purposes of the group are to achieve a reduction in production and export subsidies, increase access to protected markets, and better manage agricultural surpluses. The members of the group are Argentina, Australia, Brazil, Canada, Chile, Columbia, Fiji, Hungary, Indonesia, Malaysia, New Zealand, the Philippines, Thailand, and Uruguay. See also **General Agreement on Tariffs and Trade 1947**.

CAL See **Copyright Agency Limited**.

CALDB See **Companies Auditors and Liquidators Disciplinary Board**.

Call In company law, a demand by a company for part or all of the capital outstanding on a contributing share. Holders of shares in a limited liability company are liable for payment, while holders of shares in a no liability company may avoid payment of the call by forfeiting their shares. See also **Call on contributories; Capital; Partly-paid share; Limited company; No liability company**.

Call bull spread On the stock market, a technique which involves buying a call option with a low strike price and selling one with a high strike price. This type of strategy is appropriate when the user believes that the price of the underlying security will rise, though not by very much. See also **Call option**.

Call money Deposits placed in the money market which can be withdrawn on demand.

Call on contributories In relation to the winding up of a company, a demand made by the liquidator or the court on persons liable to contribute to the company's assets: Corporations Law ss 483(3), 506(1)(d). See also **Call; Call on shares; Contributing shareholder; Partly-paid share**.

Call on shares The process by which a company resolves that a member or members should pay a specified sum in respect of shares held. See also **Capital; Uncalled share capital**.

Call option A contract conveying for a specified period of time the right, but not the obligation, to buy at any time during the specified period ('currency of the option') a certain number of issued securities at a price fixed at the time the option is given ('exercise price'). See also **Assignment; Call on shares; Option; Property; Put option; Sale; Securities**.

Call paid A term used on a stock exchange to signify that particular securities are traded on the basis that a particular call has been paid. See also **Call; Securities**.

Call premium The premium an issuer must pay if a bond is redeemed before maturity or a preferred stock is redeemed at an amount greater than the par value. See also **Bond; Call; Par value**.

Callable issue A security that can be redeemed by the issuer before its normal maturity. See also **Security**.

Callable swap A swap agreement that is activated only at the option of one party. See also **Option; Swap**.

Called-up share capital That part of a company's share capital which the company has demanded from shareholders. Ordinarily, payments made on application for, or allotment of, shares are not calls because the payments are made by persons who are not members, or because no calls are in fact made and the payments are made in accordance with the conditions of the allotment contract: *Cameron v FCT* (1941) 64 CLR 361 at 369. However the term 'called-up share capital' may be used to include all capital that has been paid, whether called or not, plus any capital which has been called but not yet paid, in contradistinction to 'unpaid capital' which refers to that part of the capital which has not been called. See also **Call on contributories; Call on shares; Par value; Share capital; Unpaid capital**.

•**Calling** Any trade, craft, occupation or classification of an employee ((WA) Industrial Relations Act 1979 s 7) and any manufacture, undertaking, or vocation ((QLD) Industrial Relations Act 1990 s 5).

Calls in advance Where shares in a company are issued and only part of their nominal value is required at that time to be paid to the company, the payment by a member of all or part of the unpaid balance on the nominal value of shares in advance of the company calling in that amount, so long as this is authorised by its articles of association: Corporations Law s 188. The prepayment is a loan which may earn interest irrespective of whether the company has made profits, but in the absence of special provision in the articles of association there can be no repayment of the capital amount paid in advance except in a winding up. See also **Call; Issue of new shares; Liquidation; Par value; Winding up**.

Campbell committee See **Campbell inquiry**.

Campbell inquiry The inquiry into the Australian financial system conducted between 1979 and 1981 by a six member committee chaired by Sir Keith Campbell. Some of the major initiatives undertaken by the Commonwealth Government following the report included removal of controls and restrictions on bank deposit rates, deposit maturities and lending volumes and rates, granting of new bank licenses, entry of foreign banks, and changes to prudential requirements. See also **Australian banking system; Banking commission; Committee of Inquiry into the Australian Financial System; Financial deregulation; Martin review; Wallis inquiry**.

Canberra Advance Bank A bank formed in 1990 following a merger between Civic Advance Bank and the Canberra Building Society. It is a wholly-owned subsidiary of Advance Bank Australia. See also **Australian Banking System**.

•**Cancellation** The making void or annulling, particularly of an instrument or transaction.

Bills of exchange and other negotiable instruments A method of discharging a negotiable instrument by which the holder intentionally cancels it, such cancellation being apparent on the instrument: (CTH) Bills of Exchange Act 1909 s 68; (CTH) Cheques and Payment Orders Act 1986 s 78. See also **Bill of exchange; Discharge of negotiable instrument; Discharge of party; Holder; Indorser**.

Deeds and other instruments Destruction or defacement of a deed or bond, or the seal of a deed, with the intention of rendering it void: for example *Banque Nationale de Paris v Falkirk Developments Ltd* (1977) 136 CLR 177; 13 ALR 377. A deed is also cancelled if a person who is to benefit under it alters it materially. See also **Alteration; Deed; Discharge; Void**.

Cancellation clause 1. A clause contained in a contract of carriage under which the contract may be terminated by the stipulated means if the stipulated circumstances occur. **2.** A clause which allows the charterer to cancel the contract if the ship fails to arrive at the loading port by the cancelling date: for example *Cheikh Boutros Selim El-Khoury v Ceylon Shipping Lines Ltd (The Madeliene)* [1967] 2 Lloyd's Rep 224. The clause can only be acted upon once the cancelling date has arrived. If the charterer invokes the clause, it may also sue the ship owner for damages for failing to send the ship on time. The charterer is not required to notify the ship owner of any intention to exercise its rights under this clause. If the charterer does not invoke the clause, the ship owner remains obligated to deliver the ship to the loading port, even though the cancelling date has passed and the charterer is not barred from claiming damages against the shipowner for failing to send the ship on time: *Westralian Farmers Ltd v Tyneside Line Ltd* (1928) 31 WALR 14. Also known as 'cancelling clause'. See also **Cancelling date; Charterer; Charterparty; Contract of carriage; Marine insurance**.

Cancellation notice In the context of insurance, written notice required by statute, given by an insurer to notify an insured of the insurer's intention to terminate a contract of insurance: (CTH) Insurance Contracts Act 1984 s 59(1). A cancellation notice has the effect of cancelling the contract no earlier than three business days (or, in the case of life insurance contracts, 20 business days) after the insured receives the notice, unless the insured enters into a re-instatement contract at an earlier time: (CTH) Insurance Contracts Act 1984 s 59(2). See also **Insurance contract; Life insurance**.

Cancelled credit payment A redemption of credits accumulated during the course of play on a poker machine by a payment other than directly from the machine. For example, where there are insufficient funds inside a poker machine, the club may pay the participant with a cheque or by some other means: (NSW) Registered Clubs Act 1976 s 86(1).

Cancelling date The date stipulated in a charter party as being the date by which the ship is required to arrive at the loading port. If the ship fails to arrive by this date, the charterer may rescind. See also **Cancellation clause; Charterparty; Contract of carriage; Marine insurance**.

Canvassing The soliciting of subscriptions for a particular product or service. Under Queensland law, it excludes communication by post, telephone or telex: (QLD) Credit Act 1987 (repealed) s 123(5) (now replaced by Uniform Consumer Credit Code). In the other jurisdictions, it may be limited to oral representations made in person at the home or business of the debtor. See also **Credit hawker**.

Cap A put option, or a series of put options, protecting the buyer from a rise in interest rates. See also **Caption; Put option**.

•**Capable of being registered** In intellectual property, a design whose inherent characteristics answer the statutory definition of a design, disregarding requirements which are temporal or historical in quality (such as novelty or originality). See also **Copyright; Applied industrially**.

•**Capacity** The power, ability or competence of a person or body.

Agency The competence of a person to act as principal or agent. All persons of sound mind are competent to act as agents, and thus a minor may be an agent: *Re D'Angibau* (1880) 15 Ch D 228. See also **Agency; Agent; Principal**.

Economics The estimated or achieved maximum level of production from a plant on a sustained basis allowing for all necessary shutdown periods. The capacity factor is calculated: capacity factor = output for period/(rated capacity x hours in period).

Tort The ability to commit a tort. A plaintiff's capacity is a relevant issue in determining liability for intentional torts. Capacity may come into question where an alleged tort has been committed by a lunatic or a child.

See also **Incapacity; Intentional tort; Tort**.

Capacity costs Fixed or overhead costs or charges; costs and derived charges that do not vary with the total amount of goods or services produced, but only with additions to the total capacity of the system. In relation to electricity generation, capacity costs are those incurred in the initial construction of power stations, including the cost of land, the initial stockpile or charge of fuel, transmission and distribution networks, and control centres.

Capacity to contract The capacity to enter into contractual relations. There is a presumption at common law that a person who enters into a contract has full capacity to do so, and a person alleging that they are protected from the normal consequences of their actions must bear the burden of proving incapacity: *Borthwick v Carruthers* (1787) 1 Term Rep 648; 99 ER 1300. Circumstances that may lead to contractual incapacity include minority, mental disability, and intoxication.

Capacity to pay principle A wage fixing principle by which an industrial tribunal awards increases in wage rates on the basis of increases in productivity and the capacity of the economy or the industry to support wage increases: *Basic Wage Inquiry* (1931) 30 CAR 2. See also **Industrial tribunal; Wage fixation; Wage indexation**.

•**Capital** 1. In a general business or mercantile sense, the assets with which a business is carried on; the total funds provided by lenders and by owners to run a business: *Incorporated Interests Pty Ltd v FCT* (1943) 67 CLR 508 at 515; [1943] ALR 165. 2. The net value of a company's assets: *Archibald Howie Pty Ltd v Cmr of Stamp Duties* (NSW) (1948) 77 CLR 143 at 159. 3. One of the factors of production, being a commodity used in the production of other goods and services. See also **Business finance; Factors of production; Loan capital; Share; Share capital**.

Taxation and revenue 1. Expenditure establishing the business entity, structure, or organisation set up to yield a profit, or expenditure or outlays that replace or enlarge the business entity, structure or organisation: *Sun Newspapers Ltd v FCT* (1938) 61 CLR 337. 2. The owner's interest in the assets of a business, represented by the residual of total assets over total liabilities to external parties. Also known as 'owner's equity'. See also **Allowable deduction**.

Capital accumulation An increase in a stock of land, machinery, buildings and other structures, and inventories capable of being used for the production of goods and services. See also **Capital**.

Capital adequacy guidelines Guidelines for the banking system issued by the Reserve Bank of Australia in 1988, in support of the policy of the Bank for International Settlements to improve capital adequacy standards worldwide. Until 1988, Australian banks were required to support assets on their balance sheets with a six per cent capital base. Since 1988, they have been required to provide an eight per cent capital base for both off-balance and on-balance assets, on a risk-weighted basis. Of this eight per cent, at least half must comprise Tier 1 (highest quality) capital, the remainder being Tier 2 (supplementary) capital. The risk-ratio approach relates a bank's capital to its total credit risks: the higher the aggregate risks, the greater the capital resources that are required. See also **Australian banking system; Bank for International Settlements; Capital base; Reserve Bank of Australia**.

•**Capital amount** 1. An amount used in the calculation of an allowable tax deduction for certain property used in the rehabilitation of mines and quarries. 2. In relation to property, the lesser of the total expenditure of a capital nature of the taxpayer in respect of the property and the value of the property as at the date of termination of the use of the property: (CTH) Income Tax Assessment Act 1936 s 122 KA(12). See also **Allowable capital expenditure; Allowable deduction**.

Capital asset pricing model *Abbr* – CAPM A traditional method for determining the viability of business investments. The minimum return required on equity is calculated by adding a risk premium to the 'risk free' rate, that is, the 10 year government bond rate. Thus, if the bond rate is 10 per cent, the addition of a risk premium of six per cent gives a total of 16 per cent. Inflationary expectations may then be deducted to give a real rate of return on equity. The long-term bond rate is subject to changes in monetary policy and the risk premium assumed is necessarily imprecise. see also **Risk assessment**.

Capital base The capital employed in a business, essentially derived from paid-up shares, capital reserves and long-term loans. See also **Business finance; Capital; Capital reserve**.

Capital beneficiary The beneficiary of a capital fund whose rights are postponed to the rights of the income beneficiaries to receive income for a stated period. See also **Income beneficiary**.

Capital charges Charges that include interest on the amount of capital employed and provision for depreciation or repayment of principal. See also **Capital; Depreciation; Interest**.

Capital cost component In relation to production, the capital charges attributable to each unit of output, calculated: capital charges/units of output, where the capital charges are the sum of the annual interest charges on the capital employed plus the annual depreciation charges, and the units of output relate to the year under consideration. See also **Capital; Factors of production**.

Capital deepening An increase in the stock of capital relative to the quantities of all other resources, including labour. see also **Capital**.

•**Capital employed** The capital in use in a business; the total assets minus the current liabilities. See also **Capital; Factors of production; Return on capital employed**.

Capital employed, return on See **Return on capital employed**.

•**Capital expenditure** See **Capital**.

Capital formation Expenditure on fixed capital assets (land, buildings, plant, machinery and transport) either for replacing or adding to the stock of business assets. Expenditure on routine repairs and maintenance is excluded. During the year, fixed capital resources are consumed, as a result of wear and tear and progressive obsolescence. To obtain the value of net capital formation, the value of capital depreciation is deducted from the value of gross capital formation. See also **Business asset; Capital.**

Capital gain 1. A financial gain from selling assets such as land, buildings, residences, businesses, or securities at a profit over the original historic value. 2. The excess of the consideration in respect of the disposal of an asset over that asset's indexed cost base: (CTH) Income Tax Assessment Act 1936 s 160 z(1). If the asset has not been held for more than 12 months, then the capital gain is the excess of the consideration on disposal of the asset over the asset's cost base: s 160Z(3). See also **Asset; Asset disposal; Capital gains tax; Capital loss; Cost base; Indexed cost base; Listed personal-use asset; Net capital gain; Net capital loss; Non-listed personal-use asset.**

•**Capital gains tax** *Abbr* – CGT A tax imposed on the gain from the disposal or deemed disposal of an asset acquired after 19 September 1985 which is owned by a taxpayer. The tax is imposed upon the net capital gain which accrues to the taxpayer. See also **Assessable income; Asset; Asset disposal; Capital gain; Capital loss; Cost base; Income taxation; Indexed cost base; Net capital gain; Principal residence; Rollover relief.**

Capital goods Equipment made for the purpose of producing consumer goods and services, or other capital goods, for example heavy machinery, machine tools, rolling stock, steam generators and robots. See also **Capital.**

Capital growth 1. In financial markets, a return to an investor by way of an increase in capital value allowing for the negative effect of inflation. 2. In the economy generally, an increase in the value of real assets or capital allowing for inflation and the depreciation of such assets. See also **Capital; Capital growth.**

Capital guaranteed investment A financial investment in which repayment of the amount invested is guaranteed by a substantial organisation such as a leading insurance company or bank, or by a government. See also **Capital; Investment.**

Capital improvement An improvement of a fixed, permanent, and substantial character that is necessary for the beneficial, lawful occupation of land: *Re Union Bank* (1893) 3 LCC 313. See also **Capital value; Improved capital value; Improvement.**

Capital inflow The movement of capital into a country. See also **Capital.**

Capital injection The acquisition and utilisation of additional funds by an organisation. Such funds may be raised through an issue of shares or bonds or through an allocation by a parent or associated company. See also **Capital.**

Capital intensive industry An industry in which the capital to labour ratio used in production is much higher than the average ratio for industry as a whole. Examples of capital intensive industry include aluminium smelters, petroleum refineries, power stations, open-cut mines and airlines. See also **Capital to labour ratio.**

Capital lease Any lease that meets one or more of the following criteria: the lease transfers ownership to the lessee by the end of the lease term; the lease contains a bargain purchase option; the lease term is equal to 75 per cent or more of the economic life of the leased property; the present value at the beginning of the term of the minimum lease payments (excluding the portion of payments represented by executory costs such as insurance, maintenance, and taxes to be paid by the lessor, including profit) is equal to or exceeds 90 per cent of the excess of the fair value of the leased property to the lessor at the inception of the lease over any related investment tax credit retained and expected to be realised by the lesssor. A capital lease must be recorded by the lessee as both an asset and an obligation.

Capital loss A loss made on the disposal of a capital asset (that is, the asset is sold for an amount less than the book value of the asset). The excess of the reduced cost base of an asset to a taxpayer over the consideration in respect of the disposal of that asset: (CTH) Income Tax Assessment Act 1936 s 160Z(1). The capital loss is used to calculate a taxpayer's net capital gain or net capital loss for that year of income: s 160ZC. There are special rules for the treatment of capital gains or capital losses in relation to the disposal of a listed personal-use asset and a non-listed personal-use asset: ss 160ZQ, 160ZG. A capital loss is contrasted with a revenue loss, which is a loss from ordinary business operations. See also **Asset; Asset disposal; Capital; Capital gain; Capital gains tax; Cost base; Consideration in respect of disposal of an asset; Listed personal-use asset; Net capital loss; Non-listed personal-use asset.**

Capital maintenance adjustment Adjustment made under certain accounting models to an entity's capital to take account of the effects of price changes on the entity's assets and liabilities: Statement of Accounting Concepts SAC 4. See also **Capital maintenance principle; Profit and loss account.**

Capital maintenance principle See **Maintenance of capital.**

Capital market A market for both long term and intermediate financial instruments, including both the stock and futures markets, as well as markets for corporate and government bonds, and mortgages. See also **Bond; Capital market instrument; Financial market; Futures exchange; Stock market.**

Capital market instrument A financial instrument such as a company bond, debenture, share or a government and statutory authority bond. Following purchase in the primary market they may be at once sold in the secondary markets, giving them the important quality of liquidity. See also **Bond; Debenture; Primary market; Share.**

Capital market line *Abbr* – CML The line on a graph on which all efficient investment portfolios (theoretically) fall. The slope of the CML shows the current trade-off between the risk and return on the investment opportunities provided. See also **Efficient portfolio; Return; Risk.**

Capital movement The movement of money capital from one country to another to take advantage of higher interest rates or profits and perhaps political stability. Hot money moves rapidly in response to the slightest margins of gain. See also **Capital; Capital inflow**.

Capital output ratio For a given industrial technique, the ratio of the capital cost of the technique to the value added by the additional output.

Capital, partnership See **Partnership capital**.

Capital provision A provision in a will of a fixed sum of money from a deceased estate for the benefit of a specified beneficiary, as opposed to a provision based on income. See also **Annuity; Capital beneficiary; Income beneficiary**.

Capital reconstruction Alteration of the share capital of a company, if allowed by its articles of association, by creating new shares, consolidating and dividing its shares into larger or smaller amounts than those existing, converting or reconverting paid-up shares of any denominations into stock, or cancelling shares that have been forfeited: Corporations Law s 193. See also **Articles of Association; Capital; Paid-up share capital; Share capital**.

Capital redemption reserve fund Where redeemable preference shares are redeemed otherwise than out of the proceeds of a new issue of shares in a limited company, an amount of distributable profits equal to the redemption amount, put aside in its accounts as being thereafter non-distributable quasi-share capital: Corporations Law s 192(5). Thus the principle that a limited company may not reduce capital without court approval is maintained: s 192(5). The fund is not a sinking fund to provide for the redemption. Rather, it is a notional liability to cover the contingent liability to redeem the shares: *Comptroller of Stamps v Ashwick (Vic) No 4 Pty Ltd* (1987) 163 CLR 640 at 649; 76 ALR 161. See also **Authorised reduction of capital; Maintenance of capital; Preference share; Share premium account; Redeemable preference share**.

Capital reduction See **Authorised reduction of capital**.

Capital reserve An allocation of an amount in the accounts of a business or company to a reserve which is not available for profit or dividend distribution through the profit and loss account. See also **Capital; Dividend**.

Capital structure The financial resources made available for the operation of an enterprise by its proprietors and those lending to it. In a company the resources primarily made available by the proprietors are represented, in the balance sheet as 'share capital'. A company with share capital may, if authorised by its articles, alter the provisions in its memorandum relating to its capital structure by ordinary resolution: Corporations Law s 193(1). Once an operating enterprise has accumulated reserves of profits which are not intended for distribution, those form part of the capital structure. In addition to proprietors' funds, the capital structure includes loans provided by lenders (who may or may not include some or all of the proprietors themselves). See also **Capital; Official quotation; Share capital**.

Capital to labour ratio The ratio of capital equipment to labour used in production, expressed in terms of cost; for a given industrial technique, the ratio of the capital cost of the technique to the value added by the additional output. The higher the capital-to-labour ratio, the fewer workers needed per unit of output. See also **Capital; Capital goods; Capital intensive industry**.

Capital transaction The lending or borrowing of sums of money, or the transfer of assets. See also **Asset; Capital; Transaction**.

•**Capital value** In relation to the calculation of fair rent, refers to the market value: *Hume Investments Pty Ltd v Zucker* [1958] VR 623. See also **Capital improvement; Fee simple; Improved capital value; Improvement; Market value**.

Capitalisation The conversion of a company's undistributed profits into share capital: for example *Peter's American Delicacy Co Ltd v Heath* (1939) 61 CLR 457 at 496-7; [1939] ALR 124. See also **Bonus share issue; Distributable profits; Fully paid share; Issued share capital; Market capitalisation; Partly paid share; Share capital**.

Capitalisation of income In accounting, a method of determining the economic value of a firm by calculating the net present value of the firm's predicted net income. See also **Capitalised value; Economic efficiency; Net present value**.

Capitalisation of interest The adding of interest payments due to the principal of a loan, to be actually paid only when the loan itself is due to be repaid. During the 1980s, the capitalisation of interest by lenders attracted borrowers with speculative property projects with little or none of their own money to invest. With no regular payments required on loans, problems with the borrowers' projects remained camouflaged. The effect of this practice was also to reduce the lenders' cash flows. The situation was further obscured by the classification of such loans as 'performing'.

Capitalised value The present capital equivalent of a future stream of receipts; present worth or value.

Capped interest A regulation or agreement setting a maximum for the rate of interest charged on a loan. This may be guaranteed for a set period or indefinitely by government regulation. Home loans may be subject to a variable interest rate or a capped rate according to the terms of the loan. A capped rate home loan may fall, but cannot rise above the cap limit; a variable rate moves with the commercial market generally. New loans may be subject to variable, fixed or capped interest rates. See also **Home loan insurance; Interest**.

Caption An option over a cap. See also **Cap; Option**.

Captive market A market in which sellers (or buyers) are forced to accept prices and conditions imposed on them due to the availability of only one purchaser (or seller). This type of market is often the result of vertical integration and monopolisation within a small industry, and results in imperfect competition in the market. See also **Monopoly**.

•**Car** A motor car, station wagon, panel van, utility truck or similar vehicle, or any other road vehicle designed to carry a load of less than one tonne or fewer than nine passengers (other than motor cycles or similar vehicles): (CTH) Income Tax Assessment Act 1936 Sch 2 A cl 11(1). See also **Underlying business percentage**.

• **Car expense** An outgoing incurred in connection with: operating costs of a car such as registration, insurance, petrol, oil, servicing and cleaning costs; costs of borrowing money to acquire a car; costs of discharging a mortgage given as security for repayment of a car loan; interest on a car loan; lease charges; costs of preparing, registering, stamping, assigning, or surrendering a car lease; repairs; and depreciation: (CTH) Income Tax Assessment Act 1936 Sch 2A cl 11(2). Car expenses incurred by an employee or a self-employed person must generally comply with the substantiation rules in order to be deductible. See also **Allowable deduction**; **Car**; **Allowable deduction**; **Employment-related expense**; **Incurred**; **Substantiation**.

• **Car fringe benefit** A taxable fringe benefit where a car held by an employer or an associate of the employer is applied to the private use of an employee, is garaged or kept near the residence of an employee, is not at the business premises of the employer and an employee is entitled to private use of the car, or where an employee has custody and control of a car and the employee is not performing employment related duties: (CTH) Fringe Benefits Tax Assessment Act 1986 s 7. See also **Car parking benefit**; **Exempt car benefit**; **Fringe benefit**; **Fringe benefits tax**.

Car parking benefit A taxable fringe benefit payable by employers on car parking facilities provided to employees, to which special rules apply. An employer is taxed on the value (to an employee) of car parking facilities where: the facilities are provided on business premises situated within one kilometre of a commercial parking station; the car parked is owned or leased by the employee or any other person; the car is parked near the place of employment for more than four hours between 7am and 7pm, and the car is used by the employee to travel between their place of residence and employment: (CTH) Fringe Benefits Tax Assessment Act 1936 s 39A. See also **Fringe benefit**; **Fringe benefits tax**.

Carded rates Foreign currency exchange rates quoted by a trading bank each day for small foreign exchange transactions. See also **Foreign currency**; **Foreign currency exchange**; **Foreign currency transaction**; **Trading bank**.

Care and diligence The standard in relation to which an officer of a corporation must exercise his or her powers and carry out his or her duties. The degree of care and diligence is that which a reasonable person in a like position in a corporation would exercise in the corporation's circumstances: Corporations Law s 232(4). See also **Officer**; **Director**; **Director's duties**.

Care and skill, duty of See **Duty of care and skill**.

Care, employers' duty of See **Employers' duty of care**.

• **Cargo** Abbr – Cgo The goods carried on a ship, aircraft or vehicle. Unless the context otherwise signifies, 'cargo' means the entire load of the ship: *Barrowman v Drayton* (1876) 2 Ex D 15. In a policy of insurance, 'cargo' does not necessarily mean the whole loading: *Houghton v Gilbart* (1836) 7 Car & P 701; 173 ER 307. The Amended Hague Rules 1979 impose obligations to properly and carefully load, handle, stow, carry, keep, care for, and discharge cargo. See also **Amended Hague Rules 1979**; **Cargo book**; **Cargo papers**.

Cargo book A book maintained by a ship broker, ship's agent or other consignor's agent. It provides concise documentation of the goods being carried whether by land, sea or air, including records of the leading marks, numbers, types of packages, weights and measurements, shippers and consignees. See also **Cargo**; **Consignor**; **Consignee**; **Leading mark**; **Charterer**.

Cargo insurance A policy of insurance with respect to merchandise transported on a ship, aircraft, or by land vehicles. Traditionally, cargo insurance is viewed as falling into the category of marine insurance. The Australian market is dominated by procedures and policy wordings issued conjointly by the Institute of London Underwriters and the Corporation of Lloyd's. The (CTH) Insurance Contracts Act 1984 does not apply to contracts or proposed contracts of insurance to which the (CTH) Marine Insurance Act 1909 applies: (CTH) Insurance Contracts Act 1984 s 9(1)(d). Land risks incidental to sea voyages may be protected by a contract of marine insurance: (CTH) Marine Insurance Act 1909 s 8(1). See also **Cargo**; **Marine insurance**.

Cargo papers Documents required for loading or unloading cargoes. They include bills of lading, shipping orders, tally clerks' sheets, ships, stowage plans and ships' manifests. See also **Bill of lading**; **Cargo**.

• **Carriage** The transportation of passengers or goods gratuitously or for reward. See also **Carrier**; **Contract of carriage**.

Carriage by air The conveyance of passengers and goods using aircraft as the mode of transportation. Carriage by air is regulated by the common law applicable to carriers generally, by statutes such as the (CTH) Civil Aviation (Carriers' Liability) Act 1959, and by the terms of the contract of carriage. See also **Carriage by land**; **Carriage by sea**; **Carrier**; **Contract of carriage**; **Goods**.

Carriage by land The conveyance of passengers and goods using road or rail vehicles as the mode of transportation. Carriage by land is regulated by the common law applicable to carriers generally, by statute, and by the terms of the contract of carriage. See also **Carriage by air**; **Carriage by sea**; **Carrier**; **Contract of carriage**; **Goods**.

Carriage by sea The conveyance of passengers or goods using ships as the mode of transportation. Carriage by sea is regulated by the common law applicable to carriers generally, and by statutes such as the (CTH) Carriage of Goods by Sea Act 1991, and by the terms of the contract of carriage. See also **Carriage by air**; **Carriage by land**; **Carrier**; **Contract of carriage**; **Goods**.

Carriage forward An undertaking by the buyer of goods to meet the cost of delivery. See also **Contract of carriage**; **Sale of goods**.

Carriage of dangerous goods Transportation of goods that would be dangerous to life and limb, the carrier's property, other goods carried, or the environment, if not kept in some special way. A consignor impliedly warrants that goods carried are not dangerous, and may be liable regardless of knowledge of danger. A consignor must give notice of the dangerous nature of goods, and properly pack them. It is an offence to carry dangerous goods by road unlicensed: for example (NSW) Dangerous Goods Act 1975 s 11. Exceptions may apply to particular vehicles or small quantities of dangerous goods. A description of dangerous goods to be carried by sea must be distinctly marked on the container, and given to the ship owner or master when or before the goods are loaded: (CTH) Navigation Act 1912 s 249. It is an offence to knowingly send by or carry in a ship dangerous goods under a false description: (CTH) Navigation Act 1912 s 253. Goods discovered to be dangerous may be destroyed during the contract of carriage, without compensation being given to the owner: Amended Hague Rules 1979 art 4. See also **Carriage of goods; Consignor; Dangerous cargo; Dangerous goods; Dangerous load; Goods.**

• **Carriage of goods** The transportation, usually for reward, of goods by land, air or sea, from one place to another at the order of a consignor for delivery, or further delivery, to a consignee. The mere presence of goods on a travelling vehicle is not in itself sufficient to be carriage of those goods: *Baker v David Hose Pty Ltd* [1961] VR 176. See also **Cargo; Carriage by air; Carriage by land; Carriage by sea; Carriage of dangerous goods; Carrier; Consignee; Consignor; Goods.**

Carriage of passengers The transportation, usually for reward, of people by land, air or sea from one place to another. See also **Carriage by air; Carriage by land; Carriage by sea; Carrier.**

• **Carrier** One who receives passengers or goods for the purpose of carrying them for reward from one place to another, either under a special contract or as a common carrier. Carriage may be by land, air or sea. An extensive body of rules contained in the common law and statutes govern the obligations of common and private carriers. Airline operators, ship owners, bus proprietors and road hauliers are all carriers, as are courier services, taxi proprietors and the Australian Postal Corporation. See also **Carriage by air; Carriage by land; Carriage by sea; Common carrier.**

Carrier's lien The right of a carrier to withhold the goods carried at the time for delivery to the consignee, as security for the collection of the freight or other charges for carriage: for example *Kilners Ltd v John Dawson Investment Trust Ltd* (1935) 35 SR (NSW) 274. See also **Carrier; Consignee; Lien.**

• **Carry by post** In relation to an article, to carry by or through Australia Post: (CTH) Australian Postal Corporation Act 1989 s 4. It is an offence to knowingly or recklessly obstruct or hinder the carriage of an article by post. There are also various offences relating to the carriage of illegal or dangerous goods by post: (CTH) Crimes Act 1914 ss 85U, 85W, 85X, 85Y. See also **Australian Postal Corporation; Dangerous goods.**

Carry forward loss Income tax losses from previous years carried over and allowed as a deduction in the current year: (CTH) Income Tax Assessment Act 1936 s 79E. See also **Allowable deduction; Continuity of beneficial ownership; Loss; Same business test.**

Carrying charge A charge for the storage and insurance of physical commodities over a period of time. This charge may be reflected in successively higher prices for futures contracts for each succeeding future month. See also **Backwardation; Carrying charge market; Cash and carry; Contango; Futures contract; Futures exchange.**

Carrying charge market A futures market in which nearby delivery months trade at a discount to more distant contract months because of the effect of the carrying charge or interest rate. For example, in the gold market, price changes in the distant contract months tend to exceed spot price changes because of the effect of the carrying charge. See also **Backwardation; Carrying charge; Cash and carry; Contango; Futures contract; Futures exchange.**

• **Carrying on business** An element in establishing that a partnership exists. It includes establishing a place of business and soliciting or procuring any order from a person: (VIC) Business Names Act 1962 s 4. The phrase implies an element of continuity or a repetition of acts: *Hope v Bathurst City Council* (1980) 144 CLR 1; 29 ALR 577. It is in contrast to an isolated transaction which is not to be repeated; although in determining whether a person is 'carrying on business' the emphasis placed upon continuity may not be heavy. A single adventure may, depending upon its scope, amount to the carrying on of a business: *United Dominions Corp Ltd v Brian Pty Ltd* (1985) 157 CLR 1; 60 ALR 741. See also **Business; Partnership.**

Carry-over 1. A term used on the London Stock Exchange to describe an arrangement under which the completion of a contract to buy or sell securities is postponed from one settlement period to the following settlement period. A carry-over operates as a sale and repurchase or a purchase and resale of securities: *Bongiovanni v Societe Generale* (1886) 54 LT 320. **2.** In the United States, a provision in the tax law which allows a taxpayer to offset a net operating loss incurred in one year against net operating profits derived in future years. See also **Carry forward loss; Contango.**

Carte blanche *Fr* – white card. A blank sheet of paper signed by one person and given to another, allowing the latter to fill in the details at his or her discretion. Figuratively used to describe the granting of unlimited authority.

Cartel A voluntary combination of otherwise independent, competing firms who supply goods or services. In a cartel, agreements on price, output and related matters (such as allocation of customers or sales by product or territory) are substituted for independent decision making by the individual firms. See also **Acting in concert; Antitrust; Collusion; Competition law; Restrictive trade practices.**

CASAC See **Companies and Securities Advisory Committee.**

Case law The principles of law arising from judicial decisions. Case law is distinguished from statute law. Also known as 'common law'. See also **Common law**.

• **Cash 1.** In the context of credit legislation, includes cheques: for example (NSW) Credit Act 1984 (repealed) s 5; (VIC) Credit Act 1984 (repealed) s 5 (now replaced by Uniform Consumer Credit Code). **2.** In the context of corporations legislation, a particular form of benefit: Corporations Law s 9. Shares can be issued in return for both cash and non-cash consideration. See also **Allotment**.

Cash account An account recording cash transactions, of both receipts and payments of an entity. The cash account, if in debit, is an asset account, or, if in credit, is a liability account. See also **Account; Equity; Payment; Receipt**.

Cash and carry A strategy by which a commodity is purchased and stored (or carried) while selling a futures contract for that commodity. As the exercise is one of arbitrage, designed to profit from price differences in the two markets, it is undertaken when futures prices are such that profits can be made. The profit can be calculated in advance as the carrying charge and the futures contract price is known. See also **Arbitrage; Backwardation; Contango; Carrying charge; Carrying charge market; Futures contract; Money market call account**.

Cash audit The audit of cash transactions that occur during a specified period of time. A cash audit is concerned with determining the accuracy of the record of both the cash receipts and cash disbursements. It is conducted to verify the balance of cash on hand at a particular time and to ensure that the persons put in charge of cash are accountable. See also **Cash account**.

Cash basis See **Cash basis of accounting**.

Cash basis of accounting An accounting method where income is returned in the year when it is actually or constructively received and deductions are taken in the year in which the expenses are actually paid: *Federal Commissioner of Taxation v Executor Trustee and Agency Co of SA Ltd* (1938) 63 CLR 108 See also **Accruals accounting; Business income; Carry forward loss; Derived; Incurred; Personal service**.

Cash box company A company with substantial cash reserves, ready to step into the market for the purposes of acquisition at an appropriate moment.

Cash commodity Spot commodity; an actual physical commodity as distinct from a futures contract. Cash gold is gold purchased in the cash market, hence to 'purchase cash gold'. See also **Futures contract; Commodity**.

Cash cow A product within a company's marketing mix which is characterised by high market share and durability over time. Cash cows produce the revenue required to develop and support less successful or newer products. They service cross-subsidisation within the company. See also **Cross-subsidisation**.

• **Cash dealer** A financial body categorised by (CTH) Financial Transaction Reports Act 1988 s 3(1) as a cash dealer. Cash dealers have an obligation under the (CTH) Financial Transaction Reports Act 1988 to report information that may be relevant for tax evasion. See also **Approved cash carrier; Australian Transaction Reports and Analysis Centre; Identifying cash dealer**.

Cash dispenser An electro-mechanical device that permits consumers, typically using machine-readable plastic cards, to withdraw currency. See also **Automatic teller machine**.

Cash flow 1. Money a company has available to immediately reinvest in its business operations. **2.** Earnings remaining after paying all expenses including wages, interest payments, taxes and dividends plus what has been put aside to cover depreciation. A deficiency in current assets against current liabilities may result in a negative cash flow situation. See also **Asset; Liability**.

Cash flow statement A statement of cash movements resulting from transactions with external parties. Cash flow statements are required from a company as part of the consolidated financial statements of the company in accordance with accounting standards. See also **Consolidated accounts; Financial statement**.

Cash in transit insurance A type of insurance in which an insurer provides protection against loss of money in transit between specified locations. Examples of insured holding 'cash in transit' policies are finance companies, banks, insurance companies, and moneylenders who transport large sums of money and seek an indemnity if a dishonest employee embezzles money: for example *TH Adamson & Sons v Liverpool and London and Globe Insurance Co Ltd* [1953] 2 Lloyd's Rep 355. The phrase 'in transit' is not a term of art; money is 'in transit' until it is accepted by the bank: *Peter Jackson Pty Ltd v Consolidated Insurance of Australia Ltd* [1975] VR 781. Also known as 'money in transit insurance'. See also **Fidelity guarantee; Fidelity guarantee insurance**.

• **Cash management trust** *Abbr* – CMT A unit trust or fund that pools the relatively small investments of individuals, acquiring high-yielding money market instruments normally available only to professional investors with large sums at their disposal. See also **Debenture trust deed; Trustee; Unit trust**.

Cash market 1. A market in which cash is borrowed or lent for periods of less than one year and often as briefly as overnight. Market participants also trade in securities such as bills of exchange, certificates of deposit and notes that for the most part mature in less than six months. Cash and securities are traded in the money market in large parcels, generally by governments, corporations, business organisations, and cash management trusts. **2.** Spot market; a market for the immediate payment for and delivery of commodities; a market for trading in physical commodities as opposed to contracts on a futures exchange. See also **Cash; Cash rate; Commodity; Futures exchange; Securities**.

Cash matching The structuring of a portfolio of assets so that the cash flows coming in from assets are efficiently timed to match the payments of liabilities required at the present and in the future. Cash in itself is an unproductive asset, therefore minimal cash holdings are generally desired by firms, as well as for purposes of internal control. Cash matching is one means of minimising cash holdings. See also **Asset; Cash flow; Liability; Portfolio**.

•**Cash price** In consumer credit law, the price of goods, or a figure based on the market value of the goods. In relation to a contract for the hiring of goods, a figure based on the market value of the goods: (NSW) Credit Act 1984 (repealed) s 5(1) (now replaced by Uniform Consumer Credit Code). See also **Consumer credit**.

Cash rate The rate of interest earned by a bank in lending surplus cash funds to an authorised dealer in the official money market. Also known as 'official rate'. See also **Cash market; Money market; Official money market; Reserve Bank of Australia**.

•**Cash receipts** See **Cash basis of accounting**.

Cash settled futures contract A contract under which physical delivery of the subject matter of the contract is not permitted. The difference between the price paid upon opening the contract and the settlement price is paid in cash on the settlement day. A cash settled futures contract differs from a deliverable futures contract. Also known as an 'adjustment agreement': Corporations Law s 9. See also **Deliverable futures contract; Futures contract**.

Cash transaction, significant See **Significant cash transaction**.

Cashier A person who receives and disburses money in a business institution. In Australia and the United States, banks' cashiers are called tellers. In England the term cashier is used. In the United States, the term cashier in banks denotes a senior officer responsible for the custody of the bank's assets and whose signature is required on all official documents. Hence, the term 'cashier's cheque'. See also **Banker's draft; Teller**.

•**Casual employee** In general, a person employed to work on an as-required basis by the employer. The employee's hours may be regular or irregular, and the work may be short-time, or extend over a long period. See also **Permanent employment**.

Catalogue An inventory, schedule, or list of goods or services, sometimes including a description of each item in the schedule or list. Catalogues often include prices.

Catching bargain A type of unconscionable bargain where there is a material inequality between the parties, and the stronger party takes unconscionable advantage of his or her position of power in making a bargain that is disadvantageous to the weaker party. Catching bargains fall within the doctrine of unconscionable conduct, and may be set aside: for example (NSW) Contracts Review Act 1980 s 7; *Commercial Bank of Australia Ltd v Amadio* (1983) 151 CLR 447; 46 ALR 402. See also **Unconscionable**.

Causa sine qua non /kaʊsa sineɪ kweɪ noʊn/ *Lat* – a cause without which not, necessary cause. A causal factor that is essential in establishing a cause of action. A cause which is a necessary precondition of a result but plays no active part in its production.

Causal exclusion clause A clause in a contract of insurance excluding liability for loss caused by certain specified events. Where a loss is caused by an excluded event, the insured cannot recover, even if the loss was also caused by another event that was not excluded: *Hooley Hill Rubber and Chemical Co Ltd v Royal Insurance Co Ltd* [1920] 1 KB 257; *City Centre Cold Store Pty Ltd v Preservative Skandia Insurance Ltd* (1985) 3 NSWLR 739. Causation is determined by applying common sense to the facts of the case: *March v E & MH Stramare Pty Ltd* (1991) 171 CLR 506; 99 ALR 423. An insurer may also refuse to pay a claim where an act of the insured could reasonably be regarded as causing or contributing to the loss: (CTH) Insurance Contracts Act 1984 s 54(2). See also **Exclusion clause; Temporal exclusion clause**.

Causation A requirement in tort and contract that limits the defendant's responsibility for the plaintiff's loss. The plaintiff must show a sufficient connection between the breach and the loss suffered: *Wilsher v Essex Area Health Authority* [1988] AC 1074. It is sufficient for the plaintiff to prove that, but for the defendant's breach, the loss or damage in question would not have been suffered: *Reg Glass Pty Ltd v Rivers Locking Systems Pty Ltd* (1968) 120 CLR 516. The 'but for' test of causation is not the exclusive test: *March v E & MH Stramare Pty Ltd* (1991) 171 CLR 506; 99 ALR 423. See also **Breach of contract; Contract; Remoteness; Tort**.

•**Cause of action** 1. The whole set of facts which give rise to an enforceable claim. In a cause of action, the plaintiff must prove every fact which is challenged in order to obtain judgment: *Bennett v White* [1910] 2 KB 643. 2. The facts which are relied upon for judicial redress: *Read v Brown* (1888) 22 QBD 128. Also known as 'action', 'claim', 'cause', or 'matter'. See also **Claim; Right of action; Limitation of actions**.

•**Caveat** The main function of a caveat is protective, not to give notice; it is 'simply a claim by someone that he shall receive notice before any dealing with land is carried through': *J & H Just (Holdings) Pty Ltd v Bank of NSW* (1971) 125 CLR 546; [1972] ALR 323. The caveat forbids registration of any further interests that may affect the interest recorded in the caveat without the consent of the caveator.

Caveat emptor /keɪvɪət ɛmptɔ/ *Lat* – let the buyer beware. The principle that the buyer must ascertain the good quality of the goods he or she purchases. The maxim is reflected in State and Territory sale of goods legislation: for example (NSW) Sale of Goods Act 1923 s 19(2) ; (VIC) Goods Act 1958 s 19(b). See also **Caveat fabricator; Caveat venditor; Sale of goods**.

Caveat fabricator /keɪvɪæt fæbrɪkatʊə/ *Lat* – let the manufacturer beware. The maxim is reflected in Federal, State, and Territory product liability legislation, which imposes strict liability on manufacturers (and others) where products are unsafe, defective, or not fit for their purpose: for example (CTH) Trade Practices Act 1974 Pt V Div 2A, Pt VA; (NSW) Sale of Goods Act 1923 Pt 8. See also **Caveat emptor; Caveat venditor; Strict liability**.

Caveat venditor /keɪvɪət vɛndɪtɔ/ *Lat* – let the seller beware. See also **Caveat emptor; Caveat fabricator; Sale of goods; Sale of Goods Act**.

CBTCC See **Chicago Board of Trade Clearing Corporation**.

Cease and desist order An order issued by a court, tribunal or government authority directing a person to discontinue an activity or practice which is in violation of the law. A cease and desist order may also specify the action which should be taken to remedy the situation. See also **Injunction**.

Cedent An insurer who arranges to transfer all or part of the risk undertaken under a contract of insurance to another insurer, in order to reduce its exposure. Also known as the 'reinsured'. See also **Reinsurance**.

Celler-Kefauver Act 1950 A 1950 amendment to the merger provisions of the (US) Clayton Antitrust Act 1914. It was enacted to overcome what was viewed as a loophole in the original prohibition in section 7 of that Act: the failure to cover asset acquisitions. See also **Acquisition; Antitrust; Competition law; Merger**.

Central bank A bank which in any country is banker to the government, oversees the commercial banks and the monetary system, manages the issue of currency notes, implements the monetary policy of the government, conducts open market operations, intervenes in the foreign exchange market and makes available lender-of-last-resort assistance to banks and money market dealers in certain circumstances. See also **Reserve Bank of Australia**.

•**Central business district** *Abbr* – CBD The centre of a metropolitan area, city or large town. It is often the preferred location for head offices of major private and public sector organisations. It also often contains a communications centre, a cultural, educational and recreational centre, a commercial and financial centre, an entertainment, tourist and retail centre, and residential components.

Centrale de Livraison de Valeurs Mobilieres
Symbol. – CEDEL Based in Luxembourg, a worldwide organisation for the clearing of securities transactions, it is an adjunct to the Luxembourg Stock Exchange. CEDEL comprises a computerised system for the delivery, settlement and safe custody of Eurobonds and other securities. Established in 1970, it handles most of the business in the European Currency Unit. See also **Clearing house; Stock exchange; Securities exchange; Securities clearing house**.

•**Centralised cash control equipment** A system or device allowing a person to play a poker machine without inserting money into it by making a cash payment to the occupier of the premises. In hotels, the cash payment is made to the holder of the hotelier's licence: (NSW) Liquor Act 1982 s 4(1). In registered clubs in New South Wales, the cash payment is made to the registered club: (NSW) Registered Clubs Act 1976 s 4(1). See also **Club**.

Centralised system of branch accounting A system of accounting where the branch bookkeeping for each branch of a business is administered at one location. This location is usually the head office. The basic records and transactions of a business are prepared by the branch and forwarded to the main office to be processed. The centralised system of branch accounting maintains uniformity of accounting methods and procedures throughout the business, although such a system may cause some delay in processing the transactions and producing reports. See also **Accounting method**.

Centre for Industrial Development See **United Nations Industrial Development Organisation**.

Centrocon arbitration clause A clause incorporated into an arbitration agreement, usually in shipping charter parties, providing for any claim to be made in writing and the claimant's arbitrator to be appointed within three months of final discharge of the cargo. See also **Arbitration; Arbitration clause; Charterparty**.

Centrocon charter party A charter party which contains a 'centrocon' clause exempting a charterer from demurrage if the ship is unable to berth because the allotted berth is being occupied by other ships delayed by industrial action. See also **Charterparty; Demurrage**.

Cents-per-kilometre method A method for claiming the cost of running a car for business purposes as a tax deduction. An allowable deduction may be available to a person for the cost of using a motor vehicle for business purposes. A person who travels less than 5000 business kilometres in a car in a year of income has the option of claiming a deduction for that year based upon an arbitrary rate of cents-per-kilometre as set by the Commissioner of Taxation: (CTH) Income Tax Assessment Act 1936 s 82KZBC, Sch 2A ss 1-3. See also **Allowable deduction**.

Certainty A requirement of a valid contract. A contract is void for uncertainty where an important term is left to be settled at a later date or where the language used is so obscure and incapable of definite meaning that the court is unable to attribute to the parties any particular contractual intention: *Thorby v Goldberg* (1964) 112 CLR 597 at 607. See also **Contract; Severance; Term; Void**.

Certainty equivalent return The amount of benefit obtainable with certainty which one is willing to exchange for a usually larger but uncertain amount. The amount obtained with certainty is said to be the certainty equivalent of the uncertain amount. See also **Certainty**.

Certainty of object In the context of trusts, the element of a valid trust requiring ascertained or ascertainable beneficiaries. See also **Certainty of subject; Charitable trust; Discretionary trust; Fixed trust; Trust power; Trust**.

Certainty of subject In the context of trusts, the element of a valid trust requiring the property subject to the trust to be certain, that is, definitely ascertainable from the facts existing at the time the trust was created: *Herdegen v FCT* (1988) 84 ALR 271. See also **Beneficial interest; Certainty of object; Charitable trust; Trust**.

•**Certificate of competency** A certificate issued by the appropriate authority which confirms the competency and efficiency of a person to fulfil certain functions, such as the officer of a ship or a locomotive driver: for example (NSW) Commercial Vessels Act 1979 ss 30C-30Q; (QLD) Gas Act 1965 s 5; (QLD) Mines Regulations Act 1964 s 8; (VIC) Casino Control Act 1991 s 39. Usually, before the issue of any such certificate, a course of study must be undertaken, examinations passed, and a period of practical training undergone. Medical fitness may also be a prerequisite to the issue of the certificate: for example (NSW) Commercial Vessels Act 1979 s 30F.

Certificate of damage A document issued by a dock company when it receives damaged goods. It is in the form of a questionnaire to be filled in by the port authorities or by the representatives of the insurance underwriters. It addresses questions such as the cause of the damage, the day of arrival of the vessel involved, the date of unloading, when the damage was recorded in relation to its occurrence, the date and the place of the dock surveyor's survey stating the nature and cause of the damage, and the attitude of the carrier to liability. The certificate is used by the underwriters to determine whether action should be pursued for compensation. See also **Underwriter**.

•**Certificate of incorporation** A certificate which must be prepared and issued to a company by the Australian Securities Commission (ASC) on registering that company under Corporations Law Pt 2.2 Div 1: Corporations Law s 121(1). Also known as 'ASC certificate' and 'certificate of registration'.

Certificate of indebtedness A certificate signed by an authorised officer of a bank showing the amount of principal and interest due to the bank by a borrower or a guarantor. Such a certificate is prima facie or conclusive evidence of the borrower or guarantor's liability to the bank and the bank need not in addition produce its books and vouchers to prove the amount claimed. All bank guarantees and mortgages contain a clause providing for the issue of such a certificate by the bank. The validity of such clauses have been judicially recognised: *Dobbs v National Bank of Australia* (1935) 53 CLR 643; *Je Maintiendrai Pty Ltd v ANZ Banking Group Ltd* (1985) 38 SASR 70; *Bache & Co (London) Ltd v Banque Vernes et Commerciale De Paris SA* [1973] 2 Lloyds Rep 437.

•**Certificate of insurance** A document issued by an insurer setting out the main, variable, or financial terms of the contract of insurance. See also **Assured; Insurance contract; Insurer**.

Certificate of origin *Abbr* – C of O or C/O A shipping document, endorsed by the manufacturers and the original shippers, specifying the details of the goods being shipped, the name and place of manufacture, the carrying vessel, and the details of importers or consignees. The certificate of origin is used to determine whether there is any import duty payable on the goods.

•**Certificate of registration** A certificate issued as, or deemed to be, proof or confirmation that a person, body, or thing has been registered in accordance with a statutory requirement. See also **Industrial organisation**.

Certificate of shares See **Share certificate**.

•**Certificate of title** *Abbr* – CT An instrument evidencing the estate in fee simple or other estate or interest in any land, executed by the Registrar of Titles in the prescribed form: for example (QLD) Land Title Act 1994 s 4. A certificate of title only exists in relation to land under the Torrens system, including land under qualified and limited titles. See also **Old system title**.

Certificated register See **Flexible Accelerated Security Transfer**.

Certificated security A company security having an associated certificate showing the entitlement of the security holder. See also **Security; Uncertificated security**.

Certification The attestation of the truth of facts by way of a written statement.
Maritime law The issue of a certificate by an official under statutory authority or a contractual term. See also **Certificate of competency; Certificate of damage**.

Certification of transfer The process in a transfer of shares on a company's register of members where in order to effect a transfer, the relevant share certificate and a signed transfer is produced to the company. See also **Share certificate; Transfer of share**.

Certification officer A person who issues or signs a certificate that is, or purports to be, evidence of the matters contained in the certificate.

Certified agreement A memorandum of the terms of an agreement reached by parties to an industrial dispute or an industrial situation, settling or preventing the dispute, that has been certified by the Australian Industrial Relations Commission: (CTH) Industrial Relations Act 1988 s 170MA. Also known as 'registered agreement'. See also **Australian Industrial Relations Commission; Enterprise bargaining; Industrial award; Industrial dispute; No-disadvantage test; Single business**.

•**Certified copy** A copy of a public document, signed and certified as a true copy of the original by the officer to whose custody the original is entrusted, and admissible as evidence when the original would be admissible. Such copies of documents may be received in evidence if properly authenticated. See also **Certified copy of deed**.

Certified copy of deed A copy of a deed, on which has been written, by an official in whose custody the document has been kept, that the authorised person has seen the original of the document, and that the copy is a true copy of the original. Certification of copies of documents is often required for official purposes if the original is not available for production: for example *Halfpenny v Kinnelly* (1855) VLT 52. See also **Deed**.

Certiorari /sɜʃərɛərɑɪ/ *Lat* – to be informed. A type of prerogative remedy issued by a court to bring before it the decision or determination of a tribunal or inferior court to quash it on the ground of non-jurisdictional error of law on the face of the record, or for jurisdictional error or denial of procedural fairness. See also **Functus officio; Mandamus; Prohibition**.

Cesser clause A clause in a charter party which releases the charterer from liability under the charter party as soon as the vessel is loaded with the cargo. In the absence of special wording, such a clause does not prevent the charterer or the ship owner from exercising a right to the alternative remedy of a lien on the cargo for the payment of freight, dead freight or other charges. See also **Cargo; Carrier's lien; Charterer; Charterparty; Dead freight; Freight**.

Cestui que trust /sɛtɪki trʌst/ *OF* – one who trusts. Pl – *Cestuis que trustent*. A person for whose benefit a trust is created, that is, a beneficiary. A *cestui que trust* is entitled to the equitable, not legal estate. Formerly known as 'cestui que use'. See also **Beneficiary; Beneficial interest**.

CFTC See Commodity Futures Trading Commission.

Chaebol Approximately 40 dominating industrial conglomerates in South Korea, most of them family-owned and operated. They account for some 15 per cent of gross national product (GNP). The group is led by Samsung, Hyundai, Daewoo and Lucky-Goldstar. The Chaebol has become synonymous with South Korea's production and export achievements over the past 30 years. The Chaebol undergoes continual restructuring.

Chain of causation The series of events which occurs between the negligence of the defendant and the injury suffered by the plaintiff. Where the negligence of the plaintiff or a third party breaks the chain of causation, the defendant will not be liable for the injuries suffered by the plaintiff. See also **Damage; Negligence; Novus actus interveniens**.

Chain of supply The series of contractual relationships linking the manufacturer, distributor, and supplier of a product. In certain cases, the existence of a chain of supply enables liability for a defective product, which is owed by a supplier to a plaintiff, to be passed to the person at fault through a series of claims for breach of contract: for example *Kasler and Cohen v Slovaks* [1928] 1 KB 78; *Lexeme (Basingstoke) Ltd v Lewis* [1982] AC 225. The person at fault is generally the manufacturer. See also **Manufacturer; Product liability**.

Chaining In banking, a method used in certain transfer systems (mostly for securities) for processing instructions. It involves the manipulation of the sequence in which transfer instructions are processed to increase the number or value of transfers that may be settled with available funds or securities balances, or available credit or securities lending lines.

Chairman at general meeting A member elected by the other members of a company to chair a general meeting of members. Company articles usually provide that the chairman of directors presides at every general meeting or, if there is no chairman, or if he or she is not present within a prescribed time or is unwilling to act, the members present elect one of their number to be chairman: Corporations Law Sch 1 Table A art 44. A chairman should act in accordance with certain conventional standards to facilitate the functions of the meeting. The chairman's power is only for the purpose of giving members a reasonable opportunity to debate and vote: *Byng v London Life Assn Ltd* [1989] 1 All ER 560. See also **Chairman of the board; General meeting**.

•**Chairman of the board** The director appointed by the board of directors of a company (typically) having the duty of chairing meetings of directors: for example Corporations Law Sch 1 Table A art 75. The chairman will also usually chair general meetings of members, be the company's main representative to speak to outsiders to the firm about its activities, and do whatever is delegated to him or her by the board which is within the board's power to delegate. The chairman has limited ostensible authority to bind the company: *Crabtree-Vickers Pty Ltd v Australian Direct Mail Advertising & Addressing Co Pty Ltd* (1975) 133 CLR 72; 7 ALR 527. See also **Chairman at general meeting; Board of directors**.

Challenge Bank An Australian savings bank originating in 1862 as the Perth Benefit Building Investment and Loan Society, later known as the Perth Building Society. In the earlier 1980s, the Perth Building Society acquired the National Permanent Building Society and the Hotham Building Society in Victoria. In 1987, Perth Building Society became the Challenge Bank.

Chamber of commerce An association formed to preserve and promote trade and commerce in the region with which it is concerned.

Chancery One of the three divisions of the High Court of Justice in England. The functions of the Division include the administration of estates, partnership actions, actions relating to mortgages, portions, and charges on land and trusts. The Chancery Division replaced the Court of Chancery, a court presided over by the Lord Chancellor after the Court of Chancery was merged with the High Court of Justice by the (UK) Judicature Act 1873.

Change agent A management consultant employed to assist companies in identifying areas in need of change, and helping to implement those changes smoothly and effectively. Areas within the organisation which may be assessed include organisational structure, technological systems, and behaviour. See also **Management advisory service**.

Change of status An alteration of legal position of a person or body.

Corporations An alteration of the legal position or condition of a person or entity. A company incorporated under the Corporations Law can change its status to a specified alternative company pursuant to statutory conditions: Corporations Law s 167. A company can only change its status if the law expressly provides for it: *Australian Securities Commission v Marlborough Gold Mines Ltd* (1993) 177 CLR 485; 10 ACSR 230; 112 ALR 627. See also **Entity**.

Characteristic performance The doing of an act which is characteristic of a contract, other than the payment of money. A characteristic performance in a contract for the sale of goods can include supply of the goods. The concept is used to determine the proper law of the contract by reference to the residence of the party who must render the characteristic performance: (European Economic Community) Convention on the Law Applicable to Contractual Obligations 1980 art 4. See also **Contract; Performance; Proper law of contract**.

•**Charge** 1. To take control of a person or property. 2. A formal accusation of criminal conduct. 3. A judge's instructions to a jury before the jury's deliberation on the verdict in a case. 4. A periodic fee.

Real property Security for a debt or obligation attaching to property of the debtor. See also **Security; Fixed charge; Floating charge; Mortgage; Charge priorities**.

Charge priorities The order in which a number of charges over the same property are ranked for payment. When a debt is secured by a charge over the property of a company which is subject to more than one charge, the rules set out in Corporations Law ss 279-282 determine the relative ranking of the charges. Generally, a charge which has been registered with the Australian Securities Commission will have priority over an unregistered charge, and registered charges will have priority as between each other according to the time at which they were registered: Corporations Law ss 280-282. See also **Charge; Prior charge**.

Chargeable amount In consumer credit law and in relation to continuing credit contracts, the greater of the amount owing by the debtor at the commencement of the billing cycle less amounts paid during that cycle, and the sum of daily balances divided by the number of days in the billing cycle: (NSW) Credit Act 1984 (repealed) s 52(1); (VIC) Credit Act 1984 (repealed) s 52(1) (now replaced by Uniform Consumer Credit Code). See also **Billing cycle; Consumer credit; Consumer credit; Continuing credit contract**.

•**Chargeable matter** In corporations law, an action for which a fee is payable to the Australian Securities Commission (ASC) or the Minister: Corporations Law s 9. It includes the lodging of documents with the ASC, the production of documents by the ASC and the inspection of registers kept by the ASC. The fees payable are set out in the (CTH) Corporations (Fees) Regulations. See also **Lodge**.

•**Chargee** The person in whose favour a charge is created. See also **Charge; Chargor**.

•**Charging order** An order by a court restraining dealings with the shares or property of an individual: *Rainbow v Moorgate Properties Ltd* [1975] 1 WLR 788; [1975] 2 All ER 821. A charging order over shares or land is not within the concept of a registrable charge under Corporations Law s 261(1): *Re Overseas Aviation Engineering (GB) Ltd* [1963] Ch 24. See also **Charge; Charge priorities**.

Chargor The person who creates a charge. See also **Charge; Chargee; Chargor company**.

Chargor company A body corporate which gives security (a charge) over its assets, usually in return for a loan. The charge may be fixed over specific assets of the company or floating over the whole of the company's undertaking as it exists from time to time. A company creating a charge is obliged to register details of the charge with the Australian Securities Commission: Corporations Law s 263. If more than one charge is given over the assets of the company, the Corporations Law provides rules as to how priorities between the charges are to be established. See also **Charge; Fixed charge; Floating charge; Charge priorities; Register of charges; Security**.

•**Charitable purpose 1.** An object which promotes charity (within the legal meaning of the term 'charity'): *Ashfield Municipal Council v Joyce* (1976) 10 ALR 193; [1976] 1 NSWLR 455, PC. **2.** A purpose listed in the preamble to the Statute of Charitable Uses 1601, or within the 'spirit and intendment' of that statute: *Royal National Agricultural and Industrial Assn v Chester* (1974) 3 ALR 486. See also **Charitable trust; Charity**.

•**Charitable trust** A trust that is exclusively for charitable purposes (*Leahy v A-G(NSW)* (1959) 101 CLR 611; [1959] ALR 869) and of a public nature, created for a purpose, not a person: *Attorney-General (NSW) v Perpetual Trustee Co Ltd* (1940) 63 CLR 209; [1940] ALR 209. Also known as 'public trust'. See also **Charitable purpose; Charity**.

•**Charity 1.** An institution or entity that holds property upon a charitable trust and carries out the trust purposes. **2.** An institution set up for charitable purposes to carry out those activities mentioned in the preamble to the (UK) Charitable Uses Act 1601 and other activities within the spirit and intendment of the Act: *Morice v Bishop of Durham* (1804) 9 Ves 399 at 405; 32 ER 656 at 659. Also known as 'charitable trust'. See also **Charitable purpose; Charitable trust**.

Chart of accounts *Abbr* – COA In telecommunications law, one of two documents that the Australian Telecommunications Authority (AUSTEL) must prepare for telecommunications carriers, the other being the cost allocation manual. The documents provide for accounting separation of the various businesses of each carrier. Carriers are required to keep books of account and other records in accordance with the chart and the manual: (CTH) Telecommunications Act 1991 ss 80-87. See also **Australian Telecommunications Authority**.

•**Charter 1.** An instrument issued by a sovereign power in the form of a grant of rights and privileges to a city, university, or corporation. **2.** An agreement for the carriage by sea of specific goods, formulated by international organisations. **3.** The constitution of a suprastate body. An example is the Charter of the United Nations 1945. See also **Charterparty; Statute**.

Chartered company A company incorporated by royal charter which, in the past, was often created to secure self-government or local jurisdiction abroad, and to avoid breaching certain statutes as a result of its trading activity. For example, a chartered company was exempt from the offence of unlawful assembly. Chartered companies were also used to create monopolies. Today the power to create chartered corporations is within the royal prerogative exercisable by the Governor-General. It is now used generally for professional or non-profit institutions. Also known as 'regulated company'. See also **Corporation; Incorporation**.

Charterer One who enters into a contract with a shipowner for the carriage of goods. The contract of charter is known as the 'charterparty'. The rights and obligations of the charterer depend upon the type of charter party entered into. The charterer guarantees the accuracy at shipment of the marks, number, quality, and weight of the goods furnished to the carrier. The charterer must indemnify the carrier against all loss, damage, and expense arising out of inaccuracies in the particulars: Amended Hague Rules 1979 art 3(5). In any case, the charterer is not responsible for loss or damage sustained by the carrier or ship arising out of or resulting from any cause without the act, fault, neglect of the charterer or charterer's agents or servants. Also known as 'freighter' or 'shipper'. See also **Carriage of goods; Charterparty; Consignor; Freight**.

Charterer's liability The liability of a charterer under a charterparty will depend on the construction of the particular charterparty. A charterer who issues a bill of lading under a charterparty on his or her own bill of lading form becomes the contracting carrier and assumes liability for loss and damage to cargo: *Kuehne & Nagel Inc v F W Baiden* [1975] 1 Lloyd's Rep 331. Bills of lading are not required under a charter party and the (CTH) Carriage of Goods by Sea Act 1991 does not apply to a charterparty. See also **Bill of lading; Cargo; Charterer; Charterparty**.

Charterparty A contract under which a shipowner hires all or a part of a ship to a charterer for the transportation of goods from one port to another. See also **Bill of lading; Cargo; Charterer; Charterer's liability; Demurrage; Dock charter; Freight; Lay day; Time charterparty; Voyage charterparty**.

Charting The use of graphs and charts in the technical analysis of stock markets and futures markets to plot trends of price movements and other market characteristics. See also **Australian financial futures market; Charting; Chartist; Stock market**.

Chartist An American term for a person who endeavours to predict changes in the price of an item (usually corporation securities) on the basis of the past patterns of price behaviour. See also **Charting**.

Chase AMP A bank which provides banking, financial and related services to corporations, governments and statutory bodies. Established in 1985, it is jointly owned by the AMP Society and the Chase Manhattan Bank. Chase Manhattan is the third largest bank in the United States, while the AMP Society is the largest life assurance office in Australia.

Chattel *Lat – catalla* – cattle. **1.** Personal property, as distinct from real property: *Robinson v Jenkins* (1890) 24 QBD 275. **2.** Any property which is not freehold land. The property may be a leasehold (chattel real) or a movable article of property such as household furniture and jewellery (chattel personal). Chattels can, for certain purposes include interests in land less than freehold, choses in action, fixtures and growing crops when separately assigned, charged or bailed and also book debts: (WA) Bills of Sale Act 1899 s 5. See also **Bill of sale; Chattel security; Chose in action; Chose in possession; Freehold; Ownership; Personal property; Property**.

Chattel security A security interest in personal property. A chattel security may be registrable as a bill of sale. Also known as 'chattel mortgage'. See also **Bill of sale; Charge; Chattel; Inventory security interest; Personal property; Possessory lien; Security interest; Security; Wool lien**.

•**Cheque** A bill of exchange; an unconditional order in writing addressed by a person to another person (being a bank), and signed by the person giving the order, which requires the bank to pay on demand a sum certain in money to the person to whom the cheque is payable: (CTH) Cheques and Payment Orders Act 1986 s 10(1). See also **Agency cheque; Cheque book; Clearance of cheque; Collection; Counter presentation; Crossing; Negotiable instrument; Stale cheque; Stopped cheque**.

Cheque book A book containing 20-25 blank cheque leaves furnished by banks to customers who maintain cheque accounts by the use of which funds deposited may be withdrawn. See also **Cheque**.

Cheque facility test A test defining the essential characteristic of banking business as the offering of a facility to customers to draw cheques on the institution, and the institution's participation in the cheque clearance system: *United Dominions Trust Ltd v Kirkwood* [1966] 2 QB 431. In the Australian statutory framework, such a definition of banking in the context of cheques and payment orders, on its own, would be restrictive and circular. The test has been combined with the 'reputation test'. See also **Banking business; Cheque; Reputation test**.

Cheques and Payment Orders Act 1986 *Abbr* – CPOA Legislation which provides a separate law for cheques and payment orders: (CTH) Cheques and Payment Orders Act 1986. As a result Australia is the only country in the Commonwealth of nations to have a separate statute on cheques. Previously the (CTH) Bills of Exchange Act 1909 applied to all bills of exchange including cheques. The new legislation was originally to be called the Cheques Act and in fact the bill introduced to Parliament had the title 'Cheques Bill' but the opposition in the Senate refused to pass the bill unless payment orders issued by building societies were covered. Hence the current title and the statute now applies not only to cheques but also bank cheques, bank drafts, inchoate instruments, dividend warrants and payment orders issued by non-bank financial institutions. See also **Banker's draft; Bills of Exchange Legislation; Dividend warrant; Inchoate instrument; Manning Committee; Payment order**.

Cherry picking The practice in bankruptcy proceedings of selecting, for purposes of settlement, contracts that are favourable to the bankrupt in preference to the bankrupt's contracts with unsecured creditors. See also **Bankrupt; Bankruptcy**.

•**CHESS** See **Clearing House Electronic Subregister System**.

Chicago Board of Trade *Abbr* – CBT Established in 1848, the largest commodity exchange in the world and the oldest in the United States, where active trading takes place in wheat, corn, oats, soybeans, soybean oil, pork bellies, lumber and orange juice. During recent years, it has added financial contracts such as interest rates, foreign exchange and a stock market index. The stock market index includes 20 of the 30 stocks on the Dow Jones Industrial Average, and is known as the Major Market Index. Trading is conducted in trading areas called 'pits' on the exchange floor. Every offer to sell and every bid to buy must be cried-out publicly. Night sessions have been introduced to coincide with the start of Japan's business day. See also **Chicago Board of Trade Clearing Corporation; Chicago Mercantile Exchange; Commodity; Stock market**.

Chicago Board of Trade Clearing Corporation *Abbr* – CBTCC A body separate from the Chicago Board of Trade whose task is to match tens of thousands of individual sales and purchases made on the exchange. For a trade to clear, the reported purchase and reported sale must correspond in every essential detail. The corporation ensures financial integrity in the transactions. See also **Chicago Board of Trade**; **Chicago Mercantile Exchange**.

• **Chicago Convention** See also **International Civil Aviation Organisation**.

Chicago Mercantile Exchange *Abbr* – CME A commodity exchange established in 1919, which evolved from the Chicago Butter and Egg Board. The initial function of the CME was to provide a national marketplace for trading in cash and futures contracts in various agricultural commodities including live hogs, pork bellies and skinned hams. In recent years, trading has been almost entirely in futures. The CME is the second largest organised futures exchange in the world. In 1972, it established an international money market as a separate division. An index and options market was opened in 1982. The CME has introduced an automated trading system offering post-market trading. See also **Commodity**; **Chicago Board of Trade**; **Chicago Board of Trade Clearing Corporation**; **Futures contract**.

• **Chief entity** In relation to corporations, a parent entity in an economic entity that is a reporting entity: Corporations Law s 295. See also **Parent entity**; **Economic entity**; **Reporting entity**; **Entity**.

• **Chief Justice** *Abbr* – CJ The most senior judge of the High Court, Federal Court, Family Court and the Supreme Courts of the States and Territories (in a particular division of the court, for example Equity). Also known as 'Chief Judge'. See also **Bench**; **Judge**; **Justice**.

Child entity In relation to corporations, an entity which has as its parent entity or one of its parent entities a public company: Corporations Law ss 9, 243D(2). An entity is a body corporate, a partnership, an unincorporated body, an individual and a trustee of a trust that has only one trustee: Corporations Law s 243C(1). A public company is the parent entity of another entity if it is a holding company of the other entity or if it has control over the other entity: Corporations Law s 243D(1). See also **Control**; **Holding company**; **Parent entity**; **Public company**.

Child housekeeper A child of the taxpayer (including an adopted, step, or ex-nuptial, child) who is wholly engaged in keeping house for the taxpayer: (CTH) Income Tax Assessment Act 1936 s 159J(6). See also **Allowable deduction**; **Dependant**; **Dependant rebate**.

Children's tax Tax levied on certain income earned by a child. A child's income of more than $416 per annum is subject to the highest marginal rate of tax, unless the income is excepted assessable income: (CTH) Income Tax Assessment Act 1936 Div 6AA. The top marginal tax rate applies to a person under 18 years of age who is not a relevant excepted person, such as a person fully employed at the end of the financial year or employed for three months but not in full-time education. See also **Excepted assessable income**; **Excepted person**.

China International Trust and Investment Corporation *Abbr* – CITIC The overseas investment arm of the Chinese government. It has participated in Australian joint ventures.

China stock exchanges Stock exchanges established by the People's Republic of China in the southern special economic zone of Shenzhen and in Shanghai. Other centres including Guangzhou, Shenyang and Whang have limited trading facilities in bonds and other securities. Listed Chinese stocks include those of several leading enterprises such as the Shenzhen Development Bank, Vanke (technology and property), Jintian (textiles), Anda Transport and Shenzhen Campaign. See also **Stock exchange**.

Chinese wall Arrangements in a body corporate or partnership by which the passing of certain price-sensitive information to employees, officers or departments is restricted. Chinese walls constitute an exception to the Corporations Law s 1002G prohibition on insider trading: Corporations Law ss 1002M, 1002N. The possession of non-public information by an employee or officer will not mean another employee or officer liable has contravened Corporations Law s 1002G if a Chinese wall is in place (and provided no such information was communicated and no advice given). Arrangements typically involve (documented) policies and procedures to limit dissemination of information and the physical separation of departments. See also **Trading corporation**; **Insider trading**.

Chit A form of trading slip on which the details of trades are recorded by the trader who sells the contract. The buying trader initials the chit and each trader retains a copy, the original being sent to the clearing house of the exchange. See also **Clearing house**; **Futures exchange**; **Stock exchange**; **Trader**.

• **Choice principle** A principle of statutory interpretation developed concerning the application of (CTH) Income Tax Assessment Act 1936 s 260 (which provides that contracts entered into with the purpose or effect of avoiding income tax are void). The principle provides that, where (CTH) Income Tax Assessment Act 1936 specifically gives the taxpayer a choice resulting in differing income tax consequences, (CTH) Income Tax Assessment Act 1936 s 260 should not apply to deny the taxpayer any tax advantages arising from the making of that choice. The principle was applied in various cases heard in the mid 1970s such as *Federal Cmr of Taxation v Cridland* (1977) 8 ATR 169, and *Slutzkin v Federal Cmr of Taxation* (1977) 140 CLR 314; 7 ATR 166. Latter decisions of the High Court limited the principle: for example *Tuppicoff v Federal Cmr of Taxation* [1984] 4346; *Pincus Gulland & Watson v Federal Court of Taxation* [1984] 84 ATC 487.

• **Chose in action** An intangible personal property right recognised and protected by the law, which has no existence apart from the recognition given by the law, or which confers no present possession of a tangible object, such as the right to payment under a loan contract or the promise to pay on a bill of exchange: *National Trustees Executors and Agency Co of Australasia Ltd v FCT* (1954) 91 CLR 540 at 584; *Torkington v Magee* [1902] 2 KB 427 at 430. See also **Assignment**; **Chattel**; **Chose**

Cho

in possession; Future chose in action; **Intangible property**; **Personal property**; **Possession**.

Chose in possession An item of tangible personal property which is capable of physical possession by the owner and which is capable of transfer by delivery. Possession of a chose in possession is prima facie evidence of ownership: *Gatward v Alley* (1940) 40 SR (NSW) 174; 57 WN (NSW) 82. See also **Chattel**; **Chose in action**; **Movable property**; **Personal property**; **Possession**.

Churning A form of market manipulation where share traders first acquire a holding in a share and then proceed to place both buying and selling orders for that share in order to build up the turnover. The objective is to raise the price of the shares and provide an opportunity to sell at the artificially high price or alternatively to generate higher broker's commissions. Churning is prohibited by Corporations Law ss 997, 998, 1264. See also **Share**; **Excessive trading**; **Market manipulation**.

CIF See **Cost insurance freight contract**.

CIF contract See **Cost insurance freight contract**.

Circulating capital Assets of a company derived from the company's capital funds which are used to generate income by being temporarily parted with and circulated in the business in the form of money, goods or other assets: *Ammonia Soda Co Ltd v Chamberlain* [1918] 1 Ch 266 at 286-7. These assets, or their proceeds, are intended to return to the company with an increment, and are intended to be used again and again and always to return with some accretion: *Ammonia Soda Co Ltd v Chamberlain* at 286-7. Circulating capital includes trading stock and assets held for the purposes of investment: *QBE Insurance Group Ltd v ASC* (1992) 38 FCR 270 at 287; 110 ALR 301 at 318. When ascertaining whether a company has profits from which dividends can be paid, losses resulting from the depreciation of circulating capital must be taken into account and be off-set against any gains made by the company: *Verner v General and Commercial Investment Trust* [1894] 2 Ch 239 at 266. This is in contrast to the position for fixed assets, in which case the losses arising from depreciation need not be made good before the company can be said to have distributable profits: *Lee v Neuchatel Asphalte Co* (1889) 41 Ch D 1. Also known as 'circulating assets'. See also **Asset**; **Distributable profits**; **Fixed assets**; **Trading stock**.

Citibank Australia A foreign bank established in 1985, which is a wholly-owned subsidiary of the United States company, Citicorp. Citibank Australia engages in retail banking with an emphasis on mortgage and motor vehicle finance products, in international banking engaging in the foreign exchange, swaps and options markets, and in corporate finance and risk management. In 1985, the Citibank Private Bank became the first private bank in Australia.

City Panel on Takeovers and Mergers In the United Kingdom, the body which administers a self-regulatory system for takeovers, the broad principles of which are set out in the City Code on Takeovers and Mergers: *Crabtree v Hinchcliffe* [1972] AC 707 at 730, 740; [1971] 3 All ER 967 at 976, 984. See also **Merger**; **Takeover**.

Civil law 1. In contemporary terms, the Western European system of codified laws, in contradistinction to the evolutionary body of precedents associated with the common law tradition. **2.** A term formerly used to distinguish the positive laws of states from the canon law regulating the government of ecclesiastical institutions. See also **Common law**.

Civil penalty disqualification In relation to corporations, a disqualification from office resulting from an order made by the court where it is satisfied that a person has contravened a civil penalty provision. An example is the prohibition of a director from managing a corporation: Corporations Law s 1317EA(3)(a). A reference to a civil penalty disqualification is a reference to an order so in force: Corporations Law s 91(4A). See also **Civil penalty order**; **Civil penalty provision**.

•**Civil penalty order** An order which a court may make where a person has contravened a civil penalty provision: Corporations Law s 1317EA(1). An order may declare that a contravention has occurred, disqualify a contravener from managing a corporation or impose a pecuniary penalty: Corporations Law s 1317EA(3). A pecuniary penalty in an amount not exceeding $200,000 may be imposed only if the court is satisfied that the contravention is a serious one: Corporations Law s 1317EA(5). The court may also make a compensation order: Corporations Law s 1317HA. The order must be applied for within six years of the alleged contravention: Corporations Law s 1317EC. Where criminal proceedings have been commenced, any application for a civil penalty order in respect of the same contravention will be stayed: Corporations Law s 1317GB(2). See also **Civil penalty disqualification**; **Civil penalty provision**; **Corporate crime**; **Corporate offence**; **Corporate liability**; **Directors' duties**.

•**Civil penalty provision** In relation to corporations, provisions in relation to which a court may make civil penalty orders and institute criminal proceedings: Corporations Law s 1317DA. Examples, are the provisions of the Corporations Law requiring an officer of a corporation to act honestly with due care and diligence and without improperly using inside information or his or her position are civil penalty provisions: Corporations Law ss 232(2), (4), (5), (6), 1317DA. A person may also be subject to a civil penalty order if he or she contravenes a provision relating to lodging accounts, insolvent trading, or giving financial benefits to related parties: Corporations Law ss 318(1), 588G, 243ZE and 1317DA. A court may relieve a person (in whole or part) from liability for contravention of a civil penalty provision where either the person acted honestly or, having regard to all the circumstances of the case, it is fair to excuse the person for the contravention: Corporations Law s 1317JA. Criminal proceedings can be instituted where the contravener acted or omitted to act knowingly, intentionally or recklessly and, in addition, the contravener either was dishonest and intended to gain advantage for himself or herself or any other person or intended to deceive or defraud someone: Corporations Law s 1317FA. See also **Civil penalty order**; **Corporate crime**; **Corporate liability**; **Corporate offence**; **Directors' duties**.

•**Claim** The assertion of a right or demand to a right to property or to a remedy, a cause of action, the grounds in pleadings upon which relief is claimed: *Read v Brown* (1888) 22 QBD 128. Also known as 'action', 'cause', 'cause of action' or 'matter'. See also **Action; Cause of action; Counterclaim; Cross-claim; Joinder; Matter; Statement of claim; Suit**.

Class A franking account In relation to income tax, an account recording franking credits and debits relating to the 1992-93 and earlier income years: (CTH) Income Tax Assessment Act 1936 s 160APA. See also **Class B franking account; Franking account; Franking credit; Franking debit**.

•**Class action** Legal proceedings which allow the claims of many individuals against the same defendant, which arise out of the same or similar circumstances, to be conducted by a single representative: *Carnie v Esanda Finance Corporation Ltd* (1995) 182 CLR 398; 127 ALR 76.

Class B franking account In relation to income tax, the franking account that records franking credits and debits relating to the 1993-94 and later income years: (CTH) Income Tax Assessment Act 1936 s 160APA. See also **Class A franking account; Franking account; Franking credit; Franking debit**.

Class meeting A meeting of shareholders holding a particular class of shares in a company, usually distinguished by the particular rights attached to the shares. If there are not two or more classes of shares, all the shares in a body corporate constitute a class: Corporations Law s 57(1). Separate meetings of different classes of shareholders are often required in connection with a scheme of arrangement where the scheme may have a different effect on different classes of shareholders: Corporations Law s 411(1). See also **Class of shares; Scheme of arrangement**.

Class of assets or liabilities In corporations law, a category or group of assets or liabilities, which have a similar nature or similar function within a reporting entity: Corporations Regulations Sch 5 cl 12(1). Classes of assets or liabilities are disclosed in the financial statements as a single item without supplementary dissection. They will normally have notes attached giving a breakdown of the single reported figure. See also **Asset; Financial statement; Liability; Reporting entity; Reporting requirements**.

Class of shares A category of shares sufficiently different to other shares in terms of rights and benefits to make it distinguishable from any other category of shares: *Clements Marshall Consolidated Ltd v ENT Ltd* (1988) TasR (NC) N1; 13 ACLR 90. See also **Share**.

Class rights Where the share capital is divided into different classes of shares, the rights attached to that particular class: Corporations Law Sch Table A reg 4(1). See also **Class of shares; Variation of rights**.

Classification of accounts In accounting, a method of dividing accounts into various classes, each class denoting the nature of an account and whether it is a balance sheet item or a profit and loss item. The ledger accounts are classified into five categories: namely assets, liabilities, capital, revenue, and expenses. Assets are classified as current assets, fixed or non-current assets, and intangible assets. Liabilities are also classified as current or short-term liabilities, non-current or long-term liabilities. Expenses are classified as manufacturing expenses and administration expenses. See also **Asset; Balance sheet; Capital; Expense; Fixed assets; Intangible property; Liability; Loss; Profit; Revenue**.

•**Clause** For example, in a will, a clause contains the terms for a disposition made by the testator which, when removed, would leave the rest of the will intelligible and capable of being enforced: *Swinton v Bailey* (1878) 4 App Cas 70. See also **Term; Terms and conditions**.

Claused bill of lading See **Dirty bill of lading**.

Clayton's case, rule in The rule of 'first in, first out'. Payments are presumed to be appropriated to debts in the order in which the debts are incurred: *Devaynes v Noble; Clayton's Case* (1816) 1 Mer 572. See also **Account; Beneficiary; Fiduciary**.

Clean bill of lading A bill of lading that is unqualified by any statement about the order of condition of the goods: *Restitution Steamship Co v Sir John Pirie and Co* (1889) 61 LT 330. See also **Bill of lading**.

•**Clean hands** A doctrine of equity that requires a petitioner seeking equity to have acted properly. In any proceedings in equity under its inherent jurisdiction, a court will examine the conduct, in the transaction or arrangement which is the subject of the suit, of the party seeking relief: *Cory v Gertcken* (1816) 2 Madd 40; 56 ER 250. Should a petitioner be guilty of any impropriety, in the legal sense, in a matter pertinent to the suit then equity may refuse the decree sought: *Kettles and Gas Appliances Ltd v Anthony Hordern & Sons Ltd* (1934) 35 SR (NSW) 108 at 130-1.

Clean transport document A transport document which bears no clause or notation expressly declaring the goods to be transported, or their packaging, to have a defective condition. A clause will not make a bill 'unclean' unless the document to which it refers is one which exists at the time of shipment. Any such clause will result in a rejection of the bill unless the credit expressly stipulates the acceptability of the clause. See also **Letter of credit; Uniform Customs and Practice for Documentary Credits 1993**.

Clean up notice See **Clean up order**.

•**Clean up order** A notice requiring the recipient to institute a clean up program rather than specifying measures to be taken is not a valid clean up order: *Environment Protection Authority v Simsmetal Ltd* [1991] 1 VR 623; (1990) 70 LGRA 312.

•**Clearance 1.** The procedure available to the Trade Practices Commission (now the Australian Competition and Consumer Commission) prior to the 1977 amendments to the (CTH) Trade Practices Act 1974, to deem an arrangement not to be in restraint of trade. The Commission exercised this procedure if it was of the view that the restraint did not have, or was unlikely to have, a significant effect on competition. A clearance granted prior to the amendments now operates as an authorisation under (CTH) Trade Practices Act 1974 s 88. **2.** Colloquially, pre-merger consultation. Such a use is technically incorrect. See also **Australian Competition and Consumer Commission; Authorisation; Notification; Pre-merger consultation.

Clearance of cheque The procedure by which a cheque is verified by the drawee bank, which decides whether the cheque should be paid or dishonoured. Usually clearance takes place via a cheque clearing house. There are two levels of clearance; provisional and absolute clearance. Provisional clearance occurs where the deposit bank lodges the cheque with the clearing house to be directed to the drawee bank; at each day's end, account entries are totalled and balanced, and banks in debit settle their liabilities with those in credit. Absolute clearance is given after the time that a reasonable bank manager, with regard to banking practice, regards the cheque as paid because no notice of dishonour has been given. The traditional clearance procedure involved manual transfer of each cheque: *Ryan v Bank of NSW* [1978] VR 555. Electronic technology has provided a truncated means for cheque clearance. See also **Cheque; Clearing house; Collection; Deposit bank; Dishonour; Drawee bank; Exhibition; Home branch; Truncation.**

Clearance system An arrangement for the settlement of transactions in a stock exchange. See also **Clearing house.**

Cleared funds The proceeds of cheques and other payment instruments that are available to the depositor for withdrawal after a certain waiting period as regulated by the rules of the clearing system operated by the banking industry. See also **Clearance of cheque; Clearing house.**

Clearing deposit A deposit that must be paid to the futures clearing house before registration as a member of a futures exchange. For example, the Sydney Futures Exchange, in conjunction with the clearing house, determines a minimum initial margin for all futures contracts traded on the exchange. Also known as 'minimum initial margin'. See also **Futures contract; Sydney Futures Exchange.**

•**Clearing house** A central location or central processing mechanism through which financial institutions agree to exchange payment instructions or other financial obligations such as securities. See also **Clearing system.**

Bills of exchange and other negotiable instruments An association through which member banks exchange cheques drawn on each other, settling differences at the end of each day's trading. A definition is given in (CTH) Corporations Law s 9. National clearing conventions are determined from time to time by member banks of the Australian Clearing House Association. See also **Cheque; Clearance; Collection; Deposit bank; Dishonour; Drawee bank.**

Corporations An independent body which guarantees the fulfilment of all contracts traded on futures markets. The clearing house holds all deposit and margin payments and handles all cash settlements within the market, recording all business. The domestic contracts traded on the Sydney Futures Exchange are cleared in Sydney, while those contracts traded under international links are cleared by the clearing houses associated with the overseas exchanges. See also **Securities clearing house.**

Clearing House Automated Payments System
Abbr – CHAPS Introduced in 1983, a payments system enabling London clearing banks to engage in international transfers using the latest communications techniques. See also **Clearance; Clearing house.**

Clearing House Electronic Subregister System
Abbr – CHESS Introduced into Australia in 1992, a system providing for the electronic transfer of securities with the capacity to achieve a three day settlement period. The SCH maintains a subregister as an agent of issuing companies. On settlement of a transaction through the SCH there is an electronic signal on the SCH's system which brings about transfer of a parcel of securities from one holding on the subregister to another so as to effect at the same time a change in the register and the legal ownership. At the same time there will be an electronic transfer of funds between the participating member organisations. CHESS represents stage three of a plan to achieve common standards across a range of markets to facilitate cross-border investments. The plan was developed by the influential global think-tank known as the Group of Thirty (G30). Along with the Stock Exchange Automated Trading System (SEAPS), CHESS has transformed the Australian equities market, encouraging overseas investment. See also **Clearance; Clearing house; Securities clearing house; Stock Exchange Automated Trading System.**

Clearing House Interbank Payments System
Abbr – CHIPS Based in New York, a computerised telecommunications system that substantially eliminates cheques in the movement of funds. It was devised by the New York Clearing House Association, becoming operational in 1970. The system processes some 90 per cent of all international dollar transfer transactions. See also **Clearance; Clearing house.**

Clearing member A member organisation of the Australian Stock Exchange which has been approved as a clearing member for the purposes of the Stock Exchange Rules. See also **Clearance; Clearing house; Australian Stock Exchange Ltd.**

Clearing system A set of procedures by which financial institutions present and exchange data and documents relating to funds or securities transfers to other financial institutions at a single location known as the clearing house. The procedures often also include a mechanism for the calculation of participants' bilateral and multilateral net positions with a view to facilitating the settlement of their obligations on a net or net net basis. See also **Clearance; Clearing house; Netting.**

•**Client's segregated account** In relation to a futures broker, an account that is kept by the broker with a banking corporation that is designated as a client's segregated account and which does not contain money other than money deposited by the broker that was received from or on behalf of a client relating to a futures transaction involving the client: (CTH) Futures Industry Act 1986 s 86(1); Corporations Law s 9. See also **Futures broker; Futures contract.**

Clock speed In computing, the speed at which the microprocessor functions, measured in megahertz.

Within each class of microprocessor, the higher the number, the faster the microprocessor can function. However, two computers may be configured very differently, such that the one with a lower clock speed may still be faster than one with a higher clock speed due to a better memory configuration, or the inclusion of faster graphics cards and the like. See also **Microprocessor**.

Clog on the equity of redemption Any device imposed by a mortgagee upon a mortgagor to prevent or impede the mortgagor from redeeming property the subject of security. See also **Collateral advantage; Equity of redemption; Mortgage; Unconscionable**.

Clone Computer software or hardware that either looks and feels identical to that from which it is copied, or is very similar to the original in the way it functions. In computing, there is a distinction between a product that clones another (for the purpose of standardising and capitalising an existing market), and one that is a counterfeit (and thus an illegal copy of an original, sold fraudulently under a trademark belonging to a third party).

Close company A term used in United Kingdom corporation tax law to designate a company controlled by its directors or a small number of persons (five or fewer), the undistributed profits of which may for taxation purposes be treated as if they had been distributed: (UK) Income and Corporation Taxes Act 1988 s 423. See also **Close corporation; Corporation**.

Close corporation A term used in America and South Africa to describe a corporation having its shares, or at least its voting shares, owned by a small number of members: see *Brooks v Willcuts* 78 F 2d 270 at 273. See also **Close company; Closely held company; Corporation**.

•**Close out** In relation to a futures contract, to discharge the obligations of the person in the bought position or sold position under the futures contract either by matching the futures contract with a futures contract of the same kind under which the person has assumed an offsetting sold or bought position, or by any other means: (CTH) Futures Industry Act 1986 s 4; Corporations Regulations reg 1.2.03(3). Under the Corporations Law, it expressly extends discharging the obligations to whether or not they are enforceable at law or in equity: Corporations Law s 9. See also **Futures contract**.

•**Closed shop** An enterprise or workplace where all employees must be members of a particular union (or unions); that is, union membership is a condition of employment. A pre-entry closed shop exists where a person must be a union member to gain employment; a post-entry closed shop exists where a person must join the union and remain a member in order to stay in the employment. See also **Closed shop agreement; Compulsory unionism; Trade union**.

Closed shop agreement An agreement between an employer and a trade union that the employer's enterprise or workplace will be a 'closed shop'; that is, that only people who are members of that union may be employed there. See also **Closed shop; Compulsory unionism; Trade union**.

Closely held company A company with very few shareholders, all of whom are natural persons. A closely held company may, in certain circumstances, be regarded as an exempt proprietary company. The (CTH) Close Corporations Act 1989 (repealed) attempted to fashion a regime appropriate to the closely-held corporation, but has not been proclaimed. The (CTH) First Corporate Law Simplification Act 1995 dispensed with closely held corporations. See also **Exempt proprietary company**.

Closely held subsidiary Regarding a related party transaction, in relation to another body corporate, a body corporate where no member of the first mentioned body is a person other than: the other body; a nominee of the other body, a body corporate that is a closely held subsidiary of the other body because of any other application or applications of the above, or a nominee of such a body (Corporations Law s 243M(3)). It is a defence to the prohibition against related party transactions (Corporations Law s 243H) that the benefit was given to or by a closely held subsidiary: Corporations Law ss 243M(2)-(3). See also **Related party transaction; Subsidiary**.

•**Closing phase** In relation to a takeover offer, the last five trading days of the target company's home stock exchange immediately before the end of the offer period: Corporations Law s 603. See also **Offer period; Target company**.

Closing price The price of a security at the close of an exchange. See also **Australian stock exchange; Security**.

Closing purchase The sale of an option with the same characteristics as one previously bought to have the effect of cancelling each other out. A closing sale is the purchase of an option to match one sold earlier. See also **Australian stock exchange; Option**.

•**Club 1.** An association usually formed for a social object or purpose, with members sharing some common interest and meeting together as a group for mutual enjoyment and benefit: *Bohemians Club v Acting FCT* (1918) 24 CLR 334; [1918] VLR 234. **2.** An association (whether incorporated or unincorporated) of at least 30 people associated together for social, literary, cultural, political, sporting, athletic or other lawful purposes that sells or supplies liquor for consumption on its premises: (CTH) Sex Discrimination Act 1984 s 4. See also **Association; Domestic tribunal; Committee liability; Voluntary non-profit association**.

Co-agent In agency law, one of several persons given authority to act for a principal or co-principals, either jointly, or jointly and severally. A mere authority to act given to one of a number of co-agents, without further specification, is presumed to be a joint authority, and can be acted upon only by the co-agents jointly: *Brown v Andrew* (1849) 18 LJQB 153. However, an authority given jointly and severally may be acted upon by all or any of the co-agents so as to bind the principal: *Guthrie v Armstrong* (1822) 5 B & Ald 628; 106 ER 1320. A principal may also appoint co-agents giving power to a quorum to act on the principal's behalf, with the result that the principal is not bound by the act of any number less than the stipulated quorum: *Kirk v Bell* (1851) 16 QB 290; 117 ER 890. See also **Agency**; **Agent**; **Co-principal**; **Principal**.

•**Coasting trade** Sea-going trade between different ports of the same country. In Australia, it involves all trade between different Australian ports irrespective of which State or Territory the ports are situated in: *Owners of SS Kalibia v Wilson* (1910) 11 CLR 689. A ship engaged in overseas trade does not become involved in coasting trade merely because it is engaged in some coasting work as part of its voyage: (CTH) Navigation Act 1912 s 7. See also **Cabotage**.

Cocktail loan A loan drawn from various sources, at different rates of interest and probably on different terms. For example, a housing loan which proves inadequate for its purpose may be supplemented by a personal loan taken out at a much higher rate of interest. See also **Home loan insurance**; **Loan**.

•**Code** Legislation purporting to exhaustively cover a complete system of law (for example, the Code of Justinian) or a particular area of law as it existed at the time the code was enacted: for example (QLD) Criminal Code; (WA) Criminal Code; (NT) Criminal Code.

Code of Banking Practice A voluntary code of conduct established by the Australian Bankers' Association. The code seeks to foster good relations between banks and their customers, and to promote good banking practice by formalising standards of disclosure and conduct which adopting banks agree to observe when dealing with their customers. The code is voluntary, but for those institutions which agree to be bound, the provisions are contractually enforceable. Compliance with the code is monitored by the Australian Payments System Council, which provides annual reports to the Federal Treasurer. The code requires banks to have procedures for resolution of disputes between banks and customers. Also known as 'Banking Code'. See also **Australian Banking Industry Ombudsman Scheme**; **Banking practice**; **Banking custom**.

•**Code of ethics** A statement of the principles of right conduct relevant to the activities of a particular occupational group. Also known as 'code of practice'. See also **Code of practice**; **Professional misconduct**.

•**Code of practice** A code that provides guidance to industry on a particular matter, usually in relation to health and safety issues: (CTH) National Occupational Health and Safety Commission Act 1985 s 38. A code of practice is not usually binding at law. However, failure to follow a code of practice may have legal consequences under occupational health and safety legislation: for example: (NSW) Occupational Health and Safety Act 1983 ss 44A, 44B.

Trade and commerce Industry-agreed standards which form minimum terms of dealing. As arrangements are between competitors, these codes often must be authorised by the Australian Competition and Consumer Commission. See also **Arrangement**.

Co-insurance A number of persons forming a syndicate to underwrite a particular risk, reducing their exposure to that risk. See also **Average clause**.

Co-insurer An insurer who carries only part of the total risk under a contract of insurance. Under an average clause, where there is underinsurance, the insured is deemed to be a co-insurer for the uninsured portion of the loss: (CTH) Marine Insurance Act 1909 s 87. See also **Average**; **Broker's slip**; **Insurance contract**; **Underinsurance**.

•**Collar** In relation to an option, a combination of a cap and a floor. See also **Cap**; **Floor**; **Option**.

•**Collateral** 1. A subsidiary, concurrent, subordinate or additional security as opposed to primary security deposited by the borrower. 2. An item of value offered as security or pledged to secure a note or bond payable, to which the lender is entitled if the borrower does not repay the debt as agreed. See also **Agreement**; **Collateral loan**; **Collateral security**; **Security**.

Collateral advantage A stipulation forming part of the mortgage, giving the mortgagee some advantage in addition to the security: *Kreglinger v New Patagonia Meat and Cold Storage Co Ltd* [1914] AC 25. See also **Clog on the equity of redemption**.

Collateral benefit A benefit parallel but subordinate to a principal benefit. In an action for damages, collateral benefits flowing from transactions or events closely connected to the plaintiff's situation or from statutory provisions may be taken into account in assessing damages, and set off against the damages the defendant must pay, avoiding over-compensation of the plaintiff as a result: *Datson v Handley* [1980] VR 66. See also **Allocation system**; **Common law damages**; **Exemplary damages**.

Collateral contract A contract the consideration for which is the making of some other contract. See also **Consideration**; **Contract**.

Collateral loan A loan for which the borrower has deposited with the lender some kind of security as collateral, such as bonds, shares, or documents of title to land, that may be sold to satisfy the debt if it is not paid on maturity. See also **Collateral**; **Collateral security**.

•**Collateral security** 1. Property security as distinguished from the personal security of the debtor. 2. A security which is in addition to the main security to better secure the debt over which the main security exists. The mere giving of a security for a debt secured by the issue of a bill of sale does not make it necessary for the bill of sale to refer to that collateral security: *Carpenter v Deen* (1889) 23 QBD 566. See also **Collateral**; **Collateral loan**; **Charge**; **Mortgage**; **Security**.

Collateral trust bond A bond secured by specific assets. A person who issues a bond may offer security over particular assets (rather than as against their general credit standing). The assets, which may include stocks, notes, bonds or other obligations owned, are termed collateral, and the bond which they secure is a collateral trust bond. A parent company that owns bonds or stocks of its subsidiaries may use them as collateral against an issue of its own bonds. See also **Bond**; **Parent company**.

Collateral warranty See **Collateral contract**.

Collect freight Freight paid on the safe arrival of merchandise at the point of delivery. This mode of payment is advantageous to the shipper, as the carrier does not receive payment of the freight if unable to reach the destination. It is the opposite of 'advance freight'. It has a similar meaning to 'freight paid at destination' and 'freight at risk'. See also **Advance freight; Freight; Freight paid at destination.**

• **Collect, get in and receive** The terminology typically used in a court order appointing a receiver of a company, which empowers the receiver to collect, get in and receive the subject property. The receiver must use the same degree of diligence as if collecting the assets in a personal capacity: *Re Flowers & Co* [1897] 1 QB 14; *Massey v Banner* (1820) 1 Jac & W 241 at 247; 37 ER 367 at 369. Although this power authorises acts incidental to its pursuit, it does not permit sale of those assets: *Australian Industry Development Corp v Co-op Farmers & Graziers Direct Meat Supply Ltd* [1978] VR 633; (1977-78) CLC ¶40-394. See also **Court appointed receiver; Receiver.**

• **Collecting bank** A bank demanding payment of a cheque from a drawee bank on behalf of a customer or another financial institution who lodged the cheque with the collecting bank: (CTH) Cheques and Payment Orders Act 1986 s 62(1). See also **Cheque; Clearance; Collection; Deposit bank; Presentment.**

• **Collection** The crediting by the collecting bank of a cheque or a bill of exchange to the account of the holder. As regards cheques, a bank with whom a cheque is deposited for collection has a duty to present it for payment, or to make arrangements for collection to occur, as soon as is reasonably practicable, and is liable to the holder of the cheque for breach of this duty: (CTH) Cheques and Payment Orders Act 1986 s 66(1). A collecting bank which fails to reject a stale dishonoured cheque will be treated, subject to the clearing conventions, as having received the cleared proceeds and will be liable to its customer for money had and received for those proceeds: *Riedell v Commercial Bank of Australia Ltd* [1931] VLR 382. Most cheques are collected through the cheque clearing house. A deposit bank, or another bank on its behalf, will collect the cheque from the drawee bank via the clearing house. Also known as 'collecting the cheque'. See also **Bill of exchange; Cheque; Clearance; Clearing house; Collecting bank; Deposit bank; Holder; Presentment.**

Collective agreement An agreement between multiple parties where some of the parties have a common interest. Such agreements may involve an organisation acting on behalf of its members. In particular, a collective agreement is an agreement as to wages or working conditions arrived at between employers or employer organisations and trade unions. It differs from an enterprise agreement in that it is not registered with or certified by a State or Commonwealth authority, and thus its legal enforceability is unclear: *Gregory v Philip Morris Ltd* (1987) 77 ALR 79; 19 IR 258; (1988) 80 ALR 455; *Ryan (rec & mgr of Homfray Aust Pty Ltd) (in liq) v Textile Clothing and Footwear Union of Australia* (1996) 4 ACLC 555. Employers and unions may agree privately to wages or conditions exceeding those prescribed by awards or registered agreements. See also **Certified agreement; Collective bargaining; Enterprise agreement.**

Collective bargaining The decentralised system of industrial relations used, for example, in the United States. Employment conditions and dispute settlements are negotiated between the employers and the employees without reference to an arbitration authority. Parties to the bargaining may be one employer, or a group of employers, or employers' associations on one side, and employees or their representatives (such as trade unions) on the other. See also **Collective agreement; Enterprise bargaining.**

• **Collective body** In relation to an industrial organisation, the committee of management or a conference, council committee, panel or other body of or within the organisation: (NSW) Industrial Relations Act 1996 s 284. See also **Body; Industrial organisation.**

Collective boycott An agreement that restricts the persons whom the parties to the agreement may deal with. A collective boycott can also restrict the circumstances or conditions in which the parties to it deal with a person or class of persons. A collective boycott may be an exclusionary provision under (CTH) Trade Practices Act 1974 ss 4D, 45. See also **Collusion; Exclusionary provision; Secondary boycott.**

Collision Regulations 1972 *Abbr* – Colregs 1972 International rules for preventing collisions at sea. The Regulations were devised at the 1972 Convention for the Prevention of Collisions at Sea, London, and are in force in Australia: (CTH) Navigation Act 1912 ss 258(1), 258(2), 425(1)(e).

• **Collusion** In trade practices law, the common term for cooperative economic activity between firms, especially price fixing. Other collusive conduct includes concerted refusals to supply and collective boycotts in the nature of an exclusionary provision. See also **Cartel; Collective boycott; Competition law; Contract, arrangement or understanding; Exclusionary provision; Price fixing; Substantially lessening competition.**

• **Collusive bidding agreement** In relation to an auction, an agreement by two or more persons to submit a joint bid at an auction, or any other agreement that has the purpose or effect of preventing or restricting competition in respect of bidding at an auction: (TAS) Collusive Practices Act 1965 ; (VIC) Collusive Practices Act 1965 s 2(1). Also known as 'Collusive bidding contract'. See also **Auction; Bid; Collusion; Collusive tendering agreement; Competition; Knock-out agreement.**

• **Collusive tendering agreement** In Victoria, an agreement between two or more persons to submit identical tenders or a joint tender, or any other agreement having the purpose or effect of restricting competition in respect of tendering: for example (VIC) Collusive Practices Act 1965 s 2(1). See also **Collusion; Collusive bidding agreement; Competition; Fraud; Knock-out agreement.**

Colombo Plan for Cooperative Economic and Social Development in Asia and the Pacific A plan that essentially consists of an annual meeting of participating countries to discuss regional problems of economic and social development, trade and technical assistance. The Plan was officially changed to the

Colombo Plan for Economic and Social Development of Asia and the Pacific in December 1977.

Colonial Mutual Group One of Australia's oldest multi-national companies, established in 1873 by Jacques Martin and now participating in life and general insurance, superannuation and investment management. The group is also active in New Zealand, the United Kingdom, Fiji, Hong Kong, the Philippines and Singapore.

Colonial State Bank of New South Wales Ltd A bank established in its current form in 1990. It acts as an agency through which the State of New South Wales engages in State banking and, in so far as State insurance is incidental to its banking functions, as agent for State insurance: (NSW) State Bank (Corporatisation) Act 1989. Until a day to be appointed by proclamation, the payment of all money due by the corporation is guaranteed by the New South Wales Government: (NSW) State Bank (Corporatisation) Act 1989 s 12(1). The bank does not represent the State of New South Wales: (NSW) State Owned Corporations Act 1989 s 9. See also **Reserve Bank of Australia**.

Combined carriage Carriage by a carrier partly by air and partly by another mode of carriage. Where there is a combined carriage, the provisions of the Convention for the Unification of Certain Rules Relating to International Carriage by Air (Warsaw Convention) 1929 only apply to the portion of the carriage carried out by air, and even then, only if the airborne component is within art 1 of the Convention. The parties in a case of combined carriage are not prevented by the Convention from inserting conditions relating to other modes of carriage in a document of air carriage, provided that the provisions of the Convention are observed as regards the carriage by air. See also **Carrier; Combined carrier; International carriage of goods; Through bill of lading**.

Combined carrier A carrier whose business involves combined carriage partly by air and partly by other means. Also known as 'combination carrier'. See also **Carrier; Combined carriage; Through bill of lading**.

•**Comcare** A statutory body with the duty of arranging compensation and rehabilitation for employees of the Commonwealth Government, and certain other bodies. See also **Workers' compensation**.

Comfort letter 1. A formal but non-contractual assurance from a third party to a lender which represents that a particular fact is true, or that the third party is aware of the loan, or intends to act in a certain way in the future. 2. Often a recognition, addressed to a creditor, that the writer owes obligations to the creditor. See also **Creditor; Acceptance credit; Guarantee; Parent company; Subsidiary**.

Comite Maritime International Abbr – CMI The International Maritime Committee. A non-governmental organisation established in 1897 with the aim of contributing to the unification of maritime and commercial law, and maritime customs, usages and practices. Its headquarters are in Antwerp, Belgium. Membership is open to individuals and national and multinational associations concerned with maritime law. See also **International Maritime Organisation; Maritime law**.

Commencement of bankruptcy The point in time on and from which a person's bankruptcy is taken to have commenced: (CTH) Bankruptcy Act 1966 s 115. See also **Act of bankruptcy; Bankrupt; Bankruptcy; Creditor's petition; Debtor's petition; Relation-back doctrine; Sequestration**.

•**Commerce** See **Trade and Commerce**.

•**Commercial** Generally, relating to business. See also **Arbitration; UNCITRAL Model Law on International Commercial Arbitration 1985**.

•**Commercial agent** A person who, in return for payment or remuneration of some kind, undertakes tasks on behalf of another, such as serving a writ or summons, repossessing or locating goods, or collecting or requesting payment of debts. See also **Agent**.

Commercial arbitration legislation The uniform statutes passed by each State and Territory of Australia to regulate arbitration of commercial matters. The statutes are almost identical in every jurisdiction, except for some differences in the Western Australian legislation. See also **Alternative dispute resolution; Arbitration**.

Commercial bill A bill of exchange when used domestically for obtaining credit. See also **Bill of exchange; Trade bill**.

•**Commercial cause** A cause arising out of the ordinary transactions of merchants and traders, including issues relating to the construction of mercantile documents, export or import of merchandise, carriage of goods, sale of goods, building contracts, engineering contracts, insurance, banking, money lending, mercantile agency and mercantile usages: (QLD) Commercial Causes Act 1910 s 2.

Commercial contract A business contract. In practice, commercial contracts rarely, if ever, state all the primary obligations of the parties in full. Many terms are left to be incorporated by implication of law: *Photo Production Ltd v Securicor Transport Ltd* [1980] AC 827. See also **Business efficacy; Contract; Implied term**.

Commercial Court A court established to deal with commercial cases, based upon the philosophy that procedures should be formulated for cases that can most effectively minimise cost and delay. See also **Commercial Division**.

Commercial dispute resolution The application of alternative dispute resolution techniques to commercial disputes. See also **Alternative dispute resolution**.

Commercial Division A division of a supreme court created to deal with commercial disputes or disputes where there is an issue that has importance in trade or commerce: for example (NSW) Supreme Court Act 1970 s 38(b); (NSW) Supreme Court Rules Pt 14 r 2(1). See also **Supreme Court; Court of Appeal**.

Commercial judgment The assessment of risk (using financial or commercial criteria) or of character. The

Australian Banking Industry Ombudsman has no power to consider a complaint relating to a bank's commercial judgment in a decision about lending and security, unless the dispute concerns maladministration in lending matters. See also **Australian Banking Industry Ombudsman Scheme**.

Commercial law Areas of law having particular relevance to commerce and commercial transactions, such as contract, agency, banking, insurance, finance, export and import of merchandise, carriage of goods, mercantile agency and usages, company and partnership law.

Commercial List Specialist list kept in the supreme court of some jurisdictions to effect the efficient case processing required by the commercial community and made available to those proceedings arising out of ordinary commercial transactions: *Colmax Electrical Pty Ltd (in liq) v Industrial Equity Ltd* [1979] VR 577. See also **Commercial Division**.

Commercial paper Both negotiable and non-negotiable instruments. See also **Negotiable instrument; Promissory note**.

•**Commercial parking station** For fringe benefits tax purposes, in relation to a particular day, a permanent commercial car parking facility where any or all of the car parking spaces are available in the ordinary course of business to members of the public for all-day parking on that day on payment of a fee. A commercial parking station does not include a parking facility on a public street, road, lane, thoroughfare, or footpath, paid for by inserting money in a meter or by obtaining a voucher: (CTH) Fringe Benefits Tax Assessment Act 1986 s 136(1). See also **Car parking benefit; Fringe benefits tax**.

Commercial property Income producing real estate, such as office buildings, as distinguished from residential property. In the context of immunity from execution, it refers to property, other than diplomatic or military property, that is in use by the foreign state concerned substantially for commercial purposes: (CTH) Foreign States Immunities Act 1985 s 32(3). In that same context, it does not include a chose in action constituted by the credit balance in a bank account: *Alcom Ltd v Republic of Colombia* [1984] AC 580. See also **Commercial property**.

Commercial transaction A business arrangement or agreement usually involving alteration of legal rights. See also **Contract; Transaction**.

•**Commercial Tribunal** A specialist body established in New South Wales, South Australia and Western Australia to administer the relevant consumer credit legislation of each of those jurisdictions. See also **Credit provider's licence; Re-opening of contract; Unjust contract**.

•**Commission 1.** A form of remuneration for work or services. **2.** Authority granted for a particular action, function or office (for example, a judge's commission from the Crown).

Agency Remuneration paid by a principal to an agent. An agent has no right to commission unless there is an express or implied contract to that effect: *Dolphin v Harrison, San Miguel Pty Ltd* (1911) 13 CLR 271; (1911) 17 ALR 444. Also known as 'brokerage'. See also **Agency; Agent; Brokerage clause; Contract; Principal; Remuneration**.

Corporations The amount of money charged by a broker for executing trades on behalf of clients; payment of a percentage of an account involved in a transaction: Corporations Law s 9. See also **Broker**.

Equity The remuneration or compensation paid to a trustee. See also **Trust; Trustee**.

Commission broker 1. A member of a commodity or stock exchange who executes buy and sell orders. **2.** An agent who receives commission for executing orders for the purchase or sale of securities or commodities. Also known as 'commission agent' or 'commission merchant'. See also **Broker; Dealer**.

Commission merchant See **Commission broker**.

•**Commission of inquiry** A public inquiry into environmental issues provided for under various statutes: for example (CTH) Environment Protection (Impact of Proposals) Act 1974 s 11; (NSW) Environmental Planning and Assessment Act 1979 s 119.

Commissioner for Consumer Affairs A public office which gives advice on consumer affairs, investigates consumer complaints, provides information, and undertakes consumer education programmes. In Victoria, these functions are performed by the Secretary to the Department of Justice. In every other State or Territory there is an office with the title of either Commissioner for Consumer Affairs or Director of Consumer Affairs: for example (NSW) Fair Trading Act 1987 Pt 2 Div 1; (QLD) Fair Trading Act 1989 Pt II Div 1. These offices supervise the operation and enforcement of the consumer protection legislation in their jurisdiction, including the consumer credit legislation. The Commissioner's duties in relation to consumer credit transactions include reviewing and reporting on the operation of the credit legislation, advising consumers, receiving consumer complaints concerning credit contracts, negotiating variations in credit contracts on behalf of debtors experiencing hardship, taking proceedings on behalf of complainants, keeping registers of licensed credit providers and finance brokers and a register of deeds of undertakings by credit providers: for example (NSW) Fair Trading Act 1987 s 9; (NSW) Credit Act 1984 (repealed) ss 74(2), (3) (now replaced by Uniform Consumer Credit Code); (NSW) Credit (Administration) Act 1984 (repealed) ss 41(1), 43 (now replaced by Uniform Consumer Credit Code). See also **Consumer Affairs Council; Credit contract; Fair Trading Legislation; Re-opening of contract; Unjust contract**.

Commissioner of Patents A statutory office created under (CTH) Patents Act 1990 s 207. See also **Patent; Patent Office**.

•**Commissioner of Taxation** The statutory office holder, appointed by the Governor-General, who has general administration of federal taxation legislation: (CTH) Taxation Administration Act 1953 ss 2, 3A, 4. That person is also the Child Support Registrar: (CTH) Child Support (Registration and Collection) Act 1989 s

10. See also **Income taxation**; **Taxation**; **Taxation determination**; **Taxation ruling**.

•**Committee** A group of persons appointed from a larger body to attend to special business or to manage the business of a club or organisation: for example (NSW) Sydney Organising Committee for the Olympic Games Act 1993 s 3. A committee, however styled, is the body that manages the affairs of an association: for example (QLD) Associations Incorporation Act 1981 s 5(1). See also **Association**; **Committee liability**; **Constitution**; **Incorporated association**; **Officer**; **Unincorporated association**.

Committee for Inspection and Audit *Abbr* – CIA A company audit committee comprised of non-executive directors, serving as an intermediary between management and the auditor and reporting directly to the board of directors. See also **Audit committee**; **Audit**; **Auditor**.

Committee liability The doctrine by which courts hold committee members of an unincorporated association personally liable for a contract entered into, purportedly on behalf of the association, by members of the committee or persons acting with their authority: *Bradley Egg Farm Ltd v Clifford* [1943] 2 All ER 378; *Peckham v Moore* [1975] 1 NSWLR 353. The doctrine is accepted in Australia, but it is uncertain whether the doctrine applies where committee members enter a contract intended to last beyond that committee's term of office: *Carlton Cricket and Football Social Club v Joseph* [1970] VR 487. See also **Actual authority**; **Apparent authority**; **Association**; **Authority**; **Committee**; **Unincorporated association**.

Committee of creditors A committee which may be appointed during the first meeting of company creditors convened by an administrator of a company under voluntary administration. See also **Administrator**.

Committee of Inquiry into the Australian Financial System The Campbell Committee established by the Commonwealth government in 1979 to investigate the whole of the Australian financial system. It presented an interim report in 1980 and a final report in 1981. The final report recommended extensive deregulation of the financial system, with the admission of foreign banks; the abolition of controls over exchange, deposit and interest rates; a greater emphasis on the supervision of banks; the freeing of semi-government authorities to raise funds from the market rather than through government; and the issue of domestic banking licences. These and many other recommendations have since been implemented. The Committee's recommendations were subsequently reviewed by the Martin Review Group, reporting in 1984. See also **Campbell Inquiry**; **Wallis Inquiry**.

Committee of inspection 1. A group of creditors and contributories or their attorneys elected under Corporations Law s 548 by the general body of creditors and contributories to advise and superintend the liquidator: ss 548-552. 2. A committee appointed by resolution at a meeting of a bankrupt's creditors for the purpose of advising and superintending the bankrupt's trustee: (CTH) Bankruptcy Act 1966 s 70. The committee acts by a majority of its members present at a meeting: s 70(7).

See also **Bankrupt**; **Creditor**; **Contributing shareholder**; **Liquidation**; **Liquidator**; **Trustee in bankruptcy**; **Winding up**.

•**Commodity** 1. Generally, the products of agriculture or mining: for example, wool, wheat, soybeans or gold. 2. In relation to financial futures (including stock indices), financial products: for example, US Treasury Bonds. 3. In relation to a corporation, anything capable of delivery pursuant to an agreement for its delivery: Corporations Law s 9. See also **Future goods**.

•**Commodity agreement** A standardised agreement, which in effect places a person under an obligation under the futures regulations in Corporations Law Ch 8 to make or accept delivery at a particular time of a particular quantity of a particular commodity for a particular price or a price to be calculated in a particular manner: s 9; *Shoreline Currencies (Aust) Pty Ltd v Corporate Affairs Commission of NSW* (1986) 11 NSWLR 22; 10 ACLR 847; *Carragreen Currency Corporation Pty Ltd v Corporate Affairs Commission of NSW* (1986) 7 NSWLR 705; 11 ACLR 298. See also **Futures contract**.

Commodity bond Issued principally by companies and traded by banks and investment banks, commodity-linked bonds are of three kinds. A straight indexed bond has its return (interest or capital or both) linked to a commodity price index. A commodity convertible bond allows the holder to choose, on redemption day, to take either a sum of money or a commodity itself, whichever is worth more, thus limiting a buyer's possible losses. A third type of bond pays back the holder in cash, but carries a warrant, allowing the holder to buy, for instance, a certain number of bags of coffee at a certain price.

Commodity broker A trader in commodities; a broker who buys and sells contracts for future delivery of items of commerce or trade; a stockbroker. See also **Sharebroker**.

Commodity contract A contract for the sale of goods regularly dealt with on a commodity market or exchange in a State, and which is specified by a regulation made by the Governor: Commercial Arbitration Acts s 41(2). See also **Commercial Arbitration Legislation**.

Commodity futures contract A contract where the parties will make an adjustment between them at a specified future time in Australian currency according to whether a specified quantity of a specified commodity is worth more, or worth less, in Australian currency at that time than it was worth in Australian currency at the time the contract was made, the difference being determined in accordance with the business rules of the futures market at which the contract is made. Also know as 'commodity agreement'. See also **Commodity agreement**; **Futures contract**.

Commodity Futures Trading Commission *Abbr* – CFTC The United States agency formed under the (US) Commodity Exchange Act 1976 to regulate the United States commodity industry. See also **Australian stock exchange quoted security**.

Commodity swap A large transaction, generally restricted to institutional traders, involving agreements of up to 12 years' duration in which a bank typically acts as the go-between. Swaps occur on a widening range of commodities including oil, oil products including jet fuel, gold and base metals such as copper, zinc and aluminium. The simplest commodity swaps allow suppliers to fix their prices and hence incomes, while end-users are able to fix the price of their supply and hence total costs over the period of the agreement. A swap is essentially a private arrangement with no commodity market involvement. See also **Commodity**.

•**Common carrier** A carrier whose business is to be ready to carry for hire, at a reasonable price, passengers or goods for any person irrespective of who the consignor may be: *James v Commonwealth* (1939) 62 CLR 339; 13 ALJ 34. See also **Carriage by land; Carrier**.

Common cost The cost arising from operations as a whole, or from any relevant block of activities under consideration, that is unattributable to any one product or service: *Clear Communications Ltd v Telecom Corp of New Zealand* (1992) 27 IPR 481. See also **Monopoly profit**.

•**Common general knowledge** In patent law, the background knowledge and experience available to all practitioners of an industrial art in considering the making of new products, or improvements in old products. Standard texts, trade journals, and published patent specifications are possible sources of common general knowledge, but qualify only if the information they contain is generally known and accepted as a good basis for further action by the bulk of those engaged in the particular art. Only common general knowledge in the patent area can be used as evidence in invalidity proceedings based on lack of inventive step: (CTH) Patents Act 1990 s 7; *Minnesota Mining and Manufacturing Co v Beiersdorf (Aust) Ltd* (1980) 144 CLR 253 at 292; *British Acoustic Films Ltd v Nettlefold Productions* (1936) 53 RPC 221 at 250; *General Tire & Rubber Co v Firestone Tyre and Rubber Co Ltd* (1972) 89 RPC 457 at 482.

•**Common law** The unwritten law derived from the traditional law of England as developed by judicial precedence, interpretation, expansion and modification: *Dietrich v R* (1992) 177 CLR 292 at 319-20; 109 ALR 385. Generally, a statute will not be taken to have repealed the common law unless it explicitly or implicitly shows such an intention: *Fuller v R* (1994) 34 NSWLR 233; *Corporate Affairs Commission (NSW) v Yuill* (1991) 172 CLR 319 at 322, 338.

Common law and equity approach to misrepresentation In relation to contract law, the effect of misrepresentation at common law. At common law, a person who was induced to enter into a contract by a fraudulent misrepresentation could rescind the contract, but a party could not rescind on the basis of an innocent misrepresentation unless it resulted in a complete difference in substance between what was agreed and the actual subject matter of the contract, so as to constitute a failure of consideration: *Kennedy v Panama New Zealand and Australian Royal Mail Co Ltd* (1867) LR 2 QB 580. However, the equitable approach, which now prevails, is that a party who was induced by misrepresentation to enter into a contract may rescind the contract *ab initio*, provided the parties can be restored, substantially, to their pre-contractual positions: *Redgrave v Hurd* (1881) 20 Ch D 1. See also **Common law fraud; Damages; Deceit; Fraud; Fraudulent misrepresentation; Innocent misrepresentation; Misrepresentation; Negligent misrepresentation; Remedy**.

Common law and equity approach to mistake In relation to contract, the effect of mistake at common law and in equity. At common law, it was assumed that a sufficiently 'fundamental' mistake would render a contract void. This is still reflected in Sale of Goods legislation, which declares void a contract for the sale of specific goods that have, unknown to the seller, perished at the time the contract was made: for example (NSW) Sale of Goods Act 1923 s 11. However, declaring a contract void *ab initio* may defeat the rights of an innocent third party. Therefore, in equity, a mistake may only render a contract voidable and the courts will not set aside the transaction where to do so would defeat third party rights: *Taylor v Johnson* (1983) 151 CLR 422; 45 ALR 265. See also **Mistake; Rectification; Rescission; Third party; Void**.

Common law damages The principal remedy a defendant is required to pay to a plaintiff for loss suffered by the plaintiff as a result of the defendant's tort or breach of duty. See also **Damages; Measure of damages**.

Common law defence A defence to an offence where the defendant acts from an honest and reasonable mistake as to existence of facts which, if true, would have made the acts innocent. The defendant will not be guilty of the offence: *Proudman v Dayman* (1941) 67 CLR 536.

Common law fraud Dishonest conduct, the aim of which is to obtain a material advantage over another. Common law fraud is proved by showing that a false representation has been made knowingly or without belief in its truth, or recklessly, without caring whether it is true or false: *Derry v Peek* (1889) 14 App Cas 337. See also **Common law and equity approach to misrepresentation; Deceit; Fraud; Fraudulent misrepresentation**.

Common law jurisdiction The jurisdiction of courts which exercise their powers according to the principles of the common law. Common law jurisdictions are the Commonwealth, Australian Capital Territory, New South Wales, South Australia and Victoria. See also **Common law**.

Common market A general term for any multinational free trade area protected by a common external tariff. See also **European Union**.

Common rule The general application of an award to all employers and employees within a particular industry or in relation to a particular trade or occupation.

Common rule award An award that has been declared by a tribunal such as the Australian Industrial Relations Commission to be a common rule in the industry covered by the award: (CTH) Industrial Relations Act 1988 s 141. The rights and duties created by an award apply to all employers and employees in the industry, whether or not they are parties to the award, or are members of an employers' or employees' organisation. It differs from a standard award, which only binds parties to the award. See also **Common rule; Industrial award**.

Common trust fund An investment made by trustees using assets belonging to more than one trust. Trustee companies are authorised by statute to invest trust assets in common funds and, in several States, trustees are authorised by statute to invest trust assets in the common funds of trustee companies or the Public Trustee: for example (NSW) Trustee Act 1925 s 14A; (QLD) Trustee Companies Act 1968 s 36. See also **Trust; Trust fund**.

Commonwealth Bank of Australia A bank established by Commonwealth legislation in 1911 to carry on ordinary banking business. Central bank functions developed gradually until the Second World War when considerable responsibilities were conferred in areas such as exchange control and the administration of monetary and banking policy. In 1959, Commonwealth legislation created the Reserve Bank of Australia to carry on the central banking functions of the Commonwealth Bank. The bank's commercial operations were taken over by the Commonwealth Banking Corporation (CBC). See also **Central bank; Reserve Bank of Australia; Commonwealth Banking Corporation**.

Commonwealth Banking Corporation *Abbr* – CBC Formerly, a statutory corporation established by the Commonwealth government in 1959 to take over the commercial functions of the Commonwealth Bank of Australia. These functions embraced the Commonwealth Trading Bank of Australia, the Commonwealth Savings Bank of Australia and the Commonwealth Development Bank of Australia. The CBC became one of the four major banks in Australia. In 1990-91, the CBC acquired and absorbed the State Bank of Victoria. In April 1991, the CBC was converted to a public company with share capital, ceasing to be a statutory corporation. The CBC was listed on the Australian Stock Exchange in September 1991. See also **Australian Banking System**.

Commonwealth industrial authority A board, court, tribunal, body, or person having authority under a Commonwealth Act to exercise a power of conciliation or arbitration in relation to industrial disputes: (CTH) Occupational Superannuation Standards Regulations r 3(1). See also **Administrative Appeals Tribunal; Court; Australian Industrial Relations Commission**.

Commonwealth Industrial Court See **Australian Industrial Court**.

•**Commonwealth law** An Act, regulation, rule, by-law or determination made under an Act; an ordinance of a Territory, or a regulation, rule, by-law or determination made under an ordinance of a Territory; or an order or award made under any of the above laws: (CTH) Sex Discrimination Act 1984 s 4.

Commonwealth loan interest rebate A tax rebate of 10 cents for each $1 of interest on certain Commonwealth, State or semi-governmental bonds, debentures, stocks or securities (for example, Water Board loans) included in a taxpayer's taxable income: (CTH) Income Tax Assessment Act 1936 s 160AB(1). This concession is limited to interest on securities issued before 1 November 1968: (CTH) Income Tax Assessment Act 1936 s 160AB(2). See also **Rebate; Taxable income**.

•**Commonwealth of Australia** The form of government established for Australia in 1901 by the creation of the Commonwealth Constitution: (IMP) Commonwealth of Australia Constitution Act 1900 s 6. This Commonwealth of Australia is essentially federal in character. See also **Constitution; Executive**.

Commonwealth Scientific and Industrial Research Organisation *Abbr* – CSIRO A body established by the Commonwealth Government to undertake and assist in the application of scientific research for the benefit of the Australian community and industry: (CTH) Science and Industry Research Act 1949 ss 8, 9, 9AA. See also **Australian Centre for International Agricultural Research**.

Commonwealth use government inscribed stock Australian consolidated inscribed stock. General nature and capital stock issued by the Commonwealth government currently by public tender. In the case of a public tender, a prospectus is published. On issue, no document of title is provided, the entitlement to stock being 'inscribed' or recorded in a stock register. Other Commonwealth government securities such as Treasury bonds, notes, indexed bonds and bills are also currently inscribed. See also **Bond; Treasury bond; Treasury note; Treasury stock**.

Communication of acceptance Words or acts that indicate an intention to enter into a legally binding contract with the offeror on the terms contained in the offer. Generally, silence cannot constitute acceptance; some positive words or acts directed at the offeror are required: *Felthouse v Bindley* (1862) 11 CB(NS) 869; 142 ER 1037; *Empirnall Holdings Pty Ltd v Machon Paull Partners Pty Ltd* (1988) 14 NSWLR 523. See also **Acceptance; Offer; Postal acceptance rule**.

Commutation The act of substituting one thing for another.
Taxation and revenue The substitution of regular future payments under a contract in exchange for a lump sum payment. See also **Annuity; Pension**.

Companies Acts See **Companies and securities legislation**.

Companies and Securities Advisory Committee *Abbr* – CASAC A body corporate set up under (CTH) Australian Securities Commission Act 1989 s 145, 146 and charged with various functions including advising the Minister about proposed new national scheme laws, and reform of existing laws. It also has a broader function as a watchdog on the effectiveness of administration of the national scheme laws: (CTH) Australian Securities Commission Act 1989 ss 148, 148A. See also **Australian Securities Commission; Australian Securities Commission Law; Corporations Law**.

Companies and Securities Law Reform Committee *Abbr* – CSLRC Under the cooperative scheme, prior to the introduction of the Corporations Law, the body established under the 1978 agreement between the Commonwealth and the States to report to the government on matters relating to the reform of Australian companies and securities law. This role is now carried out by the Companies and Securities Advisory Committee (CASAC). See also **Companies and Securities Advisory Committee; Cooperative Companies and Securities legislation**.

Companies and securities legislation Prior to the introduction of the Corporations Law in 1991, a cooperative system of companies and securities laws throughout the States and Territories of Australia. In 1978, pursuant to a formal agreement, the Commonwealth, States and Territories agreed to a scheme where the Commonwealth's legislation was applied in each of the States. The Commonwealth regulatory body (the National Companies and Securities Commission) was empowered to regulate each State's application of the Commonwealth's laws. Legislation passed under the scheme comprised the Companies Act 1981; Securities Industry Act 1980; Futures Industry Act 1986; Company (Acquisition of Shares) Act 1980 and ancillary legislation. Also known as 'Companies Code'.

Companies Auditors and Liquidators Disciplinary Board *Abbr* – CALDB The body responsible under the Corporations Law for disciplining both auditors and liquidators: (CTH) Australian Securities Commission Act 1989 ss 202, 204. See also **Auditor; Corporations Law; Liquidator**.

Companies Code See **Companies and securities legislation**.

•**Company** An association of a number of persons with a common object or objects. It usually denotes a business or professional association. The term has no strict legal meaning: *Re Stanley* [1906] 1 Ch 131. 'Company' is broader than 'corporation', referring to unincorporated groups organised as joint ventures or joint stock companies. It can also be used to refer to unincorporated partnerships and collectives. For the purposes of the Corporations Law, the term is limited to a company registered under the Corporations Law: Corporations Law s 9. See also **Australian Securities Commission Law; Company limited by shares; Corporation; Corporations Law; Joint venture; No liability company; Partnership; Private company; Proprietary company; Public company; Unlimited company**.

•**Company auditor** See **Auditor**.

Company board See **Board of directors**.

Company buyback This practice became legal in 1991 when the buyback provisions of the Corporations Law came into effect. Buybacks can also be effected through a pro-rata offer to shareholders, or through selective purchases approved by 75 per cent of the shareholders (excluding the vendor shareholder) and with an expert opinion that the price is fair and reasonable. See also **Buyback scheme**.

Company constitution The articles of association and memorandum of association of a company. See also **Articles of association; Company; Memorandum of association**.

Company director See **Director**.

Company doctor A specialist businessman or a management expert who advises companies that have got into financial difficulties on methods of corporate reorganisation so that they may again become profitable. See also **Company; Company financial restructuring**.

Company financial restructuring The reconstruction of a company designed to meet any, some or all of the following objectives: reduce debt to manageable levels, prepare the way for the introduction of new equity, simplify the corporate structure, enable core business units to operate in a more favourable context, remove sources of cash flow drainage, and promote more effective management. The restructuring may be achieved by the sale of non-core assets or businesses, the sale and leaseback of property or intangible assets, the factoring of working capital assets, and the securitisation of specific assets by establishing a trust or other structure.

•**Company having a share capital** A company limited by shares formed on the principle of having the liability of the members limited by the memorandum of association to the unpaid amount on shares owned by them. All companies limited by shares must have a share capital: Corporations Law s 117(1)(b). A company having a share capital also includes an unlimited company with a share capital: s 9. See also **Share capital**.

•**Company law** See **Companies and securities legislation**.

•**Company limited by guarantee** A company formed on the principle of having the liability of its members limited to the respective amounts that the members undertake to contribute to the property of the company if it is wound up: Corporations Law ss 9, 115. See also **Company limited by shares; Company limited by guarantee and shares**.

Company limited by guarantee and shares A company limited by guarantee in which some members also hold shares. All members are liable to honour their guarantee if the company is wound up: Corporations Law ss 117(1)(d), 518. See also **Company limited by guarantee; Company limited by shares**.

•**Company limited by shares** A company which is funded by each member contributing, or promising to contribute when called upon to do so, a certain amount of money by way of share capital. On the winding up of the company, members are primarily liable to pay any part of the nominal value of their shares which has not been paid: Corporations Law ss 9, 115. See also **Company having a share capital; Company limited by guarantee; Company limited by guarantee and shares; Par value**.

•**Company member** See **Shareholder**.

Company name The name, apart from the Australian Company Number (ACN), which the Australian Securities Commission registers. See also **Australian company number; Incorporation**.

•**Company officer** A person who is a director, secretary, executive officer, or employee of a company; a receiver and manager of company property, not appointed by a court; an official manager, deputy manager or administrator of a company; a liquidator in a voluntary winding up, not appointed by a court; or a trustee managing a compromise or arrangement: (CTH) Corporations Law s 82A; (CTH) Bankruptcy Act 1966 s 5. See also **Company; Company secretary; Director; Executive officer**.

Company property Property acquired or held by a company. A company has power to acquire, hold and dispose of property: Corporations Law s 123(2)(e). Company property belongs to the company as an entity and not to the shareholders individually: for example *Macaura v Northern Assurance Co Ltd* [1925] AC 619; *Constitution Insurance Co of Canada v Kosmopoulas* (1987) 34 DLR (4th) 208.

Company, proprietary See **Proprietary company**.

Company, public See **Public company**.

Company rate of tax The rate of tax payable by a company on its taxable income. See also **Taxable income; Tax-free threshold; Unit trust; Year of income**.

Company seal The official seal of a company. See also **Australian Company Number; Company; Seal**.

Company secretary A person required to be appointed by a company's directors under Corporations Law s 240 and having the responsibility for all the record-keeping within the company, such as the registers required by the Corporations Law, minutes of meetings of directors and members, and also sending out notices of meetings. A company secretary is not necessarily involved in the management of a company: *Panorama Developments (Guildford) Ltd v Fidelis Furnishing Fabrics Ltd* [1971] 2 QB 711; [1971] 3 All ER 16; *Holpitt Pty Ltd v Swaab* (1992) 10 ACLC 64; 6 ACSR 488. See also **Apparent authority; Company seal; Corporations Law; Implied authority**.

Company tax See **Company rate of tax**.

Comparative advantage The principle on which international trade is substantially based, modified by protection. A comparative advantage exists when a country can produce a product at a relatively lower cost than other countries. It pays, therefore, to export such goods and to import those goods in which the country has a lesser or negative advantage. If country A can produce two commodities more cheaply than country B, country A will still tend to specialise in that commodity in which it has the greater comparative advantage and let country B specialise in the other. See also **Commodity; International trade**.

•**Comparative advertising** A form of advertising in which the advertised product or service of one trader is compared with that of another, the comparison taking various forms such as price, popularity, or effects of testing upon the product. In trade practices law, comparative advertising will generally not amount to misleading or deceptive conduct under (CTH) Trade Practices Act 1974 s 52 if factually correct information is provided and purchasers are invited to compare the product to the products of competitors: *Country Road Clothing Pty Ltd v Najee Nominees Pty Ltd* (1991) 20 IPR 419. See also **Misleading or deceptive conduct; Trade mark**.

Comparative statement A financial statement showing current period amounts together with corresponding amounts from a previous period or year. Accounting standards require that accounts and consolidated accounts contain comparative statements: Approved Accounting Standard AASB 1018. See also **Accounts; Consolidated profit and loss account; Financial statement**.

•**Compensable loss** Pecuniary and non-pecuniary loss recognised by the law as capable and worthy of remedy by a pecuniary award such as damages. A loss is compensable if it was incurred as a result of the commission of a tort, or if it is covered by a compensation scheme such as workers' compensation or motor accident compensation. Compensable losses include physical injury to the person, damage to property, and increasingly, mental distress and pure economic loss. See also **Compensation; Damage**.

•**Compensation** An amount given or received as recompense for a loss suffered. See also **Damages**.

Contract In the context of remedies for breach of contract, the objective that the plaintiff should recover what would have been received under the contract, or an equivalent. When damages are awarded in contract the plaintiff is, so far as money can do it, to be placed in the same situation, with respect to damages, as if the contract had been performed: *Wenham v Ella* (1972) 127 CLR 454; *Commonwealth v Amann Aviation Pty Ltd* (1991) 174 CLR 64; 104 ALR 1. See also **Breach of contract; Contract; Damages; Exemplary damages; Penalty**.

Compensation for loss of office In relation to a director, a benefit given to a director who retires from, or is removed from, the position of director of a company. A director may not be given a benefit on retirement from the position of director of a company unless the giving of the benefit has been approved by the members of the company (and its holding company) in general meeting: Corporations Law s 237. (NSW) Corporations Law s 227 outlines the process by which directors may be removed from office, Corporations Law s 227(11) provides that nothing in the process may deprive a person from any rights to compensations or damages they may have. See also **Director**.

•**Competition** A contest for some prize or advantage.

Trade and commerce In trade and commerce, rivalrous market behaviour. The competitive state of a market can be determined from its structure, including: the number and distribution of independent sellers, especially the degree of market concentration; the height of barriers to entry; the extent of product differentiation; the character of vertical relationships; and the nature of any stable arrangements between firms which restrict their ability to function independently: *Re Queensland Co-operative Milling Association Ltd* (1976) 8 ALR 481; ATPR ¶40-012. See also **Barrier to entry; Competition law; Concentration ratio; Market; Market power; Market structure; Monopolistic competition; Perfect competition; Substantially lessening competition; Workable competition**.

Competition code A model code inserted into the (CTH) Trade Practices Act 1974 by the (CTH) Competition Policy Reform Act 1995: (CTH) Competition Policy Reform Act 1995 Conduct Code Agreement Cl 5. See also **Competition law; Trade practices legislation**.

Competition law The general term, used mostly in Europe, for the body of law in various jurisdictions throughout the world dealing with market behaviour of corporate and business entities and industrial organisation and structure. Each jurisdiction's competition law is based on its own national and regional jurisprudence and economic and political rationale, usually with the underlying general belief (for different reasons) that free market behaviour is the ideal. Thus, each set of laws deals with a standard set of prohibitions and issues, including contracts in restraint of trade, exclusive dealing, mergers and acquisitions, and price discrimination. The seminal legislative instruments are the (US) Sherman Antitrust Act 1890, the (US) Clayton Antitrust Act 1914, and the Treaty Establishing the European Economic Community (Treaty of Rome) 1957 Competition Rules. The Australian competition legislation is contained in (CTH) Trade Practices Act 1974 Pt IV. Also known as 'restrictive trade practices law' in Australia and 'antitrust law' in the United States. See also **Acquisition; Antitrust; Competition; Contract in restraint of trade; Exclusive dealing; Market; Merger; Price discrimination; Restraint of trade; Restrictive trade practices; Trade practices legislation; Treaty Establishing the European Economic Community (Treaty of Rome) 1957 Competition Rules.**

Competition Policy Reform Act 1995 Legislation passed by the Commonwealth Parliament making substantial amendments to the scheme of regulation established under the (CTH) Trade Practices Act 1974. The legislation merges the functions of the former Trade Practices Commission and the former Prices Surveillance Authority into a new body, the Australian Competition and Consumer Commission. Through a cooperative scheme between the Commonwealth, the States and Territories, all sectors of the Australian economy, including government business functions, become subject to the restrictive trade practice provisions of the (CTH) Trade Practices Act 1974. The mechanism adopted to achieve the external coverage is by each of the Commonwealth, the States and the Territories becoming parties to the Competition Principles Agreement; Conduct Code Agreement; Agreement to Implement the National Competition Policy and Related Reforms. Each State and Territory is committed to the adoption of the Competition Code so as to apply the restrictive trade practices provisions contained in the (CTH) Trade Practices Act 1974 to entities otherwise not caught by the Commonwealth legislation due to constitutional limitations. Other important provisions include a new access regime for certain declared services thought to be essential and an expanded range of conduct for which authorisation can be granted. See also **Access regime; Conduct code agreement; National competition policy and related reforms agreement; Australian Competition and Consumer Commission; Trade Practices Commission; Prices Surveillance authority; Trade practices legislation.**

•**Competitive bidding** Any mode of sale where prospective purchasers are enabled to compete for the purchase of articles in any way, as where the price is fixed and the buyers chosen by the auctioneer nominating those who first raised their hands: *Clements v Rydeheard* [1978] 3 All ER 658.

Competitive neutrality The principle requiring all market players (whether governmental or otherwise) to be subject to the same regulatory and other requirements imposed on them when competing in the one market, such that government businesses do not enjoy any net competitive advantage by virtue of their ownership but are subject to measures that effectively neutralise any such advantage. The adoption of the principle as part of a national competition policy was recommended by the Hilmer Report in 1993. The principle of competitive neutrality is now applied to Commonwealth, State and Territory government and business enterprises under the Competition Principles Agreement: (CTH) Competition Policy Reform Act 1995 Competition Principles Agreement. See also **Competition; Competition law; Cooney Committee Report; Griffiths Committee Report; Hilmer Report; Market; Swanson Committee Report.**

•**Complainant** A person who lodges a complaint to, among other things, a tribunal, ombudsman or board: for example (NSW) Anti-Discrimination Act 1977 s 87. See also **Respondent**.

Completely constituted trust A trust constituted by a present declaration, or by the settlor transferring legal title to the intended trustee. If the intended object of a trust is a volunteer, the trust must be completely constituted. See also **Executed trust; Executory trust.**

•**Complying superannuation fund** A fund where an entity was a resident regulated superannuation fund that at all time during a year of income when that entity was in existence, and where the trustee of the fund has not contravened the (CTH) Superannuation Industry (Supervision) Act 1993, or the regulations, or if the trustee has contravened the Act or regulations but the fund has not failed a culpability test in relation to the contravention: (CTH) Superannuation Industry (Supervision) Act 1993 s 42. A complying superannuation fund receives concessional taxation treatment by the operation of (CTH) Income Tax Assessment Act 1936 ss 278-285; (CTH) Income Tax (Rates) Act 1986 s 26(1). See also **Non-complying superannuation fund; Insurance and superannuation Commissioner; Superannuation fund.**

Component part manufacturer A person or entity that manufactures or produces a part which is to be incorporated into a finished product: for example *Dransfield v British Insulated Cables Ltd* [1937] 4 All ER 382. See also **Manufacturer.**

Composite insurance A contract of insurance providing cover to different insured persons in respect of their different interests in the subject matter of the contract; for example, a contract of insurance covering both the owner of a motor vehicle and the credit provider for their respective interests: *Re an arbitration between Lombard Australia Ltd v NRMA Insurance Ltd* [1968] 3 NSWR 346; (1968) 72 SR (NSW) 45; *Australian Guarantee Corp Ltd v Western Underwriters Insurance Ltd* [1988] 2 Qd R 119. See also **Insurance.**

•**Composition** An arrangement by which creditors accept payment of their debts by instalments or less than the full amount of their debts in full satisfaction: (CTH)

Bankruptcy Act 1966 s 187(1). See also **Annulment; Bankruptcy; Creditors' meeting; Part X; Sequestration; Special resolution.**

•**Compound** To settle a debt due and owing by agreeing to accept a lesser amount. See also **Composition; Insolvency.**

•**Compromise** An agreement terminating a dispute between parties as to the rights of one or more of them, or modifying the undoubted rights of a party which he or she has difficulty in enforcing. Compromise may be reached in the absence of legal proceedings or at any stage after their commencement. It may be reached by parties filing terms of settlement and a consent order in the proceedings. See also **Arrangement; Offer of Compromise; Return of capital in a compromise; Settlement.**

Contract The party must in good faith believe that his or her claim for the compromise constitutes valuable consideration: *Callisher v Bischoffsheim* (1870) LR 5 QB 449; *McDermott v Black* (1940) 63 CLR 161. See also **Accord and satisfaction; Consideration.**

Compromise, return of capital in See **Return of capital in a compromise.**

Compulsion Coercion, extortion, exaction or use of force.

Contract To compel a person to agree to something involuntarily. Compulsion in contract law includes every species of duress, actual or threatened. See also **Duress; Unjust enrichment.**

Compulsory acquisition of shares Where a corporation has acquired more than 90 per cent of the shares in respect of which an offer under a takeover scheme or a takeover announcement was made, the purchase of any remaining shares from a dissenting offeree: Corporations Law s 701. See also **Dissenting shareholder; Part A statement; Takeover; Takeover announcement; Takeover period; Takeover scheme.**

Compulsory arbitration The power of an industrial tribunal, such as the Australian Industrial Relations Commission, to regulate terms and conditions of employment by arbitration without the agreement of some or all of the employers and employees who would be affected by the arbitration (or their representative bodies), whether after exhausting alternative means of settlement or otherwise: (CTH) Industrial Relations Act 1988 s 111(4). See also **Australian Industrial Relations Commission; Industrial dispute; State industrial system.**

•**Compulsory conference** A meeting convened by a tribunal in order to attempt conciliation between the parties to a dispute: for example (CTH) Industrial Relations Act 1988 s 119. See also **Conciliation.**

•**Compulsory insurance** In consumer credit law, and in relation to goods, any insurance that is required by law and that relates to liability in respect of death or injury arising from or caused by use of the goods: for example (NSW) Credit Act 1984 (repealed) s 5(1) (now replaced by Uniform Consumer Credit Code). See also **Regulated mortgage.**

Compulsory licence 1. In relation to designs, a licence to use a design under a monopoly without consent of the owner of the rights attached to that monopoly. An interested person may apply to a prescribed court for the grant of a compulsory licence: (CTH) Designs Act 1906 s 28(b). The only ground upon which an application may be made is that the design is applied by manufacture to any article in a country outside Australia and is not applied in Australia to such an extent as is reasonable in the circumstances of the case: (CTH) Designs Act 1906 s 28(b). The court can make orders as it considers just, providing that such orders are not at variance with any treaty, convention or arrangement with any other country: (CTH) Designs Act 1906 s 28. **2.** In relation to patents, a licence to work a patented invention granted to a person by judicial order on application to the Federal Court or a State or Territory Supreme Court. The court must be satisfied that the reasonable requirements of the public with respect to the patented invention have not been satisfied, and that the patentee has given no satisfactory reason for failing to exploit the patent. The court may grant a licence on any terms specified in the order, provided the order directs that the licence is not exclusive and that it is assignable only in connection with the enterprise or goodwill associated with the licence's use: (CTH) Patents Act 1990 s 133, Sch 1. Compulsory licences under the (CTH) Copyright Act 1968 are administered by collecting societies. See also **Copyright; Invention; Patent.**

Compulsory liquidation See **Liquidation.**

Compulsory product recall A recall of products which is compelled by force of legislation in circumstances where the Minister or a regulatory authority is of the opinion that the supplier has not taken satisfactory action to minimise the risk of injury being caused by those products: for example (CTH) Trade Practices Act 1974 s 65F(1); (NSW) Fair Trading Act 1987 s 34(2)(a); (SA) Trade Standards Act 1979 s 27a. See also **Product recall; Recall action; Voluntary product recall.**

Compulsory retirement A requirement that an employee retire from employment, or vacate an office, on or after reaching a specified age. Also known as 'forced retirement'. See also **Discrimination; Retirement.**

•**Compulsory third party insurance** *Abbr* – CTP A compulsory scheme of insurance under which a policy must be taken out in respect of all registered vehicles against liability for personal injury caused by, through or in connection with the vehicle. Some such scheme applies or formerly applied in all States and Territories: for example (NSW) Motor Vehicles (Third Party Insurance) Act 1942. Its primary purpose is to ensure victims are compensated, even if the motorist has no financial means to pay damages; it also protects motorists from financially ruinous claims. A CTP policy cannot be avoided for misrepresentation or non-disclosure, and continues in force despite change of ownership of the vehicle insured. Some jurisdictions, for example New South Wales, Tasmania and the Northern Territory, have changed to no-fault compensation systems. See also **Insurance.**

Compulsory unionism An order or award of an industrial tribunal that an employer may only employ people who are members of a particular union (or unions). See also **Australian Industrial Relations Commission**; **Closed shop**; **Industrial tribunal**; **Trade union**.

Compulsory winding up The winding up of a company pursuant to an order of the court on grounds listed in the Corporations Law. See also **Insolvency**; **Voluntary winding up**; **Winding up**.

Computer crime Using a computer to commit a criminal offence. Computer crime includes obtaining property by deception by doing an act with the intention of causing a computer system to make a response that the person doing the act is not authorised to cause the computer to make ((NSW) Crimes Act 1900 s 178BA(2)(b); (VIC) Crimes Act 1958 ss 81(1), (4)) and unlawfully accessing computer data: (CTH) Crimes Act 1914 s 76B.

Computer piracy The copying of computer software by unlicensed persons for sale, usually at lower prices than the original or licensed software.

•**Concealment** A conscious or deliberate keeping back of facts: *Clark v Esanda Ltd* [1984] 3 NSWLR 1 at 4-5. In contract law, a concealment of material facts by one party generally will not result in the contract being void or voidable at common law as silence does not usually constitute misrepresentation: *Jones v Acfold Investments Pty Ltd* (1985) 59 ALR at 622-4. Concealment may amount to a misrepresentation where it distorts a positive representation (for example *Jennings v Zilahi-Kiss, Zilahi-Kiss and M K Tremaine & Co Pty Ltd* (1972) 2 SASR 493), where the contract is one *uberrimae fidei* (for example *Dalgety and Co Ltd v Australian Mutual Provident Society* [1908] VLR 481), or where a fiduciary duty exists between the contracting parties (for example *Hill v Rose* [1990] VR 129 at 143-4). See also **Duty to disclose**; **Material fact**; **Misrepresentation**; **Uberrimae fidei**.

•**Concentration** The degree to which the control of market activity, whether on the supply or demand side, has moved into the hands of one company or a small number of companies. See also **Competition**; **Concentration ratio**; **Substantially lessening competition**.

Concentration ratio 1. A measure of the concentration occurring in a market or industry. Concentration ratios may be expressed as the percentage of value of total sales accounted for by the largest firms in the market. The concentration ratios for different industries assist in assessing their positions in the spectrum ranging from imperfect competition, oligopoly, oligopsony to monopoly. The largest corporations in Australia are found in banking, insurance and finance, wholesaling and retailing, petroleum refining and the food, beverages and tobacco industries. 2. A measure of market power. Two ratios are commonly used: the Four Firm Concentration Ratio, and the Herfindahl-Hirschman Index. See also **Competition**; **Competition law**; **Four Firm Concentration Ratio**; **Market**; **Market power**; **Market share**.

Concert party A meeting to ensure that all will act in concert. See also **Price fixing**; **Restrictive trade practices**.

•**Conciliation** A method of alternative dispute resolution in which a third party attempts to facilitate an agreed resolution of a dispute in accordance with relevant legal principles. See also **Alternative dispute resolution**; **Arbitration**; **Mediation**.

Industrial law A method of dispute resolution by which parties to a dispute reach an agreement, usually through the offices of a mediator. A body that exercises both a conciliation and an arbitration function should not use the powers available in relation to one function only for the purposes of the other function: *R v Gough; Ex parte Key Meats Pty Ltd* (1982) 148 CLR 582; 39 ALR 507. See also **Arbitration**; **Compulsory conference**.

Conciliation and Arbitration Commission See **Australian Conciliation and Arbitration Commission**.

Conciliation and arbitration power The legislative power of the Commonwealth to make laws with respect to conciliation and arbitration for the prevention of industrial disputes extending beyond the limits of any one State: Commonwealth Constitution s 51(xxxv). The power applies to industrial disputes which are either existing or threatened, impending or probable See also **Industrial dispute**; **Interstate dispute**.

•**Conciliation committee** A committee established under the (NSW) Industrial Relations Act 1991 (repealed) to operate in relation to a particular industry or enterprise. It consists of a conciliation commissioner and equal numbers of representatives of employers and employees: (NSW) Industrial Relations Act 1991 (repealed) s 328. It exercises the functions of the Industrial Relations Commission of New South Wales in respect of that industry or enterprise.

Concilio-arbitration This is a process which combines the benefits of informal conciliation with the more formal arbitration process. The concilio-arbitrator receives information from the parties at the commencement of the process, either through written submissions or individual meetings, and makes a final opinion, which is binding on the parties. See also **Alternative dispute resolution**; **Arbitration**; **Conciliation**.

Concurrent conditions In contract law, conditions that must be met by each party simultaneously. Payment and delivery are concurrent conditions in a contract of sale: for example (NSW) Sale of Goods Act 1923 s 31. See also **Condition**; **Contract of sale**.

Concurrent insurance Where the same interest in the same subject matter is covered against the same risk by two or more legally enforceable insurance policies: *Albion Insurance Co Ltd v Government Insurance Office of New South Wales* (1969) 121 CLR 342. Concurrent insurance is not unlawful, but under indemnity insurance contracts, the insured cannot recover more than his or her loss: *Albion Insurance Co Ltd v Government Insurance Office of New South Wales*; (CTH) Insurance Contracts Act 1984 s 76(2). Also known as 'double insurance'. See also **Contribution**; **Indemnity insurance**.

Concurrent interest A property interest, not being an estate, that is jointly held by more than one person as joint tenants or as tenants in common. A concurrent interest can be held at law or in equity. See also **Equitable interest; Joint tenancy; Legal interest.**

Concurrent lease A lease where the subject matter is a reversionary interest: *Stewart v Goldman & Co Pty Ltd* (1947) 64 WN (NSW) 155. See also **Lease.**

Concurrent liability Liability attracted by two or more individuals responsible for injury caused to a plaintiff, whether acting together ('joint concurrent liability') or separately ('several concurrent liability'). The plaintiff may recover the whole amount of the loss from each of the tortfeasors in the same amount: *Barisic v Devonport* [1978] 2 NSWLR 111. See also **Concurrent tortfeasors.**

Concurrent ownership Ownership by two or more persons of an interest in a parcel of land. Also known as 'co-ownership'. See also **Co-ownership; Joint tenancy; Tenancy in common.**

Concurrent tortfeasors Two or more wrongdoers who inflict one and the same damage on a plaintiff. Also known as 'joint tortfeasors'. See also **Concurrent liability; Joint concurrent tortfeasors.**

•**Condition 1.** Something demanded or required as a prerequisite to the granting or performance of something else. **2.** In its common usage (illustrated by the expression 'condition of sale') any term in a contract, whatever its nature: *Wickman Machine Tool Sales Ltd v L Schuler AG* [1972] 1 WLR 840. **3.** In contract law, a contractual term so important that any breach of it gives rise to a right to terminate the contract: *Luna Park (NSW) Ltd v Tramways Advertising Pty Ltd* (1938) 61 CLR 286. **4.** An 'essential' or 'fundamental' term: *Clifton v Coffey* (1924) 34 CLR 434; *Tramways Advertising Pty Ltd v Luna Park (NSW) Ltd* (1938) 38 SR (NSW) 632. **5.** In sale of goods legislation, a term, any breach of which may give rise to a claim for damages and to the right to reject the goods and treat the contract as repudiated: for example (NSW) Sale of Goods Act 1923 s 16(2). See also **Condition precedent; Fundamental term; Intermediate term; Term; Warranty.**

•**Condition precedent** In contract law, a stipulation that must be fulfilled before one of the parties becomes subject to a contractual obligation: *Tricontinental Corp v HDFI Ltd* (1990) 21 NSWLR 689 at 703. Satisfaction of a condition precedent may be beyond the control of both parties, or it may require a unilateral act: *Tricontinental Corp v HDFI Ltd*. See also **Condition subsequent; Contingency; Contract.**

Condition subsequent A condition, being a future event upon the occurrence of which the parties agree to terminate their obligations and the relations created by the contract, or to give either or both of the parties the right to terminate the further performance of the contract: *National Australia Bank Ltd v KDS Construction Services Pty Ltd (in liq)* (1987) 163 CLR 668; 76 ALR 27. See also **Condition precedent; Contingency.**

•**Conditional** Dependent or contingent.

Bills of exchange and other negotiable instruments In relation to bills of exchange, an acceptance of a bill may be made conditional, namely where payment by the acceptor is made dependent on the fulfilment of some stated condition: (CTH) Bills of Exchange Act 1909 s 24(3)(a). Conditional acceptances are examples of qualified acceptances: (CTH) Bills of Exchange Act 1909 s 24(3).

Contract Dependent or contingent. In contract law, a particular obligation of one party may be conditional on some event occurring, in which case the party will not be obliged to perform unless that event occurs. Where the contract itself is said to be subject to some event or condition, there may be no binding contract unless and until that event occurs or condition fulfilled. See also **Agreement; Conditional acceptance; Contract.**

•**Conditional acceptance** A qualified acceptance of a bill of exchange where payment by the acceptor to the holder is dependent on the fulfilment of a condition stated on the bill: (CTH) Bills of Exchange Act 1909 s 24(3)(a). See also **Acceptance of; Acceptor; Bill of exchange; Qualified acceptance.**

Conditional bond See **Double bond.**

Conditional contract In the context of the grant of an option contract, a contract for valuable consideration to sell upon condition that the optionee, within the stipulated time, bind himself or herself to perform the terms of the offer embodied in the contract: *Laybutt v Amoco Australia Pty Ltd* (1974) 132 CLR 57; 4 ALR 482. See also **Contract; Irrevocable offer; Option; Time stipulation.**

Conditional execution In relation to a deed, its execution by a party on condition (express or implied) that some event occur; for example, that another party will also execute the deed, constituting an escrow (a deed delivered on condition). A deed thus executed will not come into operation until the condition is fulfilled: *Federal Commissioner of Taxation v Taylor* (1929) 42 CLR 80; 35 ALR 169. See also **Deed; Escrow; Execution.**

•**Conditional indorsement** An indorsement on the face of a negotiable instrument, that is purportedly subject to the fulfilment of a condition. Where an instrument purports to be indorsed conditionally, the condition may be disregarded by the payer, and payment to the indorsee is valid whether the condition has been fulfilled or not: (CTH) Bills of Exchange Act 1909 s 38; (CTH) Cheques and Payment Orders Act 1986 s 45. See also **Bill of exchange; Indorsee; Indorsement; Negotiable instrument.**

Conditional offer In contract law, an offer that does not become operative until the occurrence of a certain event: *Jarvis v Pitt Ltd* (1935) 54 CLR 506. The offer may not be accepted so as to create a binding contract until the condition is satisfied: *Buhrer v Tweedie* [1973] 1 NZLR 517. See also **Acceptance; Condition; Offer.**

Conditional sale agreement An agreement for the sale of goods or land under which the purchase price is payable by instalments and the property in the goods or land remains in the seller until the instalments are paid: (UK) Consumer Credit Act 1974 s 189(1). Known in Australia as 'hire purchase'. See also **Hire purchase.**

•**Conditions of employment** The conditions on which, as between employer and employee, the employee works; the express or implied terms of the contract of employment: *Max Cooper & Sons Pty Ltd v Sydney City Council* (1980) 29 ALR 77. See also **Award**; **Contract of employment**; **Employment**.

Conditions of sale The terms on which an offer to sell may be made and accepted. The conditions of sale will often be stated in writing. See also **Auction**; **Implied term**.

Condonation The act of pardoning or overlooking.
Employment In relation to employment, the act of an employer condoning or forgiving an employee's breach of the contract of employment. When an employer, expressly or by conduct, condones the employee's breach, the employer loses any right to dismiss the employee summarily on the grounds of the breach: *Re Clarke and Metropolitan Meat Industry Board* (1967) SR (NSW) 16. See also **Summary dismissal**.

Conduct Behaviour, or the manner of managing one's own life.
Consumer protection Positive acts the failure or omission to act: for example (CTH) Trade Practices Act 1974 s 4(2); (NSW) Fair Trading Act 1987 s 4(4). See also **Likely to mislead or deceive**; **Misleading or deceptive conduct**.

Conduct Code Agreement An agreement made on 11 April 1995 between the Commonwealth, the States and Territories providing for the application of the Competition Code to all persons within the legislative competence of each State and Territory, the facilitation of cooperation between the parties on appointments to the Australian Competition and Consumer Commission, and a mechanism for the States and Territories to apply for exceptions from the Competition Laws: (CTH) Trade Practices Act 1974 s 4(1). See also **Australian Competition and Consumer Commission**; **Competition code**.

•**Conduct engaged in on behalf of a body corporate** Conduct of a person who has some involvement with the activities of a corporation: Corporations Law s 762. It is not limited to conduct that is authorised by the corporation, and the conduct need not be for the benefit of the corporation: *Walplan Pty Ltd v Wallace* (1985) 8 FCR 27. See also **Corporate liability**.

Confer a benefit on stranger To form a contract which contains a provision intended to benefit a person who is not a party to it. As a result of the doctrine of privity of contract, the stranger cannot sue on the contract to secure the benefit: *Beswick v Beswick* [1968] AC 58. However, this is subject to statutory modification in several Australian jurisdictions: for example (CTH) Insurance Contracts Act 1984 s 48(1). See also **Benefit**; **Privity of contract**.

•**Conference agreement** An agreement between members of an unincorporated association of two or more ocean carriers in relation to outwards liner cargo shipping services provided by them: (CTH) Trade Practices Act 1974 s 10.02.

Confession A full acknowledgment of guilt made to another by a person suspected of committing a crime. Confessions are more damaging to a person's interest than are admissions because admissions merely incriminate the person without fully acknowledging guilt: *Hazim* (1993) 69 A Crim R 371 at 380.

•**Confidential communication** The imparting or exchange of information in such circumstances that when it was made the person who made it or the person to whom it was made was under an express or implied obligation not to disclose its contents, whether or not the obligation arises under law: (CTH) Evidence Act 1995 s 117(1). See also **Breach of confidence**; **Legal professional privilege**.

•**Confidential document** A document prepared by, or for, a person who was under an express or implied obligation, legal or otherwise, not to disclose its contents: (CTH) Evidence Act 1995 s 117(1); (NSW) Evidence Act 1995 s 117(1). See also **Confidential information**; **Document**.

•**Confidential information** Facts or knowledge that are not in the public domain: *Coco v AN Clark (Engineers) Ltd* (1969) 86 RPC 41. Possessors of confidential information are often subject to fiduciary duties which prevent them misusing the information for their own advantage: *Seager v Copydex Ltd* [1967] 1 WLR 923. See also **Company officer**; **Confidential relationship**; **Duty of confidentiality**; **Fiduciary duty**; **Trade secret**.

Confidential relationship A relationship between two or more persons in which the information communicated between them is to be kept in confidence. See also **Breach of confidence**; **Confidential information**; **Fiduciary**; **Fiduciary relationship**.

•**Confidential source** A person who provides information under an express or implied pledge of confidentiality: *Department of Health v Jephcott* (1985) 8 FCR 85; 62 ALR 421. A document is exempted from the provisions of the (CTH) Freedom of Information Act 1982 if its disclosure would, or could reasonably be expected to, disclose, or enable a person to ascertain, the existence or identity of a confidential source of information in relation to the enforcement or administration of the law: (CTH) Freedom of Information Act 1982 ss 25, 37. The source need only be confidential for the document to be exempt; there need not be a 'substantial risk' that the administration of law will be impaired: *Department of Health v Jephcott*. See also **Confidential communication**; **Freedom of information**.

Confidentiality A strict contractual legal duty owed by banks to their customers. The credit of the customer depends very largely upon the observance of that confidence: *Tournier v National Provincial and Union Bank of England* [1924] 1 KB 461. The duty is, however, not absolute but qualified. Disclosure is permitted: under compulsion of law, where there is a duty to the public to disclose, where the interests of the bank require disclosure, and where the disclosure is made with the customer's express or implied consent. See also **Banker-customer relationship**; **Fiduciary duty**.

Confidentiality, duty of See **Duty of confidentiality**.

Confirmation An audit process of verifying accounting information from sources other than the books and records under review. The process of confirmation involves the auditor corresponding directly with a customer, creditor, or bank of a business to determine what a particular account balance of the business being audited should be. Positive confirmation is the process of verification where the third party is requested to reply irrespective of whether the balances being verified agree or disagree with the amount the auditor has. Negative confirmation is the process of requiring a reply only in the case of disagreement between the amount that the third party has and the amount that the auditor has. See also **Audit**; **Auditor**.

Confirming bank In relation to irrevocable documentary credits, the bank which is requested by the issuing bank to confirm the credit. See also **Draft**; **Issuing bank**; **Letter of credit**.

Confirming house An agency which provides a number of services to importers, including arranging and confirming orders with overseas suppliers and providing finance. When a confirming house 'confirms' an order with an overseas supplier, it becomes responsible for paying the supplier on presentation of the shipping documents. In effect, the confirming house acts as a guarantor for the importer. Having paid the supplier, the confirming house draws a bill of exchange on the importer for the amount due including its confirming fee and all incidental charges. It then forwards the bill with the shipping documents to the importer. Confirming houses are located in all major cities in Australia. See also See also **Bill of exchange**; **Import**.

Confiscation of profits A procedure for the recovery of money and other benefits obtained directly or indirectly from the commission of a criminal offence by the use of forfeiture and pecuniary penalty orders made by courts either as part of the criminal process or by civil proceedings: for example (CTH) Proceeds of Crime Act 1987; (NSW) Drug Trafficking (Civil Proceedings) Act 1990. See also **Civil penalty order**.

Conflict of interest A situation where a person has a personal interest in a matter the subject of a decision or duty of the person.

Corporations See **Conflict rule**.

Equity A situation in which a person owing a duty (usually fiduciary) to provide professional advice or skill, is compromised in the performance of that duty by either a like duty to another whose interests conflict with the first, or by the opportunity to make a personal profit: *Blackwell v Barroile Pty Ltd* (1994) 123 ALR 81. See also **Fiduciary**; **Fiduciary duty**.

Conflict of laws An inconsistency or 'clash' between the private law rules of different states or of the federal units of a single state.

Conflict Resolution Service A commercial organisation that offers both a range of out-of-court techniques for the resolution of disputes by appropriately trained third parties, and training in such techniques. See also **Alternative dispute resolution**; **Commercial dispute resolution**.

Conflict rule The principle that company directors must not, in any matter falling within the scope of their service, have a personal interest or inconsistent engagement with a third party, or enter into any agreement in which there either is, or is a significant possibility of, conflict between personal interest and the interests of the company, except with the company's fully informed consent: *Phipps v Boardman* [1967] 2 AC 46; *Chan v Zacharia* (1984) 154 CLR 178; 53 ALR 417. A real and sensible possibility of conflict between personal interest and duty or a conflict between the director's duty to the company and his or her duty to someone else will constitute a breach: *Phipps v Boardman* [1967] 2 AC 46 at 124; [1966] ALL ER 721. A director of a proprietary company who is directly or indirectly interested in certain transactions with a company must declare the nature of the interest: Corporations Law s 231. A director of a public company who has a 'material personal interest' in a matter that is being considered at a board meeting must not vote on the matter or be present while it is being considered: Corporations Law s 232A(1). See also **Directors' duties**.

•**Confusion** A doctrine, derived from Roman Law, relating to the intermixture of the goods of two persons such that the contributed parts can no longer be distinguished. If the intermixture is by agreement, the owners of the mingled goods will own the whole in common in proportion to their contributions: *Gill & Duffus (Liverpool) v Scruttons* [1953] 1 WLR 1407. If one person wilfully intermixes the goods without the consent of the other, the whole belongs to the latter: *Sandeman & Sons v Tyzack and Branfoot Steamship Co Ltd* [1913] AC 680 at 695. See also **Appropriation**; **Accession**.

Conglomerate See **Business combination**.

Conglomerate merger A generic term describing three types of merger: a product line extension by which non-competing products with similar marketing channels or production processes are joined; a geographic market extension by which a firm moves into an area not previously serviced; and a merger where there are no complementarities (pure conglomeration), that is where there is no production or demand substitution in relation to the goods produced by the merged entities. See also **Competition law**; **Geographic market**; **Merger**; **Substitutability**.

Connected entity A body corporate that is or has been connected with a corporation. Corporations Law s 64B sets out the circumstances in which a body corporate, natural person, partnership or trust is taken to be connected with a corporation. These include being a member of the corporation, being in a position to cast votes at a meeting of a body or having control over the body's affairs. This definition corresponds to similar definitions in (CTH) Bankruptcy Act 1966 ss 5B-5E. The definition of 'connected entity' is relevant to the definition of 'examinable affairs' in Corporations Law s 9. See also **Entity**.

Conscientious objector A person who refuses to obey a law or authorised command on the basis of a moral or ethical objection. Examples include those who resist military conscription or refuse to vote.

Industrial law A natural person whose conscientious beliefs, whether on religious grounds or otherwise, prevent him or her from participating in a course of action. A person whose conscientious belief does not allow him or her to join an industrial organisation can obtain a certificate from the Industrial Registrar: (CTH) Industrial Relations Act 1988 s 267. See also **Trade union**.

Conscious parallelism In trade practices law, interdependent behaviour among oligopolists where there is no express agreement between them. Mere interdependent parallelism does not constitute a contract, arrangement or understanding prohibited by (CTH) Trade Practices Act 1974 s 45, although inferences may be drawn from such conduct as to their existence: *Trade Practices Commission v Email Ltd* (1980) 31 ALR 53. Communication is an essential ingredient in establishing such an arrangement under (CTH) Trade Practices Act 1974 s 45, either by direct evidence or by inference: *Trade Practices Commission v Nicholas Enterprises Pty Ltd (No 2)* (1979) 26 ALR 609. See also **Contract, arrangement or understanding; Facilitating practice; Oligopoly; Parallel behaviour; Parallel pricing; Price leadership**.

Consensual contract A term originating from the civil law, denoting a contract founded upon and completed by the mere consent of the contracting parties, without any external formality or symbolic act to fix the obligations. At common law, although consensus is part of the formation of contracts, it is not of itself sufficient to give rise to contractual relations. See also **Civil law; Consideration; Contract**.

Consensus ad idem /kɒnsɛnsʊs æd ɪdɛm/ *Lat* – agreement to do the same thing. The common consent necessary for a binding contract. See also **Ad idem; Subjective theory of contract**.

Consensus facit legem /kɒnsɛnsʊs fækɪt lɛgɛm/ *Lat* – agreement makes law. The rule that parties to a contract are legally bound to perform the obligations they have undertaken or consented to perform. See also **Consent; Performance**.

•**Consent** Affirmative acceptance, not merely a standing by and absence of objection: *Bell v Alfred Franks & Bartlett Co Ltd* [1980] 1 All ER 356.

Equity A voluntary agreement or yielding of the will; an accord of mind. Consent usually involves a reasoned act in the face of a situation calling for choice: *Mercier v Holmes* 125 A2d 790. It therefore requires knowledge of the matter to which consent is said to be given: *Ex parte Ford; Re Caughey* (1876) 1 Ch D 521. Consent is sometimes contrasted with mere acquiescence or assent, as consent involves an affirmative act or attitude: *De Klyn v Gould* 9 NE 95 (1901). It also differs from agreement, which is contractual in nature. See also **Acquiescence**.

Consent award or decision An award or decision of a tribunal that is in the terms of an agreement the parties have reached between themselves. See also **Award; Decision; Tribunal**.

Consent judgment A judgment embodying terms agreed upon by the litigating parties. Until set aside or varied a judgment by consent is final and unimpeachable. See also **Settlement**.

•**Consequential loss** 1. Loss subsequent to an immediate loss incurred as a result of the commission of a tort. It often takes the form of economic loss such as loss of profits or loss of earnings. 2. Loss that arises as a result of the plaintiff's particular circumstances and which may not have been suffered by another person in the same situation. Damages may be recovered for such losses where they are not too remote: for example *Nader v Urban Transit Authority of New South Wales* (1985) 2 NSWLR 501. See also **Consequential loss insurance; Damage; Mitigation; Remoteness**.

Consequential loss insurance A policy of insurance under which the insured is protected against losses which, though consequent upon loss of property caused by an insured risk, are not covered by an ordinary contract of general insurance: *Mildara Wines Ltd v New Zealand Insurance Co Ltd* [1994] ACL Rep 235 VIC 4. Consequential losses usually relate to the period for which a business is not operational as a result of loss or damage due to an insured risk: for example *R v BC Fir and Cedar Lumber Co Ltd* [1932] AC 441. Losses may include profits and expenditures, such as rent, rates, taxes, salaries, and debentures, which continue to be payable despite the interruption of business. Consequential loss insurance may also cover the increased cost of reinstatement where the cost of new materials results in the cost of reinstatement exceeding the value of the subject matter at the time of the loss. See also **General Insurance; Insurance contract; Property insurance**.

•**Conservation** The management of human use of the biosphere so that it may yield the greatest sustainable benefit to present generations while maintaining its potential to meet the needs and aspirations of future generations: World Conservation Strategy 1980.

•**Consideration** The price, detriment, or forbearance given as value for a promise: *Dunlop Pneumatic Tyre Co Ltd v Selfridge & Co Ltd* [1915] AC 847. A contract is generally only binding if the promise is supported by consideration: *Woolworths Ltd v Kelly* (1991) 22 NSWLR 189; 4 ACSR 431. Expressed in terms of benefit and detriment, a valuable consideration may consist either in some right, interest, profit, or benefit accruing to the one party, or some forbearance, detriment, loss or responsibility given, suffered or undertaken by the other: *Currie v Misa* (1875) LR 10 Ex 153. The value of the consideration need not be adequate, but must be sufficient. See also **Acceptance; Adequacy of consideration; Agreement; Contract; Executed consideration; Failure of consideration; Illusory consideration; Nominal consideration; Offer; Past consideration; Promissory estoppel; Restitution; Sufficiency of consideration**.

Consideration in respect of acquisition of an asset For capital gains tax purposes, the amount of any money paid, and the market value of any property given, in respect of the acquisition of an asset: (CTH) Income Tax Assessment Act 1936 s 160ZH(4). Where no consideration is given for the acquisition, market value consideration is deemed to have been given: (CTH) Income Tax Assessment Act 1936 s 160ZH(9). See also **Capital gain; Capital gains tax; Capital loss; Consideration in respect of acquisition of an asset; Cost base**.

Consideration in respect of disposal of an asset For capital gains tax purposes, the amount of any money received, and the market value of any property received, in respect of the disposal of an asset: (CTH) Income Tax Assessment Act 1936 s 160ZD(1). Where there is no consideration in respect of the disposal, market value consideration is deemed to have been received: (CTH) Income Tax Assessment Act 1936 s 160ZD(2). See also **Capital gain; Capital gains tax; Capital loss; Consideration in respect of acquisition of an asset; Cost base.**

•**Consignee** The receiver of goods consigned as cargo for carriage or sale; a person to whom the consignor parts with the real control of the goods; the person to whom goods are consigned. The consignee may obtain the goods as a purchaser under a contract of sale or as a bailee under a contract of bailment. See also **Consignor; Consignment; Sale of goods; Bailment; Bailee.**

•**Consignment** *Abbr* – Consgt **1.** The delivery of goods as cargo for carriage or sale. **2.** Goods delivered by a carrier to a consignee at the direction of the consignor: *Penn Elastic Co Pty Ltd v Sadliers Transport Co (Vic) Pty Ltd* (1976) 136 CLR 28; 10 ALR 185. **3.** Goods delivered to another 'on approval' (with a view to the other purchasing the goods if satisfactory), or on 'sale or return' (with a view to the other selling the goods in the course of trade or returning them to the consignor if not sold within a given period). See also **Consignment clause; Consignment note; Consignee; Consignor; Goods; On approval; On consignment; Sale or return.**

Consignment clause A clause in a charter party stipulating whether the owner or charterer are to appoint agents at the loading and discharging ports. Usually, charterers prefer to appoint their agents for both, but sometimes the ship owner appoints an agent for the purpose of husbandry, so as to look after the ship owner's interests whenever the ship is under repair, or when disputes arise. See also **Agent; Charterer; Charterparty; Consignment; Owner.**

Consignment note *Abbr* – CN A document which accompanies a consignment of goods. It is similar to a bill of lading and is supplied by the carrier. It relates to a particular consignment of goods carried from one place to another. It contains information such as the freight to be charged and the details of the consignment. The carrier indorses the note upon delivery of the goods to it, to verify that they have been received. See also **Advice note; Bill of lading; Carrier; Consignment; Freight; Goods.**

•**Consignor** One who sends or ships goods, the recipient of which is the consignee: *Penn Elastic Company Pty Ltd v Sadliers Transport Co (Vic) Pty Ltd* (1976) 136 CLR 28; 10 ALR 185. See also **Agent; Bailment; Consignment; Consignee; Sale of goods.**

Consistency Compatibility. A statement will not form a collateral contract unless it is consistent with the main contract: *Hoyt's Pty Ltd v Spencer* (1919) 27 CLR 133; 26 ALR 21. Similarly, an implied term in a contract must be consistent with the express terms: *Summers v Commonwealth* (1918) 25 CLR 144.

•**Consolidated accounts** Financial statements of a parent company and its controlled entities prepared by treating the group for reporting purposes as a single financial entity. See also **Chief entity; Consolidated balance sheet; Consolidated profit and loss account; Control; Economic entity; General purpose financial report; Parent company.**

Consolidated balance sheet The combination of balance sheet items of subsidiaries of a holding company with those of the holding company to reflect one economic entity. A company is required to prepare a consolidated balance sheet for the economic entity constituted by itself and the entities that it controls at the end of the financial period: Corporations Law s 295B. For consolidation, assets and liabilities are transferred into one account by eliminating duplicated items and show the financial position of what would appear as a single business. See also **Balance sheet; Holding company; Subsidiary.**

•**Consolidated fund** See **Consolidated revenue fund.**

Consolidated meeting A combined meeting of members of a number of different companies within the one company group. See also **Group of companies.**

Consolidated profit and loss account The combined financial results of related companies and subsidiaries of the parent company by grouping the income and expenditure as if they were the income and expenditure of one economic entity. Company directors must prepare a consolidated profit and loss account for a company and any economic entities controlled by the parent company at any time during the accounting period: Corporations Law s 295A. See also **Parent company; Subsidiary.**

•**Consolidated revenue fund** The fund into which all revenues raised or received by the Commonwealth are paid: Commonwealth Constitution s 81. Also known as 'consolidiated fund' or 'consolidated revenue'. See also **Appropriation; Constitution.**

Consolidation Combination; unification; the consolidated whole.

Corporations **1.** In relation to shares in a registered company with share capital, the process of merging several shares of a particular nominal value into one share of a nominal value equal to the total of the nominal values of the pre-existing shares. It is the opposite of subdivision. **2.** The practice of merging two or more commercial entities into one consolidated corporation or enterprise. **3.** The bringing together of two or more accounts. See also **Consolidated accounts; Consolidation of shares; Group accounts; Merger.**

Consolidation of arbitrations The establishment of a new arbitration to deal with two or more disputes which are the subject of separate arbitrations and which have the same umpire or arbitrator. A consolidation is made by the order of an arbitrator under the Commercial Arbitration Acts s 26. Alternatively, the arbitrator may order that the arbitration proceedings be heard together or one after the other, or may stay certain proceedings until after the determination of others. A consolidation may only be ordered if there is a common question of law or fact in all proceedings, or the rights to relief in all proceedings are in respect of the same transaction, or it is desirable for some other reason. See also **Alternative dispute resolution; Arbitration; Arbitrator; Commercial Arbitration Legislation.**

Consolidation of shares The conversion of a certain number of shares of a particular nominal value into a smaller number of shares of a larger nominal value. For example, ten one dollar shares might be consolidated into five two dollar shares. A consolidation of shares does not change the aggregate value of the company's authorised capital even though the number of shares representing it decreases. A company's articles may authorise the general meeting to alter the provisions of the memorandum by consolidating all or any of its share capital into shares of larger amount than its existing shares: Corporations Law s 193(1)(b). Where a company seeks to have its shares quoted on the Australian Stock Exchange (ASX), consolidation may be necessary if the shares were initially issued with a very low par or nominal value, since shares with a nominal value of less than 20 cents cannot be quoted: ASX Listing Rules rule 2.1. See also **Authorised capital; Par value.**

•**Conspiracy** An agreement between two or more people to carry out future unlawful acts or lawful acts by unlawful means: *Nirta v R* (1983) 51 ALR 53. See also **Actus reus.**

Industrial law In industrial law, either of two torts: conspiracy to injure (or simple conspiracy); or unlawful means conspiracy. Both torts involve two or more persons conspiring to cause damage to a person's business. Either or both may arise where two or more employees engage in industrial action. See also **Industrial tort.**

Conspiracy to defraud An offence at common law and under statute in some jurisdictions involving an agreement between two or more persons to use dishonest means to inflict economic loss on another, to imperil the economic interests of another, or to influence the exercise of a public duty: *Scott v Metropolitan Police Commissioner* [1975] AC 819; *Wai Yu-Tsang* [1992] 1 AC 269; (QLD) Criminal Code s 430; (VIC) Crimes Act 1958 s 321F(2). See also **Conspiracy; Dishonest.**

•**Constituent documents** In relation to corporations, commonly used to refer to the documents by which the company was formed, for example, the constitution of a company: *Brownett v Newton* (1941) 64 CLR 439. See also **Articled clerk; Articles of association; Memorandum of association.**

•**Constitution** A document, legislatively enacted in (IMP) Commonwealth of Australia Constitution Act 1900, which lays down the structure of the judicial, executive, and legislative arms of the Commonwealth Government, outlines the powers and duties of these respective arms, and delineates the relationship between the Commonwealth and the States of Australia. Each of the States also has an enacted constitution.

Corporations The documents by which a corporation is formed and governed. The memorandum of association and articles of association together form the constitution of a corporation. See also **Articles of association; Memorandum of association.**

Voluntary associations The formal written rules of an incorporated or unincorporated association. Also known as 'rules'. See also **Incorporated association; Unincorporated association; Voluntary non-profit association.**

Constitution of trust The fulfilment of all the requirements for the creation of a valid trust, including the vesting of identifiable assets in the trustee, subject to an enforceable obligation to use those assets for the benefit of identifiable persons or purposes: *Corin v Patton* (1990) 169 CLR 540; 92 ALR 1. See also **Certainty of object; Certainty of subject.**

•**Construction 1.** The erection of a building or a structure. **2.** A building or structure. **3.** The interpretation of a document. **4.** The meaning given to expressions in a document. See also **Building; Document.**

Contract The task of extracting from contractual documents as a whole the objective intent of the parties: *Codelfa Construction Pty Ltd v State Rail Authority of NSW* (1982) 149 CLR 337 at 348, 351-3; 41 ALR 367. The construction of contractual documents is a question of law. A court will construe documents broadly, resolving ambiguity so as to give a business like meaning to the contract where the parties are business people: *Australian Broadcasting Commission v Australasian Performing Rights Associates Ltd* (1973) 129 CLR 99. See also **Actual intention; Extrinsic evidence; Factual matrix; Implied intention; Legal matrix; Term.**

•**Construction industry** The building industry, or the electrical and metal trades industry: (SA) Construction Industry Long Service Leave Act 1987 s 4. It includes the industry of carrying out the construction, installation, renovation, demolition or maintenance of works such as buildings, roads, railways, airfields, irrigation, or storage of liquids or gases: (VIC) Construction Industry Long Service Leave Act 1983 s 3.

Constructive bailment A non-consensual bailment where the law imposes on a person having possession of a chattel the obligation to deliver the chattel to another by reason of the circumstances in which the first mentioned person has possession or gained possession of the chattel: *Hope v Costello* 297 SW 100 (1927) at 103. Also known as 'extended bailment', 'involuntary bailment', or 'quasi-bailment'. See also **Bailment; Bailment by attornment; Jus tertii; Sub-bailment.**

Constructive condition A condition that the court deems or construes into an instrument or transaction in order to give effect to any obligations or rights arising out of the disposition of the property. A true constructive condition will prevent the vesting of property in the transferee unless and until he or she fulfils it. See also **Condition; equitable charge; trust.**

Constructive delivery Symbolic transfer of possession from one person to another: (NSW) Sale of Goods Act 1923 s 5; *Gamer's Motor Centre (Newcastle) Pty Ltd v Natwest Wholesale Australia Pty Ltd* (1987) 163 CLR 236; 72 ALR 321. See also **Bailee; Delivery; Possession; Sale of goods; Seller in possession after sale.**

Constructive fraud The fraudulent breach of an obligation enforced by a court of conscience. An actual intention to cheat need not be proved; this distinguishes constructive fraud from actual fraud. Conduct will be regarded as constructive fraud when a person violates, however innocently, an obligation that a court of equity will assume was known to the person: *Nocton v Lord Ashburton* [1914] AC 932. See also **Actual fraud; Fraud**.

Constructive knowledge In negligence cases, constructive knowledge is relevant mainly to the issues of reasonable foreseeability and the standard of care: *Wyong Shire Council v Shirt* (1980) 146 CLR 40; 29 ALR 217. See also **Constructive notice; Imputed knowledge; Notice**.

Constructive notice Knowledge that a person would have obtained had he or she made the inquiries that an honest and reasonable person would have made in the ordinary course of the transaction in question. The doctrine of constructive notice means that a person who has knowledge of facts which would make a reasonable person suspicious, but who consciously refrains from making straightforward inquiries for fear of learning of fraud or breach of trust, will not be able to derive advantage from his or her ignorance: *Bailey v Barnes* [1894] 1 Ch 25; *Consul Development Pty Ltd v DPC Estates Pty Ltd* (1975) 132 CLR 373; 5 ALR 231. Also known as 'imputed notice'. See also **Actual knowledge; Actual notice; Constructive knowledge; Imputed knowledge; Notice**.

Corporations Formerly, the doctrine under which all persons who dealt with a company were deemed to know the contents of a company's constitution: *Ernest v Nicholls* (1857) 6 HLC 401. The doctrine has been abolished to the extent that an outsider is not to be taken to have knowledge of a company's memorandum or articles merely because they have been lodged with the Australian Securities Commission: Corporations Law s 165(1). It still applies, however, to documents lodged with respect to registrable charges given by way of security over company property: Corporations Law s 165. See also **Articles of association; Constitution; Memorandum of association; Indoor management rule; Registrable charge**.

Constructive possession The degree of control over chattels recognised by the law as amounting to possession even though the chattel in question is not physically held by the person: for example *Kent v Parer* [1922] VLR 32; *Burns, Philp & Co v Dingle & Co* (1923) 23 SR (NSW) 240; 40 WN (NSW) 26; *Re Fada (Aust) Ltd* [1932] SASR 134. See also **Custody; Possession**.

Constructive receipt A receipt of income which is deemed to be derived by the person on whose behalf the income has been dealt with or who has directed its use even though it was not actually paid to that person: (CTH) Income Tax Assessment Act 1936 ss 19, 160D; *Gair v FCT* (1944) 71 CLR 388 at 393. See also **Derived; Income**.

Constructive trust A trust arising by operation of law, rather than the parties' intention. A constructive trust may be regarded as either: a substantive institution (a type of trust imposed by analogy with express, implied, or resulting trusts); or a remedial device to effect restitution of property, remove unjust enrichment, enable property to be traced, or enforce the trustee's equitable duty: *Stephenson Nominees Pty Ltd v Official Receiver in Bankruptcy* (1987) 76 ALR 485 at 501-6. See also **Constructive trustee; Express trust; Implied trust; Resulting trust; Tracing; Trustee de son tort; Unjust enrichment**.

Constructive trustee A person held liable by operation of law, rather than personal intention, to hold property for the use or benefit of another: *Stephenson Nominees Pty Ltd v Official Receiver in Bankruptcy* (1987) 76 ALR 485; 16 FCR 536. Also known as a 'quasi-trustee' or 'trustee de son tort'. See also **Constructive trust; Trustee; Trustee de son tort**.

•**Consul** /kɒnsʊl/ An official appointed as an agent by a state to protect and represent its commercial interests in a host country. A consul's duties generally involve commercial matters relating to shipping and trade, immigration inquiries, the issue of passports and visas, and quasi-legal matters involving the sending and receiving states. There are four types of consular officer, ranked in descending order of importance as: consul general, consul, vice consul, and consular agent. See also **Master; Minister**.

•**Consumer** One who uses a commodity or service for a non-commercial purpose; a person who acquires goods or services of any kind valued at less than $40,000, or goods or services of a kind ordinarily acquired for personal, domestic or household use or consumption, or a 'commercial road vehicle' of any value: for example (CTH) Trade Practices Act 1974 s 4B. See also **Acquisition; Consumer protection; Consumer sale; Division 2A claim; Fair trading legislation; Trade Practices legislation**.

Consumer affairs bureau Generally an administrative body established by government with the aim of promoting consumer protection. Consumer Affairs Councils or Committees have been established in Victoria, Queensland, Tasmania, and the Northern Territory, which act as advisory bodies to the responsible Minister: (NT) Consumer Affairs and Fair Trading Act 1990 Pt II Div 2; (QLD) Fair Trading Act 1989 Pt II Div 1; (TAS) Consumer Affairs Act 1988 Pt II; (VIC) Consumer Affairs Act 1972 Pt I Div 1.

Consumer Affairs Council An advisory body established in the Northern Territory, Queensland, Tasmania and Victoria: for example (QLD) Fair Trading Act 1989 Pt II Div 1; (VIC) Consumer Affairs Act 1972 Pt 1 Div 1. Each Council has business and non-business representation. Its main function is to act as an advisory body to the responsible Minister. See also **Fair trading legislation**.

Consumer Affairs, Director of See **Commissioner for Consumer Affairs**.

•**Consumer claim** A claim by a consumer for payment of a specified sum or specified services, for the relief of a payment of a specified sum for the delivery, return or replacement of specified goods, or a combination of two or more of these remedies, arising from the supply of goods or services to a consumer under a contract (or collateral contract) for the supply of goods or services: for example (NSW) Consumer Claims Tribunals Act 1987 s 3(1). See also **Consumer**.

Consumer credit The advancing of money to a person for non-commercial purposes in the expectation of repayment. See also **Credit; Uniform credit legislation**.

Consumer credit agreement In the United Kingdom, an agreement between a debtor and a creditor by which the creditor provides the debtor with credit not exceeding a prescribed amount: (UK) Consumer Credit Act 1974 ss 8, 9. See also **Consumer credit; Debtor-creditor agreement; Unrestricted-use credit agreement**.

Consumer debt See **Consumer credit**.

Consumer expectation The standard of goods which consumers are generally entitled to expect. Goods are deemed to be defective under (CTH) Trade Practices Act 1974 Pt VA if their safety does not meet consumer expectation: (CTH) Trade Practices Act 1974 s 75AC(1).

Consumer organisation A government or public interest group or body that aims to protect or enhance consumer rights. Consumer organisations include the Australian Competition and Consumer Commission (ACCC) which has extensive powers to regulate activities affecting consumers: (CTH) Trade Practices Act 1974 Pt II. See also **Australian Competition and Consumer Commission; Consumer**.

•**Consumer Price Index** *Abbr* – CPI An index which measures the rate of price increases in Australia.

Consumer product information *Abbr* – CPI The information about a pharmaceutical product required, in accordance with regulations under the (CTH) Therapeutic Goods Act 1989, to be provided with certain products. The information required to be supplied with the goods includes the name of the medicinal product, a statement of its active ingredients expressed quantitatively and excipients expressed qualitatively. The purpose for which the product is to be used and advice for using the product must also be supplied: (CTH) Therapeutic Goods Regulations reg 9A. Also known as 'patient information', or ' package insert'.

Consumer product information standard A mandatory standard prescribed by regulation (under (CTH) Trade Practices Act 1974 s 65D(2)) or declared by the Minister ((CTH) Trade Practices Act 1974 s 65E(1)), consisting of such requirements as to the disclosure of information relating to the performance, composition, contents, methods of manufacture or processing, design, construction, finishing, or packaging of products (and the form and manner in which that information is to be disclosed on or with products) as are reasonably necessary to give persons using those products information as to the quantity, quality, nature or value of them. The supply by a corporation in trade or commerce of a product that is subject to a consumer product information standard, where that product does not comply with the standard, is a criminal offence: (CTH) Trade Practices Act 1974 s 65D(1); *Miller v Fiona's Clothes Horse of Centrepoint Pty Ltd* [1989] ATPR ¶40-963; *Hamlyn v Mark Foy's Pty Ltd* [1982] ATPR ¶40-316. See also **Consumer product safety standard; Mandatory standard**.

•**Consumer product safety standard** A mandatory standard prescribed by regulation (under (CTH) Trade Practices Act 1974 s 65C(2)) or declared by the Minister ((CTH) Trade Practices Act 1974 s 65E(1)), consisting of such requirements as to the performance, composition, contents, methods of manufacture or processing, design, construction, finish or packaging of products (including the testing of products during or after the completion of manufacture or processing, and the form and content of markings, warnings or instructions to accompany them) as are reasonably necessary to prevent or reduce risk of injury to any person. The supply by a corporation in trade or commerce of a product subject to a consumer product safety standard, where the product does not comply with the standard, is a criminal offence: (CTH) Trade Practices Act 1974 s 65C(1); *Pugh v Clark Rubber Ltd* [1993] ATPR ¶41-258; *Miller v Cunninghams Warehouse Sales Pty Ltd* [1994] ATPR ¶41-321. See also **Consumer product information standard; Mandatory standard**.

•**Consumer protection** Legislative provisions designed to protect participants in transactions where goods or services are acquired by them for personal, domestic or household use or consumption, and not for resupply, use in trade or commerce, for production, manufacturing or repair purposes, or for an amount below that specified: for example (CTH) Trade Practices Act 1974 s 4B, Pt V; (NSW) Fair Trading Act 1987 Pt 3. See also **Consumer; Consumerism; Fair trading legislation; Trade practices legislation**.

•**Consumer sale** A sale of goods in the course of a business where the goods are of a kind commonly bought for private use or consumption, and where the buyer does not purchase them in the course of a business. A sale of goods by auction is excluded from the definition: for example (NSW) Sale of Goods Act 1923 s 62. See also **Consumer; Sale**.

Consumerism A widespread movement concerned with the quality and safety of consumer goods, harmful advertising, and the conduct of businesses in a manner detrimental to the consumer. In the United States the movement was greatly stimulated by the work of Ralph Nader. Consumerism has taken root in Australia spreading into such areas as investment, stockbroking, and stockmarkets. See also **Consumer; Consumer protection**.

Consumer's surplus The amount in excess of a price paid which a consumer would be willing to pay rather than go without the article. The consumer's surplus is measured by the area under the demand curve which represents the additional aggregate payment consumers would pay in excess of the amount actually paid for a good at the going price.

Consumption function Initially a Keynesian concept, a schedule that relates aggregate consumption expenditure to the level of disposable income. Keynesian theory suggested a stable relationship between current income and current consumption, so that a change in income resulted in consumption changing by a fixed proportion of that change, known as the marginal propensity to consume. However, the evidence has not been conclusive and a number of subsequent theories of the consumption function have been propounded. Also known as 'schedule propensity to consume' or 'schedule of intended consumption'. See also **Keynesian school**.

Consumption tax An indirect, retail sales or value-added tax imposed on personal and household consumption expenditure. A consumption tax may be selective or applied to the broadest range of goods and services purchased for the purpose of consumption. Also known as 'goods and services tax' or 'value-added tax'.

Contact damage Damage sustained by a ship, aircraft, vehicle, or other object through impact or collision with other objects. Also known as 'insurance collision'.

Contango A market situation in which prices are progressively higher in future delivery months than in the nearest delivery month. Contango is the opposite of backwardation. See also **Backwardation; Carrying charge; Carrying charge market; Futures contract; Cash and carry**.

Contempt of court Words or actions which interfere with the proper administration of justice or constitute a disregard for the authority of the court: *Lewis v Ogden* (1984) 153 CLR 682; 53 ALR 53. Contempt of court comprises both the physical disturbance of particular proceedings in a court that prevent the court from attending to its business, and any interference with the authority of the court that impairs confidence and respect in the court and its judgments: *Ex parte Tuckerman; Re Nash* [1970] 3 NSWR 23.

Contestable market A market in which there is perfectly free entry and exit, which are the mechanics of contestability. The theory of contestable markets de-emphasises structure (the number and size of the players in the market), and emphasises the presence or otherwise of sunk costs (those costs not recoverable should the entrant depart the market). The theory has significant implications for competition and regulatory policy. Sunk costs, that is, those expended irrecoverably in the production process, cannot be legislated away, so regulatory intervention is still called for. The object of this intervention in contestability theory is to mimic competition, that is, to bring about market behaviour in accordance with that observed in fully competitive markets. The object of the regulation is not to deter entry. See also **Competition; Competition law; Entrant; Market; Market structure**.

•**Contingency** An event or circumstance which may or may not happen, which is conditional on something uncertain; a limitation on a person's estate or interest which is not certain to occur: *Federal Cmr of Taxation v St Helens Farm (ACT) Pty Ltd* (1981) 146 CLR 336; 34 ALR 23. If it is as good as certain that the event will happen, it is a contingency without reality or substance and is no contingency at all. If the event is highly improbable, then a contingency still exists as there is a small probability that it will in fact occur. *Inland Revenue Commissioners v Trustees of Sir John Aird's Settlement* [1982] 2 All ER 929. **2.** In assessing damages in tort, an event which may be described as part of the ups and downs or vicissitudes of life, which is not specifically predictable but acknowledged as likely to occur at some time in the lives of most individuals. In the assessment of damages for non-intentional torts, the figure payable to a plaintiff in compensation will be reduced by an amount calculated by the court to represent the contingencies of life: *Malec v JC Hutton Pty Ltd* (1990) 169 CLR 638; 92 ALR 545. See also **Condition precedent; Condition subsequent; Contingent condition; Damages**.

Contingent asset An item which may in the future constitute an asset. The occurrence of a future specified event determines whether such an item will become an asset or give rise to service potential or future economic benefits: Statement of Accounting Concepts SAC 4. Contingent assets are typically reported in the notes in the company's financial report or if they satisfy the definition and recognition criteria for assets, will be recognised as such in the financial statements. See also **Asset; Financial statement**.

•**Contingent condition** In contract law, an event that may or may not occur and that neither party has promised to bring about, but on whose occurrence depends the creation or subsistence of a contract. See also **Conditional contract; Unilateral contract**.

Contingent creditor Someone who is owed an existing obligation that will or might produce a debt at a future date, or if some event happens: *Community Development Pty Ltd v Engwirda Construction Co* (1969) 120 CLR 455; [1970] ALR 173. See also **Contingent debt; Creditor**.

•**Contingent debt** A debt, based on an existing obligation, that will or might arise at a future time or if a future event occurs: *Federal Cmr of Taxation v Gosstray* [1986] VR 876; (CTH) Bankruptcy Act 1966 s 82(1). See also **Debt; Contingent creditor; Guarantee**.

Contingent interest An interest that is made to await, or depend on, the happening of some event.

•**Contingent liability** A liability which will become due only on the occurrence of an event that may or may not happen. See also **Liability; Guarantee; Financial statement.**.

•**Continuing credit contract** An arrangement in which the buyer is provided with an on-going source of credit which can be used in relation to more than one contract of sale. A credit card is a common example. Credit must be provided in the course of the credit provider's business for the purchase of goods or services or the supply of cash from time to time. Continuing credit contracts may involve only the supplier of the goods, services or cash and the debtor, or may be an arrangement where a supplier contracts with a buyer, who arranges with a credit provider to pay the supplier. There is no continuing credit contract where the only credit charge is a pre-determined credit charge or credit is to be provided by specified instalments: for example (NSW) Credit Act 1984 (repealed) s 48; (VIC) Credit Act 1984 (repealed) s 48 (now replaced by Uniform Consumer Credit Code). See also **Billing cycle; Credit card; Credit charge; Credit provider; Regulated continuing credit sale; Uniform credit legislation**.

Continuing Listing Rules The provisions in ASX Listing Rules Chapter 3 dealing with the continuing obligations imposed upon a company remaining on the official list. These obligations are directed to: the provision of information to the ASX by notice of specified events and by regular reporting; the transfer of securities, and issue of new securities; dealings with major assets; voting rights; directors' obligations; and the circumstances in which a company may repurchase its own shares. See also **Australian Stock Exchange Ltd; Australian Stock Exchange Listing Rules; Security; Asset; Directors' duties.**

Continuing trust A trust which is not extinguished upon a particular date or upon the occurrence of a particular event. The beneficiaries under the trust are not capable of directing the trustees to vest the entire trust property in their favour so as to extinguish the trust. A continuing trust must be designed so as not to offend against the rule against perpetuities.

Continuity of beneficial ownership For income tax purposes, beneficial ownership of shares in a company, which carry more than one half of the voting power, right to dividends, and the right to distributions of capital, by a person at all times during the year where a company wishes to claim a loss where the shares were similarly beneficially owned at all times during the year in which the loss was incurred: (CTH) Income Tax Assessment Act 1936 s 80A. If there is no continuity of beneficial ownership the loss from the prior year may not be deductible in the current year of income. However the loss may still be deductible after the application of the 'same business test'. See also **Beneficial ownership; Carry forward loss; Same business test.**

Continuous disability insurance A contract of insurance under which a benefit is payable on the death of the insured by accident or some other cause specified in the contract; by injury to, or disability of, the insured as a result of accident or sickness; or by the insured being found to have a specified condition or disease: (CTH) Life Insurance Act 1995 s 8. Continuous disability insurance contracts must be for a term of more than three years, during which time the benefits provided for and the premiums payable under the contract may not be altered at the insistence of the life insurance company: s 8. Continuous disability insurance is a type of life insurance policy: (CTH) Life Insurance Act 1995 s 9(1)(e).

Continuous disclosure The timely disclosure of information which is likely materially to affect security values or influence investment decisions, or in which security holders, investors and the Australian Stock Exchange (ASX) have a legitimate interest: Corporations Law s 1001B. See also **Australian Stock Exchange Ltd; Australian Stock Exchange Listing Rules; Security.**

Continuous market A market large enough to ensure securities can be sold at ease and with little price variation on two sales made at the same point in time. See also **Security.**

Continuous stocktaking A method of checking trading stock on a perpetual basis. A check to verify the trading stock amount recorded by the continuing stocktaking method is carried out periodically and adjustments are made for any discrepancies discovered to ensure that the periods of quantity of stock agree with the records of actual stock. See also **Trading stock.**

•**Contraband 1.** Goods imported or exported illegally, including in breach of a United Nations resolution prohibiting trade with a country. **2.** Goods which neutrals are forbidden to supply to belligerents in time of war: *Yangsze Insurance Assn v Indemnity Mutual Marine Assurance Co* [1908] 2 KB 504. See also **Customs duty; Goods.**

•**Contract 1.** A legally binding promise or agreement. It is an act in law where two or more persons declare their consent as to any act or thing to be done or forborne by some or one of them for use of the others or other of them: *Foster v Wheeler* (1887) 36 Ch D 695. A promise or agreement is not legally binding and enforceable as a contract unless the requirements for contract formation, including consideration and certainty of agreement, are satisfied. **2.** The body of general principle pertaining to the various branches of contract law, such as sale of goods contracts or charterparties: *Cehave NV v Bremer Handelsgesellschaft GmbH (The Hansa Nord)* [1976] QB 44. **3.** The act of entering into an agreement. **4.** The form or document that embodies the terms of an agreement between parties, for example a 'standard form contract'. See also **Acceptance; Agreement; Bargain; Consideration; Offer; Promise.**

Contract adjudicator A person appointed by the parties to a contract to monitor the performance of the contract, to give advice that might prevent disputes from arising, and to make decisions on the merits where disputes do arise. Such adjudicators are most often used in the construction industry. See also **Alternative dispute resolution; Dispute review board.**

•**Contract, arrangement or understanding** The concerted conduct prohibited by (CTH) Trade Practices Act 1974 s 45 and other sections of that Act. It includes agreements in restraint of trade and other anti-competitive agreements. See also **Arrangement; Competition law; Contract in restraint of trade; Exclusionary provision; Restraint of trade; Restrictive trade practices; Substantially lessening competition; Understanding.**

Contract by performance See **Contract for services.**

Contract carriage Carriage of goods or passengers under a contract of carriage with a carrier. See also **Contract of carriage.**

Contract debt A fixed amount payable under a contract. See also **Action of debt; Debt; Liquidated damages.**

Contract for labour A contract that is wholly or principally for the labour of a person. Under (CTH) Income Tax Assessment Act 1936 s 221A(2) payments made to a person under such a contract are 'salary or wages' within the statutory definition. A contract for labour differs from a contract by which the contractor has undertaken to produce a given result. Under a contract for labour, the contractor agrees to do the work himself or herself, whereas under a contract to produce a given result the contractor is not obliged to do the work personally but has the power to delegate the work to another: *World Book (Australia) Pty Ltd v FCT* (1992) 108 ALR 510. In a contract to achieve a certain result, the labour is undertaken not for the principal but for the contractor himself or herself to produce the result contracted for. See also **Contract for services; Contract of employment; Contractor.**

•**Contract for sale of land** A contract between a vendor and purchaser to buy and sell a specified parcel of land. Under the Statute of Frauds (reproduced in (NSW) Conveyancing Act 1919 s 54A and in similar legislation in other States) such a contract must be sufficiently recorded in writing to be enforceable, except where the doctrine of part performance would render an oral contract enforceable. See also **Part performance**; **Sale of land**; **Statute of Frauds**.

Contract for services A contractual arrangement by which one person agrees to provide workplace services to another. The contract is between two principals and neither is the employer or employee of the other; the person providing the services is an independent contractor. Also known as 'contract by performance'. See also **Contract of employment**; **Independent contractor**.

Contract formulator A manufacturer that carries out chemical formulation activities on behalf of another entity: for example *Bayer Australia Ltd v Kemcon Pty Ltd* (1991) 6 ANZ Ins Cas ¶61-026. See also **Manufacturer**.

Contract guarantee A guarantee usually issued by banks or surety companies as security for contract works. The obligation of the issuing bank to pay on demand is usually expressed to be unconditional; the obligation cannot be qualified by reference to the terms or purpose of the contract: *Wood Hall Ltd v Pipeline Authority* (1979) 24 ALR 385; 24 ALR 385. See also **Guarantee bond**.

•**Contract in restraint of trade** In a broad popular sense in contract, any contract that limits the free exercise of trade or business: *Esso Petroleum Co Ltd v Harper's Garage (Stourport) Ltd* [1968] AC 269. A contract in restraint of trade is *prima facie* void as a matter of public policy, but will be allowed where the contract is reasonable in the circumstances: *Amoco Australia Pty Ltd v Rocca Bros Motor Engineering Co Pty Ltd* (1973) 133 CLR 288; 1 ALR 385. See also **Contract, arrangement or understanding**; **Covenant**; **Illegal contract**; **Public policy**; **Restraint of trade**; **Restrictive trade practices**.

Contract injurious to public life A contract which creates a conflict between public duty and private interest. See also **Illegal contract**; **Public policy**.

Contract manufacturer A manufacturer that carries out manufacturing activities on behalf of another entity. See also **Manufacturer**.

Contract note A document issued to a client by a stockbroker who has bought securities or sold securities on behalf of the client. In the case of a buyer, the contract note shows the name of the securities, the quantity bought, the consideration, the brokerage, the stamp duty and the total amount to be paid by the client. In the case of a seller, the contract note shows the name of the securities, the quantity sold, the consideration, the brokerage and the total amount to be paid to the client. See also **Broker**.

Contract of adhesion See **Standard form contract**.

•**Contract of carriage** A contract under which a carrier undertakes to carry goods or passengers to a destination in exchange for payment of freight or the fare. See also **Bill of lading**; **Carrier**; **Charterparty**; **Fare**; **Freight**; **Goods**.

Contract of compromise An enforceable contract supported by the consideration of a bona fide abandonment of a substantive claim by a party in a dispute under a pre-existing contract: *Wigan v Edwards* (1973) 1 ALR 497. See also **Accord and satisfaction**; **Accord executory**; **Consideration**.

•**Contract of employment** A contract under which a person (the employee) agrees to work for another person (the employer) in return for some benefit or remuneration from the employer. As a general rule, if the contract gives the employer a right of control over the employee's manner of doing the work, it is an employment contract, rather than one for services: *Stevens v Brodribb Sawmilling Co Pty Ltd* (1986) 160 CLR 16; 63 ALR 513; *BWIU v Odco Pty Ltd* (1991) 29 FCR 104; 99 ALR 735. See also **Contract of service**; **Economic reality test**; **Employee**; **Employer**; **Multiple test**.

•**Contract of guarantee** A contract by which a party is obliged to answer for a debt or default of another person.

•**Contract of insurance** See **Insurance contract**.

•**Contract of sale** In consumer credit law, a contract for the sale of goods or services, including commercial vehicles and farm machinery. A sale to a body corporate is not a contract of sale. Part II of the uniform credit legislation governs a contract of sale: (NSW) Credit Act 1984 (repealed) s 20; (VIC) Credit Act 1984 (repealed) s 20 (now replaced by Uniform Consumer Credit Code). See also **Uniform credit legislation**.

•**Contract of service** A contract under which a person is engaged in the service of an employer to do such work as is contracted for and where the employer directs what is to be done. See also **Contract for services**; **Contract of employment**; **Employee**; **Employment**; **Independent contractor**.

•**Contract regulation committee** A committee established under the (NSW) Industrial Relations Act 1991 (repealed) in respect of a certain class of contracts of bailment of public vehicles (such as taxis and hire cars) and contracts of carriage. It consists of a conciliation commissioner and members representing contractors within the class of contracts. It exercises the functions of the Industrial Relations Commission of New South Wales with respect to the class of contract.

Contract subject to finance In property law, a contract for the purchase of property which permits the purchaser to avoid the contract if the purchaser cannot obtain suitable finance to enable the purchaser to complete the contract. The purchaser must act honestly and reasonably in deciding if available finance is suitable: *Meehan v Jones* (1982) 149 CLR 571; 42 ALR 463. See also **Avoid**; **Contract**; **Purchaser**.

Contract theory The underlying rationale of enforcing contractual obligations. Although contract theory has its basis in 19th century *laissez-faire* philosophy, modern contract theory is also influenced by social, political, and intellectual factors. The legal principle that a promise freely made should be performed or enforced is qualified by the movement in some areas of contract law from determining whether a contract was made and broken to determining whether, if a promise was made, it should as a matter of policy be enforced: *Air Great Lakes Pty Ltd v K S Easter (Holdings) Pty Ltd* (1985) 2 NSWLR 309. See also **Contract; Public policy**.

Contract under hand Contract executed by signature, as opposed to a contract executed under seal or by deed.

Contract under seal See **Special contract**.

Contract unit The actual amount of a commodity which is the subject matter of a futures or option contract. See also **Option**.

Contract wholly or principally for the labour of a person See **Contract for labour**.

Contracting out Expressly renouncing or excluding the operation of certain statutory provisions that would otherwise affect the terms or performance of a contract. Contracting out is often prohibited, as it nullifies the benefits the statute is intended to confer. See also **Contracts not governed by the sale of goods Acts; Disclaimer; Exclusion clause; Implied term; Limitation clause**.

•**Contracting party** In the context of plant breeder's rights, a country or an intergovernmental organisation that is a party to the International Convention for the Protection of New Varieties of Plants 1978 as reissued in 1991, a copy of which forms a schedule to the (CTH) Plant Breeder's Rights Act 1994: (CTH) Plant Breeder's Rights Act 1994 s 3(1).

•**Contractor** The builder of a construction project. See also **Construction; Contract of service; Independent contractor; Proprietor; Subcontract; Supplier; Vicarious liability**.

Contracts not governed by the sale of goods Acts A contract, other than a consumer-type transaction in which the application of sale of goods legislation has been excluded by agreement between the parties. Contracts not governed by sale of goods Acts include agency contracts, bailment, barter or exchange, gifts, hire purchase agreements where there is no agreement to buy, trading-in and contracts for services. The sale of goods Acts in each State and Territory of Australia apply to contracts for the sale of goods, which are contracts where a seller transfers or agrees to transfer the property in goods to a buyer for a money consideration or price: for example (NSW) Sale of Goods Act 1923 s 6; (VIC) Goods Act 1958 s 6; (QLD) Sale of Goods Act 1896 s 3(1). See also **Sale of goods**.

Contracts Review Act 1980 In New South Wales, legislation which enables a court to find a contract unjust and to make orders to avoid the unjust outcome. The court may make a declaration that a contract is wholly or partly void, refuse to enforce it, or vary its terms: (NSW) Contracts Review Act 1980 s 7(1). See also **Unjust contract**.

Contractual agency The appointment of an agent to contract on behalf of the principal, and the consent of both principal and agent to create the agency: *Field v Shoalhaven Transport Pty Ltd* [1970] 3 NSWR 96. See also **Actual authority; Agency; Agency by estoppel; Agent; Principal; Scope of authority**.

Contractual appropriation A loan agreement restriction imposed on a company restricting dividend payments until the retirement of the loan debt. See also **Company; Dividend; Loan**.

Contractual bailment A bailment where the terms on which the bailee has possession of the goods are governed by a contract. See also **Bailment**.

Contractual duty, standard of See **Standard of contractual duty**.

Contractual licence A licence to occupy land given on terms contained in a contract. If a contractual licence is revoked other than in accordance with the terms of the contract, the licensor may be liable to the licensee for damages for breach of contract. A contractual licence may be made irrevocable by the licensor against the licensee in some circumstances. See also **Licence**.

Contractual limitation periods The period, beginning when breach of contract occurs, during which an action in contract must be initiated.

Contractual relations, interference with See **Conspiracy; Interference with contractual relations; Intimidation**.

Contractual rights Rights arising out of a contractual relationship. See also **Contract**.

Contractual voyage A voyage by a vessel under a contract for making that voyage. In a charterparty, the contractual voyage is the stage of the voyage from the loading port to the discharging port. See also **Charterparty; Voyages in stages**.

•**Contravention** In the legal sense of the word, breach of a law, especially a failure to comply with the provision of an Act for example (CTH) Antarctic Treaty (Environment Protection) Act 1980 s 3 or subordinate instrument for example (VIC) Interpretation of Legislation Act 1984 s 38.

Contributing cause In negligence, an additional or intervening cause without which the initial negligent act or omission would not have occurred, or would not have had the effect it did, and which is held to be partly responsible for the plaintiff's loss. See also **Contributory negligence; Novus actus interveniens**.

•**Contributing member** See **Contributing shareholder**.

Contributing shareholder 1. A person holding contributing shares (shares on which only part of the capital amount and any premium has been paid). The outstanding amount is payable at a time chosen by the company. 2. In relation to a company other than a no liability company, a person who is liable, as a member or past member, to contribute to the property of the company in the event of its being wound up, including the holder of fully paid shares and, prior to the final determination of the persons who are contributories, any person alleged to be a contributory: Corporations Law s 9. 3. In the case of a company having a share capital, the holder of fully paid shares in the company: Corporations

Law s 9. Also known as 'contibuting member'. See also **Call on contributories; Partly paid share; Fully paid share; Partly paid share; Share capital; Winding up**.

• **Contribution** 1. An equitable right existing between two or more co-sureties, under which each co-surety is only obliged to contribute proportionately to the satisfaction of the principal debt. 2. The obligation of persons who are under a coordinate liability to make good a loss and share the loss pro rata: *Albion Insurance Co Ltd v GIO (NSW)* (1969) 121 CLR 342; [1970] ALR 441. See also **Contract; Coordinate liability; Co-surety; Natural justice; Principal debtor**.

Contribution assessment period A period during a bankruptcy in respect of which the bankrupt's income is assessed to see if it is large enough to require contributions from income under (CTH) Bankruptcy Act 1966 Pt VI Div 4B. The period begins on the later of the commencement of bankruptcy or when Div 4B commenced (1 July 1992) and each anniversary of that date during bankruptcy, and ends one year later or the date of discharge, whichever is earlier: (CTH) Bankruptcy Act 1966 s 139K. See also **Bankruptcy; Commencement of bankruptcy; Contribution by bankrupt; Discharge of bankruptcy; Income of bankrupt**.

Contribution by bankrupt The amount a bankrupt is required to contribute towards the bankrupt's estate out of income earned during bankruptcy. See also **Actual income threshold amount; Bankrupt; Bankruptcy; Contribution assessment period; Base income threshold amount; Income of bankrupt**.

Contribution margin The amount of a product arrived at by deducting the variable cost of a product from the selling price. The contribution margin per unit is the amount that each unit contributes towards the absorption of fixed costs and towards profits. See also **Costs of production; Fixed cost; Capacity costs**.

Contribution tax The income tax payable on contributions which are paid to superannuation funds. Broadly, contributions tax is payable on all contributions made by an employer to provide superannuation benefits for the employer's employees (regardless of whether an income tax deduction is allowed to the employer) and member contributions to the extent to which the member has received a tax deduction for those contributions. Contribution tax is payable at a concessional rate if the fund complies with the conditions set out in (CTH) Superannuation Industry (Supervision) Act 1993, or at the top marginal tax rate applicable to individuals for the year if it is non-complying: (CTH) Income Tax (Rates) Act 1986 s 26. See also **Allowable deduction; Marginal tax rate; Superannuation fund; Superannuation fund**.

• **Contributory** See **Contributing Shareholder**.

• **Contributory mortgage** A mortgage in which the money secured is advanced by more than one lender in separate amounts. Unless specifically authorised, it is a breach of trust for a trustee to lend trust money on such a mortgage without express authorisation: *Webb v Jonas* (1888) 39 Ch D 660. See also **Mortgage**.

• **Contributory negligence** A plea in mitigation of damages corresponding to the blame of the plaintiff. It consists in the plaintiff's failure to take reasonable care for his or her own safety and well-being, which contributes to the injuries suffered, or to the accident causing the damage, or to the occurrence of a situation in which injuries are foreseeable: *March v E & MH Stramare Pty Ltd* (1991) 171 CLR 506; 99 ALR 423. If contributory negligence is established, damages are reduced under apportionment legislation: for example (NSW) Law Reform (Miscellaneous Provisions) Act 1965 s 10(1). See also **Apportionment; Contributing cause; Negligence**.

• **Control** To direct, regulate or command.

Contract Physical or legal possession: *Federal Cmr of Taxation v Australia and New Zealand Banking Group Ltd* (1979) 143 CLR 499; 23 ALR 480. See also **Assessment; Custody**.

Corporations 1. The capacity or power to govern, manage, regulate or oversee. 2. In relation to an entity in Corporations Law Pts 3.2A, 3.6 and 3.7, the entity's capacity to dominate decision-making, directly or indirectly, in relation to the financing and operating policies of another entity so as to enable that other entity to operate with it in pursuing the objectives of the controlling entity: ss 9, 243E, 294B; Australian Accounting Standards AASB 1017, 1024. Where an entity has control over another, the controlled entity is a subsidiary of the other: s 46(a)(i). See also **Entity; Subsidiary**.

Tort The power of direction and command indicative of possession, rather than ownership, and of management. The degree of power may determine the rights and obligations of the person in control, in relation to other persons. The test of control is relevant in determining liability with regard to occupiers (*Kevan v Cmr for Railways* [1972] 2 NSWLR 710), vicarious liability (*Skuse v Commonwealth* (1985) 62 ALR 108; Aust Torts Rep ¶80-747), the action for trespass to chattels (*Penfolds Wines Pty Ltd v Elliott* (1946) 74 CLR 204; ALR 517), and employers. It may also assist in determining the applicability of the principle of *res ipsa loquitur* (the thing speaks for itself): *Kouris v Prospector's Motel Pty Ltd* (1977) 19 ALR 343. See also **Employer's liability; Occupier's liability; Possession; Vicarious liability**.

Trade and commerce In trade practices law, the standard by which the effect on competition of acquiring shares or assets under (CTH) Trade Practices Act 1974 s 50 was formerly judged. Control is concerned with the formal relationship between entities: *Trade Practices Commission v Arnotts Ltd* (1990) 93 ALR 657. It denotes something more than dominance: *Trade Practices Commission v Ansett Transport Industries (Operations) Pty Ltd* (1978) 20 ALR 31. See also **Acquisition; Competition; Dominance; Merger; Substantially lessening competition**.

Control day In relation to a controller of property of a corporation, the day when the receiver of that property was appointed or the day when any other person entered into possession or took control of that property for the purpose of enforcing a charge: Corporations Law s 9. However, where the controller becomes a controller alongside an existing controller of the property or in place of a controller who has ceased to act as controller of that property, the control day of the existing or original controller is deemed to be the control day of the new controller: Corporations Law s 9. See also **Control of an asset; Controller; Receiver.**

Control of an asset In corporations law, the capacity of an entity to benefit from an asset in the pursuit of the entity's objectives and to deny or regulate the access of others to that benefit: Statement of Accounting Concepts SAC 4. See also **Entity; Accounting standards; Asset.**

Control provision A clause in a contract providing that control of the contract be exercised by a person who is not a party to the contract. For example a life insurance contract for the benefit of a minor may provide that control over the contract be exercised by a particular person who has attained the age of majority.

Control risk In a company audit, the risk that a misstatement could occur in an account balance or class of transactions and not be prevented or detected by the system of internal control: Statement of Auditing Practice AUP 27 ¶15. See also **Audit risk; Statement of Auditing Standards.**

Controlled entity A natural person, company, partnership, or trust whose acts, omissions, or decisions are not, or would not reasonably be expected to be, inconsistent with the direction, instruction, or wishes of a particular person: (CTH) Bankruptcy Act 1966 ss 5, 5F(1). See also **Associated entity; Bankrupt; Bankruptcy Court; Entity; Personal services.**

Controlled foreign company Abbr – CFC A foreign company that is controlled by Australian entities and any associates of Australian entities by virtue of any one of the three control tests: (CTH) Income Tax Assessment Act 1936 s 317. These tests are the 50 per cent group control test, the 40 per cent single Australian entity test and the five or fewer Australian entities test: (CTH) Income Tax Assessment Act 1936 s 340. See also **Attributable income; Attributable taxpayer.**

•**Controller** In relation to property of a corporation, a receiver, or receiver and manager, of that property, or anyone else who (whether or not as agent for the corporation) possesses or controls that property for the purpose of enforcing a charge: Corporations Law s 9. Controllers are subject to various statutory duties under Corporations Law Pt 5.2. See also **Managing controller; Receiver.**

Controlling the composition of the board In corporations law, where an entity has power to appoint (or remove) all or a majority of the directors of another corporation, where any person cannot be appointed a director without an entity's exercise of power, or if an appointment of a person as a director 'follows necessarily' from that person being an officer of the entity: Corporations Law s 47. Where one entity has control over another, the controlled entity is a subsidiary: Corporations Law s 46(a)(i). Control must flow from a legally enforceable power; de facto control in the absence of such power is not enough: *Mount Edon Gold Mines (Aust) Ltd v Burmine Ltd* (1994) 12 ACSR 727. See also **Control; Subsidiary.**

Controlling trustee A registered trustee who is, for the time being, in control of the property of a debtor in accordance with Pt X Div 2: (CTH) Bankruptcy Act 1966 s 187(1). See also **Authority to call meeting; Composition; Deed of arrangement; Deed of assignment; Part X.**

Convention carriage Carriage of goods or passengers, usually by air, some or all of the rights and liabilities in respect of which are determined by international convention such as the Convention for the Unification of Certain Rules Relating to International Carriage by Air (Warsaw Convention) 1929, the Protocol amending the International Convention for the Unification of Certain Rules relating to International Carriage by Air (Hague Protocol) 1955, and the Convention supplementary to the International Convention for the Unification of Certain Rules relating to international carriage by Air (Guadalajara Convention) 1961. These conventions are implemented in Australia by the (CTH) Civil Aviation (Carriers' Liability) Act 1959. See also **Guadalajara Convention 1961.**

Convention Concerning International Carriage by Rail 1980 Abbr – COTIF A convention, concluded in Berne in 1980, establishing the International Organisation for Carriage by Rail, the purpose of which is to develop a uniform system of law applicable to the carriage of passengers, luggage and goods by rail between member states.

•**Convention country** Countries that are party to an international convention.

Convention Establishing the World Intellectual Property Organization 1967 A convention signed in Stockholm on 14 July 1967, creating the World Intellectual Property Organization. The Convention Establishing the World Intellectual Property Organization 1967 gives the World Intellectual Property Organization the responsibility to protect intellectual property throughout the world through cooperation among states and international organisations: art 3(i). The Convention entered into force for Australia on 10 August 1972 and was amended in Geneva on 28 September 1979.

Convention for the Unification of Certain Rules relating to International Carriage by Air 1929 A multilateral agreement, signed in Warsaw on 12 October 1929, dealing with the rights of passengers and owners or consignors of cargo and the corresponding liabilities of carriers in relation to international carriage by air. The Convention is given legislative effect in Australia by the (CTH) Civil Aviation (Carriers' Liability) Act 1959. See also **Cargo; Carriage by air; Carrier; Consignor; Contract of carriage; International carriage of goods.**

Convention on International Civil Aviation 1944 A multilateral convention concluded in Chicago in 1944, setting out the basic principles and arrangements for the development of international civil aviation in a safe and orderly manner. The Convention has been ratified in Australia: (CTH) Air Navigation Act 1920 s 3A, Schs 1-2. Its implementation is through the (CTH) Air Navigation Regulations 1947. Also known as 'Chicago Convention'. See also **International Civil Aviation Organisation.**

Convention on Limitation of Liability for Maritime Claims 1976 An international agreement allowing ship owners to limit liability for loss by claiming the benefit of a limitation of liability: Convention on Limitation of Liability for Maritime Claims 1976 art 1. See also **Maritime claim; Maritime law.**

Convention on the Inter-Governmental Maritime Consultative Organisation 1948 See **Convention on the International Maritime Organisation 1948.**

Convention on the International Maritime Organisation 1948 A Convention formerly known as the 'Convention on the Inter-Governmental Maritime Consultative Organisation 1948'. The original Convention, signed on 6 March 1948 in Geneva, aimed to provide the machinery for cooperation between governments in relation to shipping regulation and to encourage the adoption of the highest practicable standards in matters concerning marine safety and navigational efficiency. It established initially the Inter-Governmental Maritime Consultative Organisation (IMCO) for achieving the purposes of the Convention. The name, Inter-Governmental Maritime Consultative Organisation was amended in 1975 to the International Maritime Organisation (IMO) with effect from 22 May 1982. See also **International Maritime Organisation.**

Convention on the Organisation for Economic Cooperation and Development 1960 A multilateral agreement concluded in Paris on 14 December 1960 to reconstitute the Organisation for European Economic Cooperation created on 16 April 1948, as the Organisation for Economic Cooperation and Development (OECD): Convention on the Organisation for Economic Cooperation and Development 1960 Preamble. The Convention sets out the structure and goals of the OECD and outlines initiatives that contracting parties should take in pursuit of the aims of the organisation: arts 1, 2. Australia, United States, Canada, Japan, and New Zealand are parties to the Convention and are the non-European members of the OECD. Australia acceded to the Convention in 1971 and has passed the (CTH) Organisation for Economic Cooperation and Development (Privileges and Immunities) Regulations 1983, legislatively recognising its membership of the OECD.

Convention on the Prevention of Marine Pollution by Dumping of Wastes and Other Matter 1972 An international convention seeking to protect the marine environment through establishing individual and cooperative measures for the effective control of the deliberate disposal of wastes at sea from vessels, aircraft, platforms, or other manufactured structures: Convention on the Prevention of Marine Pollution by Dumping of Wastes and Other Matter 1972 arts I-III. As the disposal must be deliberate, dumping does not refer to the disposal of wastes that are incidental to the normal operations of vessels, aircraft, or platforms, nor does it apply to wastes or other matter arising from the exploration, exploitation, and associated off-shore processing of mineral resources: art III. Under the control provisions, substances on the 'black list' such as organohalogen compounds, mercury, and cadmium may not be dumped, substances on the 'grey list' such as arsenic, lead, and cyanides require special permits, while all other substances require a prior general permit: art IV, Annexures I-III. The Convention is given effect to by the (CTH) Environment Protection (Sea Dumping) Act 1981with a copy of the English text of the Convention set out in Schs 1-3 and the State Acts. Only the Commonwealth and Tasmanian legislation operate in Australia. Also known as 'London Convention 1972'.

Convention on the Recognition and Enforcement of Foreign Arbitral Awards 1958 A multilateral agreement adopted by the United Nations Conference on International Commercial Arbitration on 10 June 1958 requiring contracting parties to recognise and enforce arbitral awards made in the territory of other states where the recognition and enforcement of such awards have been sought: Convention on the Recognition and Enforcement of Foreign Arbitral Awards 1958 art 1. It is implemented in Australia by the (CTH) International Arbitration Act 1974 s 4, Sch 1. Also known as 'New York Convention 1958'. See also **International Bank for Reconstruction and Development; International Centre for Settlement of Investment Disputes.**

Convention on the Settlement of Investment Disputes between States and Nationals of other States 1965 A multilateral agreement formed under the auspices of the International Bank for Reconstruction and Development, designed to resolve investment disputes between states and nationals of other states, and which establishes the International Centre for the Settlement of Investment Disputes (ICSID): Convention on the Settlement of Investment Disputes between States and Nationals of other States 1965 art 1(1). See also **International Bank for Reconstruction and Development; International Centre for Settlement of Investment Disputes.**

Convention Supplementary to the International Convention for the Unification of Certain Rules of relating to International Carriage by Air of 12 October 1929, 1961 A Convention, supplementing the Warsaw Convention 1929, for the unification of certain rules relating to international carriage by air performed by persons other than the contracting carrier. It was opened for signature on 18 September 1961. Its terms are set out in (CTH) Civil Aviation (Carriers' Liability) Act 1959 Sch 3. Also known as ' Guadalajara Convention 1961'.

•**Conversion** An act or process transforming something from one state to another. An example is conversion in ideological belief or religion.

Tort An intentional tort to goods committed when a person intentionally and without lawful justification deals with chattels in a manner inconsistent with another's actual or constructive possession or immediate right to possession of those chattels. Conversion also protects the interest of the true owner in the absence of actual or constructive possession. It includes the disposal, destruction, or change of the nature of a chattel, and a refusal to deliver the chattel. Mere damage to the chattel is insufficient to maintain an action in conversion: *Penfolds Wines Pty Ltd v Elliott* (1946) 74 CLR 204; ALR 517. Also known as 'trover'. See also **Constructive possession; Detinue; Possession; Wrongful interference with goods.**

Conversion of cheques The collection by a bank of a cheque for someone who is not entitled to it. The cheque (that is, the piece of paper) is treated as the chattel and the value of the chattel (the amount of the cheque) converted, as the money received under it. The bank's act is inconsistent with the rights of the true owner of the cheque: *Lloyd Bank Ltd v Chartered Bank of India, Australia and China* [1929] 1 KB 40 at 55; *Marfani & Co Ltd v Midland Bank Ltd* [1968] 2 All ER 573 at 577. See also **Cheque book; Conversion.**

Convertible security A security (whether a bond, debenture, note or preference share) which gives the holder the right to receive interest periodically and repayment of the principal on maturity, with an option to convert the security to ordinary shares: Corporations Law s 9; (CTH) Income Assessment Act 1936 s 82L(1); Statement of Accounting Concepts SAC 4 ¶27. See also **Bond; Debenture; Option; Ordinary share; Security.**

Converting preference share In corporations law, a share which carries a right to a fixed rate preference dividend for a certain period of time and is then automatically converted into one or more fully paid ordinary shares of the issuing company. See also **Preference share; Preference dividend; Paid-up share capital.**

• **Convey** In property law, to do any acts during the owner's lifetime that are necessary to transfer ownership of property from the owner to another. See also **Appointment; Conveyance; Disposition.**

• **Conveyance 1.** An instrument effective to convey to another person an estate or interest in land. A conveyance includes any assignment, appointment, lease, settlement or other assurance by deed or of any property: for example (NSW) Conveyancing Act 1919 s 7. **2.** The passing of title from a purchaser to a vendor. A conveyance includes a mortgage, charge, lease, assent vesting declaration, disclaimer, release, surrender, extinguishment and every other assurance of property or of an interest by any instrument except a will: for example (VIC) Property Law Act 1958 s 18(1). See also **Assurance.**

• **Conveyancer** A person authorised to carry out the legal work involved in transactions for the conveyance of residential real property. In many Australian States only solicitors are permitted to carry out the legal work involved in property conveyances. New South Wales and South Australia permit licensed conveyancers to carry out work involved in conveyance transactions: (NSW) Conveyancers Licensing Act 1995; (SA) Conveyancers Act 1994. See also **Agreement; Conveyance; Solicitor.**

• **Conviction 1.** The complete orders made by a court after finding an accused person guilty of an offence including both the finding of guilt and the sentence passed as a consequence: *Re Stubbs* (1947) 47 SR (NSW) 329; *Attorney-General (NSW) v Dawes* [1976] 1 NSWLR 242; *R v Hannan; Ex parte Abbott* (1986) 41 NTR 37. **2.** Finding an accused person guilty of the offence charged. **3.** The recording of the finding of guilt by a court. See also **Functus officio.**

• **Cooling-off period** A period of days which commences immediately after entry into certain consumer contracts, during which the purchaser or other person assuming a financial responsibility may rescind the contract, usually subject to a small monetary payment to the other party. In domestic conveyancing, cooling-off periods have been introduced to prevent gazumping, by reducing the risk to purchasers of rapid entry into contracts: (NSW) Conveyancing Act 1919 s 66S. See also **Contract for sale of land.**

Cooney Committee Report The report entitled *Mergers, Monopolies and Acquisitions: Adequacy of Existing Legislative Controls* delivered by the Senate Standing Committee on Legal and Constitutional Affairs in December 1991. The report made recommendations about the mergers and monopolies provisions of the (CTH) Trade Practices Act 1974. Its principal recommendation was to lower the threshold by which acquisitions of shares or assets would be judged so as to prohibit acquisitions which had the effect or likely effect of substantially lessening competition. The report also recommended the incorporation into the Act of guidelines as to how a court ought to judge such conduct in determining whether it had such an effect, and a system of pre-merger notification. The Committee's recommendations have been substantially adopted. See also **Acquisition; Griffiths Committee Report; Hilmer Report; Merger; Restrictive trade practices; Substantially lessening competition; Swanson Committee Report.**

Cooperation in performance The concurrence, agreement or procurement by both parties to a contract of the fulfilment of an obligation, where performance cannot effectually occur without the concurrence of both. Where the ability of one party to perform depends on the cooperation of the other, a duty to cooperate may be found in an express term, in the construction of terms expressly agreed, or in an implied term: for example *Mackay v Dick* (1881) 6 App Cas 251. A plaintiff who fails to perform because of a failure to cooperate by the other party is entitled to damages for breach and has a valid excuse for non-performance: *Plaimar Ltd v Waters Trading Co Ltd* (1945) 72 CLR 304. See also **Construction; Express term; Implied term; Order of performance.**

Cooperative See **Cooperative company.**

Cooperative companies and securities legislation Prior to the introduction of the Corporations Law in 1991, a cooperative system of companies and securities laws throughout the States and Territories of Australia. Also known as 'cooperative scheme laws'. See also **Corporations Law.**

Cooperative company For the purposes of the (CTH) Income Tax Assessment Act 1936, a company which has objects relating to the acquisition, marketing, storage or packaging of commodities for members, has rules limiting the number of shares which may be held by each shareholder and which prohibits the quotation of its shares on a stock exchange or in any public manner: s 117. A company which was not formed for the purpose of carrying on a business, which has the required objects as its primary objects, will not be a cooperative company: *Brookton Co-op Society Ltd v FCT* (1981) 147 CLR 441; (1979) 35 ALR 293. Also known as 'Cooperative'. See also **Company.**

Cooperative Economic and Social Development in Asia and the Pacific, Colombo Plan for See **Colombo Plan for Cooperative Economic and Social Development in Asia and the Pacific**.

Cooperative scheme laws A uniform scheme of legislation enacted in each State legislature in Australia by agreement so as to create a national legislative scheme: for example Corporations Law. See also **Cooperative companies and securities legislation**; **National scheme law**.

Cooperative society A business owned by members who may also be employees, and who typically share in the profits or enjoy benefits in the form of discounted goods or services. See also **Cooperative company**.

Coordinate liability A common liability equally shared by two or more persons for one sum or debt. Discharge of the debt by one of the persons gives rise to the right of contribution. See also **Contribution**; **Co-surety**.

Co-ownership Ownership of property by more than one person, where the co-owners together hold the entire fee simple in the property. Co-ownership may exist at law or in equity, and co-owners may be joint tenants or tenants in common: *Darrington v Caldbeck* (1990) 20 NSWLR 212; (NSW) Conveyancing Act 1919 s 66F. See also **Common law**; **Equity**; **Fee simple**; **Joint tenancy**; **Tenancy in common**.

Co-principal One of two or more persons who jointly have appointed an agent to act for them. The co-principals are jointly liable to the agent and may jointly sue the agent: *Keay v Fenwick* (1876) 1 CPD 745; *Jones v Cuthbertson* (1873) LR 8 QB 504. One co-principal may ratify the action of the agent without ratifying the appointment of the agent, and therefore may not be liable for a share of the commission payable to the agent: *Hughes v Hughes* (1971) 115 Sol Jo 911. See also **Agency**; **Agent**; **Co-agent**; **Principal**; **Ratification**.

Co-promisee A person to whom a promise is given, that promise being given to two or more persons. Where a promise is made to two or more co-promisees the promise may be 'joint', 'joint and several' or 'several'. The common law presumption is that a promise to two or more is made jointly, but the question is one of intention of the parties: *Peabody v Barron* (1884) 5 LR (NSW) 72. See also **Co-promisor**; **Joint and several promise**; **Joint promise**; **Several promise**.

Co-promisor A promisor whose promise is given by two or more persons. Where a promise is given by two or more co-promisors the promise may be 'joint', 'joint and several' or 'several'. See also **Ambiguity**; **Construction**; **Co-promisee**; **Joint and several promise**; **Joint promise**; **Several promise**.

• **Copyright** Intangible property which allows the copyright owner, or those authorised by the copyright owner, the exclusive right to prohibit or to do certain acts. The rights comprised in copyright are distinct from any rights adhering in the medium in or upon which the relevant work or subject matter is recorded: for example *Pacific Film Laboratories Pty Ltd v FCT* (1970) 121 CLR 154. In Australia, copyright is governed by the (CTH) Copyright Act 1968 and constitutes personal property: s 196. See also **Literary work**; **Material form**; **Work**.

Copyright Agency Limited *Abbr* – CAL A non-profit company, limited by guarantee, established in 1974 to act as agent in respect of the reprographic copying of works in which its member authors and publishers own copyright. It has been declared by the Commonwealth Attorney-General, under (CTH) Copyright Act 1968 s 135ZZB, to be the collecting society in respect of the statutory copying scheme available to educational and certain other institutions under (CTH) Copyright Act 1968 Pt VB. On behalf of its members, CAL also offers voluntary licence schemes to churches, media monitoring services, governments, businesses and corporations, and non-profit associations. See also **Copyright**.

Corner A form of market manipulation in which a buyer, or a combination of cooperating buyers, purchase more than the available supply of a security with the intention of forcing short sellers to settle on terms dictated by the purchaser or purchasers. A corner is likely to be prohibited by Corporations Law s 997, however a corner is rare due to the regulation of short selling by Corporations Law s 846. See also **Market manipulation**; **Security**; **Short selling**.

Corporate Affairs Commission Under the former cooperative companies and securities scheme, a State or Territory government agency which was delegated powers from the National Companies and Securities Commission. In most jurisdictions this agency was called the Corporate Affairs Commission. The Commissions were primarily responsible for the day to day administration of the Companies Code and other national scheme legislation. See also **Australian Securities Commission**; **Companies and securities legislation**; **National Companies and Securities Commission**.

Corporate Affairs Office See **Corporate Affairs Commission**.

Corporate capacity The power of a company to acquire and exercise legal rights and to assume legal liabilities; for example, to make contracts. A company is deemed to have the legal capacity (including powers) of a natural person: *Northside Developments Pty Ltd v Registrar General* (1990) 170 CLR 146; 93 ALR 385; Corporations Law ss 159(b), 161. See also **Body corporate**; **Corporation**; **Directors' duties**; **Lifting the corporate veil**; **Separate legal personality**; **Ultra vires**.

Corporate crime Criminal conduct which involves a corporation; that is, committed either by or through a corporation. Corporate criminal liability is based on the doctrine of vicarious liability in that the acts of the directors, servants, or agents acting within the scope of actual or ostensible authority (*Tesco Supermarkets Ltd v Nattrass* [1972] AC 153) are deemed to have been committed by the body corporate: for example (CTH) Proceeds of Crime Act 1987 s 85. A corporation may also be criminally liable where it expressly, tacitly, or impliedly authorised or permitted the commission of the offence: (CTH) Criminal Code s 12.3 (to be proclaimed); *Universal Telecasters (Qld) Ltd v Guthrie* (1978) 18 ALR 531. See also **Civil penalty order**; **Corporate**

culture; Corporate defence; Corporate liability; Corporate offence; Crime; Director; White collar crime.

Corporate criminal liability See **Corporate liability**.

Corporate culture In legislation to be proclaimed, an attitude, policy, rule, course of conduct, or practice existing within a body corporate generally or in the part of the body corporate in which an activity takes place: (CTH) Criminal Code s 12.3(to be proclaimed). Under (CTH) Criminal Code s 12.3, evidence of a corporate culture directing, encouraging, tolerating, or leading to non-compliance may establish corporate criminal liability. An example would be a corporate culture where employees were faced with the option of either non-compliance with the law to meet a production schedule or dismissal. See also **Corporate crime**.

Corporate defence A justification which excuses a person from liability for committing a corporate offence. Proof an accused acted honestly and bona fide in the interests of a company may constitute a corporate defence: *Marchesi v Barnes* [1970] VR 434. See also **Civil penalty provision; Corporate crime; Corporate offence**.

Corporate guarantee A promise given by a corporation to answer for the debt, default, or miscarriage of another person. A corporate guarantee is usually given in favour of a creditor, in respect of a debt owed by a related corporation. See also **Debt; Guarantee; Indemnity**.

Corporate liability The attribution to a corporation of certain acts of its members and any liability attaching to those acts. See also **Conduct engaged in on behalf of a body corporate; Corporate defence; Corporate offence**.

Corporate nationality The nationality of a corporation. In general, a corporation acquires the nationality of the country where it is registered or incorporated and only that country has the right of diplomatic intervention on its behalf: *Barcelona Traction, Light and Power Co Ltd case (Belgium v Spain)* 1970 ICJ Rep 3. See also **Corporation; Foreign company**.

Corporate offence An act which contravenes the law governing the activities of corporations: for example Corporations Law s 1317FA. See also **Corporate crime**.

Corporate officer See **Officer**.

Corporate opportunity doctrine The principle that a director must not usurp or divert a business opportunity in which the company is presently interested or could reasonably be expected to be interested: *Cook v Deeks* [1916-17] All ER Rep 285; [1916] 1 AC 554; *Canadian Aero Services Ltd v O'Malley* (1975) 40 DLR (3d) 371. See also **Company officer; Director; Directors' duties; Fiduciary duty**.

Corporate paper Notes sold by large corporations in the money market as a means of obtaining funds. Such notes are secured by the general credit standing of the corporation. Firms with excess funds tend to make these available to the money market, rather than hold them as bank deposits.

Corporate personality See **Corporate capacity**.

Corporate practice A legal practitioner, sometimes referred to as 'corporate counsel' or 'in-house counsel', who is employed by and provides legal services solely to a firm or corporation. The functions of corporate counsel may be limited to providing advice to the employer or giving instructions on behalf of the firm or corporation to legal practitioners in private practice. Corporate counsel may represent or act for the employer in transactions with third parties or in court proceedings but is required in most jurisdictions to hold a practising certificate to do so. A legal practitioner in corporate practice must comply with his or her professional obligations despite any direction to the contrary from the practitioner's employer: for example (NSW) Solicitor Rules - Revised Professional Conduct and Practice Rules 1995 r 4. Also known as 'corporate counsel' or 'in-house counsel'. See also **Professional misconduct**.

Corporate presence A description of a corporation which is transacting business in a particular forum or area: *Dunlop Pneumatic Tyre Co Ltd v AG Cudell & Co* [1902] KB 342. Three requirements must be satisfied. The corporation must be carrying on business in the jurisdiction, the business must be carried on at some fixed and definite place within the jurisdiction, and the business must have continued for a sufficiently substantial period of time: *National Commercial Bank v Wimbourne* (1979) 11 NSWLR 156. See also **Foreign company; In personam**.

Corporate raider 1. A person or company which buys shares in another company with the sole object of making a bid to get controlling shares of the latter. 2. A person who is in the business of buying and selling companies rather than their products. See also **Arbitrage; Corporation; Greenmail; Takeover; White knight**.

Corporate responsibility See **Corporate liability**.

•**Corporate trustee** A trustee which is a corporate body rather than an individual. The directors of a corporate trustee may be personally liable for debts incurred by the trustee: Corporations Law s 233. Under (CTH) Superannuation Industry (Supervision) Act 1993 s 10, in relation to a fund, a corporate trustee means a body corporate that is trustee of the fund, scheme or trust. See also **Trustee; Trustee company**.

Corporate unit trust See **Unit trust**.

Corporate veil A description of the principle of the limited liability of individual members of a company, who are treated as separate legal entities and are not liable for the debts of the company. On some occasions courts have been willing to disregard the theory of the company as a separate legal entity and have 'lifted the corporate veil' to impose liability on a company's members: *Gordon v FCT* (1965) 113 CLR 604. There is no common or unifying principle which underlies a court's decision to lift the corporate veil: *Briggs v James Hardie & Co Pty Ltd* (1989) 16 NSWLR 549 at 567; 7 ACLC 841. Also known as 'piercing the corporate veil'. See also **Lifting the corporate veil; Limited company; Corporate veil**.

•**Corporation** A legal entity created by charter, prescription, or legislation. The fundamental difference between a corporation and other business entities is that the law treats a corporation as a separate legal person:

Corporations Law s 161. Also known as 'company'. See also **Australian Securities Commission Law; Body corporate; Company; Corporation sole; Corporations Law; Financial corporation; Foreign company; Incorporation; Trade Practices Legislation; Trading corporation.**

Corporation aggregate An incorporated group of coexisting persons (or an incorporated single person with whom others could associate), associated for some group enterprise. A corporation aggregate comes into being when an association of coexisting persons is recognised as a legal person distinct from its members. A registered company is an example. See also **Body corporate; Corporate capacity; Corporation sole.**

Corporation sole A corporation consisting of one person only, and that person's successors to a particular position, where that person constitutes an artificial legal person in which title to property could be vested. A corporation sole is excluded from the definition of 'corporation': Corporations Law s 9. See also **Body corporate; Corporation aggregate.**

Corporations and Securities Panel A peer review group established under (CTH) Australian Securities Commission Act 1989 Pt 10. The panel has power to conduct hearings and make declarations in respect of applications made to it by the Australian Securities Commission (ASC) when it is alleged by the ASC that unacceptable circumstances have or may have occurred in relation to the acquisition of shares in a company, or as a result of a person's conduct in relation to shares or a company's affairs: Corporations Law s 733. The panel can also make consequential orders: Pt 6.9. See also **Australian Securities Commission Law; Takeover.**

Corporations case The High Court decision in *New South Wales v Commonwealth* (1990) 169 CLR 482; 90 ALR 355. It was concerned with the constitutional validity of the provisions of the (CTH) Corporations Act 1989 dealing with the incorporation of trading and financial corporations and prohibiting their incorporation under State or Territory law. The High Court held that the Commonwealth did not have power under Commonwealth Constitution s 51(xx) to legislate with respect to the incorporation of companies, since the head of power is one with respect to 'formed corporations'. Also known as 'Incorporation case'.

•**Corporations law** The discrete body of legislation dealing with the regulation of companies and the securities and futures industries, subsumed under (CTH) Corporations Act 1989 s 82. See also **Australian Securities Commission Law; Australian Securities Commission; National scheme law.**

Corporations power The legislative power of the Federal Parliament to make laws with respect to foreign corporations, and trading or financial corporations formed within the limits of the Commonwealth: Commonwealth Constitution s 51(xx). The Federal Parliament may regulate at least the trading or financial activities of such corporations and activities undertaken for the purposes of trade (*Commonwealth v Tasmania* (1983) 158 CLR 1; 46 ALR 625) and, upon the wider view of the extent of the power, all activities of such corporations whether trading or otherwise (*Commonwealth v Tasmania* (CLR) at 148-150, 179, 269-71). This power extends to the intrastate activities of corporations (*Strickland v Rocla Concrete Pipes Ltd* (1971) 124 CLR 468; [1972] ALR 3) and, in certain circumstances, to natural persons, such as directors, (*Fencott v Muller* (1983) 152 CLR 570 at 598; 46 ALR 41). The Federal Parliament may not, however, legislate with respect to the formation of corporations: *New South Wales v Commonwealth* (1990) 169 CLR 482; 90 ALR 355. See also **Financial corporation; Foreign company; Trade and commerce power; Trading corporation.**

•**Corporatisation** An approach to improving the performance of State enterprises by creating managerial forms and structures similar to those of large private enterprises. The aim is to ensure that State enterprises perform in the interests of the owners, in this case the public. Managers are assigned full authority to manage the day to day affairs of State enterprises in accordance with a statement of commercial intent negotiated annually with the responsible Minister. The NSW government passed legislation in 1989 to facilitate corporatisation. Examples of corporatisation in NSW are the State Bank of NSW, which remains entirely owned by the NSW government under the (NSW) State Owned Corporations Act 1989, and NSW GrainCorp, which is responsible for the export of wheat and other grains.

Corporeal property Tangible property, namely property which has an actual physical existence.

Corrective advertising An order that the Minister or Australian Competition and Consumer Commission may make against a trader who has engaged in misleading or deceptive conduct, especially misleading or deceptive advertising. The trader is required to publish corrective information at the time, in a manner and in the terms specified in the order: for example (CTH) Trade Practices Act 1974 s 80A(1)(b); (NSW) Fair Trading Act 1987 s 67(b). See also **Information disclosure; Misleading or deceptive conduct.**

Correspondence with description The goods matching their description. Goods of a kind ordinarily acquired for personal, domestic, or household use or consumption, that are supplied by a manufacturer, deemed manufacturer, or importer, must correspond with the description under which they are supplied: (CTH) Trade Practices Act 1974 s 74C; for example *Newton v Mercury Power Australia Pty Ltd* (1986) ATPR ¶40-075. See also **Consumer; Deemed manufacturer; Division 2A claim; Importer; Manufacturer.**

Correspondence with sample The matching of a sample of goods with what is actually supplied. Goods of a kind ordinarily acquired for personal, domestic, or household use or consumption, that are supplied by a manufacturer, deemed manufacturer or importer, must correspond with any sample by which they were supplied, and not have a defect that renders them unmerchantable, where the defect would not be apparent on reasonable examination of the sample: (CTH) Trade Practices Act 1974 s 74E. See also **Deemed manufacturer; Division 2A claim; Importer; Manufacturer.**

Correspondent bank A bank which receives a letter of credit from another bank. The correspondent bank is generally requested to perform some service in accordance with the letter of credit. Also known as the 'remitting bank'. See also **Correspondent banking; Letter of credit.**

Correspondent banking An arrangement under which one bank ('correspondent') holds deposits owned by other banks ('respondents') and provides payment and other services to those respondent banks. Such arrangements may also be known as agency relationships in some domestic contexts. See also **Correspondent bank; Nostro account; Vostro accounts.**

•**Corroboration** Independent evidence which implicates the accused person by connecting him or her with the crime.

•**Corrupt conduct** Conduct which does or could adversely affect the honest or impartial exercise of official functions by a public official or authority. See also **Blackmail; Bribery; Corruption; Embezzlement.**

Corruption Where a person without lawful authority, offers, makes or gives to an officer, any payment, gratuity or present in consideration that the officer will do or omit any act or thing pertaining to his or her powers, authorities duties or functions: for example (NSW) National Parks and Wildlife Act 1974 s 170. See also **Bribe.**

•**Cost base** The sum of the amount of: any consideration necessary to acquire an asset; any incidental costs of acquiring or disposing of the asset (for example, advertising, stamp duty, valuation fees); non-capital costs in respect of the ownership of a non personal-use asset acquired after 20 August 1991 (for example, expenditure on maintenance, premiums to insure the asset, rates, or land tax); capital expenditure incurred to enhance the value of the asset and reflected in the state or nature of the asset at the time of disposal; and capital expenditure incurred by the taxpayer to establish, preserve, or defend the taxpayer's title to, or right over, the asset: (CTH) Income Tax Assessment Act 1936 s 160ZH(1), (6A). Determining the cost base of an asset is fundamental to calculating the capital gain or capital loss on its disposal. See also **Asset; Consideration in respect of acquisition of an asset; Capital gain; Capital loss; Indexed cost base; Non-listed personal-use asset.**

Cost insurance and freight See **Cost insurance freight contract.**

Cost insurance freight contract *Abbr* – CIF contract A contract of sale under which the seller covenants to: make an invoice of the goods sold; ship the goods to the buyer; arrange for insurance for the benefit of the buyer; and send to the buyer the shipping documents (the invoice, bill of lading and insurance policy): *Johnson v Taylor Bros and Co Ltd* [1920] AC 144. See also **Bill of lading; Contract of sale.**

Cost of capital The total amount of capital employed by a business, expressed as a rate of interest.

Cost of goods sold The cost of inventory sold during an accounting period. The cost of goods sold is calculated by adding the purchases made during the period to the opening stock and deducting the stock on hand at the end of the period. See also **Trading stock.**

Cost of plant The amount available for depreciation in relation to the acquisition of plant: (CTH) Income Tax Assessment Act 1936 s 62(1). The cost of a unit of property will include not only its purchase price or construction cost but also such items as customs duty, transportation and delivery costs, in-transit insurance, and installation costs. Where property is acquired in a non-arm's length transaction, the cost is taken as the amount that would have been paid for the property had the parties been dealing with each other at arm's length: (CTH) Income Tax Assessment Act 1936 ss 56(4), 62(3). See also **Depreciation; Plant.**

Cost or market method A method of inventory valuation where the lower of either the cost or market value of trading stock on hand is used. The market method refers to the cost of replacing goods on the inventory date and shows the lower cost of inventory on the balance sheet when prices are declining, but remains unaffected by a price rise. See also **Trading stock.**

Cost-benefit analysis *Abbr* – CBA A procedure for comparing alternative possible courses of action by reference to the net social benefits that they are likely to produce. See also **Cost-effectiveness analysis.**

Cost-effectiveness analysis *Abbr* – CEA An approach adopted when the benefits from a project or activity cannot be readily measured in monetary or other terms, yet the project or activity has political or corporate approval. See also **Cost-benefit analysis.**

•**Costs** At common law, the remuneration and disbursements incurred in relation to legal work: *Ex parte Farmers' Fertilisers Corp Ltd* (1916) 16 SR (NSW) 645; 33 WN (NSW) 182. Costs are defined as fees, charges, disbursements, expenses and remuneration for work done by a person in the capacity of a barrister or solicitor: for example (NSW) Legal Profession Act 1987 ss 3, 173; (VIC) Supreme Court Act 1986 s 3(1). See also **Assessment of costs; Costs agreement; Costs disclosure; Retainer.**

Costs agreement A written agreement between a solicitor and client permitting the solicitor to charge the client at a rate or in a manner different from that laid down by the applicable scale of costs: for example (CTH) Family Law Rules 1984 O 38 r 8. See also **Costs.**

Costs disclosure The obligation of a legal practitioner in New South Wales to make disclosure to the client of the costs of legal services to be provided to the client: (NSW) Legal Profession Act 1987 s 175(1). See also **Assessment of costs; Costs; Professional misconduct; Retainer.**

Costs of production The actual costs of producing a good or service. Explicit costs appear in the company's accounts as salaries and wages, the cost of plant and raw materials, inventories, energy and handling. Implicit costs are usually those involved in small businesses where the proprietor-manager does not receive a full salary or where interest on personal funds is not charged. Variable costs vary with output within existing plant capacity. Fixed costs are production costs which tend to be unaffected by variations in the volume of output (also known as overhead costs). Short-run costs vary with the level of production within the capacity of the existing plant. Long-run costs are those incurred when all fixed and variable costs may change.

Co-surety A surety sharing a joint and several liability to the principal creditor with one or more other guarantors. See also **Contribution; Coordinate liability; Guarantee; Guarantor**.

Co-trustee A trustee who shares the joint office of trustee with others, all of whom together form one collective trustee: *In the Estate of Just (dec'd) (No 1)* (1973) 7 SASR 508. The decisions of co-trustees must be unanimous, unless the trust is a charitable trust or the trust instrument specifically provides otherwise. A co-trustee cannot delegate his or her power to another co-trustee: *Pelham v Pelham* [1955] SASR 53. The liability of co-trustees is joint and several: *Bahin v Hughes* (1886) 31 Ch D 390. See also **Joint and several liability; Passive trustee; Trustee**.

Council of Financial Supervisors A forum chaired by the Reserve Bank, the other members being the Insurance and Superannuation Commission, the Australian Securities Commission, and the Australian Financial Institutions Commission. The Council, which was established late in 1992, provides an avenue for promoting discussion, and the exchange of information among supervisors, and for avoiding unintended overlaps, inconsistencies, and gaps in supervision of the financial system. The Council is not a supervisor in its own right. Its creation has not altered the separate statutory responsibilities of its members or replaced other channels of communication among supervisors. See also **Australian Financial Institutions Commission; Australian Securities Commission**.

•**Counsel** A person who appears as an advocate before a court. See also **Ancillary liability; Attorney; Barrister; Inducement; Solicitor**.

Counselling The process of helping individuals discover and develop their educational, vocational, psychological or inter-personal potential with a view to promoting personal happiness or social usefulness; advising or suggesting a course of action.

Consumer protection To instigate or encourage the doing or adopting of a plan: *Yorke v Lucas* (1983) 49 ALR 672; 80 FLR 143. Counselling a contravention of consumer protection legislation may be prevented by an injunction or other order.

•**Count 1.** In civil matters, the plaintiff's cause of action contained in the pleadings; historically, 'common counts' or pleading devices used to assist in debt recovery: *Pavey & Matthews Pty Ltd v Paul* (1987) 162 CLR 221 at 251; 69 ALR 577. **2.** In criminal matters, the distinct and separate offences indicated by separate paragraphs in an information or complaint. Each paragraph charges a separate offence and the particulars of that offence. An indictment may contain more than one count, but each count can be for only one offence or an allegation of conduct which would amount to a single offence: *S v R* (1989) 168 CLR 266 at 273, 280; 89 ALR 321. See also **Charge; Offence**.

Counter presentation Presentation of a cheque by a person other than a bank, by exhibiting the cheque in person to the drawee bank or home branch at a reasonable hour, on a day on which the drawee bank is open for business: (CTH) Cheques and Payment Orders Act 1986 s 63. It is so termed because presentation and payments are made 'over the counter'. See also **Cheque; Drawee bank; Home branch**.

Counter trade Barter trade. A situation where a company exports a product to another country or company and, instead of money, receives other goods in payment. The counter purchase deal is common, the seller of goods agreeing to buy a specified value of goods or services from the buying country within a specified time. A typical counter-trade deal might involve selling coal to a steel mill in South Korea, with payment in part being made in steel products. Counter trade is often the only way exporters can gain access to difficult markets, although the arranging of such trades is often a most challenging task. A substantial portion of world trade is conducted under counter-trade conditions.

•**Counterclaim** A claim or a cross-claim capable of supporting an independent action but which is pleaded in the existing action for the sake of convenience: *Stumore v Campbell & Co* [1892] 1 QB 314 at 316. A counterclaim differs from set-off in that the defendant in a set-off admits the plaintiff's claim but sets up a cross-claim excusing the defendant in whole or in part: *Re Dalco; Ex parte Dalco v DCT* (1986) 67 ALR 605. See also **Claim; Cross claim; Cross demand; Judgment debt; Offset agreement; Set-off**.

Counter-offer In contract law, an offer to contract made by one party in response to a prior offer by the other party. A conditional acceptance of an offer amounts to a counter-offer, not an acceptance. A counter-offer expressly or impliedly rejects an offer; for example, an offer to sell land at a specified price is rejected by a counter-offer to pay a smaller sum: *Baker v Taylor* (1906) 6 SR (NSW) 500. See also **Acceptance; Battle of forms; Contract; Offer; Term**.

•**Counterpart** A copy of a deed or document, usually created so that each party may have their own copy. See also **Deed; Deed inter partes**.

•**Countervailing duty** Duty that is payable on goods under (CTH) Customs Tariffs (Anti-Dumping) Act 1975 s 11, or under s 10 because of a declaration: (CTH) Customs Act 1901 s 269T(1), (2). Such a declaration is to be made where a countervailing subsidy has been given in respect of goods which causes or threatens to cause material injury to an Australian industry which produces like goods: s 269TJ. The duty is a special duty of customs imposed on importers where subsidies have been provided to the exporter of similar goods to increase the cost of imported goods in order to protect the local industry.

Countervailing power A concentration of power in one sector of the market counteracting a concentration of power in another, such as strong buyer power counteracting strong seller power. The degree of countervailing power has an impact on the level of competition in a market. It must now be taken into account in analysing the competitive effects of acquisitions of shares and assets: (CTH) Trade Practices Act 1974 s 50(3)(d). See also **Acquisition; Competition; Market; Market power; Merger**.

•**Coupon** The annual rate of interest paid pursuant to a bond, based on the bond's face value. See also **Bond**.

Coupon insurance A type of insurance used as a means of advertising in which a document (or 'coupon') is attached to, or forms part of, a purchased article and offers the purchaser personal accident or other insurance for a minimal registration fee.

Courier A carrier who travels from one place to another to provide a safe and urgent letter or parcel delivery service. See also **Carrier; Common carrier; Contract of carriage**.

•**Course of business** That which is usually done in the management of a trade or business. See also **Custom of merchants**.

•**Course of employment** The activities of an employee while performing the work for which he or she is engaged, including activities necessarily incidental to the employment undertaken during working hours. Incidental activities include rest and meal breaks taken on employer's premises, and attendance at social or sporting gatherings which the employee is required or encouraged to attend: *Re Ryan and Commonwealth* (1981) 5 ALD 131. See also **Employment**.

Tort Actions performed by an employee as part of his or her employment. An employer is vicariously liable for actions performed in the course of employment which result in the negligent infliction of injury or damage to another: *Deatons Pty Ltd v Flew* (1949) 79 CLR 370. See also **Vicarious liability**.

•**Court 1.** A place where justice is administered. **2.** The decision maker (or makers) who sits in a court. **3.** In relation to an international arbitration, a body or organ of the judicial system of a state: UNCITRAL Model Law on International Commercial Arbitration (adopted in Australia by the (CTH) International Arbitration Act 1974). See also **Arbitration; Bankruptcy Court; Commercial Arbitration Legislation; Federal Court; High Court of Australia; Supreme Court**.

Court appointed expert An independent person selected and directed by the judge to furnish the court with a scientific, technical, professional or specialised opinion which is likely to be outside the experience and knowledge of a judge or jury: for example *R v Turner* [1975] QB 834 at 841; *Murphy v R* (1989) 167 CLR 94 at 111. The expert's function is to provide the fact finder with information which will enable the fact finder to decide the case: *Minnesota Mining and Manufacturing Co v Beiersdorf (Australia) Ltd* (1980) 144 CLR 253; 29 ALR 29.

Court appointed receiver In corporations law, a receiver appointed by a court under its general equitable jurisdiction (for example (NSW) Supreme Court Act 1970 s 67) or special statutory jurisdiction (Corporations Law ss 1114(1)(e), 1268(1)(e), 1323(1)(h); (NSW) Legal Profession Act 1987 s 92). See also **Privately appointed receiver; Receiver**.

Court of Admiralty A court having jurisdiction to determine matters pertaining to proprietary maritime claims such as a claim relating to title to a ship or general maritime claims such as a claim for damage done by a ship: (CTH) Admiralty Act 1988 Pt II. See also **Admiralty law; Maritime lien**.

•**Court of Appeal** *Abbr* – CA A court that exercises the Supreme Court's appellate jurisdiction in civil matters. The Court of Appeal hears appeals from specified courts and tribunals: for example (NSW) Supreme Court Act 1970 s 48(1). It is usual for the Court of Appeal to sit with a bench of three judges of appeal, but there are certain exceptions: for example (NSW) Supreme Court Act 1970 ss 46A, 46B.

Court of Equity A court administering the jurisdiction which historically developed from the discretionary justice dispensed by the Lord Chancellor of England to mitigate, in certain cases, the rigours or deficiencies of the strict rules of the common law. See also **Common law; Equity**.

Court of Marine Inquiry A court in New South Wales, South Australia and Western Australia, the most important functions of which are to investigate casualties occurring to specified ships in specified circumstances, and to make inquiries as to charges of incompetence or misconduct on the part of masters, mates, or engineers of ships: (NSW) Navigation Act 1901 s 23; (SA) Marine Act 1936 ss 106-107; (WA) Western Australian Marine Act 1982 s 104(1). The other States and the Northern Territory have bodies, differently named, with similar functions, for example, the Marine Appeal Board of the Northern Territory: (NT) Marine Act 1981 s 10. See also **Maritime jurisdiction; Maritime law**.

•**Court of summary jurisdiction** A lower court of a State or Territory that makes summary orders or issues summary punishments: (CTH) Acts Interpretation Act 1901 s 26(d). Proceedings in a court of summary jurisdiction are conducted by a magistrate. Also known as 'local court' (New South Wales), 'magistrate's court' (Victoria and Queensland), and 'court of petty sessions' (Australian Capital Territory, Tasmania, Western Australia). See also **Justice of the peace**.

•**Court order** A direction or command of the court which, if not complied with, may result in contempt of court.

Court records The official collection of pleadings, interlocutory applications, exhibits, affidavits, orders and transcripts of testimony which have arisen during the course of proceedings. The reasons given for a particular decision do not generally form part of the record: *Hockey v Yelland* (1984) 157 CLR 124. See also **Certiorari; Court transcript**.

Court transcript A written account of the oral testimony adduced in court, summary of arguments by counsel in relation to the admissibility of evidence and propriety of directions, and orders and reasons for orders given by the judge. See also **Court records**.

•**Covenant** A formal agreement or promise in a deed or under seal: *Russell v Watts* (1885) 10 App Cas 590 at 611. Express words of covenant or agreement are not necessary, but the parties' intention to create a covenant must be clear: *Courtney v Taylor* (1843) 6 Man & G 851; 134 ER 1135.

Contract In relation to a loan agreement, a promise;

anything that forms a material provision of an agreement: *David Securities Pty Ltd v Commonwealth Bank of Australia* (1992) 109 ALR 57.

Covenant in restraint of trade A term in a contract of employment that requires the employee, after leaving the employer, not to do a particular type of work within a particular area for a particular period of time. Such agreements are prima facie void, being in restraint of trade: *Buckley v Tutty* (1971) 125 CLR 353. See also **Contract of employment**.

Covenant to repair A lease provision requiring maintenance of the structural parts of the premises during the term of the lease. Unless expressly provided there is no obligation upon a lessor to repair the premises: *Cavalier v Pope* [1906] AC 428.

Covenantee The party to whom a promise by covenant is made; the party to a covenant who is entitled to the benefit of the promise. Where the covenant relates to land, the covenantee can enforce the covenant against the successors in title to the original covenantor provided that the covenant runs with the land either at law or in equity. See also **Covenant; Covenantor**.

Covenantor The party to a covenant who promises to do or refrain from doing a particular act; the person who assumes the obligations of the covenant, who carries the burden of the covenant. The covenantor is liable to comply with the covenant as a matter of contract at the enforcement of the covenantee. See also **Covenant; Covenantee; Scheme of development**.

•**Cover** Protection against risk, loss, damage, or liability provided by a contract of insurance for the benefit of an insured. See also **Insurance contract; Interim cover; Standard cover**.

Cover note A document issued by an insurer providing interim cover to the insured pending entry into a formal contract of insurance. A cover note may expressly adopt the terms and conditions of the insurer's usual policy: for example *Steadfast Insurance Co Ltd v F & B Trading Co Pty Ltd* (1971) 125 CLR 578; 46 ALJR 10. If not, those terms will usually be implied into the interim contract: *Lotus Manufacturing Co Ltd v Sun Alliance Insurance Ltd* (1987) 4 ANZ Ins Cas ¶60-782. See also **Cover; Interim cover; Insurance contract**.

•**Covering the field** The operation of legislation governing particular subject matter completely and exhaustively to the exclusion of other legislation with respect to the same subject matter.

Craft union A union whose members work in a particular craft or trade, regardless of the industry in which the members exercise their skill: for example the Electrical Trades Union. See also **Enterprise union; General union; Industry union; Occupational union**.

Creative accounting An accounting technique in which the accountant will seek to make the financial statements of a company open to a preferred interpretation, for example to minimise tax or to impress potential investors, by taking advantage of any ambiguities in industry standards. See also **Tax avoidance**.

•**Credit** A loan or financial accommodation.

Banking and finance **1.** Belief in a person's trustworthiness; the ability of a business or person to borrow money, or obtain goods on time, in consequence of the favourable opinion held by the particular lender as to the borrower's solvency and past history of reliability. **2.** Confidence in a buyer's ability to meet financial obligations at some future time. **3.** Time allowed to the buyer of goods by the seller, in which to make payment for them; granting the use or possession of goods and services without immediate payment. It includes the delivery of goods or the advancing of money with the trust that the debtor will have the means to pay and will pay at a future date: *Herbert v R* (1941) 64 CLR 461 at 467; [1941] ALR 100. **4.** The right granted by a creditor to a debtor to defer payment of debt or to incur debt and defer its payment. See also **Credit rating; Uniform credit legislation**.

Consumer credit Any form of financial accommodation. This definition covers any advance of money in expectation of repayment. See also **Uniform credit legislation**.

Freedom of information In privacy law, a loan that is intended to be used wholly or primarily for domestic, family, or household purposes: (CTH) Privacy Act 1988 s 6(1). See also **Credit report; Credit reporting agency**.

Credit absorption tax A tax imposed by a law of a foreign country to the extent that the tax would not have been payable if the taxpayer concerned or another taxpayer had not been entitled to a credit in respect of tax under Australia's foreign tax credits system: (CTH) Income Tax Assessment Act 1936 s 6AB(6). For the purposes of the foreign tax regime it is excluded as a foreign tax and no credit is available. See also **Foreign tax credit**.

Credit Act See **Uniform credit legislation**.

Credit balance In accounting, the status of an account when the sum of the credit entries exceeds the sum of the debit entries.

Credit broker An agent or middleperson who negotiates the provision of credit or finance for a principal on a commission basis. Credit brokers are distinguishable from finance brokers, who negotiate or act as intermediaries to obtain credit for persons other than their employers or principals and whose activities are regulated by statute: for example (NSW) Credit (Finance Brokers) Act 1984; (VIC) Finance Brokers Act 1969. See also **Broker; Credit; Finance broker**.

•**Credit card 1.** A small plastic card issued to approved creditworthy persons and used to obtain cash on credit or to purchase goods and services from retailers or service providers who agree to forgo immediate cash payment. **2.** A card commonly issued by a person carrying on business to a customer for use in obtaining goods or services from that person on credit: (CTH) Trade Practices Act 1974 s 63A(3); (CTH) Privacy Act 1988 s 6(1); (NSW) Fair Trading Act 1987 s 57. See also **Credit; Credit card fraud; Debit card; Unsolicited credit card**.

Credit card fraud The dishonest use of a credit card to obtain money or other property to which the user is not entitled. The offences committed may include obtaining property by a false pretence (for example (NSW) Crimes Act 1900 s 178) or obtaining property by deception (for example (VIC) Crimes Act 1958 s 81(1)). See also **Credit card**; **False pretence**; **Obtaining property by false pretences**.

•**Credit charge** In general, the amount by which the amount payable by the borrower under a contract exceeds the amount financed. See also **Continuing credit contract**; **Credit contract**; **Credit sale contract**.

•**Credit contract** A credit sale contract, a loan contract, or a continuing credit contract: for example (NSW) Credit Act 1984 (repealed) s 5(1) (replaced by Uniform Consumer Credit Code). See also **Continuing credit contract**; **Credit sale contract**; **Regulated contract**.

Credit control The regulation of bank and other forms of lending in the interest of monetary policy normally effected by the Reserve Bank. Since the deregulation of the Australian financial system in the mid-1980s, the only type of credit control is the Reserve Bank's prime rate. See also **Credit squeeze**; **Reserve Bank of Australia**.

Credit enhancement In relation to a loan, the process of insuring risk associated with purchasing or funding a loan by means of a securitisation agreement or similar process: (CTH) Privacy Act 1988 s 6(1). See also **Securitisation arrangement**.

Credit hawker A credit provider who, either personally or through an employee, canvasses at the home or business of another person with a view to inducing the person to apply for, or obtain credit under, a regulated contract. Credit hawking is an offence in all jurisdictions except the Northern Territory and Tasmania. An exception to the prohibition arises where the credit is being offered for the purchase of goods by a supplier of the goods or for the purchase of goods from the person offering the credit. The offence is committed only by the credit provider, not by the person employed to do the canvassing: for example (NSW) Credit Act 1984 (repealed) s 122; (VIC) Credit Act 1984 (repealed) s 122 (replaced by Uniform Consumer Credit Code). See also **Canvassing**; **Credit**.

Credit insurance Insurance taken out by a debtor to cover against an inability to meet debts, particularly loan repayments. See also **Credit**; **Loan**; **Mortgage**; **Standard cover**.

Credit Licensing Authority See **Commercial Tribunal**.

Credit limit The maximum amount a customer is allowed to borrow under a lending facility such as a line of credit, overdraft or credit card. See also **Credit**; **Credit balance**; **Credit line**.

Credit line In banking and commerce, that amount of money or merchandise which a banker, merchant, or supplier agrees to supply to a person on credit and generally agreed to in advance. See also **Credit**; **Credit balance**; **Credit limit**.

Credit Lyonnais Australia Present in Australia since 1970, a subsidiary of the Credit Lyonnais Group of France, founded in 1863.

Credit note A note issued by a trader setting out that the person to whom it is directed is entitled to be credited by the issuer with a certain amount; for example for goods which the other person has returned.

•**Credit provider** A person who provides credit in the course of a business carried on by him or her. See also **Credit**; **Credit provider's licence**; **Credit report**; **Credit reporting agency**; **Credit reporting business**; **Linked credit provider**.

Credit provider's licence A licence which a person had to hold in order to carry on the business of providing credit. The licence authorised its holder to carry on business under the name or names specified in the licence. A licence continued in force until it was surrendered, cancelled or suspended. The Commercial Tribunal or similar body will refuse to grant a licence if it is not satisfied that the applicant is a fit and proper person to hold a licence: for example (NSW) Credit (Administration) Act 1984 (repealed) ss 6(1), (2), 20(1)-(4), 21(6), 22, 23(11). This licence has no present application. See also **Credit provider**; **Exempt credit provider**; **Fit and proper person**.

•**Credit purchase agreement** Generally, an agreement for the sale of goods or provision of services where the whole of the price is not paid by the purchaser at the time the agreement is made. See also **Door-to-door sale**; **Hire-purchase agreement**.

Credit rating The measurement of the creditworthiness of an individual or business; an assessment of the likelihood of an individual or business being able to meet its financial obligations. See also **Credit**; **Credit control**; **Credit report**; **Credit reporting agency**; **Credit reporting agent**; **Credit reporting business**; **Credit reporting complaint**; **Credit reporting infringement**; **Credit risk**.

Credit reference See **Banker's opinion**.

•**Credit report** Generally, any information prepared by a credit reporting agency or agent concerning a person's credit history, credit capacity, or creditworthiness for the purpose of establishing that person's eligibility for credit: (CTH) Privacy Act 1988 s 6(1). See also **Credit provider**; **Credit Reporting Agency**; **Credit Reporting Agent**.

•**Credit reporting agency** A corporation that carries on a credit reporting business: (CTH) Privacy Act 1988 s 11A. See also **Credit**; **Credit report**; **Credit reporting business**.

•**Credit reporting agent** A person who pursues the practice of providing credit reports to any person for profit or upon a regular cooperative basis: for example (VIC) Credit Reporting Act 1978 s 2. Legislation in other States contains similar definitions. See also **Credit report**; **Credit reporting business**.

•**Credit reporting business** A business or undertaking involving the preparation or maintenance of records containing personal information relating to individuals which is not publicly available and is used for the purpose of providing other persons with information on an individual's eligibility for credit, credit history, or capacity to repay credit. The essential factor is that of the preparation or maintenance of personal information. The purpose for which the collation of information is intended is not relevant: (CTH) Privacy Act 1988 s 6(1). See also **Credit; Credit provider; Credit reporting agency; Credit report**.

•**Credit reporting complaint** A complaint to the Privacy Commissioner by the subject of a credit information file regarding practices of credit reporting which are an interference with the privacy of that person: (CTH) Privacy Act 1988 ss 6(1), 36. See also **Administrative Appeals Tribunal; Credit reporting infringement**.

•**Credit reporting infringement** Any act by a credit reporting agency that violates the right to privacy of an individual in the collection, storage, access to and use of personal credit information: (CTH) Privacy Act 1988 ss 6(1), 18A, Pt IIIA. See also **Credit; Credit reporting agency; Information privacy principles**.

Credit risk The possibility that borrowers and others to whom credit has been extended will be unable to repay their obligations when due. See also **Credit rating; Risk**.

•**Credit sale agreement** See **Credit sale contract**.

•**Credit sale contract** A contract for sale of goods and services in which the supplier is also the credit provider. It excludes continuing credit contracts and lay-by sales: for example (NSW) Credit Act 1984 (repealed) s 5(1), 14; (NSW) Credit Regulation 1984 cl 4 (replaced by Uniform Consumer Credit Code). See also **Add on contract; Cash price; Continuing credit contract; Credit; Credit provider; Regulated credit sale contract**.

Credit squeeze Government policy to restrict the expansion of credit by making money scarce and more expensive to borrow, for example, by the Reserve Bank asking the commercial banks to reduce their lending. Although now most unlikely, Australia did witness such measures in 1961 and 1974. See also **Credit control**.

Credit Suisse Founded in 1856 in Zurich, the oldest of Switzerland's three big banks. Its activities in Australia include corporate lending, commercial banking, government funding business and asset management. Swiss frank capital market business is also undertaken and includes bond issues, private placements and share listings. Financing, underwriting and hedging facilities are available to the mining industry.

Credit term An arrangement made between the seller and the buyer stating the terms of payment for the goods or services. See also **Buyer; Payment; Seller**.

Credit token In the United Kingdom a card, check, voucher, coupon, stamp, form, booklet, or other document or thing given to an individual by a person carrying on a consumer credit business, the latter of whom undertakes that on the production of it cash, goods or services will be provided on credit or that on the production of it to a third party, the third party supplies cash, goods or services paid for by the individual: (UK) Consumer Credit Act 1974 (repealed) s 14(1) (replaced by Uniform Consumer Credit Code). See also **Credit; Credit card; Credit charge**.

Credit transfer The systemic granting of credit for undergraduate and non-research postgraduate studies between universities. The Australian Vice-Chancellors' Committee established the Australian Credit Transfer Agency Pty Ltd as a wholly owned subsidiary to undertake the assessment of individual applications for the granting of credit and the recognition of prior learning. See also **Australian Credit Transfer Agency Pty Ltd; Credit**.

Credit Tribunal See **Commercial tribunal**.

•**Credit union** An incorporated cooperative association in which lending members deposit money at interest and from which borrowing members borrow money at interest. See also **Building society; Financial institutions scheme; Society**.

•**Creditor** A person to whom a debt must be paid. A creditor can look directly to the debtor and assert a direct entitlement to the benefits or fruits of the order or judgment that is made against the debtor: (CTH) Bankruptcy Act 1966 ss 40, 41(2); *Abigroup Ltd v Abignano* (1992) 39 FCR 74; 112 ALR 497 at 508. See also **Credit; Debtor; Joint creditors; Judgment creditor; Preferred creditor; Secured creditor**.

Creditor broker See **Credit broker**.

Creditors' meeting A meeting of creditors at which information, business, or proposals affecting a debtor or a bankrupt are dealt with. See also **Authority to call meeting; Bankrupt; First meeting of creditors; Trustee in bankruptcy**.

Creditors' meeting, first See **First meeting of creditors**.

•**Creditor's petition** A document presented to the court by a creditor or two or more creditors jointly: (CTH) Bankruptcy Act 1966 s 5(1). See also **Act of bankruptcy; Joint creditors; Sequestration order**.

•**Creditors' voluntary winding up** A winding up of a company initiated by the company's creditors under Corporations Law Pt 5.5: s 9. A creditors' voluntary winding up may be initiated only if the company is insolvent and no declaration of solvency under s 494 has been made. See also **Voluntary winding up; Winding up**.

Creeping acquisition In corporations law, an acquisition of an additional three per cent of voting shares in each six month period. Creeping acquisitions are permitted as an exception to the blanket prohibition in Corporations Law s 615 preventing acquisitions beyond a 20 per cent threshold: s 618. The legislation calculates the increment by the use of a formula which disregards shares acquired pursuant to a *pari passu* allotment. See also **Security; Pari passu allotment; Takeover; Voting share**.

•**Crime** A wrong punishable by the state. A crime generally involves both an *actus reus* (guilty act) and *mens rea* (guilty mind). However, where the offence is one of strict or absolute liability, there is no need to prove *mens rea*: *He Kaw Teh v R* (1985) 157 CLR 523; 60 ALR

449. The prosecution must prove beyond reasonable doubt that a specific crime has been committed before the offender can be convicted: *Woolmington v DPP* [1935] All ER Rep 1; *Thomas v R* (1960) 102 CLR 584. See also **Actus reus**; **Doli incapax**.

- **Criminal law** The rules of statute and common law which direct that certain actions are punishable by the state. Each Australian jurisdiction has a body of criminal law: for example (CTH) Crimes Act 1914. See also **Common law**; **Crime**.

- **Criminal negligence** Negligence which, in the opinion of a jury, goes beyond a mere matter of compensation between subjects and shows such disregard for the life and safety of others as to amount to a crime against the state and conduct deserving punishment: *R v Bateman* (1925) 19 Cr App R 8. See also **Crime**; **Negligence**.

- **Criminal proceedings** Proceedings taken in relation to an offence against the public law; a crime, with the purpose of, or as part of the proceedings for, the punishment by the state of the person alleged to have committed the crime: *Director of Public Prosecutions (NSW) v Deeks* (1994) 34 NSWLR 523 at 47; 74 A Crim R 85; *Jago v District Court* (1989) 168 CLR 23 at 47; 87 ALR 577; *Willliams v Spautz* (1991) 174 CLR 509 at 538; 107 ALR 635. See also **Criminal law**.

- **Cross claim** A claim made by a party against a co-party, such as a co-defendant against a defendant, which arises either out of the subject matter of the original action or out of the subject matter of a counterclaim: *Re Griggs; Ex parte Auldana Ltd* (1916) 33 WN (NSW) 83; (ACT) Supreme Court Act 1933 s 28(1); (NT) Supreme Court Act 1979 s 64; (QLD) Supreme Court Act 1995 s 244(3); (SA) Supreme Court Act 1935 s 23; (TAS) Supreme Court Civil Procedure Act 1932 s 10(3); (VIC) Supreme Court Act 1986 s 29; (WA) Supreme Court Act 1928 s 24(3). Also known as 'cross action'. See also **Counterclaim**; **Cross demand**; **Set-off**.

- **Cross demand** A demand made by a party against whom the original demand was made and in answer to that original demand; a claim by a debtor against a creditor which is capable of being given a money value, but which does not amount to a set-off or counterclaim. A cross-demand has a wider ambit than a set-off or a counterclaim: *Re Smith; Ex parte Chesson* (1992) 106 ALR 359. See also **Bankruptcy notice**; **Counterclaim**; **Cross claim**; **Judgment debt**; **Set-off**.

Cross elasticity of demand The relative change in demand for commodity A resulting from a change in the price of commodity B: cross-elasticity = percentage change in the demand for A/percentage change in the price of B. If the cross-elasticity of demand between two commodities is positive, then the two commodities may well be substitutes; the increase in the price of commodity B increases the demand for commodity A, as consumers switch from B to A. On the other hand, if the cross-elasticity is negative, this suggests that the two commodities are complements; an increase in the price of B reduces the sale of A. See also **Price elasticity of demand**; **Price elasticity of supply**.

Cross offers Identical contractual offers sent by two parties to each other, both sent before the other is received. Although cross offers manifest an intention to create legal relations on identical terms, they do not of themselves create a contract because neither can be seen as acceptance with reference to the other: *Tinn v Hoffmann & Co* (1873) 29 LT 271. See also **Acceptance**; **Offer**.

Cross stream guarantee An arrangement where each company in a corporate group guarantees the debts of the others. If a new company comes into the corporate group and executes the relevant guarantee, the companies who are already existing parties to that guarantee will not automatically become guarantors of the new entity unless those existing guarantors specifically agree to do so or unless the original guarantee specifies that it covers any new entity who executes the guarantee in the future. Also known as 'mutual guarantee'. See also **Guarantee**.

- **Cross-examination** Questions addressed to a witness by a party other than the party who called the witness to give evidence: (CTH) Evidence Act 1995 s 3, Dictionary. The purpose of cross-examination is to establish the case of the cross-examining party by eliciting information from the opponent's witnesses which is relevant to a fact or facts in issue. Cross-examination may also be used to weaken the credibility of the opponent's witnesses. Cross-examination takes place after a witness has given his or her evidence in chief. Leading questions are permitted during cross-examination. See also **Evidence**; **Leading question**; **Witness**.

- **Crossing 1.** The drawing of two parallel transverse lines across the front of a cheque, with or without the addition of the words 'not negotiable' between, or substantially between, the lines: (CTH) Cheques and Payment Orders Act 1986 s 53; *Hunter v BNZ Finance Ltd v C G Maloney Pty Ltd* (1988) 18 NSWLR 420. Crossing instructs the drawee bank not to pay the cheque otherwise than to a bank: s 54. A transaction in securities where a broker acts on behalf of both buying and selling clients, or where the broker acts as principal on one side of the transaction, and where the transaction is effected in accordance with Australian Stock Exchange Business Rules 2.6(12), (14), (15), (16). See also **Australian Stock Exchange Ltd**; **Australian Stock Exchange Business Rules**; **Cheque**; **Drawee**; **Drawee bank**; **Drawer**; **Not negotiable**.

Cross-subsidisation The transfer of earnings from remunerative individual plants, products or programs to unremunerative activities within the same enterprise, including transfers of earnings between peak and off-peak outputs. Continuous cross-subsidisation tends to result in a misallocation of resources, hence a close relating of prices to costs on individual products and services ensures an efficient approach. Cross-subsidisation may be justified for limited periods only to kick start a new activity; in such a case, the cross-subsidisation should be regarded as simply a source of finance or line of credit, not otherwise justifiable.

Cross-vesting A process by which one superior court may exercise the jurisdiction of another: for example (CTH) Jurisdiction of Courts (Cross-vesting) Act 1987; (NSW) Jurisdiction of Courts (Cross-vesting) Act 1987. The cross-vesting scheme is designed to allow Supreme Courts to exercise federal jurisdiction and federal courts to exercise the jurisdiction of Supreme Courts in appropriate cases. See also **Federal jurisdiction**; **Jurisdiction**.

Crowding-out Descriptive of any group being pushed out of a market. The term has been used to describe ways in which the demand for credit by the private sector may be crowded out of the financial market by the dominant demands of the public sector. Public expenditure may sometimes be portrayed, therefore, as retarding the expansion of the economy, rather than stimulating it, as both sectors compete for funds. The situation is eased when a budget deficit moves into surplus.

• **Crown** 1. The reigning King or Queen in the capacity of Sovereign, and often signifying the entire administrative edifice of the executive government under the Crown. In the Australian federal system, the Crown acts 'in right of' the Commonwealth, and each of the States and Territories; but has only one indivisible existence, so that there is no necessary mutual immunity among the Commonwealth and States from each others' laws: *Amalgamated Society of Engineers v Adelaide Steamship Co Ltd* (1920) 28 CLR 129. 2. The prosecution in criminal matters for offences dealt with on indictment in the Supreme or District (County) Court. See also **Crown immunity**.

Crown as creditor Previously, the right of the Crown to priority over other creditors. The Crown no longer enjoys its fiscal priorities or privileges, derived from prerogative, over other creditors; it is in substantially the same position as any other creditor, and preferential payments made to the Crown by a debtor can ordinarily be avoided by a trustee in bankruptcy: (CTH) Bankruptcy Act 1966 s 8; *Re Oskar; Ex parte Commonwealth* (1984) 55 ALR 717 at 720. See also **Bankruptcy**.

Crown corporation A body corporate created by the Crown or which carries on duties on behalf of the Crown.

• **Crown holding** A holding held for the Crown by a lessee, including land held under any lease, licence, or other authority granted by the Crown under any Act: for example (QLD) Water Resources Act 1989 s 2(1). See also **Crown land**; **Crown lease**; **Holding**.

Crown immunity The presumption that a statute does not bind the Crown unless by express mention or necessary implication: *Bradken Consolidated Ltd v Broken Hill Pty Co Ltd* (1979) 145 CLR 107; 24 ALR 9. See also **Crown**.

• **Crown land** Broadly, land that is the property of the Commonwealth, a State or Territory: (CTH) Lands Acquisition Act 1989 s 6. See also **Crown lease**; **Mabo's case**.

• **Crown lease** 1. A lease of land from the Crown, granted under the Crown lands legislation. 2. An agreement to occupy or use Crown land usually in consideration for rent: for example (SA) Crown Lands Act 1929 s 147; (WA) Local Government Act 1995 s 1.4. See also **Crown land**; **Freehold**; **Licence**; **Pastoral lease**.

CS First Boston Australia A subsidiary of its United States parent, CS First Boston is a bank specialising in equity markets, international and domestic debt markets and derivative products. It has expertise in primary distribution and secondary market sales and trading.

• **CSIRO** See **Commonwealth Scientific and Industrial Research Organisation**.

• **Culpability** The extent to which an offender is morally responsible for an offence. In criminal cases, the motive for committing the crime is relevant to culpability: *R v Brown* (1987) 78 ALR 368 at 370; 32 A Crim R 162; *Neal v R* (1982) 149 CLR 305 at 324; 42 ALR 609.

Cum all With everything; a description that may be attached to the sale of a security, implying that any dividend, interest, rights, bonus or other benefit just declared or current, is retained by the purchaser.

Cum bonus With the bonus just declared; a condition that may be attached to the sale of a security.

Cum div /kʊm dɪv/ *Lat* – with or of shares. Refers to shares with the right to current dividends. Compare *ex div*. See also **Cum dividend**; **Dividend**; **Ex div**; **Share**.

Cum dividend With the dividend just declared; a condition that may be attached to the sale of a security.

Cum drawing With benefit of the current drawing; a condition that may be attached to the sale of a security. If there is no benefit, it means with liability for loss of drawing.

Cum interest With current interest; a condition that may be attached to the sale of a security, the purchaser having the right to the current or next interest payment.

Cum rights With 'rights' recently issued; a condition that may be attached to the sale of a security, the purchaser having the right to a new issue.

Cumulative 1. Growing in quantity, strength or effect by successive additions or aggregation, gained by a gradual building up of cumulative benefits. For example, the cumulative deficit is the amount formed by the successive addition of each year's deficit: (QLD) Gladstone Area Water Board Act 1984 s 166(3). In ascertaining whether the onus of proof has been discharged in any particular case, the probative force of a mass of evidence may be cumulative: *Shepherd v R* (1990) 170 CLR 573. This means that the necessary inference can be drawn having regard to the whole of the evidence, whether or not each individual piece of evidence relied upon is proved to the requisite standard, provided that the evidence can be said to consist of 'strands in a cable rather than links in a chain': *Shepherd v R* (1990) 170 CLR 573. 2. Preference shares in finance entitling the shareholder to receive any arrears in dividends before any dividends are distributed to ordinary shareholders 3. Intended to be accumulated if not paid when due. See also **Dividend**.

Cumulative dividend right A right attached to some preference shares which provides that if in any year the dividend is not declared and paid, an amount equal to the amount of the unpaid dividend is added to the dividend to be paid in the next year. See also **Preference share**; **Dividend**.

Cumulative preference share A preference share issued with a cumulative dividend right: *Re Buck* [1964]

VR 284; *Re William Bedford Ltd (in liq)* [1967] VR 490. See also **Preference share**.

Cumulative voting In an election for directors of a company, the casting by a shareholder of as many votes as he or she has, multiplied by the number of vacancies. The shareholder may not cast votes for all the directors. This is designed to promote minority shareholder representation on the board. Commonly used in the United States.

•**Curran scheme** A tax avoidance scheme where a taxpayer, who is a share trader, claims as an allowable deduction the cost of the paid up value of bonus shares that the company credits to that taxpayer. The bonus share distribution was a capital distribution and therefore was not included in the assessable income of the taxpayer: *Curran v FCT* (1974) 131 CLR 409; 4 ALR 504. Curran schemes are no longer effective for tax purposes due to legislative changes and judicial interpretation: (CTH) Income Tax Assessment Act 1936 s 6BA; *John v Commissioner of Taxation* (1989) 166 CLR 417; 83 ALR 606. See also **Allowable deduction; Assessable income; Dividend stripping; Scheme; Tax avoidance**.

•**Currency 1.** A unit of money in actual use in a country. Coin and paper money designated as legal tender: (CTH) Financial Transaction Reports Act 1988 s 3(1). See also **Exchange rate; Legal tender; Lex loci solutionis; Petty banking; Reserve Bank of Australia; Usury**.

Currency basket A combination of currencies of countries, each weighted and calculated together as a single unit against which another currency can be measured. Prior to it being floated in December 1983, the Australian dollar was pegged to a basket of currencies of countries such as the United Kingdom and the United States. See also **Exchange rate; Floating exchange rate; Trade-weighted index**.

Currency futures contract A contract by which the parties agree to make an adjustment between them at a specified future time in Australian currency, according to whether a specified amount of foreign currency is worth more, or worth less, in Australian currency at that time than it was worth in Australian currency at the time of the making of the contract, the difference being determined in accordance with the business rules of the futures market at which the contract is made. See also **Futures contract**.

Currency of option The period during which a person has, under a contract, the right but not the obligation to buy securities at a fixed price. See also **Call option; Option; Put option; Securities**.

Currency swap Changing the currency denomination of a debt into one that suits the debtor better in terms of future prospects. See also **Swap**.

Current account A bank account characterised by frequent credits as money is paid in by the customer, and frequent debits as money is paid out in accordance with orders (usually cheques) given by the customer. See also **Account**.

•**Current annual open market rental** A phrase common in modern commercial leases, used in rent review clauses to describe the level at which rent should be set for a specified period during the lease. In the absence of agreement by the lessor and lessee, it is common for such a rental to be ascertained by a qualified valuer using such criteria as comparable rents, the area in which the building is located, and the terms of the lease. See also **Lease**.

•**Current asset** Within a company or business, an asset such as cash, a short-term deposit, debtors' account or inventory that will be converted to cash within a year: Corporations Law Sch 5 cl 1(1). See also **Current ratio; Current liabilities**.

Current cost In corporations law, a value stated in terms of the present purchasing price of an item (usually an asset) based on recent transactions or estimates, rather than in terms of its historical, or acquisition, cost. See also **Historical cost; Value**.

Current cost accounting A system of accounting in which assets are recorded in the accounts of the company at their value to the business, that is the loss the business would suffer if the assets were destroyed. The balance sheet becomes a statement of current values instead of historic costs, which become progressively irrelevant due to inflation.

•**Current credit provider** For the purposes of privacy law and in relation to an individual, a credit provider who has given, to the individual, credit that has not yet been fully repaid or otherwise fully discharged: (CTH) Privacy Act 1988 s 6(1). See also **Building society; Credit union**.

Current liabilities In relation to a corporation, cash or other assets of the corporation that would, in the ordinary course of business of the corporation, be consumed or converted into cash within 12 months after the end of the last financial period: Corporations Regulations Sch 5 cl 1(1). See also **Financial period; Current asset**.

Current ratio A ratio used in financial statement analysis and calculated by dividing current assets by current liabilities. The current ratio measures the short-term solvency or liquidity of a firm. See also **Current asset; Current liabilities; Quick ratio**.

Current yield The percentage yield obtained from a financial investment by multiplying the annual coupon amount on a fixed interest security by 100, and dividing by the capital price of that security. The amount is reported as a percentage. See also **Coupon; Security**.

•**Custody** Control, responsibility for, or confinement.
Bailment The physical holding of, or control over, a thing without a right or claim to exclusiveness which is necessary to constitute possession: *Gamer's Motor Centre (Newcastle) Pty Ltd v Natwest Wholesale Australia Pty Ltd* (1987) 163 CLR 236; 72 ALR 321. See also **Constructive possession; Delivery; Possession**.

Contract Physical control, with or without legal possession: *Federal Cmr of Taxation v Australia and New Zealand Banking Group Ltd* (1979) 143 CLR 499 at 520; 23 ALR 480. See also **Assessment; Control**.

Custom A rule of conduct in society, established by long use and binding those under it. A custom must date back to time immemorial, and be certain and obligatory to constitute valid law. It may run counter to the common law but cannot contravene existing statute law.

Contract A rule of conduct which, as a result of long usage, is binding on those who come within its scope. In contract law, terms can be implied into a contract on the basis of custom: *Con-Stan Industries of Australia Pty Ltd v Norwich Winterthur Insurance (Australia) Ltd* (1986) 160 CLR 226; 64 ALR 481. Evidence of custom can be admitted to prove that a written contract was entered into subject to the existence and applicability of the custom even though it was not expressly referred to in the written document: *Hutton v Warren* (1836) 1 W & M 466; 150 ER 517. See also **Implied term; Law merchant**.

Custom and usage See **Custom of merchants**.

Custom of merchants Established commercial practice having the force of law, usually in relation to a particular locality or market. See also **Course of business**.

•**Customer generated financial transaction document** A financial transaction document relating to one of the following transactions and given to the institution by or on behalf of the customer: opening, closing or operating an account or deposit box; transferring funds by the institution on behalf of the customer; transmitting funds between Australia and a foreign country or between foreign countries on behalf of the customer; or applying for a loan ((CTH) Proceeds of Crime Act 1987 s 76). See also **Financial transaction document**.

Customer of a bank 1. A person with an account with a bank, either a current or savings account (*Hart v Sangster* [1957] 1 Ch 329; [1957] 2 All ER 208) or having a similar relationship, such as a person with a fixed or term deposit account with the bank: *Dixon v Bank of New South Wales* (1896) 17 LR (NSW) Eq 355; *Great Western Railway Co v London and County Banking Co Ltd* [1901] AC 414; [1900-3] All ER Rep 1004; *Lacave & Co v Credit Lyonnais* [1897] 1 QB 148; *Warren Metals Ltd v Colonial Catering Co Ltd* [1975] 1 NZLR 273. The relationship of banker and customer does not arise unless both parties intend to enter into such a relationship. There must be evidence to show that a bank accepted a person as a customer and dealt with that person on that footing; *Robinson v Midland Bank Ltd* (1925) 41 TLR 402; *Stewart v Bank of Australia* (1883) 9 VLR 240. A person for whom a bank merely performs a casual service is not a customer: *Great Western Railway Co v London and County Banking Co Ltd* [1901] AC 414. Once an account is opened there need not be any regular dealing in the sense of regularly visiting the bank or doing business with it. This is the essential difference between a customer of a shop and the customer of a bank: *Ladbroke & Co v Todd* [1914-15] All ER 1134; *Cmrs of Taxation v English Scottish & Australian Bank Ltd* [1920] AC 683; *Kendall v London Bank of Australia* (1918) SR (NSW) 394. Where a person deals with a bank, both parties contemplate the person becoming a customer, and an account is in fact subsequently opened, the relationship of banker and customer is deemed to have been established from the date the bank accepted the instructions of the customer even though at that time there was no account in existence: *Woods v Martins Bank Ltd* [1959] 1 QB 55. 2. An individual who alone or jointly with another acquires a banking service wholly and exclusively for his or her private or domestic use, but does not include an individual who makes a written statement to the bank in relation to a banking service, that the banking service will not be acquired wholly and exclusively for that use: Code of Banking Practice s 1.1. 3. A person who has an account with a collecting bank, which raises a contractual relationship between bank and customer: *Robinson v Oriental Bank* (1872) 3 VR L 177. The protection afforded to a collecting bank by (CTH) Cheques and Payment Orders Act 1986 s 95(2) applies if a bank is collecting on behalf of a customer, or if it is collecting on behalf of itself, having given the customer value. See also **Account; Cheque; Collecting bank; Greenwood duty; Macmillan duty**.

Customer's duty to bank The two principal duties owed by a customer to his or her bank, being to exercise reasonable care in drawing cheques so that the bank is not misled and forgery not facilitated (the Macmillan duty), and to notify the bank promptly of any forged cheque purporting to have been signed as soon as the customer when the customer learns of the forgery (the Greenwood duty). See also **Banker's standard of care; Greenwood duty; Macmillan duty**.

•**Customs** See **Customs duty**.

•**Customs duty** Monetary payments exacted from an importer of goods by a government as a condition of the grant of permission to bring the goods into the country: (CTH) Customs Act 1901 s 4. Also known as 'customs'.

Cybercrime The use of computer technology to gain a benefit in an illegal manner. See also **Hacker; Salami shaving**.

D

Dairy industry Industry in Australia that is concerned with the production, processing, manufacture, distribution, or sale, whether for export or otherwise, of dairy produce: (CTH) Dairy Produce Act 1986 s 3. See also **Dairy produce**.

Dairy produce Milk, cream, and products made from or containing milk or a constituent part of milk declared to be dairy produce by the Australian Dairy Corporation: (CTH) Dairy Produce Act 1986 s 3. Various types of cheese and yoghurt are prescribed as 'dairy produce' by the (CTH) Dairy Produce Levy Regulations 1986.

Daisy chain 1. A pattern of continuous buying or selling of commodities in the same issue, by the same customer, or with the same broker, at progressively higher or lower prices. **2.** The transfer of the ownership of a commodity through the hands of a chain of subsidiaries, tax-haven companies, affiliates and other companies and agents, being exported and imported to leave a substantial untaxed profit offshore. See also **Broker; Issue; Tax haven**.

Dalkon Shield litigation Product liability litigation commenced in the United States against the A H Robins Company, the manufacturer of the Dalkon Shield intra-uterine device, by persons seeking damages for personal injury allegedly arising out of the use of the device: for example *Palmer v A H Robins Co Inc* 684 P 2d 187 (Colo 1984).

Damage In tort, loss or injury suffered by a plaintiff as the foreseeable consequence of a defendant's negligent act or omission. In the case of physical injury, both the injury itself and other foreseeable consequences suffered by the plaintiff are considered to be damage for which damages are payable: *Mahony v J Kruschich (Demolitions) Pty Ltd* (1985) 156 CLR 522; 59 ALR 722. Also known as 'loss' or 'injury'. See also **Damages**.

Damages Compensation for damage suffered; a court-awarded sum of money which places the plaintiff in the position he or she would have occupied had the legal wrong not occurred: for example *Haines v Bendall* (1991) 172 CLR 60; 99 ALR 385.

Damages at large Damages for injury, damage, or loss estimated to occur after the trial. Damages awarded as compensation for injury to intangible interests such as reputation: *Andrews v John Fairfax & Sons Ltd* [1980] 2 NSWLR 225. Such damages are 'at large' in that there are few limits on the jury's discretion to determine the quantum of damages. Also known as 'general damages'. See also **General damages; Special damages**.

Damages for loss of bargain Damages awarded for breach of contract to protect the expectation interest of the innocent party. Damages for loss of bargain are assessed by reference to the difference between the market value of the contract (or its subject matter) at the time of contract and the price (or monetary equivalent) expressed in the contract: for example *Hoffman v Cali* [1985] 1 Qd R 253 at 260. See also **Breach of contract; Damages; Expectation interest; Loss of a chance; Loss of bargain; Measure of damages**.

Damages for loss of profits Damages awarded to a plaintiff as compensation for the amount that the plaintiff would have earned pursuant to a contract had the defendant not breached the contract. See also **Expectation interest; Reliance interest; Restitution interest**.

Damping In economics, a reducing effect. At low levels of market demand some people may withdraw from the labour market, thus damping the rise in unemployment figures. See also **Economics; Employment; Unemployment**.

Damping the sale In relation to auctions, the practice of making derogatory comments about a lot to be sold, calculated to prevent the property realising its true value. An example of damping the sale is suggesting at an auction that the property was built on an underground stream and that the cellar was waterlogged; this 'damped' the sale, the reserve price not being met: *Mayer v Pluck* (1971) 223 EG 33. Conduct by a successful bidder calculated to 'damp the sale' may constitute fraud, entitling the seller to avoid the sale, or may be relied on by the seller as a defence to proceedings for specific performance: *Twining v Morris* (1788) 2 Bro CC 326; 29 ER 182. See also **Auction; Auctioneer; Reserve price; Specific performance**.

Dangerous cargo Merchandise transported on a ship, aircraft, or by land vehicles which is of a dangerous nature: for example, acid in carboys or explosives. The carriage of certain dangerous cargo is regulated by the (CTH) Navigation Act 1912 ss 248-253A. See also **Bill of lading; Cargo; Dangerous thing**.

Dangerous goods 1. Goods harmful to life or presenting a danger to property because they are: explosive, flammable, or volatile; toxic, poisonous, or corrosive; radioactive substances; or are considered harmful to the environment: for example (NSW) Dangerous Goods Regulation 1978 cl 17. It is an offence to keep specified amounts of dangerous goods, or to transport flammable gases or combustible liquids, without a licence: for example (NSW) Dangerous Goods Act 1975 ss 9-11. **2.** Goods classified as dangerous under the Australian Code for the Transport of Dangerous Goods by Road and Rail, a classification indorsed by the Australian Transport Advisory Council: for example (QLD) Fire Service Act 1990 s 94. See also **Dangerous thing**.

Dangerous goods, carriage of See **Carriage of dangerous goods**.

Dangerous load 1. A load intrinsically dangerous, for example, explosives, corrosive chemicals etc. **2.** A load, usually on a vehicle, which is inadequately secured presenting the danger of it becoming dislodged and falling off the vehicle. See also **Dangerous cargo**; **Dangerous goods**.

Dangerous premises Real property which creates a risk of harm to individuals on or near it. Liability in negligence may be incurred by an occupier for injuries caused on dangerous premises: *Australian Safeway Stores Pty Ltd v Zaluzna* (1987) 162 CLR 479; 69 ALR 615; and for injuries caused by dangerous things escaping from premises: *Burnie Port Authority v General Jones Pty Ltd* (1994) 179 CLR 520; 120 ALR 42. See also **Negligence**; **Nuisance**; **Occupier's liability**.

•**Dangerous thing** In tort, an object that is dangerous per se, or an object capable of being used dangerously, for example a sharpened lead pencil: *R v Dabelstein* [1966] Qd R 411. The degree of danger a thing creates determines the standard of care the defendant has to maintain: *Adelaide Chemical & Fertilizer Co Ltd v Carlyle* (1940) 64 CLR 514; [1941] ALR 10. In some jurisdictions there is a duty imposed upon a person in charge of a dangerous thing to exercise reasonable care: for example (QLD) Criminal Code s 289; (WA) Criminal Code s 66.

Date of assessment In contract law, the date at which damages are assessed. Assessment is generally done on a once and for all basis at the date of the breach: *Johnson v Perez* (1988) 166 CLR 351; 82 ALR 587. However, where application of the general rule would lead to injustice, the court may choose a later date in order to, for example, accommodate inflationary factors: *Johnson v Agnew* [1980] AC 367 at 401; *Johnson v Perez*. See also **Assessment of damages**; **Late delivery**; **Non-delivery**.

Date of record In corporations law, the date on which a stockholder must own shares of a company to be entitled to a dividend paid by that company. Dividends are payable to persons registered as members as at the date of the declaration of dividends: *Re Buck* [1964] VR 284 at 290. See also **Dividend**; **Share**; **Shareholder**.

Dated security A security such as a bond or bill of exchange which has a stated date for redemption (repayment) of the nominal value. Securities without a redemption date are known as undated or irredeemable securities. See also **Securities**; **Redemption of security**.

Dawn raid An offer to buy a large block of shares in a public company at above the market price. The offer usually exists for only a limited period, disabling smaller investors from taking advantage of the attractive price offered. See also **Takeover**.

Day order In relation to securities trading, an order which is only valid for the day on which it is placed. If the order is not executed on the day on which it is placed, it lapses. See also **Broker**; **Day-night trading**; **Securities business**; **Trading floor**.

Daylight overdraft An overdraft allowed by the Reserve Bank of Australia to authorised dealers in the short-term money market to help the market function smoothly, for example, when a dealer has to repay a client before fresh funds arrive. However, a dealer's account with the RBA must be in credit or balance by the close of the day's trading. See also **Day order**; **Dealer**; **Overdraft**.

Day-night trading A developing method of global financial trading, with stock, futures, and money markets operating twenty four hours a day either by floor-trading or screen-trading. Day-night trading already exists for foreign exchange transactions and is rapidly developing in respect of equities, commodities, and debt instruments. Day-night trading developments are essentially centred around the exchanges in Tokyo, New York, Chicago, Philadelphia, Toronto, London, Zurich, Milan, Hong Kong, Singapore, Sydney, Seoul, and Johannesburg. Satellite communications play an important part in this network. See also **Day order**; **Stock exchange**; **Trading floor**.

Days of grace Three days formerly added to the time of payment fixed by a bill of exchange, unless the bill otherwise provided: (CTH) Bills of Exchange Act 1909 s 19(a) (repealed). This rule has been abolished for bills of exchange and other promissory notes created on or after 10 October 1991: (CTH) Law and Justice Legislation Amendment Act 1991 Sch. See also **Bill of exchange**; **Promissory note**.

Days on demurrage In relation to charters, the days after the expiration of lay days. Days on demurrage are an additional period of time during which the charterer is only allowed to complete the discharging operations in relation to the charter vessel in exchange for the payment of an additional consideration. Where the discharging operations exceed the permitted days on demurrage, the charterer may be liable to the ship owner for damages for detention: *Aktieselskabet Reider v Arcos Ltd* [1927] 1 KB 352. See also **Demurrage**; **Detention**; **Lay day**.

DCT See **Deputy Commissioner of Taxation**.

•**De facto** /deɪ fæktoʊ/ *Lat* – in fact. A phrase describing a situation which is accepted for all practical purposes but is not strictly legal or correct.

De facto director Any person occupying or acting in the position of director of a corporation, by whatever name called, and whether or not validly appointed to occupy or duly authorised to act in the position: Corporations Law s 60. See also **Director**; **Directors duties**; **Nominee director**.

De facto officer In administrative law, a public officer who is not validly appointed but has the reputation of being the officer he or she purports to be. A purported decision of a tribunal or other administrator may be sustained even though the tribunal was improperly constituted, on the basis of its being the act of a de facto officer: *Ellis v Bourke* (1889) 15 VLR 163. See also **De facto**.

De minimis non curat lex /deɪ mɪnɪmɪs noʊn kjuːræt leks/ *Lat* – the law is unconcerned with insignificant matters. In the performance of contracts, the rule allows minute failures and insignificant defects in performance to be excused: *Shipton Anderson & Co v Weil Bros & Co* [1912] 1 KB 574. See also **Discharge**; **Exact performance**; **Substantial performance**.

Dead freight *Abbr* – DF, D/F The freight payable by a charterer of a ship in respect of the empty space left in the ship as a result of the charterer loading a lesser quantity of cargo than that which has been booked in the charterparty. Dead freight is the difference between the freight actually earned and that which would have been earned had the charterer fulfilled its obligations. Technically, it is not freight at all, but damages for failure to load a full and complete cargo: *Aktieselskabet Reider v Arcos Ltd* [1926] 2 KB 83. Dead freight is payable because the shipowner could have sold the vacant space to another shipper. In some circumstances, short loading may be excused, and the liability to pay dead freight is not incurred. See also **Charterer**; **Charterparty**; **Freight**; **Goods**.

Dead letter Legislation no longer in force, although not formally repealed.

Dead rent The fixed amount payable as rent for a mining or quarry lease which is independent of whether any minerals are recovered or not. Further amounts or royalties are payable depending on the quantity of minerals extracted: for example (NSW) Mining Act 1992 ss 282, 284; (VIC) Mineral Resources Development Act 1990 s 12.

Dead-cat bounce Descriptive of markets with as much response as a dead cat. See also **False Trading**; **Hedging**; **Market manipulation**.

•**Dealer** Generally, a person who negotiates or arranges the purchase or sale of goods or commodities, often on behalf of another.

Dealer's duties In relation to a securities dealer, the duties imposed on the dealer under the general law or under the corporations legislation. These include fiduciary duties (*Daly v Sydney Stock Exchange Ltd* (1986) 160 CLR 371; 65 ALR 193), the duty to disclose to a client if the dealer has an interest which may influence recommendations made to the client (Corporations Law s 849), the duty to use reasonable care and skill in carrying out clients' instructions (*Hawkins v Clayton* (1988) 164 CLR 539; 78 ALR 69), the duty of confidentiality owed to the client (*Deta Nominees Pty Ltd v Viscount Plastic Products Pty Ltd* [1979] VR 167), the duty to make the best deal for the client (*Daly v Sydney Stock Exchange Ltd* (1986) 160 CLR 371; 65 ALR 193), the duty to obey the client's instructions (*Salvesen v Rederi Aktiebolaget Nordstjernan* [1905] AC 302), and the duty to not enter into a transaction as principal in relation to securities ahead of a client who has requested the dealer to deal in those securities: Corporations Law s 844(2); ASX Business Rules rule 5.6.

•**Dealer's licence** The licence that must be held to carry on or hold out that a person carries on a security business: Corporations Law ss 9, 780. The Australian Securities Commission (ASC) issues these licences: Corporations Law s 782. The conditions of the licence are found in Corporations Law s 786. See also **Dealer**; **Securities**.

•**Dealing** An act of buying or selling property, goods or commodities, or the registrable instrument that evidences such an act.

Real property An instrument other than a grant or caveat that is capable of being registered under the Torrens system, or in respect of which the Registrar of Titles is permitted or required to make a recording in the Register: for example (NSW) Real Property Act 1900 s 3. An instrument is called a dealing after it has been lodged in the Titles Office, but before it has been processed and the interest in the instrument registered or recorded, as required. See also **Grant**; **Registrable instrument**.

Dealing as a consumer See **Consumer**.

•**Dealing in securities** Subscription for, or acquisition, disposal, or underwriting of, securities; or the making, offering, or inducing to make, an agreement with respect to acquiring, disposing of, subscribing for, or underwriting the securities, or for the purpose of securing a gain to a person who acquires, disposes of, subscribes for, or underwrites the securities or to any of the parties to the agreement: Corporations Law ss 9, 109M. It includes, generally, any transaction involving securities: *Ryan v Triguboff* [1976] 1 NSWLR 588 at 601-2. See also **Dealer's licence**; **Securities**.

•**Death** The end of human life. An individual who suffers a recognisable loss as a result of the wrongful death of a relative may bring an action for compensation: for example (NSW) Compensation to Relatives Act 1897 ss 3(1), 4(1). See also **Death benefit**.

•**Death benefit** Payment to dependants of a deceased person in compensation for the loss incurred as a result of the death. Death benefits are payable if the death arose out of, or in the course of: employment (for example (NSW) Workers' Compensation Act 1987); a motor accident (for example (NSW) Motor Accidents Act 1988); or if the deceased was the victim of a criminal offence (for example (NSW) Victims Compensation Act 1987). See also **Dependant**; **Workers' compensation**.

Death duty A tax on inheritance formerly imposed by the Commonwealth or Federal Parliament on the value of a deceased person's estate: for example *Sullivan v Cmr of Probate Duties (Vic)* (1976) 135 CLR 237. Commonwealth and State death duties have been abolished: (CTH) Estate Duty Assessment Amendment Act 1978; Estate Duty Amendment Act 1978; (NSW) Stamp Duties Act 1920 Pt IV, Div 3; (VIC) Probate Duty Act 1962 s 2A (inserted by 1981 Act). The duty assessed was a charge against the assets of the estate and the executor was required to pay any death duties before distributing any assets of a deceased estate. Death duties were often progressive, increasing in proportion with the value of the estate. The value of a deceased person's estate must still be disclosed for capital gains tax purposes and to obtain probate of the estate. See also **Capital gains tax**.

•**Debenture** 1. At common law, any document which either creates a debt owed by a company or acknowledges it: *Levy v Abercorris Slate & Slab Co* [1887] 37 Ch D 260 at 264; *Handevel Pty Ltd v Comptroller of Stamps (Vic)* (1985) 157 CLR 177; 62 ALR 204. Negotiable instruments such as bills of exchange and promissory notes as well as deeds of covenant are excluded. 2. Any document issued by a body corporate that evidences its indebtedness in respect of money deposited or lent: Corporations Law s 9. See also **Company**; **Corporation**; **Debt Security**.

Debenture series The issue of several debentures securing several debts on the same property. These debentures rank for repayment in the order of their creation unless they are issued as part of the same series, in which case they rank equally. See also **Debenture; Debt**.

Debenture stock An equitable interest under an instrument (generally a debenture stock trust deed) which evidences a collective debt divided into units: *State Superannuation Board (Vic) v Trustees Executors and Agency Co Ltd* [1964] ALR 674. See also **Debenture; Debenture trust deed; Trust**.

Debenture stock trust deed See **Debenture trust deed**.

Debenture trust deed In relation to debentures, a deed defining the rights and powers of the trustee, the borrowing corporation, and the debenture holders. Before a public company can solicit subscriptions for debentures by offers not excluded by Corporations Law s 66, the company must have a debenture trust deed: Corporations Law s 1052. The trust deed must make provision for the appointment of a trustee for the debenture holders: Corporations Law s 1052(1). The prospectus soliciting subscriptions for debentures must contain a statement that subscribers' money is secured by a charge over the corporation's tangible property, which is substantial enough to meet such liability: Corporations Law ss 1045(4),(5). See also **Debenture; Liability**.

Debit 1. A book-keeping entry made in a person's account to record a sum owed by that person to the person in whose accounting records the entry is made. By convention debit entries are made in the left hand side of a double entry account. **2.** To charge a person with a sum owing; to enter a sum owing against or to a person. See also **Credit; Double entry**.

Debit balance In corporations law, the status of an account in the reporting entities books when the sum of debit entries exceeds the sum of credit entries. The result is an account with a debit balance. See also **Account; Reporting Entity**.

•**Debit card** A card intended for use by a person in obtaining access to an account held by that person for the purpose of withdrawing or depositing cash: (CTH) Trade Practices Act 1974 s 63A(3); (NSW) Fair Trading Act 1987 s 57(4). See also **Cash; Credit card; Unsolicited credit card**.

Debits tax A tax imposed on a debit over $1 made to a cheque account held with a bank or an account enabling payment orders to be drawn on a non-bank financial institution: (CTH) Debits Tax Act 1982 ss 3, 4, 5. Liability for the tax falls upon the financial institution, which has a statutory right to recover from customers an amount equal to the tax payable on a debit to their account: (CTH) Debits Tax Act 1982 ss 8, 10. See also **Cheque; Financial institution; Financial Institutions Duty**.

Debitum in praesenti, solvendum in futuro /debitum in praisenti, solvendum in futurou/ *Lat* – present debt payable in the future.

Debriefing In business, a process of questioning to extract and assess results for the purpose of gaining feedback on and assessing the assigned activity.

•**Debt 1.** An obligation to pay. **2.** A sum of money owed: *Director of Public Prosecutions v Turner* [1973] 3 All ER 124 at 126. A debt is a sum of money which is now payable or will become payable in the future by reason of a present obligation: *debitum in praesenti, solvendum in futuro*. It is a right which a creditor has to enforce by taking action in a court of law against the person who owes the money (the debtor). See also **Accruing debt; Indebted**.

Banking and finance An obligation by an individual or a business (debtor) to pay a certain sum of money to another party (creditor). See also **Debt servicing**.

Real property A legal intangible item of personal property known as a legal chose in action. An absolute assignment in writing by the creditor of any debt where express notice in writing has been given to the debtor is an effective assignment at law from the date of the notice: for example (VIC) Property Law Act 1958 s 134; (NSW) Conveyancing Act 1919 s 12. See also **Debt of record; Simple contract debt**.

Debt accruing due A debt based upon a present obligation but which is payable at a definable approaching future date and not one which is payable only on the performance of a condition precedent: *Re Australia and New Zealand Savings Bank* [1972] VR 690 at 693. See also **Accruing debt; Debt**.

Debt adjusting 1. Negotiating with a creditor or owner, on behalf of a debtor or hirer, the terms for the discharge of a debt. **2.** Taking over, in return for payments by the debtor or hirer, the obligation to discharge a debt; or any similar activity concerned with the liquidation of a debt: (UK) Consumer Credit Act 1974 s 145(5).

Debt capital The capital or funds of a company raised from loans. Debt capital may be contrasted with equity capital. See also **Bill of exchange; Debenture; Loan capital; Mortgage; Promissory note**.

Debt collecting Taking steps to procure payment of debts due under consumer credit agreements or consumer hire agreements: (UK) Consumer Credit Act 1974 s 145(7). See also **Consumer credit agreement; Debt**.

Debt counselling Giving advice to debtors or hirers about the liquidation of debts due under consumer credit agreements or consumer hire agreements: (UK) Consumer Credit Act 1974 s 145(6). See also **Consumer credit agreement; Debt**.

Debt defeasance A means of extinguishing a debt by which the debtor either irrevocably transfers into a trust sufficient assets to meet the debt servicing requirements (both principal and interest) or has a suitable entity so as to assume responsibility for those servicing requirements: Australian Accounting Standards Board (AASB) 1014 para 7. See also **Debt management; Debt rescheduling; Debt servicing; Entity; Income**.

Debt dividend A payment made by a company to a shareholder by way of a dividend which can be reasonably regarded as equivalent to the payment of interest on a loan: (CTH) Income Tax Assessment Act 1936 s 46D. In financing the activities of a company, it may be more attractive to the company or the financier for the financier to receive dividend income, which may be rebatable, rather than interest income. A debt dividend will affect the financier's ability to obtain the intercorporate dividend rebate, and the ability of the company to pay a franked dividend. There are two types of debt dividend: those paid after 7 April 1986, where the period of the loan is less than two years: ((CTH) Income Tax Assessment Act 1936 s 46C); and those paid after 10 December 1986 where there is no time requirement for the period of the loan: (CTH) Income Tax Assessment Act 1936 s 46D. A shareholder in receipt of the second type of debt dividend is entitled to a tax rebate on the dividend ((CTH) Income Tax Assessment Act 1936 ss 46 or 46A), except in relation to the unfranked portion of the dividend where the dividend was paid before 1 July 1987: (CTH) Income Tax Assessment Act 1936 ss 46D(3)(a), (b). The provisions were enacted as anti-avoidance provisions to stop the use of arrangements involving redeemable preference shares and the dividend rebate provisions. Debt dividends under (CTH) Income Tax Assessment Act 1936 s 46C are deductible to the payer company: (CTH) Income Tax Assessment Act 1936 s 67AA. See also **Dividend; Dividend rebate; Franked Dividend**.

Debt funding The gathering of funds for a commercial enterprise by way of external debt instead of issuing equity security. See also **Debt; Security**.

Debt management In contrast to fund-raising, the task of minimising the burden of debt by means of debt retirement, swaps, the matching of asset realisation with liabilities, the raising of self-financing ratios, and the variation of debt-equity ratios. See also **Asset; Debt defeasance; Liability; Swap**.

Debt moratorium An arrangement between creditors and a company to suspend the payments due on debt for the time being, to enable the company to recover its trading position. This course is an alternative to an court-imposed arrangement using an appointed administrator, or putting the company into receivership or liquidation. See also **Creditor; Liquidation; Receivership**.

Debt of record A debt which is entered by a court and is legally enforceable. It is entered in the court records and remains valid until set aside by a court of competent jurisdiction: *Bank of Athens v Royal Exchange Assurance* [1938] 1 KB 771. See also **Decree; Judgment; Recognisance**.

Debt, proof of See **Proof of debt**.

Debt ratio A mathematical expression of the relations between total liabilities and total assets of a company, which is used by long term creditors of a company in assessing the financial standing of a debtor company. A low debt ratio means that shareholders have supplied most of the funds of the company rather than creditors, so the claims of creditors against the total assets will be proportionately low and creditors are more likely to be paid. The debt ratio and equity ratio of a company are complementary and will always add to 100 per cent. See also **Asset; Equity-debt ratio; Liability**.

Debt rescheduling An arrangement between a country or company and its creditors, to spread out debt repayments over a longer period than originally scheduled. While interest charges continue to flow, the repayment of capital is delayed. The lender may be paid an extra fee for agreeing to the rescheduling. Rescheduling of official debt is negotiated through the Paris Club; that of commercial bank debt through the London Club. See also **Debt; Group of ten; London club**.

Debt security A form of assurance offered by an organisation to borrow money on agreed terms. See also **Assurance; Contract; Debt; Security; Winding up**.

Debt servicing Paying interest on a debt. See also **Debt**.

Debt servicing ratio The repayments and interest on medium and long-term debt expressed as a percentage of the value of goods and services exported. By 1994, some 20 per cent of each dollar earned from exports had to be set aside to finance Australia's foreign interest bill. See also **External debt**.

Debt subordination An agreement or declaration by a creditor of a company that in specified circumstances, the whole or part of a specified debt owed to the creditor will not be repaid until other specified debts of the company are repaid to a specified extent: Corporations Law s 563C(2). See also **Creditor; Debt**.

Debt to equity ratio In corporations law, a ratio of debt capital to share capital, showing how much of a firm's funding has been provided by long term debt compared with shareholders' equity. The higher the percentage, the greater the firm is funded by debt. See also **Capital; Equity**.

Debt waiver The relinquishing by a person of the right to require another person to repay an amount. See also **Fringe benefit; Fringe Benefits Tax**.

•**Debt waiver fringe benefit** A fringe benefit that arises when an employer waives a debt payable by an employee or releases the obligation of such a liability so that the debt owing to the employer is no longer payable: (CTH) Fringe Benefits Tax Assessment Act 1986 s 14. The benefit consists of the total debt waived plus any interest accrued but unpaid at the time of discharging the liability. See also **Debt; Fringe benefit; Interest**.

Debt-equity swap The conversion of a borrower's debt to a lender's interest.

Banking and finance The swapping of debt for bonds offering security and a higher interest rate; a response of developing countries to their problem of insurmountable debt. It became clear during the 1980s that bank loans to developing countries were not worth the face value which appeared in most banks' balance sheets. It appeared unlikely that these loans would be repaid in full, and some not at all. A solution has been to substitute bonds issued by agencies of developing countries for debt, often at a considerable discount or loss to the lenders but with the prospect of a higher and more reliable rate of interest on the reduced capital amount. See also **Bond; Equity**.

Taxation and revenue A debt-equity swap generally occurs where a person owed a debt considers the debt bad or unrecoverable, but is prepared to take an interest in the debtor, such as by way of a shareholding in a company. While this bad debt normally may be deductible for tax purposes, the value of any equity received by the debtor will adjust the amount of the deduction for the bad debt: (CTH) Income Tax Assessment Act 1936 s 63E. See also **Bad debt**.

•**Debtor** Someone who owes money to another, the creditor.

Taxation and revenue For the purposes of (CTH) Bankruptcy Act 1966 Pt X, a person who is unable to pay his or her debts as they become due out of the person's own moneys: (CTH) Bankruptcy Act 1966 s 187(1). See also **Accounts receivable; Debtor's own money; Part X; Sequestration order; Winding up**.

Debtor-creditor agreement In the United Kingdom, a consumer credit agreement to finance a transaction between the debtor and a person (the supplier) other than the creditor, but which is not made by the creditor under pre-existing arrangements with the supplier; a credit agreement to refinance any existing indebtedness of the debtor, whether to the creditor or another person; or an unrestricted-use credit agreement which is not made by the creditor under pre-existing arrangements between himself or herself and a person other than the debtor in the knowledge that the credit is to be used to finance a transaction between the debtor and the supplier: (UK) Consumer Credit Act 1974 s 13. A consumer credit agreement is an agreement between a debtor and a creditor by which the creditor provides the debtor with credit not exceeding a prescribed amount: ss 8, 9. An unrestricted-use credit agreement is a credit agreement which is not one which finances or refinances a transaction between the debtor and the creditor or another person: s 11. See also **Consumer credit agreement; Credit purchase agreement; Debtor-creditor agreement**.

Debtor-creditor relationship A relationship, contractual or otherwise, where one individual (the debtor) owes a sum of money to another (the creditor). See also **Debt; Debtor**.

Debtor's own money The money or property of a debtor available to pay the debtor's debts. For the purpose of deciding whether a payment made by a debtor is liable to be upset as a preference, at the time of payment the debtor must be shown unable to pay all the debtor's debts, as they fall due, from the debtor's own money. Money available to the debtor by borrowing it is not the debtor's 'own money': *Re Armour; Ex parte Official Receiver v Commonwealth Trading Bank of Australia* (1956) 18 ABC 69. See also **Debtor; Preference**.

•**Debtor's petition** The procedure by which a debtor asks to be made bankrupt by the court: (CTH) Bankruptcy Act 1966 ss 5(1), 55. A debtor's petition can be used by joint debtors or a partnership: ss 56, 57. See also **Creditor's petition; Debtor; Sequestration**.

Debtors' turnover A business ratio seeking to ascertain the average collection period for debtors. This ratio indicates the rate at which debts are collected. See also **Debt**.

Debts, attachment of See **Garnishment**.

Debts properly incurred in the course of receivership In corporations law, the debts properly incurred by a receiver in the course of receivership as a result of services rendered, or goods purchased, or property hired for the purpose of fulfilling the receiver's obligations in carrying on the business of the corporation. The receiver becomes personally liable for such debts as are incurred, but this does not affect the right of the receiver to be indemnified against the assets of the corporation or the debenture holder: Corporations Law s 419(1); *Knysh v Corrales Pty Ltd* (1989) 15 ACLR 629; 7 ACLC 1006. Where an express indemnity exists between the corporation and the receiver, and debts incurred as a result of neglect, default or breach of duty in improper performance of the receiver's duty, the receiver will not be entitled to be indemnified, as the debts would not have been 'properly incurred': *James v Commonwealth Bank of Australia* (1992) 37 FCR 445; 109 ALR 334. See also **Receiver; Receiver's indemnity**.

Debts still owing A sequestration order cannot be made against an allegedly bankrupt debtor unless the petitioning creditor's debt is 'still owing' when the petition is heard: (CTH) Bankruptcy Act 1966 s 52(1)(c).

Deceit The intentional tort of knowingly or recklessly making a false statement, with the intention that another will rely on it to his or her detriment. A plaintiff can recover damages for the full extent of the loss incurred as a result of relying on the misrepresentation: *Pasley v Freeman* (1789) 3 TR 51; 100 ER 450. See also **Fraudulent misrepresentation**.

•**Deceive** See **Misleading or deceptive conduct**.

•**Deception** Misleading by deliberate misrepresentation; intentionally inducing in another a state of mind which the offender knows does not accord with fact: *Corporate Affairs Commission v Papoulias* (1990) 20 NSWLR 503; 2 ACSR 655. Deception includes deception (whether deliberate or reckless) by words or conduct as to fact or law, including deception as to the present intentions of any person: for example (VIC) Crimes Act 1958 s 81(4)(a). See also **Fraudulent misrepresentation; Misrepresentation**.

•**Decision** A concluded opinion or determination.

Decision period In relation to the property of a company under administration, the period during which the holder of a charge on the whole or substantially the whole of the company's property may appoint a receiver to enter into possession of the company's property: Corporations Law s 441A. It is a period of 10 business days beginning when the administration begins, or when notice is given to the chargee, if such notice is required: Corporations Law s 9. See also **Charge; External administration; Receiver; Receivership**.

Declaration of dividend The formal act of a bankruptcy trustee which precedes any payment of dividends to creditors: (CTH) Bankruptcy Act 1966 s 140. See also **Dividend; Trustee in bankruptcy**.

Declaration of solvency A declaration by directors of a company that they have reasonable grounds for thinking that the company will be able to pay its debts in full within a period of not more than 12 months after the commencement of winding up: Corporations Law s 494(1). A director who makes a declaration of solvency without reasonable grounds commits an offence: Corporations Law s 494(4). See also **Insolvent**; **Statement of affairs**; **Voluntary winding up**; **Winding up**.

•**Declaration of trust** The manifestation of an intention to create a trust, by the creator of that trust, declaring that he or she holds property as trustee for another. A declaration of trust creates, rather than assigns, an interest if made by a person having full beneficial and legal ownership of property: *DKLR Holding Co (No 2) Pty Ltd v Cmr of Stamp Duties (NSW)* (1982) 149 CLR 431; 40 ALR 1. See also **Oral trust**; **Trust**; **Trustee**.

Declaratory judgment An authoritative but non-coercive proclamation of the court made for the purpose of resolving some legal issue. It is contrasted with court orders which are coercive, but a refusal to abide by a declaratory judgment may lead to a coercive order given against the defaulting party. Generally declaratory relief will be granted only for the determination of legal controversies and not for answering abstract or hypothetical questions, and only where the person seeking relief has a real interest in the matter: *Ainsworth v Criminal Justice Commission*. Also known as 'declaratory relief'. See also **Court order**.

Declaratory relief See **Declaratory judgment**.

•**Decree** *Lat – decretum* – decision of the emperor as judge. An order of a court made after due consideration of a case. The term 'decree' was originally used to describe the decision of a court of equity but the term 'judgment' is now used to describe the decision of any court.

Decrystallisation A floating charge which, having become fixed, returns to a floating charge. Decrystallisation would be impossible when the company is in liquidation. See also **Floating charge**; **Fixed charge**; **Automatic crystallisation clause**.

Deductible In income taxation law, amounts which are allowable as deductions from assessable income in calculating taxable income. Generally an outgoing or loss is deductible if it is incurred in gaining assessable income or is necessarily incurred in carrying on a business for the purpose of producing assessable income, and is not of a capital, private, or domestic nature: (CTH) Income Tax Assessment Act 1936 s 51. See also **Allowable deduction**; **Taxable income**.

•**Deductible amount** The undeducted purchase price of an annuity reduced by its residual capital value, if any, and apportioned over the term for which the annuity will be paid or can reasonably be expected to be paid: (CTH) Income Tax Assessment Act 1936 s 27H(2). The amount of any annuity or superannuation pension derived by a taxpayer during the year of income less the deductible amount in relation to that annuity is included in assessable income: (CTH) Income Tax Assessment Act 1936 s 27H(1). See also **Annuity**; **Assessable income**; **Derived**; **Purchase price**; **Residual capital value**; **Rebatable superannuation pension**; **Undeducted purchase price**; **Year of income**.

Deduction See **Allowable deduction**.

•**Deed** An instrument that has been signed, sealed, and delivered that passes an interest, right, or property, creates an obligation binding on some person, or is an affirmation or confirmation of something that passes an interest, right, or property: *R v Morton* (1873) LR 2 CCR 22. At common law, a deed must be written on parchment, vellum, or paper, and be sealed and delivered. Modern deeds are often less strict in their format, and in some circumstances a document may be treated as a deed if it in fact has the effect of a deed, although there may be formal deficiencies: Corporations Law s 9. Statutes in most Australian jurisdictions modify these formal requirements by adding the requirements of signing and attesting (witnessing) and reducing the requirement of sealing to a mere formality: for example (QLD) Property Law Act 1974 ss 44, 45; (VIC) Property Law Act 1958 ss 57, 73, 73A. See also **Bond**; **Contract**; **Consideration**; **Deed inter partes**; **Delivery**; **Execution**; **Indenture**; **Instrument under seal**; **Special contract**.

Deed administrator The person responsible for setting out and seeing fulfilled a deed of company arrangement. There can be more than one administrator of the deed: Corporations Law s 451B(1). The administrator of the company must be the administrator of the deed unless the creditors resolve at a meeting convened under Corporations Law s 439A to appoint someone else to be the administrator of the deed: Corporations Law s 444A(1), (2). A person can only be appointed as deed administrator if he or she has consented in writing to the appointment and is a registered liquidator: Corporations Law ss 448A, 448B. See also **Deed of company arrangement**; **Registered liquidator**.

Deed contrary to public policy A deed which is rendered void or illegal as being contrary to public policy: *Wilkinson v Osborne* (1915) 21 CLR 89; [1915] ALR 57. See also **Illegal contract**; **Public policy**; **Void ab initio**; **Void contract**.

Deed inter partes A deed made between two or more named persons. The terms 'indenture' and 'deed inter partes' are used interchangeably by the courts: for example *Re A & K Holdings Pty Ltd* [1964] VR 257. A deed that is not inter partes may or may not be a deed poll: *Chelsea v Walham Green Building Society v Armstrong* [1951] 1 Ch 853; 2 All ER 250. See also **Deed**; **Indenture**.

•**Deed of arrangement** A deed providing for the arrangement of a debtor's affairs with a view to the payment, in whole or part, of the debtor's debts: (CTH) Bankruptcy Act 1966 s 187(1). It must be in a form approved by creditors under (CTH) Bankruptcy Act 1966 Pt X. See also **Composition**; **Debtor**; **Deed of assignment**; **Part X**.

•**Deed of assignment** A deed under which a debtor assigns all of his or her divisible property to a registered trustee for the benefit of creditors: (CTH) Bankruptcy Act 1966 s 187(1). It must be in a form approved by creditors under (CTH) Bankruptcy Act 1966 Pt X. A deed of assignment does not assign 'after acquired property', but a deed containing such a provision may nevertheless be a deed of arrangement: *Re Leask and Trumbich; Ex parte Melsom* (1986) 11 FCR 305; 66 ALR 487. See also

After acquired property; Composition; Deed of arrangement; Divisible property; Official Trustee in Bankruptcy.

Deed of company arrangement In corporations law, the charter agreed upon by the creditors in a voluntary administration under Corporations Law Pt 5.3A which governs the powers of the deed administrator acting as agent for the company. The deed will release the company from a debt only in so far as the deed provides for the release and the creditor concerned is bound by the deed: Corporations Law s 444H. See also **Administrator; Winding up**.

Deed of release A release executed in the form of a deed. The general words in a release are limited to issues which are specially in the contemplation of the parties at the time when the release is given: *Grant v John Grant & Sons Pty Ltd* (1954) 91 CLR 112; 28 ALJR 217. See also **Deed; Creditor; Debtor; Discharge; Release of principal debtor**.

Deed of settlement company Historically, a large partnership which has in place a deed of settlement by which a few of the partners named in the deed are appointed trustees to conduct the business of the association on trust for the other partners in accordance with the deed. The trustees can sue and be sued. Shares in the partnership are transferable. The deed provides that stockholders should be liable only to the extent of their contributed capital. These associations may be affected by the prohibition against outsize entities: Corporations Law s 112. See also **Corporation; Outsize entity; Trustee**.

Deed under seal A deed that has been sealed. In all States and Territories (except Tasmania and the Northern Territory), legislation provides that the physical act of sealing is not necessary; it is enough that the document is expressed to be a deed or is expressed to be sealed: for example (NSW) Conveyancing Act 1919 s 38(1). See also **Deed; Seal; Sealed documents; Signed, sealed and delivered**.

•**Deem** To take to be; to treat as. Used to create a legal or statutory fiction: *Muller v Dalgety & Co Ltd* (1909) 9 CLR 693. For example, a lawyer may deem black to be white: *Barclays Bank Ltd v Inland Revenue Cmr* [1961] AC 509. Deem is also used to create a presumption of fact irrespective of reality: *R v Billick and Starke* (1984) 36 SASR 321; 11 A Crim R 452. See also **Deeming clause**.

Deemed credit sale contract Under the Uniform Credit legislation, certain consumer hire-purchase agreements and goods leases. The cash price paid for the goods or services under the contract must not exceed the prescribed amount, unless the goods are a commercial vehicle or farm machinery. Credit must be provided in relation to the goods and the contract must not be with a body corporate: (NSW) Credit Act 1984 (repealed) s 13; (VIC) Credit Act 1984 (repealed) s 13 (replaced by Uniform Consumer Credit Code). See also **Cash price; Credit sale contract; Hire-purchase agreement**.

•**Deemed dividend** Certain payments by a private company which are deemed by the Commissioner of Taxation to be a dividend, and which are then assessable as a dividend under (CTH) Income Tax Assessment Act 1936 s 44. See also **Dividend; Franked dividend; Private company**.

Deemed employee A person who performs work for another in circumstances which at common law would not be considered a relationship of employment, but who is deemed by legislation to be an 'employee' in order to receive the benefit of legislation directed at employees, such as workers' compensation or industrial relations statutes. See also **Contract of employment; Employee; Independent contractor**.

•**Deemed employer** A person who engages another to work, and who at common law would not be considered an employer, but who is deemed by a statute to be an employer for the purposes of the statute. See also **Employee; Employer; Independent contractor**.

Deemed income A level of income that one is taken to have earned on any financial investments. See also **Deeming rate; Statutory income**.

Deemed manufacturer A person or entity other than the actual manufacturer of a product who, by virtue of permitting its name, brand, or mark to be applied to a product, or by holding out or permitting another to hold out that it is the manufacturer or sponsor of a product, or by virtue of being the importer of a product or a person on whose behalf a product is imported, may attract liability in negligence in relation to that product on the basis of its close commercial association with the product: for example *Torres v Goodyear Tire & Rubber Co* 786 P 2d 939 (Ariz 1990); (CTH) Trade Practices Act 1974 ss 74A(3), 74A(4), 65C(7). See also **Division 2A claim; Manufacturer**.

•**Deemed worker** See **Deemed employee**.

Deeming clause A clause in legislation which purports to include a fact or thing within the ambit of the legislation irrespective of whether or not that fact or thing would actually be within that ambit, creating a statutory fiction as a result: *Mulle v Dalgety & Co Ltd* (1909) 9 CLR 693 at 696. The Commonwealth Parliament cannot deem a fact or thing to exist so as to acquire legislative power with respect to it: *Herald and Weekly Times Ltd v Commonwealth* (1966) 115 CLR 418 at 438; [1967] ALR 300. For example, a power to make laws with respect to lighthouses does not authorise the making of a law with respect to anything which is, in the opinion of Parliament, a lighthouse: *Australian Communist Party v Commonwealth* (1951) 83 CLR 1 at 258. Parliament may, however, enact deeming provisions with respect to evidentiary presumptions: *Williamson v Ah On* (1926) 39 CLR 95. See also **Federal powers**.

Deeming rate An assumed earning rate of interest that financial institutions like banks must credit to pensioner savings. It is determined by the Commonwealth government. See also **Deemed income**.

Deep discount bond A bond or stock on which a very low coupon interest rate is payable; nil in the case of a zero coupon bond. However, the issue price is heavily discounted, being only a fraction of the eventual redemption value. The capital gain over the life of the bond compensates for the low or non-existent income over the period. See also **Bond; Zero-coupon bond**.

Deep pocket argument In tort law, the notion that a particular defendant, because of its extensive resources or 'deep pocket', is best able to bear a loss and therefore should do so even in situations where it is not at fault. See also **Fault**; **Public policy**; **Vicarious liability**.

•**Defalcation** Any act taken in relation to property that is punishable by imprisonment, including theft, embezzlement, failure to account, and fraudulent misappropriation: for example (NSW) Commercial Agents and Private Inquiry Agents Act 1963 s 39A; (VIC) Estate Agents Act 1980 s 71. See also **Embezzlement**; **Larceny**; **Misappropriation**.

Defalcation of trust moneys Misappropriation, or wrongful diminution or reduction of trust funds or money held in a fiduciary capacity, even if the deficiency is not due to dishonesty: *Daly v Sydney Stock Exchange Ltd* (1986) 160 CLR 371 at 380; 65 ALR 193. The failure to properly account for such funds. See also **Defalcation**; **Fiduciary relationship**.

•**Default** *Fr* – failure. **1.** An omission of that which ought to be done: *Dacre v Dacre* (1798) 1 B & P 250 at 258; 126 ER 887; *Andrew v Andrew* [1875] 1 Ch D 417. **2.** The failure to perform a legal or contractual duty, or to observe a promise: *Randall v Thorn* [1878] WN 150; *Albert v Grosvenor Investment Co* (1876) LR 3 QB 123. See also **Futures contract**.

Default assessment Generally, an assessment or ascertainment of taxable income made by the Commissioner of Taxation where the taxpayer defaults in furnishing a tax return, or where the Commissioner is not satisfied with the return furnished by the taxpayer, or where the taxpayer has not furnished a return but the Commissioner has reason to believe that the taxpayer has derived taxable income: (CTH) Income Tax Assessment Act 1936 s 167. See also **Franking deficit tax**; **Fringe benefits tax**.

•**Default charge** In consumer law, a charge imposed on a debtor by a credit provider for failing to pay an amount due under a regulated contract: (NSW) Credit Act 1984 (repealed) s 72; (VIC) Credit Act 1984 (repealed) s 72 (replaced by Uniform Consumer Credit Code). See also **Credit provider**; **Regulated contract**.

Default clause A provision in a building contract entitling the proprietor to determine the contract in certain circumstances. Given the serious consequences of the application of default clauses, courts tend to construe such clauses narrowly and have been prepared to imply a term that the default clause not be implemented unreasonably: *Renard Constructions (ME) Pty Ltd v Minister for Public Works* (1992) 26 NSWLR 234; 9 BCL 40. Also known as 'forfeiture clause' in the United Kingdom. See also **Building contract**; **Default**; **Forfeiture clause**.

Default judgment A discretionary judgment or verdict given in favour of a plaintiff by virtue of the defendant's failure to comply with the procedural requirements of the court after having been served with an originating process: for example (NSW) Supreme Court Rules Pt 17 r 9; (VIC) Rules of the Supreme Court Ch I rr 21.02, 21.03. An order for default judgment may be set aside at the discretion of the court (for example (NSW) Supreme Court Rules Pt 40 r 8; (VIC) Rules of Supreme Court Ch 1 r 21.07) where the interests of justice require it (*Stollznow v Calvert* [1980] 2 NSWLR 749 at 751) and the defendant can explain the default and demonstrate a good defence on the merits (*Vacuum Oil Pty Co Ltd v Stockdale* (1942) 42 SR (NSW) 239 at 243).

Default summons In civil proceedings, a summons which gives the plaintiff the right to judgment in the event of the defendant failing to give notice of his intention to defend: *Webster & Co Ltd v Vincent* (1897) 77 LT 167; *Young v Thomas* [1892] 2 Ch 134. See also **Appearance**; **Default judgment**.

Defeasance In the context of deeds, something that defeats the operation of a deed but that, strictly, is contained in some other deed or document: *Ex parte Popplewell; Re Storey* (1882) 21 Ch D 73 at 81. A defeasance is distinguishable from a 'condition' which has a similar effect but is strictly contained in the deed itself: *Ex parte Popplewell; Re Storey*. In modern law and practice, however, this strict distinction is rarely observed, and 'defeasance' and 'condition' are used interchangeably. If a bill of sale is made or given subject to a defeasance, that defeasance must be contained in the body of the bill of sale upon registration: (NSW) Bills of Sale Act 1898 s 9. See also **Bill of sale**; **Condition**; **Deed**.

Defeasible An interest capable of being defeated or terminated.

•**Defect** A deficiency or absence of something essential to completeness: *Tate v Latham* 66 LJQB 351.

Corporations A defect in respect of a statutory demand includes an irregularity, a misstatement of the total or amount of the demand, a misdescription of a debt or other matter, or a misdescription of a person or entity: Corporations Law s 9. A demand may be set aside due to a defect: s 459J; *Re Aroora Pty Ltd* (1993) 12 ACSR 572. See also **Statutory demand**.

Industrial law In relation to any invalidity in the amalgamation of employer or employee organisations, it includes a nullity, omission, error, or irregularity: (CTH) Industrial Relations Act 1988 ss 234, 253ZD. See also **Amalgamation**; **Employee organisation**; **Employer organisation**.

Product liability A flaw that makes goods not as safe as persons generally are entitled to expect: (CTH) Trade Practices Act 1974 s 75AC(1); (NSW) Fair Trading Act 1987 s 34(1). See also **Defect in design**; **Defect in formulation**; **Defect in information**; **Defect in labelling**; **Defect in manufacture**; **Defective goods**; **Product recall**.

Defect in design A defect introduced into a product at the stage of formulating the manufacturing or processing of the product, as a consequence of an error in judgment, which creates a risk of product-related loss or damage for a person using the product in a reasonable manner, or for a person who is a bystander: for example *Vosten v Commonwealth* [1989] 1 Qd R 693; *Shepherd v S J Banks & Son Pty Ltd* (1987) 45 SASR 437; *Griffiths v Arch Engineering (Newport) Co Ltd (Newport)* [1968] 3 All ER 217. See also **Defect in formulation**; **Defect in information**; **Defect in manufacture**.

Defect in formulation A defect introduced into a product as a consequence of an error in judgment at the stage of product formulation, which creates a risk of product-related loss or damage for a person using or consuming the product in a reasonable manner: for example *Kasler & Cohen v Slavouski* [1928] 1 KB 78; *Godley v Perry* [1960] All ER 36. See also **Defect in design; Defect in information; Defect in manufacture.**

Defect in information An error or omission in the information provided with a product, which prevents safe or effective use of the product. A defect in information may take the form of a failure to warn adequately of a risk (for example *Martin v Stratman* (1994) Aust Torts Reporter ¶81-262), a failure to provide adequate instructions as to safe or effective use (for example *Milne Construction Ltd v Expandite Ltd* [1984] 2 NZLR 163), or the provision of inaccurate information that prevents safe or effective use (*Martin v Thorn Lighting Industries Pty Ltd* [1978] WAR 10). See also **Defect in design; Defect in labelling; Defect in manufacture.**

Defect in labelling An error in the labelling of a product, which renders the product as a whole unsafe or defective (for example *Martin v Thorn Lighting Industries Pty Ltd* [1978] WAR 10), or which is false, misleading, or deceptive in contravention of (CTH) Trade Practices Act 1974 ss 52, 53, 55 (for example *Narhex Australia Pty Ltd v Sunspot Products Pty Ltd* (1990) ATPR ¶41-036; 18 IPR 535). See also **Defect in information; Defect in packaging.**

Defect in manufacture A defect introduced into a product as a consequence of the fallibility of the manufacturing process, which renders the product different in some respect or respects from what was intended by the manufacturer. A defect in manufacture may result either from contamination (for example *Donoghue v Stevenson* [1932] AC 562), or faulty workmanship (for example *Woolworths Ltd v Crotty* (1942) 66 CLR 603; [1943] ALR 100) in the course of manufacture. See also **Defect in design; Defect in formulation; Defect in information.**

Defect in packaging An error in the design of the packaging of a product, which renders the product wholly unsafe or defective (for example *Adelaide Chemical & Fertilizer Co Ltd v Carlyle* (1940) 64 CLR 514; [1941] ALR 10; *O'Dwyer v Leo Buring Pty Ltd* [1966] WAR 67) or deceptive, in that the packaging deceives persons as to the quantity of product contained in the packaging (for example (CTH) Trade Practices Act 1974 ss 52, 55). See also **Defect in information; Defect in labelling.**

Defect in property A patent or latent fault in the physical nature of the improvements on land: *DTR Nominees Pty Ltd v Mona Homes Pty Ltd* (1978) 138 CLR 423; 19 ALR 223. The fault in a building or house may be patent, that is, apparent to the eye, such as cracking in the walls. On the other hand, the defect may be latent and only obvious after a period of time after the person has lived in the premises, such as subsidence or fill on the site. See also **Defective premises; Latent defect.**

Defect in title Where a person's claim to ownership of property is deficient or imperfect.

Bills of exchange and other negotiable instruments **1.** The title of a person who negotiates a negotiable instrument is defective where the person has obtained the bill or its acceptance by fraud, duress, force and fear, or other unlawful means; for an illegal consideration; or when the negotiation is in breach of faith or under such circumstances as to amount to fraud: (CTH) Bills of Exchange Act 1909 s 34(2); (CTH) Cheques and Payment Orders Act 1986 s 3(3). **2.** In relation to title to property, an irregularity indicating a want of completeness of title. See also **Acceptance; Duress; Fraud; Holder in due course; Negotiable instrument.**

•**Defect or irregularity** An absence of formal correctness or completeness. Proceedings under the (CTH) Bankruptcy Act 1966 are not invalidated by a formal defect or irregularity, unless the court is of the opinion that substantial injustice has been caused by the defect or irregularity, and that the injustice cannot be remedied by an order of the court: (CTH) Bankruptcy Act 1966 s 306. The late signing of a certificate of the passing of a special resolution is an example of an defect or irregularity which would not invalidate a proceeding under (CTH) Bankruptcy Act 1966: *Re Gagliardi; Ex parte Mount* (1984) 5 FCR 52; 57 ALR 718. See also **Irregularity.**

Defective goods Goods which are not as safe as persons are generally entitled to expect: (CTH) Trade Practices Act 1974 s 75AC(1). See also **Consumer product safety standard; Product recall; Voluntary product recall.**

Defective performance A performance which is not of the quality or quantity required by the contract, or not fit for the purpose required. An example is where underwear sold is not of merchantable quality: *Grant v Australian Knitting Mills Ltd* (1935) 54 CLR 49; [1936] AC 85. See also **Breach of contract; Failure of performance; Merchantable quality; Performance; Tender of performance.**

Defective premises Premises having a defect relating to the fabric of the premises, or to some temporary condition of the premises which makes them dangerous or defective. See also **Occupier's liability.**

Defective product A product which is flawed and therefore unfit for its intended or contemplated use or purpose, and not of merchantable quality, as a result of negligence in its design, manufacturing, or marketing. Generally, liability is owed to one who suffers loss because of the defect: *Grant v Australian Knitting Mills* (1935) 54 CLR 49; [1936] AC 85. Consumer protection against defective products may flow from the law of contract, specific legislation, or the principles of negligence. See also **Intermediate examination defence.**

Defective prospectus A document offering shares which does not comply with the Corporations Law either because it does not contain all the material required by or because it contains a false, misleading, or deceptive statement, promise, estimate, or forecast, or a material misrepresentation. Where a prospectus is found to be defective, the ASC may impose a stop order to prevent the issue of securities under the prospectus:. See also **Misrepresentation; Prospectus; Stop order**.

• **Deferral charge** In consumer law, a charge imposed upon a debtor by a credit provider for the benefit of deferring a payment that is to be made under a regulated contract: for example (NSW) Credit Act 1984 (repealed) s 71; (VIC) Credit Act 1984 s 71 (replaced by Uniform Consumer Credit Code). See also **Credit provider; Regulated contract**.

• **Deferred annuity** *Abbr* – DA An annuity, the payment of which commences at a future pre-determined date, usually the date on which the annuitant attains a certain age or retires from employment; a product offered by the roll-over market, run almost exclusively by the life insurance companies. See also **Annuity; Approved deposit fund; Fixed interest rate; Rollover fund**.

Insurance An annuity the payment of which does not begin until the annuitant reaches a certain age, usually 65 years. See also **Annuity**.

Taxation and revenue An annuity that is not presently payable where the payments are delayed until some specified future date or the happening of an event (for example, the death of the spouse of the annuitant or the attainment of a certain age by the annuitant): (CTH) Income Tax Assessment Act 1936 s 27A. A deferred annuity allows the rollover of eligible termination payments enabling the deferral of income tax until the eligible termination payment is withdrawn or the annuity commences to be paid. Deferral is not permitted beyond age 65. See also **Annuity; Eligible Termination Payment; Immediate annuity; Pension; Rollover**.

Deferred charge In relation to accounting, expenditure, other than capital expenditure, which is not recognised as an expense when incurred but rather amortised over future periods. The benefit of the expenditure is expected to yield over for several accounting periods. Also known as 'deferred asset', 'deferred cost', or 'deferred expenditure'. See also **Accounting period; Amortisation; Capital**.

Deferred credit payment A payment to which a contributor or beneficiary has a right where that right is deferred until prior conditions for the payment have been met. Examples include retirement age for superannuation, or the clearance of a personal cheque in banking. See also **Deferred annuity**.

Deferred creditor An unsecured creditor whose claim in bankruptcy administration of a company is deferred by law until the claims of other creditors have been paid in full. Examples include a claim for interest beyond a prescribed rate; or a claim by a bankrupt's spouse for money or other property lent or made available to the bankrupt. See also **Administration; Bankruptcy; Creditor; Winding up**.

Deferred debt A debt which is not repayable until all other debts that have preference or priority to it are discharged: Corporations Law s 563A. See also **Administration; Deferred creditor; Winding up**.

Deferred dividend ordinary share A share which carries the right to be paid a dividend after a designated minimum dividend has been paid on the company's ordinary shares. Deferred shares may be issued to promoters or founders of a company. The aim is usually to encourage investment in the issuer. Any shares issued to the founders or promoters of a listed company must usually be held in escrow for at least 12 months from their issue date: ASX Listing Rules LR 9.5, Ch 19. See also **Escrow; Australian Stock Exchange listing rules; Ordinary share; Preference share**.

Deferred equity financing The raising by a company of finance in the form of a loan convertible at a later date to share capital. See also **Convertible security; Debt funding; Debt management**.

Deferred income Income that is postponed until a later date for taxation purposes.

Deferred share A share that does not entitle the holder to any dividend payment until a given percentage of dividend has been paid to the holders of all non-deferred shares; the opposite of a preference share. Such shares may be taken up by promoters as a way of demonstrating confidence in a company's profitable future (hence founders' shares), or they may be given in return for otherwise unrewarded services, or even for the use of someone's name. Also known as 'founder's share'. See also **Deferred share; Preference share; Promoter; Security; Share**.

Deficiency clause A clause providing that payment of freight will be determined in accordance with the actual weight of the cargo on delivery at the place of destination. A deficiency clause is used in a contract of affreightment by sea, particularly where the goods carried are bulk commodities such as wheat or coal. See also **Affreightment**.

• **Defined benefit fund** See **Defined benefit scheme**.

Defined benefit scheme A superannuation benefit scheme under which amounts to be paid as retirement benefits are paid from an aggregated fund by reference to the member's annual salary, or are paid as a specified amount regardless of contributions made by the employer or employee: (CTH) Income Tax Assessment Act 1936 s 6E(5). Also known as 'defined benefit fund or plan'. See also **Defined contribution scheme**.

Defined contribution fund See **Defined contribution scheme**.

Defined contribution plan See **Defined contribution scheme**.

Defined contribution scheme A superannuation benefit scheme under which amounts to be paid as retirement benefits are determined by contributions made to the fund together with the investment earnings on those contributions. In relation to employed persons, contributions may be made to such schemes by employers, employees, or both. Also known as 'accummulation fund or plan'. See also **Defined benefit scheme; Superannuation fund**.

• **Defraud** To induce a person by deceit or deliberate falsehood to act to the person's detriment, or take a course of action which the person would not otherwise have taken: *Balcombe v De Simoni* (1971) 126 CLR 576; [1972] ALR 513. See also **Deceit; False pretence; Fraud**.

Defraud, conspiracy to See **Conspiracy to defraud**.

Defunct company A company that has ceased to operate or carry on business. The company itself, a member of the company, or any interested person may also apply to the ASC to have a defunct company wound up: Corporations Law s 573(1), (2). See also **Company; Deregistration; Winding up**.

Del credere agent A mercantile agent who, in return for extra commission, agrees to indemnify a principal against loss should the people with whom the agent contracts on the principal's behalf fail to honour their agreements: *Campbell v Kitchen & Sons Ltd* (1910) 12 CLR 515. See also **Agency; Agent; Commission; Contract of guarantee; Mercantile agent; Principal**.

Del credere commission Additional commission paid to an agent as consideration for the agent undertaking to pay the purchase price of the principal's goods if the third party purchaser fails to pay. See also **Agency; Commission; Del credere agent; Principal**.

•**Delay** To postpone or defer the making of a decision or the doing of some act. The word does not connote a person's knowledge of the right or ability to do the act which he or she has delayed doing; it concerns simply the facts of effluxion of time and inaction: *Koumorou v Victoria* [1991] 2 VR 265.

Contract **1.** Failure to perform contractual obligations at the appointed time. Delay may give rise to a right to terminate where: there is an express condition that time is of the essence (for example *Mehmet v Benson* (1965) 113 CLR 295; *Legione v Hateley* (1983) 152 CLR 406; 46 ALR 1); there is an implied agreement that time of performance is essential (for example *Bettini v Gye* (1876) 1 QBD 183; *Alliance Petroleum Australia NL v Australian Gas Light Co* (1985) 39 ALR 84); the delay is unreasonable, gross, and protracted, or frustrating (for example *Neeta (Epping) Pty Ltd v Phillips* (1974) 131 CLR 286; 3 ALR 151); or the defendant fails to comply with a notice requiring performance within a reasonable time: for example *Louinder v Leis* (1982) 149 CLR 509; 41 ALR 187. **2.** Laches. See also **Acquiescence; Frustration; Laches; Termination**.

Delay in acceptance In sale of goods contracts, where a buyer accepts goods but does so, in breach of contract, after the time agreed for acceptance; or, where there is no agreed time for acceptance, where the buyer fails to take delivery of the goods within a reasonable time. See also **Late delivery; Non-acceptance; Non-delivery; Sale of goods**.

•**Delegation** Handing down, granting, assigning, or relinquishing certain powers, duties and authority to another to act on one's behalf for the implementation of a specific task. See also **Agent**.

Contract In the law of agency, the entrusting to another person by an agent of the exercise of a power or duty entrusted to the agent by the agent's principal. See also **Agency; Agent; Express authority; Principal; Sub-agent**.

Tort The power of an employer to acquit itself of vicarious liability by entrusting the work to a competent independent contractor. In some circumstances the duty to provide a safe system of work cannot be delegated and the employer remains liable even for the default of an independent contractor: *Stevens v Brodribb Sawmilling Co Pty Ltd* (1986) 160 CLR 16; 63 ALR 513. See also **Independent contractor; Vicarious liability**.

Delisting The removal of a company or security from the official list of a stock exchange: Corporations Law s 779(1). See also **Official List; Australian Stock Exchange Ltd; Listed body; Public company**.

Deliverable futures contract A futures contract under which the futures exchange rules permit physical delivery of the subject matter of the contract. It contrasts with a cash settled futures contract. The Corporations Law uses the term 'eligible commodity agreement' to describe a deliverable futures contract: Corporations Law s 9. See also **Cash settled futures contract; Futures contract**.

Deliverable option An option under which delivery of the subject matter of the option is contemplated upon exercise of the option. An example is the delivery of gold under a gold option. See also **Cash settled futures contract; Option**.

•**Delivery 1.** The transfer of actual or constructive possession from one person to another. **2.** Physical or constructive expulsion.

Bailment In relation to chattels, the transfer of possession of a chattel from one person to another. Ownership may be transferred by delivery of the chattel with intent to divest ownership (rather than some lesser intent, such as to create a bailment by temporary divestiture of possession): for example *Burns Philp & Co v Dingle & Co* (1923) 23 SR (NSW) 240; 40 WN (NSW) 26; *Re Fada (Aust) Ltd* [1932] SASR 134. See also **Custody; Constructive delivery; Movable property; Ownership; Possession; Sale of goods**.

Bills of exchange and other negotiable instruments The transfer of actual or constructive possession from one person to another: (CTH) Bills of Exchange Act 1909 s 4; (CTH) Cheques and Payment Orders Act 1986 s 3(1). A bearer bill or cheque is negotiated by delivery; an order bill or cheque is negotiated by indorsement completed by delivery: (CTH) Bills of Exchange Act 1909 s 36(2), 36(3); (CTH) Cheques and Payment Orders Act 1986 s 40(2),(3). Every contract on a bill or cheque is incomplete and revocable until delivery of the instrument: (CTH) Bills of Exchange Act 1909 s 26(1); (CTH) Cheques and Payment Orders Act 1986 s 25. See also **Acceptance; Bearer bill; Cheque; Constructive possession; Indorsement; Negotiation; Order bill; Signification**.

Delivery clause A clause in a charterparty specifying the place where, and time when, a ship that is the subject of the charterparty will be ready for use. A delivery clause marks the commencement of hire of the ship. The clause normally stipulates a range of ports from which the port of delivery of the ship may be selected by one of the parties. Usually, the earliest and latest dates that the ship may be delivered, not the exact time of delivery, will be stipulated. Failure to deliver within this period may entitle the charterer to cancel the charterparty or to sue for damages for breach of contract: *Marbienes Compania Naviera SA v Ferrostaal AG (The Democritos)* [1976] 2 Lloyd's Rep 149. See also **Charterparty**.

Delivery month A specified month during which actual delivery of a commodity may be made under the terms of a futures contract. Each futures contract must state the month of delivery. Current delivery means delivery during the current month. See also **Futures contract**.

Delivery not enforceable   Abbr – DEL   A basis for selling shares so buyers will know that they cannot expect early delivery of scrip. This can arise as a result of a new issue for which the scrip has not yet been issued. These shares may sell for slightly less than existing shares to compensate purchasers for the delay in scrip delivery. See also **Scrip**; **Share**.

Delivery note   Abbr – DN   A document accompanying goods sent by a vendor, often in duplicate with one copy to be kept by the recipient of the goods and the other to be signed and returned to the vendor. The vendor's copy is evidence of due delivery of the goods. In the shipping context, a delivery note accompanies the goods to be loaded, confirms the booking of the cargo, and details the quantity and description of the goods to be carried. See also **Cargo**; **Goods**.

Delivery of award In relation to an arbitration award, making the award available to both parties to take up: *Riley Gowler Ltd v National Heart Hospital Board of Governors* [1969] 3 All ER 1401. An arbitration agreement may require delivery of the award, as does the UNCITRAL Model Law on International Commercial Arbitration 1985 art 31(4). See also **Alternative dispute resolution**; **Arbitration**; **Award**; **UNCITRAL Model Law on International Commercial Arbitration 1985**.

Delivery of mixed goods The delivery to a buyer of goods the subject of a contract of sale, together with goods of a different description not included in the contract: (NSW) Sale of Goods Act 1923 s 33(3). See also **Buyer**; **Delivery**; **Seller**.

Delivery of wrong quantity The delivery to a buyer of a quantity of goods less than or greater than the buyer contracted to buy: (NSW) Sale of Goods Act 1923 ss 33(1), (2). See also **Buyer**; **Delivery**.

Delivery to carrier The delivery of goods sold to a person (a carrier) who is to transmit those goods to the buyer, where such transmission is authorised or requested by the contract of sale: (NSW) Sale of Goods Act 1923 s 35. See also **Buyer**; **Delivery**; **Sale**; **Seller**.

Delta In corporations law, a measure of the proportional change between two items. It represents the change in the value of an option for a small change in the price of the underlying security. The delta (D) can vary between 0 and 1. See also **Option**; **Security**.

•**Demand 1.** The assertion of a legal right, requiring the receiver to do something, refrain from doing something or give something: for example *Attorney-General (NSW) v Wentworth* (1991) 24 NSWLR 347. **2.** An amount due or debt. **3.** In economics, effective demand as measured by spending on consumption of goods and services, on investment such as plant, buildings, equipment, and inventories, and on the difference between imports which satisfy home demand without adding to domestic output and exports which add to demand for domestic output. See also **Debt**; **Proceeding**.

•**Demand bill** A bill of exchange expressed to be payable on demand, at sight by the acceptor, on presentation to the acceptor, or which does not express any time for payment: (CTH) Bills of Exchange Act 1909 s 15(1). An overdue bill accepted or indorsed will be deemed a bill payable on demand, with regard to the acceptor or indorser: (CTH) Bills of Exchange Act 1909 s 15(2). See also **Acceptance**; **Acceptor**; **Bill of exchange**; **Indorser**; **Presentation for acceptance**.

Demand function In economics, the relationship between the quantity of a good which a consumer wants to buy and all the quantitative factors which determine the consumer's demand; for example, the price of the good, the prices of complementary goods, the prices of substitutes, the consumer's income and methods of payment. If all factors are held constant, save one, it is possible to study how demand will vary with changes in that one element. See also **Consumer expectation**; **Demand**.

Demand management 1. In economics, a Keynesian policy of pursuing an activist stabilisation course by regulating aggregate demand so as to minimise unemployment and curb inflation. **2.** An approach to pricing in the provision of public services such as electricity and water. The demand for water can be greatly influenced by policies adopted in respect of such matters as water charges, restrictions on peak demands, and unrestricted use of treated water. A steeply rising schedule of water charges may be adopted for those periods of the year when demand tends to be greatest. Considerable capital cost savings may be made if peak demands are not allowed to rise unhindered.

•**Demarcation dispute** In industrial law, a dispute between two or more organisations, or within an organisation, as to the rights, status, or functions of members in relation to the employment of those members. It also includes a dispute about the representation of the industrial interest of employees by an organisation of employees: (CTH) Industrial Relations Act 1988 s 4. See also **Employee organisation**; **Industrial action**.

Demise charterparty A charterparty under which the possession of the ship and the control of the master, officers and crew are completely transferred to the charterer: *Australasian United Stream Navigation Co Ltd v Shipping Control Board* (1945) 71 CLR 508; [1946] ALR 82. Whether possession and control of the ship has passed to the charterer depends on the parties' intention: *Page v Admiralty Commissioners* [1921] 1 AC 137. The charterer effectively becomes the owner for the duration of the charterparty agreement: *Colvin v Newberry* (1832) 1 Cl & Fin 283; 6 Bli NS 167; 6 ER 923. If the charterparty does not include the crew, it is a bareboat charterparty. Under a demised charterparty, the charterer assumes liability for the acts of the crew, for any collision caused by the negligence of the chartered ship, and on any bill of lading signed by the master: *Samuel, Samuel & Co v West Hartlepool Steam Navigation Co* (1906) 11 Com Cas 115. The owner, however, retains the right to receive the agreed hire for the vessel and to take redelivery of the vessel on the expiration of the charter period: *Meiklereid v West* [1876] 1 QBD 428. Demised charterparties are no longer common. See also **Bareboat charterparty; Bill of lading; Charter; Charterparty; Master**.

Demise clause A clause in a bill of lading issued by the charterer of a vessel on behalf of the owner and the master, which provides that the contract of carriage is between the ship owner and the shipper or the bill of lading holder. See also **Bill of lading; Charterer; Contract of carriage; Master**.

Demurrage 1. A sum of money agreed to be paid by a charterer, shipper, or receiver, to the shipowner as liquidated damages for delay beyond the lay days allotted in the chartered agreement for the loading or discharging operations in relation to the cargo: *Aktieselskabet Reidar v Arcos Ltd* [1927] 1 KB 352. The additional days required by the charterer for which the demurrage is paid are called days of demurrage. **2.** In motor vehicle accidents or related cases, the liability of the defendant to compensate the plaintiff for any consequential loss, such as the cost of obtaining alternative transport (for example, cost of car hire) while the damaged car is being repaired or replaced: *Moore v DER Ltd* [1971] 3 All ER 517. See also **Cesser clause; Charter; Charterer; Charterparty; Days on demurrage; Liquidated damages; Rate of demurrage**.

Denial of natural justice An act of state denying or obstructing the access of an alien to local courts or tribunals, in contravention of international law. For denial of natural justice there is no commonly accepted international standard. In Australia, a foreign judgment obtained in circumstances at odds with these principles is not enforceable. See also **Natural justice**.

•**Department** A distinctive division in an organisation.

Industrial law In relation to the Australian Public Service, a section of the Service statutorily established as a department, having responsibility for the administration of certain areas of government activity: for example (CTH) Public Service Act 1922 Sch 2. See also **Public service**.

Department of Finance Formerly part of the Commonwealth Treasury, a federal department created in 1976 for the purposes of financial management for the Commonwealth government. The Department has a pivotal role in servicing the government's budgetary requirements, involving the coordination and compilation of estimates, planning, priority setting and evaluation of expenditure initiatives. The Department also offers advice on matters related to the Commonwealth's micro-economic reform agenda, and for the natural resources and energy sectors of the Australian economy.

Department of Foreign Affairs and Trade *Abbr* – DFAT A federal government department responsible for coordinating Australia's international trade activities and foreign relations through specific Commonwealth agencies. The DFAT portfolio contains eight program areas and operates under the direction of the Minister for Foreign Affairs, Minister for Trade, and Minister for Development Cooperation and Pacific Island Affairs. DFAT administers five programs: International relations, trade and business liaison; Passport and consular services; Services for other agencies; Secure government communications and security services; and Executive and DFAT corporate services. The sixth program, Development Cooperation, is administered by the Australian Agency for International Development (AusAID), an autonomous body within DFAT. The seventh and eighth programs, are administered by the Australian Trade Commission (Austrade) and the Australian Secret Intelligence Service (ASIS). In 1994 the Australian Safeguards Office (ASO) was transferred into DFAT and a Chemical Weapons Convention Office (CWCO) was established. Associated with DFAT are cultural bodies such as the Australia-Japan Foundation and bodies advising on specific issues including trade, disarmament, and regional cooperation. See also **Australian Agency for International Development; Australian Trade Commission**.

•**Departure prohibition order** *Abbr* – DPO An order issued by the Commissioner of Taxation stopping a person from going overseas, if the Commissioner thinks that the person is intending to leave Australia without discharging their tax liability: (CTH) Taxation Administration Act 1953 ss 14R-14ZA. The Commissioner can only make such an order if the recoverability of tax will be affected by the departure of the person from Australia: *Dalco v FCT* (1987) 19 ATR 443. See also **Taxation determination; Tax planning**.

•**Dependant** A person who depends on another, wholly or substantially, for his or her survival, maintenance or financial support. It is defined differently for different purposes in various statutes. Usually some degree of kinship is also required.

Taxation and revenue For dependant rebate purposes, a person who relies on the contributions of a taxpayer for maintenance: (CTH) Income Tax Assessment Act 1936 s 159J(1). A dependant includes: a dependent spouse, child-housekeeper, invalid relative, student, or parent of the taxpayer or taxpayer's spouse: (CTH) Income Tax Assessment Act 1936 s 159J(2). See also **Child-housekeeper; Dependant rebate**.

Workers' compensation In employment and related areas of law, 'dependency' involves the notions of maintenance and support, in relation to the necessities of life for the actual life style of the worker and the dependants. The notion of maintenance and support is not limited to the bare necessities of life, to cases where there is a legal duty to support, or to some notional standard of living. The relevant standard of living is that which the worker and the dependants have established by their own incomes and expenditure: *Kauri Timber Co (Tas) Pty Ltd v Reeman* (1973) 128 CLR 177. Dependency does not arise merely from the receipt of financial assistance; one person must rely or depend on another for maintenance and support: *Affjes v Kearney* (1976) 180 CLR 199; 8 ALR 455. See also **Compensation; Workers' compensation**.

Dependant rebate A tax rebate provided to a resident taxpayer who contributes to the maintenance of a dependant: (CTH) Income Tax Assessment Act 1936 s 159J. The dependant for whom a rebate is claimed must be a resident: (CTH) Income Tax Assessment Act 1936 s 159J(1). See also **Dependant; Derived; Rebate; Separate net income.**

Dependent obligation 1. A contractual obligation of such a kind that it cannot be enforced by a plaintiff unless the plaintiff has performed his or her own obligation; that is, performance by the plaintiff is a condition precedent to performance by the defendant. Alternatively, an obligation to perform which is dependent upon the prior occurrence of an event which neither party promised to bring about: for example *Perri v Coolangatta Investments Pty Ltd* (1982) 149 CLR 537; 41 ALR 441. 2. In the context of contracts which require concurrent performance, such as contracts for the sale of land, a dependent obligation refers to the parties' obligation to be ready and willing to perform: *Foran v Wight* (1989) 168 CLR 385; 88 ALR 413. See also **Concurrent conditions; Condition precedent; Independent obligation; Performance; Term.**

Dependent spouse The spouse of a taxpayer who relies on the contributions of the taxpayer for maintenance: (CTH) Income Tax Assessment Act 1936 ss 6(1), 159J(1). See also **Dependant; Dependant rebate; Spouse.**

Depletion An accounting term for the allocation of cost to production units removed or extracted from a wasting asset. The depletion charge per unit of output is calculated by dividing the cost of the resource by the total estimated number of units available (for example, tons of coal). Depletion charges are carried as inventory until sale of the goods.

Depletion accounting An accounting practice consisting of charges against earnings based upon the amount of an asset taken out of the total reserves in the period to which the accounting relates. A bookkeeping entry, it does not represent any cash outlay nor are any funds earmarked for the purpose. It is appropriate to natural resources, such as minerals, oil, gas, and timber, which conceivably can be reduced to zero over the years. See also **Natural resource accounting.**

Depose To give evidence which is written down and sworn or affirmed: *Registrar of Melbourne County Court v Richards; Ex Parte Farrington* [1861] Wilkinson's Magistrate, 7th Ed 274 (NSW). Historically, to testify as a witness; to give evidence under oath. See also **Affidavit; Deposition.**

•**Deposit** 1. A sum of money placed into an account with a bank or other financial institution. 2. A sum of money put down to secure an article.

Consumer credit In relation to a credit sale relating to goods and services, an amount that, under the contract, is payable by the buyer to the supplier on or before supply of the goods and services: (NSW) Credit Act 1984 (repealed) s 5(1) (now replaced by Uniform Consumer Credit Code). See also **Credit sale contract.**

Contract A payment in earnest. A contract may require the payer to tender a deposit on entering the contract to signify genuineness: for example *NLS Pty Ltd v Hughes* (1966) 120 CLR 583. See also **Contract; Earnest; Forfeiture; Liquidated damages; Relief against forfeiture.**

Corporations In relation to futures and options, the amount of money (or initial margin) which the clearing house requires to be paid prior to the registration of a contract. The clearing house determines a minimum deposit for futures and option contracts. See also **Clearing house; Futures contract; Option; Clearing deposit.**

•**Deposit account** See **Savings account.**

Deposit bank The bank with whom a holder deposits a cheque for collection: (CTH) Cheques and Payment Orders Act 1986 s 66(1). The bank has a duty to present the cheque for payment, or to make arrangements for collection to occur, as soon as is reasonably practicable, and is liable to the holder of the cheque for breach of this duty: (CTH) Cheques and Payment Orders Act 1986 s 66(1). See also **Cheque; Collecting bank; Collection; Holder; Presentment.**

Deposit certificate A certificate stating that a deposit of a certain amount was made at a bank for a nominated period and at a specific rate of interest. See also **Deposit bank; Interest; Option.**

Deposit of title deeds The leaving or depositing of title deeds with a lender as security for the loan, so constituting an equitable mortgage. In the Torrens system there is some debate over whether the lender should lodge a caveat: *J & H Just (Holdings) Pty Ltd v Bank of New South Wales* (1971) 125 CLR 546; [1972] ALR 323. See also **Equitable mortgage.**

•**Deposition** A statement or declaration made by a witness under oath which is reduced to writing for subsequent use in court proceedings. It is often made pursuant to a court order: *The Oxfordshire v Owners of the Cassapedia* (1988) 4 TLR 338. See also **Presentment.**

•**Depositor** Generally, a person who lodges or places money in, for example, a bank account. See also **Bank account; Banking service.**

•**Depreciable property** An asset, being plant or articles on which depreciation is or may be allowed in relation to the cost of acquiring that asset. Depreciation is only allowable on items of plant or articles which are used or installed ready for use for the purpose of earning assessable income: (CTH) Income Tax Assessment Act 1936 s 54. See also **Depreciation; Plant.**

Depreciated value For any given time, the cost of a unit of property to the person who owns or owned the property at that time, less the total amount of depreciation (if any) allowed in respect of that unit in assessments of the income of that person for any period prior to that time: (CTH) Income Tax Assessment Act 1936 s 62(1). Also known as 'written-down value' or 'net carrying amount'. See also **Assessment; Cost of plant; Depreciation.**

Depreciation The diminution in the original value of an asset, due to use or obsolescence, over the expected life of such an asset. Various methods are used to calculate and allow for the depreciation of an asset including the reducing balance method, the sinking fund method, and the straight line method. See also **Reducing balance method; Sinking fund method; Straight line**

method.

Taxation and revenue An allowable deduction for income taxation purposes, in respect of capital assets. The asset must constitute plant or articles and be used, or installed ready for use, for the purpose of earning assessable income: (CTH) Income Tax Assessment Act 1936 s 54(1). See also **Allowable deduction; Assessable income; Depreciable property; Depreciated value; Plant**.

•**Deputy Commissioner** See **Deputy Commissioner of Taxation**.

Deputy Commissioner of Taxation *Abbr* – DCT An assistant to the Commissioner of Taxation having the powers to act as the Commissioner of Taxation in certain circumstances: (CTH) Taxation Administration Act 1953 ss 7, 8. Also known as 'Deputy Commissioner'. See also **Commissioner of Taxation**.

Deputy Registrar in Bankruptcy A person holding the office of that name under the (CTH) Bankruptcy Act 1966. A Deputy Registrar can exercise the same powers and functions as a Registrar in Bankruptcy. In that event the power or function is deemed to have been exercised or performed by the Registrar: (CTH) Bankruptcy Act 1966 s 14(2A). There is no material difference between a Registrar in Bankruptcy and a Deputy Registrar in Bankruptcy except that there must be a Registrar in Bankruptcy for each bankruptcy district, while any Deputy Registrar is to be appointed only if determined by the Minister. See also **Bankrupt; Bankruptcy court; Registrar in Bankruptcy**.

De-registration The cancellation of registration of an organisation of employers or employees: (CTH) Industrial Relations Act 1988 s 234. Registration may be cancelled in several circumstances: for example, where the organisation is no longer representative of its members, or has engaged in industrial action that has a substantial adverse effect on the safety, health or welfare of the community: (CTH) Industrial Relations Act 1988 ss 294, 296. See also **Employee organisation; Employer organisation; Registration**.

•**Deregistration** Cancellation of a company's registration by the Australian Securities Commission (ASC). See also **External administration; Incorporation; Reinstatement**.

Deregulation The removal of statutory restrictions and regulations in certain specific areas of Australian commercial and industrial life. See also **Corporatisation; Floating; Floating exchange rate; Privatisation**.

Derivation See **Derived**.

•**Derivative** A financial or investment product whose value depends on the values of underlying variables, such as commodities, interest rates, currency exchange rates, securities, or indices. Some derivatives are traded on markets, such as the Australian options market and the futures market. See also **Equity derivative; Hedging; High gearing; Option; Security; Swap**.

Derivative lease A lease where the title granted or its terms depend for efficacy upon, or originate in, those of another lease: *Brumfit v Morton* (1857) 3 JurNS 1198. Unless expressly stated to the contrary it can be assumed that derivative leases are consistent with the head lease: *Waring v Hoggart* (1824) Ry & M 39; 171 ER 935. Also known as 'under lease' or 'sublease'. See also **Sublease**.

Derivative market A market offering products derived from a mainstream market, for example the Australian Options Market and the Australian Financial Futures Market. See also **Derivative; Futures contract; Market; Option**.

•**Derived** In relation to taxation, the assessable income of a taxpayer shall include the 'gross income derived from all sources': for example (CTH) Income Tax Assessment Act 1936 s 25(1). As such, an income tax liability does not arise until such time as the income is derived by the taxpayer. See also **Assessable income; Beneficial interest; Foreign source income**.

Derived demand The demand for a commodity not required for its own sake but for its contribution to the manufacture or operation of another commodity. For example, the demand for steel creates a derived demand for iron ore and energy.

•**Description** A contractual representation rather than an explanation of quality: (CTH) Trade Practices Act 1974 s 74C(1). A description may be applied physically to a product, such as on a label (for example *Newton v Mercury Power Australia Pty Ltd* (1986) ATPR ¶40-705; ASC 55-478) or applied putatively to a product, such as through promotional or advertising material, or by other forms of communications at the point of supply. See also **Correspondence with description**.

•**Design** The features of shape, configuration, pattern, or ornamentation applicable to an article of manufacture, including a part of such an article if made separately, that can be judged by the eye in the finished article: (CTH) Designs Act 1906 s 4(1). A method or principle of construction does not constitute a design: (CTH) Designs Act 1906 s 4(1). The fact that a design is functional in that the shape or configuration serves or serves only a functional purpose is not of itself a ground for refusal of registration or invalidity: (CTH) Designs Act 1906 s 18. Certain designs are excluded by regulation. A design is not an article made according to a particular shape or pattern: *Dalgety Australia Operations Ltd v F F Seeley Nominees Pty Ltd* (1985) 10 FCR 403; 68 ALR 458. A design is applied to an article to give the article a distinctive shape or pattern which can be judged by the eye. See also **Applied to an article; Design right; Designs Office**.

Design documents The documents that must be lodged when making an application for registration at the Designs Office: (CTH) Designs Act 1906 s 20(3). The (CTH) Designs Regulations 1982 prescribe the documents which are required for an application. See also **Designs Office**.

Design right The intellectual property right of the owner of a registered design. This right is a monopoly right ((CTH) Designs Act 1906 s 25) giving the exclusive right to apply the design to an article for which the design is registered: *Parkdale Custom Built Furniture Pty Ltd v Puxu Pty Ltd* (1982) 149 CLR 191. Where there are two or more owners of the design right, each can use the design for his or her purposes without accounting to the others, unless there is an agreement to the contrary: (CTH) Designs Act 1906 s 25A(2). See also **Obvious imitation**.

•**Designs Office** The office, under the control of the Registrar of Designs, responsible for the regulation and registration of designs in Australia. A Designs Office, and a sub-office in every State, is established under (CTH) Designs Act 1906 s 9.

Desk audit An audit which checks the income tax returns of salary and wage earners, persons who derive property income, and small businesses. A desk audit is conducted by way of interview. The taxpayer is requested to attend a specified Taxation Office and is required to produce receipts or other documents to support disclosures in the taxpayer's tax return. See also **Audit; Self assessment**.

Deskilling The process by which individuals are left without appropriate skills for new employment as a result of changes in work practices or the introduction of new technology.

Detection risk In a company audit, the risk that auditors' procedures will not detect a misstatement that exists in an account balance or class of transactions that could be material, individually or when aggregated with misstatements in other balances or classes: Statement of Auditing Practice AUP 27 para 16. The level of detection risk relates specifically to auditors' procedures and some detection risk will always be present even if auditors were to examine 100 per cent of the account balance or class of transactions: AUP 27 para 16. See also **Audit risk; Control risk; Inherent risk; Statement of Auditing Standards**.

•**Detention** The keeping of persons or property in custody.

Insurance The removal from a property-owner of the power of disposition of property by a government in times of hostility, such as war.

Determinable future time In relation to a bill of exchange, a fixed period after date or sight; or the time of occurrence, or a fixed period after occurrence, of a specified event which is certain to happen (even if the time of happening is uncertain): (CTH) Bills of Exchange Act 1909 s 16. An instrument expressed to be payable on a contingency is not a bill of exchange, and the happening of the event does not cure the defect: *Baker v Efford* (1873) 4 AJR 161. See also **Bill of exchange; Contingency**.

•**Determine 1.** To make an order, direction, decision, or determination by a court or tribunal, or other authority vested with the power to so make a determination in relation to some matter: for example (VIC) Planning Appeals Act 1980 s 3; *Grace v Southern* [1978] VR 75 at 78; *Racecourse Co-operative Sugar Assn Ltd v A-G (Qld)* (1979) 142 CLR 460; 26 ALR 321. **2.** To bring to an end. For example, a lease is determined when it terminates or comes to an end. In this context a lease may be determined only in accordance with the contract of lease or where a party elects to accept the other party's repudiation of his or her obligations under the lease: *Progressive Mailing House v Tabali Pty Ltd* (1985) 157 CLR 17; 57 ALR 609. See also **Determine**.

•**Determining authority** A Minister or public authority by or on whose behalf an activity is or is to be carried out or any Minister or public authority whose approval is required in order to enable the activity to be carried out. References to determining authorities within State Acts apply to authorities and Ministers of the particular State in which the legislation was enacted but do not usually extend to Commonwealth authorities and Ministers. See also **Public authority**.

Detinue The wrongful detention of goods after the plaintiff's lawful request for their return: for example *John F Goulding Pty Ltd v Victorian Railways Cmrs* (1932) 48 CLR 157; [1932] VLR 408. Detinue arises irrespective of the manner of the original acquisition. The right of action accrues at the time of the refusal to hand over, not at the time of the original acquisition, even if that acquisition is wrongful: *John F Goulding Pty Ltd v Victorian Railways Cmrs*. See also **Conversion; Tort; Trespass**.

Deutsche Bank Australia A wholly-owned subsidiary of Deutsche Bank AG which is the largest bank in Germany and among the major banking groups in the world. Deutsche has been represented in Australia since 1973, being granted an Australian banking licence in 1986. In 1989, the bank acquired a 50 per cent ownership interest in the Australian stockbroking and investment banking firm, Bain and Company. Since 1986, the strategy of the bank has been to concentrate on wholesale and corporate banking business, with group investment banking activities being undertaken by Bain and Company. See also **Deregulation; Foreign bank**.

Devaluation A fall in the value of a nation's currency compared with others either deliberately when exchange rates are fixed, or through the effect of international influences when the exchange rate is floating. See also **Deregulation; Exchange rate; Float**.

•**Developing country** A shorthand term used in international relations to describe a country lacking comparable economic growth to its western counterparts. The developing countries embrace diverse cultural, ideological, and political backgrounds, and for the most part share the common experience of having been formerly subject to colonial domination.

Development mortgage A contributory mortgage where the land secured is to be developed using the finance raised from the mortgage. See also **Building mortgage; Contributory mortgage; Mortgage**.

Development risks defence The defence available to a manufacturer in a product liability claim that alleges a defect in design, formulation, or information, in circumstances where the product was defective when supplied, but the defect was neither known nor reasonably discoverable by the manufacturer given the state of scientific and technological knowledge at the time: *Hindustan Steam Shipping Co Ltd v Siemens Bros & Co Ltd* [1955] 1 Lloyd's Rep 167; *E v Australian Red Cross Society* (1991) 31 FCR 299; 105 ALR 53; (CTH) Trade Practices Act 1974 s 75AK(1)(c). See also **Consumer product safety standard; Product liability**.

Deviation A departure from the originally anticipated route.

Carriers 1. A departure from the originally anticipated route to be followed in performing a contract of carriage. A common carrier is bound to go by the usual route: *Hales v London and North Western Railway Co* (1863) 4 B & S 66; 122 ER 384. A private carrier is obliged to follow the route stipulated expressly or by implication in the contract. Whether or not provided for by the contract, a deviation will be excusable to save life, to avoid the stress of weather or imminent danger, if it flows from unintentionally adopting a mistaken course (*Rio Tinto Co Ltd v Seed Shipping Co Ltd* (1926) 24 Ll L Rep 316), or where the charterer has failed to provide a full and complete cargo for the vessel (*Wallems Rederej A/S v W H Muller & Co, Batavia* [1927] 2 KB 99). A deviation that is not justifiable entitles the charterer to treat the charter as at an end, or to sue for damages. **2.** In aviation, an emergency deviation from instructions given by air traffic control may only be made after the pilot has informed air traffic control of the intention to make it. See also **Contract of carriage; Deviation rule; Exclusion of liability clause.**

Deviation rule A rule applied to bailment contracts and contracts for carriage by sea, land, and rail, by which a carrier of goods who deviates from the agreed voyage as a result loses the benefit of otherwise applicable exclusion clauses: *Thomas National Transport (Melbourne) Pty Ltd v May & Baker (Aust) Pty Ltd* (1966) 115 CLR 353; [1967] ALR 3. See also **Construction; Exclusion clause.**

•**Devolution** The involuntary passing of property from one person to another by operation of law; for example, upon death, bankruptcy, or insolvency: *Australian Trade Commission v Film Funding and Management Pty Ltd* (1989) 24 FCR 595; 87 ALR 49. See also **Interest; Property.**

DFAT See **Department of Foreign Affairs and Trade.**

Diagonal privity The privity of contract, if any, that exists between an importer, manufacturer, or distributor of a product, and a person who acquires that product from its last commercial supplier. See also **Horizontal privity; Privity of contract.**

Differences In corporations law, the net change in the price of shares or futures in the period between the contract of sale and the settlement of the transaction.

Diminishing returns The principle that additional capital or labour invested will result in a smaller return, after a certain point, than the yield from the original amount invested.

DINGO bond In relation to securities, a discounted negotiable government obligation which is a type of zero-coupon bond. Investors traditionally have used DINGO bonds to deposit funds by purchasing interest coupons at a discount which at maturity yield an amount of income which would not be taxed until then, even though interest would be compounding during the term. Part of the overall general yield on DINGO bonds and other discounted and deferred interest securities is now taxed on an accruals basis under (CTH) Income Tax Assessment Act 1936 ss 159GP-GZ. See also **Accrual; Bond; Zero-coupon bond.**

Direct assignment The transference of an intangible right in property, enforceable through action, which is made directly to the person intended and not through a third party. Unlike a declaration of trust, which requires an intention to create the trust evidenced by some act to this end, a direct assignment requires an intention to assign and an act of assignment: *Shepherd v FCT* (1965) 113 CLR 385 at 391. See also **Chose in action.**

Direct cost In public administration, that cost which can be readily attributed to a specific program or activity, being incurred solely for the benefit of that program. See also **Indirect cost.**

Direct entry transactions The transmission and electronic processing of payments in bulk. Payments are exchanged either by magnetic tape or, increasingly, by direct computer-to-computer linkages. In some countries, these arrangements are centralised in an automated clearing house but in Australia, data are exchanged bilaterally. Since March 1994, banks, building societies, and credit unions have been linked in an integrated but decentralised national system. See also **Clearing house; Clearance system.**

Direct tax A tax for which the person liable is the person who in practice bears the burden of payment. Examples include income tax, wealth tax, inheritance taxes, and direct consumption taxes. See also **Consumption tax; Death duty; Income taxation; Wealth tax.**

•**Direct voting system** In relation to an election for an office in an employer or employee organisation, a method of election at which all financial members, or all financial members included in the appropriate branch, section, class, or other division of the organisation, are eligible to vote: (CTH) Industrial Relations Act 1988 s 4. See also **Employee organisation; Employer organisation.**

Directing mind and will The persons embodying the mind and will of a corporation, comprising the board of directors, the managing directors, other superior officers, and those delegated with such a high degree of responsibility for the management of the company that they can be said to be acting as the corporation rather than for the corporation: *Tesco Supermarkets Ltd v Nattrass* [1972] AC 153; [1971] 2 All ER 127. At common law, in order to fix primary liability on a company, it is necessary to consider the mental state of the person or persons who constituted its directing mind and will: *Lennard's Carrying Co Ltd v Asiatic Petroleum Co Ltd* [1915] AC 705; [1914-15] All ER Rep 280. See also **Corporate offence; Directors' duties; Managing director.**

•**Directions hearing** In relation to the Administrative Appeals Tribunal, a hearing at which orders are given in relation to the suppression of parties' names or evidence: (CTH) Administrative Appeals Tribunal Act 1975 s 35(2). See also **Administrative Appeals Tribunal.**

•**Director** A person employed as an officer of a company and having a duty to perform the duties of management of the business of the company, acting as a member of the board of directors: Corporations Law Sch 1 Table A art 66. A proprietary company must have at least one director, while a public company must have at least five directors. See also **Alternate director; Associate director; Board of directors; De facto director; Direc-**

tors' duties; **Executive director**; **Governing director**; **Managing director**; **Nominee director**; **Officer**; **Shadow director**.

Directors' duties The duties and obligations imposed personally upon directors of companies by the common law and statute, including the Corporations Law. Duties arise largely from the fiduciary position held by the director and include the duty to act in good faith for the benefit of the company as a whole (for example *Howard Smith Ltd v Ampol Petroleum Ltd* [1974] AC 821; (1974) 3 ALR 448); the duty to exercise powers only for proper corporate purposes (Corporations Law s 232(2)) the statutory duty to act honestly (s 232(4)); the duty to act with care, skill, and diligence (*Daniels v Anderson* (1995) 16 ACSR 607) and the duty to avoid certain conflicts of interest (*Phipps v Boardman* [1967] 2 AC 46; [1966] 3 All ER 721; *Chan v Zacharia* (1984) 154 CLR 178; 53 ALR 417). See also **Corporate capacity**; **Directing mind and will**; **Duty not to fetter discretions**; **Duty to act for proper purposes**; **Duty to act honestly**; **Duty to act in good faith for the benefit of the company as a whole**; **Duty to act with care, skill and diligence**; **Improper use of information**; **Improper use of position**.

Director's loan A loan from a company's funds to one or more of its directors. The provision of a loan to a director falls within the definition of 'financial benefit' in Corporations Law s 243G(4). A financial benefit may not be given to the director of a public company unless it is provided on an arm's length basis (s 24N) Corporations Law s 243N) or has been agreed to by the company's members (s 243Q). See also **Arm's length transaction**; **Financial benefit**; **Related party**.

Directors' meeting See **Board of directors meeting**.

Director's performance fee Money payable to directors if the company's performance reaches certain targeted levels. Such payments may be based on the share price which the company's shares reach or the level of profits earned. See also **Director's remuneration**; **Emolument**.

Director's qualification share See **Qualification share**.

Directors' register See **Register of directors, principal executive officers and secretaries**.

Director's remuneration The money received by a person for performing the office of director of a company. A notice sent by 10 per cent of a company's members (or members holding five per cent of the nominal value of its issued share capital) may require disclosure of the emoluments and other benefits received by the directors of the company or of a subsidiary: Corporations Law s 239. Payment of remuneration to a director is subject to the related party benefit rules unless it is reasonable for a body corporate in the circumstances of that body corporate to provide such remuneration to an officer in that person's circumstances: s 243K(1), (4). See also **Director**; **Directors' duties**; **Emolument**; **Financial benefit**.

Directors' report In corporations law, a report required to be adopted by resolution of directors of a company (dated and signed by at least two directors) and containing various details. See also **Directors' statement**; **Disclosure**; **Dividend**.

Directors' resolution A resolution passed at a meeting of the board of directors. The resolution must be the act of the directors collectively; the individual assent of the majority will not normally suffice: *D'Arcy v Tamar, Kit Hill & Calligan Railway Co* (1866) LR 2 Exch 158 at 161. See also **Board of directors' meeting**; **Resolution**.

Directors, rotation of See **Rotation of directors**.

Directors' statement In corporations law, a statement required to be attached to a company's annual accounts. It states, in the opinion of the directors, whether the profit and loss account gives a true and fair view of the profit or loss for the financial year, the balance sheet gives a true and fair view of the state of affairs as at the end of the financial year, and, at the date of the statement, whether there are reasonable grounds to believe that the company will be able to pay its debts as and when they fall due: Corporations Law ss 301-303. See also **Directors' report**; **Insolvent**; **True and fair view**.

Dirty bill of lading A bill of lading containing a qualification as to the condition or quality of the goods on their being loaded. Such conditions are necessary where the goods are defective or damaged when loaded, because they will be compared to their description in the bill of lading on discharge at their destination in order to determine if any deterioration has occurred during the voyage. A dirty bill of lading will usually be indorsed by the master of the vessel. Also known as 'claused bill of lading' or 'unclean bill of lading': *Compania Naviera Vasconzada v Churchill* [1906] 1 KB 237. See also **Bill of lading**; **Clean bill of lading**; **Goods**; **Master**.

•**Discharge** To relieve oneself, or to be relieved, of an obligation or liability.

Contract The extinguishment or release of obligations under a contract. A contract may be discharged by performance, by an agreement supported by consideration, by an implied agreement, or by estoppel: *DTR Nominees Pty Ltd v Mona Homes Pty Ltd* (1978) 138 CLR 423; 19 ALR 223. See also **Breach of contract**; **Contract**; **Discharge by agreement**; **Estoppel**; **Frustration**; **Partial discharge**; **Repudiation**; **Termination**.

Discharge by agreement A consensual discharge of contractual obligations resulting from the agreement of the parties to a contract of discharge or a contract of abandonment. The consensual nature of discharge by agreement means that it is subject to the normal rules of contract formation, including consideration. Discharge by agreement may arise from an express or an implied agreement: for example *DTR Nominees Pty Ltd v Mona Homes Pty Ltd* (1978) 138 CLR 423; 19 ALR 223. Also known as 'discharge by consent'. See also **Abandonment**; **Consideration**; **Discharge**; **Discharge by performance**; **Novation**; **Rescission**; **Variation**.

Discharge by performance The discharge of a contract as a result of each party actually performing his or her contractual obligations. As a general rule, to effect a discharge the performance should be exactly in accordance with the terms of the contract: *Cutler v*

Powell (1795) 6 TR 320; 101 ER 573. However, the courts do ignore trivial deviations (*de minimus non curat lex*): for example *Shipton, Anderson & Co v Well Brothers & Co* [1912] 1 KB 574 at 577. See also **Discharge; Divisible contract; Performance; Substantial performance**.

Discharge for breach The discharge of a contract as a result of a party breaching an essential term or condition or repudiating the contract: *Associated Newspapers Ltd v Bancks* (1951) 83 CLR 322; *Progressive Mailing House v Tabali* (1985) 157 CLR 17; 57 ALR 609. See also **Anticipatory breach; Breach of contract; Condition; Discharge; Repudiation; Term**.

Discharge of bankruptcy The process by which an individual who has been the subject of a bankruptcy order is released from the status of a bankrupt and consequently from most debts provable in the bankruptcy. The discharge affects the rights and status of the individual and not the bankruptcy itself which continues until the trustee completes the administration of the estate: (CTH) Bankruptcy Act 1966 ss 152, 153. See also **Annulment; Automatic discharge; Bankruptcy; Contribution by bankrupt; Discharge of bankruptcy; Dividend; Objection to discharge; Official Receiver; Statement of affairs; Trustee in bankruptcy**.

Discharge of deed To release a person from obligations imposed by a deed. At common law, a deed could only be discharged by performance or by another deed: *McDermott v Black* (1940) 63 CLR 161 at 187. Equity, however, allows a deed to be discharged by a simple contract, written or oral: *Slee v Warke* (1949) 86 CLR 271 at 281; *Creamoata Ltd v Rice Equalization Association Ltd* (1953) 89 CLR 286 at 306, 326. See also **Deed; Discharge; Performance**.

Discharge of negotiable instrument Complete extinguishment of all rights and liabilities on a negotiable instrument, terminating its life and negotiability: (CTH) Bills of Exchange Act 1909 s 41(1)(b). Distinguished from discharge of a party, discharge of the instrument extinguishes the instrument itself, rendering it a mere piece of paper of evidentiary value only. A negotiable instrument may be discharged by payment in due course, merger, renunciation, cancellation, or material alteration: (CTH) Bills of Exchange Act 1909 ss 64(1), 67(1), 68(1); (CTH) Cheques and Payment Orders Act 1986 s 78. See also **Cancellation; Discharge of party; Material alteration; Merger; Payment in due course; Renunciation**.

Discharge of party The release from liability of one or more parties to a bill of exchange, not resulting in discharge of the instrument. For example, an indorser may be required to reimburse a subsequent indorsee in the event of dishonour; the bill will not be not discharged because the indorser who has made payment will still have recourse to prior parties. See also **Bill of exchange; Cancellation; Discharge of negotiable instrument; Indorser; Indorsee; Renunciation**.

•**Disciplinary action** Action taken in response to misconduct or breach of discipline.

Employment Reasonable lawful action taken against an employee in the nature of, or promoting, discipline: *Commission for Safety and Rehabilitation of Commonwealth Employees v Chenhall* (1992) 37 FCR 75; 109 ALR 361. Generally, disciplinary action includes a decision by an employer to defer paying an increment to the employee, or to reduce the rank, classification, position, grade, or pay of the employee; to impose a fine or forfeit pay; to annul the appointment of an employee on probation; or to suspend or dismiss the employee: for example (NSW) Government and Related Employees Appeal Tribunal Act 1980 s 23. In other circumstances, it may involve cancelling or amending a licence: for example (NSW) Casino Control Act 1992 s 23. It does not include an action taken to determine whether or not disciplinary action is to be taken against an employee: *Commission for the Safety, Rehabilitation and Compensation of Commonwealth Employees v Chenhall* (1992) 37 FCR 75; 109 ALR 361.

Disclaim To deny a claim or to renounce a right or interest. In bankruptcy law, the trustee in bankruptcy may disclaim certain property vested in him or her and which is divisible amongst creditors, where it is unlikely to be able to be realised as a net gain to the bankrupt estate: (CTH) Bankruptcy Act 1966 s 133.

•**Disclaimer** A repudiation of liability, interest, or benefit.

Contract A term of a contract that seeks to exclude or limit a party's liability in contract or tort. Liability for even particularly serious breaches of contract may be limited: *Davis v Pearce Parking Station Pty Ltd* (1954) 91 CLR 642 at 649. However, where the disclaimer is contained in a document issued in the course of the transaction or otherwise displayed or notified, the party relying on it must show that he or she gave reasonable notice of the term to the other party: *Oceanic Sun Line Special Shipping Co Inc v Fay* (1988) 165 CLR 197; 79 ALR 9. Disclaimers are interpreted narrowly: for example *Sydney City Council v West* (1965) 114 CLR 481. A disclaimer may be invalid where it is inconsistent with a statutory provision, even if it is not expressly prohibited: for example *Australian National Railways Commission v Ranger Uranium Mines Pty Ltd* (1989) 51 SASR 475. Also known as 'exemption clause', 'exclusion clause', 'exception clause', or 'limitation clause'. See also **Disclaimer; Exclusion clause; Limitation clause**.

Deeds and other instruments A solemn and irrevocable refusal to accept a benefit under a deed or other document; an act by which the person entitled to an estate immediately, and before dealing with it, renounces it: *Bence v Gilpin* (1868) LR 3 Ex 76. Property transferred by deed vests in the grantee at once. However, when informed of the transfer, the grantee may disclaim it: *Standing v Bowring* (1885) 31 Ch D 282; [1881-8] All ER Rep 702. Upon disclaimer, the grant is avoided and the property sought to be transferred is divested from the donee and revests in the donor. See also **Deed; Grant; Vesting**.

Product liability Words or conduct that prevent liability from arising with respect to an innocent or negligent misrepresentation, or representation or conduct that otherwise might be considered misleading or deceptive within the meaning of (CTH) Trade Practices

Act 1974 s 52: for example *CBS Records Australia Ltd v Telmak Teleproducts (Aust) Pty Ltd* (1987) 8 IPR 473; ATPR ¶40-783. See also **Misleading or deceptive conduct; Misstatement.**

Disclaimer of onerous property The act of a trustee in bankruptcy which abandons the interest of the bankrupt in specified property and obligations of the bankrupt relating to that property. See also **Proof of debt; Trustee in bankruptcy.**

Disclosing entity In corporations law an entity which is a listed corporation or a listed prescribed interest scheme which raises funds pursuant to a prospectus, offers securities other than debentures as consideration for an acquisition of shares in a takeover, or whose securities are issued under a compromise or scheme: Corporations Law Pt 1.2A. A disclosing entity must cause financial statements to be made out for both the financial year and the half-year (the first six months of the financial year): s 50A. See also **Compromise; Entity; Listed body; Prescribed interest scheme; Scheme; Takeover.**

Disclosure Making available information to the public in general or to limited classes of people.

Administrative law 1. The principle of procedural fairness requires that evidence placed before a decision maker by one party must be disclosed to other parties, who must be given an opportunity to oppose it: *Sullivan v Department of Transport* (1978) 1 ALD 383; 20 ALR 323. 2. A requirement that the documents of an agency be made available to the public or to an individual requester, by means of inspection or copies: (CTH) Freedom of Information Act 1982. See also **Freedom of information.**

Agency In relation to a conflict between a fiduciary's duty and interest, provision by the agent to the principal of the information that an average commercial person would consider is required by the principal to remedy a potential breach of fiduciary duty: *Buttonwood Nominees Pty Ltd v Sundowner Minerals NL* (1986) 10 ACLR 360. Disclosure requires the agent to reveal both the nature and the extent of the conflicting interest or profit-making opportunity. See also **Conflict of interest; Fiduciary; Non-disclosure.**

Corporations An act of imparting that which is secret or not commonly known, particularly the revelation of facts that are relevant to the person to whom the declaration is made. Under the Corporations Law, a director of a proprietary company who is in any way interested in a contract with the company must disclose the nature of the interest: Corporations Law s 231. See also **Conflict rule; Profit rule; Directors' duties.**

Employment The duty on an employee to disclose to the employer information that indicates that the employee is unable to carry out the contract, or that employment of the employee would amount to breach of statutory provisions by the employer. If the employee fails to disclose such information, the contract of employment will be void or voidable for misinformation. An employee is not under a general duty to disclose adverse information about himself or herself, such as a criminal record: *Gill v Colonial Mutual Life Assurance Society Ltd* [1912] VLR 146. However, where the employee is directed to provide information, failure to do so, or to provide it honestly, is a breach of the duty to obey lawful orders: *Associated Dominion Assurance Society Pty Ltd v Andrew* (1949) 49 SR (NSW) 351. The duty is an aspect of the employee's general duty to perform well and faithfully the work contractually agreed. See also **Duty of faithful service; Duty of obedience.**

Insurance The duty imposed upon both parties to a contract of insurance to reveal in the negotiations leading up to the formation or renewal of the contract, all facts of which they are aware and which are material to the proposed insurance: *Carter v Boehm* (1766) 3 Burr 1905; 97 ER 1162. See also **Materiality; Misunderstood disclosure; Uberrimae fidei.**

Disclosure, duty of See **Duty to disclose.**

•**Discount** A reduction of a sum of money by a specified or calculated amount.

Corporations The difference between the price at which a security was issued and the price at which it now stands (the par value), if the latter is the lower. See also **Bank bill; Deliverable futures contract; Futures contract; Par value; Security; Share premium; Share.**

Damages In the context of damages, a reduction of an award to a plaintiff to take account of such factors as accelerated receipt of benefit, events subsequent to a breach of contract, and accrued rights of the defendant. For example, an award will be discounted where a creditor sues a debtor (or the debtor's guarantor) who has promised to pay a debt by instalments, in respect of the sums which had not fallen due for payment at the time the plaintiff terminated the contract: *W & J Investments Ltd v Bunting* [1984] 1 NSWLR 331. See also **Accrued right; Cause of action; Damages; Performance; Termination.**

Trade and commerce 1. A reduction in an advertised price granted to a customer or group of customers; a rebate a trader gives for prompt payment; or a reward for early settlement: *Talcott Factors Ltd v G Seifert Pty Ltd* [1964] NSWR 1205. 2. A price reduction received for prompt payment (cash discount) or for custom when paying within the stipulated trading terms (trade discount) or for bulk purchasing where the large quantity purchased enables the seller to give a lower price (quantity discount). See also **Cash price; Discount rate; Terms of trade.**

Discount a bill To sell a bill of exchange before it is due for payment. The price is calculated by applying a discount rate to the face value of the bill taking into account the time left to run to maturity and any risk of non-payment, to ascertain the present worth of the bill. See also **Discount; Bill of exchange.**

Discount broker A merchant who cashes discountable securities, usually bills of exchange, on behalf of his or her principal. The discount of a bill of exchange is a negotiation of it or the purchase of it for a sum less than its face value, and normally with a right of recourse. Discounting is a means of raising money but is not a borrowing in the way that a pledge is. See also **Bill of exchange; Broker; Discount a bill.**

Discount house 1. A United Kingdom business institution which will buy acceptances from their owners for less than their face value and hold them to maturity. The twelve members of the London Discount Market Association have a right to borrow from the Bank of England as lender of last resort should they become short of money as a result of the calling in of loans by the commercial banks who lend to them. **2.** A retailer specialising in consumer goods, both durable and soft, attracting customers with low, competitive prices, operating on low mark-ups. See also **Acceptance; Bill of exchange; Consumer sale; Markup.**

Discount issue The issuing of shares for a consideration equivalent to less than their nominal or par value: for example *Re Jarass Pty Ltd* (1988) 13 ACLR 728 at 729; 6 ACLC 767. Subject to Corporations Law s 190 a company must not issue shares at a discount: s 203(2). See also **Hawking of securities; Par value; Share premium.**

Discount rate 1. In accounting the compound annual rate by which the value of future payments must be discounted to obtain their present value or worth. Three alternative bases have been proposed for the setting of discount rates: social time preference, opportunity cost of capital, and the cost of funds. These concepts are difficult to apply; consequently, a common solution is to apply a set of real (inflation-discounted) discount rates of four per cent, seven per cent and 10 per cent, for example. Essentially, the central discount rate is seven per cent, sensitivity tests being applied with the use of the four per cent and 10 per cent rates. **2.** In foreign exchange terms, a margin by which the forward rate falls below the spot rate. See also **Foreign exchange market; Present value.**

Discounted cash flow method A method of comparing the prospective profitability of alternative investment projects. Investments are rated according to the present value or worth of future revenues discounted at compound interest, minus future costs discounted in a similar manner. This method may be applied in two ways. The yield approach is based upon the assumption that the best investment is that from which the proceeds would yield the highest rate of compound interest in equating the present value of the investment with future proceeds. In the net present value approach, an appropriate percentage rate is stipulated, the present value of the net cash flow being determined using this percentage. The initial cost of the investment is subtracted from this, the resulting surplus being the net present value of the investment. See also **Investment policy; Investment value; Present value.**

Discounted share issue See **Discount issue.**

Discounted shares See **Discount issue.**

Discounts, allowances, rebates or credits The hidden benefits which a vendor may give to a purchaser. The consideration of such benefits was important in considering whether there has been a breach of the price discrimination provision of trade practices legislation: (CTH) Trade Practices Act 1974 s 49 (repealed). See also **Discount; Price discrimination; Terms of trade.**

•**Discretionary account** In relation to securities trading, an account over which a person has conferred authority on a broker to initiate trades without prior reference to, or approval of, the person: Corporations Law s 9. Contrast non-discretionary account. See also **Broker; Non-discretionary account; Securities business.**

Discretionary income The amount of income available to spend after tax and the cost of necessities such as food and housing have been deducted.

•**Discretionary trust 1.** A trust in which the trustee has a discretion as to when any payment from the trust fund will be made, who, in a definite class of beneficiaries, will receive it, and the amount of such payment: *Federal Cmr of Taxation v Vegners* (1989) 90 ALR 547; 20 ATR 1645. **2.** A trust where property vests on the non-exercise of a discretion conferred by the trust: (NSW) Land Tax Management Act 1956 s 3(1). Where the trustee has the power to withhold income and capital altogether it is known as 'purely discretionary'. See also **Beneficiary; Express trust; Fixed trust; Trust; Trustee.**

•**Discrimination** Any distinction, exclusion, restriction, or preference made on a particular basis, such as race, sex, religion, national origin, marital status, pregnancy, or disability, which has the purpose or effect of nullifying or impairing the recognition, enjoyment, or exercise, on an equal footing, of human rights and fundamental freedoms in the political, economic, social, cultural, or any other field of life: International Convention on the Elimination of All Forms of Racial Discrimination 1966. See also **Racial discrimination; Sex discrimination; Unlawful discrimination.**

Discriminatory award A federal award that has been referred to the Australian Industrial Relations Commission (AIRC) under the (CTH) Sex Discrimination Act 1984 s 50A, and that requires a person to do any act that would be unlawful under the (CTH) Sex Discrimination legislation except for the fact that the act would be done in direct compliance with an award: (CTH) Industrial Relations Act 1988 s 113(5). If the AIRC considers that the award is discriminatory, it must remove the discrimination by setting aside or varying the award. See also **Australian Industrial Relations Commission; Award; Sex discrimination.**

Diseconomies of scale In accounting, a characteristic of growth where the long-run average costs of an enterprise or industry increase as the scale of production increases. In the case of an enterprise, the increasing costs may be due to increasing costs in the acquisition of raw materials. In the case of an industry, there may also be increasing external costs also and perhaps increases in the real cost of labour generally. Finance generally may become more expensive for both the enterprise and the industry, as risks and uncertainties increase. See also **Cost-effectiveness analysis; Economies of scale; Productivity.**

•**Dishonest** Discreditable; at variance with straightforward or honest dealing: *R v Salvo* [1980] VR 401; (1979) 5 A Crim R 1. An act is dishonest if it is done in the knowledge that it will produce adverse consequences for others: *R v Bonollo* [1981] VR 633; (1980) 2 A Crim R 431; (ACT) Crimes Act 1900 s 96(4)(b).

•**Dishonour** Refusal by a drawee to accept, or pay on, a negotiable instrument according to its terms. The holder of a bill of exchange dishonoured by non-acceptance or non-payment has an immediate right of recourse against the drawer and indorsers: (CTH) Bills of Exchange Act 1909 ss 48(2), 52(2). A cheque is dishonoured where it is duly presented and payment is refused by the drawee bank, being a refusal communicated by the drawee bank to the holder of the cheque: (CTH) Cheques and Payment Orders Act 1986 s 69. See also **Dishonour by non-acceptance; Drawee; Holder; Indorsee; Notice of dishonour.**

Dishonour by non-acceptance Dishonour of a bill of exchange where: it is duly presented for acceptance, and acceptance is refused or cannot be obtained; or presentment for acceptance is excused, and the bill is not accepted: (CTH) Bills of Exchange Act 1909 s 48(1). A bill not accepted within the customary time must be treated as dishonoured by non-acceptance, lest the holder lose the right of recourse against the drawer or indorsers: (CTH) Bills of Exchange Act 1909 s 47. See also **Bill of exchange; Dishonour; Presentation for acceptance; Presentation for payment; Qualified acceptance.**

Disintermediation By-passing intermediaries, as when lenders lend money directly to borrowers or when investors invest directly in the share market without going through brokers. The Australian financial system, however, is based largely on intermediation. See also **Finance broker; Financial corporation; Intermediation.**

•**Dismissal** The discharging of a person; the order for their departure.

Employment The termination of an employee's contract of employment by the employer, or the removal of a person from an office. It includes ending the work of the person by compulsory retirement, or by failure to provide work: for example (QLD) Anti-Discrimination Act 1991 s 15. See also **Compulsory retirement; Contract of employment; Redundancy; Retrenchment; Unfair dismissal; Wrongful dismissal.**

Disposable income The amount of income remaining after tax has been deducted.

Disposal of shares For the purposes of Corporations Law, a person disposes of shares in a body corporate if, having a relevant interest in those shares, the person ceases to have a relevant interest in those shares: Corporations Law s 51(2). See also **Body corporate; Share.**

Disposal of uncollected goods See **Uncollected goods.**

•**Dispose of** In general terms, to pass into the control of another person, to alienate, relinquish, part with, or get rid of.

Corporations In relation to shares or marketable securities of a company for the purposes of Corporations Law Ch 6, to cease to have a relevant interest in those shares or marketable securities: s 9. See also **Close out; Futures option; Marketable securities; Share.**

Real property In respect of real estate, to get rid of, sell, or leave by will. See also **Convey; Sell.**

•**Disposition** Any alienation of property for the benefit of any person, even if subject to any limitation.

•**Disposition of property** Transfer of proprietary rights.

Corporations Any act by which proprietary rights are transferred from a company to a disponee. It includes the creation of a floating charge: *Re Helmar Pty Ltd (in liq); Ex parte Verge v Reppoc Mines Pty Ltd* (1992) 8 ACSR 301. See also **Winding up.**

•**Dispute in an industry** See **Industrial dispute.**

•**Dispute order** An order made by the Industrial Relations Commission of New South Wales, ordering a person to cease or to refrain from industrial action: (NSW) Industrial Relations Act 1996 s 137. An order may only be made if conciliation has been attempted or a compulsory conference has been held in relation to the dispute. See also **Industrial action.**

Dispute resolution The settlement of a conflict between parties. 'Dispute resolution' is generally taken to comprehend the entire range of techniques used to resolve conflicts within and outside courtrooms including those that are cooperative in approach. See also **Adjudication; Alternative Dispute Resolution; Commercial dispute resolution; Conciliation; Mediation.**

Dispute review board A board established as a form of dispute resolution to oversee a particular project or operation, and to review any disputes which may arise during its course. The board becomes familiar with a contract and its performance, and conflicts can be dealt with or foreseen with a minimum of delay, while allowing performance to continue. The board usually has three members, each party to the contract appointing a member and these two members appointing the third. The method is most common in the construction industry, where the length and complexity of the work increases the potential for disputes. See also **Alternative dispute resolution; Contract adjudicator.**

Disqualification order against director An order made by the court prohibiting a person from managing a corporation: Corporations Law ss 599, 600. Managing is defined as being a director, promoter, or in any way managing a corporation: Corporations Law s 91A(3). See also **Director; Directors' duties; Promoter.**

•**Dissenting shareholder** A shareholder who, in relation to a scheme or contract, has not complied with the scheme or contract or has not transferred shares in accordance with the scheme or contract: Corporations Law s 414(1). See also **Compulsory acquisition of shares; Shareholder; Takeover scheme.**

Dissolution Generally, the termination of a registered association of two or more persons, such as a marriage, an unincorporated association, a partnership, or a corporation, which enjoyed certain legal rights or privileges. See also **External administration; Incorporation; Winding up.**

Corporations The act of undoing or breaking up of a registered company. On dissolution the company ceases to be a legal person and is removed from the register of companies. See also **Deregistration; External administration; Winding up.**

Partnerships The ending or breaking up a partnership. A partner wishing to leave the partnership must give notice to the other partners (for example (QLD) Partnership Act 1891 s 35) and must do so bona fide and not to derive some advantage: *Featherstonhaugh v Fenwick* (1810) 17 Ves 298; [1803-13] All ER Rep 89. A partnership is also dissolved by the death or bankruptcy of any partner, the expiration of the term (where it is a fixed term partnership), the firm unlawfully carrying on business, or by order of court: for example (NSW) Partnership Act 1892 ss 32-35. See also **Expulsion of partner**; **Partnership**; **Partnership agreement**; **Retiring partner**.

Voluntary associations Bringing an association to its end so that it no longer exists. The association's constitution may provide procedures for dissolution. Alternatively, the association's members may agree unanimously to dissolve the association: *Master Grocers' Assn of Victoria v Northern District Grocers Co-op Ltd* [1983] 1 VR 195. See also **Association**; **Constitution**; **Unincorporated association**; **Winding up**.

•**Distinctiveness** 1. In trade marks law, the capacity of the trade mark to distinguish the goods or services of the trade mark proprietor from the goods or services of others. Distinctiveness is determined having regard to the inherent capacity of the mark to distinguish by use and other circumstances, but may be regarded as distinctive by reason only of use: (CTH) Trade Marks Act 1995 s 41. 2. In relation to passing off, the requirement that the plaintiff establish a goodwill or reputation in the name or mark such that it distinguishes the plaintiff's goods or business: *ConAgra Inc v McCain Foods (Aust) Pty Ltd* (1992) 33 FCR 302; 106 ALR 465. See also **Market reputation**; **Passing off**; **Trade mark**.

Distinguished talent visa A permanent visa granted to a person who can show that he or she displays an exceptional record of achievement in an occupation, profession, or activity; would be an asset to the Australian community; and would have no difficulty in obtaining employment or becoming established in Australia in that occupation. The visa can also be granted if the person can show a record of outstanding achievement, and that he or she is still prominent in the arts or sports: (CTH) Migration Regulations 1994 Sch 2 visa subclasses 124, 125.

•**Distress** A self help remedy involving the right of a person ('distrainor') to seize and detain the chattel of another person for the purpose of forcing the other to perform some obligation. A lessor can distrain a reasonable amount of goods of a lessee to compensate for payment of overdue rent. See also **Intentional tort**.

Distributable profits The profits that are available for payment of dividends to shareholders. See also **Dividend**; **Buy-back scheme**.

•**Distribute** To divide and pay out from a deceased estate the legacies to beneficiaries according to the terms of the will and estate property to those entitled according to the scheme of distribution under intestacy legislation. See also **Administration**; **Distribution**.

•**Distribution** The transfer of cash or other property where the transfer does not arise from a contractual relationship but the recipient is entitled to the cash or property because of the recipient's status as a shareholder or beneficiary of a trust or under a will.

Distribution of trust assets See **Power of appointment**.

Distribution schedule A statement by a company setting out the number of holders of its shares in defined categories. For example, the listing requirements of the Australian Stock Exchange require a listed company to set out, in its annual report, the number of holders of each class of equity security in the categories: 1-1000, 1001-5000, 5001-10,000, 10,001 and over: ASX Listing Rules rule 4.10.7. See also **Equity security**.

Distributions to owners Service potential or future economic benefits distributed by an entity to all or part of its ownership group, either as a return on investment or as a return of investment: Statement of Accounting Concepts SAC 4. See also **Balance sheet**; **Profit and loss account**.

Divestiture A remedy available when the prohibition in (CTH) Trade Practices Act 1974 s 50 regarding acquisition of shares or assets has been infringed. Divestiture may occur by a declaration that the acquisition is void, an order to refund the amount paid, or a direction to dispose of assets: (CTH) Trade Practices Act 1974 s 81; *Trade Practices Commission v Australia Meat Holdings Pty Ltd* (1988) 83 ALR 299; ATPR ¶40-876. See also **Acquisition**; **Merger**.

•**Dividend** The yield or return derived from investment or some payment.

Corporations 1. A payment to creditors by a trustee in bankruptcy. Dividends are based on the net amount available for payment and the total of the debts notified to and accepted by the trustee. This usually means a declaration of a pro rata dividend for each dollar of a creditor's claim. Dividends can be declared from time to time as sufficient funds become available. The trustee of a bankrupt's estate must declare and distribute dividends among creditors who have proved their debts, with all convenient speed: (CTH) Bankruptcy Act 1966 s 140(1). 2. A distribution of part of a company's net profit to shareholders, the amount varying from year to year; it is usually expressed as cents per share: *Federal Cmr of Taxation v Slater Holdings Ltd* (1984) 156 CLR 447; 56 ALR 306. No dividend is payable except out of profits or under Corporations Law s 191; Corporations Law s 201(1). See also **Cumulative dividend right**; **Declaration of dividend**; **Dividend payout ratio**; **Dividend reinvestment plan**; **Dividend warrant**; **Dividend yield**; **Final dividend**; **Improper dividend**; **Interim dividend**; **Proof of debt**; **Trustee in bankruptcy**.

Taxation and revenue A distribution of money or property made or credited by a company to its shareholders, or the paid up value of shares issued by a company to shareholders which represent a capitalisation of profits: (CTH) Income Tax Assessment Act 1936 s 6(1). The amount of any dividend paid to a shareholder by a company out of profits derived by the company will be included in the assessable income of the shareholder: s 44(1); *MacFarlane v FCT* (1986) 13 FCR 356; 67 ALR 624. See also **Debt dividend**; **Deemed dividend**; **Dividend paid out of profits**; **Dividend streaming**; **Dividend rebate**.

Dividend bonus plan A scheme where shareholders may elect to have bonus shares issued in lieu of dividends: *BTR Nylex Ltd v Churchill International Inc* (1992) 9 ACSR 361 at 367. Dividends are declared and paid by the company only to those shareholders who do not participate in the plan, while for participants, shares are issued instead of the dividend that would otherwise have been declared on their shares: *BTR Nylex Ltd v Churchill International Inc*. The shares issued are paid up by capitalising any sum lawfully available for distribution to members by way of dividend: *BTR Nylex Ltd v Churchill International Inc*. Dividend bonus plans are distinguished from dividend reinvestment plans, the latter referring to where dividends are declared on all shares but are credited to the participants' account and used to pay for shares to be distributed to them as fully paid shares, such shares not being bonus shares: *BTR Nylex Ltd v Churchill International Inc* at 367. Also known as 'share investment plan' or 'bonus share plan'. See also **Bonus share issue**; **Dividend**; **Dividend reinvestment plan**.

Dividend cover The number of times that a company's profit covers the dividend issued. It is calculated by dividing the net profit by the dividend. See also **Dividend paid out of profits**; **Interest cover**.

Dividend imputation Introduced in 1987, an arrangement under which Australian investors who receive dividends paid out of company earnings on which full company tax has been paid receive a credit for that tax; such dividends are said to be fully franked: (CTH) Income Tax Assessment Act 1936 Pt IIIAA. Also known as 'franked dividend'. See also **Company rate of tax**; **Dividend**; **Franked dividend**; **Imputation system**.

•**Dividend paid out of profits** For income tax purposes, a dividend paid or credited to a shareholder out of profits derived by the company. It will constitute assessable income of the shareholder: (CTH) Income Tax Assessment Act 1936 s 44(1). See also **Assessable income**; **Dividend**; **Income**; **Shareholder**.

Dividend payment A distribution of company profits to shareholders. Payments are generally by way of cash but the articles of association may authorise payment of dividends wholly or partly in the form of assets: for example Corporations Law Sch 1 Table A reg 92. See also **Articles of association**; **Dividend**; **Profit**.

Dividend payout ratio The relationship, expressed as a percentage, between the amount of dividend paid by a company and the profit earned. See also **Dividend**; **Guaranteed dividend**.

Dividend per share The cash payment made by the company to shareholders on a per share basis. It is calculated by adding the interim and final dividend in terms of cents per share. See also **Dividend**; **Final dividend**; **Interim dividend**.

Dividend policy The policy of a company in respect of the distribution of net earnings between dividend distribution and the retention of earnings for the purposes of investment, or to alter the firm's debt-equity ratio. It has been argued that investors should be indifferent as between dividend pay outs and retained earnings, for when earnings are retained the value of the firm's equity rises. Probably most investors prefer a mixture of dividends and capital gain, since dividends are something in hand whereas capital gain, even if theoretically equal to sacrificed dividends, may not be realised in a timely manner due to market influences. See also **Dividend**; **Dividend reinvestment plan**; **Dividend right**.

Dividend rebate A rebate allowed to a shareholder that is an Australian resident company, equal to the amount of tax that would be payable on a dividend received from another resident company. A dividend rebate will make the receipt of the dividend effectively tax free: (CTH) Income Tax Assessment Act 1936 s 46(1). The rebate does not apply to a corporate shareholder acting as trustee: s 46(12). See also **Dividend**; **Rebate**.

Dividend reinvestment See **Dividend reinvestment plan**.

Dividend reinvestment plan Scheme implemented by some public companies under which shareholders may elect to forgo payment in cash of each dividend and to receive instead an allotment of new shares: *BTR Nylex Ltd v Churchill International Inc* (1992) 9 ACSR 361. The issue of new shares is typically made at a specified discount to market price and there are no brokerage fees or stamp duty costs payable. See also **Dividend**; **Dividend right**; **Share**.

Dividend right The right of a person registered as a member of a company to be paid dividends. Dividend rights are dependent on provisions in the company's memorandum and articles. Generally the articles provide that members are entitled to dividends only when they are declared. Usually it is the board of directors which has the power to declare dividends: for example Corporations Law Sch 1 Table A reg 86. Where the directors have a discretion whether to declare dividends or not under the articles, the courts will generally not interfere with their decisions, on the basis that it is an internal matter legitimately left for management: *Miles v Sydney Meat Preserving Co Ltd* (1912) 12 SR (NSW) 98. However a persistent refusal to pay dividends for no justifiable reason may be a factor to be looked at in determining whether the company is acting oppressively or unfairly towards members for the purposes of Corporations Law s 260. The right to dividends, like any other right attached to shares, cannot be separated from the share and assigned independently of the share: *Norman v FCT* (1963) 109 CLR 9; [1964] ALR 131. A person other than the shareholder may, however, be entitled to the dividends if a trust is created to that effect. See also **Dividend**; **Dividend policy**; **Oppressive conduct**.

Dividend streaming An arrangement entered by a shareholder to select the most satisfactory form of payment in lieu of dividends for income tax purposes. For example, a dividend which is fully franked could be diverted from shareholders who are not suited to receiving franked dividends (for example, a loss making company): (CTH) Income Tax Assessment Act 1936 s 160APA. Section 160AQCB reduces the effectiveness of many of these types of arrangements by reducing franking credits available to the company paying the dividend. Dividend imputation applies only to dividends paid out of profits subject to Australian company tax, and cannot be applied to dividends derived from foreign earnings. Commonwealth anti-dividend streaming legislation prevents overseas earnings being paid as franked dividends. No imputation credit is provided for the foreign tax paid in relation to foreign profits. See also **Dividend; Dividend imputation; Franking credit; Franked dividend.**

•**Dividend stripping** The practice of acquiring the shares in a company to give a controlling interest, distributing the company's accumulated profits as dividends, then selling the shares: *Patrick Corp v FCT* (1974) 3 ALR 251. This occurs when the calculated gain from the profit raid is thought to be greater than any loss incurred on the shares once the market finds out. Dividend stripping is a method used by taxpayers to avoid the payment of tax as it enables corporate taxpayers to obtain dividends without a substantial tax liability. Such schemes have been subsequently overcome by (CTH) Income Tax Assessment Act 1936 s 46A(1). See also **Dividend; Dividend rebate.**

Dividend warrant A warrant issued by a company to enable a shareholder to collect his or her dividend from the company's bank. Dividend warrants are used less frequently in Australia than in England. See also **Dividend.**

Dividend yield The percentage return or yield on shares, determined by the annual dividend paid by a company out of earnings and the current share price. If the price of a share is $10 and the annual dividend paid to shareholders per share is 30c, then the dividend yield is three per cent. If the price of the share falls to $5 with the same dividend, the yield becomes six per cent.

Dividends Adjustment Fund A fund ensuring that correct dividends are paid when an incorrect dividend is declared that must be established by clubs using a totalisator. Where the declared dividend is excessive, the difference between the declared dividend and the actual dividend is paid into the fund; where it is inadequate, the difference is paid from the fund to the competitors: (NSW) Totalizator Act 1916 s 10F. See also **Club; Dividend.**

Divisible contract A contract that involves several distinct performances: *Purcell v Bacon* (1914) 19 CLR 241. Where a contract is divisible, strict performance of all the terms of the contract is not required before any liability to pay is incurred: *Purcell v Bacon*. Also known as 'severable contract'. See also **Indivisible contract.**

Divisible property The property of a bankrupt which can be realised and divided by a bankruptcy trustee among the bankrupt's creditors. Except for the property listed in (CTH) Bankruptcy Act 1966 s 116(2), all the property that belonged to a bankrupt at the commencement of bankruptcy, or which has been acquired afterwards in the period until discharge, is divisible property: (CTH) Bankruptcy Act 1966 s 116(1)(a). See also **After acquired property; Bankrupt; Divisible property.**

•**Division 1 company** A company formed under Corporations Law Pt 2.2 Div 1 being a company limited by shares, by guarantee, by both shares and guarantee, or an unlimited company: Corporations Law s 115(1). See also **Incorporation; Unlimited company.**

•**Division 2 company** A company formed under Corporations Law Pt 2.2 Div 2 which is a transitional division allowing for the transfer of companies which were registered under the previous cooperative scheme to registration under the Corporations Law: Corporations Law s 126. The company is registered as the same class and type as it was before the Corporations Law registration: Corporations Law s 129. See also **Incorporation; Registration.**

Division 2A claim A strict product liability claim under (CTH) Trade Practices Act 1974 Pt V Div 2A which can be brought against a manufacturer, deemed manufacturer, or importer of goods of a kind ordinarily acquired for personal, domestic, or household use or consumption, where the goods are not fit for their purpose, do not correspond with a description or sample, are unmerchantable, where there is an unreasonable failure to provide repair facilities or parts, or where there has been non-compliance with an express warranty. See also **Deemed manufacturer; Importer; Manufacturer; Strict product liability.**

•**Division 3 company** A company formed under Corporations Law Pt 2.2 Div 3 which allows non-companies to register under the national scheme. A non-company is a body corporate other than a company, a recognised company, a corporation sole, or an unincorporated foreign company, or registrable Australian body: Corporations Law s 9. See also **Incorporation.**

•**Division 4 company** A company formed under Corporations Law Pt 2.2 Div 4, that is, having registered in another jurisdiction and wishing to transfer into the jurisdiction: Corporations Law s 142. A company which is under external administration or subject to winding up procedures may not apply for transfer of registration: Corporations Law s 143. See also **Incorporation.**

Dock charter A charterparty requiring that a ship only be regarded as an arrived ship when it has docked at the loading or unloading berth. The purpose of a dock charter is to enable the determination of when lay days will begin to run. Also known as a 'berth charterparty', 'berth charter' or 'dock charterparty'. See also **Charterparty; Lay day.**

Dock charterparty See **Dock charter.**

Dock warrant *Abbr* – D/W. A receipt given when goods are stored in a dock warehouse. A dock warrant constitutes a document of title by stating that the goods are deliverable to the person named in the warrant or to an assignee of that person. See also **Document of title; Goods.**

Doctrine of bona fide purchaser for value without notice The rule that where legal title is conveyed to a purchaser who has no notice of any prior equitable interest, that purchaser takes free from any such equitable interest: *Redman v Permanent Trustee Co of New South Wales Ltd* (1916) 22 CLR 84 at 91-2. See also **Fraud; Sale of goods.**

Doctrine of relation back See **Relation back doctrine.**

Doctrine of unanimous assent Doctrine which states that a company is bound in a matter intra vires by the unanimous agreement of all its members: *Salomon v Salomon & Co* [1897] AC 22; Corporations Law s 255(5). See also **Intra vires; Meeting**.

•**Document** Any record of information; anything on which there is writing, marks, figures, symbols or perforations having a meaning for persons qualified to interpret them; or anything from which sounds, images, or writings can be reproduced with or without the aid of anything else; or a map, plan, drawing, or photograph, ((CTH) Evidence Act 1995 s 3 Dictionary, Pt 1; (NSW) Evidence Act 1995 s 3 Dictionary, Pt 1; (NSW) Interpretation Act 1987 s 21(1)); or any other material, data, or information stored or recorded by mechanical or electronic means ((CTH) Federal Court Rules O 1, r 4). Some provisions specifically include discs and tapes: for example (NSW) Supreme Court Rules Pt 1, r 8(1).

Corporations Any paper or other material on which there is writing, printing, marks, figures or symbols which have a meaning to a person qualified to interpret them. It includes a disk or tape from which sound, images or messages can be reproduced. It specifically includes summonses, orders, legal processes and notices: Corporations Law s 9. See also **Notice; Order; Summons**.

•**Document of title** A document proving ownership of property or which is used as proof of possession and control of the property. Examples of the latter include bills of lading and dock warrants: (VIC) Goods Act 1958 s 65. The transfer of such a document effects a transfer of the property to which it relates. See also **Bill of lading; Dock warrant; Ownership**.

•**Document of title to goods** Any bill of lading, dock warrant, warehouse-keeper's certificate, or warrant or order for the delivery of the goods, and any other document used in the ordinary course of business as proof of the possession or control of goods, or as authorisation for the transfer or receipt of goods: (NSW) Sale of Goods Act 1923 s 5(1). See also **Possession; Sale; Seller in possession after sale**.

Documentary letter of credit A letter of credit in which the documents include transport documents, commercial invoices, and insurance documents. See also **Letter of credit**.

Documentary title Ownership of property proven by possession of the indicia of title relevant to the type of property held and, if necessary, proven by registration. The holder of the documentary title of property is entitled to possession of the property. Actual possession is not required for documentary title to be maintained, unless there is prolonged adverse possession, in which case rights to the property can be extinguished. To be contrasted with 'possessory title'. See also **Indicia of title; Possession**.

Doli capax /doʊli kæpæks/ *Lat* – having capacity for fraudulent conduct. See also **Doli incapax**.

Doli incapax /doʊli ɪnkæpæks/ *Lat* – not having capacity for fraudulent conduct. At common law, it is conclusively presumed that a child under the age of seven years is *doli incapax*, that is, he or she cannot commit a crime nor be guilty of an offence: *C v DPP* [1996] 1 AC 1. In many jurisdictions, this age has been raised to ten years: for example (NSW) Children (Criminal Proceedings) Act 1987 s 5; (QLD) Criminal Code s 29. Between the ages of seven (or ten) and fourteen, the Crown must prove, in addition to the elements of the offence charged, that the child was *doli capax* (capable of wrongdoing), that is, that he or she had the mental capacity to understand that he or she was doing something wrong: *R v M* (1977) 16 SASR 589. See also **Doli capax; Incapacity**.

Dollar cost averaging A system of buying securities at regular intervals with a fixed dollar amount, regardless of price. With each payment fixed, purchasers buy more securities when the price is low, and fewer when it rises. Hence, the average cost per share will be less than the average of the purchase prices over a period of time. Such an approach is not designed for short-term trading, and when opting for it an investor chooses an amount she or he can continue to invest for five years or more. See also **Securities**.

Domestic arrangement An agreement entered into by closely related persons such as a husband and wife. Domestic arrangements are enforceable where it appears that the parties intended to create legal relations: *Cohen v Cohen* (1929) 42 CLR 91. Such an intention will be more readily found where the setting of the arrangement is commercial rather than social or domestic (*Roufous v Brewster & Brewster* (1971) 2 SASR 218 at 222) or where the consequences for the plaintiffs are so serious that it is reasonable to infer that they intended to create a binding and enforceable contract: *Wakeling v Ripley* (1951) 51 SR (NSW) 183 at 187. See also **Arms length transaction**.

Domestic tribunal A body within an association appointed to adjudicate or advise on disputes between members, or on the expulsion or suspension of members according to the association's constitution. See also **Association; Constitution; Natural justice; Voluntary non-profit association**.

•**Domicile** The headquarters or home each person is required to have in order to attract legal rights and duties: *Whicker v Hume* (1858) 7 HLC 124; 11 ER 50. A person's domicile is generally the country in which they reside with an intention to remain for an indefinite period. Domicile is of three types: of origin, of choice, and of dependency.

Taxation and revenue For income tax purposes, the (CTH) Income Tax Assessment Act 1936 s 6(1) provides that a person whose domicile is in Australia is a resident of Australia unless the Commissioner is satisfied that the person's permanent place of abode is outside Australia. See also **Off-shore**.

Domicile of corporation The place in which a corporation is incorporated, as opposed to the place in which it is resident. The domicile of a corporation remains with a corporation throughout its existence: *Gasque v Cmrs of Inland Revenue* [1940] 2 KB 80. See also **Domicile; Foreign company**.

Domiciled bill A description of an acceptance of a bill of exchange which expressly states that the bill is to be paid at a particular place only, and not elsewhere: (CTH) Bills of Exchange Act 1909 s 24(4). Such a bill is then said to be 'domiciled' at the specified place. See also **Acceptance**; **Bill of exchange**; **Local acceptance**; **Qualified acceptance**.

•**Dominance** In trade practices law, a position of economic strength enjoyed by an entity or association of entities, enabling it to prevent effective competition being maintained in the market by its power to behave to an appreciable extent independently of its competitors, customers, and ultimately the consumers: *Trade Practices Commission v Arnotts Ltd* (1990) 24 FCR 313; 93 ALR 657. The 'dominance' test for determining whether a merger has breached (CTH) Trade Practices Act 1974 s 50 has been replaced by the 'substantially lessening competition' test. Unlike control, dominance is not primarily concerned with formal relationships between entities, but with their conduct toward each other in a particular market. See also **Competition**; **Control**; **Dominate**; **Griffiths Committee Report**; **Market power**; **Merger**; **Substantially lessening competition**.

Dominant position In relation to the degree of market power of an enterprise, a position where the enterprise is able to exert a commanding influence on the market: *Trade Practices Commission v Ansett Transport Industries (Operations) Pty Ltd* (1978) 32 FLR 305; 20 ALR 31. Dominance was previously used as a measure of market power and was also the test formerly used for determining whether mergers should be allowed, prior to the 1992 amendments to the (CTH) Trade Practices Act 1974. The current provision applies a test of whether the merger substantially lessens competition: s 50. The cases analysing dominance are still relevant in determining whether an enterprise has a substantial degree of market power within ss 46, 46A, but it appears that an enterprise need not be able to dominate a market in order to have a substantial degree of market power. See also **Competition**; **Control**; **Dominance**; **Dominate**; **Griffiths Committee Report**; **Market power**; **Merger**; **Substantially lessening competition**.

•**Dominate** In relation to a market, to have a commanding influence on: *Trade Practices Commission v Ansett Transport Industries (Operations) Pty Ltd* (1978) 20 ALR 31. In telecommunications legislation, a carrier is in a position to dominate a market for services only if the carrier would have been taken to be in such a position for the purposes of the (CTH) Trade Practices Act 1974 s 50 prior to the replacement of the dominance test for mergers in that section: (CTH) Telecommunications Act 1991 s 28. A carrier that is in a position to dominate a market for a particular type of service is subject to anti-discrimination rules which impose significant restrictions on its actions and pricing practices: (CTH) Telecommunications Act 1991 ss 183-188, 195, 197. See also **Dominance**; **Market**; **Market power**; **Substantially lessening competition**.

•**Donee** 1. The recipient of something given or bestowed, such as a gift. The gift may be, for example, tangible real or personal property, or an interest under a trust. 2. A person to whom a power is given; for example, the donee of a power of attorney, or the donee of a power of appointment. See also **Donor**; **Power of appointment**; **Power of attorney**.

•**Donor** A person who gives or bestows something.

Equity The creator of a power, such as a power of attorney or a power of appointment. See also **Donee**; **Power of appointment**; **Power of attorney**.

Door-to-door sale Generally, a contract between a consumer and a dealer which is made at the home of the consumer in the course of door-to-door trading, and without the free invitation of the consumer. In New South Wales, a door-to-door sale is limited to a credit purchase agreement, but in most other states it includes any contract for the sale and supply of goods that is made door-to-door: for example (NSW) Door-to-Door Sales Act 1967 s 2. Contracts made in door-to-door sales include a compulsory cooling-off period during which the purchaser may rescind the contract: for example (NSW) Door-to-Door Sales Act 1967 ss 3, 4. See also **Cooling-off period**; **Credit purchase agreement**.

Dormant account 1. A bank account that has not been accessed by or on behalf of a customer for a long time, the balance in the account thus remaining unchanged. 2. Unclaimed moneys of customers lying in a bank account which has not been operated on for a period of seven years: (CTH) Banking Act 1959 s 69(1). See also **Unclaimed moneys**.

Dormant company See **Dormant entity**.

Dormant corporation See **Dormant entity**.

Dormant entity A body corporate which, during a particular period, engages in none of the activities set out in Corporations Law s 62(1), including becoming entitled to income or liable for expenditure; purchasing or selling any goods or services; making available securities or issuing a prospectus in connection with doing so; and taking part in research and development. See also **Body corporate**; **Entity**; **Expense**; **Incorporation**.

Dormant funds A fund which is not being utilised for its intended purpose; often, it will be inactive.

Contract Any property, real or personal, that has been donated to or collected or otherwise acquired by trustees for any charitable purpose or any purpose of a public character that has not been operated by the trustees in the bona fide utilisation or application of the fund for the purposes for which it was donated, collected, or acquired for a period of six years; or may no longer be practicably used or applied for such purposes: (NSW) Dormant Funds Act 1942 ss 2(1), 5A(1). See also **Charitable purpose**; **Trustee**.

Dormant partner A person who has the rights of a partner, but contributes property without labour or contributes neither capital, nor skill, nor anything else. Also known as 'silent partner'. See also **Partner**; **Sleeping partner**; **Undisclosed principal**.

Double auction In trade and commerce, the process by which sellers and buyers are able to meet at their lowest and highest price respectively to create a market price. See also **Auction**.

Double bond A bond that consists of two parts. One is the obligation, being the formal acknowledgment of debt. The other is the condition, usually secured by some form of penalty which sets out the money to be paid or the acts to be performed; upon payment of the penalty the bond becomes void. Examples are a common money bond (or conditional bond) and a *post obit* bond. See also **Bond; Debt; Void**.

Double dipping The practice of claiming a benefit, compensation, or other payment to which one is entitled, more than once, or in more than one way, thus receiving a greater benefit than the original entitlement intended. For example, a person who receives a lump-sum compensation payment for an injury, intended in part to compensate the person for the loss of working time, and who also claims a job search allowance in respect of the time off work, can be said to 'double dip': *Re Department of Social Security and Booker* (1993) 30 ALD 510; 77 SSR 1126. See also **Job Search allowance; Workers' compensation**.

Double entry The basic accounting system of bookkeeping in which every transaction calls for entries in at least two accounts. The amounts recorded in the debit accounts will be equal to the amounts in credit accounts, and so reflecting the dual effect of each transaction.

Corporations The system of recording transactions in terms of the basic accounting equation (assets = liabilities owners equity), where each transaction has more than one effect on the equation. The amounts recorded in the debit accounts will be equal to the amounts in credit accounts, and so reflecting the dual effect of each transaction. See also **Accounting method; Credit; Debit; Transaction**.

Double indemnity Where an insured receives double the amount for which they are insured. For example in relation to life insurance, an insured may receive an accident benefit which is equal to the sum insured, so that double the amount is paid out in the event of death caused by accident. In relation to voluntary payments by third parties, an insured may receive a double indemnity if an insurer has paid a claim and the insured subsequently receives a payment from a third party in respect of the loss. If the payment is for the benefit of the insured personally rather than simply to compensate for the loss wherever it fell, the insurer is not entitled to recover that payment: for example *Transport Accident Commission v CMT Construction of Metropolitan Tunnels* (1988) 165 CLR 436; 80 ALR 545. See also **Indemnity; Life insurance**.

•**Double insurance** Insurance against the same risk with two independent insurers: *Albion Insurance Co Ltd v GIO (NSW)* 121 CLR 342; [1969] ALR 441. An insured may not recover by taking out double insurance more than the loss suffered. However, an insurance contract may not limit or exclude liability by reason that the insured is covered under other insurance: (CTH) Insurance Contracts Act 1984 s 45(1). See also **Contribution; Indemnity; Marine insurance; Overinsurance; Right of contribution**.

Double proof rule In corporations law, in relation to the distribution of funds among rival claimants in the winding up of a company, there cannot be more than one claim in respect of the same debt: *WA v Bond Corporation Holdings Ltd* (1992) 8 ACSR 352. For example, a contractual provision for more than one dividend for the same debt is invalid where less than all creditors are parties: *United States Trust Co of New York v Australia & New Zealand Banking Group Ltd* (1993) 11 ACSR 7; 11 ACLC 70. The rule can prevent a guarantor, being a contingent creditor having not paid off the principal creditor, from proving in the bankruptcy or liquidation of the principal debtor. See also **Bankruptcy; Guarantor; Proof of debt; Winding up**.

Double satisfaction rule In corporations law, where a creditor has a debt provable in the winding up of a company and a claim for the debt outside the winding up, the creditor cannot be allowed to recover more than 100 per cent of the common debt: for example *Midland Montagu Australia Ltd v Harkness* (1994) 35 NSWLR 150; 124 ALR 407; 14 ACSR 318. See also **Proof of debt; Winding up**.

Double tax treaty A bilateral agreement between two countries that relieves an international taxpayer from being taxed in both jurisdictions. The treaties to which Australia is a party are outlined in (CTH) International Tax Agreements Act 1953 s 3. Also known as 'double tax agreement'. See also **Derived; Source of income**.

Double taxation agreements Bilateral international treaties given effect in Australia by the (CTH) Income and Fringe Benefits Tax (International Agreements) Act 1953. Under these agreements, income from foreign sources is only taxed once. For example, royalties earned in Britain or the United States are not taxed in those countries, becoming taxable when in the hands of an Australian taxpayer in the same way as income received in Australia. Australia has over twenty taxation agreements with other countries. See also **Foreign investment income; Foreign source income**.

Double witching hour On the New York Stock Exchange, an event occurring once a month lasting for about one hour when millions of shares are traded through specialists. It is initiated by the simultaneous expiration of Standard and Poor's 100-Stock Index options and the Major Market Index futures and options. See also **Option; Triple witching hour**.

Doubtful debts A debt that is considered a loss because the debt's collectability is uncertain or its payment not received. A doubtful debt is expressed for accounting purposes by means of a provision taken up on the balance sheet as a liability. See also **Allowance for bad debts**.

Dow Jones averages Indices of United States security prices. The Dow Jones Industrial and Transportation averages have been regarded as significant indicators of both price and business trends. The Dow Jones Industrial Average devised in 1928 is based upon the prices of 30 component stocks. In addition to the 30 Blue-Chip Industrial Average, there is a wider 225 Blue-chip Industrial Average. See also **Blue chip security; Securities**.

Dow Jones index An index of the average price of shares on the New York stockmarket. It is named after Charles Dow and Eddie Jones who joined together in 1882 to report stockmarket news to New York's community. See also **Dow Jones averages; Share price index; Stock exchange**.

Dow theory A theory of market analysis based upon the performance of the Dow Jones industrial and transportation stock price averages. According to the theory, the market is in a basic upward trend if one of these averages advances above a previously important high, accompanied or followed by a similar advance in the other. When the averages both dip below previously important lows, this is considered an indication of a basic downward trend. The theory does not attempt to predict how long either trend will continue. Dow theory consisted originally of the analysis of stock market trends by Charles H Dow (1851-1902), founder with Edward D Jones of the financial news agency Dow, Jones and Company. Dow was the first editor of the *Wall Street Journal*. See also **Dow Jones averages; Stock market**.

Down-sizing A reduction in the size of a company or enterprise, often involving a shedding of staff and the disposal of assets. See also **Maintenance of capital; Redundancy; Re-employment**.

Downstream acquisitions exemption In corporations law, an exception to the rule prohibiting share acquisitions of more than 20 per cent: Corporations Law s 615. The exemption permits an acquisition of shares in a company (the downstream acquisition) as a result of the acquisition of shares in another body corporate (the upstream acquisition) where the acquisition of shares in the upstream company results from a takeover scheme, takeover announcement, or under permitted on-market purchases: Corporations Law s 629. This exemption applies only where the shares being acquired in the upstream acquisition are shares of a body corporate incorporated in Australia and listed on the Australian Stock Exchange: Corporations Law s 629. See also **Acquisition; Entitlement to shares; On-market buy-back; Takeover**.

Down-stream guarantee An arrangement by which the parent company guarantees the debts of one or more of its subsidiaries. See also **Cross-stream guarantee**.

Downstream processing The processing of commodities such as wool and wheat, precious stones, iron ore, and other minerals between initial production and final sale to the consumer or incorporation in another commodity. It has been argued that Australia, particularly in respect of its major exports, should undertake more downstream processing within the country instead of exporting raw materials which have undergone little or no processing. In this way, it is argued, value-added processing would increase the value of exports to the nation's overall economic advantage. Some downstream processing is already undertaken in the conversion of bauxite to alumina and aluminium before export from Australia. See also **Foreign debt**.

•**Draft** The preparation by a legal practitioner or other person of a legal document or other type of document in a rough or preliminary fashion during the course of its preparation before the final version or perfected copy of the document is produced.

Bills of exchange and other negotiable instruments A bill purchased from a bank to settle an international transaction. Also known as 'bill of exchange'. See also **Bill of exchange**.

Draft allowance A small, arbitrary allowance made to a merchant or importer, in the case of goods sold by weight or taxable by weight, to cover possible loss of weight in handling or from differences in scales. See also **Allowance; Importer**.

Draft contract A copy of a contract that has not been finalised. A draft contract may be admitted into evidence where, for example, rectification is sought on the basis that a term was unintentionally left out of the final contract: *Hoyt's Pty Ltd v Spencer* (1919) 27 CLR 133; (1919) ALR 21 at 144.

•**Draw** To make or draft, and sign, a negotiable instrument. The person who draws the instrument is the 'drawer'; the person to whom it is addressed, and is required to pay on it, is the 'drawee'. The instrument is said to be 'drawn on' the drawee. See also **Drawee; Drawer; Maker; Negotiable instrument**.

•**Drawback** The refund of duties or taxes previously charged on the importation of commodities, which is made on the exportation of the goods. A drawback includes a bounty or allowance: (CTH) Customs Act 1901 s 4. See also **Allowance; Customs duty**.

Drawdown Drawing or using money which is available to a borrower under a credit agreement or borrowing facility. See also **Credit line; Drawings**.

Drawee A person to whom a negotiable instrument is addressed: (CTH) Bills of Exchange Act 1909 s 8; (CTH) Cheques and Payment Orders Act 1986 s 10(1)(a). The drawee is required to pay a sum in money on presentment of the instrument, which is said to be 'drawn' on the drawee. The drawee must be named or otherwise indicated on a bill with reasonable certainty: (CTH) Bills of Exchange Act 1909 s 4. In the case of a cheque, the bank is the drawee of the cheque in the sense that the customer addresses to the bank the unconditional order to pay: (CTH) Cheques and Payment Orders Act 1986 s 10(1)(a). See also **Assent by the drawee; Draw; Drawee bank; Drawer**.

•**Drawee bank** The bank upon whom a cheque is drawn, which ultimately pays the cheque: (CTH) Cheques and Payment Orders Act 1986 s 3(1). The bank is the drawee of the cheque in that the customer addresses the unconditional order to pay to the bank: (CTH) Cheques and Payment Orders Act 1986 s 10(1)(a). Also known as 'paying bank'. See also **Cheque; Drawee; Paying bank**.

Drawer The person who makes (or draws), signs, and gives a negotiable instrument. By drawing a negotiable instrument, the drawer engages that on due presentment it shall be accepted or paid according to its terms, and if dishonoured, the drawer will compensate the holder or any indorser who is compelled to pay: (CTH) Bills of Exchange Act 1909 s 60(1)(a); (CTH) Cheques and Payment Orders Act 1986 s 71. A person is not liable as drawer where the instrument has not been properly signed: (CTH) Bills of Exchange Act 1909 s 28; (CTH) Cheques and Payment Orders Act 1986 s 31. See also **Dishonour; Draw; Holder; Indorser; Maker; Sign**.

Drawer-drawee contract The contract underlying the drawing of a bill of exchange by a drawer on a drawee. The contract obliges the drawee to accept one or more bills drawn by the drawer provided certain conditions are met by the drawer, such as the provision of security and the repayment with interest of amounts accepted by the drawee. A common example is a bill acceptance facility agreement. See also **Acceptance**; **Bill of exchange**; **Bill acceptance facility agreement**; **Drawee**; **Drawer**; **Indorsement**.

• **Drawings** Sums of money withdrawn from the funds of a business entity by one of its proprietors.

Partnerships and joint ventures In relation to a partnership, amounts of money withdrawn by the partners from the accumulated profits of the partnership. The entitlement of each partner to make drawings, and the amount and timing of the drawings is generally set out in the partnership agreement. See also **Partnership agreement**.

Taxation and revenue Economic benefits received from an entity by its sole proprietor or a partner during an accounting period. Drawings, although not regarded as expenses, represent a decrease to the owners' equity of a business. See also **Entity**; **Expense**.

Dry lease A lease or hire of plant and equipment, not including operation costs which are met separately by the lessee. See also **Wet lease**.

Dual registration The practice of a State branch of a federally registered trade union registering as a trade union under a State industrial relations statute. Such a branch then has two separate legal personalities, as part of a federal union, and as a State union, although it tends to operate in fact as a single body, with one membership list, one set of officers, and so on. Difficult legal questions can arise from this situation, as where one body is two separate legal entities governed by different laws: *Moore v Doyle* (1969) 15 FLR 59. See also **Industrial relations**; **Trade union**.

• **Due and payable** Required to be paid immediately: *Peacock v Commonwealth Trading Bank of Australia* [1979] 2 NSWLR 130; (1979) 29 ALR 614; (CTH) Income Tax Assessment Act 1936 s 204.

Dummy audit A mock audit designed to uncover problems in a company's accounting system, and at the same time enable executives to devise responses when dealing with a real audit. See also **Audit**; **Tax records**.

• **Dumping** The sale of goods to a purchaser in another country at a price lower than the normal value in the country of export. If the export price is below the domestic price a prima facie case of dumping exists. See also **Dumping duty**.

• **Dumping duty** A customs duty imposed on selected goods by the Commonwealth of Australia to penalise the importer so as to, usually, protect Australian producers of similar goods. Generally imported goods are regarded dumped where the goods are sold in Australia for a price that realises the importer a loss or minimal profit. Dumping duties are imposed under the (CTH) Customs Tariff (Anti-Dumping) Act 1975 s 8. See also **Customs duty**.

Dun and Bradstreet Founded in 1841, a United States firm providing information on the creditworthiness of several million companies throughout the world. Based on the credit history of each firm, financial data, and other factors, Dun and Bradstreet assigns a credit rating. The company is represented in Australia. Among other surveys, Dun and Bradstreet conduct regular reviews of business sales expectations throughout the world. See also **Credit rating**.

Duration of transit The time from which goods are delivered to a carrier or other bailee, by land or water, for the purpose of transmission to the buyer, until the buyer or the buyer's agent takes delivery of them from that carrier or other bailee: for example (NSW) Sale of Goods Act 1923 s 47(1). If the buyer or the buyer's agent obtains delivery of the goods before their arrival at the appointed destination, the transit is deemed to be at an end: for example (NSW) Sale of Goods Act 1923 s 47(2). If the carrier or other bailee acknowledges, after the arrival of the goods at the appointed destination, that the carrier or other bailee holds the goods on the buyer's behalf, and continues in possession of them as bailee for the buyer or the buyer's agent, the transit is deemed to be at an end, whether or not a further destination for the goods has been indicated by the buyer: for example (NSW) Sale of Goods Act 1923 s 47(3). Where the carrier or other bailee wrongfully refuses to deliver the goods to the buyer or the buyer's agent, the transit is deemed to be at an end: for example (NSW) Sale of Goods Act 1923 s 47(6). See also **Bailee**; **Buyer**; **Carrier**; **Delivery**.

• **Duress** An act done by one person to another for the purpose of applying pressure or undue persuasion to do something, or refrain or desist from doing something. Duress may take the form of constraint by injury, confinement, or threats.

Contract The application of illegitimate pressure to obtain a contractual promise, payment, service, or other benefit: for example *Smith v William Charlick Ltd* (1924) 34 CLR 38. The elements of common law duress are the procuring of a benefit by compulsion or pressure, and the illegitimacy of that pressure: *Universe Tankships Inc of Monrovia v International Transport Workers Federation (The Universe Sentinel)* [1983] 1 AC 366. A contract procured by duress is voidable and is binding until set aside by the victim: *Hawker Pacific Pty Ltd v Helicopter Charter Pty Ltd* (1991) 22 NSWLR 298. See also **Compulsion**; **Duress of goods**; **Economic duress**; **Vitiating factor**.

Equity Illegitimate pressure exerted upon another to induce consent to a transaction. The pressure need not constitute an overbearing of the will, but it must amount to unconscionable or unlawful conduct. Relief may be granted by way of restitution, based on the unifying legal concept of unjust enrichment: *Pavey & Matthews Pty Ltd v Paul* (1987) 162 CLR 221; 69 ALR 577. See also **Fraud**; **Unconscionable**; **Unjust enrichment**.

Duress of goods A form of duress involving the unlawful taking, detention, damaging, or destruction of a person's goods. See also **Duress**; **Economic duress**; **Unjust enrichment**.

Dutch auction An auction in which the auctioneer states a sum and proceeds in decreasing amounts until a bid is made, the first bidder becoming the purchaser: *Carroll v Solomon* (1930) 33 WALR 82; *Ex parte Hamilton* (1882) 3 LR (NSW) 89. See also **Auction**; **Auctioneer**; **Bid**.

Duties of public office The functions of a public servant or public officer consisting of things done or omitted in an official capacity. The duties of a public office include those lying directly within the scope of the office, those essential to the accomplishment of the main purpose for which the office was created, and those which, although only incidental and collateral, serve to promote the accomplishment of the principal purposes: *G J Coles & Co Ltd v Retail Trade Industrial Tribunal* (1986) 7 NSWLR 503 at 524; 17 IR 134; *Herscu v R* (1991) 173 CLR 276; 103 ALR 1 at 281, 287. A public officer who wilfully neglects the performance of a duty imposed upon him or her either by common law or statute is guilty of an indictable misdemeanour: *G J Coles & Co Ltd v Retail Trade Industrial Tribunal* (1986) 7 NSWLR 503 at 524.

•**Duty** A legal obligation owed by one person to another. A duty may require the performance of certain actions, or the refraining from certain actions. The tort of negligence is predicated on a duty of care owed by the defendant to the plaintiff. See also **Duty in contract; Duty in tort; Duty of care.**

Duty in contract The obligation imposed on any person who follows a skilled calling to exercise due care, skill, and diligence in the performance of work undertaken on behalf of the person who employs him or her: *Voli v Inglewood Shire Council* (1963) 110 CLR 74 at 84; [1963] ALR 657. The duty to exercise due care, skill, and diligence has traditionally been regarded as an implied term of the retainer between solicitor and client. Recognition that the ordinary law of negligence prima facie applies in respect of work done by a solicitor for the client removes a large part of the basis and justification for the implication of a general contractual duty of care: *Hawkins v Clayton* (1988) 164 CLR 539; 78 ALR 69. See also **Duty in tort; Duty of care.**

Duty in tort The duty owed by a solicitor to persons in a relationship of proximity with the solicitor and arising out of that relationship to exercise reasonable care to avoid negligent conduct causing damage to such persons: *Hawkins v Clayton* (1988) 164 CLR 539; 78 ALR 69. The requisite relationship of proximity must exist with respect to the allegedly negligent class of act and the particular kind of damage sustained before the solicitor will be liable for breach of the duty of care: *Hawkins v Clayton*. In the ordinary situation the relationship of solicitor and client is a relationship of proximity involving assumption of responsibility to apply expert knowledge and skill, reliance in that respect by the client, and the foreseeability of a real risk of economic loss: *Hawkins v Clayton*. It is a relationship of proximity of a kind which may well give rise to a duty of care on the part of the solicitor which requires the taking of positive steps, beyond the specifically agreed professional task or function, to avoid a real and foreseeable risk of economic loss being sustained by the client: *Hawkins v Clayton*. The scope of a solicitor's duty in tort is conditioned by the terms of the retainer: *Cousins v Cousins* (unrptd, CA(NSW), CA40366/90, Meagher JA, 18 Dec 1990). See also **Duty in contract; Duty of care.**

Duty not to fetter discretions The duty of a director of a corporation to retain, give adequate consideration to, and exercise, any active discretions conferred by the Corporations Law or company constitution: *Automatic Self-Cleaning Filter Syndicate Co Ltd v Cunningham* [1966] 2 Ch 34. See also **Constitution; Directors' duties; Fiduciary duty.**

Duty of attendance The obligation of an employee to be at work during working hours. The employee must not be absent from work without good cause during the time at which the contract requires him or her to be at work: *Adami v Maison de Luxe* (1924) 35 CLR 143. See also **Contract of employment; Duty of faithful service; Summary dismissal.**

Duty of care The obligation owed to anyone whom it is reasonably foreseeable would be injured by the lack of care of that person: *Donoghue v Stevenson* [1932] AC 562. For a duty of care to arise, there must exist a relationship of proximity between plaintiff and defendant: *Sutherland Shire Council v Heyman* (1985) 157 CLR 424; 60 ALR 1. The duty may be owed to persons in specific categories, such as by a doctor to a patient: *Rogers v Whitaker* (1992) 175 CLR 479; 109 ALR 625. The duty is breached if the defendant fails to act in accordance with the required standard of care. See also **Negligence.**

Product liability The common law obligation owed by manufacturers and other suppliers of products to take reasonable steps to minimise the risk that those products will cause injury or property damage to foreseeable users or to bystanders: *Donoghue v Stevenson* [1932] AC 562; *Suosaari v Steinhardt* [1989] 2 Qd R 477. A duty of care in negligence arises only where there is a relationship of proximity between a manufacturer or supplier and another person: *Sutherland Shire Council v Heyman* (1985) 157 CLR 424; 60 ALR 1. See also **Defect in design; Defect in formulation; Defect in information; Defect in manufacture; Duty to warn.**

Duty of care and skill The duty of an employee to perform the work agreed in the contract of employment with reasonable care and skill. An employee who accepts a job requiring a particular skill impliedly promises that he or she has, and will exercise, the skill required: *Printing Industry Employees Union of Australia v Jackson and O'Sullivan* (1957) 1 FLR 175. See also **Contract of employment; Duty of faithful service.**

Duty of confidence A duty owed by a company officer to the company not to make improper use of information obtained by virtue of the officer's position: Corporations Law s 232(5). See also **Officer; Confidential information; Fiduciary duty.**

Employment The duty of an employee not to disclose or misuse confidential information the property of the employer obtained by the employee in the course of employment: *Ansell Rubber Co Pty Ltd v Allied Rubber Industries Pty Ltd* [1967] VR 37. It is an aspect of the overall duty of faithful service which the employee owes to the employer. When the employee leaves the employment, the duty of confidentiality continues but the range of information which is covered by the duty narrows: *Riteway Express Pty Ltd v Clayton* (1987) 10 NSWLR 238. The duty is not breached where, in the public interest, the employee discloses to a proper person that the employer has committed (or proposes to commit) a crime, fraud or wrongful act: *Lion Laboratories Ltd v Evans* [1984] 2 All ER 417. See also **Duty of faithful** service.

Equity The equitable obligation of conscience to keep information confidential, arising from the circumstances in which the information was communicated or obtained; failure to do so amounts to a breach of confidence: *Moorgate Tobacco Co Ltd v Philip Morris Ltd (No 2)* (1984) 156 CLR 414; 56 ALR 193. See also **Breach of confidence; Confidential information**.

Duty of confidentiality A duty owed by a recipient of confidential information not to misuse information obtained by virtue of the recipient's relationship with the owner of the information, and to refrain from using the information for the recipient's own benefit or to the owner's detriment: *Seager v Copydex Ltd* [1967] 1 WLR 923. See also **Confidential information; Fiduciary duty**.

•**Duty of disclosure** See **Duty to disclose**.

Duty of faithful service The overall duty of an employee to perform well and faithfully the work agreed in the contract of employment. See also **Duty of attendance; Duty of care and skill; Duty of confidence; Duty of fidelity; Duty of obedience; Duty to act in best interests of employer; Employer's duty to be good and considerate**.

Duty of fidelity An aspect of the duty of faithful service which an employee owes to an employer. The employee must do the work required in good faith. The duty prohibits conduct which in respect of important matters is incompatible with the fulfilment of the employee's duty, or involves an opposition or conflict between the employee's interest and his or her duty to the employer, or impedes the faithful performance of his or her obligations, or is destructive of the necessary confidence between employer and employee: *Blyth Chemicals Ltd v Bushnell* (1933) 49 CLR 66. See also **Duty of confidence; Duty of faithful service; Duty to act in best interests of employer; Fidelity; Secret profits**.

Duty of good faith See **Duty of fidelity**.

Duty of obedience The duty of an employee to obey all lawful orders of the employer, even where the order relates to a comparatively insignificant matter: *Adami v Maison de Luxe* (1924) 35 CLR 143; [1925] VLR 147. See also **Duty of faithful service**.

Duty of utmost good faith See **Duty of fidelity; Uberrimae fidei**.

Duty paid contract A contract under which the seller of goods agrees to meet all costs attaching to the goods in the form of import duties, customs duties, and warehousing expenses. The seller does not undertake to meet labour and transport costs, the liability for which continues to be borne by the buyer. Such contracts are not common, but are sometimes used in connection with government tenders. See also **Customs duty**.

Duty paid value *Abbr* – dpv The value of goods calculated by adding to their original cost the customs duties, import duties, and warehousing expenses which they will incur prior to delivery. See also **Customs duty; Goods**.

Duty to act for proper purposes The duty of a director of a corporation to exercise powers and discretions only for the purpose for which they were given, not for collateral purposes: *Residues Treatment & Trading Co Ltd v Southern Resources Ltd* (1989) 52 SASR 54; 15 ACLR 416. See also **Directors' duties; Fiduciary**.

Duty to act honestly The duty of an officer of a corporation at all times to act honestly in the exercise of his or her powers and the discharge of the duties of office: Corporations Law s 232(2). To 'act honestly' refers to acting bona fide in the interests of the company, such that a breach of this obligation involves consciousness that what is being done is not in the interests of the company, and deliberate conduct in disregard of that knowledge: *Marchesi v Barnes* [1970] VR 434. See also **Directors' duties; Fiduciary**.

Duty to act in best interests of employer The duty of an employee to act in the employer's interests rather than in the employee's own interests. For example, an employee who works in his or her spare time for a competitor of the employer may breach the duty: *Hivac Ltd v Park Royal Scientific Instruments* [1946] Ch 169. See also **Contract of employment; Duty to act in good faith for the benefit of the company as a whole; Duty of faithful service**.

Duty to act in good faith for the benefit of the company as a whole The duty of a director of a company, due to the fiduciary relationship between the director and the company, to act bona fide in the interests of the company: *Whitehouse v Carlton Hotel Pty Ltd* (1987) 162 CLR 285; 70 ALR 251. Good faith is tested subjectively; however, many cases have held that directors may breach their duty, even if they are acting in what they genuinely consider to be an honest manner, because they have failed to give proper consideration to the interests of the company: *Bailey v Mandala Private Hospital Pty Ltd* (1987) 12 ACLR 641. See also **Directors' duties; Fiduciary**.

Duty to act with care, skill and diligence The duty of a director or officer of a company to take care, which arises from contract, from an equitable obligation, or from the common law and which is supplemented by duties imposed by the Corporations Law: *Daniels v Anderson* (1995) 37 NSWLR 438; 16 ACSR 607. Officers are required to exercise the degree of care and diligence that a reasonable person in a like position in a corporation would exercise in the corporation's circumstances: Corporations Law s 232(4). See also **Directors' duties**.

Duty to deal A general legal duty to supply goods or services to another person. In Australian competition law, a monopolist or one with a substantial degree of market power has no general duty to deal: *Queensland Wire Industries Pty Ltd v Broken Hill Proprietary Co Ltd* (1987) 17 FCR 211; 78 ALR 407. See also **Access Regime; Baumol-Willig rule; Competition Policy Reform Act 1995; Essential facility doctrine**.

Duty to deliver The duty of a carrier of goods to deliver them within a reasonable time, being a time within which a carrier using all reasonable exertions can deliver: *Taylor v Great Northern Railway Company* (1866) LR 1 CP 385. In determining a reasonable time for delivery, any strike which has occurred may be taken into account: *Sims & Co v Midland Railway Co* [1913] 1 KB 103. See also **Delivery**.

• **Duty to disclose** An obligation to make known matters likely to affect the decision making of those relying on the knowledge or good character of the person having the obligation to disclose. See also **Conflict of interest**; **Fiduciary relationship**; **Fit and proper person**.

Negligence The obligation of medical personnel to acquaint a patient with the nature and risks of a proposed treatment, to enable the individual to make decisions concerning the treatment. The duty is not limited to compliance by a medical practitioner with an accepted practice in deciding what information to disclose. Liability for breach of the duty is subject to the therapeutic privilege: *Rogers v Whitaker* (1992) 175 CLR 479; 109 ALR 625.

Duty to keep accounts The duty of agents to keep accounts of all transactions: *Gray v Haig* (1855) 20 Beav 219; 52 ER 587. The duty of certain types of agents to keep accounts is regulated by statute: for example (NSW) Farm Produce Act 1983 s 35; (VIC) Farm Produce Wholesale Act 1990 s 27. See also **Fidelity**.

Duty to know the client A stockbroker's duty to have an understanding of its client's investment objectives, financial situation (for example, assets and liabilities), and other particular needs. See also **Securities business**.

Duty to make a decision In administrative law, the requirement that an administrator make a decision or exercise a discretionary power as required or conferred by statute. At general law the remedy of mandamus is available to compel an administrator to perform a statutory duty. See also **Failure to make a decision**.

Duty to provide work, employer's See **Right to work**.

Duty to warn The legal obligation imposed on manufacturers and other suppliers of products by the law of negligence to take all reasonable steps to appraise intended users and consumers of products of risks associated with the products, particularly risks that would not be known or obvious to such persons: for example *O'Dwyer v Leo Buring Pty Ltd* [1966] WAR 67; *Halvorsen Boats Pty Ltd v Robinson* (1993) 31 NSWLR 1; Aust Torts Reports ¶81-221. See also **Failure to warn**.

E

Early completion In relation to hire-purchase agreements, the right of the hirer to complete the purchase of the goods at any time during the term of the agreement. The hirer may exercise this right by giving the owner written notice of the hirer's intention and paying the owner the net balance due under the agreement: (VIC) Hire-Purchase Act 1959 s 11; (QLD) Hire-Purchase Act 1959 s 11. See also **Hire-purchase agreement; Hirer; Net balance due; Owner**.

Earnest A deposit or some tangible thing given when a contract is made, as a guarantee that the buyer will fulfil the contract: *Farr Smith & Co Ltd v Messers Ltd* [1928] 1 KB 397. See also **Contract; Consideration; Deposit**.

Earning capacity The physical and mental ability of a person to engage in remunerative employment.

Tort A plaintiff is entitled to recover damages for any reduction in earning capacity, so far as that reduction causes financial loss to the plaintiff.

•**Earnings** The pay or remuneration a worker receives under a contract for work, in return for the worker's services. See also **Income; Wage; Remuneration**.

Earnings, attachment of See **Garnishment**.

Earnings before interest and tax *Abbr* – EBIT
A financial measure of the amount of profit or earnings of a business entity before subtracting the interest, expense and tax expense application for the period. The EBIT provides a figure that reflects the operating surplus of a business and when compared to interest costs allows an analysis of the business capacity to service debt. The EBIT can also be used to measure operating effectiveness by comparing it to the total value of assets of the business.

Earnings per share *Abbr* – EPS That portion of company profit earned for every ordinary share on issue. An EPS is calculated by taking the net operating profit after tax, deducting any preference dividend and dividing by the number of ordinary shares. See also **Bonus share issue; Dividend; Dividend per share; Earnings price ratio; Share**.

Earnings price ratio The relationship of earnings per share to the price of the share at the close of the exchange. Also known as 'earnings yield'. See also **Dividend; Earnings per share; Share**.

Earnings yield See **Earnings price ratio**.

•**Easement** A right enjoyed by a person with regard to the land of another person, the exercise of which interferes with the normal rights of the owner or occupier of that land: *Municipal District of Concord v Coles* (1906) 3 CLR 96. To be legally enforceable an easement must have four properties: a dominant tenement which practically benefits from the easement; a servient tenement which is subject to the easement; the dominant and servient tenements are owned by different persons; and the easement must be of a type recognised in law. See also **Prescription**.

Easement for light An easement giving the owner of a dominant tenement the right to continue to receive light into the dominant tenement. The easement must usually relate to a specified door or window in a building on the dominant tenement. See also **Prescription**.

East Asia and Oceania Stock Exchange Federation A federation of stock exchanges which includes the exchanges of Australia, Japan, Korea, Malaysia, the Philippines, Singapore, Taiwan and Thailand. See also **Australian Stock Exchange Ltd; Exchange; Kuala Lumpur Stock Exchange**.

EBIT See **Earnings before interest and tax**.

EBRD See **European Bank for Reconstruction and Development**.

•**EC** See **European Community**.

Econometrics The use of mathematics and statistics in economics to define economic issues and seek solutions to economic problems. The development of mathematical models is central to the discipline. See also **Economics**.

Economic and Social Commission for Asia and the Pacific *Abbr* – ESCAP A regional commission of the United Nations facilitating economic activities and development in Asian-Pacific countries.

Economic and Social Council *Abbr* – ECOSOC
A council operating under the authority of the United Nations General Assembly concerned with promoting economic and social progress and standards of human welfare, as well as the observance of human rights and fundamental freedoms.

Economic costs Costs falling into three categories: explicit costs in respect of which an actual financial liability is incurred, that is the accounting costs of running a business; implicit costs, being the costs of using resources already at the disposal of the company by way of funds and labour, and costs in the form of lost opportunities to use resources, including time, in another way; and external costs or societal costs. See also **Costs of production; Opportunity cost**.

•**Economic duress** Illegitimate economic pressure in the form of threats to a person's economic well-being, business or trade, with the result that a contract is entered or payments are made: *Hawker Pacific Pty Ltd v Helicopter Charter Pty Ltd* (1991) 22 NSWLR 298. In economic duress, the promisor's apparent consent is treated in law as revocable unless approved either expressly or by implication after the illegitimate pressure has ceased to operate on his or her mind: *Universe Tankships Inc of Monrovia v International Transport*

Workers Federation (The Universe Sentinel) [1983] 1 AC 366. See also **Duress; Duress of goods**.

• **Economic efficiency** The efficiency with which scarce resources are organised and used to achieve nominated economic, commercial, social and environmental objectives, the aim generally being to achieve best value for the dollar expended. See also **Flexible-system production; Just-in-time production**.

• **Economic entity** A group of entities comprising a parent entity and each of its controlled entities: Applicable Accounting Standard AASB 1024. See also **Chief entity; Control; Entity; Parent entity; Reporting entity**.

Economic growth An increase in the real gross domestic product of the community over time. See also **Gross Domestic Product**.

Economic impact study A study of the effect upon an economy as a whole of a major industrial development, the introduction of a new policy or regulation, or the continuation of current trends in overseas markets. Economic impact studies may be applied locally, regionally or nationally.

Economic indicators Statistics which are sensitive to changes in the state of the economy generally, industry, trade and commerce. Australian economic indicators published regularly by government, business and the universities include statistics relating to gross domestic product, the balance of payments, unemployment, demand, investment, consumer and business confidence, costs of production, housing, production, and finance. Indicators may be classified into three types: 'leaders' offering advance pointers; 'coincidents' moving in tandem with business conditions; and 'laggers' showing delayed results. See also **Index of leading indicators; Investment**.

Economic loss Injury to person or property resulting in immediate or subsequent detriment to a person's income or wealth. In negligence, loss falling into one of two categories. 'Consequential economic loss' results from negligently caused personal injury or property damage suffered by a person. 'Pure economic loss' is loss unaccompanied by personal injury or property damage. The former type of loss has generally been readily recoverable. The latter type may be recoverable in certain situations: *Caltex Oil (Australia) Pty Ltd v The Dredge 'Willemstad'* (1976) 136 CLR 529; 11 ALR 227. See also **Consequential loss; Pure economic loss**.

Economic Planning Advisory Council Abbr – EPAC A Commonwealth advisory body established following the 1983 National Economic Summit Conference. EPAC is governed by the (CTH) Economic Planning Advisory Commission Act 1983. Its primary functions are to provide for community participation in the development of economic policies, the identification of feasible and desirable economic goals, and the development of policies designed to sustain and improve economic growth. See also **Prices and Incomes Accord**.

Economic powers Those Commonwealth powers, legislative or otherwise, which allow it to generally control the national economy. The most important of economic powers include the trade and commerce power (Commonwealth Constitution s 51(i)), the taxation power (s 51(ii)), the corporations power (s 51(xx)), the banking power (s 51(xiii)), and the grants power (s 96). See also **Banking power; Corporations power; Trade and commerce power**.

Economic rationalism A widely held belief in the early 1990s that private sector markets and finance can do almost everything better than governments.

Economic reality test A test used to determine whether a person who agrees to work for another is working under a contract of employment. The economic reality test looks at the circumstances surrounding the work relationship, and asks whether or not the worker was performing the services as a person in business on the person's own account: *Market Investigations Ltd v Minister for Social Security* [1969] 2 QB 173. A person who works for himself or herself, and not on behalf of the person for whom the work is done, is not an employee. See also **Contract of employment; Contract of service; Multiple test**.

Economic rent A payment to one of the factors of production which is in excess of the minimum amount necessary to keep that unit in its present occupation or use. A firm may pay salaries sufficient to retain its present staff. However, in attempting to increase its staff the firm may find it necessary to increase salaries to attract professionals from other employment. The increase in salaries now enjoyed by the original staff is economic rent. Economic rent can be enjoyed by any factor whose supply is relatively fixed. Urban land enjoys this distinction, since values may greatly exceed those needed to draw land from its original agricultural purposes. See also **Factors of production**.

Economic system, functions of See **Functions of economic system**.

Economic theories of law Theories based on an analysis of legal systems and particular laws within them, from the perspective that they must have an economic cause and function. Economic theories of law may adopt a radical laissez-faire liberal perspective, or various Marxist perspectives. See also **Laissez-faire**.

Economic torts Torts dealing with the occasioning of harm by the intentional interference with another's economic interests. Economic torts include: the action for loss of services; action on the case for damages being the inevitable consequence of an unlawful act; conspiracy; deceit; injurious falsehood; interference with contractual relations; intimidation; and passing off. These are partly regulated by Commonwealth and State legislation, particularly the (CTH) Trade Practices Act 1974. See also **Action for loss of services; Conspiracy; Deceit; Injurious falsehood; Interference with contractual relations; Intimidation; Passing off**.

Economics A social science concerned with how people, either individually or in groups, attempt to accommodate scarce resources to their demands through the processes of exploration, exploitation, production, substitution and exchange. Economics is more specifically concerned with the allocation of the resources of society among alternative uses, the distribution of output and incomes among individuals and groups, the ways in which production and distribution change over time, the efficiencies and inefficiencies of economic systems and the alternative routes by which Australia might resolve its economic, social and environmental problems.

Economies of scale The gains by way of reduced average and marginal costs of production per unit of output often arising from increasing the size of plant, business or industry. In suitable circumstances, large-scale production leads to significant economies in the use of the factors of production namely natural resources, capital and labour and in marketing, finance and research. However, above a certain point, diseconomies may appear as management becomes more bureaucratic and inflexible, coordination is lost, and inertia takes hold of a system capable of superior performance. See also **Economics**.

Economist-Extel Index An index of industrial share prices compiled by *The Economist* in association with the Exchange Telegraph Company. The Economist-Extel Index is calculated twice daily and the index combines 50 stock prices in an unweighted arithmetic average. Each year, the constituent shares of the index are reviewed and revised as necessary. See also **All Ordinaries Index; Exchange traded option; Nikkei-Dow Index; Share price index**.

ECOSOC See **Economic and Social Council**.

EDI See **Electronic data interchange**.

EEC See **European Economic Community**.

EETO See **Eligible exchange traded option**.

Effective life In taxation law, the period over which an asset is deemed to be utilised by a taxpayer. Effective life is essential in calculating depreciation and amortisation as well as any allowable investment tax credit under the (CTH) Income Tax Assessment Act 1936: s 54A. The period cannot be longer than the estimated physical life of an asset, although it could be shorter if the taxpayer does not utilise the asset until it has been worn out. The Commissioner can make determinations as to the period which constitutes the effective life of units of property, and taxpayers may adopt such determinations. See also **Amortisation; Commissioner of Taxation; Depreciation**.

Efficient market theory The theory that the market reflects the information available to its investors. Efficient market theory implies that changes in the price of securities are due to information of a new development entering the market. See also **Australian Stock Exchange Ltd**.

Efficient portfolio The theoretical perfect portfolio. In this portfolio, for any level of risk, the portfolio produces the highest returns and for any level of return, the portfolio produces the smallest risk. See also **Australian Stock Exchange Ltd**.

•**EFIC** See **Export Finance and Insurance Corporation**.

EFT See **Electronic funds transfer**.

EFTA See **European Free Trade Association**.

EFTPOS See **Electronic funds transfer at point-of-sale**.

EFTS See **Electronic funds transfer system**.

Egg shell skull rule The rule requiring a tortfeasor to take his or her victim as the tortfeasor finds him or her, with all the victim's weaknesses, beliefs, and reactions as well as his or her capacities and attributes, physical, social, and economic: *Nader v Urban Transit Authority (NSW)* (1985) 2 NSWLR 501. Once it is established that the defendant could have foreseen some injury of the kind suffered by the plaintiff, the defendant is responsible for the full extent of damage to the plaintiff, even though, owing to some unusual weaknesses or defects peculiar to the plaintiff, the damage was greater than that which would have been suffered by the ordinary person: *Mount Isa Mines Ltd v Pusey* (1970) 125 CLR 383; *Levi v Colgate Palmolive Pty Ltd* (1941) 41 SR (NSW) 48. Also known as 'thin skull rule'.

Eggleston principles In corporations law, the set of considerations which the Australian Securities Commission must take into account when exercising its powers to exempt from, or modify the application of, Chapter 6 acquisition of shares provisions in the Corporations Law: Corporations Law s 731 See also **Australian Securities Commission; Share; Takeover**.

EGM See **Extraordinary general meeting**.

EIS See **Environmental impact statement**.

Ejectment An occupier's right to remove trespassers from the land or premises occupied, using such force as is reasonable in the circumstances: *Hackshaw v Shaw* (1984) 155 CLR 614; 56 ALR 417. Normally, even a trespasser should be asked to leave the premises before the occupier can exercise the right of ejectment, but no such request is required where the trespasser has clearly entered the premises forcibly: *Tullay v Reed* (1823) 1 C & P 6; 171 ER 1078. See also **Trespasser**.

Ejusdem generis /eɪʊsdɛm dʒɛnɛrɪs/ – of the same sort, kind, or nature. Where general words follow particular words the general words will often be construed as being limited to the same kind as the particular words. The parties may exclude the operation of the rule by using appropriate language: *Cody v J H Nelson Pty Ltd* (1947) 74 CLR 629. See also **Construction; Expressio unius est exclusio alterus; Intention; Interpretation**.

Elaborately transformed manufactures *Abbr* – ETMs Manufactured products or materials of an advanced nature such as engine components or special steels, in contrast to simply transformed manufactures (STMs) found in the processing of foods, fibre and mineral products. Manufacturing is a value-added process which may result in STMs or ETMs. For example, the conversion of bauxite into alumina involves a threefold increase in value, and its conversion into aluminium a further fivefold increase. A further step would be the transformation of aluminium billets into final products such as frames and components. ETMs account for about half of Australia's manufactured exports.

Elasticity of demand, cross See **Cross elasticity of demand**.

Elasticity of demand, income See **Income elasticity of demand**.

Elasticity of demand, price See **Price elasticity of demand**.

Elasticity of substitution A measure of the ease or difficulty of substituting between commodities by consumers or between factors of production by producers. The elasticity of substitution is equal to: the percentage change in the ratio in which two commodities are combined, divided by the percentage change in the ratio of their marginal utilities. A high value, indicating that substantial changes in the proportions of commodities combined produce little change in the relative marginal utilities, indicates a high degree of substitutability, and vice versa. See also **Cross elasticity of demand**; **Income elasticity of demand**; **Price elasticity of supply**.

Elasticity of supply, price See **Price elasticity of supply**.

•**Election** To determine in favour of a course of action, a thing, or a place. The word is used in a variety of legal contexts:

Contract An unequivocal act or clear words showing a choice between two inconsistent rights or remedies. See also **Affirmation**; **Rescission**; **Right to terminate**; **Waiver**.

Election of directors The process by which directors of a company are appointed to the Board. Generally rules governing the manner in which directors are elected will be found in the company's articles. See also **Director**; **Directors' duties**; **Election**; **Rotation of directors**.

Electronic company announcement system *Abbr* – ECAS A service provided by the Australian Stock Exchange (ASX) under which details of disclosures made to the ASX may be sent through a telecommunications system. Correspondence with the ASX which is not for public announcement is not to be sent through the ECAS. See also **Australian Stock Exchange Ltd**.

Electronic cottage A revival of the cottage-industry system whereby a fair proportion of the work force works from home, with each 'cottage' linked with a company central office by means of networked computer systems.

Electronic data interchange *Abbr* – EDI An electronic structure developed to handle the exchange of business documents including invoices and funds. The purpose of EDI is to improve commerce between suppliers and customers by reducing the costs associated with making manual payments. For example, there are approximately 20 steps involved in invoicing (including generating the invoice, sending it, approving it, writing a cheque, sending the cheque, then banking it). EDI is designed to reduce these steps to less than six. For EDI to work, all parties concerned must operate under the same EDI standard (of which there are several).

Electronic funds transfer *Abbr* – EFT Requesting and authorising the transfer of funds electronically. See also **Electronic funds transfer at point-of-sale**.

Electronic funds transfer at point-of-sale *Abbr* – EFTPOS Requesting and authorising the transfer of funds electronically at the point where a purchase is made. See also **Electronic funds transfer**.

Electronic Funds Transfer Code of Conduct A set of minimum procedures and rules governing the relationship between users and providers of electronic funds transfer (EFT) facilities. The code applies to transactions initiated by an individual through an electronic terminal by the combined use of an EFT plastic card and a personal identification number. See also **Credit card**; **Electronic funds transfer system**.

Electronic funds transfer system *Abbr* – EFTS A system which uses electronic accounting devices to transfer the right to a fund of money from one person to another, instead of using paper documentation to achieve the transfer. See also **Electronic Funds Transfer Code of Conduct**.

Electronic lodgment The lodgment of income tax returns under a scheme arranged by the Australian Taxation Office by which taxpayers (or their tax agents) lodge income tax returns using an electronic medium, such as computer disc or transmission of the information by modem. See also **Australian Taxation Office**; **Income taxation**.

Electronic mail *Abbr* – E-mail Using computers and telecommunications to transmit text and graphics messages across computer networks to others on the network or those with publicly-accessible mailing addresses (such as Internet addresses).

Electronically recorded obligations transferable in computers *Abbr* – EROTIC A system in which securities exist only as computer records, physical paper being eliminated. EROTIC move towards the 'dematerialisation' of paper. It has yet to make its appearance in Australia, where a bill of exchange is legally defined as an order 'in writing'. However, the system has been adopted increasingly overseas.

Eleven AM money market A name for the short-term money market in which interest may be earned on excess funds overnight or over the weekend. Funds can be placed any time after 11AM provided sufficient time is allowed to permit banking on the day; funds can then be withdrawn the following day any time before 11AM. The market is divided into the official and the unofficial; authorised dealers operate within the official market whereas merchant banks, building societies and others operate in the unofficial market. The various trading banks also operate an 11AM facility for their customers. Risk in the official market is generally lower than in the unofficial, while the rates offered vary between institutions. Minimum deposits are lower on the unofficial market.

•**Eligibility rules** In relation to an industrial organisation or association, the rules of the organisation or association that declare or relate to the conditions of eligibility for membership of it, or the description of the industry in connection with which the organisation is registered: (CTH) Industrial Relations Act 1988 s 4; (QLD) Industrial Relations Act 1990 s 5. See also **Industrial organisation**; **Trade union**.

•**Eligible annuity** An annuity payable under a superannuation policy under the (CTH) Income Tax Assessment Act 1936 Pt III, Div 8; an immediate annuity or a roll-over annuity; or a deferred annuity that becomes an immediate annuity no later than the 65th birthday of the taxpayer: s 27A(1). An annuity that does not meet the requirements of an eligible annuity is deemed to be an ineligible annuity: s 27A(1). See also **Annuity; Deferred annuity; Immediate annuity; Pension; Rollover annuity**.

Eligible applicant In relation to a corporation, the Australian Securities Commission (ASC), a liquidator or an administrator of the corporation, an administrator of a deed of company arrangement executed by the corporation, or a person authorised in writing by the ASC to make applications in relation to the examination of any person about a corporation's affairs and orders against a person in relation to a corporation: Corporations Law s 9; *Re AGT (Vic) Pty Ltd (in liq)* (1985) 10 ACLR 308; 4 ACLC 310. In relation to an application to the ASC for deregistration of a defunct company under Corporations Law s 573, it refers to the company or a member of the company or any other interested person: s 573(1). See also **Deregistration**.

•**Eligible commodity agreement** See **Deliverable futures contract**.

•**Eligible exchange traded option** *Abbr* – EETO A contract entered into on a futures exchange under which a party acquires an option from another party. The option may be: to buy or sell a commodity at a price determined in accordance with the contract; or to be paid an amount determined by the variation of a specific number from a certain prescribed stock index: Corporations Law s 9. See also **Futures exchange; Option**.

•**Eligible service period** The period of a person's service with an employer, employers, or an employer-sponsored superannuation fund. The eligible service period is used in calculating the income tax applicable to a person's eligible termination payment: (CTH) Income Tax Assessment Act 1936 s 27A(1). See also **Eligible Termination Payment**.

Eligible taxable income The eligible assessable income of a person under 18 on the last day of the year of income after deducting the allowable deductions relating specifically to that income. See also **Apportionable deduction; Assessable income; Excepted assessable income; Excepted person; Year of income**.

•**Eligible Termination Payment** *Abbr* – ETP A payment to an employee by an employer, a superannuation fund, or approved deposit fund (where not paid in the form of a pension or annuity) in consequence of the retirement or termination of employment of the employee. See also **Annuity; Approved deposit fund; Superannuation fund**.

Elliott review Report reviewing the Australian banking industry and monitoring the implementation of the Martin (Parliamentary) report on banking. The review was undertaken in April 1992 by the House of Representatives Standing Committee on Banking, Finance and Public Administration under the chairmanship of Mr Paul Elliott MHR. The report was issued in November 1992. See also **Australian banking system; Bank inquiry**.

E-mail See **Electronic mail**.

Embargo *Abbr* – emb Any restriction or prohibition imposed upon commerce by law.

Foreign relations A prohibition on the import or export of goods. Embargo, in international law, may be hostile and can be a method of conflict resolution and redress for perceived wrongs.

Maritime law An order restricting the movement of ships or cargo into or within a country's ports. The making of an embargo order is usually motivated by the desire to protect the country's interests, for example in times of war.

Embezzlement A statutory offence committed by a clerk or servant who misappropriates property received in the course of employment for, and under the authority of, the master or employer: (NSW) Crimes Act 1900 s 157; (SA) Criminal Law Consolidation Act 1935 s 176(1)(b). The offence occurs before the property has passed into the possession of the employee; it is distinguished from 'larceny by servant', which is committed by an employee who appropriates property entrusted to the employee's custody by the employer: (NSW) Crimes Act 1900 s 156. See also **Larceny; Misappropriation**.

Emolument A monetary advantage, whether casual or constant, arising from the occupation of an office, station or situation: *Nette v Howarth* (1935) 53 CLR 55. Under the Corporations Law s 9 emolument means the amount or value of any money, consideration or benefit given, directly or indirectly, to a director of a body corporate in connection with the management of the affairs of the body. See also **Director's remuneration; Wage**.

•**Employee** A person who works under a contract of employment with an employer, rather than under some other kind of contract for work. Under (CTH) Income Tax Assessment Act 1936 s 221A(1) an 'employee' is a person who receives or is entitled to receive salary or wages. An employee is subject, at least in principle, to the control of an employer in the way the work is done, although control may be very limited when the employee has special skills required by the employer: *Stevens v Brodribb Sawmilling Co Pty Ltd* (1986) 160 CLR 16; 63 ALR 513. See also **Contract of employment; Employer; Employer's duty of care; Independent contractor; Industry**.

Employee contribution Payment to a superannuation fund by an employee, for the purpose of providing superannuation for the employee in the future, normally payable upon the retirement, redundancy, or death of the employee. See also **Employer contribution; Superannuation fund**.

Employee incentive scheme An arrangement by which employees of a company receive certain awards over and above their usual salary, often based on the performance of the company. See also **Employee share scheme**.

•**Employee Ombudsman** In South Australia, an office established by the (SA) Industrial and Employee Relations Act 1994 advising employees on their rights and obligations under awards and enterprise agreements, and the available avenues for enforcing their rights; investigating claims of coercion in the negotiation of enterprise agreements; scrutinising enterprise agreements; representing employees in certain proceedings; advising individual home-based workers on negotiating individual contracts; investigating the work conditions of outworkers; and advising employees of their rights in occupational health and safety issues: (SA) Industrial and Employee Relations Act 1994 s 62. See also **Enterprise agreement; Industrial award; Ombudsman**.

Employee organisation An organisation of employees that has been registered under industrial relations legislation as an organisation for furthering or protecting the interests of its members: for example (CTH) Industrial Relations Act 1988 s 189(1). See also **Employer organisation; Trade union**.

Employee share buy-back See **Employee share scheme buy-back**.

Employee share plan See **Employee share scheme**.

Employee share scheme An arrangement under which shares are allotted to employees in a company, usually at a discount to market or issue price. The shares may be allotted depending on the employee's years of service with the company or as part of a benefit scheme or plan. Also known as 'employee share plan'. See also **Employee incentive scheme; Purchase of employee shares**.

Employee share scheme buy-back A type of permitted buy-back where a company buys shares held by, or for the benefit of, current or former employees, including executive directors, according to the terms of an employee share scheme: Corporations Law s 206BB, ss 206HA-206HC. A participating employee is an employee or director of the body corporate or a related body corporate: Corporations Law s 9. Formerly known as 'employee-shares purchase'. See also **Authorised buy-back; Employee share scheme**.

•**Employee shares purchase** See **Employee share scheme buy-back**.

•**Employer** A person who engages another to work under a contract of employment. Under (CTH) Income Tax Assessment Act 1936 s 221A(1) an 'employer' is a person who pays or is liable to pay salary or wages. In principle, the employer exercises control over how the work is performed, although the extent of control may be limited: *Stevens v Brodribb Sawmilling Co Pty Ltd* (1986) 160 CLR 16; 63 ALR 513. See also **Contract of employment; Employee; Employer's duty of care; Vicarious liability**.

•**Employer contribution** Payment to a superannuation fund by an employer for an employee, for the purpose of providing superannuation which is normally payable upon the retirement, redundancy, or death of the employee. See also **Employment agreement; Employee contribution; Employer sponsor; Superannuation fund**.

Employer nomination Employer sponsorship of a person overseas to migrate to Australia for the purpose of working for that employer. An employer nomination must be for a business in Australia and require a permanent full-time highly skilled person. The employer must have provision in place for the training of present employees in work related to the business. The Minister must be satisfied that an Australian citizen or permanent resident who is suitable cannot be found or that the employer should not be required to seek a suitable employee in Australia: (CTH) Migration Regulations reg 5.19. See also **Employee; Employer; Employer Nomination Scheme**.

Employer Nomination Scheme *Abbr* – ENS A program enabling employers to sponsor highly skilled workers to Australia for business purposes. See also **Employee; Employer; Employer nomination**.

Employer organisation An organisation of employers that has been registered under industrial relations legislation, such as the (CTH) Industrial Relations Act 1988. See also **Employee; Employee organisation**.

•**Employer sponsor** In relation to a superannuation fund, an employer who has contributed to the fund for the benefit of an employee: (CTH) Superannuation Industry (Supervision) Act 1993 s 16(1). See also **Employer contribution; Superannuation fund**.

Employers' association An organisation that consists wholly or mainly of employers or individual owners of undertakings, and whose principal purposes include regulating the relations between those employers and workers or trade unions. It includes combinations of employers and employers' associations. Examples are the Confederation of Australian Industry, the Business Council of Australia, the Australian Baker's Association, the Australian Merchant Bankers' Association, the Australian Chamber of Manufactures, the Australian Chambers of Commerce, the Metal Trades Industry Association, the National Farmers' Federation, the NSW Employers' Federation and the Victorian Employers' Federation. See also **Australian Chamber of Commerce and Industry**.

Employer's duty of care In negligence, the duty of care owed by an employer to its employees. An employer's duty of care comprises the duty to provide safe tools and equipment; a safe place of work; and a safe system of work, including the employment of competent fellow employees: *Wilsons & Clyde Coal Co v English Ltd* [1938] AC 57. See also **Duty of care; Employee; Employer; Employer's liability; Negligence; Non-delegable duty; Workers' compensation**.

Employer's duty to be good and considerate The duty of an employer to be good and considerate to employees, and not to do anything likely to destroy the relationship of confidence between them: *Woods v WM Car Services* (Peterborough) [1982] ICR 693. The duty has been suggested as a corollary to the employee's duty to be good and faithful, but it is not an established legal principle. See also **Duty of care and skill; Duty of confidentiality; Duty of attendance; Duty of fidelity; Duty of obedience; Misconduct**.

Employer's duty to be reasonable See **Employer's duty to be good and considerate**.

Employer's duty to provide work See **Right to work**.

Employer's liability The liability of an employer for acts or omissions of its employees which cause injury or damage to third parties, and for the failure to protect employees from injury at work. Under the first head, an employer is vicariously liable for the negligence of servants, but not generally independent contractors, acting in the course of their employment: *Stevens v Brodribb Sawmilling Co Pty Ltd* (1986) 160 CLR 16; 63 ALR 513. Under the second head, liability arises through the employer's non-delegable duty of care towards its employees, which entails a general duty to safeguard employees from unreasonable risk of injury while at work. See also **Agreement; Employee; Employer; Employer's duty of care; Independent contractor; Vicarious liability; Workers' compensation**.

Employer's liability system A type of workers' compensation system, by which liability to pay compensation to a worker injured in the course of employment falls on the worker's employer, who is required to insure against that liability: for example (NSW) Workers Compensation Act 1987. It differs from fund liability. See also **Employee; Employer; Employer's liability; Employer's personal liability; Workers' compensation**.

Employer's personal liability The liability of an employer to a third person for an employee's tortious acts that are expressly authorised by the employer, or that result from the employer's inadequate supervision of the employee, or that are ratified by the employer. In these circumstances the employer is personally liable to the third person for the tort: *Dawson v Shire of Bulli* (1927) 27 SR (NSW) 509. See also **Vicarious liability**.

•**Employment** A relationship in which parties agree that one party will perform work for another in exchange for remuneration, subject to certain terms and conditions contained in the contract of employment, and in industrial awards, agreements or legislation. The employment relationship imports certain rights and duties for the parties which do not exist in other contracts for work. Generally, 'employment' means working under a contract of service. It has different definitions in various statutes for different purposes. For example, under (CTH) Sex Discrimination Act 1984 s 4 it includes work under a contract for services. It may also include work as an unpaid worker ((ACT) Discrimination Act 1991 s 4), or work as a self-employed person ((SA) Workers Rehabilitation and Compensation Act 1986 s 3). It may refer to the work of the employee, rather than to the contract: *Hall v Centreway Cafe Co Pty Ltd* [1916] VLR 560. See also **Contract of employment; Contract of service; Employee; Employer; Employment agreement; Employment law; Employment matters; Independent contractor**.

•**Employment agreement** An agreement between an employer and employees, setting out the terms and conditions of the employment. An employment agreement may be entered into at the collective or individual level. Under (VIC) Employee Relations Act 1992 s 163, a party to the agreement must comply with every applicable provision of the agreement. See also **Enterprise agreement; Individual employment agreement**.

Employment and indemnity clause In maritime law, a clause in a charterparty providing that the master of the vessel is under the orders of the charterer, rather than the shipowner, and that the charterer must indemnify the owner against any liability arising out of the charterer's orders to the master. The shipowner may only require indemnity where there is a causal connection between the liability and the charterer's orders. Under an employment and indemnity clause, the master becomes the agent of the charterer in connection with the employment of the chartered vessel. Such a clause is often found in a time charter. See also **Charterer; Charterparty; Master; Owner**.

•**Employment contract** See **Contract of employment**.

•**Employment declaration** A declaration of details of employment such as the date of commencement of work, the title of the position, and entitlements to tax rebate and the tax free threshold. Employment declarations must be in a form approved by the Commissioner of Taxation ((CTH) Income Tax Assessment Act 1936 s 202C(5)) and are ineffective unless the tax file number of the employee is stated in the declaration: s 202CB(1). See also **Employment; Employment agreement**.

Employment law The area of law concerned with the relationship between the employer and the individual employee. It differs from industrial law. Employment law regulates the formation, performance and termination of a contract of employment as the basis of the employment relationship. See also **Employee; Employer; Employment; Industrial law; Labour law**.

•**Employment matters** The range of employment-related matters, including the recruitment procedure and selection criteria for appointing or engaging persons as employees; promoting and transferring employees; training and staff development; and conditions of service for employees: (CTH) Affirmative Action (Equal Employment Opportunity for Women) Act 1986 s 3. See also **Employee; Employer; Employment; Employment agreement; Employment law**.

Employment protection Legislation, awards and practices which specifically relate to the obligations, duties, responsibilities and rights of an employer and an employee on the termination of the employee's employment: for example (NSW) Employment Protection Act 1982. See also **Employment protection provision; Protection**.

Employment protection provision A provision that the Industrial Relations Commission (IRC) of New South Wales may be required to insert in an award: (NSW) Industrial Relations Act 1996 s 24. Employment protection provisions relate to the obligations, duties, responsibilities and rights of an employer and an employee on the termination of the employee's employment. The IRC must have regard to the principles established under the (NSW) Employment Protection Act 1982 when inserting employment protection provisions. See also **Industrial award; Redundancy**.

Employment reference 1. A written statement by an employer given to the employee upon the employee's resignation, or at the end of the employment contract, attesting to the personal suitability or otherwise of the

employee. An employment reference usually covers matters such as the employee's integrity, skills, ability and practical experience in the job. **2.** A written or oral reference given directly by the current employer to a prospective employer. At common law an employer is not obliged to give an employee a reference; however, an award or industrial agreement may require the employer to give a reference or a statement of service. See also **Employee; Employment law.**

Employment related expense An expense incurred by a taxpayer in producing salary or wages: (CTH) Income Tax Assessment Act 1936 s 82KT (1). Common examples of employment related expenses include the cost of tools and protective clothing. Other expenses which are specifically included are periodical subscriptions to professional associations, depreciation, repairs, and expenses associated with loans used to produce salary or wages: (CTH) Income Tax Assessment Act 1936 s 82KT(1). Employment related expenses exclude car expenses, travel expenses or specified expenses in relation to meal allowances or travel allowances: (CTH) Income Tax Assessment Act 1936 s 82KT(1). Also known as 'work related expense'. See also **Car expense; Depreciation; Employment; Incurred.**

Employment, scope of See **Scope of employment.**

Employment-related skill A skill used, or that may be used, by a person in the course of holding any office or appointment, performing any functions or duties, engaging in any work, or doing anything, that results in the person being an employee. It includes any business, occupation, profession or trade carried out by the person otherwise than as an employee: (CTH) Training Guarantee (Administration) Act 1990 (repealed) s 4. See also **Employee; Employment; Employment agreement; Employment matters.**

Emptio spei /ɛmptioʊ speɪ/ *Lat* – the sale and purchase of the chance of obtaining goods, rather than of the goods themselves: *Hanks v Palling* (1856) 6 E & B 659; 119 ER 1009 at 1013. Such a contract is contingent on the part of the seller but absolute on the part of the buyer.

Encryption In data transmission, encoding (scrambling) data in order to increase security during transmission. Before the data can be retrieved in its original format, it must be decrypted through the use of a password or a secret coding scheme.

•**Encumbrance** A proprietary right held by one person over the property of another that limits the ways in which the owner may use or deal with the property. Mortgages, trusts for securing money, liens, and charges are all encumbrances: for example (NSW) Conveyancing Act 1919 s 7; *Davies v Littlejohn* (1923) 34 CLR 174. See also **Charge; Charge; Equitable charge; Mortgage.**

Endorsee See **Indorsee.**

•**Endorsement** See **Indorsement.**

•**Endorser** See **Indorser.**

Endowment insurance A contract of insurance providing for a sum of money to be paid to the insured should the insured survive beyond a specified age or period of time: *Prudential Assurance Co v IRC* [1904] 2 KB 658; *NM Superannuation Pty Ltd v Young* (1993) 41 FCR 182; 113 ALR 39. See also **Insurance; Life Insurance.**

Endowment mortgage A mortgage which combines an interest-only bank loan with a life insurance policy. The bulk of the monthly repayments goes towards paying off the interest on the bank loan, while the balance attracts high earnings through the life insurance policy. When the value of the life insurance policy equals the amount borrowed, the loan is automatically cleared. Popular in Europe and the United States, endowment mortgages are gaining ground in Australia. A home bought with such a loan is an unencumbered asset. See also **Endowment insurance; Mortgage.**

•**Enforcement expense** In consumer law, an amount that a debtor is liable to pay a credit provider for expense incurred by the credit provider in exercising a right under a regulated contract which arises from the debtor's default: (NSW) Credit Act 1984 (repealed) s 76; (VIC) Credit Act 1984 (repealed) s 76 (now replaced by Uniform Consumer Credit Code). See also **Credit provider; Creditor; Debtor; Regulated contract.**

Enforcement of judgment To compel compliance with a judgment or order through means such as attachment, committal, fine, sequestration or execution. There are statutory provisions for the enforcement of judgments and orders: for example (NSW) Supreme Court Act 1970 Pt 6 Div 4; (NSW) Supreme Court Rules 1970 Pt 42; (VIC) Rules of the Supreme Court Ch I O 66. See also **Judgment; Sequestration.**

•**Engaging in conduct** Doing or not doing any act, including making or giving effect to a provision of a contract, arrangement or understanding: (CTH) Trade Practices Act 1974 s 4(2); (CTH) Industrial Relations Act 1988 s 157. See also **Conduct; Consumer protection; Contract.**

Engineering contract A contract, such as a building construction contract, entered into with an engineer for the provision of services. The Association of Consulting Engineers Australia publishes a standard form agreement for engineering contracts. See also **Building contract.**

Enhanced injury claim A product liability claim in which it is alleged that a defect in design enhanced the plaintiff's injury (but did not itself cause that injury): for example *Larsen v General Motors Corp* 274 F Supp 461 (1967); *Uner v GIO of NSW* (1987) 4 MVR 481. See also **Defect in design.**

•**Enrichment** In restitution, a benefit which has economic value to the recipient or in the market place, including property, a chose in action, a service, a payment of expense, a decrease in liability, or forbearance: *Pavey & Matthews Pty Ltd v Paul* (1987) 162 CLR 221 at 263; 69 ALR 577. See also **Free acceptance; Incontrovertible benefit; Restitution; Unjust enrichment.**

•**Enter into** To become a party to; to engage in; to accept the obligations of: Corporations Law s 206AAA. See also **Agreement.**

Entering an appearance 1. Through counsel or in person, coming to court as party to a suit. **2.** The voluntary submission to a court's jurisdiction: (CTH) Federal Court Rules O 9 r 1; *Bay Marine Pty Ltd v Clayton Country Properties Pty Ltd (No 2)* (1986) 8 NSWLR 104; 11 ACLR 326; *IAC (Finance) Pty Ltd v Murphy* (1971) 1 CCR (Vic) 189. An appearance may be entered through a memorandum or notice of appearance. If a case is heard in the absence of a party, it is said to have been heard ex parte. **3.** Failure to enter an appearance may result in a judgment being entered against a party: *Alliance Acceptance Co Ltd v Macas* (1976) 12 ACTR 19; 26 FLR 451. See also **Appearance**.

Entering judgment The formal recording of judgment in civil actions. Generally in superior courts entering judgment is a separate procedure required of a party. See also **Judgment**.

•**Enterprise** A venture or undertaking, especially one involving financial commitment.

Industrial law A business that is carried on by a single employer, a geographically distinct part of such a business, or two or more geographically distinct parts of the same business carried on by a single employer: (CTH) Industrial Relations Act 1988 s 170LC. See also **Business; Business undertaking; Entrepreneur; Enterprise agreement**.

Taxation and revenue A business and any other industrial or commercial undertaking: (CTH) Income Tax Assessment Act 1936 s 128A. Business includes any profession, trade, employment, vocation or calling but not as an employee and any other industrial or commercial undertaking: (CTH) Income Tax Assessment Act 1936 s 6. An enterprise may consist of one or more activities or one or more transactions, provided they were entered into for business or commercial purposes: *Thiel v FCT* (1990) 171 CLR 338; 94 ALR 647. It includes the means by which, or framework within which, an activity is engaged: *Thiel v FCT*. See also **Business**.

•**Enterprise agreement** An agreement between an employer and employees (or an industrial organisation of employees or a works committee) which regulates the conditions of employment of persons employed in a single enterprise in any trade or occupation: (NSW) Industrial Relations Act 1996 ss 4, 29, 30. See also **Australian Industrial Relations Commission; Employee organisation; Enterprise; Enterprise bargaining; Industrial award**.

Enterprise bargaining The process of negotiation between an employer and employees (or their representatives) in order to reach an agreement regulating the terms and conditions of employment within a particular enterprise or workplace. Also known as 'workplace bargaining'. See also **Australian Industrial Relations Commission; Arbitration; Enterprise agreement; Collective bargaining**.

Enterprise flexibility agreement Abbr – EFA An agreement between employers and employees in a single enterprise, addressing matters pertaining to the relationship between the employers and employees: (CTH) Industrial Relations Act 1988 s 170NA. An EFA differs from a certified agreement in that it is not necessary for a union to be a party. The Australian Industrial Relations Commission may approve implementation of an agreement if certain conditions are fulfilled including that the agreement does not disadvantage the employees: ss 170NB, 170NC. See also **Australian Industrial Relations Commission; Certified agreement; Enterprise; Enterprise bargaining; No-disadvantage test; Trade union**.

Enterprise flexibility clause A provision that must be inserted in a federal award by the Australian Industrial Relations Commission, so far as it thinks appropriate, establishing a process for agreements to be negotiated at the enterprise or workplace level, about how the award should be varied so as to make the enterprise or workplace operate more efficiently according to its particular needs: (CTH) Industrial Relations Act 1988 s 113A. See also **Australian Industrial Relations Commission; Award; Enterprise flexibility agreement; No-disadvantage test**.

Enterprise union A union whose membership consists entirely of the employees of one particular employer. Enterprise unions are usually found in the public and finance sectors. See also **Craft union; General union; Industry union; Occupational union**.

Entire contract A contract in which the parties have agreed expressly or impliedly that complete performance by the plaintiff is a condition precedent to the recovery of the contract price: *Cutter v Powell* (1795) 6 TR 320; 101 ER 573. See also **Condition precedent; Entire contract clause; Implied term; Performance; Severable contract**.

Entire contract clause A clause in a document to the effect that the document contains the whole contract between the parties. An entire contract clause is effective to exclude collateral agreements and implied terms, other than those which are legal incidents of the particular class of contract: *Hart v McDonald* (1910) 10 CLR 417. See also **Collateral contract; Entire contract; Estoppel; Implied term; Misleading or deceptive conduct; Representation**.

Entitlement issue The offer of new shares by a company to existing shareholders for the purpose of raising further capital for the company. It is similar in all respects to a rights issue save that the offer is non-renounceable, that is, it cannot be sold or transferred. The shareholder must choose to either take up the offer or allow it to lapse. There is no entitlement trading. See also **Non-renounceable issues; Share**.

•**Entitlement to shares** In corporations law, a person is entitled to the shares in which the person or an associate of the person has a relevant interest or to which the person is deemed to be entitled by virtue of certain facts relating to those shares pursuant to a relevant agreement: Corporations Law s 609. See also **Associate; Relevant interest**.

•**Entity 1.** A natural person, company, partnership or trust ((CTH) Bankruptcy Act 1966 s 5(1)) except for the purposes of Corporations Law Pts 3.2A, 3.6, and 3.7: Corporations Law s 64A. **2.** For the purposes of Corporations Law Pt 3.2A, a body corporate, partnership, unincorporated body, individual and a trustee of a trust that has only one trustee: Corporations Law s 242C(1). See also **Associated entity; Controlled entity; Corporation; **Chief entity**; **Disclosing entity**; **Economic entity**; **Parent entity**; **Reporting entity**.

Entity based reporting The system of reporting by the preparation and issuing of financial statements, irrespective of the original legal form of the reporting body. The reporting entity may include a company, a subsidiary company, branch, division, partnership or trust. See also **Entity**.

Entrant In trade practices law, a market participant who begins supplying goods or services in a market or market segment in which that participant has not previously supplied those goods or services. The likelihood of there being entrants or potential entrants is now seen as an especially important factor in determining the degree of competition in a market. See also **Barrier to entry**; **Competition**; **Contestable market**; **Market**; **Submarket**.

•**Entrepreneur** A person who accepts the management responsibility and financial risk of a business enterprise: for example (QLD) Second-hand Dealers and Collectors Act 1984 s 6(1). The term is often restricted to those who do so with exceptional innovative ability and flair. See also **Business**; **Enterprise**.

•**Environment** **1.** The entire context within which business is conducted embracing product viability, sales and marketing, profitability, market structure, competition, people, policies and regulations, finance, taxation, trends, the state of the economy and future opportunities. **2.** All aspects of the surroundings of humanity, whether affecting individuals or social groupings: (CTH) Environment Protection (Impact of Proposals) Act 1974 s 3; (NSW) Environmental Planning and Assessment Act 1979 s 4(1).

Environment Protection Authority (NSW) *Abbr* – EPA An agency created by the (NSW) Protection of the Environment Administration Act 1991 to protect, restore and enhance the quality of the environment in New South Wales and to administer State legislation relating to such matters as air and water quality, catchment management, noise, radiation, waste disposal, dangerous goods, and environmental offences and penalties: (NSW) Protection of the Environment Administration Act 1991 ss 4, 6(1), 7(1). See also **Environment**.

Environment related capital expenditure Expenditure incurred by a taxpayer on business to enhance or beautify an industrial site by preventing or combating pollution or removing waste produced by the business: (CTH) Income Tax Assessment Act 1936 s 82BB. For expenditure to be tax deductible as environment related capital expenditure, the costs incurred must be for the sole purpose of controlling pollution and improving the environment. See also **Allowable deduction**; **Capital**; **Environment**.

•**Environmental impact statement** *Abbr* – EIS A document describing a proposed development or activity and disclosing the possible, probable, or certain effects of that proposal on the environment: *Prineas v Forestry Commission* (1984) 53 LGRA 160. An EIS should be comprehensive, objective, and sufficiently specific for a reasonably intelligent and informed mind to examine the potential environmental consequences of carrying out or not carrying out that proposal.

Environmental study As conceived in environmental planning legislation, a study undertaken of a local government area, in whole or part, prior to the making of a local environmental plan or planning scheme. An environment study seeks information about land, the local economy, the environment and the people of the area. It aims to identify problems that may require setting special standards, for example in flood prone areas; provide a basis for varying general standards to meet local requirements; provide information to assist in making development and other applications to the council; and assist the council in its assessment of them. See also **Environment**.

Environmentally friendly product A consumer product holding itself out as incorporating high environmental standards in its production and having negligible impact on the environment in its manufacture, use and disposal. Legislative standards have not yet been developed for such products.

Equal access buy-back scheme A type of share buy-back where a company makes uniform offers to every holder of ordinary shares to buy back a particular percentage of their ordinary shares. Each holder of ordinary shares must have a reasonable opportunity to accept the offers and buy-back agreements may not be entered into until a specified time for acceptance of offers has closed: Corporations Law s 206C. Previously known as a 'Buy-back Scheme'. See also **Buy-back scheme**.

Equal opportunity A principle that requires all persons to be entitled to the same opportunities and not be subjected to artificial, irrelevant or unnecessary barriers. It is closely related to the concept of non-discrimination and is often included in or related to anti-discrimination legislation. See also **Affirmative action program**; **Anti-discrimination legislation**.

Equal pay The principle that rates of remuneration should be established without discrimination based on sex; that is, men and women workers should receive equal remuneration for work of equal value. See also **Industrial tribunal**; **Remuneration**.

Equal remuneration See **Equal pay**.

Equipment leasing Leasing of assets for a certain period of time at an agreed rental by a manufacturer seeking finance arranged with a finance company. The assets remain the property of the finance company until the lease expires and the residual value is paid in full by the manufacturer. See also **Finance company**; **Lease**.

•**Equitable** Pertaining to or valid in equity, as distinguished from the common law. See also **Common law**; **Equity**.

Equitable assets Property which is held in trust for the benefit of a person other than the legal owner. See also **Acquire**; **Notice**.

Equitable assignment An assignment of legal or equitable property, taking effect in equity, not at common law. Equitable property is assignable only in equity. See also **Assignment**; **Equity**; **Legal assignment**.

Equitable charge A security interest over property which gives the holder of the charge (the 'chargee') an equitable interest in the property to the extent necessary to satisfy the debt owed to the chargee. As a security interest, the charge will have priority over the rights of unsecured creditors. See also **Charge; Equitable lien; Equitable mortgage; Mortgage; Priority; Security; Unsecured creditor**.

Equitable compensation Equitable relief within equity's exclusive jurisdiction, granted by way of restitution for breach of a fiduciary or other equitable obligations. The measure of the relief is the loss to the plaintiff, rather than the gain to the defendant. The principles of assessment bear no necessary correlation to the assessment of common law damages: *United States Surgical Corp v Hospital Products International Pty Ltd* [1982] 2 NSWLR 766. This jurisdiction does not permit the award of equitable damages. See also **Compensation; Restitution**.

Equitable defence A bar to a grant of relief, recognised by a court of equity but not necessarily by a court of common law. Equitable defences include acquiescence, estoppel, set-off, and release. See also **Acquiescence; Equity; Estoppel; Laches; Set-off**.

Equitable interest An interest in property enforced and created by the Court of Chancery in the situation where it would have been unconscionable for the legal owner of the property to retain the benefit of the property for himself or herself. Equitable interests are 'hybrid' interests which are in between jura in rem and jura in personam. See also **Beneficial interest; Legal interest**.

Equitable lease A lease arising by virtue of the doctrine in *Walsh v Lonsdale* (1882) 21 Ch D 9 and the maxim that equity considers done that which ought to have been done: *Progressive Mailing House Pty Ltd v Tabali Pty Ltd* (1985) 157 CLR 17 at 26; 57 ALR 609. See also **Agreement for lease; Doctrine of bona fide purchaser for value without notice; Lease; Specific performance**.

Equitable lien An equitable remedy created by a court, regardless of the intention of the parties, as a remedial device to protect a party against some inequitable loss: *Stephenson Nominees Pty Ltd v Official Receiver* (1987) 16 FCR 536 at 554; 76 ALR 485. See also **Equitable charge; Equity; Hypothecation; Lien**.

Equitable mortgage A mortgage of property, enforceable in a court of equity. See also **Equity; Equity of redemption; Mortgage; Part-performance; Specific performance**.

Equitable property A right or title enforced by a court of equity but not at common law; property assignable only in equity not at law. It may be assigned for value or, except in the case of an assignment by way of security, voluntarily: *Norman v FCT* (1963) 109 CLR 9; [1964] ALR 131. See also **Beneficial interest; Equity; Equitable lien; Voluntary assignment**.

•**Equitable remuneration** The payment to trustees from trust assets, by order of a court of equity, for services performed for the benefit of the trust. The permission to remunerate trustees is normally granted by the settlor (as expressed in the trust instrument) or by statute: *Nissen v Grunden* (1912) 14 CLR 297. See also **Settlor; Trust account; Trustee**.

Equitable right to redeem The equitable right to recover property the subject of a security transaction. It is distinguished from an equity of redemption, which arises immediately upon the giving of the security: *Kreglinger v New Patagonia Meat and Cold Storage Co Ltd* [1914] AC 25. See also **Equity; Equity of redemption; Securities law**.

Equitable set-off A set-off recognised by a court of equity upon the defendant showing good equitable grounds for doing so. The defendant's claim must go to the root of the plaintiff's title, impeaching the plaintiff's right to relief. The mere existence of cross demands is insufficient: *Rawson v Samuel* (1841) Cr & Ph 161; 41 ER 451. Equitable set-off will be recognised: where a right of set-off is recognised at law; where a court of equity acts by way of analogy to the common law; by agreement; and by showing some equitable ground for being protected. See also **Equity; Retainer; Set-off**.

Equitable suretyship An obligation of suretyship in which there is a primary liability and a secondary liability of two persons for the debt of one only. Payment of the debt by the second person gives that person a right of reimbursement or indemnity from the first person. The obligation is not dependent upon a contract: *AM Spicer & Son Pty Ltd (in liq) v Spicer* (1931) 47 CLR 151; 37 ALR 357. An example is the relationship between the endorser and an acceptor to a bill of exchange. Such an obligation may also arise by estoppel. See also **Bill of exchange; Estoppel**.

Equities between debtors The equitable right of a person, who is or was a debtor in conjunction with others and has paid a disproportionately large share of the common debt, to be reimbursed by the other debtors: *Albion Insurance Co Ltd v GIO (NSW)* (1969) 121 CLR 342; [1970] ALR 441. See also **Contribution; Guarantor**.

•**Equity** *OF – equité* – fair, even **1.** The separate body of law, developed in the Court of Chancery, which supplements, corrects, and controls the rules of common law. **2.** A right recognised by a court of equity, based on ethical concepts, and justifying in certain cases the judicial intervention of that court. In a sense all equities are personal, but some may have proprietary effect: *Mercantile Mutual Life Insurance Co Ltd v Gosper* (1991) 25 NSWLR 32. The term denotes: the right to obtain an injunction or other equitable relief; an equitable interest in property; an exception to the indefeasibility of title acquired by a proprietor of Torrens title land upon registration, usually called a personal equity (*Garofano v Reliance Finance Corp Ltd* (1992) NSW Conv R ¶55-640); a 'floating equity'; and a 'mere equity': *Latec Investments Ltd v Hotel Terrigal Pty Ltd (in liq)* (1965) 113 CLR 265. See also **Common law; Equitable interest; Floating equity; Indefeasibility of title; Injunction; Mere equity**.

Corporations **1.** Funds contributed by the owners of a business. Equity contributors are entitled to the profits of the business while bearing the risks and losses. Equity comprises in the case of companies, share capital usually through the holding of ordinary shares;

in the case of partnership, partners' capital; in the case of trusts, trust capital and; in the case of sole traders, the proprietor's contributions other than borrowings. Businesses are generally financed by a combination of equity and borrowings; bonds, debentures and unsecured notes are debt rather than equity. **2.** In an accounting sense, the residual interest in the assets of an entity after deduction of its liabilities: Statement of Accounting Concepts SAC 4. **3.** The residual value of the total initial and variations margins in a futures trading account, assuming its liquidation at the current market price. See also **Equitable mortgage; Equity funding; Share capital.**

Equity accounting The accounting method that requires a company with an interest in another company amounting to control over management, or at least influencing management, to report to its members the result of the exercise of that control or influence: Australian Accounting Standard (AAS) 14. The interest does not have to be that of a holding company. According to accounting conventions, a holding of not less than 20 per cent of the particular share capital is enough for this purpose: AAS 14. Equity accounting requires consolidated accounts for the companies which are associated. In the first year that a listed company adopts equity accounting it must explain the changes in its reports caused by the change in accounting: ASX Listing Rules Appendix 4B. See also **Accounting; Australian Accounting Standards Board; Generally accepted accounting principles; Group accounts.**

Equity derivative A derivative whose value relates to the value of particular shares. For example, a put or call option over a specified quantity of an identified share; or a forward contract for the future delivery of a specified quantity of an identified share. See also **Derivative; Securities.**

Equity funding The funding of company operations through the issue of new shares at par, at premium or at discount. An alternative to debt funding. See also **At a discount; At a premium; At par; Share.**

Equity method A method of consolidated accounting for inter company investments where the investment is recorded initially at cost and the carrying value is adjusted in subsequent periods to indicate the investor's share of post acquisition earnings of the company: Australian Accounting Standard AAS 14. See also **Consolidated accounts; Equity accounting.**

•**Equity of redemption** The bundle of rights that a court of equity regards a mortgagor as having in the mortgaged property including the right to the return of mortgaged property after repayment of the relevant money to the mortgagee. See also **Clog on the equity of redemption; Equity; Equitable right to redeem; Mortgage; Mortgagee's power of sale.**

Equity security Under the listing requirements applicable for the Australian Stock Exchange Ltd, any shares (including preference shares), stock, stock units, units and rights to or options to subscribe for any of them: ASX Listing Rules rule 19.12. Normally equities do not include preference shares. See also **All ordinaries index; Australian Stock Exchange Ltd; Preference share.**

Equity trust A unit trust or managed trust which invests in shares. See also **Share; Trust; Unit trust.**

Equity-debt ratio Proprietary ratio. The ratio of shareholders' equity to total liabilities. The ratio reveals how much of the total assets of a company is financed by shareholders' funds and how much by borrowings. An equity ratio of 1:2 indicates that half of the total assets of a business are financed by shareholders' funds and half by outside creditors. The ratio will be influenced in part by the nature of the business; for example, a finance company tends to have a high dependence on borrowed funds and would operate on a lower proprietary ratio than a manufacturer. See also **Dividend policy; Gearing; Equity; Shareholder.**

Error of fact An error made by a decision maker about the existence of a particular fact. Generally, a simple error of fact is not a ground for judicial review: *Waterford v Commonwealth* (1987) 163 CLR 54; *Azzopardi v Tasman UEB Industries Ltd* (1985) 4 NSWLR 139. See also **Error of law; Finding of fact.**

•**Error of law** Misinterpretation or misapplication of a principle of law, or the application of an inappropriate principle of law to an issue of fact. It is sometimes difficult to distinguish errors of law from errors of fact in circumstances of statutory interpretation. Generally the meaning of a statutory expression is a question of law: *Australian Gas Light Co v Valuer-General* (1940) 40 SR (NSW) 126. See also **Error of fact; Finding of fact.**

Escalation clause A clause, often found in commercial contracts, which provides for an increase in the payments due under the contract on the happening of certain specified events, such as a rise in the cost of labour and materials. Sometimes, the increase to be paid is measured by an appropriate index, such as the consumer price index. See also **Contract guarantee.**

Escape clause Provision in a contract or other document permitting a party or parties to avoid liability or performance under certain conditions. See also **General Agreement on Tariffs and Trade 1947; Industry Commission.**

•**Escrow** *AF – escrowe* – a piece of cloth or parchment, a scroll A deed delivered conditionally, to take effect or become operative when a specified event occurs or some condition is fulfilled: *Monarch Petroleum NL v Citco Australia Petroleum Ltd* [1986] WAR 310. Also known as 'conditional delivery'. See also **Conditional execution; Deed; Delivery; Execution; Grantee.**

Essential facility In trade practices law, a facility to which a market competitor or potential competitor must have access in order to compete in the relevant market, and which cannot be economically duplicated. See also **Access regime; Duty to deal; Essential facility doctrine; Market.**

•**Essential facility doctrine** The legal doctrine formulated in the United States that a monopolist or one having a substantial degree of market power, who owns an essential service, has an independent duty to deal. The bases of the doctrine are that: there is a bottleneck in the market; the owner of the essential facility is analogous to the owner of a public utility; the owner's refusal to deal allows the owner to leverage his or her market power; and the owner's refusal to deal raises rivals' costs in a predatory fashion. In Australia, while the Full Federal Court has rejected an independent essential facility doctrine (*Queensland Wire Industries Ltd v Broken Hill Proprietary Co Ltd* (1987) 17 FCR 211; 78 ALR 407), legislative amendments to the (CTH) Trade Practices Act 1974 in the wake of the Hilmer Report have resulted in an access regime to declared services believed to be essential: (CTH) Trade Practices Act 1974 Pt IIIA. Under this system a person who wishes to have a particular service or facility declared essential makes an application to the Minister who, in turn, may if satisfied refer that application to the National Competition Council for a declaration: (CTH) Trade Practices Act 1974 s 44F. If the Council is not satisfied that the declaration of access would enhance competition it may not declare the facility essential: (CTH) Trade Practices Act 1974 s 44G. See also **Antitrust; Baumol-Willig rule; Competition; Competition law; Duty to deal; Essential facility; Griffiths formula; Market; Market power; Monopoly; National Competition Council.**

• **Estate** Any interest, charge, right, title, claim, demand, lien or encumbrance at law or in equity: (CTH) Acts Interpretation Act 1901 s 22.

• **Estimate** The formation of a bona fide judgment or opinion based upon reason that involves a process of approximation: *Australian and New Zealand Banking Group Ltd v FCT* (1994) 48 FCR 268; 119 ALR 727. See also **Bona fide; Mala fide; Uberrimae fidei.**

Estimating inventory A method of calculating the value of trading stock at the end of an accounting period instead of doing a physical check of inventory. Inventory is estimated by two methods: the retail inventory method and the gross profit method. See also **Gross profit method of estimating inventory; Retail method of inventory; Trading stock.**

Estoppel The doctrine designed to protect a party from the detriment which would flow from that party's change of position if the assumption or expectation that led to it were to be rendered groundless by another: *Waltons Stores (Interstate) Ltd v Maher* (1988) 164 CLR 387; 76 ALR 513. Estoppels are recognised both at common law and in equity. The concept of unconscionability has unified and rationalised the various types of estoppel, which are no longer seen as a series of independent rules: *Commonwealth v Verwayen* (1990) 170 CLR 394; 95 ALR 321. Some estoppels operate as substantive rules of law; others as evidentiary rules. See also **Acquiescence; Contract; Estoppel by convention; Estoppel by deed; Estoppel by representation; Estoppel in pais; Issue estoppel; Promissory estoppel; Proprietary estoppel; Unconscionable.**

Estoppel by conduct See **Estoppel in pais.**

Estoppel by convention An estoppel arising by reason of the parties' mutual adoption of an agreed or assumed state of facts as the basis of their relationship: *Con-Stan Industries of Australia Pty Ltd v Norwich Winterthur Insurance (Aust) Ltd* (1986) 160 CLR 226; 64 ALR 481. The assumption may also be one of law: *Commonwealth v Verwayen* (1990) 170 CLR 394; 95 ALR 321. See also **Acquiescence; Estoppel; Estoppel by deed; Estoppel by representation; Estoppel in pais; Promissory estoppel; Proprietary estoppel.**

Estoppel by deed A rule of evidence founded on the principle that a solemn and unambiguous statement in a deed must be taken as binding the party who makes it, and therefore, as not admitting any contradictory proof: *Greer v Kettle* [1938] AC 156; [1937] 4 All ER 396. Thus, where it can be gathered from a deed that the parties to it have agreed upon a certain admitted state of facts as the basis on which they contract, the statement of those facts estops the parties from averring to the contrary: *Young v Raincock* (1849) 7 CB 310; 137 ER 124. It is possibly a subset of estoppel by conduct ('estoppel in pais'). See also **Deed; Estoppel; Estoppel in pais.**

Estoppel by negligence An estoppel in which the party in whose favour it operates is the victim of the fraud of a third person, facilitated by the careless breach of duty of the second party: for example *Coventry, Sheppard & Co v Great Eastern Railway Co* (1883) 11 QBD 776. See also **Duty of care; Estoppel; Negligence.**

Estoppel by recitals Where it can be gathered from the recitals of a deed that the parties to it have agreed upon a certain admitted state of facts as the basis on which they contract, the statement of those facts estops the parties from averring to the contrary, since the recitals may amount to a direct affirmation of the facts stated: *Young v Raincock* (1849) 7 CB 310; 137 ER 124. See also **Deed; Estoppel.**

Estoppel by representation The doctrine established in both equity and common law that a person, who by representation of fact has led another to alter his or her position, may not deny that the fact is as represented: *Discount & Finance Ltd v Gehrig's NSW Wines Ltd* (1940) 40 SR (NSW) 598. See also **Estoppel; Estoppel by deed; Promissory estoppel; Representation.**

Estoppel in pais Estoppel by conduct; an estoppel arising from facts, not as a matter of record or deed. It prevents an unjust departure from an assumption of fact which the person estopped has caused another to adopt or accept for the purposes of their legal relations: *Grundt v Great Boulder Pty Gold Mines Ltd* (1937) 59 CLR 641. See also **Estoppel; Estoppel by deed; Estoppel by representation.**

Ethical trust A fund with an investment policy based on the perceived social value of the investments. Often it will take the form of a unit trust (in the United States a mutual fund) or other form of managed investment. Investments will often be made with companies who have policies relating to the preservation of the environment, or human rights. See also **Mutual fund; Unit trust.**

Euro $A bond A security issued in Australian dollars, by Australian and overseas borrowers, outside Australia. Euro $A bonds are issued in Hong Kong, London, New York, Tokyo and several other financial trading centres. The prefix euro simply means 'outside the country of origin', although originally indicating Europe. Euro $A bonds were first issued in the early 1980's. See also **Bond; Eurobond.**

Eurobond A bond denominated in the currency of one country but sold in Europe outside the country of the issuer. A borrower who sells securities in the European market denominated in Australian dollars would describe them as 'Euro-Australian Dollar Bonds'. Eurobond issues have a final maturity and either a fixed or floating interest rate. The Eurobond market covers both the primary market for new issues of Eurobonds and the secondary market on which they are traded. See also **Euro $A bond; Eurocurrencies; European currency unit; European Union.**

Eurocurrencies Currencies deposited and lent in Europe outside the country of origin. The most common Eurocurrency is the Eurodollar; others are Eurosterling, Euroyen, Eurodeutschmarks, Eurofrancs and Eurolira. The Euromarket is a financial market in Europe for such currencies, mainly centred in London. See also **Eurobond; European currency unit; European Union.**

Eurodollar The US dollar deposited in a bank outside the US, mostly in Europe. See also **London Inter Bank Offered Rate; LIBOR.**

Eurodollars United States dollar deposits placed with European banks outside the United States.

European Bank for Reconstruction and Development *Abbr* – EBRD An international financial institution established by an agreement signed on 29 May 1990 by 40 countries including the former European Economic Community countries, and the European Investment Bank. The EBRD aims to assist the transformation of the central and eastern European states from centralised economies to free market economies: Agreement Establishing the European Bank for Reconstruction and Development 1991 art 1. It also seeks to foster democracy and respect for human rights and the environment. The EBRD provides technical assistance, training, and investment in the upgrading of infrastructure, the creation of modern financial systems, and the restructuring of state industries. Australia ratified the Agreement Establishing the European Bank for Reconstruction and Development 1991 on 27 March 1991, and has passed the (CTH) European Bank for Reconstruction and Development Act 1990 to give effect to its international obligations under the agreement. See also **Agreement Establishing the European Bank for Reconstruction and Development 1991; International Bank for Reconstruction and Development; International Development Association; International Monetary Fund.**

European Community *Abbr* – EC A community of European nations founded as a move toward creating a union, and away from the previous existing situation of competing nation states. The EC contains a number of smaller specialist communities of the same member states. The community has its own revenue derived from customs duties and import levies collected at the EC external frontier. See also **European Economic Community; European Union.**

European Community Product Liability Directive A European Community (EC) directive promulgated in 1985 governing the liability of manufacturers, importers, and others for supply of defective or unsafe products within those EC member countries that have adopted the Directive. The Directive was the model upon which (CTH) Trade Practices Act 1974 Pt VA was drafted. See also **European Community; European Union.**

European currency unit *Abbr* – ECU The currency used in the European Monetary System in place of the European Unit of Account with which it is identical in value. See also **Common market; Eurodollars.**

European Economic Area The geographical area, delimited by the territory of the member states of the European Union, in which the treaty provisions are to operate among them for the removal of barriers to trade. See also **Common market; European Economic Community; European Union.**

European Economic Community *Abbr* – EEC An economic union established by treaty in 1958 to assist the member nations in their compliance with the General Agreement on Tariffs and Trade 1947. The term EEC changed on 1 November 1993 to the European Union: Treaty on European Union 1992 art G(A)(1). The Treaty on European Union 1992 also expanded and consolidated what were the EEC's areas of competency. See also **European community; European Union; Treaty of Maastricht 1992.**

European exchange rate mechanism A central feature of the European Monetary System of the European Union in which most European currency exchange rates have been pegged against each other, while being realigned from time to time. Their values are tied to neither the United States dollar nor the yen. See also **European currency unit; European Monetary System; European Union.**

European Free Trade Association *Abbr* – EFTA An international organisation created on 3 May 1960 as a rival organisation to the European Economic Community (EEC) to establish free trade in industrial goods by the abolition of customs duties and quotas, and the elimination of other indirect barriers: Convention Establishing the European Free Trade Association 1960 art 2. The EFTA aimed at creating a single market in western Europe and has been working in cooperation with the EEC and now the European Union since 1990. The original membership of the EFTA included Austria, Denmark (withdrew 1973), the United Kingdom (withdrew 1973), Portugal, Norway, Sweden, and Switzerland; Finland and Iceland joined in 1961 and 1970 respectively. The EFTA is based in Geneva. See also **European Union; Treaty of Maastricht 1992.**

European Investment Bank A bank established by the European Economic Community in 1958 to assist economic development. The bank has financed projects in the twelve member countries, and in more than 70 other countries in the Mediterranean, Africa, the Pacific and the Caribbean. See also **European Bank for Reconstruction and Development; European Economic Community; European Union; International Bank for Reconstruction and Development.**

European Monetary System *Abbr* – EMS A scheme of quasi-fixed exchange rates agreed to by members of the European Union. Exchange rates are generally allowed to fluctuate by no more than 2.5 per cent either way from rates adjusted by mutual agreement. The EMS currencies, closely aligned, form a basis for the European Currency Unit. See also **European exchange rate mechanism; European Union; European currency unit.**

European monetary union *Abbr* – EMU An ultimate step in the development of the European Union, embracing the concept of a single European central bank and a single European currency. EMU involves a three-stage process of closer economic and monetary convergence among the twelve European Union countries, climaxing with the introduction of a single currency. See also **European currency unit; European exchange rate mechanism; European monetary system; European Union.**

European Union *Abbr* – EU A supranational construct aimed at establishing a common market and an economic and monetary union for Europe, and which has as its pillars the European Economic Community; the European Coal and Steel Community; and the European Atomic Energy Community. The EU was established by the Treaty on European Union signed at Maastricht on 7 February 1992 resulting in two intergovernmental conferences being held between 1990 and 1991 on economic and monetary union, and another on political union. It aims to promote throughout the community a harmonious and balanced development of economic activities; sustainable and non-inflationary growth respecting the environment; a high degree of convergence of economic performance; a high level of employment and of social protection; the raising of the standard of living and quality of life; and economic and social cohesion between, and solidarity among, member states: Treaty on European Union 1992 art 2. The membership of the EU is identical to that of the European Economic Community, but a number of important institutional changes relating to the European Parliament and the European Court of Justice have been made to the community by the Treaty on European Union 1992 which came into effect on 1 November 1993. See also **European Community; European Economic Community; Treaty of Maastricht 1992.**

Event-tree analysis A technique used in risk assessment to find the various possible outcomes of a given initiating event.

Everett assignment In partnership law, an assignment of part of a partner's interest in the partnership to another person. An Everett assignment is a method of splitting the partner's income to reduce the partner's tax liability. See also **Chose in action; Equity; Partnership.**

Eviction *Lat* – out and conquer. The process of removing a person from occupation of premises, including legal proceedings and physical removal. See also **Lease; Relief against forfeiture.**

•**Evidence** 1. Any statement, record, testimony, or other things, apart from legal submissions, which tends to prove the existence of a fact in issue: (CTH) Evidence Act 1995. Evidence adduced at trial is subject to a number of tests to discern its admissibility, relevance, and the weight to be accorded to it: for example (CTH) Evidence Act 1995 ss 56(1), (2); (NSW) Evidence Act 1995 ss 56(1), (2). The party adducing evidence is required to make its purpose clear: *Potts v Miller* (1940) 64 CLR 282. There are several types of evidence which can be tendered or adduced at a trial: for example, direct, circumstantial, oral, documentary, real, indirect, original, derivative, primary, secondary, prima facie, expert, opinion, confessional, sworn, and unsworn. 2. The law of evidence or evidence law. This is the procedural law which is essential to the ascertainment of facts in litigation. Evidence law operates to apply (mainly exclusionary) rules of proof as a constraint upon the adduction of facts, at civil and criminal trials; hence the use of the phrase exclusionary rules of evidence, for example, hearsay evidence, similar fact evidence, illegally obtained evidence, corroborative evidence, opinion evidence, identification evidence, non-testimonial evidence. See also **Adduce.**

•**Evidential burden** Under the common law accusatorial system, the burden on the party who is under a duty to adduce evidence that is capable of being left to the jury or court. Failure to discharge the evidential burden will cause the judge to decide against the party who bears it without the need to call upon the other side. The evidential and the legal burden are known collectively as the onus or burden of proof. In criminal cases the prosecution bears the evidential burden in relation to all facts in issue which relate to the guilt of the accused: *Woolmington v DPP* [1935] AC 462 at 481. In civil cases the plaintiff generally bears the evidential burden in relation to all facts in issue which relate to establishing the cause of action. Also known as 'evidentiary burden'. See also **Balance of probabilities; Beyond reasonable doubt; Burden of proof; Evidential burden; Legal burden; Standard of proof.**

Ex aequo et bono /ɛks aɪkwoʊ ɛt bɒnoʊ/ *Lat* – on the basis of what is fair and right. The parties to an arbitration agreement may agree that the arbitrator is to determine the dispute on the basis of what is fair and right, or by reference to considerations of general justice or fairness: (NSW) Commercial Arbitration Act 1984 s 22(2); (QLD) Commercial Arbitration Act 1990 s 22(2). See also **Alternative dispute resolution; Amiable compositeur; Arbitration; Arbitrator.**

Ex ante /ɛks ænti/ A reference to the anticipated or intended, in contrast with the actual or ex post result.

Ex contractu /ɛks kɒntræktu/ *Lat* – arising out of contract. In Roman law, that which arises from contract (as distinct from quasi-contract or delict).

Ex date A term used in a stock exchange to signify the date on which the prices of securities change from being quoted 'cum' a particular benefit, such as a particular payment of dividend, to being quoted 'ex' that benefit. See also **Ex dividend.**

Ex debito justitiae /ɛks dɛbɪtoʊ dʒʊstɪtiaɪ/ *Lat* – as a debt of justice; as a legal obligation; from a lawful or just debt. See also **Ex gratia; Habeas corpus.**

Ex delicto /ɛks dɛlɪktoʊ/ *Lat* – as a result of a tort; arising out of a tort. See also **Ex contractu.**

Ex div *Lat* – without dividend. Refers to shares without a right to a dividend. Compare *cum div*. See also **Cum div; Dividend.**

Ex facie illegal On its face illegal. In relation to illegal contracts, a contract that cannot be performed without a violation of the law and is illegal whether the parties know the law or not: *Holidaywise Koala Pty Ltd v Queenslodge Pty Ltd* [1977] VR 164; [1976] 39 LGRA 338. See also **Illegal contract; Public policy**.

Ex gratia /ɛks graʃə/ *Lat* – out of grace. A payment made as a favour, not *ex debito justitiae* (as a debt of justice). See also **Ex debito justitiae; Ex gratia payment**.

Ex gratia payment *Lat – ex gratia –* from favour. Payment of money made or given as a concession, without legal compulsion.

Insurance A payment made by way of settlement of a claim without admission of liability: *Edwards v Skyways Ltd* [1964] 1 All ER 494 at 500. See also **Ex debito justitiae**.

Taxation and revenue Bonus or other payment made where management wishes to provide recompense without conceding a permanent or continuing obligation in doing so. If received during employment, such a payment may constitute assessable income: (CTH) Income Tax Assessment Act 1936 s 25(1). A pension supplement, including an ex gratia payment, is assessable income: s 27H. If received on termination of employment as a lump sum such as a golden handshake, it may be taxed as an eligible termination payment. See also **Assessable income; Eligible Termination Payment; Golden handshake; Pension**.

Ex nudo pacto non oritur actio /ɛks nudoʊ pæktoʊ noʊn ɒrɪtʊə æktioʊ/ *Lat –* from a bare promise (that is, a promise without consideration) an action does not arise.

Ex pacto illicito non oritur actio /ɛks pæktoʊ ɪlɪsɪtoʊ noʊn ɒrɪtʊə æktioʊ/ *Lat –* no cause of action arises out of an illegal agreement.

•**Ex parte** /ɛks pati//ɛks parteɪ/ *Lat –* from one side. **1.** In the absence of the other side. Ex parte applications are heard in the absence of the party against whom the order is sought: for example *Tassell v Hayes* (1987) 163 CLR 34; 71 ALR 480; (NSW) Supreme Court Rules Pt 5 r 8. **2.** An application by a non-party in the context of existing proceedings. See also **Ex parte injunction; Inter partes**.

Ex parte injunction An injunction granted by a court without notice to the party against whom it is to operate. It is distinguished from an inter partes injunction. See also **Ex parte; Injunction**.

•**Ex turpi causa non oritur actio** *Lat –* no action arises out of dishonourable cause; illegality or immorality will not ground an action. The maxim is applied by the court to protect the public by refusing to allow the machinery of the court to be used to assist the commission or furtherance of illegal acts. See also **Illegal contract; Public policy**.

Contract Illegal or immoral consideration will not support a contract, or a contract entered into to give effect to unlawful or immoral purposes will not be enforced: *Smith v Jenkins* (1970) 119 CLR 397; [1970] ALR 519.

Exact performance In the discharge of contracts, a performance which conforms exactly to the requirements of the contract: *Cutter v Powell* (1795) 6 TR 320; 101 ER 573. See also **De minimis non curat lex; Substantial performance**.

Examinable officer In relation to a corporation: a director, secretary, or executive officer of the corporation; a receiver, or receiver and manager, of property of the corporation (whether appointed under a provision contained in an instrument, or by a court); an administrator of the corporation; an administrator of a deed of company arrangement executed by the corporation; a liquidator or provisional liquidator of the corporation, whether or not appointed by the court; or a trustee or other person administering a compromise or arrangement made between the corporation and any other person or persons: Corporations Law s 9. The definition is relevant to Corporations Law ss 596A, 597A, which set out the circumstances in which an examinable officer may be examined about, or required to file an affidavit about, a corporation's examinable affairs. See also **Affidavit**.

Examination of debtors In relation to determining a debtor's solvency, the examination of all the debtor's circumstances, including the nature of the debts and the debtor's business: *Re Smith; Ex parte official Receiver* (1929) 1 ABC 186; *Rees v Bank of New South Wales* (1964) 111 CLR 210; [1965] ALR 139. A judgment creditor may orally examine the judgment debtor as to their property and other means of satisfying the judgment debt and generally as to their financial circumstances: (NSW) Local Courts (Civil Claims) Act 1970 s 41. See also **Judgment creditor; Judgment debtor; Solvent**.

Ex-bonus Without the bonus declared, the shares having passed the ex-date for a bonus issue. See also **Bonus share issue; Cum-bonus; Ex-date**.

Ex-capitalisation *Abbr –* Ex-cap Descriptive of a security when the purchaser is not entitled to the capitalisation issue attaching to the share. See also **Capitalisation; Security; Share**.

Excepted assessable income Assessable income of a minor, which is employment or business income, and other specific types of income: (CTH) Income Tax Assessment Act 1936 s 102AE(2). To determine the excepted assessable income of a minor, 'employment' income is defined as salary and wages, or as payments for services rendered: s 102AF(1). 'Business income' is defined as income from carrying on a business either alone or with others: s 102AF(3). For income tax purposes, excepted assessable income is excluded from the application of the special rates of tax which apply to income derived by persons under the age of 18. See also **Assessable income; Eligible taxable income; Excepted person**.

Excepted person For income tax purposes, a child under 18 engaged in a full-time occupation on the last day of the year of income, and a child under 18 who is in receipt of a child disability payment or a disability support pension: (CTH) Income Tax Assessment Act 1936 s 102AC (2)-(8). See also **Assessable income; Eligible taxable income; Excepted assessable income; Year of income**.

•**Exception** Exclusion or omission.

Deeds and other instruments The exclusion by the grantor of some part of what the grantor is giving; it does not pass by the grant but is excluded from it and remains with the grantor: *Cooper v Stuart* (1889) 14 App Cas 286. An exception, as distinct from a reservation, is always something granted that is presently existing; to exclude the subject matter of the exception from passing to the grantee. A so-called 'reservation' may in substance amount to an exception if what is reserved is part of an existing thing granted: *Doe d Douglas v Lock* (1835) 2 Ad & El 705; 111 ER 271. See also **Deed; Instrument under hand**.

Exception clause See **Disclaimer; Exclusion clause**.

•**Excess** The amount which an insured is not entitled to recover, which is a fixed or agreed sum. The insured may pursue a third party to recover the excess. See also **Excess clause**.

Excess clause A clause in a contract of insurance providing that an insured is only entitled to recover that part of a loss which exceeds a set amount. The amount the insured is not entitled to recover is called the 'excess' or 'deductible'. See also **Excess policy; Exclusion clause**.

Excess of loss treaty A treaty or convention enabling a shipowner to limit its liability for loss and avoid financial ruin stemming from a large number of claims arising out of one incident. See also **Convention on Limitation of Liability for Maritime Claims 1976**.

Excess of power The exercise of power by a person where the power had not been conferred on him or her. An act in excess of power is void: *ANZ Executors Trustee Co Ltd v Qintex Australia Ltd* (1990) 2 ACSR 676; See also **Abuse of power; Ratification; Ultra vires**.

Excess policy A contract of insurance in which the minimum liability amount of claim is equal to the maximum liability amount in the primary or underlying cover. The (CTH) Insurance Contracts Act 1984 s 45(1), which renders void clauses limiting or excluding liability by reason that the insured has entered into some other contract of insurance, does not apply to excess policies ((CTH) Insurance Contracts Act 1984 s 45(2)). See also **Contract; Excess clause; Insurance contract**.

•**Excess receipts of foreign currency** The amount by which a bank's surplus foreign currency exceeds the amount of its surplus foreign currency at 14 January 1960: (CTH) Banking Act 1959 s 32. See also **Mobilisation of foreign currency; Surplus foreign currency**.

Excess return A return (usually pecuniary) which goes beyond what is usual. For example, the return on an investment to the extent that it exceeds the return the investor would have received on a hypothetical risk free investment for the same amount and duration. See also **Premium**.

Excessive component In relation to an eligible termination payment paid to a person, the amount by which payment exceeds that person's reasonable benefit limit as determined by the Commissioner of Taxation: (CTH) Income Tax Assessment Act 1936 s 27A(1). The excessive component of an eligible termination payment is not subject to concessional tax rates and is taxed as ordinary income: s 27B(3). See also **Eligible Termination Payment; Reasonable benefit limit**.

Excessive trading In relation to the practice of churning, entering into securities or futures transactions by a broker using a client's account which are excessive in size and frequency in light of the character of the account. In determining whether there has been excessive trading, it may be relevant to examine the number of commissions charged as compared to the client's total investment (commission to investment ratio), the trading losses incurred by the client (commission to trading loss ratio), the average daily ledger balance for each month (commission to equity ratio), and average profits in the account in relation to average losses. Churning may also be indicated by: high liquidity and volatility of the market in which it is alleged churning took place; large percentages of day trading in the account; losses at the end of the life of the account; the broker closing out positions only to re-establish them immediately; and no discernible trading strategy on the part of the broker. See also **Churning; Market manipulation; Share**.

Excess-of-loss reinsurance A type of non-proportional reinsurance. The reinsurer covers the liability of the insurer in respect of individual losses or aggregations of losses, caused by a specified occurrence or event, in excess of a specified amount for which the insurer remains responsible. It includes various types of reinsurance, for example catastrophe reinsurance. The reinsurance itself may be subject to a limit. See also **Excess; Reinsurance**.

•**Exchange** 1. Generally, in relation to a stock exchange or securities exchange, the place where securities listed on the relevant market can be acquired or disposed of. There is a stock exchange in each capital city, with each of these being a wholly owned subsidiary of the Australian Stock Exchange Ltd. In relation to a futures exchange, the place where transactions involving futures contracts are carried out, for example the Sydney Futures Exchange Ltd. Stock exchanges and futures exchanges operate as companies limited by guarantee. 2. The Australian Stock Exchange Ltd: Corporations Law s 9. See also **Australian Stock Exchange Ltd; Stock Exchange; Sydney Futures Exchange**.

Exchange acquisition A method of exchange by which the purchaser places an order (with an intermediary, usually a broker) to buy securities (at a certain price) in the market before a seller has been determined or identified. See also **Broker; Securities**.

Exchange, bill of See **Bill of exchange**.

Exchange distribution A method of selling large blocks of stock on the floor of a stock exchange. A broker can facilitate the sale of a block of stock by inducing other brokers to solicit orders to buy. All the individual buy orders will then be lumped together with the sell order in the regular auction market. See also **Security; Share; Stock exchange**.

Exchange examining accountants A firm of accountants appointed by the committee of a stock exchange with the functions of receiving returns from members and of carrying out a special examination of a member's books as necessary. See also **Australian Stock Exchange Listing rules; Australian Stock Exchange Ltd; Exchange.**

Exchange inspector An employee of a stock exchange appointed to determine whether members of the exchange are complying with the rules of the exchange. See also **Australian Stock Exchange Ltd; Exchange; Australian Stock Exchange Listing rules.**

•**Exchange member** **1.** A natural person, partnership or corporation conducting the business of stockbroking that is admitted as a member of the Australian Stock Exchange (ASX) under ASX Articles of Association arts 35-38. These articles require that an applicant be appropriately qualified and be of good fame and character and high business integrity. Exchange members must comply with the business rules of the ASX. The board of the ASX has power to discipline members who breach the articles or the business rules: ASX Articles of Association art 51. The court also has power to enforce the business rules: Corporations Law ss 777, 1114. **2.** In relation to a futures exchange, a corporation or partnership that is a member of the futures exchange or a member of such a partnership: Corporations Law s 9. See also **Australian Stock Exchange Ltd; Australian Stock Exchange business rules; Exchange subsidiary; Sydney Futures Exchange.**

Exchange of contracts A conveyancing practice in which the vendor and purchaser physically exchange counterpart identical contracts for the sale of land, each receiving a copy executed by the other party, thus entering into a binding contract. By conveyancing convention that has become a principle of law, in some States, a binding contract for the sale of land does not come into existence unless exchange of contracts takes place. See also **Contract; Conveyance; Counterpart; Statute of Frauds.**

Exchange rate The rate at which one currency can be exchanged for another. Generally, a judgment in a court of the forum expressed in foreign currency must be converted for payment into the currency of Australia at the time the debtor pays the amount or, where there is default, immediately prior to enforcement proceedings: *Maschinenfabrik Augsburg-Nuremburg AG v Altikar Pty Ltd* [1984] 3 NSWLR 152. See also **Actual market exchange rate; Currency; Devaluation; Floating exchange rate; Purchasing-power-parity exchange rate; Rate of exchange.**

Exchange settlement accounts Accounts maintained by banks with the Reserve Bank of Australia. These accounts are used to settle balances between banks arising from the clearing of cheques and to settle transactions between the banks and the Reserve Bank arising from the purchase and sale of government securities and current exchange. Interest is not paid on these accounts. These funds are often known as official cash or same-day funds. The banks typically lend these cash funds to the authorised dealers in the short-term money market. The interest earned is known as the official or cash rate. See also **Cash rate; Short term money market.**

•**Exchange subsidiary** **1.** For the purposes of Corporations Law Ch 6 dealing with acquisition of shares, a securities exchange or a stock exchange that is a subsidiary of the Australian Stock Exchange Ltd (ASX): ss 9, 603. This includes each of the six capital city stock exchanges, for example the Australian Stock Exchange (Sydney) Ltd: s 9. **2.** For the purposes of ss 779, 920(1), a securities exchange that is a subsidiary of the Australian Stock Exchange Ltd: s 9. Under s 779, an exchange subsidiary which makes a statement in connection with a disciplinary proceeding of the ASX is entitled to qualified privilege in respect of that statement. Section 920(1) defines 'eligible exchange' as excluding an exchange subsidiary for the purposes of Pt 7.10 dealing with the National Guarantee Fund. **3.** For the purposes of Ch 7 dealing with securities except in relation to s 779, a local securities exchange that is a subsidiary of the ASX: s 9. See also **Australian Stock Exchange Ltd; Exchange member; Local securities Exchange; Stock Exchange.**

Exchange traded option An option to take up a futures position. See also **All Ordinaries Index; Australian Options Market; Option.**

Exchange traded share option In corporations law, a share option traded on the Australian Stock Exchange (ASX) which is created by buyers and sellers in the market. Once an option is created between two clearing members ('grantor' and 'taker'), it must be registered with the Options Clearing House. The other type of share option traded on the ASX is the listed company share option. See also **Listed company share option; Option; Share option.**

Exchange-for-value settlement system A system which involves the exchange of assets, such as money, foreign exchange, securities or other financial instruments, in order to discharge settlement obligations. These systems may use one or more funds transfer systems in order to satisfy the payment obligations that are generated. The links between the exchange of assets and the payment system(s) may be manual or electronic.

•**Excise** A tax on goods levied at some point in their production or distribution which has the effect of increasing the price of the goods supplied to the customer: *Capital Duplicators Pty Ltd v Australian Capital Territory* (No 2) (1993) 173 CLR 561; 118 ALR 1. The Commonwealth Parliament has exclusive legislative power over excise tax: Commonwealth Constitution s 90. See also **Consumer price index; Consumption tax; Customs duty; Taxation.**

•**Excluded corporation** Certain dealers in the short term money market as well as pastoral or life insurance companies or Australian bank which have been declared by the Australian Securities Commission to be an excluded corporation: Corporations Law s 65. An invitation by an excluded corporation to lend money to, or deposit money with, that corporation or an offer to accept money that is lent to, or deposited with, that corporation is deemed not to be an invitation or offer to subscribe for or buy debentures of the corporation: s 1061. See also **Debenture; Debenture series; Excluded issue.**

•**Excluded issue** An issue or allotment of securities that is within the definition of Corporations Law s 66(2). Included in this definition, for example, are offers or invitations to subscribe in relation to securities made to persons who are each to subscribe to at least $500,000 in the particular transaction (s 66(2)(a)) and offers to enter into underwriting agreements (s 66(2)(b)). The basic prospectus requirements contained in Pt 7.12 Div 1 do not apply in relation to an excluded issue: s 1017. Neither do the requirements with respect to notices of secondary offers (s 1043A), debentures (Corporations Law s 1044) or prescribed interests (s 1063). The Corporations Law links excluded offers and invitations very closely with excluded issues of securities. See also **Excluded corporation; Excluded offer or invitation; Securities**.

Excluded offer or invitation An offer or invitation in relation to securities that is within the definition of Corporations Law s 66(3). Included in this definition, for example, are offers or invitations to subscribe in relation to securities made to persons who are each to subscribe to at least $500,000 in the particular transaction (s 66(3)(a)) and offers to enter into underwriting agreements (s 66(3)(b)). The basic prospectus requirements contained in Pt 7.12 Div 1 do not apply in relation to an excluded offer: s 1017. Neither do the requirements with respect to notices of secondary offers (s 1043A), debentures (s 1044) or prescribed interests (s 1063). The Corporations Law links excluded offers and invitations very closely with excluded issues of securities. See also **Excluded issue; Public issue; Securities**.

•**Excluded prospectus** A prospectus in relation to securities where each offer or invitation contained in it is an excluded offer or invitation: Corporations Law s 9. The requirement that a statutory meeting must be held following the issuing of a prospectus by a public company that is a limited company and has a share capital or a no liability company, does not apply to an excluded prospectus: s 244(1). See also **Excluded offer or invitation; Prospectus; Securities**.

•**Excluded security** For the purposes of the Corporations Law, a share, debenture or prescribed interest which relates to the right to participate in a retirement village scheme: Corporations Law s 9. In the case of a share or debenture, it is a security which carries no other rights that are not merely incidental. Alternatively, a prescribed interest must be constituted by the right to participate in the retirement village scheme. See also **Participation interest; Prescribed interest**.

Exclusion clause A contractual term which operates to exclude, restrict, or qualify the rights of the parties. To be effective, an exclusion clause must: be a part of the contract; be appropriately worded to cover the breach that has occurred; reasonably be brought to the attention of the other party; and not be prohibited by statute: for example (CTH) Trade Practices Act 1974 s 68. It must operate for the benefit of one party only: *Suisse Atlantique Société d'Armement Maritime SA v NV Rotterdamsche Kolen Centrale* [1967] 1 AC 361. Where appropriate, an exclusion clause will be construed *contra proferentem* in case of ambiguity: *Darlington Futures Ltd v Delco Australia Pty Ltd* (1986) 161 CLR 500; 68 ALR 385. If the clause is so wide as to exclude any obligation, no contract might arise at all: *MacRobertson Miller Airline Services v Cmr of State Taxation (WA)* (1975) 133 CLR 125; 8 ALR 131. A term of a contract of insurance exempting or limiting the liability of the insurer to indemnify the insured: *Monarch Insurance Co Ltd v Steel Mains Pty Ltd* [1986] VR 831. The (CTH) Insurance Contracts Act 1984 ss 39-41, 46, 47 restrict the ability of insurers to rely on exclusion clauses. Also known as 'exception clause', 'exemption clause', 'disclaimer': *G H Renton & Co Ltd v Palmyra Trading Corp of Panama* [1957] AC 149. See also **Causal exclusion clause; Construction; Contract; Limitation clause; Merger clause; Temporal exclusion clause; Term**.

Exclusion of liability clause A clause used in a contract to limit the liability of a party for a responsibility which that party would normally bear. In the case of common carriers, general words of exclusion will usually be sufficient to relieve them from liability as insurers: *Price & Co v Union Lighterage Co* [1904] 1 KB 412. See also **Carrier; Common Carrier; Contract; Exclusion clause**.

•**Exclusion order** A court order by which restraints are placed on a certain class of persons or goods.

•**Exclusionary provision** A collective boycott by which a provision of a contract, arrangement, or understanding between competitors has the purpose of restricting the supply to, or acquisition of, goods or services from particular people or classes of people by the parties to the boycott: (CTH) Trade Practices Act 1974 s 4D. The restriction may apply generally, in particular circumstances, or on particular conditions. The prohibition of such a boycott does not depend on it having the purpose or effect of substantially lessening competition: (CTH) Trade Practices Act 1974 s 45. Exclusionary provisions are unenforceable in so far as they confer rights or benefits or impose duties or obligations, and corporations may not make a contract or arrangement, or arrive at an understanding, that contains an exclusionary provision: (CTH) Trade Practices Act 1974 s 45. See also **Acting in concert; Boycott; Collective boycott; Competition; Contract, arrangement or understanding; Restrictive trade practices; Secondary boycott; Substantially lessening competition**.

Exclusive dealing A range of activities by which sellers or buyers impose restrictions, directly or indirectly, on the buying or selling activities of their customers or suppliers. Activities of the seller or buyer may take many forms including: imposing restrictions on acquisitions or resupply (customer or territorial restrictions); requiring the supply or acquisition of other goods or services (tying conduct or second-line or full-line forcing); requiring the customer also to acquire goods or services from a third person (third-line forcing); and granting a lease or licence of property which includes like restrictions: (CTH) Trade Practices Act 1974 s 47. Generally, the restrictions require that there be a purpose or effect of substantially lessening competition before they are prohibited. Third-line forcing does not require this purpose or effect. A corporation proposing to engage in exclusive dealing may avoid liability by lodging a notification with the Australian Competition and Consumer Commission: (CTH) Trade Practices Act 1974 s 93(1). See also **Competition law; Full-line forcing; Minimum quantity condition; Notification; Requirements contract; Restrictive trade practices; Solus agreement; Substantially lessening competition; Tying**.

Exclusive service contract A contract which obliges a person to provide services exclusively to the other party. Such a contract may be in restraint of trade, or unenforceable because it is an unreasonable and unconscionable bargain: for example *A Schroeder Music Publishing Co Ltd v Macaulay* [1974] 1 WLR 1308. See also **Contract in restraint of trade; Restraint of trade**.

Ex-coupon Without the coupon or interest just paid.

Ex-dividend Without the current dividend or interest. A term indicating that the seller will take the current dividend or interest; otherwise the share will be sold cum-dividend. On the Australian Stock Exchange it is normal procedure for all securities to be quoted 'ex div' five business days prior to and including the companies' books closing date. See also **Cum-dividend; Dividend; Rollover; Share**.

Ex-drawing Without the benefit of the current drawing. If there is no benefit but a loss on drawing, it is without the loss. A term used in connection with the sale of securities. See also **Securities**.

Execute 1. To make valid and complete by observing the necessary formal legal requirements. 2. To give effect to or to perform acts. For example, to carry out the terms of a contract or to enforce a judgment of the court. See also **Sign**.

Executed consideration Consideration which has been actually performed, as where a promisee has performed an act in return for a promise: for example *Carlill v Carbolic Smoke Ball Co* [1893] 1 QB 256 at 275. Prior to performance, the consideration is said to be executory. See also **Consideration; Executory consideration; Past consideration; Promise; Promisee; Promisor**.

Executed contract A contract which has been formally signed, containing the final expression of the parties' will for the regulation of their relations: *J C Williamson Ltd v Lukey* (1931) 45 CLR 282; [1931] ALR 147. See also **Contract; Executory contract; Specific performance**.

Executed trust A trust in which the settlor has set out in precise detail the manner in which the general intention is to be carried out. No further act is required to give effect to it. See also **Executory trust; Trust**.

•**Execution** *OF – executer –* to follow. The exercising of some power or the fulfilling of some requirement. Execution usually refers to the signing of a document with legal requirements, such as a lease, to make it formally valid or the enforcing of a judgment of a court.

Deeds and other instruments Often used loosely to mean 'signing'; strictly it means doing all that is required to make the deed operative: signing with proper attestation, sealing and delivery. Execution may be conditional (as with an escrow). However, execution of a deed in part is generally no execution at all: *Wilkinson v Anglo-Californian Gold Mining Co* (1852) 18 QB 728; 118 ER 275. See also **Conditional execution; Deed; Delivery; Escrow**.

•**Executive** The body of people, members of the governing party or parties, that form policy and control the appropriate government departments and instrumentalities, and who are responsible to parliament for such administration. See also **Executive Council; Executive power**.

•**Executive Council** A body established to advise the Governor-General in the government of the Commonwealth: Commonwealth Constitution s 62. Its members are summoned to meetings by the Governor-General and hold office during the Governor-General's pleasure: Commonwealth Constitution s 62. Those persons who are appointed by the Governor-General as Ministers of State are ex officio members of the Executive Council: Commonwealth Constitution s 64. See also **Executive**.

•**Executive director** A director engaged by a company under a contract of employment to perform functions additional to those involved in being a member of the board of directors. A company may select its directors from senior working employees and from persons outside the company who have special knowledge. Directors chosen from outside the company are 'non-executive directors'. See also **Director; Executive officer**.

•**Executive officer** A person by whatever name called and whether or not a director of a body or entity, who is concerned or takes part in the management of the body or entity: Corporations Law s 9. An executive officer must take part in the management of all the affairs of the company, not simply the negotiation of particular contracts: *Holpitt Pty Ltd v Swabb* (1992) 6 ACSR 488; 10 ACLC 64. See also **Manage; Officer**.

Executive power That power vested in and exercisable by the Governor-General as the Queen's representative extending to the execution and maintenance of the Constitution and laws of the Commonwealth: Commonwealth Constitution s 61. See also **Executive**.

Executive share option plan An arrangement under which senior management of a company is provided with the right to acquire shares of a company in the future for a price fixed in the present. See also **Share option; Option**.

Executory consideration Consideration in the form of an as yet unfulfilled promise to do or refrain from doing something. See also **Consideration; Executed consideration; Past consideration; Promise; Promisee; Promisor**.

Executory contract A contract yet to be performed or carried out by either party. A contract is executory when all that the parties have done is exchanged promises to do something at some future time. Such a contract is enforceable because the exchange of promises is regarded as valid consideration. See also **Bilateral contract; Consideration; Executed contract; Unilateral contract**.

Executory interest An interest that arises at a future time, requiring further actions by specified persons or the occurrence of a triggering event in order to bring the interest into existence. An executory interest includes executory devises, springing uses and shifting uses. The term is sometimes used in a compendious way, being inclusive of all future interests except reversions and vested remainders.

Executory satisfaction 1. An obligation that remains to be done or satisfied in the future. **2.** An as yet unfulfilled promise to do something different from the promisee's original obligation, given as consideration for the promisor's abandonment of a claim against the promisee for the promisee's failure to perform the original obligation. The satisfaction of such a promise will operate to discharge the original cause of action. See also **Accord and satisfaction; Consideration; Executory consideration; Executory contract; Past consideration.**

Executory trust A trust in which the limitations of the estate of the trustees and beneficiaries have not been perfected and declared by the settlor, but have been left for a later declaration. See also **Completely constituted trust; Executed trust; Trust.**

Executrix Formerly, a female executor.

Exemplary damages Damages awarded in addition to general damages, where the court wishes not only to compensate the victim of a tort, but to punish the defendant. Such damages are not compensatory in nature and extend beyond the general principle of damages that the injured person should be placed, so far as money can do, in the position he or she would have been in had the tort not been committed. Also known as 'punitive damages' or 'retributive damages'. See also **Damages; General damages; Nominal damages; Special damages.**

•**Exempt body** A body corporate which is exempt from the operation of the Corporations Law. Corporations Law s 66A defines the types of body corporate which are exempt in each State or Territory, including bodies such as building societies, credit unions and co-operatives. See also **Body corporate; Corporation; Exempt foreign company; Exempt proprietary company.**

Exempt car benefit A benefit exempt from fringe benefits tax which may otherwise be assessable as a car benefit. The exempt benefit arises where the car is a taxi, panel van, utility truck, or a passenger vehicle and the only use of the vehicle by an employee is work related travel and any private use by the employee is minor or irregular: (CTH) Fringe Benefits Tax Assessment Act 1986 s 8. See also **Car fringe benefit; Car parking benefit; Fringe Benefits Tax.**

•**Exempt credit provider** A credit provider who is exempted from holding a credit provider's licence. Examples of an exempt credit provider are the Crown, banks, insurance companies, cooperative societies, building societies and credit unions: (NSW) Credit (Administration) Act 1984 (repealed) ss 4, 7(1). See also **Credit provider; Credit provider's licence.**

•**Exempt foreign company** A foreign company which is not required by the Australian Securities Commission to lodge financial statements in Australia: Corporations Law ss 9, 349(7). See also **Exempt body; Foreign company.**

•**Exempt income** Income which is exempt from income tax or which is income or statutory income but is not assessable income: (CTH) Income Tax Assessment Act 1936 s 6(1); *Federal Cmr of Taxation v W E Fuller Pty Ltd* (1953) 101 CLR 403. See also **Assessable income; Income; Income taxation.**

•**Exempt proprietary company** A proprietary company no member of which is, and no share in which is owned by, a non-exempt person: Corporations Law s 69(1) (repealed). A non-exempt person is: a body corporate other than a company, recognised company, or exempt foreign company; a public company; a private company a share in which is owned by a person other than a natural person; or a private company (other than an exempt foreign company) a share in which is owned by a body corporate that is a non-exempt person: s 69(3) (repealed). An exempt proprietary company is exempt from certain statutory provisions relating to financial disclosure, loans to directors, and the need to lodge audited company accounts. See also **Exempt body; Proprietary company; Public company.**

Exemption clause See **Disclaimer; Exclusion clause.**

•**Exhibition** A public show, exhibit or display.

Bills of exchange and other negotiable instruments In the presentment of cheques, a method of cheque clearance where the collecting bank physically displays a cheque to the drawee bank in demanding payment. Electronic technology now permits cheques to be cleared by truncation. See also **Clearance of cheque; Presentment; Truncation.**

Ex-interest When the purchaser of bonds is not entitled to receive the next interest payment; fixed interest securities usually sell ex-interest 14 days before the date of the next interest payment. See also **Bond.**

Expectation interest The benefit of promised performance to a party to a contract. Expectation interest damages in contract are what the plaintiff would have gained in money's worth if the defendant had fulfilled the obligation: *Lavarack v Woods of Colchester Ltd* [1967] 1 QB 278. See also **Breach of contract; Damages; Damages for loss of bargain; Performance; Restitution damages.**

•**Expense** Consumption or loss of service potential or future economic benefits in the form of reductions in assets or increases in liabilities of an entity, other than those relating to distributions to owners, that result in a decrease in equity during the reporting period: Statement of Accounting Concepts SAC 4. See also **Profit and loss account.**

•**Expense payment fringe benefit** A fringe benefit that is a payment in discharge, in whole or in part, of an obligation of a person to pay an amount or a reimbursement of an amount to another person in respect of expenditure incurred by the recipient: (CTH) Fringe Benefits Tax Assessment Act 1986 ss 20, 136(1). See also **Fringe benefit.**

•**Expiry date** In corporations law, the date and time by which the buyer of an option has the right to exercise the option. After the expiry date passes, the option expires and becomes worthless. Also known as 'declaration date'. See also **Call option; Option.**

•**Explanatory statement 1.** A document disclosing information to shareholders to enable them to make a properly informed judgment on a particular proposal: *Chequepoint Securities Ltd v Claremont Petroleum NL* (1986) 11 ACLR 94; 4 ACLC 711. It may relate to, for example, schemes of arrangement, inserting takeover provisions in the articles, public companies proposing to give financial benefits to related parts of the company. It should set out all relevant information relating to the proposal, in particular its effect and any interests of directors, and must be sent with every notice convening a meeting of creditors or members of a company to consider a scheme or proposal, unless an exception applies: Corporations Law ss 243v-243x, 412, 672. The level of disclosure required in the explanatory statement depends upon the nature of the scheme and whether all material information has been disclosed: *Pancontinental Mining Ltd v Goldfields Ltd* (1995) 16 ACSR 463; 13 ACLC 577. **2.** A statement given by a person who is a party to the compilation of books which are the subject of a warrant: (CTH) Australian Securities Commission Act 1989 s 37(9). See also **Scheme**; **Takeover**.

•**Exploit** In the context of patent law, the rights of a patentee to make, hire, sell, import, or deal with the invention in other commercial ways: (CTH) Patents Act 1990 s 130, Sch 1.

•**Export** To cause or occasion the carriage of goods or commodities from one country to another, typically for the purposes of commerce or trade: *Australian Trade Commission v Goodman Fielder Industries Ltd* (1992) 36 FCR 517; 15 AAR 498. See also **Dumping**; **Embargo**; **Excise**; **Export enhancement program**; **Export Guarantees**; **Export Incentive Scheme**; **Export licence**; **Export value**.

Export enhancement program *Abbr* – EEP A program for the subsidisation of uncompetitive American wheat growers. The EEP has been justified by the United States as a necessary retaliation to subsidised grain exports from the European Union. The program was authorised by the (US) Farm Act 1989. Subsidised United States grain has been exported to China and Russia. See also **Aid to production or export of goods**; **Dumping**; **Export enhancement program**; **Export Incentive Scheme**.

Export Finance and Insurance Corporation *Abbr* – EFIC A subsidiary of the Australian Trade Commission backing Australian exporters against the risks of non-payment by the buyers of their products. EFIC undertakes insurance cover that private credit insurers might consider too risky. It insures export sales contracts against the commercial, political and economic risks of non-payment. EFIC lends to overseas buyers of Australian capital goods and associated services. It also insures Australian companies with overseas investments against the risk of having profits and capital taken over by foreign governments, and against the risks of war-like operations. See also **Australian Trade Commission**; **Export**; **Export enhancement program**.

Export Guarantees Assurances or guarantees given by the Secretary of State for Trade and Industry to persons carrying on business in the United Kingdom in connection with the export and manufacture of goods. These guarantees provide British exporters with cover for a variety of risks not ordinarily insurable. The Export Guarantees Advisory Council, established under the (UK) Export Guarantees Act 1975 (repealed) and which continues to operate under the (UK) Export and Investment Guarantees Act 1991 s 13(2), is charged with advising the Secretary of State for Trade and Industry upon the granting of export guarantees. See also **Export**; **Guarantee**.

Export Incentive Scheme A scheme initiated and financed by a government designed to increase the export earnings of businesses regulated by that government. An export incentive scheme usually involves one or more mechanisms such as monetary grants, taxation or regulatory concessions made available to businesses in proportion to increased export earnings, increased devotion of resources to export of goods or produce, or increased volume of exports of goods or produce. See also **Aid to production or export of goods**; **Export**; **Export enhancement program**.

•**Export licence** A licence supplied by a government upon application permitting the export of certain goods. See also **Export**; **Licence**; **Outward bill of lading**.

Export Price Index *Abbr* – EPI An index published by the Australian Bureau of Statistics since 1901, relating to all exports of merchandise from Australia. The index numbers for each month relate to prices of those exports of merchandise that are physically shipped from Australia during that month. The current export price index was introduced in 1979. See also **Terms of trade**.

•**Export value** The fair market value of goods exported for sale by an Australian resident, less the costs of landing and selling the goods overseas that are to be met from the proceeds of sale, being the fair market value of similar goods in the principal markets in the country to which the goods are exported: (CTH) Banking (Foreign Exchange) Regulations 1946 reg 15(1). See also **Export**; **Market value**; **Reserve Bank of Australia**.

Exportation See **Export**.

Export-Import Bank of Japan Set up in 1950, a financial institution facilitating trade, particularly the export of Japanese goods and services.

Export-Import Bank of the United States Set up in 1934, a United States government agency facilitating United States trade by providing credit, financial guarantees and insurance particularly to overseas traders.

Exports integration system *Abbr* – EXIT Introduced in 1991, an electronic system for the reporting and clearance of export cargo. The system is based on electronic data interchange technology. Unless an exporter has declared an intention to export via EXIT and has obtained an export clearance number (ECN) authorising the movement of the goods overseas, the goods cannot be loaded onto a vessel or aircraft for export. EXIT superseded the earlier paper-based export return scheme.

•**Exposure** Investment or loans at risk. The degree of risk depends upon the reliability and soundness of the borrower. The implications of default by the borrower depend also on the size of the funds at risk. Banks, for example, may risk undue exposure when lending large sums to some developing countries, or when lending to corporate entrepreneurs who over extend their activities. Much depends also on whether the loans are secured over assets.

Express agency Agency by express agreement. In agency law, it is created by a principal or some person authorised by the principal, purposely appointing an agent, whether orally or in writing: *Wilson's Laundry Pty Ltd v Patmoy* [1961] NSWR 499. To be contrasted with implied agency. See also **Agency; Agent; Implied agency; Principal**.

Express authority In agency law, the actual authority of an agent conferred orally or by document. An example is the authority to act conferred by a power of attorney. To be contrasted with implied actual authority. See also **Actual authority; Agency; Agent; Apparent authority; Implied authority; Power of attorney**.

Express condition A term of a contract that is described in the contract as being essential in that breach of it gives rise to a right to terminate the contract. The right to terminate must be conferred by clear language: for example *Shevill v Builders Licensing Board* (1982) 149 CLR 620; 42 ALR 305. See also **Condition; Warranty**.

Express contract or convention A contract or agreement expressed in words or by signs that custom or usage has made equivalent to words. See also **Custom of merchants; Express term**.

Express intention The intention disclosed in the words of a contract. There is a presumption that the parties intended to say what they said: *L Schuler AG v Wickman Machine Tools Sales Ltd* [1974] AC 235. See also **Actual intention; Implied intention**.

•**Express notice** See **Actual notice**.

Express repudiation An indication by a party to a contract that he or she is unwilling or unable to perform his or her obligations under the contract: for example *Bowes v Chaleyer* (1923) 32 CLR 159 at 169; [1923] VLR 295; *Carr v J A Berriman Pty Ltd* (1953) 89 CLR 327. See also **Anticipatory breach; Frustration; Implied repudiation; Repudiation**.

Express term An expressed declaration of a particular promise or stipulation in the contract itself: *Friedlander v Bank of Australia* (1909) 8 CLR 85. To be contrasted with an implied term. A term is expressly stated in a contract by reason of what the parties have written or said. See also **Implied term; Incorporation; Term**.

Express trust A trust, expressly spelt out orally or in writing, in language evincing an intention to create a trust. See also **Implied trust; Trust**.

Express waiver A waiver which is actually declared, as opposed to an implied waiver which is implied from the actions of the party abandoning a right. See also **Waiver**.

•**Express warranty** A warranty which is specifically communicated either by words (written or spoken) or actions. An express warranty is consciously agreed to, rather than implied. See also See also **Condition; Damages; Division 2A claim; Implied warranty; Intermediate term; Product warranty; Promissory warranty; Warranty**.

Expressio unius est exclusio alterius /ɛksprɛsioʊ uniʊs ɛst ɛkskluzioʊ æltɛrsiʊs/ *Lat* – express mention of one is the exclusion of the other. A rule of statutory construction requiring the exclusion of matters not expressly mentioned. For example, the express conferral of rights precludes the implication of others not conferred: *Roughley v New South Wales; Ex parte Beavis* (1928) 42 CLR 162 at 198. See also **Express term; Implied term; Intention**.

Expropriation The taking of private property by a state by right of sovereignty, with or without compensation. See also **Compensation; Nationalisation**.

Expulsion of partner The exclusion of a partner from a partnership by a majority of partners, but only where a power to expel has been conferred by express agreement between the partners and that power is exercised in good faith: for example (SA) Partnership Act 1891 s 25. Unlike dissolution of a partnership where the business is usually wound up and assets sold, the remaining partners may be in a position to continue the partnership depending on the number of partners and the terms of the partnership agreement: *Steuart v Gladstone* (1879) Ch D 626 at 647. See also **Dissolution; Partnership**.

Ex-rights Descriptive of a share when the purchaser is not entitled to the rights issue, the ex-date having been passed.

Extension clause A clause in a motor insurance policy that affords cover to any person driving the insured's vehicle with the insured's consent, or protects the insured while he or she is driving any vehicle that does not belong to him or her.

External administration Management of a company that is no longer autonomous as the company is either in liquidation, receivership, administration, or has entered a compromise with creditors; and where the appointed administrator is in control of the company's affairs.

External auditor A qualified public or chartered accountant who is a member of a recognised accounting body. An external auditor conducts an audit in an independent capacity and gives an opinion as to the fairness of the financial statements and adherence to accepted accounting standards. See also **Auditor**.

External debt The accumulated debt owed by Australia collectively to the rest of the world. It comprises all borrowings by Australian residents from non-residents including deposits, loans, finance leases, bonds, bills, International Monetary Fund credits, and Bank for International Settlements placements. Net external debt equals the gross debt minus official reserves and Australian lending overseas. About 80 per cent of Australia's foreign debt is denominated in foreign currencies; a depreciation of the $A increases the $A value of the foreign debt. A substantial part of the increase in Australian foreign debt in recent years has been due to borrowing by the private sector. Currently about three-quarters of the debt is private (including financial institutions). See also **Bank for International Settlements; International Monetary fund**.

External economy A fall in the cost of any of the raw materials and services that a firm requires, obtained from outside sources. The fall may be due to a change in market conditions beyond the influence of the firm, for example a fall in the price of oil or rail freights. On the other hand, purchasing in bulk may enable the firm to negotiate more favourable prices and rates. These economies are also external. While an economy may be external to a firm, it may yet be internal to the industry.

External equity An interest in a company which is located outside the immediate group of companies. It can also be referred to as outside equity. For accounting purposes, outside equity is the equity interests of persons who are not members of the economic entity: Corporations Regulations 1990 Sch 5 cl 16. See also **Equity**.

External presentment A demand for payment of a cheque or payment order on the drawee bank or drawee non bank financial institution (NBFI) made by the collecting bank or collecting financial institution on behalf of a customer or other institution, where the drawee bank or drawee NBFI are not the same as the collecting bank or financial institution: (CTH) Cheques and Payment Orders Act 1986 ss 62, 106. See also **Cheque; Collecting bank; Drawee bank; Internal presentment; Non-bank financial institution; Payment order; Presentment**.

Externality A benefit or cost falling on a third party who normally cannot pay or be compensated for it through the market mechanism. For example, in the generation and supply of electricity, two externalities are costs to the community of effluent from power stations, and benefits to the community of replacing dirty fuels with clean electricity, thus reducing air pollution in cities at the point of consumption. An external benefit is often termed a positive externality; and an external cost, a negative one. An externality embraces any production or consumption process which 'spills over' such that other (third) parties are affected. Four techniques are widely used in measuring externalities: the related market (hedonic price) approach, the hypothetical market (contingent valuation) approach, the dose-response approach, and the minimum-maximum value approach. Also described as a cost not borne by the one who occasions it, and a benefit not paid for by the recipient.

•**Externally administered body corporate** A body corporate: that is being wound up; in respect of property of which a receiver, or a receiver and manager has been appointed (whether or not by a court) and is acting, or that is under administration; that has executed a deed of company arrangement that has not yet terminated; or that has entered into a compromise or arrangement with another person the administration of which has not been concluded: Corporations Law s 9. An externally administered body corporate is no longer under the control of their own shareholders and directors. See also **Body Corporate; Division 3 company**.

•**Externally administered company** See **Externally administered body corporate**.

Extinguish In contract law, to bring rights or obligations under a contract to an end. Extinguishment may occur by the act of one or both of the parties concerned (for example, performance, release by one party, or agreement of both parties) or by operation of law (for example, prescription, merger of one right into another, discharge of a bankrupt, or frustration). See also **Frustration; Merger; Performance; Prescription**.

Extinguishment of debt The process by which a debt ceases to exist. See also **Debt; Mortgage**.

Extortionate See **Unfair loan**.

Extra vires See **Ultra vires**.

Extraordinary general meeting A general meeting of members which is not an annual general meeting. So long as proper notice is given to everyone entitled to receive notice of the meeting, a general meeting of a company may be held at any time: Corporations Law s 245(9). See also **Board of directors meeting**.

Extraordinary items Gains, losses, or provisions for losses that are not a common feature of the normal business operations of a particular business. Extraordinary items are not expected to recur over subsequent periods, and are not regarded as recurring factors in evaluating ordinary business operations. For this reason extraordinary items are recorded separately in the profit and loss account of a business.

Extraordinary resolution A type of company resolution, more commonly referred to as a special resolution. Where any matter is required to be done by a company by a extraordinary resolution, it may be done by a special resolution: Corporations Law s 253(9). See also **Special resolution**.

Extrinsic evidence With regard to a contract, deed, or other instrument, evidential material that lies outside the contract or instrument. The broad purpose of the parol evidence rule is to exclude extrinsic evidence, except as to surrounding circumstances, that subtracts from, adds to, varies, or contradicts the language of the written instrument: *Codelfa Construction Pty Ltd v State Rail Authority of New South Wales* (1982) 149 CLR 337; 41 ALR 367. However, extrinsic evidence is admissible to aid interpretation of a document where it, or any of its terms, are vague or ambiguous (*White v Australian & New Zealand Theatres Ltd* (1943) 67 CLR 266), especially where the terms of the document seem to refer equally to more than one thing or person: *In re Grose (dec'd)* [1949] SASR 55. Also known as 'extraneous evidence'. See also **Ambiguity; Construction; Contract; Collateral contract; Deed; Implied term; Instrument in writing; Intrinsic evidence; Precontractual statement; Rectification**.

F

Face of document To look at a bill of exchange on its face involves looking at both sides of the bill, front and back: *Arab Bank Ltd v Ross* [1952] 2 QB 216. See also **Bill of exchange**; **Document**; **Extrinsic evidence**; **Instrument**.

•**Face value** The nominal value, as distinct from the market value, of a security, share or coin. The nominal value is the value imprinted on the share or stamped upon the coin.

Facilitating practice Activity which, although not on its face offensive to competition, increases the likelihood of other anti-competitive behaviour. In Australia, where there is no contract, arrangement or understanding, there is no prohibition, although such conduct may be evidence of strategic behaviour and thus, possibly, the use of market power within the meaning of (CTH) Trade Practices Act 1974 s 46. See also **Antitrust**; **Competition**; **Contract, arrangement or understanding**; **Misuse of market power**; **Oligopoly**.

Facilitation doctrine Doctrine prohibiting a company from giving financial assistance for the purpose of acquisition (by any person) of the company's shares. This doctrine is infringed where facilitation of the acquisition is a substantial purpose of the assistance: Corporations Law s 205(1)(a); *Independent Steels Pty Ltd v Ryan* [1990] VR 247; 15 ACLR 518. The doctrine is stricter than the 'reduction of resources doctrine' as an infringement will occur whether or not the company's resources are reduced. See also **Financial assistance for acquisition of a company's shares**; **Reduction of resources doctrine**.

Facilitation fee A fee which is paid to an arranger or intermediary to find parties to a facility or programme.

•**Fact** Any act, occurrence, or other thing deemed legally relevant to an issue at trial. Facts are required to make out the elements of an offence or claim in a case and are established by parties adducing evidence tending to show the tribunal of fact that the fact exists. With the decline of the jury trial, the judge is more frequently required to determine both questions of law and fact: *Fabre v Arenales* (1992) 27 NSWLR 437. See also **Adduce**; **Evidence**; **Material fact**.

Fact finder The person or body having the legal authority to determine questions of fact in judicial proceedings. In a trial on indictment, it is normally the jury which determines all issues of fact, although in some jurisdictions there can be trial on indictment by judge alone, so that the judge determines questions of both fact and law: (NSW) Criminal Procedure Act 1986 s 35; (SA) Juries Act 1927 s 7; (WA) Criminal Code s 651A. In summary proceedings it is the magistrate, justice, or judge who determines the facts depending upon the constitution of the court. Also known as 'trier of fact'. See also **Fact**.

Factor A commercial agent, entrusted with possession of the goods of another ('principal') to sell in his or her own name as apparent owner, remunerated by commission: *Rolls Razor Ltd v Cox* [1967] 1 QB 552. A factor is entrusted with possession and control of goods, while a broker acts as an intermediary without control or possession: (NSW) Factors (Mercantile Agents) Act 1923; (QLD) Factors Act 1892; (QLD) Sale of Goods Act 1896 s 3; (IMP) 6 Geo IV c 94 s 2; *Levi v Learmonth* (1862) 1 W & W 283. Also known as 'mercantile agent'. See also **Agency**; **Factorage**; **Agent**; **Mercantile agent**; **Principal**.

Factor loading A fee charged by a factor in a factoring arrangement for credit management and credit risk bearing. The extent of the fees depends on the level of credit management service required and the expected credit risk losses. See also **Factor**; **Factor risk**; **Factoring arrangement**.

Factor risk The risks involved with the collection activities of accounts receivables in a factoring arrangement. Credit risk is the predominant risk which arises when the accounts receivables cannot be recovered. See also **Factor**; **Factor loading**; **Factoring arrangement**.

Factorage The wages, allowance, or commission paid to a factor for his or her services. The business of a factor. See also **Factor**.

Factories shops and industries legislation Legislation that regulates the operation of factories, shops and industries in order to protect the health and welfare of workers in those businesses. See also **Occupational health and safety**.

Factoring The purchasing of invoices from a business at a percentage discount. An arrangement to eliminate payment risks in overseas sales and to ensure that the exporter receives prompt settlement. See also **Factoring arrangement**.

Factoring arrangement An arrangement for the selling of trade debts by businesses in order to arrange finance or to relieve them from administrative functions or bad debt losses. Usually the seller sells its receivables at a discount to a factor in return for immediate cash. The arrangement is profitable for both the seller and the factor. The seller profits by receiving the money early and not having to pay interest on working capital tied up in the credit arrangement. The factor profits from the difference between a discounted purchase price and the amount collected. See also **Factor**; **Factoring**; **Factor loading**; **Factor risk**.

Factors of production Natural resources, capital and labour: the three components utilised in various ratios in the production of goods and services. Natural resources include land, water, forests, fishing grounds and mineral resources. Capital includes public infrastructure as well as the physical hardware of machinery and buildings, and inventories. The labour force includes private and public employees, both full-time and part-time, employers and the self-employed. See also **Capital**; **Labour**.

• **Factory** A building or buildings where goods are made. Any building or place other than a farm or rural holding in which at least four people are engaged directly or indirectly in a manufacturing process; or at least one person is engaged directly or indirectly in a manufacturing process involving the use or handling of lead or any lead alloy or compound; or mechanical power is used in a manufacturing process; or electricity is generated or mechanically transformed; or goods are sorted, packed, frozen or chilled; or bottles are filled; or power is generated for trade, sale or gain: for example (NSW) Factories, Shops and Industries Act 1962 s 4.

Factual matrix The circumstances or setting of fact in which a contract is made, including the commercial background against which the parties contracted, and the genesis, aim, commercial purpose or object of the contract: *Codelfa Construction Pty Ltd v State Rail Authority of NSW* (1982) 149 CLR 337; 41 ALR 367. In construing a contract, the court must place itself in the same factual matrix as the one in which the parties contracted. The factual matrix may provide admissible evidence of the aim or object of the contract: *Reardon Smith Line Ltd v Hansen-Tangen* [1976] 3 All ER 570. See also **Construction**; **Legal matrix**; **Interpretation**.

Facultative reinsurance An insurance placed with, and written by, each underwriter individually rather than under a pre-existing arrangement such as a line slip or broker's slip: *Balfour v Beaumont* [1982] 2 Lloyd's Rep 493 at 496. Facultative reinsurance is a contract that is specific to the particular risk insured. The reinsured and reinsurer are free to choose whether to cede and accept respectively any particular risk. See also **Broker's slip**; **Reinsurance**; **Treaty reinsurance**.

Failing company defence An argument that a given acquisition of shares or assets will not substantially lessen competition, because the company being acquired has 'failed' and has no market power: *International Shoe Co v FTC* (1930) 280 US 291. In competition law, it is not a defence but something that will be taken into account by the Australian Competition and Consumer Commission in assessing whether it will seek to prevent the acquisition: *West Australian Newspapers Ltd (No 1)* (1990) ATPR (Com) 50-100; *West Australian Newspapers Ltd (No 2)* (1990) ATPR (Com) 50-101. See also **Acquisition**; **Authorisation**; **Competition law**; **Market power**; **Merger**; **Pre-merger consultation**; **Substantially lessening competition**.

Failure of consideration The failure by one party to a contract to perform his or her obligations under the contract. The innocent party may recover money paid in anticipation of the failed consideration: for example *McDonald v Dennys Lascelles Ltd* (1933) 48 CLR 457 at 477. Where the plaintiff received any of the performance stipulated by the contract as the agreed return for the payment the plaintiff seeks to recover, the failure of consideration will be partial not total: *McDonald v Dennys Lascelles Ltd*. See also **Consideration**; **Restitution**.

Failure of performance A breach of contract where the promisor, without lawful excuse, fails to discharge a contractual obligation at the time stipulated for performance. A breach due to a failure to perform can be distinguished from an anticipatory breach; a failure to perform can only occur when the time for performance has expired, whereas an anticipatory breach precedes the time for performance. See also **Anticipatory breach**; **Breach of contract**; **Defective performance**; **Discharge**; **Non-performance**; **Time stipulation**.

Failure of substratum The situation where a company acts in a manner entirely outside what can fairly be regarded as having been within the general intention and common understanding of the members when they became members: *Re Tivoli Freeholds Ltd* [1972] VR 445. See also **Just and equitable**; **Oppressive**; **Winding up**.

Failure to instruct A breach of the duty, imposed on manufacturers and other product suppliers by the law of negligence, to provide instructions for the safe and effective use of products: for example *Clark v Paraflight International Pty Ltd* (1987) 5 MVR 87; *Milne Construction Ltd v Expandite Ltd* [1984] 2 NZLR 163; *Grant v Cooper, McDougall & Robertson Ltd* [1940] NZLR 947. See also **Defect in information**; **Failure to warn**.

• **Failure to make a decision** In administrative law, non-compliance with a statutory duty or non-exercise of a statutory discretion within a reasonable time. A duty to exercise a power in certain circumstances may be implied from statutory prescription of the conditions in which the decision-maker may refuse to exercise the power: (CTH) Administrative Decisions (Judicial Review) Act 1977 s 3; *Public Service Association (SA) v Federated Clerks' Union of Australia* (1991) 173 CLR 132; 102 ALR 161 See also **Delay**; **Duty to make a decision**.

Failure to warn A breach of the duty, imposed on manufacturers and other product suppliers by the law of negligence, to provide warnings with a product concerning risks that are not obvious or that would not be known to users or consumers of the product: for example *Fisher v Harrods Ltd* [1966] 1 Lloyd's Rep 500; *Bryden v Chief General Manager of the Health Department* (1987) Aust Torts Reports ¶80-075; *Martin v Stratman* (1994) Aust Torts Reports ¶81-262. See also **Defect in information**; **Failure to instruct**.

• **Fair dealing** The generic term for the exceptions to infringement of copyright which depend in part upon use of the work being in all the circumstances 'fair'. The 'fair dealing' exceptions are now comprised by (CTH) Copyright Act 1968 ss 40, 41, 42, 103A, 103B, 103C. Whether a dealing is fair is a question of degree: *Hubbard v Vosper* [1972] 2 QB 84; *De Garis v Neville Jeffress Pidler Pty Ltd* (1990) 95 ALR 625; 37 FLR 99; *Commonwealth v John Fairfax & Sons Ltd* (1980) 147 CLR 39; 32 ALR 485. See also **Copyright**.

Fair trading legislation Legislation enacted in each of the States and Territories, which reproduces the consumer protection provisions of the (CTH) Trade Practices Act 1974 Part V: for example (NSW) Fair Trading Act 1987; (QLD) Fair Trading Act 1989; (VIC) Fair Trading Act 1985. See also **Consumer protection**; **Trade practices legislation**.

•**Fair trial** A court hearing which is procedurally just to both parties. It is an accused person's right to have a fair trial: *Jago v District Court of New South Wales* (1989) 168 CLR 23; 87 ALR 577. Where an indigent accused is unrepresented and as a consequence the trial is likely to be unfair, a stay of proceedings may be required to ensure a fair trial: *Dietrich v R* (1992) 177 CLR 292; 109 ALR 385. This principle does not extend to civil proceedings, committal proceedings, criminal proceedings which are not serious, or provision of legal representation for a witness: *New South Wales v Canellis* (1994) 181 CLR 309; 124 ALR 513. See also **Abuse of process**; **Trial**.

Fair trial, right to See **Fair trial**.

Fallen angel An investment-grade bond down-graded by credit-rating agencies, turning a high-grade bond into a junk bond. This has happened in the United States often as the result of a leveraged buyout, in which the increased burden of debt carried by the corporation lowers its credit-rating, with immediate losses for bond-holders. See also **Bond**; **Investment-grade bond**; **Junk bond**; **Leveraged buyout**.

Falsa demonstratio /fælsa dɛmɒnstratiou/ *Lat* – a false description or demonstration. An erroneous description of a person or thing in a written instrument is a *falsa demonstratio*.

False accounting The act of destroying, mutilating, concealing, altering, making a false entry in or omitting material from a book of account or any book relating to a company's or person's examinable affairs, or supplying false or deceptive accounting information with the intention of causing financial loss to another person or entity in favour of personal gain: for example (CTH) Bankruptcy Act 1966 s 265; (NSW) Crimes Act 1900 s 158; (QLD) Criminal Code s 441. See also **Accounting**; **Book of account**; **Falsification of accounts**; **Secret profits**.

False advertising A representation or statement in a brochure or media advertising that is contrary to fact. It is not necessary for the person to know that the term is false: *Given v C V Holland (Holdings) Pty Ltd* (1977) 15 ALR 439; 29 FLR 212. False advertising may be a breach of (CTH) Trade Practices Act 1974 s 53. See also **Advertisement**; **Advertising**; **Misleading or deceptive conduct**; **Misrepresentation**.

False name In banking and finance, the use of a name other than a name by which the person is commonly known, in opening an account, or becoming a signatory to an account: (CTH) Financial Transaction Reports Act 1988 s 24(5). It is an offence to open or operate a bank account in a false name: (CTH) Financial Transaction Reports Act 1988 s 24(6). See also **Bank account**.

•**False pretence** A representation of existing fact which is known to be untrue by the person making the representation at the time of the making of the representation. There is a distinction between a false pretence and an exaggeration: *Green & Murrells v R* (1949) 79 CLR 353; [1950] ALR 1. See also **Obtaining property by false pretences**; **Obtaining a financial advantage by deception**.

•**False representation** A representation which is not in fact correct, even if it is not false to the knowledge of the person making it: *Given v C V Holland (Holdings) Pty Ltd* (1977) 15 ALR 439; 29 FLR 212. To make a false representation in connection with particular aspects of the supply of goods and services is a criminal offence: (CTH) Trade Practices Act 1987 s 53. See also **Fair Trading legislation**; **False advertising**; **Misleading or deceptive conduct**; **New goods**; **Price**; **Sponsorship**; **Trade and commerce**; **Trade Practices legislation**.

•**False trade description** A trade description (which includes a statement specifying characteristics of a good such as quality, size, country or place of origin) which, by reason of anything contained in it or omitted from it, is false or likely to mislead in a material respect as regards the goods to which it is applied or in connection with which it is used, and which includes every alteration of a trade description which has this effect: (CTH) Commerce (Trade Descriptions) Act s 3; (TAS) Goods (Trade Descriptions) Act 1971 s 2; (VIC) Consumer Affairs Act 1972 s 33.

False trading Conduct which is intended or likely to create a false or misleading appearance of active trading in any securities on a stock market or with respect to the market for, or price of, securities. False trading is prohibited: Corporations Law s 998(1). See also **Market manipulation**.

Falsification of accounts The process of making deliberately incorrect entries in the books or accounts of the reporting entity. The falsification is either to conceal that a fraud has taken place or to present figures which show an incorrect and unfair view of the operations of the business. See also **False accounting**; **Fraud**.

Falsify Making false in any way: *R v Webber* (1988) 15 NSWLR 49; 38 A Crim R 210. The falsification of a document does not require its actual alteration: *R v Webber* (1988) 15 NSWLR 49; 38 A Crim R 210. It is an offence for an employee to falsify any accounts or other documents of an employer: for example (NSW) Crimes Act 1900 s 158; (VIC) Crimes Act 1958 s 83. See also **False accounting**; **Falsification of accounts**; **Fraud**.

Family trust See **Discretionary trust**.

•**Fare** The money paid by a passenger to a common or private carrier as consideration for the carriage of the passenger from the point of embarkation to the destination: *Baltic Shipping Co v Dillon* (1993) 176 CLR 344; 111 ALR 289 See also **Carrier**; **Common carrier**; **Contract of carriage**; **Duty of care**; **Fare paying passenger**; **Freight**.

Fare paying passenger A person who engages a carrier to transport him or her to a destination for a reward known as the fare. A contract of carriage for reward is entered into by way of a ticket issued to the passenger in exchange for payment of the fare. Payment of a fare entitles the passenger to a high standard of care from the carrier. In the case of a common carrier, on payment of the fare the passenger has a right to be carried without discrimination, so long as the passenger is not in an unfit condition. This right extends to the passenger's personal luggage. The ticket, by itself or by reference to other documents, sets the terms of the carriage. The basic term of a contract with a fare paying passenger is to carry the passenger with reasonable care to the named destination within a reasonable time. See also **Carrier; Common carrier; Contract of carriage; Fare.**

•**FAS** See **Free alongside ship.**

FAST See **Flexible Accelerated Security Transfer.**

FAST Interbroker Delivery Service *Abbr* – FIDS A service allowing same day delivery of securities by a selling broker in one capital city to the buying broker in another capital city. Following delivery of securities by the selling broker to the Australian Stock Exchange (ASX) in the first city, the ASX delivers an equivalent number of securities to the buying broker in the other city from its local office. Delivery by means of FIDS is only possible for FIDS eligible securities. FIDS deliveries are used for full or partial delivery of transfer documents for settlement of open transactions between brokers recorded under the Broker Settlement System (BBS) operated by the ASX in FIDS eligible securities, including loan or loan return transactions with the exchange supported Securities Lending Service: ASX Business Rules BR 4.40. A broker who receives an ineffective transfer through FIDS is entitled to make a claim against the National Guarantee Fund: Corporations Law Pt 7.10 Div 6C. See also; **Flexible Accelerated Security Transfer; FIDS eligible securities; National Guarantee Fund.**

Fast track arbitration An expedited arbitration process, designed to overcome the perceived length and formality of arbitrations. Under the provisions of the Commercial Arbitration legislation, the parties to the arbitration may agree to streamline or limit procedures in order to speed up the proceedings: for example, submissions may be written rather than oral, strict time limits may apply, the amount and type of expert or other evidence may be limited, the parties may forego legal representation, or the arbitrator may decide the matter *ex aequo et bono* (on the basis of what is just and fair) rather than by applying the appropriate laws. See also **Alternative dispute resolution; Arbitration; Commercial Arbitration Legislation; Ex aequo et bono; Institute of Arbitrators Australia.**

Fast track contract In building and construction, a delivery system in which the contract is let prior to completion of design. The design work is carried out contemporaneously with building work on other sections of the project in order to enable the project to be carried out in a shorter time; thus a fast track contract can be contrasted with a traditional head contract, where the proprietor engages the contractor after completion of the design. The difficulty with a fast track contract is that a contractor may be undertaking to construct something which has not been finally designed, giving rise to possible uncertainty as to the scope of the works and consequent uncertainty as to cost. Also known as 'deferred let contract'. See also **Building contract; Contractor; Proprietor.**

•**Fault 1.** Defect, blemish, flaw, or imperfection. **2.** A mistake or error in thought or action: *Doolan v Waltons Ltd* (1981) 39 ALR 408 at 414; ATPR ¶40-257. **3.** Any act or omission which gives rise to a liability.

Contract An error which may include some instances of carelessness, 'wilful ignorance or culpable neglect': *Earl of Beauchamp v Winn* (1873) LR 6 HL 223 at 234. However, this does not imply that there must be a breach of some duty of care. It is required not only that the parties' common mistake be 'fundamental' but also that the party seeking to have the contract set aside not be at fault: *Solle v Butcher* [1949] 2 All ER 1107; [1950] 1 KB 671 at 693.

Sale of goods Wrongful act or default: (NSW) Sale of Goods Act 1923 s 5(1); (VIC) Goods Act 1958 s 3(1); (QLD) Sale of Goods Act 1896 s 3(1); (SA) Sale of Goods Act 1895 s 60(1); (WA) Sale of Goods Act 1895 s 60(1); (TAS) Sale of Goods Act 1896 s 3(1); (ACT) Sale of Goods Act 1954 s 5(1); (NT) Sale of Goods act 1972 s 5(1).

Tort **1.** Negligence, breach of statutory duty, or any other act or omission which gives rise to a liability in tort (the defendant's fault): *Winter v Bennet* [1956] VLR 612 at 622; *Horkin v North Melbourne Football Club Social Club* [1983] 1 VR 153 at 158; (NSW) Law Reform (Miscellaneous Provisions) Act 1965 s 10(1) (in New South Wales fault does not mean or include a breach of statutory duty); (VIC) Wrongs Act 1958 s 25; (QLD) Law Reform (Tortfeasors Contribution, Contributory Negligence, and Division of Chattels) Act 1952 s 4.

Fault of privities The blame attaching to privity, where privity is the concurrence by the owner of a vessel in something of which it has knowledge or to which it has turned a blind eye and in relation to which there is no insurance: *Compania Maritima San Basilio SA v The Oceanus Mutual Underwriting Assoc (Bermuda) Ltd (The Eurysthenes)* [1977] 1 QB 49; [1976] 2 Lloyds Rep 171.

Faulty Not operating properly because of defects, flaws or deficiencies: *Manufacturers' Mutual Insurance Ltd v Queensland Government Railways* (1968) 118 CLR 314; 42 AJLR 181. There is no distinction between 'faulty' and 'defective': *Manufacturers Mutual Insurance Ltd v Queensland Government Railways.* See also **Default; Latent defect.**

FBT See **Fringe benefits tax.**

FCR See **Forwarded certificate of receipts.**

•**Federal court** A court with jurisdiction to exercise the judicial power of the Commonwealth, created by the Commonwealth Parliament in accordance with the Commonwealth Constitution s 75(ii). Federal courts include the High Court of Australia, the Federal Court of Australia, and the Family Court of Australia. State courts may be invested with federal jurisdiction: Commonwealth Constitution s 77(iii). See also **Court; Federal Court of Australia; High Court of Australia; Judge.**

Federal Court jurisdiction The jurisdiction exercised by the Federal Court of Australia. The jurisdiction of the Federal Court is defined by the (CTH) Federal Court of Australia Act 1976, enacted by the Commonwealth under Commonwealth Constitution ss 71, 77(i). The court has such original jurisdiction as is vested in it by statute, including jurisdiction to hear appeals from decisions of persons, authorities or tribunals other than courts: (CTH) Federal Court of Australia Act 1976 s 19. The Federal Court has appellate jurisdiction to hear appeals from judgments of the Supreme Court of a Territory and in such cases as are provided by any other Act, appeals from judgments of a court of a State, other than a full court of the Supreme Court of a State, exercising federal jurisdiction: (CTH) Federal Court of Australia Act 1976 s 24(1). See also **Appellate jurisdiction**.

Federal Court of Australia A superior court of record and a court of law and equity: (CTH) Federal Court of Australia Act 1976 s 5(2). It is not a court of unlimited jurisdiction and only has such jurisdiction as is invested in it by statute and such powers attendant upon that jurisdiction as are expressly or by implication conferred by the legislation which governs it: (CTH) Federal Court of Australia Act 1976 s 19(1); *Elna (Aust) Ltd v International Computers (Aust) Pty Ltd* (1987) 14 FCR 461 at 466; 74 ALR 232 at 237. The Federal Court of Australia replaced the Australian Industrial Court and the Federal Court of Bankruptcy. See also **Bankruptcy; Bankruptcy Court**.

Federal Court of Australia (Industrial Division) A division of the Federal Court of Australia that exercised the judicial power of the Commonwealth in relation to industrial awards under the (CTH) Conciliation and Arbitration Act 1904 (repealed), and then the (CTH) Industrial Relations Act 1988. It was established in 1977 to replace the Australian Industrial Court. It was abolished when the Industrial Relations Court of Australia was established in 1994. See also **Australian Industrial Court**.

Federal industrial system The industrial tribunal and industrial court established by the (CTH) Industrial Relations Act 1988. The system consists of the Australian Industrial Relations Commission, the Australian Industrial Registry and the Industrial Relations Court of Australia. The Commonwealth Constitution s 51(xxxv) authorises the Commonwealth government to legislate with respect to conciliation and arbitration for the prevention and settlement of industrial disputes extending beyond the limits of any one State; other constitutional heads of power also support the federal legislation. See also **Australian Industrial Relations Commission; Industrial tribunal**.

•**Federal jurisdiction** The power or authority to adjudicate controversies derived from the Constitution and Commonwealth laws: *Collins v Charles Marshall Pty Ltd* (1955) 92 CLR 529 at 562-3. Such jurisdiction, power, or authority vests in the High Court, other federal courts created by the Commonwealth Parliament, and such other courts as Parliament thinks fit: Commonwealth Constitution ss 71, 77. The Commonwealth may vest such jurisdiction in State courts (Commonwealth Constitution s 77(iii)) and has done so: (CTH) Judiciary Act 1903 s 39(2). Such jurisdiction, however, may only be conferred in respect of the matters enumerated in Commonwealth Constitution ss 75, 76: Commonwealth Constitution s 77. See also **Appellate Jurisdiction; Cross vesting; High Court of Australia; Matter**.

Federal Open Market Committee A committee of the United States Federal Reserve System which controls the sales and purchases of Federal government securities. Decisions are made in respect of open market operations which are executed by the Federal Reserve Bank. A purchase of securities by the Federal Reserve Bank adds to the cash reserves of member banks. A sale of securities reduces the cash reserves of the member banks. The committee consists of the seven members of the Board of Governors together with the heads of five of the twelve Federal reserve banks, including the head of the New York Reserve Bank which is always represented. See also **Federal reserve system**.

Federal powers The powers of the Federal Government to make laws with respect to a series of enumerated subjects. The principle list of subjects appears in the 40 paragraphs of Commonwealth Constitution s 51, but there are further grants elsewhere: Commonwealth Constitution ss 52, 76, 77, 78, 96, 105A, 122, 128.

Federal Reserve Banks The equivalent in the United States of the central banks of other countries. The (US) Federal Reserve Act 1913 divided the United States into twelve regions each of which has a Federal reserve bank. The most important is the Federal Reserve Bank of New York which conducts open market operations. The activities of the twelve banks are controlled and coordinated by the Federal Reserve Board. See also **Federal reserve system**.

Federal Reserve Board The governing body of the United States central banking system. It comprises seven full-time members appointed by the United States President with the consent of the Senate. The board determines monetary, credit and operating policies for the Federal reserve system. See also **Federal reserve system**.

Federal reserve system The central banking system of the United States, established by the (US) Federal Reserve Act 1913. The system consists of six components: the Federal Reserve Board, the federal reserve banks, the Federal Open Market Committee, the Federal Advisory Council, the Consumer Advisory Council and the commercial banks that have voluntarily joined the system. It is the responsibility of the Federal reserve system to promote the full use of human and capital resources in the United States, promote the growth of productivity, restrain inflation, contribute towards achieving balance in overseas trade and help maintain a commercial banking system that is responsive to the financial needs and objectives of the nation.

Federal state A political union, or confederation, of substantially autonomous States, designed to accommodate apparently inconsistent claims of national unity and power with the maintenance of 'State rights'. See also **Federal system; Federation**.

Federal system A political system in which governmental power is shared between a central or federal government having power over the whole country, and regional governments having power over their respective regions. The Australian federal system consists of the division of governmental powers between the Commonwealth Parliament and the State parliaments, as set out in the Commonwealth Constitution: *Amalgamated Society of Engineers v Adelaide Steamship Co Ltd* (1920) 28 CLR 129. See also **Commonwealth of Australia**.

Federal Trade Commission A United States federal regulatory agency with quasi-judicial powers, charged with the responsibility of securing compliance with the prohibition on 'unfair methods of competition in or affecting commerce, and unfair or deceptive acts or practices in or affecting commerce': (US) Federal Trade Commission Act 1914 s 5. See also **Antitrust; Competition law; Merger guidelines; Pre-merger notification; Trade Practices Commission.**

•**Federation 1.** The politico-legal process of uniting several autonomous or colonial States within (as coordinate constituent States) or under (as subordinate constituent States) a national 'federal' government, upon terms set out in a written constitution. **2.** The political entity resulting from this process. In Australia, the fundamental nature of State-Commonwealth intergovernmental relations has been altered from coordinate to subordinate, in the absence of relevant constitutional amendment, by radical judicial constitutional reinterpretation: *Federated Amalgamated Government Railway and Tramway Service Association v New South Wales Railway Traffic Employees Assn* (1906) 4 CLR; 488; *Amalgamated Society of Engineers v Adelaide Steamship Co Ltd* (1920) 28 CLR 129. The federal nature of Australia's government ensures that the Commonwealth may not interfere with the essential institutions of State government: *Queensland Electricity Commission v Commonwealth* (1985) 159 CLR 192; 61 ALR 1. See also **Federal state; Federal system.**

Fedwire Computerised communications system which links the Federal Reserve Board in Washington to its twenty four branch banks and the US Treasury. It is regarded as the central nervous system of money transfer in the United States. See also **Reserve Bank of Australia.**

Fee for service A fee or charge exacted for particular identified services provided or rendered individually to, or at the request or direction of, the particular person required to make the payment: *Air Caledonie International v Commonwealth* (1988) 165 CLR 462 at 469-70; 82 ALR 385. Where there is a direct relationship between the payment of the fee and the receipt of the service, the fee is a fee for a service: *Harper v Victoria* (1966) 114 CLR 361; ALR 731. Where there is an indirect relationship, the fee is not a fee for a service: *Parton v Milk Board (Vic)* (1949) 80 CLR 229; (1950) ALR 55. See also **Excise.**

•**Fee simple** The estate in land which is 'the most extensive in quantum, the most absolute in respect to the rights it confers of all estates known to law... and for all practical purposes of ownership, it differs from the absolute dominion of a chattel in nothing except the physical indestructibility of its subject': *Commonwealth v New South Wales* (1923) 33 CLR 1. Originated in feudal times as an estate capable of inheritance (a 'fee') which could descend to any heirs whatsoever of the original grantee. See also **Freehold.**

Fee tail A form of estate in real property where the right of an estate holder to devise the property is limited to specified members of the family. The holder of the estate has a life interest rather than a fee simple and at the death of the tenant in tail, the property passes to the class of heirs prescribed by the tail. A fee tail can still be created in South Australia, or in Tasmania if the land is under old system title: (SA) Estates Tail Act 1881; (TAS) Estates Tail Act 1853. In other States an estate in fee tail is deemed to be an estate in fee simple: for example (NSW) Conveyancing Act 1919 ss 19, 19A; (VIC) Property Law Act 1958 s 249. See also **Estate; Fee simple.**

Fellow servant rule The rule under which an employee was usually unable to sue her or his employer for injuries caused by the fault of a fellow employee. The rule was abolished by statute in England, followed by the Australian colonies: *Brown v Board of Land and Works* (1882) 8 VLR 414; (UK) (1880) 43 & 44 Vic c 42.

Fiat *Lat* – let it be done. **1.** An authoritative sanction or authorisation; a command that something should be done. **2.** An order or decree by a judge or the Attorney-General on behalf of the Crown for certain proceedings to begin. See also **Attorney-General; Justiciability.**

Fictitious bid A bid which has not in fact been made. An example is a non-existent bid invented by the auctioneer in an attempt to drive up bidding: *Futuretronics International Pty Ltd v Gadzhis* (1990) ATPR ¶41-049; ASC 56-009. See also **Auction; Auctioneer; Bid; Damping the sale; Knock down.**

Fictitious party In the context of negotiable instruments, a term having two meanings. **1.** When used disjunctively with 'non-existing', a real, existing person who was never intended by the drawer of a bill of exchange to receive the bill as payee: *Bank of England v Vagliano Bros* [1891] AC 107; (CTH) Bills of Exchange Act 1909 s 12(3). **2.** Where 'fictitious' only is used, it includes a non-existing party: *City Bank v Rowan* (1893) 14 LR (NSW) L 127; (CTH) Bills of Exchange Act 1909 s 10(2). See also **Bill of exchange; Drawer; Non-existing party; Payee.**

Fidelity The trust which exists between agent and principal that the agent will faithfully observe the duties and responsibilities owed to the principal, and that the principal will indemnify the agent against all liabilities incurred in the reasonable performance of the agency. See also **Duty to keep accounts; Indemnity.**

Fidelity, duty of See **Duty of fidelity.**

Fidelity guarantee A contract of insurance providing cover against pecuniary loss incurred as a result of fraudulent misappropriation or embezzlement.

Fidelity guarantee insurance See **Fidelity guarantee.**

FIDS eligible securities Flexible Accelerated Security Transfer System (FAST) eligible securities nominated as being eligible for delivery by means of FAST Interbroker Deliver Service (FIDS): ASX Business Rules BR 4.40. FAST eligible securities are those securities which have been approved as FAST eligible securities by the Australian Securities Commission (ASC) and are specified in the list kept by the Australian Stock Exchange (ASX) which identifies those securities and the participating companies. See also **Flexible Accelerated Security Transfer.**

Fiduciary A person who is under an obligation to act in another's interest to the exclusion of the fiduciary's own interest. See also **Fiduciary duty; Fiduciary relationship; Trust**.

Fiduciary duty An equitable duty to act in good faith for the benefit of another. A fiduciary duty arises in the context of a fiduciary relationship, such as that between trustee and beneficiary. See also **Beneficiary; Directors' duties; Equity; Good faith; Trustee**.

Fiduciary relationship A relationship of trust and confidence or of confidential relations: *Boardman v Phipps* [1967] 2 AC 46; [1966] 3 All ER 721. The critical feature of a fiduciary relationship is that the fiduciary undertakes or agrees to act for or on behalf of, or in the interests of, another person in the exercise of a power or discretion which will affect the interests of that other person in a legal or practical sense. A fiduciary relationship is a relationship which gives the fiduciary a special opportunity to exercise the power or discretion to the detriment of that other person, who is accordingly vulnerable to abuse by the fiduciary of his or her position: *Hospital Products Ltd v United States Surgical Corp* (1984) 156 CLR 41; 55 ALR 417. See also **Beneficiary; Conflict of interest; Duty to disclose; Fiduciary; Trustee**.

Fieri facias /faɪəri feɪʃəs/ *Lat* – cause to be done. A writ authorising a sheriff to recover the amount of a judgment by distraint on goods. *Abbr* – fi fa

FIFO See **First in first out valuation**.

Fill or kill order A futures market order to buy or sell a particular security that is required to be executed immediately or cancelled. It often occurs where a person intends to buy a large quantity of shares of a particular stock at a particular price. If the order is likely to affect the market price for that stock significantly it will not be executed and can be withdrawn immediately. See also **Futures contract; Securities**.

FIMBRA See **Financial Intermediaries, Managers and Brokers Regulatory Association**.

•**Final and conclusive** A phrase used legislatively in relation to certain administrative decisions meaning 'without appeal'. Designation of a decision as 'final and conclusive' renders it final on the facts but not final on the law. See also **Foreign judgment**.

Final certificate The certificate issued by the contract administrator on final completion which determines the amount of the final payment to the contractor. Under standard contracts, the issue of an unchallenged final certificate is usually conclusive as to the proprietor's liability regarding final payment. See also **Contractor; Final completion; Final payment; Progress certificate; Proprietor**.

•**Final completion** In a construction project, the stage at which everything required by the contract is finally completed, so that the contractor is discharged from all contractual obligations. Whether or not the building contract expressly requires it, the contractor must bring the work to final completion in terms of the contract. This includes work which, although not expressly specified in the contractual documents, is ancillary to that work and necessary for its performance: *Ownit Homes Pty Ltd v Batchelor* [1983] 2 Qd R 124. Final completion is marked by the giving of a final certificate; the proprietor then pays the balance of the price, including any retention moneys, and releases any performance securities held. See also **Contractor; Discharge; Performance**.

Final dividend A dividend declared out of profits as disclosed by the accounts which have been laid before the company's general meeting. The declaration gives rise to a debt payable by the company to the shareholder immediately or from a date stipulated for payment: *Industrial Equity Ltd v Blackburn* (1977) 137 CLR 567; 17 ALR 575. See also **Dividend; Interim dividend**.

Final judgment The judgment in civil proceedings that ends the action. Final judgment is usually obtained at trial unlike an interlocutory judgment which is obtained prior to trial. In bankruptcy, the quality of finality of judgment required by the (CTH) Bankruptcy Act 1966 s 40(1)(g) to ground an act of bankruptcy is not affected by an order that parties have liberty to apply as this related to enforcement of the judgment. Orders which provide for a right of indemnity of a surety against a principal debtor which only arise to constitute a debt upon the discharge of the debt by the surety are nevertheless final orders: *Abigroup Ltd v Abignano* (1992) 39 FCR 74; 112 ALR 497. See also **Interlocutory judgment**.

Final offer arbitration Arbitration in which each party submits a proposed resolution to the matter in dispute, and the arbitrator selects the most reasonable proposal and awards it without qualification or amendment: for example (WA) Industrial Relations Act 1979 s 7. See also **Ambit; Arbitration**.

•**Final payment** In relation to a building contract, payment by a proprietor to the contractor of any part of the agreed price outstanding upon final completion of the work. The amount of final payment is normally determined by the contract administrator in the final certificate which is issued at the end of the defects liability period. The assessment of the final payment must normally have regard to all claims between the parties. See also **Building contract; Final certificate; Final completion; Proprietor**.

•**Finance broker** Any person who carries on the business of negotiating or acting as an intermediary to obtain credit for persons other than his or her employer or principal: for example (NSW) Credit (Finance Brokers) Act 1984 s 4(1). The activities of finance brokers are regulated by legislation in the Australian Capital Territory, New South Wales, Victoria and Western Australia: for example (NSW) Credit (Finance Brokers) Act 1984; (VIC) Finance Brokers Act 1969. See also **Finance broker's licence; Housing loan; Regulated contract**.

Finance broker's licence A licence which a person had to hold in order to carry on the business of a finance broker: for example (NSW) Credit (Administration) Act 1984 (repealed) s 6(3) Under the uniform credit legislation, finance brokers no longer required licences. Exempted from the licensing requirements are persons who negotiate to obtain credit for their customers, for example, solicitors, company auditors, banks, insurance companies and underwriters, licensed security dealers, trustee companies, cooperative societies and credit unions: (NSW) Credit (Administration) Act 1984 (repealed) s 7(3); (VIC) Finance Brokers Act 1969 s 3(1). See also **Finance broker**.

Finance Brokers Supervisory Board (WA) A body corporate established by (WA) Finance Brokers Control Act 1975 s 6 to be the licensing and supervisory body administering the (WA) Finance Brokers Control Act 1975. The Board has the powers, duties, and functions conferred, imposed or prescribed by the Act, for example, the power to grant licences under (WA) Finance Brokers Control Act 1975 Pt III.

Finance company A business organisation which provides consumer credit and various forms of commercial finance. Finance companies obtain most of their funds from the issue of interest-bearing debentures and unsecured notes, as well as by way of share capital.

Finance, contract subject to See **Contract subject to finance**.

•**Financial accommodation** Any funds provided by means of a loan or bill facility, or funds provided under any other obligation except a lease or hiring arrangement: for example (NSW) Stamp Duties Act 1920 s 83(1). See also **Credit**; **Uniform credit legislation**.

Financial activity A transaction which has as its subject matter finance, as distinct from a transaction which, although requiring a transfer of money, has a different subject matter: *Re Ku-ring-gai Co-op Building Society Ltd (No 12)* (1978) 22 ALR 621; 36 ALR 134. See also **Financial corporation**; **Register of corporations**.

•**Financial advantage** A benefit in monetary terms. The term is to be given its ordinary meaning, and can embrace a payment of money: *Matthews v Fountain* [1982] VR 1045; *Murphy v R* [1987] Tas R 178; (VIC) Crimes Act 1958 s 82; (TAS) Criminal Code s 252A. It includes obtaining credit and avoiding payment of a debt, but not the mere deferral of payment: *Fisher v Bennett* (1987) 85 FLR 469.

Financial affairs The dealings and transactions of an associated entity which can be the subject of examination. See also **Associated entity**.

Financial analysis An analysis intended to reveal the prospective rate of return from a project and the likely demands on cash flow. It is vital to the success of commercial and public projects. Financial analysis examines a project from a narrow perspective, however, it does not take into account the effects on other enterprises or the community. In an economic evaluation these wider considerations should be taken into account. The undertaking of an economic appraisal does not, however, remove or diminish the need for a financial analysis.

•**Financial asset** A claim to money. Borrowing can be described as the sale of a financial asset, and lending the purchase of a financial asset. For example, a bank giving a loan has purchased a claim to repayments over a period of time, being repayment of the loan. See also **Asset**; **Financial Investment**.

Financial assistance for acquisition of a company's shares A company is prohibited from directly or indirectly giving any financial assistance for the purpose of, or in connection with, the acquisition by any person of shares (or units of shares) in that company or parent entities of the company: Corporations Law s 205(1)(a). Assistance includes making a loan, giving a guarantee, providing security, and forgiving a debt: s 205(2). This prohibition is an important aspect of the maintenance of capital principle. See also **Maintenance of capital**; **Facilitation doctrine**; **Reduction of resources doctrine**.

•**Financial benefit** A pecuniary advantage given directly or indirectly: Corporations Law s 243G. Giving a financial benefit can include lending money, guaranteeing a loan, providing security, or forgiving a debt: Corporations Law s 243G. See also **Related party**.

Financial benefits to related parties The prohibited act of a public company giving financial benefit to a related party: Corporations Law s 243H. Giving a financial benefit includes lending money or providing security, forgiving a debt, selling or leasing assets, acquiring or supplying services, issuing securities, giving money or property or otherwise conferring some financial advantage: Corporations Law s 243G. A related party is a director of the company or its parent entities, a spouse, parent or child of a director, an entity controlled by any of those persons or, a sibling entity of the company: Corporations Law s 243F(1). Exemptions include those relating to benefits on arm's length terms, reasonable remuneration of officers, benefits to wholly owned subsidiaries or to members in their capacity as members, and where there is approval by the general meeting: Corporations Law ss 243J-243T. These provisions supplement the general law on fiduciaries. See also **Directors' duties**; **Fiduciary**.

Financial conglomerate A group of companies under common ownership which primarily undertakes financial activities across more than one financial sector, such as banking, insurance and securities. Unlike conglomerates in some other countries, in particular, Western Europe, most large Australian conglomerates continue to be dominated by banks or insurance companies controlling nearly 80 per cent of assets and funds under management in all financial institutions.

•**Financial corporation** For the purposes of Commonwealth Constitution s 51(xx), a corporation that engages in financial activities or is intended to do so: *State Superannuation Board (Vic) v Trade Practices Commission* (1982) 150 CLR 282 at 305; 44 ALR 1. Examples of financial corporations are finance companies, credit unions, building societies, banks and insurance companies. See also **Corporation**; **Financial activity**; **Register of Corporations**; **Trading corporation**.

Financial deregulation A process which involves the removal of many restrictions from the banking and financial system, the removal of interest rate ceilings, and the floating of the dollar. Deregulation of the Australian financial system took place in the 1980's as a consequence of recommendation of the Committee of Inquiry into the Australian Financial System (Campbell Committee) which reported in 1981. The subsequent

Martin Review Group, reporting in 1984, endorsed these recommendations and supported the continuation of the process of deregulation as well as the entry of new banks into the financial system. Despite deregulation, the Reserve Bank undertakes the general supervision of the financial system with more extensive responsibilities. See also **Reserve Bank of Australia**.

Financial futures A futures contract concerned with the right to buy or sell specified financial instruments as opposed to physical commodities. See also **Futures contract; Futures adviser; Futures broker**.

•**Financial institution** An entity which accepts money as savings or investment and in turn provides funds to borrowers. In broad terms it includes banks, building societies, credit unions, life offices, superannuation funds and finance companies: Corporations Law s 111AZA. See also **Building society; Credit union; Finance company**.

•**Financial Institutions Agreement** An agreement entered into on 22 November 1991 between the States and Territories to set up a cooperative scheme for the regulation of building societies and credit unions. See also **Australian Financial Institutions Commission; Financial institutions scheme**.

•**Financial Institutions Duty** Abbr – FID A tax imposed by all States (except Queensland) and Territories on amounts credited to or deposited in accounts maintained by banks and financial institutions: for example (NSW) Stamp Duties Act 1920 Sch 2. See also **Allowable deduction; Assessable income; Debits tax**.

•**Financial institutions scheme** The scheme established and implemented by the Financial Institutions Agreement and the financial institutions legislation. See also **Financial Institutions Agreement**.

Financial Intermediaries, Managers and Brokers Regulatory Association Abbr – FIMBRA A self-regulatory British organisation which regulates the carrying on of investment business of any kind: (UK) Financial Services Act 1986 s 8(1).

Financial intermediary An institution or go-between enabling funds to flow efficiently from those who wish to lend to those who wish to borrow. In Australia, financial intermediaries include the banks and the non-bank financial intermediaries: building societies, finance companies, merchant banks, property trusts, cash management trusts and credit unions. See also **Building Society; Financial institution**.

Financial investment The purchase of shares, bonds and other financial instruments in contrast to real investment in a capital asset such as real estate or plant and equipment. See also **Financial asset; Investment**.

•**Financial journalist** A person who, in the course of the person's business or employment, contributes advice or prepares analyses or reports about securities for publication in newspapers, periodicals, or transmissions by means of an information service or sound, video or data recordings: Corporations Law s 879(1). Financial journalists are required to maintain a register containing particulars of relevant interests in securities: Corporations Law Pt 7.7. See also **Register of interests in securities; Securities; Securities business**.

Financial legislation Legislation that imposes taxation for the raising of revenue and authorises the appropriation of money from the Treasury of the Commonwealth for expenditure by the government. The Commonwealth Parliament has power under the Commonwealth Constitution to make laws with respect to taxation: Commonwealth Constitution s 51(ii).

Financial leverage A measure of financial risk that refers to an amount of money which has been borrowed against the firm's assets on a fixed financing charge in anticipation that the return achieved on the use of those assets will be greater than the financing charge. The higher the financial leverage, the higher the financial risk. See also **Leverage; Risk**.

Financial market A location where financial instruments (including money and securities) can be bought and sold. It may have a physical location such as a trading floor, or be conducted via computer or telephone links, or another communication system. See also **Financial asset**.

•**Financial period** The time over which an accounting report is made. In Australia a company's accounts must be provided in respect of a financial year, which is the period 12 months (or such longer period, not exceeding 18 months, as the directors resolve) from either the date of incorporation of a company or from the end of the previous financial year: Corporations Law s 70A. See also **Account; Financial statement; Financial year**.

•**Financial position** A monetary statement regarding the financial capacity of an entity at a given date, showing the funds available and the debts payable in order to give a true picture of the surplus funds or deficit of such an entity.

•**Financial statement** A record of the economic situation of an entity for the benefit of investors and creditors; the accounts and consolidated accounts which are required to be made out in relation to an accounting period: Corporations Law s 9. See also **Account; Accounting period; Accounting standards; Body corporate; Entity**.

Financial supermarket A financial institution that offers a diverse range of services.

Financial Times-Stock Exchange (FTSE) 100 Share Index Popularly known as the Footsie Index or Footsie 100, the pre-eminent share-price index for the British stock market. Ranked according to market capitalisation, the constituent stocks are the 100 largest listed on the London International Stock Exchange. These stocks represent some 70% of the total market value of all British equities. Introduced in 1984, the index is calculated on a minute-by-minute basis. Other *Financial Times* indices are the Financial Times Ordinary 30 Share Index (FT30), a price weighted index first calculated in 1935, and the Financial Times All Share Index (FT Actuaries), a capitalisation weighted index of 700 shares introduced in 1962.

Financial Times-Stock Exchange (FTSE) Europack 100 Share Index A stockmarket index of continental European stocks introduced by the London International Stock Exchange in 1990 in association with the *Financial Times*. It covers 100 leading continental

European stocks and was designed as a sister-product to the Financial Times-Stock Exchange 100 Share Index of British shares.

• **Financial transaction document** A document relating to a financial transaction carried out by a financial institution in its capacity as a financial institution: (CTH) Proceeds of Crime Act 1987 s 76. It includes a document relating to the opening, operation, or closure of an account held with the institution, and the opening or use of a deposit box held by the institution, but does not include cheques and payment orders. Legislation enacted by the Commonwealth, the Australian Capital Territory, and Queensland, require financial institutions to retain certain classes of documents, including financial transaction documents, for a specified minimum retention period. See also **Customer generated financial transaction document**; **Proceeds of crime**.

Financial Transaction Reports legislation
Abbr – FTR Legislation to facilitate the administration and enforcement of tax laws: (CTH) Financial Transactions Reports Act 1988 s 4(1). The legislation seeks to assist in the deterrence and detection of tax evasion and criminal activity, including offences against corporate laws, money laundering from drug trafficking and organised crime: (CTH) Financial Transaction Reports Act 1988. The agency administering the legislation is called the Australian Transaction Reports and Analysis Centre (AUSTRAC). See also **Account**; **Australian Transaction Reports and Analysis Centre**; **Laundering**.

• **Financial year** 1. An accounting period adopted by the Commonwealth Government, consisting of twelve months commencing on 1 July and ending on 30 June: (CTH) Acts Interpretation Act 1901 s 22. 2. In corporations law, a period of time not exceeding 18 months, in respect of which a profit and loss account of a company or former company is made out: Corporations Law s 70A. See also **Year of income**.

• **Find a purchaser** A phrase that describes finding and introducing a person able and willing to buy, who subsequently enters into a contract with the principal, thereby becoming a purchaser: *Turnbull v Wightman* (1945) 45 SR (NSW) 369; 62 WN (NSW) 215. The making of a contract for the sale of land is not normally part of an estate agent's business, and an estate agent authorised to 'find a purchaser' has no implied authority to enter into a contract of sale: *Williams & Co Pty Ltd v Bond* [1965] VR 610. See also **Agency**; **Agent**; **Apparent authority**; **Express authority**; **Implied authority**; **Principal**.

• **Finding** A conclusion reached by a court following an enquiry of fact.

Industrial relations 1. A determination made in the course of proceedings in a court or tribunal, usually on a question of fact. 2. Under a statute, a decision, determination or ruling made in the course of proceedings in a court or tribunal that does not finally decide, determine, or dispose of the matter to which the proceedings relate: (WA) Industrial Relations Act 1979 s 7.

Finding of fact In administrative law, a determination as to the existence of a particular fact or the drawing of an inference from evidence, as part of an administrative decision-making process. Generally, an error in making a finding of fact is not a ground for judicial review, unless there is no evidence to support the finding: *Sinclair v Mining Warden at Maryborough* (1975) 132 CLR 473; 5 ALR 513; *Hope v Bathurst City Council* (1980) 144 CLR 1; 29 ALR 577. See also **Error of fact**; **Error of law**.

• **Fine** 1. A sum paid by a tenant to a landlord for the grant, transfer or renewal of a lease. A fine is not a sum reasonably demanded to cover the landlord's expenses, rather an extortionate sum demanded by the landlord without reasonable cause: *Lord v Proctor* [1923] VLR 524. 2. A prescribed sum of money payable to the Crown or other governmental authority as punishment for a particular offence. Fines may be enforced by imprisonment, community service, or as a debt due to the Crown: for example (NSW) Justices Act 1902 s 86A-94; (VIC) Sentencing Act 1991 s 63. 3. A collusive court action used to bar an entail, made possible by the Statute of Fines (1489). A record of compromise of a court action in which one person agrees to dispose of the land in question to another. 4. A payment made by a copyholder or freeholder to the lord of the manor on his assumption of an interest in land.

Finished goods Completed goods, into which component parts or raw materials have been incorporated: (CTH) Trade Practices Act 1974 s 75AK(1)(d). Finished goods include ships, aircraft and other vehicles; animals and fish; minerals, trees and crops; and gas and electricity: (CTH) Trade Practices Act 1974 s 4(1). See also **Goods**.

FIRB See **Foreign Investment Review Board**.

• **Fire** A flame or blaze. Property is damaged by fire when it is unintentionally ignited or damaged as a direct consequence of the accidental ignition of other property: *Harris v Poland* [1941] 1 KB 462. See also **Fire insurance**; **Property insurance**.

• **Fire insurance** A policy of insurance indemnifying the insured against loss or damage of property by fire. Where property is damaged by fire, the cause of the fire is immaterial unless it was deliberately ignited by the insured or a third party acting with the knowledge or authority of the insured (*Harris v Poland* [1941] 1 KB 462), or unless the fire was caused by an excluded peril, as detailed in the contract of insurance: *Re Hooley Hill Rubber & Chemical Co Ltd & Royal Insurance Co Ltd* [1920] 1 KB 257. See also **All risks insurance**; **Exclusion clause**; **Fire**; **Indemnity**; **Indemnity insurance**; **Property insurance**.

• **Firm** 1. An unincorporated body of persons (whether consisting of individuals or of corporations or partly of individuals and partly of corporations) associated together for the purpose of carrying on business: for example (VIC) Business Names Act 1962 s 4; (QLD) Business Names Act 1962 s 3(1). 2. An undertaking providing legal services to the public for reward comprising a sole practitioner or partners or a solicitor corporation, employed solicitors and other staff, and other assets including work in progress, goodwill and liabilities. See also **Business**; **Carrying on business**; **Partner**; **Partnership**.

Firm commitment An agreement or pledge to do something which is free from conditions and uncertainties.

• **Firm of solicitors** See **Firm**.

Firm price contract See **Fixed price contract**.

Firm up A description of the increase of the price quoted by a contractor in a lump sum contract subject to rise and fall, where the contractor bears the risk of cost fluctuations. A contractor 'firms up' the tender price, in order to convert these fluctuations in price into a fixed price, by taking the extra cost into account. A proprietor, however, may prefer to assume the risk of rise and fall, rendering unnecessary the need for the contractor to firm up the price. See also **Contractor; Fixed price contract; Lump sum contract; Proprietor**.

First demand guarantee A promise to answer for a debt or default of another by which the guarantor grants a primary obligation to answer for the debt or default of another, in respect of a debt owed to the creditor. A first demand guarantee is similar in operation and effect to a standby letter of credit. See also **Guarantee; Primary obligation; Principal debtor; Standby letter of credit**.

First in first out valuation Abbr – FIFO An accounting method used for assigning the cost of trading stock and work in progress of an entity, by which the first items of trading stock purchased are assumed to have been disposed of first, with the cost of trading stock on hand at the end of the accounting period considered to be the cost of items most recently acquired. See also **Last in first out valuation; Trading stock**.

First meeting of creditors The first meeting of a bankrupt's creditors after becoming bankrupt. Under (CTH) Bankruptcy Act 1966 s 64 prior to its amendment, a first meeting of creditors had to be convened within 28 days of a person becoming bankrupt. However, for bankruptcies occurring after 3 January 1989, there is no prescribed period for the holding of the first or any meeting of creditors. See also **Bankrupt; Creditors' meeting; Trustee in bankruptcy**.

First mortgage A mortgage granted prior in time to the grant of subsequent mortgages by the same mortgagor over the same property. A first mortgagee will usually take priority over subsequent mortgagees. See also **Charge; Mortgage; Registrable charge; Second mortgage**.

Fiscal policy The policy adopted by government for the purposes of, raising revenue through taxation to meet government expenditures, influencing the level of business activity generally, and using government income and spending to achieve economic management objectives. In Australia, fiscal measures are reviewed in the annual Commonwealth Budget and in economic statements or minibudgets. Commonwealth government revenue is raised from personal and company taxes, sales taxes and excise duties, customs duties, land taxes, revenues from public sector organisations, and government charges. The States also have income from taxes including payroll taxes and petrol taxes.

Fiscal powers Those Commonwealth powers, legislative or otherwise, which allow it to control the nation's finances. The most important of these include the borrowing power (Commonwealth Constitution s 51(iv)); the currency power (s 51(xii)); the taxation power (s 51(ii)); the banking power (s 51(xiii)); and the appropriation power (s 81). See also **Appropriation; Banking power**.

• **Fiscal right** The right of the Crown to payment of its debt in priority to that of the subject in case of competition between debts of equal degree: *Commonwealth v Cigamatic Pty Ltd* (1962) 108 CLR 372. The fiscal right is a prerogative right of the Crown: *Deputy Cmr of Taxation v Jonrich* (1986) 70 ALR 357; 86 FLR 25. See also **Crown as creditor; Priority**.

• **Fiscal year** See **Year of tax**.

• **Fit and proper person** A person who is suitable, appropriate, legally eligible to undertake a particular activity.

Consumer credit The main ground on which the Commercial Tribunal must be satisfied before granting the application of a person for a credit provider's licence. In determining whether a person meets this requirement, the Tribunal may have regard to the fact that the applicant has been convicted of or served any part of a prison term for an offence involving fraud or dishonesty in the last ten years, was bound in relation to such an offence by recognisance, or had at the time of application a charge pending in relation to such an offence: for example (NSW) Consumer Credit Administration Act 1995 s 3(1). See also **Commercial Tribunal; Credit provider; Credit provider's licence**.

Fit for use Appropriate or suitable for a particular purpose. 1. Goods supplied to a consumer must be fit for their purpose: (CTH) Trade Practices Act 1974 ss 71, 74, 74B. Premises are fit for immediate occupation and use if they are free from defects and not necessarily ready for full beneficial occupation: *Ponstarn Investments v Kansallis* [1992] NPC 56. See also **Consumer; Warranty**.

Fitness for purpose Capacity for use or consumption. In consumer protection law and sale of goods law, the state of goods being reasonably fit for the particular purpose for which they were purchased: for example (CTH) Trade Practices Act 1974 s 71(2); (NSW) Sale of Goods Act 1923 s 19(1). See also **Antecedent negotiations; Deemed manufacturer; Division 2A claim; Importer; Manufacturer; Merchantable quality; Trade Practices legislation**.

Fixed assets Items of future economic benefit which are intended to be retained by the business beyond the current accounting period for the purpose of earning revenue. Fixed assets are not intended for sale in the ordinary course of business operations, and will not be readily converted to cash. Examples of fixed assets are property, plant, and equipment. Also known as 'non-current assets'. See also **Asset; Circulating capital**.

Fixed capital Any property acquired by a business that is intended to be retained and used within the business for the long term. The long term is usually defined as more than one year or one operating period, whichever is longer. See also **Capital; Fixed Assets**.

Fixed charge A specific charge or claim over an asset of a company granted by a company to a lender. It is a particular form of security involving specific pieces of property. If the debtor fails to meet the loan obligations, the creditor has the right to receive repayment of the loan out of the sale of the specific asset. See also **Fixed security; Floating charge**.

Fixed cost A cost that remains constant over a range of activity for a given period of time. It represents the cost of providing the capacity for providing a service with all associated costs, irrespective of production levels. A fixed cost may well become variable over a longer period.

Fixed debt A specific sum of money due from one person or company to another legal entity. A fixed debt may be a contract debt, a crown debt, or a secured debt. See also **Contract debt; Debt collecting**.

Fixed deposit A term or time deposit. Money placed with a bank, building society or credit union for a fixed term at a fixed rate of interest which remains unchanged during the period of the deposit. Generally the deposit cannot be withdrawn until the expiry of the agreed period. See also **Building Society; Credit union**.

Fixed interest market The market for financial instruments yielding a fixed flow return by way of interest payments. Fixed interest markets in Australia are used as a means of raising funds by the Commonwealth and state governments and their authorities, and by the corporate sector, institutions and the private investor.

Fixed interest rate An interest rate which is held constant for a given period of time following the initial advance or subsequent renewal of a fixed-rate loan. See also **Variable interest rate**.

Fixed interest trust A unit trust which specialises in bonds, debentures, other fixed interest securities and mortgages for investors seeking assured and usually high income returns. See also **Trust**.

Fixed price contract A building contract in which the contractor is required to complete the works for a lump sum, there being no 'rise and fall' clause, and thus no provision to compensate the contractor for increases in labour and material costs. Commonly, building contracts provide for payment of an agreed sum with provision for adjustment of this sum. Adjustments may be made for variations to the work, extra costs incurred as a result of certain delays, or variations in the cost of the work for certain unexpected difficulties in performing it, such as latent ground conditions: *Re Arbitration between Taylor Woodrow International Ltd and Minister of Health* (1978) 19 SASR 1. This type of contract nonetheless is known as a 'fixed price' or 'firm price' contract. See also **Building contract; Delay; Firm up; Lump sum contract**.

Fixed security A form of debt financing which attaches a specific item of property described in the instrument creating the security (the instrument of charge) in such a way that the chargor cannot dispose of the item of property for no return without the chargee's consent. See also **Charge; Security**.

Fixed sum A sum of money which is certain and readily ascertainable: *Henderson v Henderson* (1844) 6 QB 288. At common law, in an action brought in contract and tort against a specific individual, a foreign judgment is only enforceable if it is for a fixed sum. See also **Foreign judgment; Forum**.

Fixed term annuity An annuity restricted to a set term, with benefits payable to the beneficiaries if death occurs before its expiration. See also **Annuity**.

Fixed term contract A contract of employment which the parties have expressly agreed will continue for a specified period and no longer, or which will continue initially for a specified period, and if not then terminated, for a further period. A fixed term contract expires at the end of the specified period with no need for the employer to give the employee notice of termination. See also **Contract of employment; Permanent employment**.

Fixed trust A trust in which the acquisition by the beneficiary of an interest in the trust property does not depend upon the exercise of another person's discretion. The trustee of a fixed trust has no discretion to select the persons who are to benefit from the trust or the quantum of their interest: *Federal Cmr of Taxation v Vegners* (1989) 90 ALR 547; 20 ATR 1645. See also **Beneficiary; Discretionary trust; Trust; Trustee**.

Fixing prices Agreement generally by competitors to set prices at a level not below a particular price. It is prima facie unlawful to engage in the conduct of 'fixing', 'controlling' or 'maintaining' prices ((CTH) Trade Practices Act 1974 s 45A) where 'price' includes a charge of any description. See also **Contract, arrangement or understanding; Resale price maintenance**.

Flag clause A clause generally found in bills of lading providing that the carrier's liabilities are to be determined according to the laws of the country printed or shown on the bill. The term 'flag' in this context is synonymous with country or jurisdiction. See also **Bill of lading; Carrier**.

Flat interest rate A fixed rate of interest charged on the full amount of a loan, throughout the entire term of the loan, notwithstanding the progressive repayment of the capital or principal. The effective rate of interest may well be twice as much as the flat rate.

Flat tax See **Proportional tax**.

Flexible accelerated security transfer *Abbr* – FAST A scripless settlement system which permits the purchase and sale of marketable securities without the issue and redemption of share certificates, introduced into Australia in 1989. Securities are transferred to an uncertificated register. The sponsoring broker allocates a Holder Identification Number (or in the case of an institutional or trustee investor, an Institution Participant Number) to the shareholder and forwards the relevant certificates to the company for cancellation and transfer of the holding to the relevant uncertificated register. Securities on the uncertificated register are transferred (without issuing share certificates) by a transfer marked with the shareholder's Holder Identification Number (Institution Participant Number) and validated by the sponsoring broker: ASC Ins 93/729. Access to holding details is obtained through the Shareholders Uncertificated Registration Enquiry (SURE) service. FAST aims at a five-day settlement period. FAST serves the Australian Stock Exchange, brokers, share registries, and many investing institutions. Within a few years, FAST is likely to be superseded by a Settlement Transfer and Registration System (STARS), aiming at a shorter settlement period. See also **Australian Stock Exchange Ltd; Security; Clearing House Electronic Subregister System; Uncertificated security**.

Flexible system production A production system in which traditionally separate functions such as design, engineering, purchasing, manufacturing, distribution, marketing and sales are merged into a highly integrated organisation that can respond quickly to new opportunities. Flexible system production aims at higher-valued and technologically more sophisticated products. It is a system designed for change and adaptability displacing high-volume standardised production. See also **Economic efficiency; Just in time production**.

Flight capital Capital transferred from one country to another to escape deteriorating political circumstances and to take advantage of more stable, favourable and lucrative circumstances. The process of transference of capital in such circumstances is known as 'capital flight'. Also known as 'Capital flight'.

Flight insurance A form of insurance covering the person insured for damage resulting from accidents which occur whilst embarking on, travelling aboard, or disembarking from an aircraft. See also **Indemnity insurance; Life insurance**.

Flight to quality Generally a market movement towards the purchase of safer, sounder, more stable, but potentially less rewarding stocks and shares. Following the October 1987 share market crash, a flight to quality occurred in the allocation of funds with savings and trading banks deposits increasing significantly. Also known as 'flight to security'.

Flight v Booth, rule in A rule applying to contracts for the sale of land. It provides that a purchaser may avoid ('rescind') a contract where a misdescription of the property affects the subject matter of the contract so far that it may be reasonably supposed that, but for the misdescription, the purchaser might never have entered into the contract at all. The purchaser is not bound to resort to any 'error or misdescription' compensation clause in the contract: *Flight v Booth* (1834) 1 Bing (NC) 370; 131 ER 1160. See also **Contract for Sale of Land; Exclusion clause; Sale of Land**.

Float 1. An issue of shares to the public. 2. A sum of money held in a petty cash account.

Banking and finance 1. The number of cheques in the banking system waiting to be cleared. 2. A sum of money held in an imprest account. 3. A bank account used for small sundry items. 4. An interval of time between two consequential activities.

Corporations The issue by a company of securities to the public. Also known as a 'share flotation'.

Floating 1. Descriptive of the exchange rate of a currency which finds its own level in the foreign exchange markets. 2. An interest rate that is related to a given benchmark rate and moves with it. See also **Deregulation; Financial deregulation; Floating exchange rate; Reserve Bank of Australia**.

Floating assets Items of future economic benefit produced or purchased by an entity for the purpose of conversion into cash or profit within one financial year. See also **Asset; Circulating capital**.

•**Floating charge** A general charge over the assets of a company granted by the company to a lender. It is a particular form of security not involving specific pieces of property. Thus, a company ('chargor') may raise finance by granting a floating charge over its assets to the lender ('chargee'). Certain events such as the cessation of the chargor's business and the appointment of a receiver may crystallise the charge. Upon crystallisation, the charge on the company's property becomes a fixed or specific charge. Also known as 'floating security'. See also **Fixed charge; Floating charge purchase; Floating rate note**.

Floating charge purchase A business practice in which a loan, made to finance the purchase of stock, is secured against the stock and debtors of the dealer. The dealer has title to the goods, the proceeds from sales being applied to reduce the loan. See also **Fixed charge; Floating charge; Floating rate note; Floating charge**.

Floating clause A clause in a charterparty providing that a vessel must sail to a safe port or berth where it is to remain always afloat. See also **Always afloat; Charterparty**.

Floating equity An interest which a beneficiary under a will or intestacy has in a deceased's property which the beneficiary hopes to receive if that property is not required for payment of debts. See also **Equity**.

Floating exchange rate An exchange rate in which the rate of exchange is allowed to fluctuate freely on the markets, subject to occasional governmental intervention to influence its movement. See also **Financial deregulation; Floating; Reserve Bank of Australia**.

Floating rate note *Abbr* – FRN A security, often with a fixed term, that pays an interest rate subject to change in line with market conditions on a regular basis. See also **Floating charge; Floating charge purchase; Floating charge**.

Floating security See **Floating charge**.

•**Floor** 1. The surface walked upon. 2. Rooms on the same level in a building. 3. The area of a court between the judge's bench and the bar table. 4. The area of a legislative chamber where members sit. 5. The operational part of a stock exchange. 6. An interest rate level in an investment hedging agreement.

Banking and finance A financial arrangement in the form of a call option or a series of call options which guarantees a minimum rate of return, but leaves the investor free to benefit from interest rates which rise above the agreed floor level. See also **Call option; Option**.

Floor member A form of membership of the Sydney Futures Exchange (SFE) which permits a member to trade directly on the floor. A floor member can deal in a personal capacity or on behalf of clients. See also **Full associate member**; **Sydney Futures Exchange**.

•**Floor plan** 1. A commercial financing arrangement for the sale of consumer goods, for example motor cars, where a trader is allowed credit on the goods until sold, when he or she becomes liable to pay the supplier for the goods: for example *Federal Cmr of Taxation v Suttons Motors (Chullora) Wholesale Pty Ltd* (1985) 157 CLR 277; 59 ALR 688. 2. A plan that is part of a strata plan, showing the layout of each floor of a building the subject of a strata scheme, including lot designations and boundaries: (NSW) Strata Titles Act (Freehold Development) 1973 s 5. See also **Floor plan agreement**.

Floor plan agreement An agreement under which goods supplied to a dealer by a wholesaler are resold by the dealer to a finance company. Property in the goods passes to the finance company upon payment of the agreed price but the dealer takes the goods on hire and keeps them in its own possession as bailee for the finance company for display purposes. The dealer then seeks offers to purchase the goods or to take them on hire-purchase. Upon being advised by the dealer of an offer in respect of the goods, the finance company will sell the goods to the dealer. Basically, the purpose of a floor plan agreement is to finance the purchase of the stock by the dealer. They are common in the motor vehicle industry: for example *Gamer's Motor Centre (Newcastle) Pty Ltd v Natwest Wholesale Australia Pty Ltd* (1987) 163 CLR 236; 72 ALR 321. See also **Hire-purchase agreement**.

Floortion An option over a floor. See also **Floor**; **Option**.

Flotation 1. Process of offering shares on the stock exchange in a new public company. 2. Sell off of all the shares held by one company in another to the public. See also **Going public**.

Flow on The tendency of industrial awards to conform to other awards; in particular, for the contents of one key award in a particular industry to be substantially followed by other awards and agreements in the industry. The 'flow on' effect arises from the principle that awards should generally be uniform or consistent in order to reduce industrial unrest. See also **Industrial tribunal**; **Parent award**.

•**FOB** See **Free on board**.

FOB contract See **Free on board**.

FOI See **Freedom of information**.

Following trust property See **Tracing**.

Footloose industry An industry that is not tied to any existing location because of its independence from specific transport links or markets. Also known as 'mobile industry'.

•**FOR** See **Free on rail**.

FOR contract See **Free on rail**.

Forbearance to sue A promise not to sue. A forbearance to sue, whether in a court of law or some other forum for dispute resolution, is distinguishable from the giving up of a claim: *Larkin v Girvan* (1940) 40 SR (NSW) 365. See also **Consideration**; **Sue**.

Force majeure /fɔs maʒɜ/ *OF* – a coercion which cannot be resisted; a superior force. A circumstance beyond the control of a party to a contract, which enables that party to escape liability for failing to perform the contract as a result of the circumstance: *Matsaukis v Priestman & Co* [1915] 1 KB 681. First used in the Napoleonic Code, it has a more extensive meaning than the common law 'act of God' or *vis major*. It may include human acts (such as war, strikes, machinery breakdowns) as well as natural acts (such as storms, earthquakes): *Ringstad v Gollin & Co Pty Ltd* (1924) 35 CLR 303; *Matsaukis v Priestman & Co* [1915] 1 KB 681 at 686; *Lebeaupin v Crispin* [1920] 2 KB 714 at 719-721. See also **Act of God**; **Deviation**; **Frustration**; **Hardship**.

Force majeure clause *Fr* – superior strength clause. A clause, often found in commercial contracts, which excludes a party from liability for failure to perform the contract where that failure was due to forces, either natural or human, beyond that party's control. See also **Act of God**; **Frustration**; **Strict liability**.

Forcing A form of exclusive dealing involving conduct or an agreement where desired goods or services are supplied to a buyer on the condition that the buyer also acquires other goods or services. See also **Exclusive dealing**; **Full line forcing**.

Foreign acquisition 1. The acquisition of land or national estate registered pursuant to the (CTH) Australian Heritage Commission Act 1975 by a foreign person. 2. The acquisition of shares in, or assets of, a corporation which carries on an Australian business by a foreign person: (CTH) Foreign Acquisitions and Takeovers Act 1975 ss 5, 18, 19. See also **Foreign Investment Review Board**; **Foreign person**.

•**Foreign bank** A bank incorporated in another country which has a presence in Australia either through a subsidiary or a branch; a foreign corporation within the meaning of Commonwealth Constitution s 51(xx), authorised to carry on banking business in a foreign country and in Australia: (CTH) Banking Act 1959 s 5(1). Foreign banks (except the Bank of China and the Bank of New Zealand) are not subject to the provisions protecting depositors: (CTH) Banking Act 1959 ss 11D(a),(b), 11E(1). Where a foreign bank becomes unable to meet its obligations, the assets of the bank in Australia are available to meet the liabilities of the bank in Australia in priority to all other liabilities of the bank: (CTH) Banking Act 1959 s 11F. In 1985, the Commonwealth government admitted foreign banks to Australia but restricted the number of licences to sixteen. Foreign banks seeking a presence beyond this figure are restricted to opening only merchant bank offices in Australia. Australia has also prohibited foreign banks from setting up branches. The only foreign bank branches in Australia are operated by Bank of New Zealand, Banque Nationale de Paris and Bank of China.

•**Foreign bill** A bill other than an inland bill: (CTH) Bills of Exchange Act 1909 s 9(1). A foreign bill dishonoured by non-acceptance must be duly protested for non-acceptance; and a foreign bill dishonoured by non-payment must be duly protested for non-payment. See also **Bill of exchange**; **Inland bill**; **Protest**.

•**Foreign companies law** The law, or a previous law, of a State, Territory or excluded Territory relating to foreign companies within the meaning of that law or previous law: Corporations Law s 9.

•**Foreign company** A body corporate incorporated in an external Territory, or outside Australia and that Territory, which is not a corporation sole or an exempt public authority; or an unincorporated body that was formed in an external Territory or outside Australia and that Territory and, under the law of its place of formation, may sue or be sued, hold property in the name of its secretary or of an official of the body duly appointed for that purpose and which does not have its head office or principal place of business in Australia: Corporations Law s 9; (CTH) Trade Practices Act 1974 s 4(1). Commonwealth Constitution s 51(xx) gives the Commonwealth power with respect to foreign companies: for example *Nauru Local Government Council v Australian Shipping Officers Assn* (1978) 27 ALR 535.

Foreign contract A contract that is more closely associated with a jurisdiction other than Australia. The validity of a foreign contract is governed by the law of the country with which it is most closely connected: for example *Wanganui-Rangitikei Electric Power Board v Australian Mutual Provident Society* (1934) 50 CLR 581. However, a contract that is against the public policy of Australia will be unenforceable in Australia even though it is valid under the law of the jurisdiction in which it was made: *Robinson v Bland* (1760) 2 Burr 1077 at 1084; 97 ER 717; *Dynamit AG v Rio Tinto Co Ltd* [1918] AC 292.

Foreign controller **1.** In relation to a resident company, a non-resident with substantial control of the voting power in the resident company, a beneficial entitlement to receive at least 15 per cent of any dividends paid or of any distribution of capital that is made by a resident company or the capability, under a scheme, of gaining such control or such an entitlement. **2.** A non-resident, in accordance with whose directions a resident company or its directors are accustomed or obligated to act. A non-resident which has such a degree of control or influence in relation to a partnership or trust estate is a foreign controller in relation to that partnership or trust estate: (CTH) Income Tax Assessment Act 1936 s 159GZE(1)-(3). See also **Non-resident associate of a foreign controller**; **Thin capitalisation**.

•**Foreign corporation** See **Foreign company**.

•**Foreign currency** Currency other than Australian dollars. Conflict of laws principles apply to international contracts creating monetary obligations. Matters going to the substance of the debt are determined by the proper law of the contract, while matters going to its mode of performance are decided by the law of the place of performance: *Bonython v Commonwealth* (1950) 81 CLR 486; [1951] AC 201. See also **Currency**; **Proper law of contract**.

Foreign currency exchange Gains and losses arising from movements over time in the exchange rate between a taxpayer's domestic currency and the taxpayer's holdings of foreign currency or the incurring of liabilities denominated in a foreign currency. Such gains may be assessable as income under (CTH) Income Tax Assessment Act 1936 s 25(1), or deductible under (CTH) Income Tax Assessment Act 1936 s 51(1), if such gains and losses are derived or incurred as part of the taxpayers normal trading activities: see *AVCO Financial Services Ltd v FCT* (1982) 150 CLR 510; 41 ALR 225; 13 ATR 63. Where the foreign currency gains or loses are on capital account such amounts may be assessable or deductible if they satisfy the statutory requirements of (CTH) Income Tax Assessment Act 1936 Pt 111, Div 3B: (CTH) Income Tax Assessment Act 1936 ss 82U-82ZZB. The rules for converting foreign sourced income derived by an Australian resident into Australian currency are prescribed under (CTH) Income Tax Assessment Act 1936 s 20. See also **Allowable deduction**; **Derived**; **Income**.

Foreign currency hedge agreement An arrangement for insuring against changes in the relative rates of the currency of different nations. Under the agreement a rate of exchange is fixed by the parties for some time in the future. The fixed rate will apply, in respect of the currency exchanges between the parties, regardless of future fluctuations in the rate. Exchange differences on hedge transactions must be brought to account in the profit and loss account in the year in which the exchange rates change, thereby recording the hedge transaction and the underlying transaction separately: AASB 1012 para 30. See also **Foreign currency transaction**; **Hedging**.

Foreign currency loans A lending product of the early 1980s offering Australian borrowers an opportunity to avoid very high domestic interest rates. Large numbers of loans were taken out between 1982 and 1986 by farmers, private property investors and the owners of small businesses, often in Swiss francs and Japanese yen. The rates of interest were about half those prevailing in Australia. However, a dramatic change in the exchange rates between the Australian dollar and the franc and yen meant that borrowers faced a near doubling in the cost of servicing their loans. Aggrieved borrowers asserted that they had not been adequately advised of the risks involved and that promises of hedging against loss had not been honoured: *Chiarabaglio v Westpac Banking Corp Ltd* (1990) ATPR 41-024; (1991) ATPR 46-067; *Spice v Westpac Banking Corp Ltd* (1990) ATPR 41-024; *Foti v Banque Nationale de Paris* (1990) Aust Torts Reports 81-025.

Foreign currency transaction An exchange of one currency for another. The exchange may occur for the purpose of conducting a transaction or investment in another country. Other such transactions include spot deals which involve delivery of the two currencies exchanged within two business days and swaps which are agreements to exchange two currencies at one date and reverse the transaction at some future date. The phrase may also refer to a transaction denominated, or which requires settlement, in a foreign currency. See also **Foreign currency translation**; **Foreign exchange transaction**.

Foreign currency translation The process of converting financial statements from a local currency into another currency. Typically occurs where a subsidiary's accounts are initially prepared in a currency other than that of its parent company. There are accounting standards in relation to foreign currency translations: AASB Accounting Standards AASB 1012. See also **Foreign currency transaction**.

Foreign debt For taxation purposes, the balance outstanding on any amount owing by an Australian company, partnership, or trust where interest is payable to a foreign controller and that interest is or will be an allowable deduction, and the interest is not or will not be assessable income of the foreign controller or non-resident associate when it is paid: (CTH) Income Tax Assessment Act 1936 s 159GZF. See also **Allowable deduction; Assessable income; Foreign controller; Non-resident associate of a foreign controller; Thin capitalisation**.

Foreign decree A judgment or order of a foreign court. The (CTH) Foreign Judgments Act 1991 provides a regime for enforcing certain foreign judgments and decrees in Australia.

Foreign equity The sum of: the paid up value of all shares or interests in shares in an Australian company beneficially owned at the end of the year of income by a foreign controller or a non-resident associate of a foreign controller; any credit in a share premium account to which foreign controllers would be beneficially entitled; and accumulated profits available for distribution to foreign controllers and non-resident associates. For a partnership, foreign equity includes the partners' equity of the foreign controller, in the balance sheet, reduced by the balance of any outstanding amounts owed by the foreign controller. For a trust, foreign equity includes the beneficiaries equity reduced by any amount outstanding owing to the trustee of the trust by a foreign controller or non-resident associate: (CTH) Income Tax Assessment Act 1936 s 159GZG. See also **Foreign controller; Non-resident associate of a foreign controller; Thin capitalisation**.

Foreign exchange contract An agreement for the purchase or sale of a foreign currency. Use of foreign exchange contracts is the way in which investment, commercial and other transactions between countries are settled. See also **Foreign exchange forward contract; Foreign exchange transaction**.

•**Foreign exchange dealer** A person authorised by the Reserve Bank of Australia to buy and sell foreign currency: (CTH) Banking (Foreign Exchange) Regulations 1946 reg 38A. See also **Foreign exchange transaction**.

Foreign exchange forward contract A commitment to buy or sell a fixed amount of foreign currency on a future specified date at a set rate of exchange. It contrasts with a foreign exchange spot contract which is a commitment to buy or sell a fixed amount of foreign currency for delivery in the immediate future at current exchange rates. See also **Foreign currency transaction; Foreign exchange contract; Foreign exchange market**.

Foreign exchange market A market which facilitates the conversion of one currency into another. The foreign exchange market provides currencies to pay for trade, to allow overseas funds to be brought into Australia, and to allow funds to be transferred overseas. Individuals, institutions or companies can purchase foreign currencies on the spot market (at the current price) or can buy or sell on a forward basis. In respect of Australian dollars, the buy rate is the rate at which banks and other traders are willing to buy one Australian dollar in exchange for a specified foreign currency. The sell rate is the rate at which they will sell one Australian dollar in exchange for a foreign currency. In Australia, some 90 organisations are authorised under the (CTH) Banking (Foreign Exchange) Regulations to trade in foreign currencies.

Foreign exchange transaction An agreement where a currency of another country is bought or sold. See also **Foreign currency transaction; Foreign exchange contract; Foreign exchange market**.

•**Foreign insurance agent** A person who carries on the business of arranging contracts of general insurance, whether in Australia or elsewhere, as an agent for an unauthorised foreign insurer: (CTH) Insurance (Agents and Brokers) Act 1984 s 9. An unauthorised foreign insurer is one who does not have authority to carry on insurance business under the (CTH) Insurance Act 1973, is not required to have such authority, and carries on insurance outside Australia and the external territories: (CTH) Insurance (Agents and Brokers) Act 1984 s 9. Foreign insurance agents must be registered and have the prescribed professional indemnity insurance: (CTH) Insurance (Agents and Brokers) Act 1984 s 31B. Registration has effect for a year, and is recorded by the Insurance and Superannuation Commissioner in a Register of Foreign Insurance Agents: (CTH) Insurance (Agents and Brokers) Act 1984 ss 31D(3), 31E. See also **Agent; Authorised insurer; General insurance; Insurance agent**.

Foreign investment fund All income derived in non-Australian controlled foreign companies including foreign trusts and foreign life assurance policies. The amount of tax on the assessable income is determined by one of three methods: the market value method by obtaining the value from the stock exchange, the calculation method where gross income and deductions are determined for a specific accounting period and the deemed rate of return method. See also **Foreign investment income**.

Foreign investment income Income derived from investments where the source of that income is from a country other than Australia. Generally, the investor does not take an active role in the business affairs of the entity that generates the foreign income. See also **Portfolio dividend**.

Foreign Investment Review Board *Abbr –* FIRB A comprehensive bureaucracy headed by the Treasurer, and established under the (CTH) Foreign Acquisitions and Takeovers Act 1975. The main functions of the FIRB are to examine proposals by foreign interests for investment in Australia against the background of the Commonwealth Government's foreign investment policy and the national interest, make recommendations to the Commonwealth Government on those proposals, advise the Commonwealth government on foreign investment matters generally, and provide guidelines to foreign investors so that proposals may conform with policy. See also **Foreign acquisition**.

Foreign judgment A judgment rendered in a court outside the forum. In private international law terms, a judgment rendered by the court of a State or Territory is enforced in accordance with (CTH) Service and Execution of Process Act 1992 Part 6. A judgment rendered by a court to which the (CTH) Foreign Judgments Act 1991 applies must be enforced in accordance with that Act. Any other foreign judgment is only enforceable in Australia if it is enforceable at common law. See also **Foreign decree; Forum**.

•**Foreign law** The law of a jurisdiction outside the forum. The court of the forum will assume that foreign law is identical to the law of the forum unless it is proved otherwise. Foreign law must be pleaded as a matter of fact: *Asherberg, Hopwood and Crew Ltd v Casa* [1971] 1 WLR 1128. The Commonwealth Constitution s 118 in providing full faith and credit to State laws clearly overcomes the requirement of proving foreign law as between Australian States: *Koop v Bebb* (1951) 84 CLR 629.

Foreign note A promissory note which is not an inland note: (CTH) Bills of Exchange Act 1909 s 89(4). See also **Inland note; Promissory note**.

•**Foreign person** An individual who is a national of a foreign state; or a corporation registered or incorporated in a foreign state. A foreign person may be natural or artificial. An individual human being who is a citizen of and belongs to the jurisdiction of another state is a natural foreign person with respect to any third state. A corporation registered or incorporated in one state and engaged in business in another state is an artificial foreign person for the purpose of the law of the latter state. See also **Foreign acquisition**.

Foreign source income Amounts included in assessable income derived from sources in a foreign country: (CTH) Income Tax Assessment Act 1936 s 23AH(12). However, it does not include an amount included in assessable income that constitutes a capital gain under (CTH) Income Tax Assessment Act 1936 Pt IIIA. Also known as 'foreign income'. See also **Assessable income; Foreign Investment Income; Net capital gain; Source of income**.

•**Foreign tax** A tax imposed on income, profits, or gains (whether of an income or capital nature) under the law of a foreign country, including such a tax imposed by a law of any part of such a country: (CTH) Income Tax Assessment Act 1936 s 6AB(2), (6). Tax subject to a double tax treaty under the (CTH) International Tax Agreements Act 1953 is also a foreign tax. See also **Assessable income; Credit absorption tax; Double taxation agreements; Foreign source income; Foreign tax credit**.

Foreign tax credit A tax credit equivalent to the amount of foreign tax paid in respect of foreign income derived by an Australian resident taxpayer, or the amount of Australian tax payable in relation to that foreign income, if the Australian tax is less than the foreign tax paid: (CTH) Income Tax Assessment Act 1936 s 160AF. The credit will only be available to the Australian resident taxpayer if the foreign income is included in the assessable income of that taxpayer. See also **Assessable income; Foreign tax**.

Forfait finance A form of non-recourse finance that combines the ability of a party to a bill to draw or indorse it non-recourse, with the ability of the financier to become liable on the bill as a party using: for example (CTH) Bills of Exchange Act 1909 s 61. See also **Bill of exchange; Draw; Indorsement; Non-recourse finance; Sans recours**.

Forfaiters Players in international trade, forfaiters trade debts by buying at a discount from exporters in developed countries, IOUs for goods sold to importers in other countries. The debts, such as bills of exchange, are bundled into tradeable securities and sold to banks and corporate treasurers, or simply held by the forfaiters. In this way, the exporter can be completely rid of the bills.

•**Forfeiture** The immediate loss of all interest in property as well as loss of the right to possession: *Whim Creek Consolidated NL v Colgan* (1991) 31 FCR 469; 103 ALR 204.

Equity The loss or determination of an estate or interest in property or a proprietary right, which follows from the failure to observe a covenant: *Legione v Hately* (1983) 152 CLR 406; 46 ALR 1. Examples are the loss of an interest in a lease or contract for sale of land, and loss of the rights as a hirer of goods as against the owner. See also **Relief against forfeiture**.

Forfeiture clause A clause in a will which provides that a person is to forfeit a gift for some act or omission.

Forfeiture of shares The cancellation of the issue of shares, amounting to a reduction of capital. A company's constitution may stipulate that on failure to pay a valid call on shares, or an instalment of a share issue price, a member's shares to the company may be forfeited: for example Corporations Law Sch 1 Table A arts 26-32. See also **Articles of association; Call on shares; Capital; Share**.

Forfeiture of surety Action that may be taken by a court where an accused person, admitted to bail on condition that a surety be provided either by the accused person or another, fails to attend court as required by the bail undertaking. The court can require that the sum of money, or some part of it, that was guaranteed to ensure the accused's attendance, be forfeited to the state. At common law forfeiture was automatic: *R v Baker* [1971] VR 717; but there is now a discretion conferred upon the court either by inherent power or statute to determine whether to forfeit the surety or not: *Ex parte Doueihi* [1986] 2 Qd R 352; (1986) 20 A Crim R 374; (NSW) Fines and Forfeited Recognisances Act 1954 s 4A; (VIC) Crown Proceedings Act 1958 s 6. See also **Bail; Recognisance**.

Forged deed A deed that appears to have been signed or sealed by a person but that has in fact been signed or sealed by another person. A forged deed is a nullity: *Governor and Co of Bank of Ireland v Trustees of Evans' Charities in Ireland* (1855) HL Cas 389; 10 ER 950. However, a person may be estopped from denying the validity of a forged deed where he or she subsequently represents the deed as being his or hers: *Greenwood v Martins Bank Ltd* [1933] AC 51. See also **Forgery; Deed**.

•**Forgery** Counterfeit of a seal or signature; knowing falsification of a document; or unauthorised alteration of a genuine document: (CTH) Crimes Act 1914 s 63(1); (NSW) Crimes Act 1900 s 250; *Lamb v Carnovale* (1970) 19 FLR 421. It is an offence to forge certain things or documents, for example, bank notes, bills of exchange, or wills: for example (NSW) Crimes Act 1900 ss 265, 271. The forgery must be committed with intent to defraud: (NSW) Crimes Act 1900 s 250; (CTH) Crimes Act 1914 s 63(1), (3); (NSW) Crimes Act 1900 s 250. See also **Fraud**.

Forgiven debt Loans not repaid and simply cancelled as a favour or consideration to the debtor. Forgiveness has become part of the strategy in dealing with the debt of developing countries.

Formal contract A document which is sealed and delivered and intended to take effect as a deed in compliance with legislative provisions: for example (NSW) Conveyancing Act 1919 s 38(1). A formal contract must be signed as well as sealed and be attested by at least one witness not a party to the deed, and unlike simple, parol or informal contracts, it does not require consideration: for example *Leonard v Booth* (1954) 91 CLR 452; *Howard F Hudson Pty Ltd v Ronayne* (1972) 126 CLR 449. See also **Consideration; Contract; Deed; Indenture; Parol contract; Simple contract; Special contract; Specialty**.

Formal instrument of agreement In a building contract, a brief document executed by both parties, which usually records the contractor's obligation to perform the work, the proprietor's obligation to pay, and the document comprising the contract. In some cases, the instrument also lists the order of precedence of the contract documents; in other instances, this is found in the general conditions of contract. See also **Building contract; Drawings**.

Formalities of contract The manner and form in which a contract should be concluded to be valid. Formalities of contract can include requirements of writing, witnessing, notarising, or sealing. See also **Contract**.

•**Forthwith** Immediately, straightaway, as soon as possible, as soon as reasonably possible, or within a specific time limit.

Forum /fɔrʊm/ *Lat* – a market place. **1.** A place in which a dispute may be heard. A forum can include a place of jurisdiction, a court of justice, a place of litigation, and an administrative body. **2.** A court having jurisdiction to hear the matter. The *lex fori* (law of the forum) governs the procedures relied upon to resolve the dispute. See also **Lex fori**.

Forum clause A contractual clause referring a dispute to a particular jurisdiction for arbitration or adjudication. The validity of a forum clause depends on the proper law applying to the contract: *Nova (Jersey) Knit Ltd v Kammgarn Spinnerei GmbH* [1977] 2 All ER 463; 1 WLR 713. Only a choice of court clause will be taken as submission to the courts of the chosen forum: *Dunbee v Gilman & Co (Aust) Pty Ltd* (1968) SR (NSW) 219. A forum clause does not exclude the local court's jurisdiction: *Sheldon Pallet Manufacturing Co Ltd v New Zealand Forest Products Ltd* [1975] 1 NSWLR 141. See also **Forum; Proper law of contract**.

Forward delivery The delivery of purchased securities at a future date. A forward delivery transaction normally provides for the delivery of securities at the expiration of six weeks from the date of contract. See also **Forward delivery**.

Forward exchange The procedures involved in buying or selling foreign exchange for future delivery. Also, foreign currencies bought or sold for future delivery against payment on delivery. See also **Foreign exchange contract; Forward exchange contract**.

Forward exchange contract A contract between a customer and its bank to buy or sell one currency against another at an agreed future date at a set exchange rate. Such a contract enables the customer to manage and control the exchange risk exposures because the rates are set when entering into the contract and are fixed to the maturity date of the contract. See also **Foreign exchange contract; Foreign exchange forward contract; Forward exchange**.

Forward margin or points The difference between the forward rate and the spot rate of a currency. The forward margin is usually at a discount or a premium to the spot rate. Where the forward rate is the same as the spot rate, the margin is referred to as par. See also **Forward rate agreement; Spot market; Spot rate**.

Forward rate agreement *Abbr* – FRA An agreement by which the buyer is obligated to 'purchase' an agreed interest rate for a specified time period from a specific future settlement date. If the interest rate is higher at the settlement date, the buyer receives the difference between the market interest rate and the agreed interest date. If the rate is lower, the buyer has to pay out the difference. If the buyer of the FRA has an underlying floating rate liability, the risk profile is exactly matched and the buyer neither benefits nor loses, irrespective of rate movements. FRAs are straightforward with just one settlement at the specified time.

Forward swap A swap in which the start is deferred for a period. As an example, a two-year swap may begin in one year's time to match the circumstances prevailing and the risk profiles involved. See also **Swap**.

Forwarded certificate of receipts *Abbr* – FCR A form of receipt produced by a forwarding agent acknowledging receipt of specific goods to be shipped by that agent. See also **Forwarding agent; Goods**.

Forwarding agent An agent who undertakes the shipment or transmission of goods: *Lee Cooper Ltd v C H Jeakins & Sons Ltd* [1967] 2 QB 1. A forwarding agent is not a carrier and its rights and liabilities are determined according to the law of agency. A forwarding agent may be liable for failing to properly arrange carriage, but undertakes no duty to supervise the carrier where it is reasonable to expect the carrier to fulfil its obligations: *Von Traubenburg v Davies, Turner & Co Ltd* [1951] 2 Lloyd's Rep 80. The forwarding agent is not liable for a carrier's failure unless the agent knows or becomes aware of that failure and itself fails to mitigate: *Marston Excelsior Ltd v Arbuckle Smith & Co Ltd* [1971] 2 Lloyd's Rep 306 at 311. A forwarding agent is under no duty to insure, but sometimes has a duty to advise customers of the proper arrangements for transporting valuable goods: *Von Traubenburg v Davies, Turner & Co Ltd* [1951] 2 Lloyd's Rep 80. By virtue of trade custom, the forwarding agent incurs personal liability for freight charges, whether transmission is by sea or by air, even for a named principal. After paying the cost of freight, the agent can recover the payment: *Perishables Transport Co Ltd v N Spyropoulos (London) Ltd* [1964] 2 Lloyd's Rep 379. A forwarding agent's duties in relation to goods to facilitate, or at least not to impede, their safe arrival continue after their dispatch: *Langley Beldon and Gaunt Ltd v Morley* [1965] 1 Lloyd's Rep 297. The duty is to exercise reasonable care: *Pringle of Scotland Ltd v Continental Express Ltd* [1962] 2 Lloyd's Rep 80. See also **Agency**; **Agent**; **Carriage of goods**; **Carrier**; **Forwarded certificate of receipts**; **Goods**.

Foss v Harbottle, rule in 1. The proposition, identified in *Foss v Harbottle* (1843) 2 Hare 461; 67 ER 189, that the company is the proper plaintiff to bring an action in respect of a wrong done to it, and consequently that an individual member has no standing to bring proceedings complaining of a wrong done to the company. The rule in *Foss v Harbottle* is subject to various exceptions in that a shareholder can bring an action on behalf of the company if: the conduct complained of requires a special resolution of the general meeting to ratify it and there has been no such ratification (*Baillie v Oriental Telephone and Electric Co Ltd* [1915] 1 Ch 503); the conduct is ultra vires (*Prudential Assurance Co Ltd v Newman Industries Ltd (No 2)* [1982] Ch 204; 2 WLR 31); a derivative suit can be brought on the basis of fraud on the minority (*Prudential Assurance Co Ltd v Newman Industries Ltd (No2)*); or if there would otherwise be injustice (*Biala Pty Ltd v Mallina Holdings Ltd (No 2)* (1993) 11 ACSR 785; 11 ACLC 1,082). There are also statutory exceptions to the rule: for example Corporations Law s 260. 2. The rule that a member cannot bring an action to complain of an irregularity in the operation of the company if the irregularity could be rectified by an ordinary resolution of members in general meeting. Also known as the 'proper plaintiff rule' and 'internal management rule'.

Four corners rule In contract law, the rule by which the parties' intentions are to be identified from the written instrument read as a whole. See also **Contract**; **Instrument**.

Four firm concentration ratio A concentration ratio commonly used to measure market power. It is the percentage of total industry output originated by the leading four firms. It recognises that vigorous competition depends upon both the number of firms and the degree of inequality. Another commonly used measure is the Herfindahl-Hirschman Index. See also **Competition**; **Competition law**; **Market**; **Market power**; **Market share**.

Four unities The defining characteristics of a joint tenancy: unity of time; unity of possession; unity of title; and, unity of interest. Where they are present, a joint tenancy is created between the joint tenants: vesting in all of them at the same time; giving each a right to possess the whole of the property in common with the other joint tenants; created by the same deed or instrument; and, involving the same type of interest. Absence of one or more of these characteristics, results in the interest being a tenancy in common. An absence of unity of possession denies any common title altogether. See also **Joint tenancy**; **Tenancy in common**; **Unity of interest**.

Fourth market The trading in unlisted securities directly between investors.

Fractional share certificate A document under the seal of a company specifying shares held in the company by a member where part of the holding is an interest in a fraction of a share. The issue of such certificates is subject to authority in the articles (for example, Corporations Law Sch 1 Table A reg 93) and is typical in an issue of bonus shares. See also **Certification of transfer**; **Share**; **Share certificate**.

•**Franchise** 1. A business arrangement which allows an individual, partnership or company to operate under the name of an already established business. A franchise is a system in which one organisation ('franchisor') grants the right to produce, sell or use a developed product, service or brand to another organisation ('franchisee'). 2. The right to vote. See also **Franchise agreement**; **One vote one value**.

•**Franchise agreement** 1. An agreement reached directly between a land developer and government, often endorsed by an Act of Parliament at State or Federal level. The effect usually is to exempt a developer from meeting normal planning and environmental requirements and procedures, whilst making the basic decision immune from review by the courts. The agreement may make some reference to pollution control or environment protection measures, and such agreements generally, but not always, incorporate environmental assessment, compliance, and monitoring programs (known as Environmental Review and Management Programmes (ERMP) in Western Australia) tailor-made for that particular development. 2. In regard to retail sale of motor fuel, an agreement authorising a person to use a mark commonly associated with a corporation, to occupy premises of, or to supply or purchase motor vehicle fuel, in connection with the retail sale of motor fuel: (CTH) Petroleum Retail Marketing Franchise Act 1980 s 3(1). Also known as 'indenture agreement'. See also **Franchise**.

•**Franked dividend** A dividend paid out of a resident company's taxed profit. The company resolves or declares what specified percentage of the current dividend is a franked dividend: (CTH) Income Tax Assessment Act 1936 s 160AQF. A dividend paid out of profits on which company tax has not and will not be paid is an 'unfranked dividend'. The extent to which a company may frank a dividend depends on the credit balance in its franking account. See also **Franking account**; **Imputation system**.

Franking account An account that records for tax purposes the franking debits and franking credits of a class of a company arising in a franking year. If the total franking credits of a class exceed the total franking debits of that class for a franking year, a franking surplus of that class exists. If the total franking debits of a class exceed the total franking credits of that class, then a franking deficit of that class arises: (CTH) Income Tax Assessment Act 1936 s 160APJ. The amount of the surplus or deficit is the franking account balance: s160APA. See also **Class A franking account**; **Class B franking account**; **Franking credit**; **Franking debit**; **Franking deficit**; **Franked dividend**; **Franking surplus**; **Franking year**.

Franking credit An amount credited to a company's franking account which consists of one of the following: the carry forward amount of a franking account surplus from the prior franking year ((CTH) Income Tax Assessment Act 1936 s 160APL); an amount of company tax paid which has been adjusted for the purposes of (CTH) Income Tax Assessment Act 1936 ss 160APM-160APMD; the amount of franked dividends received from another company ((CTH) Income Tax Assessment Act 1936 s 160APP); and the amount of franked dividends received through trusts or partnerships ((CTH) Income Tax Assessment Act 1936 s 160APQ). A credit may arise in other very specific circumstances. See also **Franking account**; **Franking debit**; **Franking deficit tax**; **Franked dividend**; **Franking year**.

Franking debit An amount debited to a company's franking account arising in the following circumstances: where a company under-franks a dividend ((CTH) Income Tax Assessment Act 1936 s 160APX); where a company receives a refund of company income tax ((CTH) Income Tax Assessment Act 1936 ss 160APY-APYBA); and where a company pays a franked dividend: ((CTH) Income Tax Assessment Act 1936 s 160AQB). Debits may also arise in other specific circumstances. For 1994/95 and later franking years, companies are required to maintain separate class A and class B franking accounts. See also **Franking account**; **Franking credit**; **Franking deficit tax**; **Franked dividend**; **Franking year**.

Franking deficit The situation where a company's franking debits of a particular class exceed its franking credits of that class in its franking account of the same class: (CTH) Income Tax Assessment Act 1936 s 160APJ(2), (3). This may happen because the company has paid franked dividends in excess of its franking credits for the year. See also **Franking account**; **Franking credit**; **Franking deficit tax**; **Franking debit**.

Franking deficit tax A tax applied to the amount of a company's franking deficit of a particular class at the end of the franking year: (CTH) Income Tax Assessment Act 1936 s 160AQJ. Franking deficit tax is not imposed as a penalty; rather it represents a payment required to make good the amount imputed to shareholders which exceeds the amount available to be imputed. Franking deficit tax is due and payable on the last day of the month following the end of the relevant franking year: (CTH) Income Tax Assessment Act 1936 s 160ARU. For companies with a 30 June balance date, the time for payment will be 31 July. See also **Franked dividend**; **Franking credit**; **Franking deficit**; **Imputation system**.

Franking rebate See **Imputation rebate**.

Franking surplus The situation where a company's franking credits of a particular class exceed its franking debits of that class in its franking account of the same class: (CTH) Income Tax Assessment Act 1936 s 160APJ(1), (1A). See also **Class A franking account**; **Class B franking account**; **Franking account**; **Franking credit**; **Franking debit**; **Franking deficit tax**.

Franking year The period significant for franking purposes equivalent to a financial year or year of income. If a company has a year of income ending before 31 May, then its franking year will be the substituted instalment period of the company under (CTH) Income Tax Assessment Act 1936 ss 160APA, 221AB(1). The substituted instalment period ends on the last day of the month during which the year of income of the company ends, or 31 December, whichever is the later. The Commissioner of Taxation may also notify the company of a period that is specified by the Commissioner to be that company's franking year: (CTH) Income Tax Assessment Act 1936 s 160APH. See also **Financial year**; **Franking account**; **Franking credit**; **Franking debit**; **Year of income**.

Fraud An intentional dishonest act or omission done with the purpose of deceiving.

Insurance A dishonest act or omission by the insured or the insurer designed to obtain a material advantage over the other party. Fraud must be knowing (*Purcell v State Insurance Office* (1982) 2 ANZ Ins Cas ¶60-495) or reckless (*Engel v South British Insurance Co Ltd* (1983) 2 ANZ Ins Cas 60-516). See also **Insurance fraud**; **Uberrimae fidei**.

Fraud, insurance See **Insurance fraud**.

Fraud on a power An equitable doctrine prohibiting the exercise of a power, in certain circumstances, for a purpose, or with an intention, beyond the scope of or not justified by the instrument creating the power: *Vatcher v Paull* [1915] AC 372 at 378. Fraud does not mean dishonesty but action beyond the implied scope of a conferred power. When applied to exercises of powers by members of a company, the doctrine is known as fraud on the minority. See also **Fraud on the minority**.

Fraud on the minority Alteration of articles by the majority to allow expropriation of the shares of the minority or of valuable proprietary rights attaching to the shares. The alteration will be prima facie invalid unless the majority can show that the power was exercised for a proper purpose and would not operate oppressively in relation to minority shareholders: *Gambotto v WCP Ltd* (1995) 182 CLR 432; 127 ALR 417. Other alterations are prima facie valid unless the alteration is beyond any purpose contemplated by the articles or is oppressive: *Gambotto v WCP Ltd*. See also **Fraud on a power**; **Squeeze out**.

Frauds, Statute of See **Statute of Frauds**.

Fraudulent conveyance A conveyance of property made with intent to defraud the transferee, on the basis of a falsified or fraudulently concealed title: for example *Gessey v Soda Sisters Pty Ltd* (unrptd, SC(VIC), Beach J, 8802/94, 16 December 1994). A person who makes a fraudulent conveyance is guilty of a misdemeanour and is also liable in damages to the transferee for any loss sustained by the transferee: (NSW) Conveyancing Act 1919 s 183. See also **Conveyance**.

Fraudulent misrepresentation A false statement of fact, made by a person who does not believe the truth of the statement or is recklessly indifferent to whether it is true or not, to another with the intention that the other person will rely on it: *Pendlebury v Colonial Mutual Life Assurance Society Ltd* (1912) 13 CLR 676; 18 ALR 124; *Commercial Banking Company of Sydney Ltd v R H Brown & Co* (1972) 126 CLR 337; [1972-73] ALR 393. It is a misrepresentation where the representor lacks belief in the truth of the representation or makes it recklessly, not caring whether it is true or false: *Civil Service Co-op Society of Victoria Ltd v Blyth* (1914) 17 CLR 601; [1914] VLR 305. See also **Damages**; **Deceit**; **Fraud**; **Innocent misrepresentation**; **Misrepresentation**; **Negligent misrepresentation**; **Rescission**.

•**Fraudulent preference** See **Preference**.

Fraudulent trading See **Insolvent trading**.

Free acceptance In relation to restitution, the receipt of an enrichment with the knowledge that it was not offered as a gift. Free acceptance can be used to establish the enrichment of the recipient as an element of a claim for restitution of that enrichment. Free acceptance may also be used to establish that the enrichment was unjust: *Pavey & Matthews Pty Ltd v Paul* (1987) 162 CLR 221; 69 ALR 577. See also **Enrichment**; **Incontrovertible benefit**; **Restitution**.

Free alongside ship *Abbr* – FAS An arrangement under a contract for carriage by sea by which a consignor delivers the goods alongside the ship and pays all expenses up to that point. Thereafter the consignee or buyer must pay all expenses, including loading and landing expenses, freight, insurance, and all other charges involved in the process of carrying the goods to the consignee. It is the buyer's duty to organise, at its own expense, the shipping space: *Nippon Yusen Kaisha v Ramjiban Serowgee* [1938] AC 429. See also **Alongside**; **Alongside date**; **Carriage by sea**; **Contract of carriage**; **Freight**; **Loading**.

Free in and out terms *Abbr* – FIO terms A maritime expression indicating that all expenses associated with loading and unloading cargo under a contract of carriage are to be paid by the shippers or those to whom the cargo is delivered, leaving the ship owners free from liability for these expenses. See also **Cargo**; **Loading**; **Charterer**.

Free of capture and seizure An exemption clause in insurance contracts which protects the underwriters from liability for loss or damage through capture of seizure. Capture includes every act of seizing or taking by an enemy or armed forces. Seizure imports a wider meaning than capture, and includes every act of taking forcible possession either by the overpowering force of an enemy, or by lawful authority where the seizure is not for a temporary purpose, or incidental to a civil remedy or the enforcement of a civil right, or as security for the performance of some duty or obligation owed: *Cory v Burr* (1883) 8 App Cas 393 at 405. See also **Insurance**; **Insurance contract**; **Liability**; **Maritime law**.

•**Free on board** *Abbr* – FOB Such contracts are to be contrasted with cost insurance and freight contracts: *Saffron v Société Minière Cafrika* (1958) 100 CLR 231. See also **Bill of lading**; **Consignment**; **Contract of carriage**; **Cost insurance freight contract**; **Goods**; **Loading**.

Free on board contract See **Free on board**.

Free on rail *Abbr* – FOR A contract for sale of goods under which it is the seller's duty to deliver the goods to a named railway station. The seller may also agree to load the goods on to the railway wagons. Once the seller's obligation has been discharged, the risk of ownership of the goods generally passes from the seller to the buyer. See also **Goods**.

Free trade Trade which is unimpeded by tariffs, import and export quotas and other devices which obstruct the free movement of goods and services between countries. The formation of a free trade area by two or more countries, however, has not precluded the retention by those participating countries of tariffs against non-member countries. See also **Free trade area**; **General Agreement on Tariffs and Trade 1947**; **General Agreement on Tariffs and Trade 1994**.

Free trade area An international region, established by a group of countries, where trade can be conducted without discriminatory practices or interferences by governments, and where restrictions on trade, such as tariffs or duties, are minimal. The World Trade Organisation focuses on non-discrimination and free trade between trading partners, the provision of fair competition, the rational settlement of international disputes, the liberalisation of trade, and the use of tariffs rather than quotas and other barriers to trade. See also **General Agreement on Tariffs and Trade 1947**; **General Agreement on Tariffs and Trade 1994**.

Freedom of information *Abbr* – FOI The principle that administrative action should be made as open to public scrutiny as reasonably possible by permitting public access to information held by the government. FOI legislation has the expressed objects of making available to the public information about government decision-making, ensuring that policy is readily available to members of the public affected by it, and creating a general right of access to documents in the possession of decision-makers, limited only by exemptions necessary for the protection of essential public interests and the private and business affairs of individuals: (CTH) Freedom of Information Act 1982 s 3. See also **Administrative action**.

Freedom of interstate trade, commerce and intercourse The protection afforded trade, commerce and intercourse among the States from discriminatory burdens of a protectionist kind by Commonwealth Constitution s 92, the purpose of which is to create a free trade zone and eliminate protectionism: *Cole v Whitfield* (1988) 165 CLR 360 at 391, 398; 78 ALR 42. Any burden imposed upon interstate trade, commerce and intercourse is discriminatory where it involves an inequality of treatment between interstate and intrastate trade and commerce and protectionist where it confers a competitive or market advantage upon intrastate trade and commerce at the expense of interstate trade and commerce: *Castlemaine Tooheys Ltd v South Australia* (1990) 169 CLR 436; 90 ALR 371 at 379-80. See also **Absolutely free**; **Interstate trade and commerce**; **Intrastate trade and commerce**; **Trade and commerce power**.

- **Freehold** A type of land-holding originating in feudal times, being land held by a freeman and subject to services and incidents thought to be appropriate to the status of a freeman. The term is used in modern times simply to mean ownership of land. For the purposes of (VIC) Trustee Act 1958 s 3A, the term also embraces certain Crown leases. See also **Crown lease; Fee simple; Leasehold**.

- **Freight** 1. Goods carried by a carrier from one place to another. 2. Fees payable to a carrier for the carriage of goods and delivery at their destination: (CTH) Marine Insurance Act 1909 s 3. Freight includes the profit derivable by a shipowner from the employment of a ship to carry his or her own goods or movables, as well as freight payable by a third party, but does not include passage money: (CTH) Marine Insurance Act 1909 Sch 2. See also **Advance freight; Advance on freight; Back freight; Collect freight; Freight paid at destination; Freight policy; Guaranteed freight; Lump sum freight; Rate of freight**.

Freight at risk See **Freight paid at destination**.

Freight paid at destination A stipulation in a contract of carriage of goods which provides that the carrier will only be entitled to payment of the freight on the safe arrival of the goods at the stipulated destination. The term is the antonym of advance freight. Freight at risk is a similar concept, implying that the carrier accepts the risk of carriage. See also **Accident; Advance freight; Freight**.

Freight policy An insurance contract available to a carrier, protecting the insured's right to recover the freight charged where the freight is lost. The loss must be due to agreed mishaps, such as accidents in loading and unloading operations, handling, bunkering, aircraft contact, explosions, breakdowns or defects of machinery, defects in the hull, and negligence of the master or crew of the ship. See also **Freight**.

Freight rate See **Rate of freight**.

Freighter See **Charterer**.

Frequent flyer benefit Accumulated points that can be exchanged for benefits by a member of 'frequent flyer' clubs or similar programmes. Such benefits, which are generally not treated as fringe benefits, include free air travel and hotel accommodation, the value of which is considered as an assessable income to the employer. If an airline ticket is issued in the employee's name and marked as not transferable, it will not be assessed: *Payne v FCT* (1996) 96 ATC 407; 32 ATR 516.

- **Fringe benefit** A benefit provided to an employee or an employee's associate by the employer, an associate of the employer, or another person under an arrangement with the employer or the associate of the employer, in respect of the employment of the employee. For the purpose of determining an employee's fringe benefits tax liability, a fringe benefit excludes such payments as salary and wages, exempt benefits, employee share acquisition schemes, superannuation support, an eligible termination payment, and certain other benefits: (CTH) Fringe Benefits Tax Assessment Act 1986 s 136(1). An employer may have to pay tax on a fringe benefit provided under the (CTH) Fringe Benefits Tax Act 1986. See also **Car fringe benefit; Car parking benefit; Employee share scheme; Fringe Benefits Tax; Loan; Housing fringe benefit; Property fringe benefit; Residual fringe benefit; Salary; Wage**.

Fringe benefits standard year For fringe benefits tax purposes, the 12 months beginning 1 April and ending 31 March of the subsequent year: (CTH) Fringe Benefits Tax Assessment Act 1986. The first year, referred to as the transitional year, was the nine-month period from 1 July 1986 to 31 March 1987. Annual returns for the year ending 31 March must be lodged with the Australian Taxation Office by 28 April unless prior arrangements have been made for an extension of time. See also **Fringe Benefits Tax**.

- **Fringe benefits tax** *Abbr* – FBT A tax payable by employers on the value of certain fringe benefits that have been provided to their employees or to associates of those employees: (CTH) Fringe Benefits Tax Assessment Act 1986 s 136. The Act requires the identification of a number of benefits which are or have been provided to employees in respect of the employment, the definition of such benefits as taxable benefits, and the imposition of liability for tax upon such fringe benefits: *State Chamber of Commerce and Industry v Commonwealth* (1987) 163 CLR 329; 73 ALR 161. A general category of fringe benefits referred to as 'residual benefits' has been created to catch all fringe benefits not specifically categorised. See also **Associate; Benefit; Fringe benefit; Residual fringe benefit**.

Fructus naturales /frʊktus næturaleɪz/ *Lat* – fruits of nature. Produce of the ground that occurs naturally, without human cultivation, such as trees and grass. Sale of such items to a third party where that party is responsible for harvest creates a profit à prendre, as such items are fixtures. See also **Profit à prendre**.

Frustrating event An event (or series of events) which has severe ramifications on the performance of a contract; an event which brings a radical change: *Codelfa Constructions Pty Ltd v State Rail Authority of NSW* (1982) 149 CLR 337; 41 ALR 367. The event must make further performance a thing different in substance from that contracted for: *Metropolitan Water Board v Dick, Kerr & Co Ltd* [1917] 2 KB 1. A fundamentally different situation must be created by the event: *British Movietonews Ltd v London and District Cinemas Ltd* [1952] AC 166. See also **Frustration; Performance**.

- **Frustration** 1. The situation where a contractual obligation has, without the default of either party, become incapable of being performed. Frustration occurs because the circumstances in which performance is called for would render it a thing radically different from that which was undertaken by the contract: *Codelfa Constructions Pty Ltd v State Rail Authority of New South Wales* (1982) 149 CLR 337; 41 ALR 367. Frustration automatically discharges the parties from the obligation to perform, or be ready and willing to perform, their contractual duties: for example *Scanlan's New Neon Ltd v Tooheys Ltd* (1943) 67 CLR 169. Recovery at common law was restricted to a number of specified situations. This position has been statutorily modified in New South Wales, Victoria and South Australia: for example (VIC) Frustrated Contracts Act 1959. 2. For the purposes of the frustrated contracts legislation, includes the avoidance of a contract for the sale of goods: for example (VIC) Frustrated Contracts Act 1959 s 3. See also **Discharge; Frustrating event; Self-induced frustration; Supervening illegality; Failure of consideration; Unjust enrichment.**

Frustration by death Termination of a contract on the death of a party, where the party was personally involved in the contract (for example, the involvement of an employee in a contract of employment): *Taylor v Caldwell* (1863) 3 B & S 826; 122 ER 309 at 313. See also **Discharge; Frustrating event; Frustration; Personal services; Termination of agency.**

Frustration clause A contractual term which stipulates the consequences that shall flow from the occurrence of an event which, in the absence of the term, may have led to discharge of the contract by frustration. See also **Discharge; Frustrating event; Frustration.**

Full age See **Age of majority.**

Full and complete cargo The quantity of cargo which a vessel can safely carry, measured by the amount necessary to immerse any given vessel to its load lines, with a 10 per cent margin allowed for error. A charter may require the charterer to load a full and complete cargo of the kind described in the charterparty. If a precise quantity of cargo is specified in the charterparty, then nothing short of this will amount to a full and complete cargo, allowing however for a reasonable and negligible difference. See also **Cargo; Charterparty; Contract of carriage.**

Full annual value A base rate used as a means of calculating other payments such as rates or taxes associated with the relevant land. It is calculated as a net rather than a gross figure: *Rose v Watson* [1894] 2 QB 90. See also **Rent.**

Full associate member An associate member of the Sydney Futures Exchange (SFE) permitted to deal in futures contracts on her or his own behalf or on behalf of clients. Full associate members cannot trade on the floor of the SFE as all trades must be concluded through a floor member. See also **Associate member; Floor member; Sydney Futures Exchange.**

•**Full bench** See **Full court.**

•**Full court** A court conducted by a number of judges (not necessarily the entire complement of judges of the court) required to sit and determine applications for leave to appeal, appeals, references on a question of law, cases stated and in the case of the High Court, the exercise of original jurisdiction under Commonwealth Constitution ss 75, 76. A full court is frequently five or seven judges in the High Court. In the Supreme Courts and the Federal Court, it is usually three judges; however it may consist of only two judges: for example (QLD) Supreme Court of Queensland Act 1991 s 2; (VIC) Supreme Court Act 1986 s 3.

Full disclosure The presentation and disclosure of all significant and material information in financial statements. It is not enough if the information provided is only sufficient to put another person on enquiry: *Dunne v English* (1874) LR 18 Eq 524. See also **Financial statement.**

Full disclosure principle A principle requiring financial statements and notes accompanying the accounts to fully disclose all information of a material nature pertaining to the operating results and financial position of the entity. This is to ensure that a true picture of the operations and cash flow of the business is declared.

Full line forcing A mechanism involving supply of goods and services on the condition that the acquirer or a related body corporate will not, or will to a limited extent only, acquire different goods or services from a competitor. This 'tying' mechanism is also known as 'second-line forcing', and may constitute exclusive dealing under (CTH) Trade Practices Act 1974 s 47 where a second product, rather than the full range of products, is forced upon the purchaser. See also **Exclusive dealing; Tying.**

•**Full takeover scheme** A takeover scheme under which each takeover offer relates to all the shares in the target company in the relevant class that the offeree holds: Corporations Law s 603. See also **Takeover scheme.**

•**Full-time employee** Generally, an employee who works every working day during normal business hours. A person is engaged on a 'full-time' basis if the person applies so much time to the pursuit that his or her commitment is full-time in the ordinary meaning of the words: *Lane v Arrowcrest Group Pty Ltd* (1990) 27 FCR 427; 99 ALR 45. See also **Employee.**

Fully paid share A share for which the shareholder has paid the par value in consideration for becoming the shareholder of that share. The par value is the fixed amount of each share in the authorised capital: for example *Re Cork Bros Pty Ltd* (1983) 8 ACLR 371. See also **Authorised capital; Par value.**

•**Function** A use, power or event.

Functional market The functional level on which parties operate, including operation as a manufacturer, wholesaler or retailer. There may, for example, be quite distinct markets for manufacturers, wholesalers or retailers: *QIW Retailers Ltd v Davids Holdings Pty Ltd* (1993) 42 FCR 255; 114 ALR 579. However, with the growth of vertical integration, it is becoming increasingly difficult to distinguish between all these functions, and often a firm can operate on more than one functional level in a market at any given point in time. See also **Geographic market; Market; Market power; Product market.**

Functions of economic system Functions which are defined to: match supply to effective demand for goods and services in an efficient manner; determine not only what goods and services are to be produced but in what quantities and to what quality; allocate scarce resources among the industries producing and distributing goods and services; organise wholesaling, retailing and trading facilities; provide for the maintenance and expansion of capital investment; fully utilise the resources of society; convey to consumers information on what goods and services are available; and promote research and development aiming at improved, safer and new products.

Functus officio /fʌŋktəs ɒfɪʃioʊ/ *Lat* – having discharged one's duty; having completed one's term of office; having ceased to hold some public appointment; having performed the authorised act and being unable to go back to it a second time. One who is *functus officio* is precluded from again considering the matter even if new arguments or evidence are presented: *MacMillan Bloedel Ltd v Minister of Finance* (1985) 60 BCLR 145. See also **Certiorari; Prohibition**.

Fund accounting Accounting procedures that provide a complete group of accounts for each accounting entity established through legal, contractual or voluntary action. Government units account for certain types of funds separately, including the capital fund, revenue fund, sinking fund, trust funds, and special activity funds. Each entity will record the financial and other resources on one side of the account while recording the liabilities and other credits on the other side with the fund balance. Rather than profit and loss outcomes, fund accounting is concerned with the surplus or deficit position of the fund.

Fundamental breach A breach which deprives an innocent party of substantially the whole benefit of a contract: *Hongkong Fir Shipping Co Ltd v Kawasaki Kisen Kaisha Ltd* [1962] 2 QB 26. Breach of a fundamental term is a type of fundamental breach: *Suisse Atlantique Societè d'Armement Maritime SA v NV Rotterdamsche Kolen Centrale* [1967] 1 AC 361. Broadly construed, 'fundamental breach' describes any breach which provides the promisee with a right to terminate the performance of the contract: *Suisse Atlantique Societè d'Armement Maritime SA v NV Rotterdamsche Kolen Centrale*. Narrowly construed, the concept describes a total non-performance of the contract: *Yeoman Credit Ltd v Apps* [1962] 2 QB 508 at 517. It has been suggested that 'total breach' is the same thing as fundamental breach: *Farnworth Finance Facilities Ltd v Attryde* [1970] 1 WLR 1053. See also **Anticipatory breach; Breach of contract; Fundamental term**.

Fundamental mistake A misapprehension on the part of both parties to a contract as to a fundamental fact such as the existence of the goods contracted to be sold: *McRae v Commonwealth Disposals Commission* (1951) 84 CLR 377; *Svanosio v McNamara* (1956) 96 CLR 186.

Fundamental term A term that underlies a contract such that, if it is not complied with, the performance becomes something totally different from that which the contract contemplated: *Smeaton Hanscomb & Co Ltd v Sassoon I Setty Son & Co* [1953] 2 All ER 1471 at 1473; [1953] 1 WLR 1468 at 1470. The innocent party may regard breach of a fundamental term as a fundamental breach justifying termination of the contract on the ground of repudiation: *Suisse Atlantique Societè d'Armement Maritime SA v NV Rotterdamsche Kolen Centrale* [1967] 1 AC 361. See also **Condition; Exclusion clause; Fundamental breach**.

Fundraising The attempt by a commercial entity to entice investors to purchase the entity's securities. Corporations Law Pts 7.11, 7.12 require commercial entities to provide information about the securities it offers, usually in the form of a prospectus. Much of the regulation of fundraising activity in the Corporations Law is founded on investor protection.

Funds derived from operations The gain in an entity's operations resulting from improved trading conditions. The increase may be indicated as gross revenue less expenses involving the movement of funds, or as net profit adjusted for income and expense items which do not involve fund movements in a statement of changes in financial position.

Funds in court Money, debentures, stock, shares, and other forms of security or investment deposited in court to the credit of any cause, matter, or account. Funds may be deposited for the benefit of a person under a disability arising as a result of age or mental incapacity (*Smith v Reynolds* [1989] VR 309), or wherever it appears that funds should be held in neutral custody, for example, pursuant to an offer to compromise: for example (CTH) Federal Court Rules O 23. See also **Charging order; Judgment creditor; Judgment debtor; Stop order**.

Fungibility The character of certain futures and options contracts which makes securities of a particular class perfect substitutes for each other and the ability for obligations under each to be readily transferable through novation. Standardisation permits fungibility. See also **Futures contract; Novation; Option; Standardisation**.

Fungibles *Lat* – *fungibilis* – able to perform or enjoy. Chattels which are interchangeable in character and qualities: for example *Shoreline Currencies (Aust) Pty Ltd v Corporate Affairs Commission (NSW)* (1986) 11 NSWLR 11; 10 ACLR 847. See also **Bailment; Fitness for purpose; Implied warranty; Sale of goods**.

Further advance A form of security for a loan under which certain property of the debtor is identified as being charged with the debt. The debtor retains ownership of the property, but the creditor has the right to have it sold if the debt is not fulfilled. See also **Charge; Debtor; Security**.

Further assurance A promise given by a vendor to do all necessary acts to transfer the land to the purchaser. A deed of conveyance may include a covenant for further assurance: for example *Re Jones; Farrington v Forrester* [1893] 2 Ch 461. See also **Assurance; Conveyance; Covenant**.

Future chose in action A chose in action that is not yet in existence at all, or is in existence but a person has as yet no ownership rights to it. A person may own, transfer or assign a future chose in action. See also **Chose in action**.

Future debt 1. A debt that might or might not be incurred in the future and not arising out of any existing contract or obligation. **2.** A debt incurred under an existing contract or obligation but not payable until some time in the future. For example, an instalment of purchase price under a contract for sale which is not due to be paid until a future time: *Re Wills; Wills v Abram* [1993] ACL Rep 50 FC 48. Future debts are provable in bankruptcy: (CTH) Bankruptcy Act 1966 s 82. See also **Contingent debt; Proof of debt**.

Future goods Goods that are to be manufactured or acquired by the seller after the making of a contract of sale: (NSW) Sale of Goods Act 1923 s 5(1); (VIC) Goods Act 1958 s 3(1); (QLD) Sale of Goods Act 1896 s 3(1). No property in future goods can pass to the buyer unless and until the goods are manufactured or acquired by the seller: (NSW) Sale of Goods Act 1923 s 21. The parties cannot agree to the contrary: *Jansz v GMB Imports Pty Ltd* [1979] VR 581. Also known as 'unascertained goods'. See also **Goods**; **Sale of goods**.

Future interest A property right that has vested in the holder of the right, but that does not enable the holder to have the possession and use of the property. The holder of a future interest is said to be vested in interest but not vested in possession: *Walsh Bay Developments Pty Ltd v FCT* (1995) 130 ALR 415 at 427-8. To be contrasted with an 'expectancy', which gives no property rights: for example (NSW) Wills, Probate and Administration Act 1898 s 24. See also **Estate**.

Futures See **Futures contract**.

•**Futures advice business** The business of advising persons about futures contracts or a business in the course of which futures reports are published: Corporations Law ss 9, 71. A person must not carry on a futures advice business or hold out that the person is a futures adviser unless the person is a licensee or an exempt futures adviser: Corporations Law s 1143. Solicitors or accountants who give futures advice in a manner which is merely incidental to the practice of their profession are not thereby engaged in a futures advice business: Corporations Law s 71(4). Futures advice given in a newspaper, periodical or other form of media whose sole or principal purpose is not advising about futures contracts nor publishing of futures reports does not constitute a futures advice business: Corporations Law s 71(5), 71(6). Employees or agents who are acting on behalf of another person engaged in the futures advice business are not themselves carrying on futures advice business: Corporations Law s 71(8). See also **Carrying on business**; **Futures adviser**; **Futures advisers licence**; **Futures contract**; **Futures report**.

•**Futures adviser** A person who advises or counsels other persons concerning the acquisition or disposal of futures contracts. See also **Futures advice business**; **Futures advisers licence**; **Futures association**; **Futures contract**.

•**Futures advisers licence** A licence granted by the Australian Securities Commission (ASC) under Corporations Law Pt 8.3 which enables a person to lawfully conduct a futures advice business: Corporations Law s 9. A licence will be granted to a natural person if the person has the appropriate qualifications and experience, is not insolvent, and if the ASC has no reason to believe that the person is not of good fame and character or that the person will not perform the duties of a futures adviser efficiently, honestly and fairly: Corporations Law s 1144A. Where a body corporate applies for a licence, it will be granted only if the qualifications and experience of each responsible officer of the body are adequate, if the body is not being externally administered, and if the ASC has no reason to believe that the body will not perform the duties of a futures adviser efficiently, honestly and fairly: Corporations Law s 1145. See also **External administration**; **Futures advice business**; **Futures adviser**; **Futures licence**; **Insolvent**.

•**Futures association** A body corporate which has been given approval by the relevant Minister to act as a futures association: Corporations Law ss 9, 1132(1). Approval would be given only if the Minister is satisfied that the body corporate is able to properly regulate the association's affairs in the interests of the public and to administer and enforce the association's business rules, and that the body has appropriate business rules regulating the conduct of members of the association in conducting their business of dealing in futures contracts. A futures association includes a body corporate which has been given approval to act as a futures corporation by the ministerial council: Corporations Law ss 9, 1132(3). The Sydney Futures Exchange Ltd is both a futures exchange and a futures association. See also **Futures advice business**; **Futures adviser**; **Futures licence**; **Sydney Futures Exchange**.

Futures authority The authority of a futures representative to act for a futures licensee. A proper authority requires there to be a copy of the principal's futures licence on which is endorsed a statement certifying the copy to be a true copy, stating that the representative is employed by or acts for or in arrangement with the principal and signed by the principal, as well as a statement setting out details of any other futures licensee of whom the representative is also a futures representative: Corporations Law s 87(1). See also **Futures licence**; **Futures representative**; **Invalid futures authority**.

•**Futures broker** A person who deals on behalf of another person in futures contracts. See also **Broker**; **Futures broker**.

•**Futures brokers licence** A licence granted by the Australian Securities Commission (ASC) under Corporations Law Pt 8.3 to a person which enables the person to lawfully conduct a futures broking business: Corporations Law s 9, Pt 8.3 Div 1. It will be granted if the person has the appropriate qualifications and experience, and is not insolvent, and provided that the ASC has no reason to believe that the person is not of good fame and character or that the person will not perform the duties of a futures broker efficiently, honestly and fairly: Corporations Law s 1144A. Where the applicant for a licence is a body corporate, the licence will be granted if the ASC is satisfied that each responsible officer of the body possesses the necessary qualifications and experience, if the body is not being externally administered, and if the ASC has no reason to believe that the body will not perform the duties of a futures broker efficiently, honestly and fairly: Corporations Law s 1145. It is a condition of the granting of a futures brokers licence that the futures broker be a member of a futures organisation: Corporations Law s 1148. See also **Futures broker**; **Futures licence**; **Futures organisation**; **External administration**; **Insolvent**.

•**Futures contract** A commitment to deliver (in the case of a sold contract) or take delivery of (in the case of a bought contract) a specified weight or quantity of a standard grade of a commodity at a fixed price and for a specific delivery date or period, at an agreed location. Futures contracts are mainly utilised by the producers and users of commodities who wish to avoid the uncertainty which fluctuations in the prices of commodities brings. Futures contracts are traded for settlement only on four maturity dates each year and in standard contract amounts.

•**Futures exchange 1.** A body corporate which has been given approval by the relevant Minister to act as a futures exchange: Corporations Law ss 9, 1126. It has the function of administering and regulating a futures market where futures contracts can be acquired or disposed of. The Minister may give approval for a body to act as a futures exchange if the body provides for business rules which adequately regulate the admission and conduct of brokers, and if the interests of the public will be served by granting the application: Corporations Law s 1126(2). A futures exchange must take all reasonable steps to ensure an orderly and fair market for dealings in futures contracts on a futures market of the exchange: Corporations Law s 1137. A fidelity fund must be established and maintained by a futures exchange for the purpose of compensating persons who suffer pecuniary loss because of a defalcation or because of fraudulent misuse of money or other property by a member of the exchange: Corporations Law Pt 8.6, ss 1228, 1239. The court has power to make orders for the enforcement of the business rules of a futures exchange: Corporations Law s 1140. **2.** A futures exchange includes a body corporate which was a futures exchange within the meaning of a previous law corresponding to Corporations Law Ch 8: Corporations Law ss 9, 1126(3). See also **Sydney Futures Exchange**.

Futures exchange transaction A transaction by which the parties agree to buy and sell shares and those shares are to be delivered. A futures exchange transaction is not a gambling transaction: *Re Ahearn; Ex parte Palmer* (1906) 6 SR (NSW) 576; 23 WN (NSW) 188. A futures exchange transaction is not unlawful and is enforceable: Corporations Law ss 778, 1148. See also **Futures exchange**.

•**Futures industry** The industry involving the trading of futures. It performs the economic function of avoiding substantial price fluctuations in commodities which are delivered at future dates by transferring price risks to speculators: *Sydney Futures Exchange Ltd v Australian Stock Exchange Ltd* (1995) 16 ACSR 148 at 154-6; 128 ALR 417; 13 ACLC 369. Futures contracts (essentially contracts to buy or sell a specified quantity of something at a specified future delivery date) are bought and sold on a futures market. Those who deal in the physical commodities (hedgers), such as producers, dealers, and processors of the commodities, and who wish to protect against risk, enter into futures contracts in order to fix the price that would be received on delivery. The risk in changes to the values of the commodities is borne by speculators who buy or sell futures contracts and who aim to profit from correctly anticipating the direction of price changes. The futures industry originally developed when merchants and producers of rural products attempted to protect themselves from price volatility inherent in such products. The futures industry is regulated by the Sydney Futures Exchange Ltd, the Australian Securities Commission, and Corporations Law Ch 8. See also **Futures contract**.

•**Futures law** A provision of Corporations Law Ch 8; Corporations Law s 9. Corporations Law Ch 8 is concerned with the regulation of the futures industry, and contains provisions dealing with: the establishment, powers and duties of futures exchanges, clearing houses and futures associations (Corporations Law Pt 8.2); the licensing and conduct of futures brokers, futures advisers and other participants in the futures industry (Corporations Law Pt 8.3); the general conduct of futures business (Corporations Law Pt 8.4); the duties of futures brokers to keep accounts and to have those accounts audited (Corporations Law Pt 8.5); fidelity funds to be maintained by futures exchanges and futures associations (Corporations Law Pt 8.6); and offences in relation to dealings in futures contracts, such as insider dealing, market manipulation, false or misleading conduct, and fraud (Corporations Law Pt 8.7). See also **Clearing house; Futures adviser; Futures association; Futures broker; Futures contract; Futures Exchange**.

•**Futures licence** A futures broker's licence or a futures adviser's licence: Corporations Law s 9. These licences are subject to any conditions and restrictions as are prescribed: Corporations Law s 1147. In particular, these conditions may require the licensee to ensure that representatives of the licensee are adequately qualified, and conditions ensuring adequate supervision of those representatives in order to prevent contraventions of a futures law may be imposed on the licensee: Corporations Law s 1150. See also **Futures advisers licence; Futures brokers licence; Futures law**.

•**Futures option** An option over a deliverable futures contract or a cash settled futures contract. See also **Futures contract; Option**.

•**Futures organisation** A futures exchange or a futures association in respect of which an approval is in force under Corporations Law s 1126 or 1132 respectively: Corporations Law s 9. However in relation to Corporations Law Pt 8.6 dealing with fidelity funds, a futures organisation does not include a futures association each of whose members is also a member of a futures exchange: Corporations Law s 9. In relation to whether a futures organisation is entitled to qualified privilege in respect of the publication of a notice calling for claims for compensation from the fidelity fund, or in respect of a statement as to whether an insurance contract against liability for claims under Corporations Law Pt 8.6 applies to a member of the futures organisation, futures organisation includes futures exchanges and futures associations established under a previous law corresponding to Corporations Law Pt 8.2: Corporations Law ss 9, 1126(3), 1132(3). See also **Futures association; Futures exchange**.

•**Futures report** An analysis or report about futures contracts: Corporations Law s 9. See also **Futures contract**.

•**Futures representative** A person who is employed by, or acts for or in arrangement with, another person in connection with a futures broking business or futures advice business carried on by that other person: Corporations Law s 73(1). A person who holds a proper authority from a futures licensee or a person who holds an invalid futures authority from another person is also a futures representative of the licensee of the other person: Corporations Law s 73(2). A person does an act as a futures representative of another person if the person does the act in connection with a futures broking or advice business carried on by the other person, or as an employee, agent or otherwise for the benefit of the other person, provided that it is not done in the course of work of a kind ordinarily done by accountants, clerks or cashiers: Corporations Law s 73(3). A person, held out as a futures representative of another person, who purportedly does an act as a futures representative for the other person is deemed to engage in conduct as a futures representative for the other person: Corporations Law s 73(4). Generally a person must not act as a futures representative of a futures broker or futures adviser unless the broker or adviser holds a licence and unless the person holds proper authority from the broker or adviser: Corporations Law ss 1172, 1173. Futures brokers and advisers may be liable to third parties in respect of conduct engaged in by their representatives as their futures representatives: Corporations Law ss 1183, 1185. See also **Futures adviser; Futures broker; Invalid futures authority.**

Futures trading offences Offences concerning dealings in future contracts under Corporations Law Pt 8.7. These include: futures market manipulation causing artificial prices (Corporations Law s 1259); false trading and market rigging through the creation of a false appearance of active trading (Corporations Law s 1260); fraudulently inducing persons to deal in futures contracts (Corporations Law s 1262); dissemination of information about illegal transactions (Corporations Law ss 1263); and fraud in connection with futures contracts (Corporations Law s 1264).

Fuzzy logic A programming technique enabling a digital computer that only understands binary states (such as 'on' or 'off' and 'up' and 'down') to recognise analogue states that may exist between the black or white conditions. Primarily useful in computers that are programmed to offer artificial intelligence, fuzzy logic can cope with factors of truth such as 'possibly true', 'potentially true', or 'probably true'. Fuzzy logic relies heavily on heuristics.

G

Gap A situation in which something fundamental in the structure of a bill of exchange has been inserted in such a way that an unauthorised change to the item may easily be made, for example where the amount payable on a cheque is fraudulently increased: for example *London Joint Stock Bank Ltd v Macmillan and Arthur* [1918] AC 777. See also **Acceptor; Bill of exchange; Blank; Material alteration**.

Garnish To warn. The term is usually used in relation to a person who is warned by a court order to pay a debt. See also **Garnishee; Garnishment**.

•**Garnishee 1.** A debtor required by a court order to pay his or her debt, not to the debtor's creditor, but to a third party ('garnishor') who has obtained a final judgment against the creditor. **2.** An amount paid pursuant to a garnishment order. See also **Garnishment; Garnishor**.

•**Garnishee order** See **Garnishment**.

Garnishment A court order by which a third party who holds money for a judgment debtor is directed to attach certain amounts of that money to the judgment debt. A common example of a garnishment is where a court requires an employer of the judgment debtor to 'garnish' the employee's wages by paying a portion of those wages directly to the judgment creditor: for example (CTH) Public Service Act 1922 s 64; (NSW) Supreme Court Rules Pt 46 rr 3, 10A; (VIC) Rules of the Supreme Court Ch I O 71; (QLD) Supreme Court Rules O 49. Also known as 'garnishee order'. See also **Garnishee; Maintenance; Pension**.

Garnishor A judgment creditor who commences garnishee proceedings to reach the credits or property of a judgment debtor. A court may issue a garnishee order against a person ('garnishee') who owes a debt to the judgment debtor, ordering him or her to pay to the garnishor the amount owed. See also **Garnishee; Garnishment**.

GATT See **General Agreement on Tariffs and Trade 1947**.

Gearing 1. In respect of a company, the ratio of fixed interest debt to ordinary share capital; the debt to equity ratio. The greater the use of borrowing, the higher the gearing; the higher the gearing, the greater the risk of loss or the potential for profit. Debt or loan capital is incurred as a means of raising profits above a level achievable by using share capital alone. **2.** In respect of investment, the ratio of borrowed capital to equity. Investors may borrow to augment the financing of an investment such as residential property. When the interest on such a loan is greater than the income produced by the investment, the gearing is described as negative. Negative gearing presently attracts special tax concessions. An investor with $500,000 of which $400,000 is borrowed has a gearing of 80%. See also **Debt to equity ratio; Negative gearing**.

Gearing ratio A ratio expressing the amount of capital financed by external sources, such as loans, compared to total capital. See also **Capital**.

GENCON charterparty A general purpose voyage charterparty published by the Baltic and International Maritime Council. See also **Charterparty**.

•**General acceptance** An unqualified assent by a drawee to the order of the drawer: (CTH) Bills of Exchange Act 1909 s 24(1). An acceptance to pay at a particular place is a general acceptance, unless it expressly states that the bill of exchange is to be paid only in that place, and not elsewhere: (CTH) Bills of Exchange Act 1909 s 24(4). See also **Bill of exchange; Domiciled (bill); Qualified acceptance**.

General agent An agent who has authority to do acts within the ordinary course of the agent's business or profession, or who is authorised to act generally in transactions of a particular kind or incidental to a particular business: *Marriott v General Electric Co Ltd* (1935) 53 CLR 409. See also **Apparent authority; Agency; Agent; Estoppel; Special agent**.

General Agreement on Tariffs and Trade 1947 *Abbr* – GATT 1947 An international agreement which aimed to abolish trade discrimination and to foster economic development by requiring member states to treat foreign and domestic products equally. GATT 1947 was based on the concept of most favoured nation treatment which requires member states to treat all other member states equally in terms of trade restrictions. See also **General Agreement on Tariffs and Trade 1994; Marrakesh Agreement establishing the World Trade Organisation 1994; World Trade Organisation**.

General Agreement on Tariffs and Trade 1994 *Abbr* – GATT 1994 An international agreement contained within the Marrakesh Agreement establishing the World Trade Organization 1994 (the 'Marrakesh Agreement 1994'). GATT 1994 is legally distinct from the General Agreement on Tariffs and Trade 1947 (GATT 1947). The Marrakesh Agreement entered into force generally and also for Australia on 1 January 1995. GATT 1994 requires transparency of laws relating to trade, freedom of transit for commercial purposes, and equality of national treatment: General Agreement on Tariffs and Trade 1994 arts III, X. See also **General Agreement on Tariffs and Trade 1947; Transparency; World Trade Organization**.

General average contribution In maritime law, the share of loss incurred when merchants and others pay a proportionate contribution towards the losses incurred when dangerous weather at sea has required the crew to throw some cargo overboard to save the rest of the cargo and the ship. In this way, the loss is shared between all the merchants using the vessel to transport cargo: *Svendsen v Wallace Bros* (1884) 13 QBD 69. See also **Average adjuster**.

General damages A category of damages.

Contract 1. Damage presumed by law to flow as the direct consequence of a breach of contract and therefore recoverable under the first limb of the rule in *Hadley v Baxendale* (1854) 9 Exch 341; 156 ER 145: for example *President of India v La Pintada Compania Navigacion SA* [1985] AC 104 at 127. To be contrasted with 'special damages'. 2. General loss of business as a head of damage. See also **Damages; Economic loss; Hadley v Baxendale, rule in; Special damages**.

Negligence 1. In modern Australian authorities, usually damages awarded for injuries that are not capable of assessment with precise mathematical calculation: *Paff v Speed* (1961) 105 CLR 549 at 559. General damages include damages for loss that will be suffered after the date of trial and damages for immaterial injuries such as pain and suffering. The jury has a wide discretion in awarding general damages and should do so under the heads of economic loss, 'loss of amenities' or 'enjoyment of life', and pain and suffering: *Paff v Speed* (1961) 105 CLR 549 at 559. To be contrasted with 'special damages'. 2. Damages presumed in torts actionable per se and in breach of contract: *Reader's Digest Services Pty Ltd v Lamb* (1982) 150 CLR 500; 38 ALR 417. To be contrasted with 'special damages'.

General equilibrium theory A theoretical situation in which supply and demand are matched in all markets in an economy, the forces which bring about price changes being in balance. In practice, many factors such as changes in the characteristics of supply and demand and the allocation of resources result in a tendency to continuous change. General equilibrium analysis usually assumes the existence of perfect competition in which the price of every good is free to vary, and that all markets will come into balance with all goods cleared. Partial equilibrium analysis examines a small sector of the economy such as the market for a particular commodity, in which the prices of several or all other commodities are assumed to be fixed.

General equitable charge An equitable charge which secures all the property which is already subject to a security over the legal interest, such as a mortgage. See also **Equitable charge; Mortgage**.

•**General insurance** A classification used to distinguish non-life insurance contracts from life insurance contracts: (CTH) Insurance Contracts Act 1984 s 11(6). General insurance is most commonly associated with indemnity contracts, such as those for liability insurance, marine insurance, property insurance, and reinsurance, but also includes personal accident and sickness insurance which is a contingency contract: (CTH) Insurance Act 1973 s 3(1). See also **Indemnity insurance; Life insurance; Marine insurance**.

General lien 1. A lien giving a right to hold all the chattels subject to the lien until all obligations of the lienor to the lienee are performed: *Dinmore Meatworks Pty Ltd v Kerr* (1962) 108 CLR 628; [1963] ALR 54. 2. In agency law, an agent's lien extending to all claims against the principal arising out of the agency, either by express contract or by usage. A general lien has been held to be possessed by factors, bankers, insurance brokers, solicitors, sharebrokers, wharfingers and packers, but not warehousemen: for example *Mercantile Credits Ltd v Jarden Morgan Australia Ltd* [1991] 1 Qd R 407; (1990) 1 ACSR 805 (sharebrokers); *Majeau Carrying Co Pty Ltd v Coastal Rutile Ltd* (1973) 129 CLR 48; 1 ALR 1 (warehousemen). To be contrasted with a particular lien. See also **Agency; Agent; Agent's lien; Factor; Insurance broker; Lien; Particular lien; Principal; Sharebroker**.

•**General meeting** A meeting of the members (shareholders) of a company. A general meeting known as the 'annual general meeting' must be held once every year: Corporations Law s 245(1). See also **Annual general meeting; Chairman at general meeting; Extraordinary general meeting; Member; Statutory meeting**.

General obligation bond A security backed by the ability of a public authority to levy taxes on taxable real property. The bonds are repayable from the general reserves provided by such taxes and other available revenues and are backed by the full faith and credit and taxing powers of the issuing public authority. See also **Bond**.

•**General partner** A partner in a limited partnership who is not a limited partner: (NSW) Partnership Act 1892 s 49. See also **Limited partner; Limited partnership; Partner**.

General property The property rights that remain with the bailor during a bailment: *Re Bond Worth Ltd* [1980] Ch 228 at 247. Only special property passes to the bailee, entitling him or her to exercise certain possessory remedies: *Re Bond Worth Ltd*.

General purpose financial report A financial report intended to meet the information needs common to users who are unable to command the preparation of reports tailored to satisfy, specifically, all of their information needs: Statement of Accounting Concepts SAC 2. Such a report should, among other things, provide information useful to users for making and evaluating decisions about the allocation of scarce resources: SAC 2. See also **Accounting standards; Balance sheet; Consolidated accounts; Profit and loss account**.

General receivership A receivership where the property constituting the security is the company's business and the whole, or substantially the whole, of its property. See also **Receiver; Receivership**.

General release 1. The discharge of an obligation or duty: for example, where a party to a contract waives his or her rights against the other party, or where a trustee is absolved by the beneficiaries from liability in respect of trust property upon the winding up of a trust. 2. The document recording a general release. See also **Beneficiary; Trust**.

General revenue assistance Unconditional financial assistance rendered by the Commonwealth to the States from revenue raised from total tax receipts. See also **Appropriation**.

General ruling In industrial law, a ruling made by an industrial tribunal, for example the Australian Industrial Relations Tribunal, for general application in its jurisdiction. For example the national wage cases and State wage cases. See also **Australian Industrial Relations Commission; National wage case.**

General ship A ship which carries cargo consigned under bills of lading by one or more consignors. A general ship is distinguished from a chartered ship which is let to particular persons under a charterparty for specific purposes. See also **Bill of lading; Cargo; Charterparty; Goods.**

General strike A strike by a large number of workers or unions covering a variety of industries and occupations, as opposed to a strike in a particular enterprise or industry. A general strike expresses widespread popular dissatisfaction and attempts to achieve economic or political reforms on a national or regional scale. See also **Industrial action; Strike.**

General union A union whose members perform any kind of work; that is, the union does not represent workers in a particular craft, occupation, or industry; for example the Australian Workers' Union. Also known as 'conglomerate union'. See also **Craft union; Enterprise union; Industry union; Occupational union.**

Generalia verba sunt generaliter intelligenda /dʒɛnəraliə vɜbə sʊnt dʒɛnəralɪtə ɪntɛlɪdʒɛndə/ *Lat* – general words must be construed generally.

Generalised system of preferences *Abbr* – GSP A system of tariff preferences for developing countries adopted by contracting parties to the General Agreement on Tariffs and Trade. These preferences are unilateral, non-reciprocal and non-contractual. Australia has adopted the system but reserves the right to modify, withdraw, suspend, or limit these preferences especially where there is injury to domestic producers. The margins of preference are generally 10-15% below the General Tariff Rate.

•**Generally accepted accounting principles** *Abbr* – GAAP The conventions, rules, and procedures embodying the accepted accounting practices that guide accountants in the preparation of financial statements. GAAPs include both broad guidelines and relatively detailed practices and procedures and have evolved over many years in the accounting profession. See also **Financial statement.**

•**Genuine dispute** A real and genuine industrial dispute. Whether a dispute is real and genuine is a question of fact. An industrial dispute must be genuine to be within the jurisdiction of the Australian Industrial Relations Commission under Commonwealth Constitution s 51(xxxv): *R v Ludeke; Ex parte Queensland Electricity Commission* (1985) 159 CLR 178 at 183-4; 60 ALR 641. If the dispute is no more than a device to invoke the Commonwealth power it will not be a 'dispute' within s 51(xxxv). See also **Australian Industrial Relations Commission; Conciliation and arbitration power; Paper dispute.**

Geographic market The physical area in which sellers can feasibly operate to distribute their products and within which purchasers will buy the products. The extent of the geographic market can be influenced by such factors as the size and strength of the particular sellers in the market, the availability and cost of transport, the mobility of consumers, and the perishability of the products: for example *Trade Practices Commission v Australian Meat Holdings Ltd* (1988) 83 ALR 299; ATPR ¶40-876. See also **Conglomerate merger; Functional market; Market; Market power; Misuse of market power; Product market; Substitutability.**

German banking system A banking system comprising a central bank, the Deutsche Bundesbank established in 1957, a few large commercial banks which operate nationwide branch systems, and a large number of smaller banks which operate at a regional or usually local level. The largest commercial banks are the Deutsche Bank, the Dresdner Bank and the Commerzbank (the 'big three'). There are also sixteen Landesbanks co-owned by the governments of the regional states and the savings banks. The banks are required to maintain capital adequacy ratios with the Bundesbank. German banks are active in the security markets, acting as issuing houses, brokers and dealers on the stock exchange.

Gesellschaft *German* – society. A term used by the German sociologist Ferdinand Tönnies to refer to a society in which individuals are bound together by legal (usually contractual) relations, as opposed to mutual social values and interests (*Gemeinschaft*). The term is often used to describe societies based on liberal philosophies. This idea was developed by Alice Tay and Eugene Kamenka in *Law and Social Control* (1980).

Gesellschaft mit beshränkter Haftung *Abbr* – GmbH A German and Swiss legal term denoting a private association whose members enjoy limited liability.

Gilt-edged stock Marketable, fixed-interest securities, issued and guaranteed by the British government. Before maturity, 'gilts' can be bought and sold on the London International Stock Exchange. A gilt-edged security is classified as short-dated if it has five years or less to run to the maturity or repayment date, medium-dated if it has five to ten years to run, and long-dated if it has ten years or more to run. The term gilt-edged may be colloquially applied to high-grade bonds issued by a company.

Glass ceiling A term used to describe the barriers to promotion that prevent female employees from reaching upper management levels. See also **Sex discrimination.**

Glass-Steagall Act An Act passed by the United States Congress in 1933 to separate commercial banking (making loans) from investment banking (underwriting securities). The Act established the Federal Deposit Insurance Corporation. This separation resulted from the discovery that during the 1920s, many banks had sold corporate securities at inflated prices and used the proceeds to repay bank loans. The banks pressed for the right to enter the securities market and, in 1989, the Federal Reserve Board allowed a banking company to handle the sale of a new issue of junk bonds. This was approved by the Securities and Exchange Commission, representing a new policy applying to all banks.

Global debenture A document executed by a corporation issuing or raising debt which evidences or acknowledges indebtedness to each person named for the amounts noted in a register, rather than an individual document being provided to each lender. By using a global debenture in this way, debentures may be issued and sold without reliance on a document which represents title to, or ownership of, the relevant debenture. Also known as 'paperless issue of debentures'. See also **Debenture**.

Global marketing Marketing in which all markets are served which offer scope for sale, there being no rigid distinction between domestic and export markets. Global marketing offers an opportunity for a much larger volume of production in which greatly reduced costs of production may be achieved. The prospects of improved profitability in the home market are increased, while overseas falling sales in one area may be offset by increasing sales in others.

Globalisation The process by which the world becomes a single marketplace. Already many links of this global trading economy are in place including capital adequacy guidelines, money market trading arrangements, re-insurance markets, international trade in equities, and the rulings of the International Accounting Standards Committee in relation to full disclosure in accounts.

Globex A computer-based system for worldwide electronic trading of futures and options, introduced by the Chicago Mercantile Exchange (CME) in conjunction with Reuters. By complementing the regular trading hours of the open outcry market, the system provides 24-hour trading of CME products. These products include interest rate and currency futures and options, stock-index futures and options. Globex has links with the New York, London, Paris and other exchanges.

GmbH See **Gesellschaft mit beschränkter Haftung**.

God's penny Historically, earnest money given by one party to another to indicate that the giver was committed to an agreement. It was common for such earnest money to be given to a servant when hired. See also **Earnest**.

Going concern A flourishing business with favourable key financial ratios, continuity of dividends, ability to pay creditors on due dates, ease of compliance with the terms of loan agreements, and ability to raise finance. Auditors may view a firm as a going concern if, in the absence of evidence to the contrary, the entity is expected to continue in operation without any intention or necessity to liquidate or to curtail significantly the scale of its operations: Australian Accounting Research Foundation Statement of Auditing Practice.

Going private The transformation of a public company into a private company by the process of purchasing its own shares. By going private a company may replace a previously extensive list of public investors with a limited number of selected shareholders. The purpose may be to revert to family control, ward off a takeover, or execute a leveraged buyout.

Going public The transformation of a private company into a public company meeting the requirements of the Corporations Law s 1264(1)(d) and the Australian Stock Exchange. The public may be invited to invest by taking shares and becoming members or by lending to the company and becoming creditors. See also **Flotation**; **Listed body**.

Gold clause A clause that purports to secure payment of the principal amount due under a bond according to the equivalent sum rendered in gold coin of a defined weight or fineness: *Feist v Société Intercommunale Belge D'Électricité* [1934] AC 161; [1933] All ER Rep 228. For example, an obligation to pay $100 in sterling gold coin of the standard weight or fineness existing on a particular date refers to the amount required to purchase $100 in gold coin on the given date. The amount varies with fluctuations in the price of gold; if the value of gold rises, so does the equivalent value of $100 in gold coin. The purpose of a gold clause is to protect the obligee against the effects of inflation and devaluation in the currency of payment: *Treseder-Griffin v Co-op Insurance Society Ltd* [1956] 2 QB 127; 2 All ER 33. A similar financial practice is the measuring of obligations in terms of the value of a specified foreign currency. See also **Bond**; **Consumer Price Index**; **Gold standard**.

Gold standard A monetary system in which each unit of currency is worth a fixed amount of gold. Under the rules of a strict gold standard, paper currency must be convertible at its face value into gold and a gold reserve must be maintained, fully sufficient to meet all demands placed upon it.

Golden handshake A gratuity payment given to employees in recognition of their services on retirement or resignation, or as compensation for the loss of employment by retrenchment due to redundancy. A golden handshake payment is taxed as an eligible termination payment: (CTH) Income Tax Assessment Act 1936 s 27A(1). See also **Eligible Termination Payment**; **Ex gratia payment**.

Good consideration Consideration that is sufficient in law to create legal relations. Although courts will not inquire into the adequacy of consideration, consideration must be sufficient for a binding contract to be formed: *Woolworths v Kelly* (1991) 22 NSWLR 189; 41 ASCR 431. See also **Adequacy of consideration**.

•**Good faith** Propriety or honesty.

Banking and finance Good faith is based on the distinction between a person who is honestly blundering and careless, and a person who has a suspicion that something is wrong but refrains from asking questions. The latter conduct amounts to bad faith or dishonesty: *Jones v Gordon* (1877) 2 App Cas 616. See also **Banker's standard of care**.

Bankruptcy A transaction entered into by a person, with a bankrupt, in good faith, concerning property acquired by the bankrupt after bankruptcy, which the bankrupt has no right to deal with, may still be valid: (CTH) Bankruptcy Act 1966 s 126(1). See also **After acquired property**; **Bankrupt**; **Discharge of bankruptcy**; **Insolvent**; **Preference**; **Uberrimae fidei**.

Sale of goods Generally, a person who acts in good faith is protected from the consequences of dealing with another person who is acting without good faith: for example (NSW) Sale of Goods Act 1923 s 5(2). For example, a buyer may acquire good title to goods even if the seller has defective title or no title at all, as long as the buyer contracts in good faith and without notice of the seller's defective title: for example (NSW) Sale of Goods Act 1923 s 27; *Gamer's Motor Centre (Newcastle) Pty Ltd v Natwest Wholesale Australia Pty Ltd* (1987) 163 CLR 236; 72 ALR 321.

Good faith, duty of See **Duty of fidelity**.

Good faith exchange A defence to a restitutionary claim which is available to a defendant who has acquired a benefit from the plaintiff under a contract in good faith and without notice of defects in the plaintiff's intention to confer the benefit which would otherwise entitle the plaintiff to rescind the contract and recover the benefit: *Babcock v Lawson* (1880) 5 QBD 284. See also **Bona fide purchase**; **Rescission**; **Restitution**.

Good root of title In relation to old system title an instrument of disposition dealing with or proving on the face of it (without the aid of extrinsic evidence) the ownership of the whole legal or equitable estate in the property sold, containing a description by which the land can be identified, and showing nothing to cast any doubt on the titles of the disposing parties: *Re Lemon and Davies' Contract* [1919] VLR 481 at 483. Under (NSW) Conveyancing Act 1919 s 53(1) the root of title must be at least 30 years old. See also **Old system title**.

•**Goods** Movable personal property, especially merchandise used in trade and commerce and requiring carriage from one place to another. The word 'good' is of very general and quite indefinite import: *The Noordam* [1920] AC 904 at 908.

Carriers **1.** Under (CTH) Customs Act 1901 s 4, includes ships, aircraft, and all movable personal property; and under (CTH) Customs Act 1901 s 229A includes cheques, but not cash. **2.** Under (CTH) Interstate Road Transport Act 1985 s 3, goods include ships, aircraft, and vehicles (including railway vehicles), animals (including fish), minerals (including petroleum), and gas. **3.** Under the Amended Hague Rules 1979 relating to sea carriage, 'goods' includes every description of wares, merchandise, and things, except live animals, and any cargo which by contract of carriage is stated as being carried on deck, and which is so carried: (NSW) Sea Carriage of Goods (State) Act 1921 s 3. See also **Carriage of dangerous goods**; **Carriage of goods**.

Insurance For the purposes of a life insurance policy, may include money: *Prudential Staff Union v Hall* [1947] KB 685. See also **Chattel**; **Insurable interest**; **Interest**.

Product liability **1.** Under trade practices legislation, personal property, which can include ships, aircraft, animals, fish, minerals, trees, crops, gas, and electricity: (CTH) Trade Practices Act 1974 s 4(1). **2.** In other consumer protection legislation, corporeal items of personal property, other than money: (NSW) Registration of Interests in Goods Act 1986 s 3(1); (VIC) Hire-Purchase Act 1959 s 2(1). See also **Action goods**; **Hire-purchase agreement**; **Services**; **Supply**.

Sale of goods Chattels personal, emblements, and things attached to or forming part of land which are agreed to be severed before sale or under a contract of sale, but does not include things in action or money: for example (NSW) Sale of Goods Act 1923 s 5(1). See also **Chattel**.

•**Goods and chattels** *OE – god* – goods; *Lat – catalla* – cattle; items of personal property. The words 'goods and chattels' are words of most extensive import. Unless controlled by the context, they comprise all the personal estate of whatsoever nature or description: *Bartlett v Bartlett* (1857) 1 De G & J 127 at 139; 44 ER 671. This may be tangible or intangible: *Re Baldwin* (1858) 2 De G & J 230 at 238; 144 ER 977. Also known as 'goods' alone. See also **Intangibles**; **Chattel**; **Personal property**; **Freehold**; **Chose in action**.

Goods and services A collective term for all physical commodities and activities that command a price, explicit or implicit, within the economy. Ultimately, service is the fundamental economic magnitude, since goods are valued for the services they deliver.

Goods and services tax *Abbr* – GST A consumption or value-added tax. A GST is a multistage levy collected on supplies of goods, services, and sales at all or nearly all stages of production and distribution. The tax applies only on the value added at each stage; the same value is never taxed twice.

Goods, carriage of See **Carriage of goods**.

Goods in transit Items transported from one jurisdiction to another by land, sea, or air. Goods in transit are subject to principles of private international law in respect of any action arising out of transit. See also **Bill of lading**; **Law of the flag**.

Goods in transit insurance Insurance taken out by a carrier, covering goods to be transported by it for the time they are being transported. Goods in transit insurance may cover either the full value of the goods or only the personal liability of the carrier if the goods are lost or damaged: *AMEV Finance Ltd v Mercantile Mutual Insurance Ltd (No 2)* [1988] 2 Qd R 351. In the former case, if the carrier recovers more than the loss suffered, it will hold the extra amount on trust for the owners: *Hepburn v A Tomlinson (Hauliers) Ltd* [1966] AC 451. Also known as 'warehouse to warehouse insurance'. See also **In transit**; **Liability insurance**.

Goods on consignment Goods sent by a consignor to a consignee on terms that the consignee will either sell the goods to some other party and account for the proceeds of sale to the consignor in due course, or, if the goods cannot be sold, return the goods to the consignor in accordance with the agreement. See also **Goods**.

Goods used in the manufacture Goods that are, in the manufacturing process, incorporated at least to some extent in the finished goods. Goods that are merely employed in the manufacturing process do not constitute goods used in manufacture: *Alcoa of Australia Ltd v Button* (1984) 2 FCR 13; 55 ALR 101.

•**Goodwill** Every positive advantage that has been acquired in carrying on a business which would give a reasonable expectancy of preference in the face of competition; the benefit and advantage of the good name, reputation, and connection of a business: *Inland Revenue Cmrs v Muller & Co's Margarine Ltd* [1901] AC 217. Goodwill has no independent existence; it must be attached to a business. It is indivisible, though its value when realised may be shared in proportions: *Geraghty v*

Minter (1979) 142 CLR 177; 26 ALR 141. See also **Asset**; **Business**; **Contract in restraint of trade**; **Restraint of trade**.

.gov In data communications, the code used to identify an Internet user as one operating (or belonging to) a government organisation. See also **.gov**; **Internet**.

Governing director A director who is vested with all or a significant portion of the powers which the articles of association would otherwise give to the board of the company. This is common in a small enterprise where the founder of the business wishes to keep control of a company formed to conduct the business. The requirement for a minimum of three directors for a public company (Corporations Law s 221) is not contravened by the appointment of a governing director, provided that another director has been appointed who is entitled to exercise the powers of the directors if the governing director ceases to occupy that position. The other director need not be able to exercise the same powers as the governing director: *Whitehouse v Carlton Hotel Pty Ltd* (1987) 162 CLR 285; 70 ALR 251. See also **Control**; **Director**; **Public company**.

•**Governing rules** In relation to a superannuation fund, approved deposit fund or a unit trust, any trust instrument, other document or legislation, or combination of these, governing the establishment and operation of the fund or unit trust: (CTH) Superannuation Industry (Supervision) Act 1993 s 10. See also **Approved deposit fund**; **Superannuation fund**; **Trust**; **Unit trust**.

•**Governor** The Queen's representative in each State. All powers and functions of the Queen in respect of a State are exercisable only by the Governor of the State, except the power to appoint and remove the Governor and the Queen's continued exercise of any of her powers and functions in respect of a State while she is personally present in the State: (CTH) Australia Act 1986 s 7(1)-(4). However, the Governor's exercise of those powers and functions is controlled by the Premier of the State: (CTH) Australia Act 1986 s 7(2), 7(3).

•**Grant** 1. To give a particular power, right, or sum of money to a person for a specified purpose. 2. A transfer of ownership of land in contrast to livery of seisin, which was actual delivery. Formerly the word grant was required in a conveyance of an incorporeal interest in land. 3. A Crown grant of land in fee simple or by long-term lease: (WA) Transfer of Land Act 1893 s 4(1).

•**Grantee** 1. One to whom interests or estates in land, privileges, or rights have been granted. 2. A party intended to benefit under a deed or other instrument. See also **Deed**; **Grantor**.

•**Grantor** One who grants lands, powers, or privileges to another. In granting estates or interests in land to another, the grantor may reserve certain rights and conditions or interests such as easements. See also **Easement**.

Gratuitous bailment A bailment that is solely for the benefit of the bailee: *Coggs v Bernard* (1703) 2 Ld Raym 909 at 912-15; 92 ER 107. For example, there is a gratuitous bailment when free repairs are performed on goods: *Tappenden v Artus* [1964] 2 QB 185 at 201. Delivery under a gratuitous bailment at will does not extinguish the merely possessory title of a bailor who was not the true owner: *Perpetual Trustees & National Executors of Tasmania Ltd v Perkins* (1989) Aust Torts Reports ¶80-295. See also **Bailment**; **Contractual bailment**.

Gratuitous carriage The carriage of passengers, their goods, and the goods of others, other than for reward. A carrier undertaking gratuitous carriage remains subject to the liabilities of a carrier, but a lower standard of care is applied in determining the responsibility for loss or damage sustained in the course of gratuitous carriage: *Port Swettenham Authority v T W Wu & Co (M) Sdn Bhd* [1979] AC 580. See also **Carriage of goods**; **Carriage of passengers**; **Carrier**.

Gratuitous services Services provided free of charge by private individuals to a person who has suffered injury from another's negligence, to assist that person in coping with the injuries. The amount of compensation payable for the injury is not necessarily reduced to take account of gratuitous services, as what is being compensated is the need to obtain certain services, not their actual cost: *Van Gervan v Fenton* (1992) 175 CLR 327; 109 ALR 283. See also **Damages**.

•**Gratuity** A gift. Gratuities are benefits received in circumstances where the recipient had no contractual right to receive the payment. Gratuities can be of a capital or income nature to the recipient. Such amounts will be assessable as income where they arise from the provision of personal services such as tips to a taxi driver (*Calvert v Wanwright* (1947) 27 TC 475) or are incidental to the recipient's income-producing activities such as awards to professional footballers (*Kelly v FCT* (1985) 85 ATC 4283). Where the gratuity is solely referable to a personal relationship between the donor and donee, the gratuity will be capital, notwithstanding the donee may have provided personal services to the donor and had been paid for those services, provided the payments for the personal services were adequate: *Scott v FCT* (1966) 117 CLR 514; 10 AITR 367; (CTH) Income Tax Assessment Act 1936 s 26(e). Amounts received by way of gratuities involving employment or the rendering of personal services are liable to be taxed. The definition of income from personal exertion in s 6(1) includes gratuities. Tax deductions may arise from the provision of gifts, pensions, and gratuities or receipt of retiring allowances: s 78(1)(a).

Greasy Wool Index *Abbr* – GWI An index maintained by the *Australian Financial Review* which compares wool prices in 1939 with the current year to provide a notional inflation factor.

Great Depression A long period of economic and family distress from 1929-35 which followed a crash on the New York Stock Exchange in October 1929. The crash was followed by innumerable liquidations of banks, factories and mines. About 25 million workers throughout the world became unemployed. Australia was badly affected and recovery was slow.

Green slip A term used to describe the certificate of insurance which all motor vehicle owners are required to obtain from a licensed insurer to cover them against liability in respect of personal injury, or loss or damage to property, sustained by a third party as a result of a motor vehicle accident: (NSW) Motor Accidents Act

1988; (VIC) Transport Act 1988; (QLD) Motor Vehicles Insurance Act 1936. See also **Compulsory third party insurance; Third party insurance**.

Greenback A colloquialism for the US dollar. The term derived from the colour of the ink used to print US currency. See also **Currency**.

Greenmail The payment of high prices by a company in the buying back of its shares from an unwelcome corporate raider. The practice may involve a corporate raider buying a strategic stake in a company, threatening to take control and then proceeding to extract a maximum price for the sale of those shares back to the company or a group friendly to the company.

Greenwood duty The duty owed to a bank by its customer to notify the bank promptly of any forged cheques purported to have been signed by the customer when the customer becomes aware of the forgeries: *Greenwood v Martins Bank Ltd* [1933] AC 51. See also **Macmillan duty**.

Gregory effect Named after an Australian National University economist, descriptive of the large swings in Australia's terms of trade consequent to Australia being mainly a primary products exporter. In boom periods, world commodities prices increase more rapidly than the prices of finished goods. The result is a switch of real income to primary producers at the expense of the nation's manufacturing industry. In a world recession, there is a disproportionate fall in commodity prices, the primary industries finding themselves with an excessive cost structure.

Gresham's law The principle that bad money drives out the good. It was derived from Sir Thomas Gresham an English financier of the sixteenth century who argued that if two coins are in circulation and their face value differs from their gold value, the more valuable coin was melted down and taken out of circulation. See also **Money; Money supply**.

Griffiths Committee Report The report entitled *Mergers, Takeovers and Monopolies: Profiting from Competition?* delivered by the House of Representatives Standing Committee on Legal and Constitutional Affairs in May 1989. The report recommended a major redrafting of the misuse of market power provisions in (CTH) Trade Practices Act 1974 s 46. It also advised against introducing compulsory pre-merger notification, and was opposed to removing of the former 'dominance' threshold in (CTH) Trade Practices Act 1974 s 50. Contrast with the Cooney Committee Report. See also **Acquisition; Cooney Committee Report; Dominance; Hilmer Report; Merger; Pre-merger notification; Restrictive trade practices; Substantially lessening competition; Swanson Committee Report**.

Griffiths formula A formulation in United States antitrust law of the permissible limits of the use of monopoly power. It prohibits the use of monopoly power to foreclose, to gain a competitive advantage, or to destroy a competitor: *United States v Griffith* (1948) 344 US 100. The formula is one of the ways in which United States antitrust law justifies imposing a duty to deal upon monopolists, especially those holding an essential facility. See also **Antitrust; Competition law; Duty to deal; Essential facility doctrine**.

Gross assets The total assets of an entity before any liabilities are deducted. See also **Asset; Entity; Liability; Net asset value**.

Gross domestic product *Abbr* – GDP The value of final goods and services produced within a country during a specified period, usually one year. GDP measured at market prices (the expenditure method) is an estimate of the total market value of goods and services produced, excluding those used up in production and before allowing for the depreciation of fixed capital. It is equivalent to gross national expenditure plus net exports. GDP measured at factor cost (the income method) is an estimate of the total cost of producing the gross national product. It is the sum of the gross payments made to the factors of production, natural resources, capital and labour including enterprise. GDP at factor cost equals GDP at market prices minus indirect taxes plus subsidies. GDP per capita is calculated by dividing GDP by the population.

Gross farm product That part of the gross domestic product which derives from agricultural production and services to agriculture. Gross non-farm product arises from production in all other industries.

Gross fixed capital expenditure *Abbr* – GFCE A widely used measure of aggregate investment, it embraces the public and private sectors, and both economic and social capital spending.

•**Gross income** The total income derived by a taxpayer, including all amounts that are ordinary income: (CTH) Income Tax Assessment Act 1936 s 25. See also **Assessable income; Income**.

Gross national expenditure *Abbr* – GNE Total expenditure on final goods and services produced within a country during a specified period, usually one year. GNE excludes goods and services used up in the process of production. It is equivalent to the gross domestic product (GDP) plus the value of imported goods and services, minus the value of exports. It is a measure of consumption and capital expenditure by both the private and public sector adjusted for changes in stocks. GNE and GDP growth may diverge if there is a change in net exports.

Gross national product *Abbr* – GNP Gross domestic product (GDP) plus net factor incomes from overseas, that is incomes accruing to Australians from their ownership of foreign assets minus payment to foreigners for their ownership of Australian assets. The GNP-GDP ratio shifts over time.

Gross negligence A conscious and voluntary act or omission performed without intent to cause death or grievous bodily harm but which involved such a great falling short of the standard of care which a reasonable person would have exercised and such a high risk that death or grievous bodily harm would follow that the act or omission merits criminal punishment: *Nydam v R* [1977] VR 430. Gross negligence causing death may amount to manslaughter: *Andrews v DPP* [1937] AC 576; 26 Cr App R 34; *R v Buttsworth* [1983] 1 NSWLR 658. The test for gross negligence is objective rather than subjective: *R v Buttsworth*. See also **Duty of care; Negligence**.

Gross pay The total earnings of an employee for a specific period, which could be weekly, fortnightly, or monthly, before any deductions such as income tax, union dues, garnishee, or other authorised deductions are made. See also **Garnishee; Tax instalment deduction**.

Gross profit method of estimating inventory A method of estimating inventory based on the gross profit realised on sales. It is calculated by determining the cost of goods available for sale by adding the opening inventory amount to the purchases made during the accounting period. Then the cost of goods sold is calculated by deducting from sales for the period the usual gross profit rate. The estimated inventory is calculated by subtracting the cost of goods sold from the cost of goods available for sale. See also **Estimating inventory**.

Gross returns The total receipts of a business concern. Gross returns are distinguished from 'profit or gain' on the basis that 'profit or gain' can only be ascertained by deducting from the receipts of a business the expenditure or obligations to which they have given rise or from which they have arisen: *Gresham Life Assurance Society v Styles* [1892] AC 309. See also **Business**.

Gross tax payable The amount of tax payable calculated by applying the general rates of tax for the entity concerned to the taxable income. It is the amount payable before rebates and credits have been subtracted. For individuals, the relevant rates are contained in (CTH) Income Tax (Rates) Act 1986 s 12(1), Sch 7. Also known as 'prime tax assessed'. See also **Credit; Net tax payable; Rebate; Taxable income**.

Ground lease A lease of vacant land or of land exclusive of any buildings erected upon it.

Groundage A levy on ships for entering and using harbour facilities charged according to the number of days the ship stays in port, and the size and tonnage of the ship. Also known as 'harbour dues'. See also **Customs duty**.

Grounds for review The recognised bases upon which an administrative decision may be subject to judicial review. Grounds for review include: breach of the rules of natural justice; a lack of procedural fairness; a lack of jurisdiction to make a decision; the non-authorisation of the decision by the enactment in pursuance of which it was purported to be made; an improper exercise of power where the decision purports to be made in pursuance of a power conferred by an enactment; an error of law whether or not the error appears on the face of the record of the decision; fraud; no evidence or other material to justify the making of the decision; or the making of a decision which was otherwise contrary to law: (CTH) Administrative Decisions (Judicial Review) Act 1977 ss 5, 6. Review on the merits of decisions under certain statutes is also provided: (CTH) Administrative Appeals Tribunal Act 1975. See also **Administrative Appeals Tribunal; Administrative Decisions (Judicial Review) legislation**.

•**Group accounts** The accounts that a parent entity must prepare for the economic entity of which it is the parent: Applicable Accounting Standard AASB 1024 para 11. The economic entity comprises the parent entity and all the entities which it controls. Also known as 'consolidated accounts'.

Group certificate A certificate issued by an employer to an employee in respect of the salary and wages of the employee: (CTH) Income Tax Assessment Act 1936 s 221A. See also **Group employer; Group tax; Tax instalment deduction**.

•**Group company** For income tax purposes, a company related to another company where one of the companies was a subsidiary of the other company for the whole year of income, or each company was a subsidiary of the same holding company during the whole of the year of income: (CTH) Income Tax Assessment Act 1936 s 80G. A group company may transfer a tax loss, a foreign tax credit, a net capital loss, or an asset to another group company. See also **Foreign tax credit; Net capital loss; Subsidiary; Rollover relief; Tax loss**.

Group directors holding statement A statement attached to the financial statements of a group of companies. In Australia, group accounts may only be published in a consolidated form. Corporations Law s 304 sets out the requirements for the directors' report which must be made by directors of a company which is not a chief entity and sets out the requirements for a report by directors of a chief entity. See also **Entity**.

Group employer An employer who ordinarily employs 10 or more employees. A group employer must register as a group employer: (CTH) Income Tax Assessment Act 1936 s 221F. An employer who is not required to register as a group employer may apply to do so: (CTH) Income Tax Assessment Act 1936 s 221F(3). A group employer is required to pay the amounts deducted at source from employees' salary, wages, leave and other termination payments to the Australian Taxation Office and to issue a group certificate to employees after the end of the financial year. See also **Group certificate; Eligible Termination Payment; Tax stamp system**.

Group holding company The parent company in a group of companies. The definition for 'group holding company' was removed from the Corporations Law in 1991 and replaced with the concepts of parent entity (Corporations Law s 294A) and chief entity (Corporations Law s 295(2)).

Group insurance An insurance scheme in which a number of persons are insured under a single policy. The policy is issued to the person or company responsible for the group (for example an employer), and a group certificate is issued to the individual group members (for example employees). In some professions, for example the legal profession, it is compulsory to belong to a group insurance scheme. See also **Joint insurance**.

•**Group of companies** 1. A holding company and its subsidiaries: (CTH) Sales Tax (Exemptions and Classifications) Act 1992 s 3A(1). 2. In AASB Accounting Standards AASB 1005, in defining 'financial reporting by segment', in relation to financial years ending on or after 31 December 1991, it refers to entities controlled by parent entities. See also **Holding company; Subsidiary**.

Group of Eleven *Abbr* – G11 A group of nations comprising the Group of Ten plus Switzerland. The G11 has agreed to lend if requested to the International Monetary Fund for the purposes of increasing the lending resources of that body. The scheme is known as the General Arrangements to Borrow. See also **Group of Ten**.

Group of Fifteen *Abbr* – G15 Formed in 1989, a group of fifteen nations establishing a developing nations forum that is smaller and less ponderous than the Non-Aligned Movement and the Group of Seventy Seven. The G15 comprises Algeria, Argentina, Brazil, Egypt, India, Indonesia, Jamaica, Malaysia, Mexico, Nigeria, Peru, Senegal, Venezuela, Yugoslavia and Zimbabwe. See also **Group of Seventy Seven**.

Group of Five *Abbr* – G5 A smaller grouping of the world's leading financial powers, namely the United States, Japan, Germany, Britain and France. It comprises the Group of Seven minus Italy and Canada.

Group of Seven *Abbr* – G7 The world's leading financial powers, namely the United States, Japan, Germany, Britain, France, Italy, and Canada. Meetings are held regularly by the G7 finance ministers and central bankers to coordinate actions in respect of exchange rates and other matters of international concern. The G7 nations work closely with the International Monetary Fund and the World Bank.

Group of Seventy Seven *Abbr* – G77 Formed in 1964, a group of less developed nations (actually over 100) who banded together to press for better terms of trade with the richer countries.

Group of Ten *Abbr* – G10 The ten major capitalist countries of the world namely Belgium, Canada, France, Germany, Italy, Japan, Netherlands, Sweden, United Kingdom, and the United States. Although they are members of the International Monetary Fund (IMF) and a branch of that body, they act less formally. The G10 meet from time to time when the need arises. They play an important role in the allocation of large IMF loans. Also known as 'Paris Club', since its first meeting was in Paris. See also **Group of Eleven**; **International Monetary Fund**.

Group of Thirty *Abbr* – G30 A group of international experts who undertook a review of clearing and settlement systems as a contribution to improved functioning of financial markets. The G30 report *Clearance and Settlement Systems in the World's Securities Markets* (1989) recommended a number of standards which have been accepted by most countries as desirable goals. The recommendations have been indorsed by the Reserve Bank of Australia. A steering committee chaired by the Australian Securities Commission has been established to oversee the adoption of the standards in Australia's equity markets.

Group tax The amount of tax deducted by employers from the employees' salaries and wages according to a tax schedule issued by the Tax Office. Tax deductions vary and depend on whether the employee has quoted a tax file number, is claiming a general exemption, or is entitled to a rebate. See also **Group certificate**; **Group employer**; **Rebate**; **Tax file number**; **Tax instalment deduction**.

•**Guarantee** A promise to answer for the debt, default, or miscarriage of another: *Bank of New South Wales v Permanent Trustee Co of New South Wales Ltd* (1943) 68 CLR 1; *Sunbird Plaza Pty Ltd v Maloney* (1988) 166 CLR 245; 77 ALR 205. In some Australian jurisdictions, no action may be brought on a guarantee unless it has been executed in writing by the guarantor: for example (VIC) Instruments Act 1958 s 126; (IMP) Statute of Frauds 1677 s 4 (as in force in WA and NT); (QLD) Property Law Act 1974 s 56. The principal creditor has no action against the guarantor if there has been no default by the principal debtor. In consumer credit law, it includes indemnities: (NSW) Credit Act 1984 s 5(1). See also **Debt**; **Guarantee**; **Guarantor**; **Indemnity**; **Statute of Frauds**.

Guarantee bond 1. A guarantee issued by a bank or surety company to guarantee the performance of a commercial contract, for example, the sale of goods or construction work, as opposed to a loan or other financial contract. Such guarantees include a performance bond, a bid and tender bond, an advance payment bond, a retention money bond and a maintenance bond. 2. A bond on which the capital and income return (ie the principal and interest) are guaranteed by a party other than the issuer. It includes guaranteed securities which involve preferred or common stocks when dividends are guaranteed. Guaranteed bonds or stocks become, in effect, debenture (unsecured) bonds of the guarantor. Also known as 'performance bond'.

Guarantee company See **Company limited by guarantee**.

Guaranteed dividend A specified minimum dividend promised by a company to be paid on shares for a certain period: for example *Re South Llanharran Colliery Co* (1897) 12 Ch D 503. The shareholder is like a lender in so far as he or she will be entitled to receive the minimum dividend. See also **Dividend**; **Profit**; **Share**.

Guaranteed freight Freight offered to a cargo owner on the basis that its amount or method of calculation will be fixed and not varied as a result of any exigencies of the carriage. Thus, a guaranteed freight rate will continue to apply even though the costs of carriage vary as a result of factors external to the contract of carriage. In such a case, the carrier assumes the risk of cost variations. See also **Freight**.

Guaranteed investment certificate A certificate exhibiting evidence that a specified amount has been deposited at a trust company for a predetermined period of time, usually five years, at a specific interest rate. Usually, the certificate cannot be redeemed prior to maturity.

•**Guarantor** A surety; a person who binds himself or herself to answer for the debt, default, or miscarriage of another. In contracts of guarantee, any clauses that derogate from the rights of the guarantor are construed *contra proferentum*: *Chan v Cresdon Pty Ltd* (1989) 168 CLR 242 at 257; 89 ALR 522. See also **Guarantee**; **Guarantor body**; **Guarantor corporation**.

•**Guarantor body** An organisation that binds itself to answer for the debt, default, or miscarriage of another. See also **Guarantee**; **Guarantor**.

•**Guarantor corporation** A corporation that binds itself to answer for the debt, default, or miscarriage of another. It is often a related corporation. See also **Guarantee; Guarantor.**

•**Guidelines** In administrative law, a term describing policy. Other terms describing policy include 'rules', 'circulars', 'principles', and 'schemes'. As policy, guidelines do not have the force of law unless the empowering legislation provides that they are binding. By contrast, statutory rules and other forms of delegated legislation have the force of law: *Smoker v Pharmacy Restructuring Authority* (1994) 36 ALD 1; 125 ALR 577. Where a decision is made in accordance with departmental guidelines and those guidelines do not accord with the legislation under which the decision is made, the decision will be invalid: *Green v Daniels* (1977) 13 ALR 1; *Re Secretary, Department of Social Security and Bosworth* (1989) 18 ALD 373.

•**Guild** An association of masters of a particular craft or trade, formed to regulate and supervise the practice of the craft or trade. The members of a guild tend to be independent artisans or tradespersons, so that it differs from an association of employees. See also **Trade union.**

H

Habeas corpus /heɪbɪəs kəpʊs/ *Lat* – have the body. Originally a type of writ issued by a superior court allowing a prisoner to have himself or herself removed from prison and be brought before the court to have the matter for which he or she was being detained determined. This type of proceeding became the method by which the Supreme Court could review decisions of justices or magistrates refusing bail or imposing excessive bail: *R v Rochford; Ex parte Harvey* (1967) 15 FLR 140. Proceedings for habeas corpus cannot be used as a means of appealing against a sentence or as a collateral attack on a conviction: *Ex parte Williams* (1934) 51 CLR 545; [1934] ALR 422. A writ of habeas corpus may be obtained from the High Court or a State or Territory Supreme Court, but not the Federal Court: (CTH) Administrative Decisions (Judicial Review) Act 1977 s 16. See also **Bail**; **Inferior court**.

Hacker A computer user who gains unauthorised entry to computer systems for the purpose of enjoyment, causing damage, or obtaining confidential information. Some jurisdictions have legislated against hacking: for example (NSW) Crimes Act 1900 s 309; (VIC) Summary Offences Act 1966 s 9A.

Hadley v Baxendale, rule in The basic rule governing the law of remoteness of damage in contract. The plaintiff may recover such damages as may fairly and reasonably be considered as arising naturally (that is, according to the usual course of things) from such breach of contract itself, or such as may reasonably be supposed to have been in the contemplation of both parties at the time they made the contract, as the probable result of its breach: *Hadley v Baxendale* (1854) 9 Ex 341; 156 ER 145; [1843-60] All ER 461. The rule in *Hadley v Baxendale* is a single rule with two limbs: *Commonwealth v Amann Aviation Pty Ltd* (1991) 174 CLR 64; 104 ALR 1. The rule contrasts general damages on the one hand with special damages on the other. See also **Breach of contract**; **Damages**; **General damages**; **Remoteness**; **Special damages**.

Hague Rules 1924 The International Convention for the Unification of Certain Rules of Law relating to Bills of Lading 1924, a convention governing the carriage of goods by sea under contracts of carriage entered into before 31 October 1991, by identifying the rights, liabilities, and duties of carriers and owners of cargo. The Convention came into force on 25 August 1924. It was given force in Australia by the (CTH) Sea Carriage of Goods Act 1924 (repealed). It was subsequently amended by the Protocol (1979) amending the International Convention for the Unification of Certain Rules Relating to Bills of Lading of 25 August 1924, as amended by the Protocol of 23 February 1968. See also **Amended Hague Rules 1979**; **Bill of lading**; **Carriage by sea**; **Carrier**.

Haircut In banking and finance, the difference between the market value of a security and its collateral value. Haircuts are taken by a lender of funds in order to protect the lender, should the need arise to liquidate the collateral, from losses owing to depreciation in the market value of the security. See also **Collateral**; **Liquidity risk**; **Margin**.

Half-secret trust A trust whose bare existence, but not its details, is disclosed in the legal document creating it, such as a will or trust instrument. In such a trust, the beneficiaries are known but not disclosed on the face of the legal document: *Blackwell v Blackwell* [1929] AC 318; *Re Fleetwood* (1880) 15 Ch D 594; *Cullen v A-G for Ireland* (1866) LR 1 HL 190 at 198; *Voges v Monaghan* (1954) 94 CLR 231 at 233, 235. Also known as 'semi-secret trust'. See also **Incorporation by reference**; **Trustee**.

•**Half-truth** Information or a statement which is ultimately rendered incorrect as it does not set out the whole of the relevant information. Conduct may be misleading or deceptive where the overall impression conveyed is not correct: for example (CTH) Trade Practices Act 1974 s 52; *Collins Marrickville Pty Ltd v Henjo Investments Pty Ltd* (1987) 72 ALR 601; ATPR ¶40-782. See also **Misleading or deceptive conduct**; **Misrepresentation**.

Half-yearly accounts In corporations law, accounts for the first six months of a financial year: Corporations Law ss 50A(2), (5). Half yearly accounts must be prepared by a disclosing entity in addition to full year accounts: s 11AO. See also **Disclosing entity**; **Listing requirements**.

Hamburg Rules 1978 International rules relating to the liability of carriers to cargo owners for loss or damage to goods carried under a contract of carriage of goods by sea (United Nations Convention on the Carriage of Goods by Sea (Hamburg Rules) 1971 art 1), set out in the (CTH) Carriage of Goods by Sea Act 1991 Sch 2. The Hamburg Rules 1978 are scheduled to come into force in Australia on 31 October 1997 unless parliament passes a resolution that they be repealed or reconsidered: (CTH) Carriage of Goods by Sea Act 1991 s 2(3). See also **Amended Hague Rules 1979**.

Hammer 1. An announcement by the Australian Stock Exchange that a member is unable to meet his or her obligations. Such a member is said to be 'hammered' and trading by the member must cease until the debts are repaid. The hammer price is the market value of the relevant securities at the time of the default of the member firm. **2.** To sell large quantities of a share in the market at the one time, depressing the price of the share. See also **Australian Stock Exchange Ltd**; **Default**.

Hancock Committee A Committee of Review into Australian industrial relations law and arbitration systems. The 'Report of the Committee of Review on Australian Industrial Relations Law and Systems', in three volumes, was published in 1985. The Hancock Committee substantially advocated continuing a centralised, tribunal-based industrial relations system, and rejected the suggestion that constitutional powers should be used in order to increase federal legislative power. The report of the Committee led to the implementation of (CTH) Industrial Relations Act 1988 which replaced the Australian Conciliation and Arbitration Commission with the Australian Industrial Relations Commission, and also introduced a system of certified agreements, enabling parties to reach their own terms for an industrial settlement. See also **Australian Industrial Relations Commission; Certified agreement; Industrial relations; Industrial relations system.**

Hang Seng Index A composite stock index of prices on the Hong Kong Stock Exchange. See also **Hong Kong Stock Exchange.**

Harakiri bidding A practice of Japanese companies attempting to gain a market share. Software design or computer hardware is offered virtually free as a means of gaining access to a potentially large, lucrative market. One yen tenders may be submitted.

•**Hardship** Adverse repercussions, whether mental or physical, ranging from temporary discomfort or inconvenience to some permanent and unalterable evil or misfortune. See also **Undue hardship.**

Equity Courts have the discretion to refuse to grant a decree of specific performance where such a decree would cause hardship to the defendant: *Slee v Warke* (1949) 86 CLR 271. See also **Undue hardship.**

•**Harsh, unjust or unreasonable** A term used to describe the dismissal of an employee without a valid reason, or valid reasons, connected with the employee's capacity, or conduct, or based on the operational requirements of the undertaking, establishment, or service: (CTH) Industrial Relations Act 1988 s 170DE. The test is an objective one, applied using the natural meaning of the words: *AWU-FIME Amalgamated Union and Farrell v Conagra Wool Pty Ltd* (1995) ¶3-015. See also **Reinstatement; Termination; Unconscionable; Unfair dismissal; Wrongful dismissal.**

•**Hawker** A person who travels from place to place selling goods. A hawker includes a person who travels day by day from market to market but sells for some part of the day from a fixed place at each market: *Attorney-General (ACT); Ex rel Olaseat Pty Ltd v ACT Minister for Environment, Land and Planning* (1993) 43 FCR 329; 115 ALR 161. In most States and Territories, hawkers require a licence to trade: for example (NSW) Hawkers Act 1974 s 5. See also **Pedlar; Sale of goods.**

Hawking of securities The prohibited act of going from place to place offering new, or existing, securities of a corporation for subscription, or purchase: Corporations Law s 1078(1). See also **Securities; Prospectus.**

Head bailee 1. The bailee in the original bailment where there has been a sub-bailment. 2. Where there has been a series of sub-bailments, the bailee in the immediately prior bailment, that is the head bailee will be the sub-bailor in the sub-bailment in question. See also **Bailment; Head bailment; Head bailor; Sub-bailment.**

Head bailment 1. Where there has been a sub-bailment, the original bailment. 2. Where there has been a series of sub-bailments, the immediately prior bailment. See also **Bailment; Head bailee; Head bailor; Sub-bailment.**

Head bailor 1. Where there has been a sub-bailment, the bailor in the original bailment. 2. Where there has been a series of sub-bailments, the bailor in the immediately prior bailment. See also **Bailment; Head bailee; Head bailment; Sub-bailment.**

Heads of damage 1. The different categories of damages that a plaintiff may be entitled to recover in a civil action. 2. The types of loss which the law recognises as being compensable, such as loss of consortium, loss of earnings, loss of profits, loss of chance and loss of bargain.

Contract The various types of damages that a plaintiff may recover for breach of contract. The expressions 'expectation damages', 'damages for loss of profits', 'reliance damages', and 'damages for wasted expenditure' are manifestations of the principle that a plaintiff is to be put in the same position as if the contract had been performed, rather than discrete and truly alternative measures of damages that a party not in breach may elect to claim: *Commonwealth v Amann Aviation Pty Ltd* (1991) 174 CLR 64; 104 ALR 1. See also **Damages; Loss of expectation of life; Loss of bargain; Loss of a chance; Damages for loss of profits; Reliance interest; Restitution.**

Tort The various types of damage for which a plaintiff may be entitled to compensation as a result of being injured by a tortious act or omission. They are not the injuries themselves but the damage suffered as a consequence of sustaining injuries. They include loss of earning capacity, loss of competitiveness in seeking and retaining employment, hospital and medical expenses, loss of ability to perform certain domestic duties, and non-pecuniary losses (including pain and suffering, loss of amenities, and loss of expectation of life). See also **Loss of earning capacity; Damages for loss of profits; Non-pecuniary loss.**

Health insurance Liability undertaken with respect to the provision of hospital treatment or ancillary health benefits: (CTH) National Health Act 1953 s 67(4). Health insurance is most commonly associated with indemnity against the loss arising out of a liability to pay the fees associated with medical treatment. Health insurance does not include contracts for accident and sickness insurance or liability insurance: s 67(4).

•**Hearing** A proceeding, conducted by a court, tribunal or administrator with a view to resolving issues of fact or law, in which oral evidence may be taken and documentary and real evidence tendered. A hearing may be by way of oral or written submission. Legal representation may not be necessary, or even permitted. See also **Hearing rule; Trial.**

•**Hearing on the merits** A hearing in which the issues of fact or law, or both, between the parties are fought out to a final conclusion binding upon the parties: *Bridie v Messina* (1965) 66 SR (NSW) 446 at 453. There must be an investigation of the merits of the matter: *Fehon v Wallin* (1985) 17 A Crim R 364. There is no hearing on the merits where the proceedings have come to a halt because there has been a withdrawal of proceedings, want of jurisdiction, a failure to comply with some procedural step, or a defect in the information or charge. There is a hearing on the merits where a plea of autrefois acquit has been sustained, for an acquittal by direction, or the offering of no evidence on the hearing of the charge: *R v Turner* [1980] 1 NSWLR 19.

Hearing rule In administrative law, the principle that a decision maker must afford a person whose interests will be adversely affected by a decision an opportunity to present his or her case. The hearing rule is based on the maxim *audi alteram partem*. Breach of the principle by the decision maker is a denial of procedural fairness. Judicial review of the decision on this ground renders the decision void: *Kioa v Minister for Immigration and Ethnic Affairs* (1985) 159 CLR 550; 62 ALR 321. Also known as 'audi alteram partem rule'. See also **Hearing**.

Heavy cargo Cargo which has a high mass by comparison with its volume. Specifically, cargo which weighs in excess of one ton per 40 cubic feet, or in excess of one tonne per 35 cubic metres. See also **Cargo**.

Hedger See **Hedging**.

Hedging A technique of reducing or eliminating the risk of loss caused by price, interest rate or foreign currency exchange rate fluctuations, by establishing offsetting positions. See also **Buying hedge; Long hedger; Option; Securities; Switching**.

Heritage conservation rebate An income tax rebate for approved expenditure on conservation work on heritage listed buildings and structures. The rebate amount is equal to 20 per cent of the expenditure, but the expenditure must be over $5000 and a final certificate must be obtained from the relevant Minister: (CTH) Income Tax Assessment Act 1936 s 159UQ. Heritage conservation work includes the conservation, maintenance, preservation, or restoration of a building of cultural significance and listed on the heritage register: s 159UB. See also **Rebate**.

Hidden charges Required payments that are not disclosed or clearly explained to customers entering into agreements and contracts. Examples are interest charged from the date of approval of a loan rather than the date on which the loan is actually advanced, solicitors' and other fees required in addition to application and processing fees, running charges, government charges, additional stamp duties and exit charges. Some of these may be mentioned in the fine print of a contract in unquantified form.

High Court Justice A justice of the High Court of Australia: (CTH) High Court of Australia Act 1979 s 4; (CTH) High Court Justices (Long Leave Payments) Act 1979 s 3. See also **Chief justice; Judge; Justice**.

High Court of Australia Australia's highest court. The High Court of Australia is established pursuant to the Commonwealth Constitution Ch III s 71. It has original and appellate jurisdiction, set out primarily in Commonwealth Constitution ss 73, 75, 76 and (CTH) Judiciary Act 1903 ss 30-35A. The High Court of Australia has original jurisdiction over certain matters and the discretion to hear appeals from a single High Court justice exercising original jurisdiction, and other federal courts and State supreme courts: ss 73, 75, 76. The court's most prominent role is as guardian and interpreter of the Commonwealth Constitution. As the ultimate judicial arbiter in Australia, the court is a powerful organ of government. The court normally sits in Canberra, but may sit in other capital cities for short periods of each year. The High Court of Australia comprises the Chief Justice and six justices appointed by the Governor-General: (CTH) High Court Act 1979 s 5. See also **Chief Justice**.

High gearing In corporations law, the heavy reliance and use of long-term borrowing (debt) to finance the acquisition of assets by an entity. It is measured as a ratio of debt finance to equity finance and expressed as a percentage. See also **Gearing**.

High technology company A company engaged in high technology industry. A high technology company is usually associated with high risk and venture capital arrangements. See also **Seed capital**.

Hilmer Report The report of the National Competition Policy Review, entitled *National Competition Policy*, which made recommendations for sweeping structural reform of government and semi-government business. One of the most important elements of the report was the principle of competitive neutrality, requiring all market players to be subject to the same regulatory and other requirements imposed on them when competing in the one market. The Hilmer Report was implemented by the (CTH) Competition Policy Reform Act 1995 and all the States and Territories have agreed to pass complementary legislation: for example (ACT) Competition Policy Reform Act 1996; (NSW) Competition Policy Reform (New South Wales) Act 1995; (QLD) Competition Policy Reform (Queensland) Act 1996; (SA) Competition Policy Reform (South Australia) Act 1996; (VIC) Competition Policy Reform (Victoria) Act 1995. See also **Competition; Competition law; Competitive neutrality; Cooney Committee Report; Griffiths Committee Report; Market; Swanson Committee Report**.

•**Hinder** To interfere with for the purpose of delaying a person or thing.

Trade and commerce To in any way affect, to an appreciable extent, the ease of the usual way of supply of goods or services: *Tenants (Lancashire) Ltd v Wilson & Co Ltd* [1917] AC 495; *Devenish v Jewel Food Stores Pty Ltd* (1991) 172 CLR 32; 99 ALR 275. A person must not hinder the supply or acquisition of goods or services by a corporation where the conduct would have the effect of substantially lessening competition in a market: (CTH) Trade Practices Act 1974 s 45D(1). See also **Substantially lessening competition**.

Hinder or prevent In the context of (CTH) Trade Practices Act 1974 s 45D, a phrase raising a causation issue where a secondary boycott is imposed on the supply of goods and services. Conduct hindering or preventing can be engaged in by threat, verbal intimidation, or physical interference. An example is a picket. See also **Secondary boycott; Substantially lessening competition**.

•**Hire** To lend to another for consideration the possession and use of goods for a particular period or purpose. Title to the goods throughout the hire period remains with the owner: for example (VIC) Hire-Purchase Act 1959 s 2. See also **Consideration; Hire-purchase; Ownership**.

• **Hire purchase** A method of acquiring goods, normally plant and durables, by instalment payments: (NSW) Registration of Interests in Goods Act 1986 s 3. Hire purchase is governed generally by State and Territory legislation: for example (NSW) Credit Act 1984 (repealed) s 13; (VIC) Hire-Purchase Act 1959 (repealed) (replaced by the Uniform Consumer Credit Code. See also **Bailment; Hire purchase agreement; Ownership**.

• **Hire purchase agreement** A contract in which goods are to be transferred by means of hire purchase. Hire purchase involves the owner hiring the goods to another person (the hirer) who, as well as receiving possession of the goods, is given an option to purchase them at a future time: (CTH) Income Tax Assessment Act 1936 s 674(1). Until the hirer has exercised the option to purchase, property in the goods remains with the owner. All States and Territories have legislation governing the form and content of, and the rights and duties of the parties to, hire-purchase agreements: for example (VIC) Hire-Purchase Act 1959. In New South Wales and the Australian Capital Territory, a hire purchase agreement is deemed to be a credit sale contract under the consumer credit legislation: (NSW) Credit Act 1984 (repealed) s 13 (replaced by Uniform Consumer Credit Code). In most other States, separate legislation deals with hire purchase agreements: for example (VIC) Hire-Purchase Act 1959. The use of hire purchase agreements has declined with the introduction of credit legislation under which title passes at the time of sale, with the buyer then obliged to pay by instalments with interest over an agreed period. See also **Hire purchase**.

• **Hirer 1.** One who obtains the services of another or the use of something for an agreed reward: for example (NSW) Registration of Interests in Goods Act 1986 s 3; (QLD) Hire Purchase Act 1959 s 2(1); (VIC) Hire Purchase Act 1959 s 2. A hirer includes any person to whom the hirer's rights and obligations under the agreement have been assigned: (VIC) Hire Purchase Act 1959 s 2(1). **2.** One who is willing to provide his or her services or make available something for use by another for an agreed reward. See also **Dealer; Goods; Hiring; Hire-purchase agreement; Owner**.

• **Hiring 1.** The act of obtaining the services of another or the use of something for an agreed reward. **2.** The act of providing services to another, or the use of something to another, for reward: for example (NSW) Cinematograph Films Act 1935 s 2. See also **Hirer**.

Historical beta In the context of the futures and shares market, a ratio which estimates the historical variability between a specific commodity price and a related composite index. If, for example, silver was to go up 10 per cent and the precious metals index was to go up five per cent, the silver's beta would be 2:1, being the ratio 10:5. See also **Accounting beta**.

Historical cost The cost or price paid for an asset at its original purchase without any subsequent adjustment for inflation or movements in current selling or replacement costs. See also **Current cost**.

Historical cost accounting A basis of accounting where values used represent historical values or the net worth of the relevant items as at a particular date or for a particular period, being the time or times at which an item was incurred, received or made payable. A balance sheet shows in monetary terms the capital, reserves and liabilities of a company as at the date at which it is prepared. A profit and loss account shows the difference between the revenue for the period covered by the account and the expenditure chargeable in that period. Items are brought into account at their monetary value as recorded when they were received or expended: Australian Accounting Standard 2. See also **Accounting standards; Historical cost; Profit-and-loss account**.

Hi-tech industrial development Development in the areas of biotechnology, computer software, industrial ceramics, medical engineering and solar energy. Australian governments and companies have focused on these areas for strategic development and growth.

Hoardings 1. Things accumulated, held, or hidden, such as money or goods, especially in time of scarcity. **2.** Temporary fences along the side of a highway, frequently used for posting advertisements; sometimes used to refer to specific structures for posting advertisements: for example (VIC) Transport Act 1983 s 2. See also **Savings**.

• **Holder 1.** A person who has been granted something and retains it for the time being. The term arises in a number of contexts: for example (CTH) Migration Act 1958 s 4; (NSW) Mining Act 1992 s 84; (VIC) Land Act 1958 s 163; (QLD) Mineral Resources Act 1989 s 1.8. **2.** A person who is given permission to do some act by way of a licence: for example a motor dealer's licence (NSW) Motor Dealers Act 1974 s 4. See also **Prescribed interest holder**.

Bills of exchange and other negotiable instruments The payee or indorsee of a bill of exchange, promissory note or cheque payable to order, who is in possession of it; or the bearer of a bill of exchange, promissory note or cheque payable to bearer: (CTH) Bills of Exchange Act 1909 s 4; (CTH) Cheques and Payment Orders Act 1986 s 3(1). To be a holder requires a valid negotiation from the immediately preceding person in possession of the bill: *Wood v McMahon* (1877) 3 VLR (L) 282. See also **Bearer; Bill of exchange; Holder for value; Holder in due course; Payee**.

Holder for value In relation to the acceptor and all who become parties to a bill of exchange prior to such time, the holder of a bill of exchange where valuable consideration has at any time been given for the bill: (CTH) Bills of Exchange Act 1909 s 32(2); *Walsh, Spriggs, Nolan and Finney v Hoag & Bosch Pty Ltd* [1977] VR 178 at 180; (1976) 12 ALR 411. See also **Bill of exchange; Holder; Holder in due course**.

Holder in due course A holder of a negotiable instrument, taking it as complete and regular on its face. The requirements are that the person: became holder before the instrument was overdue or stale, without notice of its dishonour; took in good faith for value; had no notice of any defect in title when it was negotiated; and, in the case of a cheque, it did not bear a crossing with the words 'not negotiable': (CTH) Bills of Exchange Act

1909 s 34(1); (CTH) Cheques and Payment Orders Act 1986 s 50. See also **Bill of exchange**; **Defect in title**; **Holder**; **Holder for value**; **Not negotiable**.

Holder of a bill The payee or indorsee of a bill who is in possession of it or, in the case of a bill which is payable to bearer, the bearer of it: (CTH) Bills of Exchange Act 1909 s 4. A bearer is a person in possession of a bill which is payable to bearer: s 4. The holder of a bill, who has a right to sue, may sue in that person's own name: s 43(1)(a); *Stock Motor Ploughs Ltd v Forsyth* (1932) 32 SR (NSW) 259 at 262; 49 WN (NSW) 61. Also known as 'bearer of a bill'. See also **Holder**; **Holder for value**; **Holder in due course**; **Indorsement**.

•**Holding** 1. Possession of property that has been granted to a holder. 2. The decision of a court.

Taxation and revenue For the purposes of the substantiation rules, owning or leasing a car by a taxpayer for use in the course of gaining or producing assessable income, or using a car in carrying on a business for that purpose: (CTH) Income Tax Assessment Act 1936 ss 82KS-82KZBB, Sch 2A cll 11-13. See also **Assessable income**; **Car**; **Holding period**; **Substantiation**; **Underlying business percentage**; **Year of income**.

•**Holding company** A company holding a controlling interest in one or more other companies through the ownership of shares. Subsidiaries may be partly or wholly owned: Corporations Law s 9. See also **Approving holding company**; **Group holding company**; **Merger**; **Parent company**; **Subsidiary**.

•**Holding out** The act of a person representing themselves (or allowing themselves to be represented) as a partner of a firm, whether by words or conduct. Where a third party gives credit to the firm based on a person holding themselves out as a partner, that person is liable as a partner to that third party: for example (VIC) Partnership Act 1958 s 18(1). Whether words or conduct amount to a representation of partnership is a question of fact: *Bryant Bros v Thiele* [1923] SASR 393. Holding out is a branch of the law of estoppel. See also **Apparent authority**; **Apparent partner**; **Estoppel**.

Holding period For the purposes of determining the fringe benefit tax liability of the employer for car benefits, the time during the tax year in which a car is held by an employee: (CTH) Fringe Benefits Tax Assessment Act 1986 Pt III Div 2 ss 10, 19. See also **Holding**; **Underlying business percentage**.

Holey dollar Together with the Dump, Australia's first official coin. See also **Currency**.

Hollow log reserves Financial reserves, property and other assets accumulated by public bodies over a number of years.

Home banking An emerging arrangement allowing a person with a home computer to operate directly on a bank account over the telephone making deposits, paying bills, shifting funds between accounts, and investing, without the need to make any physical contact with a bank or to use cheques.

Home branch In the context of the presentation of a cheque, the branch of the drawee bank where the account is held on which the cheque is drawn. The home branch is a proper place to present a cheque 'over the counter' where there is no place specified in the cheque: (CTH) Cheques and Payment Orders Act 1986 s 64. See also **Counter presentation**; **Draw**; **Drawee bank**; **Presentment**.

Home equity conversion scheme An arrangement in which the owner of a residence sells equity in the residence in whole or part while retaining the right to live there. In a 'sell and stay' scheme, a person sells the family home but retains the right to live in it for life. Another arrangement involves a limited conversion of the family home into cash, with substantial ownership being retained. Interest is capitalised while the size of the loan grows. The lender's share in the equity of the home will continue to grow over time to its full market value unless preceded by the death or departure of the occupant, when the full amount outstanding must be repaid.

•**Home exchange** The exchange on which a body corporate is listed and which has been designated, for the purposes of the listing rules of the Australian Stock Exchange, as the body's home exchange: Corporations Law s 603. Where a listed organisation is required to make, or to lodge, documents for the information of the market, it is generally required that they be made to, or lodged with, the home exchange: s 674(1). See also **Australian Stock Exchange Ltd**; **Exchange**.

•**Home finance contract** A contract under which credit is provided for the acquisition, erection or alteration of a home, the acquisition of land on which to build a home, the discharging of a liability under a home finance contract, or a credit contract where a series of credit contracts are involved the first of which relates to home finance: for example (NSW) Credit (Home Finance Contracts) Act 1984 (repealed) s 4; (VIC) Credit Act 1984 (repealed) s 150 (replaced by Uniform Consumer Credit Code). Only New South Wales and the Australian Capital Territory have legislation governing aspects of home finance. See also **Credit provider**; **Housing loan**; **Mortgage**.

Home loan insurance An insurance scheme designed to provide financial support should a mortgage of an owner-occupied home be retrenched or become redundant. A typical policy will meet monthly home repayments for 12 months, the first six months at 100 per cent and the second at 50 per cent. See also **Mortgage**.

Home office A room at home set aside and used exclusively as a place of business. Taxpayers may claim deductions for expenses relating to the running of such an office. There are two categories of expenses: running expenses (which covers heating, cooling, lighting and depreciation of a professional library or equipment); and occupancy expenses (such as rent, mortgage payments, and running expenses). Occupancy expenses are claimable only if the home is used exclusively as a place of business. See also **Home office expense**.

Home office expense An expense relating to the use or ownership of a home or part of a home for business or income producing purposes: *Thomas v FCT* (1972) 3 ATR 165; *Federal Cmr of Taxation v Faichney* (1972) 129 CLR 38; 3 ATR 435. To be deductible, the part of the home used must be characterised as a 'place of business'. See also **Allowable deduction**; **Home office**.

Home unit company A company formed for the purpose of purchasing and holding land upon which a home unit building stands. Home unit company shares are divided into blocks or classes, giving the owner of a block or class the right to occupy a particular home unit within the building: *New South Wales Medical Defence Union v Crawford* (1993) 31 NSWLR 469 at 520. A home unit company's articles of association include most matters dealt with in the by-laws of the body corporate of a strata scheme. Strata schemes have been preferred to home unit companies since the early 1960s. See also **Articles of association**.

•**Honest and reasonable mistake** An incorrect judgment made without guile. An honest and reasonable mistake of fact or law may be a defence: *Davids Securities Pty Ltd v Commonwealth Bank of Australia* (1992) 175 CLR 353; 109 ALR 57; 66 ALJR 768; 24 ATR 125. An honest and reasonable mistake of fact is an exculpatory ground in cases where actual knowledge is an element of the offence: *R v Tolson* (1889) 23 QBD 168; *He Kaw Teh v R* (1985) 157 CLR 523; 60 ALR 449. See also **Mistake; Mistake of fact; Mistake of law**.

Hong Kong Bank of Australia A foreign bank and wholly-owned subsidiary of the Hong Kong and Shanghai Banking Corporation. It was established in Australia in 1985 as one of 16 foreign banks granted banking licences by the Commonwealth government. Hong Kong Bank of Australia offers a wide range of financial services to the Australian corporate market including underwriting, mining finance, stockbroking, funds management, merchant and investment banking, international trade finance and advice on privatisation. See also **Foreign bank; Merchant bank**.

Hong Kong Stock Exchange A small stock market with fewer than 300 quoted companies, of which only 12 are foreign. Established in 1989, the Securities and Futures Commission oversees the stock exchange and the futures exchange. It sets rules on capital adequacy for brokers, enforcing disclosure of all shareholdings, investigates fraud and stock manipulation and has power to proceed against inside trading. The Hang Seng Index monitors prices on the exchange. See also **Hang Seng Index**.

Honorarium *Lat* – honorary. A payment for services given voluntarily. **1.** An honorary reward as in recognition of professional services on which no price may be set. **2.** A fee for services rendered by a professional person.

Honorary trust In United States law, a trust to devote money to a non-charitable purpose, where there is no beneficiary to enforce that purpose. A court in the United States may enforce such an obligation: *Stoffels Estate* 295 Pa 248 (1929). See also **Purpose trust; Trust**.

Honour 1. An historical term synonymous with feodum. **2.** A courtesy title given to judges and justices. **3.** Acceptance of a bill of exchange for payment.

Bills of exchange and other negotiable instruments The act of the drawee accepting a bill which has been presented to him or her for acceptance or the act of the drawee or the acceptor paying the amount due on a bill which has been presented by the holder of it for payment. Non-acceptance of a bill presented for acceptance is known as 'dishonour by non-acceptance': (CTH) Bills of Exchange Act 1909 s 48(1). See also **Dishonour by non-acceptance; Presentation for acceptance; Presentation for payment**.

Honour clause A clause that declares that an agreement is not to be legally binding, with the result that the agreement is binding in honour only: for example *Rose and Frank Co v J R Crompton & Bros Ltd* [1923] 2 KB 261. Honour clauses are rare, and may be used where the parties are prepared to rely on non-legal sanctions, such as their ongoing commercial dealings with each other, as an inducement to performance. An honour clause indicates that the mutual intention of the parties was not to enter contractual relations. See also **Contract; Express intention; Intention; Term**.

Hopkinson v Rolt, rule in See **Tacking**.

Horizontal arrangement In competition law, an arrangement entered into by corporations on the same functional level in a distribution chain. It is contrasted with a vertical arrangement. See also **Arrangement; Competition; Functional market**.

Horizontal merger A merger between two or more market participants at the same functional level of the market. See also **Functional market; Merger**.

Horizontal privity The privity of contract, if any, that exists between the last commercial supplier of a product and the person who acquired it. See also **Diagonal privity; Privity of contract**.

•**Horticulture** See **Agriculture**.

•**Hostilities** Armed conflict fought without any formal declaration of war. See also **Occupation**.

Insurance Perils arising from hostilities are often excluded from the risks undertaken under insurance policies.

•**Hotchpot** A pudding; something consisting of blended parts.

Contract The bringing to account of any previous distributions when determining the current distribution of a fund. The general object of hotchpot clauses in settlements is to secure equality when advances have been made by way of appointment or otherwise: *Re Blume* [1959] Qd R 95 at 118-9. See also **Settlement**.

Equity **1.** Originally, the mixing, blending and division into equal parts among daughters, of lands given in frankmarriage and of lands descending in fee simple. Hotchpot has been abolished in New South Wales and Western Australia for both intestate and partially intestate estates and in Queensland for intestate estates. **2.** The mixing and blending of property belonging to different persons into a common fund, in order to achieve equity among various claimants against the fund. See also **Contribution; Fee simple**.

•**Hotel broker** Any person who, for reward, exercises or carries on business as an agent for selling, buying, exchanging, otherwise dealing with, or disposing of, negotiating for the sale, purchase, exchange, or any other dealing with, or disposition of, or compiling for publication, or compiling and publishing, a document that contains a list relating solely, or substantially to, the acquisition, or disposal, by any person of hotel business: (NSW) Property, Stock and Business Agents Act 1941 s 3(1). See also **Licence**.

House bill of lading A receipt for goods issued by a forwarding agent. It is not a true bill of lading: *Carrington Slipways Pty Ltd v Patrick Operations Pty Ltd* (1991) 24 NSWLR 745. See also **Bill of lading**.

House company A company formed by a sharebroking firm to act as a holder of securities acquired by the firm on its own account. See also **Company; Sharebroker**.

House of Commons In the United Kingdom, the lower house of parliament. See also **House of Lords**.

House of Lords 1. In England, the upper house of parliament. 2. The Supreme Court of Appeal in Great Britain and Northern Ireland. Until 1948, all appeals to the House of Lords were heard in the chamber of the House. Appeals are now heard by the Appellate Committee, which usually consists of three or five Lords of Appeal.

House of Representatives The lower house of the Commonwealth Parliament. The House of Representatives members represent electoral divisions across Australia. Its structure is described in Commonwealth Constitution Ch I Pt III. It is regarded as the popularly elected house because the representation of each State, except Tasmania, is in proportion to its population. The House of Representatives, because of its popular mandate, is by convention the house to which the government is responsible, and is given exclusive power to originate appropriation and taxation bills: Commonwealth Constitution s 53. See also **Lower house**.

Householder's comprehensive insurance A contract of insurance providing the insured with cover against a range of perils that may damage or destroy a residential building or its contents. The scope of cover depends on the terms of the policy which are usually quite extensive, including loss or damage caused by theft, fire, explosion, earthquake, storm or tempest, bursting and overflowing of water tanks and pipes, lightning and impact by a vehicle. Householder's comprehensive insurance will usually also cover injury or damage to a third party occurring in or about the premises. The loss may arise from the insured's negligence, accidents, or intentional or careless acts of third parties. The onus is on the insured to show that the loss suffered was due to the peril insured against: *Anderson v Norwich Union Fire Insurance Society Ltd* [1977] 1 Lloyd's Rep 253; *Winter v Weeks* (1989) 5 ANZ Ins Cas ¶60-894. The minimum cover to be provided is specified: (CTH) Insurance Contracts Act 1984 s 35. See also **Fire insurance; Insurance contract; Property insurance**.

•**Housing fringe benefit** A housing right granted by an employer or associate of the employer to an employee: (CTH) Fringe Benefits Tax Assessment Act 1986 s 25. A housing right consists of a lease or licence to occupy a house, flat, home unit, or accommodation in a hotel, motel, caravan, or mobile home: s 136(1). See also **Fringe benefit**.

•**Housing loan** In relation to legislation governing finance broking, credit, the whole or part of which is to be used for the purpose of: enabling a debtor to buy a home, or land on which to build a home; providing the debtor with funds to build or make additions to a home; discharging a debtor's liability in respect of credit in one of the above contracts; or discharging the debtor's liability under a credit contract that is one of a series of credit contracts relating to housing. The credit must not be used for the purpose of the business where the debtor is a building contractor, or in the business of building or making additions to houses or buying and selling land: for example (NSW) Credit (Finance Brokers) Act 1984 s 4(1). See also **Credit contract; Finance broker; Home finance contract; Mortgage**.

Hudson formula A formula commonly used to quantify offsite overheads and loss of profit, where a contractor can recover prolongation costs from the proprietor. The formula may be expressed as: (overhead or profit percentage/100) x (contract sum/contract period (weeks)) x delay (weeks). The overhead or profit percentage is overheads or profits expressed as a percentage of turnover or total sales for the comparable period. Contract sum is the contract price including its component for profit and overheads. Contract period is the period provided for in the contract for performance of the works. The Hudson formula is so called because it appeared in I N Wallace *Hudson's Building and Engineering Contracts* 10th ed, Sweet & Maxwell, 1970. A similar formula is the Eichleay formula. See also **Contractor; Delay; Damages for loss of profits; Offsite overhead cost; Proprietor**.

Hundred year mortgage A growing characteristic of the housing finance market in Japan. In 1988, the Nikon Mortgage Corporation announced a 99 year loan-package for house purchase. In 1990, the Nippon Housing Loan Corporation, the largest housing financier in Japan, offered a 100 year mortgage for ordinary house-buyers. The interest rates are 1 per cent above prime rate. The terms may be principal and interest, or interest only, over three generations. See also **Mortgage**.

Hyperinflation Run-away inflation in which prices increase at an astonishing rate. An example of this occurred in Germany during the 1920s when savings were destroyed in value by an astronomical rise in prices. See also **Inflation**.

Hypothecation *Abbr* – Hyp A form of security for a debt without the transfer of possession or title.

Bailment A form of security by appropriation of possession (rather than title, as with a mortgage or charge) akin to a pledge but over forms of personal property (such as a ship or its cargo) in which transfer of possession prior to default is impracticable. The security holder is entitled to possession on default by the obligor: *Askrigg Pty Ltd v Student Guild Curtin University of Technology* (1989) 18 NSWLR 738 at 744-6. See also **Lien; Pledge**.

Equity Strictly, a security interest in which the debtor retains possession of the property (in contrast, for example, to a pledge, where possession is given to the creditor). An hypothecation differs from a common law mortgage in that there is no conveyance or assurance of the property, and it differs from a pledge, in that there is no delivery of the property: *Karon Corp v Australian Mutual Provident Society* (1911) 33 NZLR 438. More generally, the term is used to indicate a charge on property which gives the chargee neither the right of possession, nor the right to sell, but merely the right to bring judicial proceedings to realise the security. Examples are an equitable charge and equitable lien. See also **Equitable charge; Equitable lien; Hypothecation agreement; Lien; Pledge.**

Maritime law The pledging of a ship or its cargo by the master of the ship to borrow money to enable completion of the voyage. Also known as 'maritime lien'. See also **Agency of necessity; Cargo; Letter of hypothecation; Lien.**

Real property A security transaction not involving an entry on the certificate of title. See also **Mortgage; Pledge.**

Hypothecation agreement An arrangement by which a security interest in property of a borrower is given to the lender. An hypothecation agreement is more commonly referred to as a charge or lien, except in the context of shipping law where a letter of hypothecation is used to refer to an agreement by which an exporter is given security over goods which have been shipped: *Cargo ex Sultan* (1859) Sw 504; 166 ER 1235 at 1238. Also known as 'respondentia bond'. See also **Charge; Hypothecation; Lien; Power of sale.**

I

IAA See **Institute of Arbitrators Australia**.

IBRD See **International Bank for Reconstruction and Development**.

ICAA See **Institute of Chartered Accountants in Australia**.

ICC See **International Chamber of Commerce**.

ICJ See **International Court of Justice**.

Icon In a graphical user interface, an object displayed on the screen to represent a file, program, or instruction. The user can select an icon by pointing to it (generally using a mouse or similar pointing device), and thereby activate the commands attached to it.

ICSID See **International Centre for Settlement of Investment Disputes**.

IDA See **International Development Association**.

Idem /ɪdɛm/ *Lat* – the same.

•**Identifying cash dealer** A cash dealer declared by the Australian Transaction Reports and Analysis Centre to be an identifying cash dealer upon giving an undertaking to promptly carry out verification procedures where required and to report if the procedures produce any information requiring reporting as a suspicious transaction: (CTH) Financial Transaction Reports Act 1988 s 8A. See also **Cash dealer**.

IFC See **International Finance Corporation**.

Illegal adventure A contract for carriage which is illegal or unlawful by common law or by statute. An insurance policy on an illegal adventure cannot be enforced: *Redmond v Smith* (1844) 7 Man & G 457 at 474. There is an implied warranty in all marine insurance policies that the adventure insured is a lawful one, and that so far as the assured can control the matter, the adventure will be carried out in a lawful manner: (CTH) Marine Insurance Act 1909 s 47. See also **Contract of carriage**.

Illegal contract A contract which the court refuses to enforce because it is expressly or impliedly prohibited by statute, or because, in cases where the impropriety is great, it infringes public policy: *Yango Pastoral Co Pty Ltd v First Chicago Australia Ltd* (1978) 139 CLR 410; 21 ALR 585; *Wilkinson v Osborne* (1915) 21 CLR 89. A contract may be void and not illegal (as in restraint of trade cases), or be both illegal and void (as in an immoral contract), or be merely unenforceable. See also **Contract in restraint of trade**; **Contract injurious to public life**; **Maintenance**; **Public policy**; **Restraint of trade**; **Supervening illegality**; **Void**.

Illusory appointment Where a person with the power to appoint property, real or personal, amongst a limited class of persons, appoints to one of that group a nominal share only. See also **Power of appointment**.

Illusory consideration A propounded consideration which is impossible to enforce: *Coghlan v S H Lock (Aust) Ltd* (1987) 8 NSWLR 88; 70 ALR 1. Consideration may be described as illusory where it is a promise, the performance of which is at the sole discretion of the promisor, a promise impossible to enforce for vagueness or uncertainty, an illegal promise, a promise to perform a contractual duty already owed to the other party, a promise binding in honour only, or a promise accompanied by an exclusion of all liability for any breach. See also **Consideration**; **Contract**.

Illusory trust An arrangement which, despite its apparent form, expresses no trust at all because of a lack of intention to transfer the beneficial interest in the property to the beneficiary. It includes a revocable mandate and directions for management. See also **Beneficial interest**; **Beneficiary**; **Trust**.

ILO See **International Labour Organisation**.

ILO Conventions Conventions adopted by the International Labour Organisation

IMF See **International Monetary Fund**.

Imitation In design law, the application of a registered design without the licence or authority of the registered owner. Imitation includes obvious imitation and fraudulent imitation. Obvious imitation involves a copy apparent to the eye notwithstanding slight differences, with the comparison being a visual one. A fraudulent imitation is a copy with differences which are both apparent and not so slight as to be insubstantial but that have been made merely to disguise the copying, something more than a visual comparison being required: *Malleys Ltd v J W Tomlin Pty Ltd* (1961) 180 CLR 120. See also **Obvious imitation**.

•**Immediate annuity 1.** An annuity for which payments commence immediately upon its purchase, and are not delayed until some specified future date or the happening of an event as for a deferred annuity: (CTH) Income Tax Assessment Act 1936 s 27A. Payments are usually made on a periodic basis, either monthly, quarterly, six-monthly, or on a yearly basis, and continue until the death of the annuitant (or of the survivor of joint annuitants), or for some other fixed period. **2.** An annuity which is presently payable: (CTH) Social Security Act 1991 s 9(1). See also **Annuity**; **Deferred annuity**; **Pension**.

Immediate holding company A company which controls a subsidiary company directly without the interposition of another company. See also **Ultimate holding company**.

Immunisation In corporations law, an asset management strategy where the manager of the portfolio matches up the duration of a bond portfolio with a specified investment horizon. The aim of the strategy is to ensure that the return is equivalent to the initial yield of the assets. See also **Asset; Portfolio**.

Immunity An exemption from liability for prosecution for a criminal offence given by the Attorney-General or the Director of Public Prosecutions, normally on condition that the person being granted the immunity gives evidence on behalf of the Crown: *R v D'Arrigo* [1994] 1 Qd R 603. It is an agreement not to prosecute rather than a pardon: *R v Milnes and Green* (1983) 33 SASR 211; *R v Georgiadis* [1984] VR 1030. An immunity can relate to the involvement of a person in a crime or crimes (a transactional immunity) or to the use of evidence given by the person in specified proceedings to prove the commission by the person of a criminal offence (a use immunity). The latter type of immunity is often called an undertaking: (NSW) Criminal Procedure Act 1987 s 14. Also known as 'indemnity'. See also **Crown immunity**.

Immunity of carrier The exemption of a carrier from liability for loss of, or damage to, goods. Such immunity is provided for in the contract of carriage and relates to specified excepted perils, such as those referred to in the Amended Hague Rules 1979. In order to obtain the benefit of the immunity, the carrier must show that the loss or damage was causally connected with an excepted peril: *Frank Hammond Pty Ltd v Huddart Parker Ltd* [1956] VLR 496. See also **Amended Hague Rules 1979; Carrier**.

•**IMO** See **International Maritime Organisation**.

Impaired assets Problem loans of banks which fall into the following categories: non-accrued loans; restructured loans; and assets acquired through the enforcement of security conditions. These loans lumped together are described as 'impaired assets'. In December 1993 the Reserve Bank of Australia exercising its powers of prudential supervision issued new guidelines to the banking industry for classifying and reporting their problem loans and impaired assets. As a general rule, when one lending facility to a customer is classified as impaired, the bank should place all other facilities to that customer on a similar status. See also **Non-accrual loans; Prudential supervision; Reserve Bank of Australia; Restructured loans**.

Imperfect competition A market situation in which neither monopoly nor perfect competition prevails; a situation closest to real life in most circumstances. It is characterised by the ability of sellers to influence demand by product differentiation, branding and advertising. The entry of competitors into various lines of production is restricted, either because of the size of the initial investment required or because of the fears of subsequent cut-throat competition. Uncertainty and imperfect knowledge of the market are features, as is the absence of price competition in varying degrees.

Implication by custom Implying a term into a contract on the basis of custom or usage. The custom must be so notorious that everybody in the trade enters into a contract with that usage as an implied term: *Nelson v Dahl* (1879) 12 Ch D 568 at 575; *Thornley v Tilley* (1925) 36 CLR 1 at 8. A term cannot be implied by custom if it is inconsistent with the express terms of the contract: *Summers v Commonwealth* (1918) 25 CLR 144. See also **Contract; Implied term**.

Implied The unexpressed intention of the maker of a legal document, such as a contract or will, which can be gleaned by reference to specific acts done or things said to facilitate that intention. See also **Express condition; Implied term; Implied trust**.

Implied agency Agency by implied agreement. Implied agency arises when the conduct of the parties towards each other makes it reasonable to infer consent to the relationship of agency: *Hook v Day* [1971] 2 SASR 440. For the purpose of inferring an agency by implied agreement, particular emphasis is placed upon what was said and done at the time the alleged agency was created: *Field v Shoalhaven Transport Pty Ltd* [1970] 3 NSWR 96. To be distinguished from express agency. See also **Agency; Agent; Express agency**.

Implied authority The actual authority of an agent arising from what is necessarily or ordinarily incidental to the express authority of the agent, or from what is customary in the place or business concerned: *Hawkins v Gaden* (1925) 37 CLR 183; 32 ALR 109. Implied authority does not extend to acts that are outside the ordinary course of the agent's business, or that are neither necessary nor incidental to the agent's express authority: *Thornley v Tilley* (1925) 36 CLR 1; 31 ALR 291. See also **Actual authority; Agency; Agent; Apparent authority; Express authority; Power of attorney; Principal**.

Implied covenant 1. A promise or term implied into a contract in order to give effect to the parties' intention. Such implication is a matter of construction for the court: *Hamly v Wood* [1891] 2 QB 488. A covenant will only be implied when it is both reasonable and necessary to give business efficacy to the contract made, and subject to the actual agreement of the parties: *BP Refinery (Westernport) Pty Ltd v President, Councillors and Ratepayers of the Shire of Hastings* (1977) 16 ALR 363; *Karaggianis v Malltown Pty Ltd* (1979) 21 SASR 381. 2. A particular covenant implied at law into all leases by virtue of the relationship between landlord and tenant. See also **Covenant; Landlord; Possession; Quiet enjoyment; Tenant; Tenant-like manner**.

Implied intention The intention the court attributes to the parties to a contract. The court is required to impute or infer intention when there is no intention expressed by the parties. The search for what the parties impliedly agreed as to the meaning or legal effect of the words is determined by ascertaining what a reasonable person in the position of the party to whom the words were addressed would have taken the speaker's intention to be: *Hutton v Watling* [1948] 1 Ch 398. See also **Actual intention; Construction; Express intention**.

Implied obligation of cooperation In contract law, the implied obligation on each party to do everything necessary to enable the other party to perform its contractual obligations, and to do nothing to impede or prevent the other party from performing these obligations: *Secured Income Real Estate (Aust) Ltd v St Martins Investments Pty Ltd* (1979) 144 CLR 596; 26 ALR 567; *William Cory & Sons Ltd v London Corp* [1951] 2 KB 476; [1951] 2 All ER 85. See also **Best endeavours clause; Implied term**.

Implied powers of partner The authority to act which one would reasonably expect a partner of a firm, as an ordinary business person, to have in order to ensure the proper functioning of the partnership business. The implied powers may include the power to: pledge or sell the partnership business; purchase, on behalf of the firm, goods of the kind usually used in the firm's business; engage and employ persons to carrying out the firm's business; borrow money, contract debts and give security for those debts; receive payment of debts due to the firm and give effective receipts or releases for those debts; and, in the case of a trading partnership, to bind the firm and all the partners by making, accepting and issuing negotiable instruments in the firm's name: *Bank of Australasia Ltd v Breillat* (1847) 6 Moo PCC 152 at 192; 13 ER 642 at 657. See also **Partner**; **Partnership**; **Powers of partner**.

Implied promise An undertaking or assurance that is not expressly stated but is sufficiently clear and unambiguous as to constitute a promise. An implied promise may found a promissory estoppel: *Legione v Hateley* (1983) 152 CLR 406; 46 ALR 1. A request for services that are subsequently rendered implies a promise to pay for the services: *Re Casey's Patents; Stewart v Casey* [1892] 1 Ch 104. See also **Promise**; **Promissory estoppel**; **Representation**.

Implied repudiation Conduct that indicates that a party to a contract is unwilling or unable to perform his or her obligations under a contract: for example *Hoad v Swann* (1920) 28 CLR 258 at 264; 21 SR (NSW) 161. Implied repudiation may involve an actual breach of a warranty or subsidiary term (for example *Associated Newspapers Ltd v Bancks* (1951) 83 CLR 322) or advance manifestation of an inability to perform the terms of the contract: for example *Rawson v Hobbs* (1961) 107 CLR 466; *Foran v Wight* (1989) 168 CLR 385; 88 ALR 413. The innocent party may either accept the repudiation or wait until performance becomes due before seeking any remedy: *Hochster v De la Tour* (1853) 2 El & Bl 678 at 691; 118 ER 922 at 927. See also **Anticipatory breach**; **Express repudiation**; **Repudiation**.

Implied term A term which the parties have not set out, but which is regarded as having been impliedly agreed to; to be contrasted with an expressed (or express) term. The court may imply a term into a contract for business efficacy, to make the contract workable (factual implication): *Codelfa Construction Pty Ltd v State Rail Authority of NSW* (1982) 149 CLR 337; 41 ALR 367. A term may be implied as being implicit from the nature of the contract itself, or from the obligation it creates (legal implication): *Con-Stan Industries of Australia Pty Ltd v Norwich Winterthur Insurance (Aust) Ltd* (1986) 160 CLR 226; 64 ALR 481. A number of terms are implied in various contracts by statute (legal implication): for example (CTH) Trade Practices Act 1974 Part V Div 2. A term may be implied because of custom or usage, or on construction of the contract. See also **Construction**; **Express term**.

Implied trust A presumed trust; a trust in which no express intention of creating a trust is spelt out, but the court presumes that the parties intended to create a particular trust. An example is a resulting trust. It is distinguished from an express trust (where the intention is spelt out by the parties), and a constructive trust (which arises without reference to the parties' intentions): for example *Schofield v Jones* (unrptd, SC(NSW), Bryson J, 1316/93, 31/3/95). See also **Constructive trust**; **Express trust**; **Resulting trust**.

Implied undertaking as to quality or fitness An implied term of a contract for the sale of goods that the goods sold are of a certain quality or reasonably fit for the purpose for which they are required: for example (NSW) Sale of Goods Act 1923 s 19(1). Originally, at common law, the maxim *caveat emptor* (buyer beware) applied to contracts of sale in the absence of any fraud or express warranty: *Parkinson v Lee* (1802) 2 East 314; 102 ER 389. The condition is only implied if the buyer made the particular purpose known to the seller so as to show his or her reliance on the seller's skill or judgment and the goods were of a description which it is in the course of the seller's business to supply: for example (NSW) Sale of Goods Act 1923 s 19(1). See also **Caveat emptor**.

Implied undertaking as to title An implied condition in every contract for the sale of goods that, unless otherwise provided, the seller has a right to sell the goods or will have a right to sell the goods when the property is to pass: for example (NSW) Sale of Goods Act 1923 s 17(1). There is also an implied warranty that the buyer will have a quiet enjoyment of the goods and that the goods will be free from charge or encumbrance in favour of any third party not declared or known to the buyer before or at the time when the contract is made: for example (NSW) Sale of Goods Act 1923 s 17(2), (3). See also **Condition**; **Quiet enjoyment**.

Implied warranty A contractual term not expressed in a written contract or in discussions forming the contract, that must nevertheless be complied with. A warranty may be implied as a matter of general law, as a result of custom or usage, or by necessary implication from the express agreement of the parties. See also **Marine insurance**; **Uberrimae fidei**; **Warranty**.

•**Import** 1. To buy or bring in goods or services from a foreign country or from an outside source. 2. To adduce foreign words into a language. 3. To convey importance or significance to something in the context of a particular situation.

Intellectual property In ordinary language, to bring into a country; also, an object brought into a country: for example *Mattel Inc v Tonka Corp* 23 IPR 91. In copyright law, importation for certain commercial purposes may constitute an infringement of copyright: (CTH) Copyright Act 1968 ss 37, 102. See also **Copyright**.

Trade and commerce Under (CTH) Customs Act 1901 s 50, goods are imported when they are 'landed or brought within a port for the purpose of landing them': *McGurk Construction and Rigging Co Ltd v Comptroller-General of Customs* (1987) 73 ALR 381.

Import penetration The ratio of imports to domestic sales. The higher the ratio, the greater the penetration of markets by imported goods. Import penetration levels in the Australian manufacturing sector have approached 30 per cent of total manufacturing domestic sales. In all, imports amount to about 15-18 per cent of Australia's gross national expenditure.

Import Price Index See **Terms of trade**.

Import quota A non-tariff form of protection that imposes an absolute restriction on the quantity, weight or value of goods that may be imported into a country in a certain period. The Commonwealth government has from time to time imposed import controls to protect employment and investment in some industries. The textile, clothing and footwear, motor vehicle and cheese industries have been assisted by import quotas which allow only restricted quantities of competing foreign goods into the country at normal rates of customs duty. The United States has imposed import quotas on steel on the grounds that the unlimited entry of foreign subsidised steel would drive most American steelmakers out of business.

Import replacement The displacement of imports by competitive domestic production. Import replacement may involve producing more of what is demanded within the Australian economy.

•**Imported goods** Goods that have been brought into Australia from another country. Goods will still be imported despite the fact that they were manufactured in Australia and then exported: (CTH) Sales Tax Assessment Act 1992 s 5. In relation to manufactured goods in the manufacture of which imported goods have been used, or imported goods that have been subjected to a process or to treatment in Australia, imported goods mean goods on which import duty has been paid and that have not been used in the Commonwealth otherwise than in the manufacture of the specified goods, or in being subjected to a process or to treatment for the purpose of producing the specified goods, or for the purpose of being inspected or exhibited: (CTH) Customs Regulations 1926 reg 131(1). See also **Goods**; **Import**; **Importer**; **Import quota**.

•**Importer** A person or entity that brings a product manufactured in a foreign country into the country in which it is to be marketed or used. An importer can be a defendant to a product liability claim in negligence: *Goodchild v Vaclight Ltd*, The Times, 22 May 1965. An importer, that is not the manufacturer of goods, is deemed, for product liability claim purposes, to have manufactured those goods where at the time of importation the manufacturer did not have a place of business in Australia: (CTH) Trade Practices Act 1974 Pt V Div 2A, Pt VA, ss 74A(4), 75AB. A person on whose behalf goods are imported into Australia is deemed, for the purposes of a product liability claim, to be the importer: ss 74A(7), 75AB. See also **Deemed manufacturer**; **Import**.

Imposition 1. A tax, levy, or rate that a government or statutory authority may require a person to pay or serve. For example, the Commonwealth Government has broad powers to impose taxes on wage earners: Commonwealth Constitution s 55; *South Australia v Commonwealth* (1942) 65 CLR 373. **2.** A pecuniary penalty or sentence imposed by a court. See also **Fine**; **Levy**; **Tax**.

Impossibility of performance The situation in which circumstances have rendered contractual obligations incapable of being discharged. Where performance is impossible because the goods contracted to be sold do not exist, no contract is in fact created: *Couturier v Hastie* (1852) 8 Exch 40; 155 ER 1250. Performance may also become impossible after the contract has been concluded. In this case, the contract may be terminated on the ground of frustration: *Codelfa Construction Pty Ltd v State Rail Authority of New South Wales* (1982) 149 CLR 337; 41 ALR 367. See also **Frustration**; **Mistake**.

Impound To seize or confiscate or to confine in an enclosed space.

Corporations To place a document in the custody of the law, generally the custody of an officer of the court.

Imprest fund A fund of a specified amount entrusted to an individual to meet future expenditure and handle disbursements of a company. The balance is maintained by periodic reimbursement from time to time. The total amount of the fund is the cash on hand or the bank balance plus the vouchers not yet reimbursed.

Improper dividend In corporations law a dividend that is payable to a shareholder of a company otherwise than out of profits or pursuant to Corporations Law s 191: Corporations Law s 201(1). A limited application of an amount in the company's share premium account is allowed: Corporations Law s 191. An executive officer who knowingly and wilfully pays (or permits to be paid), except under Corporations Law s 191, a dividend out of what he or she knows not to be profits is liable to the company's creditors for the debts due to them to the extent by which the dividends exceed profits: Corporations Law s 201(2). Improper dividends are sometimes called 'nimble dividends'. See also **Dividend**.

Improper use of information The utilisation of information by a former or a present company officer (acquired by virtue of his or her position as an officer or employee) to gain, directly or indirectly, a personal advantage or an advantage for any other person, or to cause detriment to the corporation: Corporations Law s 232(5). The fact that the information was not confidential is not relevant: *McNamara v Flavel* (1988) 13 ACLR 619. See also **Directors' duties**; **Improper use of position**.

Improper use of position The utilisation by an officer or employee of a corporation of his or her position as such an officer or employee to gain, directly or indirectly, a personal advantage or an advantage for any other person or to cause detriment to the corporation: Corporations Law s 232(6). The test of impropriety is concerned with the purpose of the use of position, rather than whether the use of position caused the advantage to the person or the detriment to the company: *Chew v R* (1992) 173 CLR 626; 107 ALR 171. The test of impropriety must be determined on objective grounds and does not depend on an alleged offender's consciousness of impropriety: *Chew v R*. See also **Directors' duties**; **Improper use of information**.

•**Improved capital value** The value of land assessed after taking into account any improvements (for example, buildings) on the land. To be contrasted with unimproved capital value of land, the latter being the basis upon which local government rates are often calculated.

•**Improvement** Enhance the value or desirability of property, real or personal. For example, something that has enhanced the value of land or made the use of land more efficient: *Brisbane City Council v Valuer General of Queensland* (1978) 140 CLR 41; 21 ALR 607; *Dampier Mining Co Ltd v FCT* (1979) 40 FLR 127; 27 ALR 579.

Taxation and revenue **1.** Expenditure on work where an assets efficiency is significantly better after it has been worked on or the assets value has increased. Alternatively if the work only restores the asset to its previous condition the work will usually be a repair unless the asset was purchased in a run down state: *Law Shipping Co v IRC* (1924) 12 TC 621. Whether expenditure amounts to an improvement determines whether the repairs are deductible: (CTH) Income Tax Assessment Act 1936 s 53. Expenditure, other than of a capital nature, by a taxpayer on capital items such as premises or plant is tax deductible: s 53. An improvement is expenditure of a capital nature. **2.** In relation to land, the construction or extension of, or the making of an alteration, or improvement to, a building or some other structure on the land: (CTH) Income Tax Assessment Act 1936 s 82KZC. See also **Allowable deduction**; **Capital**.

Imputation credit Where a shareholder receives a franked dividend, the shareholder's assessable income is 'grossed up' to include the amount of company tax paid which is attributable to the dividend (the 'imputation credit'): (CTH) Income Tax Assessment Act 1936 s 160AQT. The shareholder is then allowed a rebate equal to the credit. See also **Assessable income**; **Dividend**; **Imputation rebate**; **Imputation system**.

Imputation rebate A tax rebate allowed to a shareholder who receives a dividend which is equal to the amount of the imputation credit relating to that dividend: (CTH) Income Tax Assessment Act 1936 s 160AQU. Also known as 'franking rebate'. See also **Imputation credit**; **Imputation system**; **Rebate**.

Imputation system A system of company and shareholder taxation introduced in 1987 which imputes company tax levied on resident companies to resident shareholders who are paid a dividend. Imputation eliminates to a certain extent the previous 'double taxation' of company profits, where income tax was paid both in the hands of the company and again in the hands of the shareholder when dividends were paid. At the shareholder level imputation operates so that dividends received are included in the assessable income of the shareholder, with the amount of imputed company tax ('imputation credit'). The shareholder is entitled to a rebate ('imputation rebate') of tax of an amount equivalent to the imputed company tax. See also **Assessable income**; **Dividend**; **Imputation credit**; **Imputation rebate**; **Rebate**.

•**Impute** Deem; presume; to attribute or ascribe to a person vicariously. Knowledge of an employee or agent is, for example, generally imputed to the employer or principal: for example Corporations Law s 611. Discrimination on the grounds of characteristics generally imputed to persons of the same race, gender, age, marital status, sexuality, or disability is prohibited: for example (CTH) Sex Discrimination Act 1984 s 5. See also **Agent**; **Imputed intention**; **Principal**.

Imputed cost 1. A cost which does not incur dollar expenditures and which is not normally recognised in conventional accounting practice. For example, the use by an agency of premises owned by a government may be rent-free, but the opportunity cost should be allowed for. Its value to the agency may be imputed by assessing the rent it would be paying if comparable quality accommodation was rented commercially. **2.** An outlay contributing to the overall cost of acquired goods and services that is allocated to individual units of goods and services.

Imputed intention An implied intention attributed by a court where there is no evidence of a specific intention. See also **Impute**; **Intention**.

Contract The implication of terms into the contract between the parties by the court: *Hawkins v Clayton* (1988) 164 CLR 539; 78 ALR 69; *Bahr v Nicolay (No 2)* (1988) 164 CLR 604; 78 ALR 1. The court will only impute such an intention if it is necessary for the reasonable and effective operation of the contract: *Hospital Products Ltd v United States Surgical Corp* (1984) 156 CLR 41; 55 ALR 417. See also **Implied term**; **Impute**.

Imputed knowledge A presumption that an employer or principal was aware at a particular time of a fact within the knowledge of an employee or agent: for example Corporations Law s 611. Persons dealing with a company may assume that the officer they are dealing with has properly discharged his or her duties, unless that person has actual or imputed knowledge about matters which may prove the assumption to be incorrect: Corporations Law s 164(3). There is no need to show that the person actually did rely on this imputed knowledge: *Brick and Pipe Industries Ltd v Occidental Life Nominees Pty Ltd* [1992] 2 VR 279; (1990) 3 ACSR 649. However a person may not rely on this assumption where that person who has dealings with a company, through some relationship, ought to have known about matters relating to whether officers of a company have discharged their duties properly: *Brick and Pipe Industries Ltd v Occidental Life Nominees Pty Ltd* [1992] 2 VR 279; *Bank of New Zealand v Fiberi Pty Ltd* (1992) 8 ACSR 790. See also **Agency**; **Impute**.

In charge of carrier The state of being in the custody of a carrier for the purposes of a contract of carriage. The goods of a consignor that have been consigned to a consignee are in the charge of the carrier from the time when they are received by the carrier in accordance with the terms of the contract of carriage until the time when they are delivered by the carrier to the consignee in accordance with the terms of the contract of carriage. See also **Consignee**; **Consignor**; **Contract of carriage**.

•**In competition with each other** Supplying or acquiring substitutable goods or services, to or from a common range of customers or suppliers, or in the same market, and engaging in rivalry to that end. Agreements between persons, two or more of whom are in competition with each other and that have the purpose of preventing or restricting the supply or acquisition of goods or services to or from another are prohibited absolutely: (CTH) Trade Practices Act 1974 s 4D; *ASX*

Operations Pty Ltd v Pont Data Australia Pty Ltd (1991) 27 FCR 492: 100 ALR 125. See also **Competition; Market; Market power**.

In connection with or caused by A phrase used in insurance contracts to define the link required between the event insured against and the loss suffered. The words 'caused by' contemplate both direct and indirect causes: *Manufacturers' Mutual Insurance Ltd v Stargift* (1984) 25 NSWLR 541; 3 ANZ Ins Cas ¶60-615. The phrase 'in connection with' is ordinarily one of considerable width and consequently a loss will be connected with a cause where it is associated with or related to that cause: *Newcastle City Council v GIO General Ltd (t/a GIO Australia)* (1995) 8 ANZ Ins Cas ¶61-227. See also **Causal exclusion clause; Temporal exclusion clause**.

In contractibus tacite insunt quae sunt moris et consuetudinis *Lat* – those matters which because of manner and custom are implied in every contract.

In conventionibus contrahentium voluntas potius quam verba spectari placuit /ɪn kɒnvɛntiouɪnɪbʊs kɒntrahɛntium vɒluntas pɒtius kwam vɜbə spɛktari plækuɪt/ *Lat* – in construing contracts, the wishes of the parties, rather than the words actually used, should be considered.

• **In house expense payment fringe benefit** An expense payment fringe benefit where the expense to which the benefit relates was incurred by an employee in acquiring property or another residual benefit: (CTH) Fringe Benefits Tax Assessment Act 1986 s 136(1). See also **Benefit; Incurred; In house fringe benefit; Fringe benefits tax**.

In house fringe benefit An in house expense payment fringe benefit, an in house property fringe benefit, or an in house residual fringe benefit: (CTH) Fringe Benefits Tax Assessment Act 1986 s 136(1). The first $500 of the aggregate of the taxable values of in house fringe benefits and airline transport fringe benefits provided to an employee during a year is exempt from fringe benefits tax: s 62. See also **Airline transport fringe benefit; Fringe benefits tax; In house expense payment fringe benefit; In house property fringe benefit; In house residual fringe benefit**.

• **In house property fringe benefit** Goods and other property provided to employees which are of a kind that the employer sells in the ordinary course of business: (CTH) Fringe Benefits Tax Assessment Act 1986 s 136(1). See also **Benefit; Fringe benefits tax; In house fringe benefit**.

• **In house residual fringe benefit** A residual benefit provided to an employee of a kind that an employer provides in the ordinary course of business: (CTH) Fringe Benefits Tax Assessment Act 1986 s 136(1). See also **Benefit; Fringe benefits tax; In house fringe benefit**.

In personam /ɪn pɜsoʊnæm/ *Lat* – an action or right of action against a specific person. The right of a beneficiary is a right *in personam* against the trustee.

In rem actions *Lat* – *in rem* – against the thing. A proceeding *'in rem'* is one taken directly against property and its object is the disposition of property. The term is applied to actions between parties, where the object is to reach the property owned by them, or in which they have some interest, and dispose of it: (CTH) Admiralty Act 1988 ss 14-19; *Aichhorn & Co KG v The Ship MV Talabot* (1974) 132 CLR 449; 3 ALR 576; *General Motors-Holden Ltd v The Ship 'Northern Highway'* (1982) 29 SASR 138. See also **In personam; Jurisdiction**.

• **In situ** /ɪn sɪtu/ *Lat* – in its original place. Undisturbed.

In specie distribution The distribution of an asset. For example, the asset itself which is owned by a company or held by a trustee is distributed to a shareholder or beneficiary rather than the company or trustee realising the asset and paying the realisation proceeds to the shareholder or beneficiary. For income tax purposes a distribution in specie can be a dividend: (CTH) Income Tax Assessment Act 1936 s 6(1)(a). Where an amount would be income if paid in cash the money value of the consideration is deemed to have been given: (CTH) Income Tax Assessment Act 1936 s 21.

• **In the course of employment** See **Course of employment**.

In the money option A put option with an exercise price above the spot price, or a call option with an exercise price below the spot price. If exercised, an in-the-money option will produce a positive return. See also **Call option; Put option; Spot price**.

• **In transit** The status of goods or passengers from the time of commencing the carriage until its conclusion. Goods are in transit from the time when they are delivered to a carrier or other bailee for the purpose of transmission to the consignee until they are unloaded at their destination or delivered to the control of the consignee or his or her representative: *NEC Australia Pty Ltd v Gamif Pty Ltd* (1993) 42 FCR 410; *Bartlett and Partners Ltd v Meller* [1961] 1 Lloyd's Rep 487. See also **Consignee; Consignor; Delivery; Discharge**.

In transitu /ɪn trænzɪtu/ *Lat* – in the course of transit. See also **In transit**.

Inadequacy of consideration Consideration which is not commensurate in value to the promise which it supports. Courts will not generally inquire into the adequacy of consideration: for example *Thomas v Thomas* (1842) 2 QB 851; 114 ER 330; *Alexander v Rayson* [1936] 1 KB 169. However, although purely nominal consideration may create a binding contract (*Thomas v Thomas* (1842) 2 QB 851; 114 ER 330), the adequacy of consideration may be relevant to issues of economic duress, undue influence, unconscionability, and the enforceability of a promise in restraint of trade: for example *Bridge v Deacons* [1984] AC 705. See also **Agreement; Consideration; Illusory consideration; Past consideration**.

Incapable of being performed In relation to an arbitration agreement, its inability to be performed due to the existence of some obstacle which cannot be overcome by the parties to the agreement, who are ready and willing to perform it: *Paczy v Haendler S Natermann GmbH* [1981] 1 Lloyd's Rep 302. Mere delay or inconvenience, or some procedural bar to the performance of the agreement, do not amount to proof that the agreement is incapable of being performed: *The Merak*

[1964] 3 All ER 638. The fact that a party is unwilling or unable to satisfy an award which might be made is also insufficient: *The Tuyuti* [1984] QB 838. A court's power to grant a stay of proceedings (which would prevent the arbitration from going ahead) cannot be exercised where the court finds that the arbitration agreement is incapable of being performed: (CTH) International Arbitration Act 1974 s 7(5). See also **Alternative dispute resolution; Arbitration.**

•**Incapacity** Physically, mentally or legally unable.

Contract Legal inability to enter into a contract. Persons lacking full contractual capacity include minors or infants, mentally disabled persons, alien enemies and bankrupts. See also **Bankrupt.**

Tort A defence to intentional torts, that the defendant lacked the capacity to do the tortious act alleged. See also **Capacity.**

•**Incapacity for work 1.** A physical incapacity for doing work in the labour market in which an employee is employed, or might reasonably expect to be employed. **2.** An incapacity that diminishes a person's power to earn wages in some suitable employment: *Thompson v Armstrong & Royse Pty Ltd* (1950) 81 CLR 585. See also **Worker's compensation.**

Inchoate instrument Partial or unfinished instruments, documents or enactments. Instruments which are required to be recorded and registered are described prior to registration as inchoate, meaning they are valid only between the parties and those persons having notice of the instrument: (CTH) Bills of Exchange Act 1909 s 25; (CTH) Cheques and Payment Orders Act 1986 s 18.

•**Incidental gain** In the frustrated contracts legislation in New South Wales, any property or improvement acquired or derived by a party to a contract who suffers a detriment as a consequence of doing or suffering the acts or things that caused the detriment. An incidental gain does not include any property or improvement that is comprised in any performance under the contract, nor that is expended and disposed of in giving such performance: (NSW) Frustrated Contracts Act 1978 s 11(5). See also **Attributable cost; Frustration; Performance.**

•**Income** Income according to ordinary concepts is money, or something capable of being turned into money, received periodically, derived from rendering personal service, or from property, or the carrying on of an organised activity and depended upon to provide for the regular expenditure of the taxpayer.

Taxation and revenue A profit or gain made in the ordinary course of carrying on a business, or a gain which arises from a commercial transaction entered into by the taxpayer where the circumstances indicate the intention or purpose of making a profit or gain: *Federal Cmr of Taxation v Myer Emporium Ltd* (1987) 163 CLR 199; 71 ALR 28. See also **Annuity; Assessable income; Capital gains tax; Dividend; Gratuity; Income from personal exertion; Income from property; Interest; Net capital gain; Royalty; Statutory income.**

Income beneficiary The recipient or beneficiary of an amount of income for a stated period as opposed to a capital beneficiary. See also **Capital beneficiary.**

Income elasticity of demand The relative change in the demand for a commodity following changes in the real income of consumers: income elasticity = percentage change in quantity demanded/percentage change in income. For many commodities, increases in income will lead to increases in demand, income elasticity being positive; however, for some items such as bread and potatoes the demand may fall as they are partially replaced by more sophisticated items, the income elasticity being negative. See also **Cross elasticity of demand; Price elasticity of supply.**

Income equalisation deposit scheme A scheme that allows an eligible primary producer to deposit amounts relating to primary production income into an income equalisation account and allows the primary producer a tax deduction for the amount deposited: (CTH) Income Tax Assessment Act 1936 s 159GC. When an amount deposited into an income equalisation deposit scheme becomes repayable it is included in the assessable income of the primary producer: (CTH) Income Tax Assessment Act 1936 s 159GD. The current scheme was introduced on 1 July 1989 and is administered by the Department of Primary Industries and Energy. Although the minimum term for a tax-deductible deposit is 12 months, deposits can be withdrawn either wholly or partly if the depositor is experiencing financial hardship. Withdrawal of deposits is subject to certain conditions and rules. See also **Allowable deduction; Assessable income; Primary producer.**

•**Income from personal exertion** At common law, receipts which are the product of personal exertion.

Taxation and revenue **1.** At common law, receipts the product of personal exertion. **2.** Income including earnings, salaries, wages, commissions, fees, bonuses, pensions, superannuation allowances, retiring allowances and retiring gratuities, allowances and gratuities received in the capacity of employee or in relation to any services rendered, and various other items: (CTH) Income Tax Assessment Act 1936 s 6(1). Specifically excluded from the definition are interest (except in certain prescribed circumstances), rent, and dividends: (CTH) Income Tax Assessment Act 1936 s 6(1). See also **Commission; Income; Salary; Wage.**

•**Income from property** All income which is not income from personal exertion. Examples of income from property include interest, rent, and dividends: (CTH) Income Tax Assessment Act 1936 s 6(1). See also **Income from personal exertion.**

Income of bankrupt Any amount obtained by a bankrupt, which is income according to ordinary usages and concepts: (CTH) Bankruptcy Act 1966 s 139L. The income of a bankrupt includes the amounts such as pensions paid from a superannuation fund, but it does not include certain amounts that are not income under the (CTH) Social Security Act 1991: (CTH) Bankruptcy Act 1966 s 139L(a)-(h). See also **Bankrupt.**

Income Tax Assessment legislation *Abbr* – ITAA Legislation dealing with, but not imposing, an income tax: (CTH) Income Tax Assessment Act 1936. The imposition of tax on taxable income is covered by various rating Acts: for example (CTH) Income Tax Rates Act 1986. Also known as 'Tax Act'. See also

Allowable deduction; Assessable income; Capital gains tax; Income taxation.

Income Tax Board of Review *Abbr* – ITBR The former review body for a taxpayer objecting to a decision of the Commissioner of Taxation. The Board of Review would review the case and made recommendations. The Income Tax Board of Review has been replaced by the Administrative Appeals Tribunal. See also **Administrative Appeals Tribunal; Objection.**

Income taxation A tax levied by the Commonwealth government on the taxable income of a resident or non resident individual or entity: (CTH) Income Tax Assessment Act 1936 s 17. Certain rebates and credits may operate to reduce income taxation payable by a taxpayer. The States also have the power to levy income tax as well as the Commonwealth: *Victoria and New South Wales v Commonwealth (2nd Uniform Tax case)* (1957) 99 CLR 575. See also **Credit; Income; Pay as you earn system; Rebate; Tax; Taxable income.**

Incoming partner A person admitted into an existing firm as a partner. Unless there is express agreement to the contrary, he or she does not become liable to the creditors of the firm for anything done before the person became a partner: for example (TAS) Partnership Act 1891 s 22. See also **Partner; Partnership.**

Incontestable taxation Liability for taxation imposed without the possibility of recourse to judicial review in the event of a dispute as to liability: *Girgis Pty Ltd v FCT* (1969) 119 CLR 365 at 378-9. Such taxation is payable regardless of whether the circumstances of the case satisfy the criteria for liability and is not taxation in the constitutional sense. A law imposing such an impost is not a law with respect to taxation within Commonwealth Constitution s 51(ii) and is thus invalid: *MacCormick v FCT* (1984) 158 CLR 622; 52 ALR 53 at 65. See also **Arbitrary taxation.**

Incontrovertible benefit In restitution, an enrichment that no reasonable person would say is of no value to the recipient. The receipt of money is an incontrovertible benefit, as is the saving of a necessary expense or the discharge of a liability: for example *BP Exploration Co (Libya) Ltd v Hunt (No 2)* [1982] 1 All ER 925; *Craven-Ellis v Canons Ltd* [1936] 2 KB 403. See also **Benefit; Enrichment; Free Acceptance.**

•**Incorporate** To form a company. For the purposes of the Corporations Law, it includes forming, except with respect to s 112 (outsize partnerships): Corporations Law s 9. A company is incorporated in the jurisdiction to which the particular legislation relates, and a company incorporated by or under a law of another jurisdiction is incorporated in that other jurisdiction: Corporations Law s 76.

•**Incorporated association 1.** A non-profit association incorporated by registration as provided by State and Territory legislation: for example (NSW) Associations Incorporation Act 1984. Registration as an incorporated association gives an association separate legal status as a body corporate and gives members the benefit of limited liability: for example (NSW) Associations Incorporation Act 1984 ss 15, 16. **2.** A non-profit association incorporated pursuant to a special Act of Parliament, other legislation, royal charter, or by registration as a company limited by guarantee. See also **Association; Body corporate; Club; Company limited by guarantee; Incorporation; Unincorporated association; Voluntary non-profit association.**

Incorporated joint venture A special purpose company formed by the participants in a joint venture to carry out the joint venture project. See also **Partnership.**

Incorporation Compliance with the procedures and formalities required to establish a corporation or any other legal or political body.

Corporations The act by which an entity gains status as a corporation and inherits a separate legal personality. Incorporation generally occurs upon registration: Corporations Law s 123(1). However, incorporation can also be conferred by private statute. See also **Chartered company; Corporation; Corporations Law.**

Incorporation by notice A method of including terms in a contract where no memorandum was signed by the parties, and where one party did all that was reasonable to bring the terms to the attention of the other party: *Balmain New Ferry Co Ltd v Robertson* (1906) 4 CLR 379. Unless a course of dealing is proved between the parties, the notice must be given prior to or contemporaneous with entry into the contract: *Oceanic Sun Line Special Shipping Co Inc v Fay* (1988) 165 CLR 197; 79 ALR 9. See also **Contract; Incorporation by reference; Incorporation by signature; Term.**

Incorporation by reference A method of including terms in a contract. Incorporation by notice occurs where the parties record the bare essentials of the contract in a document which incorporates as part of the contract the terms contained in other documents, such as the standard form of trade associations, standard form contracts, the standard terms of one of the parties, or the terms of another contract related to the transaction: *Giliberto v Kenny* (1983) 48 ALR 620. See also **Contract; Incorporation by notice; Incorporation by signature; Term.**

Incorporation by signature A method of including terms in a contract by the execution (signing) of a written memorandum of the agreement. Upon signing, the terms are incorporated as express terms of the contract and actual knowledge of the terms in the document need not be established: *L'Estrange v F Graucob Ltd* [1934] 2 KB 394. See also **Contract; Incorporation by notice; Incorporation by reference; Term.**

Incorporation of terms The translation of a representation into a contractual promise or warranty. A term may be incorporated by notice when the notice is given prior to or contemporaneously with entry into the contract: *Olley v Marlborough Court Ltd* [1949] 1 KB 532; *Oceanic Sun Line Special Shipping Co Inc v Fay* (1988) 165 CLR 197; 79 ALR 9. A term may also be incorporated by a consistent and sufficiently long course of dealing: for example *Henry Kendall & Sons v William Lillico & Sons Ltd* [1969] 2 AC 31. Alternatively, terms may be incorporated by reference to, for example, the standard form of a trade association (for example *Bremer Handelsgesellschaft GmbH v J H Rayner & Co Ltd* [1979] 2 Lloyd's Rep 216) or the standard terms of one of the parties: for example *Smith v South Wales Switchgear Co Ltd* [1978] 1 WLR 165. A term may be incorporated by signature even though it has not been read by one of the parties: *L'Estrange v F Graucob Ltd* [1934] 2 KB 394.

Incorporeal hereditament An intangible interest that is inheritable, issuing out of things that are 'corporate' or 'substantial', namely land. Examples are such rights as rent, easements and profits à prendre. At common law, a deed is necessary to convey an incorporeal hereditament from one living person to another ('*inter vivos*'): for example *Bryan v Whistler* (1828) 8 B & C 288; 108 ER 1050. See also **Deed**; **Easement**; **Profit à prendre**; **Rent**.

•**Incurred** For income tax purposes, a liability is 'incurred' by a taxpayer if the taxpayer definitely commits himself or herself to the expenditure, even if an actual disbursement is not made. However, a loss or outgoing is not incurred if it is merely 'impending, threatened or expected', even if it is predictable or certain: *Federal Cmr of Taxation v James Flood Pty Ltd* (1953) 88 CLR 492; 5 AITR 579 See also **Allowable deduction**; **Prepaid expenses**.

•**Indebted** The condition of a person when there is a present debt, whether it be payable now or in future; the words 'all debts owing or accruing' mean the same thing: *Webb v Stenton* (1883) 11 QBD 518 at 529. See also **Accruing-debt**; **Debt**.

Indefeasibility of title A characteristic of Torrens title that considers the interest of the registered proprietor as paramount and protected against all prior interests and estates existing in respect of the land, except in the case of fraud or statutory exceptions: for example (NSW) Real Property Act 1900 s 42; *Breskvar v Wall* (1971) 126 CLR 376. The concept of indefeasibility of title does not apply to land under old system title and holders of legal and equitable interests do not automatically have indefeasible title. See also **Estate**; **Fraud**; **Interest**; **Old system title**.

•**Indefeasible** Unable to be brought to an end: for example *Dwight v FCT* (1992) 107 ALR 407; 92 ATC 4192. See also **Defeasible**; **Indefeasibility of title**; **Old system title**.

Indemnifying bail Taking out insurance with respect to the subject matter of a bailment. Under the law of bailment, both bailor and bailee have an insurable interest in the goods the subject of the bailment. A bailee is entitled to insure not only his or her own interest in those goods but also the owner's interest in them. If a claim is made on such an insurance policy, the bailee must be required to account to the owner for all the moneys paid out under the insurance policy which exceed the value of the bailee's own interest: *Hepburn v A Tomlinson (Hauliers) Ltd* [1966] AC 451; *British Traders' Insurance Co Ltd v Monson* (1964) 111 CLR 86; *Trident General Insurance Co Ltd v McNiece Bros Pty Ltd* (1988) 165 CLR 107; 80 ALR 574. See also **Bailor**; **Bailment**; **Bailor**; **Contractual bailment**.

•**Indemnity** 1. Security or protection against loss or injury. 2. A sum of money paid to compensate a person for liability, loss or expense incurred by the person. 3. Legal protection against liabilities arising from one's actions.

Agency An obligation on the part of a principal to protect the agent from all liabilities incurred in the reasonable performance of the agency: *Jones v Canavan* [1972] 2 NSWLR 236. See also **Agency**; **Agent**; **Fiduciary**; **Guarantee**; **Partnership**; **Principal**; **Promise**; **Trustee**; **Third party**.

Contract 1. A promise by a promisor to keep the promisee harmless against loss as a result of entering into a transaction with a third party: *Sunbird Plaza Pty Ltd v Maloney* (1988) 166 CLR 245; 77 ALR 205; *Total Oil Products (Aust) Pty Ltd v Robinson* [1970] 1 NSWR 701. 2. An obligation to protect a person against loss suffered through a third party. This narrow meaning of 'indemnity' does not include an obligation to indemnify a person in a fiduciary relationship, such as a trustee or agent; or a director to cover loss arising from performance of the director's various duties. 3. An obligation on the part of a principal to protect the agent from all liabilities incurred in the reasonable performance of the agency: *Jones v Canavan* [1972] 2 NSWLR 236. See also **Agency**; **Agent**; **Fiduciary**; **Guarantee**; **Partnership**; **Principal**; **Promise**; **Trustee**; **Third party**.

Employment In the employer-employee relationship, an employer held to be vicariously liable for the negligence of its employee may claim an indemnity from the employee. See also **Contribution**; **Vicarious liability**.

Guarantees and indemnities An agreement by a surety to make good a loss suffered by another as a result of that other person acting or forbearing to act on the request of a third party: *Mountstephen v Lakeman* (1871) LR 7 QB 196; *Yeoman Credit Ltd v Latter* 1 WLR 828. See also **Guarantee**.

Insurance A promise by one party to keep the other harmless against loss: *Yeoman Credit Ltd v Latter* [1961] 1 WLR 828 at 831. An indemnity involves making good a loss suffered by one person as a consequence of the act or omission of another: *Hunt and Baird Industries (WA) Pty Ltd v Cartwright Taylor Engineering Pty Ltd* (1984) 2 SR (WA) 198. The principle of indemnity applies to most contracts of insurance, excluding life, sickness and personal accident insurance. See also **Guarantee**; **Indemnity insurance**; **Indemnity principle**.

Negligence At common law, compensation guaranteed by one party to another for loss or damage incurred with regard to a specified event: for example *Qantas Airways Ltd v Aravco Ltd* (1996) 136 ALR 510. See also **Contribution**; **Vicarious liability**.

Indemnity insurance Insurance by which the insurer agrees to indemnify the insured against loss. The term 'indemnity insurance' covers most forms of insurance excluding life, sickness and personal accident insurance. Under a contract of indemnity insurance, the insurer's obligation to indemnify only arises when loss has actually been suffered by the insured: *British Traders' Insurance Co Ltd v Monson* (1964) 111 CLR 86. See also **Indemnity**; **Indemnity principle**.

Indemnity principle 1. The principle that an insured is entitled to be indemnified to the extent of the loss suffered: *British Traders' Insurance Co Ltd v Monson* (1964) 111 CLR 86; *Fire & All Risks Insurance Co Ltd v Rousianos* (1989) 19 NSWLR 57. **2.** The making good to a merchant or ship owner any loss arising from the destruction of property, by tempest or other sea peril, in which the assured has an interest: (CTH) Marine Insurance Act 1909 s 10. **3.** The indemnity principle does not cover losses from gaming and wagering. See also **Indemnity; Indemnity insurance**.

•**Indenture** A deed made by two or more parties that evidences some form of agreement between them.

Corporations An agreement between a corporation and a trustee, usually a bank or trust company, governing the conditions under which bonds and debentures are issued. The trustee is responsible for the enforcement of the terms of the indenture.

Deeds and other instruments The former practice of 'indenting' which involved cutting an uneven line along the paper or parchment upon which the deed was written. The practice guarded against forgery or fraudulent substitution, as each party's part of the deed would be cut similarly, and thus matched with the other part or parts at the point of indenting. Legislation in most jurisdictions has made indenture obsolete: for example (NSW) Conveyancing Act 1919 s 38(2). In some jurisdictions, a deed is given the effect of an indenture: for example (VIC) Property Law Act 1958 ss 56(2), 57. An indenture is to be contrasted with a deed poll. See also **Deed; Deed inter partes**.

Industrial law Documents or a deed signed by the parties to an indentured apprenticeship or employment, establishing a term of service for the apprentice or employee. See also **Deed**.

•**Independent contractor** A person who contracts to perform work for another person, but is not employed by that person. An independent contractor undertakes to produce a given result, the agreed payment becoming payable when the contractual conditions have been fulfilled; to be contrasted with a 'servant' or 'employee': *World Book (Australia) Pty Ltd v FCT* (1992) 27 NSWLR 377; 108 ALR 510. In principle, an independent contractor may decide how to perform a task, although in practice the extent of control exercised by the party for whom work is being done may be substantial: *Stevens v Brodribb Sawmilling Co Pty Ltd* (1986) 160 CLR 16; 63 ALR 513. See also **Contract for services; Contract of employment; Economic reality test; Multiple test**.

Independent covenants Terms of a contract that are not dependent or contingent upon each other in, that the parties did not intend that performance of the contract was to take place only if both were valid or performed. Where one independent covenant is invalid it may be severed, as severance would not alter the nature and effect of the contract: *Brooks v Burns Philp Trustee Co Ltd* (1969) 121 CLR 432. See also **Severance**.

Independent expert An expert in a particular field relevant to an issue in a trial who has not previously examined or reported on the evidence for either party. Independent experts are competent but not compellable witnesses: *Re application of Forsyth: Cordova v Philips Roxane Laboratories Inc* [1984] 2 NSWLR 327.

Independent means An economic capability for subsistence which allows the person to be financially independent of any other person's help, such as a secure source of income which may not involve the earning of a wage or salary but may be enjoyed through interest, dividends or returns generated from invested capital.

Independent obligation An unconditional or absolute obligation, where a plaintiff may call on the defendant to perform without the plaintiff first performing: for example *Wickman Machine Tool Sales Ltd v L Schuler AG* [1972] 1 WLR 840. Clear words are necessary before a relation of independency will be found: for example *Automatic Fire Sprinklers Pty Ltd v Watson* (1946) 72 CLR 435. An example which sometimes occurs is the obligation to make a periodical payment: *Shevill v Builders Licensing Board* (1982) 149 CLR 620; 42 ALR 305. See also **Damages; Debt; Dependent obligation; Order of performance; Performance**.

Independent valuation A valuation by a person who is considered an expert in relation to valuations of that type whose pecuniary or other interests could not reasonably be regarded as being capable of affecting the person's ability to give an unbiased opinion in relation to the valuation: Corporations Regulations Sch 5 cl 1(1). See also **Valuation**.

Indeur 250 Stock Index A pan-European benchmark stock index of 250 listed companies in the European Union and the European Free Trade Association, weighted by the gross domestic product and the total market capitalisation of each country. The Indeur Blue Index comprises Europe's top 75 firms, measured by market capitalisation. The Indeur Index adopted a base of 1000 points in January 1987. It is compiled by Indec Ltd.

Index arbitrage A method of trading, exploiting differences between stock index futures prices and the corresponding theoretical futures prices. If the futures price exceeds its fair value, traders will engage in cash-and-carry arbitrage. If the futures price falls below its fair value, traders can exploit the pricing discrepancy. See also **Arbitrage; Share index futures contract**.

Index fund A fund weighted in the same proportions as the components of a share price index (such as the All Ordinaries Index). The performance of a fund consisting of shares weighted in this way will mirror that of the index, thus ensuring that the index fund will not perform better or worse than the market as a whole (or the particular segment to which the index relates). See also **Mutual fund; Share price index**.

•**Index number** The All Groups Consumer Price Index number for a particular quarter, being the weighted average of the consumer price index of the eight capital cities. The indexed cost base of an asset is calculated by reference to the index number. A table of the quarterly index numbers since the introduction of capital gains tax is found at (CTH) Income Tax Assessment Act 1936 s 160ZJ(1). See also **Asset; Capital gains tax; Cost base; Indexation factor; Indexed cost base**.

Index of Leading Indicators A monthly integrated index maintained by the United States Department of Commerce embracing a wide variety of numerical and financial indicators. It is widely used in the United States as a guide to present and future economic trends. The index includes such elements as the prices of industrial raw materials, federal budget surplus or deficit, stock prices, the consumer price index, new business formation, building permits, gross weekly pay and claims for unemployment benefits.

Indexation A system of adjusting items such as wages, prices or taxation and other living costs or investments to the rate of inflation. The effect of indexation is to remove or minimise the effect of price inflation in decreasing the real value of the item. See also **Inflation**.

•**Indexation factor** A figure used to adjust an amount in accord with changes in another amount. For example, in calculating the indexed cost base of an asset, the cost base is multiplied by the indexation factor: (CTH) Income Tax Assessment Act 1936 ss 160ZH(2), 160ZJ. This factor, rounded to three decimal places, is calculated according to (CTH) Income Tax Assessment Act 1936 s 160ZJ(5), (6). See also **Asset**; **Capital gain**; **Cost base**; **Index number**; **Indexed cost base**.

Indexed annuity An annuity in which regular payments are adjusted for inflation annually. See also **Annuity**.

Indexed bond A form of investment which seeks to compensate the investor for inflation, either in the form of indexing the capital invested or the interest earned. Indexed bonds issued by corporations are essentially variable return securities. See also **Bond**.

Indexed cost base The sum of the inflation-indexed components of the cost base of an asset: (CTH) Income Tax Assessment Act 1936 s 160ZH(2). However, the non-capital costs of ownership of a non-personal-use asset are not indexed. In calculating a capital gain, where a taxpayer has held an asset for more than 12 months, the indexed cost base is deducted from the sale proceeds: (CTH) Income Tax Assessment Act 1936 s 160Z(1)(a), (3). Effectively, this compensates for the effects of inflation when calculating a capital gain. Because of the method of calculation of the indexation factor, in a situation of deflation the indexed cost base equals the cost base. The formula for calculation, set out in (CTH) Income Tax Assessment Act 1936 ss 160ZH(2), 160ZJ, is: *cost base × indexation factor = indexed cost base*. See also **Asset**; **Capital gain**; **Cost base**; **Index number**; **Indexation factor**; **Non-capital costs of ownership**; **Personal use asset**.

Indexed debenture A form of debenture on which little or no interest is payable, but where the capital amount repayable is the amount subscribed plus additions over the term of the debenture calculated by reference to a price index. See also **Debenture**.

Indicator lending rate *Abbr* – ILR In banking, the base lending rate from which interest rates are set on most variable rate overdrafts and term loans. See also **Overdraft**; **Loan**; **Variable interest rate**.

Indicia of title Evidence of a property interest. For property under the Torrens system, a certificate of title and an executed memorandum of transfer that specifies the consideration and acknowledges its receipt, are sufficient indicia of title for an incoming mortgagee: *Reliance Finance Corp Pty Ltd v Heid* [1982] 1 NSWLR 466. See also **Mortgagee**.

•**Indictable offence** An offence triable by a judge and jury: for example (NSW) Interpretation Act 1987 s 21. Whether an offence is indictable depends upon the particular jurisdiction: for example (CTH) Crimes Act 1914 s 4G. There are different classes of indictable offences in some jurisdictions. An indictable offence can be dealt with summarily by a magistrate where it is of lesser seriousness: for example (CTH) Crimes Act 1914 s 4J(1). In some jurisdictions, the accused can elect to be tried by a judge without a jury: (NSW) Criminal Procedure Act 1986 s 32; (SA) Juries Act 1927 s 7.

Indifference analysis An analysis of consumer demand based on the notion of ordinal utility. The consumer is assumed to possess a given amount of money while being faced with the prices of all the goods that might be consumed. The consumer will then decide on a set or bundle of goods to buy influenced by the money available, the prices, and the tastes, preferences and needs of the buyer. The consumer may have considered several alternative sets of goods which could be purchased. They are then ranked in order of preferences such that, given any two bundles, the consumer can judge whether one is preferred to the other, or whether there is a sense of indifference between them, both being regarded as equally desirable.

Indirect acquisition An acquisition made through an agent, nominee or trustee (*Trade Practices Commission v Australian Iron & Steel Pty Ltd* (1990) 22 FCR 305; 92 ALR 395) and any form of acquisition in an indirect way, including the interposition of a wholly-owned subsidiary (*Australia Meat Holdings Pty Ltd v Trade Practices Commission* (1989) ATPR ¶40-392). Indirect acquisition by a corporation of shares in a body corporate or assets of any person is prohibited if the acquisition would have the effect of substantially lessening competition in a market: (CTH) Trade Practices Act 1974 s 50. See also **Acquisition**.

Indirect cost That cost which cannot be readily attributed to a specific program or activity, but which is incurred for the benefit of the organisation as a whole, for example common staff services and facilities.

•**Indirect marketing arrangements** A scheme of sale whereby the manufacturer or distributor sells via a third party sale through the agency of a retailer, but the property in the goods remains with the manufacturer or distributor until sale: (CTH) Sales Tax Assessment Act (No 1) 1930 s 23(1), 23(4A); *Thorn EMI Pty Ltd v FCT* (1987) 13 FCR 491; 71 ALR 728. See also **Indirect marketing sales**.

Indirect marketing sales The retail sale of assessable goods by a person ('marketer') who is not the manufacturer of the goods. The sale is made either by a person acting for the marketer, but who is not an employee of the marketer, or from the premises used by the person, other than the principal, mainly for making retail sales: (CTH) Sales Tax Assessment Act 1992 s 20. The purpose of indirect marketing sales is to turn what would otherwise have been a wholesale sale into a retail sale. The Act operates to ensure that the taxable value of the retail sale will be the same as if it were, notionally, a wholesale sale. See also **Indirect marketing arrangements**.

Indirect self-acquisition The acquisition by a company of an interest in its own shares resulting from the acquisition of shares in its holding company. A company must not acquire shares in its holding company and any such acquisition is void: Corporations Law ss 185(3), 205(1)(b). An indirect acquisition includes the acquisition by a company of shares in another company which has substantial control over it, even though it is not a holding company. The Australian Securities Commission has power to declare such schemes unacceptable, in which case the court may make orders affecting the scheme, for example declaring the transaction void: Corporations Law Pt 2.4 Div 4A. See also **Maintenance of capital; Self-acquisition scheme; Share buy-back**.

Individual bargaining The process by which an employer and an employee negotiate an individual contract of employment, regulating the terms and conditions of employment: for example (VIC) Employee Relations Act 1992. It differs from collective bargaining, by which a collective agreement is reached that provides for the terms and conditions of employment to apply to two or more employees. See also **Collective bargaining; Contract of employment; Enterprise bargaining; Individual employment agreement; Industrial tribunal**.

Individual employment agreement An agreement between an employee and the employer on any terms they think fit: (VIC) Employee Relations Act 1992 s 9. The individual employment agreement must contain minimum terms including paid annual leave, paid sick leave, and a base rate of pay. See also **Employment agreement**.

Indivisible contract A contract that requires entire performance. Indivisible contracts usually require performance of a single specified task such as the construction of a building. Where a contract is indivisible, a party cannot recover anything under the contract unless the whole task is completed: *Phillips v Ellinson Brothers Pty Ltd* (1941) 65 CLR 221. However, if entire performance is rendered impossible by the promisee, the performing party is entitled to the value of the performance rendered: *Phillips v Ellinson Brothers Pty Ltd*. Further, if the amount of work not performed is slight or trivial, the performing party is entitled to an amount equal to the benefit received by the promisee: *Williamson v Murdoch* (1912) 14 WAR 54. The performing party may also be entitled to recover under a new contract that dispenses with the requirement of exact performance where the performance is voluntarily received by the promisee: *Steele v Tardiani* (1946) 72 CLR 386. See also **Divisible contract; Exact performance**.

Indoor management rule Persons dealing with a company in good faith may assume that acts within its constitution and powers have been properly and duly performed and are not bound to inquire whether acts of internal management have been regular: *Northside Developments Pty Ltd v Registrar-General* (1990) 170 CLR 146; 93 ALR 385. The rule is supplemented by Corporations Law s 164(1) which provides that a person having dealings with a company is entitled to make, in relation to those dealings, a number of assumptions. Also known as 'rule in Turquand's case': *Industrial Royal British Bank v Turquand* (1856) 6 El & Bl 327; 11 ER 886. See also **Constructive notice**.

Indorsee The person to whom rights are transferred by indorsement of a bill of exchange, promissory note, cheque, or payment order. See also **Indorsement; Indorser**.

•**Indorsement** The act of writing on a negotiable instrument, usually on the back, the name of the person who is the transferor, signifying the intention to transfer the right to payment. To operate as a negotiation, an indorsement must be written on the instrument, or an allonge; signed by the indorser; and be an indorsement of the entire bill or cheque: for example (CTH) Cheques and Payment Orders Act 1986 s 41. Indorsement usually makes the indorser a surety for payment. Also known as 'endorsement'. See also **Allonge; Conditional indorsement; Indorsement in blank; Partial indorsement; Special indorsement**.

Indorsement in blank The indorsement of a bill of exchange which does not specify an indorsee: (CTH) Bills of Exchange Act 1909 s 39(1). An indorsement in blank is made merely by an indorser signing the bill, usually on the back of the bill: (CTH) Bills of Exchange Act 1909 s 37. See also **Bearer bill; Indorser; Indorsement; Order bill; Special indorsement**.

Indorser The person who transfers a negotiable instrument by writing on it, usually by signing its back, and delivering it to the indorsee: for example (CTH) Bills of Exchange Act 1909 s 4. By indorsing the instrument, the indorser engages that on due presentment it will be accepted or paid according to its terms, and that if dishonoured, the indorser will compensate the holder or a subsequent indorser who is compelled to pay it: (CTH) Bills of Exchange Act 1909 s 60(2)(a); (CTH) Cheques and Payment Orders Act 1986 s 73. See also **Backer; Delivery; Dishonour; Indorsee; Indorsement; Negotiable instrument**.

•**Inducement** To persuade or influence a person to act.

Consumer protection An act of compulsion by force or threat of force, or some act of persuasion aimed at ensuring that an act is committed which amounts to a contravention. Intent, based on knowledge of the essential elements of the contravention, must be proved. Conduct which constitutes inducing a contravention of consumer protection legislation may be prevented by an injunction or other order. The conduct itself is an offence where the legislation has been contravened: (CTH) Trade Practices Act 1974 ss 75B(1), 79(1), 80A, 82, 87; (NSW) Fair Trading Act 1987 ss 61, 62, 65. See also **Ancillary liability; Counsel**.

Contract That which motivates or persuades a person to enter a contract. If a material representation is made which is calculated to induce the representee to enter into a contract and that person enters into the contract, there arises a fair inference of fact that they were induced to do so by the representation: *Gould v Vaggelas* (1985) 157 CLR 215 at 236; 56 ALR 31; *Dominelli Ford (Hurstville) Pty Ltd v Karmot Auto Spares Pty Ltd*

(1992) 38 FCR 471; 110 ALR 535. See also **Misrepresentation**; **Offer**.

Inducing breach of contract Interference with contractual relations.

• **Industrial action** A failure or refusal to work or to attend for work; or performing work in a manner different from that in which it is customarily performed; or a ban, limitation or restriction on performing work: (CTH) Industrial Relations Act 1988 s 4; (NSW) Industrial Relations Act 1996 s 4, Dictionary. See also **Lock-out**; **Strike**; **Work ban**.

• **Industrial agreement** An agreement between an employer and employees (or their representatives) about the terms and conditions of employment, or other industrial matters. An industrial agreement differs from an industrial award in that an agreement is reached by negotiations between the parties, while an award is a decision of an independent tribunal arbitrating a dispute between the parties. See also **Certified agreement**; **Enterprise agreement**; **Industrial award**; **Industrial matter**; **Industrial tribunal**.

Industrial area An area zoned in a local environmental plan or planning scheme as suitable for industrial use.

• **Industrial authority** A body or office exercising functions with respect to industrial relations, that is declared by statute to be an industrial authority. Examples are the Industrial Relations Court of South Australia, the Industrial Relations Commission of South Australia, the Industrial Relations Advisory Committee, the Employee Ombudsman and industrial inspectors: (SA) Industrial and Employee Relations Act 1994 ss 4, 7. See also **Industrial relations**; **Industrial tribunal**.

• **Industrial award** An order establishing terms and conditions of employment made under (CTH) Industrial Relations Act 1988 s 111 for the purpose of settling an industrial dispute. An award binds the parties to the dispute and proceedings (*R v Kelly; Ex parte Victoria* (1950) 81 CLR 64 at 82), successive employers (*George Hudson Ltd v Australian Timber Workers' Union* (1923) 32 CLR 413), non-disputant employees of the same union (*Burwood Cinema Ltd v Australian Theatrical and Amusement Employees' Association* (1925) 35 CLR 528) and non-unionist employees of the same employer (*Metal Trades Employers Assn v Amalgamated Engineering Union* (1935) 54 CLR 387), but must not constitute a 'common rule' for all employees and employers in an industry: *Australian Boot Trade Employees' Federation v Whybrow & Co* (1910) 11 CLR 311. See also **Conciliation and arbitration power**.

Industrial damages Court awards against trade unions for the damaging effects of industrial action. The right to strike has no status in law, whereas the right to damages is based on common law.

Industrial democracy The concept that employees should be given the opportunity to participate in the decision making processes and management of their organisation. For example by representation on decision making boards. Employee participation is seen as improving labour-management relations by increasing employee motivation and efficiency; and increasing job satisfaction for workers through greater responsibility and influence within the organisation. See also **Managerial prerogative**.

• **Industrial dispute** A disagreement or difference between people or groups of people in industry on a matter pertaining to the relationship between employers and employees. A dispute may arise when one party makes a claim and the other party rejects it. The dispute may be contrived, but it must be real and not a mere fiction: *R v Cohen; Ex parte A-G (Qld)* (1981) 157 CLR 331; 38 ALR 129. 'Industrial dispute' is not a technical or legal expression but one which is to be given its popular meaning: *R v Coldham; Ex parte Australian Social Welfare Union* (1983) 153 CLR 297; 47 ALR 225. See also **Industrial matter**; **Log of claims**; **Paper dispute**; **Social Welfare Union case**.

Industrial espionage The act or practice of spying by one company on the secrets of another. An example is the attempt by one company to obtain the results of research and development undertaken by another, hoping thereby to improve productivity at a small cost. Espionage techniques include hiring key employees of a competitor, paying a rival's employees, wiretapping, circumventing patents, and exploiting the law.

• **Industrial instrument** A contract of employment, or a law, award, determination or agreement relating to terms or conditions of employment: Corporations Law s 9. See also **Award**; **Contract of employment**; **Enterprise agreement**.

Industrial law The area of law that regulates industrial relations, that is, the relations between employers and employees and their representative organisations. Industrial law concerns the prevention and settlement of industrial disputes by conciliation and arbitration, or by agreement, or proscription, under the laws of the Commonwealth and of each State. See also **Industrial relations**; **Employment law**.

• **Industrial matter** In general, a matter pertaining to the relationship between employers and employees. Matters or things affecting or relating to work done or to be done, or the privileges, rights or duties of employers or employees in any industry ((NSW) Industrial Relations Act 1996 s 5), or anything that concerns or arises from the employment of a person: (VIC) Employee Relations Act 1992 s 4. Examples are matters relating to wages, allowance or remuneration, hours of employment, qualification or status of employees, the mode, terms and conditions of employment, and dismissals. See also **Industrial dispute**.

• **Industrial organisation** An association of employers or employees registered or recognised under an industrial relations statute: for example (NSW) Industrial Relations Act 1996 s 4, Dictionary; (QLD) Industrial Relations Act 1990 s 5. See also **Trade union**.

• **Industrial plant** Generally, any plant, melting pot or still used in industry but excluding fuel burning equipment and motor vehicles. Industrial plant includes any plant or equipment used for the manufacturing, processing, handling, moving, storing or disposing of materials in or in connection with any trade, industry or process; or any plant or equipment of a prescribed class or description: for example (NSW) Clean Air Act 1961 s 5(1); (VIC) Environment Protection Act 1970 s 4.

•**Industrial premises** Improvements on land which are used for non-residential purposes, such as manufacturing or 'secondary industry': *Gillings v Cmr of Stamps* [1983] 31 SASR 469. See also **Improvement**.

Industrial Registry See **Australian Industrial Registry**.

•**Industrial relations** Relationships between employers and employees: *Re McCarthy and Australian Telecommunications Commission* (1987) 13 ALD 1. More generally, the interaction between labour (employees or other workers and their representatives) and management (employers and their representatives) as each side attempts to improve its position. Usual subjects of negotiation between labour and management include wages, hours of work and other conditions of employment. See also **Australian industrial system; Employee; Employer; Labour**.

Industrial relations system The formal machinery and procedures by which labour and management interact to prevent or resolve conflicts concerning the employment relationship, such as the terms and conditions of employment, or the activities of trade unions. In Australia, the industrial relations system is a mixture of compulsory arbitration (resolution of disputes by an independent industrial tribunal) and collective bargaining (direct negotiations between employers and employees or their representatives). See also **Australian industrial system; Collective bargaining; Compulsory arbitration; Industrial relations**.

Industrial sabotage Wilful damage of or interference with equipment, typically done by discontented employees during an industrial dispute. See also **Industrial dispute**.

Industrial tort One of a group of torts that impose liability on trade unions or employees for the economic loss resulting from industrial action taken in the course of furthering their industrial interests. The torts are intimidation; interference with contractual relations; conspiracy to injure; unlawful means conspiracy; and unlawful interference. See also **Interference with contractual relations; Intimidation; Unlawful interference with business**.

•**Industrial tribunal** A tribunal established under Commonwealth or State law to exercise the power to regulate the terms and conditions of employment by arbitration and conciliation. The decision of a tribunal arbitrating between parties in dispute is in the form of an award. In almost all States the power may be exercised without the agreement of some or all of the employees or employers (or their representative bodies) affected by the arbitration. See also **Australian Industrial Relations Commission; Compulsory arbitration; Industrial award; Industrial law; Tribunal**.

•**Industrial waste** Generally, waste emanating from industry. Unwanted by-products from commercial, industrial or trade activities or from laboratories; or surplus to an activity, in the form of a solid, liquid, gas or energy,

whether or not of value: for example (QLD) Environmental Protection Act 1994 s 13; (VIC) Environment Protection Act 1970 s 4.

Industrial zone A zone allocated for industry within a town-planning scheme or environmental plan. The range of industries accommodated may include light industry (industry not interfering with an area's amenity), service industry premises (premises used for light industry), general industry (heavy or general industry), hazardous noxious or offensive industry (industry which could constitute a danger to persons or properties, or is offensive or noxious), waterfront industry (industry requiring direct access to a river, creek or stream), and extractive industry. Standards are defined for industrial zones.

Industrials The shares of industrial companies. The two general categories of shares traded on the Australian Stock Exchange are shares in industrial companies and in mining and oil companies. Mining and oil equities are traded in the same way as industrial shares but some are considered to involve greater risk due to the uncertainties of exploration, production and commodity prices. The industrial sector comprises companies from a variety of industries including manufacturing, retailing and finance. See also **Investment; Share**.

•**Industry 1.** All the activities of a country which provide employment in the production of goods and services. Any business, trade, manufacture, undertaking or calling of employers; and any calling, service, employment, handicraft, industrial occupation or vocation of employees; and a branch of an industry and a group of industries: (CTH) Industrial Relations Act 1988 s 4; *R v Coldham; Ex parte Australian Social Welfare Union* (1983) 153 CLR 297; 47 ALR 225. It may also include any business or activity in which workers are employed: (SA) Workers Rehabilitation and Compensation Act 1986 s 3. **2.** Specifically, an industry comprises all those activities directed to the production of a given class of goods and services. See also **Employment**.

Industry assistance Action or scheme of a government designed to facilitate the establishment, expansion or development of an industry. Typically involves one or more interrelated mechanisms including, where appropriate, monetary grants or subsidies, acquisition of land, provision of services and procurement of favourable arrangements with local authorities: for example (NSW) State Development and Industries Assistance Act 1966.

Industry Commission A body formed in 1989 from the merger of the Industries Assistance Commission, the Interstate Commission and the Business Regulation Review Unit: (CTH) Industry Commission Act 1989. The commission is the Commonwealth Government's major review and inquiry body dealing with industry matters. The initial inquiries undertaken by the commission were into mining, energy generation, railways, product liability and recycling. Concurrently, the Commission has developed techniques to evaluate industry assistance and regulation, estimating the effects of Commonwealth Government policies and formulating an approach to policy issues.

•**Industry standard** An informal and often unwritten standard or practice adopted generally within an industry. An industry standard or practice may be concerned with the design or formulation of products (for example *Cross v TNT Management Pty Ltd (t/as TNT Transport System)* (1987) 46 SASR 105), the warnings or instructions provided with products (for example *James Hardie Industries Ltd (t/as Fowler Ware) v Prenc* (unrptd SC(Vic), Full Court, 94/83, 6 December 1988); *Forbes v Olympic General Products (Qld) Pty Ltd* (1989) Aust Torts Reports ¶80-301), or with methods of manufacture (for example *Daniels and Daniels v R White & Sons Ltd* [1938] 4 All ER 258; *Greenwood v Sefton Holdings Pty Ltd* (unrptd SC(NSW), Wood J, 12235/88, 6 July 1990)). See also **Mandatory standard; Standards Association of Australia standard.**

Industry Statement 1991 The March 1991 statement by the Commonwealth government that announced the general level of protection given to industry would be reduced after 1992 from 10-15 per cent to a general rate of 5 per cent by 1996. Tariffs on passenger motor vehicles would be phased down from 35 per cent in 1992 by annual steps of 2.5 per cent to 15 per cent by the end of the century. Tariffs on textiles, clothing and footwear would be reduced to a maximum of 25 per cent by the end of the century with quotas terminated by 1993. General agricultural assistance would also be reduced in line with the pace of tariff reform in manufacturing. Financial and retaining assistance would be provided for workers displaced by these measures.

Industry union A union that represents all workers in a particular industry, whatever kind of work they do. An example is the Australian Meat Industry Employees' Union. See also **Craft union; Enterprise union; General union; Occupational union.**

Ineffective accord and satisfaction An unsuccessful attempt to discharge a contract by the plaintiff accepting something in place of his or her cause of action. Accord and satisfaction will be ineffective where the consideration offered has no tangible value or amounts to no more than part payment of the debt: *Great Fingall Consolidated Ltd v Sheehan* (1905) 3 CLR 176; *Ballantyne v Phillott* (1961) 105 CLR 379. See also **Accord and satisfaction; Compromise; Consideration.**

Ineffective contract A contract that is void or unenforceable. A contract may be inherently ineffective in that it was never valid, or it may become ineffective despite being valid in its inception. A contract may be inherently ineffective because it lacks one of the elements necessary for formation, or because it is rendered void or unenforceable by statute or public policy. A contract may become ineffective because it has been discharged or rescinded. A person may have a claim for restitution of a benefit provided in reliance on an ineffective contract: for example *British Steel Corp v Cleveland Bridge and Engineering Co Ltd* [1984] 1 All ER 504; *George v Roach* (1942) 67 CLR 253. See also **Inherently ineffective contract; Restitution; Unjust enrichment.**

Inequality of bargaining power The situation in which one party to a contract is unable to properly determine or act in his or her own best interests. A person's bargaining power may be impaired by reason of his or her own needs or desires, or by his or her own ignorance or infirmity coupled with undue influence or pressure brought to bear on him or her by or for the benefit of the other party: *Lloyds Bank Ltd v Bundy* [1975] QB 326 at 339. A transaction will not be set aside merely by reason of inequality of bargaining power: *Commercial Bank of Australia Ltd v Amadio* (1983) 151 CLR 447 at 462; 46 ALR 402. Similarly, inequality of bargaining power will not of itself give rise to a fiduciary relationship, although it may provide evidence that one party placed trust and reliance in the other: *Hospital Products Ltd v United States Surgical Corp* (1984) 156 CLR 41 at 70, 142; 55 ALR 417. See also **Fiduciary relationship; Unconscionable.**

Inertia selling The practice of sending unordered goods to consumers and billing them for the goods. Inertia selling of goods often involves the consumer being told that if the goods are not returned within a certain time the recipient will be taken to have agreed to purchase them. Inertia selling is prohibited by consumer protection legislation: for example (CTH) Trade Practices Act 1974 ss 63A, 64, 65; (NSW) Fair Trading Act 1987 ss 57, 58, 59; (VIC) Fair Trading Act 1985 ss 29, 30. See also **Unsolicited credit card.**

Infant industry A young and growing industry, often considered to need assistance in the face of foreign competition. Such industries may be afforded protection or granted a subsidy until strong enough to stand alone. See also **Industry.**

•**Inferior court** Any court which is not a superior court; that is, a court of lesser status than the Supreme Court of a State or Territory. Generally, the District or County Court, the magistrate's courts, and the children's courts of each jurisdiction are inferior courts. An inferior court has no inherent powers and must always source their power to the statute which establishes them: *Walton v McBride* (1995) 36 NSWLR 440; *Household Financial Services Ltd v Commercial Tribunal of New South Wales* (1995) 36 NSWLR 220. See also **Prerogative writs.**

Inflation A continuous increase in the level of prices as measured by the consumer price index. When running at high levels, inflation raises domestic costs of production, weakening the competitive position of Australian exports compared with those of countries with lower inflation rates, leading to a depreciation of the Australian dollar. All countries have experienced inflation since the 1939-45 war. Two principal, interrelated types of inflation are 'demand-pull' and cost-push'. Inflation may be caused by external factors such as rising import prices, and domestic factors such as the effect of prolonged drought and increases in housing costs. During the 1980s, consumer prices rose on average by 8.7 per cent per annum. In the early 1990s, the rate of inflation moderated with the onset of a recession.

Information circular A document prepared on behalf of management or in association with the solicitation of proxies to accompany the notice of a shareholders' meeting, as required by corporations and securities legislation. The document should exhibit such information as the parties making the solicitation, election of directors, auditor's appointment and other important issues to be initiated during the shareholders' meeting.

Information disclosure In consumer protection legislation, an order that may be made against a trader who has engaged in misleading or deceptive conduct, especially misleading or deceptive advertising: (CTH) Trade Practices Act 1974 s 80A(1)(a); (NSW) Fair Trading Act 1987 s 67(a). The trader is required to disclose specified information to the public, or to a particular person or group. The order is only appropriate if a number of people are likely to have been misled or deceived, and to be unaware of the deception or their remedies: *Annand and Thompson Pty Ltd v Trade Practices Commission* (1979) 25 ALR 91. See also **Corrective advertising**; **Misleading or deceptive conduct**.

Information privacy principles *Abbr* – IPP
Principles governing the use, storage and disclosure of records of personal information of which a federal agency has possession but not control: (CTH) Privacy Act 1988 s 14. The principles govern: the manner and purpose of collection of personal information (Principle 1); solicitation of personal information from an individual concerned and generally (Principles 2 and 3); storage and security of personal information (Principle 4); information relating to records kept by a record-keeper (Principle 5); access to and alteration of records containing personal information (Principles 6 and 7); record-keepers checking the accuracy of information before use (Principle 8); the use of personal information only for relevant purposes (Principle 9); and limits on use and disclosure of personal information (Principles 10 and 11). See also **Information Privacy Principles complaint**.

Information Privacy Principles complaint A complaint made to the Privacy Commissioner under the (CTH) Privacy Act 1988 about an alleged interference with privacy. Complaints usually fall into one of three categories; a breach of one or more of the eleven Information Privacy Principles, a breach of Tax File Number Guidelines, or credit reporting infringements. Certain classes of documents may be certified by the Attorney-General as not liable to disclosure to the Commissioner in the course of an investigation: (CTH) Privacy Act 1988 s 70 These are documents the production of which would be contrary to the public interest by disclosing national security information, communication between federal and state governments, Cabinet and Executive Council deliberations, or which would prejudice criminal investigation or the fair trial of a person: (CTH) Privacy Act 1988 s 70(1). See also **Information Privacy Principles**.

•**Informed consent** Consent to an act after being given full or adequate disclosure. See also **Agent**; **Conflict of interest**; **Duty to disclose**; **Fiduciary**; **Fiduciary duty**; **Principal**.

Equity A defence to a charge of breach of fiduciary duty established where the principal had been given full and frank disclosure of, and consented to, a transaction involving a conflict of interest, or the fiduciary retaining some benefit: *Boardman v Phipps* [1967] 2 AC 46; *Queensland Mines Ltd v Hudson* (1978) 18 ALR 1; 3 ACLR 176. See also **Agent**; **Conflict of interest**; **Duty to disclose**; **Fiduciary**; **Fiduciary duty**; **Principal**.

Infra *Lat* – below.

•**Infrastructure 1.** In relation to urban development, the system of essential services, utilities and public and community facilities necessary for urban areas to function. The services include water, sewerage, electricity, roads, schools, and health facilities. The framework of key facilities which supports communities and their industrial and commercial activities. Infrastructure comprises communications, transportation systems, electricity generation and distribution, water supply networks, sewerage, roads, housing, schools and universities, health services, entertainment facilities and community support services. The term may be given specific meaning in the context of a particular undertaking; for example (QLD) State Development and Public Works Organization Act 1971 s 5. **2.** The infrastructure of a telecommunications network means lines, equipment and other facilities used in connection with that network: (NSW) Government Telecommunications Act 1991 s 3.

•**Infrastructure borrowing** A loan or debenture bond made or issued after June 1992 by an incorporated company which is borrowed for the sole acquisition or use in projects which are to be used for a minimum period of 30 years to produce an assessable income. Interest received on these bonds is exempt from income tax, and the interest paid is not allowable as a deduction: (CTH) Income Tax Assessment Act 1936 s 159G$_{ZZZZE}$. See also **Allowable deduction**; **Assessable income**; **Debenture**; **Exempt income**; **Interest**; **Loan**.

Infrastructure contribution Contribution from a developer, as a condition of development consent, toward the cost of amenities and public services needed by the development. A contribution may be financial or by way of land for public purposes. Generally, local councils in Australia may levy contribution for such things as acquiring land for open space, development costs associated with open spaces and recreation, and acquiring land for, and construction of, local roads, drainage systems, and developing a range of community facilities.

Inherent risk In a company audit, the susceptibility of an account balance or class of transactions to misstatement that could be material, individually or when aggregated with misstatements in other balances or classes, assuming that there were no related internal controls: Statement of Auditing Practice AUP 27 para 14. External influences on inherent risk include economic and competitive conditions, changes in technology or accounting practices common to the industry: Statement of Auditing Practice AUP 12 para 10. Internal influences include the susceptibility of assets to loss or misappropriation and the complexity of the internal control structure: Statement of Auditing Practice AUP 12 para 11. See also **Audit risk**.

Inherent vice In relation to goods, a vice which is an innate, natural or normal quality of the goods.

Insurance An innate quality of goods that causes them to deteriorate as a result of their natural behaviour in the ordinary course of the contemplated voyage, without the intervention of any fortuitous external accident or casualty: *TM Noten BV v Harding* [1990] 2 Lloyd's Rep 283 at 288. For example, if goods are damaged because they were wet when shipped, the damage is said to be a result of inherent vice: *TM Noten BV v Harding*. Unless the policy provides otherwise, an insurer is not liable to indemnify an insured for loss caused by inherent vice: (CTH) Marine Insurance Act 1909 s 61(2)(c).

Inherently ineffective contract A contract that is void or unenforceable at the outset by reason of a defect such as failure to agree, uncertainty, incompleteness, failure of a condition precedent, absence of consideration, absence of intention to create legal relations, mistake, or illegality. Where a contract is void but one of the parties makes payments for performance in reliance on the contract, the money will be recoverable on the basis of unjust enrichment: for example *George v Roach* (1942) 67 CLR 253. See also **Ineffective contract**; **Restitution**; **Unjust enrichment**.

Initial margin requirement In corporations law, the amount a buyer is required to deposit with a broker before commencing trading. In futures trading, an initial margin is prescribed in respect of each of the different types of contract available. See also **Broker**; **Futures contract**; **Margin**.

Initial public offering *Abbr* – IPO The first offer of shares to the public. Unless the offer is an excluded issue or the company is an excluded company a prospectus must be lodged: Corporations Law ss 66(3), 1018(1). See also **Excluded offer or invitation**; **Private offer**; **Prospectus**.

Injunction A court order of an equitable nature requiring a person to do, or refrain from doing, a particular action. Injunctions may be classified as final or interlocutory; mandatory or prohibitory; ex parte or inter partes; and equitable or legal.

Contract An equitable remedy concerned with securing performance *in specie*, usually granted to restrain the violation of a provision or term of a contract: *J C Williamson Ltd v Lukey* (1931) 45 CLR 282. The court will grant an injunction where it is equitable to do so: *Pearson v Arcadia Stores Guyra Ltd* (1935) 53 CLR 571. See also **Equity**; **Inter partes**; **Negative duty**; **Positive duty**; **Remedy**; **Specific performance**.

Equity An order of a court that stops a person from doing, or demands that a person do, a particular action. An injunction is a coercive or specific (as opposed to substitutionary) remedy. It differs from specific performance, which is only granted to enforce contractual obligations. Injunctions may require ('enjoin') a particular act ('mandatory injunctions') or forbid a particular act ('prohibitory injunctions'); they may be interlocutory (or interim) or final; they may be granted ex parte or inter partes; and they may be granted to prevent wrongs currently existing or to prevent wrongs that have not been committed ('quia timet injunctions'). An injunction may be permanent, for a specified period of time, or until a proceeding in a court is determined. As the injunction is a remedy of equitable origin, an application may fail if the applicant cannot persuade the court to exercise its discretion in favour of the order being granted: for example *Re Chemists' Federation Agreement* [1958] 3 All ER 448. See also **Ex parte injunction**; **Interlocutory injunction**.

Tort A remedy available with regard to various torts including trespass to land, nuisance, and defamation. Courts are more inclined to grant injunctions where there is a likelihood that the defendant will actually do, or repeat the act complained of, and where damages might be an inadequate remedy: *LJP Investments Pty Ltd v Howard Chia Investments Pty Ltd* (1989) 24 NSWLR 490. See also **Damages**.

Injurious falsehood A false assertion calculated to injure a person in respect of the person's property, products, or business (*Sungravure v Middle East Airlines Airliban SAL* (1975) 134 CLR 1), either oral or written maliciously, that does in fact produce actual damage (*Ratcliffe v Evans* [1892] 2 QB 524; *Hall-Gibbs Mercantile Agency Ltd v Dun* (1910) 12 CLR 84). Originally protecting against attacks on title to land, the tort was widened to protect against disparagement of a trader's property, products, and business, which damaged the trader's business. Also known as 'slander of goods', 'slander of title', and 'trade libel'.

• **Injury** 1. Physical or mental damage to a person ((CTH) National Occupational Health and Safety Commission Act 1985 s 3), including aggravation or acceleration of an injury and the recurrence of a pre-existing injury (for example (CTH) Safety Rehabilitation and Compensation Act 1988 s 4; (CTH) Seafarers Rehabilitation and Compensation Act 1992 s 3), prenatal injury, psychological or psychiatric injury, and damage to artificial members such as eyes, teeth or limbs, to crutches or to other aids of a similar nature including spectacles (for example (NSW) Motor Accidents Act 1988 s 3), nervous shock (for example (VIC) Transport Accident Act 1986 s 3), death resulting from injuries (for example (QLD) Workers Compensation Act 1990 s 2.1; *Lloyds Bank Ltd v Eagle Star Insurance Co* [1951] 1 TLR 803), the invasion of the body by a virus (*Favelle Mort Ltd v Murray* (1976) 133 CLR 580; 8 ALR 649). 2. The infringement of some legal right, often considered as having a monetary value: *Hilton Hotel (1963) Ltd v Dominion Insurance Corp* (1968) 1 DLR (3d) 214. 3. In insurance law, a physiological change or physical damage to the human body as the result of the happening of the event insured against: *Deeble v Nott* (1941) 65 CLR 104. 4. Physical damage or injury to goods. See also **Accident insurance**; **Health insurance**; **Personal accident and illness insurance**; **Workers' compensation insurance**.

Inland bill A bill of exchange which is, or on its face purports to be, drawn and payable within Australasia, or which is drawn within Australasia upon a resident of Australasia: (CTH) Bills of Exchange Act 1909 s 9(1). There is no requirement to signify on the bill the place of drawing, the payment, or the place of residence of the acceptor. Unless the contrary intention appears on the face of a bill, the holder may treat it as an inland bill. See also **Acceptor**; **Australasia**; **Bill of exchange**; **Foreign bill**; **Noting**.

Inland note A note which is or on its face purports to be made and payable within Australasia: (CTH) Bills of Exchange Act 1909 s 89(4). See also **Australasia**; **Foreign note**; **Inland bill**; **Promissory note**.

Innkeeper's liability An innkeeper is strictly liable as an insurer, subject to specific exceptions and limitations, for any damage to, including the loss of, any goods of guests which are brought within the hospitium of the inn: (NSW) Innkeepers Act 1968 s 5; (VIC) Carriers and Innkeepers Act 1958 s 28: *Irving v Heferen* [1995] 1 Qd R 255.

Innkeeper's lien The legal right of an innkeeper to retain possession of a guest's property deposited by the guest at the inn, until the innkeeper is paid for the debts that the guest has incurred while at the inn: *Alldis v Huxley* (1891) 12 LR (NSW) 158; *Irving v Heferen* [1995] 1 Qd R 255. The lien does not apply to the goods of a lodger: *Alldis v Huxley*. In some jurisdictions, the lien does not extend to the guest's vehicle and its contents: (NSW) Innkeepers Act 1968 s 8; (VIC) Carriers and Innkeepers Act 1958 s 31. See also **Lien**.

Innocent misrepresentation A residual category of misrepresentation that contains all non-fraudulent misrepresentations made with an absence of moral delinquency. Equity permits the party misled to rescind the contract ab initio (from the beginning), providing the parties can be restored to their pre-contractual positions. For a purely innocent misrepresentation that is neither fraudulent nor negligent, damages are not available at common law, except where the innocent misrepresentation also falls within the concept of negligent misrepresentation. However, damages are available under statute for an innocent misrepresentation which amounts to misleading and deceptive conduct: (CTH) Trade Practices Act 1974 s 52. See also **Contract**; **Damages**; **Fraudulent misrepresentation**; **Misleading or deceptive conduct**; **Misrepresentation**; **Negligent misrepresentation**; **Rescission**.

Innocent non-disclosure In insurance law, unintentional non-disclosure of facts material to a thing insured. Non-disclosure, whether innocent or fraudulent, renders the contract voidable at the option of the insurer: (CTH) Marine Insurance Act 1909 s 24(1). See also **Disclosure**.

Innominate term See **Intermediate term**.

•**Innovation** 1. A new or improved product or method of production. 2. The process by which a new or improved product or method of production is developed: (VIC) Australian Food Industry Science Centre Act 1995 s 3. 3. In relation to whether experimental activities 'involve innovation' for the purposes of deciding whether those activities are 'research and development activities' under (CTH) Income Tax Assessment Act 1936 s 73B (1), an appreciable element of novelty is required: *AAT case 8912* (1993) 26 ATR 1262. See also **Novation**.

Innovative Agricultural Marketing Program *Abbr* – IAMP Established in 1987, a Commonwealth government program providing funds to assist innovative agricultural projects. Examples are the export of dried beef and smoked products to the Japanese market, the shipment of Australian cut flowers overseas, the export of organic produce and the marketing of North Queensland coffee.

Input output analysis The quantitative analysis of inter-industry relations. All transactions that involve the sale of products or services within an economy during a given period are arranged in a square indicating concurrently the sectors making and receiving delivery. The preparation of input-output tables has created a better understanding of how the economic system works. Input-output tables are published in conjunction with the national accounts by the Australian Bureau of Statistics, providing a basis for projections of the pattern of output and employment in the future. Also known as 'coronial inquest'.

•**Inscribed stock** Stocks and shares, the ownership of which is simply recorded in a register with no share certificates issued. Inscribed stock comprises Treasury bonds and securities issued by semi-government authorities, as in (QLD) Government Loan Act 1986 s 5; (WA) Dampier Port Authority Act 1985 s 3.

•**Inside information** See **Insider trading**.

Insider A person who possesses information that is not generally available which, if it was generally available, a reasonable person would expect to have a material effect on the price or value of the securities of a body corporate. The person must know, or ought reasonably to have known, that the information was not generally available and that it might have a material effect on the price or value of those securities if it were generally available: Corporations Law s 1002G(1). The acts from which an insider is prohibited are contained in Corporations Law s 1002G(2)-(3). See also **Insider trading**.

Insider trading Trading by any person who knows, or ought to know, that information on the price of securities in his or her possession is not generally available to other traders on the market and that if it were available, it might have a material effect on the price of those securities; and that a reasonable person would expect that information to otherwise materially affect the price of those securities: Corporations Law s 1002G. The provision precludes trading, procuring others to trade and communicating inside information to others. Corporations Law ss 1002G-1002T and (CTH) Corporations Regulations reg 7.11.01 provide various exceptions to the prohibition in s 1002G. See also **Chinese wall**.

•**Insolvency** The inability to pay debts as and when they become due and payable: Corporations Law s 95A(1). A company is insolvent if it is experiencing an 'endemic shortage of working capital' (*Hymix Concrete Pty Ltd v Garrity* (1977) 13 ALR 321; 2 ACLR 559), as opposed to a temporary lack of liquidity (*Bank of Australasia v Hall, Trustee of the Estate of Robertson (in liq)* (1907) 4 CLR 1514). Rebuttable presumptions of insolvency exist where the company fails to comply with a statutory demand, where execution is returned unsatisfied or where action is taken to enforce a floating charge by appointment of a receiver or by the chargee going into possession, personally or by agent: s 459C(2). Separate presumptions are created by Corporations Law s 588E(4) for the purpose of recovery proceedings. See also **External administration**; **Insolvent**; **Statutory demand**; **Winding up**.

•**Insolvent** 1. A debtor who is unable to pay debts as and when they fall due for payment. 2. The state of being unable to pay such debts.

Bankruptcy Inability to pay debts as they become due from a debtor's own money: (CTH) Bankruptcy Act 1966 s 122(1). A trustee who seeks to set aside a payment as a preference has the onus of proving that the debtor was insolvent at the time of payment: *Re Brechin; Ex parte Putnin and Stokes (Australasia) Ltd* (1986) 12 FCR 184. See also **Debtor's own money**; **Preference**; **Solvent**; **Trustee in bankruptcy**.

Corporations The state of being unable to pay debts: Corporations Law s 95A(2). A body corporate becomes insolvent if it commences to be wound up or ceases to carry on business, or when a receiver is appointed: s 922(1). See also **Insolvency; Insolvent trading; Insolvent transaction.**

Insolvent trading The incurring of a debt by a director at a time when the company is insolvent (or pushed by the debt into insolvency) where there are reasonable grounds for suspecting insolvency. Individual directors are under a statutory duty to prevent insolvent trading by their company: Corporations Law s 588G.This duty applies in relation to debts incurred on or after 23 June 1993, otherwise Corporations Law s 592 still governs: Corporations Law s 1384. There will be no contravention of the provision unless the director was aware of reasonable grounds for suspecting insolvency or a reasonable person in a like position in a company in the company's circumstances would have been so aware: Corporations Law s 588G(2). There are four defences to insolvent trading: Corporations Law s 588H. See also **Directors' duties; Insolvency; Insolvent transaction.**

Insolvent transaction A transaction which constitutes an unfair preference given by the company or an uncommercial transaction of the company and the transaction is entered into or an act is done or omission is made for the purpose of giving effect to the transaction at a time when the company is insolvent; or the company becomes insolvent because of, or because of matters including, entering into the transaction or a person doing an act or making an omission, for the purpose of giving effect to the transaction: Corporations Law s 588FC. See also **Uncommercial transaction; Voidable transaction; Winding up.**

•**Insolvent under administration** An undischarged bankrupt or person whose property is being dealt with under Part X of the (CTH) Bankruptcy Act 1966 : (CTH) Bankruptcy Act 1966 s 155(8). A person may not become a registered trustee if the person is an insolvent under administration: (CTH) Bankruptcy Act 1966 s 155(3A). See also **Bankrupt; Discharge of bankruptcy; Part X; Trustee in Bankruptcy.**

•**Inspector's mark** A mark indicating that a measuring instrument used for trade complies with the weights and measures legislation. An inspector appointed under the legislation must mark an instrument if it complies with the legislation: for example (NSW) Trade Measurement Act 1989 s 3(1); (QLD) Trade Measurement Act 1990 s 3(1). It is an offence to use for trade a measuring instrument that does not bear either an inspector's mark or a servicing licensee's mark.

•**Instalment contract** A contract under which the balance of the purchase price is payable by separate fixed amounts at successive fixed periods. See also **Instalment purchase.**

Contract A contract which provides for the payment of money, over time, by instalments. There are three main forms: a promise to make periodic payments for an executed consideration (for example a loan contract under which principal and interest are payable by instalments (*Moschi v Lep Air Services Ltd* [1973] AC 331); a conditional sale contract, under which the purchase price is payable by instalments and ownership in the subject matter of the contract is to be transferred on payment of the final instalment (for example *McDonald v Dennys Lascelles Ltd* (1933) 48 CLR 457); a severable contract which fixes an amount to be paid at specified intervals for the use of land or goods, for services rendered, work done or for goods supplied which are to be paid for by stated instalments (for example *O'Dea v Allstates Leasing System (WA) Pty Ltd* (1983) 152 CLR 359; 45 ALR 632). A plaintiff may sue for and recover each payment as it falls due. See also **Acceleration clause; Executed consideration; Performance; Severable contract.**

Instalment delivery A delivery of a quantity of goods sold in proportionate amounts and delivered at regular intervals over a period of time. See also **Delivery; Sale of goods.**

Instalment purchase A transaction involving the purchase of an asset by a debtor on terms that the debtor is not to acquire title to the asset until the asset has been paid for (usually by equal instalments over a specified term). The seller transfers possession immediately and, if the buyer becomes insolvent without having paid, the seller retakes possession. See also **Debtor; Possession.**

Instalment sale A credit sale in which the buyer makes a down payment and signs a contract to pay the balance of the purchase price in instalments over a period of time. Title to the goods passes to the purchaser on delivery. See also **Credit sale contract; Hire purchase; Instalment contract.**

Institute of Arbitrators Australia *Abbr* – IAA The Institute has also drawn up rules which may be adopted by the parties to an arbitration to govern the arbitration process. See also **Alternative dispute resolution; Arbitration; Fast-track arbitration.**

Institute of Arbitrators Australia, Rules for the Conduct of Commercial Arbitrations A set of rules drawn up by the Institute of Arbitrators Australia for the conduct of commercial arbitrations, designed to maintain and bring order to the arbitration process. The rules have no force in themselves, but may be incorporated in an arbitration agreement by the parties. See also **Alternative dispute resolution; Arbitration; Fast-track arbitration; Institute of Arbitrators Australia.**

Institute of Chartered Accountants in Australia *Abbr* – ICAA Established in 1928. A professional body having the object of supporting and advancing the character, status, and interests of its accountant members. See also **Australian Society of Certified Practising Accountants.**

Institute of Company Directors of Australia Formed in 1990 from the merger of the Institute of Directors and the Company Directors' Association.

Institutional investor Organisations which have funds to invest, contributed by members of the public through pension funds, unit trusts, mutual funds and insurance companies. Such investors are highly influential on the Australian Stock Exchange, with large holdings in various companies and the ability to decide the fate of a takeover bid. Institutional investors account for about one-half of the turnover on the New York Stock Exchange.

Institutional network corporation *Abbr* – INSTINET A computerised subscriber service which links institutional investors interested in trading large numbers of securities. Investors trading on it avoid paying brokerage commissions. Under the system, subscribers can indicate their volume interest and request quotes from potential sellers in the system. Also known as 'Fourth Market'.

• **Instrument** *Lat – instrumentum* – tool; implement. A formal legal document in writing: for example, a deed, will, enactment, agreement, or guarantee. A formal document of any kind, such as an agreement, deed, charter, or record, that is drawn up and executed in technical form: for example *Azevedo v Secretary, Dept of Primary Industries and Energy* (1992) 35 FCR 284 at 299-300; 106 ALR 683. Mere advice, even in documentary form, that does not confirm, create, or limit a right, will not ordinarily be an instrument: *Australian Capital Equity Pty Ltd v Beale* (1993) 41 FCR 242; 114 ALR 50. Statutory definitions may widen or narrow the general meaning. For example, an instrument includes a statutory rule made under an Act (for example (NSW) Interpretation Act 1987 s 3(1)), 'every written document' ((NSW) Stamp Duties Act 1920 s 3(1)), and may include credit cards, computer discs and tapes ((NSW) Crimes Act 1900 s 299(1)). See also **Agreement; Deed; Document; Forgery; Instrument; Instrument under hand**.

Instrument in writing An instrument in which words are permanently represented in visible form, whether by printing, lithography, or partly in one way and partly in another: for example *Geary v Physic* (1826) 5 B & C 234; 108 ER 87; (QLD) Acts Interpretation Act 1954 s 36. The writing itself may be any method of transcribing or reproducing the written word, as by ink, pencil or otherwise. Certain transactions, for example the creation or disposition of interests in land, must be evidenced by a instrument in writing containing all particulars required by statute: for example (VIC) Property Law Act 1958 s 53(1). See also **Instrument under hand; Instrument under seal**.

Instrument under hand A document in writing that creates or affects legal or equitable rights or liabilities and that is authenticated by the signature of the maker of the document: *Chadwick v Clarke* (1845) 1 CB 700; 135 ER 717. Instrument under hand includes a written contract. An instrument under hand is distinct from an 'instrument under seal', in that it is not sealed; it is also distinct from a deed, in that it need not meet the formal requirements of a deed. See also **Contract; Deed; Execution; Instrument; Instrument in writing; Instrument under seal; Simple contract**.

Instrument under seal An instrument that has a seal affixed, attached or impressed upon it. A deed is an instrument under seal that complies with the requirements necessary to constitute a valid deed: *Manton v Parabolic Pty Ltd* (1985) 2 NSWLR 361. An instrument under seal will not be a deed unless it possesses the requirements for a valid deed, although it may be a valid 'instrument under hand': *Windsor Refrigerator Co Ltd v Branch Nominees Ltd* [1961] Ch 88; [1960] 2 All ER 568. See also **Deed; Instrument in writing; Instrument under hand**.

Insurable interest An interest (usually legal or equitable) in something, the loss of which will prejudice the owner. Examples of insurable interests include a person's interest in a marine adventure ((CTH) Marine Insurance Act 1909 s 11(1)), in his or her own life ((CTH) Insurance Contracts Act 1984 s 19), or in real property (*Castellain v Preston* (1883) 11 QBD 380). See also **Indemnity principle; Insurance**.

Insurable value 1. The maximum amount payable by the insurer upon the loss of, or damage to, the subject matter of the insurance. In a valued policy, the agreed value of the subject matter insured is, in the absence of fraud, conclusive of its insurable value: (CTH) Marine Insurance Act 1909 s 33(3). **2.** In marine insurance law, under a voyage policy the value of an insured ship at the port where the voyage commences, including all her stores and money advanced for seaman's wages, the whole being covered by the premium and commission for effecting insurance: (CTH) Marine Insurance Act 1909 s 22. See also **Unvalued policy; Valued policy**.

• **Insurance** The relationship of indemnity which exists between two parties, the 'insurer' and the 'insured', irrespective of whether the relationship arises by statute or by contract: *R v Cohen; Ex parte Motor Accidents Insurance Board* (1979) 141 CLR 577; 27 ALR 263. The insurance relationship most commonly arises by a contract of insurance. A contract of insurance exists where one person (the 'insurer') undertakes, in return for some agreed consideration (the 'premium'), to pay another person (the 'insured') a sum of money, or provide an equivalent benefit, on the happening of a specified event, the occurrence or timing of which is uncertain: *Prudential Insurance Co v Cmrs of Inland Revenue* [1904] 2 KB 658. The insured must have an interest in the outcome of the specified event (an 'insurable interest'): *Prudential Insurance Co v Commissioners of Inland Revenue*. See also **Insurance contract; Insurable interest; Premium; Uberrimae fidei**.

Insurance agent A person employed to effect insurance on behalf of another. Whether a person is acting as an agent for the insurer or the insured is a question of fact: *Norwich Union Fire Insurance Society Ltd v Brennans (Horsham) Pty Ltd* (1981) VR 981. The term can include mortgage brokers, finance companies, solicitors, accountants, investment advisers, estate agents and travel agents. See also **Agent; Insurance Broker; Insurer; Insurance intermediary; Principal**.

• **Insurance and Superannuation Commissioner** *Abbr* – ISC The person responsible for administering and supervising adherence to the provisions of Commonwealth insurance legislation: (CTH) Insurance and Superannuation Commissioners Act 1987 s 4. The Commissioner is authorised to give approvals and make determinations in relation to superannuation funds, approved deposit funds and pooled superannuation trusts: (CTH) Superannuation Industry (Supervision) Act 1993 s 11.

Insurance bond A bond or life insurance policy purchased from a life insurance company by a single premium or a series of annual premiums. The premium purchases a number of investment units in a fund managed by the life insurance company. The value of the bond or policy is determined by the number of investment units purchased and their price. The funds are invested by the issuer in a range of assets.

• **Insurance broker** A person who is carrying on the business of arranging contracts of insurance as agent for intending insureds: (CTH) Insurance (Agents and Brokers) Act 1984 s 9. The primary duty of a broker is to act bona fide in all cases and to carry out the insured's instructions with reasonable skill and care: *Eagle Star Insurance Co Ltd v National Westminster Finance Australia Ltd* (1985) 58 ALR 165. This will normally involve the broker procuring suitable policies of insurance to protect his or her client against relevant risks of loss, advising on suitable options, and pointing out reasons for different premiums: *Fanhoven Pty Ltd v Bain Dawes Northern Pty Ltd* [1982] 2 NSWLR 57 at 62. See also **Brokerage**; **Insurance agent**; **Insurance intermediary**.

• **Insurance contract** A contract of speculation in which an insurer agrees, in consideration of money (a premium) paid to the insurer by the assured, to indemnify the latter against loss resulting from the happening of specified events: for example (CTH) Marine Insurance Act 1909 s 7; *Prudential Insurance Co v Cmr of Inland Revenue* [1904] 2 KB 658. The facts upon which the risk is to be computed lie mostly within the knowledge of the assured only. The concept of *uberrimae fidei* (utmost good faith) forbids either party concealing private knowledge of a fact to draw the other into a bargain entered into through ignorance of the fact and belief to the contrary: for example (CTH) Insurance Contracts Act 1984 s 13; (CTH) Marine Insurance Act 1909 s 23. An insurance contract is concluded when the proposal of the assured is accepted by the insurer: for example (CTH) Marine Insurance Act 1909 s 27; *Southern Cross Assurance Co Ltd v Australian Provincial Assurance Assn Ltd* (1939) 39 SR (NSW) 174. See also **Contract**; **Disclosure**; **Insurance**; **Insurer**; **Premium**; **Uberrimae fidei**.

Insurance fraud Acting dishonestly in making an insurance claim. A claim will be fraudulent if a false statement is made about the circumstances giving rise to the loss claimed for: *Engel v South British Insurance Co Ltd* (1983) 2 ANZ Ins Cas ¶60-516. A claim which includes a claim in respect of non-existent property will be fraudulent: *Kelwana Realty Ltd v Canadian Indemnity Co* [1978] 4 WWR 276. A claim in respect of a loss which has been deliberately caused by the insured will also be fraudulent: for example (CTH) Life Insurance Act 1995 Pt 8 Div 2; *Moriatis v Harvey Trinder (Qld) Pty Ltd* [1969] Qd R 226. At common law, an insurer is entitled to avoid a contract of insurance if an insured makes a fraudulent claim: *Britton v Royal Insurance Co* (1866) 4 F & F 905; 176 ER 844; *Moriatis v Harvey Trinder (Qld) Pty Ltd*. However, under (CTH) Insurance Contracts Act 1984 s 56(1), an insurer may not avoid the contract of insurance but may refuse to pay the claim. The insurer must prove on the balance of probabilities that the false claim was made intentionally or recklessly: *Purcell v State Insurance Office* (1982) 2 ANZ Ins Cas ¶60-495; *Barclays Bank Ltd v Cole* [1966] 3 All ER 948. See also **Arson**; **Fraud**.

• **Insurance intermediary** A person who, for reward, arranges contracts of insurance as an agent for one or more insurers or for intending insureds: (CTH) Insurance (Agents and Brokers) Act 1984 s 9. Insurance intermediary includes both insurance brokers and insurance agents. See also **Agent**; **Broker**.

Insured's duty of disclosure The duty of an insured to disclose to the insurer, prior to entry into the contract of insurance, every matter the insured knows to be relevant to the insurer's decision to accept the risk and on what terms to accept the risk, and every matter a reasonable person in the circumstances would be expected to consider relevant: (CTH) Insurance Contracts Act 1984 s 21(1). The insured's duty of disclosure does not extend to matters which diminish the risk, matters of common knowledge, matters which the insurer ought to be aware of in the ordinary course of his business as an insurer, and those matters as to which compliance with the duty of disclosure has been waived by the insurer: (CTH) Insurance Contracts Act 1984 s 21(2).

• **Insurer** A person or body who agrees in consideration for money paid, to make good a loss that an assured has suffered on the happening of specified events: *Prudential Insurance Co v Cmr of Inland Revenue* [1904] 2 KB 658. See also **Assured**; **Insurance contract**.

Insurer's knowledge, presumption of See **Presumption of insurer's knowledge**.

• **Intangible property** Property which lacks a physical presence. It is constituted by a right enforceable in a court of law or equity. An example is copyright. See also **Chattel**; **Copyright**.

Intangibles 1. The assets of a company which cannot be readily assigned a value, such as leases, franchises, goodwill, patent rights, research and development. **2.** Costs and benefits which cannot be readily quantified or priced, such as the benefits from highway safety programs and the beauty of a national park.

• **Integration** The combination or amalgamation into an integrated whole.

Contract The process by which a contractual document is entered into with the intention of superseding entirely all prior negotiations in relation to the subject matter dealt with by the document. The effect of the document is to discharge any prior oral agreement: *Gordon v Macgregor* (1909) 8 CLR 316. Under the parol evidence rule, evidence of the prior oral agreement becomes inadmissible following the integration of the contract in written form: *Air Great Lakes Pty Ltd v K S Easter (Holdings) Pty Ltd* (1985) 2 NSWLR 309.

Corporations The merging of firms engaged in the same stage of production of the same commodity (horizontal integration), or the merging of firms engaged in different stages of production of the same commodity (vertical integration) to achieve economies, greater market strength and profitability.

Intellectual property A group of legislative and common law rights affording protection to creative and intellectual effort and includes laws on copyright, design, patent, circuit layouts, plant varieties, confidential information, trade mark and business reputation (passing off and trade practices). Intellectual property encompasses both industrial property (patent, design and trade mark) as well as intellectual property. The term originally referred only to copyright. See also **Confidential information; Copyright; Patent; Trade mark.**

Intent to deceive by counterfeit signature Signing a document in a manner which is intended to induce another person to act in reliance on the signature, believing it to be the signature of another person. It is an offence to, with intent to deceive, write on a form that is given or sent to an insurer any matter that is false or misleading in a material particular: (CTH) Insurance (Agents and Brokers) Act 1984 s 13(2)(a). A counterfeit signature may constitute a matter that is false or misleading in a material particular: *Simeone v Vorreiter* (1990) 92 ALR 288. There need not be any intent to cause economic detriment: *Simeoene v Vorreiter.* See also **Deceit.**

•**Intent to defraud creditors** An intention to defeat or delay a person's creditors by making a payment or dealing with property. A disposition of property with intent to defraud creditors is void against a trustee in bankruptcy unless the person receiving the disposition acted in good faith and gave valuable consideration: (CTH) Bankruptcy Act 1966 s 121. It is sufficient that the intent relates to another of the person's creditors: s 6. It is also sufficient if the intent relates to future or anticipated creditors: *Barton v DCT (Cth)* (1974) 131 CLR 370. See also **Creditor; Good faith; Purchaser for valuable consideration; Trustee in bankruptcy.**

•**Intention** The formation of a purpose or design in mind; the mental act of determining to take some certain action or pursue some certain result.

Contract The intention of the parties to create a relationship giving rise to legal rights and obligations. Intention to contract, with agreement and consideration, is a necessary element in contract formation: *Air Great Lakes Pty Ltd v K S Easter (Holdings) Pty Ltd* (1985) 2 NSWLR 309. Intention may be express or implied, and is determined objectively. See also **Actual intention; Agreement; Consensus ad idem; Consideration; Construction; Contract; Honour clause; Implied intention; Pre-contractual statement; Representation; Subjective theory of contract.**

Intention to defraud An element of some statutory offences of dishonesty such as the offence of obtaining property by false pretences. To defraud is to deprive by deceit in order to induce a person to act to his or her injury: *R v Denning* [1962] NSWR 173. To prove such an intent, it is not necessary to show an intention to cause injury or loss: *Balcombe v De Simoni* (1972) 126 CLR 576; [1972] ALR 513. See also **Intention; Obtaining property by false pretences.**

Intention to repay An intention to pay to the owner money taken by a person without the consent of the owner or person in possession of the money. It is a relevant matter when considering whether on a charge of stealing the accused had an intention to permanently deprive the person of the money the subject of the charge of stealing, as an intent to repay the money might be considered to negative such an intent. In New South Wales, in such a situation the accused will be guilty of stealing if he or she appropriated the money regardless of whether the accused intended to repay the money taken: (NSW) Crimes Act 1900 s 118. See also **Appropriation.**

Intentional tort A tort against the person, chattels, or land. Liability for an intentional tort usually arises without proof of damage. It is sufficient to prove that an act was done deliberately which directly interfered with the plaintiff's person, chattels, or land. Various torts are also concerned with the intentional infliction of purely economic loss. See also **Pure economic loss; Tort.**

Inter alia /ɪntə eɪliə//ɪntə alia/ *Lat* – among other things. Sometimes misused with reference to persons.

Inter partes *Lat* – between parties. See also **Ex parte.**

•**Inter se** /ɪntɜ seɪ/ *Lat* – between themselves. A phrase commonly used in international treaties, making reservations operative 'between the parties themselves'.

•**Inter vivos** /ɪntə vaɪvoʊs/ *Lat* – between living persons; during life. A deed or other instrument executed inter vivos is executed between living persons. Parties to a pending court action may settle their dispute by an inter vivos or immediate transfer of assets or property, which may be dutiable: *Lockes Properties Pty Ltd v Cmr of State Taxation* (1979) WAR 133. See also **Absolute gift.**

Inter-American Development Bank *Abbr* – IADB An international institution, established in 1959, to promote economic and social development and modernisation by financing capital projects in its member countries. Until 1991, only government members in the western hemisphere were eligible for loans, although the bank's borrowings are worldwide and denominated in various international currencies.

Interbank market Short-term lending and borrowing between banks, as distinct from dealings with other financial institutions. The interbank rate is the rate of interest charged on loans between banks.

Intercompany market The movement of funds between companies with offsetting financial needs. Such movement began during the early 1950s and gave impetus to the development of merchant banks.

•**Interest** 1. Rights, advantages, duties, titles and liabilities with respect to a specific thing. An interest may be legal or equitable; a present, future or potential claim, which may be vested, conditional or contingent and may be direct or indirect. 2. A sum of money payable by a borrower to a lender in relation to the use of another capital sum called the principal and expressed as a percentage per annum of the principal.

Insurance The charge or price payable in respect of the use of another sum (the principal), usually expressed as a percentage of the principal. An insured may recover the interest on a sum payable under a contract of insurance from an insurer when the latter has unreasonably withheld payment under the policy: (CTH) Insurance Contracts Act 1984 s 57. The section cannot be excluded, restricted or modified by a term in the policy other than to the prejudice of the insurer: s 52. These provisions completely, exhaustively and conclusively cover the law on the subject: *NRMA Insurance Ltd v Tatt* (1989) 92 ALR 299 at 315. Where the Act does not apply, the common law provides that interest is generally not recoverable from the insurer unless the contract provides for such a payment or a court is empowered by statute to award interest: *Riches v Westminster Bank Ltd* [1947] AC 390. Where the interest rates are not prescribed, the court is to apply the ordinary commercial rates: *Cullen v Trappell* (1980) 146 CLR 1; 29 ALR 1. See also **Insurable interest; Risk**.

Real property A loose term for a property right. All forms of property rights, including legal and equitable rights, security rights, and rights of use or restriction over another's property, are interests. See also **Common law; Estate; Equity; Security**.

Interest arbitrage The transfer of short-term funds between countries to take advantage of differences in the rates of interest. See also **Arbitrage**.

Interest cover The number of times the earnings of a company cover the interest payments it has undertaken to make. The earnings figure is taken usually as earnings before interest and tax (EBIT). It is calculated as follows: Interest cover = EBIT / Total interest paid. A low interest cover implies high risks in times of reduced earnings. A minimum balance of between two and three is often considered desirable.

Interest only loan A loan in which repayments are calculated to cover only the interest charged each month, such that the loan balance remains the same. At the end of the loan term, usually one to five years, the loan may be renewed or rolled-over for a further term.

Interest rate The amount of money a lender receives for allowing a borrower access to a sum of money, comprising an allowance for inflation during the period of the loan, and a payment for being deprived of access to the money during that period. Interest is generally payable to a successful plaintiff in tort under varying circumstances: (NSW) Supreme Court Act 1970 s 94. See also **Compensable loss**.

Interest rate swap An exchange of interest rate obligations between two parties. If a debtor believes that interest rates will fall, it may be possible to swap a fixed rate of interest for a floating one. A swap may simply convert a yen income to a United States dollar income. Both parties need to recognise an advantage in the deal. Interest rate swaps may be arranged between banks, companies or individuals.

Interference with contractual relations The tort of interfering in a contract involving two other parties, so that one of those parties is induced to break the contract or act contrary to its terms, with resulting harm to the plaintiff. The main purpose of such interference is generally to cause economic harm to the plaintiff: *Ansett Transport Industries (Operations) Pty Ltd v Australian Federation of Air Pilots* [1991] 1 VR 637. See also **Conspiracy; Industrial action; Industrial tort; Intimidation**.

•**Interim award** A temporary or provisional award made by a court or tribunal.

Arbitration An award which disposes of only some of the matters referred to arbitration: for example, it deals only with the claim of one party without dealing with the other party's cross-claim: *Wanari Pty Ltd v Mercy & Sons Pty Ltd* [1991] ACL Rep 25 NSW 5. See also **Alternative dispute resolution; Award**.

Damages A court award made where a full and final assessment of a plaintiff's loss is not possible. An interim award acknowledges the extent of injury already known, but allows the plaintiff to return to the court at a subsequent date for further damages as appropriate. Generally, damages are awarded on a 'once and for all' basis, involving an estimation by the court of the plaintiff's future loss, so interim awards are infrequent. See also **Damages**.

Interim cover A contract of temporary insurance, whether or not it is evidenced by a cover note, that is to be superseded or replaced by another contract of insurance: (CTH) Insurance Contracts Act 1984 s 11(2). Interim cover is a complete contract of insurance, not dependant upon the completion of a contract for full cover, and thus the rules relating to the formation of contracts of insurance generally apply: *Mayne Nickless Ltd v Pegler* [1974] 1 NSWLR 228. See also **Cover; Cover note**.

•**Interim dividend** A dividend paid provisionally in anticipation of the profits to be disclosed in the final accounts. See also **Dividend; Final dividend**.

Interim receiver A person appointed by a court to take control of the property of a debtor before a sequestration order is made. An interim receiver may be appointed at any time after the presentation of a creditor's petition. The court can direct the official receiver or a registered trustee in bankruptcy to act as an interim receiver and take control of the debtor's property. However, it must be shown that appointing an interim receiver is necessary in the interests of creditors: (CTH) Bankruptcy Act 1966 s 50(1). See also **Creditor's petition; Debtor; Official Receiver; Trustee in Bankruptcy; Sequestration**.

Interlink Model of the World Economy A model containing 7000 equations developed by the Organisation for Economic Cooperation and Development. The international linkages are modelled explicitly, demonstrating, for example, the effect in one country of economic growth in another.

Interlocking companies Companies which hold substantial shareholdings in each other, providing mutual support and protection from takeovers.

Interlocking directorships Arrangements under which individual directors have seats on the boards of various companies within the same group.

Interlocutory injunction An injunction ordered by a court before the court makes a final order in the proceedings. An applicant for an interlocutory injunction must establish that there is a serious question to be tried (*Castlemaine Tooheys Ltd v South Australia* (1986) 161 CLR 148; 67 ALR 553), that he or she will suffer irreparable injury for which damages will not be an adequate compensation unless an injunction is granted, and that the balance of convenience favours the grant of relief: *Australian Coarse Grain Pool Pty Ltd v Barley Marketing Board of Queensland* (1982) 46 ALR 398; 57 ALJR 425. See also **Anton Piller order; Balance of convenience; Injunction; Mareva injunction.**

•**Interlocutory judgment** A judgment, given in interlocutory proceedings, which does not finally conclude or dispose of the substantive rights of the parties to those proceedings: *Hall v Nominal Defendant* (1966) 117 CLR 423 at 439-440, 443; [1966] ALR 705. For example, an order refusing an extension of time to begin proceedings (*Hall v Nominal Defendant*), granting leave to appeal (*Sanofi v Parke Davis Pty Ltd (No 1)* (1981) 149 CLR 147; 9 ALR 405), setting aside a default judgment (*Carr v Finance Co of Australia Ltd (No 1)* (1981) 147 CLR 246) or staying an action as vexatious or an abuse of process: *Tampion v Anderson* (1973) 3 ALR 414; 48 ALJR 11. Leave is usually required to appeal from interlocutory judgments: for example (CTH) Judiciary Act 1903 s 34(2); (CTH) Federal Court of Australia Act 1976 s 24(1A); (NSW) Supreme Court Act 1970 s 101(2)(e).

Intermarket spread swap Similtaneously purchasing on one exchange and selling on another. See also **Australian Stock Exchange Ltd.**

Intermediate examination defence A defence to a product liability claim which may be available if it can be shown that the manufacturer or a product supplier reasonably anticipated that another entity (such as a distributor or the product user) would carry out an intermediate examination of the product to reveal any defects and thus to avoid loss or damage: for example *Paine v Colne Valley Electricity Supply Co Ltd* [1938] 4 All ER 803; *Farr v Butters Bros & Co* [1932] 2 KB 606; *Hindustan Steam Shipping Co Ltd v Siemens Bros & Co Ltd* [1955] 1 Lloyd's Rep 167.

Intermediate income Refers to the source of monetary income during the intervening period of time between no income accruing and the generation of income by the final or major source of earnings.

Intermediate term A contractual term which is neither a condition nor a warranty: *Bunge Corp v Tradax Export SA* [1980] 1 Lloyd's Rep 294. Its breach gives rise to a right to claim damages. The right of a promisee to terminate a contract on breach by the promissor depends on the nature of the breach and its foreseeable and actual consequences: *Hongkong Fir Shipping Co Ltd v Kawasaki Kisen Kaisha Ltd* [1962] 2 QB 26; *Progressive Mailing House Pty Ltd v Tabali Pty Ltd* (1985) 157 CLR 17; 57 ALR 609. It is also described as an 'innominate term', on the rationale that the character of the term in question cannot be judged by construction, so that it takes on the character of a condition or a warranty in accordance with the seriousness of the actual breach established: *Ankar Pty Ltd v National Westminster Finance (Aust) Ltd* (1987) 162 CLR 549; 70 ALR 641. See also **Condition; Term; Warranty; Right to terminate.**

Intermediation The use of an intermediary especially in financial and insurance transactions. Banks, building societies and hire purchase companies are examples of financial intermediaries. See also **Disintermediation; Finance broker.**

Internal auditor An employee of an organisation, whose duties include ensuring that the financial policies and procedures prescribed by the law and management are observed. See also **Auditor.**

•**Internal control** A system ensuring that all transactions of a business are properly recorded and documented, assets are protected and an independent internal verification of records is provided. Internal control is important in assessing accounting policies, safeguarding the assets and verifying the accuracy of the financial records of the business operations.

Internal control structure The plan of the organisation and all the methods and procedures adopted by the management of an entity to assist in achieving the entity's objectives: Statement of Auditing Practice AUP 12 para 13. The structure is divided into the control environment (comprising management philosophy, organisational structure and assignment of authority and responsibility), the information system and internal controls: Statement of Auditing Practice AUP 12 para 15. Auditors must gain an understanding of the internal control structure and study and evaluate the operation of the structure or elements thereof upon which they wish to rely in determining the nature, timing and extent of other audit procedures: Statement of Auditing Standard AUS 1. See also **Audit.**

Internal equity The interest in the assets of the reporting entity as a result of monetary or other inputs of economic benefit from the proprietors or owners. Also includes past profits or reserves. See also **Asset; Proprietor.**

Internal presentment Presentation of a cheque or payment order by a drawee bank or drawee non-bank financial institution (NBFI) internally to itself as drawee, where the drawee bank or NBFI is collecting the cheque or payment order, or a bank is the agent for other collecting banks that have delivered cheques to the drawee bank via the clearing house: (CTH) Cheques and Payment Orders Act 1986 ss 62A, 106A. See also **Clearing house; Collection; Drawee bank; External presentment; Presentment.**

Internal rate of return *Abbr* – IRR The rate of return, expressed in percentage terms, generated by a project which equates the discounted future cash flows with the initial outlay. This is the percentage amount where the net present value of a project is equal to zero, and indicates the highest interest rate at which the project breaks even (that is, neither a profit or a loss results). See also **Net present value.**

International agreement For the purpose of transfer pricing, an agreement where a non-resident of Australia is supplied with property or acquired property at or through a permanent establishment of the non-resident in Australia, or an agreement where a resident of Australia carrying on business outside Australia supplied or acquired property in connection to the business carried on outside Australia: (CTH) Income Tax Assessment Act 1936 s 136AC. See also **Business; Permanent establishment.**

International Bank for Reconstruction and Development *Abbr* – IBRD An international bank created in 1946 by the Articles of Agreement of the International Bank for Reconstruction and Development 1945. The member states of the bank participate on a share basis. Originally formed to avoid the financial chaos and depression of the war years, its focus now is to encourage economic growth in developing nations. The IBRD offers financial assistance for projects incapable of being financed otherwise, and provides experts in various fields for use by member states. Loans generally have a grace period of five years and are repayable in 20 years. Also known as 'World Bank'. See also **International Monetary Fund**.

International Banks and Securities Association of Australia *Abbr* – IBSA The national organisation representing the interests of financial institutions involved in wholesale banking, securities, and financial markets such as merchant banks. Formerly it was called the Australian Merchant Bankers Association and the name change occurred in 1993 when federal legislation enabled foreign owned merchant banks to obtain licences to operate as branches of their parents. See also **Merchant bank; Money market corporation**.

International Business Development Scheme *Abbr* – IBD Administered by the Australian Trade Commission, a scheme introduced in 1988 to provide discretionary financial support to Australian firms able to exploit emerging world market opportunities. Support is provided by concessional loans, non-repayable advances and the provision of Australian Trade Commission services at concessional rates. In 1990, the scheme was augmented by the International Trade Enhancement Scheme.

International carriage of goods The carriage of goods from one country to another. The Protocol (1979) amending the International Convention for the Unification of Certain Rules of Law relating to Bills of Lading of 25 August 1924, as amended by the Protocol of 23 February 1968 (Visby Rules) *(Amended Hague Rules 1979)* apply to international sale and carriage of goods. The sale may be based on Cost, insurance and freight (CIF) or Free on board (FOB) terms or on cost and freight or free alongside terms. See also **Amended Hague Rules 1979; Carriage of goods; Cost insurance freight contract; Free on board**.

International Centre for Public Enterprises in Developing Countries An intergovernmental organisation composed of over 30 developing countries. Its objective is to assist public enterprises in developing countries to become stronger and more efficient in the conduct of their business and socioeconomic obligations. The centre has contributed to the preparation of the guarantee and warranty provisions in transfer of technology contracts. It initiates research and training, performs consultancy and documentation, and disseminates information through publications and seminars.

International Centre for Settlement of Investment Disputes *Abbr* – ICSID A centre, located in Washington DC, for resolving certain international investment disputes by conciliation or arbitration. It was established under the Convention on the Settlement of Investment Disputes between States and Nationals of Other States 1965. The Convention is implemented in Australian law by the (CTH) International Arbitration Act 1974 Pt IV. Disputes referable to ICSID are those between a state which is a contracting state and a national of another contracting state. The parties to a dispute referred to ICSID may agree on the rules of law to be applied in an arbitration, or may agree that the dispute be determined *ex aequo et bono* (on the basis of what is fair and right). In default of agreement, the arbitral tribunal applies the law of the contracting state disputant. See also **Alternative dispute resolution; Arbitration; Ex aequo et bono**.

International Chamber of Commerce *Abbr* – ICC An international commercial body composed of representatives from governments and national chambers of commerce. The ICC is actively engaged in promoting international business and international commercial arbitration, and in standardising commercial terms and practices. Its headquarters are in Paris.

International Civil Aviation Organisation *Abbr* – ICAO The most important body in international civil aviation whose aims and objectives are to develop the principles and techniques of international air navigation and to foster the planning and development of international air transport: Convention on International Civil Aviation 1944 art 43. The ICAO was established by the Convention on International Civil Aviation 1944 and came into being on 4 April 1947. It is a specialised agency of the United Nations. It is made up of an Assembly, a Council and various subordinate bodies. The Convention on International Civil Aviation 1944 provides that the ICAO is to enjoy in the territory of each contracting state such legal capacity as may be necessary for the performance of its functions and requires full juridical capacity to be granted wherever this is compatible with the laws and constitution of the state concerned: Convention on International Civil Aviation 1944 art 47. Australia has granted corporate capacity to the ICAO and has conferred extensive privileges and immunities on it and on certain persons connected with it: (CTH) International Organisations (Privileges and Immunities) Act 1963; (CTH) Specialised Agencies (Privileges and Immunities) Regulations 1986. Membership of the ICAO comprises the states which have ratified or adhered to the Convention on International Civil Aviation 1944. See also **Convention on International Civil Aviation 1944**.

International Commodities Clearing House *Abbr* – ICCH An agency for the clearing of commodity and financial futures transactions. It is owned by six British Banks, Lloyds, Midland, the Royal Bank of Scotland, Barclays, National Westminster and Standard Chartered. Prior to 1990, the ICCH provided clearing services for the Sydney Futures Exchange. These functions are now performed by the Sydney Futures Exchange Clearing House. The ICCH continues to operate in Auckland, Hong Kong, Rio de Janeiro, Paris and London.

International Convention for the Protection of Industrial Property 1883 An international agreement to form a union for protection of industrial property: International Convention for the Protection of Industrial Property 1883 art 1(1). The Convention requires Union members to protect the industrial property of persons within the jurisdiction of other members states in the same way it would its own: International Convention for the Protection of Industrial Property 1883 art 2. Industrial Property is broadly characterised to include patents, utility models, industrial designs or models, industrial designs or models, trade marks, trade names and indications of source or appellations of origin, and the repression of unfair competition: art 1(2). The Convention also applies to agricultural and extractive industries and to all manufactured or natural products: art 1(3). It was revised at Brussels on 14 December 1900; Washington on 2 June 1911; the Hague on 6 November 1925; London on 2 June 1934; Lisbon on 31 October 1958; and at Stockholm on 14 July 1967. The Paris Convention for the Protection of Industrial Property 1883 revised at Stockholm in 1967 entered completely into force for Australia on 27 September 1975 and generally on 26 April 1970. Australia is yet to enact specific legislation implementing the convention although its provision relating to patents are covered in a limited way by the (CTH) Patents Regulations 1991. Also known as 'Paris Convention'. See also **Intellectual property; Patent; Trade mark**.

International Convention for the Unification of Certain Rules of Law relating to Bills of Lading 1924 An international convention governing the carriage of goods by sea under contracts of carriage entered into before 31 October 1991, by identifying the rights, liabilities, and duties of carriers and owners of cargo. The Convention came into force on 25 August 1924. It was given force in Australia by the (CTH) Sea Carriage of Goods Act 1924 (repealed). It was subsequently amended by the Protocol (1979) amending the International Convention for the Unification of Certain Rules Relating to Bills of Lading of 25 August 1924, as amended by the Protocol of 23 February 1968. Also known as the 'Hague Rules 1924'. See also **Bill of lading; Carriage by sea; Carrier; Amended Hague Rules 1979**.

International copyright There is no 'international copyright' as such. Rather, whether material is protected by copyright in any particular country depends upon the domestic law of that country. Nonetheless, copyright protection is generally international, in so far as some 160 countries have signed one of the major conventions dealing with copyright, and have agreed to extend copyright protection under their domestic laws to material having sufficient nexus with other signatory countries. In addition, some countries which have not signed the major copyright conventions have entered into bilateral treaties with other countries. Australia is a signatory to the two major copyright conventions (Convention for the Creation of an International Union for the Protection of Literary and Artistic Works 1886 and the Universal Copyright Convention 1952) and to a number of other international copyright conventions such as the General Agreement on Tariffs and Trade 1947 Trade Related Aspects of Intellectual Property. Australia has also entered into bilateral agreements with Singapore and Indonesia. Whether material created by foreign citizens, nationals and residents, or material published first in other countries is protected by copyright in Australia is determined by reference to the (CTH) Copyright (International Protection) Regulations 1969. See also **Copyright; General Agreement on Tariffs and Trade 1947**.

International Council for Commercial Arbitration A non-governmental organisation promoting the use of arbitration as a method of solving international trade disputes. The Council does not formulate rules for commercial arbitration but encourages other relevant bodies to do so. It recognises and applies the United Nations Commission of International Trade Law's Arbitration Rules 1976 and Model Law on International Commercial Arbitration 1985. It is also involved in organising arbitration congresses and in publishing programs of action. See also **Arbitration**.

International Court of Justice *Abbr* – ICJ The principal judicial organ of the United Nations established, as a replacement for the Permanent Court of International Justice, by the Statute of the International Court of Justice 1945: Charter of the United Nations 1945 art 92. The International Court of Justice, which sits at the Hague, has both an advisory and contentious jurisdiction, the latter exercisable only with the consent of the disputing parties. Also known as 'World Court'.

International Currency Transfer Report *Abbr* – ICTR A report of currency (coin or paper money) of $A5000 or more, in Australian or foreign currency, that travellers leaving or entering Australia must make to Australian Customs Service: (CTH) Financial Transaction Reports Act 1988 s 15.

International debt crisis The crisis of the world financial system generated by the refusal or inability of some large debtor countries (initiated by Mexico in 1982), to meet the payments on their foreign debts. The crash of oil prices in the late 1970s and early 1980s contributed significantly to this crisis, posing the risk of a collapse in the international financial system. The International Monetary Fund had to assume a new role to overcome this debt crisis. See also **International Monetary Fund**.

International Development Association *Abbr* – IDA A specialised agency established under the auspices of the World Bank to promote economic development through long-term low interest loans. The assistance of the IDA is available to countries with a very low per capita gross national product. IDA credits are available to governments only and bear no interest. They have a 10 year grace period and are of a 35 or 40 year duration. IDA funds come mainly from the International Bank for Reconstruction and Development (IBRD) and contributions. The Association was established on 26 January 1960, and was created by the Articles of the International Development Association, and is an affiliate of the IBRD. See also **International Bank for Reconstruction and Development**.

International Finance Corporation *Abbr* – IFC A body established in 1956 to aid developing member countries by promoting the growth of their private sector economies. Australia is a member of the IFC: (CTH) International Finance Corporation Act 1955. The IFC aims to mobilise domestic and foreign capital for this purpose and is able to borrow in its own right as well as obtain funds from member country subscriptions.

It is based in Washington DC and is an affiliate of the International Bank for Reconstruction and Development (IBRD).

International financial institution An intergovernmental institution created in response to the devastation caused by the 1939-45 war. Examples are the International Monetary Fund and the International Bank for Reconstruction and Development, conceived by the United Nations Monetary Financial Conference in 1944. These institutions channel, mobilise, catalyse, and administer financial resources to promote agreed upon economic objectives. They also provide a forum for continuing international discussions on world financial problems. They are subjects of, and persons in, international law. See also **International Monetary Fund; International Bank for Reconstruction and Development; United Nations Monetary and Financial Conference**.

•**International funds transfer instruction** An instruction for a transfer of funds that is transmitted into or out of Australia electronically or by telegraph: (CTH) Financial Transaction Reports Act 1988 s 3(1). A cash dealer, other than a bank, who sends or receives an international funds transfer instruction must report the instruction to the Australian Transaction Reports and Analysis Centre unless the dealer is acting on behalf of a bank: (CTH) Financial Transaction Reports Act 1988 s 17B. See also **Australian Transaction Reports and Analysis Centre; Cash dealer**.

International Labour Organisation Abbr – ILO A body founded to create an international code of labour law and practice. The ILO aims to increase productive labour, improve working conditions, raise living standards, and uphold human rights in the context of work. Member states are required to bring their domestic legislation into line with ILO Conventions and make regular reports on how these are being implemented. The program in developing nations and undertakes research and development on labour related matters. The principal organs of the ILO are the International Labour Conference, the Governing Body of the International Labour Office, and the International Labour Office. The ILO was created under the Treaty of Peace between the Allied Powers and Associated Powers and Germany 1919, becoming a United Nations specialised agency in 1946. The Constitution of the ILO which was incorporated into the Treaty of Peace between the Allied Powers and Associated Powers and Germany 1919 was amended on 14 June 1923, 5 November 1945, 9 October 1946, 25 June 1953, 22 June 1962, 6 July 1964, 9 July 1964, and 22 June 1972. Australia has ratified the Treaty of Peace between the Allied Powers and Associated Powers and Germany 1919 containing the Constitution of the ILO and acceded to its amendments. The Commonwealth government has enacted legislation approving the Constitution and subsequent amendments: (CTH) International Labour Organization Act 1947; (CTH) International Labour Organisation Act 1973. Australia has also ratified and implements several of the ILO Conventions: for example (CTH) Industrial Relations Act 1988 Schs 5, 6, 10 which implements; Convention concerning Minimum Wage Fixing with Special Reference to Developing Countries 1970; Convention concerning Equal Remuneration for Men and Women Workers for Work of Equal Value 1951; and Convention concerning Termination of Employment at the Initiative of the Employer 1982, respectively. See also **ILO Conventions**.

International law of the sea Formulated and codified maritime law in international conventions. For example, the United Nations Convention on the Law of the Sea (which took place in Geneva in 1950) is the most comprehensive codification of the international law of the sea. The Convention deals with subjects such as the territorial sea, the contiguous zone, the high seas, fishing, and conservation of living resources of the high seas and the continental shelf.

•**International Maritime Organisation** Abbr – IMO An agency of the United Nations established originally as the Intergovernmental Maritime Consultative Organisation by the Convention on the Intergovernmental Maritime Consultative Organisation 1948 to offer technical advice and consultations concerning maritime activities, and to draft Conventions and agreements on matters affecting international trade, maritime safety, and marine pollution. It replaced the former Inter-Governmental Maritime Consultative Organisation on 22 May 1982. The IMO headquarters are in London. Australia is a member of the IMO. See also **Comite Maritime International; Convention on the International Maritime Organisation 1948**.

International Monetary Fund Abbr – IMF A fund created to promote international monetary cooperation, exchange stability and world trade, and eliminate foreign exchange restrictions. The IMF also advises and gives technical assistance to member states. Access to IMF resources and special drawing rights is dependent on the member's relative standing in the world economy. The IMF was established in July 1944 by the Articles of Agreement of the International Monetary Fund 1945. It is a United Nations specialised agency. The IMF is not a bank and it does not lend funds although it can provide temporary assistance by selling currency. Australia is a member of the IMF: (CTH) International Monetary Agreements Act 1947. Charges payable to the IMF by Australia may be made out of consolidated revenue: (CTH) International Monetary Agreements Act 1947 s 8. Other funds required to be paid by Australia to the IMF may be raised by loan or by the issue of securities: (CTH) International Monetary Agreements Act 1947 ss 6, 7. See also **Articles of Agreement of the International Monetary Fund 1945**.

International Monetary Fund Agreement 1945 See **Articles of Agreement of the International Monetary Fund 1945**.

International monetary obligation A financial obligation of a state or international organisation, either assigned by international law or assumed under an international treaty. An international monetary obligation is incurred by an identified infringement of an international legal duty. For example, the obligation involved in an act such as expropriation is the payment of compensation for the loss caused. An international legal right has a corresponding obligation which, if not met, entails a duty to make reparation: *Chorzow Factory case (Germany v Poland), Merits* 1928 PCIJ.

International Options Clearing Corporation
Abbr – IOCC An agency for the clearing of options transactions. In 1984, the Australian Stock Exchange became a joint owner of IOCC together with the European Options Exchange in the Netherlands and the Montreal and Vancouver Exchanges in Canada. The following year the ASX began trading in gold and silver options. This meant that options over gold, silver and United States dollar contracts could be traded in four geographic locations over a 24-hour period. By means of a unique 'travelling' electronic order book, a facility was created whereby unfilled orders are forwarded to the next centre to be matched, if possible, with buyers and sellers from that centre.

International trade The exchange of commodities by two or more states through barter or through buying and selling by wholesale or retail. The legal regime of international trade is governed by principles of the General Agreement on Tariffs and Trade 1947 and coordinated by the United Nations Commission on International Trade Law.

International Trade Organization *Abbr* – ITO An abortive intergovernmental organisation created by the United Nations Conference on Trade and Employment held in Havana, Cuba in 1948. It was designed to arrest and reverse reliance on extreme national protectionism in the era prior to the 1939-45 war, which stunted the growth of world trade. The final Act of the United Nations Conference on Trade and Employment, and the Havana Charter for the International Trade Organization 1948 of the ITO was never ratified by the United States Senate. The General Agreement on Tariffs and Trade 1947 was then conceived as an alternative interim measure to maximise world trade by minimising trade barriers. See also **General Agreement on Tariffs and Trade 1947; World Trade Organisation**.

International trade theory A body of economic theory relating to international trade. The theory of comparative advantage states that mutually advantageous trade will always be possible with trade patterns based on relative prices, rather than absolute prices, no one country having a comparative advantage in all commodities. The Heckscher-Ohlin theory maintains that a country will tend to export that commodity which uses relatively more of the factor of production that is abundant in that country. The theory assumes that countries have different quantities of the various factors of production but identical production functions. Factor-price equalisation theory states that under free international trade, the prices of traded products and the factors of production (inputs) will be equalised among countries.

Internet A network containing thousands of computer systems (including local area networks and wide area networks). The Internet serves millions of users, from enthusiasts to commercial and government institutions who wish to make their data available to the public either at no charge or for a fee.

Interperiod tax allocation See **Tax allocation**.

Interpleader A proceeding to determine the rights of claimants, by which a person who is sued regarding some property or debt can require competing claimants to that property or debt to resolve their rights: *Reading v London School Board* (1886) 16 QBD 687.

Agency A process by which an agent holding a principal's money or property pays the money into court, or agrees to abide by the court's decision in respect of the property, where two parties claim an entitlement to it. Interpleader allows an auctioneer, after being sued by a party seeking to recover money or property, to take no further part in the litigation, and for the parties contesting the right to the property to litigate which of them is entitled to it. Interpleader avoids circuity of action and the need for an auctioneer to defend proceedings against two claimants, one of whom is entitled to the money or property: *Chisholm v Richardson* (1876) 14 SCR (NSW) 334. See also **Agent; Auctioneer; Principal**.

Equity Relief by way of proceedings in which a person, from whom two or more others claim the same debt, duty or property, and who does not himself or herself claim that debt and who fears injury of conflicting claims, calls upon the others to claim against each other so that the title to the debt is decided. For example, an estate agent holding a deposit which is claimed by both parties and purchaser may 'interplead', to determine who is entitled to it. Prior to 1873, interpleader proceedings were brought in the Court of Chancery by a bill of interpleader, or in the common law courts by an action under the (UK) Interpleader Act 1831 and the (UK) Common Law Procedure Act 1860 ss 12-18. In Australia, interpleader proceedings are governed by the Supreme Court Acts: for example, (NSW) Supreme Court Rules 1970 Pt 56; (VIC) Rules of the Supreme Court Ch I O 12.

•**Interpretation** A determination or explanation of the meaning of words in a document, instrument, statute or judgment.

Contract Explaining or deciding on the meaning of words. See also **Construction; Ejusdem generis; Noscitur a sociis**.

•**Interstate contract** An agreement which contemplates the delivery of goods from one State to another as a likely means of performance: *Australian Coarse Grains Pool Pty Ltd v Barley Marketing Board (Qld)* (1985) 59 ALR 641. Interstate contracts are protected by Commonwealth Constitution s 92 which provides that trade commerce and intercourse among the States shall be absolutely free. See also **Interstate trade and commerce**.

Interstate dispute An industrial dispute that extends beyond the limits of any one State. It must be a single dispute; two different disputes in separate States do not amount to an interstate dispute. A dispute in one State that has the appearance of a local intrastate dispute may be in fact a manifestation of a larger interstate dispute: *R v Turbet; Ex parte Australian Building Construction Employees and Builders Labourers' Federation* (1980) 144 CLR 335; 33 ALR 79. A series of demands made on behalf of a number of employees to a number of employers in various parts of Australia can constitute a single industrial dispute that is interstate in nature where there is a community of interest or a common cause: *Re Australasian Meat Industry Employees' Union; Ex parte Aberdeen Beef Co Pty Ltd* (1993) 176 CLR 154; *Re Australian Education Union; Ex parte Victoria* (1995) 128 ALR 609 at 634-5. Whether such a community of interest exists will depend on a wide range of factors (*Re*

Australasian Meat Industry Employees' Union; Ex parte Aberdeen Beef Co Pty Ltd at 171), including a combination of industrial, economic and financial considerations (*Re Australian Education Union; Ex parte Victoria* at 634). A dispute in one State that causes persons in other States to take industrial action in sympathy with and support for one party to the dispute may not constitute an interstate dispute: *Caledonian Collieries v ACSEF (No 1)* (1930) 42 CLR 527; 36 ALR 61. See also **Industrial dispute**.

•**Interstate trade and commerce** The actual or contemplated movement of goods and services, tangible or intangible, interstate: *Australian National Airways Pty Ltd v Cth* (1945) 71 CLR 29 at 56. Interstate trade and commerce includes not only the actual act of transportation or movement over the border but also all the commercial arrangements of which such transportation or movement is the direct and necessary result, including the negotiations: *W A McArthur Ltd v Queensland* (1920) 28 CLR 530 at 546-7. Interstate trade and commerce begins with a contract contemplating interstate transport of the goods and services (*Australian Course Grains Pool Pty Ltd v Barley Marketing Board* (1985) 157 CLR 605 at 660-1; 59 ALR 641) and ends with the first sale after importation (*Permewan Wright Consolidated Pty Ltd v Trewhitt* (1979) 145 CLR 1; 27 ALR 182). Interstate trade and commerce must be free from discriminatory burdens of a protectionist kind: Commonwealth Constitution s 92; *Cole v Whitfield* (1988) 165 CLR 360 See also **Absolutely free; Freedom of interstate trade, commerce and intercourse; Intrastate trade and commerce; Trade and commerce power**.

•**Intestacy** The status of having died without having made a valid will, or without having effectively disposed of the whole of one's property by will. Intestacy may be partial or total. Where a will disposes of only some of the deceased's assets, there will be a partial intestacy as to those assets not disposed of by the will. Where no part of the deceased's property is disposed by will, there will be a total intestacy, usually due to no valid will being made before death or if a will was made, due to it not being duly executed or becoming otherwise inoperative.

Intimidation In relation to a witness in judicial proceedings, the offence of threatening, restraining, using violence or inflicting an injury upon, that witness. Intimidation includes causing punishment, damage, or disadvantage to such a person: (CTH) Crimes Act 1914 s 36A.

Industrial law A common law tort of intimidating a person to do an act that causes loss to another person. There must be a threat by one person (A) to use unlawful means (such as violence, a tort or a breach of contract) against another person (B) unless B does something causing loss to a third person (C). Thus, where an employer dismisses an employee as a result of a threat to strike by other employees (which would breach the contract of employment), the dismissed employee may sue the other employees for intimidation: *Rookes v Barnard* [1964] 1 All ER 367. See also **Industrial tort**.

Tort A threat to commit an unlawful act or a threat against a plaintiff or third party which coerces the party threatened into acting in such a manner as to cause economic loss to the plaintiff: *Ansett Transport Industries (Operations) Pty Ltd v Australian Federation of Air Pilots* [1991] 1 VR 637. See also **Pure economic loss**.

Intra vires /ɪntrə vaɪriz/ *Lat* – within the power. An *intra vires* act is within the legal power or authority of a person, institution, or legislation, and therefore valid. In administrative law, decisions of administrators which are within the scope of power of the administrator to make. The opposite of ultra vires. See also **Ultra vires**.

Intrastate trade and commerce Acts of trade and commerce with no interstate element, confined totally within the territory of a single particular State. The Commonwealth may not legislate with respect to intrastate trade and commerce unless it is incidental to interstate trade and commerce (*Grannall v Marrickville Margarine Pty Ltd* (1955) 93 CLR 55), that is, where the relationship between the two is direct and proximate (*Redfern v Dunlop Rubber Australia Ltd* (1964) 110 CLR 194 at 213, 219, 221, 229) or where the regulation of intrastate trade and commerce is necessary to effectuate the proper regulation of interstate trade and commerce (*Airlines of New South Wales Pty Ltd v NSW (No 1)* (1964) 113 CLR 1 at 78, 92-3, 155). See also **Freedom of interstate trade, commerce and intercourse; Interstate trade and commerce; Trade and commerce; Trade and commerce power**.

Intrinsic evidence The language of an instrument that indicates the parties' intention regarding the instrument and their legal relationship. Where a court can clearly collect the parties' intention from the language within the 'four corners' of an instrument in writing, it is bound to give effect to that intention: *NGL Properties Pty Ltd v Harlington Pty Ltd* [1979] VR 92. See also **Construction; Extrinsic evidence; Four corners rule; Instrument in writing; Intention; Term**.

Intrinsic value The amount by which the exercise price of an option is in-the-money relative to the price of the subject matter of the option. See also **Option**.

Introducing broker An associate member of the Sydney Futures Exchange (SFE) permitted to deal on its own behalf or on behalf of clients. An introducing broker cannot trade on the floor of the SFE or hold client's funds which must be held by the introducing broker's principal broker. See also **Associate member; Floor member**.

•**Invalid futures authority** The purported authority of a futures representative to act for a futures licensee which in fact is not a proper authority: Corporations Law ss 9, 87(2). It is a document which contains a statement to the effect that the representative is employed by or acts for or by arrangement with the principal and signed by the principal and which purports to be a copy of a futures licence and to be a proper authority of the representative from the principal but which is not in fact such a proper authority: Corporations Law s 87(2). See also **Futures licence; Futures representative**.

•**Invalid securities authority** The purported authority of a securities representative to act for a securities licensee which in fact is not a proper authority: Corporations Law ss 9, 88(2). It is a document which contains a statement to the effect that the representative is employed by or acts for or by arrangement with the principal and signed by the principal, which purports to be a copy of a securities licence and to be a proper authority of the representative from the principal but which is not in fact such a proper authority: Corporations Law s 88(2). See also **Securities authority**; **Securities licence**; **Securities representative**.

•**Invalidity payment** For the purposes of income tax law, a part of an eligible termination payment arising from the termination of employment of an employee because of disability. Two legally qualified medical practitioners must certify that the disability is likely to result in the employee being unable to ever be employed in a capacity for which he or she is reasonably qualified: (CTH) Income Tax Assessment Act 1936 s 27G. Termination must also have occurred before the last retirement date in relation to that employer and employment: (CTH) Income Tax Assessment Act 1936 s 27G. An invalidity payment paid after 1 July 1994 is exempt from tax ((CTH) Income Tax Assessment Act 1936 s 27CB) but may still be rolled over ((CTH) Income Tax Assessment Act 1936 s 27D). See also **Eligible Termination Payment**; **Exempt income**; **Rollover**.

•**Invention** In patent law, any manner of new manufacture, including an 'alleged invention'. This inclusion permits a patent application to proceed under the (CTH) Patents Act 1990 without first establishing that what it claims is novel, but without binding the Commissioner of Patents to accept the applicant's allegation of novelty. Furthermore, not all inventions are patentable. For example, human beings, mere admixtures or collocations of known substances or contrivances and subject matter that is contrary to law are excluded: (CTH) Patents Act 1990 ss 18, 51, Sch 1; *National Research Development Corp's Application* (1959) 102 CLR 252 at 261-2; 78 RPC 134; [1961] AOJP 2761; *Commissioner of Patents v Microcell Ltd* (1959) 102 CLR 232; *NV Philips Gloeilampenfabrieken v Mirabella International Pty Ltd* (1995) 132 ALR 117 at 120-1. See also **Manufacture**; **Patentability**.

Inventory *Lat – inventorium*. A list of articles, property or goods, enumerated in reasonable detail. The list may be used in a variety of situations, for example a record of stock held, an account of goods sold, or in relation to bills of sale or to the goods and chattels of a deceased estate. Also the amount or value of a company's current assets that consist of plant and equipment, raw materials, work in progress, stock and finished goods, or such goods individually. See also **Administrator**; **Bill of sale**; **Continuous stocktaking**; **Just-in-time production**.

•**Inventory security interest** A security interest given by a dealer in or over goods of a kind in which the dealer deals in the course of his or her business, or reserved in or over goods in the possession or control of a dealer, being goods of a kind in which the dealer deals in the course of his or her business: (VIC) Chattel Securities Act 1987 s 3(1). If a person has a registered inventory security interest in goods but is not in possession of the goods and a purchaser purchases or purports to purchase an interest in the goods for value in good faith and without notice of the security interest when the purchase price is paid, the security interest is extinguished: (VIC) Chattel Securities Act 1987 s 7. See also **Chattel security**; **Security interest**.

Inventory turnover ratio A ratio measuring the turnover of a firm's inventory, indicating the amount of inventories on hand relative to the cost of sales, that is: Cost of sales/Average inventories.

Inverted market A futures market in which the prices of distant futures are below the prices of nearer futures. See also **Backwardation**.

•**Invest** To outlay money with the expectation of a financial return through interest, profit or capital growth. Investing may take the form of the purchase of property to be held specifically for the sake of the income it will yield: *Re Wragg; Wragg v Palmer* [1919] 2 Ch 58 at 64-5. See also **Interest**; **Investment**; **Profit**.

•**Investigation** An inquiry or examination to ascertain facts; the act or process of investigating: *Taciak v Cmr of Australian Federal Police* (1995) 131 ALR 319.

Corporations **1.** A financial examination of a business conducted by accountants on behalf of a potential investor, bank, or finance company to determine the feasibility of a prospective investment and the accuracy of the financial statements and other records of the business. **2.** The examination of a company's business, property and financial circumstances by an administrator. The purpose of the administrator's investigation is to form an opinion on whether the company should be wound up: Corporations Law s 438B. **3.** In relation to the Australian Securities Commission (ASC), an investigation in the course of performing or exercising the functions and powers of the Commission: (CTH) Australian Securities Commission Act 1989 s 5(1). See also **Administrator**; **Australian Securities Commission**; **Winding up**.

•**Investment** Any mode of application of money for the purpose of gaining interest, income or profit: for example (CTH) Superannuation Industry (Supervision) Act 1993 s 10. Money invested is converted or circulated into some species of property from which an income or profit is expected. It is spending which adds to the stock of capital. Traditionally regarded as spending on capital goods such as machinery, factory buildings, information technology and infrastructure, it also includes the purchase of securities and other financial instruments. See also **Interest**; **Invest**.

•**Investment advice business** A business of advising others about securities or a business in the course of which the person publishes securities reports: Corporations Law s 77(1). Included are certain newspapers, periodicals, transmissions of sound, video or data recordings whose sole or principal purpose is to advise other persons about securities or to publish securities reports: s 77(6), (7). Acts done by solicitors or accountants which are merely incidental to the practice of his or her profession are disregarded: s 77(5). See also **Securities**; **Securities business**.

•**Investment adviser** A person who provides recommendations in respect of investment of money and other assets. For the purposes of the Corporations Law, a person who carries on an investment advice business (defined as a business of advising other persons about securities, or during the course of which a person publishes securities reports: Corporations Law ss 9, 77) must be licensed or be an exempt investment adviser: s 781. A person does not carry on an investment advice business by carrying on an act in the administration of an estate or if the person is a solicitor or accountant and the advice is incidental to the practice of their profession or the advice is published in the media: s 77(4)-(6). See also **Investment advice business; Investment adviser's licence; Securities; Securities business.**

•**Investment adviser's licence** A licence granted to a person by the Australian Securities Commission under Corporations Law Pt 7.3: Corporations Law s 9. A person must not conduct an investment advice business, or hold themselves out to be an investment adviser unless that person holds an investment adviser's licence: s 781. Certain money market dealers, public authorities and insolvency administrators are included in a category of 'exempt investment advisers' who are not required to hold a licence: s 68. See also **Investment advice business; Investment adviser; Securities licensee.**

Investment analyst A person, usually employed by a stockbroking firm, who reviews the past performance and likely future performance of an investment opportunity, such as stocks or bonds. Investment analysts look at all relevant available data with respect to a business in addition to general economic and industry conditions. See also **Security analyst.**

Investment bank A bank which advises corporations and governments on how to raise capital, and guarantees the sale of new bonds and shares, distributing them to investing institutions and individuals. It does not engage in commercial bank activity. In Australia, investment banks offer corporate finance advisory services, underwriting, sales and trading and research services in both the equity and debt capital markets to governmental, institutional and corporate clients.

Investment banker A United States term for what in Australia is more usually termed a merchant banker. Such bankers have a principal function of underwriting issues of securities but they may also engage in securities dealings, foreign exchange dealing and advisory work. US law prohibits an investment banker from taking retail customer deposits. Also known as 'merchant banker'. See also **Investment bank; Investment banking; Merchant bank.**

Investment banking In the United States, the practice of underwriting, but may also include the other activities of an investment banker such as securities dealing and advisory work. In Australia such activities are generally referred to as merchant banking, and the title 'investment bank' is prohibited without the permission of the Treasurer: (CTH) Banking Act 1959 s 66. Also known as 'merchant banking'. See also **Investment bank; Investment banker; Merchant bank.**

Investment business Dealing in, selling, subscribing for or underwriting investments. See also **Dealing; Investment banking.**

•**Investment committee** A body (often part of a company) assigned the duty of evaluating investment transactions. The managers and trustees of managed investment funds will often have formal investment committees which set guidelines and review the results of investment activity. See also **Investment policy; Managed investment.**

•**Investment company** A company which deals with or holds investments as its principal activity. Investment companies in Australia are governed by Corporations Law s 399.

•**Investment contract** Any contract, scheme or arrangement involving the investment of money whereby the investor acquires an interest in, or right in respect of, property that, in accordance with the terms of the investment, will or may be used in common with any other interest or right acquired in or under like circumstances: Corporations Law s 9. Any right to participate, or any interest in, an investment contract is a participation interest. There must be payment in the expectation or contemplation of some form of return, whether of the money itself or by way of income or profit or otherwise: *Munna Beach Apartments Pty Ltd v Kennedy* [1983] 1 Qd R 151 at 156. See also **Prescribed interest.**

Investment Convention 1965 See **International Centre for Settlement of Investment Disputes.**

Investment environment Current external factors which will impact on the likely return from investments, and which therefore contribute to determining the likely level of investments which will be made. Such factors may include the overall strength of the economy and surrounding political stability.

Investment grade bond A bond with a credit rating of BBB or higher, in contrast to a junk bond with a credit rating of BB or lower. An investment grade bond is bought by investors hoping for a reasonable amount of security. The announcement of a leveraged buyout may lead to a downgrading.

Investment grade share A share where the risk of default is minimal and is therefore suitable for investment by bodies with fiduciary responsibilities such as trustees. The Standard and Poors rating agency's highest rating of AAA is given to investment grade shares. See also **Investment grade bond.**

Investment income Income received by the owners of assets. Such income may take the form of dividends from shares, interest from deposits and loans, accounts payable and receivable, returns from discounted financial instruments, earnings from leases, patents and copyrights, and rents. See also **Income from property.**

Investment plan A plan encompassing objectives and strategies to guide the investor along a line of investment activity. A plan will vary according to the individual or group and will be influenced by whether the aim is income, capital growth or a combination of the two. It may contain a rule that not more than 10% of funds will be devoted to any one investment, and that no more than one-third of the funds shall be directed to any one kind of investment. The distribution of funds will also be influenced by the tax position of each investment.

Investment policy Guidelines as to how and when a particular investment may be made. For example, a unit trust may have a policy of investing only in securities which carry a certain rating level. The policy may also require, for example, the obtaining of independent valuations of property to be invested in. See also **Investment company; Investment grade share; Mutual fund; Unit trust.**

Investment value The theoretical price at which a convertible security would sell if it had no convertibility feature. The value is determined by estimating the price at which the convertible security would sell to provide a yield comparable to that of a non convertible security having similar investment characteristics.

•**Investment-related lottery** A lottery where the chance to win the prize arises because the taxpayer holds an investment with an investment body such as a bank. The value of any prize received under an investment-related lottery is treated as assessable income: (CTH) Income Tax Assessment Act 1936 s 26AJ. See also **Assessable income; Prize; Windfall**.

Invisible hand The influence of self-interest working through market forces which often benefits the community as a whole through the efficient delivery of goods and services. The concept was popularised by Adam Smith (1723-1790) in his work *Enquiry into the Nature and Causes of the Wealth of Nations* (1776). Smith noted that the business individual intends only personal gain but is led 'by an invisible hand to promote an end which was no part of his intention'.

•**Invitation** In relation to corporations, the act of inviting an individual. Such an invitation is not an 'invitation to the public': *Lee v Evans* (1964) 112 CLR 276 at 292. A reference to an invitation to do any act or thing includes an invitation to make an offer to do that act or thing: Corporations Law s 78(1).

Invitation to tender An invitation to treat with respect to a contract which may ultimately be entered into by the parties. An invitation to tender is not an offer capable of acceptance by the submission of the tender, although it is an offer in relation to a separate contract arising from the tender itself and which is consummated by the submission of a conforming tender: *Porter v Board of Land and Works* (1870) 1 VR (L) 207; 1 AJR 161. See also **Acceptance; Building contract; Contractor; Deposit; Forfeiture; Invitation to treat; Offer; Proprietor**.

Invitation to treat A request to others to make an offer to engage in negotiations with a contract in mind: *Carlill v Carbolic Smoke Ball Co* [1893] 1 QB 256. Contrasted with an offer which indicates an intention by the offeror to be bound without further discussion or negotiation, on acceptance of the terms set out. See also **Invitation to tender; Offer**.

•**Invoice** An itemised statement of goods sent to a consignee setting out the parties' names and addresses, date of sale, descriptions, quantities, quality, unit prices, charges, any trade discounts, terms of sale, and the total sum payable. Usually produced in multiple copies which are separated and sent to various users.

Involuntary assignment The automatic assignment by operation of law of rights and liabilities under a contract without the consent of the parties. Generally, rights and liabilities under a contract cannot be assigned without the consent of the other party to the contract or unless the parties make them assignable either expressly or impliedly. However, the rights and liabilities may be assigned involuntarily upon the death (for example *Marshall v Broadhurst* (1831) 1 Cr & J 402; 148 ER 1480) or bankruptcy (for example (CTH) Bankruptcy Act 1966 ss 58, 116) of one of the parties, or as a result of statutory provisions relating to the vesting of trust property (for example (NSW) Trustee Act 1925 ss 9, 71-78). See also **Assignment; Novation**.

Involuntary bailment See **Constructive bailment**.

Involvement in management In relation to corporations, being concerned in the running of a company. 'Managing a corporation' refers to a person who is a director or promoter of, or who is in any way (whether directly or indirectly) concerned in or taking part in the management of a corporation: Corporations Law s 91A. A person who is an insolvent under administration, or who has been convicted of certain types of offences, is prohibited from taking part in the management of a company: Corporations Law s 229. See also **Director; Insolvent; Promoter**.

IOU A written acknowledgment that a debt is owed. It derives from the statement 'I owe you'. Whether an IOU is a promissory note or some other kind of instrument is a question of the intention of the issuer of the instrument. The necessary intention to constitute a promissory note is that the issuer intends to make a contractual promise to pay on the instrument, as distinct from any promise in an underlying transaction: *Thomas v Hollier* (1984) 53 ALR 39 at 50. See also **Debt**.

IP See **Intellectual property**.

•**IPP complaint** See **Information Privacy Principles complaint**.

Ipso facto /ɪpsoʊ fæktoʊ/ *Lat* – by the fact itself. A proceeding which is ipso facto void is void for all purposes ab initio. See also **Ab initio**.

Ipso jure /ɪpsoʊ dʒʊreɪ/ *Lat* – by the operation of the law itself.

•**Irregularity** The failure to comply with a procedural formality. For example, a failure to file an objection ((CTH) Bankruptcy Act 1966 s 306(1); *Donnelly v Edelsten* (1992) 34 FLR 556; 109 ALR 651) or where the plaintiff commenced an action in the name of a firm rather than in his or her own name (*Hadley & Co v Henry* (1896) 21 VLR 646). Where an irregularity or deficiency in procedure has been disclosed, the court has extensive power (usually discretionary) to set aside the tainted proceeding in whole or in part upon terms as to costs or otherwise; set aside the tainted step in the proceeding and anything depending upon it; or make a curative order by amendment or otherwise: for example (CTH) High Court Rules O 29 r 12, O 64 r 1; (CTH) Federal Court of Australia Act 1976 s 51(1) ; (CTH) Federal Court of Australia Rules O 13 r 2; (NSW) Supreme Court Act 1970 s 81(1)(b); (NSW) Supreme Court Rules Pt 1 r 12. See also **Null and void**.

Industrial law In relation to an election or ballot of an organisation of employees or employers, an act or omission that hinders or prevents the physical recording of votes, misleading statements that may hinder the full and free recording of votes, and a departure from a rule or established practice in the conduct of elections generally: (CTH) Industrial Relations Act 1988 s 4; *R v Gray; Ex parte Marsh* (1985) 157 CLR 351. See also

Election; Employee organisation; Employer organisation.

Irrepleviable or irreplevisable That cannot be re-delivered to the rightful owner. Replevin is a way of re-delivering goods which have been taken from the owner which have been wrongfully taken from him or her. The re-delivery takes place upon his or her giving security that he will pursue an action against the person by whose orders they were taken.

Irrevocable authority In agency law, an authority given by a principal to effect a security or to secure the interest of the agent, and that cannot be revoked where the agency was created by deed or for valuable consideration: *Smart v Sandars* (1848) 5 CB 895; 136 ER 1132. See also **Agency; Agent; Authority; Consideration; Deed; Revocation of authority; Sufficiency of consideration**.

Irrevocable credit A documentary credit or standby letter of credit containing a definite undertaking by the issuing bank that it will perform its obligations according to the mode of realisation of the credit, provided that the stipulated documents are presented and that the terms and conditions of the credit are complied with. See also **Letter of credit; Revocable credit; Uniform Customs and Practice for Documentary Credits 1993**.

Irrevocable offer An offer that cannot be withdrawn. In option contracts, an offer coupled with a contract that the offer will not be withdrawn during the period, if any, specified in the option. The feature distinguishing an option from a mere offer is consideration: *Ballas v Theophilos (No 2)* (1957) 98 CLR 193. A judicial controversy persists as to whether an option is an irrevocable offer or a conditional contract: *Braham v Walker* (1961) 104 CLR 366. See also **Conditional contract; Consideration; Contract; Offer; Option contract**.

•**Issue** The act of delivery; emission; sending.

Bills of exchange and other negotiable instruments The first delivery of a negotiable instrument to a person who takes it as holder: (CTH) Cheques and Payment Orders Act 1986 s 3(1); (CTH) Bills of Exchange Act 1909 s 4. See also **Delivery; Holder; Negotiable instrument**.

Corporations The offering of securities for sale, or the distribution of offers for such a sale. In relation to prescribed interests it includes making available and otherwise circulating, distributing, and disseminating: Corporations Law s 9.

Issue estoppel A judicial determination directly involving an issue of fact or law which has disposed of the issue so that it cannot thereafter be raised by the same parties: *Blair v Curran* (1939) 62 CLR 464. When a particular matter has been decided in earlier proceedings, the party is estopped or barred from raising it in subsequent proceedings: *Parkin v James* (1905) 2 CLR 315. In deciding what issues were decided, the appellate court may consider any materials which identify the issues. Pleadings, on their own, are not decisive. Issue estoppel differs from res judicata in that res judicata relates to the entire claim, rather than just one issue: *Hoystead v Cmr of Taxation (Cth)* (1925) 37 CLR 290; [1926] AC 155; *Blair v Curran* (1939) 62 CLR 464; 13 ALJ 131; *Schattschneider v Schattschneider* [1974] 2 NSWLR 124; *Onerati v Phillips Constructions Pty Ltd (in liq)* (1989) 16 NSWLR 730; *Heid v Connell Investments Pty Ltd* (1989) 16 NSWLR 626. An issue estoppel can be based on a foreign judgment: *Carl Zeiss Stiftung v Rayner & Keeler Ltd [No 2]* [1967] 1 AC 853; [1966] 2 All ER 536; [1966] 3 WLR 125. See also **Estoppel**.

Arbitration The principle that a party is precluded from contending the contrary of a precise point which, having once been put distinctly in issue, has been with certainty decided against the party. Even if the second cause of action in which the point is raised is different from the first, the finding on the point in issue in the first action, if it is embodied in a final judgment, is conclusive and binding in a second action between the same parties. The point involved may be one of law or fact, or mixed law and fact. It must be the same point; it is not enough that it is very similar: *Co-ownership Land Development Pty Ltd v Queensland Estates* (1973) 1 ALR 201. An award made by an arbitrator resolving a dispute referred to arbitration may give rise to an issue estoppel in respect of a matter determined by the award: *Whitehead v Tattersall* (1834) 1 Ad & El 491; 110 ER 1295. See also **Estoppel**.

Issue of bonus shares An issue of free shares to existing members of a corporation: *BTR Nylex Ltd v Churchill International Inc* (1992) 9 ACSR 361 at 371. These shares must come from either the reserves of the share premium account or from profits: Corporations Law ss 191, 201(1). The power to make bonus issues is customarily given in articles: Corporations Law Sch 1 Table A reg 94.

Issue of new shares An issue of shares that have not yet been allotted by an issuer of securities. An issue of new shares follows a person subscribing to a primary offer of securities.

Issue of shares at a discount See **Discount issue**.

Issue of shares at a premium See **Premium issue**.

•**Issued share capital** The aggregate of the par or nominal value of the shares that the company has issued to its members: *Re Swan Brewery Co Ltd* (1976) 3 ACLR 164. Where the issued share capital is made greater than the authorised share capital by an issue of shares, the issue is void and the subscriber can recover the subscription price: *Bank of Hindustan, China and Japan Ltd v Alison* (1871) LR 6 CP 222. If a share has been issued for an amount greater than its nominal value, the excess or 'premium' does not form part of the company's issued capital. Also known as 'subscribed capital'. See also **Capital; Paid-up share capital; Par value; Unissued capital**.

Issuer In relation to securities, the person who creates the fractional interests as represented by the security. See also **Prospectus**.

Issues and Listings Conference A compulsory meeting between a judicial officer of the court, the parties' legal representatives and the parties themselves, which is held in the Supreme Court of NSW common law division. Its purpose is twofold; to determine whether the matter is capable of being settled, and to ascertain whether it is ready to go to hearing or arbitration. Offers of settlement are exchanged at this or prior to this conference. Attempts are made to narrow the issues in dispute: (NSW) Supreme Court Rules Practice Notes 59, 68.

Issuing bank A bank undertaking to perform the service specified in a letter of credit.

Issuing house A financial firm specialising in the issuing or floating of new securities for governments, municipalities and companies. The issuing house underwrites the whole issue, undertaking to sell the whole of a new issue of securities and to make all necessary arrangements such as advertising the prospectus. It may make arrangements with underwriters to take such part of the issue as is not subscribed to by the public if it does not take up the balance itself.

Itayose-hoh A trading method employed in some securities exchanges involving the competitive auction for a single price by the concentration of bids to buy and offers to sell. There is a single price for each trading session. This method (commonly used in Japan) contrasts with the open outcry trading. See also **Open outcry; Stock exchange.**

Itemised bill A bill of itemised legal costs. A costs agreement between client and solicitor does not entitle the solicitor to avoid delivering a bill of costs unless the agreement expressly waives the client's right to an itemised bill: *Dodd v Gillis* (1989) 16 NSWLR 623.

ITO See **International Trade Organization.**

J

J See **Judge**.

Jack Committee A three member committee appointed by the United Kingdom government in January 1987 to examine the legislation and common law relating to the provision of banking services to personal and business customers, including payment and remittance services. The committee was chaired by Professor R B Jack, and issued its report of eighteen chapters entitled *Banking Services: Law and Practice Report by the Review Committee* in February 1989. See also **Negotiability**.

Jakarta Stock Exchange A relatively small stock exchange with a limited supply of shares. For several years the number of listed companies remained unchanged at 24. In 1989, foreigners were given permission to buy up to 45 per cent of shares in Indonesian retail companies.

Japan Centre for International Finance *Abbr* – JCIF Japan's largest credit rating agency. Decisions are made in respect of a country's credit rating after an examination of government finances, public and private sector debt, imports and exports, national politics and educational standards. Despite a minor downrating in 1986, Australia has remained in the highest A category.

Japan Economic Planning Agency A Japanese government agency which analyses problems facing the Japanese economy and recommends fiscal and monetary policy measures for the promotion of economic growth with minimal inflation. The agency issues quarterly surveys covering 4400 companies, and annual reports.

Japan External Trade Organisation *Abbr* – JETRO A semi-government, non-profit organisation which promotes bilateral economic relations between Australia and Japan through publications, exhibitions, seminars and workshops aimed at promoting trade and industrial cooperation.

Japanese banking system A banking system comprising a central bank, the Bank of Japan (Nippon Ginko), 13 national commercial banks known as 'city' banks, 10 of which in 1994 ranked as the world's largest banks by assets, three long term banks (Industrial Bank of Japan, Long-Term Credit Bank, and the Nippon Credit Bank), 64 regional commercial banks, 13 trust banks and 69 mutual or sogo banks. The banking system comes under the surveillance of the Japan Ministry of Finance. By 1992, the banking system had adopted the capital adequacy guidelines recommended by the Bank for International Settlements.

Jawbone An instrument used by the United States Federal Reserve Board and the federal reserve banks to influence the activities of the commercial banks and other financial institutions. It consists of verbal appeals and recommendations which may prove sufficient to achieve monetary objectives.

J-curve A graphical representation illustrating the possible effects of a devaluation of the Australian dollar in the short and long terms. According to the J-curve, the immediate effect of a devaluation is to raise the prices of imports and reduce the prices of exports, leading to a deterioration in the balance of payments, notably in the current account. However, in the longer term the volume of imports will shrink in consequence of higher prices, while the volume of exports should grow. The hopefully anticipated effect is that the trading situation ameliorates over time, improving the balance of payments. See also **Balance of payments**; **Current account**.

JECNET An inquiry system of the Australian Stock Exchange Ltd for providing information to a network of terminals.

Job search allowance A payment made by the government to a person who is unemployed, who satisfies an activity test (unless exempt), has turned 16 years of age, is an Australian resident, and is registered as unemployed with the Commonwealth Employment Service. A person satisfies the activity test if he or she is actively seeking and willing to undertake paid work suitable to be undertaken by that person: (CTH) Social Security Act 1991 ss 513, 522.

Jobless growth The achievement of increases in productivity and production without any increase in the volume of employment through the use of more machinery, the better use of machinery and the introduction of improved work practices.

Joinder In contract law, the combination of two or more documents to find all the terms of a contract. Joinder is possible so long as the documents are part of the same transaction and are more or less contemporaneous: *Harvey v Edwards Dunlop & Co Ltd* (1927) 39 CLR 302; *Bosaid v Andry* [1963] VR 465. See also **Cause of action**; **Plaintiff**; **Presentment**.

Joint account A bank account in the names of two or more people. A sum standing to the credit of a joint account is a debt owed to the holders of that account jointly and is not enforceable by any one of them alone: *Ardern v Bank of New South Wales* [1956] VLR 569; *Jackson v White and Midland Bank Ltd* [1967] 2 Lloyds Rep 68. On the death of one party the legal interest in that party's share of the funds in the account vests in the survivors: *Russell v Scott* (1936) 55 CLR 440; [1936] ALR 375. In accordance with Australian banking practice some joint accounts are designated joint and several accounts, also referred to as '*and/or*' accounts, in which case either party to the account is authorised to operate it. See also **Account**; **Joint account clause**.

Joint account clause In relation to a loan by two persons who take security jointly and are deemed to be entitled to repayment in proportion to the lending, a clause in the security document which declares the receipt of the survivor(s) to be sufficient discharge for the money repaid without the concurrence of the personal representative of the deceased lender. It simplifies the borrower's obtaining of a good discharge on repayment of the loan The personal representative of a deceased lender, and not the co-lenders, is entitled to the share of the deceased. See also **Joint account; Security.**

Joint and several liability 1. An obligation or liability of two or more persons, so that all are liable jointly or each is liable separately. The party to whom the liability or obligation is owed may either sue one or more separately or all jointly. This means that a plaintiff is entitled to full compensation from any one of the defendants. Such a defendant may then recover contribution from any or all of the other defendants towards the amount paid to the plaintiff: for example (NSW) Law Reform (Miscellaneous Provisions) Act 1946 Pt III. 2. The basis of liability under which two or more defendants to a product liability claim are deemed to be individually and collectively liable for the whole of the damages: (CTH) Trade Practices Act 1974 s 75AM. See also **Creditor; Liability; Obligee; Obligor.**

Joint and several promise 1. In contract law, a promise which creates both an obligation incumbent on all the co-promisors (joint) and individual obligations respectively incumbent on each one (several). The several obligations are non-cumulative, so that performance by any one discharges all: *Re Broons* [1989] 2 Qd R 315. The promise is in the form, 'A and B together promise C, and A separately promises C, and B separately promises C, to pay C $1000.' The promise by A and B together is the joint promise and the two separate promises, one by A and the other by B, are the several promises. 2. A promise made to two or more co-promisees, being of the form 'A promises B and C together, and A promises B separately, and A promises C separately, to pay X $1000'. See also **Co-promisee; Co-promisor; Joint promise; Several promise.**

Joint annuity An annuity held in the names of two persons, regular payments continuing until the death of both partners or the completion of an agreed term.

Joint concurrent tortfeasors Two or more wrongdoers who act together to inflict one and the same damage on another person: *Ruffino v Grace Bros Pty Ltd* [1980] 1 NSWLR 732. Joint concurrent tortfeasors is one of two types of concurrent tortfeasors, the other being 'several concurrent tortfeasors'. See also **Concurrent tortfeasors.**

Joint cost The total cost of manufacturing in a single process two or more different products. A joint cost is allocated because the individual cost of the product cannot be identified until a later production stage has been reached. The production stage where the individual cost of the product can be determined is known as the split-off point. The joint cost concept can be applied to any single operation which produces at least two outputs.

Joint creditors Two or more creditors of a particular debtor who present a bankruptcy petition against the debtor. Although a creditor's petition requires the creditor to be owed at least $1,500, if two or more creditors join in to present a petition, it is sufficient that their debts, when taken together, amount to at least $1,500: (CTH) Bankruptcy Act 1966 s 44(1)(a). See also **Creditor's petition; Debtor; Sequestration.**

Joint debtor A person who, together with one or more others, owes the same debt. A creditor's petition can be presented against two or more joint debtors, whether or not they are partners: (CTH) Bankruptcy Act 1966 s 46(1). The court has power to make a sequestration order, or dismiss the petition, in respect of any or all of the joint debtors: s 46(2). See also **Creditor's petition; Debtor; Sequestration.**

Joint demand A situation in which the satisfaction of a want involves commodities being used in conjunction with each other. Examples are the hardware and software of computing, electrical appliances and electricity, petrol and automobiles, knives and forks, and pens and inks. See also **Joint supply.**

Joint insurance A policy of insurance in which persons enter into a contract with an insurer to indemnify them jointly in respect of a joint loss which they jointly suffer: *General Accident, Fire and Life Assurance Corp Ltd v Midland Bank Ltd* [1940] 2 KB 388. Where more than one person is insured under a policy, the duty of disclosure under (CTH) Insurance Contracts Act 1984 s 21 extends to each of those persons: *Advance (NSW) Insurance Agencies Pty Ltd v Matthews* (1989) 166 CLR 606; 85 ALR 161. See also **Composite insurance.**

Joint liability See **Concurrent liability.**

•**Joint owners** Persons who, between them, hold all ownership rights to any particular property: for example *Baird v Federal Cmr of Land Tax* (1915) 19 CLR 490. Each joint owner is entitled to possession of the whole of the property, and is not entitled to exclude the other co-owner from the use or occupation of the property. Joint owners may hold ownership rights as tenants in common or as joint tenants. See also **Co-ownership; Possession.**

Joint promise 1. A promise by two or more persons which creates a single obligation incumbent on both or all. A joint promise is of the form, 'A and B together promise C to pay C $1000'. The common law presumption is that a promise by two or more is made jointly, but the question is one of intention which is to be determined by construction of the language used, and in the case of ambiguity, by reference to the interests and relations of the parties: *Peabody v Barron* (1884) 5 LR (NSW) 72. 2. A promise made to two or more co-promisees jointly, being of the form 'A promises B and C together to pay X $1000'. See also **Ambiguity; Construction; Co-promisee; Co-promisor; Joint and several promise; Several promise.**

Joint promisee See **Co-promisee.**

Joint promisor See **Co-promisor.**

Joint receivership A receivership in which two or more persons are appointed to act together as receivers. Depending on the terms of the debenture under which they are appointed, the receivers may be appointed either jointly or jointly and severally, the latter being more convenient as each receiver may act alone in exercising the powers conferred. See also **Controller; Receiver; Receiver and manager.**

Joint stock company A company in which the stock or capital is held by a number of persons jointly, the capital being divided into shares.

Joint supply A situation in which the supply of one commodity inevitably involves the supply of one or more other commodities; for example, the provision of beef involves the simultaneous supply of hides and offal. An increased demand for any one item in a joint supply, accompanied by increased production, may result in a fall in the price of the other items if the market is to clear. See also **Joint demand**.

Joint tenancy Common ownership of property in all the co-owners together own the whole, each having an 'undivided' share, and the interest of each ceasing on his or her death for the benefit of the survivors (a right of survivorship): *Wright v Gibbons* (1949) 78 CLR 313; [1949] ALR 287. In addition to the right of survivorship, joint tenancy is evidenced by four unities: unity of time (all co-owners must have acquired their interest in the property at the same time); unity of title (all co-owners must have acquired their interest in the property from the same transaction); unity of interest (co-owners' interests in the property must be identical in nature, extent, and duration); and unity of possession (each co-owner must have a right to each part of the property and to the whole, but not an exclusive right to possess any part). Unless all four unities are present, the co-owners can only be tenants in common; if unity of possession is absent, they are separate owners. See also **Tenancy in common**.

•**Joint venture** An association of persons for particular trading, commercial, mining, or other financial undertakings or endeavours with a view to mutual profit. It is not a technical legal term with a settled common law meaning: *United Dominions Corp Ltd v Brian Pty Ltd* (1985) 157 CLR 1; 60 ALR 741. The association is usually for the participation in a single project rather than a continuing business. A joint venture may be carried out by way of a partnership, company, trust, agency, joint ownership, or other arrangement. It may include an activity carried on by a body corporate which was formed to carry on the activity by means of joint control or ownership of shares in the body corporate: (CTH) Trade Practices Act 1974 s 4J(a). See also **Agency; Business undertaking; Company; Fiduciary relationship; Incorporated joint venture; Partnership; Trust**.

Journal entry For accounting purposes, a record of debits and credits in a general journal analysing transactions which incorporate entries such as adjustments to accounts, accruals, prepayments, transfers, and closing entries.

JP See **Justice of the Peace**.

•**Judge** *Abbr* – J 1. To adjudicate, try, or pass sentence. 2. A person invested with authority to determine matters requiring the application of a legal remedy (such as the adjudication of a dispute between parties) and to award appropriate punishment to offenders. There are usually statutory eligibility criteria, such as admission to practice for some period, but otherwise appointment remains at the discretion of the government. Judges are not public servants and are not subject to supervision and control by the executive. Federal judges can only be removed by the Governor-General in Council on an address from both Houses of Parliament: Commonwealth Constitution s 72. The State Constitution Acts make similar provision, although most States merely require an address from the lower house: for example (QLD) Constitution Act 1867 s 16. Judges from inferior courts, such as magistrates, enjoy less protection because their tenure is not constitutionally enshrined.

•**Judgment** 1. The determination of a court in legal proceedings. 2. Any order of the court for the payment of an amount of money or costs or otherwise: for example (NSW) District Court Act 1973 s 84. A judgment also includes a decree or order, whether final or interlocutory, or a sentence: (CTH) Federal Court of Australia Act 1976 s 4.

•**Judgment creditor** A person the recipient of a court judgment that orders another (the judgment debtor) to pay a sum of money to that person. The judgment creditor has the right to enforce payment by execution against the judgment debtor's property. See also **Execution; Garnishment; Judgment; Judgment debtor**.

Judgment creditor's order An order of the court, on motion pursuant to a garnishment notice, that the garnishee pay to the judgment creditor the debt attached to the extent specified in the garnishment notice, or so much of the debt attached to the extent so specified as is required to satisfy the judgment or order on which the garnishment proceedings are taken: for example (NSW) Supreme Court Rules Pt 46 r 8. See also **Garnishment; Judgment creditor**.

•**Judgment debt** 1. An amount owing under a court judgment. A creditor with a judgment debt is entitled to apply for a bankruptcy notice: (CTH) Bankruptcy Act 1966 s 40(1)(g). 2. Any amount ordered by the court to be paid as costs or pursuant to the orders made by the court and any amount payable as provided by the rules as to costs without any order of the court: for example (NSW) District Court Act 1973 s 84. See also **Bankruptcy notice**.

•**Judgment debtor** A person who has a court judgment against them that orders them to pay a sum of money to the judgment creditor: for example (NSW) Supreme Court Rules Pt 46 r 1. See also **Judgment; Judgment creditor**.

Judgment in personam A judgment delivered by a competent judicial authority against a particular person or party imposing an obligation on him or her. An example is a judgment requiring a party to fulfil contractual commitments. It is contrasted with a judgment *in rem* against property. See also **In personam; Judgment in rem**.

Judgment in rem A judgment delivered by a competent judicial authority which affects or creates an interest in property, or affects the status of a person or corporation. It is contrasted with a judgment *in personam*. See also **Judgment in personam**.

Judicial discretion A discretion to be exercised according to judicial method rather than arbitrarily. An exercise of judicial discretion however does not involve the application of a strict rule of law but involves the weighing of various competing factors and making a determination according to what is fair, just, or otherwise consistent with public policy.Matters falling within the scope of judicial discretion are not subject to review except if it can be shown that the judge failed to take all relevant factors into account, took account of irrelevant factors, or reached a decision no other reasonable judge acting on the same facts would have reached.

Judicial inquiry An inquiry conducted by a member or panel of the judiciary with the function of investigating, making recommendations, or declaring and enforcing legal rights and liabilities. Judicial inquiries are not usually bound by the rules of evidence: for example (CTH) Marriage Act 1961 s 18(1)(a).

Judiciary The body of people who adjudicate upon legal disputes in what are commonly referred to as courts of law. The judiciary forms one of the three branches of the government, and under the doctrine of separation of powers must exercise its powers exclusive of the legislature and executive, although at a State level this is not a binding principle of law: *Building Construction Employees and Builders' Labourers Federation of New South Wales v Minister for Industrial Relations* (1986) 7 NSWLR 372. In Australia, the judiciary is appointed by the executive arm of government. At a Commonwealth level, its powers are designated by Commonwealth Constitution Ch III. Also known as 'judicature'. See also **Court; High Court of Australia**.

Juglar cycle A business cycle of between nine and eleven years' duration identified by Clement Juglar (1819-1905) of France. He has been credited with being the first to speak of business cycles. Juglar divided business cycles into three phases, namely prosperity, crisis and liquidation. He argued that the sole cause of the crisis was the prosperity phase that preceded it, and that depression always followed the crisis. The excesses and maladjustments of the prosperity phase made the crisis and depression inevitable. Standard business cycle theory has been mainly concerned with explanations of the Juglar theory. Clement Juglar first published his findings in 1860.

•**Junior** An employee under the age of 21 years (but not an apprentice or a trainee): for example (SA) Industrial and Employee Relations Act 1994 s 4. See also **Apprentice; Trainee**.

Junk bond A large issue of subordinated notes and debentures carrying a high risk. The increased risk of default means that they will typically offer a relatively high interest rate. The potential for repayment depends on the issuer's fortunes more than general economic bonds so they tend to be less susceptible to interest rate movements than more highly rated bonds. In the 1980s they became increasingly associated with acquisitions, takeovers and leveraged buyouts. See also **Bond; Leveraged buyout**.

Jurat /dʒuræt/ *Lat* – he or she swears. A section at the conclusion of an affidavit of documents setting out the name of the deponent, the signature of the deponent, where and when the affidavit was sworn, the name of the person before whom it was sworn, and the signature and title or description of the person before whom it was sworn. See also **Affidavit**.

•**Jurisdiction** The scope of the court's power to examine and determine the facts, interpret and apply the law, make orders and declare judgment. Jurisdiction may be limited by geographic area, the type of parties who appear, the type of relief that can be sought, and the point to be decided. The powers of courts of limited jurisdiction are generally defined by statute. Where jurisdiction is questioned, jurisdiction connotes the statutory limits imposed upon the court to hear and determine issues together with general principles requiring a clear case to be made out: *Walker v Hussmann Australia Pty Ltd* (1991) 24 NSWLR 451; 381 IR 180.

Jurisdiction clause A clause in a contract providing for the settlement of any dispute between the parties arising out of the contract to take place in a court of law of a particular jurisdiction. Where the transaction under the contract is potentially subject to the jurisdiction of two or more countries, the clause specifies the country that has jurisdiction over the contract. See also **Arbitration; Arbitration clause; Bill of lading; Charterparty; Jurisdiction**.

Jurisprudence The theory of law; the study of the principles of law and legal systems and their fundamental philosophical basis.

Juristic person See **Artificial person**.

Jury A group of people who swear to fairly determine an issue of fact. A jury in a criminal trial consists of 12 jurors while in civil trials four persons constitute a jury: (NSW) Jury Act 1977 ss 19, 20; (VIC) Juries Act 1967 s 14(2). The jury must decide questions of fact left to them by the judge and, in a criminal trial, to return a verdict of guilty or not guilty of the crime charged in the indictment.

Jus /dʒus/ *Lat* – a law or a right. In Roman law, in its widest sense, the whole of the law; more narrowly it denotes the subjective rights of a citizen; the status of a citizen as being within the paternal power of another or being independent. Pl – *Jura*.

•**Jus tertii** /dʒus tɜʃii/ *Lat* – the right of a third person. It is not possible to claim a *jus tertii* as a defence in an action for possession of property in order to defeat the claim of the person seeking possession: *Standard Electronic Apparatus Laboratories Pty Ltd v Stenner* [1960] NSWR 447; (1960) 77 WN (NSW) 833. A possessor of land must show that his or her right is superior to the right of the person claiming possession. A third party's right to possession is relevant only if it demonstrates that the claimant has no right to possession: *Oxford Meat Co Pty Ltd v McDonald* [1963] NSWR 1244; 63 SR (NSW) 423. See also **Documentary title; Possession**.

•**Just and equitable** In corporations law, a ground upon which a court may be petitioned to compulsorily wind up a company: (CTH) Corporations Law s 461(k). The provision confers upon a court a discretionary power of a very wide character and courts must be ready to apply it to new situations falling outside previous illustrations: *Ebrahimi v Westbourne Galleries Ltd* [1973] AC 360. The principal categories of application are where the company was formed for a fraudulent purpose, where there is an improper denial of information to the minority, where there is a deadlock in the general meeting, or where there is a failure of substratum: s 461. See also **Failure of substratum; Winding up**.

•**Just terms** A qualification on the power of the Commonwealth Government to acquire land or property from private companies or individuals for purposes for which the government has the power to make laws: Constitution 1901 s 51(xxxi). The general requirement of just terms is the provision of a price which a reasonably willing vendor and purchaser would have negotiated at the date of the acquisition: *Nelungaloo Pty Ltd v Commonwealth* (1948) 75 CLR 495. There is no requirement to provide compensation where the uses to which the property may be put are restricted or the property is surrendered voluntarily in pursuit of permission to conduct an activity: for example *Trade Practices Commission v Tooth & Co* (1979) 26 ALR 185; *Commonwealth v Tasmania (Australia) Ltd v Secretary, Department of Community Services and Health* (1983) 158 CLR 1; *Smith, Kline, French Laboratories* (1990) 95 ALR 87. See also **Acquisition**.

•**Justice** 1. A judge of a Supreme Court, a federal court, or the High Court. 2. A magistrate or a Justice of the Peace. In some situations, the term may be limited, as in (NSW) Crimes Act 1900 s 352, where in relation to the power of arrest the term is limited to a justice employed by the Department of Courts Administration. 3. A concept defined according to the particular philosophical school of the inquirer, as evidenced by the Platonic dialogue, *Cratylus*. Most definitions can be categorised into one of two groups: one holding that justice has a transcendental nature and is determined by God; the other maintaining that justice is a matter of convention determined by human judgment. See also **Judge**; **Justice of the peace**.

•**Justice of the Peace** A person with a commission of the Crown who is able to exercise particular judicial functions within a jurisdiction. In New South Wales, a magistrate may alone exercise any power or jurisdiction of a justice or justices and no justice other than a magistrate may adjudicate in summary proceedings in nominated police districts: (NSW) Justices Act 1902 ss 10(1), 13(1). In Queensland, Supreme Court and District Court judges, and certain court officers, are made justices of the peace by statute without further appointment: (QLD) Justices of the Peace and Commissioners for Declarations Act 1991 s 29(1). A justice of the peace may have power to restrain offenders and to take of them or of persons not of good fame surety for their good behaviour: (NSW) Imperial Acts Application Act 1969 ss 29, 30. An oath declaration or affidavit required for the purpose of any court or for the purpose of the registration of any instrument or for the purpose of any arbitration may be taken or made before any justice of the peace: for example (NSW) Oaths Act 1900 s 26. See also **Supreme Court**.

Justiciability Capable of being settled by a court of law.

Administrative law Amenability of administrative action to review by a court. At common law, the test for justiciability resembles a 'political questions' test, whose application in any particular set of circumstances remains uncertain, depending upon the status of the administrative decision-maker and the nature of the power exercised: *Peko-Wallsend Ltd v Minister for Arts, Heritage and Environment* (1986) 13 FCR 19; 70 ALR 523. Not every political issue, however, is non-justiciable: *Victoria v Commonwealth* [1993] 1 Qd R 10. Statutory powers are justiciable, subject to the operation of privative clauses. Many prerogative powers are regarded as non-justiciable. Different tests of justiciability are provided for by different statutes: for example (CTH) Adminsitrative Decisions (Judicial Review) Act 1977; (VIC) Judicial Review Act 1991; (QLD) Administrative Law Act 1978; (ACT) Administrative Decisions (Judicial Review) Act 1989. See also **Decision**; **Jurisdiction**.

Courts Suitability of a matter for adjudication by a court. The determination of issues, broadly described as 'political', relying on the exercise of non-judicial power, or adopting an executive or legislative character are non-justiciable issues and fall outside the jurisdiction of the courts: *Director of Public Prosecutions (Cth) v Toro-Martinez* (1993) 33 NSWLR 82; 119 ALR 517.

Justification A defensive plea, fact, or circumstance.

Defamation The defence that the imputation complained of is true. At common law it acts as a complete defence. Generally, the defendant must show that the imputation complained of is substantially true.

Tort The concept that it is a defence to torts involving interference with trade or business that the defendant was justified in doing the tortious act; for example, a trade union may argue that its industrial action is justified because it was protesting against dangerous conditions for workers. The scope of the 'justification' defence is uncertain, and its existence must be determined in the circumstances of each case. In general, advancement of one's own or others' interests does not suffice; it must involve 'action taken as a duty' or 'exercise of an equal or superior right': *Pete's Towing Services Ltd v Northern Industrial Union of Workers* [1970] NZLR 32. See also **Industrial tort**.

Just-in-time production An arrangement for the delivery of materials and components to a factory (or from one workstation to another inside a plant) just as they are needed. The just-in-time system obviates the need for costly inventory. Just-in-time delivery and production has been a major Japanese contribution to manufacturing techniques. See also **Inventory**.

K

KC See **Queen's Counsel**.

Keech v Sandford principle The principle, of an absolute and strict nature, that a person in a fiduciary relationship may not make an unauthorised gain in a situation of actual or potential conflict, regardless of whether the person to whom the fiduciary duty is owed could have taken the property the subject of the gain. The fiduciary holds any property so gained on constructive trust for the beneficiary: *Keech v Sandford* (1726) Cas temp King 61; 25 ER 223 The rule is sometimes also extended to those not in a strict trustee-beneficiary relationship. For example, it is extended to partners and so-called 'special' non-fiduciary relationships by analogy to the rule. In the true application of this rule the presumption of a breach of duty is irrebuttable. In the cases of analogy the presumption is rebuttable: *Chan v Zacharia* (1984) 154 CLR 178; 53 ALR 417. See also **Constructive trust**; **Fiduciary**.

Keeping house Avoiding contact with a creditor or a creditor's representative by remaining indoors. It is an act of bankruptcy if a debtor, with intent to defeat or delay creditors, begins to keep house: (CTH) Bankruptcy Act 1966 s 40(1)(c)(i). See also **Act of bankruptcy**; **Creditor**; **Debtor**.

Keiretsu Japanese conglomerates composed of banking, trading and manufacturing companies, all linked by cross shareholdings. Keiretsu companies favour trade within their groups, limiting business opportunities for outsiders.

Kennedy Round of the General Agreement on Tariffs and Trade 1947 The sixth tariff concession negotiation round under the General Agreement on Tariffs and Trade 1947 initiated by the United States President John Kennedy in 1967. The Kennedy Round of the General Agreement on Tariffs and Trade 1947 was devoted mainly to solving the trade impasse between the United States and the former European Economic Community. In negotiating the Kennedy round, it was realised that the tariff reduction on industrial products had reached its limit, and that non-tariff barriers had become more acute. It resulted in adoption of the Geneva (1967) Protocol to the General Agreement on Tariffs and Trade 1947 which was signed by Australia on 8 November 1967 and came into force generally on 1 January 1968. See also **General Agreement on Tariffs and Trade 1947**; **General Agreement on Tariffs and Trade 1994**; **Non-tariff barrier**.

Key man insurance premium Insurance cover taken out by an employer to protect the business against financial loss if a key person cannot continue in employment or complete a task due to death or disablement. Money received under such a policy is assessable income where the purpose of the insurance is to fill the place of a revenue item: *Carapark Holdings Ltd v FCT* (1966) 115 CLR 653; 10 AITR 378. See also **Allowable deduction**; **Assessable income**; **Capital gains tax**; **Capital loss**.

Keynesian school A school of economics based upon the work of John Maynard Keynes (1883-1946), most notably his *General Theory of Employment, Interest and Money* (1936). Keynes argued that there were fundamental errors in the beliefs underlying classical and neo-classical economic theory and that the automatic self-adjusting qualities that had been attributed to the economic system were fictitious. He refuted the notion that labour had only to lower its price for full employment to be restored. The Keynesian school has generally maintained that fiscal policy is a greater influence on the economy than monetary policy, an incomes policy is important in helping to limit inflation, policy instruments should be used in a discretionary manner rather than according to a set of rules, and tax rates and government expenditure should be adjusted in order to keep unemployment at a reasonable level, ensuring low inflation and a balance of payments equilibrium.

Kickback A payment of money or something given as an incentive to secure certain favours. It is usually made in secret, and can be illegal. See also **Corruption**.

Killing the bond Stripping a bond of its interest coupons so that it becomes a zero coupon. Such bonds are often considered 'better dead than alive'. See also **Bond**; **Zero coupon bond**.

King's Counsel See **Queen's Counsel**.

Kinked demand curve A demand curve that may be characteristic of a firm in certain oligopolistic industries. It occurs when a firm judges that if it cuts its prices, other firms will do likewise, but if it raises its prices, other firms may be content to leave theirs unchanged. In the first instance there may be no gain in market share and a potential loss of profit. In the second instance there is the potential complete loss of the market involved. Thus the demand curve is relatively inelastic below the going price and relatively elastic above the going price.

Kitchin cycle A concept developed in the early 1920s by the British statistician, Joseph Kitchin, that business fluctuations could be divided into two categories, namely major cycles and minor cycles. Major cycles are aggregates of two or perhaps three minor cycles, each minor cycle averaging some 40 months in length. Kitchin based his findings on commodity prices, bank clearings and interest rates in the United States and Britain for the period 1890 to 1922.

Kiting The fraudulent act of depositing a cheque in one bank account which is drawn on another bank account of the same entity and only recording the deposit on the day of the transfer. See also **Cheque**.

Knock down In relation to an auction, the acceptance of a bid by an auctioneer, marked usually by the fall of the hammer at the highest bid. Once property has been 'knocked down' to the highest bidder, an oral contract for sale of that property arises. See also **Acceptance; Auction; Auctioneer; Bid**.

Knock for knock agreement An agreement between insurance companies issuing comprehensive motor vehicle insurance under which each company agrees to bear the loss caused to its own insured as a result of a collision with a vehicle insured by another company which is also a party to the agreement. The aim of the knock for knock agreement is to reduce the companies' administration and legal costs by avoiding litigation between the owners of cars. See also **Insurance; Insurance contract**.

Knock-out agreement An agreement between potential bidders before an auction that some of them will not bid at the auction, and which deals with the sharing of property acquired by one of them at the auction or of profits on resale. Under the general law, a knock-out agreement is lawful, and the successful bidder is entitled to specific performance of the agreement for sale, as against the seller: *Harrop v Thompson* [1975] 2 All ER 94. However, in some jurisdictions, such an agreement is rendered illegal by legislation dealing with certain collusive practices at auction sales: for example (VIC) Collusive Practices Act 1965. See also **Auction; Bid; Collusive bidding agreement; Damping the sale; Restraint of trade; Specific performance**.

- **Know-how** Industrial information and techniques likely to assist in the manufacture or processing of goods and materials. In taxation law, know-how cannot be a capital asset unless the tax-payer is carrying on a business: *Brent v FCT* (1971) 2 ATR 563. In intellectual property law, for the purposes of determining whether there has been a breach of confidence, the 'know-how' acquired during a working career. The way in which a skilled worker does his or her job has a quality resulting from experience, which a worker is entitled to use for his or her own advancement in his or her chosen career: *Pioneer Concrete Services Ltd v Galli* [1985] VR 675 at 710.

Knowledge of risk The appreciation of a risk being assumed by doing or omitting to do a certain act. Where a person who voluntarily assumes the risk of participation in an activity is injured as a result of the defendant's negligence, the defence of voluntary assumption of risk may be available to the defendant. One element of this defence is the plaintiff's knowledge of the risk entailed and appreciation of the extent and nature of that risk: *Roggenkamp v Bennett* (1950) 80 CLR 292.

Kommanditgesellschaft *Abbr* – KG The German and Austrian equivalent of a limited partnership with at least one unlimited liability partner.

Kommanditgesellschaft auf Aktien *Abbr* – KGaA A German legal term denoting a form of public company certain of whose shareholders are personally liable for its debts.

Kommanditselskab *Abbr* – K/S The Danish equivalent of a limited partnership.

Kondratieff cycle Identified by the Russian economist, Nikolai D Kondratieff (1892-1938), the longest business cycle or wave found in economic history. An analysis of economic time series for England, France, Germany and the United States suggested that there existed a cycle with an average duration of some 54-60 years.

Kuala Lumpur Stock Exchange One of the leading stock exchanges in the south-east Asia region. In 1989, its long-standing ties with the Singapore Stock Exchange were ended when Malaysian companies were compelled to withdraw from that exchange. Some 182 Malaysian companies had been listed in Singapore compared with only 47 Singapore stocks in Kuala Lumpur. The Malaysian government decided that the unequal relationship with Singapore should be ended.

Kuznets cycle Long swings in economic growth rates exhibiting a duration of some 15-20 years or more. They were identified by Simon S Kuznets (1901-85) after extensive studies particularly of American economic development. The swings were most marked in the building construction industry. Kuznets identified peaks in 1873, 1892 and 1913 with troughs in 1878 and 1896. Kuznets and others also argued that these growth rate swings could be found in the 1920s and 1930s.

L

Labour The combination of all the exertions of individuals, whether physical or intellectual, directed towards the production of goods and services, although it is sometimes limited to that which tests a person's muscles and sinews: *Yarmouth v France* (1887) 19 QBD 647. See also **Contract for labour; International Labour Organisation; Labour agreement; Labour law; Labourer.**

•**Labour agreement 1.** A formal agreement entered into by the Minister and a person or organisation in Australia, authorising an employer to recruit persons (other than holders of permanent visas) for employment in Australia: (CTH) Migration Regulations 1994 reg 1.03. **2.** A formal agreement entered into by the Minister and a sporting organisation in Australia under which an employer is authorised to recruit persons (other than holders of permanent visas) to take part in the sporting activities of the sporting organisation whether as employees or otherwise: (CTH) Migration Regulations 1994 reg 1.03. See also **Labour.**

Labour costs The total cost of employing labour including both wage and non-wage costs such as social-insurance contributions, sickness benefits, payroll tax, and accident insurance. The Unit Labour Cost Index (ULCI) compares changes in Australia's nominal unit labour costs (expressed as the ratio of wages, salaries and non-wage costs to gross product) in the non-farm sector of the economy with those of our four major trading partners, after taking into account exchange rate changes. The trading partners are the United States, Japan, Britain, and Germany. See also **Absorption costing; Capital to labour ratio; Economies of scale; On-cost; Productivity.**

Labour Court See **Australian Industrial Court.**

Labour law The legal regulation of the relationship between workers and employers. The term includes the law of employment, which concerns the individual contract of employment; industrial law, which concerns the relations between employers and workers acting collectively; occupational health and safety law; and workers' compensation law. See also **Contract of employment; Employment law; Industrial law; Occupational health and safety; Trade union; Workers' compensation.**

Labourer Generally, a person engaged in manual or physical labour, especially unskilled labour, as opposed to a person whose work requires skill or training. 'What degree of skill is sufficient to raise a manual worker out of the labouring class is a question upon which widely varying opinions may be, and frequently are, held; but a man with a recognised trade or profession, or an artisan in "any art, trade or mystery" (see Lord Ellenborough's remarks in *Lewther v Radnor* (1806) 8 East 124) is not in relation to that trade, profession, art or mystery properly styled a labourer': *Hume Pipe (Australia) Ltd v Lawson* [1925] SASR 385. See also **Labour; Servant; Wharf labourer; Worker.**

Labour-intensive industry Industry in which the ratio of labour input to capital and natural resources input is higher than the average ratio for industry as a whole. Very few manufacturing processes are labour-intensive, whereas the service industries use a disproportionately large amount of labour. See also **Australian industry; Capital-intensive industry; Labour.**

•**Laches** Unreasonable delay or negligence in issuing proceedings. A court may, in its discretion, refuse to grant equitable relief if it believes that the plaintiff was unduly dilatory in instituting legal proceedings: *Orr v Ford* (1989) 167 CLR 316; 84 ALR 146; *Mehmet v Benson* (1965) 113 CLR 295; [1965] ALR 903. The defence of laches reflects the equitable maxims that equity aids the vigilant and not the indolent, and that delay defeats equities. See also **Equitable defence; Limitation of actions.**

Laffer curve In economics, a curve showing the relationship between taxation and incentives. The curve indicates that tax revenue will be zero both when tax rates are zero and when they are 100 per cent. As taxes are imposed and progressively increased, tax revenue will increase. Revenue will continue to rise as long as the marginal percentage reduction in the taxable base due to a disincentive effect is less than the marginal percentage increase in tax. At some point, higher tax rates will shrink the taxable base faster than revenues grow, and the total revenue will be reduced until at 100 per cent rate it will be zero. The curve was first developed by the French engineer A J Dupuit (1804-1866) and later developed by the United States economist Arthur Laffer. See also **Economic rationalism; Export Incentive Scheme; Supply side economics; Tax haven.**

Laissez-faire /lɛseɪ fɛə/ *Fr* – let do freely. A free enterprise economic system devoid of governmental intervention, which allows market forces (such as demand, supply, prices, and competition) to determine the operation of business and trading. Its origins are ascribed to the French business executive Aimé-François Legendre. Adam Smith incorporated the concept in his work *Lectures on Jurisprudence* (1762-64). For Smith, the economic freedoms associated with the *laissez faire* doctrine were natural rights. The doctrine is associated with utilitarian theory since *laissez faire* policies are sometimes justified by the utilitarian argument that they give rise to the greatest good for the greatest number. Many market economy countries purport to support and pursue a *laissez faire* policy. It is distinguished from the state owned and controlled economies under a socialist or communist system. See also **Demand; Perfect competition; Smith, Adam; Supply.**

•**Land** Physically, the surface of the earth, the soil beneath (arguably to the centre of the earth unless modified by the

© Butterworths

terms of the grant), the airspace above, all things growing on or affixed to the soil including buildings, trees, crops, and all minerals except the royal minerals and any other minerals excepted by the terms of the Crown grant. For statutory purposes, land 'includes messuages, tenements and hereditaments, corporeal and incorporeal, of any tenure or description, and whatever may be the estate or interest therein': (CTH) Acts Interpretation Act 1901 s 22. See also **Estate**.

•**Land and Environment Court** *Abbr* – LEC In New South Wales, a State superior court of record with limited jurisdiction: (NSW) Land and Environment Court Act 1979 ss 5(1), 16(1). The Land and Environment Court has competence to hear appeals arising from particular environmental, planning, local government and development legislation, and to decide certain native title matters: ss 17-21B. These provisions empower the court to determine whether a development application should be approved: *Shellharbour Municipal Council v Rovili Pty Ltd* (1989) 16 NSWLR 104; 68 LGRA 231. A decision of the Court is 'final and conclusive' in some matters (s 56), and in others, appeal to the Supreme Court is permitted: ss 57(1), 58(1)), mediation or neutral evaluation may be ordered where the parties to the action agree: s 61A(1). Judges of the Court are equivalent to puisne judges of the Supreme Court with respect to rank, title, status, and precedence: s 9(2). See also **Administrative appeal; Assessor; Environment**.

Land charge An interest in land to secure payment of money or performance of an obligation. Under a land charge, the debtor ('chargor') retains his or her interest in the land but is burdened by the security interest acquired by the creditor ('chargee'). The Torrens mortgage, however, does not effect a transfer of the mortgaged land and the registered mortgagee obtains a legal interest in such land: (NSW) Real Property Act 1900 s 57(1); (VIC) Transfer of Land Act 1958 s 74(2); (QLD) Land Title Act 1994 s 74. See also **Charge; Mortgage; Power of sale**.

•**Land tax** 1. A tax levied by all States and the Australian Capital Territory on the unimproved value of taxable land: for example (NSW) Land Tax Act 1956 s 3AE. Land tax is usually based on ownership of land, though in the Australian Capital Territory it is payable on leases of land. 2. Any other tax directly imposed on land by a state legislature. A rate imposed on land by the (NSW) Sydney Harbour Bridge Act 1922 was held to fall within the definition of land tax: *Levanthal v David Jones Ltd* (1930) 30 SR (NSW) 123. See also **Ad valorem; Apportionable deduction; Cost base**.

Landed costs See **Net acquisition cost**.

•**Landlord** 1. In general, an owner of land or an estate in land (including a leasehold estate) who lets premises to another person under a tenancy arrangement. 2. In residential tenancy legislation, a person who grants the right to occupy residential premises under a residential tenancy agreement: for example (NSW) Residential Tenancies Act 1987 s 3(1). See also **Leasehold; Premises; Tenancy**.

Landlord's fixtures Fixtures that cannot be removed from the premises without substantial damage to the premises: *Spyer v Phillipson* [1931] 2 Ch 183. In consequence, a tenant cannot remove them, even where the tenant is the person who affixed them. In this, they are to be contrasted with tenant's fixtures. See also **Landlord; Tenant's fixtures**.

Lapping In banking law, the fraudulent act of depositing an entity's own funds in a bank account after withdrawing those funds from another account. Lapping attempts to conceal a cash shortage by exaggerating the extent of cash deposits. See also **Fraud; Kiting**.

Lapse through abandonment The lapse of a contract of insurance that occurs when the parties to it act as if the contract has been abandoned: *Summers v Commonwealth* (1918) 25 CLR 144.

•**Larceny** The offence at common law of fraudulently, and without the consent of the owner or a claim of right made in good faith, taking and carrying away anything capable of being stolen, with the intent at the time of the taking to permanently deprive the owner of the property: *Ilich v R* (1987) 162 CLR 110; 69 ALR 231. Larceny is commonly known as 'stealing', and in some jurisdictions there is an equivalent offence known as 'theft'.

Large-case tax audit A random audit for income tax purposes aimed at Australia's top 100 companies which may involve the extensive examination of the business over a period of a few years. This practice has been accepted as within the purposes of the Income Tax Assessment Act 1936 as long as the Commissioner of Taxation is endeavouring to ascertain the taxable income of the taxpayer: *Industrial Equity Ltd v DCT (NSW)* (1990) 170 CLR 649; 96 ALR 337. See also **Audit; Taxable income; Tax Office audit strategy**.

Last in first out valuation *Abbr* – LIFO An accounting method used for assigning costs to trading stock and work in progress of an entity. LIFO cannot be used to value trading stock for taxation purposes: *Minister of National Revenue v Anaconda American Brass Ltd* [1956] AC 85; [1956] 1 All ER 20. See also **First in first out valuation; Trading stock**.

Late completion In building law, a failure by the contractor to achieve practical completion by the stipulated date in the building contract. Late completion is a breach of contract, which gives rise to an entitlement to damages and may give rise to a right in the proprietor to terminate the building contract: for example *Comco Constructions Pty Ltd v Westminster Properties Pty Ltd* (1990) 8 BCL 223; 2 WAR 335. See also **Breach of contract; Building contract; Proprietor; Time stipulation**.

Late delivery In sale of goods contracts, the tender of goods by the seller after the time appointed by the contract. The buyer is usually under no obligation to accept the goods, time of delivery being of the essence in commercial contracts. Damages for late delivery are available at common law. Prima facie the buyer may recover the difference between the market price of the goods at the time and place of actual delivery, and the market price when the goods ought to have been delivered: for example *Wertheim v Chicoutimi Pulp Co* [1911] AC 301. See also **Commercial contract; Damages; Non-delivery; Sale of goods; Tender of performance; Time stipulation**.

Latent defect A flaw, fault, imperfection or irregularity not readily observable or easily discovered; not patent. Such a defect only comes to light when it causes an accident.

Product liability A defect in a product that is not apparent on a reasonable examination of it, or that only becomes manifest after a period of use: for example *Taylor v Combined Buyers Ltd* [1924] NZLR 627. The seller of a product with a latent defect is not usually liable; the manufacturer is liable for the injury caused by those goods: (CTH) Trade Practices Act 1974 ss 75AD, 75AE, 75AF, 75AG. See also **Duty to disclose**; **Opportunity for intermediate inspection**; **Product liability**.

Laundering Directly or indirectly engaging in a transaction involving the proceeds of crime, or receiving, possessing, concealing, disposing of or bringing into any State or Territory the proceeds of crime: (CTH) Proceeds of Crime Act 1987 s 81(3). See also **Proceeds of crime**; **Smurfing**.

•**Law** The subject matter of the discipline of jurisprudence. Law is defined differently according to the particular jurisprudential school or methodology within which one is operating. For example, schools of legal sociology emphasise the social significance of the law and its relationship to politics; positivist schools of jurisprudence focus on an examination of the framework of rules and regulations and their interrelationship; and schools of natural law jurisprudence examine more metaphysical issues about the precise essence of law and the relationship between law and morality, and positive law and natural law.

Law merchant *Lat – lex mercatoria*. The customs and usages of merchants which were, as a result of judicial recognition, accepted into the common law of England. Courts will require sufficiently strong evidence of market recognition: *Commercial Bank of Australia Ltd v Skinner* (1895) 21 VLR 368. See also **Custom**; **Mercantile law**; **Negotiable instrument**.

Law of obligations An umbrella term for contract, tort, and restitution. The phrase is sometimes used to reflect the theory that there is not a general law of contract, tort, or restitution; rather, there is a general law of obligations, which is manifested in particular forms of contracts, torts, and responses to unjust enrichment. See also **Contract**; **Restitution**; **Tort**.

Law of the flag In maritime law, the law of the state whose flag is hoisted by a particular ship or vessel. The flag displays the nationality of the vessel: for example Geneva Convention on the High Seas 1958 arts 4, 5. See also **Maritime law**.

Law of the sea A core subject of international law governing various rights and obligations relative to the use of the sea. The law of the sea was codified by the United Nations in Geneva in 1958, resulting in four Conventions. Subsequently, the United Nations adopted an exhaustive new legal regime of the sea, the United Nations Convention on the Law of the Sea 1982, which came into effect in 1994.

Law officer of the Crown The Attorney-General or Solicitor-General of the Commonwealth or a State: (CTH) High Court Rules O 1 r 5.

Law Reform Commission A body established to review laws with a view to the systematic development and reform of the law: (CTH) Australian Law Reform Commission Act 1996 s 21. The Law Reform Commission consists of a president and four or more other members, each of whom must be a judge of the Federal Court or the Supreme Court of a State or Territory; a person who has been enrolled as a legal practitioner of the High Court, or the Supreme Court of a State or Territory for not less than five years; a person who is a graduate in law of a university and has had experience as a member of the academic staff of a tertiary educational institution; or a person who, in the opinion of the Governor-General is by reason of the persons specific qualifications, training or experience, suitable for appointment: s 7. All members are appointed by the Governor-General: s 7.

Law reports Published accounts of legal proceedings, usually including a statement of facts and reasoning behind the court's decision. Authorised reports (for example, the Victorian Reports) contain judgments that have been approved by the court prior to publication, and are published by official law reporting councils.

Laws of supply and demand The basic laws in respect of the marketing of goods and services in a market economy. Other things being equal, four laws or tendencies may be identified: if, at the price ruling in the market, demand exceeds supply, the price tends to rise; conversely, when supply exceeds demand the price tends to fall; a rise in price tends to lead to a contraction of demand and an expansion of supply; conversely, a fall in price tends to lead to an expansion of demand and a contraction of supply; price or prices tend to move towards a level at which demand is equal to supply, that is to an equilibrium price; and for any given price increase, the expansion or increase in the quantity supplied will be the greater, the longer the time allowed to adjust; conversely, for any given price reduction, the expansion or increase in demand will be the greater, the longer the time allowed to adjust. The term demand refers to effective demand, not to need; effective demand is demand expressed through the ability to pay. See also **Economics**; **Market economy**.

•**Lawyer** A barrister or solicitor; a person qualified to practice law. The term is used in everyday parlance to describe members of the legal profession, while the term legal practitioner, being more precise, is most commonly found in legislation. See also **Barrister**; **Solicitor**.

•**Lay** A share in the profits of an enterprise. The term was used in the first years of settlement in New South Wales and Van Diemen's Land to indicate a crew member's share of the profits of a voyage on which he sailed. See also **Share**.

Lay day A day allowed in a charterparty or bill of lading for the loading or discharge of cargo: *Inverkip Steamship Co Ltd v Bunge* [1917] 2 KB 193. If the number of lay days is exceeded, the charterers will be in breach and demurrage will be payable. See also **Bill of lading**; **Charterparty**; **Demurrage**; **Loading**; **Strike clause**.

Lay-by A means of purchasing goods by which the purchaser pays for the goods by instalments but until the last instalment is paid the goods remain in the possession of the seller. The price is allowed to be paid by three or more instalments: (NSW) Fair Trading Act 1987 s 60E(1)(b). See also **Credit; Credit sale contract; Goods; Uniform credit legislation.**

Lay-off The indefinite suspension of employment. See also **Unfair dismissal.**

Lead time 1. The time necessary in a construction program for materials, components, equipment and workforce to be assembled on a construction site. **2.** The estimated period of time from the date of the award of a purchase order or contract to the delivery of the final product. **3.** The time required to replenish a warehouse inventory or to procure a non-inventory item.

Leading mark A mark used to identify goods comprising cargo. Leading marks are documented on the bill of lading. Under the Hague-Visby Rules 1979, the shipper is entitled to demand the bill of lading showing the leading marks from the carrier. See also **Amended Hague Rules 1979; Bill of lading; Charterer; Goods.**

•**Leading question** In court, a question to a witness that directly or indirectly suggests a particular answer to the question, or that assumes the existence of a fact the existence of which is in dispute in the proceedings, and as to the existence of which the witness has not given evidence before the question is asked: for example (CTH) Evidence Act 1995 s 3, Dictionary. Generally, a leading question must not be put to a witness in examination in chief or re-examination: *Mooney v James* [1949] VLR 22; (CTH) Evidence Act 1995 s 37. However, a leading question may be put where it relates to a matter introductory to the witness's evidence (*Mooney v James*) or where no objection is made to the question and each other party to the proceeding is represented by a lawyer: s 37(1). See also **Cross examination; Objection.**

•**Lease** An interest in land given by a landowner (landlord or lessor) to another person (lessee or tenant) for a fixed duration such that the lessee has the right to exclusive possession of the premises: *Radaich v Smith* (1959) 101 CLR 209; [1959] ALR 1253. A legal lease of general law land must usually be created by deed: for example (NSW) Conveyancing Act 1919 s 24B(1); (VIC) Property Law Act 1958 s 52(1). There is an exception where a landlord orally lets premises to a tenant for a period of three years or less: for example (NSW) Conveyancing Act 1919 s 23D(2); (VIC) Property Law Act 1958 s 55. A lease of Torrens land becomes a legal lease only when it is registered at the Land Titles Office (or its equivalent): for example (NSW) Real Property Act 1900 s 41; (VIC) Transfer of Land Act 1958 s 41. Legislation governs much of the law of leases, defining leases and the terms to be implied into them. 'Lease' is to be distinguished from 'licence'. See also **Landlord; Lease covenant; Let; Licence; Rent; Sublease; Tenant; Tenant's fixtures.**

Lease back agreement An arrangement by which the owner of a property sells that property to a person or organisation, and then leases it back again for an agreed period and rental. A lease back arrangement releases the funds of the seller for other purposes. See also **Sale and leaseback.**

Lease covenant A clause in a lease setting out the rights and obligations of a lessor and lessee of land. The assignees of both parties are bound by all the covenants in the lease that 'touch and concern' the land. Some covenants are implied into every lease, such as the obligations on the lessee to pay rent and to keep the leased premises in good repair, fair wear and tear excepted. Standard covenants in leases include covenants for quiet enjoyment; to pay rent; to re-enter; to view; to keep in good repair, fair wear and tear excepted; to pay outgoings; to renew the lease; holding over at the end of the lease; for permitted use; against structural alterations; against assignment without consent of the lessor; and to insure. Many of these covenants may be incorporated by a statutory short form: for example (NSW) Conveyancing Act 1919 s 86, Sch 4, Pt 2. See also **Option to renew; Outgoings; Quiet enjoyment.**

Lease finance A flexible form of finance for the utilisation of plant and equipment. The financier advances the full cash price of the equipment necessary for a business, leaving the lessee of the equipment with no initial cash outlay. The lessee has full use of the equipment on agreed terms. Finance companies are major players in the lease finance market. See also **Equipment leasing; Finance company; Off-balance-sheet borrowing.**

Lease Premium See **Premium.**

•**Leasehold** A holding of land for a term of years or for a periodic term, including under grants from the Crown. See also **Freehold; Lease covenant.**

Leasehold reversion The interest retained in the estate held by the lessor after part of that estate has been assigned or conveyed to another: *Ex parte Henry* [1963] NSWR 1079; 63 SR (NSW) 298 at 1094-5. See also **Covenant; Estate; Interest; Lease; Rent.**

•**Leasehold strata scheme** In New South Wales, the manner of division into lots, or lots and common property, or the manner of allocating unit entitlements and rights and obligations of lessees in a lease granted by the Crown or a public authority under the (NSW) Strata Titles (Leasehold) Act 1986. See also **Site value.**

•**Leaseholder** The entity that has an interest as lessee in real property that is leased: *Sheffield Waggon Co v Stratton* (1854) 48 LJ Ex 35. The term is statutorily defined: for example (ACT) Instruments Act 1933 s 19; (NT) Instruments Act 1935 s 16. See also **Lease.**

•**Leave of absence** Permission to be absent, whether for a defined period or indefinitely.

Employment A period of time when a person is temporarily absent from their employment or duty, with the intention to eventually return to work. Leave of absence may include long service leave, extended leave, recreation leave, annual leave, or sick leave: for example Corporations Law s 9. The period of a person's absence does not normally affect his or her level of remuneration and seniority. See also **Sick leave.**

•**Legacy** A gift of personal property by will. The testator is said to bequeath a legacy to a recipient called a legatee. Originally, the term legacy was used to describe a gift of money only but now it has the meaning of any gift of personal property generally, displacing the word 'bequest', and may even include real property. A legacy may be specific, general, demonstrative, residuary, or pecuniary.

•**Legal 1.** Related to law or legal issues. **2.** Pertaining to rights that are based in law as opposed to equity. **3.** Lawful; a description of something effectual and proper and which the courts of judicature of the country will recognise and enforce: *Dufaur v Life Professional Life Assurance Co* (1858) 25 Beav 599; 53 ER 766.

•**Legal aid** Legal assistance. Legal aid is regulated by legislation in every jurisdiction.

Legal assets Representing a portion of the property held in a deceased estate, the executor or administrator of the estate is required by law to use the 'legal assets' to pay the deceased debts and legacies. See also **Asset; Estate**.

Legal assignment An assignment of legal property which complies with all legal requirements: (NSW) Conveyancing Act 1919 s 12. For example, legal assignment of a debt or other legal chose in action can only take place if express notice in writing has been given to the debtor: (VIC) Property Law Act 1958 s 134; (QLD) Property Law Act 1974 s 199. See also **Assignment; Equitable assignment**.

•**Legal burden** Under the common law accusatorial system, the duty to persuade the jury or court; the 'persuasive' burden of proof. It is distinct from the evidentiary burden. The legal burden lies on the party who alleges or asserts an issue: *Currie v Dempsey* (1967) 2 NSWR 532; 69 SR (NSW) 116 at 125. Failure to discharge the legal burden of proof on an issue will cause the trier of fact to decide against the party who bears it on that particular issue. In civil cases the plaintiff bears the legal burden in relation to all facts in issue that relate to establishing the cause of action: for example *Nominal Defendant v Haslbauer* (1967) 117 CLR 448; [1969] ALR 705. See also **Burden of proof; Evidential burden; Standard of proof**.

Legal expenses insurance Insurance in respect of legal costs and charges incurred by an assured in avoiding, or in attempting to avoid, any liability or expenditure against which the assured is insured. See also **Insurance; Statutory limitation on indemnity and insurance**.

Legal interest The legal, as opposed to beneficial, interest in property. Under the system of common law and equity, the legal title in property can be separated from its beneficial interest. A legal interest is a right in rem (that is, it is enforceable against anyone), while an equitable interest confers only a right in personam. See also **Beneficial interest**.

Legal matrix In contract law, the background of case law, statutory, and common law principles against which the parties contracted: for example *Continental Grain Export Corp v STM Grain Ltd* [1979] 2 Lloyd's Rep 460. Since it is not factual, this material is not excluded by the parol evidence rule, and is relevant where the legal effect of a contractual term is at issue. See also **Construction; Factual matrix**.

Legal mortgage A mortgage of land valid at law and in equity. A first mortgage of old system land is the only legal mortgage the mortgagor may create, all subsequent mortgages being equitable. Such a mortgage involves conveyance to a mortgagee of the legal estate in the land subject to the mortgagor's equity of redemption. In relation to Torrens land, a 'legal' mortgage only exists where the instrument creating the mortgage is registered, although the word 'legal' tends to mislead, since a mortgage of this nature is more like a statutory charge, as the legal estate is not conveyed to the mortgagee. See also **Equitable mortgage; Equity of redemption; Mortgage; Mortgagee in possession**.

Legal person An entity on which a legal system confers rights and imposes duties. A legal person includes a natural person, and an artificial or statutory body such as a company. It may also include an unborn child for specific purposes. See also **Body corporate; Corporate veil**.

•**Legal professional privilege** A common law principle which provides that confidential communications between legal practitioner and client for the sole purpose of the client obtaining, or the legal practitioner giving, legal advice or for use in existing or contemplated litigation need not be given in evidence nor disclosed by the client or by the legal practitioner, without the consent of the client: *Grant v Downs* (1976) 135 CLR 674; 11 ALR 577. Also known as 'client legal privilege'. See also **Confidential communication; Without prejudice**.

•**Legal right 1.** An interest, claim, or privilege to something which is recognised and protected by a rule of law, irrespective of whether the right has a moral basis. Legal rights are in contrast with moral rights which do not have any legal effect. **2.** Rights recognised by customary, international, and domestic law.

Legal set-off The reduction of the defendant's debt due to the plaintiff by the amount of the plaintiff's indebtedness to the defendant. In contrast with equitable set-off, legal set-off is restricted to liquidated claims at law arising between the parties to the action: for example *Smail v Zimmerman* [1907] VLR 702; 13 ALR 587. See also **Banker's lien; Counterclaim**.

•**Legal tender** The prescribed mode of lawful payment within a jurisdiction at a particular point in time: *Watson v Lee* (1979) 144 CLR 374; 26 ALR 461 at 480. In Australia, notes or coins issued by the Reserve Bank of Australia: (CTH) Reserve Bank Act 1959 s 36(1). See also **Cheque; Currency; Estoppel; Reserve Bank of Australia; Tender of performance**.

Legal title A full and complete title in regard to apparent ownership or possession. Under the Torrens system the legal title is held by the registered proprietor, as the Torrens system is a system of title by registration. Registration vests the title in the proprietor: *Breskvar v Wall* (1971) 126 CLR 376; [1972] ALR 205. See also **Equitable interest; Legal interest**.

•**Legally assisted person** A person to whom legal aid is provided: for example (NSW) Legal Aid Commission Act 1979 s 4. In Queensland, a corporation can be a legally assisted person: (QLD) Legal Aid Act 1978 s 6(1). In New South Wales, it includes a person receiving legal assistance through a community legal centre:

(NSW) Public Defenders Act 1995 s 3. Where a court or tribunal makes an order for costs against a legally assisted person, the Legal Aid Commission will normally pay those costs up to a prescribed maximum amount and the legally assisted person is not liable for payment of those costs: for example (NSW) Legal Aid Commission Act 1979 s 47. A private legal practitioner shall not, except with the approval of the Legal Aid Commission, demand or receive any payment from a legally assisted person in respect of work assigned by the Commission to the private legal practitioner on behalf of the legally assisted person: for example (NSW) Legal Aid Commission Act 1979 s 41. See also **Costs**; **Legal aid**.

Legally incompetent A person incapable of managing his or her own affairs due to mental illness or mental incapacity: *McD v McD* [1983] 3 NSWLR 81.

•**Legislation** The instruments embodying the creation and promulgation of laws by the Commonwealth and State legislatures. Law made by Parliament, that is, statute law or Acts of Parliament. Law made by other bodies under the authority of Parliament is termed delegated legislation. Delegated legislation includes regulations, rules, and by-laws. Under the principle of parliamentary sovereignty, statute law prevails and can override the common law and judge-made law: *British Railways Board v Pickin* [1974] AC 765 at 789, 793, 798. The courts have no power to declare legislation to be invalid except on constitutional grounds, namely where Parliament has no power to enact the legislation under the relevant Constitution. Subordinate legislation can be declared invalid if the enabling Act is constitutionally invalid or if the subordinate legislation is ultra vires. See also **Act of parliament**.

•**Legislative Assembly** Apart from South Australia and Tasmania, the 'lower house' of the State parliament. In South Australia and Tasmania, the lower house is known as the House of Assembly: (SA) Constitution Act 1934 s 4; (TAS) Constitution Act 1934 s 10. In Queensland, the Parliament consists of a Legislative Assembly and the Crown: (QLD) Constitution Act 1867 s 2A(1). Also known as 'Lower house'. See also **Legislative Council**; **Lower house**; **Parliament**.

Legislative authority Authority conferred by statute to do some act. Legislation may confer authority on some public authority or administrator to perform certain tasks or functions. Where action is taken that is not within the legislative authority conferred, the action is said to be ultra vires (beyond power). Action taken by administrators without legislative authority may be impugned by the courts: for example (CTH) Administrative Decisions (Judicial Review) Act 1977 ss 5(1)(d), 6(1)(d). Also known as 'statutory power'.

Legislative Council The upper house in all the State parliaments, excluding Queensland: (NSW) Constitution Act 1902 s 3; (SA) Constitution Act 1934 ss 4, 8, 56, 64, 88; (TAS) Constitution Act 1934 s 10; (VIC) Constitution Act 1975 s 15; (WA) Constitution Act 1889 s 2(2). In Queensland, the parliament consists of a Legislative Assembly and the Crown but no upper house: (QLD) Constitution Act 1867 ss 2A(1), 11A. See also **Legislative Assembly**.

Legislative powers The power to enact legislation. For both the Federal Government and State governments, legislative powers are vested in the legislature (parliament). The legislative powers of the Federal Parliament are enumerated in, and limited by, the Commonwealth Constitution: for example Commonwealth Constitution ss 51, 52. See also **Constitution**; **Legislation**.

•**Legislature** 1. The branch of government, known as the Federal Parliament, in which the Commonwealth Constitution vests the legislative power of the Commonwealth: Commonwealth Constitution s 1. 2. The legislative body, incorporating the Crown, which was established in each of the Australian colonies as they achieved self-government during the second half of the 19th century. See also **Executive**.

Lender of last resort A term applied to a country's central bank in circumstances where it provides financial accommodation to certain financial institutions like banks under strict conditions. Australia's Reserve Bank is not obliged to act as lender of last resort but may do so in cases of emergency to avert a crisis in the financial system. See also **Money market corporation**; **Reserve Bank of Australia**; **Short-term money market**.

Leonina societas /leɪoʊnɪnə sɒkiɛtəs/ *Lat* – a partnership in which one party receives all the profit and the other bears all the loss.

LEPO See **Low Exercise Price Option**.

Lerner Index An index of market power. The index measures the proportional deviation of price, at a firm's profit maximising output, from the firm's marginal cost at that output. See also **Marginal cost**; **Market power**.

•**Lessee** 1. A person to whom a leasehold estate is granted or assigned. This basic meaning is often extended by statute to include a person who proposes to become or was a lessee (for example (NSW) Landlord and Tenant (Rental Bonds) Act 1977 s 4) and derivative leases, under-lessees, sub-lessees, and their successors in title (for example (NSW) Retail Leases Act 1994; (VIC) Landlord and Tenant Act 1958 s 43(1). 2. A person to whom goods are hired or to whom a licence to use goods is granted under a lease: for example (VIC) Chattel Securities Act 1987 s 3(1). Also known as 'tenant'. See also **Lease**; **Lessor**; **Premises**.

•**Lessor** 1. A person who leases, lets, or demises premises and grants a leasehold estate in those premises to a lessee. This meaning has been extended by statute to include a person to whom the lessor assigns the reversion or the lessors heirs, executors, or administrators: for example (NSW) Retail Leases Act 1994. 2. A person who leases goods to another person: for example (VIC) Chattel Securities Act 1987 s 3. Also known as 'landlord'. See also **Grantor**; **Lease**; **Lessee**; **Sublease**.

•**Let** 1. To grant a lease but not a licence: *General Discounts Pty Ltd v Crosbie* [1968] Qd R 418; *Parker v Sowerby* (1853) 1 WR 404; 61 ER 539; *Gowen v Sedgwick* [1904] 68 JP 484; *Betts v Brookfield* [1947] NZLR 170 at 192. 2. A right to fish: *Swayne v Howells* [1927] 1 KB 385. 3. To be within control and to allow, permit, or suffer an action to take place: *Jay v Richardson* (1862) 31 LJ Ch 398; 54 ER 1008. 4. To award a contract to one of several who have submitted proposals by having chosen from amongst them. **5.** Obstruction: *Pearson v Iles* (1781) 2 Doug 561; 99 ER 352; (IMP) Perjury Act 1562 s 12. See also **Lease; Licence.**

Lettable area The total area of floor space designated for leased premises within a building is the lettable area of the building where a building comprises premises that may be separately leased and areas common to all premises. The lettable area of premises is important in calculating the proportion of outgoings to be borne by each lessee. Under (NSW) Retail Leases Act 1994 s 5(a), a shop with a lettable area of more than 1000 square metres is excluded from the operation of that Act. See also **Outgoings; Premises.**

Letter of acceptance In the United Kingdom, a letter sent by an issuing house to successful applicants for shares, indicating the number of shares allocated. In the United Kingdom an issue of shares in a public company for public offering may be made through an intermediary (the issuing house), which takes an allotment from the company and invites the public to apply for the shares. In Australia, an underwriter would be the allottee from the issuing company only in respect of shares not subscribed for by the public. See also **Allotment letter; Share.**

Letter of allotment A letter advising an applicant of the quantity of stock or shares he or she has been allotted, specifying the amounts due and the dates of payment in respect of them. See also **Allotment; Letter of acceptance; Letter of offer.**

Letter of credit An advice issued by a bank authorising the payment of money to a named person on presentation by that person of specified documents to another bank. The specified documents usually consist of evidence of transport of goods and insurance certificates in respect of goods in international trading transactions. Letters of credit are generally used as a payment mechanism in international trading transactions and operate quite independently of the underlying sale transaction. See also **Irrevocable credit; Presentment; Standby letter of credit; Transferable credit; Uniform Customs and Practice for Documentary Credits 1993.**

•**Letter of hypothecation** A letter from an exporter to a bank authorising it, in the event of the importer failing to pay, to sell the exported goods and remit the proceeds less expenses to the exporter. If the bank has made an advance to the exporter, such a letter enables it to recover the loan by selling the goods if the amount owing is dishonoured. See also **Hypothecation; Pledge; Trust receipt.**

Letter of indemnity See **Indemnity.**

Letter of intent 1. A preliminary contractual arrangement customarily used in situations where there is fundamental agreement on the main essentials of a contract with some provisions requiring further time-consuming negotiations. **2.** A letter from a proprietor to its preferred tenderer expressing an intention to enter into a contract: for example *British Steel Corp v Cleveland Bridge and Engineering Co Ltd* [1984] 1 All ER 504; (1983) 24 BLR 94. A letter of intent may be issued where the proprietor does not wish, or is not able, to enter into a formal contract with the tenderer immediately, but wishes that the preferred tenderer not withdraw its tender, but commence to ready itself for, or even make a start on, the work. Such a letter will not normally constitute an acceptance of the tender, nor oblige the proprietor to enter into a formal contract: *Turriff Construction Ltd & Turriff Ltd v Regalia Knitting Mills Ltd* (1971) 9 BLR 20. It may, however, amount to a promise by the proprietor that if the contractor undertakes some work it will receive payment even if no contract is entered into: *British Steel Corp v Cleveland Bridge and Engineering Co Ltd* [1984] All E R 504. Generally, however, a letter of intent is at most a non-promissory statement of intention: *Australian European Finance Corp Ltd v Sheahan* (1993) 60 SASR 187 at 206. Also known as 'letter of comfort'. See also **Proprietor.**

Letter of offer In relation to the offering of securities for allotment where a prospectus is not required, a letter sent describing the possibility of subscribing for securities. See also **Prospectus; Subscription.**

Letter of renunciation A method by which a shareholder may assign to someone else part or all of his or her rights to subscribe to a rights issue. See also **Renunciation.**

Leverage 1. The extent of the use by an investor of borrowed funds for investment. The greater the proportion of borrowed funds to the value of the investment, the greater the leverage. Leverage increases the return on an investment when funds borrowed for reinvestment yield profits at a rate of return greater than the borrowing cost. However, it increases the extent of the losses if the rate of return is below the borrowing cost. **2.** The ratio of loan capital to share capital in a company. **3.** In the commodities markets, the buying or selling of futures contracts on margin or the putting up of a deposit in order to trade a contract. The margin necessary to trade may represent only 5-10 per cent of the full value of the contract. Leverage is the single most important factor that permits a trader to realise a substantial gain on an investment. See also **Gearing; Loan capital.**

Leveraged buyout *Abbr* – LBO The acquisition of a company by a group of investors and managers using mostly borrowed funds. The additional debt is ultimately paid either out of earnings of the business or from the sale of some of its assets. Such buyouts are risky because of the high ratio of debt in contrast to equity. See also **Going private; Investment grade bond; Leverage.**

Leveraged investment An arrangement under which only a percentage of the value of a contract need be put down to acquire, for example, an option or futures contract. See also **Futures contract; Leverage; Option contract.**

Leveraged leasing A form of business finance involving three parties: the lessor who undertakes the purchase of equipment providing a portion of the funds, the lender or credit provider who meets the balance of the finance required to purchase the equipment by the lessor, and the lessee who pays a lease rental for the use of that equipment. Leveraged leasing differs from ordinary leasing in its capacity to accommodate the acquisition of expensive assets such as drilling rigs, aircraft, and mining equipment over a long term. See also **Hire purchase; Leverage; Lease.**

•**Levy** Generally, to raise a tax, rate, fine, or human resources.

Taxation and revenue **1.** To raise revenue where the funds raised are generally directed to a related public purpose. For example, money raised through the (NSW) Parking Space Levy Act 1992 is used to facilitate greater access to public transport. **2.** An amount of money, typically a percentage of output or import of goods taxed to ensure the protection of domestic markets by making the local product more cost competitive: for example (CTH) Australian Horticultural Corporation Act 1987 s 3(1); (NSW) Meat Industry (Meat Industry Levy) Regulations 1994 cl 3.

Lex domicilii /lɛks dɒmɪsɪlii/ *Lat* – the law of the place of residence. See also **Domicile; Legal person**.

•**Lex fori** /lɛks fɔri/ *Lat* – the law of the court in which proceedings are being conducted; the law of the jurisdiction where the suit in question has been instituted.

Lex loci contractus /lɛks loʊkaɪ kɒntræktʊs/ *Lat* – the law of a place where a contract is made. See also **Conflict of laws; Contract**.

Lex loci rei sitae /lɛks loʊki reɪ sitaɪ/ *Lat* – the law of the place where the property is situated. The law governing the transfer of title to real estate is dependent upon, and varies with, the *lex loci rei sitae*. See also **Lex situs**.

Lex loci solutionis /lɛks loʊki sɒluʃoʊnɪs/ *Lat* – the law of the place of performance. If performance is illegal under the law of the place of performance, the contract will not be enforced in Australia: *R v International Trustee for the Protection of Bondholders AG* [1937] AC 500. See also **Lex loci contractus**.

Lex loci voluntatis /lɛks loʊkaɪ vɒlʊntatɪs/ *Lat* – the law of the place of choice. Also known as '*lex loci intentionis*'.

Lex situs /lɛks saɪtʊs/ *Lat* – the law of the place in which property is situated. For example, property is subject to tax pursuant to the law of the place of the property or the domicile of its owner. See also **Lex loci rei sitae**.

•**Liability** The result of incurring a legal obligation or committing a breach, or the legal obligation itself, such as a debt. Liability can be civil or criminal, depending upon the nature of the obligation or breach.

Tort A person's present or prospective legal responsibility, duty, or obligation. Liability may arise by a party entering a contract, or through tortious or statutory obligation wholly unknown to the party at the material time: *McDowell v Baker* (1979) 144 CLR 413; 26 ALR 277. In (NSW) Law Reform (Miscellaneous) Provisions Act 1946 s 5(1)(c), the term includes ascertainment by judgment (*Bitumen and Oil Refineries (Aust) v Cmr for Government Transport* (1955) 92 CLR 200; 55 SR (NSW) 108), and does not include a temporal element: *Brambles Constructions Pty Ltd v Helmers* (1966) 114 CLR 213; [1966] ALR 981. See also **Concurrent liability; Occupier's liability; Product liability; Several liability; Strict liability; Vicarious liability**.

Trade and commerce In an accounting sense, the future sacrifices of service potential or future economic benefits that an entity is presently obliged to make to other entities as a result of past transactions or other past events: Statement of Accounting Concepts SAC 4 para 46. See also **Balance sheet; Contingent liability; Entity**.

Liability action A product liability claim brought under (CTH) Trade Practices Act 1974 Pt VA in respect of injury or death, or damage to another product or real property, caused by defective goods: (CTH) Trade Practices Act 1974 s 75AA.

Liability insurance A form of general insurance providing cover in respect of the insured's liability for loss or damage to another person: (CTH) Insurance Contracts Act 1984 s 11(7). Under a contract of liability insurance, the insurer has no obligation to indemnify the insured until he or she becomes subject to a liability covered by the policy: *Distillers Co Bio-Chemicals (Aust) Pty Ltd v Ajax Insurance Co Ltd* (1974) 130 CLR 1; 2 ALR 321. The liability must be enforceable by law: *Smit Tak Offshore Services v Youell* [1992] 1 Lloyd's Rep 154. See also **Professional indemnity insurance; Public liability insurance**.

Liability mistake A mistake that causes a person to believe that he or she is liable to pay money: *Aiken v Short* (1856) 1 H & N 210; 156 ER 1180. Where a person satisfies another's liability at the other's request, he or she is entitled to restitution unless it appears that he or she intended to make a gift: for example *Heydon v Perpetual Executors Trustees and Agency Co (WA) Ltd* (1930) 45 CLR 111; [1931] ALR 65. In some circumstances, a person satisfying another's liability without request may also be entitled to restitution: *Alexander v Vane* (1836) 1 M & W 511; 150 ER 537. See also **Mistake; Restitution**.

Liability of principal The entitlement of an agent to be indemnified by the principal for any expenses or contractual obligations incurred by the agent in the reasonable performance of the agency: *Jones v Canavan* [1972] 2 NSWLR 236. See also **Personal liability; Vicarious liability**.

Liability to third parties The liability of a professional for damages to persons other than the client in respect of the professional's breach of his or her duty of care. In terms of direct physical injury or damage, any professional person is liable to any person it could reasonably be expected might suffer such injury or damage as a result of the reasonably foreseeable consequences of the practitioner's careless or unskillful conduct: *Voli v Inglewood Shire Council* (1963) 110 CLR 74; ALR 657. In respect of pure economic loss, reasonable foreseeability is not the sole determinant of the existence of a duty of care, so that a professional may be liable for such loss suffered by a third party provided the required relationship of proximity exists with respect to the allegedly negligent class of act and the particular kind of damage sustained by the third party: *Hawkins v Clayton* (1988) 164 CLR 539; 78 ALR 69. See also **Duty in tort; Duty of care**.

•**Liable to mislead** More than 'likely to mislead'. Conduct that is liable to mislead must of necessity be likely to mislead, so a court will more readily find that conduct is likely to mislead than that it is liable to mislead: *Westpac Banking Corp v Northern Metals Pty Ltd* (1989) 14 IPR 499; ATPR 40-953; *Trade Practices Commission v J and R Enterprises Pty Ltd* (1991) 99 ALR 325. It is an offence for a person, in trade or commerce, to engage in conduct that is liable to mislead the public as to the nature, manufacturing process, characteristics, suitability for their purpose, or the quantity of goods: for example (NSW) Fair Trading Act 1987 ss 49, 50. It is an offence for a corporation, in trade or commerce, to engage in conduct which is liable to mislead the public as to these aspects of services: (CTH) Trade Practices Act 1974 ss 55, 55A; (NSW) Fair Trading Act 1987 ss 49, 50. See also **Likely to mislead or deceive; Misleading or deceptive conduct.**

•**Libel** Defamatory material expressed in print, writing, or any other mode of communication capable of being comprehended visually: *King v Lake* (1670) Hardres 470; *Meldrum v Australian Broadcasting Commission* [1932] VLR 425. Alternatively, libel has been held to be defamatory material in permanent form: *Forrester v Tyrrell* (1893) 9 TLR 257; 57 JP 532. In four Australian jurisdictions, both libel and slander now come under the general tort of defamation: (ACT) Defamation Act 1901 (NSW) s 3; (NSW) Defamation Act 1974 s 8; (QLD) Defamation Act 1889 s 9; (TAS) Defamation Act 1957 s 9(1). See also **Libel.**

LIBOR See **London Inter Bank Offered Rate.**

•**Licence** A permit to do something which would without a licence be unlawful: for example *Federal Cmr of Taxation v United Aircraft Corp* (1943) 68 CLR 525; *Sinclair v Judge* [1930] St R Qd 220. A licence may be issued by a governmental licensing authority: for example (NSW) Building Services Corporation Act 1989 s 3(1).

Corporations A right to deal in and advise in relation to securities (a 'securities licence') or to deal in and advise in relation to futures contracts (a 'futures licence'): Corporations Law s 9. See also **Futures adviser; Futures brokers licence; Investment adviser; Securities dealer.**

Environment A statutory document, issued by an environment control agency, permitting the person or organisation to whom it is issued to discharge, emit, or deposit wastes into the environment, subject to a variety of conditions relating to control measures and monitoring.

Intellectual property In copyright law, permission to use copyright material in a way that would otherwise be a breach of the copyright owner's proprietary rights: *Young v Odeon Music House Pty Ltd* (1976) 120 ALR 153; [1978] RPC 621. The word 'licence' is interchangeable with the words 'consent' and 'permission': *Computermate Products (Aust) Pty Ltd v Ozi-Soft Pty Ltd* 12 IPR 487; 83 ALR 492; 20 FCR 46.

Real property A permit issued to a person to do something on or to occupy land on particular conditions, which may or may not include payment of a regular monetary consideration. The main feature which distinguishes a licence from a lease is that a licence does not permit exclusive occupancy of the relevant land. A licence may be categorised as a bare licence, a licence coupled with a grant, or a contractual licence, which may in some cases be irrevocable. See also **Contractual licence; Lease.**

•**Licensed copy** In copyright law, a copy of a copyright work made by, or on behalf of, a body administering an educational institution under (CTH) Copyright Act 1968 ss 135ZJ, 135ZK or 135ZL; or a sound recording, or a Braille, large-print, or photographic version of a literary or dramatic work made by, or on behalf of, a body administering an institution assisting disabled readers under s 135ZP; or a reproduction of certain copyright material (defined in s 135ZC) made by, or on behalf of, a body administering an institution assisting intellectually disabled persons under s 135ZS; s 135ZB. See also **Copyright.**

•**Licensed premises** 1. Generally, the premises or part of the premises on or from which the business or activity authorised by the licence is carried on. The term is specifically used for those premises with liquor, function, and catering licences: for example (NSW) Liquor Act 1982 s 4(1). 2. In the case of an on-licence to sell liquor at a function, the premises in which the function is held. 3. In the case of any other licence to sell liquor, the premises on which the sale of liquor is authorised by the licence: (NSW) Liquor Act 1982 s 4(1). In the strict sense, there is no such thing as 'licensed premises', there are only 'licensed persons': *Electric Light & Power Supply Corp Ltd v Macquarie Club Ltd* (1952) 69 WN (NSW) 223. A licensee acquires certain duties by virtue of the licence under the various legislation. For example, a licensee cannot use the licensed premises for the purposes of prostitution, nor can a licensee permit intoxication, or any indecent, violent, or quarrelsome conduct on the licensed premises: for example (NSW) Liquor Act 1982 s 125(1). See also **Licensee; Premises; Unlicensed premises.**

•**Licensee** A person who has been granted a licence. See also **Licence.**

Licensing To require persons who seek to carry on an occupation or activity to satisfy knowledge and competency standards before they are permitted to carry on that occupation or activity. Licensing can be distinguished from certification which involves accreditation of competency but which does not prohibit those who are not accredited persons from carrying on the occupation or activity.

Licensing controls In trade law, statutory and regulatory controls affecting the performance of specific aspects of a particular task. Specific conditions or controls are imposed upon the importation of certain goods into Australia: (CTH) Customs (Import Licensing) Regulations reg 7. There is no statutory basis upon which licensing controls may be waived such that a licence can be obtained once the goods have been imported into Australia: *McGurk Construction and Rigging Co Ltd v Comptroller-General of Customs* (1987) 73 ALR 381. See also **Control; Customs duty; Licence; Licensing.**

•**Licensing Court** A court of record with the jurisdiction and power to determine complaints against licensees: for example (NSW) Liquor Act 1982 s 7. Each State and Territory has a licensing court to hear and determine complaints against licensees: for example, the New South Wales Licensing Court created by the (NSW) Liquor Act 1982, The court is responsible for regulating the sale and supply of liquor, regulating the use of premises on which liquor is sold. The court has various disciplinary powers, including reprimanding a licensee, imposing a monetary penalty, and suspending or cancelling a licence: (NSW) Liquor Act 1982 s 69(1); (VIC) Liquor Control Act 1987 s 16(2); (QLD) Liquor Act 1992 s 21. See also **Forfeiture; Licence.**

•**Licensor** A person who gives to another a licence to do, on defined terms, an action that would otherwise be prohibited: for example to enter land, to use intellectual property, to hunt certain animals, or to sell liquor. See also **Licence.**

Intellectual property In copyright law, so far as the jurisdiction of the Copyright Tribunal is concerned, either an owner or prospective owner of the copyright in a literary, dramatic or musical work, or in a sound recording, or any body of persons (whether incorporated or not) acting as an agent in relation to the negotiation or granting of licences in respect of such copyright material: (CTH) Copyright Act 1968 s 136. See also **Copyright; Licence; Licensee.**

•**Lien** *OF – loien* – to bind or hold. The right to hold the property of another as security for the performance of an obligation or the payment of a debt: *Hall v Richards* (1961) 108 CLR 84; [1964] ALR 816.

Bailment The legal right to retain possession of a chattel until a claim is satisfied or an obligation is performed: *Re Vital Learning Aids Pty Ltd* [1979] 2 NSWLR 442 at 445; *MPS Constructions Pty Ltd (in liq) v Rural Bank of New South Wales* (1980) 49 FLR 430; 4 ACLR 835. A lien may be granted by the lienor, be granted by statute, or arise by operation of law: *Fisher v Automobile Finance Co of Australia Ltd* (1928) 41 CLR 167; *Majeau Carrying Co Pty Ltd v Coastal Rutile Ltd* (1973) 129 CLR 48; 1 ALR 1. See also **Bailee's lien; Equitable lien; Lienor; Maritime lien; Unpaid seller's lien; Warehouseperson's lien; Wool lien.**

Corporations In relation to shares, a security interest over shares. An example of a lien on shares is the adoption of an article giving a company a security interest in the fully paid shares of members who are indebted to it for calls on other shares: *Allen v Gold Reefs of West Africa Ltd* [1900] 1 Ch 656; [1900-3] All ER Rep 746. See also **Charge; Equitable lien; Secured creditor.**

Insurance The right to hold the property of another as security for the performance of an obligation. In marine insurance law, the broker has a lien on the policy as against the insured for the amount of the premium and his or her charges for effecting the policy: (CTH) Marine Insurance Act 1909 s 59(2). See also **Maritime lien; Premium.**

Real property An equitable security interest held by one person over the property of another. A lien does not depend on a contract between the parties, nor upon possession of the property over which the security interest is held. A lien arises by operation of law: for example *Hewett v Court* (1983) 149 CLR 639; 46 ALR 87. A typical example is the lien of an unpaid vendor over the sold property. See also **Contract; Equitable lien; Possession; Security.**

Lien clause A clause included in a charterparty or bill of lading allowing shipowners to hold goods under a lien until the owners of the goods have paid all debts owed to the shipowners for carrying those goods. See also **Bill of lading; Carrier; Cesser clause; Charterparty; Freight; Lien; Maritime lien; Owner.**

Lien, equitable See **Equitable lien.**

Lien on award See **Arbitrator's lien.**

•**Lienee** A person to whom a lienor gives a lien, to whom a lien is assigned by statute, or on whom a lien devolves by operation of law: for example (QLD) Liens on Crops of Sugar Cane Act 1931 s 2. See also **Lien; Lienor.**

•**Lienor** The person who is the owner of the goods subject to a lien. See also **Lien; Lienee.**

•**Life insurance** A contract between a person and an insurer requiring the insurer to pay an agreed sum of money on the death of the person insured (*Williams v FCT* (1950) 81 CLR 359; (CTH) Life Insurance Act 1945 s 4(1)) or attainment of a specified age ((CTH) Australian Capital Territory Taxation (Administration) Act 1969).

Life tenant A person who holds a life estate, being an interest in land entitling the life tenant to exclusive possession and use of the land for as long as he or she lives.

Lifting the corporate veil A process by which courts look behind the legal personality which the law has given to corporate entities, to examine the purpose of its creation and the manner of its control: *Gorton v FCT* (1965) 113 CLR 604; [1969] ALR 560. For example, a court may lift the corporate veil where a company is a sham in the sense of a cloak or device to avoid or limit certain legal liabilities: *Gilford Motor Co Ltd v Horne* [1933] 1 Ch 935. See also **Corporate capacity; Corporate veil; Incorporation.**

•**Likely** Having a degree of probability greater than merely possible, but less than certain. The location of 'likely' on the probability spectrum varies according to the statutory context.

Trade and commerce In competition law, a phrase capable of various meanings. It has been held to mean 'probable', in the sense of 'more probable than not; more than a 50 per cent chance': *Australian Telecommunications Commission v Kreig Enterprises Pty Ltd* (1976) 14 SASR 303; *Tillmanns Butcheries Pty Ltd v Australian Meat Industries Employees' Union* (1979) 27 ALR 367. It does not include a mere possibility, whether real or not: *Radio 2UE Sydney Pty Ltd v Stereo FM Pty Ltd* (1982) 44 ALR 557. There must be some real and not remote chance such that the anti-competitive effect called for under the (CTH) Trade Practices Act 1974 is 'more probable than not', 'prone to', 'with a propensity', or 'liable to': *Dowling v Dalgety Australia Ltd* (1992) 34 FCR 109; 106 ALR 75. See also **Competition law; Contract, arrangement or understanding; Merger.**

Likely to deceive or confuse In trade mark law, likely to mislead. The (CTH) Trade Marks Act 1995 s 43 prohibits the registration of trade marks likely to deceive or cause confusion. The Act is construed to protect the public and the rights of traders and manufacturers. Where the likelihood of confusion or deception did not exist at the time of registration but arose subsequently, the trade mark cannot be deleted from the list of registered trade marks unless the registrar of the trade mark knew or ought to have known the mark was likely to confuse or deceive: *New South Wales Dairy Corp v Murray Goulburn Coop Co Ltd* (1990) 171 CLR 363; 97 ALR 73. See also **Likely; Misleading or deceptive conduct; Trade mark.**

•**Likely to mislead or deceive** In consumer protection law, having a capacity or tendency to mislead or deceive: *McWilliams Wines Pty Ltd v McDonald's System of Australia Pty Ltd* (1980) 33 ALR 394; 49 FLR 455. Conduct is 'likely' to mislead or deceive if there is a real or not remote chance or possibility that it will mislead or deceive: *Global Sportsman Pty Ltd v Mirror Newspapers Ltd* (1984) 2 FCR 82; 55 ALR 25. The (CTH) Trade Practices Act 1974 s 52 states that a corporation shall not, in trade or commerce, engage in conduct that is likely to mislead or deceive. See also **Liable to mislead; Likely; Misleading or deceptive conduct.**

Limit order In relation to securities trading, a type of order given by a client which specifies a minimum selling or maximum buying price. See also **Securities business.**

Limit up or down A restriction on the level which prices can move during a trading session on some futures exchanges, being the maximum increase or decrease from the previous trading session's price. See also **Sydney Futures Exchange.**

Limitation clause A contractual clause that restricts a party's liability arising from a breach of the contract to a specified sum or to a maximum amount. The rules of interpretation in relation to exemption clauses (which exclude liability altogether) apply equally to limitation clauses: *Darlington Futures Ltd v Delco Australia Pty Ltd* (1986) 161 CLR 500; 68 ALR 385. See also **Disclaimer; Exclusion clause.**

Limitation of actions The time limit on a person's right to issue legal proceedings. This principle is reflected in the equitable doctrine of laches and in the so-called statutes of limitations found in all the States and Territories of Australia: (NSW) Limitation Act 1969; (VIC) Limitation of Actions Act 1958; (QLD) Limitation of Actions Act 1974; (SA) Limitation of Actions Act 1936; (WA) Limitation Act 1935; (TAS) Limitation Act 1974; (ACT) Limitation Act 1985; (NT) Limitation Act 1981. The statutes of limitation do not apply where a specific limitation period is given in another statute: for example (CTH) Trade Practices Act 1974 s 74J. A limit is set to avoid a miscarriage of justice due to stale evidence. The court may extend the period only where it is just and reasonable to do so: *Bell v SPC Ltd* [1989] VR 170. See also **Laches; Limitation period.**

Limitation period A period during which a cause of action or prosecution may be commenced in court or an interlocutory step taken in proceedings. The period varies according to the sphere of law and the jurisdiction.

Contract Actions based on simple contract must be brought within six years of the accrual of the cause of action: for example (NSW) Limitation Act 1969 s 12(1)(a). This is the case in most jurisdictions, but in the Northern Territory the period is three years: (NT) Limitation Act s 12(1)(a).

Deeds and other instruments The period of time within which actions based on a deed or other specialty must be brought, starting from the time the cause of action accrued. The limitation period is 12 years in New South Wales, Queensland, Tasmania, the Australian Capital Territory, and the Northern Territory: for example (NSW) Limitation Act 1969 s 16. In Victoria and South Australia, the period is 15 years ((VIC) Limitation of Actions Act 1958 s 15(1C); (SA) Limitation of Actions Act 1936 s 34) and in Western Australia, 20 years ((WA) Limitation Act 1935 s 38(1)(e)(i).

Real property The period within which a person must bring an action if he or she does not wish to lose the title to real property through adverse possession. The limitation period commences when the person was first dispossessed or discontinued possession. In New South Wales, the period is 12 years: (NSW) Limitation Act 1969 s 27. The expiration of the limitation period means not only that the rightful owner is barred from commencing proceedings to recover the land, but that his or her title to the land is extinguished. The limitation period in respect of land owned by the Crown is usually longer than that applying to other persons, although this too varies from State to State. In New South Wales, it is 30 years: (NSW) Limitation Act 1969 s 27(1).

Tort The period of time within which actions in tort must be brought, starting from the time the cause of action accrued. Actions for negligence not involving personal injury must be brought within six years of the accrual of the cause of action (for example (NSW) Limitation Act 1969 s 14(1)(b)) in every jurisdiction except the Northern Territory, where the period is three years ((NT) Limitation Act 1981 s 12(1)(b)). Actions for negligence involving personal injury must be brought within six years in Victoria ((VIC) Limitation of Actions Act 1958 s 5(1A)), Western Australia, and the Australian Capital Territory. In all the other States and Territories it is three years of the accrual of the cause of action: for example (NSW) Limitation Act 1969 ss 14(1), 16, 18A.

Trade and commerce Actions under (CTH) Trade Practices Act 1974 Div 2A must be commenced at any time within three years after the day on which the cause of action accrued: s 74G. This applies regardless of the limitation period set out in the relevant jurisdiction.

Limited *Abbr* – Ltd With reference to a company, having limited liability. That is, persons with shares in a limited company are liable only to the value of their shares. A person is not able to carry on a business under a name which includes 'Limited' or 'Ltd' unless it is a properly registered company: Corporations Law s 369. Ltd also signifies a private limited company in both the United Kingdom and Ireland. See also **Limited company.**

•**Limited company** A company limited by shares, limited by guarantee, or limited by shares and guarantee, but not a no liability company: Corporations Law s 9. Limited companies have limited liability, which, in its current statutory form, prevents any right of action by the company against individual members without their consent, except to the extent of the value of the member's shares or guarantee: ss 117, 180(3). All limited liability companies must have the word 'Limited' or 'Ltd' after their names. See also **Limited partner**; **Limited partnership**.

•**Limited partner** A partner who contributes to the capital of the partnership but does not take part in its management and cannot bind the firm, and whose liability to contribute to the debts or obligations of the partnership is limited to that partner's capital contribution (or the value of any property contributed) to the partnership: for example (NSW) Partnership Act 1892 ss 49, 54(2)(g), 60. See also **General partner**; **Limited partnership**; **Partner**.

•**Limited partnership** A partnership formed in accordance with the partnership legislation and consisting of at least one general partner and at least one limited partner: for example (NSW) Partnership Act 1892 ss 49, 51(1); (VIC) Partnership Act 1958 Pt 3. A limited partner's liability to contribute to the debts and obligations of the partnership is limited by the capital he or she has contributed to the firm. The obligations of the general partners in a limited partnership are similar to those of partners in an ordinary partnership and their liability is unlimited. See also **General partner**; **Limited partner**; **Partnership**.

Limited warranty A warranty that is restricted in its operation, for example that goods purchased would be free of defects in workmanship and material for one year: *Eimco Corporation v Tutt Bryant Ltd* [1970] 2 NSWR 249; (1970) 18 FLR 50. As the warranty is collateral to the main purpose of the contract, a breach will give rise to a claim for damages but not to a right to reject the goods or service and treat the contract as repudiated. See also **Condition**; **Guarantee**; **Term**; **Warranty**.

Line of credit The extension of loans to a person by a bank. Often, the interest rate is set above the bank's prime rate such that it floats with the prime rate. This borrowing facility may be extended on an indefinite basis and may include an option to draw bank bills. See also **Acceptance fee**; **Authorised dealer**; **Credit limit**; **Prime rate**; **Retailer's card**.

•**Linked credit provider** A credit provider with whom a supplier of goods, services, or cash has a trade tie or agreement or to whom the supplier regularly refers customers to obtain credit. The supplier also makes the credit provider's forms of contract or application for credit available to customers, or has an agreement with the credit provider that these forms can be signed at the supplier's premises: (NSW) Credit Act 1984 s 5(1); (VIC) Credit Act 1984 s 5(1). The definition is the same under the (CTH) Trade Practices Act 1974 but the supplier in this context is a corporation that supplies goods and services. See also **Credit**; **Credit provider**; **Supplier**; **Trade or tie agreement**.

Liquid asset Cash, a short-term deposit, or an asset readily converted into money. See also **Asset**; **Liquidity**.

Liquid ratio 1. The ratio of liquid assets to quick liabilities. The ratio assists in the assessment of short-term solvency; it is an 'acid test'. Liquid assets consist primarily of current assets minus stock. Stock is excluded because of the time lag involved with its conversion into cash. Bank overdrafts are usually excluded from quick liabilities provided such overdrafts are secured. **2.** In a security market, the value of equity turnover for a period of 12 months divided by the market capitalisation of shares at the end of the period. See also **Asset**; **Current ratio**; **Liquidity**.

Liquidated damages Damages sought or awarded to a plaintiff, the amount being a sum fixed by the parties to a contract as a genuine pre-estimate of the plaintiff's loss in the event of the defendant's breach (*Dunlop Pneumatic Tyre Co Ltd v New Garage and Motor Co Ltd* [1915] AC 79) or ascertainable by a simple calculation or fixed by any scale of charges or other positive data: *Spain v Union Steamship of NZ Ltd* (1923) 32 CLR 138; *Alexander v Ajax Insurance Co Ltd* [1956] VLR 436; [1956] ALR 1077. A claim for unliquidated damages is not made into a liquidated demand by the plaintiff naming a definite figure: *Abbey Panel & Sheet Metal Co Ltd v Barson Products* [1948] 1 KB 493. A claim upon quantum meruit where the plaintiff states the precise sum which he claims as the value of his services is for liquidated damages: *Lagos v Grunwaldt* [1910] 1 KB 41. Historically, the action to recover a liquidated sum was one at common law in debt. A liquidated damages clause overcomes the requirement of proof of loss in a damages claim. It is to be contrasted with an agreed damages clause that is penal. See also **Action of debt**; **Agreed damages clause**; **Penalty**; **Performance**.

Liquidated sum A specific sum of money the amount of which is ascertained or capable of being ascertained by a mere calculation: for example *Re Ahearn; Ex parte Palmer* (1906) 6 SR (NSW) 576; 23 WN (NSW) 188. See also **Liquidated damages**.

•**Liquidating trade** A transaction where, for the purpose of closing out a futures contract, the person in the bought position or sold position under the futures contract assumes an off-setting sold position, or off-setting bought position as the case may be, under another futures contract: Corporations Law s 9; (CTH) Futures Industry Act 1986 s 4(1). See also **Futures contract**.

Liquidation The winding-up of a company, halting its business, realising its assets, discharging its liabilities (or a percentage of them where the liabilities outweigh the assets), and dividing any surplus assets among its members. Liquidation is undertaken by a liquidator. It may be voluntary or imposed by court order. A court may issue a winding-up order following an application to the court by a creditor, shareholder, receiver or the company itself. A company liquidation is the corporate equivalent of bankruptcy proceedings against an individual who becomes insolvent. Where a corporation is in liquidation, its liquidator may bring or defend any legal proceedings in the name of the corporation: Corporations Law s 477(2)(a). See also **Bankruptcy**; **Insolvency**; **Winding up**.

Liquidation dividend See **Dividend**.

•**Liquidator** A person appointed, in a winding up of a company, to assume control of the company's affairs and to discharge its liabilities in preparation for its dissolution. The liquidator ascertains the liabilities of the company, converts its assets into money, terminates its contracts, disposes of its business, distributes the net assets to creditors and any surplus to the proprietors, and extinguishes the company as a legal entity by formal dissolution: Corporations Law Ch 5. Only an official liquidator may be appointed for a compulsory winding up: ss 472(1), 532(8). A registered liquidator who is not an official liquidator can act as a liquidator in a voluntary winding up. See also **Official liquidator**; **Provisional liquidator**; **Registered liquidator**; **Winding up**.

Liquidity 1. The availability of cash, liquid assets and credit facilities to meet current financial liabilities. 2. A measure of the relative ease with which stocks can be traded. The ability of a market in a particular security to absorb a reasonable amount of buying and selling at reasonable price changes. See also **Balance sheet risk**; **Insolvency**; **Liquidity risk**.

Liquidity ratio See **Liquid ratio**.

Liquidity risk 1. In banking, a risk that arises from the mismatch in the final maturity of on-balance sheet assets and liabilities, plus the settlement characteristic of off-balance sheet activities. There may also be a run as a result of loss of public confidence when depositors and investors want to withdraw their funds quickly. 2. In payment systems, the risk that a counterparty (or participant in a settlement system) will not settle an obligation for full value when due. Liquidity risk does not imply that a counterparty or participant is insolvent since it may be able to settle the required debit obligations at some unspecified time thereafter. See also **Asset class**; **Balance sheet risk**; **Haircut**; **Risk**.

•**Listed body** A body corporate whose shares are listed (quoted or priced) on an official stock exchange: Corporations Law s 603; *Repco Ltd v Bartdon Pty Ltd* [1981] VR 1. Listed shares can be traded on the exchange. See also **Australian Stock Exchange Ltd**; **Quoted security**.

Listed company share option A share option traded on the Australian Stock Exchange (ASX) which is issued and listed by a company as part of its capital raising program. The Options Clearing House plays no part in trading in listed company share options. The other type of share option traded on the ASX is the exchange traded share option. See also **Exchange traded share option**; **Option**; **Share option**.

•**Listed corporation** See **Listed body**.

Listed personal-use asset A print, etching, drawing, painting, sculpture, or similar work of art; jewellery; a rare folio, rare manuscript, or rare book; a postage stamp or first day cover; a coin or medallion; an antique; or an interest in any of these assets, acquired for a consideration of over $100; or a debt owed in respect of, or an option or right to acquire, any of these assets: (CTH) Income Tax Assessment Act 1936 s 160B(2). A capital gain arising on the disposal of a listed personal-use asset is treated as an ordinary capital gain: s 160ZQ. A capital loss so arising may only be offset against capital gains arising from the disposal of other listed personal-use assets in the same year of income or in a later year: s 160ZQ. See also **Asset**; **Capital gain**; **Capital loss**; **Non-listed personal-use asset**; **Personal-use asset**; **Year of income**.

Listing requirements Requirements issued by the Australian Stock Exchange and other exchanges, that must be satisfied by a company seeking to have its shares or other securities traded on the exchange. The rules require a specified minimum number of shareholders with a specified minimum issued capital and a profitable trading record: Corporations Law ss 603, 761; *Repco Ltd v Bartdon Pty Ltd* [1981] VR 1. Also known as 'listing rules'. See also **Australian Stock Exchange Ltd**; **Public company**; **Unit trust**.

•**Literary work** Type of work which is intended to convey information or instruction, or which is intended to afford literary enjoyment: *Computer Edge Pty Ltd v Apple Computer Inc* (1986) 161 CLR 171; 6 IPR 1; 65 ALR 33; *Kalamazoo (Aust) Pty Ltd v Compact Business Systems Pty Ltd* (1985) 84 FCR 101; 5 IPR 213 at 232. For purposes of copyright, the use of the adjective 'literary' carries no requirement that the work be of any particular literary merit: *Computer Edge Pty Ltd v Apple Computer Inc*; (CTH) Copyright Act 1968 s 10(1). See also **Author**; **Copyright**; **Original work**.

Living wage The minimum wage at any particular time that is sufficient for a worker to subsist. It has been described as the amount necessary to sustain an average employee in a civilised community in a 'condition of frugal comfort estimated by current human standards': *Ex parte H V McKay* (1907) 2 CAR 1. See also **Australian industrial system**; **Minimum wage**.

Living-away-from-home allowance Abbr – LAFHA An allowance paid to an employee by an employer to compensate for additional expenses, or other additional disadvantages suffered, because the employee (with or without family) has to live away from his or her usual place of residence for employment purposes: (CTH) Fringe Benefits Tax Assessment Act 1986 s 30(1). A living-away-from-home allowance is generally subject to fringe benefits tax: ss 30, 31. A living-away-from-home allowance is exempt income to an employee recipient. It need not be shown on group certificates and is not subject to pay as you earn deductions: (CTH) Income Tax Assessment Act 1936 s 221A(1). See also **Allowance**; **Employee**; **Employer**; **Fringe benefits tax**; **Pay As You Earn system**.

Lloyd's of London The society of that name incorporated by (IMP) Lloyd's Act 1871: (CTH) Insurance Act 1973 s 3. Members consist of approved underwriters and brokers. Lloyd's functions primarily as an incorporated society of individual underwriters, and provides support and incidental services to member underwriters: *Edinburgh Assurance Co v RL Burns Corp* 479 F Supp 138 (1979). See also **Broker**; **Broker's slip**; **Insurance contract**; **Underwriting**; **Underwriting agent**.

Lloyd's Register of Shipping A register maintained by Lloyd's of London which classifies ships according to their general condition so that marine underwriters may properly assess the risk they are being asked to take. See also **A1**; **Lloyd's of London**.

Loading 1. Placing or putting on or in. 2. An extra rate paid to employees.

Industrial law An increase added to the basic wage of a worker, to recognise or compensate particular skills, responsibilities or disadvantages of the worker's employment, such as for shift work, fares, or loss of opportunity to work overtime. The term 'loadings' as used in a particular industry is a technical term or a term of art; its meaning is a question of fact to be determined by expert evidence: *Max Cooper & Sons Pty Ltd v Sydney City Council* (1980) 29 ALR 77. See also **Allowance**.

• **Loan** The temporary transfer of an asset, usually funds, from a lender who controls the funds to a borrower in return for payment usually in the form of interest. The asset must be returned either in one sum at the maturity of the loan or in periodic payments.

Taxation and revenue For fringe benefits tax purposes, a transaction involving the provision of funds to another person. A loan includes: an advance of money; the provision of credit or any other form of financial accommodation; the payment of an amount on behalf or at the request of a person where there is an obligation (whether expressed or implied) to repay the amount; and a transaction which in substance effects a loan of money: (CTH) Fringe Benefits Tax Assessment Act 1986 s 136(1). Also known as 'loan fringe benefit' or a 'loan benefit'. See also **Credit**; **Fringe benefits tax**.

Loan and charge A method for the acquisition and holding of trading stock. A fluctuating loan is made to finance the acquisition and holding of the stock, with security taken over the stock. The dealer sells the goods held and uses the proceeds to repay the loan, so the level of borrowings 'comes and goes' as do the goods over which there is security. The charge may also apply to other property of the dealer and will often be a general charge over all the property of the dealer. See also **Charge**; **Loan**.

• **Loan benefit** See **Loan**.

Loan capital Long term loans at fixed interest, commonly secured over the borrower's assets by a fixed or floating charge. The postponed date of repayment of the principal sum allows the loan to be treated for practical purposes as capital (that is, money that is not repayable while the company continues to trade). Sometimes such loans may be convertible into ordinary shares at the lender's option at a predetermined future date, and for a fixed price per share (for example convertible debentures). On conversion, the loan becomes part of the true capital of the borrowing company and is not repayable prior to liquidation. See also **Capital**; **Share capital**.

Loan note A fixed interest debt with a maturity date often falling ten years ahead of issue. According to the terms of the loan note, repayment in full must be made on the date stipulated with payments of interest in the meanwhile as agreed. A company may be bought, not with cash, but with loan notes acceptable to the vendor. The purchaser may hope to redeem those notes in due course from the profits of a rejuvenated enterprise. See also **Convertible security**; **Maturity date**; **Note**; **Unsecured note**.

• **Local acceptance** A qualified acceptance of a bill of exchange, being a promise to pay only at a specified place: (CTH) Bills of Exchange Act 1909 s 24(3)(c). An acceptance to pay at a particular place is a general acceptance, unless it expressly states that the bill is to be paid there only, and not elsewhere, in which case it is qualified acceptance: (CTH) Bills of Exchange Act 1909 s 24(4). See also **Acceptance**; **Acceptor**; **Bill of exchange**; **Domiciled bill**; **General acceptance**; **Qualified acceptance**.

• **Local agent** In relation to corporations, a natural person who is a resident of Australia appointed in relation to a foreign company: Corporations Law s 346(5). A foreign company that lodges a duly exercised memorandum of appointment or a power of attorney by or on behalf of itself is able to validly appoint a local agent who is therefore authorised to accept, on behalf of the foreign company, service of process and notices. A person continues as a local agent until he or she dies or is removed under Corporations Law s 347: Corporations Law ss 9, 346, 347. See also **Carrying on business**; **Power of attorney**.

• **Local corporation** A company or any other corporation that is incorporated in a particular jurisdiction to which the Corporations Law applies: Corporations Law s 9. The Corporations Law is applied in each of the States and the Northern Territory by legislation in each jurisdiction. See also **Corporations Law**.

• **Local futures association** A futures association that has been approved by the Minister to act as a futures association under Corporations Law ss 9, 1132. The term is used to distinguish such associations from those futures associations that were established under previous corporations legislation: ss 9, 1132(3). The latter are treated as futures associations only for the purposes of Ch 1, ss 9, 1220, 1222, 1223, 1269. See also **Futures association**.

• **Local futures exchange** A futures exchange which has been approved by the Minister to act as a futures exchange under Corporations Law ss 9, 1126. The term is used to distinguish such exchanges from those futures exchanges that were established under previous corporations legislation: ss 9, 1126(3). The latter are treated as futures exchanges only for the purposes of Ch 1, ss 9, 1220, 1222, 1223, 1269. See also **Futures exchange**.

• **Local securities exchange** A local stock exchange or an approved securities organisation: Corporations Law s 9. See also **Approved securities organisation**; **Denial of natural justice**; **International Court of Justice**; **Local stock exchange**.

• **Local stock exchange** The Australian Stock Exchange (ASX) Ltd or a State subsidiary of the ASX, the Stock Exchange of Bendigo Ltd, the Stock Exchange of Ballarat Ltd, or the Stock Exchange of Newcastle Ltd that conducts or proposes to conduct a stock market in the particular State or Territory in question, or a body corporate which has been approved by the Minister under Corporations Law s 769 to act as a stock exchange in the particular State or Territory: Corporations Law s 9. See also **Australian Stock Exchange Ltd**.

Location clause A clause in a marine insurance contract, limiting the insurance cover at any given place before the cargo is loaded. See also **Cargo**; **Loading**.

Lock-out A form of industrial action by employers, by which the employer closes the work premises and refuses to allow employees to work, with the aim of compelling or inducing employees to agree to conditions of employment, or to comply with the employer's demands, or to cause loss or inconvenience to employees: for example (CTH) Industrial Relations Act 1988 s 5. The suspension or dismissal of a particular employee does not constitute a lockout: *Meek v Minister for Water Supply, Sewerage and Drainage* (1961) 105 CLR 173. See also **Industrial action; Strike**.

Locum tenens /loʊkʊm tɛnɛnz/ *Lat* – holding someone's place; a deputy. One who holds office in place of another, or temporarily performs the professional duties of another. See also **Firm**.

Locus poenitentiae /loʊkʊs pɔɪnɪtɛntɪaɪ/ *Lat* – a place of repentance. An opportunity of withdrawing from an engagement, provided some definitive step has not been taken. For example, under the doctrine of repudiation, a promisor may retract a verbal repudiation which has not been accepted by the promisee, and call upon the promisee to perform, notwithstanding the earlier words: *Tsoa-Lee v Urban Real Property Consultants Pty Ltd* [1983] 1 NSWLR 569. See also **Repudiation**.

Locus standi /lɒkʊs stændaɪ/ *Lat* – a place to stand on. The right to appear in court and argue a case.

•Lodge To deliver and place a document or thing into the possession of a person in relation to an official procedure. Lodgment requires a degree of physical acceptance by the person to whom the thing is given and is more than the mere placing or depositing of the object with that person: *Re Angus Fire Armour Australia Pty Ltd v Collector of Customs (NSW)* (1988) 19 FCR 477; 83 ALR 449. If sent by post, a document is not lodged unless and until it is received and accepted by the intended recipient. See also **Presentment**.

Log book record 1. A record of travel details. 2. For fringe benefit tax purposes in relation to a car, a daily document setting out in respect of each business journey undertaken, details of the journey including the date, odometer reading at beginning and end of the journey, kilometres travelled, purpose, and name of the driver: (CTH) Fringe Benefits Tax Assessment Act 1986 s 136. 3. For income tax purposes, a daily log book or similar document in which details of income-producing journeys made by a car during a period are entered to determine the pattern of use of the car during that period: (CTH) Income Tax Assessment Act 1936 s 82KT (1). See also **Car; Fringe benefits tax; Income**.

Log of claims A list of demands made by an industrial organisation as to the wages and other employment conditions of particular employees. A log of claims is used as a step in creating a genuine industrial dispute and is also used as a basis for determining the 'ambit' of such a dispute in the federal jurisdiction. However, a log of claims that is fanciful or simply claims wage and allowance increases as determined by an industrial tribunal will not give rise to a genuine industrial dispute: *Re State Public Services Federation; Ex parte Attorney-General (WA)* (1993) 178 CLR 249; 113 ALR 385. See also **Ambit; Paper dispute**.

London Baltic Exchange *Abbr* – LBE A London market established in the early 18th century devoted to shipping services and cargoes. Today it is international in scope and the largest market of its kind in the world. As a commodity exchange it specialises in the grain trade with a well-established futures market: for example, wheat and barley in the European Union, potatoes and soya bean meal in the United Kingdom. Almost any business connected with ships, cargoes, and air freight is transacted.

London Club An informal group of commercial banks responsible for negotiating the rescheduling of debt with creditor countries.

London Commodity Exchange *Abbr* – LCE A commodity exchange emerging from the London Rubber Exchange founded in 1932 by the Rubber Trade Association. During the 1939-45 war, the exchange was joined by members of the London Commercial Sale Rooms. In 1954, a review resulted in the formation of a new company comprising rubber and sale room members with the name London Commodity Exchange. One of the most important of its kind, the exchange has assumed the character of a futures market.

London Discount Market *Abbr* – LDM A short-term money market. The market comprises the discount houses of the City of London, the accepting houses, the commercial banks and the Bank of England.

London Foreign Exchange Market *Abbr* – LFEM A market operating by telephone, fax and telex within the City of London and between the city and overseas financial centres. There are some 260 dealers including the banks authorised as foreign exchange dealers by the Bank of England. The market is the world's largest centre for foreign exchange dealing.

London Gold Futures Market *Abbr* – LGFM Established in 1982, a market and exchange in the City of London for trading and dealing in gold contracts for future delivery. The market is owned jointly by the London Gold Market and the London Metal Exchange.

London Gold Market *Abbr* – LGM A market served by five London bullion dealers who quote prices in US dollars. They meet twice a day to fix the price of gold on the basis of buy and sell orders from all over the world. This price provides a standard of gold value for traders in Chicago, Hong Kong, New York, Paris, Singapore, Sydney, Tokyo, Zurich and other centres.

London Inter Bank Offered Rate *Abbr* — LIBOR The benchmark interest rate charged by the major London banks when lending to other banks in eurodollars. See also **Eurodollar**.

London Interbank Bid Rate *Abbr* – LIBID The rate of interest the London prime banks will pay for the Eurodeposits of other prime banks.

London Interbank Mean Rate *Abbr* – LIMEAN The mean of the London Interbank Offered Rate and the London Interbank Bid Rate. See also **London Interbank Offered Rate; London Interbank Bid Rate**.

London Interbank Offered Rate *Abbr* – LIBOR The rate of interest charged by the major London banks on call-money loans made among themselves. This rate is used as a benchmark-rate in Eurodollar lending.

London International Commodities Clearing House *Abbr* – LICCH A clearing house owned by six major British banks which manages transactions in the futures and commodities markets. One of the tasks of the clearing house is to hold the margin exchange members are required to maintain every day. This is calculated daily in the light of their opening trading positions. This arrangement is meant to reduce the risk of loss through default. See also **Clearing house**.

London International Financial Futures Exchange *Abbr* – LIFFE A financial futures market which opened in London in 1982. In 1994 it had over 200 members. The contracts offered include twenty-year gilt interest rates, three-month sterling interest rates, US Treasury bonds, three-month Eurodollar interest rates, Sterling currency, deutschmarks, Swiss francs, Japanese yen, FT-SE 100, West German government bonds, Japanese government bonds, and a three-month European currency unit interest rate. In 1990, LIFFE merged with the London Traded Options Market, a market offering options on over 60 leading equities as well as options on the FT-SE 100 index.

London International Stock Exchange *Abbr* – LISE A single stock exchange formed in 1973 from the seven exchanges in the United Kingdom. The governing body, the Council of the Stock Exchange, is elected by the members of the exchange. In 1986, the exchange abolished fixed commissions, the previously mandatory distinction between stockbrokers (who bought and sold from the public) and stockjobbers (who traded stocks on their own account) thus permitting members to act in a dual-capacity as broker/dealers, and allowed outside firms including foreigners into the exchange.

London Metal Exchange *Abbr* – LME A physical market where metals can be bought and sold at any time. The market provides facilities for hedging. By registering daily price quotations, the market indicates world trends in both the supply and demand for metals. See also **Bullion**.

Long 1. A description of a buyer or holder of securities who has more of a particular security than the buyer has contracted to deliver. 2. Someone who has bought expecting a rise in prices. 3. A term signifying ownership of securities. 'I am long 100 US Steel' means the speaker owns 100 shares. 4. The market position of a futures contract buyer whose purchase obligates the buyer to accept delivery unless the contract is liquidated with an offsetting sale. 5. A trader who has bought futures contracts or who owns actuals that are unhedged. 'Net long' refers to a trader whose total purchases exceed the trader's total short sales. See also **Long hedger**; **Short**.

Long hedger A person who has bought a futures contract to guard against a future increase in price of a physical commodity. If people who anticipate buying a commodity in the future wish to protect themselves from a possible price increase, they may seek to hedge their position. As they are 'short' in the physical commodity (because they have not yet acquired it), they will take a long position in the futures market (that is, buy a contract). See also **Futures contract**; **Hedging**.

Long position The position of a person selling particular securities on a stock exchange when he or she actually owns the shares. A person who sells securities but does not then own them is said to have a short position. See also **Short selling**.

•**Long service leave** Leave of absence from work on ordinary pay to which an employee becomes entitled after a certain number of years of service with an employer. For example, in New South Wales an employee who has completed ten years service with the employer is entitled to two months' long service leave: for example (NSW) Long Service Leave Act 1955 s 4. The conditions depend on the particular employment contract as well as relevant legislation and industrial awards or agreements. See also **Full-time employee**; **Leave of absence**; **Provision**; **Retrenchment**.

•**Loss** 1. Damage, detriment, or suffering flowing from the act or omission of another. 2. The result when expenses exceed revenues in the same reporting period. See also **Consequential loss**; **Costs**; **Damage**; **Economic loss**; **Loss or damage**; **Losses and outgoings**; **Non-pecuniary loss**.

•**Loss leader** 1. A product sold at a price lower than cost, to attract custom. 2. The practice of selling a product at a price lower than cost to attract custom or promote the business of the vendor in some other way: *Trade Practices Commission v Orlane Australia Pty Ltd* (1984) 1 FCR 157; ATPR ¶40-437. See also **Net acquisition cost**; **Resale price maintenance**.

Loss of a chance In the assessment of damages in contract law, the loss of the plaintiff's opportunity to obtain benefits that would have resulted from the defendant's performance. Where a plaintiff contracts for profit which is not assured or quantifiable and the other party rescinds, the plaintiff cannot be said to suffer actual loss (a loss of profit), but may have lost the chance of making a profit: *McRae v Commonwealth Disposals Commission* (1951) 84 CLR 377. The concept of damages for loss of a chance frequently applies when damages are difficult to assess; the court so placed may use the loss of a chance of obtaining a benefit, such as profit, as a basis of assessment: for example *Howe v Teefy* (1927) 27 SR (NSW) 301. Loss of a chance entitles the plaintiff to expectation damages, putting the plaintiff in the position in which he or she would have been had the parties contracted: *Commonwealth v Amann Aviation Pty Ltd* (1991) 174 CLR 64; 104 ALR 1. Such an action may lie with regard to economic loss: *Johnson v Perez* (1988) 166 CLR 351; 82 ALR 587. See also **Assessment of damages**; **Damages**; **Economic loss**; **Heads of damage**; **Remoteness**.

Loss of bargain Economic loss incurred by a contracting party as a result of another party's serious breach of the contract. Damages for loss of bargain are assessed by reference to the difference between the market value of the contract (or its subject matter) at the time of breach, and the price (or monetary equivalent) expressed in the contract: for example *Hoffman v Cali* [1985] 1 Qd R 253. Discharge of the contract, by termination for repudiation or breach, is necessary before such damages can be recovered: *Sunbird Plaza Pty Ltd v Maloney* (1988) 166 CLR 245; 77 ALR 205. Where the plaintiff's termination is based on repudiation, breach of an essential term, or a sufficiently serious breach of an intermediate term, it will be presumed that the plaintiff is entitled to recover loss of bargain damages: *Foran v Wight* (1989) 168 CLR 385; 88 ALR 413. No such presumption exists where termination is pursuant to an express termination clause. See also **Breach of contract**; **Damages**; **Discharge**; **Intermediate term**; **Repudiation**; **Termination**.

•**Loss of earning capacity** Financial loss incurred as the consequence of being unable to earn income, temporarily or permanently, due to incapacity caused by the breach of a tort. The legal claim is for the loss of capacity to earn income, rather than the lost income as such: *Paff v Speed* (1961) 105 CLR 549; [1961] ALR 614. The amount compensable may be limited by statute: for example (NSW) Workers Compensation Act 1987 ss 151H, 151I. Also known as 'loss of income'. See also **Earning capacity**; **Heads of damage**.

Loss of expectation of life A head of non-pecuniary damages awarded where the plaintiff's natural life expectancy is shortened as a result of an accident. The objective is to compensate the victim for the deprivation of part of his or her life: *Skelton v Collins* (1966) 115 CLR 94; ALR 449. Generally, courts award modest sums under this head, only taking account of the fall in value of money and not the age of the victim: *Sharman v Evans* (1977) 138 CLR 563; 13 ALR 57. See also **Assessment of damages**; **Non-pecuniary loss**.

Loss of reputation Loss of a person's good name. A person whose reputation is damaged by misleading or deceptive conduct that contravenes (CTH) Trade Practices Act 1974 s 52 may recover for any loss or damage arising as a result of the contravention: (CTH) Trade Practices Act 1974 s 82; *Brabazon v Western Mail Ltd* (1985) 8 FCR 122; 58 ALR 712. See also **Damages**; **Misleading or deceptive conduct**.

Loss of vessel clause 1. A clause in a time charterparty specifying that a person is not liable to pay for the hire of the chartered vessel if it is an actual or constructive total loss. For example, a ship is an actual total loss if it is wrecked beyond repair or has sunk irretrievably to the bottom of the sea: *Roux v Salvador* (1836) 3 Bing NC 266 at 288; 132 ER 413 at 421; *Broomfield v The Southern Insurance Co Ltd* (1870) LR 5 Ex 196. Such clauses are also known as 'total loss clauses'. 2. A clause contained in a bottomry bond under which, if the ship is lost, the money lent on the security of the ship and any interest accruing on it is not payable to the lender. See also **Charterparty**.

•**Loss or damage** In trade or commerce, the disadvantage that is suffered by a person as a result of the outward fault of another: *Demagogue Pty Ltd v Ramensky* (1992) 110 ALR 608 at 625. A person who suffers loss or damage as a result of conduct that is in breach of a provision of (CTH) Trade Practices Act 1974 Pts IV and V may be awarded damages to compensate him or her for that loss or damage: s 82. A court may also make such orders as it thinks appropriate where a person has suffered, or is likely to suffer, loss or damage by the conduct of another person that breaches (CTH) Trade Practices Act 1974 Pts IV, IVA, V: s 87(1A). The expression 'loss or damage' involves a concept of quantum or assessment of damages for the purposes of s 82 that is not present in s 87: *Demagogue Pty Ltd v Ramensky*. Hence, for the purposes of s 87, it will include any detriment suffered by a person who enters into a contract induced by misleading and deceptive conduct in contravention of (CTH) Trade Practices Act 1974 s 52 or through unconscionable conduct: *Demagogue Pty Ltd v Ramensky*. See also **Misleading or deceptive conduct**; **Unconscionable**.

Loss spreading See **Allocation system**.

•**Losses and outgoings** The term 'outgoing' encompasses all types of expenditure which has an effect in gaining or producing income; for example, the purchase price of goods that are subsequently sold. However, a 'loss' merely reduces income, without any payment necessarily being involved; for example, theft or involuntary payments (*Amalgamated Zinc (De Bavay's) Ltd v FCT* (1935) 54 CLR 295). Income tax deductions are available for losses and outgoings incurred in the course of earning assessable income: (CTH) Income Tax Assessment Act 1936 s 51(1). However, no deduction is allowed for expenses to the extent that they are capital, private, or domestic in nature, or are incurred in producing exempt income: (CTH) Income Tax Assessment Act 1936 s 51(1). See also **Assessable income**; **Business**; **Capital**; **Costs**; **Exempt income**; **Incurred**.

Lost or not lost Words introduced into a policy of marine insurance to guard against the risk that the ship or cargo may be lost before the insurance is effected. Ordinarily the interest of an assured would cease to exist when the ship or goods were lost and he or she would be unable to recover on the policy, even if it had been executed in perfect good faith and in ignorance of the loss. However, the words 'lost or not lost' in a policy render the insurer liable, even though the assured may not have acquired his or her interest until after the loss, provided the assured was not aware of the loss at the time of entering into the contract: see (CTH) Marine Insurance Act 1909 s 12. See also **Insurance**; **Lien**; **Premium**.

•**Lost years** In the assessment of damages for personal injury, the number of years by which the plaintiff's life has been shortened. See also **Loss of expectation of life**.

Low exercise price option *Abbr* – LEPO Call options which typically have an exercise price of between 1 and 10 cents and are exercisable only on the last day of trading before expiry of the option. The Australian Stock Exchange (ASX) listed LEPOS for trading on the Australian Options Market in July 1994. The ASX business rules require that the securities underlying LEPOS be quoted on the stock exchange and be characterised by a substantial number of outstanding shares which are widely held and actively traded. A LEPO is not a 'futures contract' within the meaning of the Corporations Law s 72(1)(a). Nor can a LEPO be the subject of a 'commodity agreement' (as required by because the shares underlying LEPOs were not encompassed within the definition of 'commodity' in Corporations Law s 9: *Sydney Futures Exchange Ltd v Australian Stock Exchange* (1994) 126 ALR 209; affirmed in appeal in *Sydney Futures Exchange Ltd v*

Australian Stock Exchange (1995) 128 ALR 417. See also **Option; Option contract**.

Low income rebate A rebate granted to a taxpayer whose taxable income is below a certain level: (CTH) Income Tax Assessment Act 1936 s 159N. The rebate is paid when an income tax return is lodged by the taxpayer. The low income rebate is payable to a maximum of $150 and in addition to other rebates allowed to the taxpayer. See also **Rebate**.

Lower house Either the House of Representatives in the Federal Parliament or the Legislative Assembly in the State parliaments. See also **House of Representatives; Legislative Assembly**.

•**Lump sum** A payment which includes a number of items: *Secretary, Department of Social Security v Banks* (1990) 23 FCR 416; 95 ALR 605. A lump sum may consist of the aggregate of several amounts separately payable, or a total arrived at by adding amounts for different heads of damage. It may consist of a single payment which discharges liability for future payments (such as a payment to a member of a superannuation fund, or from an insurance company following a claim) or from an employer as a redundancy payment, or a payment received as a result of a court settlement. In the context of compensation, once a lump sum is paid, the amount of damages will not be reassessed by the court in the light of actual loss incurred, although if the wrong continues (such as trespass or nuisance) a new action may be brought. Many lump sum payments received in consequence of termination of employment (such as a lump sum payment made to a member of a superannuation fund) are taxed as eligible termination payments: (CTH) Income Tax Assessment Act 1936 s 27A (1). The amount of more than one lump sum payment received in relation to one or more injuries arising from the same event, at least one of which is made wholly or partly in respect of lost earnings or lost capacity to earn constitutes a lump sum compensation payment: (CTH) Social Security Act 1991 s 17(2B). See also **Award; Damages; Eligible Termination Payment; Redundancy; Superannuation fund**.

Lump sum contract 1. A building contract providing for payment of a stipulated sum for the work to be performed by the contractor. There are two types: one providing for adjustment of the agreed sum due to cost variations as the work progresses 'rise and fall'; and one without provision for 'rise and fall' ('fixed price contract'). A lump sum contract may provide for payment of the agreed sum by instalments, or for an adjustment of the agreed sum upon remeasurement on completion ('provisional lump sum contract'). A contractor may receive more than the sum stipulated in the lump sum contract, due to variations in the work, delays in its execution, and increasing building costs: *Re Arbitration between Taylor Woodrow International Ltd and the Minister of Health* (1978) 19 SASR 1. **2.** Sometimes misleadingly used to refer to an entire contract, in which performance is a condition precedent to payment. See also **Building contract; Condition precedent; Delay; Provisional lump sum contract**.

Lump sum freight Freight which is not calculated by reference to the quantity of cargo delivered but is payable for use of the means of conveyance or a portion of it. Where the contract of carriage provides for the payment of lump sum freight, the full amount is payable even if only part of the cargo is delivered for carriage: *Norway (Owners) v Ashburner* (1865) 3 Moo PCC (NS) 245;16 ER 92. See also **Cargo; Contract of carriage; Freight; Rate of freight**.

Lump sum fund A superannuation fund providing benefits in the form of a single lump sum rather than as a pension or annuity. See also **Annuity; Lump sum; Pension; Pension fund; Superannuation fund**.

Lump sum reasonable benefit limit A flat dollar amount of $ 400,000: (CTH) Income Tax Assessment Act 1936 s 140ZD(1). Where a person receives a lump sum before age 55, the limit amount is reduced by 2.5 per cent for each year that the person is under 55: (CTH) Income Tax Assessment Act 1936 s 140ZD(1). For 1995-96 and later years of income, the lump sum reasonable benefit limit is indexed on the basis of movements in the estimate of the full time adult average weekly ordinary time earnings: (CTH) Income Tax Assessment Act 1936 ss 140ZD(3), (4). See also **Reasonable benefit limit**.

M

Mabo's case A decision of the High Court of Australia in which it was held that on white settlement of Australia in 1788, the Crown acquired sovereignty and the right to alienate all land in Australia, but that native title survived: *Mabo v Queensland (No 2)* (1992) 175 CLR 1; 107 ALR 1. Native title may be established where a tribal group, clan, or (rarely) an individual, has had a continuing presence on, or occupation of, land traditionally associated with that tribe, and that presence or occupation has not been extinguished by use and possession by another or alienation by the Crown. In Mabo's case, this doctrine resulted in a decision that the Murray Islanders had the right to use and occupation of the Murray Islands. See also **Aboriginal land rights**; **Crown land**.

Machine language In computer programming, the lowest-level language that uses binary numbers recognised by the central processing unit.

Macmillan duty The duty owed to a bank by its customer to exercise reasonable care in drawing cheques so that the banker is not misled and forgery is not facilitated: *London Joint Stock Bank Ltd v Macmillan and Arthur* [1918] AC 777; *Commonwealth Trading Bank of Australia v Sydney Wide Stores Pty Ltd* (1981) 148 CLR 304; 35 ALR 513. See also **Banker-customer relationship**; **Customer of a bank**; **Customer's duty to bank**; **Greenwood duty**.

Macquarie Bank Group A bank established as an Australian licensed bank in 1985. Its predecessor, Hill Samuel Australia, was established in 1970. The equity of Macquarie Bank is held by three groups, namely Hill Samuel Bank of London, the management and staff of Macquarie Bank and various Australian institutions including superannuation funds. The bank is Australia's leading bullion dealer. It offers banking services, merger and acquisition advice, underwriting, project finance, stockbroking and investment products. In 1990, the bank acquired Boston Australia Limited, the merchant bank subsidiary of The First National Bank of Boston. See also **Acquisition**; **Merchant bank**; **Merger**.

Macro-economic policy Government or public policy concerned with the ways in which the money supply, government expenditure, and interest rates may be used to achieve desirable targets such as low rates of unemployment and inflation, or stabilising the economy in terms of employment and prices. See also **Macroeconomics**; **Micro-economics**.

Macro-economics A branch of economics concerned with the analysis of the economy as a whole including such large aggregates as savings and investment, employment and unemployment, exports and imports, external debt, inflation, interest rates and exchange rates, the balance of payments, booms, and recessions. Macro-economics embraces the study of policies that affect national economic performance, particularly monetary and fiscal policies. It is concerned with the interactions among the goods, labour and assets markets of the national economy. See also **Economics**; **Employment**; **Micro-economics**.

Macro-environment The major elements in the environment which are beyond a firm's control yet influence the firm's decision-making and have an impact on its performance. See also **Corporate capacity**; **Corporate liability**; **Macro-economics**.

•**Magistrate** A judicial officer appointed by the executive government to hear and determine civil and criminal matters arising in courts of summary jurisdiction: (NSW) Local Courts Act 1982; (NSW) Justices Act 1902; (QLD) Justices Act 1886; (QLD) Magistrates' Courts Act 1921; (SA) Magistrates' Court Act 1991; (VIC) Magistrates' Court Act 1989. See also **Court of summary jurisdiction**.

Magnetic ink character recognition cheque *Abbr* – MICR cheque A cheque incorporating a magnetic strip containing all relevant details of the drawer and its account with the drawee bank. The magnetic strip permits rapid processing of the cheque and clearance of funds. MICRs originated in England: *Burnett v Westminster Bank Ltd* [1966] 1 QB 742.

Mailbox In computing, the physical storage area on a local area network that receives and retains electronic messages for the network's users until the messages are retrieved by their respective addressees. See also **Address**; **User**.

•**Main undertaking** The dominant business activity or enterprise of a corporation, it can also refer to the property of a corporation, usually in the sense of all or substantially all of its property as a going concern: *Melville v Mutual Life and Citizens' Assurance Co Ltd* (1980) 21 ALR 649; 47 FLR 201. See also **Business**; **Corporation**; **Memorandum of association**.

•**Maintenance** 1. Provision of the means of existence or continuation. 2. The repair or upkeep of something.

Contract Assistance or encouragement to a party to litigation by a person who has no interest in the litigation or motive recognised as justifying interference: *Re Trepca Mines Ltd (No 2)* [1962] Ch 511. See also **Illegal contract**; **Public policy**.

Maintenance margin In corporations law, the money that a clearing house requires a person holding a futures position to maintain. See also **Australian Financial Futures Market**; **Clearing house**; **Margin**.

Maintenance of capital A company law doctrine that requires any payment of dividends to be made out of distributable profits: Corporations Law s 201. The doctrine prohibits a limited liability company from returning paid-up capital to shareholders before it goes into liquidation or releasing a shareholder from liability to pay the full nominal value of shares properly allotted: for example *Australasian Oil Exploration Ltd v Lach-*

berg (1958) 101 CLR 119 at 132. See also **Authorised buy-back; Authorised reduction of capital; Financial assistance for acquisition of a company's shares; Redeemable preference share; Return of capital in a compromise; Share buy-back.**

Majority, age of See **Age of majority.**

Maker A person who creates something or otherwise brings it into existence.

Bills of exchange and other negotiable instruments The person who signs a promissory note, engaging that he or she will pay the note according to its tenor: (CTH) Bills of Exchange Act 1909 s 89(1). See also **Acceptor; Holder in due course; Payee; Promissory note.**

Mala fide *Lat* – in bad faith; with intent to deceive; fraudulently.

•**Manage** To take an active part in the running of a business; to be responsible for decision making and direction of an undertaking. It is suggestive of control and not merely the carrying out of routine duties: *Barac v Farnell* (1994) 53 FCR 193; 125 ALR 241. See also **Manage a corporation.**

Manage a corporation Take part in running the operations of a corporation. The phrase 'manage a corporation' is defined in Corporations Law s 91A for the purposes of ss 229, 230, 599 and 600 to provide that a person manages a corporation if they are a director or promoter of the corporation or are in any way (whether directly or indirectly) concerned in or taking part in the management of the corporation.

Managed fund A unit trust run by a portfolio manager who actively varies the composition of the portfolio between shares, bonds, debentures and property to achieve the best returns. See also **Portfolio; Share; Trust.**

•**Managed investment** An investment in which money is paid or transferred to a body corporate or into a trust fund managed on the investor's behalf by a fund manager. The assets bought with the invested money are held in the name of the body corporate or trust fund. The money of each investor is pooled and the investor has no control over how the money is invested. However, the investor has a legally enforceable right to the income or profits derived from his or her money: (CTH) Social Security Act 1991 s 9(1A). Within certain limitations, managed investments include insurance bonds, roll-over approved deposit funds, roll-over deferred annuities, friendly society investments and public unit trusts such as cash management, property, equity and bond trusts: (CTH) Social Security Act 1991 s 9(1B), (1C). See also **Investment; Trust.**

Management advisory service A service provided by a public accountant who audits the financial affairs of a business or company and checks the accounting procedures adopted by management. The service includes recommendations, suggestions, and advice on how to improve the financial situation and strengthen the cash flow and may deal with budgeting, forecasting, stock control and other financial matters. See also **Accountant.**

Management and investment company *Abbr* – MIC A financial intermediary established under the (CTH) Management and Investment Companies Act 1983, to encourage the development of a venture capital market in Australia. See also **Business undertaking; Entity; Investment company; Venture capital.**

•**Management company** In corporations law, the body corporate by which, or on behalf of which, certain prescribed interests are, or are proposed to be, made available: Corporations Law s 9. See also **Buy-back arrangement; Prescribed interest.**

Management contracting In building and construction law, where the managing contractor manages the contractor and the designer, and the managing contractor is managed by the proprietor and has contractual ties with the proprietor, the designer and the contractor. The arrangement is different to traditional design and construct contracting, because the contractor in this arrangement is an additional party in the contractual chain in the construction phase. This contractual arrangement is often called a project management contract or a design and construct contract. See also **Building contract; Fixed price contract.**

•**Management fees** Charges incurred by holders of trust property which forms the remuneration of professional fund or trust managers.

•**Management review** In the context of the public service, an examination of any functions and activities of a government department or authority, for the purpose of assessing the extent to which its functions and activities are being carried on in an effective, efficient and economical manner: for example (NSW) Public Sector Management Act 1988 s 3. See also **Public authority; Public service.**

Management shares See **Deferred share.**

•**Manager** See **Receiver and manager.**

Managerial prerogative In industrial relations, the doctrine that some matters relating to the conduct and organisation of the employer's business or operations are inherently for the employer alone to determine: that is, that employees have no right to participate in decisions or make claims regarding those areas. See also **Industrial democracy; Industrial dispute.**

Managing controller In relation to the property of a corporation, a receiver and manager or any other controller of property of a corporation who has functions or powers in connection with managing the company: Corporations Law s 9. A managing controller is required, within two months of the control day, to prepare and lodge with the Australian Securities Commission a report on the corporation's affairs: s 421A. A court may authorise the managing controller to sell or dispose of property of the corporation even though it is subject to a prior charge: s 420B. See also **Control day; Controller; Receiver; Receiver and manager.**

•**Managing director** The director appointed by the board of directors of a company as chief executive officer of the company: for example Corporations Law Sch 1 Table A art 79. See also **Board of directors; Director; Director's duties.**

Mandamus /mændeɪmʊs/ *Lat* – we command. An order issued by a court to compel a public official to perform a public duty or to exercise a statutory discretionary power. See also **Certiorari; Prohibition**.

Mandatory Enforcing strict compliance; not directory. The use of the word 'shall' or 'must' is prima facie indicative of a mandatory provision: *Coutts v Commonwealth* (1985) 157 CLR 91 at 111-12; 59 ALR 699. Strict compliance with mandatory provisions is necessary: *Woodward v Sarsons* (1875) LR 10 CP 733.

Mandatory standard A standard for goods or anything relating to goods which, by virtue of a Commonwealth, State, or Territory law must be complied with when the product is supplied by its manufacturer: (CTH) Trade Practices Act 1974 s 75AA. See also **Consumer product information standard; Consumer product safety standard**.

Mandatum /mændatʊm/ *Lat* – delivery of goods accompanied by specific instructions to do something to the goods bailed without reward: *Coggs v Bernard* (1703) 2 Ld Raym 909 at 912-13; 92 ER 107. **2.** In Roman law, a consensual contract by which one person retained another to perform, without remuneration, a service in the interest of the first person or a third person. See also **Gratuitous bailment**.

•**Manifest** A detailed list of a ship's cargo. The manifest is extracted from bills of lading. A copy is sent to the agent at the place to which the cargo is consigned so that unloading may be planned ahead. Another copy is sent to the relevant customs authority at the port of loading so that outward clearance may be obtained. This document is termed the outward manifest. A copy of the manifest must be carried on board the ship to which it relates. See also **Agent; Bill of lading; Cargo; Customs duty**.

Manila Stock Exchange A small stock exchange with less than 150 listed companies. Trading volumes tend to be low. Foreign shareholdings in Philippine companies are usually limited to 40 per cent. The Manila Composite Stock Index comprises 25 selected issues. See also **Australian Stock Exchange Ltd; Foreign company; Stock Exchange**.

•**Manning committee** A five member committee appointed in 1962 to review the (CTH) Bills of Exchange Act 1909. The committee was chaired by Hon J K Manning, a judge of the Supreme Court of New South Wales. In its report issued in May 1964 the committee recommended separate Acts, one for cheques and another for bills of exchange and promissory notes. Its recommendations were implemented many years later. In 1971 endorsement on cheques was abolished and in 1986 a separate statute for cheques was enacted. See also **Bill of exchange; Cheque; Cheques and Payment Orders Act 1986; Payment order**.

•**Manning notice** A notice issued under (CTH) Income Tax Assessment Act 1936 that determines the number of crew members required to operate a ship in a safe and efficient manner: s 57AM. The decision to issue such a notice is reviewable under the (CTH) Administrative Decisions (Judicial Review) Act 1977: *Australian Institute of Marine and Power Engineers v Secretary, Department of Transport* (1986) 13 FCR 124; 71 ALR 73. See also **Tax records**.

•**Manufacture** To make or produce a thing which is different from that out of which it is made: *McNicol v Pinch* [1906] 2 KB 352; *Federal Cmr of Taxation v Jack Zinader Pty Ltd* (1949) 78 CLR 336; [1949] ALR 912; *Federal Cmr of Taxation v Jax Tyres Pty Ltd* (1984) 5 FCR 257; 58 ALR 138. To manufacture may also include to bring a new saleable entity into existence by skill applied to constituent elements: *Re Searls Ltd* (1932) 33 SR (NSW) 7; 49 WN (NSW) 195. To make a new article as opposed to repairing or remodelling an old one: *Federal Cmr of Taxation v Jax Tyres Pty Ltd*. See also **Manufactured**.

•**Manufactured** Made, grown, extracted, produced, processed, or assembled: (CTH) Trade Practices Act 1974 ss 74A(1), 75AA. A manufactured good may be the subject of a (CTH) Trade Practices Act 1974 Pt V Div 2A or Pt VA product liability claim. See also **Manufacture; Manufacturer**.

•**Manufacturer** A person who makes or produces goods. The term is defined differently in various statutes for different purposes. For example, it may include a person who (not as an employee) combines parts or ingredients so as to form an article or substance that is commercially distinct from the parts or ingredients: (CTH) Sales Tax Assessment Act 1992 s 5. It may include any person who causes or permits his or her name to be attached to or endorsed upon goods in a manner or form that leads reasonably to the inference that the person is the manufacturer of the goods: for example (SA) Manufacturers Warranties Act 1975 s 3.

Product liability A person or entity that transforms or assembles raw materials or component parts into a product which becomes the subject of trade. A manufacturer is under a duty of care in negligence to avoid acts or omissions, in relation to the manufacture, design, or formulation, and the provision of product information, that it can reasonably foresee will cause personal injury or damage to property: *Donoghue v Stevenson* [1932] AC 562. A manufacturer can be a defendant to a strict product liability claim: (CTH) Trade Practices Act 1974 ss 74A(1), 75AA. See also **Manufactured**.

Manufacturing defect See **Defect in manufacture**.

Mareva injunction An interlocutory court order restraining a party from removing from the jurisdiction of the court, or otherwise dealing with, assets which are the subject of the injunction: *Mareva Compania Naviera SA v International Bulkcarriers SA (The Mareva)* [1975] 2 Lloyd's Rep 509; [1980] 1 All ER 213n. The court's jurisdiction is based on the need to prevent judgments from being rendered ineffective by removal or dissipation of the assets: *Jackson v Sterling Industries Ltd* (1987) 162 CLR 612; 71 ALR 457. See also **Injunction; Interlocutory injunction**.

Margin An amount allowed beyond what is strictly necessary.

Corporations In futures trading and share purchasing, a deposit that must be placed with the broker: *Option*

Investments (Aust) Pty Ltd v Martin [1981] VR 138; (1980) 5 ACLR 124. When a trader initiates a futures position, an initial deposit must be made known as the 'initial margin'. A call for additional funds is known as a 'variation margin'. A margin requirement can be as low as five per cent in the futures market, in contrast with 30-50 per cent required for shares. See also **Futures industry; Share.**

Margin account In corporations law, a brokerage account which allows a client to buy listed securities with money borrowed from the broker. See also **Broker; Securities.**

Margin analysis A tool of analysis found in all branches of economic theory concerned with the relationships between marginal changes in related economic variables. Marginal changes are very small increments or decrements in the total quantity of a variable. See also **Economic theories of law; Economics.**

Margin call 1. In corporations law, the payment required to meet the unrealised loss resulting from an adverse movement in the price of a futures or option contract from the original contracted price. The liability of the buyer of an option is limited to the option premium, while the sellers of options and buyers and sellers of futures contracts have unlimited risk. **2.** A communication by a broker to a trader or other client requesting additional funds to cover an adverse price movement on a futures position, or in respect of a parcel of shares. The value of the investment on the market must always equal the total borrowings. See also **Futures contract; Marked to market; Option.**

Margin of safety A calculation of the difference between the amount of sales or level of production that has been budgeted for and the break-even point. See also **Break-even analysis.**

Margin trading A financing arrangement by which money is lent on the security of investments such as shares. Funds may be lent up to an agreed value of the investments. If the market value of the investment falls below the amount of the loan, the borrower is required to make a payment to the lender so that the value of the investment is not less than the loan. Margin trading is a form of gearing or borrowing to buy assets. See also **Gearing; Margin call; Market value.**

Marginal cost The cost of producing one additional unit of product or service: *Clear Communications Ltd v Telecom Corp of New Zealand* (1992) 27 IPR 481. Also known as 'incremental cost'. See also **Capital; Historical cost; Marginal product; Market.**

Marginal cost pricing A pricing strategy where the price of a good or service is set on the basis of the additional total cost incurred in producing the additional unit of output, rather than on the average cost. At times, the marginal cost may exceed greatly the average cost, particularly when the least efficient units are operating at full capacity or there is a need to add to the asset base or change the scale of operations. On other occasions, the marginal cost may be very low, as the most efficient units are used well within existing capacity. See also **Margin trading; Marginal cost.**

Marginal firm A firm which is the last to enter, or the first to leave, a particular line of production of goods or services. It is not necessarily the least efficient firm. See also **Marginal cost pricing; Marginal producer; Marginal product.**

Marginal notes Notes printed at the side of each section or clause of a Bill. They are not part of the Bill, but are inserted to explain the contents of the particular section.

Marginal producer A producer or manufacturer who would be induced to produce a certain commodity at the prevailing level of profit, but would withdraw from that line of production if profits fell slightly. See also **Marginal cost pricing; Marginal firm; Marginal product.**

Marginal product In economics, the addition to total output from using one extra unit of an input, the quantities of all other inputs remaining the same. For a time the marginal product may increase, exceeding the average product. Beyond a certain point, however, diminishing marginal returns will occur as each extra unit of input becomes progressively less effective. See also **Factors of production; Historical cost; Marginal cost.**

Marginal return on investment In economics, the change in the return on investment ratio (ROI), reflected in increases in profits, brought about by the sale of one additional unit of output. See also **Average return on investment; Marginal cost; Marginal product.**

Marginal revenue In economics, the change in total revenue resulting from varying the output sold by one unit. It equals the total revenue from N unit minus the total revenue from N-1 units. See also **Marginal cost; Marginal product; Marginal return on investment.**

Marginal tax rate In a progressive income tax system, the rate applied to the last dollar of assessable income See also **Income taxation; Progressive tax; Tax rate.**

Marginal utility In economics, the increase or decrease in the total utility of consumption of a good or service resulting from increasing or decreasing the quantity of the good or service consumed by one unit. The law of diminishing marginal utility suggests that the marginal utility of a commodity to anyone, other things remaining equal, will diminish after some point with every increase in the supply of it. See also **Marginal cost; Marginal product; Marginal revenue.**

•**Marine insurance** A contract by which the insurer undertakes to indemnify the insured in the manner and to the extent specified by the policy, against the losses incident to marine adventure: (CTH) Marine Insurance Act 1909 s 7. Contracts of marine insurance are based on the utmost good faith: s 23. See also **Assignment; Indemnity; Indorsement; Uberrimae fidei.**

Marine pollution The direct or indirect human introduction of substances or energy into the marine environment, including estuaries, which results or is likely to result in such deleterious effects as harm to living resources and marine life, hazards to human health, hindrance to marine activities (including fishing and other legitimate uses of the sea water) and reduction of amenities: United Nations Convention on the Law of the Sea 1982 art 1 para 4.

Maritime claim A claim arising out of, and in the course of, an act or contract pertaining to commerce and navigation on navigable waters. A maritime claim may arise from inquiry into the performance of functions of a passenger or merchant vessel while on navigable waters.

Maritime flag A flag hoisted on a ship identifying the ship as a commercial or military vessel, and identifying the country where the ship is registered. A ship must follow the terms and conditions set by its flag state. Landlocked states were formerly deprived of the right to a maritime flag. Now all states, regardless of their geographical disadvantages, are entitled to sail ships under their own maritime flag on the high seas: Geneva Convention on the High Seas 1958 arts 4, 5. See also **Law of the flag**.

•**Maritime jurisdiction** In international law, the jurisdiction pertaining to navigable waters and activities occurring on them. Maritime jurisdiction includes a coastal state's legislative, executive, and judicial competence over the sea, or over activities on or under it in accordance with the law of the sea. For example, a coastal state enjoys absolute jurisdiction over its internal waters by virtue of territorial sovereignty: United Nations Convention on the Law of the Sea 1982 art 2. In the contiguous zone, its jurisdiction is limited to preventing and punishing infringement of its customs, fiscal, immigration or sanitary laws: art 54. See also **Maritime law**.

Maritime law The body of law dealing with marine commerce, navigation, shipping, sailors, transportation of passengers and property by sea, and other general marine affairs. Maritime law governs civil marine torts, injuries, illegal possession and dispossession, withholding of possession, and domestic seizures of vessels. Relevant statutes are (CTH) Navigation Act 1912, (CTH) Historic Shipwrecks Act 1976, (CTH) Crimes at Sea Act 1979, (CTH) Shipping Registration Act 1981, (CTH) Admiralty Act 1988, (CTH) Limitation of Liability for Marine Claims Act 1989, (CTH) Carriage of Goods by Sea Act 1991, and (CTH) Seafarer's Rehabilitation and Compensation Act 1992. See also **Admiralty jurisdiction; Admiralty law; Affreightment; Average; Maritime claim**.

Maritime lien A proprietary interest in a ship or other maritime thing, conferred on a creditor by law as security for a debt or claim. A maritime lien is distinct from a cause of action or demand for personal judgment against the owner of the vessel. A proceeding on a maritime lien may be brought as an action in rem against the ship or property: (CTH) Admiralty Act 1988 s 15(1). See also **Cargo; Carrier's lien; Freight; Hypothecation; Lien; Maritime claim; Master**.

Marked to market 1. Valuation at market rates of securities purchased for trading purposes and off-balance sheet transactions such as foreign exchange and interest rate contracts. Gains and losses resulting from price changes are reflected in income immediately. **2.** The daily adjustment of a trader's account on a commodity exchange to reflect profits and losses on open contracts, based on closing market prices at the end of each day. **3.** A system of variation margining by which an option or futures position is compared against the market price at the close of each business day. All margins, both debits and credits, are posted daily to the clearing members' current account. Thus, profits and losses are brought to account on a daily basis. All options are marked to market. See also **Foreign exchange contract; Futures contract; Margin call; Off-balance-sheet borrowing; Option; Option position**.

•**Market** A situation, location or system of communication which provides an opportunity to sell or buy in an orderly way resources, goods, services, stocks and shares, currencies and contracts: *Arnotts Ltd v Trade Practices Commission* (1990) 24 FCR 313; 97 ALR 555. See also **Cash market; Market efficiency; Market overt**.

Intellectual property In passing off, the area of commercial activity within which a business operates. The plaintiff must establish the distinctiveness of his or her product or business in the market comprising prospective customers of the plaintiff or ultimate consumers of the plaintiff's goods or services: *ConAgra Inc v McCain Foods (Aust) Pty Ltd* (1992) 106 ALR 465. See also **Distinctiveness; Market reputation**.

•**Market** An area of close competition in which substitutable goods and services are traded; an area of close competition in particular goods and/or services and their substitutes: *Queensland Wire Industries Pty Ltd v Broken Hill Proprietary Co Ltd* (1989) 167 CLR 177 at 195; 83 ALR 577. A market may be a field of actual or potential rivalry between firms: *Re Queensland Co-Op Milling Association Ltd* (1976) 8 ALR 481 at 517; 25 FLR 169. A market for goods or services means a market in Australia and includes a market for those goods or services or other goods or services that are substitutable for, or otherwise competitive with, the first-mentioned goods or services: (CTH) Trade Practices Act 1974 s 4E. See also **Competition; Contestable market; Functional market; Geographic market; Market power; Market share; Market structure; Misuse of market power; Product market; Submarket; Substitutability**.

Market associate member In futures trading, a member of the Sydney Futures Exchange (SFE) permitted to deal on its own behalf but not on behalf of clients. Market associate members cannot deal on the floor of the SFE, and all trades are concluded through a floor member. See also **Associate member; Full associate member; Sydney Futures Exchange**.

Market capitalisation The amount that would have to be paid to acquire all of a company's issued shares at their current market price. The market capitalisation of a company is determined by multiplying the number of issued shares by the market value of each share. See also **Capital; Paid-up share capital; Share**.

Market capitalisation of shares In corporations law, the product of the multiplication of the number of a company's shares on issue by the current market price. An increase in market capitalisation may be due to either a higher price for the stock or more shares being issued by the particular company at a similar price. A bonus issue does not increase capitalisation. All things being equal, a bonus issue of shares in a company does has the effect of reducing the share price, neutralising the increase in issued shares. In the case of a rights issue in which shareholders pay for the new shares, the market capitalisation will rise. See also **Bonus share issue; Rights issue; Share**.

Market clearing A situation in which the forces of supply and demand are so in balance that all the goods and services are sold. It is a highly theoretical situation found in perfect competition. In practice, imbalances and mismatches are commonplace, particularly in the labour market. See also **Market efficiency; Market failure; Perfect competition**.

Market Court In Victoria, a court dealing with unfair conduct on the part of traders against consumers.

Market economy An economy in which many crucial economic decisions and choices are made by numerous private individuals, companies, statutory bodies, and government departments catering for the most part to competitive markets. By contrast, in a command economy, central government planning agencies make virtually all the crucial decisions. A market economy is controlled and influenced usually indirectly through legislation and monetary and fiscal policies. See also **Economic theories of law; Functions of economic system**.

Market efficiency 1. The degree to which a market economy meets the needs of society and contributes to the quality of life, encourages efficient production, and responds over time to changing requirements and tastes. **2.** In the shorter term, a measure of the extent to which the market clears, the quantity of goods and services supplied balancing those demanded. A measure of matching supply and demand. See also **Market clearing; Perfect competition**.

Market failure 1. A situation in which the market economy does not satisfy the Pareto criterion that it is possible to make someone better off without making anyone worse off. This may be a consequence of a monopoly or oligopoly situation or generally the result of imperfect competition. **2.** A situation in which the market responding only to effective demand fails to meet the needs of the poorer sections of the community. See also **Imperfect competition; Monopoly; Oligopoly**.

•**Market maker 1.** In corporations law, a broker who is prepared to quote a price at which he or she will buy or sell in all active months, and to offer any person with whom he or she has traded the opportunity to close out or off-set their position before the market maker retires as a market maker. **2.** A broker or specialist who assists in the maintenance of a fair and orderly market on a stock exchange. See also **Australian Stock Exchange Ltd; Broker; Close out**.

Market manipulation In corporations law, conduct involving entering into or carrying out two or more transactions in securities of a body corporate for the purpose of influencing the price of the securities in order to induce other persons to buy, sell or subscribe for securities of the body corporate or a related body corporate. Stock market manipulation transactions are prohibited by Corporations Law s 997(1). See also **Body corporate; False trading; Securities**.

Market order 1. An instruction to a stockbroker to buy or sell shares at the best offer price or the best bid price prevailing at the time the instruction is given. **2.** An order to buy or sell futures contracts for immediate execution at the best available price. See also **Broker; Stop-loss order**.

Market overt 1. In statute law, an open market where it is provided by statute that the buyer acquires a good title to the goods provided the buyer buys them in good faith and without notice of any defect or want of title on the part of the seller: (SA) Sale of Goods Act 1895 s 22; (WA) Sale of Goods Act 1895 s 22. In New South Wales, markets overt are deemed not to exist: (NSW) Sale of Goods Act 1895 s 4(2). **2.** A public place open to anyone and established by law, custom or the sanction of a public authority for use as a place of buying and selling: *In the Marriage of Lees; Lee v Bayes* (1856) 18 CB 599; 139 ER 1504. The trader must be selling rather than buying: *Ardath Tobacco Co Ltd v Ocker* (1930) 47 TLR 177. The goods sold must be those usually sold at that place, and the sale must occur at the customary place and time: *Hargreave v Spink* [1892] 1 QB 25. See also **Goods; Market; Trader**.

Market performance The performance of a firm or industry in a market measured against specified criteria which may include: the efficient employment of scarce factors of production to yield the greatest possible net real income; the full employment of the available factors of production; growth in enlarging and improving the flow of goods and services; and equity in the distribution of income. See also **Profit making undertaking or scheme; Profit maximisation; Profit rule**.

•**Market power** The ability of a firm to raise prices above the supply cost without rivals taking away customers in due course: *Queensland Wire Industries Pty Ltd v Broken Hill Proprietary Co Ltd* (1989) 167 CLR 177; 83 ALR 577. A body's market power may be measured by the extent to which its operation in a market is constrained by the behaviour of its competitors or potential competitors, and by its suppliers or acquirers. See also **Barrier to entry; Competition; Lerner index; Market share; Market structure; Misuse of market power; Price elasticity of demand; Substitutability**.

Market reputation The extent to which the business of a trader is known by current and prospective customers.

Intellectual property The extent to which the business of a trader is known by current and prospective customers. In passing off, the plaintiff must establish the existence of goodwill or reputation in the market in the sense that the name or mark that distinguishes the plaintiff's goods or business, the matter being a question of fact: *Cadbury Schweppes Pty Ltd v Pub Squash Co Pty Ltd* (1980) 32 ALR 387; 55 ALJR 333. See also **Distinctiveness; Market; Passing off**.

Trade and commerce In trade practices, with reference to misleading or deceptive conduct under (CTH) Trade Practices Act 1974 s 52, the public reputation of a particular trader. Market reputation is examined in order to establish the effect of the conduct on the relevant section of the public: *Taco Co of Australia Inc v Taco Bell Pty Ltd* (1982) 42 ALR 177; 2 TPR 48. See also **Market; Misleading or deceptive conduct**.

Market research Activities, questionnaires or surveys conducted for the purpose of obtaining the opinion of members of the general public of the quality, marketability, popularity, appearance, name, supply or any other such characteristics of goods or products to be sold in a commercial consumer market. It is a process by which the proprietors or manufacturers of a particular consumer item may ascertain its general appeal and profitability in a given market. See also **Market efficiency; Perfect competition**.

Market rigging See **False trading**.

Market risk In banking, the potential change in investment earnings as a result of movements in interest rates, asset prices, foreign exchange rates and the level of volatility in any or all of these areas. See also **Investment banking; Investment environment**.

Market share The percentage of the market held. Firms competing in a market may increase market share by reducing price either directly or indirectly through bonuses and discounts, offering an improvement in quality in the good or service, promoting product differentiation or by offering discounts to retailers to promote the product. Much of Japan's post-war economic performance was based on capturing market share. Japanese companies concentrated on maximising sales even at a loss; profits and returns took second place to the pursuit of market share. See also **Market reputation; Market share liability**.

Market share liability Product liability of a manufacturer calculated on the basis of that manufacturer's percentage of the market for that product at a particular date or within a particular time period: for example *Enright v Eli Lilly & Co* 533 NYS 2d 224, 77 NY 2d 577, 155 AD 2d 64, 553 NYS 2d 494 (1990); *Sindell v Abbott Laboratories* 26 Cal 3d 588, 607 P 2d 924, 163 Cal Rptr 132 (1980). Market share liability is one possible basis for the imposition of liability where a plaintiff's loss or damage arising out of use or consumption of a defective or unsafe product, such as the drug diethylstilbestrol (DES), cannot be traced or attributed to any particular manufacturer. See also **Defective product; Market share; Product liability**.

Market structure The economically significant features of a market that influence the behaviour of firms in the industry supplying that market. The main elements of market structure are concentration and concentration ratio, product differentiation, barriers to the entry of new firms, the growth rate of market demand, the price elasticity of market demand, and the ratio of fixed to variable costs. See also **Concentration; Concentration ratio**.

•**Market value** The best price reasonably obtainable for a property in the general market: *Brisbane Water County Council v Cmr of Stamp Duties* [1979] 1 NSWR 320 at 324; *Belton v London County Council* [1893] 62 LJQB 222. The market is determined by an ordinary purchaser irrespective of the circumstances of any particular purchaser (*Orchard v Simpson* (1857) 2 CBNS 299 at 305; 140 ER 431), or of any particular state of repair or value to the vendor: *Yates Property Corp Pty Ltd (in liq) v Darling Harbour Authority* (1991) 24 NSWLR 156; 73 LGRA 47; *Darbishire v Warran* [1963] 3 All ER 310 at 314. See also **Market power; Marketing; Marketing factors**.

•**Marketable parcel** The minimum number of shares necessary for a normal stock exchange transaction. See also **Australian Stock Exchange Ltd; Market value; Odd lot**.

•**Marketable securities** Debentures, stocks, shares or bonds of any government or any local government authority or of any body corporate, association or society, and includes any right or option in respect of shares in any body corporate and any prescribed interest: Corporations Law s 9. See also **Debenture; Securities; Share**.

Marketable title 1. Title that a court would compel a purchaser to accept as sufficient when asked by the vendor to decree specific performance: *Pyrke v Waddingham* (1852) 10 Hare 1; 68 ER 813 at 816. A good and marketable title is shown to a court if the facts and circumstances are so compelling to the court that it concludes beyond reasonable doubt that the purchaser will not be at risk of a successful assertion of the relevant encumbrance: *MEPC Ltd v Christian-Edwards* [1981] AC 205 at 220; *Lake Forest Inc v Bon Marche Homes Inc* 410 So 2d 362 (1982). Also known as 'good title' or 'good and marketable title'. See also **Encumbrance; Good root of title; Indefeasibility of title; Specific performance**.

Market-if-touched order A market order executed at or above a specified price when selling, or at or below a specified price when buying. The order is 'placed' above the existing market if a sell, and below the market if a buy. See also **Market; Market value**.

•**Marketing** The acts of buying, selling, financing, collecting, quality control, cleaning, grading, packing, treating, processing, carrying, storing, warehousing, handling, distributing (whether wholesale or retail), delivering and promoting: (VIC) Barley Marketing Act 1993 s 3. See also **Advertising; Market; Marketing plan**.

Marketing factors Those processes which are related to the sale of a product and not those forming an integral part of the manufacture or production of goods: *Geraldton Building Co Pty Ltd v Christmas Island Resort Pty Ltd* (1992) 11 WAR 40; *Dampier Salt (Operations) Pty Ltd v Collector of Customs* (1995) 133 ALR 502. See also **Market efficiency; Production**.

Marketing plan A plan by the Spectrum Management Agency for the issue of licences to operate radio communication devices. Each licence issued pursuant to the plan authorises the operation of devices exclusively at specified frequencies within the spectrum. A spectrum plan is one of the two kinds of plan which the Agency must prepare on receipt of a notice from the Minister which designates a specified part of the spectrum to be allocated by issuing spectrum licences, the other being a conversion plan. The spectrum licences to which the plan applies are of two types: those which do not replace apparatus licences; and those issued as a result of the failure of licensees to utilise licences offered to them: (CTH) Radiocommunications Act 1992 s 39.

Marking A word, brand or other information, attached to, on the face of, imprinted on, or borne by, goods: *Banger v Drift Fruit Juices Pty Ltd* [1974] VR 677.

Markup In relation to draft documentation, a document which has been marked to show deletions and insertions as against an earlier draft. See also **Draft contract**.

Marrakesh Agreement establishing the World Trade Organisation 1994 *Abbr* – Marrakesh Agreement 1994. A multilateral agreement that aims to increase the participation of developing countries in international trade, reduce tariffs and other barriers to trade, and eliminate discriminatory treatment in international trade relations: Marrakesh Agreement establishing the World Trade Organisation 1994. See also **General Agreement on Tariffs and Trade 1947; General Agreement on Tariffs and Trade 1994; World Trade Organisation**.

Marshalling 1. The equitable doctrine that permits the holder of a security over one fund to stand in the shoes of another secured creditor to satisfy the debt out of a different fund. **2.** The right of a surety to have access to the principal's property to make good what the surety has paid: *Heyman v Dubois* (1871) LR 13 Eq 158. **3.** The rule that where a mortgagor sells part of a property to several purchasers, the mortgagee should look first to the land retained by the mortgagor, and then to the land sold, in inverse order to the date of sale: *Harbert's Case* (1854) 3 Co Rep 116; 76 ER 647. **4.** An equitable doctrine applied in the administration of deceased estates by which those estate assets remaining after the payment of debts are adjusted or marshalled prior to distribution to ensure the distribution among the beneficiaries entitled accords with the order established under the will, statute or at law: *Re Matthews' Will Trusts* [1961] 3 All ER 869. See also **Administration; Distribution; Equity; Secured creditor; Security**.

Martin review An inquiry conducted in 1983-4 to review the Australian financial system and the findings of the Campbell Committee. The four member committee was chaired by Mr V E Martin, the executive chairman of Mutual Life and Citizens Assurance Co Ltd. It issued its report in February 1984 refining the Campbell report and endorsing continued deregulation of the financial system and the entry of new competitors into the banking sector, including foreign banks. See also **Australian banking system; Bank inquiry; Campbell inquiry**.

•**Master** A person in a position of authority or control.

Employment A term formerly used to describe a person who employs another person, the 'servant'. 'Employer' is now used instead of 'master'. See also **Contract of employment; Employer; Servant**.

Maritime law A person in command of a ship, appointed by the owner under a contract of service. The master is responsible for the navigation and management of a ship while at sea. See also **Cargo; Dangerous goods; Hypothecation; Maritime lien; Owner; Service agreement**.

Master and servant Historical term for employer and employee. An employer-employee relationship exists when an employee is employed under a contract of service. See also **Contract for services; Contract of employment; Contract of service; Independent contractor**.

Matched order A form of market manipulation involving a person placing contemporaneous buy and sell orders for substantially the same number of securities at substantially the same price. A matched order gives the deceptive appearance of a genuine transaction, or market activity, in particular securities at a particular price. A matched order may contravene Corporations Law ss 995-998. See also **False trading; Market manipulation**.

Matching principle An accounting process involving the allocation of all expenses incurred in a specified accounting period against all revenues earned in the same period. The matching principle is applied to determine the net periodic income in the most accurate manner. If revenues and expenses for an accounting period are not matched then a distorted profit and loss result will occur for a particular period. For income tax purposes, implicit recognition of the matching principle has been accepted as a basis for determining the timing of allowable deductions, particularly in relation to discounts on commercial bills: *Coles Myer Finance Ltd v FCT* (1993) 112 ALR 322; 25 ATR 95. See also **Accounting method; Accounting period; Allowable deduction; Discount**.

•**Material** Important, essential or relevant. In contract law, a misrepresentation is material if it is an inducement to enter into a contract: *Gould v Vaggelas* (1984) 157 CLR 215; 62 ALR 527. See also **Condition; Material alteration; Misrepresentation; Term**.

•**Material alteration 1.** A substantial or significant alteration to a document made by one party without the consent of the other. To be material, the alteration should affect the contractual obligations of the parties to it: *Armor Coatings (Marketing) Pty Ltd v General Credits (Finance) Pty Ltd* (1978) 17 SASR 270. See also **Acceptor; Apparent alteration; Bill of exchange; Discharge; General acceptance; Indorser**.

•**Material fact** A relevant fact. A statement of claim must contain the material facts on which the claim is based in order to show that there is a reasonable cause of action: *Do Carmo v Ford Excavations Pty Ltd* (1984) 154 CLR 234; 52 ALR 231; *H 1976 Nominees Pty Ltd v Galli and Apex Quarries Ltd* (1979) 30 ALR 181; 40 FLR 242. See also **Cause of action; Extrinsic evidence; Limitation period; Statement of claim**.

•**Material form** In copyright law, any form of storage, whether visible or not, from which a work or an adaptation of a work may be reproduced: (CTH) Copyright Act 1968 s 10(1). Copyright may subsist in a work from the time it is 'made': s 32. A work is 'made' when it is first reduced to writing or to some other material form: s 22(1). See also **Copyright; Literary work; Work**.

Material omission A non-disclosure or failure to do a thing which, if disclosed or done, would have had some influence or effect on the mind of the party or parties involved.

Corporations In relation to the information required to

be given in a Part A statement by an offeror in a takeover scheme under Corporations Law s 750, a non-disclosure which might reasonably affect, or tend to affect, the shareholder's decision as to how to act: *Re Rossfield Group Operations Pty Ltd* [1981] Qd R 372. See also **Material; Non-disclosure.**

Mortgages and securities In relation to a bill of sale, failing to state that part of the consideration is an antecedent debt: *Re Harris; Jolly v Maynard* (1930) 2 ABC 133. See also **Material; Non-disclosure.**

Material personal interest The personal interest of a director in a matter being considered by a meeting of the board. When a director of a public company has such a material personal interest in a matter that is being considered at a meeting of the board, or of directors, of the company, the director must not vote on the matter and must not be present while the matter (or a proposed resolution of that kind) is being considered at the meeting: Corporations Law s 232A, Sch 1 Table A art 71.

Materiality 1. Generally, importance; relevance; the extent to which a fact affects the essential issue. 2. An accounting disclosure requirement necessitating the presentation of certain items in situations where failure to disclose or misstatement could distort the information being presented in the financial statements. See also **Company rate of tax; Financial statement; Tax records; Tax return.**

Matrix The surrounding context. The matrix of a clause of a contract is the contract itself as well as the circumstances surrounding the contract and any relevant communications between the parties to the contract. Evidence of the factual matrix of a clause is admissible to assist interpretation in cases of genuine ambiguity, but not where the clause has a plain meaning: *Codelfa Constructions Pty Ltd v State Rail Authority of New South Wales* (1982) 149 CLR 337; 41 ALR 367. See also **Ambiguity; Extrinsic evidence; Factual matrix; Legal matrix; Seal.**

•**Matter** Substance of the claim before the court: *Flakt Australia Ltd v Wilkins & Davies Construction Co Ltd* [1979] 2 NSWLR 243; (1979) 25 ALR 605. See also **Cause of action; Issue.**

Maturity date The predetermined date on which a borrower repays a lender, the date on which a debt or borrowing is due to be repaid or the capital refunded, and the date or time on which a note, bill, bond, debenture or loan is due to be repaid.

Bills of exchange and other negotiable instruments The last date upon which a bill, other than a bill payable on demand, is payable: (CTH) Bills of Exchange Act 1909 s 19(1). The date for payment must be certain, being payable at a fixed future time, a fixed period after the date of the bill, a fixed period after sight (presentation for acceptance) or a fixed period after the occurrence of a specified event which is certain to happen (though the time of happening may be uncertain): ss 8, 15, 16. If a bill is payable at a fixed period after date, after sight, or after the happening of a specified event, the time of payment is determined by excluding the day from which the time is to begin to run and by including the day of payment: s 19(2). Additionally, in respect of a bill payable at a fixed period after sight, the time begins to run from the date of the acceptance if the bill is accepted, and from the date of noting or protest if the bill is noted or protested for non-acceptance, or for non-delivery: s 19(2). If a party pays on a bill before the maturity date, the party is treated as having bought the bill: *Morley v Culverwell* (1840) 7 M & W 174; 151 ER 727. See also **Bill of exchange; Bill payable at sight; Demand bill.**

Corporations 1. In an options market the date on which an option expires, also called the expiry date. 2. The date on which foreign exchange is to be delivered or received under contract. 3. In respect of a futures contract the date or period within which a contract will be satisfied by delivery, unless sold.

Insurance The date on which an insurance policy becomes payable with bonuses.

Maximum acceptance condition In the context of a takeover scheme, any condition which has the effect of limiting the maximum number of shares which the offeror is bound to accept. Such conditions are prohibited: Corporations Law s 642(1). See also **Condition; Minimum acceptance condition; Takeover scheme.**

Mea culpa /meɪa kʊlpa/ *Lat* – through my own fault. The phrase is from the Confession at the beginning of the Mass; now used to admit responsibility for some blunder.

Measure of damages Assessment of the amount necessary to compensate a plaintiff for the loss suffered as a result of the defendant's wrong. In contract, the measure of damages is the sum that will place the injured party in the same position as if the contract had been performed: *Robinson v Harman* (1848) 1 Ex 850; 154 ER 363; *Commonwealth v Amann Aviation Pty Ltd* (1991) 174 CLR 64; 104 ALR 1. Also known as 'assessment of damages' or 'quantum of damages'. See also **Assessment of damages; Breach of contract; Contributory negligence; Damages; Damages for loss of bargain; General damages; Heads of damage; Loss of a chance; Mitigation; Nominal damages; Special damages; Remoteness.**

Measure of recovery The basis for calculating the amount of a defendant's liability. The measure of recovery depends on the nature of the liability, for example, the fulfilment of contractual or detrimentally relied-upon expectations, compensation for loss, or restitution of unjust enrichment. Restitutionary recovery can be measured in two ways: by the benefit provided by the plaintiff or the profit earned by the defendant; and by the value received by the defendant or the value surviving: *Pavey & Matthews Pty Ltd v Paul* (1987) 162 CLR 221; 69 ALR 577. See also **Account of profits; Restitution damages.**

Measurement cargo A type of cargo where one cubic metre of its volume is less than one tonne in weight. Freight payable on measurement cargo is calculated on the basis of its cubic volume. See also **Cargo; Freight.**

•**Mediation** A method of dispute resolution which includes undertaking any activity for the purpose of promoting the discussion and settlement of disputes, bringing together the parties to any dispute for that purpose, and the follow-up of any matter being the subject of such discussion or settlement: for example (NSW) Community Justice Centres Act 1983 s 4. Generally the rules of evidence do not apply to mediation sessions: for example (NSW) Community Justice Centres Act 1983 s 11. See also **Alternative dispute resolution; Best alternative to negotiated agreement; Commercial dispute resolution; Mediator**.

Mediation-arbitration *Abbr* – Med-arb A combined mediation and arbitration dispute resolution process where a facilitator who is independent of disputants facilitates negotiation by assisting them to isolate issues in dispute and develop options for resolution: (CTH) Industrial Relations Court Rules O 72. The facilitator may recommend options for the resolution of the dispute or may impose a decision upon the parties. The role of the facilitator will usually be determined by agreement. See also **Arbitration; Mediation**.

•**Mediator** A person who mediates between parties to a dispute, to assist them to isolate issues in dispute and to explore options for settlement of the dispute. A mediator is usually an impartial third party. See also **Accredited mediator; Alternative dispute resolution; Mediation; Mediation-arbitration**.

Medicare levy A levy imposed by reference to the taxable income of a taxpayer to finance the national medical insurance scheme for Australian residents: (CTH) Income Tax Assessment Act 1936 s 251S. See also **Taxable income**.

•**Meeting** An assembly or gathering.

Corporations A coming together of persons to decide a particular issue or to discuss some issue in which they have a common interest, usually by voting. A specified number of persons as stated in the articles of association of a company or in the relevant legislation must be present to constitute a valid meeting. Under the Corporations Law, there are general meetings of shareholders and meetings of directors. See also **Adjournment; Annual general meeting; Board of directors meeting; Creditors meeting; General meeting; Minutes; Notice; Poll; Quorum; Resolution; Shareholder; Statutory meeting**.

Trade and commerce In relation to a notice given under (CTH) Trade Practices Act s 155, an arranged coming together of relevant persons held with some formality and purpose and where attendance is compulsory: *Melbourne Home of Ford Pty Ltd v Trade Practice Commission* (1979) 27 ALR 275.

•**Member** 1. In general, a registered shareholder in a corporation. 2. A person who has subscribed to a corporation's memorandum. A person is not a member until the person's name is entered on the register of members. 3. One of the persons constituting a partnership, association or guild. See also **Association; Corporation; General meeting; Member corporation; Partnership; Shareholder**.

Member corporation A shareholder which is a body corporate. For the purposes of the Corporations Law, a 'member organisation' means a member of a securities or futures exchange that carries on business otherwise than by way of a partnership (which is a 'member firm'): Corporations Law s 9. See also **Body corporate; Corporation; Member; Shareholder**.

Member of the inner bar See **Queen's Counsel**.

Members' authorisation Authorisation by shareholders at a general meeting permitting directors to engage in conduct which would otherwise be in breach of their fiduciary duty and the statutory provisions, subject to proper disclosure of the directors' interest. The company's articles may place limits on members' authorisation. The disclosure required must be of both the nature and extent of the conflicting interest or duty or the profit-making opportunity and should include information which the 'average commercial man in the street' would think the members should have: *Buttonwood Nominees Pty Ltd v Sundowner Minerals NL* (1986) 10 ACLR 360 at 362. *Abbr*

Member's personal action The right of action of a member of a company against the company arising from a breach by the company of the member's personal legal rights. The wrong giving rise to the action is a wrong done to the member personally and not to the company as a whole: for example *Grant v John Grant & Sons Pty Ltd* (1950) 82 CLR 1. A member's personal action may arise pursuant to an express contract between the member and other members or between the member and the company; pursuant to a personal cause of action conferred by statute or general law; to enforce the memorandum and articles of association as a statutory contract under Corporations Law s 180, such as to enforce the right to be protected against dilution of voting rights by the improper action of the company (*Residues Treatment & Trading Co Ltd v Southern Resources Ltd (No 4)* (1988) 14 ACLR 569; 6 ACLC 1160); or to restrain acts in disregard of restrictions in the company's constitution: for example *Ashburton Oil NL v Alpha Minerals NL* (1971) 123 CLR 614. See also **Directors' duties; Foss v Harbottle, rule in**.

Members' ratification The ratification by shareholders at a general meeting of a completed act of a director in breach of his or her duty: *Regal (Hastings) Ltd v Gulliver* [1967] 2 AC 134 at 150, 157 ; *Furs Ltd v Tomkies* (1936) 54 CLR 583 at 592. Notwithstanding that ratification by shareholders may extinguish a breach of fiduciary duty (*Winthrop Investments Ltd v Winns Ltd* [1975] 2 NSWLR 666; (1975) 1 ACLR 219 at 222), it cannot nullify the contravention of Corporations Law s 232(5), (6). See also **Directors' duties; General meeting; Members' authorisation**.

•**Members' voluntary winding up** The winding up of a company effected by special resolution of the members in general meeting: Corporations Law Pt 5.5. See also **Creditors voluntary winding up; Voluntary winding up**.

•**Memorandum** /memərændəm/ *Lat* – a note intended to refresh the memory; a record made for future reference; an informal letter from one official to another. Pl – *Memoranda* See also **Memorandum of association**.

•**Memorandum of association** The founding document of a company, often referred to as the company's memorandum. The memorandum must state the name of the company and, unless the company is an unlimited company, the amount of share capital which is proposed and the division of the share capital into shares of a fixed amount, and state that the liability of members is limited: Corporations Law s 117. The memorandum must also state the names, addresses and occupations of the subscribers to the memorandum and state that those subscribers wish to form a company pursuant to the memorandum and agree to take the number of shares in the company set out in the memorandum. Until 1984 a memorandum was required to state the objects for which the company was established. In the past, the principle of ultra vires limited a company's powers by reference to the objects set out in the memorandum. However, now that the doctrine has been abolished in Australia, it is optional for a company to include a statement of objects in its memorandum: s 117(2). See also **Articles of association**; **Company constitution**; **Objects clause**; **Ultra vires**.

•**Mercantile agent** In the factors legislation, an agent having, in the customary course of business as an agent, authority to sell goods, consign goods for the purpose of sale, buy goods, or raise money on the security of goods: (NSW) Factors (Mercantile Agents) Act 1923 s 3. An agent may be a mercantile agent even if acting in that capacity only in an isolated transaction for a single principal, or although the agent's general occupation is that of an independent dealer in the commodity entrusted to him or her, provided the agent acts in the capacity of a mercantile agent and is not a mere servant or shopkeeper: *Lowther v Harris* [1927] 1 KB 393. Formerly known as 'factor'. See also **Agency**; **Agent**; **Broker**; **Factor**; **On consignment**; **Ordinary course of business**; **Sale of goods**.

Mercantile law The law pertaining to commercial transactions. Also known as 'commercial law'. See also **Broker**; **Law merchant**; **Mercantile agent**.

Merchandise mark A description, attached or applied to goods, indicating as required such matters as the nature of the goods, the country in which they were made or produced, their suitability for any particular purpose, or the mode by which they were prepared: (VIC) Consumer Affairs Act 1972 Pt III Div I. See also **Trade description**; **Trade mark**.

•**Merchandising rights** Entertainment industry term for the exploitation of a name, persona, or image by linking an otherwise unassociated product or service to that name, persona, or image. Merchandising rights are not 'rights', as such. Rather, the granting of such 'rights' is an implied undertaking by the person associated with the name, persona or image that they will not use areas of law such as passing off, trade practices, or consumer protection to take action against the person granted the 'rights'. See also **Passing off**; **Trade mark**; **Trade practices legislation**.

Merchant bank A financial institution active mainly in the wholesale money market, described by the Committee of Inquiry into the Australian Financial System as 'operating principally in the area of wholesale, particularly short-term, finance servicing the financial needs of the larger corporations and public authorities'. A merchant bank also trades in government and public authority securities and other corporate debt instruments. It provides financial advice and services such as underwriting and placement for semi-government securities, arranging local and foreign currency loans, and participating in the foreign currency hedge market and futures market. See also **Investment bank**.

Merchant seaman A person employed as, and who performs the tasks of, a seaman on a private vessel. A merchant seaman does not include a naval rating employed as part of the defence force on a naval vessel, or a seaman employed on a public ship.

Merchant ship A merchant ship acquires the nationality of the flag state and is subject to its jurisdiction even when on the high seas: art 91, art 92(1).

Merchant shipping Shipping engaged in the carriage of cargo and passengers for reward. Merchant shipping is to be distinguished from naval and public shipping. Merchant shipping registered in a given country forms the merchant navy of that country.

•**Merchantable quality** In consumer protection law and sale of goods law, the condition of being fit for the purpose or purposes for which goods of that kind are commonly bought, having regard to their price, any description applied to them by the seller and any other relevant circumstance: (CTH) Trade Practices Act 1974 s 66(2); (NSW) Sale of Goods Act 1923 s 64(3); *Rasell v Cavalier Marketing* (Aust) Pty Ltd [1991] 2 Qd R 323; (1990) 96 ALR 375. It is an implied condition of contracts for the sale and supply of goods that the goods are of merchantable quality. See also **Deemed manufacturer**; **Fitness for purpose**; **Implied term**; **Importer**; **Manufacturer**; **Product liability**; **Sale of goods**.

Mere confusion In consumer protection law, uncertainty, misunderstanding or puzzlement. The courts have drawn a distinction between conduct which merely confuses a consumer, and conduct which misleads or deceives or is likely to mislead or deceive a consumer and therefore contravenes the consumer protection legislation: *Parkdale Custom Built Furniture Pty Ltd v Puxu Pty Ltd* (1982) 149 CLR 191; 42 ALR 1. See also **Consumer claim**; **Likely to mislead or deceive**; **Misleading or deceptive conduct**.

Mere equity A right in equity that is ancillary to an interest in land and is binding on a third party who has notice of its existence or is a volunteer. A mere equity usually takes the form of the right to have a transaction set aside for fraud or mistake: for example *Latec Investments Ltd v Hotel Terrigal Pty Ltd (In liq)* (1965) 113 CLR 265. See also **Equitable interest**; **Equity**.

Mere representation A statement or assertion that is not intended by the maker to be legally binding. The distinction between a statement that is intended to be contractual and a mere representation depends on the intention of the parties and their conduct at the time the statement was made: *Jeffrey Kenneth Gates v City Mutual Life Assurance Society Ltd* (1986) 160 CLR 1; 63 ALR 600. See also **Misleading or deceptive conduct**; **Misrepresentation**; **Pre-contractual statement**; **Puffery**; **Term**.

Merger A combination of two or more entities, rights or estates.

Bills of exchange and other negotiable instruments A method of discharging a bill of exchange by which the acceptor of the bill is or becomes its holder at or after its maturity, in the acceptor's own right: (CTH) Bills of Exchange Act 1909 s 66. The reason for discharge is that the rights and liabilities on the bill have 'merged' in one person; there is no point in the holder suing himself or herself as acceptor. See also **Acceptor; Cancellation; Rule against circuity of action; Discharge of negotiable instrument; Holder; Renunciation.**

Corporations A combination of two or more firms or corporations, usually such that one is absorbed into the structure of the other(s) and loses its separate identity. See also **Acquisition; Competition; Competition law; Conglomerate merger; Cooney Committee Report; Griffiths Committee Report; Holding company; Horizontal merger; Market; Merger guidelines; Pre-merger consultation; Pre-merger notification; Restrictive trade practices; Share; Substantially lessening competition; Takeover.**

Deeds and other instruments The process by which a lower security is absorbed into a security of a higher nature taken for the same debt. An example is the merger of a simple contract debt into a specialty for the same debt where the obligations created by the deed are considered to be of higher value than those that existed under the simple contract: *Price v Moulton* (1851) 10 CB 561; 138 ER 222. The operation of the doctrine depends on the intention of the parties, gathered from their documents. Ordinarily, where an obligor owing an existing simple contract debt gives security for its payment by a covenant under seal and a charge on property, the simple contract debt is merged into the specialty unless there is an express provision to the contrary: *Barclays Bank Ltd v Beck* [1952] 2 QB 47; [1952] 1 All ER 549. An obligation merged in this manner is said to be discharged by operation of law. Also known as 'merger by higher remedy' or 'merger in judgment' See also **Debt; Deed; Intention; Obligor; Security; Simple contract; Specialty.**

Equity The joining of one right to another such that the lesser right ceases to have an independent existence. The doctrine of merger arises in equity in three contexts: merger of estates, merger of charges, and merger in conveyance.

Merger clause A term stating that the contract represents the entire understanding of the parties with reference to the subject matter of the contract and that pre-contractual misrepresentations are superseded. See also **Acceptance; Exclusion clause; Misleading or deceptive conduct.**

Merger guidelines Guidelines issued by the regulatory bodies responsible for competition law; in Australia, the Trade Practices Commission (Draft) Guidelines issued in November 1992. In Australia, merger guidelines are not law; they indicate the Commission's view about breaches of (CTH) Trade Practices Act 1974 ss 50, 50A. In the United States, the United States Department of Justice and the Federal Trade Commission jointly issued Horizontal Merger Guidelines in 1992. See also **Federal Trade Commission; Horizontal merger; Merger; Trade Practices Commission.**

Mergers, Monopolies and Acquisitions: Adequacy of Existing Legislative Controls See **Cooney Committee Report.**

Mergers, Takeovers and Monopolies: Profiting from Competition See **Griffiths Committee Report.**

•**Merit** In relation to employment, a person's qualifications for a position, a person's aptitude for discharging the duties of the position, and the person's integrity, intelligence and good conduct: for example (NSW) Police Service Act 1990 s 3. It means the extent to which the person has abilities, aptitudes, skills, qualifications, knowledge, experience, characteristics and personal qualities relevant to carrying out the duties in question. It may include the manner in which the person carried out the functions of any position or occupation previously held or engaged in, and the extent of the person's potential for development: (SA) Public Sector Management Act 1995 s 3. See also **Discrimination; Merit principle.**

Merit goods and services Goods and services which the government considers need to be supplied and consumed in greater quantities than they otherwise would be. Examples are hospital services, educational facilities, social services, employment services and the arts. Such goods and services may be provided free or at greatly reduced prices by means of subsidies, government grants, departmental spending, or through national insurance schemes.

•**Merit principle** In relation to employment, the principle that the appointment and promotion of persons must be on the basis of individual capacity and merit, and that all employees are to receive fair and equitable treatment: for example (TAS) Tasmanian State Service Act 1984 s 4(1). The principle requires that all persons who are eligible for appointment must have a reasonable opportunity to apply for employment, and that the appointment is to be made on the basis of an assessment of the relative suitability of applicants. Appointments, promotions and so on must be made without patronage or favouritism, and without unlawful discrimination: (CTH) Public Service Act 1922 s 33(1). See also **Discrimination; Merit.**

Methods of manufacturing or processing requirements The statutory prescriptions upon the means by which a product is created. In the interests of consumer safety, the relevant Minister, either by notice published in the Commonwealth Gazette or by regulations made pursuant to the (CTH) Trade Practices Act 1974, may prescribe a consumer product safety standard consisting of any requirements as to methods of manufacture or processing: s 65C(2)(a). It is possible to patent a method of manufacture: *Uprising Dragon Ltd v Benedict Trading & Shipping Pty Ltd* (1987) 16 FCR 93. It is necessary to show a method of manufacture in order to have an invention: *Re Application of Sandoz Ltd* (1989) 14 IPR 541. See also **Patent; Invention; Manufacture.**

Metway Bank A savings bank originating in the Metropolitan Permanent Building Society formed in Brisbane in 1959 to encourage saving for home ownership. The Metropolitan became the largest financial institution based in Queensland. In 1988, it became a bank under the name of Metway. In 1990, the bank purchased Prudential Finance Limited from the Prudential Assurance Company assisting diversification of the bank's activities. See also **Building Society.**

Mezzanine debt A borrowing by a company after it has obtained its start up finance. Such loans are normally provided by specialist financiers and is aimed at consolidating a company's trading position before it is floated on a stock exchange. See also **Capital**; **Debt capital**.

MICR cheque See **Magnetic ink character recognition cheque**.

Micro-economic reform Government concerning company tax, superannuation, tariffs and quotas, industry restructuring, corporatisation, privatisation, freeing of markets, education and training, industrial relations, prices and incomes, personal taxation, statutory authorities, public administration, shipping and the waterfront, rail transport, airlines and power generation. The aim of micro-economic reform is to improve the efficiency of various sectors of the economy. See also **Micro-economics**; **Macro-economic policy**; **Macro-economics**.

Micro-economics A branch of economics concerned with the analysis of the behaviour of individual consumers and producers, particularly the optimising behaviour of individual units such as households and firms. See also **Economics**; **Micro-economics**; **Monopoly**; **Oligopoly**.

Microprocessor A computer chip that has etched on its surface thousands of microscopic programmable electronic components which include arithmetic and logic units, plus the control unit. These form the central processing unit.

MIGA See **Multilateral Investment Guarantee Agency**.

Million instructions per second *Abbr* – MIPS In computer processing, a measure of the speed of a computer's central processing unit.

Mineral exploration Exploring land or the sea-bed, whether physically or by aerial survey, to ascertain the presence of minerals in commercially exploitable quantities by conducting geological, geophysical and geochemical surveys, drilling, taking samples for the purpose of chemical or other analysis, or extracting minerals from land, other than for commercial production. Exploration activities may be regulated under mining legislation: for example (NSW) Mining Act 1992 s 13. For taxation purposes it may not include the movement of vehicles or ships between points at which exploration is carried out, although such an operation might be 'connected with' exploration: *Re BHP Petroleum Pty Ltd and Collector of Customs* (1986) 6 AAR 245. See also **Off-shore installation**.

Mingling of trust property The mixing of the property of two or more trusts in one fund. Mingling of trust property is a breach of trust and gives rise to a claim against the trustee. Where the trustee is unable to satisfy a judgment for any loss arising, the beneficiaries must resort to the rules of tracing. See also **Tracing**; **Trust**.

Minimum acceptance condition In the context of a takeover scheme, a condition requiring the offer to be accepted in respect of a specified minimum number of shares before it becomes unconditional, or subject to other conditions: Corporations Law s 642(4). A minimum acceptance condition will be void if the offer does not specify the number or percentage of shares in respect of which it must be accepted or if it purports to vary a specified number or percentage: Corporations Law s 662(3)-(6); *George Hudson Holdings Ltd v Rudder* (1973) 128 CLR 387. The percentage specified is usually 90 per cent so as to allow possible recourse to the compulsory acquisition procedures. Offers made with a minimum acceptance condition are not permissible in an on-market takeover announcement pursuant to Corporations Law Pt 6.4 since the offeror is obliged to take all shares tendered. See also **Condition**; **Maximum acceptance condition**; **Takeover scheme**.

•**Minimum credit charge** In consumer credit legislation, and in relation to a credit sale contract or loan contract, the amount that, under the contract, is the minimum amount payable to the credit provider by the debtor as a credit charge: for example (NSW) Credit Act 1984 (repealed) s 5(1) (now replaced by Uniform Consumer Credit Code). See also **Credit charge**; **Credit sale contract**.

Minimum quantity condition A condition in which the supplier specifies that it will only provide goods and services in a specific minimum quantity or for a specific minimum price. A minimum quantity condition is a variation on a requirements contract, and may constitute exclusive dealing under (CTH) Trade Practices Act 1974 s 47. See also **Exclusive dealing**; **Requirements contract**.

•**Minimum subscription** The amount to be raised by the issue of shares calculated by directors as the minimum needed to get a new company started. A public company cannot be formed unless five or more persons have subscribed their names to its memorandum: Corporations Law s 114(2). To form a proprietary company there must be one or more subscribers to its memorandum: Corporations Law s 114(1). In respect of shares offered to the public for subscription or for which the public are invited to subscribe, the minimum subscription is the amount stated in the prospectus relating to the offer or invitation as being the minimum amount that must, in the directors' opinion, be raised by the issue of shares: Corporations Law s 9. See also **Prospectus**.

•**Minimum wage** A wage rate set in an industrial award or agreement, or by legislation, below which no employee to whom the award, agreement or statute applies may be paid. See also **Industrial award**; **Enterprise agreement**; **Wage**.

•**Mining purpose** In relation to carrying on a particular activity, the aim of prospecting for, obtaining by any mode or method, selling or disposing of ores, metals or minerals, or other products of mining, including the carrying on of any business or activity necessary for, or incidental to, any of the foregoing aims: Corporations Law s 9. It does not include quarrying operations with the sole aim of obtaining stone for building, roadmaking or similar reasons: s 9. See also **No liability company**.

•**Minister** Person who holds office in the parliamentary executive with the responsibility of administering one or more departments in government, for example the Prime Minister or Premier, the Treasurer, the Minister for External Affairs or the Minister for Transport.

Ministerial Council for Companies and Securities The body with ultimate responsibility for the operation of the cooperative scheme of companies and securities regulation and the legislation which implemented the scheme. The formal agreement in 1978 which led to the formation of the co-operative scheme provided for the formation of the Council. The Council consisted of the Commonwealth and State ministers (typically the Attorneys-General) responsible for company law and securities regulation. With the introduction of the Corporations Law in 1991, the Council continued but with a slightly different role, as outlined in the Alice Springs agreement. See also **Cooperative companies and securities legislation**.

•**Minor interest** 1. An interest of minor importance or amount. 2. A relatively small share in the ownership of property.

Minority interest The equity of those shareholders who do not possess controlling interests in a subsidiary company. For example if company A owns 65 per cent of company B, the other shareholders in company B have a minority interest. It also refers to the shares held in subsidiary companies and reported in consolidated financial statements which are not owned by the chief entity or by the consolidated group of companies. The protection of minority interests forms part of the responsibilities of a board of directors. See also **Directors' duties**; **Financial statement**; **Minority shareholder**; **Subsidiary**.

Minority shareholder In corporations law, a shareholder who has voting rights that do not provide control of the general meetings of the company. See also **Corporate crime**; **Minority interest**.

•**Minute book** 1. A book kept by the clerk of a court for entering memoranda of its proceedings. 2. A record of all actions authorised at corporate board of directors or stockholders meetings as required by corporations law: for example Corporations Law s 152. See also **Minutes**.

•**Minutes** Written record required of all proceedings at general meetings and meetings of the board of directors: Corporations Law s 258. Minutes should record resolutions and the results of any voting. Minutes entered in the book are prima facie evidence of the proceedings at the meeting: s 282(2). See also **Annual general meeting**; **General meeting**; **Minute book**; **Registered office**.

Misappropriation The wrongful application or stealing, by an agent, of a principal's money or property: *Gladstone City Council v Local Government Superannuation Board* [1980] Qd R 48; 44 LGRA 175. It is an offence for an agent to misappropriate the money or goods of the principal: for example (NSW) Crimes Act 1900 ss 165-166. See also **Duty to keep accounts**; **Fidelity**; **Misconduct**.

Misappropriation rule The rule that company directors may not apply company property for their own personal benefit or for the benefit of any other person without the authority of the company. It is supplemented by Corporations Law Pt 3.2A, which prohibits a public company or its child entity from giving a financial benefit to a related party (which includes directors) of the public company. See also **Directors' duties**; **Fiduciary**; **Financial benefits to related parties**.

Miscarriage of justice Where an accused person has lost a chance which was fairly open of being acquitted by reason of a failure to apply the rules of evidence, procedure, and the relevant law: *Mraz v R* (1955) 93 CLR 493 at 514; [1955] ALR 929. Where there has been a substantial miscarriage of justice a conviction will be set aside on appeal: for example (NSW) Criminal Appeal Act 1912 s 6(1); (QLD) Criminal Code s 668E(1); (VIC) Crimes Act 1958 s 568. See also **Proviso**.

•**Misconduct** Wrongful, improper, or unlawful conduct, motivated by premeditated or intentional purpose or by obstinate indifference to the consequences of one's acts. See also **Fidelity**; **Gross negligence**; **Misappropriation**.

Arbitration In relation to an arbitrator or umpire in an arbitration, corruption, fraud, partiality, bias, or a breach of the rules of natural justice: Commercial Arbitration Acts s 4(1). It includes any breach of, or departure from, the contractual, statutory or common law requirements for arbitration: *Stannard v Sperway Constructions Pty Ltd* [1990] VR 673. It is misconduct for an arbitrator to fail to comply with the terms of an arbitration agreement, or to make an award which ought not to be enforced on the grounds of public policy: *London Export Corp Pty Ltd v Jubilee Coffee Roasting Co Ltd* [1958] 1 All ER 494. A court may remove an arbitrator on the grounds of misconduct: Commercial Arbitration Acts s 44. See also **Alternative dispute resolution**; **Arbitration**; **Arbitrator**; **Commercial Arbitration legislation**.

•**Misdemeanour** In New South Wales, an offence for which the punishment that may be imposed is no greater than imprisonment: (NSW) Crimes Act 1900 s 10. The traditional distinction between a misdemeanour and felony is now largely meaningless: *R v McHardie & Danielson* [1983] 2 NSWLR 733; 10 A Crim 51. It has been abolished in all other jurisdictions. See also **Offence**.

Misdescription An error in the description of the subject matter of a legal transaction contained in a legal instrument. If due to a misdescription of a person or thing in a testamentary disposition, putting the terms of the will as described by the testator into effect would not correspond with evidence of the surrounding circumstances at the time of making the will, the court may admit extrinsic evidence under the *falsa demonstratio* rule or the cy-prés doctrine for charitable gifts in order to ascertain the testator's intention and rectify the misdescription: *Pratt v Matthew* (1826) 22 Beav 238; *Re Price* [1932] 2 Ch 54. If the meaning of the description cannot be resolved by application of such rules of construction or if there is a patent ambiguity on the face of the will that cannot be resolved by extrinsic evidence, the misdescribed gift will be void for uncertainty. See also **Interpretation**.

•**Misfeasance** The doing of something badly or improperly.

Contract Performing one's obligations under a contract badly or improperly. Misfeasance in the performance of contractual obligations is relevant in determining whether there has been substantial performance of the contract: *Bolton v Mahadeva* [1972] 2 All ER 1322; [1972] 1 WLR 1009. See also **Nonfeasance; Substantial performance**.

• **Misleading or deceptive conduct** In consumer protection law, conduct which tends to lead a consumer into error as to its meaning: *Parkdale Custom Built Furniture Pty Ltd v Puxu Pty Ltd* (1982) 149 CLR 191; (1982) 42 ALR 1. (CTH) Trade Practices Act 1974 s 52 prohibits a corporation from engaging in trade or commerce, in conduct that is misleading or deceptive or likely to mislead or deceive. The most appropriate meaning for 'deceive' is to cause to believe what is false, to mislead as to a matter of fact, to lead into error, to impose upon, delude, or take in; the most appropriate meaning for 'mislead' is to lead astray in action or conduct, to lead into error, or to cause to err: *Weitmann v Katies Ltd* (1977) 29 FLR 336; (1977) ATPR ¶40-641; *Puxu Pty Ltd v Parkdale Custom Built Furniture Pty Ltd* (1979) 27 ALR 387; (1979) ATPR ¶40-135. See also **False representation; Liable to mislead; Likely to mislead or deceive; Mere confusion; Misrepresentation; Trade or commerce**.

Corporations A type of conduct prohibited in relation to dealing in securities: (CTH) Trade Practices Act 1974 s 52; Corporations Law s 995. See also **Prospectus; Takeover**.

Misleading price indication A statement of price that leads one who sees it into error. A corporation must not, in trade or commerce, make a false or misleading representation or indication as to price: (CTH) Trade Practices Act 1974 s 53(e). The indication need not be false to the knowledge of the person giving it, even if that person is a servant of the company of insufficient significance in the company for his or her knowledge, according to the ordinary principles of the common law, to be deemed to be the knowledge of the company. Similarly a person, not being a corporation, must not make a misleading price indication: for example (NSW) Fair Trading Act 1987 s 44(g). The indication need not be false to the knowledge of the person giving it. See also **Pricing claim**.

Misleading statement An assertion that, because of the context in which it is made or because of what it contains or omits, is capable of being misunderstood by a person or persons to whom it is made. In New South Wales, it is an offence to obtain property by a statement that is misleading in a material particular: (NSW) Crimes Act 1900 s 178BB. See also **Misleading or deceptive conduct; Misrepresentation**.

Misleading statement In the context of misleading statements as proscribed by (CTH) Trade Practices Act 1974 s 53A(1)(b), includes not only words but also pictures shown as part of any statement made: *Given v Pryor* (1979) 24 ALR 442. See also **Misrepresentation; Representation**.

Mismatch A situation arising in corporations law when assets and liabilities do not match, either in amount or in the timing of the maturity of purchases and sales. A mismatch arises when the average remaining maturity of assets in a portfolio differs from that of liabilities. Interest rate exposure results, since a change in interest rates affects asset yields and liability costs at different times. Also referred to as 'gap positions' or 'interest rate sensitivity gaps'. See also **Business finance; Liquidity risk**.

• **Misrepresentation** A representation which does not accord with the true facts (past or present). Misrepresentation will render a contract voidable. The remedy for misrepresentation is rescission of the contract. Misrepresentations may be fraudulent, negligent, or innocent.

Contract A false material statement of fact intended to induce another person to enter a contract, and relied on by that person to their detriment. Generally, a representation will not be considered a misrepresentation if it was a false statement of law (*Inn Leisure v D F McCloy* (1991) 100 ALR 447), opinion (*Bisset v Wilkinson* [1927] AC 177), or intention, unless in fact the party had no such intention: *Edgington v Fitzmaurice* (1885) 29 Ch D 459. If, prior to contract, the representee finds the representation not wholly true, the onus falls on the representor to show that the representation did not induce the contract: *Holmes v Jones* (1907) 4 CLR 1692; 14 ALR 89. This can be proved by showing that the representee relied on his or her own inquiries or observations: *Redgrave v Hurd* (1881) 20 Ch D 1. See also **Deceit; Fraudulent misrepresentation; Innocent misrepresentation; Misleading or deceptive conduct; Misstatement; Negligent misrepresentation; Representation; Rescission**.

• **Mission 1.** The business or purpose with which an agent is charged. **2.** The outpost of an agent.

Misstatement An inaccurate or misleading statement for which one cannot be held liable. For example, a government authority cannot be held liable for a misstatement of council policy: *San Sebastian Pty Ltd v Minister administering the Environmental Planning and Assessment Act 1979* (1986) 162 CLR 340; 68 ALR 161. See also **Innocent misrepresentation; Misrepresentation; Negligent misrepresentation**.

• **Mistake** Either a belief in the existence of a thing which does not exist, or ignorance of a relevant thing, or both: *David Securities Pty Ltd v Commonwealth Bank of Australia* (1992) 175 CLR 353; 109 ALR 57.

Contract The situation where a party's error or misapprehension will affect the validity or enforceability of a contract. The usual cause of a contractual mistake is reliance on a misrepresentation made by one party to another during contractual negotiations. Depending on its nature, a mistake may render a contract void ab initio, give a right to rescind a contract ab initio, or give other remedies such as relief against forfeiture. See also **Common law and equity approach to mistake; Contract; Misrepresentation; Mutual mistake; Relief against forfeiture; Rescission; Unilateral mistake; Vitiating factor; Void ab initio**.

Mistake as to identity A unilateral misapprehension as to the identity of the other party to a contract. Where the mistake is a result of a fraudulent misrepresentation, the mistaken party will be able to rescind the contract. However, a mistake as to identity will not generally render the contract void: *Lewis v Averay* [1972] 1 QB 198. See also **Mistake; Mistake of fact**.

Mistake of fact A belief regarding a particular fact which is not correct.

Restitution A mistaken belief in the existence of facts which causes a person to pay money to or confer a benefit on another. See also **Mistake; Mistake of law**.

Mistake of law Ignorance of or an inadvertence to the existence or operation of statutory provisions: *J & S Holdings v NRMA Insurance Ltd* (1982) 41 ALR 539. See also **Honest and reasonable mistake; Mistake; Mistake of fact**.

Restitution A mistaken understanding of the law as opposed to a mistake of fact; for example, a belief that an ultra vires term of a contract or statute is valid: *David Securities Pty Ltd v Commonwealth Bank of Australia* (1992) 175 CLR 353 at 376; 109 ALR 57. See also **Mistake; Ultra vires**.

Misunderstood disclosure Situation where the insurer does not understand the insured's disclosure, most commonly occurring when the insured has a poor grasp of English. Misunderstood disclosure is deemed effective where the insurer's employee or agent has failed to take reasonable care to ensure that no misunderstanding has occurred: *Dome v State Insurance General Manager* (1987) 5 ANZ Ins Cas ¶60-835. See also **Fitness for purpose; Product liability**.

Misuse defence The defence to a product liability claim that may be available if it can be shown that the plaintiff used the product in a wholly unreasonable manner: for example *Heil v Hedges* [1951] 1 TLR 512; *Decca Radar Ltd v Caserite Ltd* [1961] 2 Lloyd's Rep 301; *Poole v Crittal Metal Windows (NZ) Ltd* [1964] NZLR 522.

Misuse of market power Impermissible use of market power to harm the competition process. A corporation with a substantial degree of market power is prohibited from taking advantage of that power for certain purposes, such as eliminating or substantially damaging a competitor, preventing entry into a market, or determining or preventing competitive conduct in a market: (CTH) Trade Practices Act 1974 s 46. See also **Competition; Competition law; Griffiths Committee Report; Market; Market power; Predatory conduct; Restrictive trade practices; Substantial; Take advantage of**.

Mitigation The reduction of the severity or the effect of a wrongful act; the submission of certain facts by an offender in the hope of receiving a more lenient sentence than the court would otherwise impose.

Mitsubishi Australia A foreign bank established in Australia in 1986 and a wholly-owned subsidiary of The Mitsubishi Bank of Japan which is among the top commercial banks in the world. Mitsubishi Australia offers corporate and personal banking facilities, trade financing, project and asset-based financing, cash management, foreign exchange facilities, underwriting and investment management.

Mixed account In accounting, an account where the balance may be split between a balance sheet item and a profit and loss item. For example, stock, when it is used during an accounting period is treated as an expense. But stock on hand at the end of a period is an asset recorded on the balance sheet. See also **Accounting period; Balance sheet; Profit and loss statement; Trading stock**.

Mixed question of fact and law A question involving a combination of issues of fact and issues of law. For example, whether an accused person was insane at the time of committing the criminal act is ordinarily a question of mixed fact and law. It is for the jury to decide the factual question of whether the accused was insane at the time of committing the criminal act. However, the judge must decide the legal question of whether there is sufficient evidence establishing the existence of a disease of the mind in order to warrant the admission of such evidence: for example *Re Bromage* [1991] 1 Qd R 1 at 6; (1990) 48 A Crim R 79.

Mobilisation of foreign currency The transfer to the Reserve Bank of Australia (RBA) of certain amounts in sterling related to a bank's excess receipts of foreign currency: (CTH) Banking Act 1959 Pt II Div 4. The RBA pays an amount in Australian currency as agreed upon between the RBA and the transferring bank: s 34. See also **Excess receipts of foreign currency; Reserve Bank of Australia; Sterling**.

Modem A telecommunications device used to transmit or receive data in digital format across analogue or digital lines. Also known as 'modulator/demodulator'.

Monetary policy The use of changes in the money supply, controls on interest rates, the maintenance of reserve asset ratios, and guidance to the commercial banks on the amount and direction of lending to serve national economic objectives. The Reserve Bank of Australia implements monetary policy through its operations in the money market. Despite limitations and reservations, monetary policy has been actively employed by the Commonwealth government over recent years. See also **Interest rate; Money market; Reserve Bank of Australia**.

•**Money** Any generally accepted medium of exchange for goods, services, and the payment of debts. Examples are coin, banknotes, bills of exchange, promissory notes and claims on bank deposits: for example (NSW) Stamp Duties Act 1920 s 3. Money confers complete liquidity on its holder. It serves as a medium of exchange, a measure of value, a standard for deferred payments, a store of value, and a commodity whose worth depends upon its resale value. See also **Cheque; Currency; Legal tender**.

Banking and finance That which passes freely from hand to hand throughout the community in final discharge of debts and full payment for commodities, being accepted equally without reference to the character or credit of the person who offers it and without the intention of the person who receives it to consume it or apply it to any other use than in turn to tender it to others in discharge of debts or payment for commodities: *Moss v Hancock* [1899] 2 QB 111 at 116. In its strict legal sense it includes money in a deposit account at a bank: *Re Collings* [1933] Ch 920. See also **Credit; Good faith; Money as legal tender**.

Money as legal tender A tender for the payment of money is legal tender if made in note or coin issued by the Reserve Bank. Such notes and coin are intended for circulation as money. It is illegal for any person other than the Reserve Bank to issue any bill or note for the payment of money payable to bearer on demand which is intended for circulation as money: (CTH) Reserve Bank Act 1959 ss 36, 43, 44; (CTH) Currency Act 1965 ss 16, 22. See also **Forgery; Legal tender; Money.**

Money claim Claims where money is directly payable based on a contract as opposed to claims where money is claimed by way of damages: for example (NSW) Supreme Court Rules Pt 15 r 12; claims for money lent or for the price of goods sold. See also **Money counts.**

Money counts Types of common counts or actions formerly in use which used the formula *indebitatus assumpsit solvere* (being indebted, he undertook to pay), where money was claimed based on agreement rather than damages. The five counts were for money lent; money due for an account stated; money due as interest; money paid by the plaintiff to the use of the defendant; and money had and received by the defendant to the use of the plaintiff. See also **Money claim; Money had and received; Restitution; Unjust enrichment.**

Money had and received A cause of action whereby the plaintiff seeks to recover money from the defendant on the ground that the defendant had received the money to the use of the plaintiff to whom in justice and equity it belongs: for example *New South Wales v McCloy Hutcherson Pty Ltd* (1993) 43 FCR 489 at 506-7; 116 ALR 363. See also **Failure of consideration; Quasi-contract; Restitution; Unjust enrichment.**

Money illusion The illusion that changes in money income represent a change in real income. The changes may merely reflect changes in the cost of living and a declining purchasing power of the currency. See also **Cost benefit analysis; Income; Inflation.**

Money in transit insurance See **Cash in transit insurance.**

•**Money laundering** See **Laundering.**

•**Money lender** A person whose business is lending money at interest: (NSW) Money Lenders and Infant Loans Act 1941 s 3(1); *Cody & Willis Pty Ltd v Truman* (1967) 87 WN (NSW) 519. See also **Credit union; Moneylending; Usury.**

Money market A market comprising institutions and arrangements through which the demand for and supply of short-term funds are brought together. These funds are usually short-term financial assets which are close substitutes for money and are known as money market instruments or securities. They can be quickly converted into money. In Australia, the money market is composed of banks, merchant banks, money market dealers, finance companies, building societies, credit unions and other financial institutions. Participants in the market lend money at call, overnight or for short fixed terms. See also **Financial asset; Short-term money market.**

Money market call account A cash-at-call or cash deposit account held with a bank or non-bank institution offering high rates of interest. Deposits may be withdrawn either on a same day basis, or at 24 or 48 hours' notice. These institutions place funds in the short-term money market. Interest rates can fluctuate dramatically from hour to hour and need to be constantly monitored. See also **Interest rate; Money market; Short-term money market.**

Money market corporation A registered company recognised under the (CTH) Financial Corporations Act 1974 which makes short-term loans to authorised dealers in the short-term money market and invests in government, commercial and corporate paper and securities. The bulk of these funds are themselves short-term borrowings, perhaps obtained from other corporations also borrowing on a short-term basis. A money market corporation does not enjoy lender of last resort facilities with the Reserve Bank of Australia although it operates in a similar manner to an authorised dealer. See also **Money market call account; Short-term money market.**

Money market dealer A person who participates in the trading of short term securities or the borrowing or lending of cash for short periods of time (generally less than 12 months). An eligible money market dealer is a body corporate that is declared by the Australian Securities Commission (ASC) to be an authorised dealer in the short term money market: Corporations Law ss 9, 65(1). Money in the fidelity fund of a securities exchange may be deposited with an eligible money market dealer (s 906) as may funds of the Securities and Exchange Guarantee Fund (ss 923, 934). See also **Money market; Money market call account; Money market corporation; National guarantee fund.**

Money market deposit A deposit made with a dealer in the short term money market. In the US a money market deposit account is a high yield liquid savings account which was authorised in 1982 under the (US) Depository Institutions Deregulation Act 1980. See also **Money market dealer; Money market; Short-term money market.**

Money of account A running account of assets, usually liquid assets such as currency, which is kept between the parties with items possessed on both sides until some final event makes a conclusive reckoning. See also **Appropriation; Asset; Bank account; Money of payment.**

Money of payment Liquid assets in the form of currency used in a contract or other dealing to provide valuable consideration for obligations performed under the contract and which may be in a number of specified currencies or other form of asset. The money of payment is the currency in which the contractual obligation will be discharged. If the mode of performance is ambiguous, a presumption exists that the money of payment is also the money of account: *Parsons and Co Ltd v Electricity Trust of South Australia* (1976) 16 SASR 93. See also **Asset; Bank account; Currency; Money of account; Valuable consideration.**

Money order An instrument used to remit money to the named payee, often used by persons who do not have a cheque account relationship with a financial institution, to pay bills or to transfer money to another person or to a company. There are three parties to a money order; the remitter (payer), the payee and the drawee. Drawees are usually financial institutions or post offices: (CTH) Postal and Telecommunications Commissions (Transitional Provisions) Act 1975 s 8. Payees can either cash their money orders or present them to their bank for collection. See also **Cheque; Cheque book**.

Money paid by mistake Payment made to another under a misapprehension. A party who pays money to another by mistake may recover it if its retention is unconscionable: *South Australian Cold Stores Ltd v Electricity Trust of South Australia* (1957) 98 CLR 65 at 75; *Commercial Bank of Australia Ltd v Younis* [1979] 1 NSWLR 444. See also **Mistake; Mistake of fact; Mistake of law**.

Money paid to the defendant's use A personal claim for restitution of an unjust enrichment caused by the plaintiff's payment to a third party which discharges or reduces the defendant's liability to that third party. See also **Money counts; Restitution**.

Money supply The total stock of money in an economy. Several measures of the money stock in Australia are published on a regular basis by the Reserve Bank of Australia (RBA). These are: cash base (or money base), the sum of currency in circulation and the deposits of the banks with the RBA; M1, the cash base plus deposits in cheque accounts at commercial banks; M2, M1 plus other deposits of the private sector at commercial banks; M3, M2 plus the deposits of the public in savings accounts; and broad money, M3 plus borrowings by non-banks including cash management trusts. See also **Cash; Reserve Bank of Australia**.

Moneylender See **Money lender**.

•**Moneylending** The lending of money as a business venture. Legislation regulating moneylending is still current in the Northern Territory and Tasmania but has been repealed in the other jurisdictions: (NT) Moneylenders Act 1903 (repealed) s 3(1); (TAS) Lending of Money Act 1915 s 10(1). Under the uniform credit legislation, if a moneylending transaction falls within the definition of a loan contract, it is governed by the legislation. See also **Uniform credit legislation**.

Monopolistic competition A market structure with elements of both monopoly and perfect competition. In such a market, there are a large number of firms selling close but not completely homogeneous substitutes. See also **Competition law; Market structure; Monopoly; Perfect competition; Substitutability**.

•**Monopoly** In absolute form, a market situation in which a single seller of a good or service deals with a large number of buyers, the seller having complete control over the quantities of goods offered for sale and the price at which the goods are sold. See also **Natural monopoly**.

Monopoly power See **Market power**.

Monopoly profit A profit over and above a competitive return: *Clear Communications Ltd v Telecom Corp of New Zealand* (1992) 27 IPR 481. See also **Profit**.

Monopsony A single buyer in the market or a buyer's monopoly. See also **Market power; Market share; Monopoly**.

Moody's Investors Service A New York based agency which estimates the creditworthiness of borrowers whether they be corporations, institutions or countries. A Moody rating is a scaled evaluation of the risks of default. A top borrower is given an AAA or triple A rating. Until 1986, Australia had this rating. In respect of commercial paper or short-term debt, the ratings are A1-3, B1-3, C1-3 and lesser classifications. Australian companies carry ratings separately of this kind. Moody's was founded in 1903 by John Moody. In 1961 it merged with Dun and Bradstreet while retaining a separate identity. Both companies operate in Australia. See also **Credit rating; Credit risk; Economic indicators**.

Moral hazard In insurance law, the risk of the honesty or moral integrity of the person insured, which can be material to the risk assumed by the insurer: *Locker and Woolf Ltd v Western Australian Insurance Co Ltd* [1936] 1 KB 408. Facts relating to moral hazard, such as previous convictions in respect of motoring offences in the case of motor vehicle insurance, may be material to accepting the risk and calculating the premium: for example *Jester-Barnes v Licenses and General Insurance Co Ltd* (1939) 49 Ll L Rep 231.

Moratorium /mɒrətɔːriʊm/ The act of deferring an activity or an obligation to pay or perform. See also **Debt; Embargo**.

•**Mortgage** A lender's interest in land, secured over the land of the borrower, including a charge on property for the purpose of securing money or money's worth: (NSW) Conveyancing Act 1919 s 7. See also **Equitable mortgage; Equity of redemption; Home finance contract; Legal mortgage**.

Consumer credit An instrument or transaction under which a security interest arises. It may create a security interest in land or goods: (NSW) Credit Act 1984 (repealed) s 5(1) (now replaced by Uniform Consumer Credit Code). See also **Regulated mortgage; Security interest**.

Corporations The lien of a company, usually given by articles over the shares of members for debts due by them to the company, constitutes an equitable charge upon the shares and is a mortgage: *Everitt v Automatic Washing Machine Co* [1892] 3 Ch 506. Any charge on land for securing money or money's worth is a mortgage: (VIC) Sale of Land Act 1962 s 2(1).

Real property The transfer of legal title in old system property by a debtor to a creditor as security for a debt on condition that when the debt is fully repaid the mortgaged interest reverts to the mortgagor: *Santley v Wilde* [1899] 2 Ch 474. The interest of the mortgagor during the term of the mortgage is referred to as the equity of redemption.

Real property In relation to Torrens title land, a mortgage no longer involves the transfer of the fee simple, but instead is a registered charge on the land with statutory rights in favour of the mortgagee to take possession of, sell, and foreclose on the land on default by the mortgagor. There is an equitable mortgage over land where security is given but the interest is not registered.

Mortgage bond A bond similar to bonds or debentures issued by companies, carrying a specified maturity date of up to five years and a fixed rate of interest. The principal is repayable by the borrower on the maturity date. A mortgage bond is issued to assist home buyers. See also **Bond**; **Short-term money market**.

Mortgage expenses Costs incurred in borrowing either to be used in carrying on a business or to generate income: (CTH) Income Tax Assessment Act 1936 s 67. Expenses incurred by a taxpayer in discharging a mortgage where the borrowed money was used to produce assessable income may be claimed in full by the taxpayer. However, if only part of the money was used for business, then a proportion of the discharge expenses may be claimed. See also **Allowable deduction**; **Mortgage**.

Mortgage payable See **Mortgage**.

Mortgage trust A property trust or unit trust in which the trust asset is a mortgage of land and which gains from lending money for the purchase of land or development of property on which it holds the first mortgage. Mortgage trusts have operated in Australia since the 1970s and along with property trusts, form the main form of unit trusts. The return on a mortgage trust is linked to the mortgage interest paid by the borrower, less fees payable to the manager and the trustee and other trust expenses. See also **Investment plan**; **Mortgage**; **Trust**.

•**Mortgage-backed security** A home mortgage that has been pooled and packaged for sale as an interest-bearing instrument or security. Mortgage-backed securities are issued by the United States Federal National Mortgage Association and the United States Federal Home Loan Mortgage Corporation. Like United States Treasury bonds, they are federally guaranteed. They are liquid, being readily disposable on secondary markets, and have offered high yields. See also **Liquid asset**; **Mortgage**; **Securities**.

•**Mortgagee** A person who lends money to another where the loan is secured by taking a mortgage over the borrower's property. The term includes any person deriving title to the mortgage from the original mortgagee: (NSW) Conveyancing Act 1919 s 7. See also **Mortgagee's power of sale**; **Mortgagor**; **Receiver**.

•**Mortgagee in possession** A mortgagee of land who has entered into and taken possession of the land the subject of the mortgage: (NSW) Conveyancing Act 1919 s 7. A mortgagee may enter into possession of old system land at any time, regardless of whether default has taken place, unless there is a provision in the mortgage forbidding the mortgagee so to do. The position is very different in relation to Torrens title land, where the mortgagee may only enter into possession on default by the mortgagor and on following the procedure set out in the Torrens legislation applicable to the State, for example (NSW) Real Property Act 1900 ss 57-60. See also **Equity of redemption**; **Forfeiture**; **Legal mortgage**; **Mortgage**; **Mortgagee**.

Mortgagee's power of sale One of the rights of a mortgagee in dealing with mortgaged land after default by a mortgagor under the terms of the mortgage. See also **Duty of care**; **Equity of redemption**; **Mortgagee**.

•**Mortgagor** A borrower of money who gives a mortgage over his property to secure a mortgage debt in favour of the mortgagee. See also **Equity of redemption**; **Mortgage**; **Mortgagee**.

Motherboard *Abbr* – MB The principal circuit board in a computer. The motherboard contains (or is connected to) the central processing unit and controls vital components such as the computer's memory, hard disk, and other device controllers and cards (such as video or sound cards).

Motion 1. An application made to a court or judge to obtain a rule or order directing some act to be done: (CTH) High Court Rules O 51 r 1; (CTH) Federal Court Rules O 19 r 1. 2. A formal suggestion proposed in a meeting or legislative body that requires a vote. A motion may require a quorum before action can be taken. In parliamentary law, a motion is the formal method by which a member submits a proposed measure or resolve for the consideration and action. See also **Ex parte**; **Interlocutory injunction**; **Meeting**.

Movable property In general, property capable of being moved physically, such as goods. See also **Chattel**; **Incorporeal hereditament**; **Personal property**.

Moving average price method In accounting, an averaging method used in the perpetual inventory method to determine the value of inventory at the end of an accounting period. An average unit price is calculated each time a commodity is purchased by dividing the total unit costs by the number of units purchased. The value of the inventory at any particular time is determined by multiplying the current average unit price by the number of units on hand at that particular time. See also **Accounting period**; **Inventory**.

Moving the goal post Changing the environment so that the requirements for success are altered. In addition to a concern that business players should be presented with a 'level playing field', an apprehension that those in authority are constantly moving the goal posts, that is making it more difficult to know where to score. This view is a reaction to constantly changing rules relating, for example, to taxation, superannuation and trade. See also **Reporting requirements**; **Trade incentives**.

Multi-agents Organisations, formerly regarded as insurance brokers, who decided to act exclusively as agents for a select group of insurers in order to avoid the registration requirements of brokers under the (CTH) Insurance (Agents and Brokers) Act 1984.

Multilateral Development Bank *Abbr* – MDB A bank providing financial assistance across a broad spectrum of countries. Four major MDBs are the World Bank, the Inter-American Development Bank, the Asian Development Bank and the African Development Bank. The World Bank undertakes the greater part of MDB lending. See also **Foreign bank**; **International Bank for Reconstruction and Development**; **International Development Association**; **International Monetary Fund**.

Multilateral Investment Guarantee Agency *Abbr* – MIGA An investment guarantee agency set up under the auspices of the International Bank for Reconstruction and Development on 12 April 1988. MIGA provides long-term guarantees for certain categories of non-commercial risks, and acts as a forum for coordinating policy, improving the investment climate in developing countries, and promoting the fair and equitable treatment of investments. It is administered by the MIGA Board of Directors of the International Bank for Reconstruction and Development, with headquarters in Washington DC. See also **International Bank for Reconstruction and Development**.

Multilateral net settlement position In banking and finance, the sum of the value of all the transfers a participant in a multilateral net settlement system has received during a certain period of time less the value of the transfers made by the participant to all other participants. If the sum is positive, the participant is in a multilateral net credit position; if the sum is negative, the participant is in a multilateral net debit position. See also **Electronic funds transfer; Multilateral netting; Multilateral net settlement system**.

Multilateral net settlement system A settlement system in which each settling participant settles (typically by means of a single payment or receipt) the multilateral net settlement position which results from the transfers made and received by it, for its own account and on behalf of its customers or non-settling participants for which it is acting. See also **Multilateral netting; Multilateral net settlement position**.

Multilateral netting An arrangement among three or more parties to net their obligations. The obligations covered by the arrangement may arise from financial contracts, transfers, or both. The multilateral netting of payment obligations normally takes place in the context of a multilateral net settlement system. See also **Multilateral net settlement position; Multilateral net settlement system**.

Multimedia In computing, the combination and use of the latest technology in video, audio, graphics, and text in a single unit such as a personal computer. Multimedia personal computers incorporate hardware and software devices (such as speakers, colour monitors, and CD-Rom drives), output devices (such as colour printers), and input devices (such as microphones and scanners).

Multinational corporation A business enterprise created and owned by a group of private investors which is engaged in carrying out business and commercial activities in two or more states. A multinational corporation usually owns assets and conducts foreign trade and investment over a number of geographically, politically, and economically diverse countries. Also known as 'trans-national corporation' or 'international corporation'. See also **United Nations Conference on Trade and Development**.

Multiple directorship The state of being a director of more than one company at the same time. It is not a breach of fiduciary duty for a person merely to be a director of each of two competing companies. However, a director may be bound by an express or implied term in a contract of service which will exclude acceptance of another directorship. A director is also constrained by the law with respect to confidential information. See also **Confidential information; Directors' duties**.

Multiple rates of interest More than one rate of interest that applies to any debt or other pecuniary obligation. A credit sale contract or a loan contract will not be valid if it includes a reference to more than one annual percentage rate for the purposes of the contract; or a reference to any other rate to the effect that the credit charge under the contract is, or is to be, determined by the application of that rate to the whole or any part of the amount financed; or a reference to a right of any person to increase and take action which results in the increase of the annual percentage rate: (NSW) Credit Act 1984 (repealed) s 40(1) (now replaced by Uniform Consumer Credit Code). Where there is a reference to more than one annual percentage rate for the purposes of the contract or a reference to any other rate referred to in s 40(1), the annual percentage rate for the purposes of the contract shall be the lowest rate referred to: s 40(2). See also **Annual percentage rate; Credit; Interest rate; Principal**.

Multiple test A test to determine whether a person who contracts to work for another is an employee of the other person, or an independent contractor. The test looks at a variety of factors and indicia, rather than relying on a single factor such as the 'control test' or the 'organisation test'. In applying the test, the courts have regard to the right of control over the worker, and the worker's role in the organisation for which the work is done, but to other factors also, including whether the employer or the worker takes the chance of profit and the risk of loss, who provides the tools and equipment, and the method of payment: *Ready Mixed Concrete (South East) Ltd v Minister of Pensions and National Insurance* [1968] 2 QB 497; 1 All ER 433. Also known as 'mixed test'. See also **Contract of employment; Economic reality test; Employee; Independent contractor**.

Multiplier In economics, a ratio indicating the effect on total employment or income of a specified amount of capital investment or expenditure. Investment or expenditure represents income for the factors of production. After tax is deducted some of that income will be saved and the rest spent. This expenditure will in turn become the income of others along an almost endless chain. If the factors were previously unemployed the benefits are considerable. Through the multiplier, employing one additional person may create the equivalent of work for another. The multiplier is a crucial concept in Keynesian economics. See also **Capital; Investment**.

Multi-skilling A form of workplace training for employees, by which employees are trained to perform a variety of tasks within the enterprise, rather than continually doing a narrow range of tasks. Multi-skilling may be achieved by such things as on-the-job or formal training, job rotations or secondments, task rotation across positions, and the design of multi-functional jobs. The aim is to produce a highly skilled and flexible work force. See also **Broadbanding; Training**.

•**Municipal corporation** A body corporate with public and private characteristics and continuous succession formed for the purpose of administering local affairs as the council of a local government area.

Mutual accounts Accounts containing receipts and payments on both sides of the ledger of transactions, evidencing mutual transactions: *Phillips v Phillips*

(1852) 9 Hare 471; 68 ER 596. Where accounts exist on one side only, the issue is one of set-off. See also **Account; Account stated; Set-off**.

Mutual assent Agreement between two parties on terms and conditions of contract. A contract that is lacking mutuality is void ab initio: *Dietrich v Dare* (1980) 30 ALR 407.

Mutual credits Transactions between persons giving rise to debts owed by one to the other. Mutual credits are able to be set off where one of the parties becomes bankrupt: (CTH) Bankruptcy Act 1966 s 86. To be mutual, each transaction must be entered into in the same capacity and not, for example, in the first case as a trustee and in the second in the person's own right. See also **Bankrupt; Set-off**.

Mutual debts See **Mutual credits**.

Mutual fund A US investment company offering redeemable securities representing an undivided interest in a pool of assets invested in by the fund. Mutual funds are regulated by the US Securities and Exchange Commission (SEC) under the (US) Investment Company Act 1940, while the (US) Securities Act 1933 requires the funds shares to be registered with the SEC. In Australia, similar investments are typically organised through a unit trust structure. Also known as 'unit trust'. See also **Investment company; Unit trust**.

Mutual guarantee See **Cross-stream guarantee**.

Mutual insurance society An association of persons each of whom, in consideration of a payment, underwrites a policy for a stipulated sum. The underwriting is on the grounds that there is neither community of profit nor community of loss between the society's members, and each member is alone liable to the insured in accordance with the terms of their particular contract: *Andrews' and Alexander's case; Re London Marine Insurance Assn* (1869) LR 8 Eq 176; 20 LT 943. See also **Partnership**.

Mutual life assurance company A life assurance company whose profits are only divisible among that company's policy holders: (CTH) Income Tax Assessment Act 1936 s 110(1). See also **Life insurance; Mutuality principle**.

Mutual mistake A situation where both parties to a contract are mistaken, but each party makes a mistake different from the other. See also **Acceptance; Mistake; Offer; Unilateral mistake**.

Mutual promises Promises given in exchange for each other that are to be performed concurrently. See also **Consideration; Executed consideration; Executory consideration; Past consideration; Promise; Promisee; Promisor**.

•**Mutuality** In the context of common law set-off, the requirement for a set-off to arise that the countervailing claims must be between the same parties and in the same right. There is no similar requirement for equitable set-off. See also **Equitable set-off; Set-off**.

•**Mutuality principle** The doctrine that where a number of people associate for a common purpose and contribute to a common fund, any surplus of those contributions that remain after the fund has been applied to that common purpose is a mere return of funds and not income or profit: *Social Credit Savings & Loans Soc Ltd v FCT* (1971) 125 CLR 560. Applications of the mutuality principle include: contributions by shareholders in a company which has been incorporated as a convenient agent to perform the common purpose, so that the contributions received by the company will not be income; or where an association engages in business activities with outsiders in addition to transactions which it has with its members, the receipts from the two sources are severable, with the receipts from the members being mutual and therefore those receipts from mutual dealings are not income: *Sydney Waterboard Employees Credit Union Ltd v FCT* (1973) 129 CLR 446; 2 ALR 35. See also **Business; Business income; Income**.

N

Naamloze vennootschap *Abbr* – NV The Belgian and Dutch equivalent of a public company. See also **Aktiengesellschaft; Plc; Public company.**

NAB Business Confidence Index A business confidence index maintained by the National Australia Bank embracing many sectors of the economy including mining, manufacturing, construction, retail, wholesale, transport, finance and recreation. See also **National Australia Bank.**

NAFTA See **North American Free Trade Agreement.**

Naked bear A trader who engages in the short selling of shares, that is selling without owning the shares, in the belief that market prices will fall before delivery is due. A covered or protected bear is a trader who sells while actually owning the shares. See also **Bear; Share.**

Naked option An option sold by a trader on shares which the trader does not possess. Naked options writing is often called high-stakes gambling. See also **Bear; Naked bear; Option; Share.**

•**Name** A word or a combination of words by which a person, place, or thing, a body or class, or any object of thought, is designated or known. A given name of a person includes a reference to a diminutive form or anglicised form of a given name: (CTH) Financial Transaction Reports Act 1988 s 3(5), 3(6).

Names See **Lloyd's of London.**

National accounts Statistics prepared by the Australian Bureau of Statistics at intervals on the value of income, expenditure and production in Australia, both at current and constant prices. The transactions are summarised in four accounts, namely the domestic production account, the national income and outlay account, the national capital account, and the overseas transactions account. In addition to providing an overview of total economic activity, the national accounts provide information on the relationships between different parts of the economy and on changes in individual components over time. See also **Gross domestic product; Gross fixed capital expenditure; Gross national expenditure; Natural resource accounting.**

National Association of Securities Dealers A body which effectively runs the official United States over-the-counter market and operates the National Association of Securities Dealers Automated Quotation System (NASDAQ). It is a self-regulatory organisation setting standards for the listing of securities and for the dealers who make markets in them, and providing surveillance of trading activities. See also **National Association of Securities Dealers Automated Quotation System; Over-the-counter market; Securities.**

National Association of Securities Dealers Automated Quotation System *Abbr* – NASDAQ An automated quotation system through which the shares of over 4000 companies are traded in the United States over-the-counter-market. It provides the world's largest stock market after the New York and Tokyo stock exchanges. See also **National Association of Securities Dealers; Over-the-counter market; Securities; New York Stock Exchange.**

National Australia Bank One of the 'big four' of the Australian banking system; a bank which traces its origins back to 1834 as the Commercial Banking Company of Sydney and to 1858 as the National Bank of Australasia. In 1981 the Commercial Banking Company of Sydney and the National Bank of Australasia merged to become the National Australia Bank. See also **NAB Business Confidence Index.**

•**National Business Names Register** The register containing records of names registered as business names in the various jurisdictions: Corporations Law s 9; (CTH) Corporations Act 1989 s 70. See also **Register of Business Names.**

National Companies and Securities Commission *Abbr* – NCSC A Commonwealth body which operated between 1979 and 1990 with overall responsibility for the administration of the Companies Act and Codes. It was assisted in each State by a Corporate Affairs Commission. It was superseded by the Australian Securities Commission. See also **Australian Securities Commission; Corporate Affairs Commission.**

National Competition Council *Abbr* – NCC A body established by (CTH) Trade Practices Act 1974 s 29A. The functions of the NCC include carrying out research and providing advice on matters referred to the council by the Minister: (CTH) Trade Practices Act 1974 s 29B. The council's primary role is to make recommendations to the Minister in relation to access declarations under (CTH) Trade Practices Act 1974 Pt IIIA: s 4(1). See also **Competition Policy Reform Act 1995; Essential facility doctrine.**

National Competition Policy The report of the National Competition Policy Review which made recommendations for sweeping structural reform of government and semi-government business. One of the most important elements of the report was the principle of competitive neutrality, requiring all market players to be subject to the same regulatory and other requirements imposed on them when competing in the one market. See also **Competition; Competition law; Competitive neutrality; Cooney Committee Report; Griffiths Committee Report; Market; Swanson Committee Report.**

National Competition Policy and Related Reforms Agreement An agreement made on 11 April 1995 between the Commonwealth, the States and the Territories providing for financial assistance by the Commonwealth to the States and Territories conditional upon the States and Territories implementing competition policy reforms. See also **Competition Policy Reform Act 1995.**

National Crime Authority *Abbr* – NCA A Commonwealth authority established by the (CTH) National Crime Authority Act 1984 to collect, analyse, and disseminate information and intelligence relating to criminal activities to government and law enforcement agencies. The NCA was also established to create Commonwealth, State, and Commonwealth-State task forces to co-ordinate investigations into criminal activities: (CTH) National Crime Authority Act 1984 s 11(1)(c), (d).

National debt The total amount owed by the Commonwealth government, covering all its borrowing including the debts of government-owned enterprises.

National Guarantee Fund *Abbr* – NGF A fund administered by the National Securities Exchanges Guarantee Corporation (NSEGC) guaranteeing the obligations of payment or of provision of settlement documents in respect of trades undertaken by members of the Australian Stock Exchange (ASX): Corporations Law ss 948-954. The NGF was established under the (CTH) Australian Stock Exchange and National Guarantee Fund Act 1987. The fund guarantees the completion of all reportable transactions in quoted securities carried out through members of the Australian Stock Exchange. Clients of suspended or defaulting brokers have a direct claim against the fund in the event of not receiving payment for delivered sales or not receiving scrip for settled purchases. A selling or buying dealer can claim against the fund in respect of a default by the counterpart dealer in a transaction. See also **Australian Stock Exchange Ltd**; **National Securities Exchanges Guarantee Corporation**.

National Listing Committee A committee established by the Australian Stock Exchange (ASX) to perform functions concerning the power of the ASX under ASX Articles of Association art 74(4)(a) to admit corporations or other entities to the Official List on terms and conditions as determined by the board. The Committee has responsibility for all listing matters, including making recommendations to the board about adding or deleting a company from the Listing Rules of the ASX. A determination of the Committee binds the State branches of the ASX, who may comment upon the prospectus or require amendments to the prospectus before being required to submit it to the Committee. See also **Australian Stock Exchange Ltd**; **Australian Stock Exchange listing**; **Australian Stock Exchange Listing Rules**; **Official List**; **Prospectus**; **Public company**.

National Market System A system of trading securities which links all regional stock exchanges onto a national stock exchange, which then lists the prices of those securities simultaneously. Although the term is predominantly American, in relation to the Australian Stock Exchange (ASX) it refers to the linking of all the stock exchanges in the capital cities to the Stock Exchange Automated Trading System (SEATS). Trading can only occur between member organisations of the ASX. See also **Australian Stock Exchange Ltd**; **Securities**; **Stock Exchange Automated Trading System**.

•**National Occupational Health and Safety Commission** *Abbr* – NOHSC A federal commission established by (CTH) National Occupational Health and Safety Commission Act 1985 s 6. Its functions include formulating policies and strategies relating to occupational health and safety matters, declaring national standards and codes of practice, and providing training in knowledge and skills relevant to occupational health and safety matters. Also known as 'Worksafe Australia'. See also **Occupation**; **Occupational Health and Safety**; **Work-related trauma**.

•**National Office of Overseas Skills Recognition** *Abbr* – NOOSR A Commonwealth Government office responsible for assessing foreign qualifications and academic awards and establishing their equivalence to Australian standards and awards. For the purposes of the general points test, a person is awarded points for qualifications on the basis of the NOOSR assessment (where applicable) and not the foreign qualification: (CTH) Migration Regulations 1994 reg 1.03.

•**National scheme law** The uniform corporations legislative scheme resulting from an agreement reached in Alice Springs in June 1990 where each State and the Northern Territory agreed to pass an Act applying the companies, securities and futures law contained in the (CTH) Corporations Act 1989 (after amendment in 1990) in its jurisdiction and to confer powers on the Australian Stock Exchange. The objective of the legislative scheme is the existence of uniform laws between jurisdictions, as far as possible, as if they were a single national Corporations Law: *Australian Securities Commission v Marlborough Gold Mines Ltd* (1993) 177 CLR 485; 112 ALR 627. The Corporations Law applies as law for the Australian Capital Territory: (CTH) Corporations Act 1989 s 5. See also **Australian Securities Commission Law**; **Australian Stock Exchange Ltd**; **Corporations Law**; **Futures law**; **Securities law**.

National Securities Exchanges Guarantee Corporation *Abbr* – NSEGC A body corporate which establishes and administers the National Guarantee Fund for the purpose of dealing with claims in respect of the property of people that was, in the course of or in connection with a security dealer's business of dealing in securities, entrusted to or received by that dealer: (CTH) Securities Industry Act 1980 Pt IX Div 2; Corporations Law s 929. The NSEGC is a company limited by guarantee that is nominated by the ministerial council under (CTH) Securities Industry Act 1980 7 s 122BA. The NSEGC has a number of duties and obligations under the Act, most importantly the power to pay out on claims made by persons against security dealers in the course of or arising out of their business of dealing in securities. See also **National Guarantee Fund**.

National wage case A decision of the Australian Industrial Relations Commission (AIRC) that sets out the principles by which wages are to be fixed or adjusted. It is initiated when the Australian Council of Trade Unions (ACTU) applies to the AIRC to vary the rate of wages prescribed in a number of key federal awards, usually in the metals industry and the public service. See also **Australian Council of Trade Unions**; **Australian Industrial Relations Commission**; **Flow on**; **Parent award**; **Wage fixation**.

National Westminster Australia A subsidiary of the National Westminster Bank Plc with a network of commercial and retail branches in all Australian mainland capitals. It has a wholly-owned investment banking subsidiary, County NatWest Australia Ltd.

Nationalisation The governmental acquisition and control of privately owned foreign or domestic business or commercial installations through legislative and administrative action. Nationalisation generally occurs in a state with a new government seeking to restructure the economy in response to economic nationalism or hostility toward foreign investors. Nationalisation of foreign private investment is permissible in international law, provided it is undertaken in response to public interest in a non-discriminatory manner with appropriate compensation: for example GA Res 1803(XVII) para 4; *Aminoil case (Kuwait v American Independent Oil Co (Aminoil))* 21 ILM 976 (1982); *Amoco International Finance Corp v Iran (US v Iran)* (1987) 15 Iran-US CTR 189. The issue of appropriate compensation for the property is controversial: *Chorzow Factory case (Germany v Poland)*, Merits 1928 PCIJ ser A No 17; *Anglo-Iranian Oil Co case (UK v Iran), Preliminary Objection* 1952 ICJ 93. Also known as 'expropriation'.

Nationality of corporation See **Corporate nationality**.

Nationality of ship The state in which a ship is registered or, if it is not required to be registered, the nationality of its owners or operators: for example (CTH) Shipping Registration Act 1981 s 29(1). When a ship is on the high seas, all persons aboard the ship are within the jurisdiction of the state of its nationality: *R v Anderson* (1868) LR 1 CCR 161. Ships are entitled, and sometimes required to fly, the official flag of their state, which is known as the 'flag-state': *(UK v Iran), Preliminary Objection* 1952 ICJ 9. In marine insurance law, there is no implied warranty as to the nationality of a ship, or that its nationality will not be changed during the risk: (CTH) Marine Insurance Act 1909 s 43. To comply with a warranty of nationality, a ship must be of the nationality specified and must carry the usual documents necessary to prove it. These include the certificate of registry, flag, log book, bill of health, bill of lading and certificate of origin: *Geyer v Aguilar* (1798) 7 Term Rep 681. A ship is only bound to carry those documents prescribed by international usage or by treaty. The national character of a ship must be declared before it clears, and the customs officer must inscribe the name on the clearance. The ship may be detained until such a declaration is made: *The Princess Charlotte* (1863) Brown & Lush 75. The flag flown by a ship when there is no danger, and the nationality of the consulate on whom the master calls when in port, form strong evidence of the national character of a ship: *Arcangelo v Thompson* (1811) 2 Camp 620. (CTH) Navigation Act 1912 s 266; (CTH) Marine Insurance Act 1909 s 43.

•**Native title** A right or interest over land or waters that may be owned, according to traditional laws and customs, by Aboriginal peoples and Torres Strait Islanders. Native title is recognised by the common law of Australia: *Mabo v State of Queensland (No 2)* (1992) 175 CLR 1; (1992) 107 ALR 1. The content and nature of the rights that may be enjoyed by the owners of native title is determined by the traditional laws and customs observed by those owners. Native title may be surrendered to the Crown voluntarily, but is otherwise inalienable to persons who are not members of the relevant clan or group of Aboriginal people or Torres Strait Islanders. Native title may be extinguished by the Crown: *Mabo v State of Queensland (No 2)*. In Australia, the recognition and protection of native title is regulated by the (CTH) Native Title Act 1993. See also **Aboriginal person**; **Mabo's case**.

•**Natural justice** The right to be given a fair hearing and the opportunity to present one's case, the right to have a decision made by an unbiased or disinterested decision maker and the right to have that decision based on logically probative evidence: *Salemi v Mackeller (No 2)* (1977) 137 CLR 396; 14 ALR 1. Denial of natural justice is a ground of review against an administrative decision: (CTH) Administrative Decisions (Judicial Review) Act 1977 ss 5(1)(a), 5(1)(h)(3), 6(1)(a), 6(1)(h)(3). At common law, denial of natural justice allows a review in circumstances where the administrative decision might affect a person's rights, interests, or legitimate expectations. Also known as 'procedural fairness'. See also **Administrative Decisions (Judicial Review) legislation**; **Fair Trial**; **Good faith**; **Mandamus**.

Natural monopoly A market structure where the costs conditions dictate that the most efficient structure is a monopoly structure, that is, the total costs of production are lower when a single firm produces the entire output than when any collection of two or more produce the output. See also **Market structure**; **Monopoly**.

Natural persons Human beings in the ordinary sense, as opposed to artificial persons or entities such as companies which are recognised as legal persons under the law. See also **Corporate capacity**; **Entity**.

Natural rate of unemployment A level of unemployment in a nation considered 'normal'. It embraces those changing jobs, including seasonal workers, frictional unemployment, retrenched workers consequent to restructuring, and the long-term unemployed. The natural rate is influenced by factors such as the generosity of unemployment benefits, payroll taxes, minimum wage laws, the degree of labour mobility and the extent of competition in the economy. A recession increases the actual unemployment rate above the natural rate. There is no consensus in Australia as to the natural rate of unemployment, but is said to be perhaps increasing from about four per cent to 6.5 per cent.

•**Natural resource** The stock of naturally occurring, as opposed to man-made, tangible and intangible substances which are capable of exploitation for commercial purposes. Examples are timber, land, oil, gas, minerals and mineral ores, coal, lakes, and submerged lands.

Natural resource accounting Accounting procedures applied to the natural resources of a nation. Australia's national income accounts and estimates of gross national product do not recognise the existence or use of natural resource assets, only the flow of income from them. Hence, the flow of income from oil resources is measured, but not the depreciation or augmentation of the oil resource itself. Consequently, national income accounts present a narrow and inadequate statement of the economic health of the nation. See also **Natural resource**.

•**NCSC** See **Australian Securities Commission**.

•**Necessaries** Those things which cannot be dispensed with.

Contract Goods and services suitable to an infant's condition in life and to his or her actual requirements at the time of a sale and delivery: (VIC) Goods Act 1958 s 7. In all States except New South Wales, the only exception to the common law rule that minors are not bound by contracts is that they are liable on their contracts for necessaries. See also **Age of majority**.

Maritime law Things that are necessary to equip a ship so that it may properly participate in the service in which it is engaged. A necessary is what the shipowner would, as a prudent person, have ordered the ship to be equipped with. It covers such things as anchors, cables, and rigging. It may also cover money where this is expended upon other necessaries and the money is bona fide advanced to the master for the purpose of procuring them. The master may hypothecate the ship on behalf of the owner in order to obtain such money. The master must not undertake a voyage unless the ship is carrying water of a suitable quality and quantity, and food of suitable quality, quantity, nutritive value and variety, which are necessaries: (CTH) Navigation Act 1912 s 117. See also **Fare paying passenger; Hypothecation**.

•**Necessarily incurred in carrying on a business** The second of the two positive limbs of (CTH) Income Tax Assessment Act 1936 s 51(1) which lays down the criteria for a loss or outgoing to be an allowable deduction under s 51. This limb allows deductions of losses and outgoings incurred in a business situation. The word 'business' is defined by (CTH) Income Tax Assessment Act 1936 s 6 to include profession, trade, employment, vocation or calling, but not occupation as an employee: *Ronipibon Tin NL v FCT; Tongkah Compound NL v FCT* (1949) 4 AITR 236 at 244. See also **Allowable deduction; Assessable income; Business; Incurred; Losses and outgoings**.

Needs principle One of the early tests applied by the Commonwealth Court of Conciliation and Arbitration to determine what is a 'fair and reasonable' wage for a worker. A 'fair and reasonable' wage is one that satisfies 'the normal needs of the average employee regarded as a human being living in a civilised community': *Ex parte McKay* (1907) 2 CAR 1. The needs principle is also used to maintain the real wage of employees. See also **Living wage; Real wage; Wage fixation**.

Negative assurance A statement issued by an auditor or an accountant, indicating that an audit or examination performed by the auditor revealed no abnormalities or raised no suspicions that the matters under examination did not achieve an established standard. See also **Accountant; Auditor**.

Negative confirmation See **Confirmation**.

Negative covenant In leases, a covenant prohibiting a lessee or lessor from carrying out a specified action. The term can also refer to restrictive covenants affecting freehold title. See also **Covenant; Deed; Lease covenant; Positive covenant**.

Negative duty In the context of the granting of an injunction to restrain a breach of contract, a promise by which mere inactivity on the part of the defendant constitutes performance of the term: *Administrative and Clerical Officers Assn v Commonwealth* (1979) 26 ALR 497. See also **Contract in restraint of trade; Injunction; Positive duty; Restraint of trade**.

Negative gearing A method of reducing income tax by making a loss on an investment which can be offset against income from other sources. See also **Allowable deduction; Assessable income; Gearing; Income taxation**.

Negative pledge A contractual promise, often included in a debenture or charge, that the chargor will not create any further encumbrances over the charged property without the consent of the chargee. A negative pledge does not of itself create a security or proprietary interest in favour of the pledgee: *Howie v New South Wales Lawn Tennis Ground Ltd* (1956) 95 CLR 132; *Government Insurance Office (NSW) v KA Reed Services Pty Ltd* [1988] VR 829. See also **Bare negative pledge; Charge; Constructive notice; Debenture; Security**.

Negative prescription See **Prescription**.

Negative spread A money market situation in which a dealer earns a lower rate of interest on money out on loan (that is on fixed term assets) than is being paid out on call borrowing. Thus a money market trader may pay 12 per cent interest on borrowing while receiving only 7 per cent on investments. In this event there is a negative spread of 5 per cent. Also known as 'negative interest'. See also **Money market; Money market deposit**.

•**Neglect** To pay no attention to.

Tort To fail to perform a duty or obligation; to omit or fail to do something through carelessness or negligence: *Grimwade v R* (1990) 51 A Crim R 470. The term's precise meaning depends upon context. A failure to exercise reasonable care has been described as a form of 'neglect': *Grein v Imperial Airways Ltd* [1937] 1 KB 50. See also **Duty; Negligence**.

•**Negligence** An action in tort law, the elements of which are: the existence of a duty of care; breach of that duty; and material damage as a consequence of the breach of duty. A duty of care is a legal obligation to avoid causing harm, and arises where harm is foreseeable if due care is not taken. The type of damage, not its extent, must be foreseeable: *Hughes v Lord Advocate* [1963] AC 837. The plaintiff (as an individual or as a member of a class of plaintiff) must also be foreseeable for a duty of care to arise. The defendant breaches this duty if he or she fails to avoid the risk where a reasonable person would have done so. A proximate relationship is an additional factor to foreseeability in determining the existence of a duty of care. Proximity may be physical (the parties being close in time or space), circumstantial (due to the relationship between the parties), or causal (the injury being the direct consequence of the negligent act or omission): *Jaensch v Coffey* (1984) 155 CLR 549; 54 ALR 417. See also **Breach of duty of care; Criminal negligence; Contributory negligence; Gross negligence; Injury; Remoteness; Tort**.

Negligence clause A negligence clause is enforceable if expressed in clear and unambiguous language: *London & North Western Railway Co v Neilson* [1922] 2 AC 263;

Nisho Iwai Australia Ltd v Malaysian International Shipping Corp Bhd (1989) 167 CLR 219; 86 ALR 375. See also **Bill of lading**; **Carrier**; **Charterparty**; **Injury**; **Negligence**.

Negligence, contributory See **Contributory negligence**.

Negligence, gross See **Gross negligence**.

Negligence in manufacture Failure to ensure that a product which is supplied for use or consumption has not been made defective in the course of manufacture through, for example, contamination (for example *Donoghue v Stevenson* [1932] AC 562) or faulty workmanship (for example *Woolworths v Crotty* (1942) 66 CLR 603; [1942] 49 ALR 100). Negligence in manufacture is a breach of the duty of care imposed on manufacturers by the law of negligence. See also **Defect in manufacture**; **Duty of care**; **Negligence**.

Negligent breach of contract A breach of contract which arises by reason of the defendant's breach of a contractual duty requiring the exercise of care, giving rise to liability in tort for negligence: for example *Johnson v Perez* (1988) 166 CLR 351; 82 ALR 587. See also **Apportionment legislation**; **Breach of contract**; **Concurrent liability**; **Negligence**; **Tort**.

Negligent misrepresentation A statement of fact, advice, or opinion made in a business context which is inaccurate or misleading: *Hedley Byrne & Co Ltd v Heller & Partners Ltd* [1964] AC 465. Where the representor knew or ought to have known the representation would be relied upon, the representor owes the representee a duty of care: *Mutual Life & Citizens Assurance Co Ltd v Evatt* (1970) 122 CLR 628. At common law, persons whose business or profession it is to provide information or advice of a kind requiring a degree of skill or knowledge, owe a special duty of care to persons whom they know will rely on that information or advice: *Hedley Byrne & Co Ltd v Heller & Partners Ltd* [1964] AC 465. Also known as 'negligent misstatement'. See also **Deceit**; **Fraudulent misrepresentation**; **Innocent misrepresentation**; **Misrepresentation**; **Misstatement**; **Negligence**; **Negligent statement**.

Negligent misstatement See **Negligent misrepresentation**.

Negligent statement A statement made recklessly without knowledge of its truth or falsity. Although the statement was made without due care it may prove to be correct and thus the term is in contradistinction to negligent misrepresentation. See also **Negligent misrepresentation**.

Negotiability 1. The ability to transfer ownership of property rights represented by an instrument by simple delivery, or indorsement and delivery, of the instrument. **2.** The possession of the hallmarks or features of negotiability, characterised by: transfer by delivery, or indorsement and delivery, of an instrument being legally effective to transfer the intangible property rights represented by the instrument; the holder, being entitled to rights represented by the instrument, and being able to sue on the instrument in the holder's own name; and the transfer of the instrument not being 'subject to equities': *Crouch v Credit Foncier of England Ltd* (1873) LR 8 QB 374. See also **Holder in due course**; **Indorsement**; **Negotiable instrument**; **Not negotiable**.

•**Negotiable certificate of deposit** Abbr – NCD A document or certificate providing evidence of money on deposit at interest in a commercial bank, being negotiable and payable to the bearer. It may be sold by a holder if funds are required before maturity. Initiated in Wall Street, the secondary market for an NCD is now nationwide.

Negotiable document See **Negotiable instrument**.

•**Negotiable instrument** A document which evidences a chose in action, the rights pertaining to which can, by virtue of either custom or statute, be transferred by mere delivery of the document. The transferee who takes the instrument in good faith and for value receives a good title on it despite any defect in the title of the transferor, and can sue on it in his or her own name. Recognised negotiable instruments include bills of exchange (which include cheques), promissory notes, bearer bonds, bearer debentures and warehouse certificates. Bills of exchange, cheques and promissory notes are subject to the provisions of the (CTH) Bills of Exchange Act 1909 and the (CTH) Cheques and Payment Orders Act 1986. See also **Bearer bill**; **Bearer debenture**; **Bill of exchange**; **Cheque**; **Chose in action**; **Payment order**; **Promissory note**.

•**Negotiation** Generally, mutual discussion and arrangement of the terms of a transaction or agreement.

Bills of exchange and other negotiable instruments The process of transferring rights represented by a negotiable instrument. A bill of exchange, promissory note, cheque, or payment order is 'negotiated' when it is transferred from one person to another in such a manner as to constitute the transferee its holder: (CTH) Bills of Exchange Act 1909 s 36(1); (CTH) Cheques and Payment Orders Act 1986 s 40. See also **Delivery**; **Holder**; **Indorsement**; **Negotiability**; **Negotiable instrument**.

Negotiation credit A form of documentary credit calling for drafts drawn on the issuer or on the buyer at sight or at tenor and in the currency of the issuer or in a neutral currency.

Nem con See **Nemine contradicente**.

Nemine contradicente /nɛmɪneɪ kɒntrədɪkɛnteɪ/ *Lat* – without opposition; no one dissenting. The phrase does not imply no abstentions, and it is therefore not equivalent to 'unanimously'. Abbr – nem con.

Nemo dat qui non habet /neɪmoʊ dæt kwi noʊn hæbɛt/ *Lat* – the person who has not cannot give.

Nemo dat quod non habet /neɪmoʊ dæt kwɒd noʊn hæbɛt/ *Lat* – no person gives what he or she does not possess. A person cannot assign a greater interest than the interest possessed.

Nemo debet esse judex in propria causa /neɪmoʊ dɛbɛt ɛseɪ dʒudɛks ɪn prɒpria kaʊzə/ *Lat* – no person should be judge in his or her own cause.

Net acquisition cost In competition law, the cost of goods obtained from a supplier, consisting of the price of the goods together with freight and insurance in transit: *Trade Practices Commission v Orlane Australia*

Pty Ltd (1984) 1 FCR 157; ATRP ¶40-437. Net acquisition cost does not include costs associated with the seller's trading operations, such as the costs involved in holding and reselling the goods. 'Cost' in the context of (CTH) Trade Practices Act 1974 s 98 refers to net acquisition cost: *Trade Practices Commission v Orlane Australia Pty Ltd* (1984) 1 FCR 157. Also known as 'landed' or 'delivered' cost. See also **Goods**; **Loading**; **Loss leader**.

Net amount payable In hire-purchase legislation, the total amount payable under the hire-purchase agreement less the statutory rebates for term charges, insurance and maintenance: (VIC) Hire-Purchase Act 1959 s 15(2)(b). See also **Hire-purchase agreement**.

•**Net annual value** The financial recompense received by the holder of the capital, in a year, after all expenses incurred in receiving the recompense have been deducted. In the case of a lease, net annual value will only be a part of the net annual rent as the rent will be a gross receipts figure: *R v Tomlinson* (1829) 9 B & C 166 at 167; 109 ER 61; *R v Wistow* (1836) 5 LJMC 122; *R v Liverpool* (1851) 20 LJMC 35. See also **Capital**.

Net asset value Net worth, the difference between the total assets and the total liabilities of a company, institution or individual.

Net balance due 1. The exact amount due under an account: *Stubbs v Slater* [1910] 1 Ch 632. **2.** In consumer credit legislation, the balance outstanding of the amount financed, together with outstanding credit charges, default charges and enforcement expenses, less any payments received by a credit provider and any statutory rebates: (NSW) Credit Act 1984 (repealed) s 103 (now replaced by Uniform Consumer Credit Code). See also **Amount financed**; **Credit charge**; **Credit provider**; **Default charge**; **Enforcement expense**; **Net profit**.

Net book value See **Depreciated value**.

Net capital gain The amount of the sum of the capital gains for the year of income less any capital losses incurred during the year of income and less any net capital loss from the prior year: (CTH) Income Tax Assessment Act 1936 ss 160AY(4), 160ZC. A net capital gain is included in the taxpayer's assessable income: ss 160AY(5), 160ZO. If the losses are greater than the sum of the gains a net capital loss arises: s 160ZC(3). See also **Assessable income**; **Capital gain**; **Capital gains tax**; **Capital loss**; **Incurred**; **Net capital loss**; **Year of income**.

Net capital loss The amount of the sum of capital losses for the current year of income plus any net capital loss from the preceding year of income which exceed the sum of capital gains for the current year of income: (CTH) Income Tax Assessment Act 1936 ss 160AY(4), 160ZC. A net capital loss is not deductible from assessable income but is carried forward to the succeeding year of income for the purpose of calculating the taxpayer's net capital gain or net capital loss for that succeeding year of income: (CTH) Income Tax Assessment Act 1936 ss 160ZC, 160ZO. A net capital loss incurred by a resident company may be transferred, in whole or in part, to another resident company in the same group for offset against that company's capital gains: (CTH) Income Tax Assessment Act 1936 s 160ZP. See also **Assessable income**; **Capital gain**; **Capital gains tax**; **Capital loss**; **Incurred**; **Net capital gain**; **Year of income**.

Net carrying amount See **Depreciated value**.

Net exempt income In relation to a resident taxpayer, the excess of exempt income from all sources, whether in or out of Australia, over the non-capital expenditure incurred in deriving that income plus any foreign tax on that income: (CTH) Income Tax Assessment Act 1936 ss 79E(12), 80(3). See also **Capital**; **Exempt income**; **Foreign tax**; **Tax loss**.

•**Net income** Income remaining after the deduction of tax (*Gilchrist v R Wallace Mitchell Pty Ltd* [1972] VR 481) and any other statutory deductions. See also **Separate net income**; **Return on assets**.

Net interest income The difference between the amount that a financial institution earns on loans and securities and the amount it pays on deposits and bonds or debentures. Also known as 'net interest margin' when expressed as a percentage of average total assets. See also **Building Society**.

Net investment Total or gross investment minus depreciation or the cost of replacing existing assets due to wear and obsolescence. See also **Capital formation**; **Depreciation**; **Obsolescence**.

Net material product *Abbr* – NMP Gross domestic product minus the value of services and depreciation. See also **Gross domestic product**.

Net position In a futures market, the difference between the open contracts long and the open contracts short held in any one commodity by a trader. See also **Futures exchange**; **Futures law**; **Netting**.

•**Net present value 1.** The cost of a project where the stream of costs to be incurred (or benefits gained) over future periods are discounted back to the present using a discount rate which reflects the cost of capital to the organisation or the community. **2.** In relation to property given, accruing or derived under a deed of gift or from a deceased person, the net value of the property at the date the disposition was made or at the time of death: (SA) Succession Duties Act 1929 4(1). See also **Cost-benefit analysis**; **Present value**.

Net profit The net earnings of a company over a period calculated as gross profit minus company taxation and interest expenses. Net profit is the amount available for distribution as dividends.

Net profit ratio The ratio of net profit to net sales. The net profit ratio indicates the amount of profit or loss derived for every dollar of sales. See also **Net profit**.

Net tangible asset backing per share An indication of the value of each share in a company if all the assets were liquidated, all debts paid, and the residual distributed to ordinary shareholders on a per share basis. The net tangible assets (NTA) are calculated: NTA = Total assets − External liabilities/Number of ordinary shares. A short cut is to take the ordinary shareholders' funds in the account as net assets for calculation purposes. See also **Net tangible asset-price ratio**; **Share**.

Net tangible asset-price ratio A ratio established by dividing the net tangible asset backing per share by the market price per share. The ratio allows investors to identify shares which are selling below their stated net asset backing. See also **Net tangible asset backing per share; Share**.

Net tax payable The amount of tax payable after deducting from the gross tax payable any rebates (for example, a sole parent or zone rebate) and credits (for example, for foreign tax credit). The sum of rebates and credits of tax may not exceed the amount of tax otherwise payable: (CTH) Income Tax Assessment Act 1936 ss 160AD, 160AO. See also **Credit; Gross tax payable; Rebate; Taxable income; Zone rebate**.

Net terms *Abbr* – NT A voyage charterparty under which those with interests in the cargo pay for its loading and discharging. See also **Loading; Voyage charterparty**.

Net tonnage The total cubic capacity of the interior of a vessel available for storing cargo. The spaces occupied by the crew and by the ship's machinery are not included. Net tonnage is calculated in tons where each ton is the equivalent of 100 cubic feet. See also **Cargo; Tonnage**.

Net working capital 1. The ability of a company to meet its short-term liabilities. **2.** The excess of a company's readily realisable current assets over its current liabilities. See also **Capital employed**.

Netting In corporations law, a method used to reduce settlement and credit risk between contracting parties (for over the counter options) who have entered into multiple dealings. The main object is for each party to reduce its exposure on open contracts if its counterparty becomes insolvent before the date for performance. This is achieved by the solvent party being entitled, upon the insolvency of its counterparty, to close out or terminate all of the open contracts, and to calculate losses or profits concerning each contract. See also **Derivative; Open contract; Option**.

Netting by close-out Descriptive of a netting process involving the discounting of the cashflows produced by various contracts between two counterparties back to a single present value, the close-out figure. The close-out netting process can be used in respect of all financial risk management products. See also **Cash flow; Close Out; Derivative; Netting**.

Netting by novation Descriptive of a master contract between two counterparties under which any obligation between the parties to deliver a given currency on a given date is automatically amalgamated with all other obligations under the agreement for the same currency and value date. The result is to legally substitute a single net amount for the previous gross obligations. See also **Contract; Netting; Netting by close-out**.

Netting off In corporations law, the broker to broker settlement of obligations incurred in the trading of shares relevant to a period of trading under the Clearing House Electronic Subregister System (CHESS) or Flexible Accelerated Security Transfer (FAST) share trading systems: Australian Stock Exchange Listing Rules 4.38(5), 4.39A, 4.39B; *Sydney Futures Exchange Ltd v Australian Stock Exchange* (1995) 56 FCR 236; 128 ALR 417. It is limited to the net total due between brokers for trading, rather than on a transaction by transaction basis. The transfer of individual share bundles is effected by means of a security transfer validated by the transferor's broker. This document is then used to effect an amendment to the company's register. See also **Clearing House Electronic Subregister System; Flexible Accelerated Security Transfer; Netting off agreement**.

Netting off agreement An agreement between brokers under which the net total due from one broker to another under the Clearing House Electronic Subregister System (CHESS) or Flexible Accelerated Security Transfer (FAST) securities trading system is agreed upon. See also **Clearing House Electronic Subregister System; Flexible Accelerated Security Transfer; Netting off**.

Networking Establishing a network of contacts to draw upon when needed, typically in the course of business, to acquire information and access to particular resources. See also **Old boy network**.

Neutrality The situation of a state which is unaligned.

Insurance An express warranty in relation to insurable property, whether ship or goods. It is an implied condition that the property has a neutral character at the commencement of the risk and that its neutral character will be preserved during the risk: (CTH) Marine Insurance Act 1909 s 42(1). There is also an implied condition that the ship will be properly documented in establishing its neutrality. If loss occurs through breach of this condition, the insurer may avoid the contract: (CTH) Marine Insurance Act 1909 s 42(2). See also **Nationality of ship**.

New Economic Order See **New International Economic Order**.

New ex-interest *Abbr* – Nx A description of stock from when it is first issued until the first interest payment. The first interest payment is paid to the original subscriber and not to the buyer.

New for old policy An insurance policy which provides for the replacement of old destroyed property with new items and consequently the replaced property has a higher value than the property that existed before the damage occurred. Usually, higher premiums are payable on new for old policies. See also **All reasonable precautions; All risks insurance**.

New goods In consumer protection law, the meaning of the word 'new' in a particular case depends on its context: *Annand & Thompson Pty Ltd v Trade Practices Commission* (1979) 25 ALR 91; 40 FLR 165. In relation to a vehicle, the word 'new' has at least five possible meanings. They are that the vehicle: has not previously been sold by retail, that is, it is not second hand; is a current, and not superseded, model; has not been extensively used or suffered significant deterioration; is of recent origin; or is one that may have been repaired but is otherwise new in every respect: *Annand & Thompson Pty Ltd v Trade Practices Commission*. Federal and State consumer protection legislation prohibits a false representation that goods are new: (CTH) Trade Practices Act 1974 s 53(b); (NSW) Fair Trading

Act 1987 s 44(c); (VIC) Fair Trading Act 1985 s 12(c). See also **False representation; Misleading or deceptive conduct.**

New International Economic Order *Abbr* – NIEO A proposed new order put forward by the United Nations General Assembly's Declaration on the Establishment of a New International Economic Order 1974. The NIEO is to be based upon, among other things, the sovereign equality of states and self-determination of peoples, and the view that every state should have full permanent sovereignty over its natural resources and all economic activities carried out within its boundaries. It aims to fundamentally change the economic, legal and political order governing the relationships of the developed and socialist states on one hand, and the less developed states on the other. See also **Developing country; New International Economic Order.**

New issue An issue by a company of new securities, either debt or equity. An issue may be offered to the public including the existing shareholders. See also **Pari passu; Prospectus; Securities; Share; Share splitting; Underwriter.**

New managerialism A theory and practice of organisational management in the public sector based upon economic rationalism emphasising the goal of efficiency in increasing output with reduced input of resources. Features of a managerialist administration are corporate plans, performance conracts, performance indicators and delegation of authority.

New South Wales Industrial Commission A former industrial tribunal constituted under the (NSW) Industrial Arbitration Act 1940 (repealed). Replaced with the introduction of the (NSW) Industrial Relations Act 1991 (repealed) and by the Industrial Relations Commission of New South Wales and the Industrial Court of New South Wales.

New South Wales Treasury Corporation *Abbr* – TCORP A New South Wales Government agency established in 1983 as the State's central financing authority, it is now Australia's eighth largest financial institution. TCORP provides a broad range of corporate treasury services to the State government and its agencies. It is Australia's pre-eminent semi-government bond issuer and its stock is recognised as a benchmark in domestic fixed interest markets. A Euro-Australian dollar exchangeable bond has been issued. TCORP is independent of the New South Wales Treasury Department. The board has a performance agreement with the Premier and Treasurer. See also **Agency cheque; Non-bank financial institution.**

New York Commodity Exchange *Abbr* – COMEX Established in 1933, the world's largest commodity futures exchange in metals, notably gold, silver, copper and aluminium. Financial futures are also traded. COMEX is the third largest commodity futures exchange in the United States. COMEX trading is conducted in New York City's World Trade Centre. Along with the nation's 10 other futures exchanges, COMEX is regulated by the Commodity Futures Trading Commission, an independent government agency established in 1975 to administer the provisions of the (US) Commodity Exchange Act 1976. See also **American Stock Exchange; New York Futures Exchange; New York Mercantile Exchange; Stock Exchange.**

New York Futures Exchange Established in 1980, a subsidiary of the New York Stock Exchange. The exchange trades futures contracts based on the New York Stock Exchange Composite Stock Index, and on three sub-indices: financial, industrials and utilities. See also **American Stock Exchange; Futures contract; New York Commodity Exchange; New York Stock Exchange.**

New York Mercantile Exchange *Abbr* – NYMEX Founded in 1872, a commodity market serving the agricultural, industrial, marketing and investment communities. NYMEX currently conducts futures trading in round white potatoes, imported lean beef, platinum, palladium, heating oil and industrial fuel oil. Trade is conducted in New York City's World Trade Centre. See also **New York Commodity Exchange; New York Stock Exchange.**

New York Stock Exchange *Abbr* – NYSE The principal security market in the United States and, after the Tokyo Stock Exchange, the second largest in the world. Its beginnings may be traced back to 1792. Trading is conducted by brokers and specialists, each specialist firm being responsible for a certain number of stocks. The trading floor itself has several trading posts for particular stocks. When a broker receives an order from a client, the broker goes to the appropriate post where, in the presence of others, an auction takes place. Block trades account for about half the daily volume of shares changing hands. See also **Black Monday; New York Commodity Exchange; New York Futures Exchange; New York Mercantile Exchange.**

New York Stock Exchange Composite Stock Index A capitalisation-weighted index which includes all the 1500 common stocks traded on the New York Stock Exchange. Also, known as 'the composite'. See also **New York Stock Exchange.**

New Zealand Committee of Inquiry into the Stockmarket Reporting in 1989, a New Zealand government inquiry into the operations of the New Zealand Stock Exchange. The inquiry recommended that a compliance committee, with a majority of non-brokers, should be responsible for the enforcement of listing rules for companies and have available to it a range of sanctions embracing adverse publicity, injunctions, delisting and punitive measures. The inquiry had noted a major loss of confidence by market participants in the rule-making structure, in the observance of ethical standards, and in the general integrity of the market place. See also **New Zealand Stock Exchange.**

New Zealand Stock Exchange Located in Wellington, a stock exchange serving New Zealand and overseas stocks. The market-related indices are the Barclay's Index of Leading Industrials and the broader-based New Zealand Stock Exchange Gross Index. Following Black Monday the Barclay's Index fell 60 per cent. In 1989, the exchange established the Market Surveillance Panel to implement a revised set of listing requirements. The New Zealand Government has passed legislation to counter insider trading and to require disclosure of nominee shareholdings. The New Zealand

Securities Commission maintains a watching-brief over the securities market and its self-regulating bodies including both the New Zealand Stock Exchange and the New Zealand Futures Exchange. See also **Stock Exchange; Stock Market.**

Next-day funds Money balances that are uncleared and cannot be transferred or withdrawn from an account by the recipient until the next day.

NGF See **National Guarantee Fund.**

Niche A small, specialised segment of a market. Niche banking offers finely targeted retail products. Brokers offer services such as research, corporate financial advice and investment counselling.

NICS Newly industrialising countries in Asia, most notably the 'little dragons' South Korea, Taiwan, Singapore and Hong Kong, as well as Thailand, Malaysia, India and Indonesia. See also **Association of South East Asian Nations.**

Niemeyer statement A monthly statement by the Commonwealth Government indicating changes in the government's accounts as a result of its financial transactions. It is named after Sir Otto Niemeyer (1883-1971), an adviser to the Bank of England.

NIEO See **New International Economic Order.**

Nikkei-Dow Index A share price index calculated using the market prices of the shares of 225 selected Japanese companies listed on the Tokyo Stock Exchange. On 11 November 1987, almost a month after the October share price crisis, the Tokyo market had fallen 21 per cent. A subsequent steady upswing brought the Nikkei-Dow average back to its pre-crisis high. This was attributed to relatively stable foreign exchange rates, low interest rates, increased profits and a strong domestic economy. Also known as 'Tokyo Stock Exchange Stock Price Average'. See also **Tokyo Stock Price Index.**

Nisi /naɪsaɪ/ *Lat* – unless. A decree or order coming into force after a stated interval of time, unless some contingency occurs.

No claim bonus A lowering of the amount of the premium required to renew an insurance contract, usually motor insurance, due to the fact that no claim has been made against the policy. A no claim bonus lost due to the fault of a third party may be claimed as part of damages: *Ironfield v Eastern Gas Board* [1964] 1 All ER 544. See also **Insurance.**

No disadvantage test The test the Australian Industrial Relations Commission (AIRC) must apply when deciding whether to certify or approve an enterprise agreement. The AIRC must be satisfied that the agreement would not disadvantage the employees in relation to their terms and conditions of employment. See also **Australian Industrial Relations Commission; Award; Certified agreement; Enterprise flexibility agreement; Enterprise flexibility clause.**

No fault liability The principle that a person who has been injured by another may recover compensation from the other person, whether or not that other person was at fault (such as by negligence or recklessness). Liability flows from the event, that is, from the injury. See also **Negligence; Workers' compensation.**

No fault workers' compensation scheme A statutory scheme compensating workers or their dependants for injury or death arising out of the course of their employment, sustained in travel in the course of employment, including travel to and from work, or for work related diseases. To recover, the injured worker need not prove fault: (NSW) Workers' Compensation Act 1987; (VIC) Workers Compensation Act 1958. Common law authorities have extended the requirement 'within the course of employment' to include the mode of doing the task for which the employee is employed: *Deatons Pty Ltd v Flew* (1949) 79 CLR 370. See also **Course of employment; Work-related injury; Workers' compensation.**

•**No liability company** A company whose members do not carry any liability to pay any calls of share capital either while it is a going concern or in its winding up: Corporations Law ss 9, 117(1)(f), 385. To be so registered, the company must be a mining company: Corporations Law s 115(2). See also **Call; Company; Company limited by guarantee; Company limited by guarantee and shares; Company limited by shares; Unlimited company.**

No load fund A mutual fund which does impose a commission fee or sales charge on investors. Such funds are usually promoted direct to investors, rather than through brokers. See also **Mutual fund.**

No par value shares Shares in a company that do not have a par value. The memorandum of association of a company with share capital must state the manner in which its authorised capital is divided into shares of a fixed amount: Corporations Law s 117(1)(b). The fixed amount of each share in the authorised capital is known as its 'nominal' or 'par' value. All shares must have a par value: *Re Cork Bros Pty Ltd* (1983) 8 ACLR 371. New provisions dispense with the requirement of par value: (CTH) Second Corporate Law Simplification Bill cl 254C. See also **Par value; Share.**

•**Noise** A loud sound that would materially interfere with the ordinary comfort and convenience of residents of the neighbourhood: *Bankstown Municipal Council v Berzins* [1962] NSWLR 641. Often used in the sense of offensive noise, which by reason of its level, nature, character, or quality, or the time it is made, is likely to be harmful, offensive, and interfere unreasonably with a person's comfort: (NSW) Noise Control Act 1975 s 4(1). For example, aircraft must comply with standards setting acceptable levels of noise emission. Motor vehicles must also comply with noise emission standards set by legislation: for example (NSW) Noise Control Act 1975. The standards set noise levels and provide for the measurement of emissions. They also prescribe the equipment required to reduce noise emissions and impose penalties for failure to comply. Traffic regulations also prohibit the deliberate making of excess noise by the driver of a vehicle which otherwise complies with noise emission standards. See also **Airport; Nuisance.**

Nominal capital See **Authorised capital.**

Nominal consideration A minimal obligation undertaken as consideration to support a promise: *Caval-*

lari v Premier Refrigeration Co Pty Ltd (1952) 85 CLR 20. In contract law, a purely nominal consideration will suffice to make a promise binding: *Thomas v Thomas* (1842) 2 QB 851; 114 ER 330. See also **Adequacy of consideration**; **Consideration**; **Contract**; **Sufficiency of consideration**.

Nominal damages An award of damages to indicate the infraction of a legal right where the plaintiff proves no more than the defendant's breach: *The Mediana* [1900] AC 113; *Luna Park (NSW) Ltd v Tramways Advertising Pty Ltd* (1938) 61 CLR 286. Nominal damages is an expression used in contradistinction to substantial damages, and does not mean small: *Baume v Commonwealth* (1906) 4 CLR 97; 12 ALR 22. See also **Breach of contract**; **Damages**; **Exemplary damages**; **Special damages**; **Substantial damages**.

•**Nominal defendant** A person existing in name only who takes the place of the actual defendant, or a joint defendant not immediately liable in damages but whose presence is required for technical reasons due to his or her connection with the subject matter of the case.

Nominal interest rate The stated interest rate over a period of time. The effective rate of interest is always higher than the nominal rate due to applications fees, establishment fees, administration fees, facility fees and usage fees, and to a compounding effect as monthly nominal rates are added to the capital. See also **Flat interest rate**.

•**Nominee** An agent acting on behalf of a principal often employed in the buying and selling of securities. See also **Nominee corporation**; **Nominee director**; **Nominee shareholder**.

•**Nominee corporation** A body corporate whose principal function is to hold marketable securities as a trustee or nominee: (CTH) Corporations Law s 9. See also **Corporation**; **Nominee**; **Securities**.

Nominee director A company director appointed to represent the interests of particular shareholders or creditors on the board of directors. See also **Board of directors**; **Creditor**; **Director**; **Director's duties**; **Shadow director**; **Shareholder**.

Nominee shareholder An entity, being either a natural person or a corporation, who is registered as the holder of shares in a company in its register of members but who is a holder as nominee or trustee for another person who is the beneficial owner with the beneficial interest. See also **Nominee**; **Nominee corporation**; **Rights issue**; **Shareholder**.

Non compos mentis /nɒn kɒmpɒs mɛntɪs/ *Lat* – not of sound mind. Incompetent to transact legal business.

Non est factum /nɒn ɛst fæktʊm/ *Lat* – it is not my deed. A plea by a person who seeks to disown a deed or other document which it is alleged he or she sealed or signed, that the mind of the signer did not accompany the signature: *Foster v Mackinnon* (1869) LR 4 CP 704. See also **Contract**; **Mistake**.

Non sequitur /nɒn sɛkwətə//nɒun sɛkwɪtʊə/ *Lat* – it does not follow. An illogical conclusion.

Non-acceptance The wrongful neglect or refusal by a buyer to accept and pay for goods bought: for example (NSW) Sale of Goods Act 1923 s 52(1); (VIC) Goods Act 1958 s 56(1). In such circumstances the seller may sue the buyer for non-acceptance: for example (NSW) Sale of Goods Act 1923 s 52(1); (VIC) Goods Act 1958 s 56(1). The measure of damages is the estimated loss directly and naturally resulting in the ordinary course of events from the buyer's breach of contract; and where there is an available market, the measure of damages is prima facie the difference between the contract price and the market or current price at the time when the goods ought to have been accepted. If no time was fixed for acceptance, the time is the time of refusal to accept: for example (VIC) Goods Act 1958 s 56(2), (3). See also **Acceptance**; **Available market**; **Breach of contract**; **Buyer**; **Contract**; **Delay in acceptance**; **Late delivery**; **Measure of damages**; **Non-delivery**; **Sale**; **Sale of goods**.

Non-accrual loans 1. Loans on which principal or interest payments are contractually past due by 90 days or more or where the market value of security is insufficient to cover repayment of principal and accrued interest. 2. Loans where the accrual of interest and fees has ceased due to doubt as to full recovery. A specific provision is raised to cover the expected loss where full recovery of principal is doubtful. See also **Credit**; **Loan**; **Non-performing loan**.

Non-adjustable events Events occurring after balance date for a set of financial statements that do not require modification of the financial statements. Disclosure in the notes to the financial statements are required where non-disclosure of the events could impair the proper evaluation of results and decisions by users based on the information in the financial statements. See also **Financial statement**.

Non-bank bill A bill of exchange which does not bear the name of a bank, either as drawer, acceptor or endorser. See also **Bank Bill**; **Bill of exchange**; **Discount**; **Endorser**.

•**Non-bank financial institution** A financial institution such as a building society or credit union which is not registered as a bank under the (CTH) Banking Act 1959. Non-bank financial institutions must register with, and supply an audited balance sheet, to the Reserve Bank of Australia: (CTH) Financial Corporations Act s 9(6)(b). See also **Reserve Bank of Australia**.

Non-bank financial intermediary A financial intermediary such as a building society, finance company, merchant bank, unit trust or credit union. The (CTH) Financial Corporations Act 1974 provides for the registration and regulation of non-bank financial intermediaries. The aim of the legislation is to provide the Reserve Bank of Australia with information on the activities of these intermediaries. See also **Financial intermediary**; **Management and investment company**.

•**Non-broker** A person who is neither a futures broker nor one of two or more persons who together constitute a futures broker: Corporations Law s 9. See also **Futures broker**; **Non-dealer**.

Non-business day Christmas Day, Good Friday, Sunday, and a declared bank holiday: (CTH) Bills of Exchange Act 1909 s 98(3)-(5). A non-business day is excluded from the time count for payment of non-demand bills if the time for doing any particular act or thing is limited to less than three days: s 98(1). See also **Demand bill**.

Non-callable deposit account An account required to be maintained by each bank with the Reserve Bank of Australia (RBA) and containing a certain minimum amount calculated by reference to the non-callable deposit ratio: (CTH) Banking Act 1959 ss 21, 22. The ratio is determined by the RBA with the approval of the Federal Treasurer, but may not exceed one per cent: s 20. The RBA is required to pay interest on these accounts, but the rate is lower than the depositing bank could expect to receive from other sources. See also **Account; Reserve Bank of Australia**.

Non-capital costs of ownership Any expenditure of a non-capital nature incurred by a taxpayer, to the extent to which it is incurred in connection with the continuing ownership of the asset (for example, premiums to insure the asset), or by way of interest on a loan taken out to finance the acquisition of an asset: (CTH) Income Tax Assessment Act 1936 s 160ZH(6A). Non-capital costs do not include any amount that has been allowed or is allowable as a deduction to the taxpayer in respect of any year of income: s 160ZH(6B). See also **Allowable deduction; Capital gain; Cost base; Indexed cost base; Year of income**.

Non-cash business benefit Property or services received in an income year exceeding $300 which are provided after 31 August 1988 wholly or partly in respect of, or in relation to, a business relationship: (CTH) Income Tax Assessment Act 1936 s 21A(5). These benefits are relevant to assessment of taxation if a taxpayer receives a non-cash business benefit ((CTH) Income Tax Assessment Act 1936 s 21A), or if a taxpayer incurs expenditure under an agreement under which a non-cash business benefit is provided to the taxpayer or another person (s 51AK). See also **Assessable income; Once-only deduction**.

•**Non-company** A body corporate other than a company, a recognised company, a corporation sole, or an unincorporated body formed in an external Territory or outside Australia and the external Territories, and under the law of its place of formation which may sue or be sued, or may hold property in the name its secretary or of an officer of the body duly appointed for that purpose: Corporations Law s 9. A non-company may register as a company under Corporations Law Pt 2.2 Div 3. See also **Corporation sole; Foreign company; Recognised company; Registrable Australian body**.

Non-company corporation See **Non-company**.

Non-complying superannuation fund A provident, benefit, superannuation, or retirement fund, which is not, during the time of its existence in a particular year of income, a complying superannuation fund: (CTH) Income Tax Assessment Act 1936 s 267. Non-complying superannuation funds are liable to income tax under (CTH) Income Tax Assessment Act 1936 ss 286-288A. They do not receive the income tax concessions that apply to complying superannuation funds: (CTH) Income Tax (Rates) Act 1986 s 26. See also **Complying superannuation fund; Superannuation fund**.

Non-cumulative preference share A preference share in relation to which a dividend is payable each year, but (as dividends must be paid out of profits) where there is no profit no dividend is payable that year or out of subsequent years profits. An issuing company's memorandum or articles should indicate whether preference shares are cumulative or non-cumulative: Corporations Law s 200. See also **Cumulative preference share; Dividend paid out of profits; Preference share**.

•**Non-current asset** See **Fixed assets**.

•**Non-current liability** Liabilities of a corporation or an economic entity, for example bank loans, debentures, trade creditors, lease liabilities and employee entitlements, that would not in the ordinary course of the corporation's or entity's business, be due and payable within 12 months after the end of the corporation's or entity's last financial period, but which would be due and payable sometime after 12 months after the end of the last financial period.

•**Non-dealer** A person who is neither a securities dealer nor one of two or more persons who together constitute a securities dealer: Corporations Law s 9. A securities dealer who enters into a transaction for the sale or purchase of securities with a non-dealer must not charge the non-dealer brokerage, commission or any other fee in respect of the transaction: s 843(4). There are exceptions for transactions for the sale or purchase of an odd lot of securities that is entered into by a dealer who is a member of a securities exchange and specialises in transactions relating to odd lots of securities (s 843(5)), for transactions entered into under an approved deed within the meaning of Corporations Law Pt 7.12 Div 5 (s 843(6)), and for certain transactions involving options entered into with registered traders (reg 7.4.04)). The dealer or a representative of the dealer must inform the non-dealer that the dealer is acting as principal and not as agent before a transaction in securities can be entered into with the non-dealer: Corporations Law ss 813, 843(2), 43(3). See also **Dealer; Non-broker; Odd-lot; Registered trader**.

Non-delegable duty A duty which cannot be passed on or delegated to another and so relieve the delegator of responsibility or liability. See also **Delegation; Safe system of work**.

Non-delivery In the context of sale of goods, the wrongful neglect or refusal by the seller to deliver goods to the buyer; the buyer may sue the seller for damages for non-delivery: for example (SA) Sale of Goods Act 1895 s 50(1). See also **Available market; Breach of contract; Contract; Damages; Delivery; Measure of damages; Non-acceptance; Sale of goods**.

•**Non-disclosure** The failure to reveal, divulge or uncover.

Agency The failure of an agent to disclose either the name or the existence of the principal. This makes the agent personally liable on a contract to the third party, though the agent may in fact be acting on the principal's behalf: *McNally v Jackson* (1938) 42 WALR 27. See also **Agency; Agent; Principal; Third party; Undisclosed principal**.

Corporations The failure to disclose material or immaterial facts, usually in circumstances in which a duty of disclosure arises. In relation to companies, where bodies corporate are listed or unlisted as disclosing entities, statutory duties of disclosure arise (for example Corporations Law ss 315-317A, 335) and for listed entities, in the Australian Stock Exchange Listing Rules. There are general exemptions, the most significant of which is the requirement of 'materiality'. A duty of continuous disclosure also applies in the case of companies subject to the continuous disclosure regime: Corporations Law Pt 1.2A, Australian Stock Exchange Listing Rules 30(1). See also **Australian Stock Exchange Listing Rules; Disclosing entity; Material omission**.

Non-discretionary account In relation to securities trading, an account where all orders are initiated by the client and the broker acts as an order filler only. This contrasts with a discretionary account. See also **Discretionary account; Securities business**.

•**Non-economic loss** See **Non-pecuniary loss**.

•**Non-executive director** A director who does not take part in the day to day management of the company: *Holpitt Pty Ltd v Swaab* (1992) 6 ACSR 488; 10 ACLC 64. See also **Executive officer**.

Non-existing party A person named on a negotiable instrument who does not, as a matter of fact, have an existence physically (in the case of an individual), or in law (in the case of a company): for example *City Bank v Rowan* (1893) 14 LR (NSW) (L) 127. See also **Fictitious party; Negotiable instrument; Person**.

Non-factor risk In investment law, a risk that is unrelated to factors that affect the return on nearly all securities. It can therefore be diversified away.

Nonfeasance The omission or failure by a person or public body to do something which that person or public body has agreed or is otherwise liable to do.

Contract Where a party simply refuses to perform his part of a contract: *Boorman v Brown* (1842) 3 QB 511; 114 ER 603. See also **Contract; Misfeasance**.

Non-listed personal-use asset A personal-use asset which is not a listed personal-use asset: (CTH) Income Tax Assessment Act 1936 s 160B(3). A capital gain can only arise on the disposal of a non-listed personal-use asset if the sale proceeds exceed $5000: s 160ZG. See also **Asset; Capital gain; Capital loss; Listed personal-use asset; Personal-use asset**.

Non-negotiable instrument An instrument which lacks negotiability. An instrument is not negotiable if: it cannot be transferred by mere delivery if payable to bearer, or by indorsement and delivery if payable to order; the assignee cannot sue upon the instrument in its own name; or if the assignee does not take the instrument free from earlier equities (that is, it cannot confer a better title than it had itself): *Crouch v Credit Foncier of England Ltd* (1873) LR 8 QB 374 at 381-2. See also **Discount; Indorsement; Negotiability**.

Non-pecuniary loss A loss not easily translated into monetary terms, although such loss may be compensable.

Contract Generally in contract, mere disappointment is too remote to be recoverable, yet courts have allowed recovery for loss of reputation, inconvenience, and discomfort if it was reasonably within the contemplation of the parties at the time when the contract was made: *Burns v MAN Automotive (Aust) Pty Ltd* (1986) 161 CLR 653; 69 ALR 11. Also known as 'non-economic loss'. See also **Loss of a chance; Pecuniary loss**.

Tort Pain and suffering, loss of amenities, loss of the expectation of life, and disfigurement may be compensable non-pecuniary losses: for example (NSW) Motor Accidents Act 1988 s 68. Also known as 'non-economic loss'. See also **Distress; Loss of expectation of life**.

Non-performance In contract law, the failure to perform a contractual obligation where the promisor makes no attempt at all to perform, or has performed in a manner which is totally different from that required by the contract. For example, a seller who sends beans when the contract requires peas is guilty of non-performance: *Chanter v Hopkins* (1838) 4 M & W 399; 150 ER 1484. See also **Breach of contract; Failure of performance; Performance**.

Non-performing loan A loan in respect of which the borrower has defaulted by way of non-payment of interest or repayment of capital. See also **Loan**.

Non-portfolio dividend A dividend paid to a company where that company has a voting interest of a least 10 per cent in the company paying the dividend: (CTH) Income Tax Assessment Act 1936 s 317. Voting interest is determined by the application of the tests in (CTH) Income Tax Assessment Act 1936 s 160AFB. See also **Dividend; Share**.

Non-price competition Competition through better quality, labelling, advertising and delivery services, the ability to appeal to consumer preferences in ways other than, or in addition to, price.

Non-pro rata issue A rights issue, namely the issue of new or unissued shares to existing shareholders of a company, on a basis which is not proportional to the amount of capital already held by them in the class of shares to be issued. A company can make non-pro rata issues provided that the articles of association do not require that issues be made on a pro rata basis. A non-pro rata issue can be disadvantageous to some shareholders by resulting in a dilution of their shareholding since the company may offer proportionately more shares to others. Where the company directors have the power to make a non-pro rata offer, that power must be exercised for a proper purpose and for the benefit of the company: *Whitehouse v Carlton Hotel Pty Ltd* (1987) 162 CLR 285; 70 ALR 251. See also **Rights issue**.

•**Non-profit company** A company formed for the purpose of providing goods and services but not for the purpose of making a profit. It can include governments, charities and societies. If any profit is earned it can usually only be applied to the organisation as a whole and not to individual members. See also **Incorporated association; Voluntary non-profit association**.

Non-profit voluntary association See **Voluntary non-profit association**.

Non-provable debt A debt owed by a bankrupt to someone who is not entitled to share in the realisation of the debtor's property. The debt cannot be the subject of a proof of debt. Virtually all debts and liabilities of the bankrupt, present or future, are provable. However, there are exceptions, for example, penalties or fines imposed by a court for an offence: (CTH) Bankruptcy Act 1966 s 82(3). See also **Bankrupt; Proof of debt**.

Non-reciprocal transfer A transaction in which the entity receives assets or services or has liabilities extinguished without directly giving value in exchange to the other party or parties to the transaction: Statement of Accounting Concepts SAC 4 para 8. See also **Balance sheet**.

Non-recourse debt A debt for which the debtor is not personally liable upon default and where the creditor's recourse is limited to repossession of the property purchased with the loan moneys. See also **Creditor; Debt**.

Non-recourse finance 1. Finance provided by a finance company which, for a commission, assumes financial responsibilities on behalf of an exporter. The exporter receives any down payments and the whole of the balance remaining due within 15 days of shipment. This is without recourse once the goods have been accepted by the buyer. **2.** A loan, the repayment of which is conditional upon the project making a profit. Such a high-risk loan implies a high potential return to the lender should the project be successful.

Non-recourse signature See **Sans recours**.

Non-renounceable issues A rights issue, namely the issue of new or unissued shares to existing shareholders of a company, where the right to acquire the shares can only be exercised by the offeree member: *Consolidated Gold Mining Areas NL v Southern Goldfields Ltd* (1985) 4 ACLC 1; 13 ACLR 456 at 461. The offeree cannot trade in the rights that are contained in the offer, that is the offer; cannot be assigned. The offeree may sell or agree to assign his or her interest to another, although the offeror company is only concerned to deal with the offeree: *Consolidated Gold Mining Areas NL v Southern Goldfields Ltd*. See also **Shareholder**.

Non-reporting entity A body that is not required to comply with the Australian Accounting Standards. Entities in the private sector that the Statement of Accounting Concepts SAC 1 states would normally be considered non-reporting entities (that is, in the absence of evidence to the contrary) include sole traders, partnerships, privately owned companies (that is, exempt proprietary companies), family trusts and wholly owned subsidiaries of Australian companies. See also **Accounting standards; Australian Accounting Standards; Entity; Reporting entity**.

Non-resident associate of a foreign controller 1. Where a foreign controller is a natural person: a relative, partner, spouse, or child of that person; a trust where the foreign controller or an associate is a beneficiary; or a company where that company or a director of that company is accustomed or reasonably expected to act in accordance with directions of the foreign controller. **2.** Where the foreign controller is a company: a partner of that company; a trust where that company or an associate of the company benefits; or the company directors, or another company where the controller company directs the actions of that other company. **3.** Where a foreign controller is a trust or partnership: a person who benefits under the trust, or a partner or associate of a partner: (CTH) Income Tax Assessment Act 1936 s 159GZC. See also **Foreign controller; Thin capitalisation**.

Non-resident taxpayer A person who is not a resident of Australia: (CTH) Income Tax Assessment Act 1936 s 6(1). See also **Exempt income; Foreign tax**.

Non-tariff barrier *Abbr* – NTB A national measure directly or indirectly inhibiting importation, other than an import or export tariff. A non-tariff barrier is usually erected to protect domestic industries. Examples are a quantitative restriction, quota, service fee, or exorbitant customs fee. The General Agreement on Tariffs and Trade 1947 Pt 2 deals with the liberalisation of non-tariff barriers to international trade and contains rules, regulations, procedures, and exceptions relating to non-tariff barriers. See also **General Agreement on Tariffs and Trade 1947; Import quota**.

Non-trading partnership A partnership whose principal activities are other than buying and selling. For example, a firm of solicitors is a non-trading partnership: *Hedley v Bainbridge* (1842) 3 QB 316. See also **Partnership; Trading partnership**.

•**Non-voting share** An issued share in a body corporate which does not entitle the holder to vote at the annual general meeting of the company: (CTH) Corporations Law s 9. See also **Preference share; Voting share**.

Normal backwardation In relation to futures commodities trading, a situation where contracts with an earlier delivery date cost more than contracts with a later delivery date. This usually happens because the demand for supplies in the near future is greater than the demand for supplies at some more distant time. See also **Backwardation; Inverted Market; Normal contango**.

Normal contango In relation to futures commodities trading, a situation where contracts with a later delivery date cost more than contracts with an earlier delivery date. This premium normally represents the amount that the buyer would have had to pay as a carrying cost if the buyer had taken early delivery. See also **Cash and carry; Contango; Normal backwardation**.

Normal profit The minimum rate of profit necessary to ensure that a sufficient number of individuals or institutions will be prepared to invest, undertake risks or participate within an industry. The rate differs from industry to industry according to the degree of risk and difficulty involved. Industries with rates of reward above normal will tend to expand, while those in which the rewards are below normal will tend to contract, at least in the long-term. Costs of production include an allowance for normal profit. See also **Profit; Profit forecasts**.

North American Free Trade Agreement *Abbr* – NAFTA A free trade agreement between Canada, Mexico, and the United States effective since 1 January

1994 and governing trade and investment between the parties. See also **Free trade**; **Non-tariff barrier**.

Noscitur a sociis /nɒskɪtuə a sɒkiis/ *Lat* – it is known by its associates. The meaning of a word is known from the accompanying words.

Nostro account An account held by an Australian bank with a bank in a foreign country, being recorded in the currency of that country. See also **Australian Bank**.

•**Not negotiable** **1.** On a bill of exchange, a phrase on the bill prohibiting its transfer, or indicating an intention that the bill should not be transferable: (CTH) Bills of Exchange Act 1909 s 13(1), (4)(b). Sufficient indication of non-transferability is also evinced by the words 'not transferable' or 'pay Jones only'. **2.** On a cheque, words often written across the instrument indicating that the cheque retains its transferability, but such transfers or negotiations are subject to prior equities: (CTH) Cheques and Payment Orders Act 1986 ss 39, 55. The recipient of a cheque crossed 'not negotiable' does not receive, and is not capable of giving, a better title to the cheque than the title that the person from whom the recipient took the cheque had: *Hunter BNZ Finance Ltd v C G Maloney Pty Ltd* (1988) 18 NSWLR 420. See also **Account payee**; **Bill of exchange**; **Cheque**; **Crossing**; **Holder in due course**; **Negotiability**; **Non-negotiable instrument**.

Notarial act of honour A declaration made by the payer for honour, or the payer's agent in that behalf, declaring the payer's intention to pay a bill of exchange for honour, and for whose honour the payment is made: (CTH) Bills of Exchange Act 1909 s 73(4). See also **Acceptance or payment for honour supra protest**; **Agent**; **Bill of exchange**; **Protest**.

•**Note** Generally, a brief written or printed statement giving particulars or information.

Bills of exchange and other negotiable instruments **1.** A promissory note ((CTH) Bills of Exchange Act 1909 s 4), paper money or a banknote. **2.** A tradeable security such as the treasury note issued by the Commonwealth Government or the promissory note issued by companies and semi-government authorities. See also **Promissory note**.

•**Notice** Knowledge: *County Laboratories Ltd v J Mindle Ltd* [1957] 1 Ch 295. **2.** Something less than full knowledge. The thing of which a person is alleged to have notice must be brought clearly to that person's attention: *Goodyear Tyre and Rubber Co (Great Britain) Ltd v Lancashire Batteries Ltd* [1958] 1 WLR 857 See also **Actual notice**; **Constructive notice**.

Contract In contracts for the sale of land, the notice given (served) by a promisee when a promisor breaches a non-essential time stipulation. The effect of notice is that time becomes of the essence, and failure to comply with the notice confers a right to terminate, because it can generally be regarded as a repudiation of obligation to perform: *Ciavarella v Balmer* (1983) 153 CLR 438; 48 ALR 407. See also **Reasonable time**; **Repudiation**; **Right to terminate**; **Time stipulation**.

Notice of dishonour A notice given in writing, or by personal communication, by the holder or indorser liable on the bill of exchange or promissory note at the time of giving, intimating that the instrument has been dishonoured by non-acceptance or non-payment. The notice is given to the drawer and each indorser. It must be promptly given to those from whom the holder seeks recourse, and a drawer or indorser not notified is discharged: (CTH) Bills of Exchange Act 1909 s 53. To be effectual, notice of dishonour must be given in accordance with (CTH) Bills of Exchange Act 1909 s 54. There is no need for notice of dishonour to be communicated to the drawer or indorser of a cheque: (CTH) Cheques and Payment Orders Act 1986 s 70. See also **Bill of exchange**; **Cheque**; **Dishonour**; **Holder**; **Indorser**; **Promissory note**.

Notice of loss Notice given by the insured to the insurer of loss falling within the terms of the contract of insurance. In the absence of an express term in the contract, notice of claim must be given to the insurer within a reasonable time: *Hadenfayre Ltd v British National Insurance Society Ltd* [1984] 2 Lloyd's Rep 393. See also **Express term**; **Statement of loss**.

Notice of rescission Notice to another party to a contract that the contract is rescinded. The notice may be conditional. The general conditions of sale of land, implied in all such sales by (VIC) Transfer of Land Act 1958 Sch 7, Table A, is that, unless excluded or modified, a vendor may give notice that the contract of sale will be rescinded in seven days unless the purchaser removes requisitions or objections to title which the vendor is unable or unwilling to remove or comply with. If the purchaser persists the contract is rescinded and the purchaser is entitled to repayment of all deposits and other moneys paid: (NSW) Conveyancing Act 1919 s 66; (VIC) Transfer of Land Act 1958 Sch 7 cl 2. See also **Contract**; **Rescission**; **Termination**.

Notice of terms A document which states such details as the maximum amount of credit (if any) under the contract; the method by which the chargable amount in respect of each billing cycle is to be determined; the terms and conditions (if any) upon which, under the contract, a credit charge for a billing cycle may be made; and other terms of the continuing credit contract for example: (NSW) Credit Act 1984 (repealed) s 59(1) (now replaced by Uniform Consumer Credit Code). A credit provider must, before a debtor first incurs a debt under a continuing credit contract, give a notice in writing to the debtor stating the terms of the continuing credit contract. See also **Continuing credit contract**; **Contract**.

•**Notice to quit** The means by which a periodic tenancy is determined without mutual consent: *Pacific Loan and Finance Pty Ltd v Litmanowicz* [1960] NSWR 805.

•**Notifiable securities exchange** In relation to a listed body corporate, the body's home stock exchange and any other securities exchange or stock exchange in an official list of which the body is included other than the Australian Stock Exchange (ASX) or a subsidiary of the ASX: Corporations Law s 603. Where offers are made for the shares of a company under a takeover scheme or takeover announcement, the offeror must serve on each notifiable securities exchange of the target company before 9.30 am on the next trading day of that exchange after the first day of the takeover period (or of the offer period if takeover offers are sent pursuant to a takeover scheme), a notice setting out details of any voting shares of the target company, to which the offeror is or was entitled: Corporations Law ss 687-689, 693. Persons who are entitled to more than five per cent of the voting shares of the target company must also serve on each notifiable securities exchange similar notices: Corporations Law ss 687-688, 690-693. See also **Home exchange**; **Takeover announcement**; **Takeover scheme**.

•**Notification** Communication of notice.

Agency An agent has a duty to communicate to his or her principal any notice received or knowledge acquired by the agent of any fact material to the transaction which the agent is employed to transact on the principal's behalf: *Blackburn, Low & Co v Vigors* (1887) 12 App Cas 531. See also **Constructive notice**; **Disclosure**.

Trade and commerce The mechanism by which corporations can notify the Australian Competition and Consumer Tribunal of conduct which amounts to exclusive dealing other than third-line forcing. Once notification is lodged, the conduct is deemed not to have the effect of substantially lessening competition and the corporation is permitted to engage in that conduct until otherwise notified by the tribunal: (CTH) Trade Practices Act 1974 s 93. See also **Australian Competition Tribunal**; **Competition**; **Competition law**; **Exclusive dealing**; **Substantially lessening competition**; **Trade Practices Commission**.

Noting An entry on a dishonoured inland bill of exchange and in a journal by a notary public, providing a formal record of dishonour which has evidentiary value. The entry contains the date and place of presentation and dishonour, the identity of the parties presenting and dishonouring the bill, and the notary's initials. Subject to the Act, a bill must be noted within 48 hours after dishonour: (CTH) Bills of Exchange Act 1909 s 56(4). See also **Bill of exchange**; **Dishonour**; **Inland bill**; **Presentation for acceptance**; **Presentation for payment**.

Notional principal The principal amount upon which interest payments are calculated for certain off-balance sheet instruments such as interest rate swaps and forward rate agreements. The principal amount itself is not exchanged. See also **Forward rate agreement**; **Swap**.

•**Notional value** The amount that a person could reasonably be expected to have been required to pay in order to obtain the relevant property or benefit from the provider under an arms length transaction: (CTH) Fringe Benefits Tax Assessment Act 1986 s 136.

Novation 1. An agreement discharging a contract and entering into a new one, usually on the same terms but with one of the parties being different; a method of releasing a party from the contract and introducing a new one in his or her place: for example *Olsson v Dyson* (1969) 120 CLR 365; [1969] ALR 443. **2.** A term referring to a contract between a debtor, creditor, and third person substituting the third person for the debtor or creditor in the old contract. See also **Contract**; **Discharge by agreement**.

•**Novus actus interveniens** /nɒvʊs æktʊs ɪntəvɛniɛnz/ *Lat* – a new act intervening.

Tort An independent, intervening act which breaks the chain of causation between a defendant's negligence and a plaintiff's injury: *Haber v Walker* [1963] VR 339. A break in the chain of causation absolves the defendant from liability for the plaintiff's ultimate loss: *Mahony v J Kruschich (Demolitions) Pty Ltd* (1985) 156 CLR 522; 59 ALR 722. See also **Contributing cause**; **Remoteness**.

Noxious trade A trade or industry which, by reason of its potential to cause adverse effects upon the environment or discomfort, annoyance, or ill health to persons or in any other way substantially affect the reasonable enjoyment of their property, may be declared by a local environmental plan or planning scheme to be a noxious trade or industry for purposes of industrial zoning and development control. Such industries may also be classified as developments which require environmental impact assessment before they may be approved: for example abattoirs and fertiliser industries: for example (NSW) Ewnvironmental Planning and Assessment Act 1979 Sch 3.

Nudum pactum /nudʊm pæktʊm/ *Lat* – a nude contract; bare promise. The term, now rare, is usually confined to an agreement lacking consideration necessary to make it a contract: *Watson v Watson* (1886) 12 VLR 433. See also **Consideration**; **Contract**.

Nugatory contract A contract having no force or validity. In contract law, a nugatory payment is one involving immediate and formal loss, that is, the payment of money in return for which no service is rendered. See also **Nugatory payment**.

Nugatory payment A payment involving immediate and formal loss, that is, the payment of money in return for which no service is rendered. See also **Nugatory contract**.

•**Nuisance** An interference with a public or private interest: *Halsey v Esso Petroleum* [1961] 1 WLR 683.

Tort An unlawful interference with a person's use or enjoyment of land, or of some right over it, or in connection with it: *Hargrave v Goldman* (1963) 110 CLR 40 at 60. See also **Public nuisance**.

•**Null and void** *Lat* – *nullus* – none; *OF* – *vuide* – empty. Of no legal effect, not valid, not legally binding: *National Acceptance Corp Pty Ltd v Benson* (1988) 12 NSWLR 213; 13 ACLR 1. The two words are synonyms but in this phrase, some courts have interpreted 'void' to mean 'voidable'. See also **Contract**; **Void ab initio**.

Nulla bona /nʌla boʊna/ *Lat* – no goods. The return made by the sheriff when a debtor has no goods to be distrained.

O

Objection An expression of disapproval or complaint.

Objection to discharge Action taken by a trustee in bankruptcy or the Official Receiver to prevent the automatic discharge of a bankrupt after three years. An objection to discharge may be made where a bankrupt fails to disclose assets or income or fails to return to Australia despite the trustee's request. See also **Automatic discharge; Bankrupt; Official Receiver; Registrar in Bankruptcy; Trustee in bankruptcy.**

Objection to jurisdiction Where a defendant objects to the jurisdiction of the court which the plaintiff has chosen. A defendant may object to the jurisdiction of the court to hear the originating process on the ground that the forum is clearly inappropriate to deal with the litigation (*Oceanic Sun Line Special Shipping Co Inc v Fay* (1988) 165 CLR 197; 79 ALR 9; *Voth v Manildra Flour Mills Pty Ltd* (1990) 171 CLR 538; 97 ALR 124) or that the court has no jurisdiction to hear and determine the matter (for example *Barry v Incitec Ltd* (1991) 45 IR 143; [1992] AILR 8).

Objective test Assessing the conduct, mental state or behaviour of a person or the quality of a thing by reference to a standard external to the person who, or the thing which, is being assessed An objective test is the opposite of a subjective test. Examples of objective tests include the reasonableness test, the reasonable person test and the ordinary person test. See also **Remoteness.**

Objectivity In accounting, the requirement that asset and liability amounts stated in the accounts, and the overall effect on net profit and shareholders' equity should be recognised only when they are measured impartially. Objectivity comprises verifiability and freedom from bias.

Objects clause A clause in the memorandum of association of a company containing a statement of the objects of the company, which does not limit the company's legal capacity, but can operate like an express restriction to limit the use of corporate power by those who act for the company: Corporations Law s 162(2). The inclusion of an objects clause in the memorandum is not obligatory but in order to obtain some privileges, it is necessary for the memorandum to state objects: s 117(1), (2). For example, to be eligible to be incorporated as a no-liability company, a mining company will need a clause stating the objects of the company as being solely mining purposes: s 9. See also **Memorandum of association.**

Objects of a power The persons in whose favour a power of appointment may be exercised. Thus, where a trustee is given power by a trust deed to distribute trust income to certain specified beneficiaries, those beneficiaries are the objects of the power. See also **Power of appointment; Trustee; Trust.**

Obligee 1. In relation to a deed, the party who takes a benefit under it. 2. In relation to a bond, the person to whom the obligor is bound and to whom performance of the obligation is owed. See also **Bond; Capacity to contract; Contract; Deed; Obligor.**

•**Obligor** In relation to a bond, the person who is bound under the bond. As an obligor is liable on the bond to fulfil the obligation or condition, the obligor must have full legal capacity to contract. See also **Bond; Capacity to contract; Obligee.**

Obsolescence A condition of a product or process becoming outdated due to the availability of improved alternatives that are more cost effective, causing a declining market value for that outdated product or process. Obsolescence is a factor in determining a fixed asset's economic life which in turn decides the basis of charging depreciation on the fixed asset. See also **Depreciable property; Depreciated value; Depreciation; Plant.**

Obtaining a financial advantage See Obtaining a financial advantage by deception.

Obtaining a financial advantage by deception Receiving a monetary benefit for a false reason: *R v Ho* (1989) 39 A Crim R 145. It is an offence to obtain a valuable thing or financial advantage by deception: for example (NSW) Crimes Act 1900 s 178BA(1). See also **Deception; Dishonest; Financial advantage; Obtaining financial advantage by false statement.**

Obtaining financial advantage by false statement Receiving a monetary benefit by an untrue assertion: *Maslen* (1995) 79 A Crim R 199. It is an offence to make or publish a statement which is false or misleading in a material particular when that fact is either known or recklessly disregarded with the intention of obtaining a financial advantage: for example (NSW) Crimes Act 1900 s 178BB. See also **Financial advantage; Obtaining a financial advantage by deception.**

Obtaining property by false pretences Receiving a proprietary benefit or advantage by means of a false promise or other untrue claim. It is an offence at common law and under statute to obtain property by false pretences: for example (NSW) Crimes Act 1900 s 179; (QLD) Criminal Code s 427. See also **False pretence; Larceny; Obtaining a financial advantage by deception.**

Obvious imitation Something which is very close to the original design, the resemblance to the original design being immediately apparent to the eye looking at the two: *Dunlop Rubber Co Ltd v Golf Ball Developments Ltd* (1931) 48 RPC 268. The design right of another is infringed if a person applies any fraudulent or obvious imitation of the design to any article for which the design is registered: (CTH) Designs Act 1906 s 30(1)(a). Whether a design is an obvious imitation is a question ascertained by examining the essential features in relation to the prior art: *Dart Industries Inc v Decor Corp Pty Ltd* (1989) 15 IPR 403; AIPC 90-569. The eye that judges the fact that there is an obvious imitation is that of the judge: *Turbo Tek Enterprises Inc v Sperling Enterprises Pty Ltd* (1989) 23 FCR 331; 88 ALR 524.The word imitation does not mean it is necessary to prove the alleged infringing design was copied, consciously or unconsciously, from the registered deign: *Dart Industries Inc v Decor Corp Pty Ltd* (1989) 15 IPR 403.

Obviousness In relation to a patent, a former statutory ground of invalidity based on the idea that the invention claimed is a merely routine, rather than ingenious, advance on the prior art. It has been superseded by 'lack of inventive step', its equivalent formulation in the (CTH) Patents Act 1990. See also **Common general knowledge**.

Occupation 1. Control of a territory by foreign military forces. 2. A person's work, trade, or profession.

Industrial law A person's employment, calling or business. Any trade, vocation or craft: (QLD) Vocational Education, Training and Employment Act 1991 s 4. See also **Employee; Employer; Employment**.

Occupational health and safety *Abbr* – OHS The principle that workers should be safe and secure in their place of work. It includes matters relating to the physiological and psychological needs and well-being of persons engaged in occupations, work-related death and trauma, and rehabilitation: (CTH) National Occupational Health and Safety Commission Act 1985 s 3. Commonwealth and State legislation has aimed to establish a system to achieve and maintain health and safety improvements in workplaces, while imposing criminal sanctions on employers who infringe the standards prescribed: for example (NSW) Occupational Health and Safety Act 1983. See also **Work-related trauma**.

Occupational licensing Statutory schemes designed to ensure the competence, honesty, and fairness of those engaged in designated occupations. With respect to professional occupations there is legislation in all States and Territories governing the licensing of legal and medical practitioners (for example (NSW) Legal Profession Act 1987; (VIC) Legal Profession Practice Act 1958; (NSW) Medical Practice Act 1992; (VIC) Medical Practice Act 1994), and in most States and Territories in respect of architects, surveyors, and valuers. There has been relatively little statutory intervention in the accountancy, actuarial and engineering professions, which are largely self-regulatory. Although the Commonwealth has limited legislative power with respect to occupational licensing it has prescribed fees where possible: (CTH) Corporations (Fees) Regulations 1990 Sch. See also **Occupation; Licensing; Licence**.

Occupational union A union that represents workers in a particular occupational classification; for example, the Federated Clerks Union. See also **Craft union; Enterprise union; General union; Industry union**.

Occupier A person in actual possession of, or taking up a place in, an area. It encompasses a degree of control: *Donaldson v Bottroff* [1965] SASR 145; *Wheat v E Lacon & Co Ltd* [1966] AC 552. Occupation does not require the control to be that of ownership: *Bulong v Cohn* [1901] 3 WALR 74. See also **Control; Occupier's liability; Possession**.

Occupier's liability The legal responsibility of an occupier of premises towards visitors who have lawfully or unlawfully entered the premises and suffered injury during the course of their visit. Traditionally, occupiers owe a special duty of care to different classes of entrants onto their land, whether they be trespassers, invitees, or licensees. The old common law special duties are now assimilated with a general duty of care to all classes of entrants: *Hackshaw v Shaw* (1984) 155 CLR 614; 56 ALR 417; *Australian Safeway Stores Pty Ltd v Zaluzna* (1987) 162 CLR 479; 69 ALR 615. See also **Dangerous premises**.

Ocean waybill A document issued by a shipping line to a shipper, bearing the name of the consignee, and serving as a receipt for the goods shipped, and evidence of the contract of carriage. An ocean waybill is similar to a bill of lading but is not a document of title. It is not negotiable and is not acceptable to banks as a collateral security. The purpose of the ocean waybill is to avoid delays to ships and cargoes which occur when bills of lading are late in arriving at the port of discharge. See also **Air waybill; Bill of lading; Cargo; Contract of carriage; Consignee; Sea waybill; Charterer; Waybill**.

Odd lot Incomplete, usually pertaining to a set; odds and ends. Used in various legal contexts:

Corporations A parcel of shares that is smaller than a marketable parcel: Corporations Law ss 9, 612(1). See also **Marketable parcel**.

Odd-lot buy-back A type of permitted buy-back where a company listed on the Australian Stock Exchange buys small parcels of shares which are not marketable parcels on the exchange: Corporations Law s 206BB. See also **Odd-lot; Authorised buy-back; Share buy-back**.

OECD See **Organisation for Economic Co-operation and Development**.

Of the essence A phrase which, when used in relation to a term of a contract, refers to a condition, the breach of which allows the innocent party to treat the contract as discharged. See also **Breach of contract; Condition; Discharge for breach; Time fixed for performance; Time stipulation**.

Off the record Information given which the representor does not want to be quoted as having said.

Off-balance-sheet borrowing A financing method where the use of an asset is obtained without ownership, for example, by asset leasing. The use of an asset lease rather than borrowing to acquire the asset means that no debt is recorded on the balance sheet, even though from a legal point of view the commitment may be viewed as having a similar effect as borrowing to purchase the asset. To overcome the accounting distortions that may arise from off-balance-sheet financing, accounting standards require that certain leases that have the effect of finance borrowing are recorded in the accounts. Such a lease is known as 'finance lease'. See also **Lease**.

Off-balance-sheet financing See **Off-balance-sheet borrowing**.

Off-board Over-the-counter transactions in unlisted securities, or transactions in listed shares that are not executed on a securities exchange. See also **Australian Stock Exchange Ltd; Securities exchange.**

Offence A specified transgression of the criminal or regulatory law. An offence may be against the common law or against the provisions of statutes or subordinate legislation. See also **Crime; Indictable offence; Penalty.**

Offences against property A wide spectrum of offences relating to the unlawful taking, falsely obtaining, fraudulent conversion, unlawful possession of, unlawful interference with the possession, control, or ownership of the property of a person: for example (NSW) Crimes Act 1900 ss 93J-203. Also known as 'offences relating to property'. See also **Deception; False pretence; Conversion; Larceny.**

•**Offensive or hazardous industry** An industry which, by reason of the manufacturing method or the nature of the materials used or produced, requires isolation from other buildings and residences.

•**Offer** In contract law, the expression of willingness to contract on terms stated. One of the three elements (the others being acceptance and consideration) which form a contract. What is alleged to be an offer must have been intended to give rise, on its acceptance, to legal relations: *Australian Woollen Mills Pty Ltd v Commonwealth* (1954) 92 CLR 424; [1954] ALR 453. See also **Acceptance; Agreement; Contract; Revocation of an offer; Offer and acceptance; Term.**

Offer and acceptance The acts of the parties by which a contract is made at common law. One party, A, makes an offer by undertaking to the other, B, that if B acts in the way A describes, a contract on the terms A has described will exist between A and B. B accepts the offer by acting in the way A described. An offer and an acceptance may be oral or written, express or inferred from conduct. See also **Absolute acceptance; Acceptance; Conditional acceptance; Conditional offer; Counter offer; Invitation to treat; Offer; Postal acceptance rule.**

Offer for sale An offer of shares already on issue to the public by an existing shareholder. The documentation for such an offer is substantially the same as for a public issue, though some prospectus requirements may be waived if the selling shareholder has limited access to the company's records and there is already a well-established, well-informed secondary market for the company's shares. See also **Offer; Public issue; Share.**

Offer for supply Make available for purchase: *Wallace v Brodribb* (1985) 58 ALR 737; ATPR ¶46-404. A corporation may not advertise goods or services at a specified price if there are reasonable grounds for believing that it will be unable to offer for supply those goods or services at that price in adequate quantities and for a reasonable time, taking into account the nature of the advertisement, and also the market in which the corporation trades: (CTH) Trade Practices Act 1974 s 56(1); (NSW) Fair Trading Act 1987 s 51.

Offer of amends An offer to make redress by a person who has wronged another.

Contract An offer by a party who has breached a contract to keep the contract on foot and compensate the other party for any loss or inconvenience suffered due to the breach. See also **Breach of contract; Mitigation.**

Offer of compromise A document served by one party to a claim on the other party stating the terms on which they would be prepared to settle the claim. See also **Costs.**

Offer period The period during which offers made under a takeover scheme or under a takeover announcement for shares in a target company remain open and, in relation to an offer that has been accepted, the period during which the offer would have remained open had it not been accepted: Corporations Law s 603. In relation to takeover schemes, the offer period may be extended but the total offer period must generally not exceed 12 months: Corporations Law ss 656, 657(2). In relation to takeover announcements, offers remain open for a period of one month beginning on the first trading day of the target company's home stock exchange after the end of 14 days after the day of the announcement: Corporations Law ss 674(1), 678. However the offer period may be extended for further one month periods provided that the total offer period does not exceed six months: Corporations Law ss 678, 681(3). See also **Takeover announcement; Takeover scheme.**

Offer to the public An offer of shares in a public company made to the public, even if only to a confined section of the public, and even if it restricts ability to accept the offer: Corporations Law s 82. A public offer cannot be said to have been made if it is only: an offer to enter an underwriting agreement; an offer to someone who is ordinarily in the business of buying and selling shares, whether as principal or agent; an offer to existing members or debenture holders of a corporation and relating to shares in or debentures of that corporation; or an offer to existing members of a company in connection with a proposal referred to in Corporations Law s 507 and relating to shares in that company. Proprietary companies cannot make offers to the public.

Offeree A person who is capable of accepting a contractual offer, personally or by an agent, so as to become party to the contract on acceptance. An offer may be so phrased, or made under such conditions, as to be made to the world in general or a wide class of people, so that someone previously unknown to the offeror may accept it and make a contract: *Carlill v Carbolic Smoke Ball Co* [1893] 1 QB 256. See also **Offer and acceptance.**

Offering for subscription or purchase See **Offer for sale.**

Offering of securities See **Prospectus.**

Offeror 1. A person who makes a contractual offer, personally or by an agent, so as to become party to the contract on acceptance. **2.** In relation to the takeover of a company, the entity that is acquiring the shares and seeking to take over that company. More specifically, a person who sends or proposes to send a takeover offer, whether personally or through an agent or nominee, or makes or proposes to make offers to acquire shares in accordance with Corporations Law s 674: Corporations Law s 603. Where two or more persons act together, offeror refers to any of those persons individually as well as to those persons jointly: Corporations Law s 603. Offerors must comply with the provisions of Corporations Law Ch 6 when seeking to achieve a takeover. See also **Offer and acceptance**; **Takeover**.

Off-hire clause A clause in a time charterparty, under which the owner of a vessel is entitled to a limited time for it to be off hire in order for it to be repaired or drydocked. The permissible time is prearranged by the parties. Normally, one or two days are allowed. After the allowed time the hire charge ceases to be payable until the vessel is once again seaworthy. A vessel is not 'off-hire' if it is otherwise fully efficient but prevented from proceeding: *Actis Co Ltd v Sanko Steamship Co Ltd (The Aquacharm)* [1982] 1 All ER 390. Also known as 'breakdown clause'. See also **Time charterparty**.

Office A position of authority to which duties and functions are attached; an independent post, with some degree of permanence, to which successive people can be appointed: *Edwards v Clinch* [1982] AC 845. See also **Australian Postal Corporation**; **Business premises**.

Office automation *Abbr* – OA The use of technology (such as telecommunications and computing hardware and software) designed to be used by office personnel in order to save time and money in the areas of communications, file and information sharing, report generation, and resource management. Office automation is also useful for personnel whose job functions requires them to work away from an office environment. Ideally, a field representative should be able to remotely access files and other information without any inconvenience or penalty related to remoteness.

Officer A person who holds a position of rank or authority.

Corporations A director, secretary, or executive officer of the corporation, or a receiver, a receiver and manager, an administrator, a liquidator or a person administering a compromise or arrangement made between a corporation and its creditors: Corporations Law s 232(1). See also **Director**; **Executive officer**.

Industrial law A person who carries out, or whose duty is to carry out, the functions of an office in an organisation: (WA) Industrial Relations Act 1979 s 7. See also **Contract of employment**; **Office**.

Official assignee In New Zealand, an officer of the court in bankruptcy with the powers to administer bankrupt estates and to act as receiver or as provisional liquidator in the winding up of corporations: (NZ) Insolvency Act 1967 ss 15-18. See also **Bankruptcy**; **Official Receiver**; **Official Trustee in Bankruptcy**.

•**Official liquidator** A registered liquidator who is also registered by the Australian Securities Commission (ASC): Corporations Law s 1283(1). Only official liquidators may be appointed for a compulsory winding up or as provisional liquidators: Corporations Law ss 472(1), (2), 532(8). See also **Liquidator**; **Provisional liquidator**; **Registered liquidator**.

Official List In relation to a stock exchange, the companies which, following application by them, have been admitted so that securities issued or made available by them are eligible to be admitted to official quotation on the stock exchange. Admission to the Official List depends upon the company complying with the Listing Rules. See also **Delisting**; **Official List of Quotations and Sales**.

Official List of Quotations and Sales A list setting out, in relation to an official meeting of a stock exchange, the last buying bid and the last selling offer for and details of the high, the low and the last sale price of the securities of companies on the Official List of the stock exchange. See also **Official List**.

•**Official management** A process whereby an official manager is appointed by creditors to a company experiencing financial difficulties where there is some hope of rehabilitation: Corporations Law Pt 5.3A. Official management is an alternative to seeking liquidation of the company. See also **External administration**.

Official manager See **Receiver and manager**.

Official meeting A meeting of the members of a stock exchange, held at the time and place appointed by the committee of the stock exchange, at which the principal business is to make prices, effect sales and record quotations at sales. See also **Stock exchange**.

Official money market A market in which the Reserve Bank of Australia (RBA) deals with a limited group of specialist securities dealers. The arrangement gives the RBA scope to buy and sell securities and provides a channel through which to implement monetary policy. The RBA influences the cash rates paid by authorised dealers. Any change affects other cash rates and, by implication, securities rates paid by the rest of the market. See also **Authorised dealer**; **Reserve Bank of Australia**; **Securities**.

Official quotation The procedure by which a share is granted quotation on a stock exchange to enable those shares to be bought and sold on that stock exchange. Shares that have official quotation must be dealt with under the listing and business rules of the stock exchange on which they are quoted. Compliance with these rules can be enforced by a court: Corporations Law s 777. A company seeking official quotation of its shares must have a capital structure in which the issue price for which quotation is sought is at least 20c: ASX Listing Rule rule 12.4 Condition 2. There must also be a minimum of 500 shareholders each with a parcel of shares having a value of at least $2000: ASX Listing Rule rule 12.4 Condition 7. The company must maintain a spread of shareholdings and options holdings which, in the opinion of the exchange, is sufficient. The sanction for failure to so do even after notice has been given is discontinuance of official quotation See also **Australian Stock Exchange Ltd**; **Australian Stock Exchange Listing Rules**; **Australian Stock Exchange Business Rules**.

•**Official Receiver** The Official Receivers jointly constitute the body corporate known as the 'Official Trustee in Bankruptcy'. An Official Receiver carries out functions on behalf of the Official Trustee in Bankruptcy, but in addition has powers to, for example, gain access to all premises and books for any purpose related to the bankruptcy ((CTH) Bankruptcy Act 1966 s 77AA); review assessments made by the trustee concerning income contributions to be made by the bankrupt to the bankrupt's estate ((CTH) Bankruptcy Act 1966 s 139T);

and require the transfer of property or the payment of money from parties to transactions which are voidable against the trustee: (CTH) Bankruptcy Act 1966 s 139ZQ. Each bankruptcy district has its own Official Receiver. A reference in the (CTH) Bankruptcy Act 1966 to the Official Receiver includes a person acting as Official Receiver: (CTH) Bankruptcy Act 1966 s 5(1). See also **Bankruptcy; Official Trustee in Bankruptcy.**

Official reserves Reserves of foreign currencies, gold and special drawing rights (SDRs), held by governments as a cushion against sudden falls in export earnings or to use to defend exchange rates. See also **Exchange rate; Foreign currency; Special drawing rights.**

Official seal See **Seal.**

Official Trustee in Bankruptcy A corporation solely constituted by the person who holds the office of Secretary to the Department administering the (CTH) Bankruptcy Act 1966: (CTH) Bankruptcy Act 1966 s 18(3). The Official Trustee in Bankruptcy acts as trustee of the bankrupt estate, when there is no registered trustee, and has the same powers and obligations as a registered trustee: s 160. Its duties include the duty to notify the fact of a debtor's bankruptcy, to ascertain the assets and liabilities of the bankrupt, and to investigate the cause of bankruptcy and relevant conduct, affairs, and records of the bankrupt: ss 19, 19AA. See also **Bankruptcy; Corporation sole; Official Receiver.**

Off-line In the context of payment and settlement systems, the transmission of transfer instructions by users, through such means as voice, written or telefaxed instructions, that must subsequently be input into a transfer processing system. The term may also refer to the storage of data by the transfer processing system on media such as magnetic tape or disk such that the user may not have direct and immediate access to the data. See also **On-line.**

Off-market purchase In relation to shares, a purchase of shares made otherwise than through the stock exchange. The method of effecting a transfer of shares in an off-market transaction depends on the provisions of the articles. Usually an instrument of transfer is required to be signed by the transferor and the transferee and to be left for registration at the company's registered office, accompanied by the certificate of the shares to be transferred. The transfer of the legal title is not effective before registration. However general equitable principles in relation to transfers of choses in action may apply to make the buyer the owner in equity once the contract is made. A buyer who becomes owner in equity may not have an enforceable right to become legal owner as against the company, but if a company has no ground for refusal to register the buyer's name, it must, in general, have a certificate ready for the transferee within one month after lodgment of the transfer: Corporations Law s 1096(2). See also **Registration; Share; Share registration.**

Off-market swap A swap in which a fixed rate is adjusted above or below the prevailing market rate. In return, the swap counterparty may obtain a margin above or below the floating rate, an up-front payment, or have the floating and fixed rates calculated on different principal amounts. See also **Stock swap; Swap.**

Offset agreement An agreement between the Commonwealth government and a foreign company, requiring a certain proportion of the value of an Australian contract to be invested in Australian industries and products. By such investments, overseas companies build up offset credits which may be sold, in certain circumstances, to other companies. See also **Australian industry; Foreign company.**

Offsetting contract A futures contract which offsets or closes out an earlier obligation to deliver or take delivery of the commodity in question. For example, the buyer of a March wheat contract can sell a March wheat contract before March. The difference between the price when the trade was initiated and the price when it was offset is the gain or loss on the trade. See also **Commodity futures contract; Futures contract; Trade.**

Off-shore In financial contexts, activities conducted outside the home country of the person conducting them and usually within a country offering special terms, concessions, tax exemptions, and facilities with the aim of strengthening its own financial position: for example (CTH) Income Tax Assessment Act 1936 s 128AE; (QLD) Offshore Banking Units and Regional Headquarters Act 1993 s 3.

Offshore banking unit *Abbr* – OBU An enterprise owned by Australian residents that undertakes a wide range of banking activities outside Australia. Only 10 per cent of the income derived by an OBU from OB activities is taxable in Australia: (CTH) Income Tax Assessment Act 1936 s 121EG. The types of trading activities a OBU can undertake are set out in (CTH) Income Tax Assessment Act 1936 s 121D(1). The OBU provisions are contained in (CTH) Income Tax Assessment Act 1936 ss 121C-121EL. See also **Banking business.**

Offshore borrowing Borrowings by an Australian resident from a non-resident upon which interest is payable. Offshore borrowing may give rise to: a withholding tax liability ((CTH) Income Tax Assessment Act 1936 s 128B(2)); or be classified as a foreign debt for thin capitalisation purposes ((CTH) Income Tax Assessment Act 1936 s 159GZF); or be subject to the rules regarding the deductibility of interest payable on debts created by inter group asset transfers involving non residents ((CTH) Income Tax Assessment Act 1936 s 159GZZE(1)). See also **Thin capitalisation; Withholding-tax.**

Off-shore installation A structure or vessel that is floating or in physical contact with the sea-bed, defined with respect to its functions, and the rights and duties of states in relation to those functions. A coastal state can construct or authorise and regulate the construction, operation and use of off-shore installations in its territorial sea, exclusive economic zone and continental shelf: United Nations Convention on the Law of the Sea 1982 arts 2(1), 60(5), 80. The coastal state has exclusive jurisdiction over off-shore installations in its exclusive economic zone and continental shelf in relation to customs, fiscal, health, safety and immigration laws and regulations: arts 60(2), 80. A coastal state also has sovereign rights for the purpose of exploring, exploiting, conserving, and managing natural resources: arts 56(1)(a), 77(1).

Offshore parent A parent company of an Australian-based subsidiary located outside Australia.

Offsite overhead cost In building law, the costs of running the business of a contractor which are incurred offsite and which are not referable to any specific projects. These costs might include the salaries of management and head office staff, rental and advertising. See also **Building contract; Contractor; Hudson formula; Opportunity cost; Proprietor**.

OHS See **Occupational health and safety**.

Oil futures Futures contracts by which a trader may attempt to hedge against an adverse change in the price of oil between buying and selling a cargo. Such contracts are a specialty of the New York Mercantile Exchange and the London International Petroleum Exchange. See also **Commodity futures contract; Futures contract; Futures exchange**.

Old boy network A network said to be established by the common background of private schooling and interests, which may operate to give favours and opportunities, particularly in business and employment, to those within it. See also **Networking**.

Old Lady of Threadneedle Street A term affectionately used for the Bank of England, the central bank of the United Kingdom which is located in Threadneedle Street, London. Richard Sheridan (1751-1816), the English dramatist and parliamentarian described the Bank as an elderly lady of great credit and long standing. This description of the Bank led James Gillray, a caricaturist of the day, to depict the Bank in a cartoon as the Old Lady of Threadneedle Street in danger. It showed the English Prime Minister William Pitt (1759-1806) attacking the Bank to provide money for the conduct of the Napoleonic wars. The Old Lady was seen putting up a spirited resistance. The name stuck and has been in popular use ever since. See also **Bank of England**.

Old system title A system of land title by which a good title is established by a chain of transactions and events reaching back to a good root of title. Also called 'common law title', becoming known as 'old system' after the introduction of the Torrens title system. See also **Good root of title**.

Oligopoly A market structure characterised by a small number of firms, each of which possesses a significant degree of economic influence. Oligopolistic behaviour is interdependent, because any change in output or price affects the sales and profits of competitors. Oligopolists are thus likely to engage in parallel behaviour, not necessarily by reason of a contract, arrangement or understanding: for example *Trade Practices Commission v Email Ltd* (1980) 31 ALR 53. See also **Conscious parallelism; Parallel behaviour; Market; Monopoly; Parallel behaviour**.

Oligopsony A situation in which a market is characterised by a small number of buyers. In its most extreme form with only one major buyer the situation is one of monopsony. See also **Market; Monopoly**.

•**Ombudsman** A statutory office-holder responsible for the investigation of action relating to matters of administration, taken by a department or prescribed authority. An investigation may be conducted in response to a complaint made by any person, or on the motion of the Ombudsman. The ombudsman has no power to compel the department or authority investigated to take action in response to the report, but may make a special report to parliament if there is no adequate response. See also **Administrative action**.

Omnia praesumuntur rite et solemniter esse acta /ɒmnɪə praɪsʊmʊntʊə rɪteɪ ɛt sɒlɛmnɪtə ɛsɪ ækta/ *Lat* – all things are presumed to be correctly and regularly done.

On approval A term referring to goods delivered to a buyer for examination only, with no obligation to buy. Legislation in each State and Territory provides that property in such goods passes to the buyer when the buyer signifies approval or acceptance of the goods to the seller, or does any other act adopting the transaction, or where the buyer does not signify approval or acceptance but retains the goods beyond the agreed time for their retention, or if there is no such agreed time, beyond a reasonable time: (NSW) Sale of Goods Act 1923 s 23. See also **Acceptance; Consignment; Goods; Property**.

•**On board bill of lading** A bill of lading acknowledging that the goods to which it relates have been loaded onto the ship: *Associated Packaging Pty Ltd v Sankyo Kaiun Kabushiki Kaisha* [1983] 3 NSWLR 293. Where the bill of lading is to be used as a collateral security, the lender will often stipulate that it must be an on board bill in order to be satisfied that the goods are actually on the ship. Since the bill of lading is prima facie evidence of the receipt by the carrier of the goods described, a carrier who issues an on board bill of lading is estopped from denying that, as at the date of the bill, the goods were on board in their stated condition. The carrier is not so estopped if the holder of the bill of lading had actual notice, at the time of receiving the bill, that the goods had not been loaded. See also **Bill of lading; Cargo; Carriage of goods; Loading; Shipped bill of lading**.

•**On consignment** 1. Ordinarily, a phrase used to refer to delivery of goods to an agent for the agent to sell on behalf of the consignor as principal. 2. Sometimes used to refer to goods delivered 'on approval' or 'on sale or return' where a sale to, not by, the consignee is contemplated. Where 'on consignment' is accompanied by 'for display or return', the goods are for display only and the factors legislation does not apply: *Universal Guarantee Ltd v Metters Ltd* [1966] WAR 74. See also **Agency; Agent; Factor; On approval; Principal**.

On right and true delivery A term used in some voyage charterparties providing that freight is to be paid only when discharge of the cargo is completed. Such a clause effectively prevents a shipowner from exercising any lien over the cargo or freight. In some cases payment of the freight is agreed to be a percentage at the commencement of discharge with the balance payable upon completion or concurrently with the discharge of the cargo. See also **Cargo; Freight; Voyage charterparty**.

Once-only deduction A percentage of expenditure which is wholly deductible in a year of income and not deductible in any other year of income: (CTH) Income Tax Assessment Act 1936 s 21A(5); (CTH) Fringe Benefits Tax Assessment Act 1986 s 136(1). For example, depreciation or some other deduction spread over more than a year is not a once-only deduction. See also **Non-cash business benefit; Otherwise deductible rule; Year of income**.

On-cost An amount added to wages and salaries to cover such items as annual leave loading, workers' compensation, insurance, payroll tax, employer superannuation contributions, sick leave, provision for redundancy, and fringe benefits. The total gives a more accurate assessment of the costs of employing labour. See also **Annual holiday loading; Annual leave; Workers' compensation**.

On-costs The costs of labour that are additional to the payment of wages and salaries, for example, payroll tax and training costs. See also **Payroll tax**.

One share one vote The principle in the Australian Stock Exchange (ASX) listing rules that voting rights in respect of fully paid shares of a listed company must be one vote for one share: ASX Listing Rules rule 6.8. It is possible for a non-listed company to have non-voting shares and differential voting shares: *Amalgamated Pest Control Pty Ltd v McCarron* (1994) 13 ACSR 42; 12 ACLC 171 at 173. See also **Fully paid share**.

One vote one value The concept that every vote has the same weight. Australian voters have no constitutionally guaranteed right to one vote, one value: *Attorney-General (CTH) (Ex rel McKinlay) v Commonwealth* (1975) 135 CLR 1; 7 ALR 593.

One-name paper A description of promissory notes, bearer notes and bearer certificates which carry one name only on the security, that of the issuer. See also **Bearer security; Promissory note**.

Onerous 1. When the obligations required of a party to a covenant or condition in a lease, to a contract or to some other instrument or agreement outweigh the advantages to be obtained from it, whether ascertained objectively or with reference to the circumstances of the particular party. 2. Onerous property may be disclaimed following bankruptcy or insolvency: (CTH) Bankruptcy Act 1966 s 133; Corporations Law s 568. See also **Bankruptcy; Insolvency**.

On-line In the context of payment and settlement systems, the transmission of transfer instructions by users, through such electronic means as computer-to-computer interfaces or electronic terminals, that are entered into a transfer processing system by automated means. The term may also refer to the storage of data by the transfer processing system on a computer database such that the user has direct access to the data (frequently real-time) through input/output devices such as terminals. See also **Off-line**.

Online 1. In data communications, the immediate availability of data. 2. In computing, the readiness of peripheral devices (such as printers) to receive data for processing. 3. In data processing, the immediate and real-time processing of data by the central processing unit.

On-market acquisition The acquisition of shares in the ordinary course of stock market trading. See also **Takeover; Takeover scheme**.

On-market buy-back A type of permitted buy-back where a company listed on the Australian Stock Exchange (ASX) buys its shares in the ordinary course of trading on the stock exchange: Corporations Law s 9. See also **Authorised buy-back; Share buy-back**.

On-market offeror In relation to the takeover of a company, the offeror that is proceeding to acquire shares by way of a takeover announcement. Under a takeover announcement pursuant to Corporations Law Pt 6.4, the on-market offeror acquires shares of a listed company on the stock market itself after a dealer who is a member of the Australian Stock Exchange announces the offer at the target company's home exchange on behalf of the offeror. On-market offers are distinguished from off-market acquisitions under takeover schemes. See also **Takeover announcement; Takeover scheme**.

On-market transaction A transaction in shares carried out on the stock exchange in the ordinary course of stock market trading. To effect a transfer of shares on-market for certificated holdings, the seller's broker delivers a share certificate and instrument of transfer to the buying broker who sends them to the company for registration of the transfer: Corporations Law Pt 7.13 Div 3. For uncertificated holdings, the shares can be traded electronically on the Australian Stock Exchange under the Clearing House Electronic Subregister System (CHESS), in which case sellers need not deliver a certificate for the buyer to present to the company when seeking registration. See also **Clearing House Electronic Subregister System**.

Onus of proof See **Burden of proof**.

OPEC See **Organisation of Petroleum Exporting Countries**.

Open and accessible to the public In relation to the registered office of a company, refers to members of the public being able to attend the office, unimpeded, and conduct business with the company. The office must also be attended by a person on behalf of the company (for example the company secretary or agent of the secretary). If the office is located in a private residence, the company must make it clear to the public (for example by use of a suitably placed and worded sign) that the registered office forms part of a private house and that the public is invited to enter and should not be dissuaded from doing so by the residential nature of the premises: *Invention Finance Pty Ltd v Flavel* (1988) 13 ACLR 99; 6 ACLC 408. Notice of the hours of each business day during which the registered office is open and accessible to the public may be lodged with the Australian Securities Commission: Corporations Law ss 9, 218(2). See also **Registered office**.

Open cheque An uncrossed cheque, that is a cheque which can be cashed at a bank. See also **Cheque**.

Open contract 1. A contract that does not seek to modify or exclude the implications attaching by law to a contract of that category. **2.** In a futures market, any contract which has been bought or sold without the transaction having been completed by subsequent sale or purchase, or by making or taking actual delivery of the physical commodity or financial instrument. See also **Contract; Contracting out; Formal contract; Statute of Frauds.**

Open door policy A management style by which all employees are welcome to approach a manager directly at any time rather than through more formal routes of communication.

Open interest The total number of futures and option contracts which are registered at the clearing house of an exchange for a given month or option series as the case may be, but which have not been closed out or settled. Also known as 'open position'. See also **Clearing house; Clearing House Electronic Subregister System.**

Open market operations Abbr – OMO The purchase or sale of securities by a central bank designed to influence money supply, credit conditions or interest rate. The Reserve Bank of Australia engages in the buying and selling of government securities in the money market. If it wishes to reduce liquidity in the private sector the bank issues or sells government securities. If it wishes to increase liquidity, it repurchases government securities from the market. In the former operation, interest rates tend to increase, while in the latter, interest rates tend to decrease. See also **Reserve Bank of Australia.**

Open order An order to buy or sell shares that remains effective until the order is cancelled or completed. Also known as 'good 'til cancelled order'. See also **Australian Stock Exchange Ltd.**

Open outcry A trading method employed in some securities exchanges by which each bid to buy or offer to sell is stated aloud in such a manner that it may be heard by all other traders in the pit trading that particular contract. All those present have an equal chance to accept a bid or offer. If traders wish to accept a bid or offer they must immediately state aloud their acceptance of the bid or offer. Open outcry trading contrasts with Itayose-hoh trading. It is employed in the Australian Options Market and the Sydney Futures Exchange. See also **Itayose-hoh; Prearranged trading.**

Open position In a futures market, the total number of futures contracts entered into in a particular delivery month that have not been liquidated by an offsetting futures transaction or by actual delivery.

Open position statement A document sent once a month by a broker to a client, showing each contract the client holds as an open position, the margins paid, and the current profit or loss on each.

Open-end company An investment company, mutual fund or unit trust which makes a continuous offering of new shares and buys them back on demand. The shares of open-end funds are offered at their net asset value plus a loading fee and are redeemed at net asset value calculated daily. See also **Net asset value; Trust; Unit trust.**

Opening entry In accounting, a journal entry made to record the opening balance of an account at the start of a new accounting period. The opening entry may also refer to the record of initial assets, liabilities and owners' equity in a newly formed business. See also **Balance sheet; Consolidated profit and loss account; Journal entry.**

Opening price 1. The price or price range recorded during the period when a futures contract commences trading. **2.** The price of a share at which business first commences on the floor of a stock exchange at the official opening time. See also **Futures contract; Stock exchange.**

Opening stock For income tax purposes, the value of the inventory on hand at the beginning of a new year of income. The stock on hand or closing stock at the end of the prior year of income becomes the opening stock at the beginning of the following year of income: (CTH) Income Tax Assessment Act 1936 s 29. See also **Year of income.**

Operating efficiency A rate of return concentrating on the efficiency in the use of a company's assets. It is obtained by calculating the rate of return on total assets: Net profit before tax Interest/Total assets. Interest is added back to remove from profit the effect of financing a company's operations through borrowing.

•**Operating expenses** In the context of retail leases, the costs incurred by a landlord in operating leased premises. It includes the cost of maintaining and repairing the premises. Where those premises form part of a retail shopping complex or centre, the costs of operating the centre are also operating expenses. Operating expenses are part of a landlord's outgoings, and are usually recoverable from a tenant under the terms of a lease. Legislation regulating commercial tenancies prohibits a landlord from recouping expenses such as capital costs and depreciation from a tenant: for example (NSW) Retail Leases Act 1994 ss 23, 24. See also **Landlord; Outgoings; Retail shop premises; Shopping complex; Tenant.**

Operating revenue The amount of sales and other revenue as a result of business activities, after deducting returns, allowances, duties, and taxes or other amounts collected on behalf of third parties: Australian Accounting Standards Board (AASB) 1004; Approved Accounting Standards (AAS) 15. It is reported in the firm's profit and loss account as a means to facilitate the evaluation of the results of the firm's operations. See also **Accrual; Marginal revenue; Profit and loss account; Sale.**

Operating risk In banking, the potential inherent risks in day to day business operations. Risks include natural disaster, system failure, fraud, and forgery. See also **Balance sheet risk; Trading risk.**

Operational Functional. Its precise meaning varies significantly with context: an 'operational budget' means the expected expenditure; 'operational costs' are the costs of running a business; 'operational research' is research into methods of working. See also **Operational leasing; Operational research.**

Operational leasing A form of hiring enabling a company to employ additional equipment without additional capital expenditure. Operational lease charges include all normal maintenance and service requirements, registration and insurance charges, the lessee incurring fuel costs and labour charges only. In this way, a monthly charge replaces up-front capital expenditure for fully-serviced equipment. See also **Lease**; **Operational**.

Operational research The application of scientific and mathematical techniques to complex problems arising in the control of systems involving a workforce, machines, materials and finance, to improve the quality and cost of performance.

Operative part The main part of a formal written contract or other instrument that deals with the creation or transfer of rights by which the main object of the contract is carried into effect. See also **Deed**.

Operative words In a formal legal document such as an enactment, deed, or contract, the words that have legal operation to affect rights and liabilities of persons covered by the enactment or parties to the contract. See also **Operative part**.

Opportunity cost The cost of satisfying an objective, measured by the value those resources would have had in another attractive alternative use. See also **Common cost**; **Marginal cost**.

Opportunity for intermediate inspection A reasonable opportunity afforded to a consumer to inspect a product for the purpose of discovering any non-latent defects before using the product. See also **Chain of causation**; **Latent defect**.

•**Oppressive** In administrative law, the character of a policy, decision or action which goes beyond being merely unreasonable: *Edelston v Wilcox* (1988) 83 ALR 99.

Oppressive conduct Unjustly burdensome or harsh conduct. Oppressive conduct in the making of a contract may render that contract unjust: (NSW) Contracts Review Act 1980 s 5. See also **Oppressive, unfairly prejudicial or unfairly discriminatory conduct**; **Unjust contract**.

Oppressive, unfairly prejudicial or unfairly discriminatory conduct Actions by a company amounting to an unjust detriment to the interests of a member or members of a company but not merely prejudicial or discriminatory: *Wayde v New South Wales Rugby League* (1985) 180 CLR 959 at 472; 61 ALR 225. The court may give relief where such conduct occurs: Corporations Law s 260. See also **Winding up**.

Optimisation The achievement of the most efficient combination of resources considered in the light of objectives, for example a combination of inputs which results in profit maximisation or an allocation of resources to achieve a balance between development and environment protection. See also **Externality**; **Profit maximisation**.

Option The right to buy or sell a specified asset at a particular price. An option may be exercised on a particular date (European option) or at any time before a particular date (American option). The four components of an option are the expiry date, the exercise price, the number of shares or size of the assets involved, and the premium paid to acquire the option.

Option contract An agreement for consideration under which a party acquires a right exercisable before a specified time to buy or sell property at a given price from another party. See also **Conditional contract**; **Consideration**; **Irrevocable offer**.

Option deposit level The amount of money required to be deposited by an option buyer with the clearing house, to hold an option position. Because a buyer's liability is limited to the premium payable on the option, the buyer's option deposit will never exceed the premium. See also **Clearing house**; **Option**; **Option premium**.

Option position The number of option contracts currently registered with the clearing house which have not been closed out, exercised, or abandoned. See also **Clearing house**; **Option**.

Option premium The amount paid by an option buyer to the option seller to enter into the option. See also **Option**; **Option position**.

Option series A class of options which are identical in their major terms. These include exercise price, contract type and size, maturity date, and exchange on which they are traded. See also **Option**.

Option spread The simultaneous purchase and sale of share options within the same class of option. A technique used by the investor to reduce risks associated with a long and short position. The options may be at the same exercise price with the same or different expiry months, or at different exercise prices with the same or different expiry months. The spread, expressed in cents per share, is the difference between the buying and selling premiums. See also **Option**; **Option series**; **Spread**.

Option to purchase An agreement under which a person is granted the right to elect to buy certain property within the period of the option. Upon the exercise of the option, the parties are bound to buy and sell respectively. Until then, only the optioner is bound, the optionee being free to decide whether or not to proceed with the proposed transaction: *Laybutt v Amoco Australia Pty Ltd* (1974) 132 CLR 57; 4 ALR 482. There is a standing controversy as to whether an option to purchase constitutes a conditional contract of sale or an irrevocable offer: *Braham v Walker* (1961) 104 CLR 366 at 376; [1961] ALR 402; *Laybutt v Amoco Australia Pty Ltd* (1974) 132 CLR 57; 4 ALR 482. See also **Conditional contract**; **Irrevocable offer**; **Option**.

Option to renew A covenant, commonly found in leases, granting to the lessee the right (option) to enter into a new lease for a specified term on expiry of the current lease. See also **Lease covenant**; **Relief against forfeiture**.

Optional currency trade finance *Abbr* – OCTF In respect of imports, a flexible term finance provided by banks, available in all currencies for goods under any type of payment mechanism, the customer choosing the term and the currency. The currency of finance may be one other than that of the underlying trade obligation.

This enables the exporter to pay Australian suppliers in Australian dollars and obtain finance in the currency of the underlying export contract for the period required. In this way, a natural hedge against currency fluctuations is created. See also **Buying hedge; Currency; Foreign currency hedge agreement.**

Or nearest offer *Abbr* – ONO Commonly used where a vendor of property has indicated a price at which the property can be bought but adds that he or she will consider the offer which contains a price that is below, but nearest to, the stated price. It is a form of invitation to treat. See also **Invitation to treat.**

Oral agreement Consensus reached by words. An agreement concluded between state parties on the basis of words spoken by duly qualified and authorised representatives. An oral agreement, once properly concluded, is valid and binding on the parties: *Legal Status of Eastern Greenland (Denmark v Norway)* 1933 PCIJ ser A/B No 53.

Oral trust A trust created other than in writing. Writing is required for a declaration of trust in respect of land or any interest in land, or the disposition of an equitable interest in land: for example (NSW) Conveyancing Act 1919 s 23C. See also **Declaration of trust; Trust.**

Order A command or direction issued by a court or tribunal. Orders are issued by courts in relation to, inter alia, court procedure, relief sought by parties, and legal costs. Courts usually have wide ranging powers to make orders to enforce their judgments.

Order bill A bill of exchange expressed to be payable to order (for example, 'pay Smith or order'), or expressed to be payable to a particular person without any indication that further transfer is prohibited (for example, 'pay Smith'): (CTH) Bills of Exchange Act 1909 s 13(4). Where a bill, either originally or by indorsement, is expressed to be payable to the order of a specified person (that is, 'pay to the order of Smith'), and not to that person's order (that is, 'pay Smith or order'), it is nevertheless payable to that person's order at his or her option: (CTH) Bills of Exchange Act 1909 s 13(5). See also **Bearer bill; Bill of exchange; Indorsement.**

Order bill of lading A bill of lading made out to the order of the consignee, under which delivery of the goods is to a named consignee or to a consignee whose name is left blank or, in either case, to the order or assigns of such person: *Tully v Allanach* (1856) 1 VLT 28. See also **Bill of lading.**

Order cheque A cheque payable to a named person or to his or her order. See also **Cheque; Order bill.**

Order of payment The order in which the debts and liabilities of a bankrupt are satisfied. There are nine classes of debts that must be paid in priority: (CTH) Bankruptcy Act 1966 s 109(1). See also **Bankrupt; Creditor's petition.**

Order of performance In contract law, the order in which the parties are to perform their respective obligations under a contract. Unless the contract in expressly or impliedly stating the time for performance also states the order for performance, the order depends on whether the obligations are dependent or independent of one another. The classification of obligations as dependent or independent depends on the intention of the parties, determined on the construction of the contract: *Burton v Palmer* [1980] 2 NSWLR 878; 5 ACLR 481. See also **Construction; Dependent obligation; Independent obligation; Performance; Time stipulation.**

•**Ordinance** A rule established by an authority; a permanent rule of actions. Commonly, an ordinance is used to designate the enactments of the legislative body of a municipal corporation. See also **Executive; Mission; Municipal corporation.**

Ordinary and traded options The two broad categories of share option available on the Australian Stock Exchange. Ordinary options can be negotiated for all securities listed, while traded options are available only in the shares of a restricted list of companies. With ordinary options, the strike price is variable, being set at the ruling market price of the share. There is no secondary market in ordinary options; a fixed strike price applies. Option periods are also fixed. Contracts normally consist of 1000 shares, however they can be readily sold in the secondary market for such options. See also **Australian Stock Exchange Ltd.**

Ordinary business transaction In relation to a partnership, an act which is within the usual course of business carried on by the partnership. An unusual transaction by a partner, without the consent of the other partners, will not be binding on the partnership even though it is within the scope of the kind of business carried on by the partnership: *Goldberg v Jenkins* (1889) 15 VLR 36. See also **Partnership.**

Ordinary course of business The usual manner of carrying on trade of an enterprise. A wrongful act or omission of a partner of a firm in the ordinary course of business that causes loss or injury to a non-partner may attract liability on the part of the firm: (NSW) Partnership Act 1892 s 10; *National Commercial Banking Corporation of Australia Ltd v Batty* (1986) 160 CLR 251; 65 ALR 385. See also **Bankrupt; Good faith; Insolvent; Preference.**

Ordinary course of trading In relation to trading on a stock market, the trading in shares at an official meeting of the Australian Stock Exchange, in accordance with the business rules of the exchange: Corporations Law s 603. See also **Ordinary course of business.**

Ordinary meaning rule In statutory interpretation, the rule that words are to be interpreted in accordance with their ordinary and current meaning: *Cozens v Brutus* [1973] AC 653. An act may indicate an intention to depart from the accepted meaning of a word and in such a case the court must follow that direction: *Smoker v Pharmacy Restructing Authority* (1994) 53 FCR 287; 125 ALR 577.

Ordinary members of the public With respect to misleading or deceptive conduct under (CTH) Trade Practices Act 1974 s 52, the astute and the gullible, the intelligent and the not-so-intelligent, the well-educated as well as the poorly educated, men and women of various ages pursuing a variety of vocations: *Taco Co of Australia Inc v Taco Bell Pty Ltd* (1982) 42 ALR 177; 2 TPR 48. See also **Misleading or deceptive conduct; Objective test.**

•**Ordinary resolution** A resolution passed by the majority of those present and voting at a meeting. See also **Creditors' meeting; General meeting; Proxy; Special resolution**.

Ordinary share Share capital in a company representing a share in the ownership of the company. Such a share carries unrestricted voting rights. An ordinary share in a limited liability company usually entitles its holder to: attend and vote at general meetings; participate in any profits distributed to ordinary shareholders; have the paid up value of the share returned in a winding up after all creditors have been paid in full, and any preferential share capital has been returned; and participate rateably with other ordinary shareholders in any assets which remain after all debts have been paid, and all capital has been returned, in a winding up. See also **Preferred ordinary share; Share**.

Ordinary shareholder A shareholder who holds ordinary shares. See also **Ordinary share**.

Organic theory Theory of corporate structure based on the notion that company law vests in certain groups of people an original authority to commit the company or to delegate to others. See also **Company**.

Organisation for Economic Co-operation and Development Abbr – OECD An organisation formed in 1961 by the Convention on the Organisation for Economic Co-operation and Development 1960 which succeeded the Organisation for European Economic Cooperation. The OECD is a vehicle for international cooperation among industrialised member countries on economic and social policies, the functions of which include: to achieve the highest sustainable economic growth in member countries while maintaining financial stability, to contribute to sound economic expansion in member as well as non-member countries, and to contribute to the expansion of world trade on a multilateral, non-discriminatory basis. There are 24 members of the OECD, accounting for 16 per cent of the world's population and producing two-thirds of its output. See also **Convention on the Organisation for Economic Cooperation and Development 1960**.

Organisation for Trade Co-operation An organisation set up in 1948 to coordinate efforts to restore Europe's economy under the European Recovery Program or Marshall Plan. The Organisation for Trade Cooperation became the Organisation for Economic Cooperation and Development in 1961 which included non-European members. See also **Organisation for Economic Co-operation and Development; Trade**.

Organisation of Arab Petroleum Exporting Countries Abbr – OAPEC An Arab organisation formed in 1968 to promote international economic cooperation within the petroleum industry. Member countries include Algeria, Bahrain, Iraq, Kuwait, Lybia, Qatar, Saudi Arabia, Syria and the United Arab Emirates. Egypt's membership was suspended in 1979 and in 1987 Tunisia ceased to be a member. The headquarters of the OAPEC are in Kuwait. See also **Organisation of Petroleum Exporting Countries**.

Organisation of Petroleum Exporting Countries Abbr – OPEC A permanent organisation established by five oil producing countries (Iran, Iraq, Kuwait, Saudi Arabia, and Venezuela) in 1960. Countries that have subsequently joined OPEC are Qatar, Indonesia, Libya, the United Arab Emirates, Algeria, Nigeria, and Gabon. The organisation's principal aims are to unify petroleum policies and develop the most appropriate way to safeguard the interests of member states. See also **Organisation of Arab Petroleum Exporting Countries**.

Organised exchange The generic term for a place where goods or rights can be traded under regulated circumstances. Examples are the Australian Security Exchange and the Sydney Futures Exchange. See also **Australian Stock Exchange Ltd**.

Original bill of lading A bill of lading that has the original signature of the master of a ship and the master's agent. See also **Bill of lading; Dirty bill of lading; Order bill of lading; Through bill of lading**.

Original issue discount security A security issued at time of the initial incorporation or creation of an entity at a discount to the prevailing market value. See also **Initial public offering; Share**.

Original work For the purposes of copyright, a work which emanates from an author and which is not merely a copy from a prior work: *Computer Edge Pty Ltd v Apple Computer Inc* (1986) 161 CLR 171; 65 ALR 33. An original work is eligible for copyright protection: (CTH) Copyright Act 1968 s 32. See also **Author; Copyright; Literary work**.

Originating lender The primary lender where a borrower conducts business with an agent or branch. For example, where a person obtains funds through the Sydney branch of an overseas bank, the overseas bank is the originating bank and the Sydney branch is known as the correspondent bank. See also **Correspondent bank; Money lender**.

Originating process The method of commencing legal proceedings, including a statement of claim, a summons or cross claim: for example (CTH) High Court Rules O 1 r 5; (NSW) Supreme Court Rules 1970 Pt 1 r 8(1). Proceedings are commenced when originating process is issued (for example *Cheney v Spooner* (1929) 41 CLR 532 at 536-7; [1929] ALR 173), or under the rules of some jurisdictions, when originating process is filed: (CTH) Federal Court Rules O 4 r 1(1); (NSW) Supreme Court Rules Pt 7 r 6(1); (VIC) Rules of the Supreme Court Ch I r 5.11. See also **Cross claim; Statement of claim; Summons**.

Ors Others.

Ostensible authority See **Apparent authority**.

OTC derivative See **Over the counter derivative**.

Other insurance clause A clause commonly found in insurance contracts that excludes or restricts the insurer's liability if the loss is covered by other insurance. It is not necessary that the other insurance policy covers identical risks to attract the operation of an other insurance clause: *Australian Agricultural Co v Saunders* (1875) 10 LR CP 668. However, in the absence of clear words to the contrary, other insurance clauses are to be interpreted as only operating with respect to other insurance covering the same interest in property: *Western*

Australian Bank v Royal Insurance Co (1908) 5 CLR 533. See also **Insurance contract**.

Otherwise deductible rule 1. For fringe benefits tax (FBT) purposes, a rule reducing the FBT amount, where an employee receives a benefit, and would have been entitled to a once-only income tax deduction for expenditure on the benefit if the employee had provided the benefit, then the taxable value of the benefit for FBT purposes is reduced by the amount of that deduction: (CTH) Fringe Benefits Tax Assessment Act 1986 ss 19, 24, 34, 37, 44, 52. **2.** For non-cash business benefits purposes, where a benefit is used in circumstances such that if the recipient would have been entitled to a once-only allowable deduction, the assessable amount of the non-cash business benefit is proportionately reduced: (CTH) Income Tax Assessment Act 1936 s 21A (3). See also **Benefit**; **Fringe Benefits Tax**; **Non-cash business benefit**; **Once-only deduction** .

Ottawa Agreement 1932 A bilateral trade agreement between the United Kingdom and Australia, signed at Ottawa, Canada on 20 August 1932. The Ottawa Agreement created a sheltered market for industrial products in the Commonwealth and protected the prices of primary products at a time of general deflation. Australia's trade after the 1939-45 war was guided by this agreement in its emphasis on the protection of domestic industry, and preferential trade within the British Empire.

Out of court settlement In civil proceedings, parties to proceedings may, without reference to the court, at any time before final judgment, offer to settle or compromise all or any of the matters in issue between them. See also **Settlement**.

Out of pocket expenses Business expenses paid out of personal funds. Companies reimburse employees for the amount they are 'out of pocket', the amount they spent in conducting business. A court may also give a successful plaintiff damages for past and future out-of-pocket expenses: *Del Ponte v Del Ponte* (1987) 11 NSWLR 489.

Out of the money option A put option with an exercise price below the price of the subject matter of the option, or a call option with an exercise price above the price of the subject matter of the option. If exercised, an out of the money option will produce a negative return. See also **Call option**; **Option**; **Put option**.

Outgoings Regular financial responsibilities incidental to the use of real property, and not being in respect of repairs or maintenance (*Re Jose* [1941] SASR 26), or in compelling a lessee to effect repairs: *Re McClure's Trusts* (1906) 76 LJ Ch 52. See also **Income**; **Losses and outgoings**; **Rent**.

Outsize entity A partnership or association which has for one or more of its objects the acquisition of gain by the partnership or association, or any of its members, and consists of more than 20 persons or a number specified in an application order relating to a profession or calling: Corporations Law s 112(3). The permitted maximum for accountants and legal practitioners, for example, is 400 persons. A person must not form an outsize partnership or association, unless it is incorporated or formed under letters patent, or a law of the Commonwealth, a State, or Territory: Corporations Law ss 112(1), (2). See also **Partnership**.

Outsize partnership See **Outsize entity**.

Outstanding cheque A cheque which has not been presented for payment. If a bank terminates the relationship with the customer it must make satisfactory provision for any outstanding cheques: *Joachimson v Swiss Bank Corp* [1921] 3 KB 110 at 127; [1921] All ER Rep 92. When a bank becomes aware of a Mareva injunction all accounts known to belong to the defendant the subject of the injunction must be frozen and outstanding cheques dishonoured: *Z Ltd v A-Z* [1982] QB 558; [1982] 2 WLR 288. See also **Mareva injunction**.

Outward bill of lading A bill of lading relating to goods which are being exported from one country to another and not merely shipped from one port to another within the same country. See also **Bill of lading**; **Export licence**.

Over the counter derivative *Abbr* – OTC derivative A derivative created by negotiation between the parties to the particular derivative and not traded on any formal or organised market in the usual sense. OTC derivatives are not fungible because the parties to the particular contract ('master agreement') negotiate each derivative's terms (being terms which do not conform to a standard). An example is an OTC option, which includes caps, captions, collars, floors, floortions, and swaptions. See also **Cap**; **Caption**; **Collar**; **Derivative**; **Floor**; **Floortion**; **Swaption**.

Over the counter market *Abbr* – OTC market A market operated by security dealers for stocks not listed on the stock exchanges. An OTC market evolved in the United States during the 1920s providing facilities for transactions in securities mainly of smaller companies looking for external finance. A multi-locational OTC market comprising leading investment banks and stockbrokers now operates outside the trading floors of the stock exchanges. The stocks of most companies are traded over-the-counter. A British market developed in the 1970s. Japan also has an established OTC market run by the Japan Securities Dealers Association. See also **Over the counter derivative**.

Over the counter option See **Over the counter derivative**.

Overall impression A view gained when one assesses all relevant information. In assessing whether conduct is misleading or deceptive under (CTH) Trade Practices Act 1974 s 52, the overall impression likely to be created by the conduct on a target audience is paramount: *Taco Company of Australia Inc v Taco Bell Pty Ltd* (1982) 42 ALR 177. See also **Misleading or deceptive conduct**.

Over-award agreement An agreement or contract between an employer and employee that the employee will be paid more than the rate of payment set out in the industrial award covering the employment. The agreement may also provide for other conditions or entitlements that are more beneficial to the employee than those provided for in the award. See also **Industrial award**; **Over-award agreement**.

Overborne will In contract law and restitution, the state of mind of a person who has been subjected to coercion by another so as to vitiate that person's consent. See also **Duress; Void ab initio**.

Overbought 1. An opinion that may be held if a security has enjoyed a sharp rise in price during a period of vigorous buying and the price appears artificially high. **2.** In a futures market a market condition under which heavy liquidation of weakly-held long positions appears imminent, that is when the speculative long interest has rapidly increased and the speculative short position is sharply reduced.

Overcapitalisation The investment of more capital into a business or other asset than can be justified either in terms of the profitability of the business or in terms of what is likely to be realised on sale.

Overcarriage The carriage of goods or passengers beyond the destination to which the carrier contracted to carry them. See also **Carriage of goods; Carriage of passengers; Contract of carriage**.

Overdraft A bank lending arrangement under which a customer is allowed to make drawings in excess of any current credit balance. It is the most common form of temporary finance for businesses. The purpose of an overdraft is to provide working capital, rather than to finance capital projects. See also **Loan; Overdraft account; Overdraft facility**.

Overdraft account A current account having a debit balance. It is effectively a loan granted by a bank to its customer, thus reversing the role of debtor and creditor in the banker-customer relationship: *Re Hone; Ex parte Trustee v Kensington Borough Council* [1951] Ch 85. A bank may charge interest on the overdraft account. A customer who draws a cheque when there are insufficient funds in his or her account to meet the cheque is making an implied request to the bank to supply overdraft facilities: *Cuthbert v Robarts, Lubbock & Co* [1909] 2 Ch 226. See also **Account; Loan; Overdraft; Overdraft facility**.

Overdraft facility A facility comprising an agreement made between an individual or a company and a bank, where permission is granted by the bank to operate an account in excess of the funds on deposit. That excess, called an overdraft, is limited to a mutually agreed amount on which overdraft facility charges are imposed. See also **Account; Loan; Overdraft; Overdraft account**.

Overdue bill or note A bill of exchange or promissory note that has not been discharged on or before its maturity date. See also **Discharge; Dishonour; Dishonour by non-acceptance; Honour; Maturity date**.

Overfreight Cargo loaded in excess of the amount agreed to in the charterparty. The charterer or shipper is liable to pay for the overfreight on a pro rata basis according to the charter rate. Overfreight is the opposite of dead freight. See also **Cargo; Carriage of goods; Charterparty; Contract of carriage; Dead freight; Freight; Rate of freight; Rate of loading**.

Overheads In business, fixed costs that exist even when production equals zero, for example, rent and administrative expenses.

Overheating A term descriptive of an economy subject to excessive demand for resources in conditions in which resources are already fully employed, at least in leading sectors of the economy. See also **Demand**.

Overinsurance An insurance contract or policy providing cover for a value above that of the property or interest covered. See also **Underinsurance**.

Overmanning A situation in which the number of operators employed to operate a plant or production line, or the number of workers in a team, is higher than considered necessary as a result of comparisons with factories at home and overseas.

Overnight money A short-term money market expression for a deposit made one day for withdrawal on the next, earning one day's interest.

Overrule A court's refusal to follow the decision of another court which is at a lower or equal level in the hierarchy of courts. See also **Court**.

Overseas cargo Goods that have been carried from or are to be carried to a foreign country by sea or air. See also **Cargo**.

Overseas company See **Foreign company**.

Oversubscribe Where demand for a company's shares at the time of a public offering exceeds supply. See also **Allotment; Authorised capital; Prospectus; Share**.

Over-subscription A situation in which the value of the applications for a new issue of securities exceeds the value of the securities offered. See also **Letter of allotment**.

•**Overtime 1.** Work done outside, or in addition to, the standard hours fixed for an employee by an industrial award or agreement, or by legislation. **2.** An increased rate of remuneration paid for overtime work, provided as compensation for working non-standard hours. See also **Industrial award; Overtime ban**.

Overtime ban A form of industrial action by which workers cease to perform any overtime work, in order to pressure employers into accepting their demands relating to the terms and conditions of employment. See also **Industrial action; Overtime; Work ban**.

Over-valued currency A currency of a country whose quoted rate is higher than what financial markets believe to be the correct rate especially because of that country's balance of payments position. See also **Currency; Foreign exchange market**.

Own-brander A person or entity, often a retailer, who, by virtue of placing its own name, brand, or mark onto a product manufactured by another manufacturer, is deemed to be the manufacturer for the purposes of a strict product liability claim under (CTH) Trade Practices Act 1974 Pt V Div 2A or Pt VA. See also **Deemed manufacturer; Manufacturer**.

•**Owner** A person in whom the ownership of property is vested. Rights of ownership include the right to exclude others, to destroy or alter the property, to alienate the property, to maintain it, and to recover possession of it. Rights of ownership are divisible, in that property may be bailed, pledged, hired, mortgaged or partially transferred to another. As a consequence, an owner may not always have a right to possess and may be restricted in exercising rights such as those to alter or destroy the property.

Owner's equity See **Capital**.

Ownership The right recognised by the law, in respect of a particular piece of property (real or personal), to exercise with respect to that property all such rights as by law are capable of being exercised with respect to that type of property against all persons, including the right to possession of the property and any proceeds of its sale: *Gatward v Alley* (1940) 40 SR (NSW) 174 at 178; 57 WN (NSW) 82; *Palette Shoes Pty Ltd v Krohn* (1937) 58 CLR 1. At common law, the possession of goods or land raises a prima facie presumption that the possessor is the owner. Also known as 'title'. See also **Equitable interest; Estate; Fee simple; Legal title; Native title; Nuisance; Owner; Personal property; Possession; Property; Tenancy**.

Ownership group The group which consists of those parties with a financial interest in the net assets of an entity obtained by contributing service potential or future economic benefits to the entity in the form of contributions or by acquiring the interest from another party as a result of contributions by owners: Statement of Accounting Concepts SAC 4, para 8. See also **Accounting standards**.

P

Pac-man defence A defensive strategy of a target company in response to a takeover bid in which the target company makes a counter-takeover bid for the entity which has made the takeover bid for it. See also **Australian Securities Commission**; **Poison pill defence**.

•**Paid up** The description of a company in which the amount of authorised capital has actually been paid to a company by its shareholders: *Re Chelsea Waterworks Co and Metropolitan Water Board* [1904] 2 KB 80. See also **Paid-up share capital**.

Paid-up share capital The amount that has actually been paid by shareholders in respect of the par or nominal value of shares issued to company members. Also known as 'subscribed capital'. See also **Capital**; **Issued share capital**; **Limited company**; **Share**; **Unpaid capital**.

•**Paper dispute** The practice under which the existence of an interstate industrial dispute can be established by written demand so as to give the Australian Industrial Relations Commission jurisdiction to hear a particular dispute. A 'paper dispute' involves an industrial organisation serving a log of claims together with a letter of demand on employers in a number of States or employers' representative bodies with interstate members. See also **Ambit**; **Industrial dispute**; **Log of Claims**.

Par In relation to the par value of a share, the amount or value ascribed to each share fixed at the time the shares are initially issued to subscribers. It is an amount equal to the total share capital (authorised capital) of the company divided by the total number of shares. For a limited liability company, the par value marks the upper limit of the statutory liability of a shareholder to contribute towards the company's share capital. It also marks off that part of a member's total claim on the company which cannot be repaid to a member by way of return of capital while the company is a going concern. In addition, it provides a measure of the relative interests of shareholders.

Par forward A flat-rate forward contract or agreement with multiple deliveries over time.

Par security A security issued at par (face) value, the face value being repaid on redemption. The only return from a par security is the interest (coupon) income.

Par value The nominal or face value of a share when issued. Under the Corporations Law, a company's authorised capital must be divided into units (shares) of a fixed dollar amount (the par value). Common par values are 50c and $1. They are usually quite different from the market value of the shares. Also known as 'nominal value' or 'par exchange rate'.

Paradox of thrift A paradox that in certain economic circumstances the more frugal and thrifty individuals and households are, the lower will be the level of national income and factor employment. Conversely, the more prodigal and spendthrift individuals and households are, the higher the level of national income and factor employment. The latter statement implies some unemployment of resources, otherwise spending may simply result in inflation. Situations may thus arise in which what is 'good' for the individual and household may be 'bad' for the nation.

Paradox of value A paradox in which an essential to life, such as water, is normally little valued, but a luxury, such as diamonds, carries a high price. The explanation lies in the fact that the amount of water available is normally so great that its marginal utility is virtually zero. In respect of diamonds the stock is small and the demand great so the marginal utility is very high.

Parallel behaviour Behaviour of firms in a substantially similar manner in response to changing market forces. See also **Acting in concert**; **Collusion**; **Conscious parallelism**; **Market**; **Oligopoly**; **Parallel pricing**; **Perfect competition**; **Price leadership**.

Parallel loan The raising of capital in a foreign country to finance a project or acquire assets in that country, with reciprocal arrangements. For example, a $US loan may be made to finance an Australian extrusion factory in California. In parallel, an $A loan may be raised in Australia to finance a United States investment here, avoiding cross-border capital movements.

Parallel pricing A situation in which companies change the price of a product by the same amount at about the same time. See also **Collusion**; **Price leadership**; **Prices Surveillance Authority**; **Trade Practices Commission**.

Parent award A major award, comprehensive and detailed, in a particular industry that is seen as setting the standard for other awards ('secondary awards') in the industry or in similar industries. See also **Flow-on**; **Industrial award**.

•**Parent company** A company that is the holding company of another company or controls one or more other companies through ownership of more than half of the voting stock and majority of the shares of one or more other companies known as subsidiaries: for example Corporations Law ss 9, 243D. A company controlling the activities, resources, operations, and the composition of the board of directors of another company is also a parent company of the controlled company. See also **Holding company**; **Subsidiary**.

•**Parent entity** A company that controls the other entities in an economic entity: Corporations Law s 295. The parent entity is a 'chief entity' for the purposes of Corporations Law Pt 3.6 Div 4A if it is the parent entity in an economic entity that is a reporting entity. See also **Chief entity**; **Economic entity**; **Entity**.

© Butterworths

•**Pari passu** /pæri pæsu/ – with equal step. Equally; without preference on one side or another. See also **Pari passu allotment; Pari passu trust deed; Pro rata**.

Pari passu allotment An allotment of shares where there are no preference shares and the rights to dividends and capital return are the same for each share. See also **Pari passu**.

Pari passu trust deed The entitlement of creditors to be paid equally and without preference. In relation to debenture trust deeds, *pari passu* provisions ensure that, although debenture stock may be issued from time to time, new stock is to be considered as equal to existing stock. Stockholders are to be treated equally and to receive payment of money owed to them at the same rate: *Merchant Bills Corp Ltd v Permanent Nominees (Aust) Ltd* [1972-73] ALR 565. See also **Debenture stock; Debenture trust deed; Pari passu**.

Parity In financial terms, equality in value. When a rate of exchange is fixed against another it is described as fixed parity.

•**Parking** A term sometimes used for the holding of securities or property on behalf of someone else for a financial consideration. Such parking may be part of a plan of deception involving illegal practices and falsified records. See also **Warehousing**.

•**Parliament** An arm of government in which legislative powers are vested. The Federal Parliament consist of the Queen, the Senate, and the House of Representatives: Commonwealth Constitution s 2. Members of Parliament are elected to office by eligible voters. See also **Legislative Council**.

Parol contract A contract made by word of mouth and not put into writing: for example (NSW) Conveyancing Act 1919 s 23D(1). The term is also used to mean a contract that is written but is not in the form of a deed, that is, a 'simple' or 'informal' contract, as distinct from a 'special' contract. See also **Consideration; Deed; Simple contract; Special contract**.

•**Part** A component for a product necessary to effect its repair. Manufacturers, deemed manufacturers, and importers owe a duty to consumers and successors in title to products to ensure that parts are reasonably available: (CTH) Trade Practices Act 1974 s 74F; *Panasonic Australia Pty Ltd v Burstyner* (1993) ATPR ¶41-224.

•**Part A statement** In corporations law, in relation to a takeover offer made under a takeover scheme, a disclosure document containing various particulars including the offer period, particulars of the corporate offeror, the offeror's entitlement in the target company, transactions in the target by the offeror during the previous four months, how consideration is to be provided, and proposed benefits to officers of the target: Corporations Law s 750. See also **Part B statement; Takeover; Takeover scheme**.

•**Part B statement** In corporations law, in relation to a takeover offer made under a takeover scheme, a statement providing various particulars including the director's recommendations in relation to the offers, each director's entitlement in the target company and in the offeror, whether the directors intend to accept the offers, the interests of directors of the target in contract with the offeror, and recent changes in the target's financial position: Corporations Law s 750. See also **Part A statement; Takeover; Takeover scheme**.

•**Part C statement** In corporations law, in relation to a takeover offer made under a takeover announcement, a statement intended to provide offeree shareholders with all information material to their decision whether to accept the bid by selling on-market: Corporations Law s 750. See also **Part D statement; Takeover; Takeover announcement**.

•**Part D statement** In corporations law, in relation to a takeover offer made under a takeover announcement, a statement providing various particulars including the directors' recommendations in relation to the offers, each director's entitlement in the target company and in the offeror, whether the directors intend to accept the offers, the interests of directors of the target in contract with the offeror, and recent changes in the target's financial position: Corporations Law s 750. See also **Part C statement; Takeover; Takeover announcement**.

Part delivery The delivery of less than the whole of the goods sold under a contract for sale of goods. Under the Vienna Convention for the Sale of Goods, the buyer may declare the contract avoided in its entirety only if the failure to make delivery completely or in conformity with the contract amounts to a fundamental breach of the contract: for example (NSW) Sale of Goods (Vienna Convention) Act 1986; (VIC) Sale of Goods (Vienna Convention) Act 1987. See also **Delivery; Seller; Seller's lien; Unpaid seller's lien**.

Part payment of debt The payment of only a fraction of a debt. See also **Consideration; Contract; Creditor; Debtor; Payment**.

Part performance An equitable doctrine which enables an oral contract to be enforced in circumstances where an act or acts have been done in actual performance of a contract which in fact existed between the parties: *J C Williamson Ltd v Lukey* (1931) 45 CLR 282. See also **Specific performance; Statute of Frauds; Failure of consideration; Unconscionable**.

Part VA claim *Product liability* A strict product liability claim under (CTH) Trade Practices Act 1974 Pt VA, which can be brought against a manufacturer, deemed manufacturer, or importer of goods that have a defect. See also **Deemed Manufacturer; Defect; Importer; Manufacturer; Strict product liability**.

Part X The part of the (CTH) Bankruptcy Act 1966 that deals with arrangements between a debtor and creditors that avoid sequestration. These arrangements are frequently called Part X arrangements and include deeds of assignment and compositions. Also known as 'Part 10'. See also **Composition; Deed of arrangement; Deed of assignment; Sequestration**.

•**Partial acceptance** A qualified acceptance of a bill of exchange where the acceptance is to pay only part of the amount for which the bill is drawn: (CTH) Bills of Exchange Act 1909 s 24(3)(b). See also **Acceptor; Bill of exchange; Qualified acceptance**.

Partial assignment In copyright law, a transfer of a part only of the rights comprised in the copyright. See also **Assignment**; **Copyright**.

Partial crystallisation The process by which a floating charge over company assets becomes fixed in relation to some (as opposed to the whole) of the asset pool subject to the charge. See also **Automatic crystallisation**; **Charge**.

•**Partial discharge** A variation of a subsisting contract. A partial discharge requires consideration and is subject to the ordinary requirements of contract law. See also **Discharge**; **Variation**.

Partial indorsement An indorsement purporting to transfer to the indorsee a part only of the amount payable, or purporting to transfer a bill of exchange to two or more indorsees severally. See also **Bill of exchange**; **Indorsee**; **Indorsement**.

Partial takeover A takeover where an offer is made for only part of the outstanding shares. Partial takeover offers made on a pro rata basis for a specified proportion of all the shares in a company have been prohibited since 1986: Corporations Law s 635. Sections 635 and 636(2) have the effect that under a takeover scheme, offers must be sent to each holder of shares in the target class. However proportional partial takeover bids are allowed, having regard to s 635(b).

•**Participating employee** A person who belongs to an employee share scheme, including a salaried director of the relevant body corporate or of a related body corporate: Corporations Law s 9. See also **Employee share scheme**.

Participating preference share 1. A preference share that carries a right to a further share of profits by way of dividend, either equally with ordinary shareholders or after the ordinary shareholders have enjoyed a specified rate of dividend, where the further share of dividends is not limited to any fixed rate. 2. A preference share which carries a right to a share of the surplus proceeds after a return of capital in a winding up. See also **Dividend**; **Preference share**; **Winding up**.

Participating shares See **Participating preference share**.

Participating stock A type of preferred common stock which, in addition to a dividend at a fixed annual rate, participates with common stock in distributing profits and sometimes in the residual distribution on company liquidation. The restrictions apply generally to voting rights. See also **Participating preference share**.

•**Participation interest** In corporations law, any right to participate, or any interest, in any profits, assets, or realisation of any financial or business undertaking or scheme; or any common enterprise in relation to which the holder of the right or interest is led to expect profits, rent, or interest from the efforts of the promoter of the enterprise, or a third party; or any investment contract: Corporations Law s 9. A participation interest does not include: a right to participate in a time-sharing scheme; shares and debentures; interests in life insurance policies; interests in some partnership agreements; a cheque, money order, bill of exchange, or promissory note; a document issued by an Australian bank acknowledging indebtedness; or a document which is not a debenture by virtue of Corporations Law s 9(a) or (f): Corporations Law s 9. See also **Prescribed interest**; **Prescribed interest holder**; **Prescribed interest prospectus**; **Prescribed interest scheme**; **Prospectus**; **Security**; **Time sharing scheme**.

Participation rights 1. The rights that are attached to a share in relation to participating in certain activities. The powers to issue shares with various participation rights such as voting at general meetings, participation in profit distributions, priority as to return of capital, and participation in surplus assets on a winding up, are often expressly conferred by a company's constitution. The power is normally contained in the articles of association: for example Corporations Law Sch 1 Table A art 2; *Campbell v Rofe* (1932) 48 CLR 258; *Re Meyer Douglas Pty Ltd* [1965] VR 638. 2. An expression denoting a right given to a person to be allotted company securities of a certain kind in the event of the company deciding to make an issue. See also **Variation of rights**.

•**Particular lien** 1. A right to hold the chattel subject to lien until all obligations of the lienor to the lienee in respect of the chattel are performed: *Dinmore Meatworks Pty Ltd v Kerr* (1962) 108 CLR 628. 2. In agency law, an agent's lien for a claim arising out of or connected with the very chattels over which the lien is claimed: *Mossman v Australasian Steam Navigation Co* (1873) 12 SCR (NSW) 62. See also **Agent**; **Agency**; **Agent's lien**; **General lien**; **Lien**; **Principal**.

Particular receivership A receivership where the receiver is appointed to take control of a particular piece of property and there is no reason for the directors to relinquish direction of the company's affairs. See also **Receiver**; **Receivership**.

•**Particulars** Details of the material facts alleged in the pleadings, including details of any claim, defence, or other matter pleaded: (CTH) Federal Court Rules 1979 O 12 r 1; (CTH) High Court Rules 1903 O 20 r 5; (NSW) Supreme Court Rules 1970 Pt 16 r 6. See also **Charge**.

Partly paid share An issued share in relation to which the whole or part of the nominal value has not been paid to the issuing company. Such shared are referred to as partly paid-up. Also known as 'contributing share'. See also **Call on contributories**; **Fully paid share**; **Paid-up share capital**; **Par value**.

Partly paid-up capital See **Paid-up share capital**.

•**Partner** 1. In company law, a person who has entered into the relation of partnership with others; that is, the relationship which exists between persons carrying on a business in common with a view to profit. 2. A legal practitioner carrying on private legal practice in common with one or more other legal practitioners. De facto partners are not to be regarded as inferior to spouses: *Black v Black* (1991) 15 Fam LR 109 at 114. See also **Firm**; **General partner**; **Limited partner**; **Partnership**; **Partnership Acts**.

Partner, holding out as See **Holding out**.

Partner's duty to account for private profits The duty of a partner to account to the partnership for any benefit derived without the consent of the other partners from a transaction concerning the partnership or from any use by the partner of the partnership property, name, or business connection: (NSW) Partnership Act 1892 s 29(1). A partner may not make an exclusive profit or advantage from the conduct of the partnership business: *United Dominions Corp Ltd v Brian Pty Ltd* (1985) 157 CLR 1; 60 ALR 741. See also **Fiduciary duty**; **Partnership**.

Partner's duty to render accounts The duty of a partner to provide true accounts and full information about all things affecting the partnership to all other partners (or their legal representatives): (NSW) Partnership Act 1892 s 28; *Cameron v Murdoch (No 2)* [1984] WAR 278. A partner must disclose partnership opportunities to all other partners (or their legal representatives) while the partnership is a going concern: *United Dominions Corp Ltd v Brian Pty Ltd* (1985) 157 CLR 1; 60 ALR 741. A partner must also disclose any special knowledge about the condition of the partnership when dissolution is contemplated: *Law v Law* [1905] 1 Ch 140. See also **Fiduciary duty**; **Partnership**.

Partner's lien The right of a partner, on the dissolution or rescission of the partnership, to have the partnership's assets distributed among the partners in satisfaction of any sum of money paid by the partner for the purchase of a share in the partnership and for any capital contributed by him or her. The partnership's assets are first used to satisfy partnership liabilities; after deducting any amount due by the partner to the partnership, the surplus assets may be distributed. Each partner has an equitable lien on the shares of the co-partners to the amount of the sum owing to the partner. See also **Lien**; **Partner**; **Partnership**.

Partner's salary Partners may agree that the partnership will pay a partner a salary, for example, where the partner may undertake certain duties over and above those normally undertaken by a partner. For income tax purposes, partner's salaries are not tax deductible as a partnership is not a separate legal entity from the partners and therefore a partner cannot be an employee of a partnership of which the partner is a member: *Ellis v Joseph Ellis & Co* [1905] 1 KB 324.

•**Partnership** The relationship subsisting between partners.

Partnerships and joint ventures The relation that exists between persons carrying on a business in common with a view to profit: for example (NSW) Partnership Act 1892 s 1(1). A creditor who obtains judgment against a partnership can enforce the judgment against the partners personally. See also **Business**; **Carrying on business**; **Joint venture**; **Limited partnership**; **Partner**; **Partnership Acts**; **Profit**.

Taxation and revenue For income tax purposes, an association of persons carrying on business as partners or in receipt of income jointly: (CTH) Income Tax Assessment Act 1936 s 6(1). A partnership for income tax purposes includes the relation which subsists between persons carrying on a business in common with a view to profit: *Jolley v FCT* 86 ALR 297. However, the term also covers associations where income is received jointly, which would not otherwise be legally classified as partnerships, such as joint ventures. See also **Partner**; **Partnership Acts**.

Partnership account A bank account held by a partnership. Each partner has implied authority to open an account on behalf of the firm and may operate the account in his or her own right: (NSW) Partnership Act 1892 s 6. The partnership is not responsible for cheques or bills drawn by a partner acting outside the scope of the partnership business: *Union Bank of Australia v Fisher* (1893) 14 LR (NSW) Eq 241. See also **Account**.

Partnership Act 1890 See **Bovill's Act**.

Partnership Acts The statutes passed in each Australian State regulating the law of partnership in that State. The Acts are: (NSW) Partnership Act 1892; (QLD) Partnership Act 1891; (SA) Partnership Act 1891; (TAS) Partnership Act 1891; (VIC) Partnership Act 1958; (WA) Partnership Act 1895; (ACT) Partnership Act 1963; (NT) Partnership Act 1891 (SA). The Acts are modelled on the (UK) Partnership Act 1890. See also **Bovill's Act**; **Partnership**.

Partnership agreement A mutual agreement between two or more persons that they will carry on business in partnership on the terms stated in the agreement. Also known as 'articles of partnership'. See also **Deed**; **Partnership**; **Partnership deed**.

Partnership articles See **Partnership agreement**.

Partnership at will A partnership in which the partners have not agreed that the partnership will be for a fixed term. See also **Partnership**.

Partnership capital The aggregate of the sums contributed by members of a partnership for the purpose of commencing or carrying on the business and intended to be risked by them in that business. It is not the same as partnership property, but is a sum fixed by the agreement of the partners, while the actual assets of the firm vary from day to day and include everything belonging to the firm and having money value: *Federal Cmr of Taxation v Roberts* (1992) 37 FCR 246; 108 ALR 385 at 397. See also **Capital**; **Carrying on business**; **Partnership property**.

Partnership deed A formal contractual agreement between the partners of an entity recording matters agreed upon. Such matters include the rights and duties of each partner, the amounts to be invested, and the profit (or loss) sharing procedure. Partnership Act provisions will apply where no deed or agreement exists: for example (NSW) Partnership Act 1892. See also **Partnership**; **Partnership agreement**.

Partnership, dissolution of See **Dissolution**.

Partnership, implied powers See **Implied powers of partner**.

Partnership, limited See **Limited partnership**.

Partnership property All property, including rights and interests in property, originally brought into the stock of a partnership or acquired since formation of the partnership on account of the firm or for the purposes and in the course of the partnership business: for example

(NSW) Partnership Act 1892 s 20(1). See also **Application of partnership property; Partnership**.

Part-owner A joint tenant, a tenant in common, a parcener, or a co-parcener. See also **Joint tenancy; Tenancy in common**.

•**Part-time work** In relation to an employee, work of a lesser number of hours than constitutes full-time work under the relevant industrial award or agreement covering the employee: (NSW) Industrial Relations Act 1996 s 74. It does not include casual or temporary work. See also **Casual employee; Full-time employee**.

•**Party 1.** A person or entity who enters into an agreement with another person or entity. **2.** A participant in a transaction or in legal action or proceedings. **3.** A plaintiff, defendant, or any person against whom a claim of relief is made: for example (NSW) Supreme Court Act 1970 s 19. **4.** In relation to a legal proceeding, a party on the record: *R v Murray & Cormie; Ex parte Commonwealth* (1916) 22 CLR 437 at 469. **5.** In relation to an appeal, a direct party or a person who is entitled to be heard because he or she has a sufficient interest in the appeal: *Claridge Pty Ltd v Metropolitan Region Planning Authority (No 1)* (1981) 4 APA 334. **6.** In corporations law in relation to a scheme or transaction, it includes: where the scheme or transaction consists of an eligible agreement, a party to the eligible agreement; in so far as the scheme or transaction consists of a proposed or discharged agreement, a person who would be a party to the agreement if it were in effect; and, otherwise, a person who has entered into or carried out or proposes to enter into or carry out, the whole or a part of the scheme or transaction: Corporations Law s 206AAA. See also **Scheme; Transaction**.

Passage of title The transfer of property in the subject matter of a transaction from the transferor to the transferee. See also **Delivery; Equitable interest; Indefeasibility of title; Personal property**.

Passbook See **Bank statement**.

Passed in A description of property offered for sale by auction where the reserve price was not reached, so the property was not sold. See also **Auction; Reserve price**.

Passim /pæsɪm/ – in various places; in many passages.

Passing of risk Transfer of the possibility of loss. In the context of the sale of goods, the time at which risk passes from the vendor to the purchaser is generally when the contract is concluded. The intention of the parties is paramount as to when property, and hence generally, risk, passes: (NSW) Sale of Goods Act 1923 s 22. See also **Sale; Sale of goods; Sale of goods legislation**.

•**Passing off** An action to prevent financial loss arising from the defendant's representation that his or her own goods or services are those of the plaintiff. See also **Goodwill; Market reputation; Misleading or deceptive conduct; Misrepresentation**.

Passive management The situation in which a director of a company does not take an active role in the management of the company. For example, the director may delegate financial oversight to a fellow executive director. Such an approach may not be sufficient to be a proper exercise of directors' duties. See also **Active management; Directors' duties**.

Passive trust A trust in which the trustee has no active duties with respect to the management of the trust property. Also known as 'dry trust'. See also **Passive trustee**.

Passive trustee A trustee who is not active in the administration of the trust. **2.** Formerly, a trustee of a passive trust (that is, a trust where the trustee has no active duties to perform), commonly used before the enactment of the Statute of Uses 1535 to escape the strict feudal obligations of the common law and to preserve contingent remainders or prevent dower. See also **Trustee**.

•**Pass-through security** An asset-backed security, investors receiving income through regular coupon payments while also receiving scheduled and unscheduled repayments of the principal. These repayments of principal are 'passed through' to the investors as they occur.

Past consideration A consideration that is given and spent in an independently constituted and concluded transaction. The rule is that past consideration is no consideration: *Eastwood v Kenyon* (1840) 11 Ad & El 438; 113 ER 482. See also **Consideration; Contract**.

•**Pastoral finance company** A person whose sole or principal business is that of financing pastoral pursuits; or that of a stock or station agent to whom an order in force under (CTH) Banking Act 1959 s 11 applies; or a person, a substantial part of whose business is, in the Chief Commissioner's opinion, that of financing pastoral pursuits; or that of a stock and station agent to whom such an order applies and who is approved by the Chief Commissioner as a pastoral finance company: (NSW) Stamp Duties Act 1920 s 98(1). See also **Company; Finance company**.

•**Pastoral lease** A lease that permits the lessee to use the land or waters covered by the lease solely or primarily for maintaining or breeding sheep, cattle, or other animals, or any other pastoral purpose: (CTH) Native Title Act 1993 s 248; (NSW) Mining Act 1992 s 4(1). See also **Crown land; Lease**.

Patent A Crown grant by way of letters patent conferring upon the grantee exclusive rights, within the Commonwealth and its territories during the term of the patent, to exploit, and to authorise other persons to exploit, the invention in respect of which it is granted. A patent may be an Australian standard patent or petty patent, or a foreign patent granted upon substantially similar principles. See also **Patent application; Patent Office; Patentee**.

•**Patent application** An application for a standard patent or a petty patent comprising, in the following order: a patent request; a patent specification, comprising a description of the invention, followed, in a complete application only, by a claim or claims defining the invention; drawings, if any; and an abstract summarising the invention. See also **Patent; Patent request; Patent specification**.

Patent interest The right to exploit an invention. Subject to the provisions of the (CTH) Patents Act 1990, a patent gives the patentee the exclusive right, during the term of the patent, to exploit the invention and authorise another person to exploit the invention: (CTH) Patents Act 1990 s 13(1). Patent interests are personal property and are capable of assignment and of devolution by law: (CTH) Patents Act 1990 s 13(2). They are also susceptible to co-ownership: (CTH) Patents Act 1990 s 16. See also **Patent**.

•**Patent Office** The office established under the (CTH) Patents Act 1990 to provide the Commissioner of Patents with an administrative apparatus for exercising or performing the powers and functions of that office. See also **Advisory Council on Industrial Property; Australian Industrial Property Organisation; Commissioner of Patents**.

•**Patent request** A written request by an applicant to the Commissioner of Patents seeking grant of a patent, in respect of the invention described in the accompanying patent specification, to such person as the applicant nominates. See also **Patent; Patent application; Patent specification**.

Patent specification A document accompanying a patent request comprising a description of the invention for which monopoly protection is sought and, in the case of a complete specification, ending with a claim or claims defining the invention, and thus the scope of the desired monopoly. See also **Patent; Patent request**.

Patentability The conceptual category combining common law and statutory criteria determining whether the nature of a patent application's subject matter is appropriate to the grant of a patent. The common law criteria determine whether the subject matter is a proper subject of letters patent according to the principles which have been developed for the application of the (IMP) Statute of Monopolies 1623-4 s 6. These criteria include qualities of newness, inventiveness, and usefulness, combined with heads of excluded subject matter, such as 'generally inconvenient'. The statutory criteria expressly include the common law criteria, placing them logically prior to the distinct, though not substantively different, statutory requirements of novelty, inventive step, and utility, and the express statutory exclusions: (CTH) Patents Act 1990 ss 18, 51 (1), 64 (2); (IMP) Statute of Monopolies 1623-4 s 6; *National Research Development Corp v Cmr of Patents* (1959) 102 CLR 252 at 261-2, 269; *NV Philips Gloeilampenfabrieken v Mirabella International Pty Ltd* (1995) 132 ALR 117 at 122; *International Business Machines Corp v Cmr of Patents* (1991) 22 IPR 417. See also **Invention; Utility**.

•**Patentee** The natural or corporate person for the time being entered in the Register of Patents as the grantee or proprietor of a patent in respect of an invention. See also **Patent; Register of Patents**.

Pathfinder prospectus A prospectus that is incomplete and which is circulated to obtain responses regarding the information which is omitted, an example being a prospectus without a price to ascertain what people are willing to pay. The Australian Securities Commission (ASC) will modify the restrictions to advertising securities under Corporations Law s 1025(3) to allow pathfinder prospectuses where they are only circulated to underwriters, brokers, and those under Corporations Regulations regs 7.12.05(a), (e): ASC Policy Statement 8 para 65.

Pawnbroking A form of consumer credit in which a pawnbroker takes possession of an article as security for the repayment of money owed to the pawnbroker: *Coggs v Bernard* (1703) 2 Ld Raym 909; 92 ER 107. If the money is not repaid within a specified time, the pawnbroker has the right to sell the goods: *The Odessa* [1916] 1 AC 145. Legislation in the various jurisdictions regulates pawnbroking activities through a licensing system and prescribes formalities for loan transactions: (NSW) Pawnbrokers Act 1902; (VIC) Second-Hand Dealers and Pawnbrokers Act 1989. See also **Credit**.

Pay As You Earn system *Abbr* – PAYE A system by which tax is deducted at source from salary or wages before payment is made to employees, ensuring collection of the appropriate amount of tax: (CTH) Income Tax Assessment Act 1936 Pt VI Div 2. See also **Eligible Termination Payment; Income taxation; Prescribed Payments System; Salary; Tax instalment deduction; Wage**.

•**Payable on demand** A bill of exchange that is expressed to be payable on demand, at sight (by the acceptor), on presentation (to the acceptor), or where no time for payment is expressed on the face of the bill: (CTH) Bills of Exchange Act 1909 s 15(1).

Payable out of profits The requirement for dividends which are to be paid to shareholders. No dividend can be paid to a shareholder except out of profits: Corporations Law s 201(1); *Mackie v Clough* (1891) 17 VLR 493 at 495. As there is no relevant statutory definition of 'out of profits', the court usually turns to the company accounts and financial accounts to see if there was a profit from which dividends can be made: *Marra Developments Ltd v B W Rofe Pty Ltd* [1977] 2 NSWLR 616 at 629; (1977) 3 ACLR 185. See also **Dividend**.

Payback period The time taken for a project to recover its initial investment. Future earnings are discounted to give a present value to be matched with the initial investment. See also **Cost-benefit analysis**.

•**Pay-day** A day on which wages, salary and earnings become payable: for example (CTH) Public Service Act 1922 s 64(18).

PAYE See **Pay As You Earn system**.

PAYE deduction See **Tax instalment deduction**.

•**Payee** A person named on a negotiable instrument as the person to be paid. Where a bill is not payable to bearer, the payee must be named or otherwise indicated on the bill with reasonable certainty: (CTH) Bills of Exchange Act 1909 s 12(1). See also **Bearer; Bearer bill; Holder in due course; Negotiable instrument**.

Pay-if-paid clause A payments clause, usually found in a subcontract with a nominated subcontractor, under which it is construed that the receipt by the contractor of a progress payment is a condition precedent to the contractor's obligation to pay the subcontractor. The term originates from the United States. See also **Condition precedent; Contractor; Pay-when-paid clause; Subcontract**.

Paying bank Prior to the (CTH) Cheques and Payment Orders Act 1986, the bank upon which a cheque was drawn. The term was imprecise since a bank could pay a cheque as agent for the bank on which the cheque was drawn. Now referred to as the 'drawee bank'. See also **Drawee bank**.

•**Payment** In relation to wages, includes their provision, conferral, and assignment: (NSW) Pay-roll Tax Act 1971 s 3.

Payment for honour supra protest See **Acceptance or payment for honour supra protest**.

Payment in due course Payment made to the holder of a cheque, or to the holder of a bill of exchange at or after the maturity of the bill, in good faith and without notice that the holder's title to the instrument is defective: (CTH) Bills of Exchange Act 1909 s 64(1); (CTH) Cheques and Payment Orders Act 1986 s 79. See also **Bill of exchange; Cheque; Discharge of negotiable instrument; Good faith; Holder; Maturity date**.

•**Payment order** A form of instrument identical to a cheque but drawn on a non-bank financial institution and bearing the words 'payment order' on its face: (CTH) Cheques and Payment Orders Act 1986 s 101. See also **Agency cheque; Bill of exchange; Cheque; Non-bank financial institution; Promissory note**.

Payment system A set of instruments, banking procedures, and interbank funds transfer systems that ensure the circulation of money. A payment system covers not only retail money transfer systems used by businesses and consumers for commercial purposes but also large value interbank funds transfer systems that underpin the money and credit markets of market-oriented economies. See also **Assured payment system; Clearing system; Multilateral net settlement system**.

Payment without discount The payment of the full price for something without reduction. Discounts are frequently allowed for prompt payment of accounts. Discounts may also be demanded by a purchaser of something where some risk attaches to the thing purchased, for example, a negotiable instrument which may be sold by the holder at a discount reflecting the risk that the instrument will not be met according to its terms. See also **Without discount**.

Payout ratio The ratio of total dividends declared or paid by a company, to the profits recorded by that company in the same year. See also **Dividend**.

Payroll tax A tax levied on Australian employers by all states and territories, based on the total amount of wages and salaries, fees, commissions, and bonuses paid to employees: for example (NSW) Pay-roll Tax Act 1971 s 7. See also **Financial year**.

Pay-when-paid clause A payments clause, usually found in a subcontract with a nominated subcontractor, under which the receipt by the contractor of the payment merely fixes the time at which the contractor is obliged to discharge its obligations to pay the subcontractor. Where non-payment by the proprietor causes the payment procedure to fail, the court will imply an obligation on the part of the contractor to pay within a reasonable time: *Ward v Eltherington* [1982] Qd R 561. See also **Contract; Contractor; Pay-if-paid clause; Proprietor; Subcontract**.

PC See **Personal computer; Privy Council**.

Peak load pricing 'Time-of-day' pricing that endeavours to recover the capital costs of a facility at peak periods, recovering only operating costs or short-run marginal costs at off-peak periods. In the supply of electricity, for example, the highest charges correspond with periods of maximum demand, the effect of which is both to recover capacity charges and to discourage excessive use, reducing the amount of generating plant required. At off-peak times, charges are much lower encouraging demand while making more effective use of plant.

•**Pecuniary** *Lat – pecuniaris; pecunia* – money. Consisting of or relating to money or duties which involve the handling of money. See also **Pecuniary loss**.

•**Pecuniary loss** The loss of an easily calculated sum of money: for example *McRae v Commonwealth Disposals Commission* (1951) 84 CLR 377 at 415. However, pecuniary loss does not simply mean 'monetary outlay'; such expenditure may be a guide in the assessment of damages but is not a prerequisite of recovery: *Naum v Nominal Defendant* [1974] 2 NSWLR 14. Loss of service and other material losses are compensable as pecuniary loss. A plaintiff is entitled to recover damages in respect of pecuniary loss suffered as a result of the defendant's tortious conduct or breach of contract, subject to the rules as to remoteness of damage and the plaintiff's duty to mitigate: *Hungerfords v Walker*. See also **Compensation; Damages; Damages for loss of bargain; Non-pecuniary loss; Pure economic loss**.

Pecuniary relief Monetary relief or damages. In equity, three forms of pecuniary relief are available: equitable compensation, equitable damages, and an account of profits. Equitable compensation and an account of profits are available in the inherent jurisdiction of equity, while equitable damages are provided for by statute: (NSW) Supreme Court Act 1970 s 68. Pecuniary relief should be distinguished from non-monetary forms of relief such as injunctions, specific performance, rescission, and rectification.

Pedlar One who carries small goods for sale, usually in a bundle or pack. In its ordinary connotation, the term 'pedlar' does not apply to persons who carry unlawful goods: *Mackie v Australian Consolidated Press Ltd* [1974] 1 NSWLR 561. See also **Goods; Hawker; Sale**.

•**Penalty** 1. Punishment. 2. In contract law, an agreed damages clause which is in the nature of a punishment for non-observance of a contractual stipulation; it imposes an additional or different liability payable upon breach: *Legione v Hateley* (1983) 152 CLR 406; 46 ALR 1. A penalty is a sum *in terrorem* of the defendant; the intention is to intimidate the defendant to perform: *Dunlop Pneumatic Tyre Co Ltd v New Garage and Motor Co Ltd* [1915] AC 79. See also **Agreed damages clause; Liquidated damages; Nominal damages; Penalty clause**.

Penalty bond A double bond in which the obligation provides for payment of a higher sum than that payable by the obligor had the condition in the bond been fulfilled. See also **Bond; Double bond; Obligor.**

Penalty clause A clause imposing a penalty on default, usually unenforceable. By its nature, a penalty clause does not express the party's entitlement to recover his or her actual loss, but an exorbitant sum: *AMEV-UDC Finance Ltd v Austin* (1986) 162 CLR 170; 68 ALR 185. A penalty clause is distinguished from a clause containing a genuine pre-estimate of damages for breach of the contract. Whether a clause is a penalty clause is tested by circumstances existing at the time the contract was entered into, not at the time of the breach of contract. See also **Penalty; Relief against penalties.**

Penalty rate The higher rate that applies for those hours outside of normal working hours, including overtime, weekend work, and work on public holidays. Such rates are most commonly paid to employees in the service industries, who often work unusual hours.

•**Penalty tax** A tax is imposed by the Tax Office when a taxpayer refuses or fails to lodge a tax return relating to a year of income or makes a false or misleading statement relating to the calculation of taxable income.

Pendente lite /pɛndɛnteɪ liteɪ/ **1.** For the duration of legal proceedings. Where a cause of action survives, a proceeding does not become abated by reason of the marriage, death or bankruptcy of a party and does not become defective by the assignment, creation, or devolution of an estate or title pendente lite: (CTH) High Court Rules 1903 O 18 r 1.

Penny dreadfuls Low-priced issues of often highly speculative shares. Penny dreadfuls tend to trade at only a few cents per share. Also known as 'penny stocks'.

•**Pension 1.** A periodical payment made in consideration of past services, an injury or loss sustained, merit, or poverty. See also **Age pension; Annuity.**

•**Pension fund** A superannuation fund which provides benefits in the form of a pension or annuity rather than as a lump sum payment. See also **Annuity; Lump Sum fund; Pension; Superannuation fund.**

•**Pensioner** A person who receives a monetary benefit from either a private pension fund or, more commonly, the Commonwealth Department of Social Security. See also **Age pension; Pension.**

Peppercorn rent A nominal rent that does not reflect or equate with the market value. It is a true rent but is not regarded as a rent in kind so that it cannot be classified as a payment or as needing a receipt: *Re Moody and Yates Contract* (1885) 30 Ch D 344 at 347; *Datastream International Ltd v Oakeep Ltd* [1986] 1 WLR 404 at 406. See also **Rent.**

Per annum /pɜ ænəm/ *Lat* – by the year. A sum of money paid every year.

Per capita /pɜ kæpɪtə/ *Lat* – by heads. Individually in equal shares, according to the number of beneficiaries. Refers to the division and distribution of property based on the number of people entitled in equal shares. *Per capita* distribution makes no reference to stocks or right of representation: for example if a testator divides his or her property *per capita* amongst four children, each child will receive a one quarter share and if a child predeceases the testator, that quarter share is divided among the surviving children. To be contrasted with '*per stirpes*'.

Per capita income The real purchasing power of a community calculated as an average. In recent years, Switzerland has been ranked first, followed by Japan, Sweden, the United States, and Germany.

Per cent(um) /pɜ sɛntəm/ *Symbol* – % *Lat* – by the hundred. Percentage.

Per curiam /pɜ kjuriam/ *Lat* – by the whole court.

Per diem /pɜ diɛm/ *Lat* –by the day. A sum of money paid every day; daily; for a day's work.

Per incuriam /pɜ ɪnkuriæm/ *Lat* – through want of care. A decision given *per incuriam* is given 'in ignorance or forgetfulness' of an earlier relevant case or an inconsistent legislative provision. The doctrine of precedent may not compel a court to follow a decision made *per incuriam*.

Per proc See **Per procurationem; Procuration signature.**

Per procurationem /pɜ prɒkjuratioʊnɛm/ *Lat* – through one's manager; by proxy. By the action of an official agent or deputy. Used to indicate that a letter or document has been signed by an agent for and on behalf of the principal. The correct sequence is 'principal *per pro* agent' but the opposite sequence, 'agent *per pro* principal', is now almost universal. *Abbr* – per/pro, per pro, per proc, pp. See also **Agency; Agent; Principal; Procuration signature.**

Per se /pɜ seɪ/ *Lat* – by itself. Taken alone; essentially; without reference to anything else.

Perfect competition A theoretical concept used in economic analysis, useful for the purpose of exposing and demonstrating the basic forces and laws common to all free markets. On the supply side, the concept implies the presence of many price-taking firms competing with each other, a perfectly elastic supply of the factors of production, mobility, and complete knowledge. On the demand side, the concept implies many purchasers, complete knowledge, an absence of transport costs, and homogeneity. Perfect competition is rarely even approached in contemporary markets, but the concept is of value as a basis for comparison. See also **Economics; Imperfect competition; Monopoly; Oligopoly.**

•**Performance 1.** The doing of some act. **2.** A musical, dramatic, or other form of entertainment.

Contract The acts which a party must do to fulfil the duties created by a contract. In the frustrated contracts legislation, performance is the fulfilment, either wholly or in part, of a promise in the contract, or fulfilment wholly or in part of a condition of or in the contract: for example (NSW) Frustrated Contracts Act 1978 s 5(1). See also **Condition; Contract; Dependent obligation; Entire contract; Frustration; Independent obligation; Part performance; Promise.**

Performance bond 1. An undertaking by a person, often a corporation, to make good a contractual obligation of another, usually on proof of the failure of that other to perform the relevant obligation. **2.** In building law, an unconditional undertaking from a financial institution or insurance company, addressed to a proprietor, in which the institution or company undertakes to pay the proprietor the amount set out in the undertaking on receipt of a demand from the proprietor: *Hortico (Aust) Pty Ltd v Energy Equipment Co (Aust) Pty Ltd* (1985) 1 NSWLR 545. See also **Bond; Contractor; First demand guarantee; Guarantee; Guarantee bond; Letter of credit; Performance undertaking; Promissory note; Proprietor.**

Performance clause A clause in a time charterparty providing that if the chartered vessel is unable to achieve the agreed speed or consumes more fuel than stipulated, the charterer may recover from the shipowner the cost of the time lost or the extra fuel. The amount is usually recovered by a deduction from the hire money. See also **Charterer; Charterparty; Terms and conditions; Time charterparty.**

Performance guarantee See **Performance undertaking.**

Performance undertaking In relation to a building contract, a form of security generally used by a party which is a corporation and is a subsidiary of, or is related to, another corporation. The parent corporation guarantees the subsidiary corporation's performance under the contract, if default occurs. Also known as 'performance guarantee'. See also **Building contract; Guarantee; Performance bond; Security; Subsidiary.**

Periodic inventory method An inventory accounting procedure that records inventory acquisitions as purchases in an expense account rather than an inventory account. The cost of inventory on hand is calculated and recorded in an inventory account after the periodic physical inventory count or stocktake at the end of the period. The cost of goods available for sale is computed by adding the inventory on hand at the beginning of the period to the purchases made during the period. The cost of goods sold is determined by deducting the cost of the physical inventory at the end of the period from the cost of goods available for sale. This method can be contrasted to the perpetual inventory method. Also known as 'physical inventory method'. See also **Perpetual inventory method; Trading stock.**

Perishable goods Goods which rapidly decay. Because such goods lose their value if not put to their intended use within a short period of time, special arrangements are made for their carriage. Commonly such goods are given priority by carriers so as to reach their intended destination with the least possible delay. Where delay is inevitable and the volume of traffic warrants it, specialised vehicles or vessels may be provided for the carriage of such goods. See also **Carriage of goods.**

•**Perjury** An offence at common law of making a false statement on oath in a judicial proceeding concerning a matter material to the proceeding, while knowing that the statement is false, or not believing it to be true: *R v Traino* (1987) 45 SASR 473 at 475. In some jurisdictions, the common law offence has been substantially replicated in statute: for example (NSW) Crimes Act 1900 s 327. In other jurisdictions, the offence has been extended so that some of the restrictions of the common law offence have been removed. For example, in (QLD) Criminal Code s 123, it is immaterial whether the testimony is given on oath or under any other sanction authorised by law or whether the court or tribunal is properly constituted. See also **Witness.**

Permanent differences Differences existing between accounting income and taxable income. Permanent differences arise due to the inclusion of specific revenues, gains, expenses, or losses in accounting income that are excluded from the calculation of taxable income. Likewise, taxable income could include several items that are absent from the calculation of accounting income. For example a receipt may be a capital receipt for accounting purposes and not be accounting income, however it may be a capital gain for income tax purposes and therefore deemed to be income and included in the taxable income of the recipient. See also **Timing differences.**

Permanent employment A contract of employment of indefinite duration, with the expectation that the employee will, in the absence of illness, resignation, dismissal on notice, or dismissal for misconduct, continue to be a part of a stable workforce: *McClelland v Northern Ireland General Health Services Board* [1957] 2 All ER 129. See also **Contract of employment; Fixed term contract.**

•**Permanent establishment** For income tax purposes, a place at or through which a person carries on business including: a place where a person carries on business through an agent; a place where a person is using, or installing substantial equipment or machinery; or a place where a person is engaged in a construction project: (CTH) Income Tax Assessment Act 1936 ss 6(1), 6(6). The concept of a permanent establishment operates as a basis for determining the source of income in relation to the allocation of taxing rights in double tax treaties between Australia and other countries. See also **Double tax treaty; Source of income.**

Permitted buy-back See **Authorised buy-back.**

Perpetual inventory method An inventory accounting procedure which records inventory acquisitions and disposals in the inventory account at the time that the transactions occur. The perpetual inventory method is distinguished from the periodic inventory method and provides a continuous inventory record showing the physical quantity of trading stock and its equivalent value which is available as stock on hand. Inventory disposals and losses are transferred to the cost of goods sold account from the inventory account. See also **Periodic inventory method; Trading stock.**

Perpetual succession That characteristic of a company which makes it a continuing entity in law with its own identity regardless of changes in its membership. A registered company is declared to have perpetual succession: Corporations Law s 123(2)(c). See also **Corporation; Incorporation.**

Perpetual trustee A person who holds property in trust for another according to the principles of equity for as long as the trust exists, hence a permanent or perpetual appointment for the life of the trust. See also **Perpetuity; Trust; Trustee.**

Perpetuities, rule against See **Rule against perpetuities**.

Perpetuity A form of trust that potentially lasts forever, as the interests under a perpetuity have no identifiable vesting date. The rule against perpetuities invalidates such trusts: *Cox v Archer* (1964) 110 CLR 1. See also **Perpetuity period; Rule against perpetuities; Trust**.

Perpetuity period The period of time relevant to the rule against perpetuities or remoteness of vesting. At common law, the period is calculated according to the life or lives in being plus 21 years from the date of creation of the interest, with the possible addition of the period of gestation where an unborn child may qualify: *Hardebol v Perpetual Trustee Co Ltd* [1975] 1 NSWLR 221. See also **Future interest; Rule against perpetuities; Trust**.

Perquisite A benefit arising from and payable in the course of employment. See also **Fringe benefit**.

•**Person** A separate legal entity, recognised by the law as having rights and obligations. There are two subcategories: a natural person, being a human being; and an artificial person, being an entity to which the law attributes personality. See also **Association; Company; Incorporation; Incorporated association; Unincorporated association**.

Personal accident and illness insurance A contract of insurance providing the insured with specified benefits if he or she sustains a personal injury by accident. Personal accident insurance may pay a lump sum or a periodic amount calculated on the basis of the insured's income. Unless otherwise agreed, income protection does not extend to loss of profit: *Theobald v Railway Passenger Assurance Co* (1854) 10 Ex 45; 156 ER 349. All policies limit the events which may give rise to liability, and the words of the policy are to be read in their ordinary sense: *Australian Casualty Co Ltd v Federico* (1986) 160 CLR 513; 66 ALR 99. The (CTH) Insurance Contracts Act 1984 Pt V ss 34-36 sets out the minimum standard cover an insurer must provide under a policy. In the context of insurance, an 'accident' is an unexpected, unintended, or unforeseen happening which causes loss or hurt: *Australian Casualty Co Ltd v Federico*. It is not necessary that an accident be entirely unexpected, so long as it is not wanted or designed by the insured: *Mount Albert City Council v New Zealand Municipalities Co-operative Insurance Co Ltd* [1983] NZLR 190. An 'illness' includes not only bodily disorders sustained as a result of an identifiable traumatic occurrence but extends to sickness or disease contracted as the result of contagion or insidious disease, or the natural progression of some physical or mental defect: *Australian Casualty Co Ltd v Federico*. See also **Accident insurance; Injury; Life insurance**.

Personal action An action at common law evolving from early medieval times, the subject matter of which was not land but personal obligations, particularly contracts. A personal action is distinguishable from an action *in rem*, a claim to or against certain property in respect of which damage has been done. Also known as '*actio in personam*'. See also **In personam**.

Personal cheque as legal tender The practice of giving and accepting personal cheques in payment of debts and liabilities is now so widespread that there is a general expectation on the part of persons making payments that a personal cheque, given in payment of a debt or liability, will be accepted unless the payee objects before or at the time of receipt that the cheque does not constitute legal tender. A personal cheque, though not legal tender, is a sufficient payment if not objected to on that account: *Wexelman v Dale* [1917] 35 DLR 557; *Laidlaw v Rehill* [1943] 4 DLR 429; *George v Cluning* (1979) 28 ALR 57. An opposite view was expressed in *Blumberg v Life Interests & Reversionary Securities Corp* [1897] 1 Ch 171 at 173, where it was said that the acceptance of a personal cheque involves passing judgment on the solvency of the person who tenders the cheque. See also **Cheque; Legal tender**.

Personal computer *Abbr* – PC A self-contained computer equipped with a central processing unit, memory chips (random-access or read-only or both), software program, storage device (such as a hard disk), and the capability to receive input (such as data from a modem or a diskette) and produce output (such as data files or printed documents).

•**Personal effects** Moveable chattels, goods, and property of a distinctly personal nature such as bedroom articles, furniture, family heirlooms, and personal clothing, not including items used for business purposes or money: (VIC) Administration and Probate Act 1958 s 5(1). See also **Chattel; Legacy**.

Personal exertion, income from See **Income from personal exertion**.

Personal identification number *Abbr* – PIN A numeric code which a cardholder may need to quote for verification of identity. In electronic transactions, it is seen as the equivalent of a signature. See also **Automatic teller machine; Cash dispenser**.

Personal liability In the context of agency, a contractual liability incurred by an agent on the authority of the agent's principal that must be indemnified by the principal: *Seymour v Bridge* (1885) 14 QBD 460. See also **Vicarious liability**.

Personal loan A loan to an individual for household or other personal use and not for business purposes. See also **Business; Credit; Loan**.

•**Personal property** All property other than land and incorporeal hereditaments, which together form the category of real property. Personal property includes chattels real, which covers leasehold interests, and chattels personal which covers tangible chattels ('choses in possession'), and intangible chattels ('choses in action'). Also known as 'personalty'. See also **Chose in action; Chose in possession; Incorporeal hereditament; Leasehold**.

•**Personal service** 1. In contract law, a service which requires the personal participation of the service provider. 2. In taxation law, a service provided by professionals such as barristers, doctors, and dentists, in contrast to accountants, solicitors, and other professionals who provide professional services as a 'business'. See also **Cash basis of accounting; Frustrating event; Frustration; Specific performance**.

•**Personal services** Services provided by a bankrupt of a physical, intellectual, or other kind, whether or not as an employee and whether or they are provided to discharge the obligations of another entity: (CTH) Bankruptcy Act 1966 s 5(1). The court has power to order an entity, controlled by a bankrupt, to hand over property or money obtained as a result of the bankrupt providing personal services: (CTH) Bankruptcy Act 1966 s 139D. See also **Associated entity**; **Bankrupt**; **Bankruptcy Court**; **Controlled entity**; **Divisible property**.

•**Personal-use asset** In taxation law, an asset other than land which is kept primarily for the personal use or enjoyment of a taxpayer or associates, a debt owed in respect of such an asset, or an option to acquire an asset that would become such an asset: (CTH) Income Tax Assessment Act 1936 s 160B(1). There are two categories: listed personal-use assets and non-listed personal-use assets. There are special rules for taxing capital gains made on personal use assets. See also **Asset**; **Capital gains tax**; **Listed personal-use asset**; **Non-listed personal-use asset**.

Personenvennootschap met beperkte aansprakelijkheid *Abbr* – PVBA Belgian equivalent of a private limited liability company.

•**Petitioner** The party who issues a petition in bankruptcy. A creditor may issue a creditor's petition against a debtor who has committed an act of bankruptcy ((CTH) Bankruptcy Act 1966 s 44) or a debtor may sign for voluntary bankruptcy by filing a debtor's petition: s 55; *Deputy Commissioner of Taxation (Vic) v Boxshall* (1988) 19 FCR 435; 83 ALR 175. See also **Bankruptcy**; **Creditor's petition**; **Debtor's petition**.

Petty banking The practice of issuing promissory notes for profit in colonial New South Wales. See Historical Records of Australia, series 1, vol 7, pp 264-265. See also **Currency**; **Usury**.

Philips v Eyre, rule in An Anglo-Australian tort rule stating that both the *lex fori* and the *lex loci delicti* determine whether a plaintiff can recover damages for a foreign tort: *Philips v Eyre* (1870) LR 6 QB 1. The rule in *Philips v Eyre* suggests that the law of the place where the tort was committed, as well as the law of the municipal court, is relevant in determining the choice of the forum and the choice of the law, despite the existence of a uniform choice of law rule. See also **Lex fori**.

Physical inventory method See **Periodic inventory method**.

Piece rate See **Piece work**.

Piece work Work that is allocated by the piece, and paid for according to the number of pieces done. See also **Right to work**; **Task rate**.

PIN See **Personal identification number**.

•**Pirate** A person who without legal permission plunders other vessels indiscriminately on the high seas for the person's own ends: *Republic of Bolivia v Indemnity Mutual Marine Assurance Co Ltd* [1909] 1 KB 785. Piracy is a maritime peril which may be insured against.

Pirate copy A generic term for a copy of copyright material made without the permission of the copyright owner or the relevant exclusive licensee. A copyright owner may have remedies in detinue and conversion in respect of pirated copies of material in which he or she has copyright: (CTH) Copyright Act 1968 s 116(1). See also **Copyright**; **Licence**.

Pit In relation to securities, the areas of a trading floor used to trade contracts. See also **Stock exchange**; **Sydney Futures Exchange**.

Pit bull spread A spread which involves buying a put option at a lower strike price and selling one at a higher strike price. In a case where the user believes the price will fall, the user would use a call (put) bear spread that involves selling a low strike price call (put) and buying a call (put) with a higher strike price. See also **Spread**; **Strike price**.

Place of breach of contract The municipal jurisdiction or place where a contract's conditions and obligations are not performed or breached resulting in an action for specific performance or damages as a remedy for that breach of contract. The jurisdiction of the place of breach of contract is usually the forum where the remedies for the breach may be pursued. See also **Damages**; **Proper law of contract**; **Remedy**; **Specific performance**.

Place of making contract Generally, the place where the act or thing was done or said which finally created the contractual obligation: *Tallerman and Co Pty Ltd v Nathan's Merchandise (Vic) Pty Ltd* (1957) 98 CLR 93; [1957] SR (NSW) 466. In most cases, this will be the place where the acceptance is communicated to the offeror: *Tallerman and Co Pty Ltd v Nathan's Merchandise (Vic) Pty Ltd*. If the postal acceptance rule applies, the contract is made where the letter is posted: *Tallerman and Co Pty Ltd v Nathan's Merchandise (Vic) Pty Ltd*. See also **Acceptance**; **Offer**; **Offer and acceptance**; **Offeror**; **Postal acceptance rule**.

•**Place of origin 1.** In relation to goods, the geographical locality where goods are brought into existence and, in the case of sophisticated items produced in stages, substantially developed into their recognisable form. The description of an item as 'made in' a particular locality is a statement concerning that item's place of origin: *Netcomm (Aust) Pty Ltd v Dataplex Pty Ltd* (1988) 81 ALR 101; 11 IPR 375; (CTH) Trade Practices Act 1974 s 53. **2.** In relation to a body corporate, the State, Territory, or other location where the body is incorporated: Corporations Law s 9. See also **False representation**.

•**Placement 1.** The process of selling new issues of securities through a stockbroker or other intermediary to existing shareholders and the public. **2.** The process of selling a new issue of shares directly to an institutional investor by way of a private placement. See also **Share**.

•**Plaintiff** A person who seeks relief against any other person by any form of proceedings in a court: (CTH) Judiciary Act 1903 s 2. See also **Applicant**; **Claim**; **Complainant**; **Petitioner**.

•**Planning** A term which implies a scheme for the future incorporating some systematic plan for the development of a town intended to subject the development of

Pla

localities or areas of land to direction and restraint: *Matthews v City of Ringwood* (1963) 60 LGRA 175 at 185.

Planning controls Statutory instruments and policies of both State and municipal government determining the manner in which development occurs in a district or region. Planning controls generally require persons proposing to undertake development to apply for permission from the local planning authority. Restrictions may be imposed on development on the bases of protecting the environmental qualities of the particular area or the general quality of life in a particular neighbourhood. For example, in determining a development application, a consent authority in New South Wales must have regard to the impact of the development on the environment and the effect of that development on the landscape or scenic quality of the locality: (NSW) Environmental Planning and Assessment Act 1979 s 90.

•**Plant** Whatever apparatus is used by a person in the carrying out of business, the content of which will be resolved by considering carefully the nature or particular trade or business carried on in each case and generally would include all goods and chattels, fixed or movable, live, or dead which are kept for permanent use in the business: *Inland Revenue Cmrs v Scottish & Newcastle Breweries Ltd* [1982] 1 WLR 322. See also **Cost of plant**; **Depreciation**; **Plant or articles**.

•**Plant or articles** In taxation law, 'plant' includes whatever apparatus the taxpayer uses for the purpose of producing assessable income, such as machinery used to produce the taxpayer's trading stock and the normal tools of trade. It does not include items which merely form part of the setting within which the taxpayer's income producing activities are carried on, so that a building will rarely be plant: *Federal Cmr of Taxation v Broken Hill Proprietary Co Ltd* (1969) 120 CLR 240. (CTH) Income Tax Assessment Act 1936 s 54(2) extends the common law definition to include beasts of burden, certain structures on land used for primary production and, in certain cases, plumbing fixtures and fittings. 'Article' means a piece of goods or property: *Federal Cmr of Taxation v Faichney* (1972) 129 CLR 38. (CTH) Income Tax Assessment Act 1936 s 54 allows a deduction for the depreciation of any plant or article owned by the taxpayer that was used in the year of income for income producing purposes or has been installed and during the year of income was held in reserve ready for such use. See also **Allowable deduction**; **Depreciation**; **Plant**.

plc Abbreviation for a public limited company in the United Kingdom and the Republic of Ireland.

Plea In criminal law, an accused's answer to a charge when it is read to him or her in court. It usually takes the form of the answer 'guilty' or 'not guilty', which is known as a plea to the general issue. The accused may also make a special plea either in addition to or instead of the general plea. The accused may be permitted to change the plea during the course of the hearing. The accused may plead guilty to any count or any alternative charge whether included in the indictment or presentment or not: (NSW) Crimes Act 1900 s 394A; (VIC) Crimes Act 1958 s 390A(2).

Plea bargaining In criminal law, negotiations between the prosecution and the defence by which the accused agrees to plead guilty to an offence on condition that the prosecution not proceed with a more serious charge: *R v Marshall* [1981] VR 725 at 732. See also **Plea**.

•**Pledge 1.** A form of security over a chattel constituted by delivery by the pledgor of the chattel or documents of title to the chattel to the security holder (the pledgee) with a right to re-transfer of possession and discharge of the security on performance of the obligation secured, and an authority in the pledgee to sell the property on default by the pledgor: *Askrigg Pty Ltd v Student Guild of the Curtin University of Technology* (1989) 18 NSWLR 738 at 743-744; 1 ACSR 40; *Re Vital Learning Aids Pty Ltd* [1979] 2 NSWLR 442 at 445. See also **Bailment**; **Chattel**; **Delivery**; **Hypothecation**; **Lien**; **Possession**.

Pledge by buyer Transfer of possession of property transferred to a third person by a purchaser prior to the purchaser acquiring ownership. A pledge by a buyer does not affect the unpaid seller's rights unless the seller has allowed the buyer to make the pledge. Where a document of title has been lawfully transferred to a buyer or owner of the goods and that person transfers to a person who takes the document in good faith and for valuable consideration, if the latter transfer was by way of pledge then the unpaid seller's rights can only be exercised subject to the rights of the transferee: (NSW) Sale of Goods Act 1923 s 49; (ACT) Sale of Goods Act 1954 s 50. See also **Buyer**; **Consideration**; **Goods**; **Pledge**; **Sale**.

Pledgee The person to whom a chattel is delivered to constitute a pledge. See also **Pledge**; **Pledgor**.

Pledgor The person who creates a pledge by delivering a chattel to another as security for performance of an obligation, and who traditionally is said to retain a 'general property' in the pledged chattel. See also **General property**; **Pledge**; **Pledgee**.

Point of sale *Abbr* – POS The use of payment cards at a retail location (point of sale). The payment information is captured either by paper vouchers or by electronic terminals, which, in some cases, are designed also to transmit the information. Where this is so, the arrangement may be referred to as 'electronic funds transfer at the point of sale' (EFTPOS).

Poison pill defence A form of takeover preventative mechanism or defence which, in its basic form, involves issuing options or securities (such as convertible notes) which entitle their holders to purchase a share of the company at a specified price at some time in the future, with that entitlement immediately accelerating should, for example, a takeover be made or should a person become entitled to a specified percentage of the company's shares. Also known as 'scorched earth' tactics. See also **Greenmail**; **Pac-man defence**.

•**Poll** A method of voting at a general meeting of a company where each voter signs a paper headed 'for' or 'against' the motion, as the case may be. Members have a general right for a poll to be taken, as opposed to a simple show of hands, since any article which purports to exclude the right to demand a poll at a general meeting is void, except in relation to the election of the chairperson or adjournment of the meeting: Corporations Law s 248.

Poll tax A tax levied on the basis of the same amount being payable by each person subject to the tax.

•**Pollution** Changes in the physical, chemical, and biological characteristics of air, water, or soil which can affect the health or survival of forms of life in an undesirable way; the direct or indirect alteration of the environment to its detriment or degradation. Pollution includes effluent, litter, refuse, sewage, waste, or any other matter or thing that impairs or is likely to impair the environment: (WA) Waterways Conservation Act 1976 s 3. Forms of pollution include air, water, land, noise and marine pollution.

•**Pools** In corporations law, a form of market manipulation where a person conspires with associates to generate artificial market activity. A common scheme involves members agreeing to subscribe to a certain amount to establish a substantial pool of funds which is used by a broker for the pool to successively sell from one member of the pool to another member in order to boost reported turnover and price. Pools are prohibited: Corporations Law ss 997, 998. See also **False trading**; **Market manipulation**.

Port of entry *Abbr* – POE 1. A port equipped with a customs house administering the laws imposing duties on ships and imported goods and through which ships or merchandise are cleared. 2. A port at which immigrants arrive. See also **Customs duty**.

Portfolio The list of securities held by a person or institution. Portfolio management consists of arranging investments so as to achieve a balance of risks and rewards acceptable to the investor.

Portfolio dividend A dividend paid to a corporate shareholder where the shareholder has an interest in the payer company's voting power (for s 160AFB purposes) of less than 10 per cent: (CTH) Income Tax Assessment Act 1936 s 317.

Portfolio insurance An investment strategy using combinations of options and futures contracts. While the benefit gained from a substantial upward movement in shares prices will be somewhat less than the movement in the market, any adverse effect when share prices fall substantially will be less than the fall in the market. The portfolio is protected or 'insured' against the full consequences of wide swings in the market. Portfolio insurance was identified by the Brady Commission as the main contributor to the selling stampede on Black Monday in 1987. See also **Black Monday**.

Portfolio management The arrangement of investments in securities so as to achieve a balance of risks and rewards acceptable to the individual investor. Portfolio management involves a careful assessment of security characteristics, such as the rate of return and the likely appreciation of the security, the ability to sell a security at a good figure before maturity, the terms on which a recovered principal could be reinvested, and the effects of inflation on the value of assets. Risks may be reduced by diversification of investment into several contrasting streams and rewards may be enhanced by constant review of the investments with a view to more effective deployment.

Portfolio manager See **Portfolio management**.

POS See **Point of sale**.

•**Position** 1. An interest in a commodity market, either long or short, in the form of open contracts which have not been liquidated. 2. The balance of assets (loans and spot and forward purchases) and liabilities (deposits and spot and forward sales) in a foreign currency.

Positional good or service A good or service the market value of which is socially influenced. Many goods or services in society have hierarchical significance and personal satisfaction may be derived from being top of the tree in one respect or another. Goods and services associated with well-regarded positions may become more highly valued as basic necessities are met. Economic growth may yield less satisfaction than expected as distributional aspects become more prominent.

Positive confirmation See **Confirmation**.

Positive covenant A covenant in relation to land which imposes obligations of a positive nature, such as carrying out work or expending money on land.

Positive duty In the law of contract, a term referring to the requirement to perform a contractual obligation. A positive duty usually requires the doing of an act, rather than mere inactivity; it is thus to be contrasted with a negative duty. Also known as 'affirmative term'. See also **Injunction**; **Negative duty**; **Term**.

•**Possession** *OF – possesser Lat – possidere –* to sit on. Effective physical or manual control or occupation: *Horsley v Phillips Fine Art Auctioneers Pty Ltd* (unrptd, SC(NSW), Santow J, 3211/92, 31 July 1995). Also known as 'de facto possession' or 'detention'. See also **Chattel**; **Constructive possession**; **Conversion**; **Custody**; **Delivery**; **Detinue**; **Ownership**; **Property**.

Real property Physical occupation of, or control over, property: *Oxford Meat Co Pty Ltd v McDonald* [1963] SR (NSW) 423. In property law, possession includes intention to possess the relevant property as a mental element. The interest of a person in possession of property is recognised as a proprietary right, defeatable only by a person showing better title, which may be documentary title or title derived from prior possession. See also **Documentary title**; **Property**.

Sale of goods The right to control property, either by physical custody or by direction of the person who has physical custody: (NSW) Factors (Mercantile Agents) Act 1923 s 6(3); *Gamer's Motor Centre (Newcastle) Pty Ltd v NatWest Wholesale Australia Pty Ltd* (1987) 163 CLR 236; 72 ALR 321. See also **Constructive delivery**; **Delivery**; **Sale of goods**; **Seller in possession after sale**.

Possessory lien At common law, a right to keep possession of a chattel until a claim has been met: *Dinmore Meatworks Pty Ltd v Kerr* (1962) 108 CLR 628. The right arises by operation of law out of the relationship between the lienor and the lienee. Its essential feature is that it relates to the possession of the chattel, as it can arise only by the lienee being given possession by the owner, or a person in possession acting by the authority of the owner: *Protean Enterprises (Newmarket) Pty Ltd v Randall* [1975] VR 327. See also **Chattel; Contractor; Equitable lien; Lien; Lienee; Lienor; Proprietor**.

Post dating The dating of a document or cheque in advance, rendering it ineffective until that future date.

Post market trading *Abbr* – PMT A global electronic automated trading system operated by the Chicago Mercantile Exchange (CME). The PMT operates for the whole period when the CME is not trading, enabling 24 hour global trading in interest-rate, currency and stock-index futures contracts.

Postal acceptance rule The rule of contract that acceptance of an offer is effective immediately after a properly prepaid and addressed letter of acceptance is posted: *Adams v Lindsell* (1818) 1 B & Ald 861; 106 ER 250; *Tooth v Fleming* (1859) Legge 1152. A contract may be thus formed on posting even though the offeror is then ignorant of that fact and even though the letter is delayed in transit, or lost in the post and therefore never ultimately delivered: *Household Fire and Carriage Accident Insurance Co Ltd v Grant* (1879) LR 4 Ex 216. See also **Acceptance; Contract; Offer**.

Post-date To write on an instrument a date later than the date on which the instrument is executed. A post-dated cheque or bill of exchange is not invalid by reason only that it is post-dated: (CTH) Cheques and Payment Orders Act 1986 s 16(2)(b); (CTH) Bills of Exchange Act 1909 s 18(2). See also **Ante-date; Bill of exchange; Cheque; Instrument; Post-dated cheque**.

Post-dated cheque A cheque that is dated later than the date of execution. Post-dated cheques are not invalid: (CTH) Cheques and Payment Orders Act 1986 s 16(2). Post-dated cheques have been common commercial paper since at least the middle of the last century: *Hodgson & Lee Pty Ltd v Mardonius Pty Ltd* (1986) 5 NSWLR 496; 78 ALR 573. A bank is, however, not entitled to pay a post-dated cheque before the date which it bears and to charge the amount to the customer's account: *Brien v Dwyer* (1978) 141 CLR 378; 22 ALR 485. Where a bank pays a post-dated cheque before its date, and then dishonours another cheque of its customer (which was presented before the post-dated one) on the grounds that after payment of the post-dated cheque, the funds were insufficient to meet the other, the customer is entitled to damages for wrongful dishonour: *Pollock v Bank of New Zealand* (1901) 20 NZLR 174; *Keyes v Royal Bank of Canada* [1947] SCR 377. See also **Good faith; Post-date**.

Potior est conditio defendentis /pɒtiɔ ɛst kɒndɪtiʊ deɪfɛndɛntɪs/ *Lat* – the position of the defendant is to be preferred.

Potior est conditio possidentis /pɒtiɔ ɛst kɒndɪtiʊ pɒsɪdɛntɪs/ *Lat* – the position of the person in possession is to be preferred.

Power of advancement The power residing in a trustee to make an advance from capital for the benefit of a beneficiary who is entitled to the whole or part of the capital of the trust property. The term 'advancement' includes the payment of money to enable an infant to emigrate: *Re Dick; Dick v Dick* [1940] VLR 166 at 169 See also **Trustee**.

•**Power of appointment** In disposition of property under a will or trust instrument, a power granted by the testator or settlor to a specified person, the appointor, to select or appoint a beneficiary or beneficiaries from a general or specific class to take an interest in some property, real or personal, of the deceased estate or the trust. The power of appointment in selecting the beneficiaries or objects of the power may be general (appoint anyone including the appointor), special (appoint only from a specified class) or hybrid (appoint anyone except specified persons) and involves an exercise of discretion by the appointor in relation to distribution: (NSW) Wills, Probate and Administration Act 1898 s 9; (VIC) Wills Act 1958 s 9; (VIC) Administration and Probate Amendment Act 1994 s 6(3), (4). **2.** A term used in legislation or instruments to refer to a power to appoint a person to perform a particular function: for example (VIC) Commercial Arbitration Act 1984 s 4(1). See also **Appointment; Bare power; Trust power**.

•**Power of attorney** **1.** The authority for one person to act in the place of another as agent, conferred by an instrument (usually under seal) described as a 'power of attorney'. **2.** A formal instrument authorising a person to act for another, to sign legally binding documents on behalf of the donor of that authority. See also **Agency; Agent; Deed; Instrument under seal; Principal**.

Power of sale A power to sell property which is held as security when there is a default in the terms of repayment. A lender who has security in the form of an equitable mortgage or equitable charge will not have a power of sale unless the security document specifically gives the lender one, or unless the security document is in the form of a deed: for example (NSW) Conveyancing Act 1919 s 109(1)(a); (VIC) Transfer of Land Act 1958 s 77; (QLD) Property Law Act 1974 s 83(1)(a). A power of sale is implied in all Torrens title mortgages: for example (NSW) Real Property Act 1900 ss 57, 58; (VIC) Transfer of Land Act 1958 ss 76, 77; (SA) Real Property Act 1886 ss 132, 133. See also **Mortgage; Mortgagee**.

Powers of partner The authority a partner has in relation to the partnership. Every partner is an agent of the firm and of the other partners for the purposes of the partnership: for example (QLD) Partnership Act 1891 s 8. Any act done by a partner for carrying on business in the usual way, of the kind carried on by the partnership, binds the firm and the other partners, subject to certain qualifications as to authority: for example (NT) Partnership Act 1891 (SA) s 5. See also **Apparent authority; Carrying on business; Implied powers of partner; Partnership**.

pp See **Per procurationem; Procuration signature**.

PPS See **Prescribed Payments System**.

Prearranged trading An arrangement made by brokers outside the trading pit to execute the trade within the pit at a certain price. Prearranged trading is an alternative to trading in accordance with the open outcry system. See also **Open outcry; Pit**.

Precatory trust A trust arising from precatory words (words expressing a desire that a certain thing be done). The term 'precatory trust' is misleading since, if as a matter of construction those words are sufficient to give rise to a trust, that trust is an ordinary trust with no unusual features: *Re Williams* [1897] 2 Ch 12. See also **Trust**.

Pre-contract dealings Dealing of the parties before the contract was formed. Where the agreement is not wholly in writing, its terms may depend wholly or in part upon conversations and dealings between the parties. Evidence of dealings before the alleged contract may be led to show that no contract was in fact entered into (*Air Great Lakes Pty Ltd v K S Easter (Holdings) Pty Ltd* (1985) 2 NSWLR 309), or to show that the parties did not intend that their bargain be wholly recorded in the document: *Gordon v Macgregor* (1909) 8 CLR 316; 15 ALR 274. Even where the parties evince an intention that the agreement be wholly recorded in writing, their pre-contract dealings may be of importance to determine the true nature of the transaction (*Gurfinkel v Bentley Pty Ltd* (1966) 116 CLR 98; 40 ALJR 354), or the circumstances in which it was to apply: *Bovis Construction (Scotland) Ltd v Whatlings Construction Ltd* (1994) 67 BLR 25 at 38 See also **Building contract**; **Pre-contract work**.

Pre-contract expenditure Expenditure incurred before a contract is entered into. Generally, pre-contract expenditure cannot be recovered as a distinct head of damage; nevertheless, expenditure required under the contract, even if in fact incurred before the contract was entered into, may be recovered: *Lloyd v Stanbury* [1971] 1 WLR 535. Where the parties contemplated that pre-contract expenditure would be lost if the contract were not to be performed, and there is no way of estimating the profit which would have been made had the contract been performed, then pre-contract expenditure may be a basis for calculating compensation: *Anglia Television Ltd v Reed* [1972] 1 QB 60. See also **Damages**; **Heads of damage**; **Performance**.

Pre-contract inquiries Investigations made or questions raised made before signing of a contract: *Meehan v Jones* (1982) 149 CLR 571; 42 ALR 463. Pre-contract inquiries may lead to misrepresentation, a claim under (CTH) Trade Practices Act s 52 for misleading and deceptive conduct, or an estoppel: for example *Waltons Stores (Interstate) Ltd v Maher* (1988) 164 CLR 387; 76 ALR 513. Specific examples of pre-contractual inquiries include turnover; profit; value of premises; condition and quality of premises or repairs or renovations; and stocking capacity of rural properties. See also **Contract**; **Pre-contract work**.

Pre-contract work The work done where the contract is awarded to the contractor and the work put in hand before the formal contract is finally negotiated and executed: for example *British Steel Corp v Cleveland Bridge and Engineering Co Ltd* [1984] 1 All ER 504. Sometimes the contract is backdated to the date of its award. Subject to any statutory requirement, the contract so executed may, provided the parties agree that the contract should apply to this work (for example *Trollope & Colls Ltd v Atomic Power Constructions Ltd* [1962] 3 All ER 1035 at 1040; [1963] 1 WLR 333), have retrospective effect so that the obligations of the parties in respect of pre-contract work will be governed by the subsequent document: *City of Box Hill v E W Tauschke Pty Ltd* [1974] VR 39. See also **Building contract**; **Pre-contract dealings**.

Pre-contractual promises Promises on which a party claims to have relied in deciding to make a contract that did not in fact become terms of the contract. Pre-contractual promises may found an estoppel (*Waltons Stores (Interstate) Ltd v Maher* (1988) 164 CLR 387; 76 ALR 513) or a collateral contract: for example *L G Thorne & Co Pty Ltd v Thomas Borthwick & Sons (A'asia) Ltd* (1956) 56 SR (NSW) 81. A pre-contractual promise may also be actionable as a misrepresentation: *Alati v Kruger* (1955) 94 CLR 216. See also **Collateral contract**; **Estoppel**; **Misrepresentation**; **Representation**; **Warranty**; **Warranty of authority**.

Pre-contractual statement A statement made prior to a contract being entered into. A pre-contractual statement can be a statement intended to operate as a term whose breach gives rise to a claim for damages, a representation of fact, or a puff. The purpose of classifying pre-contractual statements is to determine those which have contractual force. See also **Contract**; **Misrepresentation**; **Representation**; **Term**.

Predatory conduct A term used in competition law to distinguish competition on its merits from impermissible business conduct. Predatory conduct sacrifices net revenues or profit that can be earned under competitive circumstances, were the rivals to remain viable, in order to induce exit or deter entry, with the expectation that monopoly profits can be earned in the absence of those rivals. An example is predatory pricing. See also **Areeda and Turner test**; **Competition**; **Competition law**; **Net profit**; **Predatory pricing**.

•**Predatory pricing** Pricing below an appropriate measure of cost for the purpose of eliminating competitors in the short run and reducing competition in the long run: *Cargil Inc v Monfort of Colorado Inc* (1986) 479 US 104. See also **Competition**; **Competition law**; **Predatory conduct**; **Restrictive trade practices**.

Pre-emption An obligation to offer the right to purchase to one person before, or in preference to, others, but at a price which may be acceptable to or set by the others: *Manchester Ship Canal Co v Manchester Racecourse Co* [1901] 2 Ch 37; *Pritchard v Briggs* [1980] Ch 338 at 364. See also **Articles of association**; **Option**.

Pre-emption defence A defence to a product liability claim based upon compliance of a product's design or information with a mandatory standard or other legal requirement: (CTH) Trade Practices Act 1974 s 75AK(b).

•**Preference** An advantage gained by a creditor over the other creditors of a person who subsequently becomes bankrupt. The advantage must result from the debtor transferring property, giving security, undertaking an obligation, or making a payment to the preferred creditor at a time when the debtor was insolvent. See also **Bankrupt**; **Creditors petition**; **Debtor's petition**; **Good faith**; **Insolvent**; **Ordinary course of business**; **Purchaser for valuable consideration**.

Preference dividend A dividend paid to a preference shareholder. See also **Preference share**.

Preference in trade, commerce or revenue The conferral, by a law of the Commonwealth relating to trade, commerce or revenue, of a tangible advantage or commercial benefit on one State or one part of a State over another State or another part of a State: *Elliott v Commonwealth* (1936) 54 CLR 657. The Commonwealth cannot give preference to one State or part of a State over another State or part of a State in a law or regulation of trade, commerce, or revenue: Commonwealth Constitution s 99. See also **Preference share**.

Preference share A share which ranks above ordinary shares but below creditors, debenture-holders and note-holders for claims on the assets, earnings and dividends of a company: (VIC) Co-operative Housing Societies Act 1958 s 3(1). See also **Ordinary share**; **Share**.

Preference shareholder See **Preference share**.

Preferential right An enforceable claim for the holder of the right to be treated in priority to others, particularly in the granting of a benefit: for example (NSW) Fisheries Management Act 1994 s 168; (VIC) Petroleum Act 1958 s 71. A statutory preferential right in respect of land may amount to an interest in land: *Duke of Bedford v Ellis* [1901] AC 1.

Preferred creditor A creditor to whom payments must be made in law before all others during the winding-up or liquidation of a company.

Preferred ordinary share A sub-class of ordinary shares with some preference or priority over another sub-class of ordinary shares: *Re Powell-Cotton's Resettlement* [1957] Ch 159. See also **Ordinary share**; **Preference share**.

Preferred stock A sub-class of ordinary stock or ordinary shares which has some preference or priority over another sub-class of ordinary stock or shares: *Re Powell-Cotton's Resettlement*; *Henniker-Major v Powell-Cotton* [1957] Ch 159. For the purposes of Corporations Law s 200,which prevents the allotment of preference shares unless particular rights of the holders of those shares are set out in the memorandum or articles, preferred stock or shares would probably be treated as preference shares.

•**Pre-incorporation contract** A contract made on behalf of a company not yet in existence. A company is empowered, within a reasonable time after incorporation, to ratify a pre-incorporation contract entered into a reasonable time before incorporation: Corporations Law s 183(2). Upon ratification, the company is bound and benefited by the contract as if it had been incorporated prior to the contract and had been a party to it: Corporations Law s 183(3). If ratification does not occur, the person or persons who purported to execute the contract on behalf of the non-existent company are liable in damages. See also **Company**; **Contract**; **Incorporation**; **Ratification**.

Pre-merger consultation An informal process adopted by the Trade Practices Commission (now the Australian Competition and Consumer Commission) involving discussing a proposed merger with the parties. The object of pre-merger consultation is to assure the parties to the merger that the Commission will not subsequently proceed with an action under (CTH) Trade Practices Act 1974 s 50. Any comments made by the Commission are strictly non-binding, and the Commission is free to adopt an alternative approach when the merger is complete. Sometimes incorrectly called a 'clearance'. See also **Authorisation**; **Clearance**; **Merger**; **Pre-merger notification**; **Trade Practices Commission**.

Pre-merger notification An obligatory notice given to the Trade Practices Commission (now the Australian Competition and Consumer Commission), or the competition law agencies in other countries such as the United States Federal Trade Commission, where a merger of a substantial nature is proposed. A pre-merger notification procedure was introduced in the United States by the (US) Hart-Scott-Rodino Antitrust Improvement Act 1976, and recommended for Australia by the Cooney Committee Report. See also **Antitrust**; **Authorisation**; **Clearance**; **Competition law**; **Cooney Committee Report**; **Merger**; **Merger guidelines**; **Pre-merger consultation**.

•**Premises** *OF* – foreplacing; setting before.

•**Premium** 1. An amount paid by way of consideration. 2. A sum or value above the nominal or par value of a thing.

Corporations 1. An amount paid in addition to the par or nominal value of a share. 2. The difference between the face value of a security and the price at which it presently stands if the latter is higher. See also **Futures contract**; **Par value**; **Security**; **Share premium**; **Spot commodity**; **Spot rate**.

Industrial law In relation to an apprenticeship, any money, goods or service paid or provided, or action done, as an inducement, reward or gift: (QLD) Vocational Education, Training and Employment Act 1991 s 4. See also **Apprentice**; **Apprenticeship**.

Insurance A sum of money paid by an assured to an insurer in consideration of his or her indemnifying the assured for loss sustained in consequence of the risks insured against: *Swain v Law Society* [1982] 2 All ER 980 at 983. See also **Insurance contract**; **Receipt of premium**; **Return of premium**.

Real property A sum of money given in consideration of the grant of any lease: (NSW) Landlord and Tenant (Amendment) Act 1948 ss 35, 36; *Regent Oil Co Ltd v Strick* [1965] 3 All ER 174 at 197. See also **Lease**.

Taxation and revenue A premium for income tax purposes has two meanings. 1. The amount in excess of the face value of a financial instrument. For example, if an investor pays $105 for a promissory note with a face value of $100, the difference of $5 is a premium. As the quantum of a premium is fixed and does not vary with time, a premium is not in the nature of interest (*Willingate v International Commercial Bank Ltd* [1978] All ER 754) unless the facts regarding the issue of the instrument suggest otherwise: *Brown v National Provident Institution* (1919) 8 TC 57. A premium may combine both an interest and a capital component: *Clowes v Federal Cmr of Taxation* (1954) 91 CLR 209. A premium is taxable as income under (CTH) Income Tax Assessment Act 1936 s 25(1) or Div 16E if the instrument is a 'qualifying security' for (CTH) Income Tax Assessment Act 1936 s 159GP(1) purposes. **2.** A payment made to a property owner for the granting or assignment of a lease, not including an amount in respect of goodwill or a licence: (CTH) Income Tax Assessment Act 1936 s 26AB defines a premium as generally of a capital nature. Premiums are assessable in accordance with the provisions of (CTH) Income Tax Assessment Act 1936 ss 26AB(2), (3), (5). If (CTH) Income Tax Assessment Act 1936 s 26AB does not apply, the quantum of premium, if granted after 19 September 1985, will be assessable under (CTH) Income Tax Assessment Act 1936 s 160ZS(1). Also known as 'lease premium'.

Premium bond A bond where interest accruing on each bond is pooled and distributed to a randomly selected few determined by a computer. See also **Bond**.

Premium issue The issue of shares where subscribers have paid, or are contractually obliged to provide, consideration which exceeds the nominal value of the shares: *Niemann v Smedley* [1973] VR 769. See also **Share premium account**.

Premium security A security where the fixed-interest payment represented by the coupon is above the current market yield, enabling the stock to be sold at a price higher than its face value, that is, at a premium. When the bond matures, however, only the face value is received.

•**Prepaid expenses** Expenditure incurred in a particular year of income for the provision or receipt of services extending beyond the end of that year. Generally, such non-capital expenditure is an allowable deduction in full in the year of income in which it is incurred: (CTH) Income Tax Assessment Act 1936 s 51(1). See also **Incurred**; **Year of income**.

Prepayment The making of a payment before such payment is legally due for payment for the purpose of bringing forward the incurring of a (CTH) Income Tax Assessment Act 1936 s 51(1) tax deduction so as to claim the benefit of the tax deduction in an earlier income tax year than would otherwise be the case. Since 25 May 1988 the deductibility of such amounts has been regulated by (CTH) Income Tax Assessment Act 1936 ss 82KZL-82KZO. Those provisions deny deductions for prepayments such as interest, rent or other services in excess of $1000 where the benefit for which the prepayment is made will extent for more than 13 months from the date of payment. Prior to 25 May 1988, many tax deferral arrangements particularly those involving agricultural businesses were based on the taxpayer obtaining significant (CTH) Income Tax Assessment Act 1936 s 51(1) deductions for prepaid business expenses.

Prepayment scheme An arrangement entered into for the purpose of bringing forward the claim for tax deductions associated with a taxpayer's income producing activities. The taxpayer prepays expenses that are deductible, usually, under (CTH) Income Tax Assessment Act 1936 s 51(1), and therefore obtains the benefit of the tax deduction in an earlier tax year than would otherwise have been the case. The effectiveness of prepayment schemes has been virtually eliminated as from 25 May 1988 by the enactment of (CTH) Income Tax Assessment Act 1936 ss 82KZL-82KZO. See also **Prepayment**.

Pre-prospectus issue promotion The publicity in relation to a proposed issue of shares prior to registration of a prospectus with the Australian Securities Commission (ASC), limited by Corporations Law ss 1025, 1026. These sections also require that any publicity relating to an issue of shares include a reference to where a prospectus may be obtained. See also **Prospectus**.

Prerogative writs Court orders providing remedies of a particular character for different kinds of administrative action. There are six in all: mandamus, prohibition, procedendo, certiorari, quo warranto, and habeas corpus. The most common are certiorari, mandamus, and prohibition. See also **Certiorari**; **Habeas corpus**; **Mandamus**; **Prohibition**.

•**Prescribed interest** A form of security which is either a participation interest or a right to participate in a time-sharing scheme, with certain regulatory exceptions: Corporations Law s 9. A prospectus must be lodged before offers or invitations for prescribed interests are made: Corporations Law ss 1018, 1022; Corporations Regulations regs 7.12.11, 7.12.12. A person must not make offers or invitations to subscribe for or purchase any prescribed interest unless that person is a public corporation and an approved deed is in force: Corporations Law ss 1064-1067. See also **Prescribed interest holder**; **Participation interest**; **Prescribed interest prospectus**; **Prescribed interest scheme**; **Prospectus**; **Time-sharing scheme**.

Prescribed interest holder One who holds a prescribed interest. A register of prescribed interest holders must be kept by the management company: Corporations Law s 1070. See also **Prescribed interest**; **Prescribed interest prospectus**; **Prescribed interest scheme**.

Prescribed interest prospectus A prospectus made available in relation to a prescribed interest. It must be provided to potential investors and lodged with the Australian Securities Commission (ASC) if a person offers for subscription, or issues invitations to subscribe for, a prescribed interest: Corporations Law ss 92(2), 1018(1). The information required to be contained in prospectuses generally under Corporations Law ss 1021, 1022 is extended by the regulations to require the disclosure of interests of the trustee or representative or management company and further details of the scheme: Corporations Regulations regs 7.12.11, 7.12.12. See also **Prescribed interest**; **Prescribed interest holder**; **Prescribed interest scheme**; **Prospectus**.

Prescribed interest scheme An arrangement, common enterprise, financial or business undertaking, investment contract or scheme under which there is an issue, offer or invitation to subscribe for or buy a prescribed interest: Corporations Regulations reg 7.12.01. Prior to the issue or offer for subscription or purchase, there must be a deed approved by the Australian Securities Commission (ASC): Corporations Law s 1065. The ASC must also approve the trustee for the purposes of the deed: Corporations Law s 1067. See also **Prescribed interest**; **Prescribed interest holder**; **Prospectus**.

Prescribed Payments System *Abbr* – PPS A system to collect instalments on account of income tax payable on payments made for work by an individual acting as an independent contractor and not as an employee: (CTH) Income Tax Assessment Act 1936 Pt VI Div 3A. See also **Pay As You Earn system**; **Provisional tax**; **Reportable Payments System**.

•**Prescription** An authorisation for supply of specified substances for administration to a particular person: (ACT) Drugs of Dependence Act 1989 s 3. See also **Acquisition**.

Prescription of standards The establishment of consumer product safety standards or consumer product information standards by regulations pursuant to the powers contained in (CTH) Trade Practices Act 1974 ss 65C(2), 65D(2). Such standards may also be declared by the Minister: (CTH) Trade Practices Act 1974 s 65E(1). See also **Consumer product information standard**; **Consumer product safety standard**; **Mandatory standard**.

Present value The sum of a series of future payments or receipts, discounted at a selected rate. The present worth method offers a general and systematic approach to the problem of making comparisons between present proposals for investments, plant, programs or policies when future streams of costs and revenues are relevant to the comparison. The present worth of a future sum may be calculated by multiplying the sum by a present worth factor. For example, for an 18 per cent discount rate, the present worth factor is given by: $(1 \div 1.18) \times m$ where m = number of years to when the future sum is received or paid. See also **Discounted cash flow method**.

Presentation for acceptance Presentation of a bill of exchange by or on behalf of the holder, to the drawee or some other person authorised to accept or refuse acceptance on the drawee's behalf, at a reasonable hour on a business day before the bill is overdue: (CTH) Bills of Exchange Act 1909 s 46(1)(a). A bill needs to be presented for acceptance when it is payable after sight, expressly stipulates such, or is drawn payable elsewhere than the drawee's residence or business place: (CTH) Bills of Exchange Act 1909 ss 44(1), (2). Presentation for acceptance may be excused; presentation by mail may be sufficient: (CTH) Bills of Exchange Act 1909 s 46. See also **Acceptance**; **Bill of exchange**; **Dishonour by non-acceptance**; **Drawee**; **Holder**; **Presentation for payment**; **Presentment**.

Presentation for payment 1. In relation to a bill of exchange or promissory note, the exhibition of the instrument by the holder to the payer at a reasonable hour on a business day at a proper place and, when the bill is paid, delivering it to the payer: (CTH) Bills of Exchange Act 1909 ss 50, 57(4). The presentation must be made on the day it falls due or, where payable on demand, within a reasonable time after issue. Presentment for payment may be dispensed with in some circumstances: s 51. Generally, a bill must be duly presented for payment, otherwise the drawer and indorsers will be discharged: s 50(1). **2.** In relation to a cheque, a demand for payment of the cheque, made in accordance with the statutory procedures, on the drawee bank, by or on behalf of the holder: (CTH) Cheques and Payment Orders Act 1986 s 61. The date of the cheque must have arrived. See also **Counter presentation**; **Drawee bank**; **Presentation for acceptance**; **Presentment**.

•**Presentment** Presentation of a bill of exchange by the holder to the drawee for acceptance, or of a bill of exchange or promissory note to the person from whom the holder is demanding payment, for payment: (CTH) Bills of Exchange Act 1909 ss 46(1)(a), 57(4). **3.** An indictment. See also **Acceptance**; **Counter presentation**; **External presentment**; **Internal presentment**; **Presentation for acceptance**; **Presentation for payment**.

•**President 1.** The Head of State of a republic. **2.** A person elected by creditors to preside at a meeting of creditors: (CTH) Bankruptcy Act 1966 s 63A(1). The bankrupt's trustee must invite creditors to nominate a person to be elected to preside at a meeting and if they do not, the trustee must make the nomination: s 64P. Until such a person is elected, the trustee must preside at the meeting: s 64K(1). See also **Bankrupt**; **Creditors' meeting**; **Trustee in bankruptcy**.

Presumed total loss A loss under a policy of marine insurance which, although not total, is deemed to be a total loss for the purpose of settling the insurance claim.

Presumed undue influence A presumption of equity which operates when a party in an antecedent relation of influence seeks to support a transaction from which he or she benefits. The presumption is raised in certain established classes of relationship, such as parent and child, solicitor and client, and trustee and beneficiary, or whenever one party occupies or assumes towards another person a special relationship of ascendancy or influence.

Presumption of innocence A rule of the criminal law that every person is presumed innocent of a criminal charge until proven guilty. The presumption can only be rebutted if the prosecution discharges the general burden of proving guilt beyond reasonable doubt. See also **Beyond reasonable doubt**; **Burden of proof**.

Presumption of insurer's knowledge In marine insurance law, the presumption that an insurer has, and contracts with reference to, knowledge of every trade usage that may operate on the subject matter of the insurance. For example, an assured is under no duty to disclose the mode of loading or unloading at the ports mentioned in the policy: (*Moxon v Atkins* (1812) 3 Camp 200; 170 ER 1354); that stowage on deck may in certain cases be in accordance with the usage of the trade: (*Gould v Oliver* (1837) 4 Bing NC 134; 132 ER 740); or the general nature and circumstance of the branch of trade to which the policy relates: (*North British Fishing Boat Insurance Co Ltd v Starr* (1922) 13 Ll L Rep 206). Even if the trade is newly established, the usages are presumed to be known to the insurer: *Noble v Kennoway* (1780) 2 Doug 510; 99 ER 326. The insurer is also presumed to know if war is imminent, or that a state of war exists in some remote part of the globe: *Schloss Bros v Stevens* [1906] 2 KB 665. A reinsurer is presumed to know that the original insurance policy may contain a continuation clause: *Charlesworth v Faber* (1900) 5 Com Cas 408. See also **Insurance**; **Insurance contract**.

Presumption of regularity The common law rebuttable presumption of law that official acts are presumed to have been done rightly and regularly. See also **Burden of proof; Evidential burden**.

Pretax profit The total of the operating profit and the extraordinary items for a given accounting period as reported in the profit and loss account before charging the related income tax expense: Applicable Accounting Standards AASB 1018. See also **Extraordinary Items; Profit and Loss Account**.

•**Price** A charge of any description: (CTH) Trade Practices Act 1974 s 4. The price of goods or services acquired by a person is the amount paid for them: (NSW) Fair Trading Act 1987 s 4. An amount for sales tax that has been or will be paid, customarily passed on by seller to buyer, is part of the 'price' of goods in common usage: *Universal Telecasters (Qld) Ltd v Guthrie* (1978) 18 ALR 531. See also **Discounts, allowances, rebates or credits; False representation; Interest; Misleading or deceptive conduct; Price discrimination; Recommended price; Rent; Specified price**.

Price control Arrangements, contracts or understandings for the purpose of fixing, controlling, or maintaining the price for goods and services: (CTH) Trade Practices Act 1974 s 45A. Price controls need not be permanent and include settling or controlling prices for a period of time: *Radio 2UE Sydney Pty Ltd v Stereo FM Pty Ltd* (1982) 44 ALR 557; 62 FLR 437. See also **Price fixing; Resale price maintenance**.

Price discrimination Selling goods of like grade and quality to different purchasers at different prices, thus discriminating between buyers. The discrimination may relate to price, discounts, allowances, rebates, credits, or the provision of services in relation to those goods. See also **Discounts, allowances, rebates or credits; Price; Substantially lessening competition**.

Price elasticity of demand The relative change in the demand for a commodity following a change in the price of that commodity: price elasticity = percentage change in quantity demanded/percentage change in price. If the price is reduced, the amount demanded normally will be increased. When the percentage increase of the amount demanded is greater than the percentage reduction of price, the demand is described as 'elastic'; if it is less, 'inelastic'. If a given percentage reduction of price results in an equal percentage increase in the amount demanded, the elasticity of demand is 'unity'. See also **Cross elasticity of demand; Income elasticity of demand**.

Price elasticity of supply The relative change in the supply of a commodity following a change in the price of that commodity: Price elasticity = Percentage change in quantity supplied/Percentage change in price. Thus, if a 10 per cent increase in the price of a commodity results in a 20 per cent increase in the quantity supplied, the elasticity of supply is two. See also **Cross elasticity of demand; Income elasticity of demand; Price elasticity of demand**.

•**Price fixing** Settling or determining a price for a period of time that is not instantaneous or merely ephemeral: *Radio 2UE Sydney Pty Ltd v Stereo FM Pty Ltd* (1982) 44 ALR 557. See also **Competition law; Contract, arrangement or understanding; Restrictive trade practices**.

Price indication, misleading See **Misleading price indication**.

Price leadership A market situation where the price policy of the dominant firm is consciously followed by the others in the market. In what is called barometric price leadership, the price leader changes the price when it judges that the climate is right.

•**Price lists** Compilations systematically listing property for sale and the prices asked, not including a guide to prices which should be paid: *Federal Cmr of Taxation v Thomson Australian Holdings Pty Ltd* (1989) 25 FCR 481; 87 ALR 682, considering (CTH) Sales Tax (Exemptions and Classifications) Act 1935 s 5(1), Sch 1 Item 51(1)(c). See also **Price**.

Price maintenance agreements See **Price control**.

Price maker A characteristic of monopoly or price leadership market situations whereby a single producer is able effectively to set the price appropriate to the market, irrespective of the actions of any competitors.

Price mechanism The system used in a market economy for the distribution of resources through the agency of price. If too much of commodity A and too little of commodity B is being produced the demand price for A falls and that for B rises, warning the productive system to make the necessary adjustments. The price mechanism theoretically leads to a point of maximum efficiency. See also **Market economy; Price**.

Price per ton system A method of calculating the price of something or the value of some work based on the weight of the thing produced or worked on.

Price risk A reference to possible losses resulting from price changes such as a decrease in the value of a portfolio of shares. See also **Risk**.

Price sensitive information Information that, if it were generally available, would have a material effect on the value of securities. For the purposes of the insider trading provisions of the Corporations Law, a reasonable person would expect information to be price sensitive if the information is likely to influence persons who commonly invest in securities in deciding whether or not to subscribe for, buy, or see: Corporations Law s 1002C. Corporations Law s 1002G(2) prohibits certain uses of price sensitive information where it is not generally available and a person is aware of this and the fact that it is price sensitive information. See also **Insider trading**.

Price taker A situation in which no one producer may set a market price higher than the prevailing price without the risk of complete loss of market share. Setting a lower price might be unprofitable and thus the producers generally accept the prevailing price. It is a characteristic of perfect competition or any market situation with many producers.

Price-cash ratio Price as a multiple of cash flow per share. The cash flow equivalent of earnings per share. The analysis of cash flow has emerged as a key element in investment during the 1990s. Measures of cash flow per share now rank with earnings per share as one of the fundamental measures of the relative costs of acquiring shares. Cash flow analysis now forms the basis for calculations of the amount of gearing which can be taken on and supported by the cash being generated by assets acquired during a takeover. The National Stocks Database publishes the cash flow per share of mainboard Australian Stock Exchange companies.

Price-earnings ratio *Abbr* – P/E Ratio A ratio calculated by dividing a company's share price by its (post-tax) earnings per share. P/E = Share price/Net earnings per share. The ratio enables investors to consider stocks on the basis of price against earnings. The earnings for each ordinary share is established by taking the total earnings of a company in a twelve month period (subtracting taxes and any provision for preference dividends) and dividing these earnings by the total number of ordinary shares. This figure may then be compared with the latest price per share. If a share is trading $12 and its earnings were 80c per share, the P/E ratio would be 15. The ratio is a useful indicator of over-priced shares.

Prices and Incomes Accord An agreement between the Australian Labor Party and the Australian Council of Trade Unions reached in February 1983 outlining an acceptable prices and incomes policy. The agreement was reaffirmed at a National Economic Summit Conference held in April 1983 between the Hawke government, representatives of Australian industry, and the trade unions. See also **Economic Planning Advisory Council; Enterprise agreement**.

Prices Justification Tribunal Tribunal established by the (CTH) Prices Justification Act 1973, the function of which was to inquire into and report upon whether the price at which a company supplied or proposed to supply goods or services was justifiable and if not to specify a price that could be justified. The (CTH) Prices Justification Act 1973 was repealed by (CTH) Commonwealth Functions (Statutes Review) Act 1981 s 231. The Australian Competition and Consumer Commission now exercises similar powers pursuant to the (CTH) Prices Surveillance Act 1983 s 17(1). See also **Australian Competition and Consumer Commission**.

Prices Surveillance Authority *Abbr* – PSA A Commonwealth statutory authority established under the (CTH) Prices Surveillance Act 1983. Its functions include reviewing notifications of price increases from declared companies, holding public inquiries, and monitoring prices: (CTH) Prices Surveillance Act 1983 s 17. The PSA and its functions have now been subsumed within the Australian Competition and Consumer Commission. See also **Australian Competition and Consumer Commission; Price**.

Pricing claim A representation with respect to the cost or value of goods or services. It is an offence to make a false or misleading representation with respect to the price of goods or services: (CTH) Trade Practices Act 1974 s 53(e). It is an offence to make a representation with respect to an amount that, if paid, would constitute a part of the consideration for the supply of goods or services, unless the cash price for the goods or services is also specified: s 53C. See also **Misleading price indication**.

•**Prima facie** /praɪma feɪsi/ *Lat* – at first sight; on the face of it.

Primage An additional duty imposed on some imported articles by a customs authority above the scheduled import duty. Also known as 'hat money'. See also **Charterer; Consignee; Customs duty; Freight; Master; Owner**.

Primary action In industrial law, industrial action by employees taken directly against their employer in order to pressure the employer into accepting their demands in relation to the terms and conditions of employment. It differs from secondary industrial action. See also **Industrial action; Secondary boycott**.

Primary award See **Parent award**.

•**Primary industry** 1. In its widest sense, all types of agricultural, pastoral, mining and quarrying activities. The term is often restricted to the production of goods from farming and livestock, forestry and fishing. 2. Any field of endeavour (other than the wool industry) whose objective is the production of agricultural or other primary produce or the extraction from the environment of minerals, substances from which energy is made available, energy or the conservation and the sustainable use of a natural resource: (CTH) Primary Industries and Energy Research and Development Act 1989 s 4. 3. In common usage, the expression secondary industry appears to be used in contradistinction to primary industry, the latter being associated with the winning of raw materials from the soil or the sea: *Davey v Brightlite Nominees Pty Ltd* [1984] VR 957; (1984) 56 LGRA 274.

Primary Industry Bank of Australia *Abbr* – PIBA A bank whose main objectives are to facilitate the provision of loans to primary producers for longer terms than are otherwise generally available, up to 30 years. It operated under the (CTH) Primary Industry Bank Act (repealed) 1977. Since 1987, the bank has been wholly-owned by the Rural and Industries Bank of Western Australia. Holding a trading bank authority, the PIBA operates throughout Australia and New Zealand with a network of branches.

Primary market The market for the raising of capital through the sale of new shares, bonds, and Treasury notes. Once acquired by traders or members of the public, such securities may then be traded on the secondary markets. The Australian Stock Exchange provides the secondary market for shares, while the money market provides the secondary market for fixed-interest securities. See also **Bond; Debenture; Share; Treasury bond; Treasury note**.

Primary obligation An obligation expressly or impliedly created by a contract. See also **Damages; Secondary obligation; Term; Termination**.

•**Primary producer** 1. Any person engaged solely or substantially in agricultural, horticultural, viticultural, dairying, pastoral or like pursuits including fishing, bee keeping and livestock production: (VIC) Dangerous Goods Act 1985 s 3(1); (SA) Motor Vehicle Act 1959 s

5. 2. A person carrying on in Australia a business of production resulting from the cultivation of land, maintaining animals or poultry for sale or for their bodily produce (including natural increase), carrying on fishing operations, forest operations, horticulture, and the manufacturing of dairy produce by the person who produced the raw materials used in that manufacture: (CTH) Income Tax Assessment Act 1936 ss 6(1), 157(2). Taxation concessions such as income averaging, indefinite carry forward losses, the exclusion of certain income from the provisional tax system, and accelerated depreciation are granted to persons who show they are 'primary producers': for example (CTH) Income Tax Assessment Act 1936 ss 70(1), 75B, 75D, 80AA; *McInness v FCT* (1977) 7 ATR 373. The general effect of classification as a primary producer renders expenses normally of a private or domestic nature tax-deductible by characterising them as business-related. See also **Business**; **Primary product**; **Primary production**.

•**Primary product** Under marketing legislation, includes products of agriculture, grazing, poultry farming or bee keeping, such as grain, fruit, vegetable, livestock, meat, hay, chaff, poultry, honey, and beeswax: for example (NSW) Marketing of Primary Products Act 1983 s 4(1). Primary products also includes articles prepared directly from the produce of agriculture such as butter and cheese, but excludes specific items such as wool: (NSW) Marketing of Primary Products Act 1983 s 4(1). See also **Primary producer**; **Primary production**.

•**Primary production 1.** Agriculture, fishing operations or forestry: (CTH) Customs Act 1901 s 164. **2.** The growing or rearing of plants (including trees, fungi, or any crop), or the breeding, rearing, or maintenance of living creatures for the purpose of sale for food or for their produce: (WA) Stamp Act 1921 s 75D. **3.** Production resulting directly from cultivating land, maintaining animals or poultry for the purpose of selling them or their bodily produce, fishing, forestry, horticulture, and the manufacture of dairy produce by persons who produce the raw product also: (CTH) Income Tax Assessment Act 1936 s 6(1). Taxation concessions are available for persons who show they are carrying on the business of primary production: for example (CTH) Income Tax Assessment Act 1936 ss 149-158A. What constitutes the business of primary production is a question of fact in each case; however, relevant matters have been held to include the purpose, scale, viability, location, and nature of the venture: *Ferguson v FCT* (1979) 9 ATR 873; 26 ALR 307. See also **Primary producer**.

Primary security market See **Primary market**.

Prime assets ratio *Abbr* – PAR A ratio that must be maintained by each domestic bank between its prime assets and its total liabilities (other than shareholders' funds) within Australia. Prime assets include notes and coins, balances with the Reserve Bank of Australia, all Commonwealth government securities, and loans to authorised money market dealers secured against Commonwealth government securities. The PAR was introduced by the Reserve Bank in 1985. In 1990, the PAR was reduced from 10 per cent to 6 per cent. The Reserve Bank regards such stocks of high-quality assets as fundamental to engendering and maintaining public confidence in the domestic banks' ability to survive a run on their funds.

Prime cost item *Abbr* – PC item A sum provided for in a building contract for work, material or specifications which, at the time of contract, the proprietor has not finally decided to include in the contract. A PC item may be provided if the cost of work is impossible to specify, such as where the final cost of excavation cannot be known until it is done. When the item is finally selected and provided, the contract price is debited with this sum and credited with the actual cost of the materials or work: *Tuta Products Pty Ltd v Hutcherson Bros Pty Ltd* (1972) 127 CLR 253. Thus, the original contract price will be adjusted up or down to reflect the PC item's true cost. Also known as 'prime cost sum' or a 'provisional sum'. See also **Building contract**; **Contractor**; **Lump sum contract**; **Proprietor**; **Provisional sum**; **Rated contract**.

Prime rate The benchmark rate charged by banks on loans to their best corporate customers. Other customers pay a margin over prime rate. Movements in the prime rate are a guide to the general trend of interest rates in the Australian economy.

•**Principal 1.** A sum of money owed as a debt, upon which interest is calculated. The sum is repayable upon maturity. **2.** The capital or main body of an estate or financial holding. **3.** A person who empowers another to act as that person's representative, for example as an agent or broker. **4.** A person having prime responsibility for an obligation.

Agency **1.** A person who confers upon an agent the authority to act on the person's behalf for the purpose of creating or affecting legal rights and duties between the person and third parties: *Petersen v Moloney* (1951) 84 CLR 91. **2.** A person giving a power of attorney; also called a 'donor of the power': (NSW) Conveyancing Act 1919 s 158. See also **Agency**; **Agent**; **Co-principal**; **Power of attorney**; **Undisclosed principal**.

Principal activities In banking, the provision of banking services, credit and access card facilities, leasing, housing and general finance, international banking, investment banking, portfolio management, life insurance, custodian, trustee and nominee, and travel services. See also **Banking business**; **Banking service**.

Principal and interest loan A loan in which repayments are calculated taking into account the amount borrowed and the interest rate so that the loan is fully paid off at the completion of the loan term. The loan term for principal and interest housing loans is usually 5-25 years. Part of each monthly loan repayment covers the monthly interest charged while the remainder is subtracted from the outstanding loan balance. These loans are sometimes called 'reducible' loans. See also **Interest only loan**.

Principal Australian register The register which, prior to amendments to the Corporations Law in 1995, was the primary register for the company, when a company could keep more than one register of members within Australia, with one register being its principal Australian register and registers in other States or Territories being branch register. Now Corporations Law s 216B(1) provides for one register of members within Australia and Corporations Law s 216K provides for an overseas branch register. See also **Register of members**.

Principal debtor The person who owes the primary obligation to the creditor in a situation where there is more than one surety in respect of a particular debt. See also **Co-surety**; **Debt**; **Debtor**; **Guarantee**.

•**Principal register** In relation to a company, previously the register that had to be kept under Corporations Law s 209 (repealed) of the members of the company: Corporations Law s 9. See also **Share register**; **Register of members**.

Principal residence For capital gains tax purposes, a dwelling, being residential accommodation, owned and occupied as the taxpayer's principal residence. The dwelling is exempt from capital gains tax if it is not used to produce income, unless another property is nominated as the principal residence. Neither a capital gain or a capital loss occurs on the disposal of a principal residence. See also **Capital gain**; **Capital loss**; **Asset disposal**.

Prior charge A charge or claim against the assets of a company that ranks ahead of other claims. For example, a first mortgage ranks ahead of a second mortgage.

Prior equity An equitable claim to property which arose before another claim to, or interest in, the same property. Where two people hold inconsistent equities in the same property, the court will consider the conduct of the claimants to see if each took adequate steps to protect the interest held. See also **Equitable interest**; **Mere equity**.

Priority The order in which interests in property are enforced. Priority is usually determined by the time of creation of the interest, an earlier interest prevailing over a later interest. Where the competing interests are equitable, priority is enshrined in the maxim *qui prior est tempore potior est jure*, meaning that, where the conduct of both parties is acceptable and both interests are full equitable interests, the one who is first in time has precedence: for example *Goldsbrough, Mort & Co Ltd v Commonwealth Agricultural Service Engineers Ltd* [1930] SASR 201 at 207. Where the property is land under the Torrens system, the prior interest is considered to deserve priority unless the prior interest holder has, by act or omission, created a situation in which it is unjust to permit that person to retain priority: *Heid v Reliance Finance Corp Pty Ltd* (1983) 154 CLR 326; 49 ALR 229. Where the competing interests are legal, priority is enshrined in the maxim *nemo dat quod non habet* (a person cannot give what he or she does not have), meaning that having disposed of a legal interest the person cannot later give that legal interest to anyone else. An equitable interest usually ranks behind a legal interest notwithstanding that it may have been created earlier. This principle is enshrined in the maxim 'where the equities are equal, the law prevails'. A later legal interest prevails over an earlier equitable interest if the party acquiring the legal interest purchased it for value, in good faith, and without notice of the equitable interest. Priority may be altered as between competing interests by agreement between the parties, or by tacking (in the case of mortgages), or where equitable considerations dictate such an alteration. See also **Mere equity**; **Prior equity**; **Tacking**.

Privacy The interest of a person in sheltering his or her life from unwanted interference or public scrutiny. At common law, there is no general right to privacy: *Victoria Park Racing and Recreation Grounds Co Ltd v Taylor* (1937) 58 CLR 479. The most comprehensive legislation protecting privacy in Australia is the (CTH) Privacy Act 1988, which gives force to the International Covenant on Civil and Political Rights 1966 art 17 and to the Organisation for Economic Cooperation and Development Guidelines on the Protection of Privacy and Transborder Flows of Personal Data and gives effect to the right of persons not to be subjected to arbitrary or unlawful interference with their privacy, family, home, or correspondence. See also **Freedom of Information Act 1982**; **Information privacy principles complaint**; **Nuisance**; **Trespass**.

Private bank 1. A specialist bank serving the needs of high-net-worth individuals. A private bank provides services such as discretionary investment management, trust and estate planning, and unsecured lines of credit. Switzerland remains the capital of international private banking concerned almost entirely with investment management. It offers secrecy in a haven of political neutrality. 2. A bank owned by partners who share unlimited liabilities in the event of losses. One of the few remaining examples is Brown Brothers Harriman and Company in Britain, founded in 1882.

•**Private company** 1. Prior to the amendment of the Corporations Law in 1995, a proprietary company of the jurisdiction or of another jurisdiction or an exempt foreign company: Corporations Law s 69(4) (repealed). 2. For income tax purposes, a company is either a 'private' company or a 'public' company. (CTH) Income Tax Assessment Act 1936 s 103A defines a private company as a company that is not a public company. See also **Deemed dividend**; **Proprietary company**; **Public company**.

Private offer An offer of securities which is not made to the public or any section of the public. The terms 'public offer' and 'private offer' were used in the Companies Codes as to whether a prospectus was required for an offer of securities. See also **Excluded offer or invitation**.

Private placement A limited distribution of securities or debt instruments to selected subscribers or purchasers, usually in large parcels of securities or in respect of securities with high individual prices. Private placements facilitate rapid, wholesale distribution of securities and debt instruments. Additionally, private placements will ordinarily allow the distributor and the company distributing the securities to avoid the prospectus and related provisions of the Corporations Law because the relevant issue, invitation or offer will be 'excluded' under Corporations Law s 66 and Corporations Regulations regs 7.12.05, 7.12.06. See also **Excluded issue**; **Excluded offer or invitation**.

Private sector The sector of an economy that is privately owned by individuals and companies, in contrast with the public sector which is owned by governments or their agencies. There are some 600,000 privately owned companies in Australia ranging in size from one-person businesses to national and international companies such as BHP, Coles Myer and General Motors-Holden. The firms that make up the private sector are classified into over 120 different industries and are responsible for some 75 per cent of the production of goods and services in Australia.

•**Private use** 1. Not for general or public use; for an individual's own use. A substantial and unreasonable interference with another's private use or enjoyment of property may constitute a private nuisance for which there is a cause of action: *Elston v Dore* (1982) 149 CLR 480; 43 ALR 577; *Hargrave v Goldman* (1963) 110 CLR 40. 2. In income tax law, a use for private purposes as opposed to being used in gaining or producing assessable income or necessarily incurred in the carrying on of a business for the purpose of producing such income. 3. For fringe benefits tax purposes, the use of a motor vehicle by an employee or employee's associate that is not exclusively in the course of producing assessable income: (CTH) Fringe Benefits Tax Assessment Act 1986 s 136(1). See also **Assessable income; Fringe Benefits Tax; Necessarily incurred in carrying on a business.**

Privately appointed receiver A receiver appointed out of court pursuant to a statutory power or an express power in an instrument. See also **Court appointed receiver; Receiver.**

Privatisation 1. The selling to the private sector of government assets in the form of enterprises, buildings, land, and investments. The privatisation of several State public enterprises and the sale of various Commonwealth assets has been pursued in Australia. 2. The contracting-out of various services to the private sector. 3. A public company reverting to private status by purchasing its own shares or having them acquired by a private company.

Privity of contract A contract law rule under which only parties to a contract are legally bound by and entitled to enforce it: *Trident General Insurance Co Ltd v McNiece Bros Pty Ltd* (1988) 165 CLR 107. The rule prevents contractual burdens being imposed on persons who are not a party to the contract. However, in some situations, a third party beneficiary of a contract to which he or she is not a party is entitled to enforce the contract which was made for his or her benefit: *Trident General Insurance Co Ltd v McNiece Bros Pty Ltd* (1988) 165 CLR 107; 80 ALR 574. See also **Consideration; Contract.**

Privy Council The principal council belonging to the Sovereign.

•**Prize** 1. A reward. 2. Something that is won. 3. Something seized or captured.

Consumer protection A reward generally won in some contest or competition. A corporation may not, in the context of trade or commerce, offer prizes or other free items without the intention of providing them as offered: (CTH) Trade Practices Act 1974 s 54; (NSW) Lotteries and Art Unions Act 1901 s 6B.

Maritime law A ship, goods, or other property captured from an enemy or neutral national at sea or within a port under the rules of prize law: *Re Genoa and its dependencies, Spezzia, Savona and other towns* (1820) 165 ER 1541.

Pro forma /proʊ fɔmə/ *Lat* – as a matter of form; as a gesture; as a formality in accordance with some legal requirement. Any stereotyped form.

Pro forma charterparty A document which sets out all of the terms of the agreement between a charterer and a shipowner but which is not actually adopted as the agreement itself. See also **Charter; Charterer; Charterparty; Contract of carriage; Terms and conditions.**

•**Pro rata** /proʊ rata / *Lat* – in proportion.

Pro rata clause An averaging clause that may be one of two types. One type of *pro rata* clause provides that, if at the time of the loss, the sum insured is less than the value of the subject matter of insurance, the insured is deemed to be his or her own insurer for the difference in value and must accordingly bear a rateable proportion of the loss. The second type of clause sets out the limits on the insurer's liability in the event of underinsurance. A *pro rata* clause will be considered ineffective unless the nature and effect of the clause is explained to the insured in writing prior to entry into the contract of insurance: (CTH) Insurance Contracts Act 1984 s 44. Also known as 'average clause'.

Pro tanto /proʊ tæntoʊ/ *Lat* – so much; to such an extent.

Pro tem(pore) /proʊ tɛmpɔreɪ/ *Lat* – for the time being; temporarily.

Procedure manual A comprehensive description of the authority and responsibilities of positions within an organisation. The procedure manual designates and explains the methods and detailed procedures necessary to perform the activities of the position.

•**Proceeding** An action commenced in a court. A proceeding is a proceeding in a court whether between parties or not, including an incidental proceeding in the course of, or in connection with a proceeding, and includes an appeal: (CTH) Federal Court Act 1976 s 4. See also **Action; Appeal.**

•**Proceeds of crime** Money or property obtained as a result of the commission of, or involvement in, a criminal offence. Property directly or indirectly derived or realised from the commission of an indictable offence: (CTH) Proceeds of Crime Act 1987 s 4(1). The object of the (CTH) Proceeds of Crime Act 1987 and complementary legislation in other Australian jurisdictions is to deprive persons of the proceeds of crime; to provide for the forfeiture of property used in connection with the commission of crime; and to enable law enforcement authorities effectively to trace such proceeds, benefits, and property: s 3(1). See also **Australian Transaction Reports and Analysis Centre; Financial transaction document; Laundering.**

•**Process** A document issued or filed with a court or tribunal in proceedings, which requires a person to attend before the court. Formerly called a writ, process may now include a writ, statement of claim, summons, subpoena, warrant, or notice of appeal. See also **Originating process; Statement of claim; Summons**.

Procuration signature A signature by an agent on a negotiable instrument which operates as notice that the agent has only a limited authority to sign, the principal being bound by such signature only if the agent in signing acted within his or her actual authority: (CTH) Bills of Exchange Act 1909 s 30; (CTH) Cheques and Payment Orders Act 1986 s 34; *Smith v McGuire* (1858) 3 H&N 554; 157 ER 589. The appropriate phrases or abbreviations are 'by procuration ', 'per procurationem', 'per proc', 'per pro', or 'pp'. See also **Actual authority; Agent; Per procurationem; Sign**.

Procured (by fraud) In a case where a bank fraudulently added property to an instrument of mortgage before registration but after the signature of one of the parties, this term in (VIC) Transfer of Land Act 1958 s 44 means 'brought about' or even at its narrowest 'brought about by care or pains': *National Australia Bank Ltd v Maher* [1995] 1 VR 318.

•**Product** In product liability, any tangible or intangible item of personal property (or personalty) other than a thing (or chose) in action or money. 'Product' does not include information (for example *ASX Operations Pty Ltd v Pont Data Australia Pty Ltd* (1990) 27 FCR 460; 97 ALR 513), financial products (for example *David Securities Pty Ltd v Commonwealth Bank of Australia* (1990) 23 FCR 1; 93 ALR 271 at 291), or real property. Also known as 'goods'. See also **Goods**.

Product endorser A person, entity, or fictional character who approves or provides a testimonial for a product on behalf of another person, such as a manufacturer. An endorser who falsely implies that a product is safe for use may be liable under (CTH) Trade Practices Act 1974 ss 52 or 53 (for example *Australian Federation of Consumer Organisations v Tobacco Institute of Australia Ltd* (1991) 27 FCR 149; 98 ALR 670; *Tobacco Institute of Australia Ltd v Australian Federation of Consumer Organisations Inc* (1992) 38 FCR 1; 111 ALR 61) and in negligence (for example *Hanberry v Hearst Corp* 1 Cal App 3d 149, 81 Cal Rptr 519 (1969); *Arnstein v Manufacturing Chemists Assn Inc* 414 F Supp 12 (Ed Pa 1976).

Product guarantee insurance Insurance under which the insurer agrees to indemnify the insured with respect to loss caused by product failures, including liability to repair or replace defective products, where the failed product has not otherwise caused personal injury or property damage. See also **Product liability insurance**.

Product liability A responsibility or onus imposed by the law of contract and tort, or by consumer legislation on a manufacturer, distributor, or supplier to warn consumers appropriately about possible detrimental or harmful effects of a product and to foresee how it may be misused. See also **Manufacturer; Negligence**.

Product liability insurance A type of liability insurance under which the insurer agrees to indemnify the insured for legal liability owed to another person as a result of personal injury or property damage caused by a defect in a product imported, manufactured, distributed, or supplied by the insured, and arising after the product has left the possession or control of the insured: for example *Vosten v Commonwealth* [1989] 1 Qd R 693. See also **Product guarantee insurance; Product recall insurance**.

Product market A market consisting of the goods or services supplied by the parties together with competing goods or services which could reasonably be used by most customers as substitutes. Factors determining the degree of substitutability include the products' peculiar characteristics, unique product facilities, distinctive customers and prices, sensitivity to price change, and the existence of specialist vendors. It is possible that a particular product is so distinctive that no competitive brand represents a realistic substitute in the mind of the consumer: *Mark Lyons Pty Ltd v Bursill Sportsgear Pty Ltd* (1987) 75 ALR 581. However, a market will rarely be found to constitute a single brand, as there will usually be realistic alternatives: for example *Aut 6 Pty Ltd v Wellington Place Pty Ltd* (1993) ¶ATPR 41-202. See also **Competition; Functional market; Geographic market; Market; Market power; Misuse of market power; Substitutability**.

Product recall A general term for action taken by the Federal or State Minister with regard to goods which are defective, may cause injury, fail to comply with a prescribed consumer product safety standard, or are the subject of a temporary or permanent ban: (CTH) Trade Practices Act 1974 s 65F(1); (NSW) Fair Trading Act 1987 s 34(1). See also **Compulsory product recall; Consumer product information standard; Consumer product safety standard; Defective goods; Recall action; Voluntary product recall**.

Product recall insurance Insurance under which the insurer agrees to pay for the expenses of removing products from the market, generally including the costs of communications and media announcements, advertisements, shipping, staff overtime, the costs of hiring additional staff, and product destruction costs. The liability of an insurer under a product recall insurance contract is not affected when the insured gives information relating to goods it supplies to a public authority: (CTH) Trade Practices Act 1974 s 65T. See also **Product liability insurance**.

•**Product safety standard** See **Consumer product safety standard**.

Product standard An informal and often unwritten standard or practice adopted within an industry; a written standard published by the Standards Association of Australia or a comparable body; or a written standard prescribed or declared and gazetted under legislation to be a mandatory standard. Product standards govern the manufacture, design, or formulation of a product, and the provision of information with a product. See also **Consumer product information standard; Consumer product safety standard; Industry standard; Mandatory standard; Standards Association of Australia standard**.

Product warranty A standard form document, produced and issued by the manufacturer or supplier of a product, which sets out the rights and obligations of the manufacturer, the supplier, and the acquirer in relation to the product. A product warranty operates subject to legislation: for example (CTH) Trade Practices Act 1974 Pt V Divs 2, 2A. Also known as 'product guarantee'. See also **Express warranty**.

•**Production** In relation to goods, the creation or manufacture of goods. It may be defined more specifically in particular legislation. For example, it may be defined to include extraction, processing, or treatment ((CTH) Development Allowance Authority Act 1992 s 6), or growing and manufacture: (CTH) Proceeds of Crime Act 1987 s 7. See also **Manufacture**.

Productive efficiency The relationship between inputs and outputs achieved when the maximum possible output is produced per unit of input. Productive efficiency must be distinguished from allocative efficiency. See also **Allocative efficiency**.

Productivity The efficiency with which the factors of production are used. Increasing productivity means the ability to produce goods at a progressively lower cost per unit of output while maintaining or improving quality. Improvements in productivity may come about through a more effective use of labour, better equipment and layout, or better use of natural resources.

•**Professional indemnity insurance** *Abbr* – PII A form of insurance that indemnifies the insured against the consequences of a breach of professional duty and particularly professional negligence. See also **Indemnity; Indemnity insurance; Product liability insurance; Professional negligence**.

•**Professional misconduct** At common law, something done in the pursuit of professional activities which would be reasonably regarded as disgraceful or dishonourable by professional brethren of good repute and competency: *Allinson v General Council of Medical Education and Registration* [1894] 1 QB 750. See also **Fit and proper person**.

Professional negligence In tort law, advice or information imparted negligently by a defendant in circumstances in which he or she realises or ought to have realised that the plaintiff was relying on the advice or information as the basis for a course of action: *Hedley Byrne & Co Ltd v Heller & Partners Ltd* [1964] AC 465; *San Sebastian Pty Ltd v Minister administering the Environmental Planning and Assessment Act 1979* (1986) 162 CLR 340; 68 ALR 161. See also **Duty in contract; Duty in tort; Duty of care; Negligent misrepresentation; Professional indemnity insurance; Professional misconduct**.

Professional partnership A category of partnership for certain professions which is allowed a higher maximum number of members under the Corporations Law. See also **Partnership**.

•**Profit** Monetary gain derived from a transaction as a result of an excess of revenues over outlays and expenses in a business enterprise: *Brandt v W G Tatham Pty Ltd* [1965] NSWR 126. In relation to a business, generally the increase in the total assets of a business between two specific dates usually separated by an interval of a year: *Re Spanish Prospecting Co Ltd* [1911] 1 Ch 92. See also **Business; Loss of a chance; Net profit; Pretax profit; Profit and loss account**.

Profit à prendre *Fr* – right to take. A right to take something off another person's land, or to take something out of the soil: *Australian Softwood Forests Pty Ltd v A-G (NSW)* (1981) 148 CLR 121; 36 ALR 257. Also known as 'right of common'. See also **Incorporeal hereditament**.

•**Profit and loss account** Financial statement giving a summary of company operations which occurred between the dates at which the periodic balance sheets are prepared: Corporations Law s 59. The basic format of a profit and loss account is set out in Corporations Regulations sch 5 cl 6(1). It must include a profit statement and an appropriation statement. The appropriation statement shows the operating profit for the financial year, the balance of retained profits at the beginning of the financial year, any transfers from reserves, and the way in which the aggregate of those amounts has been applied by way of transfers to reserves and payments of dividends. The final figure is the balance of profits retained at the end of the financial year. A company must, for every accounting period, produce a profit and loss account which gives a true and fair view of the company's profit and loss: Corporations Law s 292. See also **Accounting standards; General purpose financial report; Profit and loss statement**.

•**Profit and loss statement** An accounting statement showing the operating results of an enterprise for a stated period. The amount and type of all revenues and all expenses and the resulting net profit or loss are stated. The accounting period covered commonly consists of a month, a quarter of a year, a half year, or a year. Many transactions affect the operating results of a number of periods, requiring apportionments to be made which will be estimates rather than precise measurements. Hence any profit and loss statement is approximate and not exact. Also known as an 'income statement', 'operating statement', or 'statement of operations'. See also **Accounting standards; Profit and loss account**.

Profit centre A profitable part of an organisation, usually a division or organisational unit that is responsible both for production and selling of a product.

Profit earning chattel A real chattel such as a leasehold or a tangible article of property which is movable and has the capacity to earn money for its owner within a particular business. Where a profit earning chattel is damaged or destroyed as a consequence of another's wrong, the owner may claim damages for the loss of use of the chattel during the period of repair or reinstatement and recover the chattel's market value or the cost of repairs: *Williamson v Cmr for Railways* [1960] SR (NSW) 252; *Lonie v Perugini* (1977) 18 SASR 201. See also **Chattel**.

Profit forecasts A prediction by the management of a business of the earnings to be made in the forthcoming period. Management are not obliged to make a profit forecast but may if, for example, they wish to obtain extra finance. See also **Budget; Profit or loss**.

•**Profit making undertaking or scheme** A term used in (CTH) Income Tax Assessment Act 1936 s 25A(1). Profits from the sale of property acquired for the purpose of carrying out a profit making undertaking or scheme are taxable: s 25A. The provision does not apply to property acquired after 20 September 1985, and has limited application following the decision in *Federal Cmr of Taxation v Myer Emporium Ltd* (1987) 163 CLR 199; 71 ALR 28, where the High Court found that a profit from a once off transaction was s 25(1) income if the property generating the profit or gain was acquired for the purpose of profit making.

Profit maximisation A theoretical assumption that a firm will attempt to maximise profits, equating marginal revenue with marginal costs.While the pursuit of profit in a market economy may be regarded as the mainspring of the system, it may undergo some modification. It may prove desirable to lower profit margins to gain market share in the short-term. In the long-term, there may be an emphasis on reasonable earnings which are secure rather than on risky ventures which might be more profitable; or there may be due regard to the actions of competitors.

•**Profit or loss** The amount remaining after expenses have been deducted from revenue for an accounting period, resulting from the operations of the firm. A profit exists where revenue is greater than expense, and a loss occurs when expenses are greater than revenue. Profits and losses can be gross (the difference between sales and cost of goods sold); or operating (the difference between the gross amount and operating expenses): Applicable Accounting Standard AASB 1018. See also **Expense**; **Revenue**.

Profit rule The rule which prohibits fiduciaries, including company directors, from using their position for personal advantage or the possible advantage of a third party, except with the company's fully informed consent. A fiduciary is accountable for profits made in connection with his or her fiduciary office: for example *Boardman v Phipps* [1967] 2 AC 46; *Chan v Zacharia* (1984) 154 CLR 178; 53 ALR 417. See also **Corporate opportunity doctrine**; **Directors' duties**; **Fiduciary**.

Profit sharing An arrangement whereby employees are paid a share of the profits of the business enterprise in which they are employed, under an established scheme.

Program trading A computerised program in which orders to buy and sell are automatically placed upon the occurrence of certain events, such as a specified rise or fall in the share price index. Critics have blamed program trading for making the markets dangerously volatile in recent years. However, the Brady Commission which examined the stock market crash of 1987 found that program trading had not proved a major problem, and the banning of program trading during the crisis had actually made matters worse.

Progress certificate In relation to a building project, a certificate which records the contract administrator's determination that a specific sum is payable by the proprietor as a progress payment, based on the value of the work performed. A building contract normally requires the proprietor to pay to the contractor the sum certified by the progress certificate. The obligation is enforceable notwithstanding that the work is incomplete: *Workman Clark & Co Ltd v Lloyd Brazileno* [1908] 1 KB 968. See also **Final certificate**; **Progress payment**.

Progress payment 1. A payment made at a precise point in the carrying out of a contract at which the contractual goals have been met. Thus, payments are made sequentially over the life of the contract until completion. **2.** In relation to a building contract, payment by instalment of part of the agreed contract price, usually made upon presentation of a progress certificate given by the contract administrator. A progress payment is an interim payment on account of the contract sum. The entitlement to progress payments is the quid pro quo for the obligation to continue working: *L U Simon Builders Pty Ltd v Fowles* [1992] 2 VR 189 at 193. Also known as 'interim payment' in England. See also **Building contract**; **Progress certificate**.

Progressive tax A tax which takes an increasing proportion of the tax base as the value of the tax base increases. For example, rates of income tax with an increasing marginal tax rate as a taxpayer's income level increases, result in a progressive tax. See also **Proportional tax**; **Regressive tax**; **Taxation**.

•**Prohibition 1.** An order or decree forbidding a specified act or omission. **2.** A type of prerogative remedy issued by a court to prevent a tribunal or inferior court, which is acting in excess of its jurisdiction, from proceeding any further. See also **Certiorari**; **Functus officio**; **Mandamus**.

Project finance Financing arrangements for a major project with loan repayments and interest geared to the expected cash flow of the project. Temporary arrangements with the providers of equity and debt finance to ensure the completion of a project may be superseded by revised arrangements at a later date. Major projects often involve long construction periods in which there is no financial return. Loans are therefore linked with cash flows which may not occur for several years. Project finance may be non-recourse which means that, in the event that the project does not generate sufficient cash flow, the lenders will have recourse only against the project assets and not against the owners of the project. See also **Joint venture**.

Project management See **Management contracting**.

•**Promise** In contract law, to undertake responsibility for a state of affairs or the occurrence of an event. A term that expresses an undertaking as to an event or as to the truth of a present or past fact embodies a promise, the breach of which gives rise to a claim for damages. See also **Contingency**; **Contract**; **Damages**; **Joint and several promise**; **Joint promise**; **Promisee**; **Promisor**; **Several promise**; **Term**.

Promisee A person to whom a promise is made or given: for example (QLD) Property Law Act 1974 s 55(6)(d). See also **Co-promisee**; **Promisor**.

Promisor A person by whom a promise is made or given: for example (QLD) Property Law Act 1974 s 55(6)(e). See also **Co-promisor**; **Promisee**.

Promissory estoppel A species of equitable estoppel, arising from representations or promises (including as to the future) with respect to rights either presently existing or yet to exist between the parties. The party protected must have altered its position in reliance on an assumption induced by the representations or promises, and would suffer detriment if there was a departure from the assumption: *Waltons Stores (Interstate) Ltd v Maher* (1988) 164 CLR 387; 76 ALR 513. Promissory estoppel has been merged with proprietary estoppel into the broader doctrine of equitable estoppel. See also **Estoppel**; **Proprietary estoppel**; **Unconscionable**.

Promissory estoppel as a sword not a shield The enforcement of a non-contractual promise on the basis that the promisee has relied on that promise and would suffer a detriment if that promise was not enforced: *Walton Stores (Interstate) Ltd v Maher* (1988) 164 CLR 387; 76 ALR 513. See also **Promissory estoppel**.

•**Promissory note** An unconditional promise in writing made by one person to another, signed by the maker, engaging to pay a sum certain in money, to or to the order of a specified person, or to bearer: (CTH) Bills of Exchange Act 1909 s 89(1). Such notes are negotiable instruments, and are used mainly as security for money lending transactions. See also **Bill of exchange**; **Cheque**; **Negotiable instrument**.

Promissory warranty In insurance law, a warranty under which the insured promises to do, or refrain from doing, some particular activity. Breach of a promissory or continuing warranty does not entitle the insurer to refuse payment on the claim unless the breach could reasonably be regarded as capable of causing or contributing to the loss (CTH) Insurance Contracts Act 1984 s 54. Rather, the insurer is entitled to reduce the claim by the amount representing the prejudice actually suffered. Also known as 'continuing warranty'. See also **Proof of loss**.

•**Promoter** A person who initiates or organises a company project, or event.

Corporations 1. A person who is involved, as a principal or an assistant, in getting up and starting a business undertaking. Persons who leave it to others more active to promote the company can be promoters when they know the plan of promotion and have an agreed understanding with the active promoter that they will share any profit from the carrying out of the plan: *Tracy v Mandalay Pty Ltd* (1953) 88 CLR 215. 2. In relation to a prospectus, this means a promoter of the body who was a party to the preparation of the prospectus, but does not include a person merely because of the person acting in the proper performance of the functions attaching to the person's professional capacity or to the person's business relationship with a promoter of the body: Corporations Law s 9. See also **Corporation**; **Prospectus**.

•**Proof** Evidence which establishes the existence or non-existence of an alleged fact. See also **Burden of proof**; **Standard of proof**; **Proof of debt**.

Proof of debt A written claim by a creditor in a prescribed form containing details of the debt of a bankrupt or a company in liquidation. See also **Double proof rule**; **Double satisfaction rule**; **Insolvency**; **Provable debt**; **Set off**; **Winding up**.

Proof of loss In insurance law, a contractual requirement that the insured provide details and evidence of the loss sustained when making a claim. Partial compliance with a proof of loss provision is not sufficient: *L'Union Fire Accident and General Insurance Co Ltd v Klinker Knitting Mills Pty Ltd* (1938) 59 CLR 709. However, if non-compliance is caused by the insurer's own conduct, the insured is relieved from the requirement: *Butcher v Port* [1985] 1 NZLR 491. Insurance contracts usually contain proof of loss sand reasonable assistance clauses: for example *L'Union Fire Accident and General Insurance Co Ltd v Klinker Knitting Mills Pty Ltd*.

Proper law of contract The system of domestic law defining the obligations assumed by the parties to the contract. The proper law of contract, being the legal system under which obligations arising under the contract will be determined, may, in the absence of statutory provisions to the contrary, be expressly stipulated by the parties to the contract: *Dunbee Ltd v Gilman & Co (Aust) Pty Ltd* (1968) 70 SR (NSW) 219. See also **Contract**.

•**Proper SCH transfer** A security clearance house (SCH) regulated transfer of a quoted security or a quoted right effected in accordance with the SCH business rules or a transfer that is taken by Corporations Law s 1097D to be a proper SCH transfer. The effect of a proper SCH transfer is that the transfer of securities or rights is valid and effective for the purpose of any law governing such transfers: Corporations Law s 1109C.

•**Property** A word which can be used to describe every type of right (that is, a claim recognised by law), interest, or thing which is legally capable of ownership, and which has a value: for example *Doodeward v Spence* (1908) 6 CLR 406 at 411-12, 414-15, 416; *Commissioner of Stamp Duties (Qld) v Donaldson* (1927) 39 CLR 539 at 550. See also **Chose in action**; **Chose in possession**; **Intellectual property**; **Ownership**; **Possession**; **Personal property**.

•**Property fringe benefit** A fringe benefit resulting from the provision of property, both tangible and intangible, by an employer or associate of an employer to an employee: (CTH) Fringe Benefits Tax Assessment Act 1986 s 40. Where the property benefit is provided and consumed by the employee on a working day and on the business premises, the property benefit is an exempt benefit: (CTH) Fringe Benefits Tax Assessment Act 1986 s 41. See also **Fringe benefit**.

Property insurance A form of indemnity insurance protecting the insured against loss of or damage to property. Damage to property means disturbance of the physical integrity of the subject property: *Guardian Assurance Co Ltd v Underwood Constructions Pty Ltd* (1974) 48 ALJR 307. 'Property' has been held to include money: *Ginter v Chapman* (1969) 4 DLR (3d) 89. It is a presumed that an insured, under a contract of property insurance, intends to protect only his or her own interest. The presumption may be rebutted if the insured is under a duty to insure on behalf of others, or if it is shown the insured's intention was to insure on behalf of others: *Davjoyda Estates Pty Ltd v National Insurance Co of New Zealand Ltd* (1965) 69 SR (NSW) 381. See also **Fire**; **Fire insurance**; **Indemnity**; **Indemnity insurance**.

•**Property trust** An arrangement between persons, based on confidence, by which property is vested in or held by one person (the trustee) or persons on behalf of and for the benefit of another (beneficiary or *cestui que trust*) or others. The term also describes a category of unit trust in which the property (generally real estate) is held in trust for investors, whose interest in the trust property and any income or capital gain from that trust is calculated in proportion to the amount of units held. See also **Beneficiary; In personam; Trust; Unit trust.**

•**Proportional takeover scheme** A takeover scheme under which each takeover offer relates to a proportion of the shares in the target company in the relevant class that the offeree holds, being a proportion that is the same in respect of each offeree: Corporations Law s 603. See also **Takeover; Takeover scheme.**

Proportional tax A tax which takes the same proportion of the tax base irrespective of the level of that tax base. Also known as 'flat tax'. See also **Progressive tax; Regressive tax.**

Proportionate consolidation A form of financial statement presentation concerning the investor-investment relationship. A proportionate consolidation reflects the investor's share of each asset, liability, income, and expense item in the investor's financial statements and presents those items in the investor's balance sheet and profit and loss statement. This method of accounting can be contrasted with a method that simply states the total value of the investor's investment as a single figure in the investor's balance sheet and only records income receipts received from the investment in the profit and loss account.

•**Proposal** In an insurance contract, the offer made by the person who wants to be insured, or the form containing that offer. The usual procedure is for the intending insured to submit a completed proposal form, although, in the case of interim insurance, the applicant's offer will generally be oral. However, there are situations where insurance products are mass marketed, with the insurer not reserving any right of rejection; in this case, the offer is made by the insurer and accepted, if at all, by the insured submitting the necessary documentation to the insurer. See also **Assured; Insurance; Insurer.**

Propositus /prouppzɪtʊs/ *Lat* – the person proposed or being considered.

•**Proprietary** In computing, standards owned and strictly controlled by companies for the purpose of greater market control and superior product compatibility and interoperability. In contrast, open systems are widely published standards that can be accessed by anyone in the industry (although sometimes a fee is required).

•**Proprietary company** *Abbr* – Pty Ltd A private company whose constitution limits membership to 50 non-employee shareholders, restricts the right to transfer shares and prohibits invitations or offers to the public to subscribe for its shares or debentures: Corporations Law s 116(2). Only a company having a share capital, except for a no liability company, may be incorporated as a proprietary company: s 116(2)(a)(ii). See also **Company; Public company.**

Proprietary estoppel An equity binding the owner of property who induces another person to assume or expect that an interest in that property will be obtained by or conferred on that person, where that person relies on that assumption or expectation and alters their position to their detriment: *Waltons Stores (Interstate) Ltd v Maher* (1988) 164 CLR 387; 76 ALR 513. See also **Estoppel; Promissory estoppel.**

Proprietary restitution Restitution of unjust enrichment by means of a right *in rem*, that is, a proprietary interest in the enrichment, which arises by operation of law in favour of the person at whose expense the unjust enrichment was obtained. See also **Charge; Constructive trust; Lien; Rectification; Restitution; Resulting trust; Unjust enrichment.**

Proprietary right A right to absolute ownership and the financial interest in private property at common law: for example *Mansell v Valley Printing Co* [1908] 2 Ch 441 at 445.

•**Proprietor 1.** The owner of land. **2.** Any person seised or possessed of any freehold or other estate or interests in land at law, or in equity in possession in futurity or expectancy: (NSW) Real Property Act 1900 s 3(1). See also **Contractor; Employer; Owner; Principal.**

•**Prospectus** A written notice or other instrument inviting applications or offers to subscribe for the securities of a body corporate, or offering the securities for subscription: Corporations Law s 9. The contents of a prospectus are regulated and are based on a 'reasonable investor' standard of disclosure: Corporations Law ss 1021-2. See also **Hawking of securities; Secondary trading; Securities; Supplementary prospectus.**

•**Protected money** Money that is not divisible property because, for example, it represents the proceeds of a life assurance policy: (CTH) Bankruptcy Act 1966 s 116(2D). Even though the general rule is that property acquired by a bankrupt after the date of bankruptcy and before discharge is available to creditors, property acquired using protected money is not: s 116(3). See also **After acquired property; Bankruptcy; Discharge of bankruptcy; Divisible property.**

Protected transaction A transaction protected from the operation of the relation-back doctrine. Transactions occurring in the relation-back period before bankruptcy, in good faith, and in the ordinary course of business with someone not knowing that a bankruptcy petition has been present, are protected: (CTH) Bankruptcy Act 1966 s 123(1). For the purpose of that section, good faith can still be shown even though the person knew the debtor had committed an act of bankruptcy: (CTH) Bankruptcy Act 1966 s 123(3). See also **Act of bankruptcy; Good faith; Ordinary course of business; Relation-back doctrine.**

•**Protection 1.** In trade and commerce measures to protect companies in Australia from the competition of companies in other countries who seek to export to Australia. Such measures compromise the principle of free trade. **2.** The conservation, preservation, enhancement, and management of the environment: (WA) Environmental Protection Act 1986 s 3. See also **Free trade; General Agreement on Tariffs and Trade 1994; Industry statement 1991.**

Protective trust A statutory trust for life or for any lesser period established for a beneficiary which is to be determined upon the happening of certain specified events (such as bankruptcy of the beneficiary) whereupon the trust income is then to be applied for the maintenance of the beneficiary and his or her family at the absolute discretion of the trustees: *Re Coleman* (1888) 39 Ch D 443 at 451; *Public Trustee v Ferguson* [1947] NZLR 746 at 753. Formerly known as 'alimentary trust'. See also **Bare power**; **Beneficiary**; **Discretionary trust**; **Trust**; **Trust instrument**.

Protest In relation to bills of exchange, an internationally recognised formal record of the dishonour of a foreign bill for non-acceptance or non-payment. A protest must contain a copy of the bill, be signed by the notary or its maker, and specify the person requesting the protest. Subject to the Act, protest must be made within 48 hours after dishonour, specifying the place and date of protest, its cause or reason, any demand made and answer given, or that the drawee or acceptor were not found: (CTH) Bills of Exchange Act 1909 ss 56(4), (7). If dishonour is not protested, the drawer and indorsers are discharged. See also **Bill of exchange**; **Dishonour by non-acceptance**; **Foreign bill**; **Noting**.

•**Protocol** An international agreement which is less formal than a treaty or Convention proper.

•**Provable debt** A debt that must be recognised by a bankruptcy trustee when administering the estate of the bankrupt. A provable debt is a debt or liability to which the bankrupt was subject at the date of bankruptcy, or which arises before discharge from bankruptcy by reason of an obligation incurred before the date of bankruptcy: (CTH) Bankruptcy Act 1966 s 82(1). See also **Bankrupt**; **Discharge of bankruptcy**; **Non-provable debt**; **Proof of debt**; **Unliquidated damages**.

Provincial auctioneer An auctioneer trading in the country. A court may attribute a provincial auctioneer with a lower standard of skill and care than a leading city auctioneer when advising a seller concerning the authenticity and value of paintings: *Luxmoore-May v Messenger May Baverstock (a firm)* [1990] 1 All ER 1067. See also **Auctioneer**.

Proving a debt See **Proof of debt**.

•**Provision** An item in a balance sheet which embraces: liabilities which have accrued to employees, shareholders and others during the year, which are due to be paid in later years, for example long-service leave; and the provision of funds against the possibility of losses such as bad and doubtful debts, enabling losses to be written-off without a sudden impact on profits. Provisioning levels may be adopted routinely according to a formula, or varied according to the general economic outlook. Provision may also be general or specific, depending upon the exposure to a particular risk.

Provision for bad debts See **Allowance for bad debts**.

•**Provisional liquidator** A person appointed to safeguard the company's business and property pending the outcome of an application for a winding up order. See also **Liquidator**; **Official liquidator**; **Winding up order**.

Provisional lump sum contract A type of rated building contract in which a provisional bill of quantities is prepared, based on outline drawings, and is priced by the contractor. The resulting tender is provisional. Ultimately, the work is remeasured and the provisional sum is adjusted by applying the bill rates to the quantities as determined by remeasurement. The fundamental nature of a provisional lump sum contract is that the proprietor guarantees the bill of quantities to the contractor and the price is accordingly to be recalculated in the light of variation between the billed quantities and the 'as built' quantities: *Sist Constructions Pty Ltd v State Electricity Commission of Victoria* [1982] VR 597. Also known as 'remeasurement contract'. See also **Building contract**; **Contractor**; **Lump sum contract**; **Proprietor**; **Rated contract**.

•**Provisional sum** In building law, in general, a prime cost item. The figure inserted in a bill of quantities or tender specifications by a proprietor as the amount a tenderer should provide for a particular item of work or materials; historically distinguished from a prime cost item: *Leslie & Co Ltd v Metropolitan Asylums District Managers* (1901) 1 LGR 862. An estimate provided by a proprietor of a sum which will later be included in the subcontract as the amount to be paid to a nominated subcontractor for work to be done: *North West Metropolitan Regional Hospital Board v T A Bickerton & Sons Ltd* [1970] 1 All ER 1039; [1970] 1 WLR 607. See also **Prime cost item**; **Proprietor**; **Subcontract**.

•**Provisional tax** Tax paid in advance of a future liability to income tax which is offset against that liability when it is finally determined: (CTH) Income Tax Assessment Act 1936 Pt VI Div III. See also **Income taxation**; **Pay As You Earn system**; **Prescribed Payments System**; **Taxable income**.

Provisions 1. The contents of clauses in a legal or formal statement or document. **2.** A term used in accounting, relating to amounts written off for the purpose of providing for depreciation renewals or diminution in value of assets, or for any known but undetermined future liability. **3.** Food, water, and other necessaries with which the master of a vessel is required to stock the vessel before beginning a voyage: (CTH) Navigation Act 1912 s 117. A vessel may be inspected by the Australian Maritime Safety Authority in respect of its provisions, and detained if it fails to meet the standards: s 120. See also **Necessaries**.

Proviso /prouvaɪzou/ *Lat* – provided. **1.** A form of words beginning 'Provided that...' which is added at the end of a section to limit the operation of the section by adding exceptions. **2.** The power of an appellate court to dismiss an appeal against conviction notwithstanding that it has found that there has been an error or defect in the trial of the appellant. The proviso allows the appeal to be dismissed where a reasonable jury properly directed would on the evidence have without doubt convicted the appellant: *Driscoll v R* (1977) 137 CLR 517 at 542-3; 15 ALR 47. See also **Miscarriage of justice**.

Proximate cause In insurance law, the direct, real, dominant, operative, or efficient cause of loss or damage: *National & General Insurance Co Ltd v Chick* [1984] 2 NSWLR 86. An insurer will only be liable for loss suffered by the insured where the loss was proximately caused by a peril insured against: for example *Company v Law Investment and Insurance Corporation Ltd* [1898] 2 QB 626; (CTH) Marine Insurance Act 1909 s 61. Commonsense is the final arbiter in establishing the proximate cause of a loss: *National & General Insurance Co Ltd v Chick*. See also **Causal exclusion clause**.

•**Proxy 1.** A person authorised to do something for someone else; an agent: *Cousins v International Brick Co Ltd* [1931] 2 Ch 90. **2.** A person with authority to vote at a company general meeting or class meeting in the interest of the person who appoints the proxy. See also **Agent; Creditor; General meeting**.

Proxy fight A term used in the United States to refer to a contested vote at a company meeting.

Prudent insurer test An objective test used to determine the level of disclosure required of an insured. An insured must disclose every circumstance that would influence the judgment of a prudent insurer in fixing the premium or deciding whether he or she will take the risk: (CTH) Marine Insurance Act 1909 s 24; *Mayne Nickless Ltd v Pegler* [1974] 1 NSWLR 228. Although evidence of underwriters and brokers with respect to the materiality of the non-disclosure may be admitted, the court may decline to act on it when determining the attitude of the prudent insurer: *Protean (Holdings) Ltd (receivers & managers apptd) v American Home Assurance Co* [1985] VR 187 at 229. Also known as 'reasonable insurer test'. See also **Disclosure; Insurer**.

•**Prudential matters** Matters relating to a bank's conduct of its affairs, whether or not relating to the banking business of the bank, with integrity, prudence, and professional skill, in such a way as to keep itself in a sound financial position and not to cause or promote instability in the Australian financial system: (CTH) Banking Act 1959 s 5(1). The Reserve Bank of Australia must encourage and promote sound practices by the banks in relation to prudential matters, and should evaluate the effectiveness of those practices: (CTH) Banking Act 1959 s 11B(b), (c). See also **Reserve Bank of Australia**.

Prudential supervision Descriptive of the role of the Reserve Bank of Australia in exercising its responsibility for ensuring the efficiency and stability of the banking system. Prudential supervision is undertaken through the imposition of capital adequacy guidelines, the requirement that a prime assets ratio be maintained by the banks and a reserve assets ratio by the savings banks, and the power to monitor a bank's managerial performance and resources. Prudential supervision is also exercised by the Australian Securities Commission, the Insurance and Superannuation Commission, and State governments. See also **Prime assets ratio; Reserve Bank of Australia**.

PSA See **Prices Surveillance Authority**.

PSASB See **Public Sector Accounting Standards Board**.

Pty See **Proprietary company**.

•**Public authority** A person or body executing a function in the public interest and for the public benefit: *Federal Cmr of Taxation v Silverton Tramway Co Ltd* (1953) 88 CLR 559 at 565-6. A public authority need not be an agent or instrumentality of the Crown or subject to its control (*General Steel Industries Inc v Cmr for Railways (NSW)* (1964) 112 CLR 125), nor have been created by statute (*Western Australian Turf Club v FCT* at 310-11).

Public borrowing The difference between the total receipts of the central government, local authorities, and public enterprises and their total expenditure. See also **Public sector**.

•**Public company 1.** A company which is not a proprietary company: Corporations Law s 9. They are subject to more stringent disclosure and reporting requirements than proprietary companies. See also **Proprietary company**.

•**Public corporation** A public company or financial institution: Corporations Law s 9. In relation to a prescribed interest, it refers to a body corporate, other than a public company, that is declared by the Australian Securities Commission (ASC), in writing, to be a public corporation for the purposes of Corporations Law Part 7.12 in relation to particular purposes: s 9. A public company is a company other than a proprietary company: s 9. See also **Public company**.

•**Public document 2.** In relation to a corporation, an instrument of the corporation, or one purporting to be signed, issued, or published by or on behalf of the corporation, and which is intended to be lodged: Corporations Law s 88A. See also **Document**.

•**Public domain** In copyright law, the status of material which is not protected by copyright. See also **Author; Copyright; International copyright; Licence**.

Public examination A court hearing at which a bankrupt is examined before a judge, registrar, or magistrate about examinable affairs. See also **Bankrupt; Official receiver; Registrar in Bankruptcy; Trustee in bankruptcy**.

Public finance The financial activities of government at all levels: federal, state, territorial and local. The subject of public finance is concerned with analysing the effects of government revenue-raising and expenditure on the national economy.

•**Public fund** In taxation law, a fund which originates in a public initiative or attracts public financial participation to a substantial degree: *Bray v Federal Cmr of Taxation* (1978) 140 CLR 560; 19 ALR 309. A fund cannot be categorised as a public fund simply because of the nature of the purposes for which the fund is used or because it is available to receive public contributions: *Bray v Federal Cmr of Taxation*. A tax deduction may be claimed for donations to public funds: (CTH) Income Tax Assessment Act 1936 s 78(1)(a).

•**Public interest 1.** An interest common to the public at large or a significant portion of the public and which may or may not involve the personal or proprietary rights of individual people.

Public issue In corporations law, a method of raising new equity capital by which a company invites the public through newspapers and a prospectus to apply for stated amounts of shares at specified prices. The issue may be accompanied by an underwriting agreement which guarantees the company that all shares will be taken up. Potential investors have greater confidence in the issuer if an underwriter has agreed to take up any shortfall. However, underwriting agreements may contain some qualifications which allow the underwriter to withdraw in certain circumstances. See also **Prospectus**.

Public liability A risk of liability to the public at large against which an insurance policy may be obtained. See also **Public liability insurance**.

Public liability insurance Insurance under which the insurer agrees to indemnify the insured for legal liability owed to another person who suffers loss or damage by reason of the insured's business activities, other than the insured's supply of products. See also **Liability insurance; Product liability insurance**.

Public limited company See **Public company**.

•**Public nuisance** An unlawful act, the effect of which is to endanger the life, health, property, morals, or comfort of the public: *R v Clifford* [1980] 1 NSWLR 314. A public nuisance is a nuisance so widespread in its range or so indiscriminate in its effect that it would not be reasonable to expect one person to take proceedings to stop it on his or her own responsibility, but should be the responsibility of the community at large: *Baulkham Hills Shire Council v Domachuk* (1988) 66 LGRA 110. A public nuisance is actionable without proof of actual damage to particular individuals. See also **Nuisance**.

•**Public officer** 1. A person appointed to discharge a duty of public office, in the interests of the public, in exchange for compensation or payment out of a public fund: *R v Whitaker* [1914] 3 KB 1283. See also **Incorporated association; Officer**.

•**Public policy** A definite and governing principle which the community as a whole has already adopted, either formally by law or tacitly by its general course of corporate life: *Wilkinson v Osborne* (1915) 21 CLR 89. A court will not enforce a contract that infringes public policy (*A v Hayden (No 2)* (1984) 156 CLR 532; 56 ALR 82), such as an agreement in undue restraint of trade, even though it does not contravene any positive rule of law, if it would be injurious to the public interest: *Re Jacob Morris (dec'd)* (1943) 43 SR (NSW) 352. See also **Illegal contract; Void contract**.

Public risk insurance See **Public liability insurance**.

•**Public sector** All government agencies and public sector employees, and the operations and activities carried on by government agencies and public sector employees: for example (SA) Public Sector Management Act 1995 s 3. See also **Public service**.

Public Sector Accounting Standards Board *Abbr* – PSASB A body established in 1983 as a Board of the Australian Accounting Research Foundation (AARF) by the Australian Society of Certified Practising Accountants and the Institute of Chartered Accountants in Australia and having various functions including the implementation of a process for the formulation and maintenance of accounting standards of relevance to public sector reporting entities: for example Statement of Auditing Practice AUS 1. See also **Australian Accounting Standards Board**.

Public sector borrowing requirement *Abbr* – PSBR The total amount of funds required by all levels of government to finance their operations; the total financing requirements, budget and non-budget, of the public sector. The budget component consists of all departments and authorities whose transactions are recorded in detail in the public accounts. The non-budget component comprises those authorities, mainly state enterprises and statutory authorities, whose financial transactions are not fully reflected in the public accounts: for example, Australia Post. The net PSBR is the difference between the total expenditure of the public sector and the total receipts, with any deficit made up by borrowing.

•**Public service** The body of people engaged to carry out the work of the executive arm of government, putting into operation the legislation enacted by Parliament and any subordinate legislation. The Commonwealth Public Service is constituted by the secretaries to the departments of the service, senior executive service officers, other officers, and government employees: (CTH) Public Service Act 1922 s 10. Also known as 'civil service'. See also **Department; Executive**.

Public Trading Trust A public trading trust is defined in (CTH) Income Tax Assessment Act 1936 s 102R as a trust that in respect of a particular year was established after 19 September 1985, the trust is a 'public unit trust': s 102P, a 'trading trust': s102N, and a 'resident unit trust': s 102Q. Of critical importance in determining if a unit trust is a public trading trust is whether the unit trust is carrying on a 'trading business': s 102M, or an 'eligible investment business': s 102M. A public trading trust is taxed in a manner identical to a company. The rate of tax payable by the trustee of a public trading trust is the same as the corporate rate of tax. Distributions of income (unit trust dividends): s 102M by public trading trust are treated for income tax purposes as franked dividends: s 160ARDC. The trading trust provisions (Div 6C, ss 102M-102R) were introduced as an anti-avoidance measure.

Public trust See **Charitable trust**.

•**Public Trustee** 1. A corporation sole established by legislation in all Australian States. The Public Trustee performs a number of public functions, including acting as trustee of property in cases of incapacity, imprisonment, or where a property owner has died without appointing an executor. See also **Corporation sole; Relation-back doctrine; Trustee company**.

Puffery Representation, statement, or conduct that clearly over-exaggerates the attributes or characteristics of some product or service and is not intended to be an offer to be relied upon. The non-specific language of a puff fails to satisfy the criteria of contractual obligation for the reason that no contract was intended: *Carlill v Carbolic Smoke Ball Co* [1893] 1 QB 256; *Lambert v Lewis* [1982] AC 225.

Puffing The act of creating puffery. See also **Puffery**.

Punitive damages See **Exemplary damages**.

Purchase 1. To acquire by way of bargain and sale for money or other valuable consideration: *Hollingsworth v Lee* [1949] VLR 140. 2. To acquire real estate by any means other than descent. See also **Acquire**; **Convey**.

Purchase method A method of accounting for a business combination where the net assets acquired are recorded in the financial statements of the acquiring company at the cost to that acquiring company. Income of the acquiring company includes the income of the acquired company from the date of acquisition.

Purchase of assets A form of corporate control transaction where the offeror purchases the business undertaking and assets of the target, leaving the target as an empty shell although the shareholding of the target remains intact. The transaction needs the consent of the target's board of directors. See also **Takeover**.

Purchase of employee shares The purchase by a company of shares in itself from its employees. At common law, this was unlawful, whether on cessation of the employee's employment or otherwise: for example *Parry v Bundaberg Foundry Co Ltd* [1933] QSR 139. Corporations Law s 206C now provides for an 'employee share scheme buy-back', which means a buy-back of shares under a scheme that has as its purpose the acquisition of shares in a company by or on behalf of 'participating employees' that has been approved by the company in general meeting: Corporations Law s 9. See also **Employee share scheme buy-back**.

Purchase price 1. In relation to a superannuation pension, contributions made by a person to a superannuation fund to receive a superannuation pension only or, where the benefit to be received is only partly in the form of a superannuation pension, that part of the total consideration paid as the Commissioner of Taxation considers reasonable: (CTH) Income Tax Assessment Act 1936 s 27A(1). 2. In relation to an annuity, the sum of payments made solely to purchase the annuity, or if other benefits in addition to the annuity are obtained, so much of those payments that the Commissioner of Taxation considers reasonable to purchase the annuity: (CTH) Income Tax Assessment Act 1936 s 27A(1). 3. In relation to a lay-by sale agreement, the total amount of the money paid or payable for the goods and the value of any other consideration given to complete the purchase: (ACT) Lay-by Sales Agreements Act 1963 s 3(2). See also **Annuity**; **Lay-by**; **Pension**; **Undeducted purchase price**.

Purchaser A person who acquires an interest in property for valuable consideration by conveyance. The term 'purchaser' may have a wider meaning than 'buyer': *Re Barton; Ex parte Official Receiver v Barton* (1983) 52 ALR 95; 76 FLR 223, considering (CTH) Bankruptcy Act 1966 s 120. See also **Bona fide purchase**; **Sale of land**; **Valuable consideration**; **Vendor**.

Purchaser for valuable consideration A person who enters into a transaction and who gives or has given something of value in return. A purchaser for valuable consideration may be able to resist a claim that a payment, transfer, or charge has given rise to a preference, or that it can otherwise be set aside under the (CTH) Bankruptcy Act 1966. See also **Good faith**; **Ordinary course of business**; **Preference**; **Settlement**.

Purchaser's obligation In addition to other requirements imposed by a contract, a purchaser must: be ready, willing and able to perform his or her obligations at the due day; take delivery as required by the contract; accept the goods or property; and pay in accordance with the contract: *Foran v Wight* (1989) 168 CLR 385; 88 ALR 41.

Purchasing-power-parity exchange rate *Abbr* – PPP exchange rate An exchange rate that equates prices of similar goods between countries. Thus while gross domestic product (GDP) is probably the best available measure of prosperity, the use of current market exchange rates for currency can result in misleading results. A high GDP per person may undergo considerable modification when viewed against the cost of living in a given country. In the long run, the exchange rate between two currencies is in equilibrium when it equalises the prices of a basket of similar goods and services in both countries. In 1990, Australia ranked fourteenth in the PPP league, on a par with Britain.

Pure economic loss Pecuniary loss not consequent upon personal injury or physical damage to the plaintiff's property, often arising in the context of negligent misstatements. See also **Damages**; **Negligent misrepresentation**.

Pure endowment insurance See **Endowment insurance**.

Purpose trust A trust established for a specific purpose and not for the benefit of specific individuals. Purpose trusts established for non-charitable purposes are void, as there is no beneficiary in existence to enforce the trust: *Re Reecher's Will Trusts* [1972] Ch 526.

Put and call An option that gives the right to buy or sell a fixed number of securities at a specified price at a specified time. A put gives the holder an option to sell, a call gives the right to buy. See also **Option**.

Put option A right held by a person to sell at any time during a certain period ('currency of the option') a certain number of issued securities at a price fixed at the time the option is given ('exercise price'). A put option is an option to sell the subject matter of the option: for example *Sydney Futures Exchange Ltd v Australian Stock Exchange Ltd* (1995) 128 ALR 417; 56 FLR 236. See also **Call option**; **Option**; **Strike price**.

Putting back clause A standard clause in a time charterparty providing for hire rates to cease if a vessel deviates, delays, or puts back during its voyage. The hire is ceased until the voyage resumes. The charterer must pay the expenses if the putting back is caused by the charterer. See also **Charterer**; **Deviation**; **Off hire clause**.

Pyramid selling A trading scheme in which the promoter offers to sell to a participant both the right to sell a particular product or service, and the right to introduce others into the scheme in the same way. Consumer protection legislation prohibits the practice of pyramid selling in Australia: (CTH) Trade Practices Act 1974 s 61; (NSW) Fair Trading Act 1987 s 56; (VIC) Fair Trading Act 1985 s 24(1). See also **Fair Trading Legislation**; **Trade Practices Legislation**.

Pyramiding 1. The concentration of control over a chain of companies through a chain of majority shareholdings. **2.** When a tax is imposed at an early stage of production, the effect on the final price when a percentage increase is made at each successive stage of manufacture. **3.** The purchasing of the same security on a rising market. **4.** Additions to an initial investment or position in a commodity market, the additions being on a progressively smaller scale. **5.** The progressive acquisition of securities through borrowing funds based on the security of previous purchases, each acquisition being smaller than the one before. See also **Share**.

Q

QC See **Queen's Counsel**.

Qualification share Shares allotted to a company director for the purpose of satisfying a condition of being appointed, and retaining office, that the director hold shares in the company. A person who, as a director, signs and files with the Australian Securities Commission an undertaking to take from the company and to pay for the qualification shares is, as regards those shares, in the same position as if the director had signed the memorandum for that number of shares: Corporations Law s 222(2). See also **Director**.

•**Qualified acceptance** An acceptance of a bill of exchange where the drawee expressly varies the effect of the bill as drawn: *Guaranty Trust Co of New York v Hannay & Co* [1918] 2 KB 623. Qualified acceptance includes conditional, partial and local acceptance, acceptance qualified as to time, and acceptance by one or more drawees, but not all: (CTH) Bills of Exchange Act 1909 s 24(3). See also **Acceptance; Acceptor; Bill of exchange; Conditional acceptance; Local acceptance; Partial acceptance**.

Qualified audit report An audit report in which a qualified opinion has been expressed: Statement of Auditing Standards AUS 1 para 26. See also **Auditor's report; Qualified opinion; Unqualified opinion**.

Qualified covenant A covenant that is qualified, either by way of condition precedent or subsequent, or by way of limitation. The most common means by which a covenant is qualified is by words purporting to limit or restrict the liability of the covenantor: for example *Sanderson v Berwick-upon-Tweed Corp* (1884) 13 QBD 547. See also **Condition precedent; Condition subsequent; Covenant**.

Qualified opinion In corporations law, the opinion expressed by an auditor in an audit report when any of the following circumstances exist, and in the auditor's judgment, the effects of the matter are, or are likely to be, material: a disagreement with management regarding the financial report; a conflict between applicable financial reporting frameworks; or a significant uncertainty resulting from either a limitation on the scope of the audit, or an inherent uncertainty: Statement of Auditing Practice AUP 3 para 42. An audit report containing a qualified opinion is known as a qualified audit report. See also **Qualified audit report**.

•**Quality** The nature, kind, or character of a thing, including its attributes, properties and special features: *Ducret v Chaudhary's Oriental Carpet Palace Pty Ltd* (1987) 16 FCR 562; 76 ALR 183. See also **Conditions of sale; Defective performance; Defective product; Merchantable quality**.

Quality circle A management technique developed in Japan aimed at increasing productivity. Groups of workers responsible for their own output as an autonomous team meet together voluntarily to plan their work, ensuring improved product quality while harmonising with other autonomous groups up and down the production line. See also **Just-in-time production; Total quality management; Value added management**.

Quantity theory of money A theory evolved by the Classical School of economics and developed by later economists such as Irving Fisher (1867-1947), the essentials of which are contained in the equation: $MV = PT$ where M = the quantity of money (cash plus bank deposits); V = the velocity of circulation (the rate at which money changes hands); P = a price index covering all transactions; and T = the total volume of transactions per unit of time. From this equation it may be concluded that with V and T constant, an increase in M must result in an increase in P, the general level of prices depending on the amount of money in circulation. With V and P constant, an increase in M could be offset by an increase in T. With both P and T constant, a decrease in M could be offset by an increase in V. If T is constant, an increase in P must be due to an increase in M or V. See also **Economics**.

Quantum of damages The amount of money or compensation awarded as damages or compensation for proved losses. It refers to the amount of damages assessed in respect of an injury and not the amount of damages recoverable: (CTH) Judiciary Act 1903 s 35(4) (repealed); *Cocks v Sheppard* (1979) 25 ALR 325; 53 ALJR 591. Also known as 'assessment of damages' or 'measure of damages'. See also **Assessment of damages; Measure of damages**.

•**Quarantine** The inspection, exclusion, detention, observation, segregation, isolation, protection, treatment, sanitary regulation, or disinfection of vessels, installations, persons, goods, things, animals or plants, in order to prevent the introduction or spread of diseases or pests affecting human beings, animals or plants: (CTH) Quarantine Act 1908 s 4. The essence of quarantine is the restriction or prohibition of the movement of persons or things: *McCarter v Brodie* (1950) 80 CLR 432; [1950] ALR 385. The Commonwealth and the States enjoy concurrent powers of quarantine: Commonwealth Constitution ss 51(ix), 107, 108; (CTH) Quarantine Act 1908; (VIC) Health Act 1958.

•**Quash** To set aside ((CTH) Crimes Act 1914 s 85ZN), overthrow or annul. In criminal law, a trial court may quash an information, indictment or presentment where it is defective in substance: for example (NSW) Crimes Act 1900 s 362; (QLD) Criminal Code s 596; (SA) Criminal Law Consolidation Act 1935 s 281.

Quasi-bailment See **Constructive bailment**.

Quasi-contract For example, where a debt arose from the defendant's retention of money belonging to the plaintiff, from a sale of goods, or from the execution of work done at the defendant's request, an action in *assumpsit* would lie, *quasi ex contractu*, on an implied obligation or debt, without there being any genuine agreement to pay. The fictional promise to pay was a consequence of the plaintiff being required to plead one of the forms of action, called common counts, to succeed in a quasi-contractual action: *Pavey & Matthews Pty Ltd v Paul* (1987) 162 CLR 221; 69 ALR 577. See also **Assumpsit; Count; Action of debt; Failure of consideration; Restitution.**

Quasi-corporation Although a quasi-corporation is not a corporation, courts will sometimes regard it as possessing some degree of legal personality (for example *Knight & Searle v Dove* [1964] 2 QB 631), and it may also be a corporation for the purpose of some provisions of the Corporations Law. See also **Corporation.**

Quasi-equity funding 1. A form of funding used in the public sector where most of the equity in an enterprise is privately owned, yet the government or public body retains control through possessing a majority of voting shares. 2. A form of funding used in the private sector where a minority fundholder retains control through having a majority of voting shares. See also **Equity; Share.**

Queen's Counsel *Abbr* – QC A title or honorary rank bestowed on a barrister or legal practitioner practising in the style of a barrister. QCs no longer have a public function as advisers to the Crown. A QC is formally described as one of Her Majesty's Counsel learned in the law. QCs appointed as judges of inferior courts may retain the title 'QC'. Also known as 'silk', 'senior counsel', 'leader', or 'member of the Inner Bar'. See also **Barrister.**

Queuing A risk management arrangement where transfer orders are held pending by the originator or deliverer, or by the system, until sufficient cover is available in the originator's or deliverer's clearing account or under the limits set against the payer; in some cases, cover may include unused credit lines or available collateral. See also **Collateral; Cover; Credit line.**

Quick asset An asset which is in the form of cash or can be quickly converted into cash. A quick assets ratio is established by dividing quick assets by current liabilities. See also **Asset; Current ratio; Quick ratio.**

Quick ratio A ratio used in financial statement analysis and calculated by dividing quick assets by current liabilities. 'Quick assets' are those assets that are quickly convertible into cash and are calculated by subtracting inventories from current assets. The quick ratio measures the short-term solvency or liquidity of a firm, in particular, the ability to meet current liabilities without relying on the sale of inventory stock. See also **Current ratio; Financial statement.**

Quid pro quo /kwɪd proʊ kwoʊ/ *Lat* – one thing in exchange for another; something in exchange; a fair equivalent. See also **Remuneration.**

Quiet enjoyment A right to undisturbed occupation and possession of an estate in land. Such a right is one of the covenants for title commonly given on a conveyance of old system title land. It is also given expressly or by implication in a lease. Any physical interference with the premises will amount to a breach of the covenant for quiet enjoyment: *Martins Camera Corner Pty Ltd v Hotel Mayfair Ltd* [1976] 2 NSWLR 15. See also **Lease.**

• **Quistclose trust** A special purpose trust by which it is recognised that money held by one person is held on trust for a special purpose. If the money is paid for the special purpose, the person becomes a debtor of the settlor; but if the purpose fails, a resulting or secondary trust arises in favour of the settlor. The relationships of trustee-beneficiary and debtor-creditor are not necessarily exclusive of each other: *Barclays Bank Ltd v Quistclose Investments Ltd* [1970] AC 567. See also **Resulting trust; Settlor; Trust.**

Quorum /kwɔrʊm/ *Lat* – of which or whom. The specified minimum number of members whose presence is necessary to validate the transactions of a meeting of members of a body. The quorum is composed by those actually present at a time and place when all should and might be present as opposed to an ad hoc meeting: *Brougham v Melbourne Banking Corp Ltd* (1880) 6 VLR (Eq) 214 at 222. See also; **Part X; Proxy; Trustee in bankruptcy.**

Bankruptcy Under (CTH) Bankruptcy Act 1966 Pt X, a quorum for a meeting of creditors is two creditors who are entitled to vote and who are present in person or represented by an attorney or proxy: s 202(1). For other meetings of creditors under the (CTH) Bankruptcy Act 1966, a quorum is two creditors who are entitled to vote and who are present in person, by telephone or represented by an attorney or proxy, or only one such creditor if the trustee is present in person: s 64N(2). See also **Creditors' meeting; Part X; Proxy; Trustee in bankruptcy.**

Corporations The quorum for a meeting of the board of directors of a company is usually determined by the company's articles: for example Corporations Law Sch 1 Table A art 73. In the case of a general meeting of members, in a proprietary company, two members personally present constitute the quorum, unless the articles provide otherwise: s 249(1)(a)(ii). In any other company the statutory quorum is three members: s 249(1)(a)(iii). See also **Board of directors; General meeting.**

• **Quotation** In commodities and securities trading, the highest bid to buy and the lowest offer to sell a commodity or security in a given market at a given time. It includes the provision on a stock market of information concerning the price at which, or the consideration for which, particular persons propose, or may reasonably be expected, to sell, purchase or exchange securities: Corporations Law s 9. See also **Australian Stock Exchange quoted security; Australian Stock Exchange Listing Rules; Official quotation.**

Quoted right A marketable right, including a right in respect of shares in any body corporate, in a class of marketable rights listed for quotation on a stock market of a securities exchange, being a local stock exchange or an approved securities organisation pursuant to Corporations Law s 770: ss 9, 1097A(2). See also **Quotation; Quoted security.**

Quoted security A marketable security listed for quotation on a stock market of a securities exchange: Corporations Law s 1097A(1). Quotation enables securities to be traded on the stock market. See also **Australian Stock Exchange Ltd; Securities.**

R

•**Racial discrimination** Any act involving a distinction, exclusion, restriction, or preference based on race, colour, descent or national or ethnic origin, which has the purpose or effect of nullifying or impairing the recognition, enjoyment or exercise, on an equal footing, of any human right or fundamental freedom in the political, economic, social, cultural or any other field of public life: (CTH) Racial Discrimination Act 1975 s 9(1). See also **Anti-discrimination legislation; Aboriginal person**.

Rack-rent The rent which a property would obtain if let by the year in the open market, that is, what a tenant, taking one year with another, might fairly and reasonably be expected to pay, the tenant paying the tenants' rates and taxes and the landlord doing the repairs. Rack-rent is rent of the full value of the holding or very close to that value: *Re Sawyer & Withall* [1919] 2 Ch 333. See also **Peppercorn rent**.

Radius clause A provision contained in a contract of employment under which the employee agrees that, upon leaving the present employer, he or she, for a specified period of time, will not set up, or work for, a business of a similar nature to that of the current employer which lies within a specific geographical radius around the current employer's place of business. The legality of such clauses depends upon the reasonableness of the restraints. Also known as 'radius agreement'. See also **Restraint of trade**.

Rally In corporations law, a surge in share prices after an extended period in which the price fell.

Ranging clause 1. A clause in a charterparty defining a range of ports, either by naming them specifically or by defining a geographical area within which a number of ports are located. The ranging clause may stipulate the ports at which the vessel chartered by the charterer may commence its first voyage under charter, ports at which it might be required by the owner to finish its last voyage under charter; ports where a ship might be placed for loading and unloading, or ports at which it may be re-delivered at the end of the charter period. See also **Charterparty**.

Rate of demurrage The rate, usually calculated on a daily basis (*Yeoman v R* [1904] 2 KB 429), payable by a charterer to a shipowner, for the time taken to load or discharge cargo in excess of the time permitted in the charterparty. See also **Cargo; Charterer; Charterparty; Days on demurrage; Demurrage; Loading**.

Rate of discharge In contracts of carriage, the amount of cargo, usually calculated in tonnes, unloaded each day from a ship. A voyage charterparty will often include a term stipulating a set rate of discharge. See also **Cargo; Loading; Rate of loading; Voyage charterparty**.

Rate of exchange The rate at which one currency can be purchased in terms of another currency at any specific point in time: *Alexander Stewart & Sons Ltd v Robinson* (1920) 29 CLR 55 at 59; *LNC (Wholesale) Pty Ltd v Collector of Customs (No 2)* (1988) 77 ALR 347. See also **Currency; Exchange rate; Foreign currency transaction**.

Rate of freight The charge made by a carrier for the carriage of goods, expressed as a sum per unit of measure, for example, tonnes, cubic metres, or per container. Also known as 'freight rate'. See also **Affreightment; Charterer; Contract of carriage**.

Rate of loading The amount of cargo, usually calculated in tonnes, placed each day on a ship. A voyage charterparty will often include a term stipulating a set rate of loading. See also **Cargo; Loading; Rate of discharge; Voyage charterparty**.

Rate of return 1. The ratio of income to capital investment, expressed as a percentage; the profit of a company in relation to the level of investment used to generate it. The rate of return is usually calculated by expressing net profit after tax as a percentage of shareholders' funds. 2. In respect of fixed interest securities, either the coupon rate (interest as a percentage of face value), the current yield (interest as a percentage of current value), or the yield to maturity (a calculation which includes the redemption value). 3. In respect of ordinary shares, either the dividend yield (the dividend as a percentage of current share price), or dividend plus capital appreciation, or depreciation over a given period. See also **Shareholders' funds; Ordinary share**.

Rate variance A standard labour rate established to control direct labour. A rate variance arises when the actual wage rate and the standard labour rate vary. The variance reflects the efficiency and choice of personnel involved in direct labour.

Rated contract A contract that uses rates to calculate the contract sum and, depending on the terms of the contract, the quantity of work to be performed. A rated contract may also be an entire contract: *Ettridge v Vermin Board of District of Murat Bay* [1928] SASR 124. A contract is said to be rated where the cost is fixed per unit of material or labour, or both, and the final price is then calculated by applying this cost to the quantity of units provided. A contractor may enter into a contract for a stipulated price where this price is calculated wholly or in part by inserting unit rates in a bill of quantities, prepared on behalf of the proprietor, containing an estimated quantity for each item and by totalling the extension of the price for each item, but on the basis that, on completion, the quantities will be remeasured and the price recalculated. Such a contract is called a 'provisional lump sum contract' (*Sist Constructions Pty Ltd v State Electricity Commission of Victoria* [1982] VR 597; (1982) 1 Aust Const LR 75), a 'measure and value contract' (*London Steam Stone Saw Mills v Lorden* (1900) 2 Hudson's BC (4th ed) 30) or a 'schedule of rates contract': *Arcos Industries Pty Ltd v Electricity Com-*

378 © Butterworths

mission of NSW [1973] 2 NSWLR 186. See also **Building contract; Contractor; Provisional lump sum contract.**

Ratification The adoption by a person, entity or state of an agreement or contract that the person, entity or state was not obliged to perform prior to the act of ratification.

Agency Conduct of a principal after an unauthorised act by the principal's agent, which effectively makes the act the principal's own. Ratification allows an agent's unauthorised act to be treated as if the principal had previously given actual authority to do it: *Union Bank of Australia Ltd v Rudder* (1911) 13 CLR 152; 31 ALR 465. See also **Agency; Agent; Principal; Ratification by acquiescence; Undisclosed principal.**

Contract Where a principal adopts a contract made by an agent on his or her behalf, he or she is bound by that contract as if he or she had made it personally: *Wilson v Tumman* (1843) 6 Man & G 236; 134 ER 879. See also **Actual authority; Agent; Principal.**

Corporations In the case of a company, ratification cures the defect that the original act was performed without authority and has the effect that the company is bound by the act and entitled to take advantage of the act as if the agent had been authorised when he or she acted. See also **Actual authority; Directors' duties; Members' ratification; Pre-incorporation contract.**

Ratification by acquiescence In agency law, ratifying conduct of an intended principal who, having knowledge of all material facts and that he or she is regarded as having accepted the position of principal, takes no steps to disown that character within a reasonable time, or adopts no means of asserting his or her rights at the earliest period possible: *Lapraik v Burrows (The Australia)* (1859) 13 Moo PCC 132; 15 ER 50; *McLaughlin v City Bank of Sydney* (1912) 14 CLR 684. A principal who knowingly accepts benefits that flow from an allegedly unauthorised act of an agent is taken to have ratified the agent's act, except in very special circumstances: *Australian Blue Metal Ltd v Hughes* [1962] NSWR 904; (1962) 79 WN (NSW) 498. See also **Acquiescence; Agency; Agent; Principal; Ratification.**

RBL See **Reasonable benefit limit.**

Re *Lat* – in the matter (of); in relation to; in reference to; concerning. Re is frequently used to designate proceedings in which there is only one party.

Readily realisable asset An asset which can be realised in time to enable a debtor to pay debts falling due and to satisfy the test of solvency. The court has power to dismiss a creditor's petition if satisfied by the debtor that the debtor is able to pay the debts: (CTH) Bankruptcy Act 1966 s 52(2). A debtor's interest as a joint tenant in a residential property, which can only be realised after an application to the court and a favourable exercise of the court's discretion, is not a readily realisable asset for this purpose: *Re D'Onofrio; Ex parte Blyth* (1983) 65 ALR 545. See also **Creditor's petition; Debtor; Solvent.**

Ready and willing Possessing both intention and capacity to perform one's contractual obligations. A party may terminate a contract for anticipatory breach where it appears that the other party is not ready and willing: *Foran v Wight* (1989) 168 CLR 385; 88 ALR 413. Also known as 'ready, willing and able'. See also **Anticipatory breach; Breach; Performance; Repudiation; Specific performance; Settlement.**

Real debt A debt that is in reality owed by a debtor to a creditor. In bankruptcy law, the court will go behind a judgment debt to determine whether that judgment was founded on a real debt; that is, whether the debtor in reality owed to the creditor the moneys which the judgment held that he or she owed: *Re Ferguson; Ex parte E N Thorne & Co Pty Ltd (In liq)* [1970] ALR 177; (1969) 14 FLR 311. See also **Debt.**

Real interest rate The nominal or market interest rate adjusted for inflation. With an inflation rate of 5 per cent per annum, a nominal or market rate of interest of 10 per cent would be equal to a real interest rate of 5 per cent. A combination of inflation and taxation may readily reduce an apparently high interest rate to virtually zero in real terms. See also **Inflation; Interest.**

Real investment Resources tied up in physically productive and tangible assets such as plant and machinery or motor vehicles. The opposite to investment in securities and intangibles.

Real return A figure that is calculated by adjusting the rate of return according to changes in inflation. See also **Consumer price index; Rate of return; Return.**

Real security A security in respect of real as opposed to personal property. The term refers to both the legal and equitable interest in real estate. Trustees may be given powers to invest only in real securities. See also **Securities; Trust.**

Real wage The purchasing power of the wage an employee receives; it involves a comparison between the general cost of living and the amount of pay the worker receives. If the cost of living increases, and the actual wage paid stays the same, the worker's real wage has decreased, as the worker can purchase fewer goods or services than before. See also **Inflation; Wage fixation; Wage indexation.**

Realisation In economics, conversion of an asset into cash or receivables.

Realisation account An account which records the profit or loss on the realisation of an asset. The amount recorded in the realisation account is determined by offsetting the amount realised on the sale of asset against the recorded book value of the asset. A realisation account is also used when liquidating an estate or business.

Reasonable benefit limit *Abbr* – RBL An amount determined by the Commissioner of Taxation representing the maximum amount of superannuation and retirement benefits (including payments from approved deposit funds, superannuation pensions, annuities, and golden handshake payments made by an employer on termination of employment) that a person is entitled to receive during that person's lifetime on a concessionally taxed basis: (CTH) Income Tax Assessment Act 1936 Div 14 Part III, ss 140-140zQ. Amounts in excess of the reasonable benefit limit may be paid to a taxpayer but are taxed at the top marginal rate of tax plus the Medicare levy, regardless of the taxpayer's level of income: (CTH) Income Tax Assessment Act 1936 s 27B(3). There are two types of reasonable benefit limit: a lump sum reasonable benefit limit and a pension reasonable benefit limit. See also **Annuity; Approved deposit fund; Golden handshake; Lump sum reasonable benefit limit; Marginal tax rate; Medicare levy; Pension.**

Reasonable care The standard of care owed by those who have a duty to take care such as that owed by employers to their employees. In determining what constitutes reasonable care in a particular situation, regard should be had to: the degree of risk of an accident; the degree of injury likely to result from such an accident; and the nature and extent of the remedial action suggested: *Raimondo v South Australia* (1979) 23 ALR 513. See also **Duty of care; Negligence.**

Reasonable dispatch An obligation on a carrier when carrying goods to take no more time than is necessary in all the circumstances. There is an implied undertaking in a voyage charterparty that the ship will proceed on a voyage with reasonable dispatch having regard to the normal port clearance times and the speed of the ship during the charter. Similarly, time charterparties often provide that all voyages are to be prosecuted with utmost dispatch. See also **Charterer; Charterparty; Contract of carriage; Voyage charterparty.**

Reasonable fitness for purpose Where a seller supplies goods to a consumer, a condition implied that the goods shall be reasonably fit for the particular purpose for which they are required: for example (NSW) Sale of Goods Act 1923 s 19(1). Such a condition will only be implied when the buyer made that particular purpose known to the seller, the purpose was made known as to show reliance on the seller's skill and judgment, and the goods are of a description which it is in the course of the seller's business to supply.

• **Reasonable man** The ordinary person. A person with the characteristics of an ordinary man in the defendant's position. A fictitious, imaginary, or hypothetical person of ordinary prudence, intelligence, and skill under the circumstances: *Heaven v Pender* (1883) 11 QBD 503; *King v Phillips* [1953] 1 All ER 617. The reasonable man is now known as the 'reasonable person'.

Reasonable notice Notice given within a period of time which is adequate and sufficient, taking into account all the circumstances. For example, in employment law, reasonable notice of termination might be determined by reference to the frequency of payment of earnings and the nature of the employment, with a tendency to extend the period of notice for more senior and responsible employees: for example *Thorpe v South Australian National Football League* (1974) 10 SASR 17; *Quinn v Jack Chia (Aust) Ltd* [1992] 1 VR 567. See also **Dismissal; Termination.**

Reasonable reliance on information supplied Use of information supplied by another person when there is no reason to doubt its authenticity or correctness. It is a defence to a contravention of (CTH) Trade Practices Act 1974 Pt V where it can be established that the person placed such reliance on information supplied: (CTH) Trade Practices Act 1974 s 85(1)(b); *Adams v ETA Foods Ltd* (1987) 19 FCR 93; 78 ALR 611; *Thorp v CA Imports Pty Ltd* (1990) ATPR ¶40-996.

Reasonable rent A rental that is reasonable having regard to all the circumstances: *Email Ltd v Robert Bray (Langwarrin) Pty Ltd* [1984] VR 16. In a given fact situation, reasonable rent will not necessarily be equal to market rent: *Email Ltd v Robert Bray (Langwarrin) Pty Ltd*. See also **Lease; Rent.**

Reasonable skill and diligence A fair, proper and due degree of care and ability as might be expected from an ordinarily prudent person with the same knowledge and experience as the defendant engaging in the defendant's particular conduct or omission and under the particular circumstances: *Australian Securities Commission v Gallagher* (1994) 11 WAR 105; 10 ACSR 43. A person who fails to exercise reasonable skill and diligence may be guilty of negligence.

• **Reasonable time** The time for performing an obligation under a contract which does not contain a time stipulation: *Perri v Coolangatta Investments Pty Ltd* (1982) 149 CLR 537; 41 ALR 441. What is a reasonable time must necessarily depend on the circumstances of the case, and is a question of fact: *Brien v Dwyer* (1978) 141 CLR 378; 22 ALR 485; *Rudi's Enterprises Pty Ltd v Jay* (1987) 10 NSWLR 568. See also **Notice; Performance; Time stipulation.**

Reasonable wear and tear Wear and tear to rented premises attributable to reasonable use by the tenant (wear) and the ordinary operation of natural forces (tear). It is usually exempted from the tenant's covenant to repair: for example (NSW) Conveyancing Act 1919 s 84(1). The onus is on the tenant to show that any want of repair comes within the exception to the covenant to repair: *Haskell v Marlow* [1928] 2 KB 45. Under a reasonable wear and tear exemption, a tenant is released only from an obligation to repair what is directly due to wear and tear; the tenant remains bound to carry out whatever repairs are necessary to prevent indirect damage flowing as a consequence of the wear and tear: *Bunyip Buildings Pty Ltd v Gestetner Pty Ltd* [1969] SASR 87. Wilful damage is not reasonable wear and tear: *Julian v McMurray* (1924) 24 SR (NSW) 402. Also known as 'fair wear and tear'. See also **Covenant to repair; Landlord; Tenant.**

Rebatable eligible termination payment annuity A superannuation eligible termination payment (ETP) annuity the recipients of which receive a rebate of part of the tax that would otherwise be payable: (CTH) Income Tax Assessment Act 1936 s 159SM. A rebatable ETP annuity is a qualifying annuity purchased wholly with rolled-over amounts, and which does not fall within the definition of 'superannuation pension': s 159SJ(1). See also **Annuity; Eligible Termination Payment; Rebatable superannuation pension; Rollover.**

Rebatable superannuation pension A superannuation pension paid by a fund which is or has been a complying superannuation fund (or its equivalent) in the year in which the first payment occurs or any earlier year of income: (CTH) Income Tax Assessment Act 1936 s 159SJ(1). Recipients of rebatable superannuation pensions may receive a rebate of part of the tax that would otherwise be payable: s 159SM. See also **Complying superannuation fund**; **Pension**; **Rebatable eligible termination payment annuity**; **Rebate**; **Superannuation fund**.

•**Rebate** Something paid by way of reduction, return, or refund on what has already been paid or contributed: *Brookton Co-op Society Ltd v FCT* (1977) 16 ALR 93; 7 ATR 587. See also **Allowable deduction**; **Dependant rebate**; **Dividend rebate**; **Gross tax payable**; **Imputation rebate**; **Zone rebate**.

Recall See **Product recall**.

Recall action Action taken by a supplier to recall products, which may include: the calling back or withdrawal of products from the market or distribution chain; the making of a request to consumers or to other suppliers to return products for refund, replacement, or modification or to contact the supplier to arrange for a replacement product or part to be sent to the consumer; the sending of a service agent to a person's home or place of business to repair or modify a product; or the making of a request to a service agent that the agent repair or modify a product when it is next presented for servicing. See also **Compulsory product recall**; **Product recall**; **Voluntary product recall**.

Recall insurance See **Product recall insurance**.

Recapitalisation An adjustment made to a company's capital structure incorporating changes in the nature and value of the share capital. The procedure of recapitalisation occurs when a company changes the par value of its shares and issues new share certificates to replace the old certificates that have been called in. A recapitalisation has no bearing upon the assets or liabilities of the company. See also **Capital**; **Company**; **Par value**; **Share**.

•**Receipt** 1. A document which acknowledges or expresses the receipt, deposit, or payment of money or goods: *Attorney-General (UK) v Northwood Electric Light and Power Co Ltd* [1947] KB 511. 2. Taking physical possession or acquiring goods. See also **Debt**; **Estoppel**; **Seal**.

Receipt of premium The receiving of money due under a contract of insurance. A contract of insurance may provide that the insurer's liability is conditional upon actual receipt of the premium: *Equitable Fire and Accident Office Ltd v The Ching Wo Hong* [1907] AC 96. See also **Insurance contract**; **Premium**; **Return of premium**.

Receivables Debts currently owing to a company or individual; payments due from others.

Received bill of lading A bill of lading confirming only that the goods have been delivered into the shipowner's custody: *The Marlborough Hill v Alex Cowan and Sons Ltd* [1921] 1 AC 444. See also **Bill of lading**.

Receiver A person who is given property for safe keeping or to administer, usually for the benefit of the giver.

Corporations A person appointed by a creditor or court to investigate the affairs of a company which has run into financial difficulties. A receiver has power to do all things necessary or convenient to be done for or in connection with, or as incidental to, the attainment of the objectives for which the receiver was appointed: Corporations Law s 420. See also **Controller**; **Court appointed receiver**; **Privately appointed receiver**; **Receiver and manager**; **Registered liquidator**.

•**Receiver and manager** A receiver who is given the power to manage the business of the company where the continued operation of that business is desirable: *Re Newdigate Colliery Ltd* [1912] 1 Ch 468; *Re Custom Card (NSW) Pty Ltd and the Companies Act* [1979] 1 NSWLR 241. A person appointed as a receiver of a company will also be a receiver and manager by virtue of the powers conferred by Corporations Law s 416. See also **Managing controller**; **Official receiver**; **Official trustee in bankruptcy**; **Receiver**.

Receiver's indemnity A receiver's security over the assets of the corporation for liabilities properly incurred in the ordinary course of the receiver's duties and for which the receiver is personally liable. The receiver prima facie only has a right to be indemnified out of those assets: *Rosanove v O'Rourke* [1989] 1 Qd R 171. Personal liabilities incurred by a receiver include those set out in Corporations Law s 419(1). The indemnity has priority over every other claim in the receivership, with some exceptions: Corporations Law s 443E(1). See also **Receiver**.

Receiver's profit The amount of money that a receiver acting for a secured creditor can make over and above current asset values by completing unfinished work of the debtor whose business the receiver is managing. See also **Receiver**; **Secured-creditor**.

Receivership The process in which a receiver is appointed to a company to collect or protect property for the benefit either of the appointor or the persons ultimately held entitled to that property. Receivership is typically instituted where a company is at or near insolvency. See also **Insolvency**; **Receiver**.

Receiving carrier A carrier that is responsible for accepting goods from another carrier and then shipping those goods. See also **Carrier**; **Charterer**; **Common carrier**.

Recession A significant reduction in employment and production, trade and investment. It is often defined as two consecutive quarters of negative growth in the gross domestic product. See also **Employment**; **Gross Domestic Product**; **Recovery**.

Reciprocity agreement An agreement for the mutual exchange of commercial, legal, or other privileges, for the benefit of all the parties concerned. Reciprocity agreements are to be enforced in tandem. See also **Agreement**; **Exchange**.

Recognisance *Lat – recognitio* – acknowledgment. An acknowledgment by a person that the person is indebted to the state for a certain a sum of money where the debt is extinguished on a certain happening, for example where the person appears in court or has for a certain period been of good behaviour: *In the matter of a claim by the Mayor, Aldermen and Burgesses of the Borough of Nottingham* [1897] 2 QB 502. See also **Bail**.

Recognised company A body corporate that, because of the definition of 'company' of another jurisdiction, is a company for the purposes of Corporations Law s 9. A company registered in the home jurisdiction is a local corporation, and thus each local company is a recognised company in jurisdictions other than its State or Territory of origin. See also **Local corporation**.

Recognised futures exchange A body corporate that conducts a futures market outside Australia and which is a prescribed body corporate under Corporations Regulations reg 8.2.02: Corporations Law s 9. The prescribed body corporates are listed in Corporations Regulations Sch 1: Corporations Regulations reg 8.2.02. See also **Australian financial futures market**.

Recommended price A price stated by the supplier of a good as the price at which the good might be supplied. Making a price recommendation does not infringe the resale price maintenance provisions of the (CTH) Trade Practices Act 1974, so long as it does not become a specified price, that is, a price below which the good is not to be sold if supply to that person is to continue: (CTH) Trade Practices Act 1974 s 96. See also **Price; Resale price maintenance; Specified price**.

Reconstruction 1. Structural changes, transformation, renewal, or alteration of premises that are not insignificant. 2. In commercial language, the preservation and transfer of a company's business, not to outsiders, but to another company (consisting of substantially the same shareholders) so that the business may be continued by the company taking over: *Webb v FCT* (1922) 30 CLR 450. See also **Amalgamation**.

Recourse The right to claim against a debtor or guarantor where a default has occurred, or against a drawer or an endorser in respect of a dishonoured bill of exchange. See also **Bill of exchange; Non-recourse finance**.

Recovered or preserved property In bankruptcy law, property of a bankrupt which has been recovered, realised, or preserved under an indemnity for costs of litigation provided by a creditor: (CTH) Bankruptcy Act 1966 s 109(10)(a). See also **Bankrupt; Bankruptcy Court; Order of payment**.

Recovery The regaining of something lost, or wrongfully appropriated.
Corporations A phase of renewed economic activity and growth following a recession or depreciation; an upturn in the business cycle. On the stock market, an upward movement of prices after a decline. See also **Business cycle; Recession; Stock market**.

Rectification An equitable remedy involving variation of a document to record the terms of an agreement as fully and accurately as all parties originally intended it to: *Maralinga Pty Ltd v Major Enterprises Pty Ltd* (1973) 128 CLR 336; 1 ALR 169. See also **Mutual mistake; Rescission; Settlement; Specific performance; Unilateral mistake**.

Red The debit or loss side in finance and accounting. To be 'in the red' means one is in debit or showing a loss. See also **Credit balance; Debit**.

Red Book An authoritative reference work published in 1993 on the payment systems in the Group of Ten (G-10) compiled in consultation with the central banks of the G-10 countries. Similar 'Red Books' are published by the central banks of countries where important developments in payment systems are occurring. Australia's Red Book is published by the Reserve Bank. See also **Reserve Bank of Australia**.

Red clause credit A letter of credit where the advising bank is authorised to make advances to the entity for working capital before receiving the commercial documents stipulated in the credit. Traditionally the clause authorising advance payments is printed in red. See also **Letter of credit**.

•Redeemable preference share A preference share which may be bought back by a company from the shareholder before liquidation. See also **Distributable profits; Preference share; Share**.

Redelivery *Abbr* – Re-del In maritime law, the return of a ship by the charterer to the owner. A time charter will contain a clause requiring redelivery at the end of the period of charter. Usually, the redelivery clause stipulates that the ship must be returned in the same condition as on delivery. Breach of the redelivery clause does not entitle the shipowner to insist on the charterer putting the ship in proper repair, but gives rise to a right to damages if any deterioration in the ship was due to the charterer's own contractual default: *Attica Sea Carriers Corp v Ferrostaal Poseidon Bulk Reederei GmbH* [1976] 1 Lloyd's Rep 250 at 253. See also **Time charterparty; Withdrawal; Charterer**.

Redemption fee An amount payable at the time when shares or units in a trust or mutual fund are redeemed (bought back) from the fund. In the United States it relates specifically to a fee which is paid to compensate the fund for expenses directly related to the redemption of fund shares: (US) Investment Company Act 1940 s 270.11a-3(a)(7).

Redemption of security Satisfaction of an obligation resulting in the discharge of a security given for that obligation. In bankruptcy law, where a secured creditor lodges a proof of debt that estimates the value of security held by the creditor, the trustee can redeem that security at any time by paying its estimated value to the creditor: (CTH) Bankruptcy Act 1966 s 91(1). See also **Proof of debt; Secured creditor; Trustee in bankruptcy**.

Rediscount rate The penalty rate at which the Reserve Bank of Australia will buy back a Treasury note before maturity. See also **Reserve Bank of Australia; Treasury note**.

Redress clause A clause in a charterparty limiting the owner's liability to excess cargo claims: (CTH) Carriage of Goods by Sea Act 1991. See also **Cargo; Charterer; Charterparty**.

Reducing balance method A method for calculating and allowing for the depreciation of an asset. In the reducing, diminishing or declining balance method a constant percentage of the remaining book value of an asset is written off each year. See also **Asset; Depreciation; Historical cost**.

Reduction of capital See **Maintenance of capital**.

Reduction of resources doctrine The doctrine providing that a transaction will infringe the Corporations Law prohibition on financial assistance for acquisition of a company's shares where the company has diminished its financial resources, including future resources, in connection with the sale and purchase of its shares: Corporations Law s 205(1)(a); *Burton v Palmer* [1980] 2 NSWLR 878; (1980) 5 ACLR 481. Providing indirect financial assistance to a company to acquire shares as an inducement to enter into a joint venture constitutes a diminution of financial resources of the joint venture partner: *Darvall v North Sydney Brick & Tile Co Ltd* (1987) 12 ACLR 537; 6 ACLC 191. It contrasts with the 'facilitation doctrine'. Also known as 'impoverishment doctrine'. See also **Facilitation doctrine; Financial assistance for acquisition of a company's shares**.

Redundancy In relation to employment, the termination of an employee's employment on the ground that the employer does not need the employee's work. Redundancy procedures are usually regulated by industrial awards or legislation: for example (CTH) Public Service Act 1922; (NSW) Industrial Relations Act 1991 (repealed).

Re-employment The act of employing a former employee under a new contract of employment. The power of a court or industrial tribunal to order reinstatement includes the power to order re-employment of, for example casual employees: *Orange City Bowling Club v Federated Liquor and Allied Industries Employees Union of Australia (NSW Branch)* [1979] AR (NSW) 90. Re-employment differs from reinstatement in that a new contract of employment is created when an employee is re-employed, whereas reinstatement returns the employee to employment under the original contract of employment. See also **Reinstatement**.

•**Re-entry 1.** The right of a landlord to re-enter premises to terminate a lease for breach of covenant. At common law, there is no right to re-enter for breach of covenant unless that right has been reserved by the lease: *Doe d William v Phillips* (1824) 2 Bing 13; 130 ER 208. In equity, the right to re-enter exists as security for the payment of rent, with the tenant generally being entitled to relief against forfeiture once the rent is paid; since a landlord's right of re-entry under a lease is seen as security for the payment of rent, it is not enforceable once the rent and any costs incurred by the landlord have been paid by the tenant: *Howard v Fanshawe* [1895] 2 Ch 581; *Direct Food Supplies (Vic) Pty Ltd v DLV Pty Ltd* [1975] VR 358. **2.** The right of a landlord to recover possession of premises once a lease has otherwise been terminated. This right is enforceable by court action, or by self-help. The tenant having become a trespasser, the landlord is entitled to use reasonable force to evict him or her: *Housing Commission (NSW) v Allen* [1967] 1 NSWR 776. See also **Breach of covenant; Landlord; Possession; Relief against forfeiture; Rent; Tenant**.

Re-exchange The exchange of two commodities, usually money, that have previously been exchanged for each other. An interest rate and currency swap agreement involves an initial exchange of an amount of money between two different currencies and final re-exchange at the end. There are a series of intervening payments based on interest rates in the relevant currencies. See also **Rate of exchange**.

Refer to drawer *Abbr* – R/D Words written by a bank on a cheque which has been dishonoured for lack of funds in the drawer's account. In their ordinary meaning these words amount to a statement by the bank, 'we are not paying; go back to the drawer and ask why' or else 'go back to the drawer and ask the drawer to pay': *Flach v London and South Western Bank* (1915) 31 TLR 334. 'A cheque is presented to the bank and the answer is "Refer to drawer". Everyone knows that that means there are no funds to meet it': *Braidwood v Turner* [1908] 10 WALR 105 per Burnside CJ. The modern cases take the view that the words are capable of conveying a defamatory meaning: *Hill v National Bank of New Zealand* [1985] 1 NZLR 736; *Raafbye Corporation Pty Ltd v Westpac Bank* (unrptd, SC(NSW), Levine J, 21 Oct 1994). See also **Dishonour; Notice of dishonour**.

Referee in case of need In banking law, a person to whom the holder of a bill of exchange may resort in case the bill is dishonoured by non-acceptance or non-payment. The drawer of a bill, and any indorser, may insert the referee's name on the bill, with the phrase 'in case of need' inserted following the name. The referee in case of need in effect becomes a form of surety. It is at the option of the holder to resort to the referee in case of need as the holder may think fit: (CTH) Bills of Exchange Act 1909 s 20. See also **Dishonour by non-acceptance; Drawer; Holder; Indorser**.

•**Reference** See **Employment reference**.

Referral selling A selling technique where a trader induces a consumer to purchase goods and services by representing that the consumer will, after the contract is made, benefit financially or otherwise in return for supplying the seller with names and addresses of other customers. However, receipt of the benefit is contingent upon an event occurring after the contract is made, normally a completed purchase by the customers nominated by the original consumer. Referral selling is prohibited in Australia under consumer protection legislation: (CTH) Trade Practices Act 1974 s 57; (NSW) Fair Trading Act 1987 s 52. See also **Fair Trading legislation; Trade Practices legislation**.

Refinancing The replacement of an existing loan, which is due to be repaid, by a new loan either from the same or different source on the same or different terms. See also **Loan**.

Refinancing credit contract A credit contract entered into by a debtor in return for a credit-provider agreeing to discharge any existing regulated contract. The new contract need not be a regulated contract: (NSW) Credit Act 1984 (repealed) s 69(1) (replaced by Uniform Consumer Credit Code). See also **Credit provider; Regulated contract**.

Refund to satisfy An offer by a seller to remove liability for unsatisfactory goods which is, in effect, an attempt to cancel the transaction. The offer does not remove the rights available to the purchaser to recover the amount of any relevant loss or damage: (CTH) Trade Practices Act 1974 s 68. See also **Product liability**.

Refusing delivery Failure to accept goods as agreed. Where the buyer's failure to take delivery signifies an intention to reject the goods, the seller may pursue remedies for non-acceptance. See also **Delivery; Non-acceptance; Possession**.

Register of business names The register in each jurisdiction in which all firm names under which partnerships trade are entered. Registration is required, under the Business Names legislation, for all firm names which consist of more than the surname of all of the partners together with their given names or initials. See also **Business name; Partnership**.

Register of buy-backs A register previously required to be held by companies which were permitted by their articles of association to buy back their own shares or which had at any time bought back their own shares: Corporations Law s 206VA (repealed). See also **Buy-back**.

Register of charges The register kept by the Australian Securities Commission (ASC), containing notifications of charges created by companies, and charges over property acquired by companies: Corporations Law Pt 3.5. See also **Charge; Registrable charge**.

Register of corporations A register kept by the Reserve Bank of Australia (RBA) containing the name, address of the registered office, and other particulars the RBA considers appropriate to be entered, of every corporation that has furnished the RBA with documents as required by (CTH) Financial Corporations Act 1974 s 9. In general, corporations subject to this Act are foreign, trading, or financial corporations formed within the limits of Australia whose principal business activity or source of revenue is the provision of finance: (CTH) Financial Corporations Act 1974 s 8. See also **Financial corporation; Reserve Bank of Australia**.

Register of debenture holders A register required to be kept by all companies and all registered Australian bodies of their debenture holders: Corporations Law s 1047. It must contain particulars of the names and addresses of the debenture holders and of their respective loans. Registered debenture holders and shareholders are entitled to inspect the register free of charge: s 1047. See also **Debenture**.

Register of directors, principal executive officers and secretaries The register that a company must keep under Corporations Law s 242(1) containing the name, address, business occupation and date of birth of each company secretary, director and secretary: s 242(3). The Australian Securities Commission (ASC) has the power to ask a person to inform the ASC, in writing, whether the person is a director or secretary of a particular company: s 242A . See also **Director; Officer**.

Register of interests in securities A register containing details of relevant interests in, and changes in, interests in securities: Corporations Law s 881. Persons who hold a licence or a proper authority from a person who holds a licence and financial journalists must maintain this register: s 880. The Australian Securities Commission (ASC) must be notified as to where the register is kept and changes in details of persons who hold proper authority or start or cease to be financial journalists: ss 882, 883. See also **Financial journalist; Securities; Securities business**.

Register of members A register required to be kept by a company which includes names and addresses of the members of the company, dates at which persons ceased to be members during the previous seven years, and statements of the shares held beneficially and non-beneficially by members: Corporations Law s 209(1). See also **Share; Shareholder**.

Register of options A register required to be kept by all companies that grant options to take up unissued shares: Corporations Law s 215(1). The company must enter various particulars, including the name and address of the holder, the date the option was granted, the number and description of the shares in respect of which the option was granted, the option exercise period, and any consideration payable for the grant or exercise of the option: s 215(2). The register does not contain details of transferees of options. See also **Authorised capital; Option**.

Register of patents A database comprising particulars relating to the patents maintained at the Patent Office. The Register of Patents is prima facie evidence of the particulars it contains. In relation to a patent, the registered particulars include: number, term and any extension granted, the name of the patentee and particulars of entitlement, the name of the inventor, details of any patents of addition granted, details of court orders filed or served on the Commissioner, amendments after grant, and cessation. Notice of a trust relating to a patent is not registrable. The register is open to public inspection during Patent Office business hours: (CTH) Patents Act 1990 ss 186, 187, 188, 190, 195; (CTH) Patents Regulations 1991 regs 19.1, 19.2. See also **Commissioner of Patents; Patent Office; Patentee**.

Registered Australian body A registrable Australian body that is registered under Corporations Law Pt 4.1 Div 1: Corporations Law s 9. That is, a body that is not a company, or a foreign company, but which has been registered under the Corporations Law because it is carrying on business outside the jurisdiction from which it originates. See also **Australian Registered Body Number; Registrable Australian body**.

Registered capital See **Authorised capital**.

Registered company A company registered under the Corporations Law: Corporations Law s 118. Generally, the term refers to companies registered under Corporations Law Pt 2.2 Div 1 but it can also refer to companies registered under Pt 2.2 Div 2 or Pt 2.2 Div 4. Non-companies may be registered as companies under Pt 2.2 Div 3. See also **Company; Division 1 company; Division 2 company; Division 3 company; Division 4 company**.

Registered company auditor See **Auditor**.

Registered foreign company A foreign company that is registered under Corporations Law Pt 4.1 Div 2: Corporations Law s 9. This is a company incorporated outside Australia but which is registered under the procedures provided in Corporations Law s 344 because it is carrying on business within Australia. See also **Foreign company**.

Registered insurer A company registered by the Insurance and Superannuation Commissioner to carry on a life insurance business: (CTH) Life Insurance Act 1995 s 21.

•**Registered liquidator** A person registered by the Australian Securities Commission (ASC) as a liquidator under Corporations Law Pt 9.2 Div 2: s 1282. Registration is granted on proof of professional and academic qualifications and experience in external corporate administrations. Bodies corporate cannot be registered as liquidators: s 1279. Persons registered as liquidators must lodge security with the ASC: s 1284. See also **Liquidator; Official liquidator; Winding up**.

•**Registered office** The office required for each company to which all communications and notices may be addressed and which is to be open during business hours: Corporations Law s 217. See also **Corporation**.

Registered representative In corporations law, a person who is a director, partner or employee of a Sydney Futures Exchange (SFE) member and is registered with the SFE. A person is prohibited, by the SFE Business Rules, from advising clients concerning futures or option contracts unless registered as a registered representative of the SFE member: art 37.2. See also **Sydney Futures Exchange**.

Registered securities Securities listed, together with the names of their owners, in a register which is maintained by the organisation that issued the shares.

Registered trader A person approved by the board of the Australian Stock Exchange for the purpose of making transactions as a dealer on the floor of the Exchange in accordance with the provisions of ASX Business Rule 7.1.24. A registered trader includes a registered trader's partnership and a registered independent options trader: Corporations Regulations reg 7.4.04; ASX Business Rule 7.1.24.

Registered trustee See **Official Trustee in Bankruptcy**.

Registrable Australian body A body corporate, not being a company, or a recognised company, or an exempt public authority, or a corporation sole, or an unincorporated body that, under the law of its place of formation, may sue or be sued, or may hold property in the name of its secretary or of an officer of the body duly appointed for that purpose, but not including a financial institution or a foreign company: Corporations Law s 9. These bodies are required by Corporations Law s 340 to register under the Corporations Law before carrying on business in any jurisdiction which is not their place of incorporation. See also **Registered Australian body; Registrable body**.

Registrable body A registrable Australian body or a foreign company: Corporations Law s 9. These bodies are required to register under the Corporations Law before carrying on business in a jurisdiction which is not the place in which they are incorporated or formed: ss 340, 343. See also **Foreign company; Registrable Australian body**.

Registrable charge In corporations law, a legal or equitable charge on property of a company which must be registered to maintain priority over later charges. Registrable charges include floating charges over all or part of a company's assets or undertaking, charges over uncalled share capital, charges over goodwill, charges over book debts, and charges over crops or wool: Corporations Law s 262(1). See also **Charge; Debenture; Floating charge**.

•**Registrable instrument** Any written document or instrument capable of being registered as an interest in land. Registrable instruments may arise under the Deeds system or under the Torrens system. See also **Registration**.

•**Registrable interest** In relation to goods, the interest in the goods of the person to whom an obligation is owed of which the performance is secured by a security interest in the goods, the lessor of the goods, the owner of the goods under a hire-purchase agreement relating to the goods, or any other prescribed interest in the goods: for example (NSW) Registration of Interests in Goods Act 1986 s 3(1). See also **Goods; Registration of Interests in Goods legislation**.

Registrar in Bankruptcy A person appointed under the (CTH) Bankruptcy Act 1966 to hold the office bearing that name. There is a Registrar in Bankruptcy for each bankruptcy district: s 14(1). The Registrar in Bankruptcy exercises various powers and functions such as the giving of certificates to the court as to whether, in the opinion of the Registrar, the provisions of the Act and Rules have been complied with in relation to a creditor's petition: (CTH) Bankruptcy Rules r 22. See also **Creditor's petition**.

Registration 1. The act of making a list in a register, particularly of an official character in which the existence of some thing or state of affairs is recorded; for example, the ownership of land, or the ownership, existence and particulars of ships, aircraft, or motor vehicles. **2.** The fact of being entered in a register. See also **Owner**.

Registration of interests in goods legislation Legislation which establishes the public Register of Interests in 'prescribed goods', maintained by the Commissioner for Consumer Affairs. At present, motor vehicles are the only goods covered by the legislation, for example: Registration of Interests in Goods Act 1986. A security interest in a motor vehicle must be registered by a creditor or it cannot be enforced against a purchaser who buys the vehicle in good faith. There is similar legislation in all jurisdictions of Australia: for example (VIC) Chattel Securities Act 1987. See also **Goods**.

Regressive tax A tax which takes a decreasing proportion of the tax base as the tax base increases. Indirect taxes, such as sales tax, are usually regressive taxes since low income earners tend to spend a higher proportion of their incomes on the taxed goods than do high income earners and consequently attract proportionally higher taxes. See also **Progressive tax; Proportional tax; Sales tax**.

Regulated continuing credit sale A continuing credit contract in which credit is supplied by way of: cash, where there is a charge of greater than 14 per cent; or payment for goods and services, where either a non-account charge is made, or an amount is not required to be paid within a period of four months after it is first owed, or an amount owing will be payable by five or more instalments. See also **Continuing credit contract**; **Credit**.

• **Regulated contract** A credit sale contract, loan contract or continuing credit contract which is regulated under Part III of the uniform credit legislation. This Part stipulates the way in which the contract is to be entered and the form of the contract: (NSW) Credit Act 1984 (repealed) s 5(1) (replaced by Uniform Consumer Credit Code). See also **Continuing credit contract**; **Credit contract**; **Credit sale contract**; **Uniform credit legislation**.

• **Regulated credit sale contract** A credit sale contract in which the cash price paid for the goods or services under the contract does not exceed the prescribed amount, unless the goods are a commercial vehicle or farm machinery: (NSW) Credit Act 1984 (repealed) s 30(1) (replaced by Uniform Consumer Credit Code). See also **Credit sale contract**.

Regulated loan contract A loan contract in which the amount financed is less than a prescribed amount and there is an interest rate exceeding 14 per cent, unless at the time of contract, the debt is secured by a mortgage over farm machinery or a commercial vehicle: (NSW) Credit Act 1984 (repealed) ss 5(1), 30(2) (replaced by Uniform Consumer Credit Code).

• **Regulated mortgage** A mortgage given by a person who is not a body corporate which secures the performance of an obligation to pay money arising under a regulated contract. Part IV of the uniform credit legislation regulates both the form of the mortgage transaction and the operation of the mortgage contract: (NSW) Credit Act 1984 (repealed) s 89; (VIC) Credit Act 1984 (repealed) Pt IV (replaced by Uniform Consumer Credit Code). See also **Chattel security**; **Mortgage**; **Regulated contract**; **Uniform credit legislation**.

Regulated superannuation fund A superannuation fund where the trustee has irrevocably elected that the (CTH) Superannuation Industry (Supervision) Act 1993 will apply to the fund: (CTH) Superannuation Industry (Supervision) Act 1993 ss 10, 19. The advantage of electing to be a regulated superannuation fund is that it enables the superannuation fund to qualify as a complying superannuation fund if it meets further requirements and this allows the fund to receive certain income tax concessions. See also **Complying superannuation fund**; **Superannuation fund**.

• **Reimbursement 1.** Repayment to a person of an amount that the person has spent. **2.** In income tax law, the receipt of an amount that compensates a taxpayer for an amount previously expended for which a tax deduction may have been claimed under (CTH) Income Tax Assessment Act 1936 s 51(1). Such an amount may be income under ordinary concepts being the ordinary proceeds of a business: *H R Sinclair & Sons Pty Ltd v FCT* (1966) 10 AITR 3.

Reinstatement To return to or establish a former state or condition.

Corporations The re-registration of a company whose registration had been cancelled. See also **Deregistration**; **External administration**.

Employment The act of returning to employment an employee who had been dismissed, whether the employee returns to the position from which he or she was dismissed, or to another position within the organisation. See also **Industrial tribunal**; **Re-employment**.

Insurance The restoration of property to the state in which it was before being damaged. If the property is destroyed, reinstatement means replacing the property: *Anderson v Commercial Union Assurance Co* (1885) 55 LJQB 146. See also **Consequential loss insurance**; **Fire insurance**; **Insurance contract**; **Property insurance**; **Variation**.

Reinsurance A contract of insurance taken out by the original insurer (the reinsured) with another insurer (the reinsurer) to indemnify the reinsured against liability or payments under the original or underlying contract of insurance. General insurers are required to enter into reinsurance arrangements approved by the Insurance Commissioner: (CTH) Insurance Act 1973 s 34. See also **Facultative reinsurance**; **Treaty reinsurance**.

Reinsurance treaty See **Treaty reinsurance**.

Reinsured See **Cedent**.

Reinsurer See **Cedent**.

Re-investment rate risk The possibility that during the life of a bond, the rate at which the periodical interest rate payments made on the bond (the coupon) can be reinvested in the bond might decline. See also **Bond**; **Interest rate**.

Re-issue 1. In relation to shares, the issuing back to a shareholder of shares which have been forfeited because the shareholder has failed to pay a valid call or an instalment of a share issue price. A company is normally empowered to re-issue forfeited shares and offset the proceeds against the unpaid liability which led to the forfeiture: Corporations Law Sch 1 Table A cll 28, 31. **2.** In relation to debentures, the issue of debentures which have been redeemed by the company. A company has power to re-issue debentures by re-issuing the same debentures or by issuing other debentures in their place, unless provided otherwise by the articles or by contract: Corporations Law s 1051. See also **Call paid**; **Debenture**; **Forfeiture of shares**.

Rejection of goods Refusal to accept goods. Rejection of goods may occur where permitted by an express or implied term of a contract, by a course of dealing, where the seller breaches an express or implied condition, or where the seller repudiates the contract. See also **Refusing delivery**; **Rescission**.

• **Related body corporate** A body corporate that is a holding company of a second body corporate, a subsidiary of that second body corporate, or a subsidiary of a holding company of a second body corporate: Corporations Law s 50. See also **Body corporate**; **Holding company**; **Subsidiary**; **Takeover**.

• **Related company** A company which controls or is controlled by or is under joint control with another company via ownership of subsidiaries. See also **Related corporation**.

Related corporation A corporation which is the holding company or subsidiary of another corporation, or two corporations that are subsidiaries of the same holding company: Corporations Law s 50; (CTH) Trade Practices Act 1974 s 4A(5); *Trade Practices Commission v Bowral Brickworks Pty Ltd* (1984) 2 FCR 552; 55 ALR 733. See also **Holding company**; **Related body corporate**; **Subsidiary**.

Related entity A body, including a promoter of the body, a director or member, a relative or de facto spouse of a director or member, a relative of a spouse or of a de facto spouse of a director or member and a body corporate that is related to the first-mentioned body: Corporations Law s 9. The Corporations Law prohibits a company from giving a benefit to a related entity except as provided for in Corporations Law ss 243J-243PB. See also **Entity**; **Related party**.

Related party A party which has the ability to control another party or exercise significant influence over finance and operating decisions. Parties can also be related because they are subject to a common outside interest or control. See also **Financial benefits to related parties**; **Related corporation**; **Related entity**.

Related party transaction A transaction that a public company makes with directors of the public company or its parent entities, a spouse or de facto spouse of those directors, a parent, son, daughter of such directors or their spouses or de facto spouses, entities controlled by any of these persons or a parent or sibling entity of the company: Corporations Law s 243F(1). Pt 3.2A regulates related party transactions. A public company must not give a financial benefit to a related party and a child entity of a public company must not give a financial benefit to a related party of the public company: s 243H. There are a series of exceptions to this: ss 243J-243PA. For example, financial benefits given on arm's-length terms: s 243N. See also **Child entity**; **Director**; **Public company**; **Financial benefits to related parties**.

Relation-back day In relation to a winding up of a company or a Corporations Law Pt 5.7 body, the day on which the application for winding up was filed: s 9. Certain voidable transactions of the company can be set aside or otherwise affected if they occurred within a certain period before the relation-back day: Pt 5.7B. See also **Insolvency**; **Winding up**.

Relation-back doctrine An expression of the retrospective operation of bankruptcy. According to the doctrine, bankruptcy starts earlier than the actual date that a debtor or creditor applied for bankruptcy. The bankruptcy is taken to have 'related back to' the time of the earliest act of bankruptcy up to six months before the petition was presented: (CTH) Bankruptcy Act 1966 s 115; for example *Rae v Samuel Taylor Pty Ltd* (1964) 110 CLR 517; [1965] ALR 102. From that time on, transactions involving the debtor can later be set aside. See also **Act of bankruptcy**; **After acquired property**; **Creditor**; **Commencement of bankruptcy**; **Debtor**.

Release of principal debtor Discharge of a principal debtor's obligations to a creditor, usually by payment of the debt by the principal debtor to the creditor, or by payment of the debt by one or more co-sureties to the creditor. A creditor may agree to release a debtor from his or her obligations in the absence of full payment of the debt by a deed of release. See also **Creditor**; **Debtor**; **Deed of release**; **Discharge**; **Principal debtor**.

•**Relevant interest** The interest of a person to exercise a vote in respect of a voting share or to dispose of a share: Corporations Law s 31(1). If a director has a relevant interest in, or rights or options over, shares or debentures in a company the relevant securities exchange must be notified: s 235. It does not matter that the power is indirect, or exercisable by means of, or in breach of, trusts, agreements, arrangements, understandings or practices, whether enforceable or unenforceable: s 30(4). Relevant interests have been found to arise, depending on the particular circumstances, in a variety of situations including pre-bid understandings, issues of options, common directorships, interposed companies, and articles restricting transfer of shares: ss 30-45. See also **Entitlement to shares**; **Takeover**.

Reliance interest A contracting party's right, upon the termination of the contract for breach by the other party, to be compensated for expenses and losses incurred in reliance on the anticipated performance of the contract by the other party: *Gates v City Mutual Life Assurance Society Ltd* (1986) 160 CLR 1; 63 ALR 600. A plaintiff may only claim in respect of his or her reliance interest to the extent that he or she would have recovered the expenses and losses if the defendant had performed the contract: *Amann Aviation Pty Ltd v Commonwealth* (1990) 22 FCR 527; 92 ALR 601. Where the expenditure has resulted in the acquisition of assets whose value is retained, that value must be offset against the expenditure: *McRae v Commonwealth Diposals Commission* (1951) 84 CLR 377. Expenses incurred must be reasonable, contemplated by the other party, and capable of proof. Reliance damages do not usually form the basis of an award, because normally a plaintiff is adequately compensated by damages awarded on an expectation basis for loss of the bargain. See also **Damages**; **Estoppel**.

Relief The remedy sought by a plaintiff in a court action. For instance, the plaintiff could ask for specific performance of a contract and, in lieu of specific performance, damages. The relief available in any particular action may be limited by statute: for example (NSW) Real Property Act 1900 Pt XIV; which limits the range of civil rights and remedies available. See also **Remedy**; **Court order**.

•**Relief against forfeiture** Relief granted by a court of equity against the forfeiture of property or a proprietary interest. See also **Forfeiture**; **Unconscionable**.

Contract The relief available in equity's inherent jurisdiction to a promisor against the forfeiture of property which would occur on exercise of a right of termination and forfeiture: for example *Scandinavian Trading Tanker Co AB v Flota Petrolera Ecuatoriana* [1983] 2 AC 694. See also **Equity**; **Mistake**; **Option contract**.

Relief against penalties Relief granted by a court of equity against penalty clauses in a contract. Courts of equity regard penalty provisions as unenforceable, and leave the party trying to enforce them to whatever remedy that party might have at common law (such as damages) for the defaulter's breach. See also **Penalty**; **Penalty clause**; **Unconscionable**.

Remedy The means available at law or equity by which a right is enforced or the infringement of a right is prevented, redressed, or compensated. Remedies may be obtained by four different methods: by the act of the person injured (including self-defence, recaption, distress, entry, abatement, and seizure); by operation of law (as in the case of retainer and remitter); by agreement between the parties (as in the case of accord and satisfaction, and arbitration); or by judicial process (such as an action or suit). The first three categories are extra-judicial remedies, while the last are judicial remedies. Civil remedies include damages, an injunction, an order for specific performance, or a declaration. The basic common law remedy in tort actions is damages, the aim of which is to put the plaintiff, in so far as is possible, into the position he or she was in before the tort was committed: *Todorovic v Waller* (1981) 150 CLR 402; 37 ALR 481. See also **Abatement**; **Accord and satisfaction**; **Damages**; **Distress**; **Injunction**; **Retainer**; **Specific performance**.

Remitting bank See **Correspondent bank**.

Remoteness A factor in contract and tort which limits a defendant's responsibility for the loss suffered by a plaintiff. To obtain compensation the loss must not be too remote. Whether the loss or damage suffered by the plaintiff is too remote depends on the knowledge possessed by or imputed to the defendant: for example *Burns v MAN Automotive (Aust) Pty Ltd* (1986) 161 CLR 653; 69 ALR 11. In contract, the plaintiff may recover such damages 'as may fairly and reasonably be considered either arising naturally, that is according to the usual course of things, from the breach of contract itself, or such as may reasonably be supposed to have been in the contemplation of both parties, at the time they made the contract, as the probable result of the breach of it': *Hadley v Baxendale* (1854) LR 9 Ex 341; 156 ER 145. In tort, the test is 'reasonable foreseeability', that is whether the kind of injury or damage suffered by the plaintiff was reasonably foreseeable as a consequence of the defendant's negligence: *Overseas Tankship (UK) Ltd v Morts Dock & Engineering Co Ltd (The Wagon Mound No 1)* [1961] AC 388; *Overseas Tankship (UK) Ltd v Miller Steamship Co Pty Ltd (The Wagon Mound No 2)* [1967] 1 AC 617; *Mount Isa Mines Ltd v Pusey* (1970) 125 CLR 383. See also **Contract**; **Damages**; **General damages**; **Hadley v Baxendale, rule in**; **Mitigation**; **Special damages**; **Tort**.

•**Remuneration** Payment, reward, or recompense for services rendered: *Chalmers v Commonwealth* (1946) 73 CLR 19. See also **Consideration**; **Salary**; **Wage**.

Renounceable option In corporations law an assignable option to have an allotment of shares in a body corporate made to the holder of the option: Corporations Law s 603. A renounceable right to securities permits a member to sell or assign a contractual right to accept an offer of securities. See also **Allotment**.

•**Rent** A period payment, usually in money, due by the tenant of land or premises to the landlord in consideration for the tenant's right to occupy the land or premises: for example (SA) Residential Tenancies Act 1995 s 3(1); *Junghem v Wood* [1958] SR (NSW) 327. Traditionally, rent was that payment or charge for which distress may be levied by the landlord, as distinct from other charges related to the tenant's occupation, such as outgoings. A tenant is obliged to seek out the landlord to pay rent: *Harrison v Petkovic* [1975] VR 79. See also **Consideration**; **Landlord**; **Occupation**; **Outgoings**; **Tenant**.

Renunciation The abandoning of a right or interest.

Bills of exchange and other negotiable instruments A method of discharging a negotiable instrument by which its holder absolutely and unconditionally abandons his or her rights against the acceptor of a bill of exchange at or after its maturity, or the drawer, indorser, or all other persons liable on a cheque: (CTH) Bills of Exchange Act 1909 s 67; (CTH) Cheques and Payment Orders Act 1986 ss 78, 80, 84. See also **Acceptor**; **Discharge of negotiable instrument**; **Discharge of party**; **Holder**; **Maturity date**; **Waiver**.

Contract The giving back, or giving away, of property that another person attempted, or the law has operated, to vest in the renouncing party, so as to prevent the vesting from being effective: for example *Re Paradise Motor Co Ltd* [1968] 1 WLR 1125; [1968] 2 All ER 625.

Re-opening of contract In consumer credit law, the variation of the terms of a regulated contract, regulated mortgage or guarantee by the Commercial Tribunal if the tribunal regards the contract as unjust in the circumstances. See also **Commercial Tribunal**; **Regulated contract**; **Unjust contract**.

Reorganisation The process of realigning a company's capital structure where creditors and shareholders relinquish their rights and claims on the organisation. The company's assets and capital structure have to be revalued to reflect current operating conditions, and the retained earnings account is started anew. Reorganisation is a remedy taken by a company which is unable to pay its creditors' claims. Court approval must be sought before any reorganisation occurs: Corporations Law s 195. See also **Amalgamation**; **Arrangement**; **Scheme of arrangement**.

Replacement cost accounting A method of inflation accounting which values assets at the current cost to replace or reproduce an item, or its realisable value, rather than at the cost at which the item was originally purchased. This method can effect accounting for assets, depreciation, investments, cost of goods sold, and inventories and aims to ensure that the resources of the entity are realistically measured and that the financial statements are of maximum value to users. See also **Depreciation**; **Inventory**.

Reportable Payments System *Abbr* – RPS A tax file number based system designed to ensure compliance with the taxation laws by taxpayers outside the Pay As You Earn (PAYE) and prescribed payments (PPS) collection systems: (CTH) Income Tax Assessment Act 1936 Pt VI Div 1AA. The reportable payments system requires payers of specified payments in particular industries to deduct tax and remit those deductions to the Australian Taxation Office. The industries currently covered by the RPS system are the clothing and fishing industries. See also **Pay As You Earn system**; **Prescribed Payments System**.

Reported earnings The amount of revenue shown in the profit and loss account of a business. The amount reported in the annual report will normally have separate notes detailing the revenue contributions. See also **Profit and loss account**; **Revenue**.

Reporting bond dealer A member of a group of dealers established in 1985 by the Commonwealth government authorised to trade directly with the Reserve Bank of Australia in government bonds with more than one year to maturity.

•**Reporting entity** An economic entity in regard to which it is reasonable to expect that the general purpose financial reports of the economic entity will be depended upon to assist users of information in their decision-making: Statement of Accounting Concepts SAC 1. For company accounts ending on or after 30 June 1992, compliance with accounting standards will be compulsory for reporting entities: Applicable Accounting Standard AASB 1025. See also **Entity**.

Reporting requirements The obligation of the management of the firm to supply financial data to shareholders, government agencies, and the public. The reports should be prepared at least yearly for corporations (Corporations Law ss 292, 293) and may sometimes be more frequently required.

Repossession The taking of possession of something that is the subject of a contract, by a person who has a right to possession of that thing on a breach of the contract. See also **Possession**.

•**Representation** In contract law, an oral or written statement made by one party relating to a past event or existing fact, but not as to law, which induces a course of action such as entry into a contract. A representation may be inferred from conduct: *Simos v National Bank of Australasia Ltd* (1976) 10 ACTR 4. See also **Misrepresentation**; **Negligent misrepresentation**.

Repudiation A term used in various senses in contract law: *Shevill v Builders Licensing Board* (1982) 149 CLR 620; 42 ALR 305. **1.** An absence of readiness or willingness to perform contractual obligations by the promisor, sufficiently serious to give the promisee a right to terminate (repudiation of obligation). **2.** A statement that no contract is in existence is repudiation in this sense: for example *Australian Coarse Grains Pool Pty Ltd v Barley Marketing Board* [1989] 1 Qd R 499. **3.** Termination of the performance of a contract: for example *Hongkong Fir Shipping Co Ltd v Kawasaki Kisen Kaisha Ltd* [1962] 2 QB 26. See also **Anticipatory breach**; **Condition**; **Discharge**; **Locus poenitentiae**; **Ready and willing**; **Repudiatory breach**; **Right to terminate**.

Repudiatory breach A breach which gives rise to a right to terminate the performance of a contract, being of a kind that the promisee may treat as a repudiation of the whole contract: *Antaios Compania Naviera SA v Salen Rederierna AB* [1985] AC 191. See also **Repudiation**; **Termination**.

Repurchase agreement *Abbr* – REPO **1.** An agreement between two parties in the money market, whereby the first party sells securities to a second party, while at the same time agreeing to buy them back at a specified price at a fixed time in the future. **2.** A deal between the Reserve Bank of Australia (RBA) and an authorised dealer to buy or sell stock. The RBA buys stock on days on which there is a shortfall of cash in the market (thus putting cash into the banking system), while agreeing to sell that stock back (taking cash out of the system) on a day when there is a surplus of funds. See also **Open market operations**.

Reputation test In banking law, a test used to determine whether an institution conducts a banking business. Under the test, the institution conducts a banking business if it is accepted by the community as doing so. Indications include: the institution's payment orders are accepted through the clearing system for cheques; crossed cheques presented for collection by the institution are paid to it; the institution called and regarded itself a bank, and was so regarded by the revenue raising authorities; and the institution has power in its constitution to conduct the banking business. The institution must exhibit the 'stability, soundness and probity' usually associated with (or at least expected from) banks: *United Dominions Trust Ltd v Kirkwood* [1966] 2 QB 431. This test has been combined with the 'cheque facility test'. See also **Banking business**; **Cheque facility test**.

Requirements contract A contract by which a party, who needs supplies of a particular product for a business, undertakes to buy all the requirements of the business for a fixed period from a particular supplier in return for the latter's promise to supply: *Dominion Coal Co Ltd v Dominion Iron & Steel Co Ltd* [1909] AC 293. A requirements contract may constitute an exclusive dealing under (CTH) Trade Practices Act 1974 s 47. See also **Contract**; **Exclusive dealing**.

Resale price maintenance *Abbr* – RPM In competition law, the supplier's maintenance of the resale price of its goods by restricting or refusing supply unless the purchaser (most commonly a retailer) agrees not to resell below the price specified by the supplier: (CTH) Trade Practices Act 1974 s 96. The practice is prohibited: (CTH) Trade Practices Act 1974 ss 48, 96-100. See also **Competition law**; **Loss leader**; **Recommended price**; **Restrictive trade practices**; **Specified price**.

•**Rescission 1.** Strictly speaking, putting an end to a contract in a way that treats the contract as if it never existed (rescission *ab initio*). Rescission (in this sense) totally discharges the parties from the duty to perform their contractual obligations. A vitiating factor in the events prior to contract formation may give a right of rescission in this sense: *McDonald v Dennys Lascelles Ltd* (1933) 48 CLR 457. **2.** Terminating a contract for breach or repudiation: for example *Shevill v Builders Licensing Board* (1982) 149 CLR 620; 42 ALR 305 ('rescission *in futuro*'). This is a looser usage: *Photo Production Ltd v Securicor Transport Ltd* [1980] AC 827. **3.** A right to put an end to a contract, conferred expressly by a statute: for example (CTH) Trade Practices Act 1974 s 75A. See also **Ab initio**; **Breach of contract**; **Discharge**; **Discharge by agreement**; **Repudiation**; **Right to terminate**; **Termination**; **Vitiating factor**.

Reservation of title A clause in a contract for the sale of goods providing that ownership in the goods is retained by the seller until payment is made for the goods: for example *Aluminium Industrie Vaassen BV v Romalpa Aluminium Ltd* [1976] 2 All ER 552; *Chattis Nominees Pty Ltd v Norman Ross Homeworks Pty Ltd (in liq)* (1992) 28 NSWLR 338; *Puma Australia Pty Ltd v Sportsman's Australia Ltd (No 2)* [1994] 2 Qd R 159. Also known as 'Romalpa clause'. See also **Accession; Confusion; Ownership; Romalpa clause**.

Reserve Bank of Australia The central bank of Australia: (CTH) Reserve Bank Act 1959 Pt IV. The Reserve Bank is a preservation and continuance of the Commonwealth Bank of Australia as a body corporate with its own seal under a new name: (CTH) Reserve Bank Act 1959 s 7. When required to do so by the Commonwealth, it must act as banker and financial agent for the Commonwealth: (CTH) Reserve Bank Act 1959 ss 26, 27. Major functions of the Reserve Bank include prudential supervision of banks, protection of depositors, mobilisation of foreign currency, regulation of foreign exchange, oversight of the gold reserves, control of interest rates, and management of the note issue. See also **Central bank**.

• **Reserve fund** An accounting allocation to a reserve account comprised of a pool of certain assets which are readily realisable and retained for a specific purpose. For example, a sinking fund for the redemption of shares or bonds. The assets usually comprise cash and investment securities. Also known as 'statutory required reserve fund'. See also **Realisation account; Redemption of security**.

• **Reserve price** A minimum price fixed or 'reserved' by a vendor, below which the vendor is not prepared, and an auctioneer is not authorised, to sell. Also known as 'upset price'. See also **Auction; Auctioneer; Authority; Vendor**.

• **Residual capital value** In relation to an annuity or superannuation pension, the capital amount payable on the termination of the annuity or superannuation pension: (CTH) Income Tax Assessment Act 1936 s 27A (1). See also **Annuity; Deductible amount; Purchase price**.

• **Residual fringe benefit** For the purposes of fringe benefits tax, a benefit not covered by any other specific valuation rule: (CTH) Fringe Benefits Tax Assessment Act 1986 s 45. For a residual benefit to be a fringe benefit, there must be something that can be identified as a benefit, and the necessary employment relationship must exist: (CTH) Fringe Benefits Tax Assessment Act 1986 s 136(1). Examples include: free or discounted services, such as travel or the performance of work; the use of property; the provision of insurance cover; the provision of reticulated gas or electricity (s 156), or taxi travel provided by an employer to its employee (*National Australia Bank v FCT* (1993) 26 ATR 503). Certain residual benefits are exempt from fringe benefits tax, such as employee use of an employer's equipment: (CTH) Fringe Benefits Tax Assessment Act 1986 s 47. See also **Fringe benefit; Fringe benefits tax**.

Resignation In corporations law, the formal giving up of membership of an association, upon which act membership ceases. A person may expressly resign in the manner set out in the association's constitution: *Finch v Oake* [1896] 1 Ch 409. If the constitution does not provide for resignation, a member may resign by notifying the secretary orally or in writing that he or she intends to resign; resignation will then take effect immediately, unless its formal acceptance is required by the rules. See also **Association; Committee; Constitution; General meeting; Member**.

Resolution A formal expression of the collective will.

Resource development financing Making funds available to enable exploitation of natural resources such as minerals and agricultural resources. See also **Capital; Investment**.

Resources rent tax *Abbr* – RRT A tax based on profits in excess of a level considered necessary for the commencement or continuation of a natural resource project or the encouragement of exploration.

Respondent 1. A party to court proceedings against whom relief is claimed by an applicant or an appellant: for example (CTH) Federal Court Rules O 4 r 2; *Lumley Life Ltd v IOOF of Victoria Friendly Society* (1991) 36 FCR 590; 100 ALR 600 at 604. For example it has been held that an application under the (CTH) Customs Act 1901 in the Federal Court of Australia should have described the persons against whom the proceedings were brought as respondents rather than defendants: *Commissioner for Australian Federal Police v Hatfield* (1992) 106 ALR 335; 34 FCR 190. It is analogous to the term defendant, which is used in many State jurisdictions. See also **Applicant**.

Restitution A remedy by which a plaintiff is restored to his or her original position before the loss or injury. The rationale for the remedy is unjust enrichment. Restitution obliges the defendant to make fair and just repayment for a benefit received at the plaintiff's expense: *Pavey & Matthews Pty Ltd v Paul* (1987) 162 CLR 221; 69 ALR 577. See also **Compensation; Damages; Quasi contract; Failure of consideration; Unjust enrichment**.

Restitution damages Damages requiring the defendant to pay for the benefit obtained from the plaintiff's partial performance of the contract. Restitution damages are available where the plaintiff has conferred benefits on the defendant but is unable to claim the contract price on breach: for example *Automatic Fire Sprinklers Pty Ltd v Watson* (1946) 72 CLR 435. An example of restitution damages is where a buyer of goods pays the price in advance of delivery, but the seller does not deliver, or does not have title; the buyer is entitled to recover as damages a sum equal to the amount paid. See also **Damages; Expectation interest; Reliance interest; Restitution**.

Restitution interest The right of a party to a contract to the return of any benefit conferred on the defendant where the defendant has not performed his or her obligations under the contract. For example, where a buyer of goods pays the purchase price in advance of delivery but the seller does not deliver, or delivers worthless goods, the buyer is entitled to recover the sum equal to the amount paid, less the value of any benefit in fact obtained. See also **Damages; Expectation interest; Reliance interest; Restitution**.

Restraining order An enforceable direction by a court that an offender be prevented from dealing with all, or some, of his or her property except as provided by the court where that property was derived from unlawful activity: for example (CTH) Proceeds of Crime Act 1987 s 43; (NSW) Confiscation of Proceeds of Crime Act 1989 s 43; (NSW) Environmental Offences and Penalties Act 1989 s 6. See also **Exclusion order; Proceeds of crime**.

Restraint In marine insurance law, a restraint is the act of preventing goods from being removed by laying hands upon them: *Rodoconachi v Elliott* (1873) LR 8 CP 649. In a standard form marine policy, one of the hazards or perils covered is 'arrest, restraints and detainments of all kings, princes, and people'. The term refers to executive acts, including embargoes, but excludes riots or the ordinary judicial processes of law. See also **Embargo; Restraint of trade**.

•**Restraint of trade** An agreement in which a party agrees with any other party to restrict his or her liberty in the future to carry on trade with other persons not parties to the contract in such manner as he or she chooses: *Petrofina (Great Britain) Ltd v Martin* [1966] 1 Ch 146 at 180. The common law prohibits unreasonable restraints, based on public policy: *Quadramain Pty Ltd v Sevastapol Investments Pty Ltd* (1976) 133 CLR 390; 8 ALR 555. A corporation may not make a contract or arrangement in restraint of trade or commerce and such contracts are unenforceable: (CTH) Trade Practices Act 1974 s 45(2). Restraints of trade are prima facie void unless the restraint can be justified as reasonable in the interests of the parties in that it affords no more than adequate protection to the covenantee while at the same time it is not injurious to the public: *Amoco Australia Pty Ltd v Rocca Bros Motor Engineering Co Pty Ltd* (1973) 133 CLR 288; 1 ALR 385; *Petrofina v Martin* [1966] Ch 146; *Lindner v Murdoch's Garage* (1950) 83 CLR 628. See also **Competition law; Contract, arrangement or understanding; Contract in restraint of trade; Covenant in restraint of trade; Restrictive trade practices**.

Restricted list A list of securities which a brokerage firm does not trade in on its own account, and about which it does not make recommendations to clients in respect of purchasing, selling or retaining, for the purpose of avoiding contravention of the insider trading rules: Corporations Law Pt 7.11 Div 2A; ASX Business Rules r 3.5. Securities firms commonly adopt the practice of establishing such a restricted list of securities when they come into possession of material non-public information concerning the security, even if a Chinese wall is in place, in order to avoid the possibility, for example, of a representative of the firm recommending a purchase of securities to a client on the basis of publicly available information while another department of the firm possesses non-public information indicating that the recommendation is ill-advised. See also **Chinese wall; Insider trading; Security**.

Restricted trading day Good Friday, Christmas Day, and any day declared by the Governor by proclamation and published in the *Gazette* to be such: (NSW) Liquor Act 1982 s 4(1). See also **Annual holiday loading; Australia Day**.

Restrictive indorsement An indorsement prohibiting further negotiation of a bill of exchange, or expressing that it is a mere authority to deal with the bill as directed, and not a transfer of ownership. Examples are bills endorsed 'pay D only' or 'pay D for the account of X', or 'pay D or order for collection': (CTH) Bills of Exchange Act 1909 s 40(1). A restricted indorsee has the right to receive payment, and to sue any party to the bill that the indorser could have sued, but not the power to transfer rights as indorsee unless it so authorises expressly: (CTH) Bills of Exchange Act 1909 s 40(2). See also **Bill of exchange; Indorsee; Indorsement; Indorser**.

Restrictive trade practices The making of certain contracts, arrangements or understandings, and the practices of secondary boycotts, misuse of market power, exclusive dealing, resale price maintenance, price discrimination, and anticompetitive mergers and acquisitions: *Refrigerated Express Lines (Australasia) Pty Ltd v Australian Meat and Livestock Corp* (1980) 29 ALR 333. These are practices or activities prohibited ((CTH) Trade Practices Act 1974 Pt IV) in order to protect and advance a competitive environment and competitive conduct: *Queensland Wire Industries Pty Ltd v BHP Co Ltd* (1989) 167 CLR 177; 83 ALR 577. See also **Acquisition; Antitrust; Competition law; Exclusive dealing; Merger; Misuse of market power; Price discrimination; Resale price maintenance; Restraint of trade; Secondary boycott; Trade Practices legislation**.

Restructured loans In banking, loans on which the original contractual terms have been concessionally modified due to the financial difficulties of borrowers, and on which interest continues to be so accrued at a rate which is equal to or greater than the bank's coverage cost of funds at the date of restructuring. See also **Credit; Loan; Non-accrual loans; Non-performing loan**.

Rests Agreed points in time at which interest payable on a principal sum can be calculated and either paid or added to that principal, or at which repayments of principal are deducted leaving a new balance on which interest runs for the ensuing period ending at the next rest. Rests are commonly monthly, quarterly, or half-yearly. See also **Bullet loan; Instalment contract; Interest; Refinancing**.

Resulting trust A trust arising where an express trust fails in whole or in part; where an express trust is fully performed without exhausting the trust property; and where the purchaser of property directs the vendor to convey the property to another person: *Re Vandervell's Trusts (No 2)* [1974] Ch 269. See also **Constructive trust; Express trust; Implied trust**.

Retail banking Banking business conducted between a bank and its customers through its branch network, as opposed to wholesale banking relating to the banks' financial dealings with other banks and major corporate customers. See also **Banker's standard of care; Banking business; Banker-customer relationship; Merchant bank**.

Retail method of inventory A method used by retailers to calculate the value of stock on hand at the end of an accounting period, based on a predetermined ratio between the cost of the goods and their retail selling price. This ratio is applied to the inventory to calculate the cost of inventory at the end of a financial period. See also **Average cost method**; **Depletion**; **Gross profit method of estimating inventory**; **Periodic inventory method**; **Perpetual inventory method**; **Weighted average inventory method**.

Retail sale Where goods are sold more than once between coming onto the market in a consumable state and consumption, the final sale to the consumer. The purchaser need not be an ordinary member of the public, nor need the quantity be small: *Collector of Customs v Chemark Services Pty Ltd* (1992) 42 FCR 585; 114 ALR 531. See also **Consumer**.

•**Retail shop lease** An agreement granting a right to occupy for value retail shop premises, including an implied or oral agreement, provided the lease is for a term of not less than six months and not greater than 25 years: for example (NSW) Retail Leases Act 1994 ss 3, 6. See also **Lease**; **Occupation**; **Retail shop premises**; **Shop premises**.

Retail shop premises Premises in a retail shopping centre, or premises used wholly or predominantly for carrying on a specified retail shop business: for example (NSW) Retail Leases Act 1994 s 3. Certain retail shops, such as those with a lettable area of 1000 square metres or more, are generally excluded from the operation of the Act: for example (NSW) Retail Leases Act 1994 s 5. See also **Retail shop lease**; **Shop premises**; **Shopping complex**.

Retail transaction account *Abbr* – RTA An account operated by a personal customer into which funds are deposited and against which withdrawals are permitted from time to time, as distinct from being fully withdrawn after a set period. Interest may or may not be repayable on these accounts. Each type of transaction is a different service for the customer and has different cost and revenue implications for the financial institution. See also **Bank account**; **Bank passbook**; **Banker-customer relationship**; **Retail banking**.

Retailer A person who supplies goods to consumers in the course of business, not for the purpose of resupply. Retailers are liable to consumers who suffer loss or damage as a result of such things as: the retailer's breach of an express or implied warranty; goods which are not fit for the purpose for which they were purchased; goods which are of unmerchantable quality; goods which do not correspond with a description or sample; and goods which do not have adequate repair facilities or spare parts: (CTH) Trade Practices Act 1974 Part V Div 2A. See also **Seller**; **Supplier**; **Merchantable quality**.

Retailer's card A card issued by non-banking institutions, to be used in specified stores. The holder of the card has usually been granted a line of credit. See also **Credit card**; **Debit card**.

Retained profit Profits carried forward by a company from past financial periods to the present, namely the accumulation of profits recorded by an entity over a number of accounting periods. The level of retained profits at the beginning of a financial year must be included in the profit and loss statement: Corporations Law Regulation Sch 5 cl 6. If the closing balance of retained profits is higher than that brought forward at the beginning of the year, then shareholders' equity has increased. See also **Accumulated losses**.

Retainer A contract for the provision of specialised services.

•**Retirement** A departure from employment or working life permanently and voluntarily, usually on the ground of age or ill health. By statute, it may mean ceasing (otherwise than by reason of death) to be employed by an employer: for example (NSW) Public Authorities Superannuation Act 1985 s 5. See also **Dismissal**; **Redundancy**; **Retrenchment**.

Retirement accounting An accounting procedure entailing no charge to expense being made for a fixed asset until that time in which the asset is removed from service. The historical cost of the fixed asset is charged against operations in the year of the retirement of the asset. See also **Fixed charge**; **Historical cost**; **Obsolescence**.

Retiring partner A partner who voluntarily leaves the partnership. This causes a dissolution of the original partnership and the creation of a new one. The retirement of a partner raises indebtedness between all or some of the members of the continuing partnership, who are buying out the retiring partner, and the retiring partner whose interest is being bought out: for example (NSW) Partnership Act 1892 s 42. A retiring partner remains liable for all the partnership debts and obligations incurred before the effective date of retirement, but may be discharged from such liability by an agreement with the remaining partners and the firm's creditors: for example (SA) Partnership Act 1891 s 17(3). A retiring partner cannot enforce debts that were due to the firm at the date of retirement: *Sobel v Boston* [1975] 2 All ER 282. See also **Dissolution**; **Partnership property**.

•**Retrenchment** The compulsory termination of the service of an employee for the reason that his or her service is no longer necessary, or the work for which he or she was engaged is finished, or to reduce the number of employees because the quantity of work has diminished: for example (CTH) Long Service Leave (Commonwealth Employees) Act 1976 s 4(1). See also **Dismissal**; **Redundancy**.

Retrocession 1. When a reinsurer (retrocedent) cedes the reinsurance to another reinsurer (retrocessionaire). 2. The vesting of title to property in the original owner who had lost it.

Retrospectivity The operation, or purported operation, of a statute prior to the time of its enactment. Statutory provisions, particularly those imposing criminal penalties, are presumed to operate only for the future. However, an Act will operate retrospectively if parliament has made that intention unmistakably clear. See also **Legislative powers**; **Retrospectivity**.

Return In relation to an investment, any increase in the value or amount of the investment, whether of a capital or income nature and whether or not that amount was distributed: (CTH) Social Security Act 1991 s 9(1). See also **Abnormal return**; **Annuity**; **Average return on investment**; **Excess return**.

Return of allotments A document which must be lodged by a corporation within one month after making an allotment of its shares: Corporations Law s 187(1). The return must state: the number and nominal amounts of the shares comprised in the allotment; the amount (if any) paid, deemed to be paid or due and payable on the allotment of each share; and, if the capital of the company is divided into shares of different classes, the class of shares to which each share comprised in the allotment belongs: Corporations Law s 187(1)(a)-(c). See also **Allotment**; **Share capital**.

Return of capital A payment or distribution in kind of assets by a company or unit trust to shareholders or unitholders where the payment or distribution represents a return of the capital, including any premium, originally subscribed for the shares or units. A return of capital so paid is not assessable as a dividend ((CTH) Income Tax Assessment Act 1936 s 6(1) 'dividend' (d), (e)) or assessable as a trust distribution ((CTH) Income Tax Assessment Act 1936 s 99B(2)(a)). If the shares or units are assets subject to capital gains tax the return of capital will reduce the indexed cost base of the shares ((CTH) Income Tax Assessment Act 1936 s 160ZL(2)), or units ((CTH) Income Tax Assessment Act 1936 s 160ZM(2)) by the quantum of the non assessable distribution. See also **Maintenance of capital**.

Return of capital in a compromise The refund to a shareholder of any money paid on issued shares as part of a genuine compromise of a dispute over membership of the company: *Commonwealth Homes and Investment Co Ltd v MacKellar* (1939) 63 CLR 351; ALR 470; *Woodgers and Calthorpe Ltd (in liq) v Bowring* (1935) 35 SR (NSW) 483; 52 WN (NSW) 153. Such payments are valid if the contract to take the shares is void or voidable, for example where the condition precedent to the contract coming into existence is not fulfilled, or where the contract is voidable for misrepresentation. However a return of capital is invalid where there is a valid contract to take shares in existence, and there has only been a breach of a term of the contract: *Commonwealth Homes and Investment Co Ltd v MacKellar*; *Woodgers and Calthorpe Ltd (in liq) v Bowring*. A valid return of capital is made as an exception to the maintenance of capital principle. See also **Compromise**; **Maintenance of capital**.

Return of premium The giving back of all or part of the premium to an insured by the insurer. See also **Premium**.

Return on assets *Abbr* – ROA Net income expressed as a percentage of average total assets in a company. ROA is used along with return on equity (ROE) as a measure of profitability and as a basis for intra-industry performance comparisons. This ratio measures the overall return on the assets used in a business. See also **Return on equity**.

Return on capital employed The relating of profit to an estimate of the average capital employed in a business to give a ratio, commonly called the primary ratio, calculated as net profit after tax/shareholders' funds. It is essential that the long-run return on capital employed in a business should be sufficient to ensure a fair return to the proprietor or shareholders, provide for the normal conduct and expansion of the business, attract new capital when required and retain the confidence of creditors and employees. See also **Capital employed**.

Return on equity *Abbr* – ROE Net income expressed as a percentage of average shareholders' equity. It is used along with return on assets as a measure of profitability. See also **Return on assets**.

Returns and allowances A reduction in the invoiced selling or purchase price of goods either when the goods are returned to the seller or due to the incorrect order received by the purchaser. The seller issues a credit note detailing the reduction in price. The adjusting amounts are recorded by the seller in a short term contra revenue account known as sales returns and allowances, and recorded by the purchaser in the purchase returns and allowances account. See also **Discount**; **Terms of Trade**.

•**Revenue** In the accounting context, an inflow or other enhancement, or saving in outflows, of service potential or future economic benefits in the form of an increase in assets or reduction in liabilities of an entity, other than that relating to contributions by owners, that results in an increase in equity during the reporting period: Statement of Accounting Concepts SAC 4 para 95. See also **Income**; **Profit and loss account**.

Revenue debt A charge or sum of money owing by an individual or company to the government such as a tax debt, administrative debt, or a commercial debt owing to a government organ or other instrumentality. Revenue debt is usually referred to as a Crown debt for which no statute of limitation applies. Australian courts will not assist governments from outside Australia in recovering a revenue debt: *Bath v British and Malayan Trustees Ltd* [1969] 2 NSWR 114. See also **Debt**; **Revenue**.

Revenue law The body of legislative and case law dealing with the assessment, levy, and collection of all forms of tax. Through revenue law, a government imposes and collects at periodic intervals taxes, excise, customs, dues, or rents to be appropriated for the payment of government expenses. See also **Custom**; **Excise**; **Foreign judgment**; **Legislation**; **Tax**.

Revenue received in advance A revenue item characterised by an inflow of cash and an incomplete earnings process. It includes an income received in advance and belongs to a future period. See also **Revenue**.

Reversal The setting aside or annulment of a decision of a lower court by a higher court to which an appeal was brought. A reversal of the original decision means that the appellate court considers the case to have been wrongly decided, the appellant wins the case and the appellate court either substitutes its own judgment or returns the case to the lower court with instructions on how to proceed: for example (NSW) Supreme Court Act 1970 ss 105-107.

Reverse stock split Where the total number of shares outstanding is lowered without reducing the total value of the issue by issuing one new share for the revocation of two or more old shares. Also known as 'stock split down'. See also **Securities exchange**; **Issue of new shares**; **Value**.

Reverse takeover A takeover where the consideration for the acquisition of shares is the issue of new shares in the offeror to target shareholders in exchange for their shares in the target. In this case, the target shareholders will hold the majority of the offeror's shares, while the target becomes a subsidiary of the offeror. See also **Takeover**.

Reversionary lease A lease which takes effect in the future after the expiration of a lease which has already commenced in occupation. See also **Estate**; **Rule against perpetuities**.

Review of assessment The process involved when the Inspector-General in Bankruptcy reviews a decision by a trustee to assess a bankrupt's liability to make contributions. The Inspector-General can review the trustee's decision to make an assessment on the Inspector-General's own initiative or if requested to do so by the bankrupt for justifiable reasons: (CTH) Bankruptcy Act 1966 s 139ZA(1). See also **Contribution by bankrupt**; **Trustee in bankruptcy**.

Revocable credit A documentary credit or standby letter of credit which may be amended or cancelled by the issuing bank at any moment and without prior notice to the beneficiary. An issuing bank is bound to reimburse a bank which, in reliance on the credit and prior to any notice of amendment of cancellation, has made any payment or has accepted or negotiated a draft in accordance with the terms of the credit. See also **Irrevocable credit**; **Letter of credit**; **Uniform Customs and Practice for Documentary Credits 1993**.

Revocation of an offer A withdrawal or termination of an offer so that it can no longer be accepted. Generally, an offer is capable of acceptance until its revocation is communicated to the offeree; there is no 'postal revocation rule', even if the offer sought to be revoked was capable of postal acceptance: *Byrne & Co v Leon Van Tienhoven & Co* (1880) 5 CPD 344. If an offer can be accepted by performing acts, it may become irrevocable once an offeree has performed some of the acts: *Abbott v Lance* (1860) 2 Legge 1283; *Veivers v Cordingley* [1989] 2 Qd R 278. See also **Acceptance**; **Consideration**; **Offer**; **Postal acceptance rule**.

Revocation of authority The termination of an agency relationship by a principal: for example *Walder v Cutts* [1909] VLR 261; (1909) 15 ALR 352. A revocation of authority may be made before the authority has been completely exercised by giving notice of revocation, either written, orally or by conduct. See also **Agency**; **Agent**; **Authority**; **Irrevocable authority**; **Principal**; **Termination**.

Revolving credit A contractual agreement between a commercial bank and a customer to provide funds up to a specified limit at an agreed interest rate. The customer is not obliged to defray the debt within a specified time and, upon repaying some of the amount owing, may borrow again to the specified limit. This arrangement applies to credit cards where borrowing may continue indefinitely within a defined upper limit. See also **Banker**; **Commercial bill**; **Credit card**.

Revolving fund A fund replenished periodically from business activities or from transferring amounts from other funds. It serves a particular purpose, for example, as a working capital fund created to finance the operations of a department, or an imprest petty cash fund. See also **Net working capital**.

Revolving underwriting facility *Abbr* – RUF An arrangement whereby a customer issues short-term notes supported by an undertaking by a bank that, if the customer is unable to issue the notes at a predetermined price, the bank will buy them at a prescribed price, or alternatively guarantee the availability of funds by providing standby credit. On the other hand, the bank may offer to underwrite only on a 'best efforts basis' with no undertaking to buy unsold notes or make funds available; this is known as a note issuance facility. See also **First demand guarantee**; **Standby letter of credit**; **Underwriter**.

Right in personam A right or class of rights against a person or class of persons. A right in personam is distinguished from a right in rem, which is a right against property. It is also known in Hohfeld's scheme of fundamental legal conceptions as a 'paucital right'. See also **In personam**; **Right in rem**.

Right in rem A right against property. Also known, in Hohfeld's scheme of fundamental legal conceptions, as a 'multital right'. An example is the right of a purchaser in the land the subject of a contract for sale, or the right of an mortgagee in the mortgaged property. See also **Right in personam**.

• **Right of action** The right to bring an action. See also **Chose in action**; **Intangible property**.

Right of combination The entitlement of a bank to combine or set-off accounts kept by a customer (even if they are kept at different branches) and to treat the balance as a single amount either due to the customer or owing to the bank: *Garnett v M'Kewan* (1872) LR 8 Exch 10. See also **Account**; **Trust account**; **Set-off**.

Right of contribution The right of an insurer, where an assured has double insurance on a risk, to proportional contribution from the other insurer: *Albion Insurance Co Ltd v GIO (NSW)* (1969) 121 CLR 342; [1970] ALR 441; (CTH) Marine Insurance Act 1909 s 86(1). See also **Contribution**; **Double insurance**.

Right of indemnity In the context of the law of trusts, the equitable right to be reimbursed for expenses incurred on behalf of or for the benefit of another: for example (NSW) Trustee Act 1925 s 59(4). The expenses must have been incurred while the person entitled to reimbursement (for example a trustee) was executing his or her powers and duties. The right is based on the equitable principle that the one who gets the benefit of trust property should bear its burden: *Hardoon v Belilos* [1901] AC 118. It creates a charge on trust property: *Re Exhall Coal Co Ltd* (1866) 35 Beav 449; 55 ER 970. See also **Equity**; **Trustee**.

• **Right of redemption** The right of a mortgagor of property to have an unencumbered title to the property restored once the mortgage is paid out. See also **Equity of redemption**; **Encumbrance**; **Mortgage**; **Mortgagor**; **Old system title**.

Right of stoppage in transitu The right of an unpaid seller of goods, who has parted with possession of the goods sold on credit, to stop delivery if the buyer becomes insolvent. When the buyer of goods becomes insolvent, the unpaid seller who has parted with the goods has the right of stopping them *in transitu*; that is, the seller may resume possession of the goods as long as they are in the course of transit and may retain them until payment or tender of the price: for example (NSW) Sale of Goods Act 1923 s 46. The seller cannot exercise the right after the goods are delivered to the buyer or an agent for the buyer. See also **Constructive delivery**; **Delivery to carrier**; **Duration of transit**.

Right to payment An entitlement to recoup moneys.

Trade and commerce In trade practices law, a corporation must not, in trade or commerce, assert a right to payment from a person for unsolicited goods or services unless the corporation has reasonable cause to believe that there is a right to such payment: (CTH) Trade Practices Act 1974 s 64(1), 64(2A).

Right to strike The right of employees collectively to withdraw their labour, breaking the contract for work. Various controls and degrees of liability, under statute and tort or contract law, are imposed on industrial action in different jurisdictions. It has been said that 'the right of workmen to strike is an essential element in the principle of collective bargaining' (*Crofter Harris Tweed Co Ltd v Veitch* [1942] AC 435); that is, withdrawal of labour is the major bargaining tool for workers to promote and protect their industrial interests. See also **Collective bargaining**; **Industrial action**; **Industrial tort**; **Strike**.

Right to terminate A right to put an end to a contract for breach. When exercised the parties to the contract are discharged from the obligation to perform their respective contractual duties, but not from liability for breaches occurring before the termination. The right to terminate at common law is conferred where there is a breach of condition, a sufficiently serious breach of an intermediate term, or where there is a repudiation or anticipatory breach: *Shevill v Builders Licensing Board* (1982) 149 CLR 620; 42 ALR 305. The right to terminate is to be distinguished from the right to rescind, which strictly applies only in respect to events occurring before entry into the contract. See also **Anticipatory breach**; **Breach of contract**; **Condition**; **Discharge**; **Intermediate term**; **Repudiation**; **Rescission**; **Termination**.

Right to work 1. An entitlement of an employee to have work provided by his or her employer. There is no right to work at common law; an employer may refuse to give an employee any work, as long as the employer continues to pay the employee's wages. There are some exceptions: for example, where the failure to provide work may lead to a loss of reputation or publicity for an employee whose career depends on displaying his or her talents: *White v Australian and New Zealand Theatres* (1943) 67 CLR 266. The existence of an implied term in the employment contract establishing a right to be provided with work has been suggested: *Langston v AUEW* [1974] 1 All ER 980. See also **Association**; **Employee**; **Employer**; **Restraint of trade**.

Rights issue The offer to existing shareholders of a company issue of new or unissued shares in the company, usually at an issue price lower than the market price. A rights issue is a method of raising non-loan finance from its own members. There is no rule of law that a company must offer shares to its existing members when increasing its share capital (*Mutual Life Insurance Co of New York v Rank Organisation Ltd* [1985] BCLC 11) but the articles may require otherwise: for example Corporations Law Sch 1 Table A reg 38. The articles may also provide that the shares must be issued to the members on a pro rata basis in proportion to the amount of capital already held by them in the class of shares to be issued, in order to protect their voting power and relative interests in the company: for example Corporations Law Sch 1 Table A reg 38. Where the rights offer is non-renounceable, the right to acquire the shares can only be exercised by the offeree member: *Consolidated Gold Mining Areas NL v Southern Goldfields Ltd* (1985) 4 ACLC 1; 13 ACLR 456 at 461. Where it is renounceable, members may sell their rights to take up the new shares, with the result that they can obtain financial compensation for the reduction in their relative interests in the company which occurs when others exercise their rights to acquire the new shares: for example *Allina Pty Ltd v FCT* (1991) 28 FCR 203; 99 ALR 295. Where the company directors have the power to make a non-pro rata issue, that power must be exercised for a proper purpose and for the benefit of the company: *Whitehouse v Carlton Hotel Pty Ltd* (1987) 162 CLR 285; 70 ALR 251. Prospectuses are required for rights issues: Corporations Law s 1018. Restrictions on rights issues are also imposed by the Australian Stock Exchange Listing Rules: ASX Listing Rules rule 7.7. Also known as 'rights offer'. See also **Directors duties**; **Prospectus**.

•**Risk** A possibility, chance, or likelihood of harm, hazard, or loss. A person is at risk when he or she is exposed to danger, peril, or injury. A risk may be moral, physical, or economic. If a person has created a real risk and not taken reasonable steps to eliminate it, he or she has breached his or her duty of care and will be liable for any damage caused by that breach: *Wyong Shire Council v Shirt* (1980) 146 CLR 40; 29 ALR 217. On the other hand, a person who has voluntarily assumed a risk will not be able to recover damages for another's tortious acts or omissions: *Insurance Cmr v Joyce* (1948) 77 CLR 39; [1948] 2 ALR 356.

•**Risk assessment** The identification and evaluation of loss or injury that may be sustained by an insured. A contract of insurance provides protection against factors which may threaten the assets, profitability or liability of the insured. The amount of the premium payable is related to the insurer's assessment of the potential risk the insured faces: *Re George and Goldsmiths and General Burglary Insurance Association Ltd* [1899] 1 QB 595 at 611. See also **Average**; **Public liability insurance**.

Risk, knowledge of See **Knowledge of risk**.

Risk note A contract signed by a consignor that limits the liability of a carrier, often to loss or injury resulting from the wilful misconduct of the carrier or its servants. See also **Affreightment**; **Carrier**; **Consignor**; **Contract of carriage**.

Risk, passing of See **Passing of risk**.

Risk transference The insurer's assumption of responsibility for the insured person's liability for damage or loss. The expression is the commercial equivalent of the legal principle of indemnity. There is no legal transfer of risk because the loss or legal liability remains with the insured. See also **Indemnity; Indemnity principle; Risk assessment.**

Risks clause See **All risks policy.**

Rolling strike A form of industrial action, by which workers in different groups strike at different times; so workers in one section may strike for one day and return to work the next day, when it will be the turn of another section of workers to strike. See also **Industrial action; Strike; Wildcat strike.**

Rollover To move funds directly from one investment into another, similar or identical one.

Banking and finance 1. The extension of an investment or renewal of a loan facility on its maturity date. 2. The capture of a dividend by buying stock up to the eve of its ex-dividend date, such rollovers generating extra income.

Taxation and revenue The election to transfer all or part of an eligible termination payment (ETP) into a complying superannuation fund or approved deposit fund (ADF), or to purchase an eligible annuity. See also **Approved deposit fund; Eligible annuity; Eligible Termination Payment; Pension; Rollover fund; Rollover relief; Superannuation fund.**

Rollover annuity A deferred annuity, the purchase price of which consists wholly of a rolled over amount or amounts: (CTH) Income Tax Assessment Act 1936 s 27A(1). See also **Annuity; Deferred annuity; Eligible annuity; Purchase price; Rollover.**

Rollover fund A fund into which eligible termination payments (ETPs) are transferred. A rollover fund includes complying superannuation funds, approved deposit funds, or eligible annuities issued by a life office or similar institution. See also **Approved deposit fund; Eligible annuity; Eligible Termination Payment; Rollover; Superannuation fund.**

Rollover immediate annuity An immediate annuity the purchase price of which consists wholly of a rolled-over amount or rolled-over amounts: (CTH) Social Security Act 1991 s 9(1). See also **Immediate annuity; Purchase price.**

Rollover relief A deferral of a capital gains tax liability. Rollover relief may be available where: businesses are reorganised in specified ways; assets are compulsorily disposed of, lost, damaged, or destroyed; statutory licences are renewed or extended; or the ownership of a building is converted to strata title: (CTH) Income Tax Assessment Act 1936 Pt IIIA Div 17. In some cases rollover relief only applies if an election is made and the Commissioner of Taxation is duly notified. See also **Capital gains tax; Rollover.**

Romalpa clause A clause in a contract for the sale of goods, reserving rights of title in the goods in the vendor until a certain event occurs, such as payment of the purchase price. It is named after the clause in *Aluminium Industrie Vaassen BV v Romalpa Aluminium Ltd* [1976] 2 All ER 552. See also **Contract; Reservation of title; Security.**

Rotation of directors The process by which directors, who are generally appointed for terms of a number of years under the articles of association, retire from the board. Each year a certain number of directors will be due to retire; for example Corporations Law Sch 1 Table A art 58 provides for the election of directors for terms of three years and the retirement of one third of the total number of directors each year. The articles may provide that a person who is appointed as managing director is not subject to retirement by rotation so long as he or she holds that position, although his or her appointment as managing director may cease if he or she ceases to be a director: Corporations Law Sch 1 Table A reg 79(2). A director of a listed company must not hold office (without re-election) past the third annual general meeting following the director's appointment or three years, whichever is longer: ASX Listing Rule LR 14.4. See also **Director; Director's duties.**

Round lot The unit of shares traded on an exchange; a marketable parcel of shares. Less than a round lot is an odd lot. See also **Odd lot.**

Round tripping The movement of funds to profit by slight margins of gain; for example, interest-rate arbitrage. See also **Arbitrage.**

Round turn In a futures market, a completed transaction involving both a purchase and a subsequent sale, or a sale followed by a liquidating purchase.

Royal Commission into the Monetary and Banking System The first official inquiry into the Australian financial industry established in 1936. The main reason for the Commission was a history of bank failures in the 1890s and 1930s which suggested that banks were not always managed in an efficient manner and consequently required some form of regulation. See also **Australian banking system; Campbell inquiry.**

•**Royalty** A payment made in respect of the exercise of a right to take a substance, and calculated either in respect of the quantity taken or the value of the substance taken, or the occasions upon which the right is exercised: *Stanton v FCT* (1955) 92 CLR 630; 6 AITR 216. See also **Copyright; Patent.**

•**Rule** 1. A principle of common law, settled by authority and forming part of the common law. 2. Regulations made by courts, government departments or statutory authorities pertaining to the conduct of business within those bodies, such as rules of court prescribed by judges regulating practice and procedure. 3. An order or direction made by a court during proceedings. See also **Statutory rules.**

Rule against circuity of action The rule that where a negotiable instrument is negotiated back to the drawer, to a prior indorser, or to the acceptor, that party may reissue and further negotiate it, but is not entitled to enforce payment of it against any intervening party to whom the reissuing party was previously liable: (CTH) Bills of Exchange Act 1909 s 42; (CTH) Cheques and Payment Orders Act 1986 s 47. See also **Acceptor; Bill of exchange; Indorser; Negotiable instrument.**

Rule against perpetuities A common law rule that no interest is good unless it must vest (if it vests at all) not later than 21 years after some life in being at the creation of the interest (the 'new' rule against perpetuities). It was laid down in the *Duke of Norfolk's Case* (1681) 3 Ch Cas 1; 22 ER 931. The effect of the rule is that a future interest will be void at the outset as at the date of the death of the testator if there is any possibility, however unlikely, that it will vest outside the perpetuity period: *Re Moore* [1901] 1 Ch 936; *Hardebol v Perpetual Trustee Co Ltd* [1975] 1 NSWLR 221. The common law perpetuity period of a life or lives in being plus 21 years has been subject to substantial modification in all states except South Australia. It has been abolished and replaced with a fixed period of 80 years in New South Wales and the Australian Capital Territory but remains a possible period in Queensland, Victoria and Western Australia (although provisions may be made for a period up to 80 years): (NSW) Perpetuities Act 1984; (VIC) Perpetuities and Accumulations Act 1968; (QLD) Property Law Act 1974 Pt XIV; (TAS) Perpetuities and Accumulations Act 1992; (WA) Property Law Act 1969 Pt XI. Also known as 'old rule against perpetuities' or 'rule in *Whitby v Mitchell*', 'new rule against perpetuities' or 'rule against remoteness of vesting'. See also **Beneficiary**; **Charitable purpose**; **Charitable trust**; **Common law**; **Perpetuity**; **Perpetuity period**; **Trust**.

•**Running account** A series of transactions where repayments are made in respect of past debts in order to ensure that the creditor continues to deal with the debtor. A creditor does not receive a preference if the debtor makes a repayment under a running account to ensure a continuing relationship: *Queensland Bacon Pty Ltd v Rees* (1966) 115 CLR 266; [1966] ALR 855. For example, if a debtor pays something off a grocer's account to ensure that the grocer will continue to give further supplies of groceries: *Richardson v Commercial Banking Company of Sydney Ltd* (1952) 85 CLR 110; [1952] ALR 315. Transactions for commercial purposes that are part of a continuing business relationship (for example, a running account) are required to be regarded as if they constituted a single transaction for the purposes of determining whether an unfair preference has been given: Corporations Law s 588FA(2). It is the ultimate effect of the course of dealing after looking at the whole relationship that is to be considered, not the individual transactions in isolation. See also **Account**; **Creditor**; **Debtor**; **Preference**; **Unfair preference**; **Voidable transaction**.

Running days Those days on which a ship is ordinarily engaged in discharging its cargo. Running days are used in a charterparty to calculate lay days. Running days comprise consecutive days of 24 hours, including weekends and holidays: *Nielsen & Co v Wait, James & Co* (1885) 16 QBD 67. Also known as 'running hours' or 'consecutive days'. See also **Lay day**; **Loading**.

Rural and Industries Bank of Western Australia Wholly-owned by the Western Australian government, a bank which had its origins in the Agricultural Bank of Western Australia established in 1904 to promote rural enterprise in the colony. In 1945, the charter of the bank was widened and it became the Rural and Industries Bank of Western Australia operating as a full trading bank. The bank is the largest financial institution based in Western Australia.

S

Safe aground A charterparty term permitting a charterer to take the vessel to a port where it may contact with the bottom depending on the tide. The term is often part of the expression 'not always afloat but safe aground.' See also **Always afloat; Charterer; Charterparty**.

Safe place of work A place of employment as free from danger as the nature of the work permits and which the exercise of reasonable care should remove or guard against danger: *Australian Oil Refining Pty Ltd v Bourne* (1980) 28 ALR 529; 54 ALJR 192. See also **Safe system of work**.

Safe system of work A system or mode of work which in the circumstances makes adequate provision for the safety of workers and which, if carried out with reasonable care, will protect the workers from foreseeable risks of injury: *Winter v Cardiff Rural District Council* [1950] 1 All ER 819. See also **Occupational health and safety; Safe place of work**.

Safety audit A critical examination of all, or part, of a total operating industrial system, with relevance to safety.

Salami shaving Computer crime that involves removing a very small amount of money from a series of bank accounts and depositing it into the criminal's account. See also **Cybercrime; Hacker**.

Salaried partner A person who is paid a fixed remuneration instead of an entitlement to participate in a distribution of partnership profits, but who is held out by the partners to the world to be a partner. See also **Partner; Partnership**.

•**Salary** A fixed amount paid regularly to an employee as remuneration for work done. It is sometimes used in contradistinction to 'wage', which may vary in amount from pay period to pay period according to the type or amount of work done, depending on the type of employment. See also **Allowance; Commission; Wage**.

•**Sale** The transfer, or agreement to transfer, property to a buyer for a price: for example (NSW) Sale of Goods Act 1923 ss 5(1), 6; (VIC) Goods Act 1958 s 6(1). See also **Buyer; Price; Sale of goods; Seller**.

Sale and leaseback A method where a business or company may sell an asset to a finance or an insurance company and lease it back at an agreed amount for a specific period of time.

Sale by description A contract in which goods are sold or supplied according to a consumer's description. If the sale is by reference to a sample as well as by description, the bulk of the goods must comply with both the sample and the description: (CTH) Trade Practices Act 1974 s 70; (NSW) Sale of Goods Act 1923 s 18. See also **Correspondence with description; Description; False trade description; Trade description**.

Sale by person not the owner A contract for the transfer of goods by a person who has no title. It is an established principle of law that a person can transfer no better title than he or she possesses under the maxim *nemo dat quod non habet*. In such circumstances the owner is entitled to recover possession unless precluded by his or her own conduct from denying the seller's authority: *Mercantile Credit Co Ltd v Hamblin* [1965] 2 QB 242; *Eastern Distributors Ltd v Goldring* [1957] 2 QB 600; [1957] 2 All ER 525; (NSW) Sale of Goods Act 1923 s 26; (VIC) Goods Act 1958 s 27. See also **Nemo dat quod non habet**.

Sale by sample The sale of goods pursuant to a contract, an express or implied term of which is that the quality of the bulk of the goods will correspond with that represented by the sample exhibited to the purchaser.

Sale of goods The transfer, or agreement to transfer, property in goods to a buyer for a price: for example (NSW) Sale of Goods Act 1923 s 6(1). See also **Buyer; Price; Property; Sale; Sale of goods legislation; Seller**.

Sale of goods legislation Legislation whose purpose is to 'codify' or 'codify and amend' the law relating to the sale of goods. Sale of goods legislation is substantially uniform across States and Territories as it was modelled on English legislation passed at the end of the 19th century to codify sale of goods law. See also **Sale; Sale of goods; Trade practices legislation**.

Sale of land A disposition of land, or an interest in land for consideration. All Australian States and Territories have systems for the registration of transfers made following sales of land: for example (NSW) Real Property Act 1900; (VIC) Transfer of Land Act 1958. See also **Old system title**.

Sale on approval A conditional sale to an individual consumer, only becoming absolute when the buyer, on trialing the goods, approves or is satisfied with the article sold.

•**Sale or return** A contract for the sale of goods where the goods are delivered to the prospective buyer on the understanding they will be returned within a certain time if the recipient does not want to buy them. Property in the goods passes to the buyer when he or she signifies acceptance to the seller, does anything to adopt the transaction, treats the goods in a manner which is inconsistent with his or her option to return them, or keeps the goods without giving notice of rejection before the expiry of the time for their return or, where no time limit is fixed, retains the goods beyond a reasonable time: (NSW) Sale of Goods Act 1923 s 23 r 4. See also **On approval; Sale of goods**.

Sale under voidable title A contract for the transfer of goods where the vendor has a title which may be rescinded as being obtained by fraud, misrepresentation, non-disclosure, duress, or undue influence. In such circumstances, where title has not been avoided at the time of sale, a buyer in good faith without notice of the defect acquires good title: *Lewis v Averay* [1972] 1 QB 198; (NSW) Sale of Goods Act 1923 s 27; (VIC) Goods Act 1958 s 29. Where the voidable title is acquired by a fraud perpetrated on the original seller, an innocent third party will acquire good title provided that the original seller has not rescinded prior to the subsale. See also **Sale of goods**.

•**Sale value** Amount for which goods are sold: (CTH) Sales Tax Assessment Act (No 2) 1930 s 4. The sale value consists of the sale price of goods or the total of all moneys which the buyer promises to pay to the seller to obtain title in goods.

•**Sales tax** A federal tax imposed on imported goods and the last wholesale sale of goods which are manufactured and consumed in Australia: *Brayson Motors Pty Ltd (in Liq) v FCT* (1985) 156 CLR 651. See also **Chose in action; Intangible property**.

Sales tax exemption Freedom from the obligation to pay sales tax. An exemption can be obtained when a registered person quotes a sales tax number or when an unregistered person quotes an exemption certificate: (CTH) Sales Tax (Exemptions and Classifications) Act 1992 s 4, Sch 1. Incorrect quotation is an offence and a penalty is imposed for improperly claiming exemption to acquire goods free of sales tax: (CTH) Sales Tax Assessment Act (No 1) 1930 s 15.

Salvage agreement An agreement for the provision of salvage services. Before a master of a ship can bind the owner under a salvage agreement, there must be an agency: *Re The Elise* (1859) 5 Wab 436; 166 ER 1203. As the salvage operations are not voluntary where an agreement has been made, the services, once performed, will not give rise to a common law salvage claim, but only to a claim based on the agreement. Proof of the agreement must be clear and satisfactory, but the agreement itself need not be in writing: *Re The Graces* (1844) 2 W Rob 294; 166 ER 765. However, most salvage agreements are made under standard forms and the Lloyd's open form is the one generally recognised world wide. The Lloyd's form places an obligation on both the salvor and the salvee to use their best endeavors and leaves the eventual award to be determined by arbitration in London. The contract is based on the principle of 'no cure, no pay'. See also **Master**.

Same business test The requirement that the same business is carried on after a change in the beneficial ownership of shares in a company as it was prior to that change, so that an income tax loss from a prior year for that company may be deductible in the current year of income. See also **Beneficial ownership; Carry forward loss; Continuity of beneficial ownership**.

•**Same or some comparable employment** A phrase used in workers' compensation legislation in calculating the reduction in earnings experienced by an injured worker during a period of partial incapacity. The reduction in the workers' weekly earnings is the difference between the weekly amount which the worker would probably have been earning as a worker if he or she had not been injured and continued to be employed in the same or some comparable employment, and the average weekly amount the worker is earning or would be able to earn in some suitable employment after the injury: for example (NSW) Workers Compensation Act 1987 s 40(2). The term does not refer to a comparable employer, or to a comparable contract of employment, but to a comparable occupation: *Johnston v Cmr for Railways* (1973) 1 ALR 481. See also **Suitable employment**.

Sanction A penalty or punishment imposed for a breach of the law.

Criminal law **1.** An authorisation, ratification, or approval. **2.** A penalty or punishment imposed by the criminal law. See also **Penalty**.

Tort A penalty or punishment for a breach of the law. Sanctions imposed in tort are usually damages, aiming to compensate the plaintiff for losses suffered or rights violated. See also **Exemplary damages; Fine**.

Sans frais *Fr* – without expense.

Sans recours *Fr* – without recourse. An expression frequently used on a bill of exchange by the drawer or indorser, or on a cheque by an indorser, who signs the instrument to negative or limit the drawer's or indorser's own liability on the instrument: (CTH) Bills of Exchange Act 1909 s 21(a); (CTH) Cheques and Payment Orders Act 1986 s 17(2). See also **Drawer; Holder; Indorser**.

•**Satisfaction 1.** At common law, the discharge by a different performance, or some other substitute consideration, of a personal obligation, instead of strict performance. If there has not yet been a breach of obligation, the obligor and obligee may agree (an accord executory) that a different performance, or some other substitute consideration, will discharge the obligation. If the obligor provides the agreed substitute, this satisfaction discharges the original obligation. If the obligor does not provide it, the original obligation revives and is enforceable by the obligee. The substitute may be a new promise to act, rather than the act itself, so that satisfaction occurs although the promised substitute is never provided: *Tallerman & Co v Nathan's Merchandise (Vic) Pty Ltd* (1957) 98 CLR 93 at 114. See also **Accord and satisfaction; Accord executory; Ademption; Election; Inter vivos**.

Savings That part of income not consumed; the withholding of money from expenditure on goods and services.

Savings account An interest bearing account opened with a bank. Unlike a current account it cannot usually be drawn upon by cheque. An overdrawn savings account cannot exist at law: *Barclays Bank v Okenarhe* [1966] 2 Lloyd's Rep 87. Also known as a 'deposit account'. See also **Account; Current account; Savings bank**.

Savings and loan association *Abbr* – S&L A United States financial institution similar to an Australian building society taking deposits and making loans to its members for the purpose of home-buying. S&Ls in effect borrow short and lend long. During the 1980s, with increasing money market competition, many ran into difficulties. Out of 4000 in 1980, some 835 closed their doors during the following decade. In 1989, the United

States Congress created the Resolution Trust Corp to bail out struggling S&Ls. In 1990 it issued a 40 year bond to raise funds for the process.

•**Savings bank** A banking institution aiming at encouraging and facilitating the small saver.

Scalper In relation to securities, an adviser who purchases securities, then advises others to do the same, and upon the price rise caused by the advice to buy these securities the advisor sells at a profit. See also **Securities adviser; Security**.

Schedule of investments A schedule required by the business rules of the Australian Stock Exchange (ASX) showing investments owned by members. A broker is required to furnish, at the end of its financial year, a schedule of investments: Australian Stock Exchange Business Rules BR 1.5.1. A broker is also required to prepare a schedule showing amounts held in its trust account on behalf of clients as at 31 March, 30 June, 30 September and 31 December in each year and furnish a copy of the schedule to the broker's auditor: BR 1.5.2. See also **Australian Stock Exchange Business Rules**.

•**Scheme** A policy or plan adopted in relation to certain business interests or bodies.

Corporations Form of corporate control transaction which makes use of the arrangements and reconstructions provisions of Corporations Law Pt 5.1: Corporations Regulations Sch 8 Pt 1(1). These provisions allow corporate assets and capital to be rearranged in a manner which is binding on members and creditors, provided that a procedure is followed involving disclosure and advertising, shareholder approval by special majority, and the approval of the court. See also **Takeover**.

Taxation and revenue A scheme includes any plan, proposal, action, course of action, or course of conduct by one or more people: (CTH) Income Tax Assessment Act 1936 s 177A(1). See also **Agreement; Arrangement; Understanding**.

Scheme of arrangement A reorganisation of a company's capital structure or rescheduling of its debts, following a period of financial difficulties. The purpose is to meet the demands of creditors while avoiding liquidation.

Scheme of development A series of limitations or restrictions imposed on purchasers, including subsequent purchasers, of land that has been subdivided. The restrictions relate to each block in a subdivision. Equity developed specific rules that apply to schemes of development in order to overcome the problems of mutual enforceability of covenants. Where a scheme of development exists the covenants will be enforceable against all owners regardless of the date of acquisition: *Re Louis and the Conveyancing Act* [1971] 1 NSWLR 164. See also **Covenant**.

Scope of authority In agency law, the extent of the nature and type of acts an agent is authorised to do on the principal's behalf that affect the legal liability of the principal. Generally, the principal cannot escape liability for acts done by the agent within the scope of actual or apparent authority, in the absence of notice of any particular instructions to the agent limiting the authority: *Bacon v Purcell* (1916) 22 CLR 307. See also **Actual authority; Agency; Agent; Apparent authority; Authority; Express authority; Implied authority; Principal**.

•**Scope of employment** A term of delimitation indicating the extent of an employer's vicarious liability. An employer generally is liable for any torts an employee commits in the course of the work being performed for the employer. See also **Vicarious liability**.

Scott v Avery clause A contractual term which prevents the parties from suing on the contract until the dispute is submitted to arbitration and an award is obtained: *Scott v Avery* (1856) 5 HLC 811; 10 ER 1121; *Codelfa Construction Pty Ltd v State Rail Authority of NSW* (1982) 149 CLR 337 at 422. Such a provision does not oust the jurisdiction of the court to determine the dispute: *Czarnikow v Roth, Schmidt and Co* [1922] 2 KB 478. See also **Alternative dispute resolution; Arbitrator**.

Screen trading A concept of world-wide 24 hour automated trading in stocks and futures where orders will be entered, matched and cleared by punching buttons on a computer keyboard; an order-matching system where trading and execution would be virtually instantaneous and at the price seen on the screen. The vision is controversial being a threat to market-makers and specialists. At present, screens are used to disseminate information while most trading is done over the telephone or face-to-face.

•**Scrip** Documents that are securities, or documents of title to securities: Corporations Law s 9. Companies must produce scrip certificates on demand by members: *Ardlethan Options Ltd v Easdown* (1915) 20 CLR 285. See also **Scrip lending; Securities; Share certificate**.

Scrip lending A scrip or stock loan, the lending of scrip by one party to another, usually in a case of short selling. Australian banks often lend scrip to major institutional and broking clients. Scrip lending grew in Australia during the 1970s to overcome late settlement problems. It has traditionally allowed institutions to meet settlement on short transactions and exploit arbitrage opportunities over the settlement period. Banks generally lend scrip against the security of cash deposits. See also **Scrip; Short selling**.

Sea cargo agent An agent such as a forwarding agent dealing in the consignment or receipt of cargo for carriage by sea on behalf of consignors or consignees. A sea cargo agent will frequently have to make arrangements for the provision of stevedores and other facilities such as lighters for the loading and unloading of cargo. See also **Agent; Air cargo agent; Cargo**.

Sea carriage That portion of international commerce which transports goods, whether exports or imports, from one country to another by the medium of the oceans and seas, usually by means of modern containerised shipping, bulk oil carriers, or cargo vessels. Sea carriage is performed by charterparties and is governed by private international law rules. See also **Amended Hague Rules 1979; Export; Import**.

Sea waybill A receipt issued by a shipping line to a shipper for the merchandise shipped. A seaway bill is evidence of the contract of carriage and resembles a bill of lading, but is not a document of title. It is not a negotiable document. It bears the name of the consignee who has only to prove his, her, or its identity in order to receive take delivery of the cargo. The purpose of a seaway bill is to avoid the delays to ships and cargoes that occur when bills of lading are late in arriving at the port of discharge. See also **Air waybill; Bill of lading; Charterer; Consignee; Contract of carriage; International Convention for the Unification of Certain Rules of Law relating to Bills of Lading 1924; Ocean waybill; Waybill.**

•**Seal 1.** An impression or mark attached to a document. **2.** An implement used to impress such a mark. **3.** To impress such a mark as an authorisation or agreement.

Corporations The Corporations Law provides for three types of company seals, the common seal, official seals and a share seal: ss 123(2)(d), 182(10), 1088. See also **Australian Company Number; Company seal.**

Deeds and other instruments A mark or symbol attached to a document to indicate authenticity or as a formal requirement. See also **Deed; Deed under seal; Sealed documents.**

Sealed documents Documents which have been sealed to indicate their authenticity or as a formal requirement (as in the case of deeds). See also **Deed; Deed under seal; Seal.**

Seat of corporation The place, in company law, where the corporation or firm is first incorporated. See also **Incorporation; Articles of association; Jurisdiction; Memorandum of Association.**

Seaworthy trim clause A clause in a charterparty providing that in the event that the vessel loads or discharges at two or more ports, it must be left, during the loading or discharging operation, in seaworthy trim to the master's satisfaction to enable the ship to shift between the ports. The seaworthy trim clause is important to meet the 'perils of the sea on the passage to the next port': *Britain SS Co Ltd v Louis Dreyfus & Co* (1935) 51 Ll L Rep 196 at 199. See also **Charterparty.**

•**Second hand goods 1.** Goods that have been previously used or owned by another person: *L R McLean and Co Ltd v Cmr of Inland Revenue* [1994] 3 NZLR 33. **2.** Any goods that have been worn or otherwise used: (VIC) Second-Hand Dealers and Pawnbrokers Act 1989 s 3(1); (QLD) Second-hand Dealers and Collectors Act 1984 s 6(1).

Second mortgage A mortgage granted by a mortgagor over specified property, subsequent to a first mortgage granted by the same mortgagor over the same property which has not yet been discharged. See also **First mortgage; Mortgage.**

Second or subsequent bankruptcy 1. A bankruptcy of the same person which occurs after discharge from an earlier bankruptcy. **2.** A bankruptcy of the same person which occurs while the person is still a bankrupt.

See also **After acquired property; Bankrupt; Discharge of bankruptcy; Trustee in bankruptcy; Vesting of property.**

Secondary boycott Conduct targeted against a third party in order to place pressure on another.

Industrial law A boycott or other ban on work taken against one person, to place pressure on another person. The target of the action is not the employer of the workers engaging in the action, but some third party dealing with the employer. See also **Boycott; Boycott contravention; Industrial action; Strike; Work ban.**

Trade practices Conduct by persons that hinders or prevents the supply of goods or services by persons who are neither the supplier nor consumers of such goods and services: (CTH) Trade Practices Act 1974 s 45D. Secondary boycotts are prohibited under s 45D where the conduct is engaged in for the purpose, and would have the effect of, causing a substantial lessening of competition in the relevant market. See also **Acting in concert; Collective boycott; Collusion; Contract, arrangement or understanding.**

•**Secondary industry** An industry involved in the production of manufactured goods: *Davey v Brightlight Nominees Pty Ltd* [1984] VR 957. Also known as 'manufacturing industry'. See also **Primary industry; Tertiary industry.**

•**Secondary meaning** In passing off, a meaning of a descriptive name or mark where the plaintiff can show that the name or mark is not only descriptive but also has a meaning that is distinctive of the plaintiff's business, in the sense of indicating a particular trade source: *B M Auto Sales Pty Ltd v Budget Rent-A-Car System Pty Ltd* (1976) 12 ALR 363; 51 ALJR 254. See also **Distinctiveness; Market reputation.**

Secondary obligation In contract law, an obligation which arises by operation of law on the breach of a primary contractual obligation. The chief example is the obligation to pay damages for breach of contract. See also **Breach of contract; Damages; Primary obligation; Termination.**

Secondary picketing Picketing which is not in furtherance of a trade dispute or not near or at a person's place of work. Secondary picketing is not protected by statute. A person involved in secondary picketing may be liable to civil action or criminal prosecution for conspiracy or obstruction: *Sid Ross Agency Pty Ltd v Actors and Announcers Equity Assn of Australia* [1971] 1 NSWLR 760; *Australian Builders' Labourers' Federated Union of Workers (WA Branch) v J-Corp Pty Ltd* (1993) 42 FCR 452; 114 ALR 551.

•**Secondary prospectus** The prospectus required for the offer or invitation of securities that have been issued before, that are not quoted on the stock market of a stock exchange and that are not excluded offers or invitations: Corporations Law s 1043B. If 30 per cent or more of the voting shares in a company or the voting shares in a class are being sold, the secondary prospectus must comply with Corporations Law s 1043C. If the Corporations Law does not apply, the secondary prospectus need only comply with the less rigorous provisions in s 1043. See also **Prospectus; Secondary trading.**

Secondary trading Trading in existing securities. Secondary sales of quoted securities are not subject to the prospectus requirements in the Corporations Law. However, the prospectus requirements are applicable where such securities have been allotted for the purpose of on-sale (s 1030), or if the sales constitute hawking of securities (s 1078). Secondary sales of unquoted securities are subject to special information requirements. Where the sale is for more than 30 per cent of the securities of a corporation, a notice containing prospectus-like disclosure must be lodged: Corporations Law Pt 7.12 Div 3A; Corporations Regulations reg 7.12.08A, Sch 9A. If the sale is for less than 30 per cent of the securities of a corporation, the seller must give the buyer a notice containing certain basic information: Corporations Law s 1043D(2); Corporations Regulations reg 7.12.08C. See also **Prospectus; Secondary prospectus; Securities; Hawking of securities.**

Secret commission Any gift or valuable consideration accepted by or given to an agent as an inducement or reward for any act done, forbearance observed, or favour shown in relation to the principal's affairs or business or on the principal's behalf or for obtaining an agency or contract for or with the principal: (CTH) Secret Commissions Act 1905 s 4(1). Accepting secret commissions is a breach of an agent's duty to the principal (*Jordan v Walker* (1885) 11 VLR 346) and the agent is liable to the principal for the amount (*Lunghi v Sinclair* [1966] WAR 172). In New South Wales, a secret commission is also known as a 'corrupt commission' or 'secret profit'. See also **Agency; Agent; Bribe; Fiduciary duty; Principal; Secret profits.**

Secret profits Pecuniary profits made by an employee from third persons during employment, without the employer's approval. See also **Duty of faithful service; Secret commission.**

Secret reserve The amount of under statement in an organisation's owners' equity due to asset under valuation or omission, or overstated liabilities in the financial statements. Secret reserve refers to a condition in existence in the business rather than an account in the financial statements.

Section 1210 document The document which Corporations Law s 1210 requires a futures broker to give to a person before accepting that person as a client. The document comprises an explanatory document, a risk disclosure statement, a document which sets out the specifications, and details of the essential terms of each kind of futures contract in which the broker deals. See also **Futures broker; Sydney Futures Exchange.**

•**Secured creditor** A creditor who holds some kind of security over the property of his or her debtor. Arrangements such as a mortgage, charge, or lien, confer on the creditor the means of satisfying the debt owing by the debtor out of what is in truth the property of the debtor: (CTH) Bankruptcy Act 1966 s 5; *Re Florence: Ex parte Turimetta Properties Pty Ltd* (1979) 28 ALR 403; 36 FLR 256. A secured creditor will take priority over unsecured creditors upon the bankruptcy or insolvency of the debtor. Although a secured creditor can present a creditor's petition, the secured creditor can only claim to be a creditor for the difference between the debt and the value of the security. Otherwise, the petition must state that the secured creditor is willing to surrender the security in the event of a sequestration order being made: (CTH) Bankruptcy Act 1966 ss 44(2), 44(3). These provisions apply even though the secured property is not in the debtor's name but is held in trust for the debtor: *Re Florence; Ex parte Turimatta Properties Pty Ltd*. A company receiver appointed by the court is a secured creditor in respect of his or her expenses, remuneration and costs: *Re Central Commodities Service Pty Ltd* [1984] 1 NSWLR 25. See also **Charge; Creditor; Creditor's petition; Lien; Mortgage; Security; Unsecured creditor.**

Secured liability A liability or debt which is sustained by specific assets pledged to the creditor or person to whom the debt is owed. See also **Secured loan.**

Secured loan A loan in respect of which the borrower offers assets as collateral to the lender. If the borrower defaults on the repayment of the loan, the lender has the right to sell those assets and retain the proceeds up to the amount of the loan. A secured loan is generally less risky to the lender than an unsecured loan and commands a lower rate of interest.

•**Securities** Government debentures, stocks, or bonds; shares in, or debentures of, a body; prescribed interests; units of such shares, or of prescribed interests; or an option contract: Corporations Law s 92. See also **Derivative; Excluded security; Prospectus; Securities dealer; Security.**

•**Securities adviser** A securities dealer, an investment adviser or a securities representative of a dealer or of an investment adviser: Corporations Law s 9. See also **Investment advice business; Securities business.**

Securities and Exchange Commission *Abbr* – SEC Established by the United States Congress in 1934 to help protect investors, a body which administers legislation relating to the securities exchanges and the financial and corporate sectors. The SEC is concerned with such matters as disclosure of adequate information regarding new issues, insider trading, stock manipulation, fraud, and the use of credit in security speculation. Brokers and dealers must be registered with the SEC. The US securities regulator established in 1934. It is responsible for matters such as the making of offers of securities, regulation of members of the securities industry and accounting requirements. It administers the (US) Securities Act 1933, (US) Securities and Exchange Act 1934, (US) Public Utility Holding Company Act 1935, (US) Trust Indenture Act 1939, (US) Investment Company Act 1940 and the (US) Investment Advisers Act 1940. It also exercises powers under the (US) Securities Investor Protection Act 1970 and has advisory functions in corporate reorganisations under the (US) Bankruptcy Act 1978.

Securities authority The authority of a securities representative to act for a securities licensee. A proper authority requires a copy of the principal's securities licence on which is indorsed a statement certifying the copy to be a true copy, stating that the representative is employed by or acts for or in arrangement with the principal and signed by the principal, as well as a statement setting out details of any other securities licensee of whom the representative is also a securities representative: Corporations Law s 88(1). See also **Invalid securities authority; Securities licence; Securities representative.**

Securities business A business of dealing in securities: Corporations Law s 93(1). See also **Securities; Securities adviser; Securities dealer; Securities licence; Securities representative.**

•**Securities clearing house** *Abbr* – SCH A body corporate approved under Corporations Law s 779B to provide clearing house facilities for a stock market, including facilities for the registration of transfers of, and the settlement of transactions involving, quoted securities or quoted rights: Corporations Law Pt 7.2A. See also **Clearing house; Clearing House Electronic Subregister System.**

Securities Clearing House business rules The business rules of the Securities Clearing House (SCH). The business rules govern the settlement of transactions and the corresponding duties of issuers of quoted securities and quoted rights: Corporations Law s 779F. Where business rules apply, they prescribe the method and registration of transfer of shares rather than the company's articles: s 1085(1)(b). See also **Clearing House Electronic Subregister System; Securities clearing house.**

Securities Clearing House participant A person, or partnership, entitled to participate in the facilities provided by the Securities Clearing House (SCH): Corporations Law s 9. An SCH participant is contractually bound by the business rules of the SCH: s 779F. See also **Clearing house; Securities Clearing House; Securities Clearing House business rules.**

Securities conduct Activities related to dealing or advising in securities. Under Corporations Law s 9, 'eligible securities conduct' is conduct in the course of, for the purposes of, or otherwise in connection with dealing in securities, advising a person about securities or giving a person a securities report. See also **Dealing; Investment adviser; Securities report.**

•**Securities dealer** A person who carries on, or holds out that the person carries on, a securities business: Corporations Law s 780. A securities dealer is required to hold a dealer's licence. See also **Securities; Securities adviser; Securities business; Securities representative.**

•**Securities exchange** A place where securities may be bought and sold. It may or may not have a physical location. For the purposes of Corporations Law Ch 6, it refers to the Australian Stock Exchange (ASX), the State subsidiaries of the ASX or a body corporate declared by the regulations to be a securities exchange: Corporations Law s 9. Also known as 'securities market'. See also **Local stock exchange; Approved securities organisation; Stock market.**

Securities Exchange Guarantee Corporation *Abbr* – SEGC The guarantor of trading on the Australian Stock Exchange. It is a body corporate in respect of which a nomination as the SEGC is in force under (CTH) Corporations Act 1989 s 67(1), or is taken to be in force because of that Act: s 9. It administers the National Guarantee Fund which guarantees obligations of payment, or the provision of settlement documents, in respect of trades undertaken by members of the SEGC. See also **Australian Stock Exchange Ltd; National Guarantee Fund; Securities exchange.**

Securities industry The business of buying and selling shares and other instruments such as futures and options. See also **Securities exchange; Securities licensee.**

Securities industry development account An account maintained by the Australian Stock Exchange (ASX) compromising payments made from the National Guarantee Fund (NGF) where the amount held in the NGF exceeds the minimum amount required to be maintained by the NGF: Corporations Law ss 943-945. The account may be applied to purposes relating to the development of the securities industry or to a prescribed purpose, if that purpose has been approved by the Minister. See also **Australian Stock Exchange Ltd; National Guarantee Fund.**

Securities Industry Protection Corporation *Abbr* – SIPC An American compensation scheme for investors in the event of failure of market makers or dealers. The (US) Securities Investor Protection Act 1970 requires that every broker or dealer registered with the Securities and Exchange Commission (SEC) is a member of the SIPC. It is not a government agency but was created by Congress and operates under some supervision by the SEC, by an annual assessment of the members and by backing from the US Treasury. All members of the US National Association of Securities Dealers belong to this scheme. See also **National Guarantee Fund.**

•**Securities law** The regulation of dealings involving securities by the Corporations Law, including the offering of securities (for example Pts 7.11, 7.12), the licensing of security dealers and investment advisers (for example Pt 7.3), practices deemed as improper in connection with security markets (for example Pt 7.11) and the creation and function of such markets. See also **Australian Securities Commission; Australian Stock Exchange Ltd.**

•**Securities licence** A dealer's licence or an investment adviser's licence: Corporations Law s 9. See also **Investment advice business; Securities business; Securities dealer; Securities licensee.**

•**Securities licensee** A person who holds a securities licence: Corporations Law s 9. Under Corporations Law s 780 a person must not carry on, or hold out that they carry on, a securities business unless the person holds a dealer's licence or is an exempt dealer. Corporations Law s 781 prohibits the carrying on of an investment advice business, or the holding out that a person carries on an investment advice business, unless the person is a securities licensee or an exempt investment adviser. See also **Dealer's licence; Licensee; Investment adviser's licence.**

Securities market See **Securities exchange.**

Securities professional A person who is employed in the securities industry, such as a broker or investment adviser. See also **Securities licensee; Securities industry.**

•**Securities recommendation** A recommendation with respect to securities or a class of securities whether made expressly or by implication: Corporations Law s 9. An investment adviser is required to disclose certain matters before making a securities recommendation and to have reasonable grounds for making a securities recommendation: ss 849, 851. See also **Investment adviser**.

•**Securities report** An analysis or report regarding securities: Corporations Law s 9. The report will usually contain an analysis of whether the market price of the security is likely to rise or fall given the current financial position of the company. The Corporations Law s 781 prohibits a person from giving investment advice unless they are a licensee. The publication of a securities report falls within the definition of an investment advice business (s 77(1)) which is relevant in determining whether a licence is required. See also **Investment adviser; Investment adviser's licence; Securities licensee**.

•**Securities representative** A person who is employed by, or acts for or by arrangement with, another person in connection with a securities business or investment advice business carried on by that other person: Corporations Law s 94(1). A securities representative excludes a person who does acts or engages in conduct of a kind ordinarily done by accountants, clerks, or cashiers: s 94(3). A natural person is prohibited from doing an act as a representative of a securities dealer or investment adviser unless the dealer or adviser holds a licence and the person holds a proper authority: ss 806, 807. See also **Investment advice business; Securities business**.

Securitisation The substitution of loans by marketable financial instruments. An example is when bank assets, such as loans and mortgages, are sold to a company which raises funds by issuing negotiable securities. See also **Securitisation arrangement**.

Securitisation arrangement An arrangement involving the funding, or proposed funding of, loans that are provided by a credit provider, or the purchase of loans by a credit provider, by issuing instruments or entitlements to investors and under which payments are principally derived, directly or indirectly, from such loans: (CTH) Privacy Act 1988 s 6(1). See also **Credit enhancement; Loan; Securitisation**.

•**Security** Something that secures or makes safe.

Corporations **1.** Any right or interest in property which renders the repayment of a debt more secure and certain: *Batchelor & Co Pty Ltd v Websdale* [1962] NSWR 1441. **2.** An asset offered by a borrower to a lender as collateral. If the borrower defaults on the repayment of the loan, the lender has the right to sell the asset and retain the proceeds up to the amount owing. **3.** A document issued by a government, semi-government body, statutory body, or public company in return for funds invested for a specified purpose by purchasers. Also known as 'charge'. See also **Charge; Hypothecation agreement; Lien; Mortgage; Security interest**.

Security analysis A review of all relevant data about a company for the purposes of investors and creditors that looks at the intrinsic value of the investment and risk characteristics and produces information about current and prospective borrowers who trade in secondary capital markets. See also **Investment analyst; Security analyst**.

Security analyst One who seeks to determine the intrinsic value of a marketable security as distinct from its market value. See also **Security analysis**.

•**Security interest** In consumer credit law, an interest or power over goods or other property which secures the performance of an obligation. See also **Bill of sale; Chattel security; Credit sale contract; Inventory security interest; Mortgage**.

Seed capital Initial start-up capital for a new venture, often associated with venture capital financing in high technology industries. Such capital may be provided in the form of an equity investment or a loan, and sometimes takes the form of a subordinated loan. See also **Capital; Subordinated loan; Venture capital**.

Selective buy-back A type of authorised buy-back where a company buys shares back from a particular member, otherwise than in either an equal access buy-back scheme, on-market buy-back, odd-lot buy-back, or employee share scheme buy-back: Corporations Law ss 9, 206B, 206C. A selective buy-back must be approved by all ordinary shareholders at a general meeting or by a special resolution passed at a general meeting with no votes being cast in favour of the resolution by any person whose shares are to be bought back: ss 206C, 206E. Once the shares are bought back they must be cancelled: ss 206C, 206I. See also **Authorised buy-back; Buy-back; Employee share scheme buy-back; Equal access buy-back scheme; Odd-lot buy-back; Share buy-back**.

Self-acquisition scheme A scheme or transaction for the purpose of a company obtaining a relevant interest in itself: Corporations Law s 206AAB. It is a self-acquisition scheme, for example, if the company gets control of another company that has a right to vote, voting shares in the company or a right to dispose of shares in the company: s 206AAB(1)(a). A scheme which causes the acquiring company to obtain an interest of more than 10 per cent in itself may be declared unacceptable by the Australian Securities Commission with the effect that the court can make orders setting aside the scheme: ss 206AAD, 206 AAG. See also **Maintenance of capital; Relevant interest; Share buy-back**.

Self-appointed agent In the law of agency, a person who takes action through necessity to protect the interests of an alleged principal. See also **Agency; Agent; Agency of necessity**.

Self-assessment A system of taxation assessment under which tax returns are not subject to scrutiny before or as part of assessment. Self-assessment applies to individuals, partnerships, trusts, companies, superannuation funds, approved deposit funds, and pooled superannuation trusts. See also **Assessment; Audit; Tax return**.

Self-education expenses All expenses (other than higher education contributions, open learning charges, or debt repayments under the tertiary student financial supplement scheme) incurred by a taxpayer in connection with a course provided by a place of education, undertaken by the taxpayer to gain qualifications to be used in carrying on a profession, business, trade, or any employment: (CTH) Income Tax Assessment Act 1936 s 82A. The first $250 of self-education expenses for an income year are not deductible: (CTH) Income Tax Assessment Act 1936 s 82A(1). See also **Income taxation**.

•**Self-employed person** A person who works for gain or reward other than under a contract of employment (that is, as an employee) or of apprenticeship, whether or not he or she employs another person: (NSW) Occupational Health and Safety Act 1983 s 4. See also **Apprenticeship; Contract of employment; Employee**.

Self-financing ratio The amount of capital for a new investment, obtained by an organisation from its own earnings (from depreciation funds, profits and surpluses), expressed as a percentage of total capital requirements.

Self-help An action undertaken by a person who has suffered injury from another's wrong to obtain redress without recourse to a court.

Contract Rights which are enforceable without the need to have recourse to the courts. In the law of contract, most remedies are self-help remedies: for example, termination for breach or repudiation, and rescission for misrepresentation or mistake. See also **Breach of contract; Misrepresentation; Mistake; Penalty; Relief against forfeiture; Repudiation; Rescission; Termination; Termination clause**.

Self-induced frustration The frustration of a contract by a frustrating event that occurs because of default arising from an act or omission of one of the parties: for example *Maritime National Fish Ltd v Ocean Trawlers Ltd* [1935] AC 524. A contract cannot be discharged by a party who relies on self-induced frustration. See also **Discharge; Frustration**.

Self-liquidating advance A bank advance to a customer for the purpose of tiding over a temporary shortage of funds only. It may be given, for example, when a farmer is faced with a heavy outlay of wages during the 'seed-time to harvest' period, the loan being repaid once the crop is sold.

Self-reducing loan package Abbr – SLP A home loan financing arrangement in which the home buyer takes out both a loan secured against residential property and a separate investment loan, the total amount borrowed being used to finance the purchase of a home and a portfolio of blue-chip Australian shares. Once the property and shares are purchased, the dividend stream generated by the shares helps to partly finance the ongoing interest costs of the loans. The borrower gets the benefit of both dividend imputation and the negative gearing of the share portfolio, as well as a projected capital gain on the shares.

Self-regulation The process of allowing industry to correct systemic problems within that industry without government intervention.

•**Sell** To barter or exchange; offer, agree or attempt to sell; expose, send, forward or deliver for sale; cause or permit to be sold or offered for sale: for example (NSW) Liquor Act 1982 s 4.

Seller Person who sells; a vendor.

Corporations In the context of a short sale of securities, the person selling the securities. If the person selling is an agent, seller means the principal: Corporations Regulations reg 7.4.08. See also **Ordinary and traded options; Short selling**.

Sale of goods A person who transfers, or agrees to transfer, property to a buyer: for example (NSW) Sale of Goods Act 1923 s 5(1); (VIC) Goods Act 1958 s 3(1). See also **Buyer; Sale; Sale of goods**.

Seller in possession after sale A person who has sold goods and retains possession of those goods, or documents of title to those goods: for example (NSW) Sale of Goods Act 1923 s 28(1). See also **Delivery; Document of title to goods; Possession; Sale of goods; Seller**.

Seller's lien The right of an unpaid seller to retain possession of goods sold until payment in circumstances where there is no continuing credit available to the buyer: for example (NSW) Sale of Goods Act 1923 s 43(1). See also **Possession; Seller; Seller in possession after sale**.

Selling and distribution expense An expense in connection with the sale of goods and distribution of the company's products to its customers. Selling and distribution expenses cover salaries and wages of the sales team and storage costs involved in the distribution of products.

Selling out The sale of securities by a broker where a buyer on the exchange fails to pay for them by the due date for settlement. The original buyer is liable to pay any loss that is incurred.

Semi-government security A security issued by a semi-government authority or government agency for the purposes of financing major works such as power stations, dams, sewage treatment works, freeways, airports, communications, transport and community services such as schools and hospitals. See also **Securities**.

Senior executive appraisal A method of dispute resolution for commercial disputes between corporate entities, developed by Sir Laurence Street. It is an adaptation of the United States mini-trial. Senior executives of the corporations which are in dispute meet with a neutral adviser in a conference where they appraise the dispute and attempt to formulate a possible basis for settlement. Representatives of each party prepare a brief position paper which is forwarded to the other party, the executives and the adviser. At the conference, the parties respond to the papers and may make a short oral presentation. The senior executives and the adviser meet after the conference to attempt to negotiate a settlement. The appraisal is considered less adversarial and confrontational than the mini-trial. See also **Alternative dispute resolution**.

Seoul Stock Exchange A stock exchange with some 500 listed companies and daily trading volumes exceeding those of the stock exchanges in Hong Kong and

Singapore. In 1989, there were no foreign listings. Non-resident foreigners are barred from owning South Korean stocks except indirectly through nine 'trust' funds which are similar to investment trusts. Notwithstanding, a number of foreign stockbroking firms have set up office in Seoul.

Separate entity doctrine The principle that a company is a legal person with its own legal personality separate from that of its members. Directors of a company which is part of a group should, in deciding what transaction their company should enter into, consider the interests of that company rather than the interests of the group as a whole: *Walker v Wimborne* (1976) 137 CLR 1; 3 ACLR 529. See also **Corporate capacity; Separate legal personality**.

Separate legal personality The distinct legal existence of an incorporated body apart from the individuals who are from time to time its members: *Salomon v A Salomon and Co Ltd* [1897] AC 22; [1895-99] All ER Rep 33. See also **Corporate capacity; Corporation; Incorporation**.

•**Separate net income** The income of a dependant, after the deduction of expenses regarded, in accordance with ordinary and commercial principles, as direct charges against that income. This does not include deductions from previous years: *Case 3* (1981) 25 CTBR. Separate net income includes both assessable and exempt income: *AAT Case 4468* (1988) 19 ATR 3631. A taxpayer's dependant rebate is generally reduced $1 for every $4 of the dependant's separate net income over $282: (CTH) Income Tax Assessment Act 1936 s 157J(4). See also **Assessable income; Dependant rebate; Exempt income; Gross income; Losses and outgoings; Taxable income**.

Sequestration The action by which a person's property is taken out of the person's control. When a debtor commits an act of bankruptcy, the court has power, on a creditors' petition, to make a sequestration order against the estate of the debtor: (CTH) Bankruptcy Act 1966 s 43(1). See also **Act of bankruptcy; Bankrupt; Bankruptcy Court; Creditor's petition; Debtor; Trustee in bankruptcy; Vesting of property**.

Sequestration order A court order made against a debtor's assets upon the making of which the debtor becomes a bankrupt: *RA Ringwood Pty Ltd v Lower* [1968] SASR 454; (CTH) Bankruptcy Act 1966 s 43(2). See also **Bankruptcy**.

•**Serious credit infringement** Action on the part of the receiver of credit which is a serious infringement of credit legislation. A serious credit infringement includes fraudulently obtaining credit, attempting to fraudulently obtain credit, or acting in a manner which is designed to evade obligations made under a credit agreement or that a reasonable person would consider to constitute an evasion of obligations made under the credit agreement: (CTH) Privacy Act 1988 s 6(1). See also **Credit; Credit card**.

Serious fraud offence An offence against any law involving fraud or dishonesty, which is punishable by imprisonment for a period of three months or more: Corporations Law s 9. See also **Fraud**.

•**Servant** A person in the service of another. A term formerly used to describe a person employed by another person, the 'master'. See also **Contract of employment; Employee; Master**.

Contract The employed party to a contract of employment. In statutory formulas such as 'director, servant or agent' (for example (CTH) Trade Practices Act 1974 s 84(2)), there is generally no implication that only servants whose status and authority would make their acts the acts of the master (employer) at common law are included: *Given v C V Holland (Holdings) Pty Ltd* (1977) 15 ALR 439.

Employment A person employed by others to do work such as manual labour, clerical work, or otherwise. A servant may be the agent of his or her employer or master: *Federal Cmr of Taxation v Barrett* (1973) 129 CLR 395; 2 ALR 65. A servant must obey the lawful orders of the employer. See also **Master; Master and servant**.

Service agreement 1. An agreement under which one party agrees to provide specified services for another in return for remuneration. **2.** An agreement between a liner conference and a shipper providing that the shipper consign specified quantities of cargo for a specified period to conference line ships in exchange for service and an agreed freight rate schedule. Some agreements require that minimum quantities of cargo are consigned over the contract period. Also known as 'service contract'. See also **Affreightment; Cargo; Charterer; Contract of carriage; Freight; Rate of freight**.

Service company A company or trust established to provide administration services to other companies in its group or to a professional partnership such as a partnership of accountants or lawyers or doctors. The service entity charges the group companies or partnership a fee based on cost plus a profit margin, which is a legal form of income splitting: *Federal Cmr of Taxation v Phillips* (1978) 78 ATC 4169. Also known as 'service trust'.

•**Services 1.** Assistance or accommodation from one person to another: *Adamson v New South Wales Rugby League Ltd* (1991) 31 FCR 242; 100 ALR 479. **2.** Any rights, benefits, privileges, or facilities provided in trade and commerce: (CTH) Trade Practices Act 1974 s 4. It extends to services in relation to real, personal and intellectual property. See also **Contract for services; Contract of employment; Contract of service; Goods; Supply**.

Services rendered Work done for another person on the basis of a contract or otherwise: *Employers' Mutual Indemnity Assn Ltd v FCT* (1943) 68 CLR 165. The expression 'services rendered' contemplates acts done for the benefit of another which are more than the mere making of a contract and which go beyond the performance of an obligation undertaken in the course of an ordinary commercial contract: *Revesby Credit Union Co-op Ltd v FCT* (1965) 112 CLR 564. The assessable income of a taxpayer includes the value to the taxpayer of all allowances, gratuities, compensations, benefits, bonuses and premiums allowed, given, or granted to him or her in respect of or in relation to services rendered by him or her: (CTH) Income Tax Assessment Act 1936 s 26(e).

Services standard An informal and often unwritten standard or practice adopted within an industry; a written standard published by the Standards Association of Australia or a comparable body; a written standard prescribed or declared and gazetted under legislation to be a mandatory standard. Queensland and South Australia have legislation prescribing and enforcing standards with respect to services: (QLD) Fair Trading Act 1989 Pt 4 Divs 1, 2; (SA) Trade Standards Act 1979 Pts III-V. See also **Industry standard; Mandatory standard; Standards Association of Australia standard**.

Set Where a bill of exchange is used as a means of payment in international trade, multiple copies of the bill, produced with each part numbered and referring to the other parts, so that each part can be sent by a different means (for example, 'first of exchange' by facsimile confirmed by airmail of hard copy, 'second of exchange' by surface mail). See also **Bill of exchange; Split bill of exchange**.

•**Set-off** A claim made by a defendant against a plaintiff by way of defence and cross claim: *Stehar Knitting Mills Pty Ltd v Southern Textile Converters Pty Ltd* [1980] 2 NSWLR 514. See also **Counterclaim; Cross claim; Equitable set off**.

Banking and finance A common law right by which a debtor is entitled to take into account a debt owed to him or her by the creditor when sued for a debt due to the creditor. Also known as 'combination'. See also **Banker's lien; Lien; Right of combination**.

Bankruptcy The process of adjusting claims in a bankruptcy by which a debt owed by a bankrupt to a creditor is reduced or extinguished by a mutual claim which the bankrupt has against that creditor. See also **Act of bankruptcy; Bankruptcy; Bankruptcy notice; Counterclaim; Cross demand; Debtor; Mutual credits**.

Corporations The reduction of the debt claimed by a creditor to the extent of any amount owed by that creditor to the debtor. Set-off is allowed where there have been 'mutual credits, mutual debts or other mutual dealings' between the insolvent company and the other party, except if, at the time of giving credit to (or receiving credit from) the company, the person had notice of the fact that the company was insolvent: Corporations Law s 553C. See also **Proof of debt; Winding up**.

Settle 1. To resolve a dispute or proceedings. A settlement of a dispute or proceedings may be documented by terms of settlement, a deed of release or consent orders. 2. To check and finalise the contents of a document. See also **Deed of release; Settlement; Terms of settlement**.

Settled price 1. The price which a clearing house of a futures exchange uses to mark open positions to the futures market each business day. 2. The price used by a clearing house on the settlement day of a futures or option contract. Also known as 'settlement price'. See also **Clearing house**.

•**Settlement** A disposition of property; the compromise or resolution of a claim or dispute.

Bankruptcy The act of disposing of property with the intention that the property will be retained in some form by the person receiving it. Settlements of property by someone who becomes a bankrupt and which lack good faith or valuable consideration in return, can be void against a trustee in bankruptcy: (CTH) Bankruptcy Act 1966 s 120(1). See also **Good faith; Purchaser for valuable consideration**.

Practice and procedure The compromise of a claim: for example (NSW) Commercial Arbitration Act 1984 s 27. A party may make an open offer to settle or compromise either in court during the hearing of an action (*Bates v Nelson* (1973) 6 SASR 149 at 158) or out of court at any stage of the proceedings before final judgment (*Watt v Watt* (1988) 12 Fam LR 589). See also **Without prejudice**.

Real property 1. A transfer of property to be held by persons in succession, such as a life estate and remainder: for example (NSW) Conveyancing Act 1919 s 7(2). See also **Conveyance**.

Trusts 1. A procedure by which a person (the 'settlor') can create a trust. The settlor disposes of his or her interest in the property by vesting the property in a trustee, following necessary steps to pass the legal interest to the trustee, and the trustee agrees to hold the property subject to trusts for nominated beneficiaries. The settlor must intend to create a trust if it is to be enforceable in a court of equity: *Aboriginal Development Commission v Treka Aboriginal Arts and Crafts Ltd* [1984] 3 NSWLR 502. 2. Every non-testamentary disposition of (or in relation to) property that may take effect after the death of the disponor, made without consideration or for a consideration of less than the monetary value of the property: (VIC) Probate Duty Act 1962 s 4. See also **Beneficiary; Settlor; Trust; Trustee**.

Settlement day The day upon which persons holding an open position make or take delivery under deliverable futures contracts, or settle in cash in the case of cash settled contracts. See also **Cash settled futures contract; Futures contract; Open position**.

Settlor A person who creates a trust by manifesting a sufficiently certain intention that a trust was intended in favour of one or more beneficiaries or purposes recognised as valid objects of a trust. See also **Beneficiary; Donee; Donor; Trust**.

Severable contract 1. A contract which is not entire, and from which it is possible to sever terms. 2. A contract in which the parties have divided the contract price into a number of instalments each corresponding to a definite proportion of the other party's performance. See also **Entire contract; Performance; Severance**.

Several liability Legal responsibility which is divisible or separable; liability capable of being severed, separated, or divided between two or more tortfeasors so that each tortfeasor is only partially responsible for the damage caused. See also **Concurrent liability; Concurrent tortfeasors**.

Several promise 1. A promise made by two or more co-promisors which is cumulative, so that if it takes the form 'A separately promises C, and B separately promises C, to pay C $1000', then A and B each promise to pay $1000, that is, $2000 in all. 2. A promise made to two or more co-promisees which is cumulative, being of the form 'A promises B to pay B $1000 and A promises C to pay C $1000', there being two promises, obliging A to pay $2000 in all. See also **Co-promisee; Co-promisor; Joint and several promise; Joint promise**.

•**Severance** The act of dividing or breaking off into parts.

Contract Removal from a contract of a term or part of a term that is void or illegal so as to save the remainder of the contract. See also **Qualified covenant**.

Real property The division of an interest in property into two or more parts. For example, fixtures can be severed from the land of which they form a part and a joint tenancy can be severed to become a tenancy in common. In a joint tenancy, all of the owners of the property hold the property between them, but are not considered to hold individual shares in the property. In a tenancy in common, the owners of the property hold specific apportioned shares of the property. Severance of a joint tenancy can be effected in several ways: *Corin v Patton* (1990) 169 CLR 540; 92 ALR 1. See also **Co-ownership; Joint tenancy; Tenancy in common**.

Sex discrimination The less favourable treatment of a person than another because of their sex, marital status or pregnancy or potential pregnancy or family responsibilities. The (CTH) Sex Discrimination Act 1984 gives effect to the Convention on the Elimination of all Forms of Discrimination Against Women 1979. Discrimination on the basis of sex is also unlawful pursuant to all Australian State and Territory anti-discrimination legislation: (NSW) Anti-Discrimination Act 1977 s 24; (VIC) Equal Opportunity Act 1995 s 6; (QLD) Anti-Discrimination Act 1991 s 7; (SA) Equal Opportunity Act 1984 s 29(2); (WA) Equal Opportunity Act 1984 s 8; (ACT) Discrimination Act 1991 s 7; (NT) Anti-Discrimination Act 1992 s 19. See also **Discrimination**.

•**Sexual harassment** An unwelcome sexual advance or an unwelcome request for sexual favours or engaging in other unwelcome conduct of a sexual nature in circumstances in which a reasonable person, having regard to all the circumstances, would have anticipated that the person harassed would be offended, humiliated, or intimidated. Sexual harassment is unlawful: (CTH) Sex Discrimination Act ss 28A, 28B, 28L; (VIC) Equal Opportunity Act 1995 ss 85-95; (QLD) Anti-Discrimination Act 1991 ss 118-120; (SA) Equal Opportunity Act 1984 s 87; (WA) Equal Opportunity Act 1984 ss 24-26; (ACT) Discrimination Act 1991 ss 58-64; (NT) Anti-Discrimination Act 1992 s 22. See also **Anti-discrimination legislation**.

Shadow director A person who has not been appointed to the board of directors of a company, but is a director because the duly appointed directors follow his or her instructions. A shadow director includes a person in accordance with whose directions or instructions the directors are accustomed to act: Corporations Law s 60(1)(b). See also **Director; Directors' duties; Executive director; Nominee director**.

Sham transaction A transaction in which the parties intend not to create those legal rights and obligations that they give the appearance of creating: *Sharrment Pty Ltd v Official Trustee in Bankruptcy* (1988) 13 FCR 449; 82 ALR 530 at 537. A sham transaction is used to conceal a real transaction: *Scott v FCT (No 2)* (1966) 40 ALJR 265 at 279.

•**Share 1.** A security issued by a company representing part ownership in the company, entitling the holder to participate in the distribution of the company's profits and, when the company is wound up, its surplus assets. **2.** The interest of a shareholder in a company, measured by a sum of money: *Borland's Trustee v Steel Bros & Co Ltd* [1901] 1 Ch 279. When allotted, a share is regarded as a legal chose in action and is affected by the laws applicable to dealings with personal property. See also **Ordinary share; Preferred ordinary share; Securities**.

Share buy-back The acquisition by a company of its own shares or interests in them. Share buy-backs may contravene the maintenance of capital principle and are, subject to exceptions, prohibited: Corporations Law s 205(1)(b). Self-acquisition schemes are regulated by Corporations Law Pt 2.4 Div 4A. See also **Authorised buy back; Maintenance of capital; Self-acquisition scheme**.

•**Share capital** The money subscribed for the shares of a company, or what is represented by that money: *Verner v General and Commercial Investment Trust* [1894] 2 Ch 239 at 265; [1891-94] All ER Rep Ext 409. The amount stated in the memorandum is known as the 'authorised' or 'nominal' share capital of the company. It can be any amount, and it can be subsequently altered: s 193. See also **Authorised capital; Par value**.

Share capital clause See **Share capital**.

•**Share certificate** A document under the seal of a company specifying shares held in the company by a member, the nominal value of the shares and the extent to which they are paid-up: Corporations Law s 1087(1). See also **Certification of transfer; Fractional share certificate; Share**.

Share classes In relation to corporations, groups of shares which have the same rights attached to them. A common share class are preference shares, where the common right is that the holder receives interest in priority to other shareholders of different classes: *Re Brighton & Dyke Railway* (1890) 44 Ch D 28 at 38. See also **Preference share**.

Share dividend See **Dividend**.

Share, forfeiture of See **Forfeiture of shares**.

Share, founder's See **Deferred share**.

Share index futures contract A contract by which the parties agree to make an adjustment between them at a specified future time in Australian currency according to whether a specified share index figure (such as the Australian Stock Exchanges All Ordinaries Price Index figure) at that time is greater or less than that index figure at the time of the making of the contract. The difference is determined in accordance with the business rules or the futures market at which the contract was made. All Ordinaries Share Index futures contracts traded on the Sydney Futures Exchange (SFE) can be made for settlement at the end of any month of March, June, September, or December during a period of 18 months from the time of the trade. See also **Futures contract; Sydney Futures Exchange.**

Share index option An option (either put or call) concerning the All Ordinaries Share Price Index or the Twenty Leaders Index. See also **All Ordinaries Index; Call option; Option; Put option; Twenty Leaders Index.**

Share investment plan See **Dividend bonus plan.**

Share option A contract under which one party has a right to decide whether or not to purchase the shares at some future time or to require the other party to purchase those shares at the future time. See also **Option.**

Share premium In company accounting, the amount of the excess of the issue price over the par value of a share. The amount of premium received by a company is transferred to a 'share premium account': Corporations Law s 191(1). See also **Share; Share premium account.**

•**Share premium account** 1. In company accounting, an account comprising amounts transferred representing the aggregate of the premiums received by a company on its share issues: Corporations Law s 191(1). 2. An account recording amounts representing premiums received on the issue of shares by a company, and for income tax purposes no other amount: (CTH) Income Tax Assessment Act 1936 s 6(1). See also **Dividend; Share premium.**

Share price futures contract index *Abbr* – SPI futures contract A major futures contract listed on the Sydney Futures Exchange (SFX) based on the All Ordinaries Index. The SPI futures contract is a broad based index representing the weighted index of all shares traded on the Australian Stock Exchange (ASX) and is calculated and disseminated by the ASX. The SFX has listed a futures contract on this index since 1983. See also **Futures contract; Share price index.**

Share price index *Abbr* – SPI An index of Australian shares calculated daily by the Australian Stock Exchange (ASX). It is calculated as an average of the market prices of over 200 listed shares, and expressed in index form. Also known as 'All Ordinaries Index'; 'Australian All Ordinaries Share Price Index' or 'Australian Share Price Index'. See also **Hedging; Share price futures contract index.**

•**Share register** The register that a company must keep showing its members and the shares that each member holds: Corporations Law s 216B(3). See also **Register of members; Share registration.**

Share registration The registration of persons holding shares in a company in the company's register of members. The company must generally register the names of all members: Corporations Law s 216B. A listed public company may introduce a provision in its articles empowering the directors to refuse to register shares acquired by a partial takeover offer unless shareholders have approved the bid by ordinary resolution in general meeting: ss 671-672. See also **Register of members.**

Share seal See **Seal.**

Share splitting The subdivision of shares into shares of smaller value. For example, an authorised capital of $1 million shares divided into 100,000 shares of $10 each may be subdivided into 500,000 shares of $2 each. Share splitting is useful to a listed company whose shares trade at a high market price restricting their marketability and the company would like ownership of its shares to be spread more widely. A company may subdivide its shares only if authorised by the articles: Corporations Law s 193(1). See also **Authorised capital.**

Share subscription prospectus See **Prospectus.**

Share transfer See **Transfer of share.**

Share transmission See **Transfer of share.**

Share warehousing The 'storing' of shares by a friendly shareholder for a person who wishes to acquire a controlling interest without detection. The parties to such actions are sometimes referred to as 'concert parties'. See also **Substantial shareholding; Takeover.**

Share warrant A negotiable instrument which evidences legal ownership of shares. Shares are transferable simply by delivery of the document so that a person who takes it for value in good faith is entitled to the shares it represents free from any defects in the title of the person from whom it is taken: *Webb Hale & Co v Alexandra Water Co* (1905) 21 TLR 572. Companies must not issue share warrants: Corporations Law s 189. Where a body corporate that was not originally a company, but becomes registered as one under Pt 2.2 Div 3, has issued share warrants before its registration day, the bearers of the share warrants are entitled to have their names entered as a member in the company's register of members on surrendering the share warrant: s 141.

Sharebroker A member of a stock exchange or a partner in a partnership that is recognised as a member firm by a stock exchange: (CTH) Securities Industry Act 1980 s 133(1)(b). Sharebrokers buy and sell shares as an agent for a client. As payment for a deal carried out on behalf of a client, a sharebroker receives commission proportionate to the price of the goods sold ('brokerage'). Since 1984, the rates of brokerage have been negotiable. A sharebroker contracts in his or her principal's name and merely acts as a negotiator between the parties and therefore does not have direct physical control or possession of the shares sold. A sharebroker cannot sue or be sued on a contract unless he or she signs a written memorandum with his or her own name: *Fleet v Murton* (1872) LR 7 QB 126; *Fairlie v Fenton* (1870) LR 5 Ex 169. The client who employs a sharebroker must indemnify the sharebroker for any liability he or she incurs under them while acting in execution of his or her authority: *W Noall & Son v Wan* [1970] VR 683. Orders are placed with a broker either at limit, at market, at discretion, or at best. On completion of a purchase or sale, the broker provides a contract note which itemises the number of shares and the price for which they were bought or sold, together with a statement of commission and stamp duty. If selling, the old share certificate must be returned for forwarding to the share register of the company so that a new share certificate may be made out in the name of the new owner. The transferor may sign a transfer form or authorise the broker to validate all transfer forms on the transferor's behalf. Compensation is available under the National Guarantee Fund in respect of losses arising from unauthorised transfers. Also known as 'stockbroker'. See also **At best; At discretion; At limit; At market; Australian Stock Exchange Ltd; Brokerage; Share certificate.**

•**Shareholder** 1. A person registered in a company's register of members as the holder of shares; it does not include an unregistered beneficial owner: *Federal Cmr of Taxation v Patcorp Investments Ltd* (1976) 140 CLR 247; 10 ALR 407. 2. In the (CTH) Income Tax Assessment Act 1936, a shareholder may include a person who is entitled as against the company to be registered, and whom the company is absolutely entitled to register as a member: *Federal Cmr of Taxation v Patcorp Investments Ltd.* Also known as 'company member' or 'member'. See also **Company; Member; Register of members; Share.**

Shareholder listing See **Principal register.**

Shareholder value analysis *Abbr* – SVA An analytical method for establishing the present worth of shareholder value, calculated by discounting the future net earnings of the enterprise to give a net present value. Any estimate of future company earnings must contain a range of qualifications and assumptions.

Shareholders' dividend plan Any plan or scheme which provides the opportunity for holders of securities to accept securities in lieu of dividends or interest payments either in part or in full, at the election of the holder: ASX Listing Rules Definitions. Securities issued by a company pursuant to a shareholder dividend plan must rank pari passu with the class of security in respect of which the dividend has been declared: ASX Listing Rules rule 7.8. The terms of the plan must provide for all shareholders to be able to elect to participate in the plan for either all or only part of their shareholding: rule 7.8.2. Shareholder dividend plans include both dividend reinvestment plans and dividend bonus plans. See also **Class of shares; Dividend; Dividend bonus plan; Dividend reinvestment plan.**

Shareholders' equity See **Equity.**

•**Shareholders' funds** A common description of share capital, comprising a company's paid-up share capital, any amounts held in any share premium account, capital redemption reserve or revenue reserve of the company, and undistributed profits: (CTH) Pooled Development Funds Act 1992 s 4(1). Also known as 'share capital'.

Shareholders' meeting One of the two institutions of corporate governance, the other being the board of directors. The shareholders at these meetings, through voting rights attached to their shares, may vote on resolutions and rectify the company articles. Also known as 'general meeting'. See also **Annual general meeting; Board of directors; General meeting; Statutory meeting.**

Shareholders' rights The rights of a shareholder derived from a series of mutual covenants, such as the articles of association, entered into by all shareholders: *Borland's Trustee v Steel Bros & Co Ltd* [1901] 1 Ch 279. These rights vary according to the specific shareholding but there are statutory constraints on the variation of these rights: Corporations Law ss 197, 198. See also **Articles of association; Memorandum of association; Variation of rights.**

Shares, consolidation of See **Consolidation of shares.**

Shares issued at par Shares issued at face or par value, neither at a premium nor at a discount. One dollar shares in a company are issued (offered for sale) for $1. See also **Discount; Par value; Share premium; Share.**

Shares, subdivision of See **Share splitting.**

Shares, surrender of See **Surrender of shares.**

•**Sheer commercial necessity** A ground in relation to invalidation of a contract. To invalidate a transaction on the ground of economic duress, it is not enough to prove that a party was confronted with a commercial necessity to act and that the necessity is caused by another party's threat or pressure. The pressure must be illegitimate. Whether illegitimacy is shown merely by the overwhelming force of degree of pressure, or requires another element such as the unlawfulness of the threatened action, is unclear at common law: *Barton v Armstrong* [1976] AC 105; *Crescendo Management Pty Ltd v Westpac Banking Corp* (1988) 19 NSWLR 40; *Dimskal Shipping Co SA v International Transport Workers Federation, 'The Evia Luck'* [1992] 2 AC 152. See also **Duress.**

Shelf company A company formed but not actually engaged in any business activities: *Fencott v Muller* (1983) 152 CLR 570; 46 ALR 41. See also **Shelf registration; Shell company.**

Shelf prospectus An American expression denoting a prospectus, usually in respect of debt securities, which has been approved by the regulatory authority but has not been issued. It is incomplete as to details such as the rate of interest offered and awaits the company's decision to complete and issue it when the time is right for borrowing. The purpose is to avoid delays between the decision to borrow and the issue of a prospectus caused by requirements of registration. See also **Pathfinder prospectus.**

Shelf registration The incorporation of a company which is not intended to be used immediately for the conduct of business. Shelf-companies are registered in advance to avoid delays in registering a new company. See also **Shelf company.**

Shell company An expression used in the United Kingdom to denote what in Australia is known as a 'shelf company'. See also **Shelf company.**

Ship broker An agent who transacts business between shipowners and charterers or others who ship cargo. The functions of a ship broker include negotiating terms on behalf of a seller or buyer of a ship, negotiating for the charter of a ship on behalf of a charterer or shipowner, attracting cargo to the ships of the broker's principal, and taking care of the needs of the master, crew and ship on behalf of the shipowner while in port. See also **Brokerage clause; Cargo; Charter; Charterer; Master.**

Shipped bill of lading A bill of lading in which the shipowner acknowledges that the goods are loaded on board: *Associated Packaging Pty Ltd v Sankyo Kaiun Kabushiki Kaisha* [1983] 3 NSWLR 293. Also known as 'on board bill of lading'. See also **Bill of lading**; **On board bill of lading**.

Shipping conference An association of shipowners, the purpose of which is to fix transport rates to be charged, and often the capacity allowable, on each trade route. These cartel arrangements are frequently threatened by non-conference outsiders who seek a larger share of the trade, particularly the more lucrative parts of it.

Shipping note *Abbr* – SN A document prepared by a shipper setting out the consignment being sent forward for carriage and sent to the shipowner or its agent. Also known as 'shipping order'. See also **Advice note**; **Charterer**; **Consignee**; **Consignment**; **Consignor**.

• **Shop** Any building or place, or portion of a building or place, in which goods are exposed or offered for sale by retail: for example (NSW) Factories, Shops and Industries Act 1962 s 9. See also **Shop premises**.

• **Shop premises** 1. Generally, premises at which goods are retailed to the public. 2. In some of the legislative schemes regulating commercial tenancies, premises at which services are provided to the public, or at which the supply of services is negotiated: (NSW) Retail Leases Act 1994 s 3; (SA) Retail Shop Leases Act 1995 s 3. Also known as 'retail shop'. See also **Business premises**; **Retail shop lease**; **Retail shop premises**; **Shop**; **Shopping complex**.

Shop steward An active union member in a particular enterprise or workplace who is a representative of the union in that workplace. The shop steward acts for the workers in dealings with management and with the union leadership. The steward's functions also include encouraging union membership and collecting dues. See also **Trade union**.

• **Shopping complex** A group of two or more retail shops located in one building or in adjacent buildings and subject to the same ownership, management, or control: (SA) Retail Shop Leases Act 1995 s 3(1). In New South Wales a 'retail shopping centre' is similarly defined, save that it requires a cluster of at least five retail shops: (NSW) Retail Leases Act 1994 s 3. Also known as 'shopping centre'. See also **Shop premises**; **Retail shop premises**.

Short One who sells futures assuming they will be able to repurchase the futures later at a lower cost. See also **Short selling**.

Short delivery In maritime law, delivery of a lesser amount of cargo than that shown in the bill of lading. The contract of carriage may allow the charterer to deduct a specified amount from the freight payable for such short delivery. See also **Bill of lading**; **Cargo**; **Charterer**; **Contract of carriage**; **Freight**; **Rate of freight**; **Shortage**.

Short hedger The sale of a future to hedge against holdings of commodities. See also **Futures contract**; **Buying hedge**.

Short interest 1. In short selling, the total amount of shares that have been sold short but are not yet purchased to cover the short position. 2. In marine insurance law, the shipping of less than the full cargo insured for. Where there is a short interest the assured becomes entitled to a return of the premium proportionate to the shortage: *Forbes v Aspinall* (1811) 13 East 323; 104 ER 394. See also **Short position**; **Short selling**.

Short position Descriptive of a situation in which a trader sells securities not actually owned.

Short selling 1. The contracting to deliver at some future time more of a particular stock than is actually held at the time of the contract. 2. A sale of an item by a seller who does not own it but who believes that it can be acquired at a cost lower than the sale price before the due date for delivery. See also **Arbitrage transaction**.

Shortage 1. A quantity of cargo not delivered or short delivered. 2. Goods shown on a ship's manifest which cannot be found when the cargo is discharged. See also **Cargo**; **Goods**; **Short delivery**.

• **Shortfall** 1. The amount by which a thing is deficient or inadequate. 2. Where a company makes a rights issue of securities to its shareholders or when a company offers securities to the public, the failure of offerees to take up all the securities offered. In order to ensure the success of a public issue, the company will have entered into an agreement with an underwriter who is bound to take up any shortfall. In a rights issue by any sizeable company, there is usually a technical shortfall because a small percentage of persons on the register of members are dead or neglectful of business. If there is an underwriter in a rights issue, he or she may gain from that technical shortfall where, as is usually the case, the post-offer market price is higher than the issue price. See also **Prospectus**; **Underwriter**.

Shortlanded cargo Cargo, shown on a ship's manifest, which is not discharged at the port to which it was consigned. The ship's agent usually makes inquiry at other ports of discharge during the voyage to ascertain whether the missing cargo has been discharged at one of those ports. The inquiry is made by a document known as a cargo tracer. See also **Cargo**.

• **Short-term employee** A person employed for a short term only, such as a period of less than three months: (CTH) Public Service Act 1922 s 82AD(4). Such employees are taken on when the employer requires temporary assistance in the performance of particular duties. The employment may be extended in accordance with the needs of the employer.

Short-term money market A money market comprising an authorised dealer based money market and an unofficial money market. The authorised dealer based market was established in 1959 by the Reserve Bank of Australia, making available 'lender of last resort' facilities to selected dealers. The dealers may borrow from the Reserve Bank for a minimum seven days, but at a rate designed to discourage excessive use of that facility. The authorised dealers must have at least 70 per cent of their assets in Commonwealth government securities. Every day, financial institutions place money with the short-term money market dealers, who buy bonds and other securities while offering a rate of interest to the depositor. Money placed with the market is available at call, or up to seven days' notice. The dealers are required to consult regularly with the Reserve Bank on all money market matters, furnishing detailed information about their portfolios, operations, interest rates, balance sheets, and profit and loss accounts. The Reserve Bank may sell short-dated Commonwealth government securities to the authorised dealers by way of open market operations. See also **Authorised dealer; Money market; Money market dealer; Reserve Bank of Australia.**

Show of hands A method of voting on a resolution at a general meeting of a company where hands held up are counted and the result is declared, regardless of the number of votes to which each member is entitled, and without considering proxies. Unless excluded by the articles, the common law rule that questions arising at a meeting are to be decided in the first instance by a show of hands applies. The articles may provide that, on a show of hands, every person present who is a member or a representative if a member is to have one vote: for example Corporations Law Sch 1 Table A art 49. Members may demand for voting on a poll instead of a show of hands: s 248. See also **Articles of association; General meeting; Poll; Shareholder.**

Sick leave A paid leave of absence from work while an employee is temporarily unable to work by reason of illness or injury. Provision for sick leave may be contained in an industrial award or agreement. See also **Workers' compensation.**

Sight bill An instrument, equivalent to a bill of exchange, payable on demand. See also **Bill of exchange.**

•**Sign** To affix a person's name to a document: *Geo Thompson (Aust) Pty Ltd v Vittadello* [1978] VR 199. A person can sign a bill with a rubber stamp, and by analogy a computer printed name or other printed script. 2. A device used to convey information or a command to people by words, pictures or lights. See also **Acceptor; Bill of exchange; Company seal; Drawer; Indorser; Signature.**

Signature A person's mark on a document which indicates his or her intention to be bound by its contents. See also **Procuration signature; Sign; Signed, sealed and delivered.**

•**Signed, sealed and delivered** A formula typically found at the end of a deed, indicating that the parties have signed it, sealed it (that is, have affixed their seals), and delivered it (that is, regard it as presently binding on them). See also **Deed; Deed under seal; Delivery; Seal; Sealed documents; Signature.**

•**Significant cash transaction** A cash transaction involving the physical transfer of currency from one person to another in an amount of not less than $10,000: (CTH) Financial Transaction Reports Act 1988 s 3(1). See also **Approved cash carrier; Australian Transaction Reports and Analysis Centre; Cash dealer; Identifying cash dealer.**

Signification Notification or communication by a drawee to the person entitled to a bill of exchange of the drawee's acceptance of the bill. See also **Acceptance; Acceptor; Assent by the drawee; Bill of exchange; Delivery; Drawee; Drawer.**

Signing of a charterparty The execution of a contract of charterparty. The agreement may be signed by the shipowners and charterers, or by a broker or agent. In the latter case, care must be exercised as to the capacity in which the broker or agent signs the contract, otherwise the agent may be legally liable for any misrepresentation or inaccuracies which the agreement contains or on which it is based. There are various titles under which a broker or agent may sign a charterparty: for example, 'as agent for the charterer', 'as agent for the shipowner', 'as agent', 'as agent only'. See also **Affreightment; Charterer; Charterparty; Contract of carriage; Sea cargo agent; Ship broker.**

Silence Failure to communicate. A contract is not made simply by an offeree's silence after an offeror informs an offeree that silence in reply to the offer will be taken as acceptance, even if the offeree forms, but does not attempt to communicate, an intention to accept: *Felthouse v Bindley* (1861) 11 CB(NS) 869; 142 ER 1037. See also **Acceptance; Bilateral contract; Offer; Unilateral contract.**

Silent partner A member of a partnership by virtue of a capital contribution who does not play an active role in the day-to-day operation and administration of the business. A silent partner is jointly and severally liable for any debts incurred by the partnership and equally entitled to share in the profits of the business. Also known as 'sleeping partner'. See also **Dormant partner.**

Simple contract A contract that is not special. Consideration is an essential element of a simple contract, unlike contracts which are described as 'special', 'specialty', 'formal' or 'under seal'. See also **Consideration; Formal contract; Simple contract debt; Special contract.**

Simple contract debt A debt arising out of a contract not made under seal (a deed), but orally or in writing. See also **Simple contract.**

Singapore Interbank Offered Rate *Abbr* – SIBOR The rate of interest charged among banks in the Singapore interbank market. Funds are advanced to customers at a rate above SIBOR. See also **London Interbank Offered Rate.**

Singapore International Monetary Exchange *Abbr* – SIMEX An offspring of the old Gold Exchange in Singapore, an international financial futures exchange trading in gold, foreign currencies, and United States Treasury bond futures. It was established in 1984 being linked with the Chicago Mercantile Exchange. Traders are able to buy and sell futures contracts under a 'mutual offset' arrangement between the two exchanges. The exchange is supported by the Monetary Authority of Singapore.

Singapore Stock Exchange An international stock exchange with substantial share capitalisation. The capitalisation was substantially reduced by a decision of the Malaysian government in 1989 to sever the long-standing ties between the Kuala Lumpur Stock Exchange and the Singapore Stock Exchange. It was felt that the Kuala Lumpur exchange was too vulnerable to events in Singapore. Consequently, Malaysian companies were compelled to withdraw from the Singapore Exchange. Singapore had until then listed Malaysian companies, with Singapore handling about 50 per cent of the total turnover of Malaysian shares traded on both exchanges. In losing Malaysian stocks, turnover in Singapore fell by about 40 per cent. The Straits Times Industrial Index monitors prices on the Singapore exchange.

Single bond A bond for the payment of a certain sum of money without any condition in, or annexed to, the deed. It is contrasted with a double or conditional bond. The expression 'single bond' now usually signifies a bond given by one obligor only. See also **Bond; Double bond; Obligor**.

•**Single business** A business carried on by a single employer, or by two or more employers as a joint venture or common enterprise, or a single project or undertaking. A single business includes activities carried on by the Commonwealth, a State or a Territory, or a body, association, office or other entity established for a public purpose by a Commonwealth, State or Territory law: (CTH) Industrial Relations Act 1988 s 170LB. See also **Certified agreement; Enterprise bargaining**.

Single entry A simple system of accounting and record keeping usually associated with small businesses in which most transactions are recorded in a single record. Formal journals and ledgers which are the basis of the double-entry system are not maintained, nor are general journal entries made. See also **Double entry**.

•**Sinking fund** An interest bearing investment in securities set aside to provide resources to pay a debt or redeem a capital stock upon conversion of the investment into cash. A sinking fund is kept separate from the organisation's other assets. See also **Sinking fund method**.

Sinking fund method A method for calculating and allowing for the depreciation of an asset. The purpose is to build up a fund by equal periodic instalments in order to accumulate a certain sum by a given date for the replacement of an asset (or other specific purpose). The interest or other earnings on the fund are periodically reinvested and allowed to accumulate with the periodic contribution of principal. The sinking fund instalment, consisting for example of an annual payment, is equal to the original or historic capital cost of the asset multiplied by a sinking fund factor. See also **Reducing balance method; Straight line method**.

•**Site value** The sum of money that an owner could reasonably be expected to obtain in the market for a parcel of land held in fee simple, free of any lease, mortgage or other charge and assuming that any improvements to the land had not been made: (NSW) Strata Titles (Leasehold) Act 1986 s 180(8)(e), Sch 2; (VIC) Subdivision Act 1988 s 3(1). See also **Fee simple**.

Skill and judgment Professional or trade expertise, practical or familiar knowledge. A consumer is entitled to expect that goods are fit for the purpose for which they are sold except where the circumstances show that the consumer does not rely on the skill and judgment of the seller, or it would be unreasonable for the consumer to do so, in relation to the purpose for which the goods are proposed to be used: for example (CTH) Trade Practices Act 1974 s 71; (NSW) Sale of Goods (Vienna Convention) Act 1986 Sch 1 Art 35. See also **Fitness for purpose; Merchantable quality**.

Sleeping partner A partner who takes no active part in the management of the partnership business, but who is a full partner in every other respect. A sleeping partner may contribute nothing to the partnership: *Pooley v Driver* (1876) 5 Ch D 458; 11 ER 431. Also known as 'dormant partner'. See also **Dormant partner; Partnership agreement**.

Slip An insurance document in the form of a slip of paper setting out the basic terms of the proposed insurance, describing the risk to be insured: *General Accident, Fire and Life Assurance Corp Ltd v Tanter (The Zephyr)* [1984] 1 All ER 35. A slip is subsequently taken to various insurers who accept proportions of the total risk.

Small business employer In industrial law, an employer of not more than 20 employees, or an employer with a management structure under which all people employed are subject to the direct supervision and control of the employer (or the employer's chief executive): (NSW) Industrial Relations Act 1991 (repealed) s 187.

Smith, Adam (1723-90) Scottish Enlightenment philosopher and author of *Lectures on Jurisprudence* (1762-64), *The Theory of Moral Sentiments* (1759) and *The Wealth of Nations* (1776). His ideas provide the foundations for certain schools of economic rationalism. Smith divided history into four ages: those of hunters, shepherds, agriculture, and commerce. This concept was developed by Friedrich von Hayek, who conceived of the free market as the result of the evolution of legal, social and religious customs. See also **Economic theories of law**.

Smithsonian Agreement An agreement reached by the Group of Ten countries in Washington DC in 1971 to re-establish a system of fixed rates of exchange. The gathering was held at the Smithsonian Institution. Under the agreement, the US dollar was devalued in terms of gold. Within the total permitted range of fluctuations against the dollar of 4.5 per cent (the tunnel), the rates for the participating European currencies at any one time were restricted to a band of 2.25 per cent (the snake); hence the expression 'the snake in the tunnel'. Thus, the European currencies were tied much more tightly to each other and the US dollar compared with other world currencies. However, as a result of exchange market pressures, first the tunnel and then the snake disappeared. The snake was succeeded in 1979 by the European Monetary System and a new currency, the European Currency Unit was created. The Smithsonian Agreement emerged as a result of a breakdown in the original Bretton Woods Agreement. See also **Bretton Woods Agreement**.

Smurfing The conversion of small denominations of 'street money' ($5 or $10 notes) into more easily portable currency and monetary instruments such as $100 notes, bank cheques, money orders, and travellers cheques. Smurfing is normally resorted to for the purpose of money-laundering. See also **Laundering**.

Société à Responsabilité Limitée   *Abbr* – SARL
Fr. The French, Luxembourg and Swiss equivalent of a private limited liability company.

Société Anonyme *Abbr* – SA *Fr.* The Belgian, French, Luxembourg and Swiss equivalent of a corporation.

Social Welfare Union case A case concerned with the nature of an 'industrial dispute'. The question was whether project workers employed to run a Community Youth Support Scheme (CYSS) could be said to work in an 'industry' and so be parties to an industrial dispute. The High Court held that an industrial dispute had arisen. The words 'industrial dispute' are not a technical or legal expression; the words are to be given their popular meaning, which includes disputes between employers and employees about the terms and conditions of work: *R v Coldham; Ex parte Australian Social Welfare Union* (1983) 153 CLR 297; 47 ALR 225. Also known as 'CYSS case'. See also **Industrial dispute**.

Sociedad Anonima *Abbr* – SA *Sp.* The Spanish equivalent of a public corporation.

Sociedade Anonima de Responsibilidade Limitada *Abbr* – CSA *Portuguese*. The Portuguese equivalent of a corporation.

Sociedade pro Quotas *Abbr* – Limitada *Portuguese*. The Portuguese equivalent of a limited company.

Società per azioni *Abbr* – SpA *Italian*. The Italian equivalent of a public corporation.

•**Society** A financial cooperative whose objects include raising funds by subscription, deposit, or otherwise as authorised, for example under the (QLD) Financial Institutions Code 1992), applying funds in providing financial accommodation to its members within the confines of the Code and the society's own rules, encouraging savings among members; and promoting cooperative enterprise, providing programs and services to its members, and assisting its members to meet their financial needs: for example (QLD) Financial Institutions Code 1992 s 109(2). A building society, credit union, or other body registered as a society under, for example, Australian Financial Institutions Commission Code 1992 s 3 or (QLD) Financial Institutions Code 1992 s 3 is a society regulated by the financial institutions scheme. See also **Association**; **Building society**; **Credit union**; **Financial institutions scheme**.

Society for Worldwide Interbank Financial Telecommunications *Abbr* – SWIFT A cooperative organisation created and owned mainly by European and American banks that operates a network which facilitates the exchange of payment and other financial messages between financial institutions (including broker-dealers and securities companies) throughout the world. A SWIFT payment message is an instruction to transfer funds; the exchange of funds (settlement) subsequently takes place over a payment system or through correspondent banking relationships. The system serves more than 1000 banks in Western Europe, North America, Latin America, Japan, Hong Kong, Singapore, Australia and South Africa. SWIFT members are able to transmit transactions among themselves.

Socio-technical management system *Abbr* – STMS A system of production in which most management decisions are delegated to employees. Workers are formed into teams with responsibility for certain parts of an operation. Each team hires and fires, sets working hours, decides on holidays, overtime, the training of new members, identifying and solving problems, ordering supplies, and is responsible for delivering its goods to the next team in the plant. Group managers act as counsellors and advisers with the board of directors still responsible for corporate strategy and future directions. The system has been used in Europe and North America; some Australian companies are now applying the principle.

Soft currency A currency that is weakening in its exchange rates with other currencies; or weaker than previously quoted.

Soft dollars A practice on Wall Street where part of the commission earned by brokers is spent on market research for the benefit of clients; this expenditure is known as soft dollars. Soft dollar brokers in effect provide a rebate to their customers. Indirectly, the money managers who pay the brokerage commission also buy research data without writing a cheque. Money managers are said to be credited with one soft dollar for every two hard dollars.

Soft landing The easing of an over-heated economy through the use of monetary policy and fiscal policy into a more balanced state, without initiating a recession.

Soft loan Money lent on concessional terms, usually at lower interest rates or with longer maturity periods than could be obtained in the commercial lending market.

Soft sell A low-pressure approach to selling, in which the buyer has no feeling of being coerced. In contrast, the hard sell involves pressure, manipulation, and aggression.

•**Sold** Given in exchange for consideration. Although the term 'sold' generally implies the consent of the person giving the property and taking the consideration, compulsory acquisition often also falls within statutory provisions applying to property 'sold'. For example, shares compulsorily acquired under takeover schemes are 'sold' within (CTH) Income Tax Assessment Act 1936 s 26AAA: *Federal Cmr of Taxation v Salenger* (1988) 19 FCR 378; 81 ALR 25.

Sole corporation An entity consisting of one person only and his or her successors. These types of corporations were limited to ecclesiastical or royal office and were not relevant to the development of the modern business corporation: *Archbishop of Perth v 'AA' to 'JC' inclusive: 'DJ' v Trustees of Christian Brothers* (1995) 18 ACSR 333. See also **Corporation sole**.

•**Sole trader 1.** A person who trades alone, without the use of a company structure or partners, and who bears alone full responsibility for the activities of the business. **2.** A person who is a member organisation of a securities exchange: Corporations Law s 9.

•**Solicitor** A class of legal practitioner. Generally, a solicitor will be a member of a local association of legal practitioners practising as solicitors, usually known as a law society. See also **Bar Council**; **Solicitor**.

•**Solicitor-General** The government's most senior law officer after the Attorney-General: (CTH) Law Officers Act 1964 s 5. The statutory functions of the office include acting as counsel for the executive government, the provision of opinions to the Attorney-General on matters of law and such other functions ordinarily performed by counsel as may be requested by the Attorney-General: s 12. See also **Attorney-General**; **Counsel**.

Solus agreement An agreement by which a buyer agrees to buy all goods for resale from another person, and to sell the goods of that other person and no other at the buyer's premises. See also **Contract in restraint of trade**; **Exclusive dealing**; **Restraint of trade**.

Solvency margins A specified margin, which insurance companies must maintain, between the value of their assets and the amount of their liabilities, to ensure their ability to pay debts as and when they become due. A solvency margin of the greater of $2m, 20 per cent of its premium income during the last preceding financial year, or 15 per cent of its outstanding claims provision for the last preceding financial year must be maintained by insurance companies in order to be granted authority to carry on an insurance business: (CTH) Insurance Act 1973 s 29.

•**Solvent** Able to pay all of one's debts, as and when they become due and payable: Corporations Law s 95A. This indicates that the total value of the assets exceeds the amount of liabilities. See also **Bankruptcy**; **Insolvency**; **Preference**; **Readily realisable asset**; **Trustee in bankruptcy**.

Source of income For income tax purposes, the source of an item of income which is determined by common law principles as modified by any applicable legislation. See also **Assessable income**; **Derived**; **Income**.

Special agent An agent who has authority to act on some particular occasion or purpose that is not within the ordinary course of the agent's business or profession: *Robinson v Tyson* (1888) 9 LR (NSW) 297; *Marriott v General Electric Co Ltd* (1935) 53 CLR 409. See also **Agency**; **Agent**; **Apparent authority**; **Estoppel**; **General agent**; **Principal**; **Universal agent**.

Special cargo In shipping, cargo needing extraordinary attention or supervision due to its value or fragility. Freight on valuable cargo is often paid in proportion to the value, and is known as ad valorem freight. See also **Ad valorem freight**; **Cargo**; **Dangerous cargo**; **Freight**; **Perishable goods**.

•**Special contract** A contract expressed in an instrument under seal (that is, in the form of a deed). A special contract is enforceable despite the absence of consideration. A contract which is not 'special' is referred to as a 'simple contract'. Also known as 'contract under seal'. See also **Deed**; **Formal contract**; **Simple contract**; **Specialty**.

•**Special damages** In contract law, damages awarded under the second limb of the rule in *Hadley v Baxendale* (1854) 9 Ex 341; 156 ER 145 for losses reasonably supposed to have been in the contemplation of both parties, at the time they made the contract, as the probable result of the breach: for example *President of India v La Pintada Compania Navigacion SA* [1985] AC 104; 2 All ER 773. See also **Breach of contract**; **Contract**; **Damages**; **General damages**; **Hadley v Baxendale, rule in**; **Tort**.

Tort **1.** Damages awarded for loss actually suffered and expenditure actually incurred. Common examples are medical expenses and loss of income. **2.** Damages in respect of a tort that is not actionable per se: *Lachoume v Broughton* (1903) 3 SR (NSW) 475. **3.** Damages that are peculiar to a particular plaintiff in that they are over and above those suffered by the public at large: *Benjamin v Storr* (1874) LR 9 CP 400. See also **Damages**; **Damages at large**; **General damages**.

Special drawing rights *Abbr* – SDRs An international reserve currency system created by the International Monetary Fund. It provides for a new type of money (known as paper gold) to serve as the first international legal tender. The first allocation of SDRs took place in 1970. SDRs are in effect supranational money whose value is pegged to the currencies of the Group of Seven countries. See also **International Monetary Fund**; **Official reserves**.

Special facts doctrine An American rule which relates to a director's duty of disclosure to shareholders. Where there are special circumstances or facts present which might make it inequitable if the director were not to provide information to the shareholders, a duty to disclose will arise and concealment of relevant information may amount to fraud: *Taylor v Wright* 69 Cal App 2d 371; 159 P 2d 980 at 985.

•**Special indorsement** An indorsement specifying the person to whom, or to whose order, a bill of exchange is payable: (CTH) Bills of Exchange Act 1909 s 39(2). See also **Bill of exchange**; **Indorsee**; **Indorsement**; **Indorsement in blank**; **Payee**.

•**Special notice** The notice that must be given to the members of a company when a special resolution is put before the company. Where such a resolution is proposed, 21 days notice of the meeting must be given (Corporations Law s 253) unless 95 per cent of members otherwise consent: s 253(4). See also **General meeting**; **Ordinary resolution**; **Special resolution**.

Special offering In the United States, an offering of securities so large it requires approval from the Securities and Exchange Commission and has specific rules relating to the offer. See also **Securities and Exchange Commission**.

Special price A reduced or discounted price which must be a genuine price in that the retailing corporation must be able to show that the normal price indicated was the price at which the good or service had been sold for a reasonable period of time in a reasonable quantity, or otherwise it may constitute illegal 'bait advertising': (CTH) Trade Practices Act 1974 s 56; (NSW) Fair Trading Act 1987 s 51. See also **Bait advertising**; **Misleading or deceptive conduct**; **Retail sale**.

•**Special resolution 1.** In corporations law, a resolution passed by a majority in number and at least 75 per cent in value of the creditors present personally (or by attorney or by proxy) at a meeting of creditors, and voting on the resolution: for example (CTH) Bankruptcy Act 1966 s 5(1). **2.** In relation to voluntary associations, a resolution in a meeting for which 21 days notice of the meeting and terms of the resolution to be given is required, and which must be approved by three-quarters of the members present and voting (whether in person or by proxy if the association's rules so allow): for example (NSW) Associations Incorporation Act 1984 s 5. See also **Association; Creditors' meeting; Ordinary resolution; Proxy; Resolution.**

Special service providers *Abbr* – SSPs In finance law, entities incorporated under the Australian Financial Institutions Commission's Code, owned by building societies for their mutual benefit. Typically, SSPs are established to access and provide services to member societies which would be uneconomic or otherwise unavailable for individual societies to source, particularly in the area of settlement and electronic funds transfer. See also **Australian Financial Institutions Commission.**

Specialisation A division of labour. The advantage of specialisation lies in the fact that individuals gain greater skill and dexterity by doing one job rather than several. This division of labour also facilitates the use of machinery, resulting in a substantial improvement in productivity. However, labour through becoming specialised faces difficulties if suitable avenues of employment decline.

Specialist block purchase An American term denoting a transaction where a specialist on a stock exchange buys a large block of securities either to sell for his or her own account or to try and place with another block buyer and seller. United States exchange rules require that such transactions be executed only when the securities cannot be absorbed in the regular market. See also **Specialist block sale.**

Specialist block sale The sale of a block of securities from a trader to another block purchaser. It is the opposite of a specialist block purchase. See also **Specialist block purchase.**

Specialists' book An American term denoting the records maintained by a specialist on the stock exchange. Such records include the specialist's own inventory of securities, market orders to sell short, and limit and stop orders that other stock exchange members have placed with the specialist. The orders are listed in chronological sequence. See also **Exchange distribution; Market maker; New York Stock Exchange.**

•**Specialty 1.** A contract under seal; a deed. Also known as 'agreement by specialty', 'formal contract' or 'special contract': *Rann v Hughes* (1778) 7 TR 350n; 101 ER 1014. **2.** A debt secured by a promise contained in a deed. In some circumstances, a debt need not be evidenced by a deed in order to be a specialty; a debt owed by the Crown or arising under statute is a specialty even though it is not evidenced by a deed: for example *Royal Trust Co v A-G (Alberta)* [1930] AC 144. **3.** Any money payable by a member of a company to the company under the company's constitution is a specialty debt from the member to the company: Corporations Law s 180(2). Also known as 'specialty debt'. See also **Debt; Deed; Formal contract; Merger; Special contract.**

•**Specific goods** Under the uniform Sale of Goods Acts, goods agreed upon and identified at the time the contract of sale is made, all other goods being termed 'unascertained': for example (NSW) Sale of Goods Act 1923 s 5(s). See also **Fitness for purpose; Future goods; Merchantable quality; Sale of goods legislation; Unascertained goods.**

Specific performance 1. An equitable remedy to compel the execution *in specie* (in its own form) of a contract which requires some definite thing to be done before the transaction is complete and the parties' rights are settled and defined in the manner intended: *J C Williamson Ltd v Lukey* (1931) 45 CLR 282; VLR 221. **2.** In its strict or technical sense, the enforcing of an executory contract by compelling the execution of an assurance to complete it: *Stern v McArthur* (1988) 165 CLR 489; 81 ALR 463. **3.** An order applied to an executed contract requiring the defendant to perform his or her contractual obligation: *Australian Hardwoods Pty Ltd v Cmr for Railways* [1961] 1 All ER 737. Specific performance is available where the common law does not provide a remedy, or where the common law remedy is inadequate: *J C Williamson Ltd v Lukey* (1931) 45 CLR 282; [1931] ALR 157. See also **Damages; Equity; Executed contract; Executory contract; Injunction; Performance.**

•**Specified price** The price below which a good must not be sold, as stipulated by the supplier. See also **Recommended price; Resale price maintenance.**

•**Speculator** In relation to securities, a person who purchases interests in securities with a short term view of selling them later at a price exceeding that originally paid. See also **Dealer; Short selling.**

Spens formula A name given in the United Kingdom to a provision in the terms of issue of a preference share providing that, in the event of a return of capital by the company, the holder will receive the market value of the share if that value is above par value. See also **Maintenance of capital principle; Par value; Valuation.**

Spin-off A separable part of a company which, due to its individual performance, has its activities moved to a new company called the spin-off company. Normally this is done so the new company can raise money by offering shares to the members of the original company or to the public. See also **Company.**

Split bill of exchange A bill of exchange which has been produced in a set of multiple copies, the various indorsed parts being given to different persons by the holder of more than one part. The holder who splits the set is liable on every such part, but subsequent parties are liable only on the part they have indorsed, as if the parts were separate bills: (CTH) Bills of Exchange Act 1909 s 76(2). See also **Bill of exchange; Holder; Indorsement; Set.**

•**Sponsorship** Vouching for or indorsing a person or product.

Consumer protection The action of a commercial or other organisation or a person standing behind some activity and perhaps wholly or partly financing it: *10th Cantanae Pty Ltd v Shoshana Pty Ltd* (1987) 18 FCR 285; 79 ALR 299; 10 IPR 289. See also **Approval; Affiliation; False representation; Misleading or deceptive conduct.**

Spot commodity An actual commodity as distinguished from a future contract. Also known as 'cash commodity' or 'actuals'.

Spot contract On a foreign exchange market, a contract to deliver one currency in exchange for another, usually within two business days from the date of the deal. Also known as 'spot exchange'. Se also **Spot rate**.

Spot market A market for immediate delivery of the product and immediate payment.

Spot price The current market price for a given futures contract or option series. See also **In the money option**; **Option**.

Spot rate The rate of exchange quoted in foreign exchange markets in relation to contracts under which funds must be paid over within two working days. See also **Spot contract**.

•**Spouse** Either member of a married couple in relation to the other.

Taxation and revenue The husband or wife of another person. A spouse includes a de facto husband or wife, but not a divorced husband or wife: (CTH) Income Tax Assessment Act 1936 ss 6(1), 160K(2). See also **Associate**; **Dependant**.

Spread 1. In relation to commodities, the gap in a quotation between buying and selling prices. 2. In relation to foreign exchange, the difference between the buying and selling rates of currencies. 3. In relation to banking, the difference between the borrowing and lending rates for funds. 4. In relation to dealers, the margin between the rate at which they buy from borrowers and the rate at which they sell to investors. 5. In relation to securities, the amount by which the offering price exceeds the face value of the issue. 6. In relation to futures markets, a market position which is simultaneously long and short for the equivalent amount of the same or related commodities.

Spreadsheet A display of financial information into rows or columns to facilitate financial calculations, particularly for accountants. Computer software for spreadsheets allows the information entered into those rows and columns to interact to a prescribed formula so that when the information in one 'cell' changes, the resultant outcomes are also displayed.

Squaring the day The selling by the Reserve Bank of Australia (RBA) on any day of just enough securities to absorb surplus cash in the market, or the buying of just enough to cover a shortfall. The RBA may oversquare or undersquare on any day. To influence the system, the RBA may buy less when the system is 'down', or sell more when the system is 'up' and in surplus. This latter forces the authorised dealers to look for funds in the bank cheque market, either to sell securities or to borrow funds. This may force up interest rates. This action is reversed if the RBA wishes to ease conditions. See also **Reserve Bank of Australia**.

Squeeze out A technique adopted by majority shareholders in a company to exclude minority shareholders from corporate management and to encourage them to dispose of their investment. Common techniques include withholding information about the company's affairs, dismissal of minority members from executive positions, appointing additional directors to reduce the minority's influence at board level, withholding dividends, amendment of articles in terms unfavourable to the minority and allotting share capital to dilute the minority's holding. Minority shareholders may in some circumstances seek redress against squeeze out techniques. Remedies may be available if the action complained of is oppressive and infringes Corporations Law s 260, if it constitutes fraud on the minority, or if it involves a breach of directors' duties. See also **Directors' duties**; **Fraud on the minority**; **Minority interest**; **Oppressive, unfairly prejudicial or unfairly discriminatory conduct**.

St George Bank Formerly a major building society ranking among Australia's top 10 financial institutions, becoming a licensed Australian bank in 1992. St George began as a terminating building society in 1937, converting to a permanent building society in 1954. As a building society, its financial resources far outstripped any other in Australia. In 1990, it became the first building society to enter the corporate bond market by way of a transferable certificate of deposit program.

•**Staff** A body of people employed in some undertaking or carrying out the work of an establishment. People on leave, for example on leave without pay or long service leave, are ordinarily regarded as still being on the staff of their employer: *Johns v Australian Securities Commission* (1992) 35 FCR 146; 108 ALR 409. It includes officers and temporary employees: (NSW) Public Sector Management Act 1988 s 3. See also **Employee**.

Stag In relation to shares an applicant for shares to be issued by a company who does not intend to retain the shares but expects to sell them on a stock exchange for a price exceeding the total of the issue price and the brokerage on the sale. See also **Short selling**.

Stakeholder A person or corporation holding money as a deposit in a conveyancing transaction pending completion of the contract, or holding moneys pending determination of a wager or a claim. See also **Contract**; **Contract for sale of land**; **Conveyance**.

Stale bill of lading A bill of lading received after the vessel to which it refers has arrived at its discharging port and the consignees have already received delivery of the goods covered by the bill. See also **Bill of lading**; **Consignee**; **Waybill**.

Stale cheque A cheque which on its face appears to have been drawn more than 15 months previously: (CTH) Cheques and Payment Orders Act 1986 s 3(5). When a cheque becomes stale, the duty and authority of the drawee bank to pay the cheque are terminated. See also **Cheque**; **Drawee bank**; **Drawer**.

Stale prospectus A prospectus under which no securities are to be allotted or issued as it is greater than 12 months old: Corporations Law s 1040. The same applies to secondary prospectus notices under ss 1040, 1043C. This prohibition does not apply where the issue offer or invitation are excluded, or the prospectus is an excluded prospectus: s 1040(2). A replacement prospectus becomes stale when the prospectus it replaces would be so: s 1024D(3). See also **Prospectus**.

•**Stamp duty** A tax imposed by all Australian States on documents or transactions that affect or record the transfer of the ownership of assets (for example, conveyances of real property, shares and business assets) or the creation of rights in respect of assets (for example, the granting of a lease).

Standard and Poor's A United States corporate rating agency which estimates the likelihood that corporations, institutions or countries may default on their debts.

Standard and Poor's indices *Abbr* – S&P's indices Capitalisation-weighted New York Stock Exchange share market price indices. The S&P500 comprises 500 different companies made up of 400 industrials, 40 utilities, 20 transportation, and 40 financial institutions. Stocks included in the S&P500 account for some 80 per cent of all stocks listed on the New York Stock Exchange. The S&P100 is made up of 92 industrials, one utility, two transportation, and five financial institutions. All the stocks in the S&P100 are included in the S&P500.

Standard cover The minimum cover provided by an insurer in a contract of insurance. The (CTH) Insurance Contracts Act 1984 prescribes the classes of insurance contracts that require standard cover, defines the risks covered, and the minimum amount to be paid by the insurer: (CTH) Insurance Contracts Act 1984 ss 34-36. See also **Cover; Cover note; Interim cover.**

Standard form contract A contract that is not individually negotiated by the parties but contains the same terms for all transactions of that type. Also known as 'contracts of adhesion'.

Standard of contractual duty The degree of care which a promisor must exercise in performing a contractual obligation. See also **Absolute liability; Breach of contract; Reasonable care; Strict liability.**

Standard of liability Either civil or criminal liability, depending on whether it is enforced by civil or criminal courts. The standard of liability is civil in tort or negligence: *Northern Territory v Mengel* (1995) 129 ALR 1. Liability may also be strict, for example in the case of certain statutory offences. See also **Economic loss; Liability; Loss; Negligence; Strict liability; Tort.**

Standard of proof An objective measure for determining whether or not a fact or issue has been proved. See also **Legal burden.**

Tort The degree of certainty with which disputed facts in a criminal or civil action must be established in order to be accepted as proved. In civil actions, the standard of proof is 'on the balance of probabilities': (CTH) Evidence Act 1995 s 140(1); *Rejfek v McElroy* (1965) 112 CLR 517; [1966] ALR 270. See also **Balance of probabilities; Burden of proof.**

Standardisation Where a futures or option contract conforms to a particular standard. For example, exchange traded options often have predetermined exercise prices, expiry dates, types (put or call), and the subject matter of the option is of a specified quality or grade. Standardisation permits fungibility. See also **Fungibility; Futures contract;; Option; Put option.**

•**Standardised agreement** An agreement that is one of two or more agreements, each of which is an agreement of the same kind as the other, or as each of the others, as the case may be: Corporations Law s 9; *Shoreline Currencies (Aust) Pty Ltd v Corporate Affairs Commission (NSW)* (1986) 11 NSWLR 22; 10 ACLR 847; *Carragreen Currency Corp Pty Ltd v Corporate Affairs Commission* (1987) 7 NSWLR 705; 11 ACLR 298.

Standards Association of Australia standard A standard developed under the aegis of the Standards Association of Australia. A Standards Association standard has no particular legal standing (*O'Connor v Hansen Wilckens Hornibrook Constructions Ltd* (1968) 42 ALJR 239; *Chicco v Corporation of the City of Woodville* (1990) Aust Torts Reports ¶81-028) unless it is declared by the Minister, pursuant to (CTH) Trade Practices Act 1974 s 65E(1), to be a consumer product safety standard for the purposes of s 65C or a consumer product information standard for the purposes of s 65D. See also **Consumer product information standard; Consumer product safety standard; Industry standard; Mandatory standard.**

Standby agreement An agreement where options are issued by a company entitling shareholders to purchase additional shares and an investment bank agrees to purchase any unsubscribed rights for resale to the general public.

Standby credit 1. Finance available if it is required. A standby letter of credit may be issued by a bank in support of a commitment which the bank's customer has made to another person. 2. An agreement with the International Monetary Fund (IMF) that funds will be provided by the IMF if required. See also **Letter of credit; International Monetary Fund; Standby letter of credit.**

Standby letter of credit A form of letter of credit, under which the paying bank undertakes to pay a specified sum of money to a named beneficiary on presentation of specified documents by the beneficiary, to another bank. It protects one party against the other party's failure to fulfil his or her obligations. The documents specified usually include a certificate that the primary debtor has defaulted under an underlying contract. The obligation of the paying bank to pay the named beneficiary on presentation of the relevant documents exists independently of the underlying contract. A standby letter of credit is similar in operation and effect to a first demand guarantee. See also **Beneficiary; First demand guarantee; Letter of credit.**

Standing offer A form of tender in which an offer is made to provide goods or services to the inviter of the tender if and when required. Acceptance of the standing offer does not bind the inviter to accept all or any part of the goods or services in question: *Colonial Ammunition Co v Reid* (1900) 21 LR (NSW) 338; 17 WN (NSW) 192. See also **Offer and acceptance.**

Standing order In banking, an instruction from a customer to his or her bank to make a regular payment of a fixed amount to a named party. See also **Banking authority.**

Standover tactics In business, bullying measures, usually threats and intimidation, used to achieve a desired outcome through coercion.

State Bank of South Australia A body corporate managed by a board of directors appointed by the Governor and authorised to carry on the general business of banking within and outside South Australia: (SA) State Bank of South Australia Act 1983 ss 6(2), 7(1), (2). The bank has wide powers and functions which it must manage, realise and otherwise deal with 'to the best advantage of the State': s 19. The bank's liabilities are guaranteed by the State Treasurer: s 21. In some contexts, the bank is the South Australian Asset Management Corporation: s 3. The (SA) State Bank (Corporatisation) Act 1994 provides for the transfer of part of the undertaking of the bank to a public company. See also **Reserve Bank of Australia**.

State Bank of Victoria Until 1991, a bank wholly owned by the Victorian government when it became wholly owned by the Commonwealth Banking Corporation: (VIC) State Bank (Succession of Commonwealth Bank) Act 1990 s 9. Earlier in 1985, the State Bank of Victoria had acquired ownership of the merchant bank Tricontinental. Subsequently, Tricontinental sustained considerable losses, forcing the sale of its parent to the Commonwealth Bank. A Royal Commission into the Tricontinental Group was held in 1990. See also **Commonwealth Bank of Australia; Reserve Bank of Australia**.

•**State industrial authority** A board or court of conciliation or arbitration, or a tribunal, body or person, having authority under a State Act to exercise any power of conciliation or arbitration in relation to industrial disputes within the limits of the State. It includes a special board constituted under a State Act relating to factories: (CTH) Industrial Relations Act 1988 s 4. See also **Industrial dispute; State industrial system**.

State industrial system The system of industrial tribunals established by each of the six States in order to resolve industrial disputes. Most States have structured their industrial systems along the same lines as the Commonwealth, so that conciliation and arbitration functions are exercised by a permanent industrial tribunal and judicial functions are exercised by a court. See also **Federal industrial system; Industrial tribunal; State industrial authority**.

Statement of account A document forwarded monthly by a creditor to a debtor setting out the opening balance, plus additional sales for the month less any payments received during the month, and the outstanding balance as at the end of the month.

Statement of accounting and auditing standards *Abbr* – AAS A statement depicting accounting and auditing methods and indorsed by the national councils of both the Institute of Chartered Accountants in Australia and the Australian Society of Certified Practising Accountants. A statement of accounting and auditing standards requires members of both accounting bodies to adhere to the accounting standards stipulated. Any material departure from the standards must be disclosed in the financial statements.

Statement of Accounting Concepts *Abbr* – SAC Approved statements of the Australian Accounting Standards Board (AASB) which articulate the conceptual framework for general purpose financial reporting. SACs are used to develop accounting standards, and to set out the principles by which matters not presently the subject of specific accounting standards should be resolved. Four SACs have been released: SAC 1 (Definition of the Reporting Entity), SAC 2 (Objective of General Purpose Financial Reporting), SAC 3 (Qualitative Characteristics of Financial Information), SAC 4 (Definition and Recognition of the Elements of Financial Statements). See also **Accounting standards**.

Statement of affairs 1. A document prepared by a debtor or bankrupt giving personal particulars and detailing the person's assets and liabilities: (CTH) Bankruptcy Act 1966 s 6A(2). **2.** In corporations law, a mandatory annexure to a director's declaration of insolvency that must be lodged in order to effect a member's voluntary winding up. See also **Bankrupt; Debtor; Insolvency; Voluntary winding-up**.

Statement of Auditing Standards *Abbr* – AUS Professional standard describing the basic principles which govern the auditor's professional responsibilities and which must be complied with whenever an audit is carried out: Statement of Auditing Standards AUS 1 para 3. In particular, paras 8-13 outline the principles governing the scope of an audit in the public sector. Guidance on the practical application of the principles comprising the standards of auditing is given in Statements of Auditing Practice (AUPs). AUS 1 is prepared by the Auditing Standards Board of the Australian Accounting Research Foundation. See also **Audit guide; Auditing Guidance Release; Auditing standards**.

Statement of changes in financial position A financial statement summarising the funds generated from the operations and others resources applied and changes occurring during the period. The statement details the source of funds received by a business or company and how such funds have been expended.

Statement of changes in net assets A statement showing the changes in financial position adapted to meet the requirements of investment companies. The statement details a reconciliation of the net assets at the beginning of a period with the net assets at the end. Emphasis is placed upon transactions and market value changes which affect the investment portfolio.

•**Statement of claim** A method of commencing proceedings (for example (NSW) Supreme Court Rules 1970 Pt 4 r 1), which consists of a written statement by the plaintiff in an action showing the facts which are to be relied upon to support the claim against the defendant, and the relief claimed. See also **Originating process**.

Statement of financial circumstances See **Affidavit or statement of financial circumstances**.

Statement of loss The notification by an insurance policyholder to the insurer of a loss which may lead to a claim under the policy. Also known as 'notice of loss'.

Statement of material facts A corporate document filed with the Australian Securities Commission (ASC) detailing a proposed allocation of securities, not subject to prospectus requirements as required under securities legislation. A statement of material facts comprises information relating to the securities, financial data and reasons for the issue of the securities.

Statement of net balance The total of all debits and credits at a particular point in time accepted by the giver of the statement. In the context of insolvency, it represents the net account to a debtor or a creditor, taking into account all set-offs or amount owing and owed. It is usually the figure given in settlement or finalisation of contractual relations. Under uniform credit legislation, a credit provider must furnish a debtor with a statement of the net balance within seven days of the request: (ACT) Credit Act 1985 (repealed) s 104; (NSW) Credit Act 1984 (repealed) s 104; (QLD) Credit Act 1987 (repealed) s 105; (VIC) Credit Act 1984 (repealed) s 104; (WA) Credit Act 1984 (repealed) s 104 (replaced by Uniform Consumer Credit Code). See also **Set-off**; **Uniform credit legislation**.

•**Statement of price** Specification of the cost of goods which is applied by being woven in, impressed on, worked into, annexed or affixed to the goods, which is applied to a covering, label, reel or thing in or with which goods are supplied, or which is used in a sign, advertisement, catalogue or other document or otherwise in a manner likely to lead to the belief that it refers to goods: (CTH) Trade Practices Act 1974 s 99(1). The use of a price statement by a manufacturer likely to be understood by the subsequent retailer as the price below which goods may not be sold constitutes the offence of resale price maintenance: ss 48, 96(3)(f): *BP Australia Ltd v Trade Practices Commission* (1986) 12 FCR 118; 66 ALR 148; *Trade Practices Commission v Penfolds Wines Pty Ltd* (1991) 104 ALR 601; ATPR ¶41-071. See also **Resale price maintenance**.

Statex-Actuaries Index Published in the *Australian Financial Review* with the Australian Share Price Index and the Australian Accumulation Index, an index designed specifically to assist portfolio managers. It is composed of fifty leading stocks, containing two per cent of each stock so that it is equally weighted. The stocks included are reviewed regularly. See also **Australian Accumulation Index**.

•**Statistician** One who works with statistics. The Australian Bureau of Statistics and an Australian Statistician are established under (CTH) Australian Bureau of Statistics Act 1975 s 5. The functions of the bureau and the statistician include the collection, compilation, analysis and dissemination of statistics, formulating statistical standards and ensuring coordination in the operation of official bodies with regard to the information they collect: s 6. See also **Statistics**.

•**Statistics** Numerical data or facts, collected or arranged. Within each jurisdiction there is legislation facilitating the collection of statistics: for example (SA) Statistics Act 1935. See also **Statistician**.

Status quo The state of things as they are or were. Compensation in tort law is based on the principle of *restitutio in integrum* which requires a plaintiff to be restored to his or her status quo, that is, to be placed in the position he or she would have been in if the tort had not been committed. See also **Damages**.

•**Statute** An act passed by parliament. See also **Act of Parliament**.

Statute barred action An action which cannot be maintained, where the period of time provided by statute within which a plaintiff must commence legal proceedings (for example (NSW) Limitations Act 1969) has lapsed. See also **Limitation of actions**; **Limitation period**.

Statute law Law created by legislation. Contrasted with common law. See also **Act of parliament**; **Common law**; **Legislation**.

Statute of Frauds (1677 29 Car 2 c 3) A statute enacted to prevent perpetration of fraud by requiring certain contracts to be evidenced in writing and authenticated by signature to be enforceable; for example, contracts for the sale of land. See also **Contract for sale of land**.

Statute of Limitation (1623 21 Jac 1 c 16) The original English statute which placed a limitation period on the time for a plaintiff bringing an action. See also **Limitation of actions**; **Limitation period**.

Statute of repose The overall time period within which a product liability claim must be commenced, beginning from the time of first supply of the product to a consumer ((CTH) Trade Practices Act 1974 s 74J(3)) or the time of supply of the product by its manufacturer ((CTH) Trade Practices Act 1974 s 75AO(2)). See also **Consumer**; **Manufacturer**; **Product liability**.

Statutory arbitration Arbitration of a dispute otherwise than by an agreement between the parties to arbitrate. A statute may provide that any dispute must be settled by arbitration: for example (VIC) Retail Tenancies Act 1986. See also **Alternative dispute resolution**; **Arbitration**.

Statutory contract A contract deemed to exist by statute. See also **Members' personal action**.

•**Statutory corporation** A corporation created by, or pursuant to, a statute: for example (CTH) Commonwealth Bank Act 1959. See also **Corporation**.

•**Statutory declaration** A declaration made by virtue of any Act of the Commonwealth, of a State or of a Territory authorising a declaration to be made otherwise than in the course of a judicial proceeding: Corporations Law s 9. It is a written statement of facts in the name of the declarant that is solemnly declared to be true. A statutory declaration is usually signed before a legal practitioner or a person authorised by legislation for taking statutory declarations: (CTH) Statutory Declarations Regulations 1993 Sch; (VIC) Evidence Act 1958 s 107; (QLD) Oaths Act 1867 s 13.

•**Statutory demand** The demand in writing which a creditor who is owed more than a prescribed amount ($2000) may serve on a debtor company, so that if the company fails to pay the amount due or to give security or compound for it within a prescribed time (21 days after service), the company will be deemed to be unable to pay its debts: Corporations Law ss 459E, 459F. The inability to meet debts (or insolvency) is a ground for the court to order the winding up of a company: s 459A. The court may set aside the demand if, for example, there is a genuine dispute about the existence of the debt, the company has an offsetting claim or there is a substantial defect in the demand: s 459G. See also **Compound; Debt; Insolvency; Security; Set-off; Winding up.**

Statutory duty A liability or duty imposed by statute to do or not do something. See also **Breach of statutory duty.**

Statutory income An amount specifically included in the assessable income of a taxpayer that is not generally considered to be ordinary income. For example, a net capital gain is deemed to be assessable income even though generally a capital gain is distinguished from what would ordinarily be income: (CTH) Income Tax Assessment Act 1936 s 160ZO(1). See also **Assessable income; Income; Net capital gain.**

Statutory insurance schemes A scheme of insurance which gives a right of recourse to a statutory insurer or guarantor to recover losses. See also **Building contract.**

•**Statutory interest account** An account by that name kept by the law society or law institute in each State or Territory with a bank in that jurisdiction: for example (NSW) Legal Profession Act 1987 s 67(1). The law society or institute is required to deposit to the credit of that account all interest received on the investment of money paid to it by solicitors being a prescribed part of each firm's total trust account money: for example (NSW) Legal Profession Act 1987 s 64. See also **Bar Council; Trust account.**

Statutory limitation on indemnity and insurance A legislative provision which states that a company or related body corporate must not indemnify present or former officers or the auditor against a liability incurred by that person: Corporations Law s 241(1). There are two exceptions; in the case of third party liability (s 241(2)) and legal expenses (s 241(3)). A company is prohibited from paying, or agreeing to pay, a premium in respect of a contract insuring a present or former officer or auditor against liability incurred in that position, arising out of conduct involving wilful breach of duty in relation to the company, or a contravention of ss 232(5)-(6): s 241A. The prohibition does not prevent insurance with respect to the costs of defending legal proceedings: s 241A(3). See also **Directors' duties.**

•**Statutory meeting** A meeting of company members required to be held in the case of a public company that is a limited company with share capital and which issues a prospectus for the first time: Corporations Law s 244(1). All no liability companies which issue prospectuses for the first time must also hold statutory meetings. Meetings must be held within three months after the date on which the company allots shares. At least seven days before the meeting, a statutory report must be sent to every member giving various details including details about shares allotted and about the officers of the company: s 244(3). The members at this meeting may 'discuss any matter relating to the formation of the company or arising out of the statutory report': s 244(7). See also **Annual general meeting; General meeting.**

Statutory minimum Any minimum that is set down in legislation: an amount fixed by statute in relation to, for example, minimum rates of pay, minimum fines or minimum outstanding debts. For example, the minimum debt amount prescribed for which a person is permitted to serve a demand for payment: Corporations Law ss 9, 459E. The minimum amount will vary from statute to statute.

•**Statutory report** A report required to be sent at least seven days before the holding of the statutory meeting of a company, to every member of the company: Corporations Law s 244(2). The report provides various details including details about shares allotted and about the officers of the company: s 244(3). The members present at the statutory meeting may discuss any matter relating to the formation of the company or arising out of the statutory report: s 244(7). See also **Statutory meeting.**

•**Statutory rules** Abbr – SR Delegated legislation made pursuant to a statute enacted by parliament. Statutory rules are made with the authority of the Minister and tabled in the respective parliament but are not debated before the House. See also **Instrument.**

•**Statutory trustee** A corporation established by legislation in all States enabling it to act as a personal representative, executor and trustee. See also **Perpetual succession; Trustee.**

Stay order An order of a court which has the effect of suspending the operation of an earlier order, generally pending the occurrence of some specified event such as the hearing of an appeal against the original order. See also **Appeal.**

•**Sterling** Currency that is legal tender in the United Kingdom: (CTH) Banking Act 1959 s 32. See also **Mobilisation of foreign currency.**

•**Stevedoring** The business or activity of loading or unloading the cargo of a vessel, and incidental activities such as handling or storing cargo or stevedoring equipment at any site: (NSW) Marine Port Charges Act 1989 s 3(1). The Commonwealth has power to make laws in respect of stevedoring operations under the trade and commerce power: Commonwealth Constitution 1900 s 51(i). See also **Cargo; Loading; Stowage.**

Stock dividend See **Dividend.**

•**Stock exchange 2.** The Australian Stock Exchange and its branches: Corporations Law s 9. See also **Australian Stock Exchange Ltd; Stock market.**

Stock Exchange Automated Trading System Abbr – SEATS An electronic share trading system serving the Australian Stock Exchange. The network enables stockbrokers to trade securities directly, away from the trading floor. With a SEATS trading terminal, a stockbroker can make or accept bids and confirm sales, in most cases while the investor waits on the telephone. The system shows exactly how many buyers and sellers there are for a stock, as well as a complete rundown on how the stock was traded over the day. Sales are effected by an 'electronic handshake'. See also **Australian Stock Exchange Ltd.**

Stock exchange listing See **Australian Stock Exchange listing.**

Stock exchange transaction A transaction by which the parties agree to buy and sell shares and those shares are to be delivered. Such a transaction is not a gambling transaction: *Re Ahearn; Ex parte Palmer* (1906) 6 SR (NSW) 576; 23 WN (NSW) 188. See also **Futures exchange transaction**.

•**Stock in trade** Property or chattels acquired for the purpose of being sold, let or hired in a person's trade: *Re Richardson* (1881) 44 LT 404. Stock in trade may include raw materials, work in progress, and land: *Federal Cmr of Taxation v St Hubert's Island Pty Ltd (In Liq)* (1978) 138 CLR 210; 19 ALR 1; *Collins Marrickville Pty Ltd v Henjo Investments Pty Ltd* (1987) 72 ALR 601; (NSW) Stamp Duties Act 1920 s 243B(1)(a); (CTH) Income Tax Assessment Act 1936. Also known as 'stock on hand'. See also **Inventory**.

Stock lien See **Wool lien**.

•**Stock market** A market, exchange or other place at which, or a facility by means of which, securities are regularly offered for sale, purchase or exchange: Corporations Law s 9. A stock market may only be conducted by an approved stock exchange: ss 767, 769. See also **Floor member; Securities; Stock exchange**.

Stock split An increase in the number of shares in a given share capital stock without changing the total dollar value of the stock. A stock split has the effect of decreasing the par value of the shares and is accomplished by replacing one old share with a certain number of new shares. See also **Par value; Share capital**.

Stock swap An exchange of shares by shareholders in one company for shares in another company, as part of a merger or takeover. See also **Swap**.

•**Stockbroker** See **Sharebroker**.

Stockpiling of bills The storing of bills which have been rejected by the upper house of parliament, with the intention of re-submitting them to be passed at a later time. Also known as 'storehouse of bills'.

Stop limit order An order to buy at a price above, or to sell at a price below, the current value that becomes an order with a limited sale or purchase price once a specified price has been achieved.

•**Stop order** In relation to corporations, a direction by the Australian Securities Commission (ASC) forbidding the allotment or issue of securities under a prospectus: Corporations Law s 1033(1). See also **Prospectus**.

Stop price The price which the market must reach before an order to buy or sell is revoked.

Stop-loss order An order placed with a broker that becomes a market order when the market reaches the designated price (being the price at which the stop-loss order is placed). Also known as 'stop loss' or 'stop order '. See also **Broker; Market order; Securities business**.

Stoppage in transitu The right of an unpaid vendor to retake possession of goods sold while they are still in transit (that is, in the hands of the carrier), to enforce the vendor's lien for the price: for example (NSW) Sale of Goods Act 1923 s 42(1). See also **Bailment; Carrier's lien; Consignee; Consignment; Consignor; Contract of carriage; Goods; In transit; Insolvency; Possession; Repossession; Sale of goods**.

Stopped cheque A cheque on which the duty and authority of a bank to pay a cheque drawn on it is terminated by countermand of payment: (CTH) Cheques and Payment Orders Act 1986 s 90(1)(a). The countermand must be unambiguous and must be made to an appropriate officer of the drawee bank: *Commonwealth Trading Bank of Australia v Reno Auto Sales Pty Ltd* [1967] VR 790. See also **Cheque; Drawee bank**.

Stowage The storing, packing, and arranging of cargo in a ship in such a manner as to protect it from damage or contamination, and to facilitate its unloading at various ports of discharge. Under a voyage charterparty, stowage is the responsibility of the shipowner. A shipowner employing a stevedore remains liable for negligent stowage by the stevedore. Article 3 of the Amended Hague Rules 1979 prescribes a duty to properly and carefully stow cargo. To determine whether a breach of this duty has occurred, regard must be had to all the circumstances, including the nature of the particular goods and the conditions of the weather and sea likely to be encountered on the voyage: *Shipping Corp of India Ltd v Gamlen Chemical Co (A'asia) Pty Ltd* (1980) 147 CLR 142; 32 ALR 609. See also **Cargo; Carrier; Contract of carriage; International Convention for the Unification of Certain Rules of Law relating to Bills of Lading 1924; Loading; Stevedoring; Voyage charterparty**.

Straddle See **Trading spread**.

Straddle option A right held by a person to exercise both a call option and a put option. See also **Call option; Put option**.

Straight credit A documentary credit in which the issuing bank promises to pay only the seller a certain sum for the tender of the documents. The term is used in contrast to a credit in straight-line depreciation where the promise is also made to negotiators and bona fide holders of the seller's drafts. See also **Documentary letter of credit; Draft; Issuing bank; Letter of credit**.

Straight line method A method for calculating and allowing for the depreciation of an asset. The straight line or fixed instalment method distributes the cost of an asset uniformly over its depreciable life. The amount to be set aside each year may be calculated from the formula: P - L / n where P is the initial asset cost (the historic cost), L the expected salvage or residual value at the end of the useful life of the asset and n is the plant life expressed in years. See also **Reducing balance method; Sinking fund method**.

Strata title A type of land title providing Torrens title to parts of buildings. First introduced in New South Wales in 1961, strata title provides a more secure alternative to company title and tenancy in common methods of owning parts of a building. See also **Body corporate; Floor plan**.

Straw company A company which is in such a weak financial position that it is not worthwhile suing, since any remedy granted in court requiring the payment of money will probably not be able to be complied with.

Straw man A person not worth suing because they lack financial substance. Also known as 'man of straw'.

•**Street trading** The selling, offering, or exposing for sale of any article if the selling or offering or exposing for sale is done in a public place, not including the occasional selling of articles if the net proceeds are wholly applied for the benefit of a church or school or for a cultural or charitable purpose: for example (WA) Child Welfare Act 1947 s 4. See also **Sale of goods**.

Strict liability Liability for damage without the need to prove negligence or fault. The defendant is liable irrespective of an absence of negligence or intention on his or her part and even if he or she took reasonable care to prevent the damage. See also **Absolute liability**; **Liability**; **Vicarious liability**.

Strict product liability The basis of liability under (CTH) Trade Practices Act 1974 Pt V Div 2A and Pt VA and under certain State and Territory product liability legislation, in which proof of negligence is not an element of a claim. See also **Division 2A claim**.

•**Strike** A form of industrial action by which employees, acting together, cease work in order to compel their employer to improve wages or conditions, or in order to give vent to a grievance or make a protest, or to support or sympathise with other striking workers. See also **Industrial action**; **Lock-out**; **Work ban**.

Strike clause A clause in a charterparty or bill of lading that details the options available to the parties if a strike interrupts the loading or unloading of cargo. Such clauses vary with each contract, and are strictly construed. For example, there are strike clauses which are confined in their operation to strikes by certain kinds of workers: *Dampskibsselskabet Torm A/S v Australian Wheat Board* [1981] VR 145. See also **Bill of lading**; **Centrocon charter party**; **Charterparty**; **Lay day**; **Strike**.

Strike price The price at which the buyer of an option has the right to buy (in the case of a call option) or sell (in the case of a put option) the subject matter of the option. Also known as 'striking price' or 'exercise price'. See also **Call option**; **Put option**.

•**Structure** Includes a tank or other structure for the storage or supply of water; sewerage or effluent drains; a bridge, viaduct, aqueduct or tunnel; a chimney stack or cooling tower; a silo; and a dock, jetty, pier or wharf: for example (SA) Construction Industry Long Service Leave Act 1987 s 4. See also **Building**.

Structure conduct performance model The generally accepted model of the factors influencing economic performance and industrial organisation, conceived by Edward Mason of Harvard University during the 1930s and elaborated by numerous scholars since. The model postulates that the basic conditions in the market (supply conditions including availability of raw materials, technology and the legal framework, and demand conditions including price elasticity, substitutability and cyclical conditions) influence market structure (such as numbers of sellers and buyers, product differentiation, and barriers to entry), which in turn influences conduct (pricing behaviour, research and innovation, and legal tactics), which in turn influences performance. Each in turn has a feedback influence on the prior element. See also **Barrier to entry**; **Competition**; **Demand**; **Market**; **Market structure**; **Price elasticity of demand**; **Price elasticity of supply**; **Substitutability**; **Supply**.

Stub stocks A small amount of equity in a company overwhelmed by debt. In this situation the company's assets are dwarfed by its liabilities, giving its assets a negative net worth. Many stubs are created by leveraged buyouts. If the company goes into liquidation, stubs stand behind a long line of bond and debenture holders, and only after such debt is satisfied may stub holders make a claim on assets and earnings.

Subagent 1. In a strict legal sense, a delegate and appointee of an agent. In general, a subagent is accountable only to the agent who employs the subagent, and that agent in turn to the agent's principal: *Stephens v Babcock* (1832) 3 B & Ad 354; 110 ER 133. **2.** A person who acts for or is employed by an 'agent' (used in a non-legal sense) and who exercises any of the functions of that 'agent'. See also **Agency**; **Agent**; **Delegation**; **Principal**.

Sub-bailment A situation arising when a person (the sub-bailee) receives temporary possession of goods from a prior bailee (the sub-bailor or intermediate bailor) rather than from the original bailor: *Gilchrist Watt & Sanderson Pty Ltd v York Products Pty Ltd* [1970] 2 NSWR 156; *Brambles Security Services Ltd v Bi-Lo Pty Ltd* (1992) Aust Torts Reports ¶81-161. A series of bailments may involve a series of sub-bailments. However, where the existing bailee ceases to owe any duty to the bailor, with or without attornment to the bailor by the new bailee, there is not a sub-bailment but what is known as a 'springing bailment' or 'substitutional bailment': for example *Roufos v Brewster* (1971) 2 SASR 218. See also **Bailment**; **Bailment by attornment**; **Bailor's remedies**; **Head bailee**; **Head bailment**; **Head bailor**; **Sub-bailment**.

•**Subcontract** An agreement by a contractor and a third party for the performance by the third party of some or all of the contractor's obligations under its contract with a proprietor. See also **Building contract**; **Contract**; **Contractor**; **Proprietor**.

•**Subject to contract** A formula in an agreement, creating the presumption that the parties intend not to make a concluded bargain unless and until they execute a formal contract: *Masters v Cameron* (1954) 91 CLR 353. See also **Condition precedent**; **Contract**; **Contract of sale**.

Subject to equities In relation to assets, affected by an equitable claim. A person who acquires property other than as a bona fide purchaser for value (especially an assignee in bankruptcy) takes the property subject to the equities, that is, subject to all the equitable claims to that property which would have prevailed against the person from whom that property was acquired: *Ex parte Dumas* (1754) 2 Ves Sen 582; 28 ER 372; *Official Receiver in Bankruptcy v Klau* (1987) 74 ALR 67.

Subject to valuation A phrase indicating that there is no intention of the parties to a contract to make a concluded bargain at all, unless and until a valuation on terms satisfactory to the party inserting this clause is obtained: *Meehan v Jones* (1982) 149 CLR 571; 42 ALR 463; *Masters v Cameron* (1954) 91 CLR 353 at 360. See also **Condition precedent**; **Contract of sale**.

Subjective theory of contract The theory that the true consent of the parties is essential to a valid contract, to be contrasted with the objective theory: *Taylor v Johnson* (1983) 151 CLR 422; 45 ALR 265. See also **Consensus ad idem**; **Consideration**; **Contract**; **Intention**.

•**Sublease** A lease of a leasehold interest (known as the headlease). A sublease may be in respect of the whole or part only of the premises, and must terminate before the termination date of the headlease, or it will in fact be an assignment of the headlease. Also known as 'underlease'. See also **Assignment**; **Derivative lease**; **Lease**; **Privity of contract**; **Sublessee**; **Sublessor**.

Sublessee A person who holds a leasehold estate derived from another leasehold estate. A sublessee's estate may not be of the same or greater duration as the lease from which it is derived, as it will in that case be an assignment of the lease. A sublessee does not have any legal relationship with the owner of the freehold land, but may apply to a court for relief if the lease from which the sublease is derived is to be forfeited by the headlessor: for example (NSW) Conveyancing Act 1919 s 130. Also known as 'under-lessee'. See also **Forfeiture**; **Leasehold**; **Sublease**.

Sublessor A person who has created in favour of another person a leasehold estate derived from the sublessor's own leasehold estate. The sublessor is one to whom the sublessee pays rent and in favour of whom the covenants of the sublease are observed. A purported sublease will be invalid if the sublessor's own tenancy is a tenancy at will, a tenancy at sufferance or (generally) a statutory tenancy. The sublessor remains liable to the head lessor for any breaches of the head lease committed by the sublessee. Also known as 'underlessor'. See also **Sublessee**; **Sublease**.

Sublicence The grant by a licensee of a subsidiary licence which derives from the licence held by the grantor and depends for performance on the head licence as held by the grantor. See also **Licence**.

Submarket A segment within the boundaries of a more broadly defined market. A submarket has within it closer and more immediate substitutes; competition in it is especially close. The products may have peculiar characteristics or uses, unique production facilities, distinct customers, distinct prices, sensitivity to price changes, and specialised vendors. The concept of a submarket has no explicit statutory role in Australian competition law. Rather, it is a tool of analysis: *Singapore Airlines Ltd v Taprobane Tours WA Pty Ltd* (1991) 33 FCR 158; 104 ALR 633. See also **Competition**; **Market**; **Substitutability**.

Subordinated creditor A creditor ranking lower than a secured creditor, and likely to receive less from a liquidation. also known as 'junior creditor'. See also **Secured creditor**.

Subordinated debenture A debenture which is intended to rank behind other debts. See also **Debenture**; **Subordinated loan**; **Subordination of debt**.

•**Subordinated loan** An unsecured loan which ranks behind other debts in the event of a company being liquidated: (NSW) Trustee Companies Act 1964 s 3. Subordinated debt is often provided by major shareholders or a parent company. Financial institutions may use this path to increase their borrowing potential; in company balance sheets, subordinated debt may appear as equity being described as a subordinated debenture issue. See also **Subordination of debt**.

Subordination of debt The ranking of the unsecured debt of a company so as to postpone the claim of another creditor. It occurs when an unsecured creditor agrees not to be repaid until another unsecured creditor is repaid in full. It is sanctioned under Corporations Law s 563C, which allows a creditor of a company to enter into a debt subordination agreement with the company if the creditor so desires, provided that the subordination would not disadvantage any other creditor. See also **Subordinated loan**; **Subordination trust**.

Subordination trust A device or mechanism used to subordinate the debt of a company. Under a subordination trust, the subordinated creditor (junior creditor) agrees, in consideration for the new lender (senior creditor) making the loan to the debtor, to claim the subordinated debt when it matures but to hold the proceeds of that debt on trust for the senior creditor until the senior creditor's debt is paid in full. The use of such a trust effectively avoids the *pari passu* allotments that usually take place when paying out unsecured debt. A subordination trust does not affect the liquidator's distribution of dividends to creditors who have proved their debts. Both the junior creditor and the senior creditor will rank equally from the liquidator's viewpoint but, where the company is insolvent, the junior creditor will be accountable to the senior creditor. See also **Pari passu allotment**; **Pari passu trust deed**; **Subordinated loan**; **Subordination of debt**.

Subpartner A person who purchases part of a partner's interest in the partnership, or who agrees with a partner to share the partner's profits. Such an agreement does not make the person a partner of the original firm. The parties to the agreement become partners between themselves without affecting the other members of the original firm: *Australia and New Zealand Banking Group Ltd v Richardson* [1980] Qd R 321. The purchase money benefits the partner selling the interest, not the partnership. The agreement does not give the purchaser any rights against the partnership: *Hocking v West Australian Bank* (1909) 9 CLR 738. See also **Partner**; **Partnership**.

•**Subpoena** /sʌbpinə/ *Lat* – under a penalty. A document by which a court compels a person to attend court to give evidence or to produce documents within that person's possession: for example (CTH) High Court Rules O 37 r 25.0; (CTH) Federal Court Rules O 27 r 2; (NSW) Supreme Court Rules 1970 Pt 37 r 2; (VIC) Rules of the Supreme Court Ch I r 42.02. A subpoena must be properly served on the person required to attend court: (CTH) High Court Rules O 37 r 32; (CTH) Federal Court Rules O 27 r 8; (NSW) Supreme Court Rules 1970 Pt 37 r 7; (VIC) Rules of the Supreme Court Ch I r 42.04. See also **Document**; **Evidence**.

•**Subrogation 1.** A doctrine by which an insurer is entitled to have the rights of the insured substituted to him or her so as to be entitled to the rights and remedies the insured possesses against third parties in relation to a claim: *Castellain v Preston* (1883) 11 QBD 380; *Meacock v Bryant and Co* [1942] 2 All ER 661. Subrogation applies inherently to all contracts of indemnity, although it can be restricted or expanded by express terms of the contract: *State Government Insurance Office (Qld) v Brisbane Stevedoring Pty Ltd* (1969) 123 CLR 228. The right of subrogation only arises when the insurer has fully indemnified the insured: *Santos Ltd v American Home Assurance Co* (1986) 4 ANZ Ins Cas ¶60-795. **2.** The right of an insurer to recover a payment made by him or her in respect of a loss when the assured also receives a payment from a third party in respect of that loss: *John Edwards and Co v Motor Union Insurance Co Ltd* [1922] 2 KB 249. The use of the term 'subrogation' to describe this right has been doubted in Australia: *British Traders' Insurance Co Ltd v Monson* (1964) 111 CLR 86 at 94. See also **Indemnity**; **Personal accident and illness insurance**.

Subsale One sale that forms part of an overall group of sales within one contract. See also **Sale**.

•**Subscriber 1.** In relation to prescribed interests, any person accepting an offer, or making an offer pursuant to an invitation, in respect of, or subscribing for or buying, any such prescribed interests: Corporations Law s 9. **2.** In relations to securities generally, any person who takes or agrees to take securities from an issuing company, the taker assuming the liability to pay for the securities: *Government Stock and Other Securities Investment Co v Christopher* [1956] 1 WLR 237 at 242. **3.** A person who has put their name to a memorandum so that a company can be incorporated (one or more for proprietary companies, five or more for public companies): Corporations Law ss 114(1)(a), 114(2)(a). See also **Invitation**; **Offer**; **Prospectus**; **Subscription**.

•**Subscription** Taking or agreeing to take newly issued shares (a 'primary allotment' or 'primary issue') from an issuing company for cash, the taker assuming liability to pay for the shares. The terms 'purchase' and 'sell' refer to dealings with previously allotted or issued shares. See also **Prospectus**.

Subscription moneys The money that is paid when subscribing for shares. There are many cases in which this money must be returned. A person who claims to have been induced to subscribe for shares in a company by misrepresentation or fraudulent conduct of the company may rescind the membership contract and recover the subscription moneys, and possibly interest: *Commonwealth Homes and Investment Co Ltd v MacKellar* (1939) 63 CLR 351 at 366. An issue of shares in excess of a company's authorised capital is void, and the subscriber is entitled to recover the subscription moneys because the consideration of the company has failed: *Bank of Hindustan, China and Japan Ltd v Alison* (1871) LR 6 CP 222. See also **Authorised capital**; **Subscription**.

Subscription warrant A document issued by a company with a debenture entitling the holder to subscribe for a number of shares proportionate to the face value of the debenture on or after a specified date. In the United Kingdom, the warrant may be detached from the debenture and dealt with as a separate item. A subscription warrant differs from a convertible debenture in that a holder of a subscription warrant who wishes to take up shares must pay the company the issue price. See also **Convertible security**.

•**Subsidiary** A company under the control of another company which controls the composition of the board of directors of the subsidiary, or holds more than one half of the voting shares, or holds more than one half of the ordinary share capital of the company: Corporations Law s 46. See also **Holding company**; **Parent company**.

•**Subsidiary company** See **Holding company**.

Subsidiary ledger A ledger comprising the individual accounts for a specific asset or liability account. The total balance of all the accounts in the subsidiary ledger for the asset or liability is presented in a control account within the general ledger. For example, the control account may be 'accounts receivable' which is the general ledger account summarising the total amount owed by trade creditors to the business, with each individual trade creditor having an individual subsidiary account showing the amount that each individual trade creditor owes the business.

•**Subsidy** A grant, bounty or payment made to industries to assist the production of various goods and services and help domestic industry remain competitive. See also **Protection**.

Taxation and revenue For income tax purposes, a financial grant made by the state for the purpose of encouraging a particular activity in the field of trade, commerce, or business: *Reckitt and Colman v FCT* (1974) 23 FLR 58; 3 ALR 381. Also known as 'bounty'.

•**Substantial 1.** Real or of substance, as distinct from ephemeral or nominal: *Tillmanns Butcheries Pty Ltd v Australasian Meat Industry Employees' Union* (1979) 27 ALR 367 ('substantial loss or damage'). **2.** Large, weighty or big: *Palser v Grinling* [1948] AC 291; *Re Queensland Co-operative Milling Assn Ltd; Re Defiance Holdings Ltd* (1976) 8 ALR 481 ('substantial public benefit'). **3.** In a relative sense, considerable: *Radio 2UE Sydney Pty Ltd v Stereo FM Pty Ltd* (1982) 44 ALR 557 ('substantially lessening competition'); *Dowling v Dalgety Australia Ltd* (1992) 34 FCR 109; 106 ALR 75 ('substantial degree of power'). **4.** Greater rather than less: *Dandy Power Equipment Pty Ltd v Mercury Marine Pty Ltd* (1982) 44 ALR 173 ('substantially lessening competition'). See also **Collusion**; **Competition**; **Contract, arrangement or understanding**; **Exclusionary provision**; **Exclusive dealing**; **Merger**; **Misuse of market power**; **Substantially lessening competition**.

•**Substantial damages** Damages compensating the plaintiff for harm or loss actually suffered as the result of a tort or breach of contract. The term is used in contrast to nominal damages, and is synonymous with 'real' damages: *Baume v Commonwealth* (1906) 4 CLR 97. See also **Breach of contract**; **Damages**; **Nominal damages**.

Substantial performance The doctrine concerning the performance of contracts, which allows a plaintiff to recover the contract price despite a minor failure in performance by the plaintiff: *Bolton v Mahadeva* [1972] 2 All ER 1322. See also **Entire contract; Performance; Severable contract**.

•**Substantial shareholder** A person who is entitled to not less than the prescribed percentage (Corporations Law s 708(5)) of the voting shares or a class of voting shares in a body corporate: s 708(4). See also **Substantial shareholding**.

•**Substantial shareholding** An entitlement to not less than five per cent of the relevant class of shares: Corporations Law Pt 6.7. A substantial shareholder of a listed public company must disclose the interest (and variations to that entitlement) to the company and serve a copy of the disclosure notice on the stock exchange. Contravention of the provisions enables the court to make an order, including cancellation of contracts and divestment of shares. The Australian Securities Commission may trace the beneficial ownership of that company's shares, whether or not the beneficial owner has reached the five per cent threshold. See also **Entitlement to shares; Share warehousing; Substantial shareholder; Takeover**.

Substantially lessening competition Restricting or hindering the competitive forces and conditions of the market, not necessarily lessening the number of competitors in that market. The formula is sometimes referred to as the 'competition test', and is applied as a threshold test in (CTH) Trade Practices Act 1974 Pt IV, most recently to mergers and acquisitions: s 50. See also **Collusion; Competition; Contract, arrangement or understanding; Exclusive dealing; Hinder or prevent; Market; Merger; Misuse of market power; Substantial**.

Substantiation For income tax purposes, proving in the way required by (CTH) Income Tax Assessment Act 1936 Pt III Div 3F that a taxpayer incurred deductible expenses. See also **Allowable deduction; Assessable income; Car expense; Employment-related expense; Incurred**.

Substitutability The measure of interchangeability of goods or services in response to changes in relative prices, thus setting limits to the market and the ability of any one firm in it to influence prices (and hence, to exercise market power). Substitutability must be measured from both the supply and the demand side, that is, the response of both suppliers and buyers to a change in relative prices. 'The basic test involves the ascertainment of the cross-elasticities of both supply and demand, that is, the extent to which the supply of or demand for a product responds to a change in the price of another product': *Queensland Wire Industries Pty Ltd v Broken Hill Proprietary Co Ltd* (1989) 167 CLR 177; 83 ALR 577. See also **Competition; Contestable market; Cross elasticity of demand; Elasticity of substitution; Functional market; Geographic market; Market; Market power; Product market**.

Substituted accounting period An accounting period of 12 months ending on a date other than 30 June, adopted by a person with the Commissioner of Taxation's leave. The substituted accounting period ends on the corresponding date of succeeding years, unless with the Commissioner's leave some other date is adopted:

(CTH) Income Tax Assessment Act 1936 s 18. Tax returns are usually prepared on the basis of a year of income ending 30 June. See also **Year of income; Year of tax**.

Substitution In the maritime context, the replacement of one ship with another. In a voyage charter, a shipowner usually has the option of hiring out a ship other than the one named in the charterparty. The value of such an option is that the shipowner may not know which of its ships will be capable of performing the voyage at the time the contract is made, particularly if this happens well before loading. See also **Carriage by sea; Charterparty; Contract of carriage; Voyage charterparty**.

Substratum In corporations law, the intention and common understanding of the members (shareholders). The Supreme Court has the power to compulsorily wind a company up if it is of the opinion that it would be just and equitable to do so: Corporations Law s 461(k). One of the categories where the court has found such an opinion is where there has been a failure of the substratum: *Re Tivoli Freeholds* [1972] VR 445. See also **Failure of substratum; Objects clause**.

Subtrust A trust created where the owner of equitable property declares himself or herself owner of it for another, under a trust in which the owner imposes active duties on himself or herself. The law is uncertain where the owner places no active duties on himself or herself. A declaration of subtrust is distinguished from an assignment of the interest under the original trust. In the latter case no new interest in property is created. See also **Declaration of trust; Trust**.

Subunderlease A lease derived from a sublease, in the same manner that a sublease is derived from a head or chief lease. It is theoretically possible to have a series of subunderleases to any number of degrees (known as 'sub-subunderleases', 'sub-sub-subunderleases' and so on) but this is rare in practice, as a sublease usually contains a covenant prohibiting further subleasing. See also **Leasehold; Sublease**.

Subunderwriter An entity which takes some of the underwriting risk of the primary underwriter to a public offer of shares in return for a portion of the underwriting fee. The underwriting agreement is usually between the primary underwriter and the subunderwriter. Subunderwriters benefit from the same exceptions as underwriters regarding takeover provisions (Corporations Law s 622(3)) and insider trading (s 1002J(1)-(2)). See also **Underwriter**.

Successive carriage The carriage of goods or passengers to their place of destination by more than one carrier, by a later carrier taking over the carriage from an earlier one. Where the carriage is by air, successive carriage is deemed to be one undivided carriage if it is regarded by the parties as a single contract or a series of contracts, and the carriage does not lose its international character merely because one contract is within one sovereignty: Convention for the Unification of Certain Rules relating to International Carriage by Air 1929 art 1(3). See also **Carriage by air; Carriage of goods; Carriage of passengers; Convention for the Unification of Certain Rules relating to International Carriage by Air 1929**.

Successor corporation A corporate entity that has succeeded a predecessor corporation, and which may be held liable in certain circumstances for the tortious acts or omissions, including product liabilities, of the predecessor: for example *Shannon v Samuel Langston Co* 379 F Supp 797 (WD Mich 1974); *Cyr v B Offen & Co Inc* 501 F 2d 1145 (1st Cir 1974); *Kloberdanz v Joy Manufacturing Co* 288 F Supp 817 (DC 1969); *Ramirez v Amsted Industries Inc* 431 A 2d 811 (1981).

•**Successor in title** 1. A person who holds title after another. 2. In product liability law, a person who acquires or derives title to a product through or under a person who is a consumer for the purposes of a (CTH) Trade Practices Act 1974 Pt V Div 2A claim. See also **Consumer**.

•**Sue** To bring a civil proceeding against a person. According to the circumstances, a party sues or is sued either personally or in a representative or other capacity, for example as trustee or executor. See also **Action**; **Originating process**; **Suit**.

Sue and labour clause A clause in marine insurance establishing the right of the insured to recover the expenses incurred in order to avert or minimise a loss recoverable under an insurance policy: for example (CTH) Marine Insurance Act 1909 s 36, Sch 2.

Sufficiency of consideration A synonym for the validity or effectiveness of consideration. Sufficient consideration is often described as 'good' or 'valuable' consideration: *Wigan v Edwards* (1973) 1 ALR 497. See also **Adequacy of consideration**; **Consideration**; **Contract**; **Executed consideration**; **Executory consideration**; **Nominal consideration**; **Valuable consideration**.

Suicide clause A clause in a life insurance contract relieving the insurer of all liability in the event that the person insured, whether sane or insane, dies by suicide within a given period of the policy commencing: for example (CTH) Life Insurance Act 1995 s 228.

•**Suit** Any action or original proceeding between parties: (CTH) Judiciary Act 1903 s 2. The term encompasses any civil legal proceeding brought by one person against another to enforce a right or claim, or to obtain redress for damage sustained. It has largely been replaced by the term 'action', which includes an action of any kind, both at law and in equity. See also **Action**; **Proceeding**.

•**Suitable employment** Work for which an employee is suited, having regard to the employee's age, experience, training, language and other skills, the employee's suitability for rehabilitation or vocational retraining, the employee's place of residence, the nature of the employee's incapacity and pre-injury employment, the length of time the employee has been seeking suitable employment, and any other relevant matter: for example (CTH) Safety Rehabilitation and Compensation Act 1988 s 4; (NSW) Workers Compensation Act 1987 s 43A. See also **Employment**.

Sum insured The amount of insurance specified in an insurance contract which indicates the maximum amount for which the insurer will be liable: for example (CTH) Insurance Contracts Act 1984 s 49.

Sum of the years digits method A method of allocating the total depreciation for an asset to the accounting periods in that assets' useful life. Unearned income is allocated to specific periods on a declining basis by multiplying it by a fraction. The numerator of the fraction equates with the number of periods remaining plus one, that is, the number of years in the asset's life in their reverse order, while the denominator is the sum of the numbers of a succession of periods.

Summary dismissal The dismissal of an employee immediately, without notice of termination by the employer. See also **Condonation**; **Contract of employment**; **Unfair dismissal**.

Summary termination See **Summary dismissal**.

•**Summons** Process issued by a court requiring a person to appear at a particular court at a particular time and place, either to give evidence or produce documents (for example (NSW) Justices Act s 26) or to attend to answer a charge, information or complaint (for example (NSW) Justices Act 1902 ss 24, 60; (QLD) Justices Act 1886 ss 53(1), 58(1); (VIC) Magistrates' Court Act 1989 s 28). The purpose of a summons is to notify the defendant of the proceedings so that he or she may answer the charge: *Plenty v Dillon* (1991) 171 CLR 635 at 644; 98 ALR 353. See also **Arrest**.

Sunrise industry A growth industry, usually based on technology, which is seen to have enormous potential, and which has been identified by the government as an area for future export growth. See also **Sunset industry**.

Sunset clause A legislative provision under which legislation will automatically expire after a certain number of years.

Sunset industry An industry seen to be in decline or stagnation, with a limited future and declining potential. See also **Sunrise industry**.

Super voting share A voting share which entitles the holder to more than one vote. A listed company may not issue fully paid shares otherwise than with voting rights on a 'one-for-one' basis: (CTH) Australian Stock Exchange Listing Rules rule 3K(2)(a). Company law does not, however, prevent an unlisted company from creating differential voting rights, provided proper procedures are followed. See also **Australian Stock Exchange listing rules**; **Voting share**.

•**Superannuation fund** A provident, benefit, superannuation, or retirement fund that is indefinitely continuing, or a public sector superannuation scheme: (CTH) Superannuation Industry (Supervision) Act 1993 s 10. Superannuation funds are established as a trust, with the trustee holding the fund for the benefit of the members, who in legal terms are the beneficiaries of the trust. A superannuation fund must be maintained solely for the purpose of providing retirement benefits or death benefits for the fund members: s 62. See also **Beneficiary**; **Complying superannuation fund**; **Defined contribution scheme**; **Defined benefit scheme**; **Trust**.

•**Superannuation guarantee charge** *Abbr* – SGC A charge imposed under (CTH) Superannuation Guarantee (Charge) Act 1992 s 5 on an employer who fails to make the minimum level of superannuation contribution as calculated under (CTH) Superannuation Guarantee (Administration) Act 1992 ss 20, 21 in respect of each of the employer's employees. The minimum level of support increases each year until the year 2002. After that date, the level of support will be nine per cent of the employer's annual national payroll. The employer's contributions must be made to a complying superannuation fund. Employers are required to self-assess their SGC obligation. Certain classes of employee payments are exempt from the SGC provisions: ss 27-29. The SGC has three components: the sum of the employer's individual SGC shortfall (ss 18-19); the interest; and the administration: s 32. SGC is not tax deductible: (CTH) Income Tax Assessment Act 1936 s 51(9). See also **Complying superannuation fund**.

Superannuation guarantee scheme A scheme imposed by statute requiring most employers to contribute an amount equal to a prescribed percentage of each employee's salary and wages to a complying superannuation fund: (CTH) Superannuation Guarantee Charge Act 1992 ss 5, 6; (CTH) Superannuation Guarantee (Administration) Act 1992 ss 16, 18. Failure to comply with this obligation results in a liability being imposed on the employer, excepting the Commonwealth and tax-exempt Commonwealth Authorities, to pay a charge or tax to the Commissioner of Taxation: (CTH) Superannuation Guarantee (Administration) Act 1992 s 50. See also **Commissioner of Taxation; Complying Superannuation fund; Employee; Employer; Superannuation fund; Superannuation guarantee charge**.

•**Superannuation guarantee shortfall** A shortfall arising when the percentage sum of superannuation support actually paid by an employer in respect of an employee is less than the minimum percentage level of support provided under the superannuation guarantee scheme: (CTH) Superannuation Guarantee (Administration) Act 1992 ss 17-19. See also **Superannuation guarantee scheme**.

Supercargo A person employed by a shipowner, shipping company, or charterer to oversee cargo handling operations, obtain additional cargo on a voyage, sell cargo to the best advantage, purchase return cargo and if authorised, receive freight. See also **Cargo; Freight; Sea cargo agent**.

Supervening illegality In contract law, where the performance of a contract becomes illegal after its formation but before it has been discharged by performance. See also **Frustration; Illegal contract**.

Supplemental deed A deed (or other instrument) which is read as supplemental to an earlier deed, so that the two operate jointly to achieve a purpose, only if an intention appears from the deeds. See also **Incorporation by reference**.

Supplementary prospectus A prospectus issued by a corporation to either correct a deficiency in the original prospectus or to provide particulars about something that has occurred since the original prospectus was prepared: Corporations Law s 1024A(1). A corporation may lodge a replacement prospectus instead of a supplementary prospectus if it prefers to include all of the up-to-date prospectus information in a single document: s 1024B(1).

A corporation must lodge a supplementary or replacement prospectus if it becomes aware of a significant change affecting a matter included in the prospectus or a significant new matter has arisen which would have been required to be included in the prospectus had it arisen earlier: s 1024(1). See also **Prospectus**.

Supplier One who provides goods or services by way of sale. In relation to a contract of sale, credit sale contract or contract for the hiring of goods, a person who supplies goods or services. In relation to a continuing credit contract, it means a person who supplies goods, services, or cash: (NSW) Credit Act 1984 (repealed) s 5(1); (VIC) Credit Act 1984 (repealed) s 5(1) (replaced by Uniform Consumer Credit Code). See also **Continuing credit contract; Contract of sale; Credit sale contract**.

Consumer protection **1.** A person who, in the course of a business, supplies goods or services: for example (NSW) Fair Trading Act 1987 s 4. **2.** Any person who is part of a business that makes a product available to consumers. This includes all persons in the chain of production and distribution of a consumer product including the distributor, retailer, and manufacturer. A supplier is under a duty to bring to a consumer's attention any defective or dangerous qualities of a chattel which are not a matter of common knowledge and which are known to the supplier: *Clarke v Army & Navy Co-Operative Society Ltd* [1903] 1 KB 155. Where a consumer expressly or impliedly makes known the purpose for which the goods or services are required and it appears that he or she is relying on the supplier's skill and judgment, there is an implied warranty that the goods or services will be reasonably fit for the purpose for which they are supplied: for example (CTH) Trade Practices Act 1974 s 74(2); (NSW) Sale of Goods Act 1923 s 19(1). See also **Manufacturer; Retailer**.

Supply To furnish or provide. In relation to goods, includes supply by way of sale (including resupply), exchange, lease, hire or hire purchase. In relation to services, 'supply' includes to provide, grant, or render services for valuable consideration. In relation to goods and services, it includes donating for promotional purposes: (CTH) Trade Practices Act 1974 s 4(1); (NSW) Fair Trading Act 1987 s 4(1). See also **Goods; Services**.

Supply by sample A contract for the supply or sale of goods to a consumer in which there is an express or implied term that the goods are supplied by reference to a sample. A sale by sample has three implied conditions: that the bulk will correspond with the sample in quality; that the consumer will have a reasonable opportunity of comparing the bulk with the sample; and that the goods will be free from any defect rendering them unmerchantable that would not be apparent on reasonable examination of the goods: for example (CTH) Trade Practices Act 1974 s 72; (NSW) Sale of Goods Act 1923 s 20. See also **Correspondence with sample; Merchantable quality**.

Supply of capital 1. The amount of capital available, usually for investment. **2.** Making available funds as an equity investment (although it may be a loan) to a particular entity or for a particular project. See also **Capital; Investment**.

Supply schedule A numerical tabulation of the mathematical relationship between the quantity supplied and the price. Generally, as the price increases the supply of any particular good or service will increase.

Supply side economics A philosophy that an economy should be managed by controlling those forces that influence output; for example, the availability of capital and labour, and the level of productivity. The money supply should grow in line only with the growth of output generated by capital accumulation and the growth of the labour force. Flexible wages and prices should automatically ensure full employment and an appropriate level of aggregate demand. There would still be a natural rate of unemployment due to structural and technological change and friction, but no more. The level of, and changes to, the tax burden would also affect economic activity; while tax cuts could produce such an increase in activity as to be self-financing. See also **Economics**.

Supply time The time at which a product was supplied by its actual manufacturer; or the time, prior to transmission or distribution, at which electricity was generated: (CTH) Trade Practices Act 1974 s 75AK(2).

•**Supreme Court** The superior court of record in each State and Territory which continues to exist under the relevant statutory provisions in each State and Territory: for example (NSW) Supreme Court Act 1970 s 22; (VIC) Constitution Act 1975 s 75(1). The Supreme Court is the highest court in the judicial hierarchy of each State or Territory. The Supreme Courts are, unlike any other trial courts in Australia, courts of general jurisdiction so that every matter is within the jurisdiction of a Supreme Court unless expressly excluded.

Surcharge and falsify 1. An additional or excessive charge for payment or taxes. 2. To show an omission (for example in an account) of something that operates as a charge against the accounting party. See also **False accounting**.

•**Surety** A person who is answerable for the obligation of another, either under a contract or as an equitable surety. The surety's liability is secondary to the primary liability of the principal debtor, in the sense that it is contingent upon the principal debtor's continuing liability and default. See also **Co-surety; Equitable suretyship**.

Surety bond A financial bond held in trust to protect people or companies against losses resulting from the non-performance of a contract.

•**Surplus assets** 1. An amount of assets in excess of what is required to cover liabilities. 2. The excess of assets over liabilities accumulated through the existence of a business, excepting assets against which stock certificates have been issued. See also **Asset; Liability; Share certificate**.

•**Surplus foreign currency** The amount by which a bank's assets outside Australia, but attributable to or acquired by virtue of its Australia business, exceeds the amount of its similar liabilities outside Australia: (CTH) Banking Act 1959 s 32. See also **Excess receipts of foreign currency; Mobilisation of foreign currency**.

Surrender of shares The voluntary giving up of shares to the company by a shareholder. See also **Acquire; Maintenance of capital principle**.

•**Surrender value** The amount payable to a life insurance policyholder who surrenders or cancels their policy.

Surtax A tax formerly payable in the United Kingdom in respect of incomes exceeding a certain amount per annum. It was last charged in 1972-73 and was replaced by a higher tax rate.

•**Suspension** 1. A postponement of execution of a sentence or the deferring of a judgment after legal proceedings have been concluded. 2. A temporary extinguishment in a person's right or title in something. 3. Cessation of payment of business debts as a result of insolvency 4. The temporary removal from a particular post or office for whatever reason. See also **Extinguish**.

Suspension of payment The action of a debtor who decides to stop paying creditors in general. A debtor commits an act of bankruptcy if the debtor gives notice that the debtor has suspended or is about to suspend payment of debts: (CTH) Bankruptcy Act 1966 s 40(1)(h). See also **Act of bankruptcy; Debtor**.

Suspension of performance Withholding performance of a contractual obligation pursuant to a right to suspend. The right to suspend performance may be expressly conferred by statute, by the contract, or it may be implied. An unfulfilled condition precedent, for example, confers on the plaintiff a right to suspend his or her performance until its fulfilment, as there is no obligation on the plaintiff to perform during this period: *Hare v Nicholl* [1966] 2 QB 130. Suspension of performance differs from termination; where the contract is merely suspended the parties can resume performance under the original contract. See also **Condition precedent; Termination of performance**.

Sustainable debt Debt which can readily be supported by the individual, group, company, institutions, government or nation, whatever the level of debt in absolute or relative terms. As long as lenders are willing to lend more at the going rate of interest then mounting debts may be regarded as sustainable even though increasingly burdensome; when they are not, then it is not sustainable. If debt rises indefinitely as a proportion of income, the rate of borrowing that underpins that income cannot last. See also **External debt**.

Sustainable earnings Money or other items of valuable or economic benefit expected to be received by an accounting entity to meet present needs while also taking into account costs that may arise in the future. See also **Accounting earnings**.

Swanson Committee Report The report by the Trade Practices Review Committee on the operation of the (CTH) Trade Practices Act 1974, delivered to the Minister for Business and Consumer Affairs in August 1976. The report was the first major review of the operation of the then new Act. It examined all of the major competition provisions of the Act and recommended amending or abolishing various sections. See also **Competition law; Cooney Committee Report; Griffiths Committee Report; Hilmer Report; Restrictive trade practices; Trade practices legislation**.

•Swap In corporations law, a contract under which the parties agree to exchange cash flows over a period of time. A currency swap is the exchange of a fixed rate liability in one currency for a fixed rate liability in another currency. In an interest rate swap, each cash flow represents a stream of interest payments on a certain principal sum over a certain period; in one instance at a fixed rate, and in the other, at a variable interest rate. See also **Derivative**.

Swaption An option over a swap. See also **Option**; **Swap**.

Sweatshop A workplace, particularly in the clothing and textile industries, where the employees are made to work in cramped, overcrowded or dirty surroundings for long hours and low wages. Legislation such as the (NSW) Factories, Shops and Industries Act 1962 is designed to eliminate such practices. See also **Factories shops and industries legislation**.

SWIFT See **Society for Worldwide Interbank Financial Telecommunications**.

Switching The transfer of investment between different classes of securities. Switches are of four fairly distinct kinds: policy switching, which may involve the redistribution of a portfolio to take advantage of immediate possibilities of profit; anomaly switching between securities of comparable maturity to profit from some fleeting anomaly in their prices; and in futures markets, closing a position in one delivery month of a commodity with the simultaneous inflation of a similar position in another contract month of the same commodity. When used in hedging, this tactic is referred to as 'rolling forward' the hedge.

Sydney Arbitration Centre See **Australian Centre for International Commercial Arbitration**.

Sydney Computerised Overnight Market *Abbr* – SYCOM The computerised trading system which is used for screen trading of futures contracts on the Sydney Futures Exchange (SFX). The system executes trades automatically by matching orders to buy and sell on a price and time priority basis, so that bids at a certain price are matched in chronological sequence with offers at the same price. Futures trading is conducted on the trading floor of the SFX during the day while night trading is carried on via screens using SYCOM. Inaugurated in 1989, SYCOM's function was substantially extended in 1991 where, in conjunction with the floor, it had a capacity for 24 hour trading. See also **Sydney Futures Exchange**.

Sydney Futures Exchange *Abbr* – SFE Established in 1960 as the Sydney Greasy Wool Futures Exchange, a commodity exchange trading futures contracts on wool, live cattle, 90 day bank accepted bills, the All-Ordinaries Share Price Index, three year Treasury bonds, 10 year Treasury bonds, semi-government bonds and Australian dollars, and exchange-traded options on 90 day bank accepted bills. See also **Sydney Futures Exchange Clearing House**.

Sydney Futures Exchange Business Rules *Abbr* – SFE Business Rules. Provisions of the constitution of the Sydney Futures Exchange Ltd (SFE) and other rules made by the SFE which bind members of the SFE: Corporations Law s 761. Where a person fails to comply with, observe, enforce or give effect to those rules, a court may, on the application of the SFE or of a person aggrieved by the failure, make an order giving directions concerning compliance with, observance of or enforcement of, or giving effect to, those rules: s 1140. See also **Sydney Futures Exchange; Trading etiquette**.

Sydney Futures Exchange Clearing House *Abbr* – SFECH Inaugurated in 1990, a clearing house for the Sydney Futures Exchange (SFE). Prior to 1990, its functions were performed by the International Commodities Clearing House. SFECH is a wholly-owned subsidiary of the SFE but a separate legal entity with its own board.

Sydney Futures Exchange Fidelity Fund A fund managed by the Sydney Futures Exchange under the Futures Industry Code for the compensation of clients who suffer loss as a result of defalcation or fraudulent misuse of money or other property by a member of the exchange. The fund is not available to clients who suffer loss solely as a result of trading in futures contracts. The fund is sustained by a levy on contracts traded. The Corporations Law imposes an obligation on a futures organisation and securities exchange to maintain a fidelity fund: ss 1128, 895.

Synallagmatic contract A contract in which reciprocal obligations are imposed on the parties. See also **Bilateral contract**.

•Syndic An agent or attorney who acts for a corporation or university.

•Syndicate A group of persons working together for a common purpose; for example, to purchase property such as land, or a racehorse. It is not a technical legal term. A syndicate may be a partnership if the requisite elements of a partnership are present in the arrangements between the persons. See also **Partnership**.

Syndicated loans Loans involving several banks or financial institutions joining together to raise massive sums for, quite often, a single borrower. Usually, one of the lenders takes the leading role in managing the loan. Syndicates have supported debt-financed takeovers and management buyouts as well as credit restructuring by corporations. Industrial borrowers have predominated.

Synthetic agreements for foreign exchange *Abbr* – SAFE A generic term covering two separate instruments: foreign exchange agreements and exchange rate agreements. In a SAFE contract, the two parties (a buyer and a seller) agree on a forward foreign exchange margin (forward points) on a notional amount, for a specified maturity at a specific future date (the settlement date). On the settlement date, the difference is calculated between the agreed rate on the SAFE (the contract rate) and the reference rate specified in the contract (the settlement rate). The amount due is then calculated and paid by one party to the other. No principal amounts are exchanged. The contracts are settled in cash by a payment to the counterparty whose contract is 'in the money'.

Synthetic liquidity The deft shuffling of securities among issuers, brokers, traders and buyers to stimulate prices.

Synthetic product A combination of futures contracts and physical (cash) positions and sometimes different currencies, offering a better return than is available in the cash market. An example might involve bank bill futures in combination with the physical purchase or sale of bank bills, creating a synthetic position or instrument which earns the investor a higher yield than that available from either the physical or the futures market.

T

Table A articles A set of standard form articles of association for a company limited by shares: Corporations Law Sch 1 Table A. The articles of any company, other than a no liability company, may adopt any or all of the regulations contained in Table A: s 175(1)(a). See also **Articles of association; Table A company; Table B articles**.

Table A company A company that has adopted Corporations Law Sch 1 Table A as its articles of association. See also **Articles of association; Division 1 company; Table A articles; Table B articles**.

Table B articles A model set of articles of association contained in Corporations Law Sch 1 Table B which may be adopted in whole or in part by a no liability company: Corporations Law s 175. See also **Articles of association; Table A articles**.

Tacking 1. The process by which a holder of an equitable interest can prevail over a prior equitable interest by obtaining the legal estate, provided he or she had no notice of the prior equitable interest at the time of acquiring his or her interest. Tacking is not possible if the equitable interest holder's acquisition of the legal estate involved the legal holder in a bare trust. This form of tacking has been abolished in Queensland, Victoria, and Tasmania: (VIC) Property Law Act 1958 s 94; (QLD) Property Law Act 1974 s 82; (TAS) Conveyancing and Law of Property Act 1884 s 38. It is permitted, however, if an arrangement has been made to this effect with subsequent mortgagees, if the prior mortgagor had no notice of such subsequent mortgages or if the prior mortgage imposes an obligation to make such further advances. See also **Mortgage; Priority**.

Tainted income Classes of income and gains of a controlled foreign company (CFC) such as commodity gains, exchange gains, interest income, royalty income, sales income, and service income: (CTH) Income Tax Assessment Act 1936 s 317. The calculation of a CFC's total tainted income is required in determining the attributable foreign source income derived by the controlled foreign corporation. If a CFC passes the active income test then there is no attribution of that CFC income to its Australian controller. One of the factors used in calculations the active income test is the quantum of tainted income derived by the CFC.

Taiwan Leading Composite Index An index compiled by the Taiwan Council for Economic Planning and Development. It seeks to forecast economic activities for the coming three to five months. In contrast, a coincident composite index measures economic activity for the current month.

Taiwan Stock Exchange A highly active stock market located in Taipei. The average daily trading value in shares has grown substantially in recent years. Foreigners are not allowed to buy shares directly in listed companies.

•**Take advantage of** In trade practices law, to use; the phrase is morally indifferent. In the context of (CTH) Trade Practices Act 1974 s 46, 'take advantage of' does not require any proof of hostile or predatory intent. The use need not be reprehensible, nor morally or socially undesirable: *Queensland Wire Industries Pty Ltd v Broken Hill Proprietary Co Ltd* (1989) 167 CLR 177; 83 ALR 577. See also **Market power; Misuse of market power**.

Takeover The acquisition of a controlling interest in a target company by another company through the acquisition of a sufficient proportion of the target company's shares. Corporations Law Ch 6 imposes a blanket prohibition on the acquisition of voting shares beyond a 20 per cent threshold, unless certain methods are used, including the making of offers under a takeover scheme or takeover announcement, a creeping acquisition, and shareholder approved acquisitions: ss 615-633, Pts 6.3, 6.4. See also **Acquire; Compulsory acquisition of shares; Corporations and Securities Panel; Creeping acquisition; Purchase of assets; Scheme; Takeover scheme; Takeover announcement; Voting share**.

•**Takeover announcement** A takeover procedure by which a stockbroker for the offeror makes an announcement to the market that after 14 days the broker will stand in the market for a month and will acquire all shares of the stated class of target shares which are made available by sellers at the price specified in the announcement: Corporations Law Pts 6.4, 6.5. A takeover offer is allowed as an exception to the prohibition on the acquisition of more than 20 per cent voting shares: Corporations Law s 615. On the day of the takeover announcement, a Part C statement is served on the target by the targeting company with copies to the Australian Stock Exchange (ASX), the Australian Securities Commission (ASC), and to each shareholder. The target company is then required to serve a Part D statement on the ASX, lodge a copy with the ASC, and give a copy to the offeror. Also known as 'takeover bid' or 'on-market offer'. See also **Part C statement; Part D statement; Takeover; Takeover period**.

Takeover defensive actions Strategies employed by the management of a target company during a hostile takeover bid to avoid a successful takeover, such as introducing takeover approval provisions, the use of employee share plans, or amending the articles to restrict the transfer of shares by including pre-emptive rights: *North Sydney Brick and Tile Co Ltd v Darvall* (1986) 5 NSWLR 681. Parts B or D statements in response to the takeover must not contain materially false statements: Corporations Law s 704(3). Similarly these defensive actions must not be a breach of directors' fiduciary duties: *Howard Smith Ltd v Ampol Petroleum Ltd* [1974] AC 821; [1974] 1 NSWLR 68; (1974) 3 ALR 448. See also **Directors' duties; Takeover scheme; Target company**.

Takeover period 1. In relation to a takeover scheme under Corporations Law Pt A, the period beginning when the Corporations Law Pt A statement was served on the target company and ending at the end of 28 days after the day on which the statement was served or, if offers are sent pursuant to the statement before the end of those 28 days, at the end of the offer period. 2. In relation to a takeover announcement under Corporations Law Pt C, the period beginning when the announcement was made and ending at the end of the offer period: Corporations Law s 603. See also **Takeover scheme; Takeover announcement; Part A statement; Part C statement.**

•**Takeover scheme** A formal takeover procedure by which an offeror files and dispatches a disclosure document (Part A statement) together with written offers, and the target responds with a Part B statement: Corporations Law Pts 6.3, 6.5. The procedure is structured as an exception to the prohibition in s 615 on acquisitions of shares beyond the 20 per cent threshold. The Part A statement along with one of the offers must first be registered by the Australian Securities Commission (ASC), then served on the target company and sent to the target shareholders. The Part B statement is given to the offeror, sent to the target company's shareholders, served on the stock exchange, and lodged with the ASC. See also **Acquire; Compulsory acquisition of shares; On-market acquisition; Part A statement; Part B statement; Takeover; Takeover period.**

Taker In corporations law, the purchaser of an option contract. The taker pays a consideration to the seller (writer) and receives the right under the option contract. See also **Option; Writer.**

Target audience The group of persons to whom particular conduct, statements, or representations are directed. Whether conduct is misleading or deceptive is tested according to the likely effect of the conduct in question on the target audience or the group of persons at whom the conduct would ordinarily be directed: (CTH) Trade Practices Act 1974 s 52; *Taco Company of Australia Inc v Taco Bell Pty Ltd* (1982) 42 ALR 177; 2 TPR 48. See also **Misleading or deceptive conduct.**

•**Target company** In relation to a takeover offer, the company for the acquisition of shares in which that offer has been, or is proposed to be sent; in relation to a takeover scheme, the company shares in which are proposed to be acquired under the scheme; and in relation to a takeover announcement, the company in relation to shares in which the takeover announcement has been, or is proposed to be, made: Corporations Law s 603. Also known as 'target firm'. See also **Takeover scheme; Takeover announcement.**

•**Tariff** The imposition of a tariff has the effect of increasing the price of the imported commodity, and may allow domestic producers of the same good to increase their prices also. However, the actual effect of a tariff depends upon a number of factors: the response of consumers to a higher import price and possibly higher domestic prices; the availability and price of close substitutes; the actual response of domestic producers individually who may seek to increase market share against immediate rivals; and the reaction of those firms who use the commodity as an input to production. See also **Industry Statement 1991; Protection.**

Task rate Wages paid to a worker once the worker has completely performed a task. For example, a radio play artist who is paid a fixed fee for performance is paid by task rates: *Federal Cmr of Taxation v J Walter Thompson (Aust) Pty Ltd* (1944) 69 CLR 227; 18 ALJ 178. See also **Piece work.**

•**Tax** See **Taxation.**

•**Tax Act** See **Income Tax Assessment Legislation.**

Tax agent A person registered with the Tax Agents' Board in his or her State and who is allowed to charge a fee for preparing income tax returns and transacting business on behalf of taxpayers in income tax matters: (CTH) Income Tax Assessment Act 1936 s 251L. A tax agent must be a fit and proper person, have appropriate qualifications, be able to prepare income tax returns, deal competently with taxation queries, and must not have been convicted of a serious taxation offence during the last five years, or be an undischarged bankrupt: (CTH) Income Tax Assessment Act 1936 ss 251JA(1), 251BC(1). See also **Tax return.**

Tax allocation A process of accruing income tax in respect of accounting income derived in a specified period. A tax allocation is used where the difference in the timing of revenue or expenses for accounting and income tax purposes cause differences between accounting and taxable income. The difference in amount between the accounting provision for current income tax payable on the accounting income and the income tax currently payable represents the recognition of current tax expected to be recovered or payable in the future. The taxable income of an organisation may differ from the accounting income shown on the financial statements due to the different methods used in determining each.

Tax avoidance A scheme or arrangement where a taxpayer enters into a transaction that complies with the letter of the tax law but has the effect of obtaining a tax benefit. The tax benefit of a tax avoidance scheme may be nullified under the anti-avoidance provisions in the (CTH) Income Tax Assessment Act 1936 Pt IVA. Traditionally, tax avoidance was distinguished from tax evasion because avoidance does not involve active or passive fault by the taxpayer: *Australasian Jam Co Pty Ltd v FCT* (1953) 88 CLR 23; 5 AITR 566. See also **Assessable income; Derived; Tax evasion; Tax planning; Attributable taxpayer.**

Tax base The measure to which tax rates are applied in calculating tax liability. The tax base may be expressed in value terms (for example, income, the value of retail sales) or as a physical quantity (for example a kilogram of sugar). The most common tax base is income.

•**Tax benefit** In relation to the anti-avoidance provisions of the (CTH) Income Tax Assessment Act 1936 Pt IVA, either an amount not included as assessable income that would have been included if the tax avoidance scheme had not been entered into, or a deduction allowed to the taxpayer where the whole or part of that deduction would not be allowed if the scheme had not been entered into: (CTH) Income Tax Assessment Act 1936 s 177C(1). See also **Allowable deduction; Assessable income; Scheme; Non-resident taxpayer.**

Tax determination See **Taxation determination.**

Tax effect accounting The method of calculating income tax expense where the tax is considered to be an expense incurred by the entity in earning income, and is accrued in the same period as the revenues and expenses to which it relates: Applicable Accounting Standard AASB 1020; Australian Accounting Standard AAS3. The tax expense is calculated by applying the tax rate to pre-tax accounting profit instead of to taxable income. The amount of income tax attributable to the transactions in the profit and loss account is recognised irrespective of whether the tax is currently payable, has already been paid, or will become payable in the future. The approach therefore gives rise to a provision for deferred income tax to recognise the effect of timing differences, and to future income tax benefits in respect of both timing differences and tax losses. See also **Assessment; Deferred annuity; Pretax profit; Timing differences.**

Tax evasion The illegal non-payment of tax that would be properly payable if a full and true disclosure of assessable income and allowable deductions had been made. Tax evasion involves a breach of legal obligations. Tax evasion must be distinguished from tax avoidance, which does not involve active or passive fault by the taxpayer: *Australian Jam Co Pty Ltd v FCT* (1953) 88 CLR 23; [1953] ALR 855. See also **Assessable income; Allowable deduction; Incurred; Tax avoidance; Tax planning.**

Tax exemption See **Exempt income.**

• **Tax file number** *Abbr* – TFN A unique number issued by the Australian Taxation Office for each taxpayer: (CTH) Income Tax Assessment Act 1936 s 202A. The purposes of a tax file number include detecting non-disclosure of income and enabling the Australian Taxation Office to 'match' the details of income disclosed in a taxpayer's return with details it receives from other sources: (CTH) Income Tax Assessment Act 1936 s 202. Employers and other tax file number recipients must comply with guidelines under the (CTH) Privacy Act 1988 to ensure the security of tax file number information. Penalties apply where tax file number information is misused: (CTH) Taxation Administration Act 1953 ss 8WA, 8WB. See also **Australian Taxation Office.**

Tax haven A country offering low tax rates, or zero tax, and other incentives to foreign companies and investors. Tax havens can be used by companies to shift income from high to low taxing countries, usually with the assistance of a subsidiary as an intermediary. The use of tax havens by Australian companies is less common since 1 July 1990 when the foreign accruals taxation system was introduced: (CTH) Income Tax Assessment Act 1936 Pt III, Div 6AAA; Pts X, XI. See also **Accruals tax; Company rate of tax; Tax rate.**

Tax holiday A period, usually of years, during which a corporate taxpayer is not required to pay any income or company tax. Tax holidays are usually granted by governments when trying to promote new development in a particular area.

Tax instalment See **Tax instalment deduction.**

Tax instalment deduction An amount of tax deducted by an employer under the pay as you earn system. Every employer, including government bodies, is generally required to withhold tax instalment deductions at prescribed rates from each payment of salary or wages made to an employee: (CTH) Income Tax Assessment Act 1936 s 221C(1A). The tax instalment deductions withheld by employers are not a final liability, but operate as an estimate of tax payable on the current income. The total tax instalment deductions made during the year are applied against the tax liability ascertained after the end of the income year. See also **Pay As You Earn system; Salary; Wage; Year of income.**

Tax loss The excess of allowable deductions (other than any unrecouped losses brought forward from an earlier year) over the sum of assessable income and net exempt income for a taxpayer for a year: (CTH) Income Tax Assessment Act 1936 ss 79E(1), 80(1). See also **Allowable deduction; Assessable income; Exempt income; Loss; Net exempt income; Taxable income.**

Tax minimisation See **Tax avoidance.**

Tax office See **Australian Taxation Office.**

Tax office audit strategy A policy aimed at increasing audit activity to ensure that taxpayers comply with the rules. The Australian Taxation Office (ATO) conducts various types of audit programmes on big companies, small businesses, and individuals. While the ATO offers advice to taxpayers on what is required, it can also impose penalties for breaches of tax laws and for income tax offences. The strategy extends to assisting other enforcement agencies in the investigation of criminal activities. See also **Australian Taxation Office.**

Tax planning The arrangement of a taxpayer's affairs in such a way as to minimise the amount of tax to be paid. The underlying assumption in tax planning is that there is no obligation on any citizen, legal or moral, to pay more tax than is required by law and affairs may be so arranged as to minimise tax payable. See also **Tax avoidance; Tax evasion; Tax shelter.**

Tax rate The rate of tax applicable for a year as specified in (CTH) Income Tax (Rates) Act 1986. Income tax payable is a function of the taxable income and the applicable tax rates. The (CTH) Income Tax (Rates) Act 1986 ss 5-20 contain rates of tax applicable to individuals, beneficiaries, and trustees. Sections 21-28 contain rates of tax applicable to companies, superannuation funds, prescribed unit trusts, and certain other trusts. The tax rate applied to an individual's income increases as the taxable income level increases: (CTH) Income Tax (Rates) Act 1986 sch 7. See also **Income taxation; Progressive tax; Tax base; Tax free threshold; Taxable income.**

Tax records Records which are required to be kept under the (CTH) Income Tax Assessment Act 1936, including any documents that are relevant for the purpose of ascertaining the person's income and expenditure, and documents containing particulars of any election estimate, determinations, or calculations made by the person under the Act: s 262A(2). In general a person who has possession of tax records which are kept or obtained under or for the purposes of the Act must retain those records for five years after the records were prepared or obtained, or five years after the completion of the transactions or acts to which those records relate, whichever occurs later: s 262A(4)(a). See also **Tax return.**

Tax reimbursement arrangement A system under which the Commonwealth Government collects all income taxes in Australia and then reimburses the States through State grants, determined according to size and need. This arrangement has been employed since the introduction of the Uniform Income Tax Scheme. See also **Uniform Income Tax Scheme**.

Tax return A form supplied by the Australian Taxation Office in which taxpayers must accurately disclose their income from all sources, claim tax deductible expenses incurred during the financial year. Tax returns must be lodged according to the relevant due date. See also **Tax records**.

Tax shelter An arrangement where the derivation of assessable income is deferred until a latter income tax year, or the incurring of a tax deduction is brought forward into an income tax year earlier than the income tax year in which the deduction would have been normally claimed. See also **Tax avoidance; Tax evasion; Tax planning**.

•**Tax stamp** See **Tax stamp system**.

Tax stamp system A system which previously operated for non-group employers who maintained a tax deduction sheet for each employee and purchased tax stamps equal to the amount of any income tax deductions which were required to be made from the salary, wages, or eligible termination payments made to the employee. The tax stamp system was phased out and all employers are now covered by the group employer system. See also **Eligible termination payment; Group employer**.

Taxable asset See **Asset**.

•**Taxable income** The excess of assessable income over allowable deductions for a taxpayer, for a period, calculated in accordance with the provisions of the applicable income tax laws: (CTH) Income Tax Assessment Act 1936 ss 6(1), 48. See also **Allowable deduction; Assessable income; Tax loss**.

•**Taxation** A compulsory exaction of money by a government for public purposes, being neither a pecuniary penalty nor a fee for services rendered: *Matthews v Chicory Marketing Board (Vic)* (1938) 60 CLR 263. Taxation in Australia is levied at three levels of government: Federal, State, and local. Examples of Federal taxes include income tax, fringe benefits tax, sales tax, customs and excise duty, and departure tax. State taxes include land tax, payroll tax, stamp duty, financial institutions duty, and debits tax. Local government taxes include property rates. Taxes may be classified as either progressive, regressive, or proportional. Taxes on income such as wages, salaries, profits, dividends, rent and interest, and on capital gains are known as direct taxes. Taxes on commodities or services are known as indirect taxes. In the early 1990s, the Commonwealth government obtained over 90 per cent of its revenue from direct and indirect taxation. Some four per cent of its revenue came from customs duties and tariffs. State and local government taxes include payroll taxes, land taxes, and indirect taxes. Total tax revenues in Australia amount to about 33 per cent of gross domestic product, higher than in the United States and Japan, but lower than in Britain, Sweden, and Germany. See also **Customs duty; Debits tax; Excise; Financial institutions duty; Fringe benefits tax; Income taxation; Land tax; Payroll tax; Progressive tax; Proportional tax; Regressive tax; Sales tax; Stamp duty**.

Taxation, arbitrary See **Arbitrary taxation**.

Taxation Board of Review Formerly, a federal administrative body with power to review specified decisions on objections against assessments of tax by the Commissioner of Taxation. The powers of the Board were amalgamated into the Administrative Appeals Tribunal in 1986. See also **Administrative Appeals Tribunal**.

Taxation, Commissioner of See **Commissioner of Taxation**.

Taxation Determination A guideline of the Australian Taxation Office's (ATO) interpretive and administrative policy, issued by the Commissioner of Taxation. A Taxation Determination usually addresses only one particular taxation issue and is not intended to be a comprehensive analysis of the overall impact of general tax provisions. See also **Commissioner of Taxation; Taxation Determination System; Taxation Ruling**.

Taxation Determination System A system under which taxation determinations are released. The Taxation Determination System was introduced to complement the Taxation Rulings System. See also **Taxation Determination**.

•**Taxation offence** An offence against a taxation law or an offence relating to an offence against a taxation law: (CTH) Taxation Administration Act 1953 s 8A; (CTH) Crimes Act 1914 ss 6, 7, 7A, 29A, 29B, 29D, 86(1). For example, it is an offence to recklessly make a false or misleading statement to a taxation officer: (CTH) Taxation Administration Act 1953 s 8N. A person may be guilty of a taxation offence even though he or she is merely an accessory after the fact to a taxation offence: (CTH) Crimes Act 1914 s 6. Taxation offences may be punished by administrative penalty only or may be prosecuted and a penalty of fine or imprisonment imposed: *R v Whitnall* (1993) 42 FCR 512; 120 ALR 449. See also **Offence**.

Taxation Ruling A new or revised guideline issued by the Commissioner of Taxation on some taxation matter of public importance. From 1 July 1992, a system of public and private rulings was introduced: (CTH) Taxation Administration Act 1953 Pts IVAAA, IVAA. The system enables the Commissioner to fulfil his or her obligations under the (CTH) Freedom of Information Act 1982 by making documents used in decisions publicly available. See also **Taxation Determination**.

•**Tax-free threshold** The portion of an individual taxpayer's income subject to a zero tax rate under the ordinary rates scale: (CTH) Income Tax (Rates) Act 1986 s 12(1), Sch 7 Pt 1(1). Taxable income in excess of the tax-free threshold is taxed at progressive rates. Where a taxpayer first ceases full-time education, a pro-rating of the tax-free threshold applies: (CTH) Income Tax (Rates) Act 1986 Pt II, Div IV. The tax-free threshold does not apply to non-residents: (CTH) Income Tax (Rates) Act 1986 s 12(1), Sch 7 Pt II(1). Also known as 'general exemption'. See also **Income taxation; Progressive tax; Pro-rata; Tax rate; Taxable income**.

Technology transfer 1. The transfer of development and design work from a parent company to a subsidiary, often in another country where it will be paid for through royalties and repatriated profits. The Commonwealth Government has endeavoured to reduce the dependence of overseas firms in Australia on scientists and engineers in their parent companies by making offset arrangements a part of large contracts. 2. The passage of technical, scientific, and industrial knowledge and information from one state to another, as an integral part of trade deals and development activities. See also **United Nations Industrial Development Organisation**.

Teller 1. A bank officer who receives or pays out money or may do both. In England and the Commonwealth countries such an officer is called a cashier. Such an officer has general authority to part with the property in the bank's money as well as the possession of it. 2. A member of parliament appointed by the Speaker to collect and tally votes arising from a division. See also **Cashier**.

Telstra Corporation Limited A wholly government-owned telecommunications carrier. It was previously called the 'Australian and Overseas Telecommunications Corporation', and is now known domestically as 'Telstra'. Telstra is licensed as a general telecommunications carrier and as a public mobile carrier. It is subject to ministerial direction, and to a range of price capping and price control arrangements: (CTH) Telstra Corporation Act 1991 ss 8(1), 9, 19-25.

Temporal exclusion clause An exclusion clause that excludes liability for a loss suffered while specified circumstances exist. For example, a clause in a motor vehicle policy excluding liability for loss sustained at a time when the vehicle is being used in an unsafe condition: *Bashtannyk v New India Assurance Co Ltd* [1968] VR 573. Temporal exclusion clauses apply irrespective of whether the circumstances directly cause a loss. However, the courts may allow recovery when the relevant circumstances could not have caused or contributed to the loss: *Bashtannyk v New India Assurance Co Ltd* [1968] VR 573. See also **Causal exclusion clause**; **Clause**; **Exclusion clause**.

•**Tenancy** Originally, any right of occupation and seisin of land, including freehold. In modern times, the term is still used in this sense when referring to a joint tenancy, a tenancy in common or a tenancy for life. However, the modern usage is more often in the context of a landlord and a tenant, meaning a right to occupy the land of another, usually (though not only) for a term of years. Some statutes extend its meaning to a right of occupancy which is not necessarily exclusive, as in (NSW) Residential Tenancies Act 1987 s 3(1). The term is also used to refer to other types of arrangement such as sharefarming: (NSW) Agricultural Tenancies Act 1990 s 4. See also **Joint tenancy**; **Tenancy agreement**; **Tenancy in common**; **Tenant**.

•**Tenancy agreement** An agreement, whether or not in writing and either express or implied, under which a lease is created. The term is restricted in its operation in various statutes to leases for residential purposes: for example (VIC) Residential Tenancies Act 1980 s 2. See also **Lease**.

Tenancy in common A type of co-ownership where two or more persons own distinct interests in the same piece of property. The tenants in common hold undivided shares, possessing the property in common and without exclusive possession of any part of it. The shares may be in different proportions. Tenants in common may deal with their respective shares as they wish during their lifetime, and usually may devise them by will. Joint tenants or tenants in common are each regarded as having the same sufficient title to sue a trespasser or even another joint tenant or tenant in common if the co-tenant expels him or her from the land or destroys the subject of the co-tenancy without his or her consent: *Greig v Greig* [1966] VR 376. See also **Aliquot share**; **Joint tenancy**; **Undivided share**.

•**Tenant** 1. A term originating in feudal times, referring to a person who held 'tenure' of land either from the Crown or a mesne lord. The term was not restricted to those who held a leasehold interest only, but applied to a person who held any interest in land, even in fee simple. The use of the term in this sense has become much less common over time, although it is still seen in such terms as 'tenant in common', 'joint tenant', and 'life tenant'. 2. In modern times, the term is used almost exclusively to refer to a person who holds land under a tenancy from a landlord, whether for a term of years, or under a periodical tenancy, or at will, or at sufferance. During the currency of a tenancy, a tenant is entitled to exclusive possession of the premises the subject of the tenancy against all the world, including the landlord (with limited exceptions): *Radaich v Smith* (1959) 101 CLR 209; [1959] ALR 1253. See also **Landlord**; **Lease**; **Lessee**; **Tenancy**.

Tenant at will A lessee who is granted possession (often by implication) by the lessor, subject to either party having a right to terminate the resulting lease at any time: *Commonwealth Life (Amalgamated) Assurance Ltd v Anderson* (1945) 46 SR (NSW) 47 at 49; 62 WN (NSW) 240. Usually, the lessee does not pay rent: *Ex parte Rooney* (1873) 11 SCR (NSW) 381. See also **Lease**; **Rent**.

Tenant by sufferance A person who is in possession of land without the assent or dissent of the person entitled to possession, or without statutory imprimatur, and whose initial entry into possession was by consent. See also **Lease**; **Possession**; **Trespass**.

•**Tenant in possession** A person who is in actual possession or occupation of land: *Burke v Dawes* (1938) 59 CLR 1; [1938] ALR 135. See also **Tenant**; **Term of years**.

Tenantable repair A state of repair which, taking into account the age, character, and locality of the leased premises, would make the premises reasonably fit for occupation by a reasonably minded tenant of the class likely to rent them: *Proudfoot v Hart* (1890) 25 QBD 42. It is synonymous with good repair and habitable repair: *Anstruther-Gough-Calthorpe v McOscar* [1924] 1 KB 716. See also **Premises**; **Covenant to repair**; **Tenant**; **Tenant-like manner**.

Tenant-like manner A standard of repair for a tenant which amounts to taking care of the leased property on a day to day basis having regard to the length of the lease.

Tenant's fixtures Items affixed to leased premises by a tenant which the tenant may remove at or before the end of the lease. They are an exception to the rule that fixtures run with the reversion. Tenant's fixtures must be intended for trade, domestic or ornamental purposes. The tenant is obliged to make good any damage caused in removing the fixtures. See also **Chattel**.

• **Tender** The calling for others to make an offer, usually for the supply or purchase of goods or services. The seeking of tenders is an invitation to treat. The submission of the tender to the inviter is an offer which the inviter is subsequently free to accept or reject: *Meudell v Mayor of Bendigo* (1900) 26 VLR 158; 6 ALR 174. If the tender is for the definite supply or purchase of goods or services, acceptance of the tender creates a binding contract. If the tender is for supply of goods or services which may or may not be required, the tender constitutes a standing offer. In such a case, acceptance by the inviter of a submitted tender does not bind the inviter to accept all or any part of the goods or services in question. Instead, a separate contract is created every time the inviter orders goods or services in accordance with the tender: *Colonial Ammunition Co v Reid* (1900) 21 LR (NSW) 338 at 346; 17 WN (NSW) 192. The tenderer can revoke the standing offer at any time and in doing so will not be bound to deliver any goods or services that have not at that stage been ordered: *Colonial Ammunition Co v Reid* (1900) 21 LR (NSW) 338 at 346; 17 WN (NSW) 192. See also **Offer and acceptance; Standing offer**.

Tender of performance The offer of performance made by the promisor to the promisee. The promisor must tender the performance within the time required by the contract, unless the promisee has dispensed with the requirement: *Foran v Wight* (1989) 168 CLR 385; 88 ALR 413. See also **Legal tender; Order of performance; Performance**.

• **Tenure** The mode of holding land, derived from feudal times, under which a person (the 'tenant') holds land 'of' or from another. All land in Australia and the United Kingdom that has been granted by the Crown, even that in fee simple, is held by tenure rather than absolute ownership, as the Crown alone is the source of all tenure. Land held under native title is an exception, since native title rights do not derive from any Crown grant: *Mabo v Queensland (No 2)* (1992) 175 CLR 1; 107 ALR 1. See also **Crown land; Estate**.

Term 1. In general, any clause or provision in a contract. Terms are also described as clauses, stipulations, provisions, covenants, and obligations. Apart from the terms expressly stated in the contract, by reason of what the parties have written or said, implied terms may also exist to impose obligations on either or both of the parties or to qualify the terms of their bargain. 2. A contractual statement which amounts to an undertaking or guarantee by the maker of the statement, that it is true or that the maker had reasonable grounds for making it: for example *Ellul v Oakes* (1972) 3 SASR 377. Also known as 'warranty'. See also **Contract; Incorporation by notice; Incorporation by reference; Incorporation by signature; Pre-contractual statement; Puffery; Representation; Warranty**.

Term annuity An annuity that guarantees an income for a set number of years, commonly five or 10. If the retiree dies before the term is complete, the income goes to that person's estate. See also **Annuity**.

Term bill A bill of exchange which is expressed to be payable at a fixed or determinable future time. A bill is payable at a determinable future time if it is expressed to be payable at a fixed period after date or sight or on the occurrence, or at a fixed period after the occurrence, of a specified event which is certain to happen, even though the time of happening may be certain: Bill of Exchange Act 1909 s 16; *Korea Exchange bank v Debenhams (Central Buying) Ltd* [1979] 1 Lloyd's Rep 548 See also **Bill of exchange**.

Term deposit An investment by which a customer can place funds on deposit with a bank for a specified period in exchange for a fixed rate of interest for the full term: for example (CTH) Commonwealth Bank Sale Act 1995 s 117(4). See also **Deposit**.

Term insurance A life insurance policy where the sum insured is only payable if the death of the person whose life is insured occurs during the term of the policy. Term insurance premiums do not contain an investment component and the insurer incurs no liability if the insured is alive at the end of the term. Term insurance is also called 'temporary insurance'. See also **Life insurance**.

Term lease A lease for a specified period of time. This period must be certain and upon its conclusion the lease ceases automatically: *Right Flower v Darby* (1786) 1 TR 159; 99 ER 1029. The lease will still be regarded as having a specified duration even when it can also be determined upon a specified event happening prior to the specified date of conclusion: *Porter v Williams* (1914) 14 SR (NSW) 83; *Withers v Evans* [1967] 2 NSWR 187. See also **Lease**.

• **Term loan** A borrowing of money for a fixed period, which must be repaid by the end of the specified period: *State Bank of South Australia v Nicholls* [1993] 1 VR 259.

Term of years An interest in land which lasts for a fixed term, nearly always a leasehold estate in land. See also **Leasehold**.

Term subordinated debt A fixed term subordinated loan. With a minimum maturity at issue of seven years it has limited recognition as tier two capital under the capital adequacy guidelines of the Reserve Bank of Australia.

Term to maturity The number of days, months or years until a loan, bill of exchange, bond, insurance policy or other security becomes due for repayment. See also **Bond; Loan**.

Termination To bring to an end a contract or contractual obligation. A contractual obligation may be terminated by performance, consent (for example *Fitzgerald v Masters* (1956) 95 CLR 420), breach (for example *Associated Newspapers Ltd v Bancks* (1951) 83 CLR 322), nonfulfilment of a contingent condition (for example *Perri v Coolangatta Investments Pty Ltd* (1982) 149 CLR 537; 41 ALR 441), or frustration (for example *Codelfa Construction Pty Ltd v State Rail Authority of New South Wales* (1982) 149 CLR 337; 41 ALR 367). On termination, both parties are discharged from the further performance of the contract, but rights are not divested or discharged which have been unconditionally acquired: *McDonald v Dennys Lascelles Ltd* (1933) 48 CLR 457. The right to damages survives termination. Termination is distinct from rescission; but sometimes termination is called 'rescission in futuro', to distinguish it from rescission proper, 'rescission ab initio' (rescission from the beginning). See also **Accrued right; Breach of contract; Damages; Performance; Repudiation; Rescission; Right to terminate; Suspension of performance.**

Termination benefits Under the Australian Stock Exchange (ASX) Listing Rules, any payments, property and advantages of every description convertible into money which are receivable upon termination of the office or employment of any director or employee, but not including payments from any superannuation or provident fund or payments required by law to be made: ASX Listing Rules rule 10.18. A listed company or any entities with which it is associated is prohibited from entering into a service agreement making available or increasing termination benefits upon a change in control of the company, that prohibition being directed against the adoption by listed companies of 'golden parachute' defences against takeovers: ASX Listing Rules rules 10.19, 14.11. Any service agreement must receive the prior approval of shareholders in general meeting if the termination benefits receivable under that agreement, aggregated with termination benefits receivable under all other service agreements then in force, exceed five per cent of the total share capital and reserves of the company. See also **Director.**

Termination clause A contractual right of termination or discharge. A termination clause may expressly confer a power to terminate, or it may clarify when a power to terminate arises, by defining contractual terms or classifying the breach of particular terms. An express contractual right of termination is strictly interpreted, in that the right may not be exercised in advance of the stipulated time, and a party may not act on the clause before giving any notice required to be given under it: for example *Rawson v Hobbs* (1961) 107 CLR 466. See also **Breach of contract; Discharge; Notice; Right to terminate; Term; Termination.**

Termination of agency The bringing to an end of a relationship of principal and agent. Termination may occur by an act of the parties, which includes: agreement to terminate, and revocation of the agent's authority by the principal (*Tynan v A'Beckett* [1923] VLR 412 at 421; (1923) 44 ALT 189) renunciation of the agency by the agent (*Hochster v De La Tour* (1853) 2 El & Bl 678; 118 ER 922) and dismissal of the agent for accepting secret commissions. It may also occur by operation of law, which includes: completed performance by the agent: (*Bell v Balls* [1897] 1 Ch 663); the expiration of the time for which the agent was appointed; the death, bankruptcy, or mental incapacity of the agent: (*Re Overweg; Haas v Durant* [1900] 1 Ch 209; *Gibbons v Wright* (1954) 91 CLR 423 at 445), the principal becoming an enemy alien; the subject matter of the agency becoming illegal or being destroyed; and the performance of the agency becoming impossible or illegal. See also **Agency; Agent; Power of attorney; Principal; Special agent; Universal agent.**

Termination of performance The discharge of a promisor's obligation to perform, or to be already and willing to perform, contractual duties. The discharge may occur: automatically, either pursuant to an express term of the contract, or under the doctrine of frustration; by an election to treat the contract as discharged, or pursuant to an express clause, either under common law principles governing discharge for breach or repudiation; or by the exercise of a statutory right. See also **Discharge; Performance; Repudiation; Termination.**

Termination of receiver The discharge of a receiver or the resignation of a receiver upon completion of the task for which the receiver was appointed. The company's existence continues and control of its property, if any, reverts to its directors, unless a liquidator or other insolvency administrator is acting, or the receiver is replaced. A court-appointed receiver must apply to the court for a discharge unless the court order provides for the automatic termination of the appointment: Corporations Law ss 434, 434B. See also **Court appointed receiver; Privately appointed receiver; Receiver.**

Terms and conditions 1. The stipulations in a contract or agreement. **2.** In the maritime context, the expression 'term' refers to the general nature of the contract of carriage, for example, free on board. The expression 'condition' refers to the kind of payment such as 'cash against documents', 'letter of credit' or 'payment after 30 days'. See also **Bill of lading; Charterparty; Cost insurance freight contract; Free on board.**

Terms charge In a hire-purchase agreement, any charge payable under the agreement other than a charge for insurance, maintenance of the goods, delivery, vehicle registration fees, and stamp duty: (VIC) Hire-Purchase Act 1959 s 3(2)(e)(ix); (QLD) Hire-Purchase Act 1959 s 3(2)(e)(viii). See also **Hire-purchase agreement.**

•**Terms contract** An executory contract for the sale and purchase of land under which the purchaser is required to make two or more payments to the vendor before the purchaser is entitled to a conveyance or transfer, or is entitled to possession or occupation of the land before being entitled to a conveyance or transfer: (VIC) Sale of Land Act 1962 s 2. See also **Conveyance; Executory contract; Instalment contract; Possession.**

Terms of settlement The terms of an agreement to settle out of court. To record and give expression to the terms of a settlement the parties may enter into a formal agreement or deed, taking effect as a contract, and providing for the discontinuance of the proceedings. The terms of a settlement or compromise may also be expressed in a consent order pronounced in open court, known in these circumstances as a 'rule of court': *Re Hearn; de Bertodano v Hearn* (1913) 108 LT 452; *Ashenden v Stewarts & Lloyds (Aust) Ltd* [1972] 2 NSWLR 484. Where parties reach an agreement and the agreement is not filed, the court may note that the parties have reached an agreement and have decided to keep the terms confidential: (CTH) Practice Note No 4 (Federal Court) (1994) 45 FCR 5; 121 ALR 702. See also **Settlement**.

Terms of trade The ratio of a country's export prices to its import prices. It measures the purchasing power of its exports in terms of the imports they can buy. If the ratio worsens, that is, if export prices fall relative to import prices, a given volume of exports will buy fewer imports. The terms of trade figure is calculated by comparing the export price index (an index of export prices received in foreign currency) and the import price index (an index of the cost of imports in Australian dollars).

Tertiary industry The provision of services required by the primary and secondary industries and by individual consumers; for example, the provision of transport, communications, health, finance, education, entertainment, and the wholesale and retail trades. The development of the service sector has been a leading feature of most industrial economies. See also **Primary industry; Secondary industry; Services**.

TFN See **Tax file number**.

Thailand Stock Exchange Located in Bangkok, the securities exchange of Thailand. Prices are monitored by the Securities Exchange of Thailand (SET) Index. Restrictions on foreign ownership continue; no foreigner may own more than 49 percent of a company or more than 25 percent of a bank.

Thin capitalisation For income tax purposes, the capitalisation of an Australian entity where the foreign debt of that Australian company, trust, or partnership if it has a foreign controller, exceeds the ratio of the foreign equity of that entity by more than 3:1, or 6:1 in the case of an Australian bank. The interest allowable as a deduction is reduced to the extent that the foreign debt to foreign equity ratio exceeds the permitted level: (CTH) Income Tax Assessment Act 1936 ss 159GZS-159GZW. See also **Capitalisation; Foreign controller; Foreign debt; Foreign equity; Non-resident associate of a foreign controller**.

•**Third party** A person who is not a principal to an agreement, proceeding or transaction.

Agency In agency law, a person who is neither a principal nor agent. The third party is usually the person brought into a legal relationship with the principal by the agent. Also referred to as 'third person', 'outside party' or, 'stranger': *Hely-Hutchinson v Brayhead Ltd* [1968] 1 QB 549. See also **Agency; Agent; Principal**.

Contract In relation to a contract, a person who is not a party to that contract. Generally, according to the doctrine of privity of contract, only the parties to a contract are bound by and entitled to enforce its terms: *Trident General Insurance Co Ltd v McNiece Bros Pty Ltd* (1988) 165 CLR 107; 80 ALR 574. See also **Compulsory third party insurance; Jus tertii; Privity of contract**.

Third party cheque Where the name of the payee of the cheque is different from the name of the account to which the cheque is sought to be credited. A cheque in the business or trade name of a customer or a name which is so similar to the customer's name that it is reasonable in all the circumstances for the bank to have assumed that the customer was the person intended by the drawee to be the payee is not a third party cheque: (CTH) Cheques and Payment Orders Act 1986 s 95(2). See also **Cheque; Conversion of cheques**.

Third party insurance 1. A contract of insurance in which the insurer promises to indemnify the insured against liability to third parties. Certain types of third party insurance, such as third party motor vehicle insurance, are compulsory. 2. A contract of insurance in which a third party has an interest. For example, a third party may claim under a contract of insurance if he or she is specified or referred to, by name or otherwise, in the contract as a person covered by the contract: (CTH) Insurance Contracts Act 1984 s 48; *Trident General Insurance Co Ltd v McNiece Bros Pty Ltd* (1988) 165 CLR 107; 80 ALR 574. See also **Assignment; Insurance contract; Liability insurance; Workers' compensation insurance**.

Third party mortgage A mortgage provided by a borrower to secure advances of money made by the mortgagee to the borrower; *Commercial Bank of Australia Ltd v Amadio* (1983) 151 CLR 447; (1983) 46 ALR 402. A mortgagee should ensure that a guarantor providing a third party mortgage is given full legal advice as to the potential that may arise before entering into the transaction. See also **Guarantee; Mortgage**.

Third person See **Third party**.

Third World Countries of Africa, South America, Asia and the Pacific regions which are poor and not highly industrialised. The term is attributed to the French geographer Rene Dumont who first used it in 1947 to describe underdeveloped countries as opposed to the advanced industrialised nations which he categorised as First World and the Eastern European nations, which though poor had promising economies, which he categorised as Second World. See also **International Bank for Reconstruction and Development**.

Thro B/L See **Through bill of lading**.

Through bill of lading *Abbr* – TBL A bill of lading issued when more than one carrier is required for the carriage to be completed and the sea journey only forms one part of the complete carriage of the goods from the consignor to the consignee: *Sidney Cooke Ltd v Hapag-Lloyd Aktiengesellschaft* [1980] 2 NSWLR 587. Such a contract requires at least one transhipment for its performance. The issuers of the bill may be responsible for the goods throughout the carriage, or for only one leg, acting as agent of the carriers undertaking the on-carriage. Also known as 'combined transport bill'. See also **Bill of lading; Carriage by sea; Carriage of goods; Contract of carriage; On board bill of lading; Successive carriage; Transit**.

•**Ticket** 1. A document or voucher entitling a person to travel on a train, bus, ferry or other mode of transport for a particular journey or type of journey: for example (QLD) Transport Infrastructure (Railways) Act 1991 s 3A(1). A ticket may represent a binding contract between the parties. Any conditions on the ticket must be reasonably brought to the notice of the other party: *Parker v South Eastern Railway Co* (1877) 2 CPD 416.

2. In connection with a totalisator, a card, token, or thing entitling a person to an interest in any dividend or distribution in money as the consequence of the operation of a totalisator: for example (VIC) Gaming and Betting Act 1994 s 3(1). A ticket can be construed as an instrument of gaming: *Jennings v Yet Ching* (1931) 48 WN (NSW) 248. See also **Contract**; **Ticket cases**.

Ticket cases A line of cases which stand for the principle that, where one party makes an offer to contract on terms stated in or referred to in a document received by the other party, that party's decision to keep the document indicates assent to the contract on the terms stated or referred to: *McCutcheon v David MacBrayne Ltd* [1964] 1 All ER 430. For the principle to apply, the party relying on the ticket must give reasonable notice that the ticket is a contractual document: *Causer v Browne* [1952] VLR 1. See also **Acceptance**; **Contract**; **Exclusion clause**; **Incorporation**; **Offer**; **Term**.

•**Tied continuing credit contract** A continuing credit under which a linked credit provider provides credit in respect of payment to a supplier by a person receiving the supplier's goods or services: for example (NSW) Credit Act 1984 (repealed) s 12(2); (VIC) Credit Act 1984 (repealed) s 12(2) (replaced by Uniform Consumer Credit Code). See also **Continuing credit contract**; **Credit provider**; **Linked credit provider**; **Supplier**.

Tied insurance Where particular goods or services, or goods and services at a particular price, or discounts, allowances, rebates or credit, are offered on the condition that the person accepting the offer also enters into a particular insurance policy or a policy of insurance with a particular insurer. In Australia, tied insurance is prohibited: (CTH) Trade Practices Act 1974 s 47(6). However, a supplier may propose to arrange insurance for a purchaser if the supplier complies with certain disclosure requirements: (CTH) Insurance Contracts Act 1984 s 73. See also **Exclusive dealing**.

•**Tied loan contract** A loan contract entered into by a credit provider who is a linked credit provider with a supplier, and a buyer of goods and services from the supplier. The credit provider must know or ought reasonably to have known that the buyer entered into the loan contract wholly or partly for the purpose of paying the supplier for the goods or services: for example (NSW) Credit Act 1984 (repealed) s 12(1); (VIC) Credit Act 1984 (repealed) s 12(1) (replaced by Uniform Consumer Credit Code). See also **Credit provider**; **Linked credit provider**; **Supplier**.

Tiers of debt The classification of debt within an organisation according to its status; a measure particularly important in times of financial adversity. For example, debt might be classified as primary debt, which is serviced from the cash flow of the business, zero-coupon debt, where the interest is inferred at maturity, or subordinated unsecured notes, which only become worth something if the business is sold for more than the sum of the first two tiers.

Time bar A clause or condition which limits the time within which an action may be taken under a contract: for example *Jennings Construction Ltd v QH & M Birt Pty Ltd* (1986) 8 NSWLR 18; 6 Aust Const LR 1. Provided it is clearly expressed, a time bar will be given effect. The contractual provision will prevent the bringing of a claim to which it refers by a party to the contract or, possibly, a non-party for whose benefit the provision is expressed to have been concluded: for example *Scruttons Ltd v Midland Silicones Ltd* [1962] AC 446 at 474; [1962] 1 All ER 1. See also **Exclusion of liability clause**.

Time charterparty A charterparty under which a ship is hired from a shipowner for a set period of time. Under a time charter, the shipowner places the ship, complete with crew and equipment, at the disposal of the charterer in return for the hire money. Unless otherwise agreed, the charterer decides on the type and quantity of cargo to be carried and the ports of loading and discharging. The charterer must bunker the ship, pay for cargo handling operations, and satisfy all port, pilotage, towage, and ship's agency charges. The operation of the ship's machinery and its navigation remains the responsibility of the shipowner who must meet the cost of maintaining the ship and paying wages to the crew: *Strang Patrick Stevedoring Pty Ltd v The Owners of the Motor Vessel Sletter (formerly the Hibiscus Trader)* (1992) 38 FCR 501. See also **Charterparty**; **Loading**; **Trading limits clause**.

Time fixed for performance The time at which contractual obligations must be fulfilled. The time fixed for performance under a contract is decided by reference to the intention of the parties as expressed in the contract. The time may be expressly stipulated by reference to a specified date or time period. Alternatively, the time may be fixed by reference to an event, such as delivery of the goods to the buyer's place of business. Generally, where a contract does not specify the time of performance, the obligation in question must be performed within a 'reasonable' time. What constitutes a reasonable time is a question of fact to be determined at the time when the performance is alleged to be due rather than at the moment of contractual formation, and the time fixed must be fair to both parties: *Perri v Coolangatta Investments Pty Ltd* (1982) 149 CLR 537 at 567-8; 41 ALR 441. See also **Anticipatory breach**; **Breach**; **Performance**; **Time stipulation**.

•**Time sharing scheme 1.** In corporations law, a scheme, undertaking, or enterprise in which participants are entitled to use or occupy certain property, for two or more periods during the period of operation of the scheme, undertaking, or enterprise: Corporations Law s 9; Australian Securities Commission Policy Statement 66. A time sharing scheme must operate for a period of at least three years in which the participants are entitled to use property to which the scheme relates at least twice: *Australian Softwood Forests Pty Ltd v A-G (NSW)* (1981) 148 CLR 121; 36 ALR 257 (broad interpretation); Corporations Law s 9. **2.** A scheme for the division of the total use and occupational rights in a parcel of real property in terms of time among a number of persons. Each of those persons becomes entitled to the use and occupation of that parcel for a pre-determined period of time annually, with such rights recurring each consecutive year for a specified number of years. In certain circumstances a time share could create an interest in the property: *Commissioner for Corporate Affairs v Lake Eildon Country Club Ltd and Neville Kay Pty Ltd* (1980)

ACLC ¶40-655 at 34,358; *Wade v A Home Away Pty Ltd* [1981] VR 475. See also **Co-ownership; Fee simple; Participation interest; Prescribed interest; Prospectus; Security.**

Time stipulation In contract law, a term under which the parties fix the time at which their contractual obligations are to be performed: for example *Foran v Wight* (1989) 168 CLR 385; 88 ALR 413. A time stipulation may specify a date, a period, refer to a specified event which may or may not be an element of either party's performance, or it may be a combination of these: for example *Sunbird Plaza Pty Ltd v Maloney* (1988) 166 CLR 245; 77 ALR 205. When a contract does not specify a time for performance, a stipulation will be implied requiring the obligation to be performed within a reasonable time: *Perri v Coolangatta Investments Pty Ltd* (1982) 149 CLR 537; 41 ALR 441. See also **Condition; Express term; Notice; Performance; Reasonable time; Right to terminate.**

Timing differences Differences existing between accounting income and taxable income that occur due to the different period in which an item is included or deducted in the accounting income and taxable income. Timing differences are distinguished from permanent differences by the fact that timing differences will ultimately be included or deducted from both the accounting income and the taxable income, even though the amounts included or deducted in the current accounting period or income tax year do not correspond with the other amount. For example, the depreciation rate for an asset may be different for accounting and tax purposes, therefore a timing difference will arise in relation to the amount of depreciation deducted in a particular period. However the total amount of depreciation that will be deducted over the life of the asset in both accounting and income tax terms will be the same. See also **Accounting period; Depreciation; Taxable income; Year of income.**

Tippee A person who obtains price sensitive information regarding the value of securities from someone he or she knows, or ought to know, is under an obligation under Corporations Law s 1002G(3) not to communicate the price sensitive information. See also **Chinese wall; Insider trading; Price sensitive information.**

Tokyo Commodity Exchange for Industry *Abbr* – TOCOM A commodity exchange which trades gold, silver and platinum futures, and gold in the form of warehouse receipts. Each receipt (or lot) represents one kilo of gold held in the exchange's warehouses. It is more a warrant than a true physical market.

Tokyo Futures Market Opened in 1988, a futures market based on the Tokyo Stock Price Index (TOPI), a composite index of stocks listed on the Tokyo Exchange first section. The market is widely used for speculation, hedging and arbitrage. See also **Tokyo Stock Exchange; Tokyo Stock Price Index.**

Tokyo Stock Exchange *Abbr* – TSE The world's largest stock exchange. In 1990, share turnover greatly exceeded that of the New York Stock Exchange and the London International Stock Exchange, which ranked second and third respectively in the world. In 1990, the TSE had 114 authorised traders, including some 25 foreign dealers. Only since 1986 have foreigners been admitted to the exchange; in that year seats were awarded to Merrill Lynch, Morgan Stanley, and three British brokers.

Tokyo Stock Price Index *Abbr* – TOPIX An index which includes all stocks listed on the Tokyo Stock Exchange first section (first section stocks account for 96 per cent of total Tokyo market capitalisation). TOPIX was introduced in 1989 to overcome criticisms of the Tokyo Stock Exchange Stock Price Average (Nikkei-Dow Index), namely excessive influence by high priced stocks and inadequate market representation. TOPIX is a capitalisation weighted share price index, calculated on a minute by minute basis. See also **Tokyo Futures Market; Tokyo Stock Exchange.**

Tolls and charges Money payable in respect of the use or maintenance of ports, harbours, canals or navigational aids, such as lights or lighthouses. Under (CTH) Admiralty Act 1988 s 4(3) claims to tolls and charges may be dealt with as general maritime claims. See also **Groundage.**

Tombstone A black-edged announcement appearing in the press advertising the completed sale of securities, the announcement appearing as a matter of record only. The notice discloses the number of shares involved, the par value of the shares, the names of the distributors, and the markets in which the securities were sold. See also **Securities; Par value.**

• **Tonnage 1.** The cubic capacity of a ship expressed in tons where one ton equals 100 cubic feet of internal space. Tonnage may be calculated in various ways depending upon the spaces measured within the ship. Hence, the terms deadweight, gross, and net tonnage. Tonnage may refer to the cargo capacity of ships of a particular country or trade. It may also refer to the available cargo space of a ship. Statutes may confine the term to one particular measurement for statutory purposes. For example, (TAS) Marine Act 1976 s 4 confines the term to gross tonnage unless otherwise expressly stated. Tonnage dues are payable when a ship enters or leaves a port. See also **Net tonnage.**

Tontine A financial arrangement where subscribers to a loan each receive an annuity for life, which is increased as other subscribers die, until the last survivor receives the whole sum of annuities. See also **Annuity; Loan.**

Tools of the trade 1. Items used by a person in order to carry on that person's trade. Ordinary tools of trade with a value not exceeding the prescribed amount are not divisible property in a bankruptcy: (CTH) Bankruptcy Act 1966 s 116(2)(c). **2.** Equipment used by a tradesperson in the carrying out of work to produce assessable income. Although the cost of replacing, repairing, and insuring tools of trade is fully tax deductible, the equipment must be depreciated if the cost of such equipment is $300 or more. See also **Allowable deduction; Depreciation; Divisible property; Trade.**

• **Tort** *LF* – wrong. A civil wrong distinguished from the law of contract, law of restitution, and the criminal law. A tort is a breach of a duty, potentially owed to the whole world, imposed by law: *Macpherson & Kelley v Kevin J Prunty & Associates* [1983] 1 VR 573. Torts serve to protect a person's interest in his or her bodily security, tangible property, financial resources, or reputation.

Tor — *Butterworths Business and Law Dictionary*

Interference with one of these interests is redressable by an action for compensation, usually in the form of unliquidated damages. The law of torts therefore aims to restore the injured person to the position he or she was in before the tort was committed: *Todorovic v Waller* (1982) 150 CLR 402; 37 ALR 481. See also **Conversion; Deceit; Negligence; Nuisance; Injurious falsehood; Passing off; Tortfeasor; Trespass; Unliquidated damages**.

Tort of inducing breach of statutory duty A tort arising when one person induces another to breach a duty imposed on the second person by a statute. The tort has not yet been adopted in Australia. See also **Industrial tort**.

• **Tortfeasor** Wrongdoer. A person responsible in law for damage caused to another: *Macpherson & Kelley v Kevin J Prunty & Associates* [1983] 1 VR 573. A person vicariously liable for the tort of another is also a tortfeasor. Where the tortfeasor's vicarious liability arises from statute, he or she is still a tortfeasor within the meaning of contributory negligence legislation: *Soblusky v Egan* (1960) 103 CLR 215. See also **Tort; Vicarious liability**.

Total quality management *Abbr* – TQM The efficient utilisation of existing assets and resources. This implies the elimination of waste and error in business systems and processes so that the full potential of the assets and resources can be realised. As a concept, total quality management extends to every aspect of the activities of an enterprise: marketing, design, engineering, manufacturing, finance, administration and management systems.

Total wage A wage rate consisting of a single wage that is equal to or higher than the prescribed minimum wage rate. In 1967, the total wage concept replaced the dual wage system of a basic wage with additional margins for skill: *Basic Wage, Margins and Total Wage case 1966* (1966) 115 CAR 93; *National Wage case 1967* (1967) 118 CAR 655. See also **Margin**.

Towage 1. The charge made for the services of a tug in towing a vessel. Towage gives rise to a general maritime claim which can be enforced in the Admiralty Courts: (CTH) Admiralty Act 1988 s 4(3)(j). 2. The service provided by one vessel, such as a tug, in assisting another vessel on its way, as by accelerating its progress during a voyage. Examples are the towing of a becalmed sailing vessel and the towing of any vessel in confined waters where it would be impracticable for the towed vessel to rely upon its own machinery or resources. Towage is to be contrasted with salvage, since towage may be performed when the vessel towed is neither in danger nor difficulty. See also **Admiralty court**.

TPC See **Trade Practices Commission**.

Tracing 1. The equitable right of a beneficiary to 'follow' property into the hands of the person who holds it, unless that person is a bona fide purchaser for value without notice. Trust property which has been converted into other property may still be traced: *Taylor v Plumer* (1815) 3 M & S 562; 105 ER 721. 2. Less precisely, action at common law for conversion, detinue, or money had and received. The common law had no remedy for specific recovery of chattels, although (UK) Common Law Procedure Act 1854 s 78 gave the court a discretionary power to order specific restitution. Otherwise, an action in trover enabled the plaintiff to recover damages only, while in an action for detinue the plaintiff could recover either chattels or damages. See also **Account; Clayton's case, rule in; Constructive trustee; Conversion; Detinue; Notice; Right in rem**.

Trade Operations of a commercial character by which the trader provides to customers for reward some kind of goods or services: *Ransom v Higgs* [1974] 1 WLR 1594 at 1600. Trade consists of traffic by way of sale or exchange or commercial dealing: *Re Ku-ring-gai Co-operative Building Society (No 12) Ltd* (1978) 22 ALR 621 at 625; 36 FLR 134 at 139. The practice of some occupation, business or profession habitually carried on, especially when practised as a means of livelihood or gain, is a trade: *Cooney v Ku-ring-gai Corporation* (1963) 114 CLR 582 at 602; [1964] ALR 98. See also **Trade and commerce; Trader**.

Trade and commerce All those commercial transactions, dealings, and exchanges between people encompassing either tangible or intangible goods and services (*Bank of New South Wales v Commonwealth* (1948) 76 CLR 1 at 381-2) including their transport (*W & A McArthur Ltd v Queensland* (1920) 28 CLR 530 at 546-7). Production or manufacturing, however, are not trade and commerce but rather a necessary preliminary: *Grannall v Marrickville Margarine Pty Ltd* (1955) 93 CLR 55 at 71-2. The Commonwealth may legislate with respect to interstate and overseas trade and commerce: Commonwealth Constitution s 51(i). See also **Freedom of interstate trade, commerce and intercourse; Interstate trade and commerce; Intrastate trade and commerce; Trade and commerce power; Trade or commerce**.

Trade and commerce power The legislative power of the Commonwealth to make laws with respect to trade and commerce with other countries, and among the States: Commonwealth Constitution s 51(i). The Commonwealth may directly regulate the export trade of Australia (*O'Sullivan v Noarlunga Meat Ltd* (1954) 92 CLR 565) and interstate trade and commerce, but not intrastate trade and commerce (*W & A McArthur Ltd v Queensland* (1920) 28 CLR 530 at 548), nor production and manufacture (*Grannall v Marrickville Margarine Pty Ltd* (1955) 93 CLR 55) other than incidentally (*Redfern v Dunlop Rubber Australia* (1964) 110 CLR 194). See also **Absolutely free; Freedom of interstate trade, commerce and intercourse; Interstate trade and commerce; Intrastate trade and commerce; Trade and commerce**.

Trade bill A bill of exchange used for the settlement of debts between parties arising from the supply of goods and services. See also **Bill of exchange**.

Trade commission A rate of remuneration of an agent that is implied by usage in the trade: *Drielsma v Manifold* [1894] 3 Ch 100. See also **Del credere commission**.

Trade debtor See **Accounts receivable**.

Trade description Any description, statement, or indication as to the nature, quantity, quality, purity, class, grade, origin, manufacturer and mode of manufacturing, ingredient, patent, privilege, or copyright of good or goods: (CTH) Commerce (Trade Descriptions) Act 1905 s 3. False descriptions of such criteria are illegal and are likely to constitute misleading or deceptive conduct or false representations for the purposes of (CTH) Trade Practices Act 1974 ss 52, 53. See also **Misleading or deceptive conduct**.

Trade effluent Wastes of organic and inorganic origin discharged by industrial and commercial enterprises. Trade effluent forms part of the prohibited solids and liquids that contribute to pollution: for example (NSW) Clean Waters Act 1970 s 16; (NSW) Environmental Offences and Penalties Act 1989 s 8B. See also **Pollution; Trade waste**.

Trade fixture An item which has all the other characteristics of a fixture combined with the right for a lessee to remove it: *Byrnes v Macarthur* (1881) 2 NSWR 57; *Registrar of Titles v Spencer* (1909) 9 CLR 641. This right will be conferred when, as a question of fact, the item was required by the lessee for the purpose of carrying on the trade or manufacture of that lessee. This will be demonstrated by factors such as portability: *Neylon v Dickens* [1979] 2 NZLR 714. The items need not have as their sole purpose use within the trade or manufacture: *Lawton v Lawton* (1743) 3 Atk 13; 26 ER 811. Excluded from the definition are agricultural items which have a separate regime, and items which are only ancillary to the trade: *Weller v Everitt* (1900) 25 VLR 683; *Whitehead v Bennett* (1858) 27 LJ Ch 474; 6 WR 351.

Trade incentives An arrangement made by a manufacturer for the supply and purchase of goods. Although the selling price of goods is the amount of goods sold, there are other components which affect the real sale value of these goods. The negotiated arrangements are known as incentives and include trade discounts, trade price rebates, volume rebates, promotional rebates, incentive rebates, cooperative advertising allowances and deferred credits. These incentives modify the sale value of goods which are subject to sales tax.

Trade libel A tort available to a trader where false and disparaging statements are made which injure the trader in the course of his or her trade, the trader having to establish that the false statements were made with malice and that there has been damage: *Hanimex Pty Ltd v Kodak (Australasia) Pty Ltd* (1982) ATPR ¶43-593. Trade libel is otherwise referred to as injurious falsehood, slander of goods, slander of title, and disparagement of property. See also **Injurious falsehood**.

•**Trade mark** A sign used, or intended to be used, to distinguish goods or services dealt with or provided in the course of trade by a person from goods or services so dealt with by any other person: (CTH) Trade Marks Act 1995 s 17. Trade marks may be registered: (CTH) Trade Marks Act 1995 s 19. Registered trade marks are the personal property of the registered owner: (CTH) Trade Marks Act 1995 s 21. See also **Passing off**.

Trade Measurement Agreement 1990 An agreement between the Commonwealth of Australia and the States and Territories of Australia in relation to the adoption of uniform trade measurement legislation. In this agreement, all the States and Territories agreed to enact uniform trade measurement legislation, to promote commercial certainty and greater efficiency in the trade measurement industry, and to reduce business costs. At present, all States and Territories except Victoria, Tasmania, and Western Australia have uniform legislation, for example (NSW) Trade Measurement Act 1989; (NSW) Trade Measurement Administration Act 1989.

•**Trade or commerce** The words are to be construed widely: *Re Ku-ring-gai Co-op Building Society (No 12) Ltd*. Private dealings, as opposed to business dealings, are not in trade or commerce: *O'Brien v Smolonogov* (1983) 53 ALR 107. The relevant conduct must be a part of the corporation's trading or commercial activities, and not merely incidental to them: *Concrete Constructions (NSW) Pty Ltd v Nelson* (1990) 169 CLR 594; 92 ALR 193. See also **False representation; Misleading or deceptive conduct; Trade practices legislation**.

•**Trade or tie agreement** Any agreement between supplier and credit provider relating to the supply to the supplier of goods and services in which the supplier deals, the supplier's business of supplying goods, or the provision of credit to consumers to pay for goods and services supplied by the supplier: (NSW) Credit Act 1984 (repealed) s 5(1); (VIC) Credit Act 1984 (repealed) s 5(1) (replaced by Uniform Consumer Credit Code). See also **Credit; Credit provider; Linked credit provider; Supplier**.

Trade practice See **Trade usage**.

Trade Practices Commission *Abbr* – TPC Formerly, the authority principally responsible for enforcement of the (CTH) Trade Practices Act 1974. See also **Australian Competition and Consumer Commission; Authorisation; Clearance; Hilmer Report; Injunction; Market; Notification; Pre-merger consultation; Trade Practices Commission Guidelines; Trade Practices Tribunal; Trade practices legislation**.

Trade practices legislation Legislation intended to regulate various restrictive trade practices (anti-competitive behaviour) and provide for certain consumer protection: for example (CTH) Trade Practices Act 1974. The (CTH) Trade Practice Act 1974 (TPA) is primarily concerned to regulate the activities of corporations but s 6 provides an extended jurisdiction based on a variety of heads of Commonwealth power: *R v Australian Industrial Court; Ex parte CLM Holdings Pty Ltd* (1977) 136 CLR 235; 13 ALR 273. See also **Consumer protection; Restrictive trade practices**.

Trade Practices Tribunal Formerly, the federal administrative body whose principle function was to review a determination of the Trade Practices Commission in relation to authorisation applications and notifications, and to affirm, set aside, or vary that determination. In 1995 the body was renamed the Australian Competition Tribunal. See also **Trade Practices Commission; Australian Competition Tribunal; Australian Competition and Consumer Commission**.

Trade receivables Money received by a company from its normal operations, such as the supply of goods and services. Trade receivables, along with cash and other contractual rights to receive cash from another entity, are sometimes described as financial instruments. Trade receivables must be included in the consolidated accounts of a company: Corporations Regulations Sch 5 cl 13. See also **Negotiable instrument; Receivables**.

Trade secret Any formula, pattern, device, or compilation of information that is used in a person's business and that gives that person an opportunity to derive an advantage over other persons who do not know or use it: *Bacchus Marsh Concentrated Milk Co Ltd (in liq) v Joseph Nathan & Co Ltd* (1919) 26 CLR 410. Trade secrets are a form of property and may be sold. See also **Confidential information; Duty of confidentiality; Restraint of trade**.

• **Trade union** An organisation of employees; or an association of employees that is registered or recognised as a trade union under the law of a State or Territory; or an association of employees, the principal purpose of which is to protect and promote the employees' interests in matters concerning their employment: (CTH) Industrial Relations Act 1988 s 4; (NSW) Industrial Relations Act 1996 s 304. If a trade union is divided into branches (whether or not the branches are themselves trade unions), persons who are members of the respective branches are taken to be members of the trade union: (CTH) Social Security Act 1991 s 16(3). See also **Australian industrial system; Employee organisation; Industrial organisation ; Employer organisation**.

Trade usage Usual behaviour employed by those in business. See also **Antitrust; National Competition Policy; Uncompetitive practice; Unfair competition**.

Trade variants In relation to designs, a common matter of taste or choice within a trade: *Macrae Knitting Mills Ltd v Lowes Ltd* (1936) 55 CLR 725. The courts have been reluctant to find the novelty or originality required in designs which are merely trade variations: *J Rapee & Co Pty Ltd v KAS Cushions Pty Ltd* (1989) 90 ALR 288; 15 IPR 577. Whether a feature is commonly used in the relevant trade is a matter for expert evidence of trade witnesses: for example *J Rapee & Co Pty Ltd v KAS Cushion Pty Ltd* (1989) 90 ALR 288; 15 IPR 577.

Trade waste Any matter or thing, whether solid, liquid, or gaseous or a combination of states, which is refuse from any industrial, chemical, trade, or business process or operation, including building or demolition work: (NSW) Waste Recycling and Processing Service Act 1970 s 5(1). Applications for approval to discharge trade waste into a sewer may be obtained: (NSW) Local Government (Approvals) Regulation 1993 reg 71. Also known as 'trade refuse'. See also **Pollution; Trade effluent**.

Trade weighted index *Abbr* – TWI A measure of the value of the Australian dollar against a basket of other currencies, the proportions or weightings of the other currencies in the basket (such as the US dollar, yen, and pound sterling) being based on the proportion of Australia's trade which is carried on with those countries. Consequently, the TWI weightings vary according to the level of trade. The TWI provides guidance on whether the Australian dollar is rising or falling against the included currencies, and not just the US dollar. See also **Share price index; Share price futures contract index**.

Trader A person engaged or about to engage in the business of selling by retail any goods, wares or merchandise but not including a farmer: for example (NSW) Bills of Sale Act 1898 s 3. See also **Trade; Trade and Commerce**.

• **Trader's bill of sale** A type of bill of sale, given in New South Wales by an unincorporated retailer over business chattels, which requires public registration before it has legal validity and takes its priority from the time of lodgment for registration: (NSW) Bills of Sale Act 1898 ss 3, 5C(1); *Franov v Deposit and Investment Co Ltd* (1962) 108 CLR 460. An unsecured creditor of the grantor of a trader's bill of sale may, by lodging a caveat, require its debt to be paid: (NSW) Bills of Sale Act 1898 ss 5G-5K. See also **Bill of sale**.

Trading activities Activities that a corporation engages in, or will engage in, in the course of carrying on its business. In determining whether a corporation is a trading corporation for the purposes of Commonwealth Constitution s 51(xx), a 'substantial' or 'a sufficiently significant proportion of the corporation's overall activities' must be trading activities: *R v Federal Court of Australia and Adamson; Ex parte Western Australian National Football League (Inc) and West Perth Football Club (Inc)* (1979) 143 CLR 190; 23 ALR 439. Trading is not limited to buying or selling goods and trading activities are not necessarily profit-making or profit motivated activities: *R v Trade Practices Tribunal; Ex parte St George County Council* (1974) 130 CLR 533; 2 ALR 371. See also **Trading corporation**.

• **Trading bank** A bank authorised to carry on general banking business. Earlier legislation distinguished between trading and savings banks, the latter being more restricted as to the types of accounts kept and the loans permitted. For most purposes, the distinction is no longer relevant, although savings banks are still subject to certain investment and deposit restrictions which do not apply to trading banks.

Trading certificate Under English law, a certificate or licence issued by the Registrar of Companies enabling a public company to begin trading. There is no such requirement under the Corporations Law, although upon registration of a corporation in Australia, the corporation is issued with a certificate of registration by the Australian Securities Commission. The certificate operates as conclusive evidence that all the requirements of the Corporations Law in respect of registration of the body corporate as a company have been complied with, the body corporate is duly registered as a company under the Corporations Law, and the day of commencement of registration is the day specified in the certificate: Corporations Law ss 121, 122. See also **Registered company**.

Trading corporation For the purposes of Commonwealth Constitution s 51(xx) a corporation, incorporated within the limits of the Commonwealth, undertaking trading activities which constitute a sufficiently significant proportion of its overall activities: *R v Federal Court of Australia; Ex parte Western Australian National Football League (Inc)* (1979) 143 CLR 190 at 208; 23 ALR 439. Trading for this purpose is not limited to buying or selling at a profit but extends to undertaking business activities with a view to earning revenue: *R v Federal Court of Australia; Ex parte Western Australian National Football League (Inc)* (1979) 143 CLR 190 at

235; 23 ALR 439. A purely manufacturing corporation will not be a trading corporation (*Huddart Parker and Co Pty Ltd v Moorehead* (1909) 8 CLR 330 at 393), nor will every corporation which trades (*R v Federal Court of Australia; Ex parte Western Australian National Football League (Inc)* (1979) 143 CLR 190 at 225; 23 ALR 439). A corporation's trading activities may be so incidental to some other principal activity, such as the provision of education, that the corporation could not be described as a trading corporation: *R v Federal Court of Australia; Ex parte Western Australian National Football League (Inc)* at 234. The fact that a corporation undertakes extensive non-trading activities which might properly warrant its being categorised as a corporation of some other type will not prevent it from being properly categorised as a trading corporation if it also engages in significant trading activities: *State Superannuation Board (Vic) v Trade Practices Commission* (1982) 150 CLR 282 at 304; 44 ALR 1. The trading activities need not be profitable and may be undertaken purely for charitable purposes: *E v Australian Red Cross Society* (1991) 99 ALR 601; 27 FCR 310. The characterisation of a corporation as a trading corporation is a question of fact and degree: *R v Federal Court of Australia; Ex parte Western Australian National Football League (Inc)* (1979) 143 CLR 190 at 234; 23 ALR 439. A wide range of sequential and related activities may be considered when determining whether trading is 'substantial': *Commonwealth v Tasmania* (1983) 158 CLR 1; 46 ALR 625. See also **Corporations power**; **Financial corporation**; **Trade and commerce**; **Trading activities**.

Trading etiquette *Abbr* – TE Business Rules of the Sydney Futures Exchange ('SFE') which prescribe the manner of trading in futures contracts. For example futures contracts are quoted and traded on the floor of the SFE by the open outcry method, which involves each bid to buy or offer to sell being stated aloud in a manner that it may be heard by all other traders in the pit trading that particular futures contract: TE 6.3. If a trader wishes to accept a bid or offer they must state aloud their confirmation, usually by stating 'right' although this is not required: TE 6.3.2. At that point the futures contract is concluded. The trader who sells the contract then records the details of the trade on a trading slip known as a 'chit'. The buying trader then initials the chit and each trader retains a copy, and the original is sent to the clearing house of the SFE: TE 10.1, TE 10.2, TE 10.3. See also **Sydney Futures Exchange**; **Sydney Futures Exchange Business Rules**.

Trading floor In relation to a stock exchange, the place where official meetings are held. See also **Official meeting**; **Trading post**.

Trading hours In relation to a securities exchange, the hours of a trading day during which a stock market of that securities exchange is open for trading in securities: for example Corporations Law s 603.

Trade and commerce The period between two fixed times in a day during which persons or companies pursuing the business or occupation of trade or a trader open their premises or make themselves available to the public for the purpose of trading. Those two fixed times are often regulated or specified by a legislature of a State or Territory: for example (VIC) Liquor Licensing Act 1987 s 3. Various trading hours may be permitted according to the nature and location of the particular business or trade. In Queensland, the full bench of the Industrial Relations Commission has jurisdiction to make an order fixing the trading hours of non-exempt shops of its own motion or upon application by or on behalf of an industrial organisation or other organisation: (QLD) Trading (Allowable Hours) Act 1990 s 21.

Trading limits clause A clause usually appearing in a time charterparty setting out the geographical limits within which the subject vessel is permitted to operate. Usually the limits will confine a vessel to visiting safe ports only. Sometimes, it may be agreed that the voyage may take the vessel outside the trading limits on payment of an extra insurance premium: for example *Maritime Transport Overseas GmbH v Unitramp (The Antaios)* [1981] 2 Lloyd's Rep 284. See also **Charterparty**.

Trading partnership A partnership whose principal activities are buying and selling: *Wheatley v Smithers* [1906] 2 KB 321; *Higgins v Beauchamp* [1914] 3 KB 1192. See also **Non-trading partnership**; **Partnership**.

Trading post 1. An area or position of a stock exchange trading floor where particular shares or stocks assigned to that area are traded. 2. A general store often located in a remote or sparsely populated area or region. See also **Trading floor**.

Trading profit The amount of gain made by a business in a given period, usually a year: *Federal Cmr of Taxation v Slater Holdings Ltd* (1984) 156 CLR 447 at 460; 56 ALR 306 at 314. In relation to whether a company has profits from which dividends can be paid, a method of ascertaining profits is to find the total trading revenue over the trading period (including for example proceeds of sale of the company's products) and then subtract total trading expenses, namely those expenditures over the trading period that are referable to the routine conduct of the company's business (such as wages, power, stationery). The next step is to compare the value of the stock of those assets which are consumed or turned over in the conduct of the company's business, as held at the beginning of the trading period, and the value of the similar assets held at the end of that trading period, and to add or deduct the difference to or from the difference between revenue receipts and revenue expenditure as the case requires. Taxes payable may also have to be taken into account: *Commonwealth v O'Reilly* [1984] VR 931; (1984) 8 ACLR 804. See also **Trading stock**.

Trading risk In banking, the potential risk to earnings resulting from changes in interest rates, currencies and equity and commodity prices. See also **Balance sheet risk**; **Market risk**; **Operating risk**.

Trading scheme A group of unrelated individuals working together on a commercial enterprise. In the context of pyramid selling, participants are regarded as being engaged in a trading scheme: (CTH) Trade Practices Act 1974 s 61. A corporation contravenes s 61 if the corporation is the promoter of, or a participant in, a trading scheme and a person who is a participant in the trading scheme makes a payment for the benefit of the corporation: s 61. See also **Pyramid selling**.

Trading spread A strategy to reduce risks in trading. Spreads are market transactions that enable the trader to profit not from the rise or fall of a single commodity futures contract, but from a widening or narrowing in the price differential (carrying charge or contango) between two futures contract months. In spread trading, one futures contract is bought while, simultaneously, another is sold. The change in the differential between the two contract months determines the trader's profit or loss. Also known as 'straddle'. See also **Contango**; **Futures contract**.

•**Trading stamp** A coupon or token printed by a trading stamp company and sold in bulk to traders, to be issued free to consumers. Consumers then exchange the stamp for goods or services provided by the trading stamp company. In all States and Territories except Queensland, trading stamp operations and schemes are prohibited: for example (NSW) Fair Trading Act 1987 s 60B. See also **Fair trading legislation**.

•**Trading stock** Goods held by a trader for sale or exchange in the ordinary course of trade. The goods need only to be held in the possession of the trader as part of the body of stock; the trader does not need to own or to have paid for the stock: *Federal Cmr of Taxation v Suttons Motors (Chullora) Wholesale Pty Ltd* (1985) 157 CLR 277; 59 ALR 688. Trading stock includes things such as the produce of agriculture when harvested, or coal, ores, sand, gravel, and stone when removed from the earth. It includes land where it is part of a trading activity (*Federal Commissioner of Taxation v St Hubert's Island Pty Ltd (in liq)* (1978) 138 CLR 210; 19 ALR 1), or shares in the hands of a sharetrader (*Investment & Merchant Finance Corp Ltd v FCT* (1971) 125 CLR 249; 2 ATR 361). See also **Trader**; **Trading activities**; **Trading stock on hand**.

Trading stock on hand Goods held for sale rather than investment, but not necessarily physically delivered into possession or physically available for sale in the ordinary course of business: *All States Frozen Goods Pty Ltd v FCT* (1990) 21 FCR 457; 92 ALR 511 (considering (CTH) Income Tax Assessment Act 1936 s 28). Anything produced, manufactured or purchased for the purposes of manufacture, sale or exchange, including livestock: (CTH) Income Tax Assessment Act 1936 s 6(1). See also **Manufacture**; **Sale**.

Trading trust A trust over goodwill and business assets by which a trustee or some third person conducts a business in accordance with and under the authority of the terms of a trust instrument. In Australia there is a distinction between private and public trading trusts: *Elders Trustee and Executor Co Ltd v EG Reeves Pty Ltd* (1987) 78 ALR 193. The trustee is given extensive powers of trading, being able to incur debts on behalf of the trust. Also known as 'business trust' in the United States.

Traditional security Any security acquired after 10 May 1989, provided it is not trading stock or a prescribed security such as Commonwealth non-bearing interest securities, nor a qualifying security having certain attributes. See also **Security**; **Trading stock**.

•**Trainee** 1. A person who undertakes a traineeship, that is on-the-job training combined with a course of studies to become qualified in a particular calling: for example (NSW) Industrial and Commercial Training Act 1989; (ACT) Vocational Education and Training Act 1995. It differs from an apprenticeship in that the training tends to relate to a clerical or service vocation (such as bookkeeping, computer programming or hospitality) rather than a particular trade (such as electrical fitting, plumbing or cooking). See also **Apprentice**; **Apprenticeship**.

•**Training** Educating a person; developing desired skills or abilities in the person. Training includes instruction and closely supervised practice: (CTH) Training Guarantee (Administration) Act 1990 s 4.

Training guarantee charge A charge imposed on employers who fail to spend the equivalent of 1.5 per cent of their payroll on eligible training. It applies to each resident employer with a minimum specified annual payroll. Also known as 'training guarantee levy'. See also **training guarantee scheme**.

Training guarantee scheme A scheme, administered by the Australian Taxation Office, which required employers whose national payroll was equal to or exceeded a specified threshold to spend a minimum amount on structured training each financial year: (CTH) Training Guarantee Act 1990 (repealed); (CTH) Training Guarantee (Administration) Act 1990 (repealed). An employer who failed to spend the minimum amount had a training guarantee shortfall, and was required to either pay a training guarantee charge equivalent to the shortfall or make up the shortfall through additional training expenditure in the next two years: (CTH) Training Guarantee (Administration) Act 1990 (repealed) ss 15B, 71. See also **Australian Taxation Office**; **Training guarantee charge**.

Tranche A portion or segment of an available loan; the slices or segments into which drawing rights available to members of the International Monetary Fund are divided. These tranches include a gold tranche and four credit tranches. See also **International monetary fund**.

•**Transaction** The carrying out of negotiation, dealings or affairs, usually in the context of business; a business deal or arrangement.

Corporations In relation to a body corporate pursuant to Corporations Law Pt 5.7B, in relation to a body corporate or Pt 5.7 body, (which includes a registrable body: s9) a transaction to which the body is a party, including a conveyance, transfer, or other disposition by the body of property of the body, a charge created by the body on its property, a guarantee given by the body, a payment made by the body, an obligation incurred by the body, a release or waiver by the body, and a loan to the body: Corporations Law s 9. See also **Compulsory acquisition of shares**; **Voidable transaction**.

Trade and commerce A dealing or series of dealings between two or more parties, often in the course of business, that affects the rights of the parties: *Gorton v FCT* (1965) 113 CLR 604; *Palmer v Cmr of State Taxation (WA)* (1976) 136 CLR 406; 11 ALR 637.

Transaction cost The cost incurred in undertaking a business arrangement in addition to actual differences in buying and selling prices. For example, the brokerage or commission over and above the actual purchase or sale price in a securities transaction, or the many legal, statutory and other expenses incurred in buying or selling a house. See also **Transaction**.

Transfer, certification of See **Certification of transfer**.

Transfer in blank See **Blank transfer**.

• **Transfer of a business** In industrial law, the transfer, transmission, conveyance, assignment, or succession, whether by agreement or by operation of law, of the whole or any part of a business, undertaking, or establishment: (NSW) Industrial Relations Act 1996 s 101.

Transfer of business agreement For the purposes of the (CTH) Petroleum Retail Marketing Franchise Act 1980, an 'arrangement' or 'understanding' for the assignment of an interest in a business or franchise: *Ampol Ltd v Calaby Pty Ltd* (1991) 110 ALR 343. The agreement may be formal or informal, oral or written, legal or equitable: (CTH) Petroleum Retail Marketing Franchise Act 1980 s 3. It need not give rise to rights or obligations at law or in equity: *Ampol Ltd v Calaby Pty Ltd*. See also **Franchise**.

Transfer of share The changing of legal title to a share by way of sale or gift. Shares may be transferred subject to any restrictions in a company's articles of association. For a transfer to be effective, there must be a change made to the register of members. The legal title does not pass merely on delivery by a transferor to a transferee of the share certificate. Transfers may be made on-market or off-market. A share is transferable as provided by the articles or, in the case of on-market transfers, the SCH (securities clearing house) business rules: Corporations Law s 1085(1). See also **Off-market purchase**; **On-market transaction**.

Transfer pricing A tax minimisation technique involving the manipulation of the price of goods or services such that profits, and hence assessable income, is transferred between entities. Transfer pricing can also be achieved with any good or service that has some value, for example, raw materials, management fees, charges for the use of intellectual property such a royalty payments, and any other commodity or service that is exported or imported. Transfer pricing can occur at both a domestic and international level. International transfer pricing involves the transfer of profits from a high tax country to a low tax country. Legislation seeks to control international transfer pricing: for example (CTH) Income Tax Assessment Act 1936 ss 38-43 (importation and manufacture of goods), Div 13 (international agreements and determination of source of certain income) and Pt IVA (schemes to reduce income tax). At the domestic level similar principles apply in that profits are transferred from a high taxpayer to a low tax payer, for example a taxpayer with accumulated tax losses. Provisions that attack domestic transfer pricing include the trading stock provision (ss 31C, 36(1), 36(8)) and payments to associated persons and relatives (s 65). See also **Tax minimisation**.

Transferability In banking, the quality of an instrument by which all existing rights and obligations of the transferor may be passed by delivery or by indorsement and delivery. See also **Negotiability**.

Transferable credit A documentary credit or standby letter of credit under which the original beneficiary has the right to request that the credit be made available in whole or in part to another party. The request is made to the bank which is authorised to pay, to incur a deferred payment undertaking, or to negotiate. In the case of a freely negotiable credit, it is made to a bank specifically authorised as a transferring bank. See also **Letter of credit**; **Uniform Customs and Practice for Documentary Credits 1993**.

Transferor by delivery An anonymous bearer who negotiates a bill of exchange by delivery without indorsing it: (CTH) Bills of Exchange Act 1909 s 63(1). A transferor by delivery may from time to time hold bills payable to bearer, or those having become payable to bearer by indorsement in blank, since these bills are transferable by delivery alone. The transferor is not liable on the bill, not signing it as a party; the transferor is only liable to the immediate transferee by virtue of the relationship underlying the transfer: *Commercial Bank of Australia Ltd v Barnett* [1924] VLR 254; (CTH) Bills of Exchange Act 1909 ss 28(1), 63(2). See also **Bearer bill**; **Bill of exchange**; **Delivery**; **Indorsement in blank**.

Transhipment The transfer of cargo or passengers from one means of conveyance to another. The transfer may be from one ship to another, one vehicle to another, or one train to another. For example, transhipment may involve direct transfer from one means of conveyance to another, or off-loading onto a wharf or into a goods shed or warehouse prior to re-loading. Depending on whether or not the goods are dutiable, customs regulations may apply to a transhipment. See also **Cargo**; **Customs duty**; **Loading**.

Transit 1. The fact of going across or through; the passage of something from a point of departure to a point of arrival; the transportation of goods or people from one place to another. 2. The right of free access and stopover in the territory of a foreign state by a carrier on a continuous journey. It is guaranteed by a number of international instruments. For example the Convention on Transit Trade of Land-locked States 1965 guarantees the freedom of transit of goods. Ships of all states have the right of transit for the purpose of traversing the sea or travelling to or from internal waters: United Nations Convention on the Law of the Sea 1982 arts 17, 18; (CTH) Seas and Submerged Lands Act 1973 Sch. The General Agreement on Tariffs and Trade 1994 proclaims the right of transit for commercial purposes through the territory of members via the route most convenient for international transit. See also **Carriage of goods**; **Carriage of passengers**; **Carrier**; **Contract of carriage**; **Goods in transit**; **In transit**.

Transmission of share See **Transfer of share**.

Transparency The requirement that important trade-related matters of a member of the World Trade Organisation be published for the information of other members. Specifically, transparency requires that members' laws, regulations, judicial decisions and administrative rulings of general application pertaining to certain matters, must be published promptly in such a manner as to enable governments and traders to become acquainted with them: General Agreement on Tariffs and Trade 1994 art X(1). Transparency also requires the publication of agreements affecting international trade policy which are in force between members' governments or governmental agencies: art X(1). No measure of general application taken by any member which effects an advance in a rate of duty or other charge on imports under an established and uniform practice or imposes a new or more burdensome requirement, restriction or prohibition on imports, or on the transfer of payments for imports, is to be enforced before such measure has been officially published: art X(2). See also **General Agreement on Tariffs and Trade 1994; Marrakesh Agreement establishing the World Trade Organisation 1994; World Trade Organisation.**

Travel insurance A guarantee of indemnity that is undertaken with respect to a specific journey. Travel insurance must include cover for financial loss in respect of transportation or accommodation expenses where the insured had to cancel the journey due to unforeseen circumstances, loss or damage of personal belongings incurred during the journey and sickness, disease, injury, or death incurred during the journey: (CTH) Insurance Contracts Act 1984 s 35; (CTH) Insurance Contract Regulations 1985 regs 25-29.

•**Treasury bond** A bond issued by the Commonwealth government when it wishes to raise money from the public: (CTH) Commonwealth Inscribed Stock Act 1911 ss 51A-51G. See also **Bond; Treasury indexed bond.**

Treasury indexed bond *Abbr* – TIB First issued in 1985, an inflation-indexed bond, available in two types: capital-indexed, where the capital value is indexed to the inflation rate; and interest-indexed, where the interest payments are indexed to inflation. Inflation is measured by the consumer price index. See also **Treasury bond.**

Treasury note A Commonwealth government short-term security, issued through the Reserve Bank of Australia, with terms to maturity of three to six months. They do not pay interest but are issued at a discount (below face value). The Reserve Bank has conducted treasury note tenders since 1979. Weekly tenders are conducted, usually on a Wednesday. The Reserve Bank stands ready to rediscount (buy) treasury notes which are within 90 days of maturity. Treasury notes are highly negotiable and are aimed at short-term money market investors. They were introduced in 1962 to help manage within-year fluctuations in liquidity.

Treasury stock Shares held by a company in itself. The shares or stock are held by the company's treasury as an investment.

Treaty Establishing the European Economic Community 1957 Competition Rules Competition rules accompanying the Treaty Establishing the European Economic Community (Treaty of Rome) 1957. The rules governing competition are set out in arts 85-94. The aims of the treaty are: the creation of a true common market in which goods, services, labour, and capital move as freely throughout the community as they do within the national territory of each member state; and the progressive coordination of the economies of the member states. See also **Competition law.**

Treaty of Maastricht 1992 A multilateral agreement to further the economic convergence of national economies, of former European Economic Community. It gives greater powers to the European Parliament, makes the Western European Union the Economic Community's defence arm, and introduces two new pillars to form the European Union. It consists of two parts: the Economic and Monetary Union Treaty; and the Political Union Treaty. The treaty was signed on 7 February 1992 and came into effect on 1 November 1993. See also **European Economic Community; European Union.**

Treaty reinsurance A contract of reinsurance in which the reinsured agrees to place all reinsurance of a specified kind with the reinsurer and the reinsurer agrees to accept all such reinsurance. See also **Excess-of-loss reinsurance; Facultative reinsurance; Reinsurance.**

Trespass *OF* – to pass across. **1.** Wrongful entry on to the land of another, without the consent of the person who has rightful possession of the land. **2.** One of the earliest forms of tort: a direct, forcible, and wrongful interference with the person, land, or chattels of a person. The tort gave rise to the forms of action known as trespass, from which numerous specific writs arose to recover possession of goods, land, or damages for trespass. See also **Conversion; Detinue; Tort.**

•**Trespasser** A person who intentionally or negligently commits a trespass or directly interferes with the land of another by entering premises without any express or implied invitation, licence, permission, lawful authority, or consent of the person in possession of land: *Lincoln Hunt Australia Pty Ltd v Willesee* (1986) 4 NSWLR 457. A person who initially enters land with lawful authority becomes a trespasser if the consent is revoked and he or she refuses to leave the premises after a reasonable period of time has elapsed: *Cowell v Rosehill Racecourse Co Ltd* (1937) 56 CLR 605; *Barker v R* (1983) 153 CLR 338; 47 ALR 1. See also **Trespass; Occupier's liability.**

Trial A fact finding process, by which a court resolves disputed issues of fact presented by the parties and applies appropriate legal rules, culminating in a judgment.

•**Tribunal 1.** Generally, a body appointed to adjudicate disputes. **2.** A person or body (who or which is not a court of law but may be presided over by a judge) who (or which), in arriving at the decision in question, is expressly or indirectly required by law to act in a judicial manner to the extent of observing one or more of the rules of natural justice: (VIC) Administrative Law Act 1978 s 2. Under (VIC) Administrative Law Act 1978 s 3, any person affected by a decision of a tribunal may apply for review to the Supreme Court of Victoria. While it is doubtful whether the Governor in Council falls within the expression 'tribunal', this does not mean that the rules of natural justice need not or cannot be complied with: *FAI Insurances Ltd v Winneke* (1982) 151 CLR 342; 41 ALR 1. The Administrative Appeals Tribunal has jurisdiction to hear appeals from specified decisions by the Environment Protection Authority: (VIC) Environment Protection Act 1970 s32(1). **3.** In administrative law, a body which reviews administrative action or makes primary decisions. A tribunal may conciliate or determine disputes or complaints or administer a regulatory scheme. Tribunals may be vested with jurisdiction to review the merits of administrative action, as well as the legal issues involved in it. At the federal level, a tribunal may not exercise the judicial power of the Commonwealth, (that is, make enforceable determinations of legal rights and obligations,) due to the doctrine of separation of powers: *Attorney-General (Cth) v R and Boilermakers' Society of Australia* [1957] AC 288; (1957) 95 CLR 529; *R v Trade Practices Tribunal; Ex parte Tasmanian Breweries Pty Ltd* (1970) 123 CLR 361. See also **Administrative action; Annulment; Court.**

Tripartite collateral contract A contractual relationship that arises between A and B when A makes a promise to B who, in reliance on that promise, enters into a contract with C, that contract being of some benefit to A. For example, where a person purchases goods on hire-purchase from a finance company on the strength of an assurance from the vendor of those goods, a collateral contract exists between the purchaser and vendor even though there is no direct contractual relationship: *Andrews v Hopkinson* [1957] 1 QB 229; *Irwin v Poole* (1953) 70 WN (NSW) 186. The same result may now be achieved through legislation: for example (CTH) Trade Practices Act 1974 Pt V Div 2A; (SA) Misrepresentation Act 1972 s 7(1), (2). See also **Collateral contract.**

Triple witching hour An American company law term denoting the last trading hour on the third Friday of March, June, September and December, being the date options and futures on stock indexes expire concurrently. It is characterised by massive trades in index futures, options and underlying stocks by hedge strategists and arbitragers, causing abnormal activity and volatility. Smaller scale witching hours occur in the other eight months, usually on the third Friday, when index futures or options expire. See also **Double witching hour; Option; Triple witching hour.**

True and fair accounts In relation to the duty of a company's directors, the production of a profit and loss statement and a balance sheet which give a true and fair view of the state of the company: Corporations Law ss 292, 293. In satisfying this requirement, directors must ensure compliance with all the requirements of the Corporations Law and applicable accounting standards: s 298. If, despite compliance with all relevant legal and accounting standards, the accounts still do not give a true and fair view, the directors must add such further information and statements as are necessary to give a true and fair view of the accounts and state of the company: s 299. See also **True and fair view.**

True and fair view In relation to corporations, a phrase describing the standard of reporting expected from company directors in relation to a range of matters. The words 'true and fair' refer to the mode of presentation, not the mode of derivation or calculation. Directors must produce accounts which give a true and fair view of the state of the company (Corporations Law ss 292, 293), and add such information and explanations to the company's financial statements as will give a true and fair view of matters required to be dealt with (s 299). The auditor must state whether or not the accounts have been drawn up so as to give a true and fair view of the state of affairs and profit position of the company: s 331B. A balance sheet will not give a true and fair view of the affairs of the company if notes to the balance sheet are false and misleading: *Guss v Veenhuizen* (1976) 136 CLR 34; 9 ALR 461. Generally, if all applicable accounting and auditing standards have been complied with, the accounts will give a true and fair view of the state of the company: Accounting Standards Review Board (ASRB) Release 100, para 11. See also **Accounting standards ; Financial statement; True and fair accounts.**

Truncation 1. In accounting, a shortening of process steps, in an effort to reduce paperwork and operating costs. **2.** In relation to the presentment of cheques, communicating the specific details of a cheque, usually by electronic means, to enable cheque clearance. Truncation may be contrasted with 'exhibition' of a cheque. See also **Clearance of cheque; Exhibition; Presentment.**

•**Trust** A fiduciary relationship where a person holds the title of property for the benefit of another.

Corporations An arrangement in which investors entrust their capital to a trustee who, under a trust deed, places the management of the trust's assets in the hands of a management company. The trustee's role is to hold legal title to the assets of the trust and to protect the interests of the investors. The trustee's duties are fiduciary and include ensuring that the management company properly carries out its duties, investing trust money so as to derive income, preserving trust property, avoiding conflicts of interest, complying with instructions in the trust instrument, and administering the trust personally with care. The type of investments in which a trust may invest include equity and property. The interest of an investor takes the form of units in the trust; units may be quoted on the stock exchange, or they may be sold back to the manager in accordance with the trust deed. Listed trusts are traded on the Australian Stock Exchange in the same way as shares in public companies. See also **Unit trust.**

•**Trust account 1.** A record of a trustee's stewardship of a trust. It includes the records required by a court of equity to be kept, and the statutory records required by the trustee legislation: for example (QLD) Trust Accounts Act 1973 s 6. A trustee is obliged to keep full and accurate accounts, to render accounts, and to allow the beneficiary to inspect the accounts and other trust documents. **2.** A bank account in which solicitors, accountants, estate agents, and other similar professionals, hold funds on behalf of another person, such as a client. For example (NSW) Legal Profession Act 1987 s 61(2)(a). The bank will incur no liability to the beneficiary for a breach of trust by the trustee unless the bank has notice that the account is a trust account and has knowledge of the improper or fraudulent design: *New South Wales v Commonwealth (No 3)* (1932) 46 CLR 246. See also **Account; Blind trust; Fiduciary; Trustee; Trust.**

Trust asset An item of real property or personal property which is the subject of a trust agreement where a person, the trustee, holds property on behalf of another, the beneficiary or cestui que trust. The trustee has a right in rem in the property, the beneficiary has a right in personam against the trustee. See also **Beneficiary; Cestui que trust; Trust; Trustee.**

Trust Bank Tasmania A bank established in 1991 from a merger of the State Bank of Tasmania (SBT) and the Tasmania Bank. The SBT was established initially in 1845 as the Hobart Town Savings Bank. The Tasmania Bank was established in 1987 following the merging of the Launceston Bank for Savings (trading as Statewide Bank) originating in 1835 and the Tasmanian Permanent Building Society originating in 1858. The Trust Bank Tasmania is Tasmania's largest financial institution, and engages in wholesale and retail banking.

• **Trust fund** An amount of property or money that is administered by a person for the benefit of another. For example, after a deceased estate has been fully administered, a trust fund consisting of the assets of the estate comes into existence, and a beneficial interest or interests in each and all of the assets constituting the trust fund exists in favour of a beneficiary or beneficiaries: for example *New Zealand Insurance Co Ltd v Cmr of Probate Duties* [1973] VR 659; *Burns Philp Trustee Co Ltd v Viney* [1981] 2 NSWLR 216. Specific trust funds are defined by legislation, for example (VIC) Religious Successory and Charitable Trusts Act 1958 s 63(1) defines 'trust fund' as any property subject to any public charitable trust and applicable for the benefit of a public charity. See also **Trust; Trust account; Trust fund investment**.

Trust fund investment An investment made by a trustee in securities or other permissible property for the benefit of the trust beneficiaries: *Low v Bouverie* [1891] 3 Ch 82. It is usually made pursuant to powers set out in the trust instrument. See also **Security; Trust; Trust instrument**.

• **Trust instrument** A document expressing a trust. Generally, it spells out the rights, powers, and obligations of the trustee, and the kinds of investments the trustee may make pursuant to his or her trust obligation. See also **Trust**.

Trust power The fiduciary power given to a trustee under a discretionary trust and which the trustee is obliged to exercise. For a trust power to be valid, it must be possible to say with certainty whether any individual is a member of the class under the trust. It must also be practicable such that it can be executed under the control of the court. That is, it must not be so wide as not to form anything like a class: *McPhail v Doulton* [1971] AC 424. A trust power is distinguished from a bare power. See also **Bare power; Power of appointment**.

• **Trust property** Property forming the subject of a trust. It may be real or personal, corporeal or incorporeal, tangible or intangible, a chose in possession or a chose in action, and legal or equitable. Property held in trust by a bankrupt for another person is not divisible property in a bankruptcy: (CTH) Bankruptcy Act 1966 s 116(2)(a). See also **Bankrupt; Chose in action; Chose in possession; Divisible property; Property; Trust**.

• **Trust receipt** A form of personal property security where a finance institution, having security (by way of pledge, letter of hypothecation, mortgage, charge, or otherwise) over documents of title to chattels, releases the documents of title to allow the goods to be sold and the sale proceeds to be dedicated to repaying the money secured. The letter of offer or release of security constitutes the trust receipt and retains the institution's security over the chattels and their sale proceeds in the event of the obligor's insolvency, but does not protect against dishonest conduct by the obligor: *Askrigg Pty Ltd v Student Guild of the Curtin University of Technology* (1989) 18 NSWLR 738 at 746; 1 ACSR 40. See also **Insolvency; Security**.

• **Trustee** A person to whom property is conveyed, devised, or bequeathed in trust for another (the beneficiary). The trustee owes a fiduciary duty to the beneficiaries under the trust. A person can be appointed or constituted trustee by an act of the parties concerned, by order or declaration of a court, or by operation of law. A trustee may be a natural person or, under the trustee legislation, a body corporate. Duties are imposed on a trustee, either by statute or by case law, to ensure that the terms of the trust are carried out, that the trustee acts prudently with regard to trust property and makes proper distribution in the right amount to those entitled: for example (NSW) Trustee Act 1925; (VIC) Trustee Act 1958 ; (QLD) Trusts Act 1973. See also **Beneficiary; Cestui que trust; Constructive trustee; Co-trustee; Fiduciary; Passive trustee; Public Trustee; Statutory trustee; Trust; Trustee company; Trustee in bankruptcy**.

Trustee company A corporate body authorised by trustee companies legislation to carry on business as a trustee company: for example (NSW) Trustee Companies Act 1964. Unless authorised by the trust instrument or by statute or court order, a trustee or executor is not entitled to remuneration for carrying out the duties of office. See also **Corporate trustee**.

Trustee de son tort *OF* – trustee by one's own wrong. A person who is not a trustee and has no authority from a trustee, but whom the law saddles with trustee obligations because he or she voluntarily meddles with trust property or does acts characteristic of the office of trustee: *Mara v Browne* [1896] 1 Ch 199. See also **Constructive trustee; Trustee**.

Trustee in bankruptcy A person with functions and duties under the (CTH) Bankruptcy Act 1966 who represents the interests of a bankrupt's creditors. Only the Official Trustee in Bankruptcy and a natural person registered as a trustee, can act as a trustee of the estate or affairs of an insolvent person or a bankrupt: s 155(6). Also known as 'trustee'. See also **Bankrupt; Bankruptcy; Insolvent; Official trustee in bankruptcy; Official Trustee in Bankruptcy; Trustee**.

Twenty Leaders Index An Australian Stock Exchange (ASX) Share Price Index summarising the movements in share values concerning trading on the ASX of the top 20 companies (as ranked by market capitalisation). See also **Share Price Index**.

Twisting In life insurance, the writing of the same business a second time allowing the agent to earn fresh commission. After the sell of an insurance policy issued by one company, the policy holder is persuaded by the attractiveness of an apparently superior product to change companies. As the commission earned by an agent is received mainly during the first year or two on any policy, a change of company enables the commission to be earned again. See also **Life insurance**.

Two dollar company A company incorporated with a two dollar share capital relying entirely for its initial working funds on loans from, or guaranteed by, its backers.

Two-tier system A principle for fixing wages, by which a general increase in pay is awarded by an industrial tribunal to all wage and salary earners (the first tier); Increases above this general increase (up to a ceiling) may be awarded on a case by case basis depending on factors such as productivity and efficiency (the second tier). This system was introduced in 1987: *National Wage case 1987* (1987) 17 IR 65. The increases may be a percentage of the current wage, or a flat rate, or both. See also **National Wage case**; **Wage fixation**; **Wage indexation**.

Tying The practice of selling or offering to sell a good or service only on the condition that the purchaser also purchases another good or service. The tied good may be either the good or service of the seller ('second-line forcing'), or that of a third party ('third-line forcing'). Tying is a species of exclusive dealing under (CTH) Trade Practices Act 1974 s 47. See also **Exclusive dealing**; **Full-line forcing**.

U

Uberrimae fidei /ubɛrɪmeɪ fɪdeɪ/ *Lat* – of the utmost good faith.

Contract The obligation of the promisee to communicate to the promisor every fact and circumstance which might influence the promisor's decision whether or not to enter into the contract. Where only one of two parties know the material facts, a duty is imposed upon that party to disclose them to the other party: *Greenwood v Greenwood* (1863) 2 De GJ & Sm 28; 46 ER 285. See also **Contract; Insurance; Misrepresentation**.

Insurance Under the (CTH) Insurance Contracts Act 1984 s 13, the duty of utmost good faith is an implied term of each contract of insurance. The law imposes a duty on the proponent to disclose to the insurer, whether asked or not, all facts which a prudent insurer would reasonably consider material to the decision whether to undertake the insurance at all and if so, on what terms and at what premium: *Khoury v Government Insurance Office of NSW* (1984) 165 CLR 622; 54 ALR 639. The duty applies to all contracts of insurance: *Godfrey v Britannic Assurance* [1963] 2 Lloyd's Rep 515. It applies to entry into the contract and arguably during the period of cover: *NSW Medical Defence Union Ltd v Transport Industries Insurance Ltd* (1985) 4 NSWLR 107. It applies to both insurers and insureds: *Moraitis v Harvey Trinder (Qld) Pty Ltd* [1969] Qd R 226; and extends to third parties if they are necessarily involved in the insurance: *CE Heath Casualty & General Insurance Ltd v Grey* (1993) 32 NSWLR 25. At common law the only remedy for breach of this duty is to rescind the contract and recover the premium. A statutory remedy of damages is, however, provided by (CTH) Insurance Contracts Act 1984 s 13. See also **Disclosure; Fraud; Fraudulent misrepresentation**.

• **Ultimate holding company** A body that is a holding company of another but which is a subsidiary of no body corporate. See also **Holding company; Immediate holding company**.

Ultra vires /ʌltrə vaɪriz/ *Lat* – beyond the power. An ultra vires act is beyond the legal power or authority of a person, institution, or legislation, and therefore invalid. The opposite of ultra vires is *intra vires*.

Corporations Beyond power. A corporation with limited capacity acting through natural persons, that purports to do something beyond its capacity, (which is usually set out in its memorandum and articles of association) is said to act ultra vires. At common law, ultra vires acts were void (*Directors of Ashbury Railway Carriage and Iron Co (Ltd) v Riche* (1875) LR 7 HL 653) and included abuses of power by directors or shareholders: *Rolled Steel Products (Holdings) Ltd v British Steel Corp* [1986] Ch 246; *ANZ Executors and Trustee Co Ltd v Qintex Australia Ltd* [1991] 2 Qd R 360; (1990) 2 ACSR 676. However, under Corporations Law ss 159-162, persons who deal with companies in good faith cannot be met with an assertion by the company that it is not bound because it had no capacity to enter the transaction. These provisions do not bind a company in respect of a transaction where the persons who purport to act for it lack authority: Corporations Law s 162. See also **Articles of association; Authority; Corporate capacity; Intra vires; Memorandum of association**.

Restitution A term used to describe an unlawful claim by a public authority for the payment of money from a person subject to that authority, such as a demand for taxes under an invalid regulation. A person who submits to an ultra vires demand may be entitled to restitution on the basis that the public authority is unjustly enriched by the payment: *Woolwich Equitable Building Society v IRC* [1993] AC 70. See also **Ultra vires**.

Unascertained goods Goods that cannot be identified with any certainty. Property in unascertained goods does not pass until they are ascertained: for example (NSW) Sale of Goods Act 1923 s 21. This occurs when either buyer or seller, with the other's assent, unconditionally appropriates goods, of the contract description and in a deliverable state, to the contract: for example s 23 rule 5. See also **Appropriation; Future goods; Specific goods**.

• **Unauthorised futures market** A futures market that is not a futures market of a futures exchange approved under the Corporations Law, nor an exempt futures market: s 9. A person must not establish or conduct, or hold him or herself out as conducting, an unauthorised futures market: s 1123. See also **Australian Financial Futures Market; Futures exchange**.

• **Unauthorised stock market** A stock market that is not a stock market of a securities exchange approved under the Corporations Law, nor a stock market approved under s 770A, nor an exempt stock market: s 9. A person must not establish or conduct, or hold him or herself out as conducting, an unauthorised stock market: s 767. See also **Securities exchange; Stock market**.

Uncalled share capital See **Called-up share capital**.

Uncertificated security A company security for which no certificate is issued by the participating company, and which is evidenced by a unique holder identification number recorded in the appropriate register of holders of securities maintained by the participating company: Australian Stock Exchange Listing Rules, Definitions Section. See also **Flexible Accelerated Security Transfer**.

UNCITRAL Model Law on International Commercial Arbitration 1985 A model law for regulating international commercial arbitration, adopted by the United Nations Commission on International Trade Law, and implemented in Australia by the (CTH) International Arbitration Act 1974. It was adopted by the United Nations General Assembly on 21 June 1985. The model law operates in Australia to regulate international commercial arbitrations where the place of the arbitration is within Australia: UNCITRAL Model Law on

International Commercial Arbitration 1985 arts 1(1), (2). The model law will apply to the arbitration unless the parties to the arbitration agreement otherwise agree in writing: (CTH) International Arbitration Act 1974 s 21. See also **Arbitration**.

• **Unclaimed moneys** Money legally payable by a bank but in respect of which the time within which recovery proceedings must be taken by the customer has expired. See also **Account; Dividend; Interest; Principal; Profit**.

Unclean bill of lading See **Dirty bill of lading**.

Uncollected goods Goods of which the owner has failed to take delivery or give direction for their delivery, and the bailee of the goods is unable to trace or communicate with the owner: for example (NSW) Uncollected Goods Act 1995 s 5. In New South Wales uncollected goods are able to be disposed of by the bailee, provided that they meet the minimum time stipulation of three months: (NSW) Uncollected Goods Act 1995 s 6. See also **Refusing delivery; Rejection of goods**.

Uncommercial transaction A transaction that a hypothetical reasonable person in the company's circumstances would not have entered into, having regard to any benefits and detriments to the company in entering the transaction and to any benefits to other parties: Corporations Law s 588FB(1). An uncommercial transaction is liable to be set aside or varied as a voidable transaction if it is an insolvent transaction that occurred within a prescribed time frame, and provided that the other party cannot show that: it became a party in good faith; it lacked reasonable grounds for suspecting objectively that the company was insolvent; and it provided valuable consideration, or changed position, in reliance on the transaction: s 588FG(1). See also **Voidable transaction; Winding up**.

Uncompetitive practice Actions or conduct having the purpose or effect of preventing, distorting, or restricting competition. Uncompetitive practices are prohibited by (CTH) Trade Practices Act 1974 Pt IV, which aims to procure and maintain competition in trade and commerce. See also **Antitrust; Restrictive trade practices**.

Unconditional delivery The delivery of a deed that makes it take effect as such, as opposed to conditional delivery or delivery in escrow. See also **Deed; Delivery; Escrow**.

• **Unconscionable** Unfair, unjust, unscrupulous, unreasonable, or excessive; against the dictates of conscience as recognised by a court of equity. Conduct is deemed unconscionable where it can be seen in accordance with the ordinary concepts of humanity to be so unfair and against conscience that a court would intervene (*Zoneff v Elcom Credit Union Ltd* (1990) 94 ALR 445; ATPR ¶41-058) or so unreasonable and oppressive so as to affront minimum standards of fair dealing (*Commonwealth v Verwayen* (1990) 170 CLR 394; 95 ALR 321). A transaction will be set aside as being unconscionable wherever one party by reason of some condition or circumstance is placed at a special disadvantage vis-a-vis another and unfair or unconscientious advantage is then taken of the opportunity thereby created: *Commercial Bank of Australia Ltd v Amadio* (1983) 151 CLR 447; 46 ALR 402; *Blomley v Ryan* (1956) 99 CLR 362. Also known as 'unconscientious'. See also **Bargaining power; Harsh unjust or unreasonable; Part performance; Unjust contract**.

• **Undeducted contributions** In relation to an eligible termination payment (ETP) made to a taxpayer, contributions made by a taxpayer or other person (other than an employer) after 30 June 1983 to a superannuation fund for which no deduction is allowed: (CTH) Income Tax Assessment Act 1936 s 27A (1), 27A(7)(b). From 1 July 1994, the unused, undeducted purchase price of a commuted pension or annuity forms part of an ETP and is included as undeducted contributions: s 27A(1). Where there has been a rollover of an ETP from one superannuation fund to another, the amount of the undeducted contributions does not include the amount of that rollover payment: s 27A(7) (CTH) Income Tax Assessment Act 1936 s 27A(7). Undeducted contributions are not included in assessable income. See also **Assessable income; Commutation; Eligible Termination Payment; Rollover; Superannuation fund**.

• **Undeducted purchase price** Abbr – UPP The non-assessable component of a pension or annuity. In relation to an annuity or pension first payable after 1 July 1983, or a rebatable superannuation pension or rebatable eligible termination payment (ETP) annuity, the sum of a person's undeducted contributions plus so much of the cost of the annuity or pension to the recipient which was not an allowable deduction or a rebatable amount or for which no rebate was allowable: (CTH) Income Tax Assessment Act 1936 s 27A(1). In the case of a rebatable superannuation pension or rebatable ETP annuity first payable on or after 1 July 1994, it means only a person's undeducted contributions: s 27A(1). See also **Allowable deduction; Annuity; Pension; Rebate; Rebatable superannuation pension; Rebatable eligible termination payment annuity; Undeducted contributions**.

Under bond In the custody of the customs authorities. Goods are said to be under bond when they are left in the custody of the customs authorities against the payment of customs or excise duties. Goods may be released from bond without payment of the duties if they are to be dealt with in a way that would not attract customs or excise duty, for example re-exporting imported goods or supplying such goods to vessels as ship's stores. See also **Customs duty**.

Under tenant A lessee who holds title derived from a lessee and so holds a leasehold interest in a leasehold estate. The under-tenant has no privity of contract or of estate with the lessor: *Holford v Hatch* (1770) 1 Doug KB 183; 99 ER 119; *Johnson v Wild* (1890) 44 Ch D 146; *Fuller's Theatre and Vaudeville Co Ltd v Rofe* [1923] AC 435. Also known as 'sub-tenant'. See also **Distress; Landlord; Lease; Leasehold; Sublease; Tenant**.

Underinsurance An amount of insurance effected for less than the full value of the interest or property insured. See also **Marine insurance; Overinsurance**.

Underlease See **Sublease**.

• **Underlying business percentage** In relation to a car held by a taxpayer during a holding period in a year of income, the number of business kilometres the car travelled during the holding period, expressed as a percentage of total kilometres travelled during the holding period: (CTH) Income Tax Assessment Act 1936 s 82KT(1); (CTH) Fringe Benefits Tax Assessment Act 1986 s 136(1). See also **Car; Cents per kilometre method; Holding period; Year of income.**

Undermargined account An account when the amount of money a client deposits with a stock broker in the account against which the client can borrow to buy securities drops below the margin requirements. See also **Margin account.**

•**Understanding** In competition law, where the minds of the parties are at one that a proposed transaction between them should proceed on the basis of maintaining a particular state of affairs, or adopting a particular course of conduct: *Top Performance Motors Pty Ltd v Ira Berk (Qld) Pty Ltd* (1975) 5 ALR 465. There must be a communication between the parties and an expectation raised in each mind: *Trade Practices Commission v Nicholas Enterprises Pty Ltd (No 2)* (1979) 26 ALR 609. See also **Arrangement; Contract; Contract, arrangement or understanding; Estoppel.**

Undertaking by credit provider In consumer credit law in New South Wales and Western Australia, a promise of a credit provider made at the request of the Commissioner when the credit provider has repeatedly engaged in unjust conduct. The undertaking is contained in a deed executed by the credit provider. The credit provider undertakes to discontinue the unjust conduct, to refrain from it in future, and to rectify the consequences of the past unjust conduct. While the credit provider observes the undertaking, the Commissioner may not bring proceedings against it, or seek an order against it from the tribunal: (NSW) Consumer Credit Administration Act 1995 s 14; (WA) Credit (Administration) Act 1984 ss 28, 29. See also **Commercial Tribunal; Commissioner for Consumer Affairs; Unjust conduct.**

Undervalued security 1. In relation to share trading, a security that is selling at less than its liquidation value or its market price. The reasons for this may be that the industry in which it is engaged has fallen out of favour with investors or that the company is not well known. **2.** Property subject to a security interest, such as a mortgage, being sold at a low value. See also **Securities; Security.**

Underwriter A person who guarantees the funds sought by a company when issuing shares or bonds, taking up the balance should the public not subscribe for all the issued shares: for example *Anemtech Ltd v Eyres Reed McIntosh Ltd* (1986) 10 ACLR 780; 4 ACLC 520. See also **Excluded issue; Shortfall.**

Insurance A person who issues an insurance policy, or a person who signs an insurance policy, thus guaranteeing payment. An underwriter may join with others in entering into a policy of insurance as an insurer. Underwriting may be effected by taking a line of a broker's slip which amounts to an offer to accept a proportion of the risk to be insured. Once a slip is fully subscribed it is binding on all parties to it: *Jaglom v Excess Insurance* [1972] 2 QB 250. See also **Broker's slip; Underwriting agent; Underwriting agreement; Underwriting commission.**

Underwriting agent One who acts as the intermediary of an insurer to solicit, arrange, effect, or enter into contracts of insurance in return for remuneration. See also **Underwriter; Underwriting agreement; Underwriting commission.**

Underwriting agreement A contract between an insurer and an intermediary for the intermediary to be an underwriting agent for the insurer. See also **Underwriter; Underwriting agent; Underwriting commission.**

Underwriting commission The remuneration paid to an underwriting agent by an insurer. See also **Underwriter; Underwriting agent; Underwriting agreement.**

•**Undischarged bankrupt** A bankrupt who has yet to be discharged (for example (NSW) Companies Act 1961 s 5(1)), and who may be subject to bankruptcy proceedings. Such a person has few rights, being entitled solely to the tools of a trade and necessary wearing apparel for the bankrupt and immediate family. Among other restrictions, an undischarged bankrupt may not act as a company director or take part in any other company management, or take up public office. See also **Annulment; Discharge of bankruptcy.**

Undisclosed principal In agency law, a principal whose name or existence is not known to a third party at the time the principal's agent contracts with the third party. The doctrine of the undisclosed principal states that where an agent contracts on behalf of an undisclosed principal within the scope of the agent's authority, the authorised contract may as a general rule, be enforced by or against the principal: *Mooney v Williams* (1906) 3 CLR 1; 11 ALR 437. However, if the agent contracts in terms that imply that the agent is the real and only principal, evidence to contradict the terms of the contract will not be admitted: *Perpetual Trustee Co Ltd v Bligh* (1940) 41 SR (NSW) 33. See also **Agency; Agent; Authority; Non-disclosure; Principal; Scope of authority.**

Undivided share A term used to describe the interest of a tenant in common, especially of land. An undivided share is not physically distinct, as unity of possession always exists between tenants in common. The share may be an equal or unequal portion of the whole; for example, two tenants in common may own in equal shares, or one as to two-thirds and the other as to one-third. An undivided share may be dealt with as its owner desires, and may be devised by will. See also **Joint tenancy; Tenancy in common.**

Undue concentration of ownership Ownership by a small number of entities of most or all of the business in an industry. 'Undue concentration of the ownership or control of a media' was an expression used in the (CTH) Broadcasting Act 1942 that does not appear in the current Act ((CTH) Broadcasting Services Act 1992). See also **Monopoly.**

•**Undue hardship** A defence to a decree for specific performance of a contract. The hardship must amount to an injustice inflicted upon the defendant by holding him or her to the bargain: *Slee v Warke* (1952) 86 CLR 271. The time to determine whether there is sufficient hardship to justify the defence is the date at which the decree is sought by the plaintiff: *Hewett v Court* (1983) 149 CLR 639; 46 ALR 87. See also **Equity**; **Specific performance**.

•**Undue influence** Unconscientious use of any special capacity or opportunity that may exist to affect another's will or freedom of judgment: *Johnson v Buttress* (1936) 56 CLR 113; [1963]ALR 390. The doctrine of undue influence is equitable in origin, and remedies for undue influence are rescission or an order by the court setting aside the contract. The onus is on the party seeking to have the contract set aside to establish that a relationship of undue influence existed except in the context of certain relationships, such as that between parent and child, where a relationship of undue influence will be presumed: *Johnson v Buttress* (1936) 56 CLR 113; [1963]ALR 390; *Powell v Powell* [1900] 1 Ch 243. In New South Wales contracts are open to review and one of the circumstances the court must consider is whether undue influence, unfair pressure, or unfair tactics, were exerted against a contracting party: (NSW) Contracts Review Act 1980 s 9(2)(j). See also **Contracts Review Act 1980**; **Presumed undue influence**; **Unjust contract**; **Vitiating factor**.

Undue preference See **Unfair preference**.

•**Unemployment** A condition of involuntary idleness; a situation in which a person is able and willing to work but cannot find suitable paid employment: *Director General of Social Services v Thomson* (1981) 38 ALR 624. The direct and indirect economic and social costs to society of unemployment include the cost to the nation in social security payments, and the loss of tax revenue, the loss in contribution to the Gross Domestic Product (GDP), the adverse effect on health adding to the costs of the health service, and social, family and individual impacts. See also **Natural rate of unemployment**.

Unenforceable Not able to be enforced. The term is meaningless unless qualified by the precise alleged obligation, the party seeking to enforce, and the remedy sought. For example many contracts of sale of goods are unenforceable by equitable remedies, but all can be enforced by common law action for damages or debt. The (IMP) Statute of Frauds 1677 and its modern equivalents (for example (NSW) Conveyancing Act 1919 s 54A) can render a contract for the sale of land unenforceable. A claim that is unenforceable because of the Statute of Frauds cannot in law or equity be enforced by counterclaim or defence: *Perpetual Executors & Trustees Association of Australia Ltd v Russell* (1931) 45 CLR 146. See also **Void**.

Unenforceable contract A legal and valid contract that has come into being, but which is not enforceable due to a rule of public policy, or as a result of non-compliance with a statutory requirement that does not render the agreement void. The main examples are statutory, for example where writing is required for the enforceability of a contract. The categories of contracts that are unenforceable at common law include some cases of lack of contractual capacity (for example *Gibbons v Wright* (1954) 91 CLR 423 at 441-3; [1954] ALR 383); agreements contrary to public policy; and contracts where performance of the contract has been postponed by the agreement of the parties. See also **Ineffective contract**.

•**Unfair competition** Misappropriation of what equitably belongs to a competitor through underhand or sharp conduct: *Hexagon Pty Ltd v Australian Broadcasting Commission* (1975) 7 ALR 233. There is no tort of unfair competition recognised by Australian courts: *Moorgate Tobacco Co Ltd v Philip Morris Ltd (No 2)* (1984) 156 CLR 414; 56 ALR 193. However, the term may be used generally to describe a variety of torts and statutory offences which protect a plaintiff's business from interference. Also known as 'unfair trading'. See also **Injurious falsehood**; **Trade mark**.

Unfair contract In relation to employment, a contract of employment liable to be declared void on the ground that it is unfair, harsh, or unconscionable, provides a total remuneration that is less that a person performing the work would receive as an employee performing the work, is against the public interest, or is designed to avoid the provisions of an industrial instrument: for example, (NSW) Industrial Relations Act 1996 ss 105, 106. A contract could be unfair whether or not it tended to subvert industrial awards and agreements: *Stevenson v Barham* (1977) 136 CLR 190; 12 ALR 175. See also **Contract of employment**; **Unjust contract**.

Unfair dismissal The termination of a contract of employment in circumstances that are unfair, harsh, unjust, or unreasonable. What is 'fair' depends on the circumstances of the case. To be 'fair' may include warning the employee that dismissal may result from the conduct; notifying the employee clearly of what was being said against him or her; giving the employee an opportunity to answer the allegations; and a right for the employee to receive on request a written statement of the reasons for the dismissal: *Termination Change and Redundancy case* (1984) 9 IR 115; 295 CAR 673; *Byrne v Australian Airlines Ltd* (1994) 120 ALR 274; 47 FCR 300. A dismissal need not be wrongful to be unfair. See also **Contract of employment**; **Wrongful dismissal**.

Unfair loan A loan to the company where the interest on the loan or charges in relation to the loan are or were extortionate: Corporations Law s 588FD(1). Whether the interest or charges were extortionate requires consideration of such matters as the lender's risk, the value of any security, the term of the loan, the payment schedule and the amount of the loan: s 588FD(2). See also **Usury**; **Voidable transaction**; **Winding up**.

Unfair money See **God's penny**.

Unfair practice An action or practice that is prohibited in the interests of consumer protection. Misleading and deceptive conduct, unconscionable conduct, and unfair sales techniques such as bait advertising and pyramid selling are all prohibited as constituting unfair practices: (CTH) Trade Practices Act 1974 Pt V Div 1. See also **Bait advertising**; **Misleading or deceptive conduct**; **Pyramid selling**; **Unconscionable**.

Unfair preference A payment or transfer of property made by a company, when insolvency is imminent, to a particular creditor where the creditor receives more for an unsecured debt than would have been received if the creditor had had to prove for it in the winding up: Corporations Law s 588FA(1). See also **Insolvent transaction**; **Running account**; **Voidable transaction**; **Winding up**.

•**Unfairness** Unconscionable (or unconscientious) conduct. Unfairness is judged not by some generalised or colloquial sense of unfairness, but by the general principles of equity acting upon a person's conscience. Thus, inadequate consideration under a contract is evidence of unfairness, but is not itself unfairness: *Blomley v Ryan* (1956) 99 CLR 362. The fact that a contract has been induced by unfair conduct in the equitable sense is a defence to a decree of specific performance. See also **Specific performance; Unconscionable**.

Unfranked dividend See **Franked dividend**.

Unfunded liabilities Current future obligations and liabilities, provision for which has not yet been made; liabilities that can only be met from current cash flow or future earnings or revenues. Superannuation schemes may often be unfunded or only partially funded. Claims on such schemes require funding in whole or part from financial sources other than the pension fund. Fully funded schemes have sufficient funds set aside and invested to meet all expected liabilities as they arise.

Unidentified manufacturer The person who made, grew, extracted, produced, processed, or assembled a product whose supply and defect may be alleged in a strict product liability claim under (CTH) Trade Practices Act 1974 ss 75AD-75AG, but whose identity is not known to the intending plaintiff. If the manufacturer of action goods is unknown, a person who wishes to institute a liability action may serve on the supplier or each supplier of the action goods a written request to provide particulars of the corporation that manufactured the goods or that was a supplier of the goods. If after 30 days the person making the request still does not know who manufactured the action goods, then each corporation to whom a request was made and who did not comply with the request is deemed to have manufactured the action goods: (CTH) Trade Practices Act 1974 s 75AJ. See also **Action goods; Manufacturer**.

Uniform companies legislation Legislation that came into effect in the early 1960's and which represented efforts by the States, and Commonwealth of Australia to achieve uniform companies legislation. Acts based on the same draft bill were passed in each of the States and the Commonwealth made Companies Ordinances for the Australian Capital Territory, the Northern Territory, and Papua New Guinea. This legislation was superseded in 1981 by the cooperative scheme. See also **Companies and Securities Legislation; Cooperative scheme laws**.

Uniform credit legislation The Credit Acts of the Australian Capital Territory, New South Wales, Queensland, Victoria and Western Australia. The legislation is not strictly uniform, but the provisions in each jurisdiction are comparable. The uniform credit legislation regulates three main types of credit contract: credit sale contracts, loan contracts and continuing credit contracts: Uniform Consumer Credit Code. See also **Continuing credit contract; Credit; Credit sale contract**.

Uniform Customs and Practice for Documentary Credits 1993 *Abbr* – UCP A body of rules published by the International Chamber of Commerce for the regulation of documentary credits. The UCP is binding on banks, applicants for credits (documentary credits and standby letters of credit), and beneficiaries of credits, where the rules have been incorporated by reference to the UCP in letters of credit: *Goldetz (M) & Co Inc v Czarnikow-Rionda Co Inc (The Galatia)* [1979] 2 All ER 726. See also **Autonomy; Clean transport document; International Chamber of Commerce; Letter of credit; Revocable credit; Transferable credit**.

Uniform Income Tax Scheme A scheme devised by the Commonwealth government in 1942 by which it gained control of State income taxation. It was implemented by four Acts: (CTH) State Grants (Income Tax Reimbursement) Act (repealed) 1942; (CTH) Income Tax (War-Time Arrangements) Act (repealed) 1942; (CTH) Income Tax Assessment Act (repealed) 1942; and (CTH) Income Tax Act 1942. These Acts were held to be a valid exercise of the Commonwealth Parliament's legislative powers (*South Australia v Commonwealth* (1942) 65 CLR 373; 2 AITR 275; *Victoria v Commonwealth* (1957) 99 CLR 575), although in effect they deprived the States of their right to collect income taxes. See also **Income taxation**.

Unilateral contract A contract in which an offer is made in the form of a promise to be accepted by the performing of an act: *Carlill v Carbolic Smoke Ball Co* [1893] 1 QB 256. Performance of the act called for with the intention of accepting the offer constitutes both the acceptance of the offer and the furnishing of consideration by the offeree: *R v Clarke* (1927) 40 CLR 227. Typical examples are offers of reward for the giving of certain information or offers of reward for the return of lost property. See also **Acceptance; Bilateral contract; Consideration; Contract; Offer**.

Unilateral mistake A mistake by only one party to a contract. If it is acknowledged that the understanding of one party was correct, the case is one of unilateral mistake: *Goldsbrough Mort & Co Ltd v Quinn* (1910) 10 CLR 674. See also **Mistake; Mutual mistake**.

Unincorporated association A non-legal entity, formed by the mutual understanding of its members, consisting of nothing more than the aggregate of all its members at a particular time: *Leahy v A-G(NSW)* (1959) 101 CLR 611; [1959] ALR 869; *Conservative and Unionist Central Office v Burrell* [1980] 3 All ER 42. An unincorporated association has no separate legal status: *Carlton Cricket & Football Social Club v Joseph* [1970] VR 487. Also known as 'unincorporated body'. See also **Association; Club; Incorporated association; Voluntary non-profit association**.

•**Union** A group of people, organisations, or States, for example, who join together and act collectively to advance the interests of the members of the group, or for some common purpose. 'Union' is often used to mean 'trade union'; that is, a group of workers or employees who organise to protect and improve their conditions of employment. The terms 'union' and 'trade union' have generally been replaced in Australian industrial legislation with other terms that reflect the status of unions as formal institutions with a recognised and regulated role in the industrial relations system: for example, 'organisation of employees' ((CTH) Industrial Relations Act 1988), 'industrial organisation of employees' ((NSW)

Industrial Relations Act 1996, or 'recognised association': (VIC) Employee Relations Act 1992). See also **Employee organisation**; **Trade union**.

Union fee deductibility The right to subtract union fees from taxable income. Union fees and other periodical subscriptions to trade, business, or professional associations are generally deductible to a taxpayer, provided the association's services have a direct link to the derivation of the taxpayer's assessable income: (CTH) Income Tax Assessment Act 1936 ss 51(1), 73. See also **Assessable income**; **Derived**.

Unissued capital The difference, if any, between a company's issued capital and its authorised capital. See also **Authorised capital**; **Capital**; **Issued share capital**.

•**Unit** A fraction or an incomplete or inchoate part of a greater whole. A unit of a share, debenture or other interest (including a prescribed interest) is a right or interest (whether legal or equitable) in the share, debenture or other interests, including an option to acquire such a right or interest, and a unit in a unit trust is a proportional share in the unit trust: Corporations Law s 9. See also **Share**; **Unit trust**.

•**Unit holder** A beneficiary under a unit trust. See also **Beneficiary**; **Unit trust**.

•**Unit trust** A trust in which the beneficial interest in the trust property is divided in the trust instrument into fractions ('units') which are typically offered to the public. It is an express, fixed trust since all the beneficiaries ('subscribers' or 'unit holders') are ascertainable at any given time. The net income of a unit trust is regarded as trust income for taxation purposes, and tax is generally payable by the beneficiaries: (CTH) Income Tax Assessment Act 1936 Pt III, Div 6. However certain public unit trusts, called 'corporate unit trusts' and 'public trading trusts' are treated as companies for tax purposes, with the trusts being taxed at the company rate of tax and distributions to unitholders being assessable on the same basis as dividends: (CTH) Income Tax Assessment Act 1936 Pt III, Divs 6B-6C. See also **Express trust**; **Fixed trust**; **Public trading trust**; **Trust**; **Unit holder**.

United Nations Conference on Trade and Development *Abbr* – UNCTAD A United Nations conference held once every four years since 1964. The United Nations Conference on Trade and Development was institutionalised by a resolution of the United Nations General Assembly: UN GA Res 1995(XIX). Its focus has been on the formulation of new economic policies and on the law of international development. Projects of UNCTAD include promoting commodity agreements, actively trying to change the rules of private maritime law, and promoting the New International Economic Order. The General Assembly established the Trade and Development Board as the 'permanent organ of the Conference': GA Res 1995(XIX) art 4. See also **New International Economic Order**.

United Nations Convention on Contracts for the International Sale of Goods 1980 A multilateral agreement that establishes a uniform set of laws for the regulation of international contracts for the sale of goods. The convention only applies to contracts for the sale of goods between parties whose places of business are in different states: United Nations Convention on Contracts for the International Sale of Goods 1980 art 1.

United Nations Economic and Social Council *Abbr* – ECOSOC One of the six principal organs of the United Nations dealing with the coordination and direction of economic, social, cultural, and humanitarian activities as carried out by other specialised agencies of the United Nations.

United Nations Industrial Development Organisation *Abbr* – UNIDO A body established by the General Assembly in 1966 as an organ to promote and accelerate the industrialisation of developing countries. It became a fully autonomous specialised agency in 1986. It is now the central coordinating body of the United Nations in industrial development and its responsibilities include organising industrial training programs and providing advisory services to states in obtaining external financing. A body established in 1966 as an arm of the General Assembly, and since 1986 a United Nations specialised agency. It was originally called the Centre for Industrial Development. See also **Developing country**; **Technology transfer**.

United Nations Monetary and Financial Conference An international conference held in Bretton Woods, United Nations, in July 1944 by 44 states to discuss the world economic order in the period following the 1939-45 war. The aim was to create a new international monetary order and credit system for reconstruction purposes. The outcome was the creation of the International Monetary Fund, the International Bank for Reconstruction and Development, and the abortive International Trade Organisation replaced by the General Agreement on Tariffs and Trade 1947. Also known as 'Bretton Woods Conference'. See also **Bretton Woods Agreement**; **International Bank for Reconstruction and Development**; **International Monetary Fund**; **International Trade Organization**.

Unity of interest In property law, one of the 'four unities' which are the indicia of a joint tenancy. Unity of interest requires that the interests held by the joint tenants be identical in their legal nature (for example, all joint tenants holding a freehold estate, or all holding a leasehold estate), identical in extent (for example, one-third each in the case of three joint tenants) and identical in duration (for example, all holding for the same term of years, or all holding an interest in fee simple). If unity of interest is absent, the parties hold as tenants in common. See also **Four unities**; **Joint tenancy**; **Tenancy in common**.

Universal agent An agent whose authority is to act for the principal in all matters. Usually, a universal agent is appointed by power of attorney. See also **Agency**; **Agent**; **Power of attorney**; **Principal**; **Special agent**; **Termination of agency**.

Universal offer An offer made to the world. A universal offer will ripen into a contract with any person who performs the conditions for acceptance: *Carlill v Carbolic Smokeball Co* [1893] 1 QB 256. See also **Acceptance**; **Offer**; **Offer and acceptance**; **Offeree**; **Offeror**; **Unilateral contract**.

•**Unjust conduct** In consumer credit law, conduct of a credit provider that is dishonest or unfair, in breach of contract, or that contravenes the consumer credit legislation. When a credit provider has repeatedly engaged in unjust conduct, the Commissioner for Consumer Affairs may apply to the Commercial Tribunal or its equivalent for an order to restrain the conduct or request the credit provider to execute a deed giving undertakings as to the credit provider's conduct: (NSW) Consumer Credit Administration Act 1995 s 14; (QLD) Credit Act 1987 (repealed) s 141 (replaced by Uniform Consumer Credit Code). See also **Commercial Tribunal; Commissioner for Consumer Affairs; Credit provider; Undertaking by credit provider; Uniform credit legislation**.

Unjust contract In New South Wales, a contract which the court has jurisdiction to review on the basis that it is harsh, oppressive and unconscionable: (NSW) Contracts Review Act 1980 s 4(1); *Beneficial Finance Corp Ltd v Karavas* (1991) 23 NSWLR 256; ASC ¶56-042. The court must have regard to criteria set out in the (NSW) Contracts Review Act 1980 s 9(2). A contract may be unjust because its terms, consequences or effects are unjust ('substantive injustice') or because of the unfairness of the methods used to make it ('procedural injustice'): *West v AGC (Advances) Ltd* (1986) 5 NSWLR 610; ASC ¶55-500. See also **Contract; Unconscionable**.

Unjust enrichment A benefit for which the recipient is required to make restitution to the person at whose expense it was obtained. An enrichment is unjust if for example, the enrichment was provided by mistake, under duress or undue influence, or the enrichment was obtained as a result of breach of fiduciary duty: *David Securities Pty Ltd v Commonwealth Bank of Australia* (1992) 175 CLR 353 at 378-9; 109 ALR 57. See also **Benefit; Quasi contract; Restitution**.

•**Unlawful discrimination** Discrimination on specified grounds in specified areas that is prohibited by legislation. Most States prohibit discrimination on grounds including race, ethnic or national origin, sex, marital status, pregnancy, disability, and political affiliation. The legislation exempts certain areas from anti-discrimination laws; for example, religious bodies, and insurance and superannuation providers: (NSW) Anti-Discrimination Act 1977; (VIC) Equal Opportunity Act 1995. See also **Discrimination**.

•**Unlawful industrial action** Industrial action that is based on a demarcation dispute; or 'sympathy' industrial action taken for the purpose of supporting another industrial organisation involved in industrial action; or industrial action based on a claim for wages or benefits in respect of time spent engaging in other industrial action: for example (NSW) Industrial Relations Act (repealed) 1991 s 215. See also **Demarcation dispute; Industrial action**.

Unlawful interference with business A tort arising when a person does an unlawful act directed at another person and interfering with that person's business. The unlawful act may involve procuring a breach of contract or interfering with the performance of a contract (*Merkur Island Shipping Corp v Laughton* [1983] 2 AC 570) or fraudulent statements (*Lonrho plc v Fayed* [1990] 2 QB 479) or (in certain circumstances) breach of a statutory prohibition: *Lonrho Ltd v Shell Petroleum Co Ltd* [1981] 2 All ER 456. The tort is relatively new, and has not yet been adopted in Australia. It seems to subsume other torts such as interference with contractual relations, unlawful means conspiracy, and intimidation. See also **Industrial tort; Interference with contractual relations; Intimidation**.

•**Unlicensed premises** Premises in respect of which a licence to sell or dispose of liquor is not in force under the relevant licensing legislation. Penalties attach to persons selling liquor on such premises: for example (NSW) Liquor Act 1982 s 123. See also **Licensed premises; Licensee**.

•**Unlimited company** A company formed on the principle of having no limit placed on the liability of its members on winding up of the company: Corporations Law s 9. The liability of each member is several and a single member could be liable to contribute the full amount needed, but would have a right in equity to contribution from other members: *Albion Insurance Co Ltd v Government Insurance Office of NSW* (1969) 121 CLR 342. See also **Company limited by guarantee; Company limited by guarantee and shares; Company limited by shares; No liability company**.

Unlimited liability Where there is no limit placed on liability. In the context of the Corporations Law, companies with members who have unlimited liability are called unlimited companies: Corporations Law s 9. In the context of partnerships, a partner who has unlimited liability is liable for all debts of the partnership: for example (QLD) Partnership Act 1891 s 12. See also **Unlimited company; Partnership**.

•**Unliquidated damages** Damages for a loss whose existence is certain, but whose worth in damages can of its nature only be estimated, not calculated exactly. The modern criterion is that if the common law has not classified the cause of action as sounding in liquidated damages, damages are unliquidated unless they can be calculated by reference to a scale of charges or other positive data: *Spain v Union Steamship Co of NZ Ltd* (1923) 32 CLR 138. See also **Default judgment; Liquidated damages; Non-provable debt**.

Unlisted company A company that is not a listed company as defined in (CTH) Income Tax Assessment Act 1936 s 103(4). See also **Private company; Public company**.

Unlisted security market A market established in 1980 by the London Stock Exchange to trade in the shares of small companies not listed on the main exchange. It is cheaper for a company to list on this market and the listing requirements are less stringent. See also **Primary market**.

Unofficial money market An avenue for the deployment of surplus funds additional to that provided by the authorised dealers in the short-term money market. The unofficial money market includes the banks and money market corporations. See also **Reserve Bank of Australia; Short term money market**.

Unpaid capital In corporations law the issued or subscribed capital which has not actually been paid to the company or been credited as paid. See also **Paid-up share capital**.

Unpaid seller's lien The equitable lien of a vendor who has parted with the legal title to property, to the extent of any purchase money which has not been paid. Also known as 'unpaid vendor's lien'. See also **Equitable lien**.

•**Unpaid worker** A person who performs work for an employer for no remuneration: (SA) Equal Opportunity Act 1984 s 5. Also known as 'voluntary worker'. See also **Employee**; **Employer**; **Remuneration**.

Unpublished price sensitive information In relation to insider trading, information that is not generally available to the public that would have a material effect on the price or value of securities if it was so available: Australian Securities Commission Policy Statement 105 (issued 26 February 1996); *ICAL Ltd v County Natwest Securities Aust Ltd* (1988) 6 ACLC 467; 13 ACLR 129 at 500. Information will only be generally available if it consists of readily observable matter or has been disseminated in a manner likely to bring it to the attention of investors: Corporations Law s 1002B. See also **Chinese wall**; **Insider trading**; **Price sensitive information**.

Unqualified opinion Opinion expressed by an auditor in an audit report when the auditor is satisfied in all material respects with the matters upon which Statement of Auditing Standards AUS 1 requires an overall conclusion to be formed: Statement of Auditing Practice AUP 3 para 41. The audit report should express this satisfaction in a clear, affirmative and unambiguous manner: AUP 3 para 41. See also **Qualified audit report**.

Unrealised capital gain For taxation purposes, an increase in the value of an asset that has not been sold and shown in the financial reports because the asset is still owned and used by the business. See also **Unrealised capital loss**.

Unrealised capital loss For taxation purposes, a decrease in the value of the asset has decreased to below that reported in the balance sheet, yet this loss has not been reported as the asset has not been sold. See also **Unrealised capital gain**; **Upstream guarantee**.

•**Unreasonable delay** In contract law, a protracted delay in performing an express time stipulation: *Neeta (Epping) Pty Ltd v Phillips* (1974) 131 CLR 286; 3 ALR 151. Whether delay is unreasonable is a question of fact, depending on the nature of the contract and the detriment, loss, or disadvantage suffered by the promisee: for example *Laurinda Pty Ltd v Capalaba Park Shopping Centre Pty Ltd* (1989) 166 CLR 623; 85 ALR 183. See also **Repudiation**; **Right to terminate**; **Time stipulation**.

Unrestricted-use credit agreement In the United Kingdom, a consumer credit agreement which is not one which finances or refinances a transaction between the debtor and the creditor or another person: (UK) Consumer Credit Act 1974 s 11. See also **Consumer credit agreement**;; **Credit purchase agreement**; **Debtor-creditor agreement**.

Unsafe goods Products that are defective in such a way as to be likely to cause injury: (CTH) Trade Practices Act 1974 Pt VA. Goods have a defect if their safety is not such as persons are generally entitled to expect: s 75AC (1). The subsequent supply by a corporation in trade or commerce of such goods is a criminal offence: s 65C(1)(b). See also **Goods**.

Unsecured creditor A creditor who has lent money to a company or individual without holding a mortgage, charge, or lien on the property of the debtor as security for that debt. See also **Debt**; **Secured creditor**; **Security**.

Unsecured note A security issued by a company which is not secured by any of the company's assets or property. In the event of default, receivership, or liquidation it ranks after secured creditors in respect of claims on the company's assets. See also **Note**; **Secured loan**; **Unsecured creditor**.

Unsolicited credit card A credit card that is sent to a consumer without the consumer's request or authority. Consumer protection legislation prohibits the forwarding of unsolicited credit and debit cards to a person, except where the card is a replacement or renewal card: for example (CTH) Trade Practices Act 1974 s 63A; (NSW) Fair Trading Act 1987 s 57. See also **Credit card**; **Debit card**.

Unvalued policy A contract of insurance that does not specify the value of the subject matter insured but rather leaves the insurable value to be subsequently determined, subject to certain limits: *Berger and Light Diffusers Pty Ltd v Pollock* [1973] 2 Lloyd's Rep 442; (CTH) Marine Insurance Act 1909 s 34. See also **Valued policy**.

Unwinding A procedure followed in certain clearing and settlement systems in which transfers of securities or funds are settled on a net basis, at the end of the processing cycle, with all transfers provisional until all participants have discharged their settlements obligations. If a participant fails to settle, some or all of the provisional transfers involving that participant are deleted from the system and the settlement obligations from the remaining transfers are then recalculated. Such a procedure has the effect of transferring liquidity pressures and possibly losses from the failure to settle to other participants, and may, in the extreme, result in significant and unpredictable systemic risks. See also **Clearing system**; **Payment system**.

Upset price See **Reserve price**.

Upstairs dealer market The sale of securities within a dealer's firm, without using a securities market. See also **Securities exchange**.

Upstream guarantee An arrangement by which a wholly-owned subsidiary guarantees the obligations of the parent company or another company in the group. The giving of such a guarantee would constitute a related party transaction prohibited by Corporations Law Pt 3.2A unless it is at arm's length or has been approved by the company in general meeting: Corporations Law ss 243F(1), 243G(4), 243H, 243N, 243QA. See also **Guarantee**.

Up-tick An American term denoting a transaction that is executed at a price higher than the preceding transaction in that security. A plus sign will be displayed throughout the day next to the last price of each stock that traded on an up tick at the trading post of the specialist on the floor of the New York Stock Exchange. Short sales may only be executed on up ticks. See also **Short selling**.

US dollar bankers' acceptances Bills denominated in United States dollars traded on the United States market, New York being the major trading centre in that country. It is a discount market, restricted to trade related items only. Each bill must show details of the underlying transaction. The market is used to finance both importer and exporter transactions.

Use of market power See **Misuse of market power**.

Used for the purpose of gaining or producing assessable income In taxation law, a phrase which describes the requirement by which an expense qualifies as an allowable deduction. Deductions for depreciation of plant or articles are available in respect of property used by the taxpayer during the year of income for the purpose of producing assessable income, and in respect of property which has been installed ready for use for that purpose and is during the year held in reserve: (CTH) Income Tax Assessment Act 1936 s 54. The gaining or producing of assessable income need not be the sole purpose of use: *Federal Cmr of Taxation v Faichney* (1972) 129 CLR 88; 3 ATR 435. See also **Allowable deduction**; **Assessable income**; **Depreciation**; **Plant**; **Year of income**.

•**Used in the manufacture** Incorporated in goods in the course of a manufacturing process. It excludes goods merely employed in the process such as fuel: *Alcoa of Australia Ltd v Button* (1984) 2 FCR 13; 55 ALR 101. See also **Manufacture**.

•**User 1.** A person who employs or utilises some good or service: for example (VIC) Health Services (Conciliation and Review) Act 1987 s 3; (WA) Electricity Corporation Act 1994 s 91, Sch 6. **2.** The use of property.

Product liability A person who suffers personal injury or property damage as a consequence of using or consuming a product, but who has neither acquired property in nor title to the product: for example *Donoghue v Stevenson* [1932] AC 562; *Clark v Paraflight International Pty Ltd* (1987) 5 MVR 87; *Griffiths v Arch Engineering Co Ltd (Newport)* [1968] 3 All ER 217.

•**User pays** The concept that consumers are charged the marginal cost of providing a product or service. Such consumers are charged the whole marginal cost of providing that service, both capital and running. Each consumer theoretically pays the difference in the costs to the system incurred with and without that consumer. The concept has considerable merit in relation to the main body of consumers in ensuring a rational and efficient use of resources in respect of any service, for an undue disparity between costs and prices will lead to a distortion in demand and, if prices are too low, an undue allocation of community resources through an inflated demand. See also **Demand**; **Economic rationalism**; **Marginal cost**.

USM See **Unlisted security market**.

Usual covenants A shorthand expression to incorporate those provisions in a lease that are ordinarily expected to occur (as a question of fact) in a lease of that kind: *Blake v Lane* (1876) 2 VLR (L) 54; *Tooth & Co Ltd v Bryen (No 2)* (1922) 22 SR (NSW) 541; *Hampshire v Wickens* (1878) 7 Ch D 555. What will ordinarily occur can be established by a course of dealing by one lessor: *McGarrity v Condy* (1927) 27 SR (NSW) 217 at 223-4. See also **Covenant**; **Lease**; **Rent**.

•**Usual terms and conditions** The terms upon which a party to a contract usually contracts, such as the terms of a standard form contract. Where such a standard form contract in fact exists, the contract will not be void for uncertainty: *Trustees Executors & Agency Co Ltd v Peters* (1960) 102 CLR 537; [1960] ALR 327. They are distinct from special terms and conditions, or those merely commonly used: *Trustees Executors and Agency Co Ltd v Peters*. See also **Standard form contract**.

Usury The act or practice of lending money at an exorbitant or illegal rate of interest. See also **Currency**; **Petty banking**.

Utility The condition or quality of being useful, of satisfying human needs and wants.

Economics The amount of satisfaction that a consumer derives from using a product or service. Utility cannot be measured, however, in any definite quantitative form, but consumers display preferences in the market place clearly ranking goods according to need, cost and utility, seeking the maximum satisfaction at the least cost. See also **Marginal utility**.

Utmost good faith See **Uberrimae fidei**.

V

Vacant possession That which is conferred on a purchaser of real property where that property is free from occupation by the vendor or a third party (such as a lessee or licensee). Where a person takes vacant possession of property, the property is both unoccupied and free from any claim to a right to possession from anyone else. See also **Lessee**; **Lessor**.

• **Valuable consideration** The giving, in good faith, of a right, forbearance, or benefit in return for the acquisition of a right, forbearance or benefit from another.

Bills of exchange and other negotiable instruments Valuable consideration for a bill of exchange or cheque under (CTH) Bills of Exchange Act 1909 s 4 is constituted by consideration sufficient to support a simple contract, or an antecedent debt or liability: (CTH) Bills of Exchange Act 1909 s 32(1); (CTH) Cheques and Payment Orders Act 1986 s 35. If valuable consideration is given for the creation or negotiation of a bill, it is usual to write 'value received' on it in the appropriate place. Every party whose signature appears on a bill is prima facie deemed to have become a party to the bill for value: (CTH) Bills of Exchange Act 1909 s 32(2). See also **Bill of exchange**; **Consideration**; **Holder in due course**.

Contract In contract law, consideration which the law accepts as being equivalent in value to the promise or act for which it is given. It may consist either in some right, interest, profit, or benefit accruing to the one party, or some forbearance, detriment, loss, or responsibility, given, suffered, or undertaken by the other: *Currie v Misa* (1875) LR 10 Ex 153 at 162. See also **Adequacy of consideration**; **Consideration**; **Executed consideration**; **Executory consideration**; **Past consideration**; **Sufficiency of consideration**.

• **Valuation 1.** The act or process of ascertaining the worth of a thing. **2.** The assigning of a value to land, property, or assets, in principal to establish the current likely market price: *Woolf v City of Camberwell* [1931] VLR 162.

Valuation of trading stock Generally, the value, however assessed, of a business's goods kept on hand for the supply of customers. There are four methods for valuing trading stock: the cost price method which includes all costs and overheads in cost of production connected with the stock; the replacement cost which is the price of replacement at the end of the financial year; the market selling price which is the current selling value of the closing stock applicable at the end of year of income; the special method where the Commissioner of Taxation agrees to a much reduced value given to the stock at the time. See also **Continuous stocktaking**; **Cost or market method**; **Trading stock**.

• **Value 1.** The market price of a good or service as determined by the price mechanism. **2.** The total utility or satisfaction that is obtained in the consumption or use of a good or service. See also **Market**; **Price mechanism**; **Utility**; **Valuable consideration**.

Value added The value added to a commodity at each stage of its manufacture; for example the value added by the flour miller to the final value of the flour. In this example, it is the value of the flour minus the cost of the wheat. The value added at each stage of processing equals the final value of the bread sold. See also **Discount rate**; **Retail method of inventory**; **Retail sale**.

Value-added management *Abbr* – VAM Management of enterprises aimed at raising the value of the final product through improved quality, lower rejects and returns, reduced inventories, better production efficiency and the elimination of other wastes which do not contribute to the value added. See also **Just-in-time production**; **Total quality management**; **Value added**.

Value-added tax *Abbr* – VAT Levied by more than 40 countries, a broad-based sales tax on goods and services imposed on the value added at each stage of the production and distribution chain. A value-added tax has been adopted throughout the European union; it was invented in France and introduced there in 1954. Standard rates vary from 5 per cent in Taiwan to 25 per cent in Ireland, while luxury goods may attract higher rates. See also **Consumption tax**; **Goods and services tax**.

Valued policy An insurance policy in which the insurer and insured agree on the value of the subject matter insured: *British Traders' Insurance Co Ltd v Monson* (1964) 111 CLR 86; [1964] ALR 845; (CTH) Marine Insurance Act 1909 s 28(2). Valued policies avoid the difficulties of assessing the market value of the insured property by establishing the value of the assured's interest in the property insured before any loss occurs. Such an agreed value insurance policy is an indemnity policy: *British Traders' Insurance Co Ltd v Monson*. In the event of a partial loss, the insured is entitled under the policy to recover an amount proportionate to the loss: *Elcock v Thomson* [1949] 2 KB 755. See also **Insurance contract**; **Unvalued policy**.

Variable interest rate In banking, a rate of interest that can fluctuate with the general trend in interest rates or with movements in a specific interest rate. See also **Accrued interest**; **Fixed interest rate**; **Interest only loan**.

• **Variation** An amendment of a contract with the consent of all of the existing parties to the contract which modifies some of the rights or obligations of the parties without amounting to a rescission of the original contract and formation of a new one: *Electronic Industries Ltd v David Jones Ltd* (1954) 91 CLR 288. See also **Contract**; **Discharge by agreement**; **Novation**; **Party**; **Partial discharge**; **Rescission**; **Variation of a regulated contract**; **Variation of mortgage**; **Variation of rights**.

Variation of a regulated contract In consumer credit law, alteration of the terms of a regulated contract.

There may be variation of the amount financed or the method of payment between the parties, variation by discharge and entering into a new contract, or variation due to hardship as negotiated by the Commissioner or ordered by the Commercial Tribunal: (NSW) Credit Act 1984 (repealed) ss 70, 73, 74; (VIC) Credit Act 1984 (repealed) ss 70, 73, 74 (replaced by Uniform Consumer Credit Code). See also **Commercial Tribunal**; **Commissioner for Consumer Affairs**; **Regulated contract**.

Variation of mortgage The alteration of a mortgage contract by the creation of new rights or duties. A variation can be effected in one of the following ways: by partial rescission of the contract; by partial rescission and an alteration of terms; or by the addition of new terms without rescission of any terms: *Tallerman and Co Pty Ltd v Nathan's Merchandise (Vic) Pty Ltd* (1957) 98 CLR 93. See also **Fixed security**; **Mortgage**; **Rescission**.

Variation of rights In corporations law, alteration of rights attached to a class of shares. These rights vary according to the specific shareholding but there are statutory constraints on the variation of these rights: Corporations Law ss 197, 198. Any condition in the memorandum or articles regarding variation of rights must be followed and cannot be abrogated: ss 197(3), 198(3). Otherwise three quarters of those having their rights varied must agree: ss 197(2), 198(2). There is an appeal to the court if the memorandum or articles are amended so that rights are varied: ss 197(4), 198(4). See also **Class of shares**; **Memorandum of association**; **Articles of association**.

Veil of incorporation See **Corporate veil**.

• **Vendor** A seller. The term is most commonly used in relation to a party selling land, and includes any person to whom the rights of a vendor under a contract have been assigned: for example (VIC) Sale of Land Act 1962 s 2(1). See also **Contract of sale**; **Purchaser**; **Seller**.

Vendor securities Non-cash consideration shares issued to promoters and vendors. If a no liability company ceases to carry on business within 12 months of incorporation, vendor shares rank behind shares issued for cash in priority for the winding up: Corporations Law s 396(1). The Australian Stock Exchange (ASX) has special listing rules relating to vendor securities and ASX Listing Rules rule 19.12 gives a wide definition of vendor securities. The company must also enter into an escrow agreement in respect of the securities with the vendor: ASX Listing Rules rule 9.1. See also **Business day**; **Escrow**; **Winding up**.

Vendor shares Company shares received in return for the sale of a property to a company; sometimes both vendor shares and cash are received. See also **Share**; **Sale of land**.

Venture capital Equity capital invested in high risk projects, with the prospect of high returns; such investment is commonly made in new businesses or in existing businesses which are undertaking major changes. The uncertainties may be of an economic, political, social or environmental kind. With a view to encouraging the public to invest funds with venture capitalists, the Commonwealth government has provided tax advantages for investments with licensed Management and Investment Companies (MICs). Ventures may be financed in a variety of ways in terms of the debt/equity mix, perhaps with special features such as convertible notes or options, subordination of loan capital, deferred rights attached to shares, the distribution of profits, and the terms of the shareholder agreement. On the other hand, investment in MICs or venture projects is usually by way of a subscription to shares pursuant to a prospectus. Also known as 'risk capital'. See also **Management and investment company**.

Verbal contract 1. Formerly, a contract expressed by the parties in words, whether oral or written, as opposed to one made wordlessly but whose terms are words supplied by the law. **2.** The term is increasingly used to mean a contract made entirely by spoken, not written, words; 'Verbal contract' is not a technical term. See also **Contract**; **Oral agreement**.

Versus /vɜsʊs/ *Lat* – against. Especially of the two parties in an action at law. *Abbr* – v.

Vested interest 1. An interest in which the identity of the person who takes the interest is known and there is no condition precedent to the interest falling into possession other than determination of the prior particular estate; an immediate fixed right of present or future enjoyment: *Glenn v Federal Cmr of Land Tax* (1915) 20 CLR 490. **2.** An estate is vested in interest where there is a present right of future enjoyment: *Walsh Bay Developments v FCT* (1995) 31 ATR 15; 130 ALR 415. For example, in the grant 'to A for life, remainder to B in fee simple', B's interest is vested (vested 'in interest'), although it is not yet vested in possession. See also **Contingent interest**; **Future interest**.

• **Vesting** A provision within an employer-sponsored superannuation fund, entitling a fund member to part or all of the employer's contributions which have been paid in on the member's behalf, upon leaving. This vesting occurs either immediately, after a specified number of years, or progressively over the years, increasing the size of a departure benefit. However, a resignation benefit with full vesting often remains less than the benefit received on retirement, death or disablement.

Vesting of property The transfer of property ownership rights from one person to another. Where a debtor becomes a bankrupt the divisible property of the bankrupt vests immediately in the trustee in bankruptcy: (CTH) Bankruptcy Act 1966 s 58(1)(a). After acquired property automatically vests in the same way as soon as it is acquired by the bankrupt: (CTH) Bankruptcy Act 1966 s 58(1)(b). See also **After acquired property**; **Bankrupt**; **Debtor**; **Divisible property**; **Trustee in bankruptcy**.

Vesting of trust property The transfer to the trustee of the property subject to the trust. Where the trust is created by assurance inter vivos, the vesting must generally be contemporaneous with the creation of the trust if the trust is a voluntary one: *Milroy v Lord* (1862) 4 De GF & J 264; 45 ER 1185. When the trust is created by declaration, the property is ex hypothesi vested in the trustee: *Garrett v L'Estrange* (1911) 13 CLR 430. See also **Constitution of trust**; **Vesting of property**.

Vicarious liability The liability imposed on one person for the wrongful act of another on the basis of the legal relationship between them, usually that of employer and employee.

Agency The liability imposed on a principal who employs another person to perform work on the principal's behalf for tortious acts performed by the person within the scope of his or her authority. If an unlawful act was done by the agent within the scope of his or her authority, it is immaterial that the principal directed the agent not to do it: *Colonial Mutual Life Assurance Ltd v Producers and Citizens Cooperative Assurance Co of Australia Ltd* (1931) 46 CLR 41. See also **Agent; Personal liability; Principal; Liability of principal**.

Employment The liability of an employer to third persons for the tortious acts of an employee which the employer actually or impliedly authorises. The acts must be committed in the course of employment, while the employee is acting within the scope of his or her authority and performing the employment duties, or be acts incidental to the employment duties: *Kooragang Investments Pty Ltd v Richardson and Wrench Ltd* [1981] 2 NSWLR 1; *Darling Island Stevedoring and Lighterage Co Ltd v Long* (1957) 97 CLR 36. See also **Course of employment; Employer's personal liability**.

Vicarious performance In contract law, the performance of an obligation by the promisor through the acts of a third party. See also **Subcontract**.

Vitiating factor A factor which affects a person's assent to a contract or intention to confer a benefit on another. Vitiating factors include misrepresentation, mistake, duress, undue influence, and unconscionable conduct. See also **Duress; Misrepresentation; Mistake; Unconscionable**.

•**Void 1.** Legally non-existent; having no legal effect; lacking the intended legal effect: *Brooks v Burns Philip Trustee Co Ltd* (1969) 121 CLR 432. An act, decision, deed or transaction that is void cannot be enforced or relied upon. Whether an act, decision, deed or transaction such as a contract or a marriage, is void or voidable, depends on the principles applied in the particular area of law. **2.** In administrative law, a decision reached in breach of the duty to observe procedural fairness. It may be the subject of an appeal: *Calvin v Carr* [1980] AC 574; (1979) 22 ALR 417; [1979] 1 NSWLR 1. See also **Void ab initio**.

Void ab initio *Lat* – of no effect from the beginning. A contract or other transaction void ab initio is treated as never having had legal effect; this is the usual meaning of 'void'. Court proceedings are unnecessary to deprive a contract void ab initio of effect; rights and liabilities will not be recognised to the extent that the existence of a void contract must be asserted to prove them. See also **Void; Void contract**.

Void contract An apparent contract which is non-existent because it is invalidated from the outset, such as where it is illegal, contrary to public policy, prohibited by statute, or ultra vires one of the parties. Restitution of benefits conferred under a void contract may be possible on the basis of failure of consideration, mistake, incapacity, or public policy: *Guinness Plc v Saunders* [1990] 2 AC 663. See also **Ineffective contract; Ultra vires; Void ab initio**.

Voidable A contract or other transaction is valid until a party with the right to set it aside ('avoid' it) does so. The right may be legal or equitable. In each case the avoidance makes the transaction void from the outset (void ab initio). At common law avoidance is the act of a party, called in the case of contracts 'rescission', and permitted only if the parties can return to their pre-contractual position (*restitutio in integrum*); equity makes common law rescission available, and offers equitable rescission, on wider grounds, although complete *restitutio in integrum* is not possible: *Alati v Kruger* (1955) 94 CLR 216. See also **Rescission; Unenforceable; Void; Void ab initio**.

Voidable instrument A formal legal document creating rights and duties that can be set aside and rendered null and void at the suit of a party to the instrument, or by a third party. An instrument may be voidable due to faults intrinsic to the document, the conduct of one or all of the parties to the document (fraud, for example), or the mental incapacity of one of the parties: *Gibbons v Wright* (1954) 91 CLR 423. See also **Fraud; Instrument; Void**.

Voidable preference See **Unfair preference**.

Voidable transaction A transaction which is liable to be set aside, varied or made the subject of a court order where the transaction is an insolvent transaction of the company entered into within a prescribed time frame: Corporations Law s 588FE. See also **Insolvent transaction; Transaction; Uncommercial transaction; Unfair loan; Unfair preference; Winding up**.

Voluntary assignment 1. The assignment of contractual rights or obligations with the consent of both contracting parties. **2.** A gift; an intentional, gratuitous, immediate transfer of an existing proprietary right, vested or contingent, from the assignor to the assignee: *Norman v FCT* (1963) 109 CLR 9 at 26. See also **Assignment; Involuntary assignment; Novation**.

•**Voluntary body** An association or other body (whether incorporated or unincorporated) whose activities are not engaged in for the purpose of making a profit. It does not include a club, a body established by the Commonwealth or State governments, or an association that provides grants, loans, credit or finance to its members: (CTH) Sex Discrimination Act 1984 s 4. See also **Association; Corporation; Unincorporated association**.

Voluntary non-profit association The association formed where two or more persons come together voluntarily to pursue common aims or purposes, agreeing to be bound by mutual undertakings as association members: *Conservative and Unionist Central Office v Burrell* [1982] 2 All ER 1; [1982] 1 WLR 522. Also known as 'voluntary association' or 'non-profit voluntary association'. See also **Association; Club; Domestic tribunal; Incorporated association; Unincorporated association**.

Voluntary product recall A voluntary recall of products undertaken by a supplier without compulsion of legislation, either because the products may or will cause personal injury or property damage, or because of a defect in their quality. Where goods will or may cause injury to any person, the supplier must within two days after recalling the goods, give written notice to the

Minister stating that the goods are subject to recall, and detailing the nature of the defect: for example (CTH) Trade Practices Act 1974 ss 65R(1), 65F(7); (NSW) Fair Trading Act 1987 s 34(9), (10); (SA) Trade Standards Act 1979 s 27c(1). Also known as 'voluntary recall'. See also **Compulsory product recall; Product recall; Recall action.**

Voluntary winding up A winding up of a company which is initiated by either members or creditors, rather than the court: Corporations Law Pt 5.5. A members' voluntary winding up is possible only for companies able to pay all their debts. If the company is insolvent, a voluntary winding up must be a creditors' voluntary winding up: s 497(1). See also **Creditor; Creditors' voluntary winding up; Contributing shareholder; Liquidator; Members' voluntary winding up; Winding up.**

Vostro accounts The accounts of foreign banks with Australian banks denominated in Australian currency. The vostro account of one bank is the nostro account of the other. See also **Foreign bank; Nostro account.**

Voting rights The powers which holders of shares in a company have to vote at meetings of the company. Shares may be 'non-voting shares' and thus carry no voting rights. For the purposes of the Corporations Law s 9 a voting share is one that confers a right to vote, but does not include a share which only gives a right to vote in relation to a period where a dividend is in arrears, on a proposal to reduce the company's share capital, on a resolution to approve a buy-back, on a proposal that affects the rights attached to the share, on a proposal to wind up the company, on a proposal for the disposal of the whole of the company's property business or undertaking, or during the winding up of the body. Where each member in a company holds one vote, irrespective of the number of shares held by the member, the shares they hold are not voting shares for the purposes of the Corporations Law: *Westel Co-operative Ltd v Foodland Associated Ltd* (1987) 12 ACLR 308; 5 ACLC 979; *Re Darling Downs Co- operative Bacon Association Ltd* (1988) 12 ACLR 709; 6 ACLC 355.

• **Voting share** An issued share in a body corporate that confers a general right to vote: Corporations Law s 9. Excluded are shares which have a right to vote exercisable only in certain specified circumstances, namely the right to vote during a period when a dividend is in arrears, on a proposal to reduce the body's share capital, on a proposal that affects rights attached to the share, on a proposal to wind up the body, on a proposal for the disposal of the whole of the body's property and undertaking, or during the winding up of a body. Consequently, typical preference shares are not normally voting shares. See also **Non-voting share; Redeemable preference share; Super-voting share; Takeover.**

Voting trust A trust originating in the United States and sometimes declared to be illegal. Under a voting trust the shareholder of a corporation assigns his or her voting rights to a controlling group of trusts, and in return, receives a distribution of income by way of dividend, for the purpose of separating control from ownership. See also **Voting rights; Trust.**

Voucher A document which evidences a transaction, usually a payment.

Voyage charterparty A document amounting to a contract setting out the terms and conditions agreed to by a charterer and a shipowner for the use of a ship's cargo space for one or more voyages. See also **Act of God; Carriage of goods; Charter; Charterer; Charterparty; Common carrier; Contract of carriage; Deviation; Lay day; Loading; Reasonable dispatch** .

Voyages in stages The stages of a sea voyage. Each voyage consists of four stages, namely the loading voyage under which the vessel travels from wherever it is to the point of loading, the loading operation, the carrying voyage under which the vessel travels to the point of discharge, and the discharging operation. A voyage in stages is also a voyage divided into a number of parts, either naturally (for example, where the voyage is partly by river and partly by sea), by agreement between the parties, or by necessity of the circumstances of the voyage (for example, to take on more fuel). See also **Loading.**

Vulture fund A financial fund created and maintained by a company or financial institution to be used swiftly at an appropriate moment for the acquisition or seizure of a vulnerable business, which may offer rich pickings.

W

Wage A monetary amount that an employer agrees to pay to an employee for the employee's services (*Terry Shields Pty Ltd v Chief Cmr Pay-Roll Tax* (1989) 17 NSWLR 493) especially for manual labour. See also **Fringe benefit; Income; Remuneration; Salary; Taxable income.**

Wage fixation In industrial relations, the practice of having minimum wage rates set for an industry by an independent industrial tribunal, such as the Australian Industrial Relations Commission. The aim of wage fixation is to produce fairness, consistency and stability in wage levels. See also **Compulsory arbitration; Industrial award; Industrial tribunal; National wage case.**

Wage indexation The practice of increasing wages in accordance with increases in the cost of living, as measured by the Consumer Price Index: for example *National Wage case 1983* (1983) 291 CAR 3. See also **Australian Conciliation and Arbitration Commission; Real wage; Wage fixation.**

Wages freeze A bar placed on any increase in the wages of employees. The wage freeze of 1982 was implemented by the (CTH) Salaries and Wages Pause Act 1982 which prevented any increase in the wages of Commonwealth and Northern Territory government employees. It was followed by the *National Wage Case December 1982* (1982) 287 CAR 82, in which the Australian Conciliation and Arbitration Commission introduced a general pause in wage increases. The freeze ended in 1983. See also **National wage case; Wage fixation.**

Waiver An intentional relinquishment of a right or interest. Waiver can describe an election or an estoppel, and the distinction will not always be clear: *Commonwealth v Verwayen* (1990) 170 CLR 394. See also **Election; Estoppel.**

Bills of exchange and other negotiable instruments **1.** The act of a drawer or indorser of a bill of exchange in dispensing with some or all of the holder's duties: (CTH) Bills of Exchange Act 1909 s 21(b). **2.** An express stipulation written on a cheque by its drawer or indorser dispensing with, as against the drawer or indorser, the right of presentment of a cheque: (CTH) Cheques and Payment Orders Act 1986 s 17. See also **Bill of exchange; Cheque; Drawer; Holder; Indorser; Presentment; Renunciation.**

Contract **1.** The election by a party not to enforce a right conferred by a contract, indicated by words or conduct. The abandonment of a right: for example *Gange v Sullivan* (1966) 116 CLR 418. **2.** An estoppel, by which a party is, by words or conduct, disentitled to enforce a right conferred by a contract: *Finagrain SA Geneva v Kruse* [1976] 2 Lloyd's Rep 508. See also **Abandonment; Acquiescence; Affirmation; Discharge; Election; Estoppel; Proprietary estoppel.**

Tort **1.** The legal grounds on which a person is precluded from asserting one legal right when he or she is entitled to alternative rights inconsistent with each other: *Sargent v ASL Developments Ltd* (1974) 131 CLR 634 at 655; 4 ALR 257 at 273. For example, where a plaintiff chooses not to exercise a right to forfeit a lease or rescind a contract of sale for wrongful repudiation or breach of condition, he or she may be said to have waived that right and will not be permitted to assert it against the defendant at a later date: *Kammins Ballrooms Co Ltd v Zenith Investments (Torquay) Ltd* [1970] 2 All ER 871. See also **Election; Estoppel; Repudiation.**

Waiver clause A clause in a policy of insurance providing that any waiver on the part of the insurer will not be binding unless explicitly stated in writing. A waiver clause may be overridden if the insurer's conduct gives rise to an estoppel: *Craine v Colonial Mutual Fire Insurance Co Ltd* (1920) 28 CLR 305; 26 ALR 326; *Reece v Pearl Assurance Co Ltd* (1934) 34 SR (NSW) 124; *Barr-Brown & NIMU Insurance Co, Re an Arbitration* [1942] NZLR 444. In marine insurance, a waiver clause ensures that the policy continues to protect both the underwriter and the insured during the process of negotiation over abandonment claims. It may state that measures taken by the assured or the underwriters with the object of saving, protecting, or recovering the subject matter insured are not to be considered as a waiver or acceptance of abandonment or otherwise to prejudice the rights of either party. See also **Abandonment; Waiver.**

Wall Street A reference to the New York financial community concentrated in the Wall Street area of Manhattan. See also **Black Monday.**

Wallis inquiry The five member committee chaired by Mr Stan Wallis, managing director of Amcor Ltd, appointed by the Federal Treasurer on 30 May 1996, to evaluate the deregulation of the Australian financial system since the Campbell Report of 1981. The Wallis inquiry examined and reported on: choice, quality and cost of financial services to consumers, the efficiency and competitiveness of the financial system, the effects of deregulation on growth, employment and savings; the technological and marketing advances and integration of financial markets; and regulatory arrangements affecting the financial system. The committee's final report was presented to the Commonwealth Treasurer on 18 March 1997. Also known as 'the Daughter of Campbell'. See also **Campbell inquiry; Deregulation.**

War clause 1. A clause contained in a bill of lading or charterparty stipulating the course of action open to the master of the vessel if the vessel, its cargo or crew is put at risk because of war, should the voyage proceed. The terms of such clauses vary, but always allow the master to avoid putting the ship or crew at risk. **2.** A clause contained in a policy of insurance, typically marine or aviation insurance, which covers the insured against losses arising from capture, seizure, hostilities, or other warlike operations. See also **Bill of lading; Cargo; Charterparty; Master.**

• **Warehouse** A place or building in which goods are sold or offered or exposed for sale by wholesale: (NSW) Factories, Shops and Industries Act 1962 s 74.

Warehouse to warehouse insurance See **Goods in transit insurance**.

Warehouseperson A person who stores goods as a bailee for hire or reward, even if only for one person: *Griffith Laboratories Pty Ltd v Meat Industry Suppliers and Agents Pty Ltd* (1983) 34 SASR 172.

Warehouseperson's lien A lien on goods deposited with a warehouseperson for storage, whether deposited by the owner of the goods, or by authority, or by any person entrusted with possession of the goods by the owner or by his or her authority: (NSW) Warehouseman's Liens Act 1935 s 3. See also **Lien**.

Warehousing 1. Arranging for someone to hold an asset or shareholding to ensure that the actual owner remains anonymous, for example a nominee shareholding in which the identity of the beneficial owner is masked. 2. The pledging of a long-term mortgage as security for a short-term loan from a financial institution. 3. An arrangement between a broker or dealer and a customer for a sale with a provision for repurchase on a future date at a present price. This form of warehousing is prohibited by the United States Securities and Exchange Commission. See also **Parking**.

Warning A caution; anything pointing out or alerting to the existence of danger. In tort, a warning includes a label, sign, notice, alarm, or advice. An occupier of premises owes a duty to entrants to bring to their attention any foreseeable danger: *Nagle v Rottnest Island Authority* (1993) 177 CLR 423; 112 ALR 393. If a warning would prevent injury, the warning is usually sufficient to show an occupier has met the required standard of care: *Commissioner for Railways (NSW) v Anderson* (1961) 105 CLR 42; ALR 865. See also **Defect in information**; **Failure to warn**; **Notice**; **Sign**.

Warning notice In consumer protection law, a notice published in the Gazette by the Minister stating that certain goods are being investigated to determine whether they cause injury, and/or warning of possible risks involved in using the goods: (CTH) Trade Practices Act 1974 s 65B(1). See also **Product recall**; **Consumer product safety standard**; **Warning**; **Unsafe goods**.

Warranty 1. A guarantee or assurance. An express or implied promise that certain facts are as they are represented to be. In its common usage, any contractually binding promise, whatever its nature: *Oscar Chess Ltd v Williams* [1957] 1 All ER 325; 1 WLR 370. 2. A contractual term, breach of which gives rise to a right to claim damages, but not to a right to reject the subject matter of the contract or to treat the contract as repudiated: (NSW) Sale of Goods Act 1923 s 5(1); (VIC) Goods Act 1958 s 3(1); *Associated Newspapers Ltd v Bancks* (1951) 83 CLR 322. Warranties are distinguishable from conditions, breach of which gives rise to the right to terminate and claim damages. 3. Sometimes used to describe an executory undertaking or promise in a collateral contract: *Gardiner v Grigg* (1938) 38 SR (NSW) 524. 4. The promise of a manufacturer of goods in relation to its obligations if the goods prove defective (such as a promise to repair or replace the goods): *Mihaljevic v Eiffel Tower Motors Pty Ltd* [1973] VR 545. 5. An oral statement which induces a person to enter a contract: *Van den Esschert v Chappell* [1960] WAR 114; *Ellul v Oakes* (1972) 3 SASR 377. 6. In marine insurance law, an undertaking by an assured of a promissory nature. See also **Condition**; **Contract**; **Damages**; **Damages**; **Express warranty**; **Implied warranty**; **Intermediate term**; **Promissory warranty**.

Warranty of authority A representation that a company officer or agent has authority to bind a company or principal. If the officer or agent did not have such authority, and a person acts on the warranty of authority and suffers loss, then the office or agent may be personally liable: *Brownett v Newton* (1941) 64 CLR 439; *Black v Smallwood* (1966) 117 CLR 52; [1966] ALR 744. See also **Actual authority**; **Agent**; **Directors' duties**; **Principal**; **Ultra vires**; **Warranty**.

Warranty of value A warranty in an insurance policy that at all times the sum insured will represent the full value of the property insured. See also **Underinsurance**.

Wash sale The sale and repurchase of the same security losses for tax purposes. A wash sale allows an investor to lock-in capital losses for tax purposes even though the fall in share or asset price may be temporary. A wash sale may contravene Corporations Law ss 995-998. See also **Market manipulation**.

Wasting property Property which only lasts for a limited time. Any asset or property which perishes or becomes worn out, either with use or by lapse of time, is of a wasting nature, including buildings and machinery erected for trade purposes: *Worrall v Commercial Banking Co of Sydney* (1917) 17 SR (NSW) 457 at 463, 464; 34 WN (NSW) 206.

Waterside employer A person who engages people for employment as waterside workers for work on a wharf or ship; or a ship's agent or shipowner who directs the method or time of working of a stevedoring employer or contractor; or a master or officer of a ship engaged in stevedoring: (CTH) Industrial Relations Act 1988 Sch 1. See also **Contractor**; **Employee**; **Waterside worker**.

Waterside worker A person who works loading or unloading cargo into or from ships, including a person who is a member of the Waterside Workers' Federation of Australia who works doing stevedoring operations.

Waybill A document prepared by a carrier at the point of origin of a shipment, showing the point of origin, destination, route, consignor, consignee, description of shipment and amount charged for the transportation service: for example (WA) Stock (Brands and Movements) Act 1970 Pt VIII. A waybill is forwarded to the carrier's agent at the destination or point of transfer. It constitutes written evidence of the shipment of the described goods in the event of any claim by or against the carrier and, in that respect, resembles a bill of lading. However, unlike a bill of lading, it is not a document of title and is not negotiable. A waybill is used in the maritime context to avoid the delays which may occur to ships and cargos when bills of lading are late in arriving at the discharge port. A 'blanket waybill' is a waybill covering more than one consignment of freight.

See also **Air waybill; Bill of lading; Consignee; Consignor; Contract of carriage; Ocean waybill; Sea waybill.**

Wealth tax A tax levied on the assets of the individual, as distinct from income. A wealth tax is usually applied to the net assets of the taxpayer (that is, assets minus liabilities) with a threshold level below which no tax is payable. Several countries have adopted a wealth tax. France introduced a wealth tax for the first time in 1981, though with numerous exemptions. Australia has no wealth tax.

Weight, contents and value unknown A clause in a bill of lading providing that the weights and other descriptions of the cargo are those stated by the consignor and are unconfirmed by the master or the agents signing the bill of lading: *New Chinese Antimony Co Ltd v Ocean Steamship Co Ltd* [1917] 2 KB 664. Under such a clause, the consignee may be exonerated from liability in case of any discrepancy in the weight, contents or value of the closed packages if disclosed after unloading. See also **Bill of lading; Loading; Master; Charterer.**

Weighted average inventory method An inventory valuation method which considers the fluctuating prices and quantities of acquired goods in the computation of the cost of inventory. The weighted average method takes the prices of units at the beginning inventory and the varying prices of purchases made and are weighted by the number of units to determine the weighted average cost per unit. It may be computed as the weighted average cost of all available goods present in a given period, or as a weighted moving average cost adjusted when new goods are delivered. See also **Cost or market method; Trading stock.**

Welsh mortgage A mortgage with no condition or proviso for the repayment of the capital at any time. The agreement is that the mortgagee, to whom the estate is conveyed, will receive the rents until the debts are paid, when the mortgagor is at liberty to redeem at any time.

Westpac Banking Corporation One of the 'big four' of the Australian banking system, a bank tracing its history back to the Bank of New South Wales established in 1817 and the Commercial Bank of Australia founded in Melbourne in 1866. In 1982, these two banks merged to become the Westpac Banking Corporation; the name being chosen because of the area of prime interest to the bank, the Western Pacific. In 1986, Mase Westpac Limited, a wholly-owned subsidiary of Westpac, became one of the five members of the London Gold Market. Westpac is currently represented in 30 countries. Australia's largest finance company, Australian Guarantee Corporation Limited (AGC) is a wholly-owned subsidiary of Westpac. See also **Australian banking system.**

Westpac letters Confidential correspondence between Westpac Bank and its solicitors during the period November to December 1987. The letters related to detailed investigations carried out by the solicitors about foreign currency loans arranged for several customers by Partnership Pacific Ltd (PPL), Westpac's merchant bank subsidiary. The letters disclosed that Westpac's subsidiary had acted negligently causing loss to several borrowers. The letters were highlighted by the media and Westpac's attempt to restrain their publication by injunction was unsuccessful: *Westpac Banking Corp Ltd v John Fairfax Group Pty Ltd* (1991) 19 IPR 513. See also **Foreign currency loans.**

Westpac-Melbourne Institute Index of Consumer Sentiment An index constructed by the Melbourne University Institute of Applied Economics and Social Research to reflect the expectations of consumers in relation to personal finances, the national economy, market conditions and future prospects. A changing pessimism/optimism ratio emerges over time. The index is based on telephone interviews conducted by an independent research and polling group.

Westpac-Melbourne Institute Indices Indices construed by the Melbourne University Institute of Applied Economics and Social Research which include a range of widely used leading and coincident economic indicators, together with some relatively obscure measures such as the number of telephone connections, to reflect the state of the Australian economy.

Wet lease A lease of plant, equipment, and the labour used to operate it, excluding payment of outgoings, which are met by the lessor, but which are usually built in to the hire price. See also **Dry lease.**

Wharf labourer A person who works in loading, discharging and coaling ships. The work may also involve operations to take the goods from where they have been put ready to be transferred from the loading place up to at least the time when they have been finally secured on board the ship: *Brooks v South Australian Stevedoring Co Ltd* [1920] SALR 207. See also **Labourer; Waterside worker.**

Wharfage The charges payable for the use of a wharf by a vessel for the purposes of loading or unloading goods, embarking, or disembarking passengers. See also **Loading; Wharfinger.**

Wharfinger The owner, operator, or occupier of a wharf who receives merchandise on the wharf, either for the purpose of forwarding or for delivery to the consignee on the wharf. The wharfinger will often provide warehousing facilities. See also **Wharfage.**

White collar crime A broad category of crimes committed by persons from a middle or upper class socio-economic background in the course of their occupations. White collar crimes include tax fraud, misrepresentation in financial statements, corporate crime, environmental offences, and medifraud. See also **Corporate crime; Taxation offence.**

White knight An organisation or person who comes to the rescue. In greenmail, a white knight is a third party who is asked by a company being threatened by a corporate raider to purchase the shares held by the raider, thus saving the threatened company from takeover. See also **Greenmail.**

Whole of life insurance A life insurance policy under which the sum insured is only payable on the death of the person whose life is insured. Whole of life insurance premiums have an investment element, in that surplus profits of the insurer are distributed as bonuses or added to the value of the policy, which the insured may redeem if he or she elects to surrender the policy. See also **Life insurance.**

Wholesale sales tax *Abbr* – WST A tax imposed on a limited range of goods manufactured in, and imported into, Australia: (CTH) Sales Tax Assessment Act 1992 s 5. It is imposed on about six categories of goods; services are excluded. It is levied at rates of 10 per cent, 20 per cent and 30 per cent, with a general rate of 20 per cent and a higher rate of 30 per cent for luxury goods such as watches, clocks, radios and television sets. As a proportion of Commonwealth revenue, the WST accounts for about 10 per cent of total taxation receipts and about 30 per cent of total federal indirect taxes. The administration costs of the WST are low, partly due to the low number of taxpayers. The WST is collected at the wholesale level, and is only imposed on about 20 per cent of final consumer spending.

Wholly mutual company A life insurance company having no share capital and limited by guarantee. The liability of its members is limited to payment of a prescribed amount in the event of the company going into liquidation. See also **Company limited by guarantee; Share capital**.

• **Wholly-owned subsidiary** A body corporate is a wholly owned subsidiary of another body corporate if its only member (shareholder) is the parent, the parent's nominee, another wholly owned subsidiary of the same parent or the nominee of such another wholly owned subsidiary: Corporations Law s 9.

Wildcat strike A form of industrial action in which workers strike suddenly without following the procedures established by legislation, industrial tribunals, union rules, or other means. See also **Industrial action; Rolling strike; Strike**.

Wilful default In the law of trusts, deliberate and purposeful conduct of a trustee which the trustee knows to be a breach of trust consisting of a failure to perform his or her duty: *Re Trusts of Leeds City Brewery Ltd* [1925] Ch 532n. The trustee's statutory indemnity is inapplicable in cases of loss caused by wilful default: for example (NSW) Trustee Act 1925 s 59(2). See also **Trust; Trustee**.

Wilful misconduct Intentional or reckless misbehaviour.

Willingness-to-pay A principle underlying the valuation of benefits from a project or activity. Benefits are usually of two kinds: services to consumers for which a price is paid, and services to consumers and benefits for the broader community for which a price is not paid. A valuation needs not only a summation of the prices actually paid but an assessment of what people might be expected to willingly pay for the free services and benefits, rather than do without them. A variety of techniques have been developed for the assessment of willingness-to-pay values. Some non-traded benefits such as travel time savings in the case of road construction have well-established methods of valuation.

Winch clause A clause in a charterparty providing for the use of the ship's winches by the charterer. A winch clause often includes a stipulation as to how many winch operators are to be made available by the shipowner and who is responsible for payment for the use of shore winches if they are employed. See also **Charterer; Charterparty**.

Windfall An unexpected gain or profit, generally not related to the efforts and expenditures of the entity that benefits. For taxation purposes, windfalls, such as winning a prize in a lottery or in a competition, are generally non-assessable: for example (CTH) Income Tax Assessment Act 1936 s 160ZB(2). See also **Assessable income; Income taxation**.

Winding up In Corporations law, a form of external administration under which a person called a 'liquidator' assumes control of a company's affairs in order to discharge its liabilities in preparation for its dissolution. The liquidator ascertains the liabilities of the company, converts its assets into money, terminates its contracts, disposes of its business, distributes the net assets to creditors and any surplus to the proprietors and extinguishes the company as a legal entity by formal dissolution. Corporations Law Ch 5 governs the winding up of companies incorporated under Pt 2.2 Div 1, bodies corporate registered under Pt 2.2 Divs 2, 3, 4 and certain other bodies referred to in Pt 5.7. Also known as 'liquidation'. See also **Compulsory winding up; External administration; Voluntary winding up**.

Winding up order A court direction that a company be dissolved under Corporations Law Pt 5.4B: Corporations Law s 465B(1). A winding up order acts in favour of all creditors and contributories of the company as if it had been made on the joint application of all the creditors and contributories: Corporations Law s 471(1). This order can be made even if a voluntary winding up is in progress: Corporations Law s 467B. See also **Compulsory winding up; Voluntary winding up; Winding up**.

Withdrawal The process of retracting or cancelling.

Contract An offer may be withdrawn or revoked any time before it has been accepted: *Dickinson v Dodds* (1876) 2 Ch D 463. An acceptance of an offer can be withdrawn any time before it has been communicated to the offeror.

Partnerships and joint ventures The retirement of a partner from the partnership, or if the partnership is of only two persons, then it refers to a dissolution of the partnership: *Van der Waal v Goodenough* [1983] 1 NSWLR 81 at 89.

Withholding tax 1. A tax that is deducted from income at its source rather than from income in the hands of the taxpayer. In relation to non-resident taxpayers, withholding tax is imposed on dividends, interest, and royalties paid to non-residents: (CTH) Income Tax Assessment Act 1936 s 128B. 2. In relation to resident taxpayers, the term is sometimes used to describe a tax withheld from salary or wages paid under the pay-as-you-earn system or payments made under the prescribed payments system. See also **Assessable income; Non-resident taxpayer; Pay-As-You-Earn system; Prescribed payments system**.

Within scope of employment The test used to determine the extent to which an employer is legally responsible for wrongful acts of his or her servant. An employer is only responsible for acts which the servant committed within the scope of his or her employment. If the servant acts beyond these limits, he or she is said to be 'on a frolic of his own', for which an employer is not vicariously liable: *Joel v Morison* (1834) 6 Car & P 501; 172 ER 1338. See also **Vicarious liability**.

Without discount 1. In relation to the hire due under a time charterparty, the absence of a reduction in the amount of hire for early payment: *Compania Sud Americana de Vapores v Shipmair BV, The Teno* [1977] 2 Lloyd's Rep 289 at 292. 2. In relation to the price asked for the transfer of a negotiable instrument, the absence of a reduction of the face value of the instrument as a compensation to the purchaser for the risk that the instrument will not be met according to its terms when it falls due. See also **Payment without discount; Time charterparty**.

Without prejudice A statement made without an intention to affect the legal rights of any person.

With-profits annuity An annuity which, for a smaller guaranteed income, pays the annuitant a share in the profits achieved by the annuity fund. See also **Annuity**.

Witness 1. A person who sees or hears material relevant to an enquiry.

Woodchip industry An industry involving the procurement of timber and its mechanical reduction to chips.

Wool lien Security over the next season's wool clip, to ensure the payment of loans made to the owner of sheep. The (NSW) Preferable Liens Act 1844 (7 Vic No 3) (no longer in force) allowed squatters to borrow money to finance their businesses, secured on the wool clip from season to season. See also **Bill of sale**.

Work 1. Effort or energy exerted to achieve a result; labour. 2. That on which effort is expended; something to be done. 'Work' is defined differently in various statutes for different purposes. In relation to discrimination legislation, it includes work done in a relationship of employment, work under a contract for services, work remunerated wholly or partly by commission, work under a statutory appointment, work experience, apprenticeship or traineeship, voluntary or unpaid work, and work by a person in a sheltered workshop: (QLD) Anti-Discrimination Act 1991 s 4. It includes work done as a self-employed person: (NSW) Occupational Health and Safety Act 1983 s 4. It may include any form of service or activity: (NSW) Children (Community Service Orders) Act 1987 s 3. See also **Contract for services; Contract of employment; Employment; Literary work; Self-employed person**.

Work and materials contract A contract in which the substance of the bargain is the skill and labour involved in the production of the article the subject of the contract, and where the transfer of materials in addition to the skill involved is merely ancillary: *Robinson v Graves* [1935] 1 KB 579. See also **Contract**.

Work ban A form of industrial action, by which employees cease to perform a particular part of their duties but do not cease work altogether. See also **Industrial action; Strike**.

Work in progress Tangible goods that are in the process of conversion by manufacture from raw materials to business trading stock: *Henderson v Cmr of Taxation* (1969) 119 CLR 612. See also **Business; Trading stock**.

Work rules Detailed rules formulated by employers to regulate the conduct of employees. The rules may be incorporated as terms of the contract of employment, in which case they may only be altered by the mutual agreement of the employer and employees. However, if the rules are no more than instructions on how to do the work, they are not part of the terms of employment and may be altered unilaterally by the employer (*Secretary of State for Employment v Associated Society of Locomotive Engineers Firemen (No 2)* [1972] 2 QB 455), as such instructions are seen as part of the employer's managerial prerogative.

Work value change principle A principle of wage fixation by which an industrial tribunal grants an increase in wage rates where it is shown that the value of the work performed has increased. Changes in work value are changes in the nature of the work, the skill and responsibility required, or the conditions under which the work is performed: *National Wage case April 1975* (1975) 167 CAR 18. To warrant a wage increase, the changes should constitute a significant net addition to work requirements. See also **Wage fixation**.

Workable competition A concept of competition which moves away from theoretical concepts of perfect competition, recognising that competition is never perfect and that policy makers need a more practical definition. The term was first used by J. M. Clarke. In a situation of Workable Competition, no one seller, and no one group of sellers acting in concert, has the power to choose its level of profits by giving less and charging more (that is, by exercising market power). Workable competition is characterised by rivalrous conduct and the threat of entry. There are no predatory practices. See also **Competition; Competition law; Market power; Perfect competition; Predatory conduct**.

Worker A person who works; especially a manual or industrial labourer. 'Worker' is defined differently for different purposes; for example, it may mean a person who works under a contract of employment, excluding a person who works as an independent contractor, or a casual employee ((NSW) Workers Compensation Act 1987 s 3), or an outworker ((VIC) Workers Compensation Act 1958 s 3), or a public servant ((ACT) Workers' Compensation Act 1951 s 6). It may include a self-employed person ((SA) Workers Rehabilitation and Compensation Act 1986 s 3), or any person engaged in manual work or personal service ((SA) Workers Liens Act 1893 s 2). See also **Contract of employment; Independent contractor; Work**.

Workers' compensation A statutory system of compensation for work-related injuries. It does not depend on the existence of any fault by the employer. The statute specifies amounts of compensation payable according to the nature or consequences or the injury. In some cases, the statutory scheme is an alternative to common law damages for negligence or other torts: for example (NSW) Workers Compensation Act 1987. In other cases, it replaces common law damages, either wholly or in part. Also known as 'accident compensation'. See also **Accident pay; Award; Comcare; Course of employment; Sick leave**.

•**Workers' compensation insurance** A form of insurance that indemnifies employers against liability to their workers arising under the relevant workers' compensation legislation: for example (NSW) Workers Compensation Act 1987; (VIC) Accident Compensation Act 1985; (QLD) Workers' Compensation Act 1990. Workers' compensation policies usually also provide indemnity against an employer's common law liability to his or her workers. In all States and Territories of Australia it is compulsory for employers to obtain workers' compensation insurance, unless the employer is a self insurer: for example (NSW) Workers Compensation Act 1987 s 155; (VIC) Accident Compensation (Workcover Insurance) Act 1993 s 7; (QLD) Workers' Compensation Act 1990 s 44. See also **Insurance contract; Indemnity; Liability insurance**.

Worker's lien A statutory lien, held by a worker doing work for an owner or occupier of land, over the owner's estate or interest in the land, to protect wages owing to the worker. The lien may extend to all the goods on the land belonging to the owner or occupier, but is limited in amount to four weeks' wages: (SA) Worker's Liens Act 1893 s 4. See also **Lien**.

Workplace Any premises where employees or self-employed people work: (ACT) Occupational Health and Safety Act 1989 s 5. See also **Employee; Self-employed person; Work**.

Workplace agreement An agreement made between employers and employees that provides for some or all of the rights and obligations that employers and employees have in relation to one another, including rights and obligations that are to take effect after termination of employment: for example (WA) Workplace Agreements Act 1993 s 5. See also **Enterprise agreement; Enterprise bargaining; Workplace**.

Workplace bargaining See **Enterprise bargaining**.

•**Work-related injury** Any injury, disease, disability, loss of artificial limb or medical aid, or death that is attributable to work, including the aggravation, exacerbation or recurrence of a prior work-related injury: (SA) Occupational Health, Safety and Welfare Act 1986 s 4. Any personal injury arising out of or sustained in the course of employment is compensable under workers' compensation legislation: for example (NSW) Workers Compensation Act 1987 Pt 3; (VIC) Accident Compensation Act 1985 Pt IV Div 2. See also **Workers' compensation**.

Work-related trauma The injury of a person (including the aggravation, acceleration or recurrence of an injury); or the contraction, aggravation, acceleration or recurrence of a disease of a person; or the loss or destruction of, or damage to, an artificial limb or other artificial substitute, or a medical, surgical or other similar aid or appliance; or the coming into existence (or aggravation, acceleration or recurrence) of any other condition, circumstance, occurrence, activity, form of behaviour, course of conduct or state of affairs that is harmful or disadvantageous to a person or the community, where any of the above is (or may be) related to the occupation of the person or the occupational activities of another person: (CTH) National Occupational Health and Safety Commission Act 1985 s 3. See also **Occupational health and safety; Work related injury**.

Worksheet An accounting document which simplifies the preparation of financial statements but is not normally recognised as part of the set of financial statements. A worksheet sorts out the adjusted accounts into columns to be used in the preparation of the profit and loss statement and balance sheet. The document does not account for year end adjustments or closing entries. The entries are officially completed at some future time in the accounting records by using the general journal. See also **Accounting; Balance sheet; Profit and loss statement**.

World Bank See **International Bank for Reconstruction and Development; International Development Association; International Monetary Fund**.

World Court See **International Court of Justice**.

World Trade Organisation *Abbr* – WTO An international organisation established on 15 April 1994 by the Marrakesh Agreement establishing the World Trade Organisation 1994. The function of the WTO is to facilitate the implementation, administration and operation, and to further the objectives, of the Marrakesh Agreement establishing the World Trade Organisation 1994 and of the Multilateral and Plurilateral Trade Agreements: Marrakesh Agreement establishing the World Trade Organisation 1994 art III(1). The WTO has legal personality, and must be accorded by each of its members such legal capacity as may be necessary for the exercise of its functions: art VIII(1). The WTO must provide the forum for negotiation among its members concerning their multilateral trade relations in certain matters: art III(2). The WTO must co-operate, as appropriate, with the International Monetary Fund and with the International Bank for Reconstruction and Development and its affiliated agencies, with a view to achieving greater coherence in global economic policy-making: art III(5). The three principal organs of the WTO are the Ministerial Conference, the General Council and the Secretariat: arts IV, VI. See also **General Agreement on Tariffs and Trade 1994; International Bank for Reconstruction and Development; International Monetary Fund; Marrakesh Agreement establishing the World Trade Organisation 1994**.

Writ of execution An order directing an officer of the court to enforce a judgment in a specified manner: (NSW) Local Courts (Civil Claims) Act 1970 s 59. The writ of execution derives from 'the old common law process by which the sheriff, in obedience to one of the common law writs, procures for a judgment creditor the fruits of his judgment': *Re a Company* [1915] Ch 520 at 527. A writ of execution now extends to mean a writ of levy for property, a writ for possession, a writ for delivery, a writ of sequestration or a writ in aid of any of these writs: (NSW) Supreme Court Rules 1970 Pt 44 r 1. Writs of execution have been replaced in Victoria by warrants of execution: (VIC) Rules of the Supreme Court Ch I r 68.01. See also **Execution**.

Write-off method A method of writing off money owed to a business when the money cannot be collected. The write-off method is to debit the value to bad debt expense and credit debtors to reduce current assets on the balance sheet. This method is called the direct write-off method. The allowance method is also used where the amount is written-off against the allowance for uncollectible accounts. See also **Accounts receivable; Balance sheet**.

Writer The seller of an option contract. The purchaser (taker) pays a consideration to the seller (writer) and receives the right under the option contract. See also **Option**.

Written authorisation In the law of agency, express authority in writing given by a principal for an agency relationship to be created. Written authorisation is sometimes required for a valid agency relationship to be formed. For example, writing may be required: where the contract of agency is to continue for a period exceeding one year ((TAS) Mercantile Law Act 1935 s 6), for the principal to be liable on a sale or purchase of a business ((NSW) Property, Stock and Business Agents Act 1941 s 50D), or to confer authority to create or dispose of an interest in land ((NSW) Conveyancing Act 1919 s 23C). Written authority is construed more liberally than authority conferred under seal, and regard is to be had to the object of the authority and the circumstances of the business: *Donaldson v Noble* (1888) 14 VLR 1021 at 1035-6. See also **Authority; Express authority; Irrevocable authority**.

Written down value See **Depreciated value**.

Wrong 1. The violation or infringement of a legal right. 2. Any injury, especially civil injuries which are independent of contract and are not breaches of trust. See also **Tort**.

Wrongdoer A person who commits an offence and violates the law by invading or infringing the rights of another or by causing damage to another's person, property, or goods. A wrongdoer who commits a tort is known as a 'tortfeasor'. See also **Tortfeasor**.

Wrongful dishonour A refusal or failure of a bank to pay a customer's cheque in spite of the customer having sufficient funds in the account to meet it. See also **Good faith**.

Wrongful dismissal The termination by an employer of the employment of an employee otherwise than in accordance with the terms of the contract of employment, or in contravention of an award or statute applying to the employment. An employee who has been wrongfully dismissed has a cause of action against the employer. See also **Summary dismissal; Unfair dismissal**.

Wrongful distribution In the law of trusts, overpayment by a trustee to a beneficiary or third party, of moneys in a trust fund. See also **Beneficiary; Trust; Trustee**.

Wrongful interference with goods Conversion of goods, trespass to goods, or negligence or any other tort (except detinue) in so far as it results in damage to goods or to an interest in goods: (UK) Torts (Interference With Goods) Act 1977 ss 1, 2. In the United Kingdom, legislation provides that a court may order delivery of goods and payment of consequential damages where the goods have been wrongfully interfered with and detained: (UK) Torts (Interference With Goods) Act 1977 s 3. In Australia, remedies in respect of wrongful interferences with goods lie at common law. See also **Conversion; Detinue; Negligence; Tort**.

Wrongful payment Any payment under a bill of exchange other than a payment to the legal holder or endorsee of the bill. Where a bill payable to order or on demand is paid by a banker in good faith and in the ordinary course of business to a person whose endorsement has been forged or made without authority, the banker is deemed to have paid the bill in due course and is not further liable in respect of the wrongful payment: (CTH) Bills of Exchange Act 1909 s 65(1). See also **Bill of exchange**.

Wrongful termination An attempt by a promisor to cancel the contract or its performance in circumstances where there is no legal right to do so. A wrongful termination is not an effective termination and is termination of a contract or its performance is usually a repudiation: *Sibbles v Highfern Pty Ltd* (1987) 164 CLR 214; 76 ALR 13. See also **Repudiation; Rescission; Termination**.

WTO See **World Trade Organisation**.

Y

• Year of income The financial year during which income is received. For taxation purposes, the year of income of a company is the financial year preceding the year of tax: (CTH) Income Tax Assessment Act 1936 s 6(1). Consequently, tax levied on a company for the year of tax ended 30 June 1996 is based upon taxable income of the company derived during the year ended 30 June 1995. However, the year of income for an individual is the financial year on which tax is levied: (CTH) Income Tax Assessment Act 1936 s 6(1). Consequently, tax levied on an individual for the year ended 30 June 1996 is based upon taxable income of the individual derived during the year ended 30 June 1996. The distinction arises because individuals are taxed under the pay as you earn system on salary and wages and provisional tax on other income, while companies are not. See also **Company rate of tax; Financial year; Income taxation; Pay As You Earn System; Substituted accounting period; Year of tax**.

• Year of tax The financial year for which income tax is levied: (CTH) Income Tax Assessment Act 1936 s 6(1). In Australia, the year of tax is normally the year ended 30 June. An exception to this is the year of tax for Fringe Benefits tax purposes, being the year ended 31 March: (CTH) Fringe Benefits Tax Assessment Act 1986 s 136(1). See also **Financial year; Fringe Benefits Tax; Income taxation; Year of income**.

Year to year The use of, or a lease of, property the term of which extends for one year to the next year. Entry into occupation, followed by payment of rent under an agreement for a future lease, brings into existence a common law tenancy from year to year, so long as the payment of rent is referable to a yearly tenancy: *Chan v Cresdon Pty Ltd* (1989) 168 CLR 242; 89 ALR 522. The amount of notice that must be given to a yearly tenant is six months, expiring on the day of the end of the term of the lease. If notice is not correctly given then another term of the lease is given. See also **Term lease**.

Yearly value An estimate of worth or value obtained every year. See also **Annual value**.

Yen interest-rate swap Known in Tokyo as yen-yen swaps, the exchanging of interest payments between two parties, usually banks or companies, on each other's yen debt. This allows each party to obtain the sort of loans they want more cheaply than they could themselves, or are prevented from raising by, for example, government regulation. For example, a company might want to turn a floating rate short term debt into a fixed rate long term debt. Yen-yen swaps began in 1986.

Yield to maturity The effective rate of return on a debenture or security realised at maturity. Computation of the rate of return involves a comparison between the price and the expected fund flow, or its equivalent of the principal and interest charges.

Yield up To give possession up or to return to the owner or lessor. This may occur after service of a notice to quit. See also **Possession**.

York-Antwerp Rules 1974 Rules governing the adjustment among persons interested in a ship, freight and cargo of the general average payable to the person suffering loss. The York-Antwerp rules were produced by the International Law Association conferences at York (1864) and Antwerp (1877), revised in 1890, 1924, 1950, and 1974 with minor amendments since. The rules apply to the extent that a charter party or bill of lading specifies. The rules were formulated in 1974 and amended in 1990. The 1994 version of the rules was agreed to at the 35th conference of the Comite Maritime International at Sydney in October 1994. They are not part of Australian law and only apply when they are included in a contract such as a charterparty, bill of lading, or policy of marine insurance. See also **Bill of lading; Charterparty**.

Z

Zero based budgeting *Abbr* – ZBB A management accounting system that reassesses all programmes for each new budget period. Zero based budgeting is primarily used by government. Each budget objective is assessed in terms of the benefits created for varying expenditure levels.

Zero coupon bond A fixed value security offering no interest payment during its term: for example *Alliance Holdings Ltd v FCT* (1981) 37 ALR 430; 12 ATR 509. This type of security is usually issued at a discount from its redemption value, the difference between the issue price and face value being the form of return. See also **Debenture; DINGO bond**.

Zone pricing A pricing method in which all customers within a defined zone or geographical region are charged the same price, more distant customers being asked to pay a higher price than those closer to a company's dispatch point. Zone pricing also applies to much public transport where all fares within a zone are uniform, but stepped up between zones. Local telephone calls in Australia within a given zone, perhaps an entire metropolitan area, are uniform irrespective of time, while more distant calls attract higher charges increasing with time. However, with Australia Post ordinary mail is carried anywhere in Australia for the same price regardless of distance.

Zone rebate A tax rebate available to residents of specified remote areas of Australia: (CTH) Income Tax Assessment Act 1936 s 79A (1). These areas consist of two zones: Zone A and Zone B. Zone A represents areas where the factors of isolation, uncongenial climate and the high cost of living are more pronounced. Zone B comprises less badly affected areas. Accordingly, the rebate for ordinary Zone A residents is higher than the rebate for ordinary Zone B residents. A special category of zone rebate is available to residents of particularly isolated areas (called the 'special area') within either Zone A or Zone B: (CTH) Income Tax Assessment Act 1936 s 79A. See also **Income taxation; Rebate**.

Appendix A — International Currency Units

Country or Territory	Currency Unit (Smaller Unit)	Abbreviation or Symbol
Afghanistan	Afghani (100 puls)	Af or Afs
Albania	Lek (100 quindars)	Lk or L
Algeria	Dinar (100 centimes)	Da or AD or DA
American Samoa	Currency is that of USA	
Andorra	Currencies are those of France and Spain	
Angola	New Kwanza (100 lwei)	Kz
Anguilla	East Caribbean dollar (100 cents)	EC$
Antigua and Barbuda	East Caribbean dollar (100 cents)	EC$
Argentina	Peso (10,000 australes)	
Armenia	Dram (100 couma)	dram
Aruba	Florin	Afl
Australia	Dollar (100 cents)	A$
Austria	Schilling (100 Groschen)	ASch or Sch
Azerbaijan	Manat (100 Gopik)	AM
Bahamas	Dollar (100 cents)	Ba$
Bahrain	Dinar (1000 fils)	Bd or BD
Bangladesh	Taka (100 poisha)	Tk
Barbados	Dollar (100 cents)	Bd$ or BD$
Belarus	Rouble (100 kopecks)	Rbl
Belgium	Franc (100 centimes)	FB or Bfr or Bf
Belize	Dollar (100 cents)	BZ$
Benin	Franc CFA	CFA Fr
Bermuda	Dollar (100 cents)	Bda$ or BD$
Bhutan	Ngultrum (100 cheltrum)	N
Bolivia	Boliviano (100 centavos)	$b or B$
Bosnia-Hercegovina	Dinar (100 paras)	
Botswana	Pula (100 thebe)	P or Pu
Brazil	Cruzeiro	Cr or Cr$
British Virgin Islands	Currency is that of USA	
Brunei	Dollar (100 sen)	Br$ or B$
Bulgaria	Lev (100 stotinki)	Lv
Burkina Faso	Franc	CFA Fr
Burundi	Franc (100 centimes)	Bur Fr or FrBr
Cambodia	Riel (100 sen)	CR
Cameroon	Franc CFA	CFA Fr
Canada	Dollar (100 cents)	C$ or Can$
Cape Verde	Escudo Caboverdiano (100 centavos)	Esc or CV Esc
Cayman Islands	Dollar (100 cents)	CI$
Central African Republic	Franc CFA	CFA Fr
Chad	Franc CFA	CFA Fr
Chile	Peso (100 centavos)	Ch$
China	Renminbi or Yuan (100 fen)	Y
Christmas Island	Currency is that of Australia	

© Butterworths

Country or Territory	Currency Unit (Smaller Unit)	Abbreviation or Symbol
Cocos Islands	Currency is that of Australia	
Colombia	Peso (100 centavos)	Col$
Comoros	Franc CFA	CFA Fr
Congo	Franc CFA	CFA Fr
Cook Islands	Currency is that of New Zealand	
Costa Rica	Colon (100 centimos)	CR¢ or ¢
Croatia	Kuna (100 lipas)	HRD
Cuba	Peso (100 centavos)	Cub$
Cyprus	Pound (100 cents)	C£
Czech Republic	Koruna (100 haleru)	Kc
Denmark	Krone (100 ore)	DKr or DKK
Djibouti	Franc (100 centimes)	DF
Dominica	East Caribbean Dollar (100 cents)	EC$
Dominican Republic	Peso (100 centavos)	DR$
Ecuador	Sucre (100 centavos)	Su
Egypt	Pound (100 piastres)	E£
Equatorial Guinea	Franc CFA	CFA Fr
Eritrea	Currency is that of Ethiopea	
Estonia	Kroon (100 sents)	Ekr
Ethiopia	Birr (100 cents)	Br
Falkland Islands	Falkland pound (100 pence)	
Faroe Islands	Currency is that of Denmark	
Fiji	Dollar (100 cents)	F$ or $F
Finland	Markka (100 pennia)	Fmk
France	Franc (100 centimes)	Fr or F or FF
French Guiana	Currency is that of France	
French Polynesia	Franc CFP	
Gabon	Franc CFA	CFA Fr
Gambia	Dalasi (100 butut)	D
Georgia	Georgian Coupon	
Germany	Mark (100 pfennig)	DM
Ghana	Cedi (100 pesewas)	
Gibraltar	Gibraltar pound (100 pence)	
Greece	Drachma (100 leptae)	Dr
Greenland	Currency is that of Denmark	
Grenada	East Caribbean Dollar (100 cents)	EC$
Guadeloupe	Currency is that of France	
Guam	Currency is that of USA	
Guatemala	Quetzal (100 centavos)	Q
Guinea	Syli (cauris)	Sy
Guinea-Bissau	Peso (100 centavos)	GBP
Guyana	Dollar (100 cents)	G$ or Guy$
Haiti	Gourde (100 centimes)	Gde
Honduras	Lempira (100 centavos)	La

International Currency Units

Country or Territory	Currency Unit (Smaller Unit)	Abbreviation or Symbol
Hong Kong	Dollar	HK$
Hungary	Forint (100 filler)	Ft
Iceland	Krona (100 aurar)	IKr
India	Rupee (100 paisa)	R or Re or Rs
Indonesia	Rupiah (100 sen)	Rp
Iran	Rial (dinar)	RI
Iraq	Dinar (1000 tils)	ID
Ireland, Republic of	Punt (100 pence)	IR£
Israel	Shekel (100 agora)	IS
Italy	Lira (100 centesimi)	L
Ivory Coast	Franc CFA	CFA Fr
Jamaica	Dollar (100 cents)	J$ or Jam$
Japan	Yen (100 sen)	Y
Jordan	Dinar (1000 fils)	JD
Kazakhstan	Tenge (tiyn)	T
Kenya	Shilling (100 cents)	Ksh or Sh
Kiribati	Australian dollar	
Korea, North	Won (100 zeuns)	Wn
Korea, South	Won (100 chon)	SK W
Kuwait	Dinar (1000 fils)	KD
Kyrgyz	Som (tyin)	KS
Laos	Kip (100 at)	K or Kp
Latvia	Lats (100 santimes)	Ls
Lebanon	Pound (100 piastres)	L£
Lesotho	Loti (100 lisente)	M
Liberia	Dollar (100 cents)	L$
Libya	Dinar (1000 dirhams)	LD
Liechtenstein	Currency is that of Switzerland	
Lithuania	Litas (centas)	LTL
Luxembourg	Franc (100 centimes)	LF
Macao	Pataca (100 avos)	P or $
Macedonia	Denar (100 deni)	Den
Madagascar	Franc malgache (100 centimes)	FMG
Malawi	Kwacha (100 tambala)	K or MK
Malaysia	Ringgitt or Malaysian Dollar (110 sen or cents)	M$
Maldives	Rutiyaa (10 laaris)	MvRe
Mali	Franc CFA	MFr or MF
Malta	Lira or pound (100 cents)	LM
Marshall Islands	Currency is that of USA	
Martinique	Currency is that of France	
Mauritania	Ouguya (5 khoums)	U
Mauritius	Rupee (100 cents)	Mau Rs or R
Mayotte	Currency is that of France	
Mexico	Peso (100 centavos)	Mex$
Moldova	Leu (bani)	MDL

Country or Territory	Currency Unit (Smaller Unit)	Abbreviation or Symbol
Monaco	Currency is that of France	
Mongolia	Tugrik (100 mongo)	Tug
Montserrat	East Caribbean Dollar (100 cents)	EC$
Morocco	Dirham (100 centimes)	DH or Dh
Mozambique	Metical (100 centavos)	M
Myanmar (Burma)	Kyat (100 pyas)	K
Namibia	Dollar (100 cents)	N$
Nauru	Currency is that of Australia	
Nepal	Rupee (100 paisa)	NY or NR¢
Netherlands	Guilder (100 cents)	Hfl or Dfl or Gld or Fl
Netherlands Antilles	Guilder (100 cents)	NAf
New Caledonia	Franc CFP	
New Zealand	Dollar (100 cents)	NZ$
Nicaragua	Cordoba (100 centavos)	C$ or C
Niger	Franc CFA	CFA Fr
Nigeria	Naira (kobo)	N
Niue	Currency is that of New Zealand	
Norfolk Island	Currency is that of Australia	
Northern Mariana Islands	Currency is that of the USA	
Norway	Krone (100 ore)	NKr
Oman	Rial Omani (1000 baiza)	RO
Pakistan	Pakistan rupee (100 paisa)	R or Pak Re
Palau	US dollar (100 cents)	US$
Panama	Balboa (100 centesimos)	Ba
Papua New Guinea	Kina (100 toea)	K or Ka
Paraguay	Guarani (100 centimos)	G
Peru	New Sol (100 cents)	S
Philippines	Philippine peso (100 centavos)	P or PP
Poland	Zloty (100 groszy)	Zl
Portugal	Escudo (100 centavos)	Esc
Puerto Rico	Currency is that of the USA	
Qatar	Qatar riyal (100 dirhams)	QR
Reunion	Franc (100 centimes)	CFA Fr
Romania	Leu (100 bani)	L
Russia	Rouble (100 Kopecks)	Rbl
Rwanda	Rwanda franc (100 centimes)	Rw Fr
St Christopher and Nevis	East Caribbean dollar (100 cents)	EC$
St Helena	St Helena pound (100 pence)	£
St Lucia	East Caribbean dollar (100 cents)	EC$
St Pierre and Miquelon	Franc (100 centimes)	Francs
St Vincent and the Grenadines	East Caribbean dollar (100 cents)	EC$
El Salvador	El Salvador colon (100 centavos)	ES¢
San Marino	Lira (100 centesimi)	Lire
Sao Tome and Principe	Dobra (100 centavos)	Dobra

International Currency Units

Country or Territory	Currency Unit (Smaller Unit)	Abbreviation or Symbol
Saudi Arabia	Saudi riyal or rial (20 qursh or 100 halalah)	SA R
Senegal	Franc CFA (100 centimes)	CFA Fr
Seychelles	Seychelles rupee (100 cents)	Sre or R
Sierra Leone	Leone (100 cents)	Le
Singapore	Singapore dollar (100 cents)	S$ or Sing$
Slovak Republic	Koruna (100 haleru)	Sk
Slovenia	Tolar (100 stotin)	SIT
Solomon Islands	Solomon Islands dollar (100 cents)	SI$
Somalia	Somali shilling (100 cents)	Som Sh or So Sh
South Africa	Rand (100 cents)	R
Spain	Peseta (100 centimos)	Pta
Sri Lanka	Sri Lankan rupee (100 cents)	SC Re
Sudan	Sudanese dinar (10 pounds), Sudanese Pound (piastres)	SD, Sud£ £S
Surinam	Surinam guilder (100 cents)	Sf
Swaziland	Lilageni (100 cents)	E
Sweden	Krona (100 ore)	SKr
Switzerland	Swiss franc (100 rappen or centimes)	SFr or SW Fr
Syria	Syrian pound (100 piastres)	S£
Taiwan	New Taiwan dollar (100 cents)	T$ or NT$
Tajikistan	Rouble (100 Kopecks)	
Tanzania	Tanzanian shilling (100 cents)	TSh
Thailand	Baht (100 satang)	Bt
Togo	Franc CFA	CFA Fr
Tokelau	Currency is that of New Zealand	
Tonga	Pa'anga (100 seniti)	T$
Trinidad and Tobago	Trinidad and Tobago dollar (100 cents)	TT$
Tunisia	Tunisian dinar (1000 millimes)	TD
Turkey	Turkish lira (100 kurus)	TL
Turkmenistan	Manat (tenge)	TMM
Turks and Caicos Islands	US dollar (100 cents)	US$
Tuvalu	Australian dollar (100 cents)	$A
Uganda	Uganda shilling (100 cents)	USh
Ukraine	Hryvnia (karb-ovanets)	Ka or URK
United Arab Emirates	UAE dirham (100 fils)	Dh or UD
United Kingdom	Pound sterling (100 pence)	£
United States of America	US dollar (100 cents)	US$
Uruguay	Uruguayan new peso (100 centesimos)	N$
Uzbekistan	Sum (tijins)	
Vanuatu	Vatu (100 centimes)	VT
Vatican City State	Lira (100 centesimi)	Lire
Venezuela	Bolivar (100 centimos)	B
Vietnam	Dong (10 hao or 100 xu)	D
Virgin Islands (US)	US dollar (100 cents)	US$

Country or Territory	Currency Unit (Smaller Unit)	Abbreviation or Symbol
Wallis and Futuna Islands	Franc CFP	
Western Samoa	Tala (100 sene or cents)	WS$
Republic of Yemen	Riyal (100 fils)	YR
Yugoslavia	Dinar (100 paras)	Din or DN
Zaire	Zaire (100 makata)	Z
Zambia	Kwacha (100 ngwee)	K
Zimbabwe	Zimbabwe dollar (100 cents)	Z$

Appendix B — Currencies traded by Australian banks

Country	Currency	Abbreviation
Austria	Schillings	ATS
Belgium-Common	Francs	BEF
Canada	Dollars	AD
China	Renminbi	CNY
Denmark	Kroner	DKK
Fiji	Dollars	FJD
Finland	Markka	FIM
France	Francs	FRF
Germany	Marks	DEM
Greece	Drachmae	GRD
Hong Kong	Dollars	HKD
India	Rupees	INR
Indonesia	Rupiah	IDR
Ireland	Punts	IEP
Italy	Lire	ITL
Japan	Yen	JPY
Kenya	Shillings	KES
Kuwait	Dinah	KWD
Malaysian	Ringgit	MYR
Malta	Lira	MTL
Netherlands	Guilders	NLG
New Caledonia/Tahiti	CFP Francs	XPF
New Zealand	Dollars	NZD
Norway	Kroner	NOK
Pakistan	Rupees	PKR
Papua New Guinea	Kina	PGK
Philippines	Pesos	PHP
Portugal	Escudos	PTE
Saudi Arabia	Riyals	SAR
Singapore	Dollars	SGD
Solomon Islands	Dollars	SBD
South Africa	Rand	ZAR
Spain	Pesetas	ESP
Sri Lanka	Rupees	LKR
Sweden	Kronor	SEK
Switzerland	Francs	CHF
Thailand	Bahts	THB
United Kingdom	Pounds	BP
USA	Dollars	USD
Vanuatu	Vatu	VUV

© Butterworths

Appendix C — World Central Banks

Country	Central Bank
Afghanistan	Islamic State of Afghanistan Bank (Central Bank of Afghanistan)
Albania	Bank of Albania
Algeria	Banque Centrale d'Algerie
Angola	Banco Nacional de Angola
Argentina	Banco Central de la Republica Argentina
Armenia	Central Bank of the Republic of Armenia
Aruba	Central Bank of Aruba
Australia	Reserve Bank of Australia
Austria	Oesterreichische Nationalbank (Austrian National Bank)
Azerbaijan	Azerbaijan Republican Bank
Bahamas	Central Bank of the Bahamas
Bahrain	Bahrain Monetary Agency
Bangladesh	Bangladesh Bank
Barbados	Central Bank of Barbados
Belarus	National Bank of the Republic of Belarus
Belgium	Banque Nationale de Belgique
Belize	Central Bank of Belize
Benin	Banque Centrale des Etats de l'Afrique de l'Ouest
Bermuda	Bermuda Monetary Authority
Bhutan	Royal Monetary Authority
Bolivia	Banco Central de Bolivia
Botswana	Bank of Botswana
Brazil	Banco Central do Brasil
Bulgaria	Bulgarska Narodna Banka (Bulgarian National Bank)
Burkina Faso	Banque Centrale des Etats de l'Afrique de l'Ouest
Burma	Union of Burma Bank
Burundi	Banque de la Republique du Burundi
Cambodia	National Bank of Cambodia
Cameroon	Banque des Etats de l'Afrique Centrale
Canada	Bank of Canada
Cape Verde	Banco de Cabo Verde
Cayman Islands	Cayman Islands Currency Board
Central African Republic	Banque des Etats de l'Afrique Centrale
Chad	Banque des Etats de l'Afrique Centrale
Chile	Banco Central de Chile
China	Chung-kuo jen min yin hang (People's Bank of China)
Colombia	Banco de la Republica
Congo	Banque des Etats de l'Afrique Centrale (BEAC)
Costa Rica	Banco Central de Costa Rica
Croatia	Narodna banka Hrvatske (National Bank of Croatia)
Cuba	Banco Nacional de Cuba
Cyprus	Kentrike Trapeza Kyprou (Central Bank of Cyprus)
Czech Republic	Ceska Narodni Banka (Czech National Bank)

© Butterworths

Country	Central Bank
Denmark	Danmarks Nationalbank
Djibouti	Banque Nationale de Djibouti
Dominican Republic	Banco Central de la Republica Dominicana
Ecuador	Banco Central del Ecuador
Egypt	Bank al-Markaz al-Misr (Central Bank of Egypt)
El Salvador	Banco Central de Reserva de El Salvador
Eritrea	National Bank of Eritrea
Estonia	Eesti Pank (Bank of Estonia)
Ethiopia	Ya'Ityopya behrawi bank (National Bank of Ethiopia)
Fiji	Reserve Bank of Fiji
Finland	Suomen Pankki (Bank of Finland)
France	Banque de France
Gabon	Banque des Etats de l'Afrique Centrale
Gambia	The Central Bank of the Gambia
Georgia	Georgian Central Bank
Germany	Deutsche Bundesbank
Ghana	Bank of Ghana
Greece	Trapeza tes Hellados (Bank of Greece)
Guatemala	Banco de Guatemala
Guinea	Banque Centrale de la Republique de Guinee
Guinea-Bissau	Banco Nacional de Guinea-Bissau
Guyana	Bank of Guyana
Haiti	Banque de la Republique d'Haiti
Honduras	Banco Central de Honduras
Hong Kong	Hong Kong Monetary Authority
Hungary	Magyar Nemzeti Bank (National Bank of Hungary)
Iceland	Sedlabanki Islands (Central Bank of Iceland)
India	Reserve Bank of India
Indonesia	Bank Indonesia (Bank of Indonesia)
Iran, Islamic Republic of	Bank Markazi Jomhouri Islami Iran (Central Bank of the Islamic Republic of Iran)
Iraq	Bank al-Markazi al-Iraqi (Central Bank of Iraq)
Ireland	Bank Ceannais na hEireann (Central Bank of Ireland)
Israel	Bank Yisrael (Bank of Israel)
Italy	Banca d'Italia
Jamaica	Bank of Jamaica
Japan	Nippon Ginko (Bank of Japan)
Jordan	Bank al-Markaz al-Urdun (Central Bank of Jordan)
Kazakhstan	National State Bank of Kazakhstan
Kenya	Central Bank of Kenya
Korea (North)	Central Bank of the Democratic People's Republic of Korea
Korea (South)	Bank of Korea
Kuwait	Bank al-Kuwayt al-Markazi (Central Bank of Kuwait)
Kyrgyz Republic	National Bank of Kyrgyz Republic
Laos	Banque d'Etat de la Republique Democratique Populaire Lao
Latvia	Latvijas Banka (Bank of Latvia)

Country	Central Bank
Lebanon	Banque du Liban (Central Bank of Lebanon)
Lesotho	Central Bank of Lesotho
Liberia	National Bank of Liberia
Libya	Central Bank of Libya
Liechtenstein	Liechtensteinische Landesbank
Lithuania	Lietuvos Bankas (Bank of Lithuania)
Luxembourg	Institut Monetaire Luxembourgeois
Macau	Autoridade Monetaria e Cambial de Macau (Monetary and Foreign Exchange Authority of Macau)
Macedonia	National Bank of the Republic of Macedonia
Madagascar	Banque Centrale de la Republique Malagache (Central Bank of Madagascar)
Malawi	Reserve Bank of Malawi
Malaysia	Bank Negara Malaysia (Central Bank of Malaysia)
Maldives	Maldives Monetary Authority
Mali	Banque Centrale des Etats de l'Afrique de l'Ouest
Malta	Central Bank of Malta
Mauritania	Banque Centrale de Mauritanie
Mauritius	Bank of Mauritius
Mexico	Banco de Mexico
Moldova	National Bank of Moldova
Mongolia	The State Bank of Mongolia
Morocco	Bank al-Maghrib
Mozambique	Banco de Mocambique (Bank of Mozambique)
Myanmar	Central Bank of Myanmar
Namibia	Bank of Namibia
Nepal	Nepal Rastra Bank
Netherlands	de Nederlandsche Bank
Netherland Antilles	Bank van de Nederlandse Antillen
New Zealand	Reserve Bank of New Zealand
Nicaragua	Banco Central de Nicaragua (Central Bank of Nicaragua)
Niger	Banque Centrale des Etats de l'Afrique de l'Ouest
Nigeria	Central Bank of Nigeria
Norway	Norges Bank (Bank of Norway)
Oman	Bank al-Markazi al-Umani (Central Bank of Oman)
Pakistan	State Bank of Pakistan
Palestine	Palestine Monetary Authority
Panama	Banco Nacional de Panama
Papua New Guinea	Bank of Papua New Guinea
Paraguay	Banco Central del Paraguay
Peru	Banco Central de Reserva del Peru
Philippines	Bangko Sentral ng Pilipinas (Central Bank of the Philippines)
Poland	Narodowy Bank Polski (National Bank of Poland)
Portugal	Banco de Portugal
Qatar	Masrif Qatar al-Markazi (Qatar Central Bank)
Romania	Banca Nationala a Romaniei (National Bank of Romania)

World Central Banks

Country	Central Bank
Russia	Bank Rossii (Central Bank of the Russian Federation)
Rwanda	Banque Nationale du Ruanda (National Bank of Rwanda)
Saudi Arabia	Muassasat al-Nadq al-Arab al-Saudi (Saudi Arabian Monetary Agency)
Senegal	Banque Centrale des Etats de l'Afrique de l'Ouest
Seychelles	Central Bank of Seychelles
Sierra Leone	Bank of Sierra Leone
Singapore	Monetary Authority of Singapore
Slovak Republic	N rodn Banka Slovenska (National Bank of Slovakia)
Slovenia	Banka Slovenije (Bank of Slovenia)
Solomon Islands	Central Bank of Solomon Islands
Somalia	Bankiga Dhexe ee Soomaaliya (Central Bank of Somalia)
South Africa	South African Reserve Bank
Spain	Banco de España
Sri Lanka	Central Bank of Sri Lanka
Sudan	Bank al-Sudan (Bank of Sudan)
Surinam	Centrale Bank van Suriname (Central Bank of Surinam)
Swaziland	Central Bank of Swaziland
Sweden	Sveriges Riksbank (Bank of Sweden)
Switzerland	Schweizerische Nationalbank (Banque Nationale Suisse)
Syria	Masrif Suriyah al-Markaz (Banque Centrale de Syrie) (Central Bank of Syria)
Taiwan	Chung yang yin hang (Central Bank of China)
Tajikistan	National Bank of the Republic of Tajikistan
Tanzania	Bank of Tanzania
Thailand	Bank of Thailand
Togo	Banque Centrale des Etats de l'Afrique de l'Ouest
Tonga	National Reserve Bank of Tonga
Trinidad and Tobago	Central Bank of Trinidad and Tobago
Tunisia	Bank al-Markazi al-Tunisi (Banque Centrale de Tunisie)
Turkey	Turkiye Cumhuriyet Merkez Bankasi (Central Bank of the Republic of Turkey)
Turkmenistan	State Central Bank of Turkmenistan
Uganda	Bank of Uganda
Ukraine	National Bank of Ukraine
United Arab Emirates	Masrif al-Markaz (Central Bank of the United Arab Emirates)
United Kingdom	Bank of England
United States of America	Federal Reserve System
Uruguay	Banco Central del Uruguay
Uzbekistan	State Bank of Uzbekistan
Vanuatu	Reserve Bank of Vanuatu
Venezuela	Banco Central de Venezuela
Vietnam	State Bank of Vietnam (Vietbank)
Western Samoa	Central Bank of Samoa
Yemen	Central Bank of Yemen (Bank al-Markazi al-Yamani)
Yugoslavia	Narodna Banka Jugoslavije (National Bank of Yugoslavia)

Country	Central Bank
Zaire	Banque du Zaire
Zambia	Bank of Zambia
Zimbabwe	Reserve Bank of Zimbabwe

Appendix D — World Stock Exchanges

Country	Stock Exchange
Argentina	Mercado de Valores de Buenos Aires
Australia	Australian Stock Exchange, Adelaide
	Australian Stock Exchange, Brisbane
	Australian Stock Exchange, Hobart
	Australian Stock Exchange, Melbourne
	Australian Stock Exchange, Perth
	Australian Stock Exchange, Sydney
Austria	Wiener Börsekammer, Vienna
Bangladesh	Dhaka Stock Exchange
Barbados	Barbados Securities Exchange, Bridgetown
Belgium	Bourse de Fonds Publics de Bruxelles
Bermuda	Bermuda Stock Exchange
Brazil	Bolsa de Valores do Rio de Janeiro
	Bolsa de Valores de São Paulo
Canada	Alberta Stock Exchange, Calgary
	Montreal Stock Exchange
	Toronto Stock Exchange
	Vancouver Stock Exchange
	Winnipeg Stock Exchange
Chile	Bolsa de Comercio y Valores de Santiago
	Bolsa de Corredores y Valores de Valparaiso
China	Shenzhen Stock Exchange
Colombia	Bolsa de Bogota
	Bolsa de Medellin
	Bolsa de Occidente
Costa Rica	Bolsa National de Valores, San José
Croatia	Zagreb Stock Exchange
Czech Republic	Prague Stock Exchange
Denmark	Kobenhavns Fondsbors
Ecuador	Bolsa de Valores de Quito
Egypt	Cairo Stock Exchange
	Alexandria Stock Exchange
El Salvador	Bolsa de El Salvador, San Salvador
Finland	Helsinki Stock Exchange
France	Bourse de Paris
Ghana	Ghana Stock Exchange
Germany	Wertpapierbörse Frankfurt
	Bremer Wertpapierbörse
	Berliner Börse
	Rheinisch-Westfalische Börse, Dusseldorf
	Börse, Hamburg
	Niedersächsische Börse, Hanover
	Bayerische Börse, Munich

Country	Stock Exchange
Germany (ctd)	Baden-Wurttembergische Wertpapierbörse, Stuttgart
Greece	Athens Stock Exchange
Hong Kong	Hong Kong Stock Exchange
Hungary	Budapest Stock Exchange
India	Bangalore Stock Exchange
	Bombay Stock Exchange
	Calcutta Stock Exchange
	Delhi Stock Exchange
	Madras Stock Exchange
Indonesia	Badan Pelaksana Pasar Modal, Jakarta
Iran	Teheran Stock Exchange
Ireland	The Stock Exchange, Dublin
Israel	Tel Aviv Stock Exchange
Italy	Borsa Valori, Genoa
	Borsa Valori, Milan
	Borsa Valori, Naples
	Borsa Valori, Rome
	Borsa Valori, Turin
Jamaica	Jamaican Stock Exchange, Kingston
Japan	Fukuoka Stock Exchange
	Hiroshima Stock Exchange
	Nagoya Stock Exchange
	Osaka Securities Exchange
	Sapporo Stock Exchange
	Tokyo Stock Exchange
Jordan	Amman Financial Market
Kenya	Nairobi Stock Exchange
Korea	Korea Stock Exchange
	Seoul Stock Exchange
Kuwait	Kuwait Stock Exchange
Lebanon	Beirut Stock Exchange
Luxembourg	Bourse de Luxembourg
Malaysia	Kuala Lumpur Stock Exchange
Mexico	Bolsa Mexicana de Valores, Mexico
Morocco	Bourse des Valeurs de Casablanca
Nepal	Securities Exchange Centre, Kathmandu
Netherlands	Vereniging voor de Effectenhandel, Amsterdam
New Zealand	Auckland Regional Stock Exchange
	Christchurch Regional Stock Exchange
	Dunedin Stock Exchange
	Wellington Regional Stock Exchange
Nigeria	Nigerian Stock Exchange, Lagos
Norway	Oslo Bors
	Bergens Bors
Pakistan	Karachi Stock Exchange
	Lahore Stock Exchange

Country	Stock Exchange
Panama	Panama City Stock Exchange
Peru	Bolsa de Valores de Lima
Philippines	Manila Stock Exchange
Poland	Warsaw Stock Exchange
Portugal	Bolsa de Valores de Lisboa
	Bolsa de Valores do Porto
Singapore	Singapore International Monetary Exchange
	Stock Exchange of Singapore
Slovenia	Ljubljana Stock Exchange Inc.
South Africa	Johannesburg Stock Exchange
Spain	Bolsa de Bilbao
	Bolsa de Madrid
	Bolsa de Valencia
	Oficial de Comercio de Barcelona
Sri Lanka	Colombo Securities Exchange
Sweden	Stockholm Stock Exchange
Switzerland	Basle Stock Exchange
	Berne Stock Exchange
	Bourse de Genève
	Bourse de Lausanne
	Effekten Börsenverein, Zurich
Taiwan	Taiwan Stock Exchange
Thailand	Securities Exchange of Thailand, Bangkok
Trinidad and Tobago	Trinidad and Tobago Stock Exchange, Port of Spain
Turkey	Istanbul Menkul Kiymetler Borsasi
UK	London Stock Exchange
USA	American Stock Exchange, New York
	Arizona Stock Exchange
	Boston Stock Exchange
	Midwest Stock Exchange, Chicago
	New York Stock Exchange
	Pacific Stock Exchange, San Francisco
	Philadelphia Stock Exchange
Uruguay	Bolsa de Valores de Montevideo
Venezuela	Bolsa de Valores de Caracas
Zimbabwe	Zimbabwe Stock Exchange, Harare

Appendix E — Australian Stock Exchange Addresses

Adelaide
Santos House
Level 19 91 King William Street
Adelaide SA 5000
GPO Box 547 Adelaide SA 5001
Tel: (08) 8216 5000
Fax: (08) 8216 5099
DX 766 Adelaide

Brisbane
Riverside Centre
123 Eagle Street Brisbane QLD 4000
PO Box 7055 Riverside Centre
Brisbane QLD 4001
Tel: (07) 3835 4000
Fax: (07) 3832 4114
DX 9000 Brisbane

Hobart
AMP Building Level 12
86 Collins Street Hobart TAS 7000
GPO Box 100A Hobart TAS 7001
Tel: (03) 6234 7333
Fax: (03) 6234 3922
DX 213 Hobart

Sydney
Exchange Centre
20 Bond Street Sydney NSW 2000
PO Box H224 Australia Square
Sydney NSW 2000
Tel: (02) 9227 0400
Fax: (02) 9233 5836
DX 10439 Stock Exchange

Perth
Exchange Plaza
Mezzanine Level
2 The Esplanade Perth WA 6000
GPO Box D187 Perth WA 6840
Tel: (08) 9224 0000
Fax: (08) 9221 2020

Melbourne
Stock Exchange Centre
530 Collins Street Melbourne VIC 3000
GPO Box 1784 Melbourne VIC 3001
Tel: (03) 9617 8611
Fax: (03) 9614 0303
DX 30892 Melbourne

Appendix F — Recognised Futures Exchanges

(Source: Corporations Regulations Sch 11)

Belgium Futures and Options Exchange (Belfox)
Board of Trade of the City of Chicago (CBOT)
Board of Trade of Kansas City, Missouri, Inc
Bolsa de Mercadorias and Futuros (Commodities and Futures Exchange, Brazil) (BM & F)
Chicago Mercantile Exchange (CME)
Chicago Rice and Cotton Exchange
Coffee, Sugar and Cocoa Exchange, Inc
Commodity Exchange Inc (COMEX)
Deutsche Terminbörse (German Futures Exchange) (DTB)
European Options Exchange (EOE)
Financial Futures Exchange Barcelona (MFB)
Financial Futures Exchange Madrid (MFM)
Hong Kong Futures Exchange Ltd (HKFE)
Italian Futures Exchange (MIF)
The International Futures Exchange (Bermuda) Ltd (INTEX)
The International Petroleum Exchange of London Ltd (IPE)
London Futures and Options Exchange (FOX)
The London International Financial Futures Exchange Ltd (LIFFE)
March a Terme International de France (The French International Futures Market) (MATIF)
Mercados de Futuros Financieros, SA (Spanish Financial Futures Market) (MEFFSA)
The Metal Market and Exchange Company Ltd (London Metal Exchange) (LME)
Mid America Commodity Exchange (MIDAM)
Minneapolis Grain Exchange
The Montreal Exchange (ME)
New York Cotton Exchange (NCE)
New York Futures Exchange, Inc (NYFE)
New York Mercantile Exchange
New Zealand Futures & Options Exchange Ltd (NZFOE)
OM Stockholm AB
Osaka Securities Exchange (OSE)
Philadelphia Board of Trade (PHLX)
The Singapore International Monetary Exchange Limited (SIMEX)
Swiss Options and Financial Futures Exchange (SOFFEX)
Tokyo Commodity Exchange for Industry (TOCOM)
Tokyo Grain Exchange
Tokyo International Futures Exchange (TIFFE)
Tokyo Stock Exchange (TSE)
The Toronto Futures Exchange (TFE)
The Winnipeg Commodity Exchange (WCE)

Appendix G — Australian Prime Ministers

Edmund Barton	1 Jan 1901 — 24 Sept 1903
Alfred Deakin	24 Sep 1903 — 27 Apr 1904
John Watson	27 Apr 1904 — 17 Aug 1904
George Reid	18 Aug 1904 — 5 Jul 1905
Alfred Deakin	5 Jul 1905 — 13 Nov 1908
Andrew Fisher	13 Nov 1908 — 2 June 1909
Alfred Deakin	2 Jun 1909 — 29 Apr 1910
Andrew Fisher	29 Apr 1910 — 24 Jun 1913
Joseph Cook	24 Jun 1913 — 17 Sep 1914
Andrew Fisher	17 Sep 1914 — 27 Oct 1915
William Hughes	27 Oct 1915 — 9 Feb 1923
Stanley Bruce	9 Feb 1923 — 22 Oct 1929
James Scullin	22 Oct 1929 — 6 Jan 1932
Joseph Lyons	6 Jan 1932 — 7 Apr 1939
Earle Page	7 Apr 1939 — 26 Apr 1939
Robert Menzies	26 Apr 1939 — 29 Aug 1941
Arthur Fadden	29 Aug 1941 — 7 Oct 1941
John Curtin	7 Oct 1941 — 5 Jul 1945
Francis Forde	6 Jul 1945 — 13 Jul 1945
Joseph (Ben) Chifley	13 Jul 1945 — 19 Dec 1949
Robert Menzies	19 Dec 1949 — 26 Jan 1966
Harold Holt	26 Jan 1966 — 18 Dec 1967
John McEwen	19 Dec 1967 — 10 Jan 1968
John Gorton	10 Jan 1968 — 10 Mar 1971
William McMahon	10 Mar 1971 — 5 Dec 1972
E Gough Whitlam	5 Dec 1972 — 11 Nov 1975
J Malcolm Fraser	11 Nov 1975 — 5 Mar 1983
Robert Hawke	5 Mar 1983 — 19 Dec 1991
Paul Keating	19 Dec 1991 — 2 Mar 1996
John Howard	2 Mar 1996 —

© Butterworths

Appendix H — Australian Federal Treasurers

Treasurer	Date sworn in
G Turner	1 January 1901
J C Watson	27 April 1904
G Turner	18 August 1904
J Forrest	5 July 1905
W J Lyne	30 July 1907
A Fisher	13 November 1908
J Forrest	2 June 1909
A Fisher	29 April 1910
J Forrest	24 June 1913
A Fisher	17 September 1914
W G Higgs	27 October 1915
A Poynton	14 November 1916
J Forrest	17 February 1917
W A Watt	27 March 1918
J Cook	28 July 1920
S M Bruce	21 December 1921
E C G Page	9 February 1923
E G Theodore	22 October 1923
J H Scullin	9 July 1930
E G Theodore	29 January 1931
J A Lyons	6 January 1932
R G Casey	3 October 1935
R G Menzies	26 April 1939
P C Spender	14 March 1940
A W Fadden	28 October 1940
J B Chifley	7 October 1941
A W Fadden	19 December 1949
H E Holt	10 December 1958
W McMahon	26 January 1966
L H E Bury	23 November 1969
B M Snedden	22 March 1971
E G Whitlam	5 December 1972
F Crean	19 December 1972
J F Cairns	11 December 1974
W G Hayden	6 June 1975
P R Lynch	11 November 1975
J W Howard	19 November 1977
P J Keating	11 March 1983
J C Kerin	4 June 1991
R Willis	9 December 1991
J Dawkins	27 December 1991
R Willis	23 December 1993
P H Costello	11 March 1996

Appendix I — Reserve Bank Governors

Governors of the Reserve Bank since 1960

Dr H C Coombs[1]   14 January 1960 — 22 July 1968
Sr John Phillips   23 July 1968 — 22 July 1975
Sir Harold Knight   23 July 1975 — 13 August 1982
Mr R A Johnston   14 August 1982 — 18 July 1989
Mr B W Fraser[2]   18 September 1989 — 17 September 1996
Mr I J Macfarlane   18 September 1996 —

Notes

1. Dr Coombs was appointed Governor of the Commonwealth Bank of Australia (the central bank) from 1 January 1949 and continued as Governor on 'Separation' in January 1960.

2. Mr M J Phillips, Deputy Governor, performed the duties of Governor from 19 July 1989 to 17 September 1989.

Notes

Notes

Notes

Notes